ENCYCLOPEDIA OF

DRUGS, ALCOHOL & ADDICTIVE BEHAVIOR

EDITORIAL BOARD

ENCYCLOPEDIA OF

DRUGS, ALCOHOL & ADDICTIVE BEHAVIOR

THIRD EDITION

Volume 1

A–C

Pamela Korsmeyer and Henry R. Kranzler

EDITORS IN CHIEF

MACMILLAN REFERENCE USA
A part of Gale, Cengage Learning

GALE
CENGAGE Learning

Detroit • New York • San Francisco • New Haven, Conn • Waterville, Maine • London

Encyclopedia of Drugs, Alcohol, & Addictive Behavior, 3rd edition

Pamela Korsmeyer and Henry R. Kranzler, Editors in Chief

For product information and technology assistance, contact us at
Gale Customer Support, 1-800-877-4253.
For permission to use material from this text or product, submit all requests online at **www.cengage.com/permissions.**
Further permissions questions can be emailed to
permissionrequest@cengage.com

Since this page cannot legibly accommodate all copyright notices, the acknowledgments constitute an extension of the copyright notice.

While every effort has been made to ensure the reliability of the information presented in this publication, Gale, a part of Cengage Learning, does not guarantee the accuracy of the data contained herein. Gale accepts no payment for listing; and inclusion in the publication of any organization, agency, institution, publication, service, or individual does not imply endorsement of the editors or publisher. Errors brought to the attention of the publisher and verified to the satisfaction of the publisher will be corrected in future editions.

Library of Congress Cataloging-in-Publication Data

Encyclopedia of drugs, alcohol & addictive behavior / Pamela Korsmeyer and Henry R. Kranzler. -- 3rd ed.
    p. cm.
    Includes bibliographical references and index.
    ISBN 978-0-02-866064-6 (set) -- ISBN 978-0-02-866065-3 (vol. 1) -- ISBN 978-0-02-866066-0 (vol. 2) -- ISBN 978-0-02-866067-7 (vol. 3) -- ISBN 978-0-02-866068-4 (vol. 4)
    1. Drug abuse--Encyclopedias. 2. Substance abuse--Encyclopedias. 3. Alcoholism--Encyclopedias. 4. Drinking of alcoholic beverages--Encyclopedias. I. Korsmeyer, Pamela, 1945- II. Kranzler, Henry R., 1950-

HV5804.E53 2009
362.2903--dc22   2008012719

Gale
27500 Drake Rd.
Farmington Hills, MI 48331-3535

ISBN-13: 978-0-02-866064-6 (set)   ISBN-10: 0-02-866064-1 (set)
ISBN-13: 978-0-02-866065-3 (vol. 1)   ISBN-10: 0-02-866065-X (vol. 1)
ISBN-13: 978-0-02-866066-0 (vol. 2)   ISBN-10: 0-02-866066-8 (vol. 2)
ISBN-13: 978-0-02-866067-7 (vol. 3)   ISBN-10: 0-02-866067-6 (vol. 3)
ISBN-13: 978-0-02-866068-4 (vol. 4)   ISBN-10: 0-02-866068-4 (vol. 4)

This title is also available as an e-book.
ISBN-13: 978-0-02-866114-8; ISBN-10: 0-02-866114-1
Contact your Gale sales representative for ordering information.

Printed in the United States of America
1 2 3 4 5 6 7 12 11 10 09 08

EDITORIAL AND PRODUCTION STAFF

Project Editors
Douglas Dentino, Angela Doolin, Alan Hedblad, Jeffrey Lehman, Mark Mikula

Art Editor
Donna Batten

Contributing Editors
Ken Wachsberger, Jeffrey Wilson

Editorial Assistants
Caitlin Cowan, Amy Kwolek, Jacyln Setili, Darcy Thompson

Manuscript Editors
Patti Brecht, Judy Clinebell, Laurie Edwards, Lauren Grace, Peter Jaskowiak,
Melodie Monahan, Pam Revitzer, Ann Shurgin

Proofreaders
Rebecca J. Frey, Andrea Fritsch, Carol Holmes, Donna Wright

Custom Graphics
GGS Book Services, PMG, York, Pennsylvania

Indexer
Laurie Andriot

Technical Support
Mark Drouillard,
Mark Springer

Composition
Evi Seoud

Page Design
Pamela A. E. Galbreath

Imaging
Lezlie Light

Permissions
Margaret Chamberlain-Gaston, Jackie Jones, Kelly A. Quin, Robyn V. Young

Manufacturing
Wendy Blurton

Product Manager
Kate Hanley

Director of Publishing
Hélène Potter

Publisher
Jay Flynn

CONTENTS

PREFACE

The first edition of the *Encyclopedia of Drugs and Alcohol* (as it was first titled), published in 1995, was the product of a massive effort on the part of Jerome H. Jaffe and a group of distinguished colleagues that he, through his long experience and many friends in the various fields of addiction studies, was able to bring together. The result of the collaboration among the members of this original group was a compendium of information from every viewpoint and specialty having to do with the use and abuse of psychoactive substances. We, the editors of this third edition of the *Encyclopedia*, have attempted to remain true to Dr. Jaffe's original purpose as described in the preface to the first edition.

> The Macmillan *Encyclopedia of Drugs and Alcohol* has been written as a comprehensive source of information for non-specialists who have an interest in any of the diverse topics that are included under the broad general heading of substance use and abuse. While many of the entries are devoted to the actions of drugs on the body, the work as a whole is intended to serve the wider interests of social science and includes articles on social policy, history, politics, economics, international trafficking, law enforcement, scientific and medical research, treatment and prevention of drug abuse, and epidemiology.

The title of the second edition, published in 2001, was modified to include addictive behaviors that did not involve drugs or alcohol. While paying close attention to the original vision and the broader scope reflected in the title change, we have tried to update and expand the work to include new and emerging topics and important developments in the many fields of addiction studies. We have included information on recent scientific discoveries and theories in behavioral neuroscience, which help to illuminate how addictive substances and behaviors affect the brain and the impact of these effects on behavior. This new scientific information also includes a growing number of discoveries in genetics, which have emerged following the sequencing of the human genome. In addition, recent advances in neuroimaging have made it possible to examine events occurring in the healthy and addicted brains of animals and humans, further elucidating the underlying processes. The results of new, large-scale population studies inform much of the epidemiologic coverage of substance use, abuse, and dependence. We have gone to some lengths to reorganize the sections on treatment in as intuitive a way as possible and to include new developments in the use of medications, which increasingly are being combined with psychosocial interventions in the treatment of individuals with addictive disorders.

Recognizing the cultural importance of how addiction is perceived both in the United States and in societies and political systems throughout the world, the editorial board obtained authoritative essays on such popular subjects as drugs in the movies, the effect of the Internet on drug use, and the coverage of addiction issues in the media. In order to give the reader a broad view of how these issues are understood and dealt with in cultures other than that of the United States, we commissioned articles on drug use and trafficking in a representative group of countries and regions.

We have tried to maintain standards of objectivity in the treatment of controversial subjects and to provide enough information on competing theories and points of view so that readers may draw their own conclusions. One of the main challenges in compiling these volumes was to ensure that the language used by the contributors was not so technical as to make the entries obscure. In reviewing entries prior to publication, a concerted effort was made to use lay language whenever possible and, when technical terms were required, to define them. We, the editors in chief, are satisfied that the finished work provides an authoritative source of information that will help to educate the general public on a variety of complex and controversial issues.

This third edition contains 545 entries, of which nearly 70 percent are either completely new (133 articles) or substantially revised and updated (236 articles). Early on, the editors decided, and Macmillan Reference personnel agreed, that the extensive list of treatment programs included in the fourth volume of the first two editions should be dropped. It was the board's judgment that such a list would fall out of date so fast as to be of little use to the reader.

In early 2006, Kate Hanley of Macmillan Reference invited Pam Korsmeyer and Henry Kranzler to consider sharing the task of editor in chief of a third edition of the *Encyclopedia*. Both were pleased and honored to accept the invitation. Ms. Korsmeyer had worked for many years as an editor and writer on the history of use, abuse, and control of psychoactive substances, and she was happy to be able to reengage the field after several years' absence. Dr. Kranzler has been a clinician and investigator in addictions for more than twenty years and welcomed the opportunity to survey the biological and medical aspects of the field comprehensively, as required by a thorough revision of the *Encyclopedia*.

At the beginning of the *Encyclopedia* project, the editors in chief and the Macmillan Reference project managers agreed that the work of constructing the table of contents, developing "scopes" for each article, and reviewing the finished essays should be divided among six fields of interest. A prominent scholar was then invited to take responsibility for each of the six fields, and the two editors in chief oversaw three fields apiece. Henry Kranzler worked with Deborah Hasin (epidemiology), Kathleen Carroll (treatment), and Michael Kuhar (neuroscience and pharmacology). Pam Korsmeyer guided the efforts of Nancy Campbell (history, society, and culture), Eric Wish (public policy), and Virginia Berridge (international issues). Howard Kushner also participated in the initial development of the table of contents, contributing first-rate work to the coverage of history, society, and culture. When he found that he was unable to remain on the editorial board, Nancy Campbell stepped in, much to the good fortune of the project and the editors.

The substantial organizational effort could not have been possible without the contributions of the staff at Macmillan/Gale, who were ably led by Kate Hanley, Jeffrey Lehman, and Alan Hedblad. Their tireless dedication kept the editorial board and editors in chief focused on the task of identifying suitable authors for the many revised and new entries, providing direction in the preparation of initial draft entries, and thoroughly editing the entries to ensure their suitability for inclusion in the *Encyclopedia*.

PAMELA KORSMEYER
HENRY R. KRANZLER

ARTICLES

Glutethimide
Golden Triangle as Drug Source

Jews and Alcohol
Jimsonweed

H

Hair Analysis as a Test for Drug Use
Hallucination
Hallucinogenic Plants
Hallucinogens
Harm Reduction
Harrison Narcotics Act of 1914
Hashish
Hemp
Hepatitis C Infection
Heroin
Hispanic Americans, Alcohol and Drug Use Among
HIV Risk Assessment Battery (RAB)
Homelessness, History of Association with Alcohol
      and Drugs
Hookah
Hydromorphone

I

Iatrogenic Addiction
Ibogaine
Imaging Techniques: Visualizing the Living Brain
Immunoassay
Impulsivity and Addiction
India and Pakistan
Industry and Workplace, Drug Use in
Inhalants
Inhalants: Extent of Use and Complications
Injecting Drug Users and HIV
International Classification of Diseases (ICD)
International Control Policies
International Drug Supply Systems
Internet: Impact on Drug and Alcohol Use
Intimate Partner Violence and Alcohol/Substance
      Use
Ireland, Republic of
Italy

J

Japan
Jellinek Memorial Fund

K

Kava
Kenya
Khat

L

L-Alpha-Acetylmethadol (LAAM)
Laudanum
LD50
Legal Regulation of Drugs and Alcohol
Legalization vs. Prohibition of Drugs: Historical
      Perspective
Legalization vs. Prohibition of Drugs: Policy
      Analysis
Limbic System
Lysergic Acid Diethylamide (LSD) and
      Psychedelics

M

Mandatory Sentencing
Marijuana (Cannabis)
MDMA
Media
Memory, Effects of Drugs on
Meperidine
Meprobamate
Mescaline
Methadone Maintenance Programs
Methamphetamine
Methanol
Methaqualone
Methedrine
Methylphenidate
Mexico
Michigan Alcoholism Screening Test (MAST)
Middle East
Military, Drug and Alcohol Abuse in the United
      States
Mini International Neuropsychiatric Interview
      (MINI)

O

N

P

R

S

T

T-ACE
Tax Laws and Alcohol
Tea
Temperance Movement
Terrorism and Drugs
Tetrahydrocannabinol (THC)
Theobromine
Tobacco
    A History of Tobacco
    An International Overview
    Tobacco Industry
    Dependence
    Medical Complications
    Smokeless
    Smoking Cessation and Weight Gain
Tolerance and Physical Dependence
Toughlove
Treatment
    An Overview
    An Overview of Alcohol Abuse/Dependence
    An Overview of Drug Abuse/Dependence
    A History of Treatment in the United States
Treatment, Behavioral Approaches to
    An Overview
    Cognitive Therapy
    Cognitive-Behavioral Therapy
    Contingency Management
    Couples and Family Therapy
    Group Therapy
    Long-term versus Brief
    Minnesota Model
    Motivational and Brief
    Self-Help and Anonymous Groups
    Traditional Dynamic Psychotherapy
    Twelve-Step and Disease Model Approaches
Treatment, Pharmacological Approaches to
    An Overview
    Anticonvulsants
    Antidepressants
    Antipsychotics
    Aversion Therapy
    Acamprosate
    Buprenorphine
    Clonidine
    Disulfiram
    Long-Acting Preparations
    Methadone
    Naltrexone

    Serotonin-Uptake Inhibitors
    Vaccines
Treatment, Specialty Approaches to
    Acupuncture
    Hypnosis
    Adolescents
    Older Adults
    Therapeutic Communities
Treatment, Stages/Phases of
    Initiation of Abstinence
    Medical Detoxification
    Non-Medical Detoxification
    Screening and Brief Intervention
    Relapse Prevention
    Stabilization
    Aftercare
Treatment: Outpatient versus Inpatient Setting
Treatment Accountability for Safer Communities
    (TASC)
Treatment Outcome Prospective Study (TOPS)

U

U.S. Government
    The Organization of U.S. Drug Policy
    Agencies in Drug Law Enforcement and
        Supply Control
    Agencies Supporting Substance Abuse
        Prevention and Treatment
    Agencies Supporting Substance Abuse
        Research
U.S. Government Agencies
    Bureau of Narcotics and Dangerous Drugs
        (BNDD)
    Center for Substance Abuse Prevention (CSAP)
    Center for Substance Abuse Treatment
        (CSAT)
    National Institute on Alcohol Abuse and
        Alcoholism (NIAAA)
    National Institute on Drug Abuse (NIDA)
    Office of Drug Abuse Law Enforcement
        (ODALE)
    Office of Drug Abuse Policy
    Office of National Drug Control Policy
    Special Action Office for Drug Abuse
        Prevention (SAODAP)
    Substance Abuse and Mental Health Services
        Administration (SAMHSA)

CONTRIBUTORS

CAROLINE JEAN ACKER
Department of History
Carnegie Mellon University
Opium: International
Overview
Opium: U.S. Overview

EFRAT AHARONOVICH
Assistant Professor of Clinical
Psychology
Columbia University College of
Physicians & Surgeons
Complications: Neurological
Minnesota Multiphasic
Personality Inventory
(MMPI)

ANALUCIA ALEGRIA
New York State Psychiatric
Institute
Gambling Addiction:
Epidemiology

F. JAVIER ÁLVAREZ
Faculty of Medicine
University of Valladolid, Spain
Spain

CHARLES AMBLER
University of Texas at El Paso
Africa
South Africa

ALBERT J. ARIAS
Assistant Professor, Department of
Psychiatry
University of Connecticut School of
Medicine
Delirium Tremens (DTs)
Opioid Complications and
Withdrawal
Withdrawal: Alcohol
Withdrawal: Benzodiazepines
Withdrawal: Nonabused Drugs

E. ERIN ARTIGIANI
Deputy Director, Policy and
Governmental Affairs
Center for Substance Abuse
Research, University of Maryland,
College Park
Driving Under the Influence
(DUI)
Prescription Drug
Monitoring Program
Prevention, Education and
U.S. Government: Agencies
in Drug Law
Enforcement and Supply
Control

THOMAS BABOR
Professor and Chair, Department
of Community Medicine &
Health Care
University of Connecticut School of
Medicine

Addiction (Journal)
Alcohol, Smoking, and
Substance Involvement
Screening Test (ASSIST)
Diagnosis of Substance Use
Disorders: Diagnostic
Criteria
Diagnostic and Statistical
Manual (DSM)
International Classification of
Diseases (ICD)
Michigan Alcoholism
Screening Test (MAST)
Treatment, Stages/Phases of:
Screening and Brief
Intervention

JERALD G. BACHMAN
Institute for Social Research
University of Michigan, Ann
Arbor
Religion and Drug Use

JOHN A. BAILEY
Clinical Assistant Professor,
Department of Psychiatry
University of Florida, College of
Medicine
Iatrogenic Addiction

BETH A. BAILEY
(NORDSTROM)
Associate Professor of Family
Medicine

East Tennessee State University
Fetal Alcohol Syndrome

JUDY K. BALL
*Director, Division of Faculty
Surveys, Office of Applied Studies
Substance Abuse and Mental
Health Services Administration,
U.S. Department of Health and
Human Services*
Drug Abuse Warning
Network (DAWN)

ROBERT L. BALSTER
*Professor of Pharmacology
University of Michigan Medical
School*
Phencyclidine (PCP):
Adverse Effects

JOAQUIN BARNOYA
*Research Director and Assistant
Adjunct Professor
Cardiovascular Unit of
Guatemala and Department of
Epidemiology, University of
California, San Francisco*
Tobacco: Medical
Complications

JAMES E. BARRETT
Drexel University
Reinforcement
Research: Drugs as
Discriminative Stimuli

ADAM E. BARRY
*Assistant Professor, Department of
Health & Kinesiology
Purdue University*
Alcohol Use Disorders
Identification Test
(AUDIT)
Alcohol: History of Drinking
(International)

PATRICIA BARTON
University of Strathclyde
India and Pakistan

LANCE BAUER
*School of Medicine
University of Connecticut*
Psychomotor Effects of
Alcohol and Drugs

JIM BAUMOHL
*School of Social Work and Social
Research
Bryn Mawr College*
Homelessness, History of
Association with Alcohol
and Drugs
Treatment: A History of
Treatment in the United
States
Welfare Policy and Substance
Abuse in the United States

SUSAN E. BECKERLEG
University of Warwick
Khat

NEAL L. BENOWITZ
*Tobacco Control Program, Helen
Diller Family Comprehensive
Cancer Center
University of California, San
Francisco*
Nicotine

MATS BERGLUND
*Clinical Alcohol Research,
Department of Health Sciences
Lund University*
Treatment, Pharmacological
Approaches to: Aversion
Therapy

CHERYL BESELER
*New York State Psychiatric
Institute, Columbia University
Assistant Professor, Department of
Epidemiology, University of
Nebraska Medical Center*
Adult Children of Alcoholics
(ACOA)
Risk Factors for Substance
Use, Abuse, and
Dependence: Sensation
Seeking and Impulsivity

WARREN K. BICKEL
*Professor and Director, Center for
Addiction Research
University of Arkansas for
Medical Sciences*
Behavioral Economics

BERT BIELEMAN
*Director
Intraval Foundation, Groningen,
The Netherlands*
Netherlands

CARLOS BLANCO
*Department of Psychiatry, College
of Physicians and Surgeons of
Columbia University
New York State Psychiatric
Institute*
Gambling Addiction:
Epidemiology

FLOYD E. BLOOM
*Professor Emeritus
The Scripps Research Institute, La
Jolla, CA*
Acetylcholine
Catecholamines
Endorphins
Enkephalin
Monoamine
Neuron
Neurotransmission
Neurotransmitters
Norepinephrine
Synapse, Brain

RICHARD J. BONNIE
*Harrison Foundation Professor of
Medicine and Law
University of Virginia,
Charlottesville*
Controlled Substances Act of
1970
National Commission on
Marihuana and Drug
Abuse:
Recommendations on
Decriminalization

National Commission on
    Marihuana and Drug
    Abuse

MARC N. BRANCH
Department of Psychology
University of Florida, Gainesville
    Behavioral Tolerance

SAMANTHA BRANDFON
School of Social Work
University of Michigan
    Movies

GREGORY W. BROCK
Department of Family Studies
University of Kentucky, Lexington
    Toughlove

KIRK J. BROWER
Associate Professor of Psychiatry
University of Michigan Medical
School
    Anabolic Steroids

RICHARD H. BUCHER
Adjunct Professor
George Mason University, Fairfax,
VA
    Accidents and Injuries from
        Drugs
    Advertising and Tobacco Use
    Industry and Workplace,
        Drug Use in
    Internet: Impact on Drug
        and Alcohol Use
    Productivity: Effects of
        Alcohol on
    Productivity: Effects of
        Drugs on
    Social Costs of Alcohol and
        Drug Abuse
    U.S. Government Agencies:
        National Institute on
        Drug Abuse (NIDA)
    U.S. Government: The
        Organization of U.S.
        Drug Policy

KATHLEEN KEENAN
BUCHOLZ
Professor, Department of
Psychiatry
Washington University School of
Medicine, St. Louis, MO
    Antisocial Personality
        Disorder

ALAN J. BUDNEY
Professor, Center for Addiction
Research, Department of
Psychiatry and Behavioral Sciences
University of Arkansas for
Medical Sciences
    Marijuana (Cannabis)

GERHARD BÜHRINGER
Professor for Addiction Research,
Technische Universität Dresden
Director, IFT Institut für
Therapieforschung, Munich
    Alcoholism: Abstinence
        versus Controlled
        Drinking

ELLEN BURKE
Mental Health Counselor,
Lecturer in Child and Family
Studies
Berea College, Berea, KY
    Toughlove

DAVID BURROWS
AIDS Projects Management
Group
    Eastern Europe

SHANE BUTLER
School of Social Work & Policy
Trinity College, Dublin
    Ireland, Republic of

JEAN LUD CADET
Molecular Neuropsychiatry
Branch, NIH/NIDA,
Intramural Research Program
Baltimore, MD
    Methamphetamine

NANCY D. CAMPBELL
Associate Professor, Department of
Science and Technology Studies
Rensselaer Polytechnic Institute
    Woman's Christian
        Temperance Union
    Women and Substance Abuse

FABIO CAPUTO
Department of Internal Medicine
SS Annunziata Hospital, Cento
(Ferrara), Italy
    Italy

MOLLY CARNEY
    Treatment, Behavioral
        Approaches to: Cognitive
        Therapy

NEIL CARRIER
Wellcome Unit for the History of
Medicine
University of Oxford
    Kenya

KATHLEEN M. CARROLL
Professor of Psychiatry
Yale University School of Medicine
    Treatment, Behavioral
        Approaches to: An
        Overview
    Treatment, Behavioral
        Approaches to:
        Cognitive-Behavioral
        Therapy
    Treatment: An Overview

MARILYN E. CARROLL
Department of Psychiatry
University of Minnesota,
Minneapolis
    Phencyclidine (PCP)

REBECCA CARROLL
Professor of Rhetoric
St. Mary's College of California
    Anslinger, Harry Jacob, and
        U.S. Drug Policy

ASHLEE C. CARTER
Doctoral Candidate in Clinical Psychology
University of South Florida
Expectancies

MARY CARVLIN
Drug Metabolism
Street Value

JONATHAN P. CAULKINS
Professor of Operations Research and Public Policy
Carnegie Mellon University, Qatar Campus & Heinz School of Public Policy and Management
Harm Reduction
Legalization vs. Prohibition of Drugs: Historical Perspective
Legalization vs. Prohibition of Drugs: Policy Analysis

ARTHUR I. CEDERBAUM
Professor, Pharmacology and Systems Therapeutics
Mt. Sinai School of Medicine, New York, NY
Drug Interactions and Alcohol

KAREN CHAN OSILLA
RAND Corporation
Treatment, Behavioral Approaches to: Motivational and Brief

JOHN N. CHAPPEL
Department of Psychiatry
Univeristy of Nevada School of Medicine, Reno
Sobriety

CHERYL J. CHERPITEL
Associate Director, National Alcohol Research Center
Senior Scientist, Public Health Institute, Alcohol Research Group
Accidents and Injuries from Alcohol

PIERRE-ARNAUD CHOUVY
Research Fellow
National Center for Scientific Research (CNRS), Paris
Golden Triangle as Drug Source

DOMENIC A. CIRAULO
Division of Psychiatry
Boston University School of Medicine
Benzodiazepines

PATRICK R. CLIFFORD
School of Public Health
University of Medicine and Dentistry of New Jersey
Treatment, Stages/Phases of: Initiation of Abstinence

GREG COHEN
Stanford University
Childhood Behavior and Later Substance Use

SANDRA D. COMER
College of Physicians & Surgeons
Columbia University
Phencyclidine (PCP)

WILSON M. COMPTON
Director, Division of Epidemiology, Services and Prevention Research
National Institute on Drug Abuse
Epidemiology of Drug Abuse

FELINA MARIE CORDOVA
MPH Candidate, Family and Child Health, Research Assistant Mel and Enid Zuckerman College of Public Health, University of Arizona
Complications: Endocrine and Reproductive Systems
Complications: Immunologic

LINDA B. COTTLER
Professor of Epidemiology; Director, Epidemiology and Prevention Research Group Department of Psychiatry, Washington University School of Medicine
Computerized Diagnostic Interview Schedule for DSM-IV (C DIS-IV)

LIRIO S. COVEY
Professor of Clinical Psychology in Psychiatry and Research Scientist Clinical Therapeutics, Department of Psychiatry, Columbia University Medical Center and the New York State Psychiatric Institute
Tobacco: Dependence

KATHRYN A. CUNNINGHAM
Professor and Interim Chair, Department of Pharmacology and Toxicology; Director, Center for Addiction Research University of Texas Medical Branch
Serotonin

STEPHANIE DALL VECCHIA-ADAMS
Amygdala
Dynorphin
Ventral Tegmental Area

DEIDRE E. DAVIS
Menninger Department of Psychiatry and Behavioral Sciences Baylor College of Medicine
Treatment, Pharmacological Approaches to: Serotonin-Uptake Inhibitors

VALINA DAWSON
Johns Hopkins University
Neuroleptic
Receptor: NMDA (N-Methyl D-Aspartic Acid)

GEORGE DE LEON
*Center for Therapeutic
Community Research
New York, NY*
Treatment, Specialty
Approaches to:
Therapeutic
Communities

JAYME A. DELANO
*Senior Program Associate
Institute for Governmental Service
and Research*
Drug Courts
Treatment Accountability for
Safer Communities
(TASC)

NICHOLAS DeMARTINIS
*Formerly Department of
Psychiatry
University of Connecticut Health
Center*
Psychoactive Drug
Psychoactive
Psychopharmacology
Sedative-Hypnotic

LARA DePADILLA
*Department of Behavioral Sciences
and Health Education
Rollins School of Public Health,
Emory University*
Military, Drug and Alcohol
Abuse in the United States

DON C. DES JARLAIS
*Edmond De Rothschild Chemical
Dependency Institute
Beth Israel Medical Center*
Injecting Drug Users and
HIV
Needle and Syringe
Exchanges and HIV/
AIDS
Substance Abuse and AIDS

STEPHEN L. DEWEY
*Senior Scientist, Medical
Department*

Brookhaven National Laboratory
Gamma-Aminobutyric Acid
(GABA)

FRANK DIKÖTTER
*Chair Professor of Humanities,
Department of History, The
University of Hong Kong
Professor of the Modern History of
China, SOAS, University of
London*
China

DAVID J. DROBES
*Professor, University of South
Florida
Senior Member, Moffitt Cancer
Center, Tampa, FL*
Craving
Withdrawal: Nicotine
(Tobacco)

ROBERT L. DuPONT
*President, Institute for Behavior
and Health, Inc.*
Physicians and Medical
Workers, Substance
Abuse Among

STEVEN I. DWORKIN
*Department of Psychology
University of North Carolina at
Wilmington*
Limbic System

LINDA DYKSTRA
*Department of Psychology
University of North Carolina,
Chapel Hill*
Pain: Behavioral Methods for
Measuring Analgesic
Effects of Drugs
Research: Measuring Effects
of Drugs on Behavior
Sensation and Perception and
Effects of Drugs

HOWARD J. EDENBERG
*Chancellor's Professor and
Director, Center for Medical
Genomics*

*Department of Biochemistry and
Molecular Biology, Department of
Medical and Molecular Genetics,
Indiana University School of
Medicine*
Genome Project

ELLEN LOCKARD EDENS
Antisocial Personality
Disorder

EVERETT H. ELLINWOOD
*Department of Psychiatry
Duke University Medical Center,
Durham, NC*
Risk Factors for Substance
Use, Abuse, and
Dependence: Drug
Effects and Biological
Responses

ROSEMARY ELLIOT
*Lecturer, Department of Economic
and Social History
University of Glasgow*
Germany

NANCY E. FAERBER
Canton, MI
Beers and Brews
College on Problems of Drug
Dependence (CPDD),
Inc.

WILLIAM FALS-STEWART
*University of Rochester
Rochester, NY*
Treatment, Behavioral
Approaches to: Couples
and Family Therapy

CINDY FAZEY
*Visiting Professor, School of
Sociology and Social Policy
University of Liverpool*
Crop Control Policies

MICHAEL B. FIRST
Professor of Clinical Psychiatry

Columbia University
New York State Psychiatric Institute
Structured Clinical Interview
for DSM-IV (SCID)

MARIAN W. FISCHMAN
College of Physicians and Surgeons
Columbia University
Amphetamine
Benzoylecognine
Coca Paste
Coca Plant
Dextroamphetamine
Freebasing
Methedrine
Methylphenidate
Pemoline
Psychomotor Stimulant

JOHN L. FITZGERALD
Associate Professor
University of Melbourne
Sport, Drugs in International

**CARLOS ANTONIO FLORES
PÉREZ**
Researcher
Center of Investigation and
Superior Studies in Social
Anthropology
Mexico

ALICE B. FREDERICKS
Nicotine

DANIEL X. FREEDMAN
Formerly Professor of Psychiatry
and Pharmacology
UCLA School of Medicine
Dimethyltryptamine (DMT)
DOM
Hallucinogenic Plants
Lysergic Acid Diethylamide
(LSD) and Psychedelics
Mescaline
Morning Glory Seeds
Nutmeg
Peyote
Psilocybin

REBECCA J. FREY
New Haven, CT
Amobarbital
Calcium Carbimide
Drug Interactions and Alcohol
Phencyclidine (PCP):
Adverse Effects
Sobriety
Tetrahydrocannabinol (THC)

WILLIAM A. FROSCH
Professor Emeritus of Psychiatry
Cornell University Medical School
Psychoanalysis
Treatment, Behavioral
Approaches to:
Traditional Dynamic
Psychotherapy

KENNETH FURTON
International Forensic Research
Institute, Department of
Chemistry and Biochemistry
Florida International University,
Miami
Dogs in Drug Detection

MARC S. GALANTER
Department of Psychiatry
New York University School of
Medicine
Association for Medical
Education and Research
in Substance Abuse
(AMERSA)

DEVANG H. GANDHI
University of Maryland School of
Medicine, Baltimore
Treatment, Stages/Phases of:
Medical Detoxification

JAMES C. GARBUTT
Professor of Psychiatry
Department of Psychiatry and
Bowles Center for Alcohol Studies,
University of North Carolina at
Chapel Hill
Treatment, Pharmacological
Approaches to: Disulfiram

Treatment, Pharmacological
Approaches to: Long-
Acting Preparations

TRACIE J. GARDNER
Assistant Professor, Division of
Alcohol and Addictive Disorders
Menninger Department of
Psychiatry and Behavioral
Sciences, Baylor College of
Medicine
Research: Developing
Medications to Treat
Substance Abuse and
Dependence
Treatment, Pharmacological
Approaches to: An
Overview
Treatment, Pharmacological
Approaches to:
Buprenorphine
Withdrawal: Cocaine

CORAL E. GARTNER
Postdoctoral Research Fellow,
School of Population Health
University of Queensland
Australia

PAUL F. GAVAGHAN
Chevy Chase, MD
Distilled Spirits Council

JEFFREY A. GERE
Immunoassay

JOSEPH GFROERER
Office of Applied Studies
Substance Abuse and Mental
Health Services Administration
National Survey on Drug Use
and Health (NSDUH)

NICHOLAS E. GOEDERS
Professor and Head, Department
of Pharmacology, Toxicology and
Neuroscience
Louisiana State University Health
Sciences Center, Shreveport
Agonist
Agonist-Antagonist (Mixed)

Alkaloids
Antagonist
Aphrodisiac
Designer Drugs
Dose-Response Relationship
Drug Interaction and the Brain
Drug Types
Drug
ED50
Ethnopharmacology
LD50
Pharmacology
Plants, Drugs From
Psychoactive Drug
Psychoactive
Psychopharmacology
Receptor, Drug

MARK S. GOLD
*Distinguished Professor and
Chairman
University of Florida, College of
Medicine*
Iatrogenic Addiction

BRUCE A. GOLDBERGER
*Professor
University of Florida College of
Medicine, Gainesville*
Hair Analysis as a Test for
Drug Use

MARK S. GOLDMAN
*Distinguished Research Professor
University of South Florida*
Expectancies

RONALD GOLDSTOCK
*Adjunct Professor of Law
Cornell University Law School*
Money Laundering

JON E. GRANT
*Associate Professor, Department of
Psychiatry
University of Minnesota*
Gambling Addiction:
Assessment

ALAN I. GREEN
*Raymond Sobel Professor of
Psychiatry, Professor of
Pharmacology and Toxicology
Chairman, Department of
Psychiatry, Dartmouth Medical
School*
Treatment, Pharmacological
Approaches to:
Antipsychotics

JOHN GREENAWAY
*Senior Lecturer in Politics,
Research Director
School of Political, Social and
International Studies (PSI),
University of East Anglia*
Britain: Alcohol Use and
Policy

IVELAW LLOYD GRIFFITH
*Professor of Political Science,
Provost, and Senior Vice President
for Academic Affairs
York College, The City University
of New York*
Caribbean, Illicit Drugs in

ROLAND R. GRIFFITHS
*Professor, Departments of
Psychiatry and Neuroscience
Johns Hopkins School of Medicine,
Baltimore, MD*
Coffee
Tea

FREDERICK K. GRITTNER
*Adjunct Professor
Hamline University School of Law*
Asset Forfeiture
Border Management
Civil Remedies
Controls: Scheduled Drugs/
Drug Schedules, U.S.
Crime and Alcohol
Crime and Drugs
Distilled Spirits Council
Dramshop Liability Laws
Drug Interdiction
Drug Laws, Prosecution of

Drug Laws: Financial
Analysis in Enforcement
Economic Costs of
Alcohol and Drug
Abuse
Exclusionary Rule
Foreign Policy and Drugs,
United States
Legal Regulation of Drugs
and Alcohol
Mandatory Sentencing
New York State Civil
Commitment Program
Paraphernalia, Laws Against
Rockefeller Drug Laws
Tax Laws and Alcohol

JOEL GROW
*Addictive Behaviors Research
Center
University of Washington*
Treatment, Behavioral
Approaches to: Self-
Help and Anonymous
Groups
Treatment, Stages/Phases of:
Aftercare
Treatment, Stages/Phases of:
Stabilization

STEVEN W. GUST
*National Institute on Drug Abuse
Rockville, MD*
Employee Assistance
Programs (EAPs)

MAHLON HALE
*Associate Professor, Department of
Psychiatry
University of Connecticut Health
Center*
Anhedonia

WAYNE HALL
*Professor of Public Health Policy
School of Population Health, The
University of Queensland,
Brisbane, Australia*
Australia

CARL L. HART
Department of Psychology,
Department of Psychiatry
Columbia University
> Risk Factors for Substance
> Use, Abuse, and
> Dependence: Learning

DEBORAH S. HASIN
Professor of Clinical Public
Health, Department of
Epidemiology, Columbia
University
New York State Psychiatric
Institute
> AUDADIS
> Complications: Mental
> Disorders
> Risk Factors for Substance
> Use, Abuse, and
> Dependence: An
> Overview

MARK L. HATZENBUEHLER
Yale University
> Alcohol and AIDS

WANDA HAUSER
Center for Substance Abuse
Research
University of Maryland
> Hookah

DWIGHT B. HEATH
Professor Emeritus of Anthropology
Brown University
> Peru

SARAH H. HEIL
Assistant Research Professor
University of Vermont
> Treatment, Behavioral
> Approaches to:
> Contingency
> Management

SCOTT HENGGELER
Professor of Psychiatry and
Behavioral Sciences

Medical University of South
Carolina
> Treatment, Specialty
> Approaches to:
> Adolescents

VICTOR M. HESSELBROCK
Professor, Department of
Psychiatry
University of Connecticut School of
Medicine, Farmington
> Semi-Structured Assessment
> for the Genetics of
> Alcoholism (SSAGA)

TIMOTHY A. HICKMAN
Lecturer in History, Department
of History
Lancaster University
> Fashion Industry,
> International

STEPHEN T. HIGGINS
Professor, Departments of
Psychiatry and Psychology
University of Vermont
> Treatment, Behavioral
> Approaches to:
> Contingency
> Management

RILEY HINSON
Department of Psychology
University of Western Ontario,
London, Canada
> Conditioned Tolerance

LEO E. HOLLISTER
Professor Emeritus
University of Texas Medical School
at Houston
> Bhang
> Cannabis Sativa
> Ganja
> Hashish
> Hemp
> Tetrahydrocannabinol
> (THC)

MATTHEW O. HOWARD
Frank A. Daniels Distinguished
Professor, School of Social Work
University of North Carolina at
Chapel Hill
> Inhalants: Extent of Use and
> Complications
> Inhalants

SHARON HSIN HSU
Addictive Behaviors Research
Center
University of Washington
> Amotivational Syndrome
> Chinese Americans, Alcohol
> and Drug Use Among
> Processes of Change Model
> Treatment, Behavioral
> Approaches to: Long-
> term versus Brief

ROBERT L. HUBBARD
Research Triangle Institute
Triangle Park, NC
> Drug Abuse Treatment
> Outcome Studies
> (DATOS)

KEITH HUMPHREYS
Professor (Research) of Psychiatry
and Behavioral Sciences and
CHP/PCOR Associate
Stanford University
> Alcoholics Anonymous (AA)

DANA E. HUNT
Principal Scientist
Abt Associates, Inc.
> Arrestee Drug Abuse
> Monitoring (ADAM and
> ADAM II)

RICHARD G. HUNTER
Postdoctoral Fellow
Laboratory of Neuroendocrinology,
Rockefeller University
> Ayahuasca
> Betel Nut
> Club Drugs
> Rohypnol

SERENA IACONO
President, Board of Directors
The Joy Project
  Anorexia Nervosa
  Anorexia
  Bulimia Nervosa

WILLIAM (BILL) G. IACONO
Distinguished McKnight
University Professor, Professor of
Psychology, Psychiatry,
Neuroscience, and Law
University of Minnesota
  Anorexia Nervosa
  Anorexia
  Bulimia Nervosa

TED INABA
Professor Emeritus, Department of
Pharmacology
University of Toronto
  Drug Metabolism

T. RON JACKSON
Affiliate Professor, School of Social
Work
University of Washington, Seattle
  Methadone Maintenance
    Programs

ARTHUR E. JACOBSON
National Institute on Drug Abuse
Rockville, MD
  College on Problems of Drug
    Dependence (CPDD),
    Inc.

FAITH K. JAFFE
Towson, MD
  U.S. Government Agencies:
    Special Action Office for
    Drug Abuse Prevention
    (SAODAP)

JEROME H. JAFFE
Department of Psychiatry,
Division of Alcohol and Drug
Abuse

University of Maryland School of
Medicine, Baltimore
  Ibogaine
  Narcotic Addict
    Rehabilitation Act
    (NARA)
  Propoxyphene
  Secular Organizations for
    Sobriety (SOS)
  Treatment, Specialty
    Approaches to:
    Therapeutic
    Communities
  U.S. Government Agencies:
    Special Action Office for
    Drug Abuse Prevention
    (SAODAP)
  Wikler's Conditioning
    Theory of Drug
    Addiction

WILLIAM JAFFEE
McLean Hospital
Harvard Medical School
  Treatment, Behavioral
    Approaches to: Group
    Therapy

RENE JAHIEL
University of Connecticut Health
Center
  France

JURIS JANAVS
Assistant Professor of Psychiatry,
Depression and Anxiety Disorders
Research Institute
University of South Florida
College of Medicine, Tampa
  Mini International
    Neuropsychiatric
    Interview (MINI)

DAVID H. JERNIGAN
Associate Professor, Department of
Health, Behavior and Society
Johns Hopkins Bloomberg School of
Public Health
  Advertising and the Alcohol
    Industry

JOHN JIGGENS
Queensland University of
Technology
  International Drug Supply
    Systems

CHRIS-ELLYN JOHANSON
Professor and Associate Director,
Substance Abuse Research
Division
Wayne State University, Detroit,
MI
  Polydrug Abuse

BETHANN N. JOHNSON
Department of Pharmacology and
Experimental Therapeutics
Boston University School of
Medicine
  MDMA

HAROLD KALANT
Professor Emeritus, Department of
Pharmacology, University of
Toronto
Research Director Emeritus
(Biobehavioral), Centre for
Addiction and Mental Health,
Toronto, Ontario, Canada
  Addiction: Concepts and
    Definitions
  Physical Dependence

PETER W. KALIVAS
Professor and Chair of
Neurosciences
Medical University of South
Carolina
  Brain Structures and Drugs
  Glutamate

CHARLES KAPLAN
Research Professor and Associate
Dean of Research, Center for
Drug & Social Policy Research
(CDSPR), University of Houston
Scientific Advisor, Intraval
Foundation, Groningen/
Rotterdam, The Netherlands
  Netherlands

RICHARD F. KAPLAN
Professor of Psychiatry and Neurology
Department of Psychiatry, University of Connecticut Health Center
> Complications: Cognition
> Memory, Effects of Drugs on

BHUSHAN K. KAPUR
Department of Laboratory Medicine and Pathobiology University of Toronto
> Drug Testing Methods and Clinical Interpretations of Test Results

STEVEN B. KARCH
Consultant Pathologist and Toxicologist
> Coca/Cocaine, International

HILA KATZ
Assistant Research Scientist New York State Psychiatric Institute
> Complications: Mental Disorders

HELEN KEANE
Senior Lecturer, School of Humanities
Australian National University
> Models of Alcoholism and Drug Abuse
> Rhetoric of Addiction
> Values and Beliefs: Existential Models of Addiction

GEORGE A. KENNA
Assistant Professor, Department of Psychiatry
Brown University
> Blood Alcohol Concentration, Measures of

Blood Alcohol
> Concentration
Breathalyzer
Pharmacodynamics
Pharmacokinetics
> of Alcohol
Pharmacokinetics: General
Pharmacokinetics:
> Implications for Abusable Substances

KATHERINE M. KEYES
Pre-doctoral Fellow, Psychiatric Epidemiology Training Program, Department of Epidemiology, Columbia University New York State Psychiatric Institute
> Epidemiology of Alcohol Use Disorders
> Gender and Complications of Substance Abuse
> Risk Factors for Substance Use, Abuse, and Dependence: Gender

LORI KEYSER-MARCUS
Department of Psychiatry Virginia Commonwealth University
> Caffeine

E. J. KHANTZIAN
Clinical Professor of Psychiatry, Harvard Medical School Cambridge Health Alliance and Tewksbury Hospital
> Risk Factors for Substance Use, Abuse, and Dependence: Psychodynamic Perspective

BEAU KILMER
RAND Drug Policy Research Center
> Seizures of Drugs

GEORGE R. KING
> Risk Factors for Substance Use, Abuse, and Dependence: Drug Effects and Biological Responses

GERNOT KLANTSCHNIG
St. Antony's College, Oxford
> International Control Policies

AUKJE KLUGE
Emory University
> Laudanum

CLIFFORD KNAPP
Department of Pharmacology and Experimental Therapeutics Tufts University School of Medicine, Boston, MA
> Benzodiazepines

GEORGE F. KOOB
Professor and Chair, Committee on the Neurobiology of Addictive Disorders
The Scripps Research Institute
> Reward Pathways and Drugs

PAMELA KORSMEYER
Independent Scholar New Haven, CT
> Epidemics of Drug Abuse in the United States
> Operation Intercept
> Parent Movement, The

THERESE KOSTEN
Associate Professor of Psychiatry Baylor College of Medicine
> Research: Developing Medications to Treat Substance Abuse and Dependence

THOMAS KOSTEN
Jay H. Waggoner Chair and Professor of Psychiatry and Neuroscience

Menninger Department of Psychiatry and Behavioral Sciences, Baylor College of Medicine
  Amantadine
  Treatment, Pharmacological Approaches to: An Overview
  Treatment, Pharmacological Approaches to: Buprenorphine
  Treatment, Pharmacological Approaches to: Serotonin-Uptake Inhibitors
  Treatment, Pharmacological Approaches to: Vaccines
  Withdrawal: Cocaine

HENRY R. KRANZLER
Professor of Psychiatry and Program Director, General Clinical Research Center University of Connecticut School of Medicine
  Semi-Structured Assessment for Drug Dependence and Alcoholism (SSADDA)
  Treatment: An Overview of Drug Abuse/ Dependence

JANINE KREMLING
Department of Criminology University of South Florida
  Prisons and Jails, Drug Treatment in
  Prisons and Jails, Drug Use and HIV/AIDS in Prisons and Jails

MICHAEL J. KUHAR
Chief, Neuroscience Division, and Charles Howard Candler Professor Yerkes National Primate Research Center of Emory University
  Antidote
  Chocolate
  Chromosome
  Gene

  Ginseng
  Norepinephrine
  Nucleus Accumbens
  Poison
  Receptor, Drug
  Theobromine
  Treatment, Pharmacological Approaches to: Antidepressants
  Vitamins

KAROL L. KUMPFER
Professor, Department of Health Promotion and Education University of Utah
  Prevention

PHYLLIS A. LANGTON
Professor Emerita of Sociology George Washington University
  Temperance Movement

STEPHEN E. LANKENAU
Assistant Professor of Research Department of Pediatrics, Keck School of Medicine, University of Southern California
  OxyContin

JULIA LEAR
Research Officer, LSE Health London School of Economics and Political Science
  European Union

JILL LECTKA
  Drug Interaction and the Brain

KELLEY LEE
Reader in Global Health London School of Hygiene and Tropical Medicine
  Tobacco: An International Overview

LORENZO LEGGIO
Brown University, Center for Alcohol and Addiction Studies, Providence, RI

Catholic University of Rome, Institute of Internal Medicine, Rome, Italy
  Treatment, Pharmacological Approaches to: Acamprosate

ANNA LEMBKE
Staff Physician and Senior Research Scientist Department of Psychiatry and Behavioral Sciences, Stanford University
  Alcoholics Anonymous (AA)
  Childhood Behavior and Later Substance Use

KENNETH E. LEONARD
Senior Research Scientist and Research Professor, Research Institute on Addictions and Department of Psychiatry University at Buffalo, The State University of New York
  Intimate Partner Violence and Alcohol/Substance Use

CARL G. LEUKEFELD
Professor, Bell Chair in Alcohol and Addictions University of Kentucky
  Civil Commitment

ARON H. LICHTMAN
Department of Pharmacology and Toxicology Virginia Commonwealth University
  Cannabinoids

HOWARD A. LIDDLE
Professor, Department of Epidemiology and Public Health and Department of Psychology; Director, Center for Treatment Research on Adolescent Drug Abuse

University of Miami Miller School
of Medicine
    Families and Drug Use

ANDREW K. LITTLEFIELD
*Alcohol, Health, and Behavior
Laboratory*
University of Missouri, Columbia
    Codependence
    Risk Factors for Substance
        Use, Abuse, and
        Dependence: Personality

DIANE E. LOGAN
*Graduate Research Assistant,
Clinical Psychology*
University of Washington
    Abstinence Violation Effect
        (AVE)
    Relapse
    Research: Clinical Research
    Treatment, Stages/Phases of:
        Relapse Prevention

R. LOOSE
Dublin Business School of Arts
    Freud and Cocaine

MARSHA F. LOPEZ
*Division of Epidemiology, Services,
and Prevention Research*
*National Institute on Drug Abuse /
NIH*
    Epidemiology of Drug Abuse

LIN LU
*Professor, National Institute on
Drug Dependence*
Peking University, China
    Treatment, Specialty
        Approaches to:
        Acupuncture

SUSAN E. LUCZAK
*University of Southern California,
Los Angeles*
    Jews and Alcohol

ARNOLD M. LUDWIG
Adjunct Professor of Psychiatry
Brown University, Providence, RI
    Creativity and Drugs

SCOTT E. LUKAS
Harvard Medical School
McLean Hospital, Belmont, MA
    Amobarbital
    Barbiturates
    Beers and Brews
    Chloral Hydrate
    Chlordiazepoxide
    Distillation
    Distilled Spirits, Types of
    Ethchlorvynol
    Ethinamate
    Fermentation
    Glutethimide
    Meprobamate
    Methanol
    Methaqualone
    Moonshine
    Phenobarbital
    Rubbing Alcohol
    Secobarbital
    Sedative
    Sedative-Hypnotic
    Sleeping Pills
    Still

XINGGUANG LUO
*Assistant Professor, Department of
Psychiatry, Yale University School
of Medicine*
    Risk Factors for Substance
        Use, Abuse, and
        Dependence: Genetic
        Factors

MICHAEL T. LYNSKEY
Department of Psychiatry
*Washington University School of
Medicine*
    Risk Factors for Substance
        Use, Abuse, and
        Dependence: Sexual and
        Physical Abuse

DAVID MACDONALD
*International Drug Demand
Reduction Consultant*
    Afghanistan

LISA MACHOTKA
Research Assistant
University of Washington
    Treatment, Stages/Phases of:
        Relapse Prevention

DORIS LAYTON MacKENZIE
*Professor, Department of
Criminology and Criminal
Justice, University of Maryland*
    Shock Incarceration and
        Boot-Camp Prisons

JAMES F. MADDUX
*Retired from Department of
Psychiatry*
*University of Texas Health Science
Center, San Antonio*
    Narcotic Addict Rehabilitation
        Act (NARA)
    U.S. Government Agencies:
        U.S. Public Health
        Service Hospitals

G. ALAN MARLATT
*Director, Addictive Behaviors
Research Center*
*Professor, Psychology, University of
Washington*
    Abstinence Violation Effect
        (AVE)
    Amotivational Syndrome
    Chinese Americans, Alcohol
        and Drug Use Among
    Processes of Change Model
    Relapse
    Treatment, Behavioral
        Approaches to: Cognitive
        Therapy
    Treatment, Behavioral
        Approaches to: Long-
        term versus Brief
    Treatment, Behavioral
        Approaches to: Self-Help
        and Anonymous Groups

Treatment, Stages/Phases of:
Aftercare
Treatment, Stages/Phases of:
Stabilization

DOUGLAS B. MARLOWE
Senior Scientist
Treatment Research Institute,
University of Pennsylvania
Criminal Justice System,
Treatment in the

GRAEME F. MASON
Associate Professor of Diagnostic
Radiology and Psychiatry,
Division of Bioimaging Sciences,
Magnetic Resonance Research
Center
Yale University, School of
Medicine
Imaging Techniques:
Visualizing the Living
Brain

SHAHRZAD MAVANDADI
Research Investigator, Mental
Illness Research, Education, and
Clinical Center
Philadelphia Veterans Affairs
Medical Center
Aging, Drugs, and Alcohol

MATTHEW MAY
Independent Scholar
American Society of
Addiction Medicine
(ASAM)
Cola/Cola Drinks
Mothers Against Drunk
Driving (MADD)

LINDA MAYES
Special Advisor to the Dean, Yale
School of Medicine
Arnold Gesell Professor, Child
Psychiatry, Pediatrics, and
Psychology, Yale Child Study
Center

Pregnancy and Drug
Dependence

MICHAEL R. McCART
Assistant Professor of Psychiatry
and Behavioral Sciences
Medical University of South
Carolina
Treatment, Specialty
Approaches to:
Adolescents

JAMES T. McDONOUGH
Editor, Lexicographer, Researcher
Ardmore, PA
Abuse Liability of
Therapeutic Drugs:
Testing in Animals
Jimsonweed
Myths About Addiction and
Its Treatment

A. THOMAS McLELLAN
Director, Treatment Research
Institute
Professor, Department of
Psychiatry, University of
Pennsylvania
Addiction Severity Index
(ASI)

HAYDEN McROBBIE
School of Public Health and
Psychosocial Studies
Auckland University of
Technology, New Zealand
Nicotine Delivery Systems for
Smoking Cessation

LAURA A. MEIS
VA Medical Center
Minneapolis, MN
Treatment, Behavioral
Approaches to: Couples
and Family Therapy

CATHARINE MENNES
Washington University School of
Medicine

St. Louis, MO
Computerized Diagnostic
Interview Schedule for
DSM-IV (C DIS-IV)

DAVID METZGER
Department of Psychiatry
University of Pennsylvania,
Philadelphia
HIV Risk Assessment Battery
(RAB)

KATHRYN MEYER
Wright State University
Japan

STEPHEN MICHAEL
Director, Arizona Smokers'
Helpline
University of Arizona Zuckerman
College of Public Health
Tobacco: A History of
Tobacco
Tobacco: Tobacco Industry

PAMELA V. MICHAELS
Forensic Psychologist, Lerner &
Lerner (Lerner Media, Lerner
Communications)
Abuse Liability of Drugs:
Testing in Humans
Alcoholism: Origin of the
Term
Automation of Reports and
Consolidated Orders
System (ARCOS)
Fetus, Effects of Drugs on the
Funding and Service Delivery
of Treatment
National Council on
Alcoholism and Drug
Dependence (NCADD)
National Forensic Laboratory
Information System
(NFLIS)
Professional Credentialing
Public Intoxication
Racial Profiling
Remove Intoxicated Drivers
(RID-USA, Inc.)

Slang Terms in U.S. Drug
   Cultures
Sleep, Dreaming, and Drugs
SMART Recovery and
   Rational Recovery
Students Against Destructive
   Decisions (SADD)
Tolerance and Physical
   Dependence
Treatment Outcome
   Prospective Study
   (TOPS)
U.S. Government Agencies:
   Center for Substance
   Abuse Prevention (CSAP)
U.S. Government Agencies:
   Center for Substance
   Abuse Treatment
   (CSAT)
U.S. Government Agencies:
   National Institute on
   Alcohol Abuse and
   Alcoholism (NIAAA)
U.S. Government Agencies:
   Office of National Drug
   Control Policy
U.S. Government Agencies:
   Substance Abuse and
   Mental Health Services
   Administration
   (SAMHSA)
U.S. Government Agencies:
   U.S. Customs and
   Border Protection (CBP)
U.S. Government: Agencies
   Supporting Substance
   Abuse Prevention and
   Treatment
U.S. Government: Agencies
   Supporting Substance
   Abuse Research
Zero Tolerance

KLAUS A. MICZEK
Moses Hunt Professor of Psychology,
Psychiatry, Pharmacology and
Neuroscience
Tufts University
   Aggression and Drugs:
      Research Issues

JAMES H. MILLS
Vice-Dean (Research), Faculty of
Law, Arts and Social Sciences
University of Strathclyde
   Cannabis, International
      Overview

F. GERARD MOELLER
Department of Psychiatry and
Behavioral Sciences
University of Texas Health Science
Center at Houston
   Cocaine

MARK MOFFETT
Postdoctoral Fellow, Yerkes National
Primate Research Center
Emory University
   Dopamine

ALEX MOLD
Centre for History in Public
Health, Department of Public
Health and Policy
London School of Hygiene and
Tropical Medicine
   Britain

TIMOTHY H. MORAN
Department of Psychiatry
Johns Hopkins University,
Baltimore, MD
   Anorectic

HERBERT MOSKOWITZ
Professor Emeritus, California
State University, Los Angeles
Research Psychologist, University
of California, Los Angeles
   Driving, Alcohol, and Drugs

ELIAS A. MOSSIALOS
Research Director, European
Observatory on Health Care
Systems
Director, LSE Health, The London
School of Economics and Political
Science
   European Union

PETER L. MYERS
International Coalition for
Addiction Studies Education
   Cults and Drug Use

ETHAN NADELMANN
Founder and Executive Director
Drug Policy Alliance
   Drug Policy Alliance (DPA)

HELEN NAVALINE
Center for Studies of Addiction
University of Pennsylvania,
Philadelphia
   HIV Risk Assessment Battery
      (RAB)

DARRYL NEILL
Professor of Psychology
Emory University, Atlanta, GA
   Research, Animal Model: An
      Overview

ERIC J. NESTLER
Nash Family Professor of
Neuroscience, Psychiatry, and
Pharmacology
Mount Sinai School of Medicine
   Gene Regulation: Drugs

JENNA NIENHUIS
The University of Michigan
   Treatment: Outpatient versus
      Inpatient Setting

PRASHANT NIKAM
Product Strategy Manager
GlaxoSmithKline R&D,
Collegeville, PA
   Advertising and the
      Pharmaceutical Industry

JOSEPH NOWINSKI
Supervising Psychologist,
Correctional Managed Health
Care Division
University of Connecticut Health
Center

Treatment, Behavioral
Approaches to: Twelve-
Step and Disease Model
Approaches

JOHN I. NURNBERGER
*Joyce and Iver Small Professor of
Psychiatry, Institute of Psychiatric
Research
Department of Psychiatry,
Indiana University School of
Medicine, Indianapolis*
Diagnostic Interview for
Genetic Studies (DIGS)

ISIDORE S. OBOT
*Professor, Department of Psychology
University of Uyo, Nigeria*
Nigeria

TIMOTHY J. O'FARRELL
*Families and Addiction Program
Harvard Medical School
Department of Psychiatry at the
VA Boston Healthcare System,
Brockton, MA*
Treatment, Behavioral
Approaches to: Couples
and Family Therapy

MAYUMI OKUDA
*New York State Psychiatric
Institute*
Gambling Addiction:
Epidemiology

ANN O'LEARY
*Senior Behavioral Scientist
Centers for Disease Control and
Prevention*
Alcohol and AIDS

GRACE O'LEARY
Freebasing

JASON A. OLIVER
*University of South Florida
The Moffitt Cancer Center*
Withdrawal: Nicotine
(Tobacco)

SARAH S. OLSON
*Department of Psychiatry
University of California, San
Francisco*
Treatment, Specialty
Approaches to: Older
Adults

PATRICK M. O'MALLEY
*Institute for Social Research
The University of Michigan*
Monitoring the Future

STEPHANIE S. O'MALLEY
*Professor of Psychiatry
Yale University School of Medicine*
Tobacco: Smoking Cessation
and Weight Gain

CAROLYN YORK O'NEIL
*Department of Psychiatry
Indiana University School of
Medicine, Indianapolis*
Diagnostic Interview for
Genetic Studies (DIGS)

DAVID OSLIN
*Associate Professor of Psychiatry
University of Pennsylvania
Geriatric and Addiction Psychiatry
The Philadelphia VA Medical
Center*
Treatment, Pharmacological
Approaches to:
Naltrexone

ESA ÖSTERBERG
*Alcohol and Drug Research
National Research and
Development Centre for Welfare
and Health, Helsinki, Finland*
Nordic Countries (Denmark,
Finland, Iceland, Norway
and Sweden)

MARK PARASCANDOLA
*Epidemiologist
National Cancer Institute*
Tobacco: Smokeless

KAREN PARKER
Anxiety
Hallucination
Overdose, Drug (OD)
Over-the-Counter (OTC)
Medication
Schizophrenia

THEODORE V. PARRAN
*Associate Clinical Professor of
Medicine
Case Western Reserve University
School of Medicine, Cleveland, OH*
Multidoctoring

GAVRIL W. PASTERNAK
*Anne Burnett Tandy Chair in
Neurology and Laboratory Head,
Program of Molecular
Pharmacology and Chemistry
Memorial Sloan-Kettering Cancer
Center*
Analgesic
Codeine
Dihydromorphine
Heroin
Hydromorphone
L-Alpha-Acetylmethadol
(LAAM)
Meperidine
Morphine
MPTP
Naloxone
Naltrexone
Narcotic
Opiates/Opioids
Oxycodone
Oxymorphone
Papaver Somniferum
Paregoric
Treatment, Pharmacological
Approaches to:
Methadone

DEV S. PATHAK
*Affiliate Professor, College of
Public Health, University of South
Florida*

Professor Emeritus, The Ohio State University
   Advertising and the
      Pharmaceutical Industry

JOHN E. PEACHEY
   Calcium Carbimide

ROBERT N. PECHNICK
Associate Director, Psychiatry Research
Cedars-Sinai Medical Center, Los Angeles
   Dimethyltryptamine (DMT)
   DOM
   Hallucinogenic Plants
   Lysergic Acid Diethylamide
      (LSD) and Psychedelics
   Mescaline
   Morning Glory Seeds
   Nutmeg
   Peyote
   Psilocybin

BRIAN F. PERRON
Assistant Professor, School of Social Work
The University of Michigan
   Inhalants: Extent of Use and
      Complications
   Inhalants
   Movies
   Treatment: Outpatient versus
      Inpatient Setting

ROGER H. PETERS
Chair and Professor, Department of Mental Health Law and Policy
Louis de la Parte Florida Mental Health Institute, University of South Florida, Tampa
   Prisons and Jails, Drug
      Treatment in
   Prisons and Jails, Drug Use
      and HIV/AIDS in
      Prisons and Jails

ANTHONY G. PHILLIPS
Department of Psychology

University of British Columbia, Vancouver, Canada
   Research: Motivation

SVETLANA POPOVA
Centre for Addiction and Mental Health, Toronto, Canada
   Cancer, Drugs, and Alcohol

MARC N. POTENZA
Associate Professor of Psychiatry and Child Study Center
Yale University School of Medicine
   Compulsions
   Gambling Addiction:
      Assessment
   Gambling
   Impulsivity and Addiction

KENZIE L. PRESTON
Johns Hopkins Bayview Medical Center
Baltimore, MD
   Research: Measuring Effects
      of Drugs on Mood

RUMI KATO PRICE
Associate Professor and Principal, Innovative Psychiatric Research and Methods (IPRAM)
Department of Psychiatry, Washington University, St. Louis, MO
   Hair Analysis as a Test for
      Drug Use
   Risk Factors for Substance
      Use, Abuse, and
      Dependence: Race/
      Ethnicity
   Vietnam Era Study (VES),
      Washington University

PETR PROTIVA
Division of Gastroenterology and Hepatology
University of Connecticut Health Center
   Hepatitis C Infection

MARIE RAGGHIANTI
Center for Substance Abuse Research
University of Maryland
   Coerced Treatment for
      Substance Offenders

NICOLAS RASMUSSEN
Associate Professor, School of History and Philosophy
University of New South Wales
   Amphetamine Epidemics,
      International

JÜRGEN REHM
Professor and Chair, Addiction Policy, Dalla Lana School of Public Health, University of Toronto, Canada
Senior Scientist and Co-Head, Section Public Health and Regulatory Policies, Centre for Addiction and Mental Health, Toronto
   Cancer, Drugs, and Alcohol

PETER REUTER
School of Public Policy and Department of Criminology
University of Maryland, College Park
   Street Value

ELIZABETH K. REYNOLDS
Center for Addictions, Personality, and Emotion Research
University of Maryland, College Park
   Pregnancy and Drug
      Dependence

SOO HYUN RHEE
Assistant Professor
Department of Psychology, University of Colorado, Boulder
   Conduct Disorder and Drug
      Use

LEE N. ROBINS
Department of Psychiatry
Washington University School of
Medicine, St. Louis, MO
  Vietnam War: Drug Use in
    U.S. Military

ROGER A. ROFFMAN
Professor, School of Social Work,
University of Washington
Director, Innovative Programs
Research Group, University of
Washington
  Marijuana (Cannabis)

RANDALL ROGERS
Addiction Treatment Program
Team Leader
Harry S. Truman Memorial
Veterans' Hospital, Columbia,
Missouri
  Treatment, Behavioral
    Approaches to:
    Contingency
    Management

MYROSLAVA ROMACH
Associate Professor of Psychiatry
Faculty of Medicine, University of
Toronto
  Anxiety
  Hallucination
  Overdose, Drug (OD)
  Over-the-Counter (OTC)
    Medication
  Schizophrenia

PIA ROSENQVIST
Nordic Centre for Alcohol and
Drug Research
Helsinki, Finland
  Nordic Countries (Denmark,
    Finland, Iceland, Norway
    and Sweden)

INGEBORG ROSSOW
Norwegian Institute for Alcohol
and Drug Research

Prevention of Alcohol
    Related Harm: The Total
    Consumption Model

BELINDA M. ROWLAND
Voorheesville, NY
  Chronic Pain

IHSAN M. SALLOUM
Professor of Psychiatry
Department of Psychiatry and
Behavioral Sciences, University of
Miami Miller School of Medicine
  African Americans, Ethnic
    and Cultural Factors
    Relevant to Treatment
    for
  Treatment, Pharmacological
    Approaches to:
    Anticonvulsants
  Treatment: An Overview of
    Alcohol Abuse/
    Dependence

SHARON SAMET
Research Scientist
New York State Psychiatric
Institute
  Depression
  Personality Disorders
  PRISM

BILL SANDERS
Associate Professor, School of
Criminal Justice and
Criminalistics
California State University, Los
Angeles
  Gangs and Drugs
  Hallucinogens
  Rave

DEREK D. SATRE
Assistant Adjunct Professor,
Department of Psychiatry,
University of California, San
Francisco
Kaiser Division of Research,
Oakland, CA

Treatment, Specialty
    Approaches to: Older
    Adults

HARRY SHAPIRO
Director of Communications and
Information
DrugScope, London
  Music

SHOSHANA H. SHEA
Veterans Administration San
Diego Healthcare System
University of California, San
Diego
  Jews and Alcohol

KENNETH J. SHER
University of Missouri, Columbia
  Codependence
  Risk Factors for Substance
    Use, Abuse, and
    Dependence: Personality

LEO SHER
Associate Clinical Professor of
Psychiatry, Columbia University
College of Physicians & Surgeons
Research Psychiatrist, Division of
Molecular Imaging and
Neuropathology, New York State
Psychiatric Institute
  Suicide and Substance Abuse

KENNETH SILVERMAN
Department of Psychiatry and
Behavioral Sciences
Johns Hopkins Bayview Medical
Center
  Coffee
  Tea

D. DWAYNE SIMPSON
S. B. Sells Distinguished Professor
of Psychology and Addiction
Research
Director, Institute of Behavioral
Research, Texas Christian
University

Drug Abuse Reporting
Program (DARP)
Drug Abuse Treatment
Outcome Studies
(DATOS)

LYNN TWAROG SINGER
*Professor of Pediatrics, General
Medical Sciences, and Psychology
Case Western Reserve University*
Alcohol- and Drug-Exposed
Infants

RANA A. SINGH
*Department of Neurology
Baylor College of Medicine*
Treatment, Pharmacological
Approaches to: Vaccines

RAJITA SINHA
*Professor of Psychiatry & Director
Yale Stress Center*
Risk Factors for Substance
Use, Abuse, and
Dependence: Stress

HARVEY SKINNER
*Dean, Faculty of Health
York University, Toronto*
Drug Abuse Screening Test
(DAST)

GREGORY E. SKIPPER
*Fellow, American Society of
Addiction Medicine
Medical Association of the State of
Alabama*
Physicians and Medical
Workers, Substance
Abuse Among

REG SMART
*Centre for Addiction and Mental
Health, Toronto*
Canada
Crack

JAMES E. SMITH
*Department of Physiology and
Pharmacology*

*Wake Forest University, Winston-
Salem, NC*
Limbic System
Nucleus Accumbens

ROBERT J. SOKOL
*Director, C.S. Mott Center for
Human Growth and Development
Distinguished Professor of
Obstetrics and Gynecology, Wayne
State University School of
Medicine*
Fetal Alcohol Syndrome
T-ACE

SUSAN L. SPEAKER
*Historian, Digital Manuscripts
Program
History of Medicine Division,
National Library of Medicine*
Addictive Personality and
Psychological Tests
Media

DAVID SPIEGEL
*Department of Psychiatry and
Behavioral Science
Stanford University School of
Medicine, Stanford, CA*
Treatment, Specialty
Approaches to: Hypnosis

STEFANIE A. STERN
RAND Corporation
Treatment, Behavioral
Approaches to:
Motivational and Brief

GERSON STERNSTEIN
*Medical Director, Paragon
Behavioral Health
Kensington, Connecticut*
Sexuality and Substance Abuse

VERNER STILLNER
*Emeritus, Department of
Psychiatry
University of Kentucky, Lexington*
Dover's Powder

MAXINE STITZER
*Professor, Psychiatry and
Behavioral Sciences
Johns Hopkins Bayview Medical
Center, Baltimore, MD*
Reinforcement

TIMOTHY R. STOCKWELL
*Centre for Addictions Research of
BC, University of Victoria
British Columbia, Canada*
Treatment, Stages/Phases of:
Non-Medical
Detoxification

DACE SVIKIS
*Virginia Commonwealth
University*
Caffeine

BETTY TAI
*Director, Center for the Clinical
Trials Network
National Institute on Drug
Abuse, NIH/DHHS*
Clinical Trials Network

KALOYAN TANEV
*Department of Psychiatry
University of Connecticut Health
Center*
Delirium

RALPH E. TARTER
*Professor of Pharmaceutical
Sciences, Psychiatry, and Psychology
University of Pittsburgh School of
Pharmacy*
Adolescents and Drug Use
Attention Deficit
Hyperactivity Disorder
Coping and Drug Use

WINIFRED TATE
*Assistant Professor of Anthropology
Colby College*
Colombia

W. KENNETH THOMPSON
Bureau of International Narcotics Matters
Chevy Chase, MD
> Foreign Policy and Drugs, United States

SIMON THORNLEY
Public Health Medicine Registrar
Auckland District Health Board, New Zealand
> Nicotine Delivery Systems for Smoking Cessation

CHRISTINE TIMKO
Research Career Scientist
Department of Veterans Affairs and Stanford University
> Narcotics Anonymous (NA)

ANTHONY C. TOMMASELLO
Associate Professor and Director
University of Maryland School of Pharmacy, Office of Substance Abuse Studies
> Opioid Dependence: Course of the Disorder Over Time

J. SCOTT TONIGAN
Research Professor, Department of Psychology
University of New Mexico
> Al-Anon

MICHAEL TONRY
University of Minnesota Law School
> Rockefeller Drug Laws

LORAINE TOWNSEND
Health Systems Research Unit
Medical Research Council, South Africa
> Dropouts and Substance Use

SARAH W. TRACY
McClendon Honors College
University of Oklahoma

Alcohol: History of Drinking in the United States
Prohibition of Alcohol

HARRISON M. TRICE
Formerly Professor Emeritus
Cornell University, Ithaca, NY
> Alateen

GEORGE R. UHL
Johns Hopkins Bayview Medical Center, Baltimore, MD
> Neuroleptic
> Receptor: NMDA (N-Methyl D-Aspartic Acid)

THOMAS C. VARY
Distinguished Professor
Penn State University College of Medicine, Hershey, PA
> Complications:
> Cardiovascular System (Alcohol and Cocaine)

ALEXANDER C. WAGENAAR
Professor, Department of Epidemiology and Health Policy Research
College of Medicine & Institute for Child Health Policy, University of Florida
> Minimum Drinking Age Laws

TAMARA L. WALL
Professor, Department of Psychiatry
University of California, San Diego
> Jews and Alcohol

JOHN M. WALLACE
Institute for Social Research
University of Michigan, Ann Arbor
> Religion and Drug Use

SHARON L. WALSH
Francis Scott Key Medical Center

Baltimore, MD
> Research: Measuring Effects of Drugs on Mood

GENE-JACK WANG
Senior Medical Scientist & Chair
Medical Department, Brookhaven National Laboratory
> Obesity
> Overeating and Other Excessive Behaviors

RONALD ROSS WATSON
Professor, University of Arizona
Division of Health Promotion Sciences, Mel and Enid Zuckerman College of Public Health, and School of Medicine, Arizona Health Sciences Center
> Complications: Endocrine and Reproductive Systems
> Complications: Immunologic
> Tobacco: A History of Tobacco
> Tobacco: Tobacco Industry

DAVID WEINSHENKER
Associate Professor, Department of Human Genetics
Emory University
> Clone, Cloning
> Treatment, Pharmacological Approaches to: Clonidine

LISA WEISS
Epidemiologist, Department of Epidemiology
Mailman School of Public Health, Columbia University
> Prescription Drug Abuse

ROGER WEISS
Professor of Psychiatry, Harvard Medical School
Clinical Director, Alcohol and Drug Abuse Treatment Program, McLean Hospital
> Freebasing

Treatment, Behavioral
Approaches to: Group
Therapy

JOHN WELSHMAN
History Department
Lancaster University
Britain: Tobacco Use and
Policy

HARRY K. WEXLER
National Development and
Research Institutes
New York, NY
New York State Civil
Commitment Program

MARNEY A. WHITE
Assistant Professor of Psychiatry
Yale University School of
Medicine, New Haven, CT
Tobacco: Smoking Cessation
and Weight Gain

DEAN WHITTINGTON
Birkbeck College
London
Bolivia
Harrison Narcotics Act of
1914
Middle East
Terrorism and Drugs
World Health Organization
Expert Committee on
Drug Dependence

CATHY SPATZ WIDOM
Psychology Department
John Jay College, City University
of New York
Child Abuse and Drugs

RICHARD L. WILLIAMS
U.S. Government Agencies:
Bureau of Narcotics and
Dangerous Drugs
(BNDD)
U.S. Government Agencies:
Office of Drug Abuse

Law Enforcement
(ODALE)
U.S. Government Agencies:
Office of Drug Abuse
Policy

WENDOL A. WILLIAMS
Assistant Professor of Psychiatry
Yale University School of Medicine
Gambling

KEN C. WINTERS
Professor, Department of
Psychiatry
University of Minnesota,
Minneapolis
Treatment, Behavioral
Approaches to:
Minnesota Model

FRIEDNER D. WITTMAN
Project Director, Prevention by
Design
Alcohol- and Drug-Free
Housing

GEORGE WOODY
University of Pennsylvania,
Philadelphia
HIV Risk Assessment Battery
(RAB)

WILLIAM WOOLVERTON
Professor and Associate Chairman
for Research, Department of
Psychiatry and Human Behavior
The University of Mississippi
Medical Center
Abuse Liability of
Therapeutic Drugs:
Testing in Animals

BRYAN YAMAMOTO
Department of Pharmacology and
Experimental Therapeutics
Boston University School of
Medicine
MDMA

JAMES P. ZACNY
Professor, Department of
Anesthesia and Critical Care
The University of Chicago
Pain, Drugs Used for

ROBERT ZACZEK
Group Director, Neuroscience
Biology
Bristol-Myers Squibb
Pharmaceutical Research
Institute
Fly Agaric
Jimsonweed
Kava
Scopolamine and Atropine

LEAH R. ZINDEL
Registered Pharmacist
Alcohol: Chemistry and
Pharmacology
Alcohol: Psychological
Consequences of
Chronic Abuse
Allergies to Alcohol and
Drugs
Antagonists of Alcohol and
Drugs
Barbiturates: Complications
Benzodiazepines:
Complications
Cocaethylene: Immunologic,
Hepatic, and Cardiac
Effects
Complications: Liver
(Clinical)
Complications: Liver
(Metabolic)
Complications: Medical and
Behavioral Toxicity
Overview
Complications: Nutritional
Complications: Route of
Administration
Jellinek Memorial Fund
Research: Aims, Description,
and Goals
Sedatives: Adverse
Consequences of
Chronic Use

ABSTINENCE VIOLATION EFFECT (AVE).

The abstinence violation effect (AVE) describes an individual's affective and cognitive reaction following a lapse, or initial return to an undesired behavior. When an individual makes a commitment to abstain from or moderate a specific behavior (for example, substance use, eating, or sexual behaviors) and then re-engages in that behavior, the emotional response and cognitive attributions may mediate the potential for a full relapse, or return to the original pattern. The AVE refers to both the affective responses (pleasure, guilt) as well as the cognitive judgments of locus and controllability, which in turn may affect the emotional response. The AVE surfaces primarily when the initial affective response is not pleasant and when the cognitive appraisals support stable, internal traits such as lack of willpower. Whereas any lapse may increase the chance of relapse, lapses mediated by the AVE have an increased probability to lead to full relapse.

In relapse prevention (RP), the goal is to redirect attention and attribution from the internal locus and uncontrollability of the AVE to more external or situational factors that can be anticipated and managed. Essentially, cognitive restructuring may be used to shift attribution from those stable, internal traits to situational or temporary states. RP focuses on identifying high-risk situations, defining alternative coping skills, and altering outcome expectancies. These strategies, combined with more general techniques of stimulus-control and urge-management, reduce the likelihood of a lapse leading to a full relapse. Although the definitions and mechanisms may vary, researchers have found empirical support for the AVE in various behaviors, including addiction to alcohol and drugs, eating disorders, and sexual offenses.

See also **Relapse; Treatment: A History of Treatment in the United States.**

BIBLIOGRAPHY

Curry, S., Marlatt, G. A., & Gordon, J. R. (1987). Abstinence violation effect: Validation of an attributional construct with smoking cessation. *Journal of Consulting and Clinical Psychology, 55,* 145–149.

Hudson, S. M., Ward, T., & Marshall, W. L. (1992). The abstinence violation effect in sex offenders: A reformulation. *Behaviour Research and Therapy, 30,* 435–441.

Larimer, M. E., Palmer, R. S., & Marlatt, G. A. (1999). Relapse prevention: An overview of Marlatt's cognitive-behavioral model. *Alcohol Research & Health, 23,* 151–160.

Marlatt, G. A., & Gordon, J. R. (1985). *Relapse prevention: Maintenance strategies in the treatment of addictive behaviors.* New York: Guilford Press.

Shiffman, S. Hickcox, M., Paty, J. A., Gnys, M., Kassel, J. D., & Richards, T. J. (1997). The abstinence violation effect following smoking lapses and temptations. *Cognitive Therapy and Research, 21,* 497–523.

Stephens, R. S., Curtin, L., Simpson, E. E., & Roffman, R. A. (1994). Testing the abstinence violation effect construct with marijuana cessation. *Addictive Behaviors, 19,* 23–32.

Wheeler, J. G., George, W. H., & Marlatt, G. A. (2006). Relapse prevention for sexual offenders: Considerations for the "Abstinence Violation Effect." *Sexual Abuse: Journal of Research and Treatment, 18,* 233–248.

DIANE E. LOGAN
G. ALAN MARLATT

ABUSE LIABILITY OF DRUGS: TESTING IN HUMANS.

There is virtually no drug used to treat illness that does not also pose certain risks. One such risk, generally limited to drugs that have actions on the central nervous system, is that the drug will be misused or abused because of these effects. Drugs such as these are said to have abuse potential or abuse liability. If the drugs have an important therapeutic use that is believed to outweigh the abuse liability, they will probably be made available, but they will be subject to certain legal controls under various federal and state laws. Between the 1960s and the early 2000s, a number of methods were developed to test new drugs to determine their abuse liability, so that both the public and the medical profession could be warned about the need for appropriate caution when using certain drugs. These methods involve preclinical testing in animals and clinical testing in humans.

There are myriad reasons that testing with humans is useful and necessary in the development of safer and more effective pharmacological agents. When research on laboratory animals demonstrates some degree of abuse liability for a specific drug, it must be validated with human research studies. Doing so reduces the likelihood of error in assessing potential risks. Moreover, self-reported changes associated with the subjective effects of medicinal drugs can be more readily evaluated in the humans for whom they were developed. Human clinical studies are also important in determining appropriate dose levels and dosage forms to ensure safety and efficacy while minimizing unwanted side effects. Finally, comprehensive and effective testing with humans helps to determine how best to reduce the availability of drugs that are likely to be abused to those who are likely to misuse them and to provide for the legitimate medical and scientific use of such pharmacological agents.

HUMAN VOLUNTEER SELECTION

One important factor in drug abuse liability testing with humans is the manner in which the volunteer subjects are chosen to participate in the assessment procedures. In most studies, the human volunteer subjects have some experience with drug use, but wide variations exist in the nature and extent of their drug use and abuse. Some studies, for example, use students and other volunteers whose misuse and abuse of drugs has been mostly recreational; other studies involve people with histories of more intensive drug use and abuse over extended periods. Also, the settings in which the tests are conducted vary widely, from residential laboratory environments, where the subjects live for several days or weeks at a time, to laboratories, where the subjects do not remain in residence but continue their daily routine after drug ingestion. Variations also occur in the age of the subjects tested and the time of day that the drug is administered. Often subjects have been selected for specific human drug-abuse-liability tests on the basis of some special features (e.g., anxiety levels, level of alcohol consumption) to determine the extent to which such factors influence the outcome of the tests.

Convincing evidence exists that many of these factors—particularly the subject's prior experience using drugs or alcohol—play an important role in the assessment of abuse liability. The obvious value in using subjects with prior exposure to the drug in question lies in the fact that these individuals are similar to those most likely to misuse drugs with abuse liability—for example, drug abusers who help determine whether a new drug has a greater or lesser chance for abuse than the one they already know. It is also important to carry out abuse liability testing with people who, for example, do not usually abuse drugs but are light social drinkers, to assess the likelihood of abuse (and potential interactions with alcohol) of certain generally available medications, such as sleeping pills or appetite suppressants.

DRUG COMBINATIONS

The prediction of a drug's abuse liability, based on a wide variety of testing procedures with humans, is further complicated by the fact that drugs of abuse are often used in combination with other pharmacological agents. This situation creates some very difficult challenges for the testing of abuse liability because of the large number of possible drug combinations that need to be tested and their unknown, potentially toxic, effects. While it has long been known that drug abusers use drugs simultaneously, such as cocaine and heroin or marijuana and alcohol, few testing procedures have been developed to assess their interactions. Even more puzzling is the fact that some drugs with opposite effects (e.g.,stimulants such as amphetamines and depressants such as barbiturates) are known to be used simultaneously by polydrug abusers (people who abuse more than one drug at a time), suggesting that unique subjective effects may be important factors in such abuse patterns.

PRINCIPLES OF ABUSE LIABILITY TESTING

Based on extensive research undertaken between about 1970 and the early 2000s, some important general principles governing abuse liability testing with humans were established. First, a meaningful assessment requires that the test drug be compared with a drug of known abuse liability to provide a standard for evaluation. Second, the assessment procedure must involve the indicated comparison over a range of doses of both the test drug and the standard drug of abuse. This principle permits both a quantitative and a qualitative comparison of the drugs, while guarding against the possibility of overlooking some unique high- or low-dose effects. Third, the testing procedures should include measures of drug effects in addition to those found in the laboratory, which directly predict the likelihood of abuse. With these additional measures, it is often possible to obtain reliable estimates of abuse liability by comparing test drugs with a drug of abuse across a range of effects as a standard for evaluation. Fourth, confidence in conclusions regarding the abuse liability of a drug can be enhanced by utilizing a range of measures and experimental procedures. This is because the present level of knowledge in this area does not permit a firm determination of the best or most valid predictor of the likelihood of abuse. Finally, a population of test subjects with a history of drug use appears to be the most appropriate selection for predicting the likelihood of abuse of a new test drug, since this is the population who might use such a drug in that way.

DEVELOPMENT OF ABUSE LIABILITY TESTING PROCEDURES

Since the mid-nineteenth century, literary accounts of the use and misuse of opium, marijuana, and cocaine, among other substances, have emphasized their mood-altering effects and their potential for abuse. Only in more modern times, however, have systematic methods for measuring such subjective effects been refined through the use of standardized questionnaires. When volunteers who are experienced drug users complete questionnaires after they have taken a drug, their answers to the subjective-effects questions—how they feel, their likes and dislikes—readily distinguish between the various drugs and doses, as well as between the presence of the drug or its absence (i.e., placebo).

This basic subjective-effects methodology has been further refined by using a training procedure to ensure that the human volunteer can differentiate a given drug (e.g., morphine) from a placebo (i.e., non-drug). New drugs are then tested to evaluate their similarity to the trained reference drug of abuse. This behavioral drug discrimination method permits the volunteer to compare a wide range of subjective and objective effects of abused drugs with those of new drugs. These procedures have proven to be highly reliable and, therefore, very useful in identifying drugs with potential abuse liability.

Among the most important factors in assessing abuse liability is the determination of whether humans will take the drug when it is offered to them and whether such drug taking is injurious to the individual or society. These cardinal signs of drug abuse have provided an important focus for laboratory animal self-injection experiments, but systematic studies in which humans self-administer drugs of abuse have been less common. Methods have been developed with humans, however, for comparing the behavioral and physiological changes produced by self-administration of a known drug of abuse with the changes produced by other self-administered drugs. In addition to the questionnaires, physiological measures—such as changes in heart rate, blood pressure, changes in the blood or different types of tissue, levels of systemic arousal, and other, more sophisticated physiological measures such as CT scans, MRIs, functional MRIs, and the like—are used to make comparisons between subjective sensation and bodily changes associated with abuse liability. Changes in brain chemistry and cortical arousal can be potent indicators of abuse potential.

The measure that has proven most useful in this approach to human drug abuse liability assessment is the ability of a drug to reinforce and maintain self-administration behaviors much like the behaviors used to obtain food and water. Such reinforcing effects of drugs are an important determinant influencing the likelihood that a particular drug will be abused. Laboratory studies with volunteers who are experienced drug users, for example, have shown that they will perform bicycle riding exercises to obtain doses of abused drugs (e.g., pentobarbital). There is a systematic relationship between the amount of exercise performed and the amount of drug available (i.e., higher doses and shorter intervals between doses produce more exercise behavior than lower doses and longer interdose intervals). When a placebo or a drug that is not abused (e.g., chlorpromazine) is made available for bicycle riding, by contrast, the rate of self-administration declines to near zero.

Differences between drugs in abuse liability can also be assessed by determining whether humans prefer one drug of abuse to another. During a training period, for example, experienced drug users sample coded capsules containing different drugs or different doses of a drug. Then, during subsequent test sessions, they are presented with the coded capsules and allowed to choose the one containing the drug or drug dose they prefer. This blind procedure (i.e., the volunteers are not told what drugs the capsules contain) prevents biases that might be introduced by using the drug names. When neither the volunteer subject nor the person conducting the test knows what drug the capsules contain, the procedure is referred to as *double-blind*.

Not surprisingly, it has also been shown that the preference for one drug over another or one drug dose over another agrees well with ratings of drug-liking made independently of the choice tests just described. In self-administration studies in which volunteers show a preference for one drug of abuse over another, subjective ratings of liking and positive mood changes were clearly more frequent for the preferred drug than for the drug chosen less often. Such self-reports have inherent limitations, however, because of variations in individual verbal skills, which make it necessary to confirm such findings with other measures.

In addition to the self-administration and subjective-effects measures that are of obvious value in testing the abuse liability of drugs in humans, other quantitative drug effect measurements have proven useful. When, for example, observer ratings (e.g., nurses watching the patients) and performance tests (e.g., speed of movement) are measured

after different drugs are administered to volunteers, the results can be compared to determine whether the behavioral changes produced by a test drug are the same as or different from those of a known drug of abuse. When a number of different performance tests (e.g., arithmetic calculations, memory for numbers and letters, speed of reaction) are given following such drug administration, it is possible to construct a behavioral profile showing the performance effects of different drugs. Comparisons between different drugs and test drugs with regard to the similarity of such profiles across their respective dose ranges increase confidence in assessments made of the abuse liability of unknown drugs.

EFFECTIVENESS OF ABUSE LIABILITY TESTING

Given the availability of procedures for abuse liability testing in humans it is reasonable to ask how well they work. That is, it is worth asking if it has been possible to predict from the results of these tests whether a new drug will be abused when it becomes generally available. The two major sources available for checking the effectiveness of human abuse liability testing procedures are case reports by clinicians of patient drug abuse and epidemiological surveys of large numbers of individuals as well as of specific target sites (e.g., hospital emergency rooms). Both of these approaches have shortcomings, as they lack the precision and focus that human laboratory testing can provide. Despite the drawbacks, they can detect abuse liability problems in both specific groups of individuals and the population at large, in a manner that has generally validated the results of human laboratory testing procedures.

ETHICAL CONSIDERATIONS

Several codes and regulations agreed on by scientists, regulatory bodies such as federal agencies, and the lay public provide norms for the conduct of research and testing with human volunteers. In general, they require a clear statement, understandable to the volunteer, of the risks and benefits of the testing procedure, as well as an explicit consent document in written form. After it is clear that the participant thoroughly appreciates all that is involved and the potential consequences of participation, the volunteer signs the consent form in the presence of a witness who is not associated with the research. These required procedures ensure both the autonomy and the protection of volunteers for drug abuse liability testing.

See also **Abuse Liability of Therapeutic Drugs: Testing in Animals; Controlled Substances Act of 1970; Reinforcement; Research, Animal Model: An Overview.**

BIBLIOGRAPHY

Bigelow, G. E. (1991). Human drug abuse liability assessment: Opioids and analgesics. *Addiction, 86* (12), 1615–1628.

Bond, A., Seijas, D., Dawling, S., & Lader, M. (1994). Systemic absorption and abuse liability of snorted flunitrazepam. *Addiction, 89* (7), 821–830.

Busto, U. E., & Sellers, E. M. (1991). Anxiolytics and sedative/hypnotics dependence. *Addiction, 86* (12), 1647–1652.

Campbell, N. D. (2006). A new deal for the drug addict: The addiction research center, Lexington, Kentucky. *Journal of the History of the Behavioral Sciences, 42* (2), 135.

De Wit, H. (1991). Preference procedures for testing the abuse liability of drugs in humans. *Addiction, 86* (12), 1579–1586.

Evans, S. M., Critchfield, T. S., & Griffiths, R. G. (1991). Abuse liability assessment of anxiolytics/hypnotics: Rationale and laboratory lore. *Addiction 86* (12), 1625–1632.

Farré, M., & Camí, J. (1991). Pharmacokinetic considerations in abuse liability evaluation. *Addiction, 86* (12), 1601–1606.

Fischman, M. W., & Foltin, R. W. (1991). Utility of subjective-effects measurements in assessing abuse liability of drugs in humans. *Addiction, 86* (12), 1563–1570.

Foltin, R. W., Marian, W., & Fischman, M. W. (1991). Methods for the assessment of abuse liability of psychomotor stimulants and anorectic agents in humans. *Addiction, 86* (12), 1633–1640.

Griffiths, R. R., Bigelow, G. E., & Ator, N. A. (2003). Principles of initial experimental drug abuse liability assessment in humans. *Drug and Alcohol Dependence, 70* (3, Suppl. 1), S41–S54.

Henningfield, J. E., Cohen, C., & Heishman, S. J. (1991). Drug self-administration methods in abuse liability evaluation. *Addiction, 86* (12), 1571–1577.

Kelly, T. H., Robbins, G., Martin, C. A., Fillmore, M.T., Lane, S.D., Harrington, N.G., et al. (2006). Individual differences in drug abuse vulnerability: D-Amphetamine and sensation-seeking status. *Psychopharmacology, 189* (1) 17.

Parasrampuria, D.A., Schoedel, K.A., Schuller, R., Silber, S.A., Ciccone, P.E., Gu, J., et al. (2007). Do formulation differences alter abuse liability of methylphenidate? *Journal of Clinical Psychopharmacology, 27* (5), 459.

Preston, K. L. (1991). Drug abstinence effects: Opioids. *Addiction, 86* (12), 1641–1646.

Preston, K. L. (1991). Drug discrimination methods in human drug abuse liability evaluation. *Addiction, 86* (12), 1587–1594.

Roache, J. D. (1991). Performance and physiological measures in abuse liability evaluation. *Addiction 86* (12), 1595–1600.

Sellers, E. M., Otton, S. V., & Busto, U. E. (1991). Drug metabolism and interactions in abuse liability assessment. *Addiction, 86* (12), 1607–1614.

Sughondhabirom, A., Diwakar, J., Gueorguieva, R., Coric, V., Berman, R., Lynch, W. J., et al. (2005). A paradigm to investigate the self-regulation of cocaine administration in humans. *Psychopharmacology, 180* (3), 436.

White, T. L., Lott, D. C., & De Wit, H. (2006). Personality and the subjective effects of acute amphetamine in healthy volunteers. *Neuropsychopharmacology, 31* (5), 1064.

JOSEPH V. BRADY
REVISED BY PAMELA V. MICHAELS (2009)

ABUSE LIABILITY OF THERAPEUTIC DRUGS: TESTING IN ANIMALS.

Determining the probability that a new drug will be abused is an important step in reducing the overall abuse of therapeutic drugs. Since the likelihood that a drug will be abused by a patient must be carefully weighed against the benefit provided by the drug, it is important that research outline any and all reinforcing effects a drug may have which could lead to subsequent abuse. Prediction of the likelihood of abuse has historically been based upon human experiments and observation. This method, however, is increasingly being replaced with experimentation on animals.

Research conducted since the early 1960s has shown that animals such as monkeys and rats will, with very few exceptions, repeatedly self-administer the same drugs that human beings are likely to abuse. Moreover, test animals do not self-administer drugs that human beings do not abuse.

Research based on animal testing is conducted in a slightly different manner and often requires laboratory procedures not needed for research based on human test subjects. Provisions must be made to allow the animal a means by which to self-administer the drug. Since animals frequently are not physically able to administer a drug in the same way a human would, alternate methods are employed. Animals may be taught to push levers or do similar actions in order to get a dose of a drug. The results of these drug self-administration studies in animals play a critical role in the prediction of the likelihood of abuse of new drugs in human beings.

The liability that a drug will be abused is often evaluated by what has been termed a "substitution procedure." Such research begins with the administration of a known drug, which is then substituted with a new drug under investigation. The first phase in the substitution procedure is designed to establish a baseline of how much effort an animal is willing to make to obtain a drug dose in general. Each day an animal is allowed to give itself a drug of known potential for abuse. The researcher notes how frequently the animal takes a dose and how much effort it is willing to make to get a dose of the drug. The researcher can make a lever harder to push, make the animal push it repeatedly, or make the animal follow a complicated set of actions to get a dose. This provides a baseline against which to compare the effects of the new drug which will be studied.

For example, a monkey may give itself cocaine or codeine via intravenous injections during sessions that last several hours. When session-to-session intake of the known drug is stable (that is, stays about the same, thus showing the dosage which is sufficient to satisfy the animal and reduce its drive to obtain more), the liquid in which it was dissolved is substituted for the baseline drug for several consecutive sessions. Since this liquid is usually neutral, with no positive or negative effects, the animal gives itself fewer and fewer injections until it hardly bothers pushing the lever at all. The animal is briefly returned to baseline conditions, followed by a substitution period during which a dose of the test drug is made available. This continues for at least as many sessions as were required for the animal to stop bothering with pushing the lever for the neutral liquid. This process is repeated with different concentrations of the new drug until the experimenter has tested a range of possible doses of the new medicine.

The rates at which the animal gives itself the test drug, neutral liquid, and known addictive drug are then compared. A new drug that the animal prefers to the neutral liquid is considered to be a substance that reinforces the desire for itself (a "positive reinforcer") and would thus be predicted to have abuse liability.

Such substitution procedures provide information which indicates whether or not a drug is liable to be abused, but do not allow a comparative estimate as to whether or not a new drug is more addictive or less addictive than other known drugs. These procedures measure how frequently the animal gives itself a dose, a measure that reflects both the direct effects of the drug and the effects of the drug's reinforcement of the desire for itself. Another method must be used to measure the reinforcing effect of a drug separately from its other effects. To compare drugs, it is useful to know how big the maximum reinforcing effect is—termed its *reinforcing efficacy*. Several procedures have been developed to measure reinforcing efficacy. Most either allow an animal to choose between the new drug and another drug or non-drug reinforcer (choice procedures), or they measure how hard an animal will work to obtain an injection (progressive-ratio procedures).

In choice procedures, the measure of reinforcing efficacy is how often the new drug is chosen in preference to the other drug (or non-drug). In progressive-ratio procedures, the number of times the animal must push the lever in order to get a drug injection is increased until the animal no longer bothers to push the lever. At some point the animal determines that it is not worth the extra effort to get another dose. This point is called the break point and is a measure of the reinforcing efficacy of the drug.

The fact that animals given a choice between different strengths of the same drug show a propensity to choose the higher dose most often is evidence that these procedures provide a valid measure of reinforcing efficacy. In addition, break points are higher in progressive-ratio experiments involving higher stable doses and lower for experiments involving lower doses. Results of both the choice and the progressive-ratio procedures in animal research are consistent with what is known about abuse of drugs in human beings—that is, drugs such as cocaine, a highly preferred drug in choice studies, maintain higher break points in progressive-ratio studies than other drugs, and are frequently abused.

These experiments show how animals discriminate among drugs, and the extent to which they prefer certain drugs over other drugs. The results may be used to predict potential subjective effects in human beings. Since subjective effects play a major role in drug abuse, such experiments are an important tool used in the evaluation of the likelihood of abuse in new drugs. A new drug with subjective effects similar to those of a known, addictive, and often abused drug is likely to be abused itself. Additionally, drug-discrimination experiments not only identify the potential for abuse but also provide important information which allows researchers to classify new drugs based on their predicted subjective effects, something that drug self-administration experiments cannot do. Thus, drug discrimination provides additional information relevant to the comparison between the new drug and drugs that we already know are addictive and frequently abused. For example, a monkey shows a similar discrimination pattern using a new drug as it has shown previously using a known drug such as cocaine. This new drug is likely to be abused and to have subjective effects similar to those produced by cocaine.

ABUSE LIABILITY OF THERAPEUTIC DRUGS: TESTING IN ANIMALS: CONCLUSION
Researchers have improved methods for predicting the likelihood that a new drug will be abused. Using animals in substitution, choice, and progressive-ratio procedures has greatly enhanced researchers' understanding of factors involved in determining the liability that a new drug or chemical compound will be abused. Current research techniques allow the evaluation of likely preference and the reinforcing efficacy of a new compound based on experiments with animals such as monkeys and rats. This information is then used to reliably predict whether a drug is likely to be abused and to which known drugs it is likely to be similar, both in terms of how addictive it is and what its subjective effects will be. Such information is clearly valuable in deciding how much to restrict a new drug and is a critical tool in the effort to reduce the abuse of therapeutic drugs.

See also **Abuse Liability of Drugs: Testing in Humans; Controlled Substances Act of 1970; Reinforcement; Research, Animal Model: An Overview.**

BIBLIOGRAPHY

Ator, N. A., & R. R. Griffiths (2003). Principles of drug abuse liability assessment in laboratory animals. *Drug and Alcohol Dependence, 70* S55A, S72.

Brady, J. V., & S. E. Lukas (1984). Testing drugs for physical dependence potential and abuse liability. NIDA Research Monograph no. 52. Washington, D.C.: U.S. Government Printing Office.

Schoedel, K. A., & E. M. Sellers (2008). Assessing abuse liability during drug development: Changing standards and expectations. *Clinical Pharmacology and Therapeutics.* Advance online publication, doi:10.1038/sj. clpt.6100492.

Thompson, T., & K. R. Unra, Eds. (1977). *Predicting dependence liability of stimulant and depressant drugs.* Baltimore: University Park Press.

WILLIAM WOOLVERTON
REVISED BY JAMES T. MCDONOUGH JR. (2001)

ACAMPROSATE. *See* **Treatment, Pharmacological Approaches to: Acamprosate.**

ACCIDENTS AND INJURIES FROM ALCOHOL. Trauma (bodily injury) is a major social and medical problem in both developed and developing countries. Injuries are among the leading cause of death and disability in the world, and affect all populations, regardless of age, sex, income, or geographic region. In 1998 about 5.8 million people died of injuries worldwide, and injuries caused 16 percent of the global burden of disease (Krug et al., 2000). In developed countries injuries are the leading cause of death between the ages of one and forty, and in the United States population injuries are the fourth leading cause of death (exceeded only by heart disease, stroke, and cancer). Of all deaths from injury in the United States, about 65 percent are classified as "unintentional" (which excludes deaths from suicide and homicide). Unintentional injury is the leading cause of death in the United States among those under forty-four years of age. More than a hundred

Year	BAC = .00 Number	BAC = .00 Percent	BAC = .01–.07 Number	BAC = .01–.07 Percent	BAC = .08+ Number	BAC = .08+ Percent	Total number	Total fatalities in alcohol-related crashes Number	Total fatalities in alcohol-related crashes Percent
1994	23,409	57	2,322	6	14,985	37	40,716	17,308	43
1995	24,085	58	2,490	6	15,242	36	41,817	17,732	42
1996	24,316	58	2,486	6	15,263	36	42,065	17,749	42
1997	25,302	60	2,290	5	14,421	34	42,013	16,711	40
1998	24,828	60	2,465	6	14,207	34	41,501	16,673	40
1999	25,145	60	2,321	6	14,250	34	41,717	16,572	40
2000	24,565	59	2,511	6	14,870	35	41,945	17,380	41
2001	24,796	59	2,542	6	14,858	35	42,196	17,400	41
2002	25,481	59	2,432	6	15,093	35	43,005	17,524	41
2003	25,779	60	2,427	6	14,678	34	42,884	17,105	40
2004	25,918	61	2,325	5	14,593	34	42,836	16,919	39
2005	25,920	60	2,489	6	15,102	35	43,510	17,590	40
2006	25,040	59	2,480	6	15,121	35	42,642	17,602	41

SOURCE: National Highway Traffic Safety Administration Fatality Analysis Reporting System, U.S. Department of Transportation.

Table 1. Alcohol content and alcohol-related accidents, 1994–2006. ILLUSTRATION BY GGS INFORMATION SERVICES. GALE, CENGAGE LEARNING

thousand Americans die annually as a result of accidental injuries, nearly half of which are from motor vehicle crashes, and the remainder from falls, burns, poisonings, and drownings, among other causes. Unintentional injury accounts for an even higher rate of morbidity, with the rate of serious injury estimated to be over three hundred times the mortality rate (Vyrostek et al., 2004), and it is estimated that more than seventy million Americans annually require medical treatment for non-fatal unintentional injuries. Intentional injuries, those resulting from violence-related events (homicides and assaults) and from suicide (attempted and completed), also account for substantial proportions of fatalities and of those requiring medical intervention.

Globally, alcohol is among the most important risk factors for both morbidity-related disability and mortality. Injuries constitute 46 percent of the deaths attributable to alcohol and 42 percent of the Disability-Adjusted Life Years (DALYs) (Rehm et al., 2004), with unintentional injuries accounting for over twice the DALYs as intentional injuries. The problem of alcohol-related injuries is particularly alarming in many developing countries, where alcohol consumption is rapidly increasing, injury rates are extremely high, and appropriate public policies have not been implemented.

The first documentation of alcohol's involvement in injury dates to 1500 BCE, with an Egyptian papyrus warning that excessive drinking leads to falls and broken bones. The scientific study of alcohol and injuries was the subject of much investigation throughout the twentieth century. Data from both coroner and emergency room (ER) studies indicate that a large proportion of victims of both fatal and nonfatal injuries test positive for blood alcohol—this proportion is greater than one would expect to find in the general population on any given day. The consumption of alcohol has been highly associated with fatalities and serious injuries, but whether or not alcohol is more common in injuries of greater severity has been an issue of ongoing debate (Li et al., 1997). Alcohol may be significantly associated with increased risk of serious injury, possibly due to other factors that are associated with alcohol use, such as speeding, not wearing seat belts or helmets, and other risk-taking behaviors. Studies of alcohol, injury, and risk-taking dispositions in the general population have shown risk-taking, impulsivity, and sensation-seeking to be associated with both injury occurrence and alcohol consumption (Cherpitel, 1999). However, alcohol intoxication itself can bias injury severity scores upward, and those more severely injured are also more likely to reach the ER sooner, and consequently more likely to have a positive (and higher) blood alcohol concentration (BAC) than those less severely injured who arrive later.

Although alcohol cannot be said to cause the accident in most cases, alcohol consumption is thought to contribute to both fatal and nonfatal injury occurrence, primarily because it is known to diminish motor coordination and balance and to

| Year | Male | | | Female | | |
| | Total | Percent | | Total | Percent | |
		BAC = .01+	BAC = .08+		BAC = .01+	BAC = .08+
1994	40,233	30	26	13,567	17	14
1995	41,235	30	25	14,184	16	13
1996	41,376	29	25	14,850	16	13
1997	40,954	28	24	14,954	15	12
1998	40,816	28	23	15,089	15	12
1999	41,012	28	23	14,835	14	12
2000	41,795	29	24	14,790	16	13
2001	41,901	29	24	14,919	15	13
2002	42,377	29	25	14,999	15	12
2003	42,586	28	24	15,211	14	12
2004	42,250	28	24	15,384	15	12
2005	43,282	28	24	15,059	16	13
2006	41,975	28	24	14,655	18	15

SOURCE: National Highway Traffic Safety Administration Fatality Analysis Reporting System, U.S. Department of Transportation.

Table 2. Fatal accidents by sex and blood alcohol concentration, 1994–2006.
ILLUSTRATION BY GGS INFORMATION SERVICES. GALE, CENGAGE LEARNING

impair attention, perception, and judgment with regard to behavior, placing the drinker at a higher risk of accidental injury than the nondrinker. The residual or hangover effects of alcohol consumption may also contribute to injury occurrence. It should not be overlooked that the use of alcohol in combination with other drugs may potentiate the effects of alcohol and increase the risk of injury.

ESTIMATES OF ALCOHOL'S INVOLVEMENT

In U.S. studies, the proportion of injured patients testing positive for estimated BAC at the time of admission to the ER has ranged from 7 percent to 22 percent, while data from other countries show ranges from 4 percent (Canada and the Czech Republic) to 59 percent (South Africa) (Cherpitel, 2007). Reviews of these studies suggest that the variation in BAC may be due to differences in the time that elapsed between the injury and arrival in the ER, as well as to individual characteristics of the particular ER populations studied (such as age, sex, and socioeconomic status—all known to be associated with alcohol consumption in the general population), and also to the mix of various types of injury in the ER caseload (Cherpitel, 1993). For example, alcohol consumption is more commonly associated with injuries resulting from violence than from any other cause. In studies that have been restricted to weekend evenings, when one would expect a large proportion of the population to be consuming alcohol, the proportion of those

testing positive for alcohol at the time of ER admission was particularly high. In coroner studies, such as those conducted by Haberman and Baden (1978), alcohol-related fatalities were estimated to account for about 43 percent of all unintentional injuries. Studies that have compared estimated BAC between fatal and nonfatal injuries in the same geographic locality have shown higher rates of positive BACs among fatal injuries (57%) than nonfatal injuries (15%) (Cherpitel, 1996). It is well known that many who drink also consume other psychoactive drugs, so it is not possible to ascertain the independent effect of alcohol on both fatal and nonfatal accidents.

TRAUMA RELATED TO MOTOR VEHICLES

Motor Vehicle Accidents. Motor vehicle accidents are the leading cause of death from injury—and the greatest single cause of all deaths for those between the ages of fifteen and thirty-four in the United States. Almost 50 percent of these fatalities are believed to be alcohol related, and alcohol's involvement is greater for drivers in single-vehicle nighttime fatal crashes (U.S. Department of Health and Human Services, 1997). The risk of a fatal crash is estimated to be from three to fifteen times higher for those with a BAC of at least 0.10 percent (100 milligrams of alcohol per 100 milliliters of blood), than for drivers with a zero BAC (Roizen, 1982). Alcohol is more frequently present in fatal than in nonfatal crashes. It is estimated that 25 percent to 35 percent of drivers requiring ER care for injuries resulting from such crashes have a BAC of 0.10 percent or greater.

Motorcycle Accidents. Motorcyclists are at a greater risk of death than automobile occupants, and it has been estimated that up to 50 percent of fatally injured motorcyclists have a BAC of at least 0.10 percent (Romelsjö, 1995).

Pedestrian Accidents. Pedestrians killed or injured by motor vehicles are also more likely to have been drinking than those not involved in such accidents (Romelsjö, 1995). It is estimated that 31 percent to 44 percent of fatal injuries to pedestrians are due to alcohol intoxication, with 14 percent of the fatal pedestrian accidents involving an intoxicated driver and 24 percent involving an intoxicated pedestrian.

Aviation Accidents. Flying skills are impaired at BACs as low as 0.025 percent, and a BAC of 0.015 percent or greater has been found in 18 percent to 43 percent of pilots deceased from accidents (Romelsjö, 1995).

HOME ACCIDENTS
Among all nonfatal injuries occurring in the home, an estimated 22 percent to 30 percent involve alcohol, with 10 percent of those injured having BACs of over 0.10 percent at the time of the accident. Coroner data suggest that alcohol consumption immediately before a fatal accident occurs more often in deaths from falls and fires than in motor vehicle deaths.

Falls. Falls are the most common cause of nonfatal injuries in the United States (accounting for over 60%) and the second leading cause of fatal accidents (Baker et al., 1992). Alcohol's involvement in fatal falls has been found to range from 21 percent to 77 percent, and in nonfatal falls from 17 percent to 57 percent. Alcohol may increase the likelihood of a fall as much as sixty times in those with high BACs, compared with those having no alcohol exposure.

Fires and Burns. Fires and burns are the fourth leading cause of accidental death in the United States (Baker et al., 1992). Alcohol involvement

has been estimated in 12 percent to 83 percent of these fatalities (with a median value of 46%), and up to 50 percent of nonfatal burn injuries (with a median value of 17%). In a review of studies of burn victims, Hingson and Howland (1993) estimated that about 50 percent of burn fatalities were attributed to intoxicated individuals and that alcohol exposure was most frequent among victims of fires caused by cigarettes.

RECREATIONAL ACCIDENTS
Drownings. Drownings rank as the third leading cause of accidental death in the United States for those aged five to forty-four, and the fourth leading cause across all age groups (Howland et al., 1995). Haberman and Baden (1978) reported that 68 percent of drowning victims had been drinking, but other estimates have ranged from 30 percent to 54 percent (with an average of 38%) (Hingson & Howland, 1993). Alcohol is consumed in relatively large quantities by many of those involved in water-recreation (especially boating) activities, and studies suggest that those involved in aquatic accidents are more likely to be intoxicated than those not involved in such accidents. In a review of the literature on those who came close to drowning, Roizen (1982) found that about 35 percent had been drinking at the time.

Bicycle Injuries. Bicycling is the leading cause of recreational injuries, resulting in over 500,000 ER visits, 20,000 hospitalizations and 1,000 deaths annually in the United States (Li et al., 1996). Among those fatally injured, 32 percent have been found to be BAC positive and 23% had BACs of 0.01 percent or above. A comparison of fatal bicycle injuries with non-fatal injuries found fatal injuries more likely to have positive BACs (30% vs. 16%) and to have BACs of 0.10 percent and above (22% vs. 13%) (Li et al., 1996).

Snowmobiles and Mopeds. Forty percent of snowmobile injuries (Smith & Kraus, 1988) and 30 percent of moped injuries (Roizen, 1989) were found to involve alcohol.

Hypothermia and Frostbite. Alcohol has been found greatly to increase the risk of hypothermia and frostbite. Among exposure-related fatalities, 63 percent were found to be BAC positive, with 48

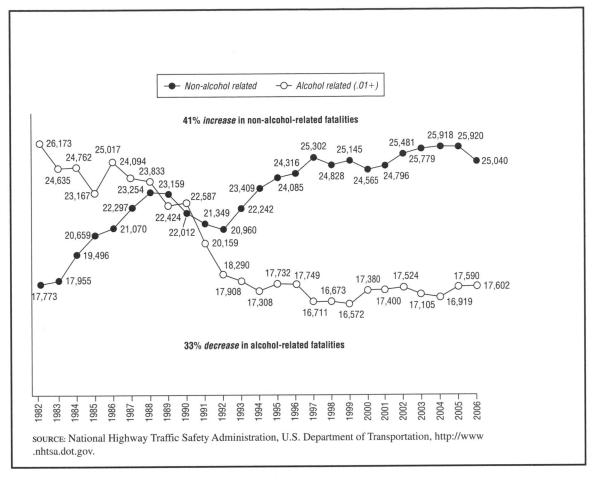

Figure 1. Crash fatalities by alcohol involvement. ILLUSTRATION BY GGS INFORMATION SERVICES. GALE, CENGAGE LEARNING

percent at 0.15 percent or higher (Luke & Levy, 1982), while 53 percent of frostbite patients have been found to be alcohol positive (Urschel, 1990).

WORK-RELATED ACCIDENTS

Alcohol's involvement in work-related accidents varies greatly by type of industry, but the proportion of those testing positive for blood alcohol following a work-related accident is considerably lower than for other kinds of injuries, particularly in the United States, since drinking on the job is not a widespread or regular activity. Among work-related fatalities, an estimated 15 percent were positive for blood alcohol, and a range of 1 percent to 16 percent has been estimated for nonfatal injuries (Roizen, 1989; Stallones & Kraus, 1993).

INTENTIONAL INJURIES

Violence-Related Injuries. Both fatal and nonfatal injuries commonly result from violence, and these

injuries are more likely to be alcohol-related than injuries from any other cause, for both men and for women, regardless of age. Such injuries are considered intentional and include those nonfatal injuries resulting from assaults and fights, as well as fatal injuries from homicides. Alcohol is more likely to be involved in fatal injuries from violence than in nonfatal injuries treated in an ER in the same geographic locality (Cherpitel, 1996). A review of ER studies showed that between 22 percent and 70 percent of violence-related injuries were BAC positive, compared to 7 percent to 22 percent of non-violence-related injuries attending the same ERs during the same period of time (Cherpitel, 1994). These figures refer to alcohol involvement among the victims of violence-related events, and less is known about alcohol involvement of the perpetrator of such events, but the correlation is thought to also be high. ER patients with violence-related injuries are also more likely to be heavier drinkers and to report alcohol-related problems than those with injuries from other causes.

Suicide. A review of suicides found a range of 10 percent to 69 percent for alcohol positive cases among completed suicides (with an average of 33%) and a range of 10 percent to 73 percent for alcohol positive cases among attempted suicides (Cherpitel et al., 2004). About 20 percent of suicide victims have been identified as alcohol dependent, and are at increased risk of suicide compared to those in the general population. The suicide risk among alcoholics is estimated to be almost twice as high as for non-alcoholics.

ALCOHOLISM, VOLUME OF DRINKING, AND DRINKING PATTERN

The available literature on the role of alcoholism in injury occurrence suggests that problem drinkers and those diagnosed as alcoholics are at a greater risk of both fatal and nonfatal injuries than those in the general population who may drink prior to an accident. Alcoholics and problem drinkers are significantly more likely to be drinking, and to be drinking heavily, prior to an accident than others. Haberman and Baden (1978) found that among fatalities from all causes, alcoholics and heavy drinkers were more than twice as likely as non-problem drinkers to have a BAC of 0.10 percent or above. Alcoholics have also been found to experience higher rates of both fatal and nonfatal accidents, even when sober. Analysis of national mortality data found that those who died of injury drank more frequently and more heavily than those who died of disease, and that daily drinking, binge drinking (consuming five or more drinks per occasion), and heavier drinking (fourteen or more drinks per week) increased the likelihood of injury as the underlying cause of death (Li et al., 1994). Chronic alcohol abuse has long-term physiological and neurological effects that may increase the risk of accidents. Chronic drinking also impairs liver function, which plays an important part in injury recovery. Heavy drinking also compromises the immune system, predisposing the alcoholic to bacterial infections following injury. The risk of accidental death has been estimated to be from three to sixteen times greater for alcoholics than for non-alcoholics, with the highest risk being death from fires and burns. Haberman and Baden (1978) found that among all fatalities from fires, 34 percent involved alcoholics.

A *dose-response relationship* may also be important in risk of injury; that is, the more alcohol consumed, the greater the likelihood of injury occurrence. Reviews of fatal vehicular crashes have found that risk increases exponentially with increasing BAC (Perrine et al., 1989), and a summary of U.S. findings show a dose-response relationship, with a BAC of 0.08 percent, 0.10 percent, 0.15 percent and 0.20 percent associated with a twofold, sevenfold, tenfold, and twentyfold increased risk, respectively, for a road traffic accident (Brismar & Bergman, 1998). A Finnish ER study also found a dose-response relationship between BAC and the likelihood of injury from falls, with those having BACs between 0.06 percent and 0.10 percent being three times more likely to be injured than those with non-detectable blood alcohol; while those with BACs between 0.10 percent and 0.15 percent were ten times more likely, and those with BACs over 0.15 percent were sixty times more likely to have suffered a fall injury (Honkanen et al., 1983).

Although the amount of drinking on any particular occasion is an important risk factor in injury occurrence, the pattern of usual drinking may also play a part in risk of injury. Data from the U.S. general population found the risk of injury increased with an average of one drink a day for both men and women, regardless of age. The risk of injury also increased with the frequency of consuming five or more drinks a day more often than twice a year (Cherpitel et al., 1995). A study of crash-involved drivers showed more frequent drinkers to be at lower risk than less frequent drinkers at all BAC levels (Hurst et al., 1994). Other analysis of drinking and driving in the United States, however, found that the highest risk of injury was associated with those who only occasionally drank heavily, but who drank more than their usual amounts at the time of the event (Gruenewald et al., 1996), suggesting that heavy episodic drinking may be more strongly related to injury than usual volume of drinking. This is supported by data from an ER study showing that those who usually drank little but on occasion drank heavily were at greater risk for injury (Gmel et al., 2006).

See also **Driving, Alcohol, and Drugs; Driving Under the Influence (DUI); Industry and Workplace, Drug Use in; Social Costs of Alcohol and Drug Abuse.**

BIBLIOGRAPHY

Baker, S. P., O'Neill, B., & Karpe, R. (1992). *The injury fact book*. Lexington, MA: Lexington Books.

Brismar, B., & Bergman, B. (1998) The significance of alcohol for violence and accidents. *Alcoholism: Clinical and Experimental Research, 22*(7), 299S–306S.

Cherpitel, C. J. (1993). Alcohol and injuries: A review of international emergency room studies. *Addiction, 88,* 923–937.

Cherpitel, C. J. (1994). Alcohol and injuries resulting from violence: A review of emergency room studies. *Addiction, 89,* 157–165.

Cherpitel, C. J. (1996). Alcohol in fatal and nonfatal injuries: A comparison of coroner and emergency room data from the same county. *Alcoholism: Clinical and Experimental Research, 20,* 338–342.

Cherpitel, C. J. (1999). Substance use, injury, and risk-taking dispositions in the general population. *Alcoholism: Clinical and Experimental Research, 23,* 121–126.

Cherpitel, C. J. (2007). Alcohol and injuries: A review of international emergency room studies since 1995. *Drug and Alcohol Review, 26,* 201–214.

Cherpitel, C. J., Borges, G. L. G., & Wilcox, H. C. (2004). Acute alcohol use and suicidal behavior: A review of the literature. *Alcoholism: Clinical and Experimental Research, 28*(5), 18S–28S.

Cherpitel, C. J., Tam, T. W., Midanki, L. T., Caetano, R., & Greenfield, T. K. (1995). Alcohol and non-fatal injury in the U.S. general population: A risk function analysis. *Accident Analysis and Prevention, 27,* 651–661.

Gmel, G., Bissery, A., Gammeter, R., Givel, J.-C., Clames, J.-M., Yersin, B., et al. (2006). Alcohol-attributable injuries in admissions to a Swiss emergency room: An analysis of the link between volume of drinking, drinking patterns and pre-attendance drinking. *Alcoholism: Clinical and Experimental Research, 30*(3), 501–509.

Gruenewald, P. J., Mitchell, P. R., & Treno, A. J. (1996). Drinking and driving: Drinking patterns and drinking patterns. *Addiction, 91*(11), 1637–1649.

Haberman, P. W., & Baden, M. M. (1978). *Alcohol, other drugs, and violent death*. New York: Oxford University Press.

Hingson, R., & Howland, J. (1993). Alcohol and non-traffic unintended injuries. *Addiction, 88,* 887–883.

Honkanen, R., Ertama, L., Kuosmanen, P., Linnoila, M., Alha, A., & Visuri, T. (1983). The role of alcohol in accidental falls. *Journal of Studies on Alcohol, 44,* 231–245.

Howland, J., Mangione, T., Hingson, R., Smith, G., & Bell, N. (1995). Alcohol as a risk factor for drowning and other aquatic injuries. In R. R. Watson (Ed.), *Drug and alcohol abuse reviews: Vol. 7. Alcohol and accidents*. Totowa, NJ: Humana Press.

Hurst, P. M., Harte, D., & Frith, W. J. (1994). The Grand Rapids DIP revisited. *Accident Analysis and Prevention, 26*(5), 647–654.

Krug, E. G., Sharma, G. K., & Lozano, R. (2000). The global burden of injuries. *American Journal of Public Health, 90,* 523–526.

Li, G., Baker, S. P., Sterling, S., Smialek, J. E., Dischinger, P. C., & Soderstromm C. A. (1996) A comparative analysis of alcohol in fatal and nonfatal bicycling injuries. *Alcoholism: Clinical and Experimental Research, 20*(9), 1553–1559.

Li, G., Keyl, P. M., Smith, G. S., & Baker, S. P. (1997). Alcohol and injury severity: reappraisal of the continuing controversy. *The Journal of Trauma, 42,* 562–569.

Li, G., Smith, G. S., & Baker, S. P. (1994). Drinking behavior in relation to cause of death among US adults. *American Journal of Public Health, 84,* 1402–1406.

Luke, L. I., & Levy, M. E. (1982). Exposure-related hypothermia deaths–District of Columbia 1972–1982. *Morbidity and Mortality Weekly Report, 31*(50), 669–671.

Perrine, M.W., Peck, R. C., & Fell, J. C. (1989). Epidemiologic perspectives on drunk driving. In *Surgeon General's Workshop on Drunk Driving: Background Papers* (pp. 35–76). Washington, DC: U.S. Department of Health and Human Services.

Rehm, J., Room, R., Monteiro, M., Gmel, G., Graham, K., Rehn, N., et al. (2004). Alcohol use. In M. Ezzati, A. D. Lopez, A. Rodgers, & C. J. L. Murray (Eds.), *Comparative quantification of health risks: Global and regional burden of disease attributable to selected major risk factors* (Vol. 1, pp. 959–1108). Geneva, Switzerland: World Health Organization.

Roizen, J. (1982). Estimating alcohol involvement in serious events. In *Alcohol consumption and related problems [Alcohol and Health Monograph 1. DHHS Publication (ADM) 82–1190]* (pp. 179–219). Rockville, MD: U.S. National Institute on Alcohol Abuse and Alcoholism.

Roizen, J. (1989). Alcohol and trauma. In N. Giesbrecht, R. Gonzales, M. Grant, et al. (Eds.), *Drinking and casualties. Accidents, poisonings and violence in an international perspective* (pp. 21–66). London: Croom Helm.

Romelsjö, A. (1995). Alcohol consumption and unintentional injury, suicide, violence, work performance, and intergenerational effects. In H. D. Holder & G. Edwards (Eds.), *Alcohol and public policy: Evidence and issues* (pp. 114–142). New York: Oxford University Press.

Smith, G. S., & Kraus, J. F. (1988). Alcohol and residential, recreational, and occupational injuries: A review of the epidemiologic evidence. *Annual Review of Public Health 9,* 99–121.

Stallones, L., & Kraus, J. F. (1993). The occurrence and epidemiologic features of alcohol-related occupational injuries. *Addiction, 88*, 945–951.

Urschel J. D. (1990). Frostbite: Predisposing factors and predictors of poor outcome. *The Journal of Trauma, 30*(3), 340–342.

U.S. Department of Health and Human Services. (1997). Ninth Special Report to the U.S. Congress on Alcohol and Health. NIH Publication No. 97–4017.

Vyrostek, S. B., Annest, J. L., & Ryan, G. W. (2004). Surveillance for fatal and nonfatal injuries—United States, 2001. *Morbidity and Mortality Weekly Report, 53*(SS-7), 1–59.

CHERYL J. CHERPITEL

ACCIDENTS AND INJURIES FROM DRUGS.

CENTRAL NERVOUS SYSTEM EFFECTS

The effects of drugs, including alcohol, may be divided into three categories: acute, carryover, and chronic. Acute effects are those that occur while the person is directly under the immediate effects of the drug (intoxicated or high), and it is during these times that individuals become very vulnerable to accidents and injuries. Carryover effects are effects that occur after the drug has been essentially eliminated from the system, but the effects of the drugs remain to some degree. A hangover from alcohol use is an example of a carryover effect. Even low dose use can have carryover effects. A seminal study on the ability of airplane pilots to successfully land their aircraft after smoking a single marijuana cigarette showed that 8 and even 24 hours after smoking the marijuana, the ability of pilots to safely land their aircraft was measurably diminished. In each instance of carryover effect, the alcohol or drug has dissipated from the system but clarity of thought, decision-making, and attentiveness may be negatively affected, often in more subtle but equally impacting ways. Chronic effects generally are those advanced medical problems that result from continued intermittent or intensive use of drugs.

Accidents and injuries associated with drug and alcohol use generally occur during the acute or carryover phases of drug use because the conditions that cause the accidents are often due to limited mobility and depth perception, slow reaction time, unawareness of setting, and limited ability to make decisions. Most accidents from drugs and alcohol occur either on the highway or at work.

HIGHWAY ACCIDENTS

According to Car-Accidents.com, there were nearly 6,420,000 auto accidents in the United States in 2005. The financial cost of these crashes was more than $230 billion, with 2.9 million people injured and 42,636 people killed. About 115 people die every day in vehicle crashes in the United States, one death every 13 minutes.

Alcohol. According to the Centers for Disease Control (CDC), during 2005, 16,885 people in the United States died in alcohol-related motor vehicle crashes, representing 39 percent of all traffic-related deaths. In 2005, nearly 1.4 million drivers were arrested for driving under the influence of alcohol or narcotics. Drugs other than alcohol (e.g., marijuana and cocaine) were involved in about 18 percent of motor vehicle driver deaths. These other drugs are generally used in combination with alcohol.

In 2006, the National Highway Transportation Safety Administration (NHTSA) reported that there were 16,005 people killed in the United States in alcohol-related motor vehicle traffic crashes (with individuals having a blood alcohol concentration [BAC] of .01 or higher) and 13,470 fatalities in crashes involving an alcohol-impaired driver (BAC of .08 or higher). These 13,470 alcohol-impaired-driving fatalities in 2006 numbered just slightly more than the 13,451 alcohol-impaired-driving fatalities reported in 1996.

The NHTSA report also noted that the 13,470 fatalities in alcohol-impaired-driving crashes during 2006 represent an average of one alcohol-impaired-driving fatality every 39 minutes and that the rate of alcohol impairment among drivers involved in fatal crashes was four times higher at night than during the day. Other highlights of the report are given below:

> The percentage of drivers with a BAC of .08 or above in fatal crashes was highest for motorcycle operators (27%), followed by drivers of light trucks (24%), and then passenger cars (23%). The percentage of drivers with

BACs of .08 or higher in fatal crashes was the lowest for large trucks (1%).

In fatal crashes in 2006, the highest percentage of drivers with a BAC of .08 or higher was for drivers ages 21 to 24 (33%), followed by ages 25 to 34 (29%) and 35 to 44 (25%).

Drivers with a BAC of .08 or higher involved in fatal crashes were eight times more likely to have a prior conviction for driving while impaired (DWI) than were drivers with no alcohol (8% and 1%, respectively).

In 2006, more than 8,200 (55%) of the drivers involved in fatal crashes who had been drinking had a BAC of .15 or greater.

Both females and males had significantly higher death rates in fatal crashes in which the BAC was .08 or greater, 83 percent and 86 percent, respectively.

According to the Insurance Institute for Highway Safety, alcohol involvement is much lower in crashes involving nonfatal injuries, and it is lower still in crashes that do not involve injuries at all.

These results occurred through several years when there was a declining rate of alcohol-related accidents in the United States.

A 2003 report by the National Center for Statistics and Analysis estimated that of the approximately 3 million people who were injured on U.S. public roads, about 250,000 were involved in alcohol-related crashes. Over 60 percent of those injured were vehicle drivers, 30 percent were vehicle passengers, 3 percent involved motorcycles, and 5 percent included non-occupants (pedestrians and others). While estimates vary, according to David Hanson (2008), between 2 and 3 percent of these injury-producing crashes involve intoxicated drivers.

Drugs. Until the late 1990s, there was little investigation into the impact of drugged drivers on highway accidents. Most of the focus on highway accidents and substance abuse pertained to alcohol use. In the early 2000s, however, studies increasingly showed that an unexpected percentage of highway accidents are caused by drugged driving, that is, driving under the influence of drugs other than alcohol. Some studies have shown that many drivers who test positive for alcohol also test positive for the psychoactive chemical in cannabis (THC), making it clear that consuming alcohol and using other drugs are often linked behaviors that combine to affect people's driving.

The Institute for Behavior and Health (IBH) has studied extensively the impact of drug use on highway accidents, and it reports that "Drugged Driving [is a] leading cause of traffic accidents, injuries, and fatalities." Its report cites the following:

10.2 million Americans drove under the influence of drugs in 2006. This corresponds to 4.2 percent of the population aged 12 or older, similar to the rate in 2005 (4.3%), but lower than the rate in 2002 (4.7%). In 2006, the rate was highest among young adults aged 18 to 25 (13%).

Drugged driving causes $33 billion in damages every year based on estimates by the American Automobile Association and IBH.

In any two week period, 1 out of 3 high school seniors has driven after using drugs or ridden with someone who was.

8,600 people died in 2005 as a result of drugged driving.

20 percent of motor vehicle accidents are attributable to drugged driving.

580,000 people were injured in car crashes as a result of drugged driving.

A study by Walsh and colleagues (2004) indicated that 34 percent of motor vehicle crash victims admitted to a Maryland trauma center tested positive for "drugs only"; about 16 percent tested positive for "alcohol only." Approximately 9.9 percent (or 1 in 10) tested positive for alcohol and drugs, and within this group, 50 percent were younger than age 18.

In a large study of almost 3,400 fatally injured drivers from three Australian states (Victoria, New South Wales, and Western Australia) between 1990 and 1999, Drummer and colleagues determined that drugs other than alcohol were present in 26.7 percent of the cases (Drummer et al., 2003). Almost 10 percent of the cases involved both alcohol and drugs.

ACCIDENTS IN THE HOME
An estimated 22 to 30 percent of all nonfatal injuries that occur in the home involve alcohol. One U.S. study showed that people with medically identified alcohol problems had an elevated risk of injury and that 46 percent of problem drinkers required

treatment for at least one injury in a three-year period compared to 38 percent of controls without alcohol problems (Miller et al., 2001). In addition alcohol users sustained an average of two injuries over a three-year period compared to 1.6 injuries for controls. Subjects with a combined alcohol and drug problem had a much higher risk of injury. Women problem drinkers over the age of twenty had a significantly higher risk of injury compared to controls, and by the age of fifty female injury rates exceeded male rates. However, there exists only a modest amount of comprehensive research in the United States on this subject, and where it exists, it almost always relates only to alcohol-related home accidents. Falls are the most common cause of nonfatal injuries in the United States, accounting for over 60 percent and the second-leading cause of fatal accidents. Alcohol is involved in 21 to 48 percent of fatal falls and 17 to 53 percent of nonfatal falls. Alcohol may increase the likelihood of a fall as much as sixty times in those well over the legal limit for intoxication, compared with those having no alcohol exposure.

Fires and burns are the fourth-leading cause of accidental death in the United States. Studies show that alcohol is involved in as many as half of these deaths. Alcohol exposure is most frequent among victims of fires caused by cigarettes (Book Rags, 2008).

One study of injury morbidity, based on emergency room visits to a Massachusetts general hospital from October 1966 to September 1967, identified alcohol-positive breathalyzer readings of 0.01 percent and higher among 22 percent of 620 persons treated for injuries in the home (Wechsler et al., 1969). And reflecting an area often overlooked in these discussions, the study also noted that positive readings were associated with 56 percent of 188 persons reporting because of injuries from fights and assaults. Positive readings were found for 9 percent of a comparison group admitted for non-injuries.

Research from the United Kingdom may be more helpful in determining the extent of impact. According to the Institute for Alcohol Studies (IAS), there are approximately 4,000 deaths from home accidents annually. Approximately 2.6 million home accidents each year result in the victim visiting an emergency room for treatment. There are similar numbers of cases in which the victim is treated by a general practitioner. In addition, there are millions of minor cases in which no medical assistance is sought.

The IAS report noted that a 2002 UK study found that being under the influence of alcohol emerged as the single most important form of contributory behavior in regard to fatalities and a major factor in regard to serious injuries. Based on this study, the IAS estimated that alcohol is a causal factor in around 10 percent of fatalities from home accidents (Institute of Alcohol Studies, 2007).

A 1998 UK study of accidents, which considered statistics in various countries in the West, noted that the most common form of alcohol-related accident in 1998 was a fall, either on stairs or on the same level. Falls accounted for 41 percent of all alcohol-related home accidents. The next most common form of alcohol-related accident was striking a stationary object (11% of alcohol-related home accidents). The most common type of injury from alcohol-related home accidents in 1998 was an open wound (30%) followed by injury to soft tissue (19%) and bone injuries (13%). Sixty-two percent of alcohol-related accidents in the home involved men and 38 percent involved women (Institute of Alcohol Studies, 2007).

BOATING ACCIDENTS

More than 80 percent of the people who die in boating accidents are drowning victims (State of California, 2003). Because alcohol reduces coordination and balance, the chances of falling overboard as well as drowning are increased in those who have been drinking. In addition, depth perception, reaction time, and night vision are all affected by drinking and increase the chances of accidents on the water. A summary of selected reports indicates the following:

- A 2006 Coast Guard report stated that while alcohol use was a contributing factor in 7 percent of boating accidents, it accounted for nearly twenty percent of all reported fatalities and was the leading cause of boating fatalities (U. S. Coast Guard, 2006).
- According to the Florida Fish and Wildlife Conservation Commission and the Oregon State Marine Board (2008), alcohol contributes to about one-third of all fatal boating accidents.

- About half of all boating accidents involve drugs or alcohol (Boat U. S. Foundation, 2008).
- A study of water traffic accidents in Finland between 1969 and 1995 concluded that alcohol intoxication was a contributing cause of death in 63.0 percent of the fatalities (Lunetta et al., 1998).

THE WORKPLACE

According to the U.S. National Institute for Occupational Safety and Health (NIOSH), 5,734 workers died in 2005 from an occupational injury and more than four million workers had a nonfatal injury or illness. As NIOSH reported:

> Private-sector workers, daily, experience 11,500 nonfatal work-related injuries/illnesses; more than half of these injuries/illnesses require job transfer, work restrictions, or time away from their jobs as a result. Among all workers, not just the private sector, 9,000 workers are treated in emergency departments each day, and approximately 200 of these workers are hospitalized. In 2004, this resulted in an estimated 3.4 million nonfatal injuries and illnesses among civilian workers that were serious enough to be treated in hospital emergency departments.

While there is no one comprehensive study as of 2008 on the impact of drugs, including alcohol, on workplace accidents and injuries, the following information provides a general landscape from which to draw conclusions.

- A two-year study of railroad occupational accident investigations and analysis of post-accident tests showed that approximately one-third of the accidents were associated with positive drug test results, and alcohol and/or drug use was determined to be casually related to the accident (Gust et al., 1990).
- Up to 40 percent of industrial fatalities and 47 percent of industrial injuries can be linked to alcohol use and alcoholism (Bernstein & Mahoney, 1989).
- Employees who use drugs are 3.6 times more likely to be involved in a workplace accident and five times more likely to file a workers' compensation claim (U. S. Department of Health and Human Services, Substance Abuse and Mental Health Services Administration, 2000).

- The risk of job-related injury associated with substance use increases by 50 percent to 100 percent depending upon the substance used and the frequency and amount of use. (See Zwerling, Ryan, & Orav, 1990; Hingson, Lederman, & Walsh, 1985; Gutierrez-Fisac, Regidor, & Ronda, 1992; Pollock et al., 1998; Moll van Charante & Mulder, 1990; Lewis & Cooper, 1989).
- According to the National Federation of Independent Businesses, one in six workplace deaths and one in four workplace injuries involve drugs or alcohol use (Gaudio, 2006).

There is strong, continuing evidence that drug and alcohol use has a significant causal impact on accidents and injuries.

See also **Accidents and Injuries from Alcohol; Alcohol: History of Drinking in the United States; Dover's Powder; Driving, Alcohol, and Drugs; Fetus, Effects of Drugs on the; Social Costs of Alcohol and Drug Abuse.**

BIBLIOGRAPHY

Bernstein, M., & Mahoney, J. (1989). Management perspectives on alcoholism: The employer's stake in alcoholism treatment. *Occupational Medicine, 4*(2), 223–232.

Boat U.S. Foundation. Online boating study safety guide. Available from http://www.boatus.com.

Book Rags. (2008). Accidents and injuries from alcohol. Available from http://www.bookrags.com/research/.

Centers for Disease Control and Prevention. (2008). Impaired driving. Available from http://www.cdc.gov/.

Centers for Disease Control, National Institute on Occupational Safety and Health. (2008). Traumatic occupational injuries. Available from www.cdc.gov/.

Drummer, O. H., Gerostamoulos, J., Batziris, H., Chu, M., Caplehorn, J. R. M., Robertson, M. D., et al. (2003). The incidence of drugs in drivers killed in Australian road traffic crashes. *Forensic Science International, 134,* 154–162.

Florida Fish and Wildlife Conservation Commission. (2008). The legal requirements of boating alcohol and drugs. Available from http://www.boat-ed.com/fl/.

Gaudio, B. (2006). 10 Reasons to implement a drug-free workplace. National Federation of Independent Business: Tools and tips. Available from http://www.nfib.com/.

Gust, S. W., Walsh, J. M., Thomas, L. B., & Crouch, D. J. (Eds.). (1990). Drugs in the workplace: Research and evaluation data (Vol. 2). (National Institute on Drug Abuse, Research Monograph 100). Available from http://www.nida.nih.gov/.

Gutierrez-Fisac, J. L., Regidor, E., & Ronda, E. (1992). Occupational accidents and alcohol consumption in Spain. *International Journal of Epidemiology, 21*(6), 1114–1120.

Hanson, D. J. (2008). Alcohol consumption and traffic crashes. Alcohol: Problems and solutions. Available from http://www2.potsdam.edu/.

Hingson, R., Lederman, R. I., & Walsh, D. C. (1985). Employee drinking patterns and accidental injury: A study of four New England states. *Journal of Studies of Alcohol, 46*(4), 298–303.

Institute of Alcohol Studies. (2007). Alcohol and accidents. IAS Factsheet. Available from http://www.ias.org.uk/.

Institute for Behavior and Health. (2008). Stop drugged driving: Facing the facts. Available from http://druggeddriving.org.

Insurance Institute for Highway Safety. (2008). Available from http://www.iihs.org/research/.

Lewis, R. J., & Cooper, S. P. (1989). Alcohol, other drugs, and fatal work injuries. *Journal of Occupational Medicine, 31*(1), 23–28.

Lunetta, P., Penttilaand, A., & Sarna, S. (1998). Water traffic accidents, drowning and alcohol in Finland, 1969–1995. *International Journal of Epidemiology, 27*, 1038–1043.

Miller, T. R., Lestina, D. C., & Smith, G. S. (2001). Injury risk among medically identified alcohol and drug abusers. *Alcoholism: Clinical and Experimental Research, 25*(1), 54–59.

Moll van Charante, A., & Mulder, P. G. (1990). Perceptual acuity and the risk of industrial accidents. *American Journal of Epidemiology, 131*(4), 652–663.

National Center for Statistics and Analysis. (2003). Motor vehicle traffic crash injury and fatality estimates: 2002 early assessment (DOT HS 809 586). Available from http://www-nrd.nhtsa.dot.gov/.

National Highway Traffic Safety Administration. (2007). Traffic safety facts research note (U.S. Department of Transportation Report No. DOT HS 810 821). Washington, D.C. Available from http://www-nrd.nhtsa.dot.gov/.

Pollock, E. S., Franklin, G. M., Fulton-Kehoe, D., & Chowdhury, R. (1998). Risk of job-related injury among construction laborers with a diagnosis of substance abuse. *Journal of Occupational and Environmental Medicine, 40*(6), 573–583.

State of California, Department of Boating and Waterways. (2003). Facts about boating and alcohol: A deadly mix. Available from http://www.dbw.ca.gov/.

U.S. Coast Guard. (2006). Boating statistics (Commandant Publication No. P16754.20). Available from http://www.uscgboating.org/.

U.S. Department of Health and Human Services Substance Abuse and Mental Health Services Administration. (2000). 1999 National household survey on drug abuse. Rockville, MD: Author.

Walsh, J. M., Flegel, R., Cangianelli, L. A., Atkins, R., Soderstrom, C. A., & Kerns, T. J. (2004). Epidemiology of alcohol and other drug use among motor vehicle crash victims admitted to a trauma center. *Traffic Injury Prevention 5*(3), 254–260.

Wechsler, H., Kasey, E. H., Thum, D., & Demone, H. W., Jr. (1969). Alcohol level and home accidents. *Public Health Report, 84*, 1043–1050.

Yesavage, J. A., Leirer, V. O., Denari, M., & Hollister, L. E. (1985). Carry-over effects of marijuana intoxication on aircraft pilot performance: A preliminary report. *American Journal of Psychiatry, 142*, 1325–1329.

Zwerling, C. (1993). Current practice and experience in drug and alcohol testing in the workplace. *Bulletin of Narcotics, 45*(2), 155–196.

JAMES E. RIVERS
REVISED BY RICHARD H. BUCHER (2009)

ACETYLCHOLINE. Acetylcholine (ACh) is a major neurotransmitter in the central and peripheral nervous systems. It is the ester of acetate and choline, formed by the enzyme choline acetyltransferase, from choline and acetyl-CoA. This was the first substance (c. 1906) to meet the criteria of identification for a neurotransmitter. Later, acetylcholine was shown to be the general neurotransmitter for the neuromuscular junctions. In all vertebrate species, it is the major neurotransmitter for all autonomic ganglia and the neurotransmitter between parasympathetic ganglia and their target cells. Acetylcholine neurotransmission occurs widely within the central nervous system. Collections of neurons arising within the brain—the medulla, the pons, or the anterior diencephalon—innervate a wide set of cortical and subcortical targets; some of these circuits are destroyed in Alzheimer's disease.

See also **Neurotransmission; Neurotransmitters; Scopolamine and Atropine.**

BIBLIOGRAPHY

Cooper, J. R., Bloom, F. E., & Roth, R. H. (1996). *The biochemical basis of neuropharmacology*, 7th ed. New York: Oxford University Press. (2002, 8th ed.)

Webster, R., Ed. (2002). *Neurotransmitters, drugs and brain function*. Chichester, U.K.: John Wiley & Sons.

FLOYD BLOOM

ADDICTED BABIES. *See* Alcohol- and Drug-Exposed Infants.

ADDICTION: CONCEPTS AND DEFINITIONS.

This entry deals with concepts related to the basic nature of addiction that are widely used but often misused, and that have undergone significant changes since the term *addiction* first came into the common vocabulary. In the following discussion, the terms are grouped according to themes, rather than being arranged in alphabetic order.

ABUSE AND MISUSE

In everyday English, *abuse* carries the connotations of improper, perverse, or corrupt use or practice, as in child abuse or abuse of power. As applied to drugs, however, the term is difficult to define and carries different meanings in different contexts. In relation to therapeutic agents, such as benzodiazepines or morphine, the term *drug abuse* is applied to their use for other than medical purposes or in unnecessarily large quantities. With reference to licit but non-therapeutic substances such as alcohol, it is understood to mean a level of use that is hazardous or damaging, either to the user or to others, or both. When applied to illicit substances that have no recognized medical applications, such as phencyclidine (PCP) or mescaline, any use is generally regarded as abuse. The term *misuse* refers more narrowly to the use of a therapeutic drug in any way other than what is regarded as good medical practice.

Substance abuse means essentially the same as drug abuse, except that the term *substance* (shortened form of *psychoactive substance*) avoids any misunderstanding about the meaning of drug. Many people regard as drugs only those compounds that are, or could be, used for the treatment of disease, whereas *substances* also includes materials such as organic solvents, salvinorins (magic mint), or toad

venoms, that have no medical applications at present but are abused in one or more of the senses defined above.

The best general definition of *drug abuse* is the use of any drug in a manner that deviates from the approved medical or social patterns within a given culture at a given time. This is probably the concept underlying the official acceptance of the term *abuse* in such instances as the names of the National Institute on Drug Abuse (USA) and the Canadian Centre on Substance Abuse. Such official acceptance, however, does not prevent the occurrence of ambiguities such as those mentioned in the next section.

RECREATIONAL OR CASUAL DRUG USE

The two terms, *recreational* and *casual*, are generally understood to refer to drug use that is small in amount, infrequent, and without adverse consequences, but these characteristics are not in fact necessary parts of the definitions. In the terminology recommended by the World Health Organization (WHO), the two terms are synonymous as of 2008. However, *recreational use* really refers only to the motive for use, which is to obtain effects that the user regards as pleasurable or rewarding in some way, even if that use also carries some potential risks. *Casual use* refers to occasional as opposed to regular use and, therefore, implies that the user is not dependent or addicted, but it carries no necessary implications with respect to motive for use or the amount used on any occasion. Thus, a casual user might become intoxicated or suffer an acute adverse effect on occasions, even if these are infrequent.

Occasional use may also be circumstantial or utilitarian, if employed to achieve some specific short-term benefit under special circumstances. The use of amphetamines to increase endurance and postpone fatigue by students studying for examinations, truck drivers on long hauls, athletes competing in endurance events, or military personnel on long missions, are all instances of such utilitarian use. Many observers also consider the first three of these to be abuse or misuse, but some would not regard the fourth example as abuse because it is or was prescribed by military authorities under unusual circumstances, for necessary combat goals. Nevertheless, in all four instances the same drug effect is sought for the same purpose (i.e., to increase endurance). This example illustrates the complexities and ambiguities of definitions in the field of drug use.

INTOXICATION

Intoxication is the state of functional impairment resulting from the actions of a drug. It may be acute (i.e., caused by consumption of a high dose of drug on one occasion); it may be chronic (i.e., caused by repeated use of large enough doses to maintain an excessive drug concentration in the body over a long time). The characteristic pattern of intoxication varies from one drug to another, depending upon the mechanisms of action of the different substances. For example, intoxication by alcohol or barbiturates typically includes disturbances of neuromuscular coordination, speech, sensory functions, memory, reaction time, reflexes, judgment of speeds and distances, and appropriate control of emotional expression and behavior. In contrast, intoxication by amphetamine or cocaine usually includes raised blood pressure and heart rate, elevation of body temperature, intense hyperactivity, mental disturbances such as hallucinations and paranoid delusions, and sometimes convulsions. The term may be considered equivalent to *overdosage*, in that the signs of intoxication usually arise at higher doses than the pleasurable subjective effects for which the drug is usually taken.

HABIT AND HABITUATION

In everyday English, a *habit* is a customary behavior, especially one that has become largely automatic or unconscious as a result of frequent repetition of the same act. In itself, the word is simply descriptive, carrying no fixed connotation of good or bad. As applied to drug use, however, it is somewhat more judgmental. It refers to regular persistent use of a drug, in amounts that may create some risk for the user, and over which the user does not have complete voluntary control. Indeed, an *alcohol habit* has been defined in terms very similar to those used to define dependence. In older writings, *habit strength* was used to characterize the degree of an individual's habitual drug use, in terms of the average amount of the drug taken daily. Reference to a drug habit implies that the drug use is the object of some concern on the part of the user or of the observer but that it may not yet be sufficiently strongly established to make treatment clearly necessary.

Habituation refers either to the process of acquiring a drug habit or to the state of the habitual user. Since habitual users frequently show increased tolerance (decreased sensitivity to the effects of the drug), habituation is also used in the earlier literature to mean an acquired increase in tolerance. In its early reports, the World Health Organization Expert Committee on Drug Dependence (as it is known as of 2008, after several changes of name) used the term *habituation* to refer to a state arising from repeated drug use, that was less serious than addiction in the sense that it included only psychological and not physical dependence, and that harm, if it occurred, was only to the user and not to others. Drugs were classified according to whether they caused habituation or addiction. These distinctions were later recognized to be based on misconception, because (1) psychological (or psychic) dependence is even more important than physical dependence with respect to the genesis of addiction; (2) any drug that can damage the user is also capable of causing harm to others and to society at large; and (3) the same drug can cause effects that might be classed as *habituation* in one user and *addiction* in another. The WHO Expert Committee later recommended that both terms be dropped from use and that *dependence* be used instead.

PROBLEM DRINKING

In an effort to avoid semantic arguments and value judgments about abuse or addiction, clinical and epidemiological researchers have increasingly made use of objective operational definitions and measures. *Problem drinking* is alcohol consumption at an average daily level that causes problems, regardless of whether these are of medical, legal, interpersonal, economic, or other nature, to the drinker or to others. The actual level, in milliliters of absolute alcohol per day, obviously varies with the individual, the type of problem, and the circumstances. The advantage of this term is that a drinker who may not meet the criteria of dependence or who is reluctant to accept a diagnostic label of alcoholism or addiction can often be led to acknowledge that a problem exists and requires intervention.

ADDICTION AND DEPENDENCE

The term *addiction* was used in everyday and legal English long before its application to drug problems. In the sixteenth century, it was used to designate the state of being legally bound or given over (e.g., bondage of a servant to a master) or, figuratively, of being habitually given over to some practice or habit; in both senses, it implied a loss of liberty of action. At the beginning of the twentieth century, it came to be used more specifically for the state of being given over to the habitual excessive use of a drug, and the person who was given over to such drug use was described as an addict. By extension from the original meanings of addiction, *drug addiction* meant a practice of drug use that the user could not voluntarily cease, and loss of control over drinking was considered an essential feature of alcohol addiction. The emphasis was placed upon the degree to which the drug use dominated the person's life, in such forms as constant preoccupation with obtaining and using the drug and inability to discontinue its use even when harmful effects made it necessary or strongly advisable to do so.

During the first half of the twentieth century, however, the pharmacological and social consequences of such use came increasingly to be the defining criteria. In 1957, the WHO Expert Committee defined addiction as,

> a state of periodic or chronic intoxication produced by the repeated consumption of a drug (natural or synthetic). Its characteristics include (1) an overpowering need (compulsion) to continue taking the drug and to obtain it by any means; (2) a tendency to increase the dose [later said to reflect tolerance] (3) a psychic (psychological) and generally a physical dependence on the effects of the drug; and (4) detrimental effect on the individual and on society.

Physical dependence is an altered physiological state arising from the regular heavy use of a drug, such that the body cannot function normally unless the drug is present. This state is recognizable only by the physical and mental disturbances that occur when drug use is abruptly discontinued or withdrawn, and the constellation of these disturbances is known as a *withdrawal syndrome.* The specific pattern of the withdrawal syndrome varies according to the type of drug that has been used and usually consists of changes opposite in direction to those originally produced by the action of the drug. For example, if opiate drugs cause constipation, their withdrawal typically produces diarrhea; if cocaine causes prolonged wakefulness and

euphoria, the withdrawal syndrome will include profound sleepiness and depression; if alcohol decreases the reactivity of nerve cells, the withdrawal syndrome will include signs of over-reactivity, such as exaggerated reflexes or convulsions. In all cases, however, the withdrawal syndrome is quickly abolished by resumption of administration of the drug or of a substitute drug with a very similar pattern of actions.

It has long been recognized that a person can become physically dependent on a drug given in high doses for medical reasons (e.g., morphine given repeatedly for relief of chronic pain) and yet not show any subsequent tendency to seek and use the drug for non-medical purposes. The WHO Expert Committee revised its definitions and concepts to reflect this knowledge in 1973, substituting the single term *dependence* for the two terms *addiction* and *habituation.* Unfortunately, this change has not yet led to uniform terminology or concepts.

In essence, *dependence* is a state in which the individual cannot function normally—physically, mentally, or socially—in the absence of the drug. A simple definition given in the fourth edition of the *Diagnostic and Statistical Manual of Mental Disorders* published in 1994 by the American Psychiatric Association (*DSM-IV*) includes only one fundamental element: "compulsive use of the drug despite the occurrence of adverse consequences." However, a more detailed description of the *dependence syndrome* includes both physical components (increased tolerance to the drug; repeated experience of withdrawal symptoms; use of the drug to prevent or relieve withdrawal symptoms) and behavioral signs of loss of control over drug use (e.g., increasing prominence of drug-seeking behavior, even at the cost of disruption of other important parts of the user's daily life; use of larger amounts than intended; inability to cut down the amount used, despite persistent desire to do so; and awareness by the user of frequent craving).

Psychic dependence or *psychological dependence* refers to those components of the dependence syndrome other than tolerance and withdrawal symptoms, in particular the urgency of drug-seeking behavior, craving, inability to function in daily life without repeated use of the drug, and the inability to maintain prolonged abstinence. It has been attributed to a distress or tension, especially during periods of abstinence from the drug, which the user seeks to relieve by taking the drug again. This is, however, really a description, rather than an explanation.

Because of these differences in definition of dependence by different authorities, the term has proven to be less clear than intended and has not displaced the term *addiction* from common use. The latter carries a clearer emphasis on the behavior of the individual, rather than the consequences of that behavior, as in the concept of nicotine addiction. A committee report of the Academy of Sciences of the Royal Society of Canada (1989) concluded that the only elements common to all definitions of addiction are a strongly established pattern of repeated self-administration of a drug in doses that reliably produce reinforcing psychoactive effects and great difficulty in achieving voluntary long-term cessation of such use, even when the user is strongly motivated to stop. It has been suggested by some highly experienced researchers in the field of substance use problems that the next edition of the *DSM* (*DSM-V*) and of the WHO *International Classification of Diseases* (*ICD-11*) should revert to the use of *addiction* in place of *dependence*, because the latter term is more likely to confuse physicians and deter them from giving adequate doses of analgesics to patients with terminal cancer, for example. Others have argued equally strongly against abandoning the term *dependence*, in part because *addiction* carries with it a stigma that discourages patients from seeking treatment, and the question is not yet entirely resolved.

Some studies of the *DSM-IV* criteria for dependence have shown them to be highly reliable and reproducible for nicotine and opioids, good for alcohol and cocaine, and only fair for cannabis, sedatives, and psychostimulant drugs. Some authors have questioned whether separate substance-specific diagnostic criteria for dependence are required, whereas others have argued that despite the differences in reliability for different drugs, overall the patterns of dependence on different substances are more similar than different and that a single set of criteria should be retained. However, several investigators have argued for the inclusion of additional criteria related to severity, such as the number of

dependence criteria present in a given case or the frequency of consuming more than five standard drinks of alcohol on a given drinking occasion or comparable measures for other substances. An additional topic of debate is whether behaviors not related to drug use, such as compulsive gambling or compulsive eating, should be regarded as addictions. It is generally accepted that there are many close resemblances between these behaviors and those seen in drug dependence and that the same reinforcement system is involved, but as of the first decade of the twenty-first century, there was not complete agreement that the processes are entirely analogous.

Genetic Factors in Dependence. It has been known for many years that family members of alcohol-dependent patients have a significantly greater risk of becoming dependent themselves than members of the general population do. Although the family environment plays an important role in this greater risk, there is abundant evidence that hereditary factors are also important contributors. Exploration of the genetic mechanisms is an important part of research in the early twenty-first century, not only on alcoholism but on other types of drug dependence as well. A few general principles derived from this research can be stated here.

First, there is not one single gene that determines the risk of dependence; rather, there are a very large number of genes, each encoding one component of the total picture. For example, there are different genes that determine the initial sensitivity to the actions of a drug on first exposure to it, the degree of reinforcement produced by a given dose of a drug, the ability to develop sensitization of the reinforcing effects, the intensity of withdrawal effects if the drug is stopped, the ability to develop tolerance to various effects of the drugs, and so forth. There are also genes that determine the degree of unpleasant or punishing effects of a drug, which may constitute a genetic protection factor against using enough of it to cause problems. Structural variations have been found in many of these genes that can cause both quantitative and qualitative differences in the various drug effects in different individuals and populations.

A second principle is that the degree to which a gene is expressed, that is, the degree to which its action is allowed to proceed or is held in check, can be affected by non-genetic influences either within the individual's metabolism or in the environment. Therefore, a person who has a gene variant that would increase the risk of some aspect of dependence if it is expressed, but who is not exposed to the environmental risk factor, does not necessarily show such a change and, therefore, does not necessarily become dependent.

A third principle is that even if the person carrying such genetic risk factors does become dependent, the consequences can be strongly affected by environmental influences. For example, both dependent and non-dependent persons use less of a drug if the price is increased or the availability is otherwise decreased. This correlation has been shown not only with alcohol, but also with tobacco, heroin, cocaine, cannabis, and other drugs. Therefore, the impact of dependence on the user, and to a considerable extent on those in contact with the user, can be influenced by social interventions that do not directly treat the dependence itself. This fact has given rise to the philosophy of harm reduction, according to which society can take a variety of measures to decrease the overall harm resulting from drug dependence even if it is not possible to prevent or cure the dependence in many cases.

Subtypes of Dependence. Despite the validity of the general diagnostic criteria, it has been recognized for many years that dependence varies greatly from patient to patient, with respect to the relative prominence of the various features of the clinical picture. This variability has perhaps been examined most in relation to alcohol dependence, where it gave rise many years ago to the concept that there are different subtypes of alcoholism. Later class analyses of large numbers of respondents in epidemiological studies have provided some evidence for the existence of several clusters of patients differing, for example, in frequency of binge drinking, family history, concurrent psychiatric disorders (comorbidity), and use of other drugs. Some attempts have been made to correlate different patterns of gene variations with these different clinical pictures. However, no consistent patterns have been found in different studies as of 2008, and the concept of subtypes has not found wide acceptance, nor has it had significant impact on diagnostic or therapeutic practices.

REINFORCEMENT AND ITS RELATION TO DEPENDENCE

No drug can give rise to dependence unless (1) it produces some effect that causes the user to make efforts to obtain and use the drug again and (2) it is taken frequently enough to establish a strong pattern of drug-related behavior that is resistant to eradication. The effect that leads to repetition of drug-taking is a psychoactive effect, that is to say, an effect that alters the user's perceptions, thoughts, and emotions in a manner that is usually (but not always) experienced as pleasurable or rewarding. The various drugs that are potentially abused or addictive are all thought to act in different ways to stimulate a set of nerve-cell pathways referred to in scientific shorthand as the *reward system*. Activation of this system leads to an increased probability that the behavior that caused the activation (in this case, the drug-taking) will be repeated or reinforced, and the drug is called a *reinforcer*. A drug must have a reinforcing effect if it is to become addictive, but it is important to recognize that reinforcement is not the same as addiction. Reinforcement is an essential mechanism for survival, learning, and adaptation. The satisfaction of thirst by drinking water, of hunger by eating food, and the avoidance of harm by escape are all examples of types of reinforcement by natural and necessary behaviors. Addictive drugs are regarded as *usurpers* of the reward system that produce reinforcement by direct drug action on it without serving any necessary biological function.

Nevertheless, drug-induced reinforcement, like reinforcement by food, water, sexual activity, or escape from harm, simply means that the behavior that caused it has an increased likelihood of being repeated. Some other process or processes must enter into play if that behavior is to become so strongly entrenched that it comes to dominate the individual's thinking and activities. Various hypotheses have been put forward concerning the nature of such additional processes. One suggestion is that activation of the reward system is controlled by something analogous to a thermostat regulating the set-point of the system, and that frequent repetition of drug-taking leads to a change in set-point so that reinforcement grows progressively stronger over time. Another, perhaps related, hypothesis is that the degree of reinforcement by a given drug is regulated by genetic factors; therefore, vulnerability to addiction is greater in those who inherit either an abnormally high sensitivity to the reward system or a low sensitivity to the aversive (punishing, disagreeable) effects of the drug. Another view holds that the essential feature leading to addiction is not reward (i.e., pleasure or liking for the drug) but drug-induced sensitization of the process of incentive saliency (i.e., the subjects' awareness of, and wanting for, drug-related stimuli becomes progressively greater, so that they have a steadily increased probability of controlling behavior). Yet another, and closely related, hypothesis is that drug-taking generally occurs within certain specific environmental or social contexts, and cues arising from these contexts can become linked to the drug effects as conditional stimuli, which then become able to elicit drug-taking behavior and further reinforcement. This concept of the conditioned stimulus is analogous to the role of the bell in Pavlov's experiments in which salivation, at first elicited by the feeding of meat to a dog, could eventually be elicited by the bell alone if the bell was always sounded just before the presentation of the meat. In this view, when the drug-taking comes under the control of such extraneous stimuli and is no longer a purely voluntary act, the transition to addiction has occurred. These various hypotheses, and possibly others, require much further research before the relation of reinforcement to addiction can be fully explained. Moreover, all such hypotheses must recognize that the degree of risk that any given individual will become addicted to a particular drug, even a strongly reinforcing one such as cocaine, is strongly influenced by environmental, social, economic, and other factors.

Neurobiological Elements of the Reward System. The first link in the set of nerve cell pathways constituting the reward system is a group of cells in the midbrain (ventral tegmental area or VTA) that give rise to fibers running to cells in the base of the forebrain (Nucleus accumbens or NAc) and in the prefrontal cortex (PFC), where they release the transmitter chemical dopamine. This chemical stimulates cells in both the NAc and the PFC, and fibers from these cells in turn release chemical transmitters that act upon other cells in various parts of the brain. Many of them send fibers back to the VTA, where they release glutamate, which increases the activity of the dopamine cells; in contrast, cells in the NAc send fibers back to the VTA

that release gamma-aminobutyric acid (GABA), which decreases the activity of the dopamine cells. In addition, the activity of the VTA dopamine-releasing cells and of the NAc cells is normally influenced by a variety of chemicals (including histamine, serotonin, orexin, morphine-like peptides, cannabis-like fatty materials, corticotropin releasing factor, and others) formed in and released from other nerve cells, some of which stimulate cell activity whereas others inhibit it. Thus, the level of activity of the dopamine cells, and hence of the other cell types that they act upon, is controlled by the changing balance among a variety of influences that adjust it in response to changes within the body and in the surrounding environment.

Different addictive drugs affect the dopamine cells in the VTA by different mechanisms. For example, cocaine and amphetamine directly stimulate the release of dopamine from the endings of the nerve fibers in the NAc and the PFC, or inhibit the reuptake of dopamine into the nerve endings; morphine-like drugs inhibit the release of GABA and thus free the dopamine cells from GABA inhibition, so that they become more active. Orexin from the hypothalamus and cannabis-like fatty materials (endocannabinoids) act directly on target sites (receptors) on the VTA cell bodies, the former to stimulate the dopamine cells and the latter to inhibit them.

It was formerly thought that the release of dopamine from the endings of the VTA cell fibers onto cells in the NAc directly resulted in reinforcement, but there is as of 2008 much evidence that its effect is to alert other parts of the brain to a novel stimulus, such as a drug effect, that may or may not be rewarding. The effects of the released dopamine on the activity of the cells in the NAc, the PFC, and other sites in the brain, as well as the actions of the drugs directly at those other sites, are presumably responsible for producing the rewarding or reinforcing effects.

The research in the 2000s on neurobiological factors in reinforcement and in addiction has provided some rational basis for the identification and testing of potential therapeutic agents for the treatment of dependence. For example, endogenous opioid peptides (e.g., endorphins, enkephalins) act through inhibitory receptors found on GABA-releasing nerve endings that affect both VTA dopamine neurons and their fiber endings that activate cells in the NAc; by inhibiting the release of GABA, they allow the VTA and NAc cells to become more active. Therefore, an opioid receptor blocker such as naltrexone, which prevents the action of opioid peptides as well as that of heroin or morphine, will also block the first steps of the reinforcement or reward process, regardless of which drug is initiating the VTA cell activation. Thus, naltrexone has been found to be moderately useful in treating patients with alcohol dependence, as well as those with heroin dependence. Similar basic neurobiological discoveries have given rise to therapeutic trials with acamprosate in alcohol dependence, with serotonin 5-HT3 receptor blockers such as ondansetron in nicotine and alcohol dependence, and with activators of GABA receptors such as baclofen and topiramate in alcoholism and in cocaine dependence.

Progression from Drug Use to Dependence. Reinforcement can occur as a result of the first exposure to a drug, yet the great majority of occasional users, even of drugs such as cocaine or heroin, do not become dependent or addicted. Therefore, some additional change must occur as a result of repeated drug exposure in those users who do become dependent. Many neurobiologists believe that the additional change is a process known as synaptic plasticity, that is, adaptive changes in synapses (functional cell-to-cell contact sites) on cells such as those in the VTA and NAc that render them more easily stimulated and increase their output of neurotransmitter substances. According to this view, the result of such changes would be that the reinforcing effect of the drug is increased and, therefore, comes to control the person's behavior and direct it increasingly toward drug-seeking and drug use. An alternative concept is that the balance of the various stimulatory and inhibitory influences on the activity of the dopamine cells in the VTA is regulated by something analogous to a thermostat and that with repeated use of a drug, the set point is shifted in such a manner that the user gets less reward from the usual dose and is thus motivated to increase the amount used. Among young adult users of alcohol, for example, those who experience relatively little effect from an ordinary sized drink are much more likely to have become dependent five years later.

These concepts imply that the actions of the drugs themselves initiate adaptive changes that convert drug use into dependence. Yet epidemiological studies have found that as many as 34 percent of patients with a diagnosis of dependence according to *DSM-IV* criteria did not have a preceding history of abuse (usually implying bouts or binges of heavy use), and patients with a diagnosis of abuse do not always progress to dependence. These findings suggest that production of dependence may require some additional causal factor that is independent of those factors giving rise to abuse. The additional causal factor could be a separate genetic risk factor, or some influence in the person's physical or psychological environment. This question clearly requires considerably more research.

RELAPSE AND REINSTATEMENT

As noted earlier, addiction or dependence is not characterized by an inability to stop using the drug, but by an inability to maintain the cessation of use. A high proportion of dependent patients do make efforts to stop drug use and, in fact, do stop for varying periods of time, but then they resume drug use even though they would wish not to do so. This pattern of behavior is known clinically as relapse, and patients may have many short periods of abstinence followed by relapse. Much research into the causes of relapse has been carried out in both clinical and laboratory settings. In humans, relapse most commonly occurs either when the social setting provides an opportunity to take a small amount of the drug, or when the patient experiences sudden emotional or physical stress.

Animal research has made increasing use of a model in which the animal is taught to press a lever in order to obtain a small dose of a drug (e.g., morphine, alcohol, cocaine) when a signal light informs it that the drug is available. Most (but not all) of these animals will then steadily increase their total intake per session when given the opportunity to do so, until they take the drug in preference to food or water, and will develop a drug withdrawal syndrome if the drug is suddenly stopped. These animals are regarded as a model of dependent humans. They are then subjected to a procedure known as extinction, in which they are allowed to press the lever in response to the drug-availability signal, but the drug is not delivered.

After a varying number of such trials, they learn that the lever-pressing response to the signal is not rewarded, and they stop pressing the lever. This is regarded as an animal model of treatment-related abstinence in the human. If the animal is then given a small intravenous dose of the drug, or a stressful stimulus such as a small electric shock to the feet, it will rapidly resume pressing on the drug lever in response to the drug-availability signal, even if the drug is still not made available as a result. This is regarded as an animal model of relapse in humans. However, since it is impossible to know whether the animal is experiencing the same types of internal disturbance as the human patient does in relapse, the operational term *reinstatement of drug-seeking behavior* is generally used in place of *relapse*. This animal model can then be used to test the ability of various drugs or procedures to prevent reinstatement, so that effective ones can be explored for possible therapeutic use to prevent relapse in humans.

CRAVING AND RELATED CONCEPTS

Craving refers to an intense desire for the drug, expressed as constant, obsessive thinking about the drug and its desired effects, a sense of acute deprivation that can be relieved only by taking the drug, and an urgent need to obtain it. This state is probably induced by exposure to bodily sensations and external stimuli that have become conditional stimuli by being linked in the past to circumstances and situations in which drug use has been necessary, such as self-treatment of early withdrawal symptoms by taking more drug. If those sensations or external stimuli are then produced by other means, they can give rise to the same mental states and behaviors as those that had formerly been brought about by drug withdrawal, including craving, and thus can cause a relapse. *Drug hunger* is essentially synonymous with craving, and *urge* represents the same phenomenon but of lesser intensity.

The behavioral consequence of an urge or craving is usually a redirecting of the person's thoughts and activities toward obtaining and using a new supply of drug. All the behaviors directed toward this end, such as searching drawers and cupboards for possible remnants of drug, getting money (whether by legal or illegal means), contacting the sources of supply, purchasing the drug, and preparing it for use, are included under the term

drug-seeking behavior. The more intense the craving, the more urgent, desperate, or irrational this behavior tends to become.

TOLERANCE AND SENSITIZATION

The term *tolerance*, which has long held a prominent place in the literature on drug dependence, has a number of different meanings. All of them relate to the degree of sensitivity or susceptibility of an individual to the effects of a drug. *Initial tolerance* refers to the degree of sensitivity or resistance displayed on the first exposure to the drug; it is expressed in terms of the degree of effect (as measured on some specified test) produced by a given dose of the drug or by a given concentration of drug in the body tissues or fluids: The smaller the effect produced by that dose or concentration, the greater is the tolerance. Initial tolerance can vary markedly from one individual to another or from one species to another, as a result of genetic differences, constitutional factors, or environmental circumstances.

The more frequent meaning of *tolerance*, however, is *acquired tolerance* (or acquired increase in tolerance), that is, increased resistance or decreased sensitivity to the drug as a result of adaptive changes produced in the body by previous exposure to that drug. This factor is expressed in terms of the degree of reduction in the magnitude of effect produced by the same dose or concentration, or (preferably) the increase in dose or concentration required to produce the same magnitude of effect. Acquired tolerance can be due to two quite different processes. *Metabolic tolerance* (also known as *pharmacokinetic tolerance* or *dispositional tolerance*) is produced by an adaptive increase in the rate at which the drug is inactivated by metabolism in the liver and other tissues. This response results in lower concentrations of drug in the body after the same dose, so that the effect is less intense and of shorter duration. *Functional tolerance* (also known as *pharmacodynamic tolerance* or *tissue tolerance*) is produced by a decrease in the sensitivity of the tissues on which the drug acts, primarily the central nervous system, so that the same concentration of drug produces less effect than it did originally.

Acquired functional tolerance can occur in three different time frames. *Acute tolerance* is that which is displayed during the course of a single drug exposure, even the first time it is taken. As soon as the brain is exposed to the drug, compensatory changes begin to develop and become more marked as time passes. As a result, the degree of effect produced by the same concentration of drug is smaller in the later part of the exposure than it was in the early part; this phenomenon is sometimes called the *Mellanby effect*. A second time pattern of tolerance development is known in the experimental literature as *rapid tolerance*. This term refers to an increased tolerance seen on the second exposure to the drug, if this occurs not more than one or two days after the first exposure. *Chronic tolerance* is that form of acquired tolerance that develops progressively over an extended period of time in which repeated exposure to the drug takes place. There is suggestive evidence that these three forms may involve the same or very similar mechanisms. As of 2008, all experimental interventions tested produced virtually identical effects on rapid and chronic tolerance, and chronic tolerance is accompanied by an increase in the rate of development of acute tolerance.

Although acquired tolerance involves important physiological changes in the nervous system, it is also markedly influenced by learning. Tolerance develops much more rapidly if the individual is required to perform tasks under the influence of the drug than if the same dose of the same drug is experienced without any performance requirement. Similarly, environmental stimuli that regularly accompany drug administration can come to serve as Pavlovian conditional stimuli that elicit tolerance as a conditional response, so that tolerance is demonstrated much more rapidly in the presence of these stimuli than in their absence.

Sensitization refers to a change opposite to tolerance that occurs with respect to certain effects of a few drugs (most notably, central stimulant drugs such as cocaine and amphetamine, or low doses of alcohol that produce behavioral stimulation rather than sedation) when these are given repeatedly. The degree of effect produced by the same dose or concentration grows larger rather than smaller. For example, after repeated administration of amphetamine, a dose that initially produced only a slight increase in physical activity can come to elicit very marked hyperactivity, and a convulsion can be produced by a dose that did not initially do so. This fact does not apply to all effects of the drug, however; tolerance can occur toward some effects (such as the inhibition of appetite) at the same time that sensitization develops to others. The reason for this difference was not yet known in the early twenty-first century.

CROSS-TOLERANCE AND CROSS-DEPENDENCE

The term *acquired tolerance* is applied to tolerance developing to the actions of the same drug that has been administered repeatedly. However, if a second drug has actions similar to those of the first, an individual who becomes tolerant to the first drug is usually also tolerant to the second drug, even on the first occasion when the latter is used. This phenomenon is called *cross-tolerance*, and it may be partial or complete: It may extend to all the effects of the second drug or only to some of them. The adaptive changes in the nervous system that give rise to acquired tolerance are believed by most researchers (though not all) to be responsible also for the development of physical dependence. Thus, an adaptive change in cell function, opposite in direction to the effect of the drug, will offset the latter when the drug is present (tolerance) but will give rise to a withdrawal sign or symptom when the drug is removed. The term *neuroadaptive state* has been proposed to designate all the physiological changes underlying the development of tolerance and physical dependence. If the second drug, to which cross-tolerance is present, is given during withdrawal from the first, it can prevent or suppress the withdrawal effect; this response is known as *cross-dependence*. A related concept is that of *transfer of dependence*, from a first drug on which a person has become dependent to a second drug with similar effects that has been given therapeutically to relieve the withdrawal signs produced by the first.

See also **Models of Alcoholism and Drug Abuse.**

BIBLIOGRAPHY

Ahmed, S. H., & Koob, G. F. (1998). Transition from moderate to excessive drug intake: Change in hedonic set point. *Science, 282,* 298–300.

American Psychiatric Association. (1994). Substance-related disorders. *Diagnostic and statistical manual of mental disorders* (4th ed., pp. 175–272). Washington, DC: Author.

Babor, T. F., & Caetano, R. (2006). Subtypes of substance dependence and abuse: Implications for diagnostic classification and empirical research. *Addiction, 101* (Suppl.1), 104–110.

Begleiter, H., & Kissin, B. (Eds.). (1995). *The genetics of alcoholism*. New York: Oxford University Press.

Bock, G. R. & Whelan, J (Eds.). (1992). Cocaine: Scientific and social dimensions. In *Ciba Foundation Symposium: 166*. Chichester, England: Wiley.

Chaudron, C. D., & Wilkinson, D. A. (Eds.). (1988). *Theories on alcoholism*. Toronto: Addiction Research Foundation.

Edwards, G., & Gross, M. M. (1976). Alcohol dependence: Provisional description of a clinical syndrome. *British Medical Journal, 1,* 1058–1061.

Epstein, D. H., Preston, K. L., Stewart, J., & Shaham, Y. (2006). Toward a model of drug relapse: An assessment of the validity of the reinstatement procedure. *Psychopharmacology, 189,* 1–16.

Glass, I. B. (1991). *The international handbook of addiction behaviour*. London: Routledge.

Goldstein, A. (1994). *Addiction: From biology to drug policy*. San Francisco: Freeman.

Goudie, A. J., & Emmett-Oglesby, M. (1989). *Psychoactive drugs: Tolerance and sensitization*. Clifton, NJ: Humana Press.

Hasin, D., Hatzenbuehler, M. L., Keyes, K., & Ogburn, E. (2006). Substance use disorders: *Diagnostic and Statistical Manual of Mental Disorders* (4th ed.) (*DSM–IV*) and *International Classification of Diseases* (10th ed.) (*ICD–10*). *Addiction, 101* (Suppl. 1), 59–75.

Johnson, B. A. (2005). Recent advances in the development of treatments for alcohol and cocaine dependence: Focus on topiramate and other modulators of GABA or glutamate function. *CNS Drugs, 19,* 873–896.

Kalant, H. (1996). Current state of knowledge about the mechanisms of alcohol tolerance. *Addiction Biology, 1,* 133–141.

Kalant, H. (1989). The nature of addiction: An analysis of the problem. In A. Goldstein (Ed.), *Molecular and cellular aspects of the drug addictions* (pp. 1–28). New York: Springer-Verlag.

Kalant, O. J. (1973). *The amphetamines: Toxicity and addiction* (2nd ed.). Toronto: University of Toronto Press.

Kalant, O. J. (1987). *Maier's cocaine addiction / Der Kokainismus*. Toronto: Addiction Research Foundation.

Kauer, J. A., & Malenka, R. C. (2007). Synaptic plasticity and addiction. *Nature Reviews Neuroscience, 8,* 844–858.

Keller, M., & McCormick, M. (1968). *A dictionary of words about alcohol*. New Brunswick, NJ: Rutgers Center of Alcohol Studies.

Moss, H. B., Chen, C. M., & Yi, H.-Y. (2007). Subtypes of alcohol dependence in a nationally representative sample. *Drug and Alcohol Dependence, 91,* 149–158.

O'Brien, C. P., Volkow, N., & Li, T.-K. (2006). What's in a word? Addiction versus dependence in *DSM–V. American Journal of Psychiatry, 163,* 765–766.

Poulos, C. X., Hinson, R. E., & Siegel, S. (1981). The role of Pavlovian processes in drug tolerance and dependence: Implications for treatment. *Addictive Behaviors, 6,* 205–211.

Rigter, H., & Crabbe, J. C., Jr. (Eds.). (1980). *Alcohol tolerance and dependence*. Amsterdam: Elsevier/North-Holland Biomedical.

Robinson, T. E., & Berridge, K. C. (1993). The neural basis of drug craving: An incentive-sensitization theory of addiction. *Brain Research Reviews, 18,* 247–291.

Royal Society of Canada (1989) Tobacco, nicotine, and addiction. Ottawa: Author.

Schuckit, M. A., Smith. T. L., Danko, G. P., Pierson, J., Hesselbrock, K. K., Bucholz, J. K., et al. (2007). The ability of the self-rating of the effects of alcohol (SRE) scale to predict alcohol-related outcomes five years later. *Journal of Studies on Alcohol and Drugs, 68,* 371–378.

U.S. Surgeon General (1988). The health consequences of smoking. Nicotine addiction. Rockville, MD: U.S. Public Health Services/Department of Health and Human Services.

Wikler, A. (1977). The search for the psyche in drug dependence: A 35-year retrospective survey. *Journal of Nervous and Mental Disease, 165,* 29–40.

World Health Organization (1952, 1957, 1973 and others). Reports of the Expert Committee on Problems of Drug Dependence (various). *Technical report series of the World Health Organization*. Geneva: Author.

HAROLD KALANT

ADDICTION (JOURNAL). *Addiction* is

a monthly, peer-reviewed scholarly journal that has been in continuous publication since 1884. Addiction publishes peer-reviewed research reports on alcohol, illicit drugs, tobacco, and gambling. Its research reports cover epidemiology, treatment, prevention, policy, medical consequences, as well as social, psychological, and genetic causes. In addition to original research, the journal publishes editorials, commentaries, reviews, historical articles, letters, book reviews, and interviews. As an international medium of scientific exchange, the journal has its head office in Great Britain with regional offices in the United States and Australia.

THOMAS BABOR

ADDICTION SEVERITY INDEX (ASI).

The Addiction Severity Index (ASI) is a semi-structured interview designed to provide important information about the nature and severity of substance use as well as information about other life problems that may contribute to or result from that substance use. Developed by A. Thomas McLellan and coworkers in 1980, the ASI has been translated into twenty-two languages (Japanese, French, Spanish, German, Dutch, and Russian among them) and was designed to be administered by a technician or counselor. Consistent guidelines for each question on the ASI have been compiled in training materials including two videos and three instructional manuals. Self-training can be accomplished by using the video along with the administration manual, although a one-day formal training seminar is recommended. The instrument is in the public domain, and so there is no charge for it; only a minor fee is charged for copies of the administration materials and the computer scoring disk.

The interview is based on the idea that addiction to drugs or alcohol is best considered in terms of the life events that preceded or resulted from the substance-abuse problem. The ASI focuses on seven functional areas, or subscales, that have been widely shown to be affected by the substance abuse: medical status, employment and support, drug use, alcohol use, legal status, family and social status, and psychiatric status. Each of these areas is examined individually by collecting information regarding the frequency, duration, and severity of symptoms or problems, both historically over the course of the patient's lifetime and more recently during the thirty days prior to the interview. Within each of the problem areas, the most recently published version—ASI-5—provides both a 10-point, interviewer-determined severity rating of lifetime problems as well as a multi-item composite score (computer-calculated) that indicates the severity of problems in the past thirty days.

The ASI-5 contains 164 items in the seven problem areas. It requires approximately 45–75 minutes to administer initially, depending upon the number and nature of the problems presented, and about 20–25 minutes to administer at follow-up because the follow-up version excludes the lifetime items. The most reduced form of the instrument is the ASI-Lite: a shortened form that provides composite scores and historical information but not the interviewer severity ratings nor the grid of questions asking about family/genetic heritability. It contains 111 questions and requires approximately 30–40 minutes to administer initially as a semi-structured interview, and about 15–20 minutes to administer at follow-up to measure change. The ASI has been used in over 300 studies in the United States and the European version (EuropASI) has been used in about 100 more. The updated normative information for U.S. adults in addiction treatment was presented in a study conducted by McLellan and colleagues in 2005.

Despite the wide use and historical reliability and validity of the ASI, by 2005 there had been many changes in the kinds of drugs used and in the kinds of additional problems seen among drug users. Moreover, the instrument had become popular among a wide range of new users and was being used for different agencies and populations including welfare, criminal justice, employment, the homeless, and primary psychiatric populations. In addition there were problems with the instrument, such as significant training requirements for interviewers, very few cost-relevant items, and low reliability for two of the composite scores. Thus the 2005 group completed a thorough revision, under the direction of John Cacciola, published in 2006. The new version—called the ASI-6—is still designed primarily for use with substance-abusing adults who are in substance abuse treatment or research settings, though use with other populations might also be appropriate in certain circumstances. Interviewer severity ratings have been eliminated, and a 6-month time frame has been added to the 30-day frame for cost estimation purposes. While items have been added to update coverage, there are now branching questions that, if answered negatively, allow the interviewer to skip all subsequent questions related to that topic. This helps to keep administration time at less than one hour. Finally, training is substantially reduced because, as they are written, the items are now designed for administration.

Following more than 25 years of use in the field, there appear to be three reasons for acceptance of the ASI. First, the ASI is able to validly characterize and quantify the severity of the multiple health and social problems found among those with substance use disorders. Knowledge about the nature and severity of these health and social problems is key to developing an appropriate treatment plan for predicting the course of treatment and for fully evaluating treatment interventions. The second reason is that the ASI is free and in the public domain, which accounts for the wide commercial interest in developing software and training products to support its use. Finally, there has been an ongoing effort to refine, validate, and improve the ability of the ASI to measure contemporary issues in addiction treatment. As indicated, availability of the sixth version of the ASI is imminent, and this has been necessary to keep the instrument contemporary with the new discoveries in the addiction field and to correct problems in earlier versions.

See also **Addiction: Concepts and Definitions; Risk Factors for Substance Use, Abuse, and Dependence: An Overview.**

BIBLIOGRAPHY

Alterman, A. I., McDermott, P. A., Cook, T. G., Metzger, D., Rutherford, M. J., Cacciola, J. S., et al. (1998). New scales to assess change in the Addiction Severity Index for the opioid, cocaine, and alcohol dependent. *Psychology of Addictive Behaviors, 12*(4), 233–246.

Alterman, A. I., McDermott, P. A., Cook, T. G., Metzger, D., Rutherford, M. J., Cacciola, J. S., et al. (2001a). A comparison of the predictive value of four ASI summary indices. *Psychology of Addictive Behaviors, 15*(2), 159–162.

Budman, S. F., Golldman, R. J., Newman, F. L., Beckley, K. E., Trottier, D, & Cacciola, J. S. (2001). Initial validation of a computer-administered addiction severity index: The ASI-MV. *Psychology of Addictive Behaviors, 15*(1), 4–12.

Cacciola, J. S., Alterman, A. I., & McLellan, A. T. (2006). Initial evidence for the reliability and validity of a "Lite" version of the ASI. *Drug and Alcohol Dependence, 38*, 87–89.

Carey, K. B., Cocco, K. M., & Correia, C. J. (1997). Reliability and validity of the addiction severity index among outpatients with severe mental illness. *Psychological Assessment, 9*(4), 422–428.

Carise, D., McLellan, A. T., Cacciola, J., Cook, T., Love, M., Lam V., et al. (2002). Suggested specifications for a standardized Addiction Severity Index database. *Journal of Substance Abuse Treatment, 20*(3), 239–244.

Hall, G. W., Carriero, N. J., Takushi, R. Y., Montoya, I. D. (2000). Pathological gambling among cocaine-dependent outpatients. *American Journal of Psychiatry, 157*, 1127.

Kokkevi, A., & Hartgers, C., (1995). EuropASI: European adaptation of a multidimensional assessment instrument for drug and alcohol dependence. *European Addiction Research, 1*, 208–210.

McLellan, A. T., Luborsky, L., O'Brien, C. P., Woody, G. E. (1980). An improved diagnostic instrument for substance abuse patients: The Addiction Severity Index. *Journal of Nervous and Mental Disease, 168*, 26–33.

McLellan, A. T., Luborsky, L., Woody, G. E., Druley, K. A., O'Brien, C. P. (1983). Predicting response to alcohol and drug abuse treatments: Role of psychiatric severity. *Archives of General Psychiatry, 40*, 620–625.

McLellan, A. T., Luborsky, L., Cacciola, J., Griffith, J. (1985). New data from the Addiction Severity Index: Reliability and validity in three centers. *Journal of Nervous and Mental Disease, 172*, 84–91.

McLellan, A. T. (1991). Using the ASI to compare cocaine, alcohol, opiate and mixed substance abusers. In L. Harris (Ed.), *Problems of drug dependence 1990* (NIDA Research Monograph). Washington, DC: U.S. Government Printing Office.

McLellan, A. T., Cacciola, J., Kushner, H., Peters, R., Smith, I., & Pettinati, H. (1992). The fifth edition of the Addiction Severity Index: Cautions, additions and normative data. *Journal of Substance Abuse Treatment, 9*(5), 461–480.

McLellan, A. T., Cacciola, J., Alterman, A. I., Rikoon, S., Carise, D. (2005). The ASI at 25: Origins, contributions and transitions. *American Journal on Addictions, 28*(2), 36–45.

Rounsaville, B. J., Dolinsky, Z. S., Babor, T. F., Meyer, R. E. (1987). Psychopathology as a predictor of treatment outcome in alcoholism. *Archives of General Psychiatry, 44*, 505–513.

A. Thomas McLellan
Revised by Rebecca Marlow-Ferguson (2001)
A. Thomas McLellan (2009)

ADDICTIVE PERSONALITY AND PSYCHOLOGICAL TESTS. The term *addictive personality* has been used in various ways since the 1940s, usually to refer to a pattern of traits

commonly observed in alcoholics and other substance abusers. The traits include impulsivity, immaturity (dependency and neediness), poor frustration tolerance, anxiety, and depression. Long-term studies of addicts have shown that these characteristics often diminish during abstinence. This suggests that they are produced by the drugs—or by the life that drug use imposes—or are a response to social conditions, rather than caused by inherent personality. However, the term has also been used to describe related personality traits (e.g., early difficulties with impulse control and submission to authority) that may predate drug abuse/dependence and hence serve as predictors of such behaviors. Although addiction researchers have repeatedly correlated several types of personality disorders with alcohol and drug abuse, they have largely rejected the concept of addictive personality, and it is not a recognized diagnostic term in the *Diagnostic and Statistical Manual* (*DSM*) or the *International Classification of Diseases* (*ICD*). Substance use research during the past 50 years has made it clear that the etiology of addictive behaviors is enormously complex, involving an array of physiological, social, demographic, and situational factors in addition to individual personality traits. Psychological approaches to addiction have come to focus more heavily on understanding how addictive behavior is motivated. Motivational models include positive reinforcement (drugs make the user feel good), negative reinforcement (drugs reduce or remove the experience of feeling bad), and the roles played by various other cognitive processes, such as expectations and beliefs. Such models are gradually being clarified by ongoing research in brain science, which elucidates the neuropharmacological processes of behavioral responses to abused substances.

That said, psychological testing—including that focused on personality—has been and remains a key part of the assessment process for alcohol and drug abuse/dependence. Psychological tests and measurements (psychometrics) are structured ways of evaluating an individual's inner mental life and external behaviors. They present subjects with more or less standard stimuli, to which the subjects respond. Depending on the test, these responses reveal something about subjects' intelligence, abilities and skills, educational and vocational interests and achievements, and personality. Often the tests are especially helpful in diagnosing organic brain disease—its presence, its presumed location, and the particular resulting functional deficits. The tests themselves range from structured questionnaires or interviews to written tasks, to obtaining responses to purposely ill-defined stimuli such as ink blots (Rorschach test). They have been used (1) to evaluate the probability of the presence of a substance abuse problem, (2) to examine the impact of substance use on behavior and brain function, both acutely and chronically, and (3) to assess personality features—profiling those predisposed to drug use and abuse or those that are the results of such use.

There are dozens of such testing instruments available to clinicians and researchers. Some of them are broadly applicable, and others are designed for specific populations (e.g., adolescents). Some assess underlying personality traits; others track recent drug use patterns, and yet others reflect long-term chronic use patterns. They vary in their utility in different stages of assessment and treatment (i.e., screening, diagnosis, assessment of substance-using behavior, treatment planning, treatment and process assessment, and outcome evaluation). Psychometric instruments also vary in their reliability (how generalizable the instrument is across different times, settings, scale versions, evaluators, etc.) and their validity (e.g., ability to comprehensively sample the domain of interest, the relation of test scores to subjects' real-world behavior, and the degree to which the test reveals an underlying causal or explanatory dimension of behavior). During the first few decades that they were used to identify possible personality correlates of alcohol and drug abuse, the tests often yielded inconsistent results. Depending on the test, drug-user personality traits could include low self-esteem, sensitivity to disapproval, anxiety, depression, low frustration tolerance, hedonism, helplessness, gregariousness, being a loner, shyness, aggressiveness, impulsiveness, immaturity, and a number of others. Such discrepancies likely stem from differences in the way the groups of substance abusers were defined, the fact that many patients abuse more than one drug, differences in the severity of substance abuse among patients, and the frequency of coexisting psychiatric disorders in many of those tested.

The Minnesota Multiphasic Personality Inventory (MMPI) has been and continues to be the personality test most frequently used to assess substance abusers. Because some MMPI test items that correlate well with substance abuse also correlate with other disorders, three supplementary scales, the MacAndrew Alcoholism Scale (MAC), the Addiction Admissions Scale (AAS), and the Addiction Potential Scale (APS), were designed specifically to detect substance abuse. Of these, the MAC, developed in 1965, has been the most extensively used and studied. MacAndrew constructed the scale by contrasting MMPI responses of male alcoholics with those of nonalcoholic male psychiatric patients and then selecting the test items that differentiated the two groups. None of the items directly assesses substance abuse behavior; rather, they tap personality factors often associated with such behavior, such as rebelliousness, aggressiveness, risk-taking, and pleasure-seeking. A recent review of studies using the MAC found that the test correlates well with measures of alcohol and substance abuse in adults and adolescents (both male and female) across a diverse spectrum of use and abuse patterns. It works well in differentiating substance abusers from nonabusing nonpatient populations, but it does not discriminate nearly as well between substance abusers and psychiatric patients who are not substance abusers. Some studies have found that individual MAC scores remain fairly consistent even after treatment. Because the MMPI was of limited use in assessing the likelihood of drug abuse, subjective effects questionnaires such as the Addiction Research Center Inventory (ARCI) were developed. The ARCI, developed in the early 1960s at the National Institute of Mental Health, measures a broad range of physical, emotive, cognitive, and subjective effects of drugs. Patients are generally tested before and repeatedly after administration of a single dose of a given drug.

Future addiction research and assessment may well refine the accuracy of psychometric instruments, providing more information about the role of such factors as age, gender, ethnicity, culture, and even genetics in substance abuse problems. Such problems, as one author has noted, remain complex, multidimensional, multidetermined, nonlinear, and dynamic entities that resist attempts to reduce them to personality profiles.

See also **Addiction: Concepts and Definitions; Minnesota Multiphasic Personality Inventory (MMPI).**

BIBLIOGRAPHY

Allen, J. P. (Ed.). (2003). *Assessing alcohol problems: A guide for clinicians and researchers* (2nd ed.; NIH Publication No. 03-3745). National Institute on Alcohol Abuse and Alcoholism.

Conway, K. P., Kane, R. J., Ball, S. A., Poling, J. C., & Rounsaville, B. J. (2003). Personality, substance of choice, and polysubstance involvement among substance dependent patients. *Drug and Alcohol Dependence, 71,* 65–75.

Craig, R. C. (2005). Assessing contemporary substance abusers with the MMPI MacAndrews Alcoholism Scale: A review. *Substance Use & Misuse, 40,* 427–450.

Gifford, E., & Humpreys, K. (2007). The psychological science of addiction. *Addiction, 102,* 352–361.

Vaillant, G. E. (1995). *The natural history of alcoholism revisited.* Cambridge, MA: Harvard University Press.

WILLIAM A. FROSCH
REVISED BY SUSAN L. SPEAKER (2009)

ADOLESCENTS AND DRUG USE.

Adolescence, generally defined as the teenage years, bridges childhood and adulthood. During this period, pubertal development is concluded, the brain undergoes reorganization of functional circuitry, intellectual capacities attain plateau, and physical growth is completed. These biological processes are complemented by the assumption of adult roles (e.g., working), accompanied by expansion of the behavior repertoire concomitant to attaining majority age (e.g., sex, driving a car, substance use).

EPIDEMIOLOGY

A 2007 epidemiological survey indicated that 48.2 percent of high school seniors had tried an illicit drug, 56.4 percent had experienced alcohol intoxication, and 47.1 percent had smoked cigarettes (Johnston et al., 2007). Notably, thirty-day prevalence of tobacco use among high school seniors declined from 19.6 percent in 1975 to 6.2 percent in 2005 in boys and from 16.1 percent to 5.2 percent in girls. Social policies limiting access, increasing the cost of cigarettes through taxation, and social marginalization of users have had significant impact on reducing smoking prevalence. Although adolescents recognize the harmfulness of tobacco, this attitude change has not generalized to consumption of other widely used drugs. Results obtained in the Monitoring the Future Survey in 1975 indicated that occasionally smoking marijuana was perceived as harmful by 18.1 percent of the twelfth grade population, which rose to 25.9 percent in 2006. Despite the increased perception of harmfulness, 10.2 percent of youths smoked marijuana to get "very high" in 1975 compared to 10.5 percent in 2006. These findings illustrate that there has been no change in the subset of the population that is at highest risk for developing problems consequent to drug use.

Substance use is one facet of initiating adult behaviors. Consumption does not, however, invariably portend long-term problems or addiction. The results of longitudinal research indicate that youths who experiment with drugs may even have better long-term social adjustment than abstainers (Tucker et al., 2006). This finding should not be interpreted to imply that substance use is safe or inconsequential, but rather to underscore the point that exposure does not inevitably presage lasting severe disorder.

ETIOLOGY

Whereas prevalence of substance use disorder consequent to use of illegal drugs is higher in adult males than females (10.3% vs. 6.4%) a much smaller gap is observed in adolescents (5.4% vs. 4.9%) (SAMHSA, 2003). Notably, significant heritability of substance use disorder has been reported in male and female adolescents (Silberg et al., 2003). Moreover, the genetic factors contributing to risk are largely the same across the different classes of illicit drugs in males (Tsuang et al., 1998) and females (Karkowski et al., 2000).

Genetic factors alone cannot cause drug use or addiction. A facilitating environment that affords the opportunity for consumption is a necessary condition. During adolescence, peers exert a critical influence on substance use initiation. Consequently, most youths receive their first drug offer and have their first substance use experience in the context of peer interactions. A pattern of habitual substance use is most likely to develop when the friendship network consists of socially non-normative youths.

Genetic and environmental factors interact to produce biobehavioral phenotypes (observable characteristics) during adolescence that potentiate the risk for drug use initiation, habitual consumption, and subsequent diagnosis of a substance use disorder. The key characteristics promoting this

trajectory from initiation to diagnosis of disorder are noted below.

Neurological Maturation. Dramatic neurological changes occurring during adolescence strongly influence the risk for substance abuse. During this period, the brain undergoes reorganization of neural circuitry, especially in the frontal cortex, which subserves regulation of emotion and behavior as well as the higher cognitive capacities integral to strategic thinking, self-monitoring of behavior, and appraisal of future consequences (Spear, 2000). The constellation of high emotion reactivity, behavior undercontrol and limitations in consequential thinking is overtly expressed as a propensity for risk taking and indifferences to societal norms, which, in a facilitating environment (e.g., high drug availability, peer drug use), predisposes to substance use.

Sexual maturation. Precocious onset and rapid progression of puberty are also associated with increased risk of substance abuse (Kirillova et al., 2001). The emergence of secondary sex characteristics (e.g. facial hair in boys, breast development in girls) evokes the appearance of maturity beyond chronological age that may lead to acceptance into an older peer cluster that introduces the youngster to abusable substances. In addition, elevation in testosterone level in adolescent boys is associated with a propensity toward social dominance and low adherence to social norms that, in turn, promotes substance abuse (Reynolds et al., 2007).

Interpersonal Adjustment. Adolescence is a critical period of socialization. Multiple roles and responsibilities of adulthood are increasingly adopted as the youngster transitions from the primarily family sphere of influence to the influences of peers in the workplace, school, and recreation settings. Driving a car provides mobility, and earning money yields resources, to access and purchase abusable substances in these environments. Susceptibility to peer pressure, combined with the desire for acceptance in the popular peer cluster, further amplifies risk for substance use.

Psychological Characteristics. The most prominent psychological characteristic predisposing to substance use is undercontrolled behavior. This is manifest broadly as conduct problems and indifference to societal norms. A temperament disposition in early childhood marked by poor self-regulation (e.g., restlessness, irritability, excitability) in severe cases commonly precedes attention deficit hyperactivity disorder (ADHD) and conduct disorder (CD) by late childhood that, in turn, leads to substance abuse in early adolescence. The same genetic factors largely underlie CD, ADHD, and substance use disorder. Moreover, drug/alcohol exposure during fetal development, and having parents with poor childrearing skills, or low investment in the child, hampers the child's development of self-regulation. The dysregulated adolescent domiciling in a family where there is inadequate supervision is prone to engage in risky behaviors. Specifically, the ubiquity of drugs in the social environment, combined with high offer rates from peers, potentiates substance abuse in psychologically dysregulated youths.

Psychological dysregulation in late adolescence amplifies risk for antisocial personality disorder in boys and borderline personality disorder in girls. These are the most frequent gender-related personality disturbances presaging and co-occurring with substance use disorder. Concomitant to mating assortment, occurring commonly by late adolescence, both members of the couple evincing poor self-regulation are prone to substance abuse and substance use disorder. Conflict and violence in the relationship is exacerbated by the acute disinhibiting effects of drugs. Their children are also at elevated risk for substance use disorder at a young age concomitant to high genetic loading, disrupted family milieu, and parents who have low skill or investment in child rearing.

DEVELOPMENTAL PERSPECTIVE

Substance use among adolescents is a developmental outcome. Consumption may be experimental and thus transitory. Alternatively, it may remain nonproblematic, but habitual behavior throughout life. However, onset of substance use at an early age, especially where there is also disruptive behavior, augments risk for substance use disorder during adolescence.

Recognition of the adverse impact of addiction on physical and mental health and social adjustment has catalyzed research directed at delineating the characteristics of vulnerable youths and the natural history of addiction. One long-standing view of etiology has been framed as the "gateway hypothesis" (Kandel, 2002). In this theory, consumption of legal drugs is conjectured to provide the impetus to use "soft" illegal drugs, specifically marijuana, which in turn predisposes to "hard" drug use. The pharmacological characteristics of the drug earlier in the sequence and associated risk factors related to consumption of the next drug in the sequence are argued to comprise the mechanisms promoting transitions from one type of drug to the next. The notion of a gateway sequence is, however, not substantiated by empirical evidence. Rather, research findings point to common liability (Vanyukov et al., 2003). A trait integral to this liability, termed *neurobehavior disinhibition,* consisting of cognitive competence, behavior control, and emotion modulation predicts substance abuse in adolescents and diagnosis of a substance use disorder by young adulthood (Tarter et al., 2003).

ASSESSMENT

The Drug Use Screening Inventory was developed and subsequently revised (DUSI-R) to quantify the processes that predispose to and correlate with adolescent substance abuse (Tarter & Kirisci, 2001). This 149-item self-report questionnaire evaluates severity of disturbances in ten domains: (1) substance use, (2) behavior problems, (3) health, (4) psychiatric status, (5) school, (6) family, (7) peers, (8) social competence, (9) work, and (10) leisure/recreation. The respondent's profile readily informs about the areas of disturbance that require intervention. Because administration takes only about fifteen minutes, and scoring is automatic using a Web-based format, it is widely used to identify high-risk youths who require prevention intervention as well as to document changes during treatment and aftercare.

PREVENTION

Prevention interventions have yielded only limited long-term benefit primarily because programs target one or only a few aspects of the risk for substance abuse and have insufficient duration and intensity. Effective prevention needs to target parents who have a substance use disorder so that they can be inculcated with the skills needed to raise a child who is at elevated genetic and environmental risk. Prevention also needs to be directed at women who are pregnant because alcohol and drug consumption during gestation may compromise neurological development in the fetus, which manifests postnatally as disinhibited behavior. This psychological propensity amplifies risk for early age onset substance abuse and substance use disorder. Furthermore, preventions need to be implemented in the early postnatal period to strengthen parent-infant attachment. Bonding is the foundation of parental motivation to supervise the child. Preventing neglectful parenting is especially important as the child transitions into adolescence when the opportunities for substance abuse sharply increase. Notably, providing parental support, such as home visitations by nurses, has a long-term positive impact on the child's outcome (Olds et al., 2003).

Social, educational, and health institutions need to be utilized, therefore, in a coordinated manner to identify and ameliorate the cognitive, emotional, and behavioral characteristics that render the youngster susceptible to initiating substance consumption. Accordingly, effective prevention requires a sustained effort directed at promoting healthy psychological development. Youths having attitudes and a behavior disposition that align with societal norms can be restrained from participating in environments where there is high drug availability (e.g., unsupervised parties, affiliation with socially deviant peers). Hence, a key feature of effective prevention is long-term commitment to the child's welfare such that the ubiquity of drugs in the environment can be managed through effective parenting complemented by inculcation of normative values and behaviors in the child.

See also **Conduct Disorder and Drug Use; Coping and Drug Use; Monitoring the Future.**

BIBLIOGRAPHY

Johnston, L., O'Malley, P., Bachman, J., & Schulenberg, E. (2007). *Monitoring the future: National survey results on drug use, 1975–2006: Volume 1, Secondary school students* (NIH Publication No. 07–6205). Bethesda, MD: National Institute on Drug Abuse.

Kandel, D. (2002). Examining the gateway hypothesis. In Kandel, D. (Ed.), *Stages and pathways of drug involvement. Examining the gateway hypothesis* (pp. 3–15). New York: Cambridge University Press.

Karkowski, L. M., Prescott, C. A., & Kendler, K. S. (2000). Multivariate assessment of factors influencing illicit substance use in twins from female-female pairs. *American Journal of Medical Genetics, 96,* 665–670.

Kirillova, G., Vanyukov, M., Gavaler, J., Pajer, K., Dunn, M., & Tarter, R. (2001). Substance abuse in parents and their offspring. The role of sexual maturation and sensation seeking. *Journal of Child and Adolescent Substance Abuse, 10,* 77–89.

Olds, D. L., Hill, P. L., O'Brien, R., Racine, D., & Moritz, P. (2003). Taking preventive intervention to scale: The nurse-family partnership. *Cognitive and Behavioral Practice, 10*(4), 278–290.

Reynolds, M., Tarter, R., Kirisci, L., Kirillova, G., Brown, S., Clark, D., et al. (2007). Testosterone level and sexual maturation predict substance use disorders in adolescent boys: A prospective study. *Biological Psychiatry, 61*(11), 1223–1227.

SAMHSA (Substance Abuse and Mental Health Services Administration). (2003). *Results from the 2002 national survey on drug use and health: National findings.* NHSDA Series H-22, DHHS Publication No. SMA 03-3836. Rockville, MD: Office of Applied Studies.

Silberg, J., Rutter, M., D'Onofrio, B., & Eaves, L. (2003). Genetic and environmental risk factors in adolescent substance use. *Journal of Child Psychology and Psychiatry, 44,* 664–676.

Spear, L. (2000). Neurobehavioral changes in adolescence. *Current Directions in Psychological Sciences, 9,* 111–114.

Tarter, R. (1990). Evaluation and treatment of adolescent substance abuse: A decision tree method. *American Journal of Drug and Alcohol Abuse, 16,* 1–46.

Tarter, R., & Kirisci, L. (2001). Validity of the Drug Use Screening Inventory for predicting DSM-III-R substance use disorder. *Journal of Child and Adolescent Substance Abuse, 10,* 45–53.

Tarter, R., Kirisci, L., Mezzich, A., Cornelius, J., Pajer, K., Vanyukov, M., et al. (2003). Neurobehavior disinhibition in childhood predicts early age onset substance disorder. *American Journal of Psychiatry, 160,* 1078–1085.

Tsuang, M. T., Lyons, M. J., Meyer, J. M., Doyle, T., Eisen, S. A., Goldberg, J., et al. (1998). Co-occurrence of abuse of different drugs in men: The role of drug-specific vulnerabilities. *Archives of General Psychiatry, 55,* 967–972.

Tucker, J. S., Ellickson, P. L., Collins, R. L., & Klein, D. J. (2006). Are drug experimenters better adjusted than abstainers and users?: A longitudinal study of adolescent marijuana use. *Journal of Adolescent Health, 39*(4), 488–494.

Vanyukov, M. M., Tarter, R. E., Kirisci, L., Kirillova, G. P., Maher, B. S., & Clark, D. B. (2003). Liability to substance use disorders: 1. Common mechanisms and manifestations. *Neuroscience and Biobehavior Review, 27,* 507–515.

RALPH TARTER

ADULT CHILDREN OF ALCO-HOLICS.

Individuals over the age of eighteen with at least one biological parent with a history of severe, chronic alcohol problems are labeled "adult children of alcoholics" (ACOA). This label is generally stigmatizing, but studies have shown that this stigmatization may be unwarranted. A 2000 review of the literature by S. L. Harter found that studies have noted greater depression, anxiety, stress-related disorders, maladjustment, and relationship problems in ACOA compared to adult children of nonalcoholics (ACONA). However, Harter also found that many of these studies were based on a clinical or convenience sample, lacked appropriate comparison groups, and had poor measurements.

RISKS INVOLVED WITH ACOA

According to L. Chassin and colleagues (1991), ACOA are predisposed to alcohol and drug problems beginning in adolescence, while children of alcoholics are 5.1 times more likely to report dependence symptoms related to substance use than children of nonalcoholics. Longitudinal cohort studies by J. Knop and colleagues (2007) show that drinking problems continue into adulthood. In addition, compared to ACONA, ACOA may be more likely to choose alcoholic spouses, and they are less likely to reduce their drinking when they enter the workforce, marry, and become parents (Jackson et al., 2001; Flora & Chassin, 2005). However, these problems are not consistently observed in ACOA, and they might apply equally well to dysfunctional families generally.

Alcohol's influence on ACOA is difficult to isolate because alcohol-related familial dysfunction is intertwined with antisocial personality disorder (ASPD), aggression, and affective disorders. A parental alcohol use disorder (AUD) may not be the proximal cause of an AUD in an adult offspring, as this condition may be due to a familial transmission of externalizing or internalizing disorders. Often, however, AUDs are correlated with

ASPD. For example, a 1997 study by R. C. Kessler and colleagues determined that ASPD is found in 17 percent of alcoholic men and 8 percent of alcoholic women, compared to 3.6 percent among nonalcoholic individuals, as reported by B. F. Grant and colleagues in 2004. In a 2004 study of 1,116 twin pairs by S. R. Jaffee and colleagues, the odds of physical maltreatment were found to increase threefold when a mother or father had antisocial behavioral traits. Further, physical maltreatment predicted antisocial behavior several years later. The maltreatment was not influenced by genetic factors, and the effects of maltreatment on antisocial behavior remained significant after controlling for parental antisocial behavior and genetic transmission of antisocial behavior. This finding supports previous longitudinal studies showing that physical maltreatment plays a role in an offspring's antisocial behavior (Lansford et al., 2002; Keiley et al., 2001). Thus, maltreatment may partially explain an AUD whether an ACOA or not. In a 1997 study, T. Jacob and S. Johnson found that maltreatment, lack of affection, high levels of criticism and hostility, inconsistent discipline or supervision, and a lack of involvement can all result in aggressive, antisocial children. Likewise, maltreatment can promote deviant behavior and juvenile delinquency, and it can affect children of alcoholics and nonalcoholics similarly.

Men and women are affected differently by abuse and neglect in childhood. In a 1995 study of severely abused and neglected children, C. S. Widom and colleagues found no significant association between childhood victimization and later alcohol use in men. However, having one or more alcoholic parent predicted both *DSM-III-R* dependence criteria and an AUD. In women, a significant relationship was found between childhood abuse or neglect and alcohol-dependence criteria. Much like the men in this study, women with an alcoholic parent were significantly more likely to endorse alcohol-dependence criteria. A 2007 follow-up study found that child abuse was a significant factor for heavy drinking in middle-aged women. However, the significant effect disappeared after controlling for parental alcohol or drug problems. For men there was no significant effect of childhood abuse on later drinking behavior. This study and several others demonstrate differential effects by gender on the relationship between a parental history of alcohol problems and the development of an alcohol problem when parental abuse is also a factor. In order to adequately study AUDs in ACOA, both parent-child and child-sibling relationships—including standardized measures of abuse and neglect—need to be taken into account.

In addition to the family dysfunction associated with parental alcoholism, a susceptibility to alcohol-use disorders in ACOA may involve shared polymorphic alcohol-metabolizing genes, a vulnerability to comorbidities, and inherited personality traits such as impulsivity and novelty-seeking. The genetic effects, when coupled with the psychosocial modeling by parents of positive alcohol expectancies and drinking behavior, result in a complex interplay of genes and environment. A family history of alcohol problems in first- or second-degree relatives is an established risk factor for an AUD, and such a history has been shown to interact with many other factors, such as expectancies about alcohol and motives for drinking.

Parental alcoholism has been linked to low self-esteem, anxiety, depression, and a perceived lack of control in ACOAs. However, adverse events in childhood may lead to resilience and improved coping mechanisms in some individuals. Studies on coping styles and resilience have been conducted to find the protective factors that might explain the heterogeneity of functioning in ACOA. Coping has been classified into two styles: approach (positive) and avoidance (negative). In a 2007 study of 128 male and female African Americans, J. C. Hall found no differences in self-esteem and coping responses between ACOA and ACONA. Hall attributes this finding to strong relationships with extended family members. However, in a 2007 sample of 209 Caucasian and African American women, M. Amodeo and colleagues found that African American women with alcoholic parents, low self-esteem, and a history of early family conflict were more likely to report avoidant coping responses.

Expectancies are beliefs about the effects of alcohol; they form early in childhood and are based, in part, on parental modeling. In 2008, A. Agrawal and colleagues completed an adult female twin study, and they found that environmental influences shape alcohol expectancies, while genetics influence motives for drinking. Heritabilities for social, coping, and conformity motives ranged from 11 percent to 22 percent. In a 2006 study of Asians, C.-Y. Hahn and colleagues found that the aldehyde dehydrogenase gene mediated the relationship between alcohol expectancies and alcohol consumption. Thus, alcohol expectancies and motivations to drink are likely to be grounded in both environment and genetics.

There is obviously still a great deal of work to be done to explain whether parental alcoholism leads directly to an increased risk of an AUD in ACOA, or whether the effects are indirect and correlated with comorbidity and maltreatment.

See also **Alcohol; Alcoholics Anonymous (AA); Treatment, Behavioral Approaches to: Twelve-Step and Disease Model Approaches.**

BIBLIOGRAPHY

Agrawal, A., Dick, D., Bucholz, K. K., Madden, P. A .F., Cooper, M. L., Sher, K. J., et al. (2008). Drinking expectancies and motives: A genetic study of young adult women. *Addiction, 103*(2), 194–204.

Amodeo, M., Griffin, M. L., Fassler, I., Clay, C., & Ellis, M. A. (2007). Coping with stressful events: Influence of parental alcoholism and race in a community sample of women. *Health & Social Work, 32*(4), 247–257.

Chassin, L., Rogosch, F., & Barrera, U. (1991). Substance use and symptomatology among adolescent children of alcoholics. *Journal of Abnormal Psychology, 100*(4), 449–463.

Flora, D. B., & Chassin, L. (2005). Changes in drug use during young adulthood: The effects of parent alcoholism and transition into marriage. *Psychology of Addictive Behaviors, 19*(4), 352–362.

Grant, B. F., Hasin, D. S., Stinson, F. S., Dawson, D. A., Chou, S. P., Ruan, W. J., et al. (2004). Prevalence, correlates, and disability of personality disorders in the United States: Results from the National Epidemiological Survey on Alcohol and Related Conditions. *Journal of Clinical Psychiatry, 65*(7), 948–958.

Hahn, C.-Y., Huang, S.-Y., Ko, H.-C., Hsieh, C.-H., Lee, I.-H., Yeh, T.-L., et al. (2006). Acetaldehyde involvement in positive and negative alcohol expectancies in Han Chinese persons with alcoholism. *Archives of General Psychiatry, 63*(7), 817–823.

Hall, J. C. (2007). An exploratory study of differences in self-esteem, kinship social support, and coping responses among African American ACOAs and Non-ACOAs. *Journal of American College Health, 56*(1), 49–54.

Harter, S. L. (2000). Psychosocial adjustment of adult children of alcoholics: A review of the recent empirical literature. *Clinical Psychology Review, 20*(3), 311–337.

Jackson, K. M., Sher, K. J., Gotham, H. J., & Wood, P. K. (2001). Transitioning into and out of large-effect drinking in young adulthood. *Journal of Abnormal Psychology, 110*(3), 378–391.

Jacob, T., & Johnson, S. (1997). Parenting influences on the development of alcohol abuse and dependence. *Alcohol Health and Research World, 21,* 204–209.

Jaffee, S. R., Caspi, A., Moffitt, T. E., & Taylor, A. (2004). Physical maltreatment victim to antisocial child: Evidence of an environmentally mediated process. *Journal of Abnormal Psychology, 113*(1), 44–55.

Keiley, M. K., Howe, T. R., Dodge, K. A., Bates, J. E. & Pettit, G. S. (2001). The timing of child physical maltreatment: A cross-domain growth analysis of impact on adolescent externalizing and internalizing problems. *Development and Psychopathology, 13*(4), 891–912.

Kessler, R. C., Crum, R. M., Warner, L. A., Nelson, C. B., Schulenberg, J., & Anthony, J. C. (1997). Lifetime co-occurrence of *DSM-III-R* alcohol abuse and dependence with other psychiatric disorders in the National Comorbidity Survey. *Archives of General Psychiatry, 54*(4), 313–321.

Knop, J., Penick, E. C, Nickel, E. J., Mednick, S. A., Jensen, P., Manzardo, A. M., et al. (2007). Paternal alcoholism predicts the occurrence but not the remission of alcoholic drinking: a 40-year follow-up. *Acta Psychiatrica Scandinavica, 116*(5), 386–393.

Lansford, J. E., Dodge, K. A., Pettit, G. S., Bates, J. E., Crozier, J., & Kaplow, J. (2002). A 12-year prospective study of the long-term effects of early child physical maltreatment on psychological, behavioral, and academic problems in adolescence. *Archives of Pediatric and Adolescent Medicine, 156,* 824–830.

Widom, C. S., Ireland, T., Glynn, P. J. (1995). Alcohol abuse in abused and neglected children followed-up: Are they at increased risk? *Journal of Studies on Alcohol, 56*(2), 207–217.

Widom, C. S., White, H. R., Czaja, S. J., & Marmorstein, N. R. (2007). Long-term effects of child abuse and neglect on alcohol use and excessive drinking in middle adulthood. *Journal of Studies on Alcohol & Drugs, 68*(3), 317–326.

CHERYL BESELER

ADVERTISING AND THE ALCOHOL INDUSTRY.

Beer and distilled spirits dominate alcohol consumption in the United States, accounting for approximately 56 percent and 30 percent of total consumption (in terms of absolute alcohol), respectively (Impact Databank, 2007). The U.S. alcohol industry is highly concentrated. Two companies—Anheuser-Busch and the merged groups SABMiller and Molson–Coors—account for approximately 80 percent of the beer sold in the United States. Ten distilled spirits companies account for 80 percent of spirits sales; the top five are responsible for 62 percent of total sales.

In a mature market dominated by large multinational alcohol marketing firms, beer and distilled spirits products are by necessity marketed products (Jernigan, 2001; Lopes, 2003). Alcohol companies spend heavily on them: In 2006, alcohol companies spent nearly $2 billion marketing alcoholic beverages on radio and television, in print, and on the Internet. According to Federal Trade Commission estimates, they spend two to three times this amount on "unmeasured" marketing activities, such as product placements, sponsorships, point of purchase advertising, on-premise promotions, and so on, for a conservative total of $6 billion per year in marketing expenditures (Federal Trade Commission, 1999).

ALCOHOL USE BY AMERICANS

In a survey conducted in 2006, 125 million Americans age twelve and older had used alcohol in the previous month (51% of the population). About 57 million people (23%) engaged in binge drinking, defined as five or more drinks on the same occasion. Of these, about 17 million Americans (6.9%) were heavy drinkers, defined as five or more drinks on the same occasion on at least five different days in the past month (Substance Abuse and Mental Health Services Administration [SAMHSA], 2007).

The percentage of college undergraduates who say they have had alcohol in the past 30 days was 65.4 percent in 2006, while 47.6 percent reported having been drunk in the past month (Johnston et al., 2007a). Among college students, 40.2 percent reported binge-drinking in the past two weeks. This is the same percentage as was reported in 1993 and 1994.

Among high school students in 2007, 15.9 percent of eighth graders, 33.4 percent of tenth graders, and 44.4 percent of twelfth graders drank alcohol in the past month, while 5.5 percent, 18.1 percent, and 28.7 percent respectively had been drunk. The percentage of high school seniors who reported having five or more drinks in a row in the last two weeks was 25.9 percent in 2007, down from a high of 31.5 percent in 1998 (Johnston et al., 2007b).

The *Diagnostic and Statistical Manual, Fourth Edition* (*DSM-IV*) defines alcohol abuse as including one or more of the following symptoms: recurrent drinking resulting in failure to fulfill major role obligations; recurrent drinking in hazardous situations; recurrent drinking-related legal problems; and continued drinking despite recurrent social or interpersonal problems caused or exacerbated by drinking. *DSM-IV* defines alcohol dependence using seven diagnostic criteria: tolerance; the withdrawal syndrome or drinking to relieve or avoid withdrawal symptoms; drinking larger amounts or for a longer period than intended; persistent desire or unsuccessful attempts to cut down on drinking; spending a great deal of time obtaining alcohol, drinking, or recovering from the effects of drinking; giving up important social, occupational, or recreational activities in favor of drinking; and continued drinking despite a physical or psychological problem caused or exacerbated by drinking (Grant et al., 2006). According to these definitions, in 2001 to 2002, 4.65 percent of adults 18 and above were alcohol abusers, and 3.81 percent were alcohol dependent. One in four children under the age of eighteen is exposed to alcohol abuse or dependence in the family (Grant, 2000), and more than half of American adults have or have had a family member who is alcohol dependent (Dawson & Grant, 1998).

Underage alcohol use has been the subject of major reports from the National Research Council and Institute of Medicine, and the Surgeon General, who in 2007 issued the first-ever *Surgeon General's Call to Action to Reduce Underage Drinking*. Both sets of recommendations endorsed the United States' relatively high legal purchase age for alcohol of twenty-one and encouraged greater action among adults to reduce youth access to alcohol (U.S. Surgeon General, 2007).

Alcohol use is also a significant contributing factor in crime: nearly one in four (2.7 million persons) of the 11.1 million victims of violent crime reported that the perpetrator had been drinking at the time of the crime (Greenfeld, 1998). Approximately 17.6 million Americans have an alcohol use disorder, and of these 2.3 million have alcohol and drug use disorders. The relationship between the two was statistically significant for all but three of twenty-five drug use disorders studies (Stinson et al., 2006).

THE ADVERTISING PROBLEM

The high level of alcohol use by those under the age of twenty-one creates an advertising problem for the companies that market alcoholic beverages. The question for them is how to advertise to the twenty-one-and-older group and also appear not to be appealing to the under-twenty-one group. Since teenagers have a strong desire to grow up fast or at least participate in activities they view as adult, they are vulnerable to anything they believe would help them achieve adulthood.

Critics accuse the alcoholic beverage companies of making their advertising and promotional programs inviting to teenagers, who are already receptive to the ideas of engaging in adult activities, being successful, being more confident, and being more attractive to the opposite sex. The alcoholic beverage companies respond that they follow the industry voluntary advertising guidelines and do not target teenagers. They point to programs such as the public service initiatives sponsored by the U.S. beer industry, which encourage drinkers to "know when to say when," "drink smart or don't start," "think when you drink," or "drink safely." They also purchase branded "responsibility" advertising which has as its primary message drinking in moderation, safety, or not drinking before age twenty-one. Between 2001 and 2006, approximately 2.2 percent of alcohol advertising dollars on television were spent on these advertisements (Center on Alcohol Marketing and Youth, 2008).

FEDERAL OVERSIGHT OF THE ALCOHOL INDUSTRY

The U.S. Bureau of Alcohol and Tobacco Tax and Trade (TTB) in the Department of the Treasury is the federal agency with responsibility for overseeing the alcohol industry. Its rules discourage advertising claims that are obscene or misleading, as well as those that associate athletic ability with drinking. Also, the TTB takes the position that "unqualified health claims on products that pose increased health risks are deceptive." Alcoholic beverages sold in the United States have to carry a warning on the container that states: "GOVERNMENT WARNING: (1) According to the Surgeon General, women should not drink alcoholic beverages during pregnancy because of the risk of birth defects. (2) Consumption of alcoholic beverages impairs your ability to drive a car or operate machinery, and may cause health problems."

Until the 1990s, the alcohol content of beer could not be included on the labeling of the container or in any associated advertising. As a result of a suit by Adolph Coors, a federal court decision overturned this restriction on labeling, and so companies are permitted to label their beers and malt liquors with the alcohol content. Beer averages 5 percent alcohol, ales average 6 percent, malt liquors average 4.1 percent, wine 12 percent to 20 percent, and distilled spirits from 40 percent (80 proof) to 50 percent (100 proof). Beer is usually sold in twelve-ounce containers, whereas malt liquors are usually sold in forty-ounce bottles.

The Federal Trade Commission (FTC) also reviews advertising, with emphasis on instances of false or misleading ads. At the request of Congress, the FTC issued reports on self-regulation in the alcohol industry in 1999 and 2003 (Federal Trade Commission, 2003; Federal Trade Commission, 1999). On the day that the 2003 report was released, trade associations for the beer and distilled spirits industries announced that they would tighten their standards for maximum youth audience composition of media vehicles where their members place their advertising from 50 percent to 30 percent. Since the proportion of youth ages twelve to twenty (the group at primary risk of underage drinking) is only 15 percent, the new standard still left many vehicles with disproportionate youth audiences available to alcohol advertising. In 2006, advertising in such vehicles accounted for 77 percent of youth exposure to alcohol advertising in magazines, 58 percent of youth exposure to radio advertising for alcohol, and 34 percent of youth exposure to alcohol advertising on television (Center on Alcohol Marketing and Youth, 2008).

The Food and Drug Administration (FDA) in the Department of Health and Human Services has no jurisdiction over alcohol advertising, with the exception of wines with less than 7 percent alcohol. Unlike pharmaceuticals, there is no mandate that labels or advertising materials for alcoholic products provide a list of either risks/consequences or possible health benefits. Americans regularly see ads, company logos, and billboards that encourage people to drink, but such advertising fails to provide information about the down side of drinking, especially excessive drinking.

ADVERTISING

Merriam-Webster's Collegiate Dictionary defines the verb *advertise*: "to call public attention to especially by emphasizing desirable qualities so as to arouse a desire to buy or patronize." The noun *advertising* includes "by paid announcements." The broad umbrella of advertising—in addition to television, radio, and print media—uses billboards, point-of-purchase signs and displays, and increasingly, sponsorship of special events such as music festivals; auto, bicycle, and boat racing; and other sports.

THE ROLE OF ADVERTISING

Advertising is used as a major tool in marketing. When a company first introduces a new product, the goals generally are:

1. To inform potential purchasers that a particular product is available and why they might like to try this new product.
2. To persuade people that they should go out and buy the product.
3. To let people know where the product can be purchased.
4. To reassure people who buy the product that they have made a wise choice in doing so.

When more than one company sells products in a given category, the goals generally become the following:

1. To increase market share by taking business away from a competitive product, which can be done by offering a better product or a better value and/or by increasing the level of advertising and promotion to out-shout the competition.
2. To increase the size of the market by inducing more people to start using the product. In the case of alcoholic beverages, market size increase can be accomplished by aggressively promoting features that will appeal to the potential

purchaser, that is, makes consumers more confident, more outgoing, more appealing to the opposite sex, and, in the case of minors, leads to participation in adult-type activities.

3. To increase the size of the market by inducing people to increase their usage of the product(s), which can be accomplished by tying the product to occasions such as spring break and by promoting the product heavily to the target audiences.

4. To keep reassuring heavy drinkers that they are in good company by drinking the particular brand of beer or liquor being advertised. Since the 10 percent of those who drink most heavily account for about 50 percent of all alcohol consumed in the United States, this factor is an important reason to advertise.

CORRELATION OF ADVERTISING WITH CONSUMPTION

Concern about alcohol advertising is particularly strong regarding its effects on young people. When the U.S. Federal Trade Commission looked at the issue of alcohol advertising and youth in 1999, it concluded that "while many factors may influence an underage person's drinking decisions, including among other things parents, peers and media, there is reason to believe that advertising also plays a role" (Federal Trade Commission, 1994). In 2000, a special report to the U.S. Congress on alcohol decried the lack of longitudinal studies assessing the effects of alcohol advertising on young people's drinking behavior; it concluded: "survey studies provide some evidence that alcohol advertising may influence drinking beliefs and behaviors among children and adolescents. This evidence, however, is far from conclusive" (U.S. Department of Health and Human Services, 2000).

However, the intervening six years have witnessed an outpouring of new studies, looking particularly at alcohol advertising's impact on youth. One review of the research concluded: "There is now sufficient evidence on the constituent elements of this [alcohol] marketing to say that the balance of probabilities now favours the conclusion that it is having an effect" (Hastings et al., 2005).

EFFECTS OF YOUTH EXPOSURE TO ALCOHOL MARKETING

Perhaps the most significant research development as of 2008 has been the publication of the findings of several longitudinal studies of alcohol marketing's effects on young people. One finding of these studies was that other factors such as positive expectations about alcohol use or peer effects did not predict awareness of alcohol advertising, but what best predicted awareness of alcohol advertising was actual exposure to that advertising (Collins et al., 2003) and that this awareness is evident in children as young as age nine and prevalent among fourteen-year-olds (Collins et al., 2005). All these longitudinal studies found statistically significant relationships between exposure to alcohol advertising and subsequent drinking behavior among young people. The one national study among them found that found that youth exposure to every additional alcohol ad above a monthly average of twenty-three predicted a 1 percent increase in youth drinking, while every additional dollar spent per capita on alcohol advertising in a given media market above an average of $6.80 predicted a 3 percent increase in youth drinking (Snyder et al., 2006). Other longitudinal studies found significant relationships between youth drinking behavior, on the one hand, and exposure to alcohol use in motion pictures or ownership of alcohol promotional items, on the other (McClure et al., 2006; Sargent et al., 2006).

Researchers have sought to discover how alcohol advertising affects young people's decision-making regarding alcohol use. According to one review of the neuroscience, psychology, and marketing literatures relevant to this question (Pechmann et al., 2005), understanding the biological and psychosocial context of adolescence is critical to understanding this interaction. Key to this are three distinctive vulnerabilities of adolescence: impulsivity, linked to a temporal gap between the onset of hormonal and environmental stimuli into the amygdala and the more gradual development of inhibitory control through the executive planning and decision-making functions of the pre-frontal cortex; self-consciousness and self-doubt, attributable at least in part to the emergence of abstract thinking, but evident in the greater frequency and intensity of negative mood states during adolescence; and elevated risk from product use, including impulsive behavior such as drinking and driving, but also greater susceptibility to toxins because of the plasticity of the developing brain as well as greater sensitivity to the brain's so-called stamping functions identifying pleasure and reward. These vulnerabilities lead adolescents to be especially attracted to risky branded products that promise immediate gratification, thrills, and/or social status.

Early work on alcohol advertising and youth tended to rest on a simple theoretical basis: Exposure to alcohol advertising influences youth drinking behavior. However, subsequent studies have pointed to the importance of alcohol advertising in shaping youth attitudes, perceptions, and particularly expectancies about alcohol use, which then influence youth decisions to drink. Survey research studies on alcohol advertising and youth have found small but significant correlations between young people's awareness of this largely positive environment and drinking beliefs and behaviors among young people (Grube & Waiters, 2005).

Another question to answer concerns whether alcohol advertising targets young people. A highly contested body of research has attempted to answer the question of whether youth exposure to alcohol advertising results from intentional practices on the part of alcohol companies, or from the incidental effects of companies trying to reach a legal-aged audience. A 2003 article in the *Journal of the American Medical Association* alleged that magazine advertising by beer and liquor companies is associated with adolescent readership (Garfield, Chung, & Rathouz, 2003), but an economist who had worked as a consultant to law firms representing tobacco and alcohol interests charged that the variables in their model were too highly correlated with each other (Nelson, 2005; Nelson, 2006). Others have found, however, that this economist's own variables are too highly correlated and replicated the finding that alcohol advertisements were more likely to be placed in vehicles with disproportionately youthful audiences (Siegel et al., 2008). Others have attempted to use content analysis to assess whether alcohol advertising targets youth. They found that one of six magazine ads and one in fourteen television ads appeared to target underage drinkers (Austin & Hust, 2005).

Another concern is the effectiveness of regulatory restrictions on marketing in reducing youth drinking. One contribution to this debate examined the impact of alcohol advertising on drinking among American youth between 1996 and 1998 by combining market-level data for alcohol advertising in five media with data from two major surveys of underage drinking behavior in the United States (Saffer & Dave, 2006). Based on these data, the authors estimated that a 28 percent reduction in alcohol advertising would reduce the percentage of adolescents who drink monthly from 25 percent to between 24 and 21 percent and the percentage who engage in binge drinking monthly from 12 percent to between 11 and 8 percent.

Another study estimated the effects of several interventions—increased alcohol excise taxes; restriction of alcohol advertising; counter advertising; school-, community-, and college-based programs; family-based interventions; and interventions to prevent driving while intoxicated—on youth drinking behavior and thence on alcohol-attributable future mortality in the U.S. population. According to their analysis, the most effective intervention would be a complete ban on alcohol advertising, which would reduce deaths from harmful drinking by 7,609, equivalent to a 16.4 percent decline in alcohol-related life-years lost. A partial advertising ban (defined as a reduction in total alcohol advertising expenditures of one-third) would result in a 4 percent reduction in alcohol-related life-years lost (Hollingsworth et al., 2006).

BEVERAGE ALCOHOL PER CAPITA CONSUMPTION

In the United States, per capita consumption of all alcoholic beverages combined reached its peak in 1980 to 1981 at 2.76 gallons of pure alcohol. Per capita consumption dropped to a low of 2.15 gallons in 1995, but climbed back up to 2.24 gallons by 2005 (Lakins, Williams, & Yi, 2007). The U.S. Department of Health and Human Services has an objective for the year 2010: to reduce the per capita alcohol consumption to no more than 1.96 gallons of ethanol per person per year. However, given an increasing trend in per capita consumption since 1999, per capita alcohol consumption would need to decrease by approximately 3 percent per year from 2006 through 2010 for this objective to be met.

BEVERAGE ALCOHOL SALES

Beer ranks fourth (behind soft drinks, milk, and coffee) in per capita consumption of any kind of beverage, a position it has held for many years. Beer sales, at retail in 2004, were reported by Adams Beverage Group to be $82.2 billion, compared to $81.8 billion for soft drinks. This statistic represents 6.4 billion gallons of beer or approximately 68 billion bottles/cans of beer.

The alcoholic spirits market in 2004 tallied $49.4 billion in retail sales and totaled 394 million gallons. Wine came in third in 2004 with retail sales of $23 billion, but second by measure at 635 million gallons. The combined retail sales of all three totaled $154.2 billion (Adams Beverage Group, 2005)

THE INDUSTRY'S VOLUNTARY MARKETING CODES

Alcohol companies have answered their critics' charges by pointing to the self-regulatory codes of the three principal trade associations: the Beer Institute, the Distilled Spirits Council of the United States (DISCUS), and the Wine Institute. These codes have been expanded and strengthened in regard to placements of advertising, with both the Beer Institute and DISCUS issuing detailed guidelines regarding how the 30 percent maximum on youth audiences for alcohol advertising should be implemented and monitored. In January 2006, the Beer Institute substantially weakened the content provisions of its code. In late 2007, DISCUS issued detailed guidelines for Internet advertising. Both bodies have also improved the transparency of their code review procedures and have added third-party review processes, although the third parties involved are paid by the relevant trade associations for their work. However, there is little research evidence that content provisions of the voluntary codes are effective or enforceable. Australian researchers have examined code operations and compliance in that country and have found the self-regulatory system ineffective and fundamentally inadequate (Donovan et al., 2007; Jones & Lynch, 2007).

The issue of the correct standard for the size of youth audiences of alcohol advertising has drawn the attention not only of the Federal Trade Commission but also of state attorneys general. Attorneys general from twenty states wrote to the FTC in 2006 and requested the agency to "explore with the industry and others the reduction of the industry standard from 30 percent to 15 percent, which standard would require that alcohol advertising be limited to media where no more than 15 percent of the audience is age 12–20" (Rowe et al., 2006). A test of this lower standard using 2004 television data found that implementing it would have reduced youth exposure by 20 percent and alcohol company advertising expenditures by 8 percent, with virtually no effect on the industry's ability to reach young adults ages twenty-one to twenty-four or twenty-one to thirty-four with its advertising (Jernigan, Ostroff, & Ross, 2005).

THE COSTS OF ALCOHOL PROBLEMS

According to the U.S. Centers for Disease Control and Prevention, excessive alcohol consumption (defined as greater than 3.1 drinks per day for men and greater than 1.6 drinks per day for women) was responsible for 75,766 deaths in 2001, the latest year for which data are available as of 2008 (ARDI). According to the National Institute on Alcohol Abuse and Alcoholism, alcohol abuse and alcoholism cost an estimated $185 billion in 1998, the latest year for which estimates were available, whereas drug abuse cost the nation $148.4 billion (Office of National Drug Control Policy, 2001).

See also **Alcohol: History of Drinking in the United States.**

BIBLIOGRAPHY

Adams Beverage Group. (2005). *Adams liquor handbook 2005.* Norwalk, CT: Author.

Austin, E. W., & Hust, S. J. (2005). Targeting adolescents? The content and frequency of alcoholic and nonalcoholic beverage ads in magazine and video formats November 1999–April 2000. *Journal of Health Communication, 10* (8), 769–785.

Center on Alcohol Marketing and Youth. (2008). *Alcohol marketing and youth: an overview.* Washington, DC: Author.

Collins, R. L., Ellickson, P. L., McCaffrey, D. F., & Hambarsoomians, K. (2005). Saturated in beer: Awareness of beer advertising in late childhood and adolescence. *Journal of Adolescent Health: Official Publication of the Society for Adolescent Medicine, 37* (1), 29–36.

Collins, R. L., Schell, T., Ellickson, P. L., & McCaffrey, D. (2003). Predictors of beer advertising awareness among eighth graders. *Addiction, 98,* 1297–1306.

Dawson, D. A., & Grant, B. F. (1998). Family history of alcoholism and gender: Their combined effects on

DSM–IV alcohol dependence and major depression. *Journal of Studies on Alcohol, 59* (1), 97–106.

Donovan, K., Donovan, R., Howat, P., & Weller, N. (2007). Magazine alcohol advertising compliance with the Australian Alcoholic Beverages Advertising Code. *Drug and Alcohol Review, 26* (1), 73–81.

Federal Trade Commission. (1999). *Self-regulation in the alcohol industry: A review of industry efforts to avoid promoting alcohol to underage consumers.* Washington, DC: Author.

Federal Trade Commission. (2003). *Alcohol marketing and advertising: A report to Congress.* Washington, DC: Author.

Garfield, C. F., Chung, P. J., & Rathouz, P. J. (2003). Alcohol advertising in magazines and adolescent readership. *Journal of the American Medical Association, 289* (18), 2424–2429.

Grant, B. F. (2000). Estimates of U.S. children exposed to alcohol abuse and dependence in the family. *American Journal of Public Health, 90* (1), 112–115.

Grant, B. F., Dawson, D. A., Stinson, F. S., Chou, S. P., Dufour, M. C., & Pickering, R. P. (2006). The 12-month prevalence and trends in *DSM–IV* Alcohol abuse and dependence. *Alcohol Research & Health, 29* (2), 79–93.

Greenfeld, L. A. (1998). Alcohol and crime: An analysis of national data on the prevalence of alcohol involvement in crime: Report prepared for the Assistant Attorney General's National Symposium on Alcohol Abuse and Crime. Washington, DC: U.S. Department of Justice.

Grube, J. W., & Waiters, E. (2005). Alcohol in the media: Content and effects on drinking beliefs and behaviors among youth. *Adolescent Medicine Clinics, 16* (2), viii, 327–343.

Hastings, G., Anderson, S., Cooke, E., & Gordon, R. (2005). Alcohol marketing and young people's drinking: A review of the research. *Journal of Public Health Policy, 26*, 296–311.

Hollingsworth, W., Ebel, B. E., McCarty, C. A., Garrison, M. M., Christakis, D. A., & Rivara, F. P. (2006). Prevention of deaths from harmful drinking in the United States: The potential effects of tax increases and advertising bans on young drinkers. *Journal of Studies on Alcohol, 67* (2), 300–308.

Impact Databank. (2007). *The U.S. beer market: Impact databank review and forecast, 2006 edition.* New York: M. Shanken Communications.

Jernigan, D. H. (2001). Cultural vessels: Alcohol and the evolution of the marketing-driven commodity chain (Doctoral dissertation, University of California at Berkeley). *Dissertation Abstracts International, 62*, 349–350A.

Jernigan, D., Ostroff, J., & Ross, C. (2005). Alcohol advertising and youth: A measured approach. *Journal of Public Health Policy, 26* (3), 312–325.

Johnston, L. D., O'Malley, P. M., Bachman, J. G., & Schulenberg, J. E. (2007a). *Monitoring the future national survey results on drug use, 1975–2006 Vol. 2: College students and adults ages 19–45.* Bethesda, MD: National Institute on Drug Abuse.

Johnston, L. D., O'Malley, P. M., Bachman, J. G., & Schulenberg, J. E. (2007b). *Overall, illicit drug use by American teens continues gradual decline in 2007.* Ann Arbor: University of Michigan News Service.

Jones, S. C., & Lynch, M. (2007). Non-advertising alcohol promotions in licensed premises: Does the Code of Practice ensure responsible promotion of alcohol? *Drug and Alcohol Review, 26* (5), 477–485.

Lakins, N. E., Williams, G. D., & Yi, H.-Y. (2007). *Surveillance report #82: Apparent per capita alcohol consumption: National, state, and regional trends, 1977–2005.* Arlington, VA: National Institute on Alcohol Abuse and Alcoholism.

Lopes, T. D. S. (2003). The growth and survival of multinationals in the global alcoholic beverages industry. *Enterprise & Society, 4* (4), 592–598.

McClure, A. C., Dal Cin, S., Gibson, J., & Sargent, J. D. (2006). Ownership of alcohol-branded merchandise and initiation of teen drinking. *American Journal of Preventive Medicine, 30* (4), 277–283.

Nelson, J. P. (2005). *Advertising, alcohol and youth.* Washington, DC: Cato Institute.

Nelson, J. P. (2006). Alcohol advertising in magazines: Do beer, wine and spirits ads target youth? *Contemporary Economic Policy, 24* (3), 357–369.

Office of National Drug Control Policy. (2001). The economic costs of drug abuse in the United States, 1992–1998. Executive Office of the President (Publication No. NCJ–190636).

Pechmann, C., Levine, L., Loughlin, S., & Leslie, F. (2005). Impulsive and self–conscious: Adolescents' vulnerability to advertising and promotion. *Journal of Public Policy & Marketing, 24* (2), 202–221.

Rowe, G. S., Shurtleff, M. L., Goddard, T., Blumenthal, R., Danberg, C., Bennett, M. J., et al. (2006). *Re: Alcohol reports, paperwork comment* (FTC File No. P064505). A communication from the chief legal officers of the following states: Arizona, Connecticut, Delaware, Hawaii, Idaho, Illinois, Iowa, Maine, Maryland, New Jersey, New Mexico, New York, Ohio, Oregon, Rhode Island, Utah, Vermont, Washington, Wyoming [California Subsequently Signed on].

Saffer, H., & Dave, D. (2006). Alcohol advertising and alcohol consumption by adolescents. *Health Economics, 15* (6), 617–37.

Sargent, J. D., Wills, T. A., Stoolmiller, M., Gibson, J., & Gibbons, F. X. (2006). Alcohol use in motion pictures and its relation with early-onset teen drinking. *Journal of Studies on Alcohol, 67* (1), 54–65.

Siegel, M., King, C., Ostroff, J., Ross, C., Dixon, K., & Jernigan, D. H. (2008). Comment: Alcohol advertising in magazines and youth readership: Are youths disproportionately exposed? *Contemporary Economic Policy, 26.* Available from http://www.blackwell-synergy.com/. (Online subscription service).

Snyder, L. B., Milici, F. F., Slater, M., Sun, H., & Strizhakova, Y. (2006). Effects of alcohol exposure on youth drinking. *Archives of Pediatrics and Adolescent Medicine, 160* (1), 18–24.

Stinson, F. S., Grant, B. F., Dawson, D. A., Ruan, W. J., Huang, B., & Saha, T. (2006). Comorbidity between *DSM-IV* alcohol and specific drug use disorders in the United States: Results from the National Epidemiologic Survey on Alcohol and Related Conditions. *Alcohol Research & Health, 29* (2), 94–106.

Substance Abuse and Mental Health Services Administration (SAMHSA). (2007). *National survey on drug use and health.* Rockville, MD: Office of Applied Studies.

U.S. Department of Health and Human Services. (2000). Alcohol advertising: What are the effects? In *Tenth special report to the U.S. Congress on alcohol and health* (pp. 412–414). Washington, DC: Author.

U.S. Surgeon General. (2007). *Surgeon General's call to action to prevent and reduce underage drinking.* Washington, DC: Department of Health and Human Services, Office of the Surgeon General.

CHARLES M. RONGEY
G. BORGES
REVISED BY DAVID H. JERNIGAN (2009)

ADVERTISING AND THE PHARMACEUTICAL INDUSTRY.

The pharmaceutical industry, which researches, develops, produces, and markets prescription drugs in the United States, is the most heavily regulated of all industries when it comes to the advertising and promotion of its products. Through its Drug Marketing, Advertising, and Communications Divisions (DDMAC), the Food and Drug Administration (FDA) regulates all advertising and promotional activities for prescription drugs, including statements made to physicians and pharmacists by pharmaceutical sales representatives. Advertising of over-the-counter (OTC) drugs, which are not regulated by the FDA, are under the jurisdiction of the Federal Trade Commission (FTC).

Before a new prescription drug is approved for marketing, the FDA and the pharmaceutical company must agree on the "full prescribing information" that will accompany the product and that must be included in all ads, brochures, promotional pieces, and samples. This full prescribing information must include, in the correct order, the following information about the drug: its trade name, its assigned name, the strength of its dosage form, a caution statement (noting that a prescription is required), a description of its active ingredients, the clinical pharmacology of the drug, indications for its usage, contraindications for usage, precautions, adverse reactions, instructions on what to do in case of overdose, correct dosage and administration, how the drug is supplied (e.g., in pill or capsule form), and storage information. Typically, this information is very detailed, and even when it is given in six-point type, it can run to two printed pages. The pharmaceutical companies pay to have this information published in the *Physician's Desk Reference*, which is sent to U.S. medical professionals free of charge. The book is also sold in bookstores or is available on library reference shelves for use by consumers who want to know more about specific drugs.

All promotional pieces and ads used to market a new drug must first be approved by the FDA to ensure that the statements being made are consistent with those in the official labeling. After a new drug has been introduced, copies of all subsequent ads and promotional pieces must be sent to the FDA at the time of their first use, too, but they do not have to be preapproved. The FDA reviews ads, brochures, direct-mail pieces, and sales aids to ensure that they maintain a "fair balance" in presenting both the benefits and risks of a medication. In the 1990s the FDA directed its attention to scientific symposia and other medical meetings at which information about new drugs, or new indications for drugs, are presented. They ensure that the meetings are not just promotional programs for a single drug. In no other industry are advertising and promotion required to meet such strict standards.

THE CHANGING ROLE OF PHARMACEUTICAL ADVERTISING

Traditionally, companies advertised and promoted pharmaceutical products primarily to physicians, with some limited advertising and promotion being directed to pharmacists. With the expiration of patents on some major drugs in the 1980s and 1990s, generic versions of the drugs became available from competing manufacturers. The generic drugs were priced lower than the brand-name products, so pharmacists lobbied for laws allowing them to substitute generic products for brand-name products. This gave pharmacists more control over which generic company's products to purchase and dispense. Advertising and promotion to pharmacists increased. When committees, usually composed of pharmacists, became very important in deciding which drugs could, or could not, be prescribed or reimbursed under third-party payment programs (Medicaid, HMOs, and other insurance programs), advertising and promotion were also directed to the decision makers in those organizations. Since 1981, advertising is also being directed to the consumer.

DIRECT-TO-CONSUMER ADVERTISING (DTCA)

Since the 1980s, pharmaceutical manufacturers have used DTCA to educate and foster an informed conversation between patients and their health care practitioners about health, disease, and treatments. Since the 1980s Lisa A. Foley and David J. Gross (2000) point out that DTCA comprises direct mail solicitations, radio and television commercials, magazine and newspaper advertisements, and messages on billboards and mass transit kiosks. Both the United States Government Accountability Office (2006) and Matthew Arnold (2008) show that DTCA expenditure has increased multifold from $791 million in 1996 to $4.7 billion in 2006, mainly due to the relaxation of FDA rules governing such advertisements in 1997 (The Henry J. Kaiser Family Foundation, 2001).

In addition to FDA regulations on promotional practices of the pharmaceutical industry, the member companies of the Pharmaceutical Research & Manufacturers of America (PhRMA) worked together to create a code on interactions with healthcare professionals. In addition, PhRMA established a set of voluntary guiding principles for DTCA of prescription medicines, which they posted on their Web site.

MERITS AND DEMERITS OF DTCA

DTCA is currently one of the most controversial public policy issues in the health care arena. Several claims are made about its benefits and harmful effects to society (Table 1). While proponents emphasize that DTCA informs consumers about new drug therapies and enhances patient-physician relationships, opponents state that consumers lack the expertise to assess the quality of the content of the promotional claims. Further, opponents of DTCA also believe that it will lead to increases in prescription drug costs and inappropriate health care resource utilization. In summary, stakeholders have divergent viewpoints regarding DTCA. However, studies by Barbara Mintzes (2001) and Prashant Nikam (2003) reveal that little scientific evidence exists to support hypotheses that DTCA provides potential health benefits or excludes potential harm.

DTCA AND FEDERAL REGULATIONS

The U.S. FDA regulates all prescription drug advertising under the Food, Drugs, and Cosmetic Act (US FDA CFR 202.1[e]). Prior to the early 1980s, companies did not promote prescription drugs directly to consumers. Instead, product sponsors disseminated drug information materials to healthcare professionals. In 1981 only one prescription drug was advertised to the public. By 1989, 21 pharmaceutical companies had advertised over 30 products, and estimated annual spending on consumer-directed promotion had grown to 80 million dollars. However, most advertising campaigns were disease-oriented and did not mention specific product names. The first full advertising campaign, including brand name, indication, and fine print labeling information (referred to as the "brief summary" in FDA regulations) began in 1983. Later that year the FDA asked industry to respect a voluntary moratorium on DTCA to research the impact of DTCA and to develop appropriate legislation, if required. On September 9, 1985, Kenneth R. Feather (1986) reported, the FDA ended the moratorium, stating that they had adequately studied the DTCA issue, and there was no need to provide new regulations or revise existing ones.

During the early 1990s pharmaceutical manufacturers increasingly used consumer magazines to advertise their products. These advertisements typically included a promotional message together with the brief summary of adverse effects. The brief summary appeared in small print and was not easily understood or seldom completely read by the consumers. In the 1990s pharmaceutical manufacturers

Merits	Demerits
Consumer behavior	
• Plays a valuable role in educating and informing the public about health matters and specific drug treatments • Allows consumers to participate actively in the healthcare decision making process • Improves patient-physician communication	• Confuses patients into believing that minor difference in drugs represents a major therapeutic advance; the public lacks the educational framework to judge the claims • Encourages 'doctor shopping' to obtain a desired prescription; pressures doctors to prescribe • Wastes doctors' time by having to re-educate the patients about misinformation and appropriate therapy
Healthcare resource utilization	
• Applies more appropriate use of medicines, saving lives and improving the quality of life • Encourages healthcare-seeking behavior for untreated and under treated disease states • Reduces overall healthcare costs; lowers overall drug prices due to increased competition	• Encourages inappropriate demand for medicines and/or demand for inappropriate medicines • Leads to excessive demands on physicians, over-medication, and drug abuse • Increases overall healthcare costs due to unnecessary use of expensive drugs; causes higher drug prices due to increased expenditure on drug promotion
Health outcomes	
• Leads to early symptom recognition and improved treatment outcomes • Improves compliance	• Exaggerates disease risks and promotes anxiety • Encourages 'off-label' drug use
Social and legal issues	
• Helps remove the social stigma associated with certain diseases • Increases disease and health awareness • Promotes freedom of information and commercial communication	• Creates unrealistic expectations of drugs • Takes advantage of vulnerable populations and leads to increased "medicalization" of healthy life stages • Infringes on personal privacy; weakens the learned intermediary defense, thus increasing legal liability of manufacturers

Table 1. Merits and demerits of DTCA. (Adapted from Mintzes, 2001, Nikam, 2003a.) ILLUSTRATION BY GGS INFORMATION SERVICES. GALE, CENGAGE LEARNING

also started using television advertisements in a limited fashion. By the mid-1990s, product sponsors started placing "reminder" advertisements on television. These advertisements only mentioned the drug name and were extremely confusing to consumers as no health claims were disclosed.

In response to increasing consumer demand for information, the FDA began to consider regulations for broadcast (television and radio) DTCA. The FDA announced draft guidance on broadcast advertising on August 8, 1997, allowing the advertisement to omit the brief summary. Instead, manufacturers were required to state the product's major risks and provide additional sources of information (such as a toll-free phone number viewers could call to request full labeling by mail, fax, or recorded phone message; an Internet site; a simultaneous DTC print advertisement that included the brief summary; or brochures in doctors' offices, libraries, and stores). The prescription drug advertisements cannot be false or misleading, cannot omit material facts, and must present a fair balance between effectiveness and risk information. Further, the regulations specified that print advertisements must disclose every risk addressed in the

product's approved labeling (US FDA FR 62:43171–43173). In August 1999 the FDA issued a final "Guidance to Industry" that specifically addressed DTCA for broadcast advertising (radio and television), but it only included minor changes to the 1997 draft (US FDA FR 64:43197–43198).

To enforce the DTC regulations, the FDA can take a variety of regulatory actions including sending letters to pharmaceutical manufacturers notifying them that they are violating the prescription drug advertisement rules. However, the number of such regulatory actions taken by the FDA has declined significantly in recent years. Wayne L. Pines (1999) and Julie M. Donohue, Marisa Cevasco, and Meredith B. Rosenthal (2007) indicate this could be either due to better compliance with promotional regulations or to a reduction in FDA oversight due to a decrease in their capacity to enforce the regulations.

DTCA IMPACT ON CONSUMER BEHAVIOR

The rate of DTCA of prescription drugs has rapidly increased from 1997 to 2006. However, only a few recent cross-sectional empirical studies (including survey research) have assessed outcomes associated with DTCA, such as that done by Mintzes (2001). Two empirical studies showed that varying amount and format of risk information in DTCA does appear to affect consumer attitudes toward the drug advertisement in both print (Tucker & Smith, 1987) and television (Morris, Ruffner, & Klimberg, 1985). Research by William R. Doucette and John C. Schommer in 1998 also showed that variations in amount, specificity, and format of risk information had an impact on awareness and knowledge pertaining to drug-related risks. However, most studies evaluating outcomes associated with DTCA were based on observational analyses and survey-based research. Survey methodology is associated with limitations concerning the validity and reliability of responses, recall biases, and lack of ability to control extraneous variables. There is significant need for theoretically rigorous experimental research that evaluates the impact of DTCA on consumer behavior and public health.

A recent experimental study in a sample of the elderly suggests that when consumers are exposed to specific risk statements in DTC print advertisements, they were less likely to look for additional information or to adopt the advertised drug. Additionally, they held less favorable attitudes toward the advertised drug as compared to those presented with general risk statements. When risk statements were presented individually, they had no significant effect on attitudes or behaviors. However, Prashant Nikam, Dev S. Pathak, H. Rao Unnava, and Joseph F. Dasta (2003a, 2003b, 2004) found that, when exposed to four risk statements, study participants were less likely to adopt the advertised drug. Another randomized controlled trial by Richard L. Kravitz and colleagues (2005) concluded that patient's DTCA-related requests had a profound impact on physician prescribing behavior for major depression and adjustment disorder.

DTCA is one of the fastest growing forms of advertising and is expected to continue to increase because of recent FDA regulatory changes in 1997. Since the late 1990s the amount of public exposure to DTCA has significantly increased, but as Deborah J. Cook and colleagues (1992) point out, the controversy around DTCA continues to grow in the absence of credible empirical evidence

meeting the scientific criteria for evaluating the quality of a study.

FUTURE OF DTCA

In 2007 healthcare spending in the United States reached $2.3 trillion, representing 16 percent of the gross domestic product (GDP) and is projected to reach $3 trillion in 2011 (Poisal, 2007, p. w243). Per projections, hospital care accounted for 31 percent, physician and clinical services 21 percent, and prescription drugs 10.3 percent of the total national health expenditure (Keehan et al., 2008, p. w146). On the pharmaceutical industry side, total spending on pharmaceutical promotion grew from $11.4 billion in 1996 to $29.9 billion in 2005. In 2005, $4.2 billion (2.6% of total sales) and $7.2 billion (4.4% of total sales) were spent on DTCA and promotion to physicians respectively. The total promotional spending, including free samples, accounts for approximately 18.2 percent of total sales revenue (United States Government Accountability Office Report, 2006, p. 13; Donohue et al., 2007, p. 676).

In the light of increasing spending on DTCA, critics charge that prescription drug advertising may lead to over-prescribing or cause pharmaceutical prices to increase, whereas advocates counter that DTCA serves an educational purpose, fosters patients-physician interactions, and assists in early detection of health conditions. On the issue of pharmaceutical pricing, empirical evidence of such a correlation is ambivalent. Overall, there is paucity of scientifically rigorous empirical research evaluating the impact of DTCA on patient-physician behavior, public health, and utilization of healthcare services.

See also **Tobacco: Smoking Cessation and Weight Gain.**

BIBLIOGRAPHY

Arnold, M. (2008, April). DTC Report: Steady Migration, *Medical Marketing and Media*, 42–47. Available from http://www.mmm-online.com/.

Cook, D. J., Guyatt, G. H., Laupacis, A., & Sackett, D. L. (1992). Rules of evidence and clinical recommendations on the use of antithrombotic agents. *Chest*, 102 (Suppl. 4), 305–11S.

Donohue, J. M., Cevasco, M., & Rosenthal, M. B. (2007). A decade of direct-to-consumer advertising of prescription drugs. *New England Journal of Medicine, 357*(7), 673–681.

Doucette, W. R., & Schommer, J. C. (1998). Consumer preferences for drug information after direct-to-consumer advertising. *Drug Information Journal, 32*(4), 1081–1088.

Feather, K. R. (1986). Direct to the consumer advertising: How close can we come? *Journal of Pharmaceutical Marketing and Management, 2*(1), 67–71.

Foley, L. A., & Gross, D. J. (2000). Are consumers well informed about prescription drugs?: The impact of printed direct-to-consumer advertising. *AARP Public Policy Institute Report.* Washington, DC: AARP.

The Henry J. Kaiser Family Foundation. (2001). *Understanding the effects of direct-to-consumer prescription drug advertising: Kaiser Family Foundation survey report.* Menlo Park, CA: Kaiser Family Foundation.

Keehan, S., Sisko, A., Truffer, C., Smith, S., Cowan, C., Poisal, J., et al. (2008, February 26). Health spending projections through 2017: The baby-boom generation is coming to Medicare. *Health Affairs Web Exclusive,* w145–w155.

Kravitz, R. L., Epstein, R. M., Feldman, M. D., Frantz, C. E., Azari, R., Wilkes, M. S., et al. (2005). Influence of patients' requests for direct-to-consumer advertised antidepressants. *Journal of American Medical Association, 293*(16), 1995–2002.

Mintzes, B. (2001). *An assessment of the health system impacts of direct-to-consumer advertising of prescription medicines* (Volume II). *Literature review, direct-to-consumer advertising of prescription drugs: What do we know thus far about its effects on health and health care services?* Vancouver: Health Policy Research Unit, University of British Columbia.

Morris, L. A, Ruffner, M., & Klimberg, R. (1985). Warning disclosures prescription drugs. *Journal of Advertising Research, 25*(5), 25–32.

Nikam, P. T. (2003). *Impact of risk disclosures through direct-to-consumer advertising on elderly consumers' behavioral intent* (Doctoral Dissertation at The Ohio State University.) Available from http://www.ohiolink.edu/.

Nikam, P. T., Pathak, D. S., Unnava, H. R., & Dasta, J. F. (2003a). Impact of risk disclosures in prescription drug advertising on elderly consumers' health seeking behavior: A consumer welfare and public policy perspective. Presented at *AcademyHealth 2003 Annual Meeting*, Nashville, TN.

Nikam, P. T., Pathak, D. S., Unnava, H. R., & Dasta, J. F. (2003b). Impact of risk disclosures through direct-to-consumer advertising on elderly consumers' behavioral intent. *Value in Health, 6*(3), 210–211:PHP10.

Nikam, P. T., Pathak, D. S., Unnava, H. R., & Dasta, J. F. (2004). How risky is risk information?: Empirical evidence from direct-to-consumer prescription drug advertising and its impact on consumer behavior. *Applied Health Economics and Health Policy, 3* (I Suppl), S49.

Pharmaceutical Research and Manufacturers of America. (2004, January). Code on interactions with healthcare professionals. Available from http://www.phrma.org/.

Pharmaceutical Research and Manufacturers of America. (November 2005). PhRMA guiding principles: Direct to consumers advertisements about prescription medicines. Available from http://www.phrma.org/.

Pines, W. I. (1999). A history and perspective on direct-to-consumer promotion. *Food Drug Law Journal, 54,* 489–518.

Poisal, J. A., Truffer, C., Smith, S., Sisko, A., Cowan, C., Keehan, S., et al. (2007, February 21). Health spending projections through 2016: Modest changes obscure Part D's impact. *Health Affairs,* w242–w253.

Schommer, J. C., & Hansen, R. A. (2001). A problem well defined is half solved: Methodological issues related to the study of direct-to-consumer advertising (DTCA) for prescription drugs. Presented at *Department of Health Human Services Conference*, May 30, 2001.

Tucker, G. K., & Smith, M. C. (1987). Direct-to-consumer advertising: Effects of different formats of warning information disclosure on cognitive reactions of adults. *Journal of Pharmaceutical Marketing and Management, 2*(1), 27–41.

United States Food and Drug Administration. (1997). *Guidance for industry.* Rockville, MD: Center for Drug Evaluation and Research: Office of Training and Communications Division of Communications Management Drug Information. 21 CFR 202.1(e).

United States Food and Drug Administration. (1997, July). *Draft guidance for industry on consumer-directed broadcast advertisements. Federal Regulation August 12, 1997.* Rockville, MD: Center for Drug Evaluation and Research: Office of Training and Communications, Division of Communications Management Drug Information, *62,* 43171–43173.

United States Food and Drug Administration. *Guidance for industry on consumer-directed broadcast advertisements, Federal Regulation August 9, 1999.* Rockville, MD: Center for Drug Evaluation and Research: Office of Training and Communications, Division of Communications Management Drug Information, *64,* 43197–43198.

United States Government Accountability Office Report. (2006, December 14). Prescription drugs: Improvements needed in FDA's oversight of direct-to-consumer. GOA-07-54.

Charles M. Rongey
Revised by Prashant Nikam (2009)
Dev Pathak (2009)

ADVERTISING AND TOBACCO USE.

Tobacco companies spend more than $13 billion annually to advertise and promote cigarettes and other tobacco products (Lindblom, 2008). The companies claim that the purpose and desired effect of marketing are to provide information and to influence brand selection among current smokers, although only about 10 percent of smokers switch brands in any one year. Because in 2007 an estimated 19.2 million adult smokers stopped smoking for at least one day during the preceding year because they were trying to quit and almost 400,000 other smokers die from smoking-related diseases, the tobacco companies must recruit thousands of new young smokers every day to replace those who die or otherwise stop smoking (Centers for Disease Control and Prevention [CDCP], 2007).

Tobacco companies contend that smoking is an "adult habit" and that adult smokers "choose" to smoke. However, medical research has clearly established that most smokers become addicted to the nicotine in cigarettes and that quitting such addiction is very difficult, according to the U.S. Department of Health and Human Services (2000).

Unlike the pharmaceutical companies, which are tightly regulated as to their advertising and promotion, the tobacco industry historically had few regulations. The basic restrictions have been that companies cannot use paid advertising on television or radio, they cannot claim what they cannot prove (e.g., that low-tar cigarettes are less hazardous to health), and they must include one of four warnings on cigarette packages and ads. The fact that warning labels are printed on a pack of cigarettes has been successfully used by the tobacco companies as a defense against tobacco victims' lawsuits.

The whole picture changed when Florida, Minnesota, Mississippi, and Texas reached an agreement in 1997 and early 1998 with the major tobacco companies and won compensation for health-care expenses incurred due to smoking. Minnesota obtained copies of long-secret memos, reports, letters, and other documents that were made public as part of the $6.6 billion settlement reached in their lawsuit against cigarette makers.

On November 23, 1998, the major tobacco companies entered into an agreement with the other forty-six states. This agreement, known as the Master Settlement Agreement (MSA), settled litigation brought by the states and other entities seeking reimbursement of expenditures related to smoking and health. Under this agreement, the states and tobacco companies jointly agreed to concrete provisions to reduce youth smoking, implement new public health initiatives, and set important new rules for governing the tobacco companies' ways of doing business.

The cigarette companies agreed to pay $368.5 billion over 25 years. Of this, $246 billion goes to the states, and they have started to receive payments under this agreement. The state of Florida receives $450 million each year under this agreement, Iowa $54.9 million, and the other states differing amounts. Iowa, Kansas, and Washington set aside this money entirely for health care. Iowa passed a law that their money will go to three areas: access to health care, public health and smoking prevention, and substance-abuse treatment and prevention. In other states, this newfound money created hot political battles over how much to spend on tobacco prevention programs.

The impact of the Master Settlement Agreement has been mixed. A 2001 study by Charles King III and Michael Siegel concluded: "The Master Settlement Agreement with the tobacco industry appears to have had little effect on cigarette advertising in magazines and on the exposure of young people to these advertisements."

A study in 2004 by Sloan, Mathews, and Trogdon concluded the MSA did no major harm to tobacco companies, and some features of the agreement may have increased company value and profitability. The report stated that profits from domestic sales rose from levels prevailing immediately before the MSA and that there was no indication that the MSA caused an increase in tobacco exports. Another 2004 study noted that whereas expected changes included reduced total expenditures and reductions for outdoor advertising, specialty promotional items identified with a brand and public entertainment used for advertising and promotions increased 96 percent between 1995 and 2001, with large increases in 1998 and 1999, as the MSA took effect. It noted that, whereas outdoor advertising declined 98 percent between 1997 and 2001, public entertainment expenditures increased 45 percent. However, in 2001 these categories represented only a small fraction of the total budget. Of greater significance was that expenditures for retail value-added efforts increased 344 percent between 1997 and 2001 (to 42.5% of the total advertising budget), and by 2001 the incentives-to-merchants and retail value-added categories comprised more than 80 percent of total expenditures. This conclusion was supported in another study that observed large increases in promoted sales following implementation of the MSA as well as during periods of sustained cigarette excise tax increases (Loomis, Farrelly, Nonnemaker, & Mann, 2006). In 2002 the Massachusetts Department of Public Health reported that one of the smokeless tobacco companies that signed the MSA increased advertising expenditures aimed at youth by 13 percent after the agreement, although three others had decreased such advertising by 11 percent.

The MSA changed the way cigarette companies can market, advertise, and promote their cigarettes. The agreement specifically includes the following:

- No participating manufacturer may take any action, directly or indirectly, to target youth in the advertising, promotion, or marketing of tobacco products. It also prohibits any action whose *primary purpose* is to initiate, maintain, or increase the incidence of youth smoking.

- Effective April 23, 1999, billboards, stadium signs, and transit signs advertising tobacco were banned. However, this does *not* apply to retail establishments selling tobacco. They may have signs up to 14 square feet (4.3 square meters) inside or outside their stores.

- Effective May 22, 1999, the use of cartoon characters in advertising, promoting, packaging, or labeling of tobacco products was banned. (This applies only to "exaggerated depictions, or depictions of entities with superhuman powers." It does *not* cover the standard camel logo or simple drawings of a camel. It does not prohibit the continued use of the Marlboro man or other human characters.)

- Beginning July 1, 1999, participating manufacturers and others licensed by them may no longer market, distribute, offer, sell, or license any apparel or merchandise bearing a tobacco brand name.

- Free product sampling is banned anywhere, except in a facility or enclosed space where an operator can ensure that no minors are present.

- Manufacturers could not sell or distribute cigarette packs containing less than twenty cigarettes until the year 2001.

- There shall be no payment for the use of tobacco products in movies, TV programs, live performances, videos, or video games. (Does not apply to media viewed in an adult-only facility or to media not intended for distribution to or display to the public.)

- There shall be no licensing of third parties to use or advertise any brand name in a way that would constitute a violation of the MSA if done by the participants.

- No nonbranded item may be given in exchange for the purchase of tobacco products, for redemption of coupons, or for proof of purchase without proof of age.

- No use of a tobacco brand name as part of the name of a stadium shall be allowed.

- Tobacco sponsorships are limited to one per year, after a three-year grace period (from November 1998). Such brand-name sponsorship may not include concerts, events in which any paid participant or contestants are youth, or any athletic event between opposing teams in any football, basketball, baseball, soccer, or hockey league.

The previous voluntary cigarette advertising and promotion code rules are also still in effect:

1. Cigarette smoking is an adult custom. Children should not smoke. Laws prohibiting the sale of cigarettes to minors should be strictly enforced. The cigarette manufacturers may advertise and promote their products only to adult smokers. The manufacturers support the enactment and enforcement of state laws prohibiting the sale of cigarettes to persons less than 18 years of age.

2. Cigarette advertising shall not appear in publications directed primarily to those less than 21 years of age, including school, college, or university media (such as athletic, theatrical, or other programs). Comic books or comic supplements are included in this ban.

3. No one depicted in cigarette advertising shall be or appear to be under 25 years of age.

4. Cigarette advertising shall not suggest that smoking is essential to social prominence, distinction, success, or sexual attraction, nor shall it picture a person smoking in an exaggerated manner.

5. Cigarette advertising may picture attractive, healthy-looking persons provided there is no suggestion that their attractiveness and good health are due to cigarette smoking.

6. Cigarette advertising shall not depict as a smoker anyone who is or has been well known as an athlete, nor shall it show any smoker participating in, or obviously just having participated in, a physical activity requiring stamina or athletic conditioning beyond that of normal recreation.

7. No sports or celebrity testimonials shall be used or those of others who would have special appeal to persons less than 21 years of age.

The agreed-on advertising and promotional restrictions spelled out in the MSA should curb underage smoking, but tobacco companies have found ways to bypass the bans and advertise in other venues. Billboard advertising is banned, but tobacco companies have increased their level of advertising in magazines, many of which are read by teenagers.

A California suit against R. J. Reynolds Tobacco, filed on May 11, 2000, charged that the company violated the legal settlement with state governments by improperly distributing large quantities of free cigarettes by mail. This case marked the first time an attorney general took a cigarette company to court to enforce the terms of the MSA. Reynolds said it was part of a program of "consumer testing" and was therefore allowable under the agreement. The attorney general alleged Reynolds mailed the free cigarettes "under the guise of consumer testing or evaluation in order to market and advertise its products." According to the suit, Reynolds sent more than 900,000 multi-pack cigarette mailings to more than 115,000 California residents during 1999; some people received as many as ten packs at a time.

In his memoirs, former Surgeon General C. Everett Koop said about the tobacco industry, "After studying in depth the health hazards of smoking, I was dumbfounded—and furious. How could the tobacco industry trivialize extraordinarily important public-health information: the connection between smoking and heart disease, lung and other cancers, and a dozen or more debilitating and expensive diseases? The answer was—it just did. The tobacco industry is accountable to no one" (Koop, 1991).

WHO SMOKES?

In 2006 an estimated 72.9 million Americans aged 12 or older were current users of a tobacco product. This represents almost 30 percent of that population. In addition, 61.6 million persons (25% of the population) were current cigarette smokers; 13.7 million (5.6%) smoked cigars; 8.2 million (3.3%) used smokeless tobacco; and 2.3 million (0.9%) smoked tobacco in pipes. Young adults aged 18 to 25 had the highest rate of current use in all tobacco products, including cigarettes, compared to adults aged 26 or older. Among youths aged 12 to 17 in 2006, 2.6 million (10.4%) used cigarettes. The rate of cigarette use among 12- to 17-year-olds declined from 13 percent in 2002 to 10.4 percent in 2006. Statistics showed 2.4 million people aged 12 or older smoked cigarettes for the first time in 2006, which was similar to the 2005 estimate (2.3 million), but significantly greater than the 2002 estimate (1.9 million). Most new smokers in 2006 were under age 18 when they smoked their first cigarettes (61.2%) (Substance Abuse and Mental Health Services Administration, 2007).

UNDERSTANDING THE SMOKING HABIT

Almost all smokers started before the age of 21, most before the age of 18, and many before the age of 14. Young people who learn to inhale cigarette smoke and experience the mood-altering effects from the inhaled nicotine quickly become dependent on cigarettes to help them cope with the complexities of everyday life. Having developed nicotine dependence, they must continue smoking to avoid the downside of nicotine withdrawal. The earlier they start to smoke, the more dependent they become—and the sooner they experience smoking-related health problems. Six years of research at the National Center on Addiction and Substance Abuse at Columbia University revealed that a child who reaches age 21 without smoking, using illegal drugs, or abusing alcohol is virtually certain never to do so. Conversely, the 2007 national survey of students indicated that more students perceive the risk of smoking but "by the time most youngsters fully appreciate the hazards of smoking, many have already initiated the behavior" (Johnston, O'Malley, Bachman, & Schulenberg, 2008).

PURPOSE OF CIGARETTE ADVERTISING

The tobacco companies are adept at using advertising and different promotional programs to help them accomplish several major objectives:

1. To reassure current smokers. To offset the effect of thousands of studies showing the adverse health effects of smoking and the requested warning labels on cigarette packages, the tobacco industry has continued to claim that no one has yet "proven" that smoking "causes" health problems—that these are just "statistical associations." But, on April 7, 2000, in Florida, a six-person jury decided that cigarettes were a "deadly, addictive, and defective product" and caused cancer for three smokers who sued the industry in a class-action lawsuit. The companies were legally obligated to award $12.7 million to the plaintiffs. In a later phase of the trial, the jury awarded $17.6 billion in punitive damages to the plaintiffs, but this ruling was contested and the case stalled in court. The state of Florida, to protect its tobacco payments in the future ultimately, passed a law capping the amount of bond the companies would have to post to appeal such punitive damages at $100 million or 10 percent of the company's net worth, whichever is less.

2. To associate smoking with pleasurable activities. In their ads, tobacco companies show healthy young people enjoying parties, dancing, attending sporting events, having picnics at the beach, sailing, and so on. The implication is that those who smoke will experience the good times enjoyed by the smokers in the ads.

3. To associate smoking with other risk-taking activities. Since as indicated by the warning labels on every package of cigarettes, smoking involves risk to one's health, tobacco companies attempt to counter this by showing in their ads such risk-taking activities as ballooning, mountain climbing, sky diving, and motorcycle riding. This is the industry's not so subtle way of saying: "Go ahead and take a risk by smoking. You are capable of deciding the level of risk you want to assume." The tobacco companies are betting on the fact that most young people consider themselves immortal and do not believe any of the negative consequences of smoking will ever affect them.

4. To associate cigarette smoking with becoming an adult. Realizing that teenagers desire to be considered adults, to be free to make their own decisions, and to be free from restrictions on what they can and cannot do, tobacco companies go to great lengths to stress that smoking is an "adult habit"—that only adults have the right to choose whether or not to smoke. Since teenagers are in a hurry to grow up and be free, the simple act of smoking cigarettes can be their way of showing to the world that they are indeed adults.

5. To associate cigarette smoking with attractiveness to the opposite sex. Many ads for cigarettes imply that if you smoke, you will also be attractive to members of the opposite sex. In fact, surveys of young people and adults show that most people prefer to date nonsmokers.

6. To associate smoking with women's liberation. "You've come a long way, baby" was the theme of the early ads for Virginia Slims cigarettes. What these ads did not say is that women who smoke like men will die like men who smoke. The slogan "Torches of Freedom" coupled with an image of women smoking cigarettes while marching down Fifth Avenue in the Easter Parade was a cigarette company's public relations ploy years ago to influence women to start smoking. In the 1990s, lung cancer became the number one cancer found in women, exceeding the incidence of breast cancer.

7. To show that smoking is an integral part of our society. The sheer number of cigarette ads—those on advertising cards, on articles of clothing, on signs at sporting events—leave the impression that smoking is socially accepted by the majority of people. This image is supported by movies that include scenes of cigarette smoking. Many events sponsored by

tobacco companies include the name of a major brand of cigarettes or smokeless tobacco, such as the Kool Jazz Festival, the Benson & Hedges Blues Festival, the Magna Custom Auto Show, the Winston Cup (stock car racing), the Marlboro Cup (soccer), the Marlboro Stakes (horse racing), and the Virginia Slims Tennis Tournament, just to name a few. Although tobacco advertising is legally prohibited on television, the ban has been ignored by the strategic placement of tobacco-product ads in baseball and football stadiums, basketball arenas, and hockey rinks, around auto racetracks, and at tractor pulls and other sporting events.

8. To discourage articles in magazines about the health risks of smoking. Ads for cigarettes, beer, food, and other products, which are marketed by the major cigarette companies or their parent companies, are so important to magazines that many publishers are reluctant to antagonize cigarette producers by running articles on the health risks of smoking. This is especially true with women's magazines.

9. To gain legitimacy. Tobacco companies seek public acceptance and recognition by supporting worthwhile groups and programs. Many groups receive significant amounts of funding from tobacco companies to support their programs. One especially large grant, from RJR Nabisco, was a contribution of $30 million for "innovative education programs" to schools across the country. In 1989 Philip Morris made arrangements to sponsor the Philip Morris Bill of Rights Exhibit, which toured the United States in celebration of the 200th anniversary of the Bill of Rights. In this way, Philip Morris tried to associate its company—including its tobacco subsidiary—with the Bill of Rights and to reap positive press coverage as the exhibit went on display in each city.

HISTORY OF TOBACCO ADVERTISING
Tobacco companies' advertising, before restrictions were implemented, focused on television, radio, newspapers, and magazines. The advertising was represented by ads such as "I'd walk a mile for a Camel" or the "Call for Phillip Morris" or "More doctors smoke Camels" or "Not a cough in a carload." This evolved into the "Joe Camel" ads, the "Kool Penguin" ads, and the "Newport Menthol" cigarette ads.

Tobacco advertising and promotional expenses have steadily increased. Advertising budgets in 2008 reached $13 billion, more than twice the expenditures of a decade before. In 1997 the tobacco companies spent $5.66 billion to promote their products, up from $5.11 billion in 1996. The largest category of spending was for promotional allowances to wholesalers and retailers, $2.4 billion, more than double their spending in 1990. Next were expenditures for retail value-added. At $970 million, this category includes non-cigarette items given away with cigarettes. Coupons and multiple pack offers were an additional $552 million, followed by specialty item distribution, $512 million; point of sale advertising, $305 million; outdoor advertising, $295 million; magazines, $236 million; public entertainment, $195 million; and $130 million for all other forms of advertising.

There were no restrictions on cigarette advertising in the United States until the first *Report of the Surgeon General* was released on January 11, 1961. Because of the health hazards described therein, the report led to the Federal Cigarette Labeling and Advertising Act of 1965 and, beginning in 1966, Congress mandated that a health warning appear on all cigarette packages, although not in advertisements. On June 2, 1967, the Federal Communications Commission (FCC) ruled that the Fairness Doctrine in advertising applied to cigarette ads on television and radio and required broadcasters who aired cigarette commercials to provide "a significant amount of time" to citizens who wished to point out that smoking "may be hazardous to the smoker's health." This rule went into effect on July 1, 1967. The FCC required that there be one free public-service announcement (PSA) for every three paid cigarette commercials. During the three-year period of 1968 to 1970, in which the PSAs were mandated by the Fairness Doctrine, per capita cigarette sales decreased by 6.9 percent.

In January 1970 the cigarette industry voluntarily offered to end all cigarette advertising on television and radio by September 1970—a move that would also eliminate any PSAs, which were hurting sales. Ultimately, Congress approved the

Public Health Cigarette Act of 1969, which prohibited cigarette advertising in the broadcast media as of January 1, 1971.

In September, the Little Cigar Act of 1973 banned broadcast advertising of little cigars (cigarette-sized cigars). During the three-year period of 1971 to 1973, following the end of the PSAs required by the Fairness Doctrine and the beginning of the broadcast advertising ban, cigarette sales increased by 4.1 percent.

More than a decade later, smokeless-tobacco advertising in the broadcast media was banned by the Comprehensive Smokeless Tobacco Health Education Act of 1986. This ban took effect on August 27, 1986. The Federal Trade Commission (FTC) Bureau of Consumer Protection ruled in 1991 that the Pinkerton Tobacco Company violated the 1986 statute banning the advertising of smokeless tobacco and prohibited it from "displaying its brand name, logo, color, or design during televised (sports) events" of its Red Man Chewing Tobacco and snuff. This was the first action of its kind by the FTC. STAT (Stop Teenage Addiction to Tobacco), at their 1991 STAT-91 Conference, addressed the problem of tobacco companies' efforts to encourage tobacco addiction in young people. It was learned that the RJR Nabisco cartoon camel was at the center of the most extensive advertising campaign ever created to influence the values and behavior of young people. Camel's share of the teenage market rose from almost nothing to almost 35 percent in just three years by using "this sleazy dromedary."

See also **Advertising and the Alcohol Industry; Nicotine; Risk Factors for Substance Use, Abuse, and Dependence: Stress; Tobacco: Dependence; Tobacco: Tobacco Industry; Tobacco: Smokeless.**

BIBLIOGRAPHY

American Society of Addiction Medicine. (1996). *Public policy statement on nicotine dependence and tobacco.* Atlanta, GA: U.S. Department of Health and Human Services, Centers for Disease Control and Prevention. Available from http://americ20.temp.veriohosting.com.

Centers for Disease Control and Prevention. (2006, September) *Smoking-Attributable Mortality, Morbidity, and Economic Costs* (SAMMEC online report). Available from http://www.cdc.gov/tobacco/.

Centers for Disease Control and Prevention. (2007, November 9). Cigarette smoking among adults—United States, 2006. *Morbidity and Mortality Weekly Report, 56*(44), 1157–1161. Available from http://www.cdc.gov/.

Davis, R. M., Novotny, T. E., & Lynn, W. R. (1988). *The reports of the surgeon general: The health consequences of smoking.* Atlanta, GA: Center for Health Promotion and Education, Office on Smoking and Health.

Johnston, L. D., O'Malley, P. M., Bachman, J. G., & Schulenberg, J. E. (2008). *Monitoring the future— National results on adolescent drug use: Overview of key findings, 2007.* (NIH Publication No. 08-6418). Bethesda, MD: National Institutes on Drug Abuse.

King, C., III, & Siegel, M. (2001, August 16). The Master Settlement Agreement with the tobacco industry and cigarette advertising in magazines. *New England Journal of Medicine, 345*(7), 504–511.

Koop, C. E. (1991). *Koop: Memoirs of America's Family Doctor.* New York: Random House.

Lindblom, E. (2008, June 9). Toll of Tobacco in the United States of America. *Campaign for Tobacco-Free Kids.* Available from http://www.tobaccofreekids.org/.

Loomis, B. R., Farrelly, M. C., Nonnemaker, J. M., & Mann, N. H. (2006). Point of purchase cigarette promotions before and after the Master Settlement Agreement: Exploring retail scanner data. *Tobacco Control, 15,* 140–142. (doi:10.1136/tc.2005.011262). Available from http://tobaccocontrol.bmj.com/.

Massachusetts Department of Public Health. (2002, May). *Smokeless tobacco advertising expenditures before and after the Smokeless Tobacco Master Settlement Agreement.* Available from http://www.tobaccofreekids.org/.

Sloan, F. A., Mathews, C. A., & Trogdon, J. G. (2004). Impacts of the Master Settlement Agreement on the tobacco industry. *Tobacco Control 13,* 356–361. Available from http://tobaccocontrol.bmj.com/.

Substance Abuse and Mental Health Services Administration. (2007). *Results from the 2006 National Survey on Drug Use and Health: National findings* (Office of Applied Studies, NSDUH Series H-32, DHHS Publication No. SMA 07-4293). Rockville, MD: Author.

U.S. Department of Health and Human Services. (1998). *The health consequences of smoking: Nicotine addiction: A report of the Surgeon General.* Rockville, MD: Author. Available from http://profiles.nlm.nih.gov/.

U.S. Department of Health and Human Services, Centers for Disease Control and Prevention. *2000 Surgeon General's report—Reducing tobacco use.* Atlanta, GA: Author. Available from http://www.cdc.gov/tobacco/.

CHARLES M. RONGEY
REVISED BY RICHARD H. BUCHER (2009)

AFGHANISTAN. Afghanistan has a long history of both medical and nonmedical drug use. Hashish and opium have been constituents of medicines prepared by *hakims* (traditional healers), and they are still used for this purpose. A tradition of hashish manufacture and use stretches back several thousand years, and opium arrived in the area over 1,000 years ago, either as a trade commodity from Egypt or Greece, where it was a popular medicine, or imported by the armies of Alexander the Great. In 1905, reports from the British Indian government noted that opium was cultivated in districts of what are now the provinces of Herat, Nangarhar, Kabul, and Qandahar. By 1932, Afghanistan was producing 75 tons of opium, although production did not start to increase significantly until the 1980s. Home-brewed alcohol was also reportedly produced and consumed in some areas, particularly the area of Nuristan, whose inhabitants were converted to Islam in 1896. While homemade wine is still produced in a few areas, this has mainly been supplanted by Russian vodka, which is illegally imported from the Central Asian Republics. Tobacco products such as *naswar*, a local form of green chewing tobacco, and proprietary brands of cigarettes are also used, contributing to health problems in a population where respiratory diseases are endemic.

TRADITIONAL USE PATTERNS
Afghanistan presents a paradox: It is a conservative Islamic country in which the use of all intoxicants is strictly *haram* (forbidden), yet cultural attitudes regarding the production and consumption of hashish, and to a lesser extent opium, has traditionally been relatively tolerant in some sections of the Afghan community. However, those who become dependent on a drug or display drug-related problems risk social opprobrium and stigma.

During the late 1960s and early 1970s, the lure of cheap and easily available hashish and opium led young Western travelers on the "hippie trail" to stay in Afghanistan while en route to India and other Eastern destinations. At the time, an Afghan psychiatrist noted that there were significant numbers of hashish users in the country, mostly from the lower classes and income groups, yet there were few associated health or social problems. He

also estimated that there were around 100,000 opium addicts in Badakhshan Province, representing nearly 80 percent of the country's opiate dependent population. Many of these users originally became involved with the drug through self-medication.

WAR AND DRUGS
Thirty years of almost constant war, conflict, civil disorder, and social disruption, however, have eroded the cultural constraints and social rules that once helped to prevent occasional recreational and social drug use from lapsing into problem use and dependency. Severe impoverishment and deprivation, social displacement, loss of family members, and other war-related traumas have resulted in an increase in chronic mental health problems such as depression, anxiety and post-traumatic stress disorder (PTSD), which has led many to self-medicate with a wide range of drugs. While some use drugs recreationally (particularly hashish), and others may be influenced or coerced by peers, many use drugs simply to cope with the physical and psychological pain of daily existence.

A compounding problem is that most of the population has minimal access to reliable information on the risks and dangers of drugs, not only those traditionally available, such as hashish and opium, but also "new" drugs like heroin and a wide range of cheap and easily available psychotropic drugs, such as analgesics, hypnosedatives, and tranquilizers—particularly diazepam (Valium). In Kabul alone there are over 2,000 pharmacies where diazepam can be bought without a medical prescription for less than one dollar for a month's supply. Typically, a person will be given a medical prescription for such a drug and when this supply is finished the person will then purchase it without a prescription from a pharmacy or other shop in the bazaar. The market in psychotropics and other pharmaceuticals is largely uncontrolled and unregulated, with an estimated 80 percent of the drugs traded in the private sector being smuggled in from neighboring countries. Low-quality, out-of-date, and counterfeit pharmaceutical drugs are common.

A GROWING PROBLEM
While there are few reliable statistics in Afghanistan, all indicators and estimates suggest a substantial

increase in problem drug use since the 1970s. In 2005 a survey from the United Nations Office of Drugs and Crime (UNODC) of 1,480 key informants and 1,393 drug users in both rural and urban locations estimated that around 920,000 people, representing 3.8 percent of the population, were problem drug users. This was probably an underestimate, however, for many people who regularly use opium consider it a medicine rather than an intoxicating drug. Hidden populations of drug users—such as injecting drug users (IDUs), remote rural dwellers, police and military personnel, and female drug users—may also have been underestimated. The estimated numbers of people using drugs were: 520,000 hashish users; 180,000 pharmaceutical users; 160,000 alcohol users; 150,000 opium users; 50,000 heroin users (with 14 percent of these being injectors); and 200,000 users of other drugs, such as cough medicines, volatile liquids, and various preparations made from the cannabis plant and opium poppy capsule. Polydrug use was reportedly common, with nearly half of all drug users consuming more than one drug. A smoking mixture of opium and diazepam has also been reported in several areas of the country. This combination is popular because it prolongs the effect of the drugs and helps the user sleep better.

Injecting drug use has increasingly become a concern. In 2007 evidence from Kabul indicated that HIV prevalence among IDUs was less than 5 percent, and had thus not reached the level of a concentrated epidemic. Hepatitis C prevalence was 36.6 percent, however. High-risk behaviors are common among IDUs in Kabul, with 50.4 percent of this population sharing syringes and 76.2 percent having engaged the services of a sex worker. Similar high-risk behaviors have been reported in other Afghan cities, such as Herat and Mazar-e Sharif, where measurable IDU populations have been detected. A disproportionate number of these IDUs are returnees from Iran, where they were first introduced to heroin. A new drug designed specifically for injecting has also emerged: "crystal," allegedly a crystalline form of heroin, is reputedly easier to prepare for injecting than powder heroin, and its effects last longer.

OPIUM CULTIVATION

In general, since 1980 there has been a substantial increase in the availability of both opium and heroin, and this has been a contributing factor in the increase in problem drug use. During the 1980s and the *jihad* against the Soviet invaders, opium was cultivated to buy arms for the *mujahideen* (Afghan "holy warriors," or rebel fighters), although this was not their only source of income. While the dynamics of opium cultivation and drug production are complex, after the Soviets left in 1989, cultivation and production increased sharply, providing a source of income for many impoverished farmers and their families, for mujahideen groups (who were now fighting with each other), and for individual commanders, who used the money to expand their power base.

By 1995, when the Taliban controlled most of the country, opium production stood at 2,300 tons, and it continued to rise until 2001, when a Taliban edict banning opium cultivation dropped production to a mere 200 tons. Such a drastic decrease had the effect of further impoverishing the poorest debt-ridden farmers and increasing the price of opium, benefiting groups that held opium stocks—such as traders, traffickers, and the Taliban itself. Since 2002 and the demise of the Taliban, opium cultivation and production have increased significantly, with production in 2006 put at 6,100 tons and a record production in 2007 of 8,200 tons, with an estimated value of US $1 billion. By 2007, 14 percent of the population was estimated to be involved in opium cultivation in some capacity.

At the same time, heroin has been increasingly produced in Afghanistan, rather than over the porous eastern border in Pakistan. Large protected heroin "factories," established during the Taliban's reign, have now given way to smaller, more mobile, home-based production units. Large-scale drug bazaars have also declined, although in 2007 the Shaddle Bazaar in eastern Nangarhar province had around 30 shops trading in opium, with farmers traveling from neighboring provinces to sell their opium. Most opioids—such as opium, morphine base, and heroin—are still trafficked through Iran and Pakistan, while the rest passes through the "northern route" via the Central Asian Republics to Russia and Europe. Indicators suggest that Afghanistan's thriving drug trade has exacerbated corruption among both low- and high-level government officials, led to a building boom in several urban areas, and funded antigovernment insurgency groups and criminal gangs.

PUNISHMENT AND TREATMENT

Under Article 27 of the Counter Narcotics Law of 2005, any person using or possessing an opioid drug or hashish for personal consumption can be imprisoned and fined. If the amount of the drug is over one gram, then penalties should also be imposed for trafficking. Paradoxically, if a medical doctor certifies that a person is addicted to a drug, the court can exempt the person from imprisonment and fine and instead order attendance at a detoxification or drug treatment center.

In reality, the weak justice system and the lack of "secure" treatment centers means that while some drug users are arrested and imprisoned, often without trial, a few attend the 40 treatment centers developed since 2002, when only two such centers existed in the whole country. Typically, these centers are underfunded, have largely unqualified and untrained staff, and are able to offer treatment and rehabilitation to only a fraction of those who need it. Most function as detoxification centers. Community-based aftercare and relapse prevention are difficult in a context of severe family impoverishment and high unemployment. Yet while drug use is seen as a criminal act, national policy now endorses the development of a wide range of treatment options, including harm reduction for IDUs, who are at risk of transmitting HIV and other blood-borne diseases.

The National Drug Control Strategy (NDCS) for Afghanistan, which was signed by President Hamid Karzai in 2003, approves treatment, rehabilitation, and harm-reduction services for individuals and families with drug problems. In May 2005 the ministers for public health and counter narcotics jointly approved the Harm Reduction Strategy for IDU and HIV/AIDS Prevention. But although such a policy framework exists for tackling drug use as a bio-psychosocial problem, there has been limited available funding for service development, and drug users are still criminalized. In Afghanistan, therefore, it is likely that, for the foreseeable future, continuing drug availability, insecurity, conflict, and impoverishment will only lead to an increase in drug consumption among many vulnerable groups, such as returning refugees, ex-combatants, the unemployed, disaffected youth, and widows.

See also **Benzodiazepines; Foreign Policy and Drugs, United States; Heroin; India and Pakistan; Injecting Drug Users and HIV; International Drug Supply Systems; Middle East; Opiates/Opioids; Opium: International Overview.**

BIBLIOGRAPHY

Gobar, A. H. (1976). Drug abuse in Afghanistan. *Bulletin on Narcotics, 28(2),* 1–5.

Macdonald, D. (2007). *Drugs in Afghanistan: Opium, outlaws and scorpion tales.* London: Pluto Press.

Todd, C. S., Abed, A. M. S., Strathdee, S. A., Scott, P. T., Botros, B. A., Safi, N., et al. (2007). HIV, hepatitis C, and hepatitis B infections and associated risk behavior in injection drug users, Kabul, Afghanistan. *Emerging Infectious Diseases, 13(9),* 1327–1331. Available from http://www.cdc.gov/.

United Nations Office on Drugs and Crime (UNODC), and Government of Afghanistan Ministry of Counter Narcotics. (2005). *Afghanistan Drug Use Survey 2005.* Kabul: UNODC Country Office for Afghanistan. Available from http://www.unodc.org/.

United Nations Office on Drugs and Crime (UNODC), and Government of Afghanistan Ministry of Counter Narcotics. (2007). *Afghanistan Opium Survey 2007 Executive Summary.* Kabul: UNODC Country Office for Afghanistan. Available from http://www.unodc.org/.

DAVID MACDONALD

AFRICA. Africa is enormously diverse, with more than 900 million people living in approximately fifty countries (if surrounding island nations are included). The continent encompasses a wide-range of ecological zones, including the massive Sahara Desert in the north and the West African forest belt. These diverse ecological zones and the numerous more localized environments located within them have exerted, and continue to exert, a powerful impact on the patterns of trade and consumption of drugs and alcohol across Africa. Spread over the continent are a huge number of ethnolinguistic groups, whose cultures and belief systems often involve drug use or its proscription. In addition, much of North Africa came under Muslim control during Islam's first century, the eighth century, and spread across the Sahara and along the East African coast. Historically, Christianity has only been important in a few areas, such as Sudan and Ethiopia, but that faith grew very rapidly during the twentieth century, as did Islam. This geographical and cultural diversity was further complicated by the expansion of international commerce into the continent and the linked colonial partition of the continent by the European powers in the decades around 1900. Beginning in the 1950s, the transition to independence or majority rule once again redefined the African map. Thus, Africa has had no common or single drug history or experience, but a multiplicity of such histories.

Each community existed within a highly articulated environment of intoxicants and stimulants, derived from locally produced or gathered agricultural products and imports. Surprisingly little research has been done on indigenous drugs other than alcohol and little is known about their histories. They had and continue to have a variety of uses, including recreational, ceremonial, and medicinal. Certainly, the boundary was not always clear between plants that might be stimulants and others that were primarily used as medicines. More recently these have been supplemented by imported crops, such as coffee and tea.

HISTORY OF ALCOHOL USE

Alcoholic drinks of various kinds were widely distributed and virtually universal, but distillation was unknown in sub-Saharan Africa before the twentieth century. African alcohols probably date at least to the introduction of grains more than 2,000 years ago. The term "beer" is used to describe these beverages, but they bear little resemblance to European-style beers. A wide range of such drinks were produced, depending on local economies and ecologies. The drinks produced from grains, honey, and fruits or from palm wine had diverse and often overlapping purposes. They were the essential lubricants on many social occasions, but the pouring of libations and ceremonial consumption had powerful ritual importance as well. As in many other areas of the world, alcohol also was often an important ingredient in medicines. Offering drinks was an inducement to labor, and in many areas tribute payments were made in the form of alcohol.

The most common forms of alcohol were drinks made from fermented grains, honey, fruit juice, sugar cane, or the liquid extracted from palm trees. The production processes differed depending on the raw materials involved, as did the division of labor involved in brewing. Women typically did most of the work involved in producing grain beers in the areas where these predominated, reflecting the central role of women in the production of these crops. They brewed millet, sorghum, and maize beers in labor-intensive methods that involved the germination of some grain to stimulate fermentation. The resulting beers were thick, porridge-like drinks, which had substantial food value. The fermentation of honey and sugar-cane juice produced thinner drinks as did the wine derived from tapping palm trees. Men generally did the work of gathering and fermenting these drinks. Maize beer only became common in the nineteenth and twentieth centuries as this imported crop spread widely. It is difficult to estimate the levels and patterns of consumption historically. Certainly all of these drinks, notwithstanding the later claims of European observers, had low alcoholic content, probably rarely exceeding four or five percent.

Strict rules generally governed the consumption of alcoholic drinks, as well as other drugs, and hierarchies typically determined drinking etiquette. At the same time, drinking also apparently provided the occasion for "time outs," in which the rules of obeisance and propriety might be suspended temporarily. Only men with considerable wealth could afford to produce grain beers on a large scale or to obtain palm wine. For most people the agricultural seasons determined the availability of drink, and only those men with the ability to amass substantial grain supplies or to command the labor to tap trees could afford to produce and distribute liquor the year round. The offering of drinks was often regarded as a critical element of generosity—an important characteristic for leaders. Among the most well-known illustrations of this phenomenon was the *odwira* festival sponsored by the King of the Asante kingdom, located in present-day Ghana. This highly orchestrated annual ritual involved a generous distribution of alcohol in gestures that reinforced the authority and stature of the king. There are many other reports of the prominent role played by alcohol in enhancing royal power, for example, in the East African kingdom of Buganda in the middle of the nineteenth century and in the Zulu kingdom in southern Africa in the 1820s.

HISTORY OF DRUG USE

The traditional alcohols produced in Africa were all in the active process of fermentation, so they could not be stored for more than a few days. As a result, extensive trades in liquor did not develop, although there were often local markets in palm wine in West African communities. In contrast, two drug products, kola and khat, could be stored and traded, although in the case of khat, only for a limited time. The kola nut was a mild stimulant harvested in the forest zones inland from the West African coast and traded to the north and east. The nut itself was not only consumed for pleasure, but its offering became a critical element in domestic hospitality. The profits from the trade were substantial, and control over it represented, for example, a crucial element in the wealth and power of the Asante king, who controlled merchant communities that monopolized the trade. The demand came largely from Muslim areas, and its popularity may have developed initially as an alternative to alcohol as communities converted to Islam.

Khat is a leafy plant chewed as a mild stimulant, again often in Muslim areas. Production centers in the Meru highlands east of Mount Kenya, from where it is distributed to communities along the Indian Ocean coast. Cannabis was also widely distributed across Africa, but seems to have been used extensively only in a few areas. At the same time, kola and khat traders took advantage of new transportation options, such as railways, trucks, and steamships, to transform the trades. Kola is a legal substance, but in the case of khat there was and continues to be official ambivalence about its acceptability.

ALCOHOL AND THE SLAVE TRADE

The expansion of international commerce with Africa introduced distilled alcohol to the continent beginning in the fifteenth century, if not before. Brandy and other spirits were mainstays of ships' cargoes from the earliest period of the Atlantic commerce, although other goods were more important in trade. With the development of the American colonies, rum emerged as a vital trade good in the transatlantic slave trade; in particular, traders used it to cement commercial deals with local middlemen and rulers along the West African coast. Further south, *aguardente*, the sugarcane liquor produced in Brazil, entered the slave trade

in large quantities. Given the high cost of transport, these distilled drinks did not penetrate far beyond the coast. But in Ghana, in particular, imported rum had become deeply integrated into the social and ritual life of communities before the nineteenth century.

DRUG AND ALCOHOL ABUSE RESEARCH

Much of the earlier scholarship on precolonial or traditional African alcohol and drug use characterized such activities as "integrated" practices that reflected and reinforced social and political norms. In such circumstances social controls would make alcohol abuse virtually impossible. More recent research (see Willis, 2002) suggests that, at the very least, African communities were aware of the potential dangers associated with excessive consumption. Certainly the capacity of wealthier people to command the food resources to produce beer could undermine the food supply and accentuate hunger during certain seasons and in bad harvest years.

At the same time, the many European accounts of wild African drinking clearly reflect as much the assumptions of the observers as any objective assessment of African drinking. The perishability of fermented beers encouraged types of drinking that were typical in agricultural communities. Since these drinks had to be consumed quickly, communal beer drinks were common, and guests were encouraged to keep drinking until the liquor was finished. Thus, African concepts of moderation differed sharply from those that developed in the West, where daily drinking was the norm and the ability to hold one's liquor admired. In contrast, Africans usually drank only sporadically and often aimed at some degree of inebriation. These drinking styles probably contributed, however, to excessive drinking when alcohol became commercialized and continuously available.

INTERNATIONAL TRADE AND INTERNATIONAL CONTROL

During the late nineteenth century, the mass production of cheap gin in Holland and Germany, together with the reduction in transport costs, opened up a lucrative trade supplying *schnapps* gin to Nigeria and other areas of the West African coast—a zone where the rum trade was already established. The growth in this trade converged with the expansion of Christian missionary activity in the region and the development of global temperance movements. As the new colonies along the coast became increasingly dependent upon the revenue derived from this trade, an active and vociferous campaign developed to challenge the so-called liquor traffic. Part of an international effort to protect indigenous peoples from the supposed ravages of the trade, for a time beginning in the 1880s, the West African liquor traffic was a major humanitarian controversy. The question was briefly discussed at the 1884 Berlin Conference, but became the focal point of the 1890 Brussels antislavery meeting.

There, in the first of a series of agreements, the major powers agreed to ban the production of spirits in tropical Africa and to ban the spread of the trade in spirits beyond those areas where it was already established. In addition, the powers increased duties on alcohol imports, purportedly to limit imports into the West African coastal region. As West African trade expanded, however, gin imports expanded as well, causing the anti-liquor trade forces to make increasingly dramatic, if largely unsubstantiated, claims regarding the destructive impact of gin imports on West African communities. Successive increased tariffs did little to stem the trade, however, and only wartime prohibition effectively reduced gin imports after 1917. This prohibition was written into international law in the 1919 Treaty of St. Germain-en-Laye, which moved beyond previous regulations to define the cheap imported gin, known as "trade spirits," as a dangerous drug, following the model of the recent international narcotics accords. The Brussels Convention had been a model for the 1911 Hague conference. Imports of more expensive spirits were still allowed, however.

The colonial regimes established in Africa beginning in the late nineteenth century passed laws that mirrored their European counterparts, gradually expanding the range of drugs declared dangerous and illegal. In contrast, their approaches to alcohol control varied. Generally, the West African colonies adopted relatively liberal approaches to liquor control, focusing attention on regulating imports but controlling locally-produced drinks through gradually expanding licensing systems. In the 1930s the first industrial breweries were established with the goal, soon realized, of creating a large African market for bottled, European beer. At the same time, a substantial illicit trade in locally produced spirits emerged. In the British colonies of eastern and central Africa as well as in South Africa, Africans were forbidden entirely to consume spirits; European beer and wine were also prohibited. In those areas, regulation focused on controlling production and consumption of traditional African beers, although some of it was now commercially produced. Although household production continued relatively unimpeded in rural areas, in cities throughout most of the region, beer sales were confined to state-owned establishments, which produced substantial revenues for the state. In fact, one of the obvious themes in the history of the alcohol commerce in Africa is its close tie to state revenue, a tie that has possibly become even stronger in the twenty-first century.

The period of decolonization brought gradual liberalization of alcohol regulations and, with independence and majority rule, all elements of racial discrimination in alcohol distribution were eliminated. Independence also brought a rapid increase in levels of production and consumption as well as the emergence of large-scale and powerful brewing and distilling concerns, many of which had ties both to international liquor capital and to the state. The expansion of production and consumption also brought increased public health concern about excessive alcohol use, and denunciations of drunkenness became mainstays of political discourse in many countries. Few countries had the resources to devote to treatment facilities, and alcohol experts conceptualized African drinking and alcohol abuse in collective terms, an approach at odds with the individualized disease models that predominated in the West. The newly independent governments also generally followed the lead of the United States in the adoption of severe restrictions on illegal drugs and harsh penalties for drug trading and possession.

CANNABIS PRODUCTION AND USE

Cannabis production is widespread in Africa and has expanded substantially since the 1960s. There is a surprising dearth of information on what is increasingly a major crop, reflecting perhaps the dangers of researching a trade that is illegal, but involves the complicity of many state officials and legitimate businesspersons. It is estimated that by the 1990s 15 percent of the population of Ghana were regular users of cannabis, but that 50 percent of the local crop was exported to other African countries and to Europe. The decline in the 1980s of markets for many of Africa's key agricultural resources created the economic context for a shift to cannabis production in a number of countries in addition to Ghana, because the crop produced healthy profits even when the costs associated with illegal activity were considered. At the same time the general economic decline provided both a ready supply of transporters and dealers and a growing market.

Consumers typically fell into two categories: those who used the drug for pleasure and those who used it because of strenuous or stressful work. An extreme example of this is the systematic provision of cannabis and other drugs to the "boy soldiers" and other combatants in the civil conflicts in Sierra Leone, Liberia, and other countries. Through the 1980s cannabis entirely dominated the African drug economy, but beginning in the 1990s the use of imported drugs became much more common. Predictably, the growing role of African countries in international drug trafficking has attracted much more interest from scholars and the news media than the production and distribution of drugs within Africa itself.

INTERNATIONAL TRADE IN ILLEGAL DRUGS

Before the 1980s Africa did not usually surface in discussions of international drug trafficking. With its close proximity to Spain, Morocco had developed a substantial cannabis production industry and exported the product, especially in the form of hashish, across North Africa and into Europe. During the late 1980s and early 1990s, however, a number of African countries became involved in the global drugs trade. In some cases, for example Ghana and especially Nigeria, local entrepreneurs built substantial international trading enterprises. In other cases, external cartels built connections with local interests, as the international trade shifted and diversified to maintain profits. Initially, African countries were largely transit points, funneling drugs produced elsewhere to markets in Europe and the United States.

In these circumstances it was often difficult to attract the political support and resources to attack the trade. Occasionally, African commentators even noted an ironic reversal, in which the continent that had been exploited by external powers was now profiting from a vast commerce that ultimately fed on demand largely concentrated in the former imperial states. By the late 1990s, however, the transit trade had begun to spill over into local cultures and economies, and the drugs trade became a hot button political issue.

In a number of key respects, African countries were fertile ground in the 1980s and 1990s for the development of drug trafficking. Colonialism had bequeathed economies highly oriented toward production for export and dependent on foreign investment. The economic downturn of the late 1970s had a devastating impact across the continent, as country after country was forced into structural adjustment programs to encourage more open economies and reduce the state role in the economy. Whatever the long-term impact of such programs, in the short run unemployment and under-employment grew rapidly, and the ranks of the desperately poor expanded. Increasing numbers of formerly middle class and educated people found themselves living hand to mouth, with few prospects. Migration to towns and cities accentuated these problems, as a formerly overwhelmingly rural continent became urbanized.

Structural adjustment policies resulted in reductions in government expenditures, and weaker states were unable to combat increasingly sophisticated drug syndicates. Impoverished bureaucracies and officials were highly susceptible to corruption in environments where ineffectual state regulation made money laundering and evasion of customs relatively easy. In many countries, privatization and democratization accentuated a shift toward a culture of private entrepreneurship that sometimes ignored illegality. In an extreme example, West Africans have established their own international drug distribution concerns and have become important players in the global drug trade. In this environment, unfortunately, drug policies on the continent have been driven as much by United States pressure as by the assessment of local needs and realities. It is a sobering fact that the international economy has produced heroin at prices that are within reach of addicts in poor African communities along the East African coast and elsewhere, but cannot deliver cheap pharmaceuticals that would combat epidemics of HIV and malaria.

See also **Alcohol: History of Drinking (International); Foreign Policy and Drugs; International Drug Supply Systems; Kenya; Khat; Nigeria; South Africa.**

BIBLIOGRAPHY

Abaka, E. (2005). *Kola is God's gift: Agricultural production, export initiatives, and the kola industry of Asante and the Gold Coast, c. 1820–1950.* Oxford: James Currey.

Akyeampong, E. (1996). *Drink, power, and cultural change: A social history of alcohol in Ghana, c. 1800 to recent times.* Portsmouth, New Hampshire: Heinemann.

Akyeampong, E. (2005). Diaspora and drug trafficking in West Africa: A case study of Ghana. *African Affairs, 104,* 429–447.

Allen, C. (1999). Editorial: Africa and the drugs trade. *Review of African political economy, 26,* 5–11.

Ambler, C. (2003). Alcohol and the slave trade in West Africa, 15th–19th centuries. In D. Bradburd & W. Jankowiak (Eds.), *Drugs, labor, and colonial expansion* (pp. 73–87). Tucson: University of Arizona Press.

Anderson, D., Haidu, D., Beckerleg, S., & Klein, A. (2007). *The khat controversy: Stimulating the debate on drugs.* Oxford: Berg.

Bernstein, H. (1999). Ghana's drug economy: Some preliminary data. *Review of African political economy, 26,* 13–32.

Bryceson, D. (Ed.). (2002). *Alcohol in Africa: Mixing business, pleasure, and politics.* Portsmouth, New Hampshire: Heinemann.

Curto, J. (2004). Enslaving spirits: The Portuguese-Brazilian alcohol trade at Luanda and its hinterland, c. 1550–1830. Leiden: Brill.

Crush, J., & Ambler, C. (Eds.). (1993). *Liquor and labor in southern Africa.* Athens: Ohio University Press.

Lovejoy, P. (1995). Kola nuts: The "coffee" of the central Sudan. In J. Goodman, P. E. Lovejoy, & A. Sherratt, (Eds.), *Consuming habits: Drugs in history and anthropology* (pp. 103–125). London: Routledge.

Van den Bersselaar, D. (2007). *The king of drinks: Schnapps gin from modernity to tradition.* Leiden: Brill.

Willis, J. (2002). *Potent brews: A social history of alcohol in East Africa, 1850–1999.* Athens: Ohio University Press.

CHARLES AMBLER

AFRICAN AMERICANS, ETHNIC AND CULTURAL FACTORS RELEVANT TO TREATMENT FOR.

Leading experts (Helms & Cook, 1999; Pinderhughes, 1989) defined ethnicity as the historical cultural patterns and the collective identity shared by groups from specific geographic regions of the world, and culture is defined as the commonly shared beliefs, values, and norms of groups. Sufficient evidence (Jones-Saumty, 2002; Mallow & Cameron-Kelly, 2006) supports the importance of cultural congruency or competency in substance abuse treatment with ethnically and culturally diverse populations. Cultural congruency is synonymous with cultural competency, a widely recognized term in mental health care. Cultural competency assumes that mental health providers should possess knowledge and skills of a particular culture to deliver effective interventions to members of that culture. Three areas generally determine cultural competency (Sue, 2006): (a) Cultural awareness and beliefs: Providers' sensitivity to their own personal values and biases and how these may influence perceptions of the client, client's problem, and the counseling relationship; (b) Cultural knowledge: Counselor's knowledge of the client's culture, worldview, and expectations for the counseling relationship; and (c) Cultural skills: Counselor's ability to intervene in a manner that is culturally sensitive and relevant.

BACKGROUND

African Americans are an ethnically and culturally diverse group, and their cultural values and norms reflect this diversity. Historically, many of the cultural values and norms shared by African Americans have been shaped by the experiences this group has had from slavery to contemporary society. Racial pride and identity are values passed down from generation to generation along with socialization skills that serve as the foundation for the development and survival of African Americans in the United States.

Moral codes of behavior are primarily derived from enduring spiritual and religious beliefs and practices that influence individual character and collective interactions. Moreover, African Americans express firm ties to family whether biological or surrogate, social support networks, and even in the early twenty-first century, remain consistent in their communal aspects of daily existence. For example, in Black religious organizations the term *church family* is often used; or, when individuals are in treatment, fellow program participants are viewed as a *recovery family*, with whom aftercare support relationships are created.

African Americans have demonstrated flexibility in altering certain cultural values and norms when adapting to different needs and demands of the group and society. For instance, research by Neighbors and colleagues (2007) documented increases in access to and utilization of mental health treatment and substance abuse treatment services, which shows that African Americans have progressively evolved in attitudes and behavior about these services.

Periodically, notable cultural issues and drug use trends impact how African Americans view and respond to treatment. The crack epidemic is a prime example. The crack epidemic emerged during the late 1980s, and a number of African American communities experienced its devastating effects. Many African Americans addicted to crack made a marked departure from traditional cultural values and norms indicated by a rise in risky sexual behaviors and diseases, dramatically altered family lifestyles, a sharp increase in criminal activity and violence, and weakened and sometimes dismantled community cohesiveness.

Crack dependency introduced different members of the African American community into the mental health and substance abuse treatment systems. Researchers and treatment providers responded slowly to the crack crisis, but eventually these efforts accelerated and intensified. The result was that drug treatment demonstrated more interest in culturally based approaches for minority groups, and treatment services tailored for the growing number of women who abused crack also grew. This coordinated response to the crack epidemic remained active into the early twenty-first century and is an indication that attention to cultural issues and drug use trends and treatment patterns must be an ongoing process.

TREATMENT PATTERNS

As treatment data from the Substance Abuse and Mental Health Services Administration-Drug and Alcohol Information Services (SAMHSA-DASIS) revealed in 2002, African Americans as a group usually sought and received treatment services for both illicit and legal chemical dependency. According to data from the 1999 Treatment Episode Data

Set (TEDS) and DASIS report, although non-Hispanic Blacks made up 12 percent of the U.S. population in 1999, this group represented 23 percent of admissions to publicly funded substance abuse treatment facilities (SAMHSA-TEDS, 2006).

Treatment seeking and utilization patterns of African Americans must be assessed on both an individual and community-wide basis. The idea that African Americans are a homogenous group is flawed. For example, Waggoner and Brinson (2007) documented differences in rates of drug use trends and treatment patterns for rural and inner-city dwellers along with emerging data on ethnic intergroup variability in treatment utilization.

Despite the non-uniform character of African Americans as a group, most still manifest resistance to drug treatment. The National Survey on Drug Use and Health (NSDUH) provided information on the general population's five most often reported reasons for not receiving illicit drug or alcohol use treatment. Although this report did not indicate specific data on any particular ethnic group, it is still useful information when applied to African Americans. This information may provide insight into why African Americans do not seek treatment (2006).

This report, based on combined data of 2004 to 2006, gave an overview of persons who needed, but did not receive, treatment at a specialty facility and their perceived need for treatment. The five main reasons for not seeking treatment were: (a) not ready to stop using (37.2 percent); (b) no health coverage and could not afford cost (30.9%); (c) possible negative effect on job (13.3%); (d) not knowing where to go for treatment (12.6%); and (e) fear of neighbors' or community's negative opinions (11.0%) (SAMHSA-NSDUH, 2006).

POST-TREATMENT SUPPORT: RECOVERY GROUP PARTICIPATION

African Americans participate in substance abuse recovery or mutual-help groups, but the exact type and rates of participation can only be roughly estimated as an independent source of data was not found. In general, of the four million persons aged 12 or older (1.6% of the population) who received treatment for a problem related to the use of alcohol or illicit drugs in 2006, more than half (2.2

million) received treatment at a self-help group (SAMHSA, 2006).

The two categories for aftercare drug treatment and recovery groups are traditional and non-traditional/alternative. The most common traditional recovery groups are Alcoholics Anonymous (AA) and Narcotics Anonymous (NA). These two groups are based on the twelve-step philosophy of the individual's spiritual awareness of a higher power and admission of powerlessness over the substance(s). Alternative drug recovery groups (e.g., women- or health-specific) similar to these traditional ones are modeled after the self-help movement, which encourages personal responsibility and action to prevent relapses.

African Americans utilize both traditional and alternative drug recovery and relapse prevention groups; however, participation at mutual-help groups has a different meaning and outcome for them because of cultural factors such as segregation and racism. In 1993 Smith, Buxton, Bilal, and Seymour attributed African Americans' resistance to the twelve-step model to the perception that these fellowships were exclusive; some also confused them with religion, and confusion over surrender versus powerlessness was also an issue. Other concerns included low self-esteem, dysfunctional family structure, communication difficulties, and institutionalized and internalized racism.

CULTURAL RISK AND PROTECTIVE FACTORS

African Americans have multiple cultural risk and protective factors that influence patterns of substance abuse as well as the type and quality of treatment received. Research by Terrell (1993) suggests that acculturation experiences, sources of stress, coping mechanisms, social support variations, and beliefs about substance use are key factors associated with differential patterns of substance abuse among some ethnic groups, particularly African Americans, Hispanics, and Native Americans.

Cultural strengths and barriers promote or impede treatment utilization and outcomes for substance abusers. For example, they may be encouraged or discouraged by peers, spiritual leaders, or circumstances to deny the need for treatment or to change drug-using lifestyles once in treatment. Furthermore, there is a growing recognition that for maximum engagement of women in treatment,

providers must have an understanding of sociocultural factors, gender needs and differences, and an awareness of childhood problems some women may have experienced, including childhood sexual and/or physical trauma.

The most prominent ethnocultural factors that have an impact on substance abuse treatment for African Americans include personal or individual motivation, education/employment/economics, religion/spirituality, family/social support, racism (internal and external) including diversity and cultural identity, neighborhood/environment, and legal criminal justice status. A summary of these factors follows.

Motivation. Motivation for drug use treatment is widely regarded as crucial to a client's engagement in treatment and also in success in quitting drug use. Motivation is typically measured with items reflecting high treatment readiness (e.g., perceived need for treatment and commitment to participate) and low treatment resistance (e.g., skepticism regarding benefits of treatment).

MET or Motivational Interviewing (MI) is an approach wherein motivation to change substance use can be achieved by increasing individual awareness of negative consequences using a nonconfrontational approach. Motivation can affect treatment retention results for specific drug users and types. Cocaine-dependent patients (African Americans accounted for less than 10% of the sample) with low initial motivation to change reported less cocaine and alcohol relapse and use days and fewer alcohol problems than Motivational Enhancement Therapy (MET) patients with higher initial motivation. One possible explanation for this phenomenon, offered by the authors of the study, is that the more permissive message used in MET is maladaptive for the more motivated patients who may respond to a more directive approach.

Education/Employment. Education and employment status are also important factors for marginalized substance abusers. Among substance abusers admitted to treatment for illicit drug use (2003–2004), a significant number of African Americans had at least a high school education (SAMHSA-NSDUH, 2006). A study of treatment retention for urban, uninsured, adult African Americans in substance abuse treatment done by Mitchell

Hampton (2006) shows that education did not have any significant influences on retention other than an indication that those with higher levels of education are likely to stay longer.

Employment has no significant relation with retention, although studies indicate that employed people, full-time or part-time, tend to stay longer than those who are unemployed. The majority of U.S. adults with substance abuse or dependence problems, however, are gainfully employed. Research data on employment status and trends for African American substance abusers are limited and, when included, the numbers are extremely low. For example, in a 2006 study by Slaymaker and Owen on employment status of substance abusers in treatment, the sample size for African Americans was negligible (less than 3%).

The available research (Brown, Melchior, Slaughter, & Huba, 2005) was based on African American women, and the cultural implications of this should be considered by researchers. Employment was one of three indicators that women (66.3% African American) seeking to enter substance-abuse treatment were ready to modify several types of risky behaviors. Other indicators are seeking mental health counseling, reducing risky sexual behaviors, reducing risk of physical violence, and improving vocational or educational skills. Results demonstrated that, when these factors were present, significant increases occurred in women's readiness for behavior change. The interaction between initial readiness to modify substance-abuse behaviors and longitudinal change also was significant.

Religion and Spirituality. Religion and spirituality play a significant role for African Americans seeking drug treatment. Religion is an organized social system of beliefs and practices, whereas spirituality refers to an individual's unique, subjective sense of meaning and/or transcendent experiences. Religion can produce positive higher resolve to consume less drugs, or it can cause distress when struggling to make independent choices.

In 2007 Michalak, Trocki, and Bond investigated the relative importance of three religion variables (religious preference, religiosity, and alcohol proscription) and eight demographic variables (gender, ethnicity, education, income, marital status, age, region, and employment status) as predictors of drinking versus abstention and moderate versus heavy drinking in a representative racial sample. Religion variables were strongly associated with abstention in that study.

Likewise, religion and spirituality is strong for African Americans regardless of gender. Heinz, Epstein, and Preston reported that women and African American heroin and cocaine abusers were more likely to report religious and spiritual beliefs or experiences on several individual religion-based items than men and non-African Americans (2007). African Americans had higher scores on the Index of Spiritual Experience (INSPIRIT)—a questionnaire that assesses both spirituality and religiosity—than Caucasians. These findings suggest that spiritual and religious experiences in substance-abuse recovery, along with demographic characteristics, should be considered in the design of spiritually oriented behavioral interventions for addiction.

Family and Social Support. The majority of African Americans have strong connections to family and social support networks that directly influence both positive and negative treatment outcomes, but gender differences exist. For example, the leading referral source of African American males is the criminal justice system, whereas for females it is self or a family member (SAMHSA, 2006). Unfortunately, most mental health facilities still lack family education services.

Racism: Internal and External. African Americans cope with racism both internally and externally. The difficulty of dealing with both of these stressors is perhaps amplified for substance abusers. External racism or oppression has been strongly correlated with race-related stress and negative emotional reactions. Internalized racism is a form of racial hatred associated with poor mental health outcomes such as low self-esteem and depression. Institutional racism occurs but is often hard to identify; nevertheless, it is felt by many who still believe that white society is "out to get them," a central long-standing idea in the so-called *conspiracy theory*. The prevalence of conspiracy theories among African Americans is associated with the historical patterns of systematic discrimination and racism from slavery to the Jim Crow laws in the South to the current disenfranchisement and inequities such as those found in the criminal justice system.

Understanding and integrating diversity and recognition of cultural identity needs will help break down barriers to effective treatment and research on substance dependence. One large study (Jacobson, Robinson, & Blumenthal, 2007) on racial disparities examined intake and discharge records from all publicly funded outpatient and residential alcohol-treatment recovery programs in Los Angeles County during 1998 to 2000. Study participants (N = 10,591) were African American, Hispanic, and white patients discharged from these programs, ages 18 or older, who reported alcohol as their primary substance abuse problem. African Americans had significantly lower completion rates (17.5%) relative to whites (26.7%). These large differences in completion rates between African American and white patients are partially explained by economic differences (i.e., employment, homelessness, and usage of Medi-Cal rather than private insurance), but these factors remain largely unexplored.

Legal/Criminal Justice Status. Frequently, the judicial system will use legal coercion to provide treatment to substance users, with the expressed intent of diverting them from incarceration. Legal or criminal justice involvement of African Americans with substance abuse problems is considered a typical outcome for this ethnic group, but the system is often seen as unfairly biased against them.

The question is: How effective is mandated treatment for this population? The answer is mixed. Perron and Bright found that legal coercion reduced the risk of dropout across three treatment modalities—short-term residential, long-term residential, and outpatient (2008). Alternatively, in a sample that was 60.7 percent African Americans, 33.5 percent non-Hispanic Whites, and 21.2 percent women whose ages ranged from 16 to 63 years old, readiness (but not resistance) predicted treatment retention during the six-month period. Resistance (but not readiness) predicted drug use, especially among offenders for whom the treatment referral was coercive. These findings suggest that readiness and resistance should both be assessed among clients entering treatment, especially when the referral is coercive.

Neighborhood/Environment. The link between poor health outcomes such as depression and other psychiatric disorders, substance abuse, and the quality of neighborhoods and environment of African Americans has been firmly established. Many African Americans must contend with the marketing of substances, living in high-stress environments (e.g., low income, crime-ridden, high unemployment areas), and other risk factors. The interface of addiction and treatment in this context is equally disturbing. Society expects oppressed groups to seek help from social institutions where alienation and segregation is perceived as the norm. This inherent contradiction and the mistrust generated by perceived and real racism often results in underutilization of treatment services by this group even when such services are available.

CULTURALLY CONGRUENT TREATMENT MODELS

For successful engagement and retention of clients, providers of treatment programs need to understand the role that culture plays in the daily lives of African Americans. As previously discussed, multiple ethno-cultural factors contribute to the success or failure of treatment. Treatment models that use this information offer African Americans with substance abuse problems diverse program options. Two culturally congruent substance-abuse-treatment models are the African American Extended Family Program and the Sande Society.

The African American Extended Family Program is a good example of how the precepts of twelve-step recovery can be adapted to the needs of a specific community. It takes African American cultural mores and traditions into consideration and makes them primary to recovery. Culturally, African Americans strongly value communalism, or a collective identity (Longshore & Grills, 2000). The Haight-Ashbury Free Clinics, Inc. (HAFCI)/ Glide Memorial Methodist Church African American Extended Family Program (AAEFP), described in detail in Reverend Cecil William's book, *No Hiding Place*, offers this family program. This program represents an important collaboration that has established an effective intervention in the inner-city crisis of crack-cocaine use. This intervention is an adaptation of the traditional twelve-step principles of supported recovery for African

American inner-city culture. In the *HAFCI-Glide* program, the basic practicalities of recovery are utilized in a model that is uniquely meaningful in terms of the African American experience.

The Big Book of Alcoholic Anonymous (AA) uses the terms *spiritual experience* and *spiritual awakening*, manifesting in many different forms, to describe what happens to bring about a personality change sufficient to induce recovery. While some of these may involve an "immediate and overwhelming God consciousness," most are what William James called an "educational variety" of revelation, developing slowly over time. According to a *Big Book* appendix titled "Spiritual Experience," the core of this process is tapping an "unexpected inner resource" by members who identify this resource with "their own conception of a Power greater than themselves." African-centered approaches offer an alternative conceptual framework for understanding the culturally normative behavior of African Americans in drug abuse treatment and recovery. They are based on an appreciation of core African-centered beliefs. The program developers proposed seven fundamental constructs to serve as the basis of a model for African-centered transformative healing: consciousness, character, conduct, collectivity, competence, caring, and creed.

The Sande Society is another example of an African-centered substance abuse program. It is a *rite-of-passage* approach involving highly developed ritual based on that of the Bundi society in Sierra Leone. This treatment approach with its African-centered themes was developed with special consideration for holding together and rebuilding the families of African American women. This program integrates four treatment phases (each four months long) linked to four principles for a balanced life: (1) *Genesis/Restraint*; (2) *Initiation/Respect*; (3) *Transformation/Responsibility*; and (4) Sande Society/ Reciprocity. These are the basis for participants and family members to make personal life changes and to grow mentally, spiritually, and physically healthy.

Family preservation is a primary factor in this treatment process. The communal environment has individual apartments equipped with kitchens, communal group and meeting rooms, a fully equipped childcare center, a recreational and exercise gym, a vocational training room, a medical/health area, and staff offices. It promotes positive social interactions between families and decreases isolation and functioning outside the collective. Ultimately, Sande Society members participate in sharing their experiences and stories of challenges and success in supportive empowerment and teaching sessions.

SUMMARY

Ethnic and cultural factors relevant to substance abuse treatment for African Americans are complex and require constant review. African Americans, similar to other ethnic and cultural groups, have specific cultural values and norms regarding treatment for substance abuse. Researchers and treatment providers need to understand and integrate relevant ethnocultural factors in the development of effective culturally congruent interventions. This specialized information when combined with scientific data on drug-use trends and treatment patterns has the potential to improve treatment utilization and outcomes for this population. While significant progress is evident in the ethnoculutural attitudes and behaviors of African Americans regarding treatment for substance abuse problems, more emphasis should be placed on the development of community-based prevention and outreach efforts. Culturally-based treatment appears to be making some progress with African Americans. The immediate challenge to researchers and treatment providers is to establish evidenced-based treatment models and to demonstrate the effectiveness of the programs for African Americans.

See also **Alcoholics Anonymous (AA); Coerced Treatment for Substance Offenders; Crack; Ethnopharmacology; Gender and Complications of Substance Abuse; Narcotics Anonymous (NA); National Survey on Drug Use and Health (NSDUH); Prevention; Religion and Drug Use; Risk Factors for Substance Use, Abuse, and Dependence: Gender; Risk Factors for Substance Use, Abuse, and Dependence: Race/Ethnicity; Treatment, Behavioral Approaches to: Self-Help and Anonymous Groups; Treatment, Behavioral Approaches to: Twelve-Step and Disease Model Approaches; Treatment, Stages/Phases of: Aftercare; Treatment: An Overview; U.S. Government Agencies: Substance Abuse and Mental Health Services Administration (SAMHSA); Welfare Policy and Substance Abuse in the United States.**

BIBLIOGRAPHY

Brown, V. B., Melchior, L. A., Slaughter, R., & Huba, G. J. (2005). Stages of multiple behavior change as a function of readiness for substance abuse treatment among women at risk. *Journal of Addictions Nursing, 16* (1–2), 23–29.

Heinz, A., Epstein, D. H., & Preston, K. L. (2007). Spiritual/religious experiences and in-treatment outcome in an inner-city program for heroin and cocaine dependence. *Journal of Psychoactive Drugs, 39*(1), 41–49.

Helms, J. E., & Cook, D. A. (1999). *Using race and culture in counseling and psychotherapy: Theory and process.* Needham Heights, MA: Allyn & Bacon.

Jacobson, J. O., Robinson, P. L., & Blumenthal, R. N. (2007). Racial disparities in completion rates from publicly funded alcohol treatment: Economic resources explain more than demographics and addiction severity. *Health Services Research, 42* (2), 773–797.

Jones-Saumty, D. (2002). Substance abuse treatment for Native Americans. In G. X. Ma & G. Henderson (Eds.), *Ethnicity and substance abuse: Prevention and intervention* (pp. 270–283). Springfield, IL: Charles C. Thomas.

Longshore, D., & Grills, C. (2000). Motivating illegal drug use recovery: Evidence for culturally congruent intervention. *Journal of Black Psychology, 26*(3), 288–301.

Mallow, A., & Cameron-Kelly, D. (2006). Unraveling the layers of cultural competence: Exploring the meaning of meta-cultural competence in the therapeutic community. *Journal of Ethnicity in Substance Abuse, 5*(3), 63–74.

Michalak, L., Trocki, K., & Bond, J. (2007). Religion and alcohol in the U.S. National Alcohol Survey: How important is religion for abstention and drinking? *Drug and Alcohol Dependence, 87*(2–3), 268–280.

Mitchell Hampton, M. (2006). Factors associated with the retention of urban uninsured adult African Americans in outpatient substance abuse treatment. In *Dissertation Abstracts International: Section B: The Sciences and Engineering, 67*(1-B), pp. 214.

Neighbors, H. W., Caldwell, C., Williams, D. R., Nesse, R., Taylor, R. J., Bullard, K., et al. (2007). Race, ethnicity, and the use of services for mental disorders: Results from the National Survey of American Life. *Archives of General Psychiatry, 64*(4), 485–494.

Perron, B. E., & Bright, C. L. (2008). The influence of legal coercion on dropout from substance abuse treatment: Results from a national survey. *Drug and Alcohol Dependence, 92,* 123–131.

Pinderhughes, E. (1989). *Understanding race, ethnicity and power: The key to efficacy in clinical practice.* New York: Free Press.

Slaymaker, V. J., & Owen, P. L. (2006). Employed men and women substance abusers: Job troubles and treatment outcomes. *Journal of Substance Abuse Treatment, 31*(4), 347–354.

Smith, D., Buxton, R., Bilal, R., & Seymour, R. (1993). Cultural points of resistance to the 12-step recovery process. *Journal of Psychoactive Drugs, 25*(1), 97–108.

Substance Abuse and Mental Health Services Administration (SAMHSA) (2006). The Drug and Alcohol Information Services (DASIS) Report. *Black admissions to substance abuse treatment: 1999.* Available from http://www.oas.samhsa.gov/.

Sue, S. (2006). Cultural competency: From philosophy to research and practice. *Journal of Community Psychology, 34*(2), 237–245.

Terrell, D. M. (1993). Ethnocultural factors and substance abuse: Toward culturally sensitive treatment models. *Psychology of Addictive Behaviors, 7*(3), 162–167.

Waggoner, E., & Brinson, J. (2007). Prevalence of substance abuse within the African- American community: Mental health implications and interventions. In S. M. L. Logan, R. W. Denby, & P. A. Gibson (Eds.), *Mental health care in the African-American community* (pp. 113–135). New York: Haworth Press.

Williams, C. (1992). *No hiding place: Empowerment and recovery for our troubled communities.* San Francisco: Harper Collins.

CARLEEN ROBINSON
REVISED BY IHSAN SALLOUM (2009)

AGGRESSION AND DRUGS: RESEARCH ISSUES.

Alcohol, more than any other drug, has been linked to aggressive and violent behavior. Alcohol, opioids, hallucinogens, and psychomotor stimulants differ markedly from each other in terms of their pharmacology and neurobiological mechanisms, dependence liability, legal and social restraints, expectations, and cultural traditions. Each of these substances triggers, escalates, and disrupts aggressive behavior via distinctly different mechanisms, and it would be misleading to extrapolate from the conditions that promote violence in individuals under the influence of alcohol to those with other drugs. Different types of drugs interact with aggressive and violent behavior in several ways including (1) direct activation of brain mechanisms that control aggression, mainly in individuals who have been aggressive in the past; (2) drug states, such as alcohol or hallucinogen intoxication, serving as license for violent and aggressive behavior; (3) drugs such as heroin or cocaine serving as commodities in an illegal distribution system, drug trafficking, which relies on violent enforcement tactics; and (4) violent behavior representing one of the means by which an expensive cocaine or heroin habit is financed. Systematic experimental studies in animals represent the primary means to investigate the proximal and distal causes of aggressive behavior, whereas studies in humans most often attempt to infer causative relationships mainly by correlating the incidence of violent and aggressive behavior with past alcohol intake or abuse of other drugs. The ethical dilemma of research on aggression in animals and humans is the need to reduce harm and risk to the research subject, on the one hand, and on the other, to capture clearly the essential features of human violence, which is by definition injurious and harmful.

HOW TO MODEL VIOLENT BEHAVIOR IN EXPERIMENTAL RESEARCH WITH ANIMALS
Methodologically, aggression research stems from several scientific roots, the experimental-psychological, ethological (focusing on the evolutionary biology of behavior), and neurological traditions being the most important. The use of aversive environmental manipulations to produce defensive and aggressive behavior has been the focus of the experimental-psychological approach. During the 1960s models of aggression were developed that rely on prolonged isolated housing or crowding; exposure to noxious, painful electrical shock pulses; omission of scheduled rewards ("frustration"); or restricted access to limited food supplies as the major aversive environmental manipulations. The behavioral endpoints in these models are defensive postures and bites in otherwise placid, domesticated laboratory animals. Animal models of aggressive behavior become relevant to the human condition when they successfully capture the escalated nature of aggressive behavior such as after social provocation and after frustrating experiences. Aggression research using human subjects studied under controlled laboratory conditions has employed aversive environmental manipulations, such as the administration of electric shocks, noxious noise, or loss of prize money to a fictitious opponent. This type of experimental aggression research highlights the dilemma of attempting to model essential features of violence under controlled laboratory conditions without risking the harm and injury that are characteristic of such phenomena. Because it is unethical to conduct

experimental studies that involve realistic violent behavior, competitive behavior in laboratory situations is often used to model violence in the laboratory. However, the validity of this model to violence in the real world has rarely been tested.

In addition to environmental manipulations, histopathological findings of brain tumors in violent patients prompted the development of experimental procedures to destroy tissue in areas of the brain such as the septal forebrain, medial hypothalamus, or certain midbrain regions of laboratory rats and other animals. Such experimental manipulations most often result in rage-like defensive postures and biting, often called rage, hyperreactivity, and hyperdefensiveness. Alternatively, electrical stimulation of specific brain regions can evoke predatory attack, and aggressive and defensive responses in certain animal species. When animals are given very high, near-toxic doses of amphetamines and similar drugs, bizarre, rage-like responses may emerge. Similarly, aggressive and defensive behavioral elements are induced by exposure to very high doses of hallucinogens and during withdrawal from opiates. The inappropriate context, the unusually fragmented behavioral response patterns, and the inclusion of only domesticated laboratory rodents make aggressive and defensive reactions that are induced by lesions, electrical brain stimulation, drugs, and toxins difficult to interpret or generalize to the human situation.

In contrast to the emphasis on aversive environmental determinants or on neuropathology, the ethological approach to the study of animal aggression has focused on adaptive forms of aggressive behavior. Defense of a territory, rival fighting among mature males during the formation and maintenance of a group, defense of the young by a female, and antipredator defense are examples of these types of aggressive, defensive, and submissive behavior patterns, often referred to as agonistic behavior.

Sociobiological analysis portrays these behavior patterns as having evolved as part of reproductive strategies ultimately serving the transmission of genetic information to the next generation. The focus on aggressive behavior as it serves an adaptive function in reproductive strategies, however, complicates the extrapolation to violent behavior as it is defined at the human level. How the range of human violent acts relates to the various types of animal aggression and how it may share common biological roots remain to be specified.

ALCOHOL

How have these ethological, neurological, and experimental-psychological research traditions contributed to our understanding of the link between drugs of abuse and alcohol to human aggression and violence? Epidemiological and criminal statistics link alcohol to aggressive and violent behavior in humans. The pattern of this association is large in magnitude, consistent over the years, widespread in the types of aggressive and violent acts, massive in cost to the individual, family, and society, and serious in the suffering and harm caused. Systematic experimental studies have identified the early phase after a low acute (short-term) alcohol dose as a condition that increases the probability of many types of social interactions, including aggressive and competitive behaviors, and high-dose alcohol (with intoxication) as the condition most likely to be linked to many different kinds of violent activities. Yet, most alcohol drinking is associated with acceptable social behavior. This is because individuals differ markedly in their propensity to become intoxicated with alcoholic beverages and subsequently to engage in violent and aggressive behavior, rendering population averages poor representations of how alcohol causes individuals to behave violently. The sources for the individual differences derive from interactions among genetic, developmental, social, and other environmental factors. Genetic association between antisocial personality, possibly diagnosed with the aid of certain electrophysiological measures, and alcoholism remains to be firmly established.

In the early 1990s the neurobiological mechanisms of alcohol action for a range of physiological and behavioral functions began to be identified; it appears that the actions of alcohol on ionophoric (regulating the movement of ions into the neuron and its action potential threshold) serotonin, glutamate, and GABA receptor subtypes are particularly relevant to alcohol's effects on aggressive and violent behavior. For example, studies in rodents and primates indicate that subtype-selective benzodiazepine-receptor antagonists prevent the aggression-heightening effects of alcohol. Molecular mutations of GABA receptor subunits provide

further insight into the mechanisms via which alcohol heightens aggressive behavior in certain individuals. Similarly, the actions of alcohol on neuroendocrine events that control testosterone and adrenal hormones appear important in the mechanisms of alcohol's aggression-heightening effects. Among the environmental determinants of alcohol's effects on violence that are of paramount significance are social expectations and cultural habits as well as the early history of the individual in situations of social conflict. Impaired appraisal of the consequences, inappropriate sending and receiving of socially significant signals, and disrupted patterns of social interactions are characteristics of alcohol intoxication that contribute to its violence-promoting effects. A particularly consistent observation is the high prevalence of recent alcohol ingestion in victims and targets of aggression and violence. In contrast to heroin and cocaine, because alcohol is not an illicit drug, its link to violence is not a characteristic of the economic distribution network for this substance.

OPIOIDS

Violence in the context of drug addiction is due largely to securing the resources to maintain a drug habit as well as to establishing and conducting the business of drug dealing. Neither animal nor human data suggest a direct, pharmacological association between violence and acute or chronic administration of opiates. Although measures of hostility and anger are increased in addicts seeking methadone treatment, these feelings usually do not lead to aggressive or violent acts. Rather, the tendency to commit violent crimes correlates with preaddiction rates of criminal activity. However, experimental studies in animals point to the phase of withdrawal from chronic heroin as the period during which the individual is most vulnerable to being provoked to heightened levels of aggressive behavior. Nevertheless, although humans undergoing opioid withdrawal may experience increased feelings of anger, there is no evidence suggesting that they are more likely to become violent as a result.

PSYCHOMOTOR STIMULANTS

The most serious link of amphetamine to violence occurs in individuals who, after taking intravenous amphetamine—most often chronically—develop a paranoid psychotic state during which they commit violent acts. Most psychiatric reports and police records do not support the commonly held psychiatric opinion of the early 1970s that amphetamines, more than any other group of drugs, may be related specifically to aggressive behavior. The prevalence of violence by individuals who experience amphetamine paranoid psychosis may be less than 10 percent in general population samples and as high as 67 percent among individuals who showed evidence of psychopathology prior to amphetamine use. Low acute doses of amphetamine can increase various positive and negative social behaviors; higher doses often lead to disorganizing effects on social interactions and to severe social withdrawal. In the early twenty-first century the neurobiological mechanisms for the range of amphetamine effects on aggressive and social behavior remain unknown.

Surprisingly few pharmacological and psychiatric studies exist on cocaine's effects on aggression and violence; the available evidence points to psychopathological individuals who may develop the propensity to engage in violent acts. Cocaine has also been shown to induce a paranoid state, which may heighten the risk of violence. However, the far more significant problem is the violence associated with the supply, dealing, and procurement of cocaine, as documented in epidemiological studies.

HALLUCINOGENS
Most experimental studies with animals and humans, as well as most data from chronic cannabis users, indicate that preparations from the plant (e.g., marijuana and hashish) or the active agent tetrahydrocannabinol (THC) decreases aggressive and violent behavior. Owing to the drug's relatively widespread access, lower cost, and characteristic pattern of use, socioeconomic causes of violence in cannabis dealing and procurement are less prominent than with cocaine or heroin. Novel molecular pharmacological tools will enable a more adequate characterization of the endocannabinoid system in modulating aggressive behavior.

LSD has not been in widespread use since the 1980s, but older data suggest that rarely certain psychopathological individuals while using LSD may engage in violent acts. Phencyclidine (PCP) cannot be causally linked to violent or assaultive

behavior in the population as a whole. It appears that personality traits and a history of violent behavior determine whether or not PCP intoxication leads to violence. PCP violence is a relatively rare phenomenon, although when it occurs, the violence stands out because of its highly unusual form and intensity. The risk for such violence depends on the individual's social and personal background.

The impact of genetic predispositions to the susceptibility to become involved with dependence-producing drugs—such as alcohol, heroin, or cocaine—and to act violently has not yet been delineated in terms of specific neural mechanisms. Similarly, the modulating influences of learning, social modeling, or parental physical abuse on the neural substrate for drug action and for aggressive behavior have only recently begun to be specified. Because these critical connections remain incompletely understood, it is not possible at present to identify specific modes of intervention on the basis of neurobiological data.

See also **Alcohol: Psychological Consequences of Chronic Abuse; Crime and Alcohol; Crime and Drugs.**

BIBLIOGRAPHY

Evans, C. M. (1986). Alcohol and violence: Problems relating to methodology, statistics and causation. In P. F. Brain (Ed.), *Alcohol and aggression,* (pp. 138–160). London: Croom Helm.

Miczek, K. A., Faccidomo, S., de Almeida, R. M. M., Bannai, M., Fish, E. W., & DeBold, J. F. (2004). Escalated aggressive behavior: New pharmacotherapeutic approaches and opportunities. In J. Devine, J. Gilligan, K. A. Miczek, D. Pfaff, & R. Shaikh (Eds.), *Youth violence. Scientific approaches to prevention* (pp. 336–355). Annals of the New York Academy of Sciences, Vol. 1036.

Miczek, K. A., Faccidomo, S. P., Fish, E. W., & DeBold, J. F. (2007). Neurochemistry and molecular neurobiology of aggressive behavior. In J. D. Blaustein (Ed.), *Behavioral neurochemistry, neuroendocrinology and molecular neurobiology. Handbook of neurochemistry and molecular biology* (pp. 285–336). New York: Springer-Verlag.

Miczek, K. A., Fish, E. W., de Almeida, R. M. M., Faccidomo, S., & DeBold, J. F. (2004). Role of alcohol consumption in escalation to violence. In J. Devine, J. Gilligan, K. A. Miczek, D. Pfaff, & R. Shaikh (Eds.), *Youth violence. Scientific approaches to prevention* (pp. 278–289). Annals of the New York Academy of Sciences, Vol. 1036.

KLAUS A. MICZEK

AGING, DRUGS, AND ALCOHOL.

Despite the aging of the U.S. population and the resultant increase in the proportion of adults living to an advanced age, relatively little research has examined the correlates, predictors, and consequences of substance use among older adults. Thus, substance misuse in later life—which includes the use of alcohol and illicit, prescription, and over-the-counter drugs—has been called an "invisible epidemic" (Widlitz & Marin, 2002). Although older adults report lower levels of substance use than their younger counterparts, demographic changes and cohort trends suggest that substance misuse in later life is a pressing public health matter, and that older adults represent a group in need of specialized substance treatment programs and services (Gfro-erer et al., 2003). Not only are older adults the fastest-growing segment of the U.S. population, but over the first decades of the twenty-first century, the aging population will include the "baby boomers," or individuals born between 1946 and 1964. The aging of the baby boom cohort presents unique challenges to both health and social service sectors, for in addition to reporting higher rates of illicit drug and alcohol use and abuse, the baby boom cohort is significantly larger than previous cohorts (Koenig et al., 1994).

An examination of rates of substance use and misuse among older age groups helps shed light on the potential public health impact of these demographic trends. Although alcohol misuse is often underreported and, accordingly, underestimated in later life, epidemiological work shows that alcohol use and misuse are common among older adults. In 2006, the National Survey on Drug Use and Health (NSDUH) reported that 48 percent of adults aged 60 to 64 had consumed alcohol in the past month. Further, 35.2 percent reported non-binge or non-heavy use, 10.1 percent reported binging behavior (more than 5 drinks at one time on at least 1 day in the past 30 days), and 2.7 percent reported heavy use (over 5 drinks at one time on 5 or more days in the past 30 days) (SAMHSA, 2006). Problematic drinking among the baby boomers was notably higher, however, with 22 percent of adults aged 50 to 54 categorized as heavy or binge drinkers. Adults aged 65 and above reported slightly lower rates of use, with 38.4 percent reporting past-month alcohol use,

with 30.8 percent, reporting non-binge or non-heavy use, 6.0 percent reporting binging behavior, and 1.6 percent reporting heavy use. Moreover, epidemiological studies estimate that from the early 1990s until 2002, the prevalence of alcohol abuse or dependence tripled among adults aged 65 and older, with 2.36 percent of older men and 0.38 percent of older women meeting diagnostic criteria for alcohol abuse, and an additional 0.39 percent of older men and 0.13 percent of older women meeting criteria for alcohol dependence (Grant et al., 2004).

In addition, analyses of adults aged 65 and above who completed the 2001–2002 National Survey on Alcohol and Related Conditions (NESARC) yielded 12-month prevalence estimates of 1.5 percent, 1.2 percent, and 0.2 percent for alcohol use disorder, alcohol abuse, and alcohol dependence, respectively (Hasin et al., 2007). Given that substance misuse is more likely to be presented in health care settings, rates of alcohol misuse are often high among primary care (Kirchner et al., 2007), mental health (Holroyd & Duryee, 1997), and nursing home (Oslin et al., 1997) samples. For example, in a 2007 study of older adults in primary care settings, Kirchner et al. reported that of the 24,863 individuals screened, 21.5 percent drank within recommended levels (1–7 drinks per week), 4.1 percent were at-risk drinkers (8–14 drinks per week), and 4.5 percent were heavy (more than 14 drinks per week) or binge drinkers.

Compared to alcohol use, illicit drug use among older adults is relatively rare. For example, data from the Epidemiological Catchment Area (ECA) study imply that in the early 1980s, the lifetime prevalence of drug abuse and dependence was 0.12 percent for older men and 0.06 percent for older women, while the lifetime history of illicit drug use was 2.88 percent and 0.66 percent for men and women, respectively (Anthony & Helzer, 1991). Other work, however, suggests that illicit substance use is more common among older adults than previously estimated (McBride et al., 1992; Schonfeld & Dupree, 2000). Data from the 2001–2002 NESARC, for instance, yielded 12-month prevalence estimates of 0.20 percent for drug use disorder, 0.10 percent for drug abuse, and 0.10 percent for drug dependence (with lifetime prevalence estimates of 0.6%, 0.5%, and 0.2%, respectively) for adults aged 65 and older (Compton et al., 2007). Drug use among the baby boomers is of particular concern. According to the National Household Survey on Drug Use and Health (NSDUH), the percentage of adults in this age cohort that reported having used illicit drugs in the past month increased from 3.4 percent to 6.0 percent between 2002 and 2006 (SAMHSA, 2006). Thus, rates of illicit drug use and abuse will likely continue to rise as the baby boomers age.

When exploring alcohol and drug use among older populations, it is important to address the use of legal drugs. Given that aging is accompanied by an increased susceptibility to multiple diseases, which may be chronic, acute, infectious, or degenerative in nature, older adults use pharmacological and health services more often than any other segment of the population. For example, older adults are more likely to take multiple medications relative to their younger counterparts, with 71 percent regularly taking at least one prescription medication and 10 percent reporting taking five or more medications (Lassila et al., 1996). Further, it has been estimated that the average older patient takes 5.3 prescription medications each day (Golden et al., 1999). The use of over-the-counter drugs, such as aspirin, diet aids, and decongestants, is also quite common. In one study, 87 percent of older adults reported regular use of over-the-counter medications and 5.7 percent reported the concurrent use of five or more over-the-counter medications (Stoehr et al., 1997). *Polydrug abuse* (also known as *polypharmacy*), or the concurrent use of multiple drugs, is of particular concern in situations where complex medication regimens are not carefully and appropriately adhered to by patients or monitored by physicians. Older adults often see multiple health care providers, and if a clinician is unaware of the medications prescribed by all the other clinicians treating the patient, two or more of these medications may interact, sometimes with fatal results (Monane, Monane & Semla, 1997; Stein, 1994). It is therefore imperative to be cautious when prescribing or recommending a treatment. Both risks and benefits should be taken into account when determining a treatment plan, and guidelines for appropriate use should be clearly communicated to patients.

In light of the high prevalence of pharmaceutical drug use in later life, the risk of misusing prescription and over-the-counter medications increases with age.

Although the literature on this topic is sparse, a review of existing work suggests that 11 percent of older women misuse prescription drugs, with projections that 2.7 million adults will be using prescription drugs for nonmedical purposes by the year 2020, (Simoni-Wastila & Yang, 2006). According to Rummans, Evans, Krahn, & Fleming (1995), a large proportion of the medications prescribed to older adults include psychoactive, mood-altering drugs (e.g., drugs for psychosis, depression, anxiety, and sleep problems). For example, the use of benzodiazepines, which are among the most commonly prescribed medications in the United States, increases with age and tends to be chronic in later life (Simon et al., 1996). This is troubling, given that psychotherapeutic medications are subject to improper use and can lead to negative health outcomes, whether used alone or in combination with other drugs or alcohol. Thus, both alcohol and prescription-drug misuse may result in physical, psychological, and social problems and premature death among older adults as a result of factors such as severe withdrawal symptoms, medical complications, and suicide. Furthermore, all these factors taken together—alcohol, old age, multiple diseases, and multiple medications—can lead to poisonous, even fatal, interactions if not closely assessed and monitored. The complexities of age, alcohol, and drug interactions are discussed in the sections that follow.

GUIDELINES AND CLASSES OF SUBSTANCE USE IN LATER LIFE

To properly identify and care for individuals with drug or alcohol problems, it is important to understand both drinking guidelines and the full range of substance use behavior seen among older adults. Due to physiological changes, which are outlined below, guidelines and recommendations for use of these substances by older adults differ from those applied to younger adults. The Treatment Improvement Protocol (TIP) for older adults developed by the National Institute on Alcohol Abuse and Alcoholism (NIAAA) and the Center for Substance Abuse Treatment (CSAT) states that people aged 65 and above should consume no more than one standard drink per day (Blow, 1998; National Institute on Alcohol Abuse and Alcoholism, 1995). In addition, older adults should not consume more than two standard drinks on any one occasion (i.e., binge drinking).

Disulfiram (Antabuse)

Hypoglycemic agents
   chlorpropamide (Diabinese)
   tolbutamide (Orinase)

Other drugs
cefamandole (Mandole)

cefmetazole (Zefazone)

cefoperazone (Cefobid)

Cefotetan (Cefotan)

chloramphenicol (Chloromycetin)

furazolidone (Furoxone)

griseofulvin (Fulvicin)

ketoconazole (Nizoral)

Metronidazole (Flagyl)

monoamine oxidase inhibitors (e.g., phenelzine and tranylcypromine)

moxalactam (Moxam)

procarbazine (Matulane)

quinacrine (Atabrine)

Alcohol sensitizing mushrooms

Coprinus atramentarius (inky cap mushroom)

Clitocybe clavipes

Table 1. Drugs producing antabuse-like reactions with alcohol. ILLUSTRATION BY GGS INFORMATION SERVICES. GALE, CENGAGE LEARNING

There are no set recommendations for prescription and over-the-counter drugs, however, for the appropriate prescription and use of these medicines must be considered on a case-by-case basis. Lastly, there are no safe limits for the use of tobacco, marijuana, or other illicit drugs.

In spite of these recommendations, there is still a great deal of variability in the degree to which older adults use alcohol and drugs. As outlined by Frederic C. Blow (1998), using both the clinical experience and research findings of addiction specialists, a number of categories have been created to capture this variability. Individuals who report drinking less than one to two drinks in the previous year are described as *abstainers*. This is the most common drinking pattern in later life, with approximately 50 percent to 70 percent of older adults reporting abstinence. *Low-risk, social,* or *moderate drinkers* include individuals who drink within the recommended guidelines and do not demonstrate any alcohol-related problems. Individuals with *low-risk medication/drug use* adhere to physicians' prescriptions. It is still important, however, to monitor

the number and types of medications being used, as harmful medication interactions may still occur among this group.

Older adults who consume substances above recommended levels (e.g., more than 1 drink/day, high medication doses or durations that exceed reasonable clinical practice), yet experience minimal or no substance-related health, social, or emotional problems represent *at-risk or excessive substance users.* When the use of alcohol or drugs is at a level at which adverse medical, psychological, or social consequences have occurred or are significantly likely to occur, older adults are said to follow a pattern of *problem use.* According to the *Diagnostic and Statistical Manual of Mental Disorders, Fourth Edition (DSM-IV), substance abuse* is a maladaptive pattern of substance use that results in clinically significant impairment or distress (within a 12-month period), as evidenced by difficulty in one or more of the following domains: reduced ability to fulfill common roles (i.e., social, educational, and/or occupational); continued substance use in physically dangerous situations; repeated substance-related legal problems, and continuation of use regardless of substance-related social or interpersonal problems (American Psychiatric Association, 1994). Finally, according to *DSM-IV* criteria, older adults with *alcohol or drug dependence* have a medical disorder marked by clinically significant distress or impairment coupled with preoccupation with alcohol or drugs, loss of control, continued substance use despite adverse consequences, and/or physiological symptoms such as tolerance and withdrawal. Although there has been some debate regarding the validity of *DSM* diagnostic criteria for older adults, identifying older adults with alcohol or drug dependence is essential, as this represents a group in need of specialized treatment and services. Indeed, understanding patterns of use, as a whole, can help inform the proper screening, diagnosis, and counseling of older adults in numerous settings.

CORRELATES AND CONSEQUENCES OF SUBSTANCE MISUSE IN OLDER ADULTHOOD

A great deal of work has focused on identifying factors that are related to increased susceptibility to substance misuse and the maintenance of problematic substance-use patterns in later life. Results suggest that gender, medical comorbidity, a history of past substance use, and social and family environment represent just a few of these factors. For example, older men tend to drink greater quantities of alcohol than older women, and they are more likely to have alcohol-related problems (Moore et al., 2005) and a longer history of problem drinking (D'Archangelo, 1993). Women who abuse alcohol, however, are more likely than their male counterparts to have been married to a problem drinker, report negative life events and ongoing difficulties with spouses and other family members, and have a history of depression (Brennan & Moos, 1990). Age-related losses in social, physical, and occupational domains (such as widowhood and the death of family and friends); reduced physical function; and retirement also contribute to the adoption or maintenance of abusive drinking patterns in later life among both men and women (Blow, 1998).

Factors such as declining physical health and age-related physiological changes will increase both exposure and reactivity to medications, thus increasing the possibility of misusing these substances in later life. Moreover, women are more likely to use and misuse psychoactive medications (Simoni-Wastila & Yank, 2006), especially if they have a lower socioeconomic status (e.g., lower levels of education and income), are divorced or widowed, or have been diagnosed with a psychiatric disorder (such as depression) or an anxiety disorder. Generally, comorbid psychiatric diagnoses increase the risk for prescription drug abuse and dependence, regardless of gender. Finally, incorrect prescribing practices and inadequate monitoring of drug reactions and patient adherence by health care providers also increase the odds of problematic drug use (Montamat & Cusack, 1992).

While there is some evidence that low to moderate alcohol use (i.e., drinking within recommended guidelines), is associated with health benefits among older adults (Djousse et al., 2007; Rimm et al., 1991), it is important to recognize that there is no evidence that initiating drinking reduces health risks. Furthermore, abstinence should be recommended for older adults who present with a history of alcohol or drug abuse, are taking certain medications, or have been diagnosed with certain acute or chronic conditions. For example, patients with liver disease and gastrointestinal ulcers should not drink alcohol. Alcohol should also be avoided by patients with damage to the heart or other muscles (which may be the result of previous heavy drinking).

The negative consequences of problematic substance use span multiple social and health domains. Severe addiction or dependence harms the user physically, mentally, emotionally, and spiritually. Many people with substance dependence die from physical complications, accidents, and suicide. Alcohol and drug abuse causes thousands of premature deaths, and the cost of complications contributes billions of dollars to any large nation's health expenditure. Health care costs for a family with an alcoholic member are typically twice those for other families, and up to half of all emergency room admissions are alcohol related. Alcohol abuse also contributes to the high healthcare costs of elderly beneficiaries of government-supported health programs.

In general, the medical complications of alcohol abuse observed in older individuals are the same as those seen in younger individuals. These complications include liver disease; acute and chronic inflammation of the pancreas; inflammation, bleeding, and diseases of the gastrointestinal tract; an increased risk of infections; and disturbances in metabolism. Furthermore, alcohol is primarily a drug that depresses or deadens the central nervous system (CNS). The toxic effects of alcohol abuse can cause brain tissue to shrink or waste away, unsteadiness and lack of coordination in movement, and damage to nerves throughout the body. Even moderate use can lead to adverse health outcomes. Low to moderate alcohol consumption impairs one's ability to drive, and it may increase the risk of accidents and fatal injuries due to falls, motor vehicle crashes, and suicide (Sorock et al., 2006). Depression, memory problems, liver disease, cardiovascular disease, cognitive changes, and sleep problems have also been linked to moderate alcohol use.

These negative effects of alcohol are particularly exacerbated in later life due to normal physiological changes that accompany aging. For example, older adults tolerate gastrointestinal bleeding and infection less well than do younger persons. Older adults are particularly prone to vitamin deficiencies, malnutrition, anemia, loss of bone mass, diseases of the central and peripheral nervous systems, heart conditions, and cancer. Alcohol-induced degeneration of the CNS is compounded by the normal loss of nerve cells that occurs with advancing age.

Finally, alcohol use represents one of the leading risk factors for the occurrence of adverse drug reactions, and it is known to interfere with the metabolism of certain medications. As a result it can lessen the effectiveness of routine drug therapy or even create new medical problems. Among older adults, excessive alcohol use together with medications can severely compromise and complicate a well-planned therapeutic program. Thus, even casual use of alcohol may be a problem for older individuals, particularly if they are taking medications that interact with alcohol. Difficulties can also arise from the interaction of alcohol and over-the-counter medications.

AGING AND ALTERED PHYSIOLOGICAL RESPONSE

As previously mentioned, physiological factors render older adults more sensitive to alcohol, illicit drugs, and over-the-counter and prescription medications, so that guidelines and recommendations for use of these substances differ for older and younger adults. Physiological differences stem from age-related changes in pharmacokinetics—the bodily processes that absorb, distribute within the body, make use of, and excrete substances—which affect the levels of alcohol and drugs in blood and tissues (Vestal & Cusack, 1990). For example, with aging, the percentage of water and lean tissue (mainly muscle) in the body decreases, while the percentage of fat tissue increases. These changes affect the distribution of alcohol and drugs to different parts of the body, the length of time that they stay in the body, and the amount of these substances absorbed by body tissues. One reason that drinking the same amount of alcohol has a greater effect on older adults is that there is a smaller volume of total body fluids, resulting in higher blood-alcohol levels than in young persons (Vestal et al., 1977).

Changes in metabolism, kidney function, and the CNS also are responsible for differential age-related physiological responses. Most substances are eliminated from the body by metabolism in the liver followed by excretion by the kidney. Although enzymes continue to metabolize at the same rate in the old as in the young, both the total

weight of the liver (as a percentage of total body weight) and the total blood flow through the liver decrease with age (Loi & Vestal, 1988). As a result, the overall capacity of the liver to convert substances into their inactive by-products declines with age. Furthermore, both the rate at which the kidney filters the blood and the total flow of blood through the kidneys decline with age. Substances are thus excreted more slowly in older adults' urine, and hence build up more quickly in the bloodstream. Finally, nerve-cell sensitivity increases with age, causing drugs that act on the CNS to produce a stronger effect in older patients.

Given the physiological changes outlined above, it comes as little surprise that older adults are more susceptible than younger adults to unintended, adverse drug reactions (ADRs). The overall incidence of ADRs in this age group is two to three times that found in young adults. Although the results of studies vary, about 20 percent of all adverse drug reactions occur in elderly persons (Korrapati, Loi, & Vestal, 1992). ADRs are more severe in older individuals than among young adults. For instance, any drug that affects alertness, coordination, and balance will likely cause more falls and other accidents in older persons than in younger ones. Furthermore, hangover effects of sedative-hypnotic drugs and other mind-altering medicines—such as antipsychotics, antidepressants, and anxiolytics—are common and often more serious for older adults. These hangover effects suggest, in part, that the receptors in older adults' nerve cells are more sensitive, and perhaps supersensitive, to the presence of these medicines, though such effects could also be due to the reduced clearance of medications in older adults, as described above.

Adverse effects of medications may be caused or increased by age-related chronic diseases, by intake of alcohol, and/or by incompatibilities between the foods and medicines that are taken. For example, older adults who drink regularly, even if they are not alcoholic, and/or who use illicit drugs place themselves at increased risk for adverse effects. Consuming alcohol in combination with prescription or over-the-counter drugs may lead to exaggerated or negative effects or, conversely, a blunting of the effectiveness of some medications due to alcohol's effects on metabolism (Moore et al., 2007). The combination of alcohol and prescribed or over-the-counter sleeping pills, for instance, could decrease intellectual function by producing an organic brain syndrome; frequent results include confusion, falls, wild swings in emotions, and other ADRs (Adams, 1995). Finally, there is some evidence to suggest that women and persons living alone, suffering from multiple diseases, taking multiple drugs, with poor nutritional habits, and with decreased sensory perception or mental clarity are at increased risk of ADRs.

ALCOHOL AND DRUG INTERACTIONS AMONG OLDER ADULTS

It is very difficult to determine the actual incidence of combined drug and alcohol use among adults in later life, but it is likely to be reasonably high for the following reasons: (1) the average adult over sixty-five takes from two to seven prescription medicines daily, in addition to over-the-counter medications; (2) most older persons do not view alcohol as a drug, and they therefore falsely assume that modest amounts of alcoholic beverages can do little harm to an already aged body; and (3) few older persons hold to the traditional notion that mixing alcohol and medications will have bad consequences.

The underreporting, underrecognition, and underestimation of alcohol-drug interactions may lead to dangerous and adverse health consequences, particularly because older adults have an increased sensitivity to both alcohol and drugs, due to the physiological changes outlined above. Interactions between alcohol and over-the-counter or prescription medications, which are commonly used by older adults for a variety of acute and chronic medical conditions, may be especially harmful. Among older adults, the consumption of alcohol in combination with prescription or over-the-counter drugs may lead to exaggerated or adverse therapeutic effects, or to a blunting of the effectiveness of some medications (Moore et al., 2007). For example, antihistamines, including diphenhydramine (Benadryl), dimenhydrinate (Dramamine), and most cold medications and anticholinergics, such as scopolamine, can cause confusion in the elderly, which is exacerbated by concurrent alcohol use. Moreover, alcohol consumed in combination with drugs used to treat type II diabetes (e.g., sulfonylureas), a common condition in older adulthood, may cause dangerously low levels of blood sugar, especially in patients whose diet calls for decreased carbohydrates.

- Elderly patients are advised to avoid alcohol consumption just before going to bed in order to avoid sleep disturbances.
- Because of the potential for alcohol–drug interaction, alcohol ingestion should be avoided before driving.
- Abstinence from alcohol by older patients receiving CNS depressants, analgesics, anticoagulants, antidiabetic drugs, and some cardiovascular drugs is recommended.
- A doctor or pharmacist should be consulted about alcohol–drug interactions.
- Any side effect or loss of energy should be immediately reported to the physician.
- Older individuals who want to drink, have no medical contraindications, and take no medications that interact with alcohol may consider one drink a day to be a prudent level of alcohol consumption. Alcohol when taken in moderation may be useful.

Table 2. Guidelines for use of alcohol by older adults. (Adapted from M. C. Dufour, L. Archer, & E. Gordis. (1992). Alcohol and the elderly. *Clinical Geriatric Medicine, 8*(1), 127–141.) ILLUSTRATION BY GGS INFORMATION SERVICES. GALE, CENGAGE LEARNING

Finally, alcohol use has been shown to interfere with older adults' metabolism of prescribed medications such as digoxin and warfarin, drugs for which modest changes in blood levels can transform therapeutic effects into dangerous adverse effects (Hylek et al., 1998; Onder et al., 2002).

Although not every medication reacts dangerously with alcohol, a variety of drugs do so consistently. The most dangerous of these reactions occurs when alcohol is combined with another CNS depressant. Since alcohol itself is a potent CNS depressant, its use with barbiturates, sedative-hypnotics, or other sedating drugs adds to and reinforces their CNS-depressant effects, which further decreases mental alertness, consciousness, and control of movement (Gerbino, 1982). In one study of older adults, diazepam (Valium), codeine, meprobamate (Equanil), and flurazepam (Dalmane) were the top four agents responsible for drug-alcohol interactions (Jinks & Raschko, 1990). The interaction of alcohol with benzodiazepine drugs may be especially harmful among older adults. This is especially true for diazepam (Valium) and chlordiazepoxide (Librium), due to their long duration of effects. Commonly observed side effects of these medications when combined with alcohol include high blood pressure, sleepiness, confusion, and depression of the CNS, which may lead to slowed or stopped breathing. Similarly, excessive or acute alcohol use increases the CNS effects of tricyclic antidepressants, thus increasing the chances of falls, broken bones, and, in extreme cases, severe drowsiness, lowered body temperature, coma, and death.

CONCLUSION

It is projected that by the year 2020, the number of older adults requiring substance abuse treatment will increase to 4.4 million, a number that far exceeds the estimated 1.7 million that were in need of treatment in 2000 and 2001 (Gfroerer et al., 2003). The capacity of older adults to handle alcohol and drugs differs from that of the young because of age-related changes in various systems of the body. Alcohol abuse among older adults can lead to falls, fractures, and other similar medical complications. The combination of prescription and over-the-counter medications with alcohol consumption can lead to disastrous complications and even premature death. Thus, older adults and their families or caregivers are encouraged to seek the advice of their pharmacist or family physician in regard to mixing alcohol and medications, and to follow the guidelines given in Table 2.

Although substance misuse among older adults represents a pressing public health issue, individuals in need of treatment or at risk for future problems often go unidentified and untreated. To meet the special needs of older adults experiencing problems with alcohol and drugs, it is important that social service and health care professionals learn to recognize age-specific signs and symptoms of substance misuse, and to be informed regarding available treatment options for older adults. The literature on treatment outcomes among older adults, though scant, is promising. Specifically, treatment outcomes for older adults have been shown to be comparable or significantly better than outcomes among younger adults (Lemke & Moos, 2003; Oslin et al., 2002; Satre et al., 2004). Thus, despite popular belief, older adults are amenable and responsive to treatment, particularly when they are in programs that offer age-appropriate care and include providers who are aware of aging issues. Further research and clinical efforts directed towards identifying and reducing problematic substance use will foster improvements in overall quality of life among older adults with substance use problems.

See also **Diagnostic and Statistical Manual (DSM); Drug Interactions and Alcohol; Drug Metabolism;** National Survey on Drug Use and Health (NSDUH); Polydrug Abuse; Social Costs of Alcohol and Drug Abuse; U.S. Government Agencies: Center for Substance Abuse Treatment (CSAT); U.S. Government Agencies: Substance Abuse and Mental Health Services Administration (SAMHSA).

BIBLIOGRAPHY

Adams, W. L. (1995). Interactions between alcohol and other drugs. *International Journal of the Addictions, 30*(13–14), 1903–1923.

American Psychiatric Association. (1994). *Diagnostic and statistical manual of mental disorders* (4th Rev. ed.), Washington, DC: Author.

Anthony, J. C., Helzer, J. E. (1991). Syndromes of drug abuse and dependence. In L.N. Robins & D. A. Regier (Eds.), *Psychiatric Disorders in America: The Epidemiologic Catchment Area Study.* New York: Free Press.

Blow, F. C. (1998). *Substance abuse among older adults.* Treatment Improvement Series Protocol (TIP) Series No. 26. Rockville, MD: US Department of Health and Human Services, Center for Substance Abuse Treatment.

Brennan, P. L., & Moos, R. H. (1990). Life stressors, social resources, and late-life problem drinking. *Psychology and Aging, 5*(4), 491–501.

Compton, W. M., Thomas, Y. F., Stinson, F. S., & Grant, B. F. (2007). Prevalence, correlates, disability, and comorbidity of DSM-IV drug abuse and dependence in the United States: Results from the national epidemiologic survey on alcohol and related conditions. *Archives of General Psychiatry, 64*(5), 566–576.

D'Archangelo E. (1993). Substance abuse in later life. *Canadian Family Physician 39,* 1986–1988, 1991–1993.

Djoussé, L., Biggs, M. L., Mukamal, K. J., Siscovick, D. S. (2007). Alcohol consumption and type 2 diabetes among older adults: The cardiovascular health study. *Obesity, 15*(7), 1758–1765.

Dufour, M. C., Archer, L., & Gordis, E. (1992). Alcohol and the elderly. *Clinical Geriatric Medicine, 8*(1), 127–141.

Gerbino, P. P. (1982). Complications of alcohol use combined with drug therapy in the elderly. *Journal of the American Geriatric Society, 30*(11 Supplement), S88–S93.

Gfroerer, J., Penne, M., Pemberton, M., & Folsom, R. (2003). Substance abuse treatment need among older adults in 2020: The impact of the aging baby-boom cohort. *Drug and Alcohol Dependence, 69*(20), 127–135.

Golden, A. G., Preston, R. A., Barnett, S. D., Llorente, M., Hamdan, K., & Silverman, M. A. (1999). Inappropriate medication prescribing in homebound older adults. *Journal of the American Geriatrics Society, 47*(8), 948–953.

Grant, B. F., Dawson, D. A., Stinson, F. S., Chou, S. P., Dufour, M. C., & Pickering, R. P. (2004). The 12-month prevalence and trends in DSM-IV alcohol abuse and dependence: United States, 1991-1992 and 2001-2002. *Drug and Alcohol Dependence, 74*(3), 223–234.

Hasin, D. S., Stinson, F. S., Ogburn, E., & Grant, B. F. (2007). Prevalence, correlates, disability, and comorbidity of DSM-IV alcohol abuse and dependence in the United States: Results from the National Epidemiologic Survey on Alcohol and Related Conditions. *Archives of General Psychiatry, 64*(7), 830–842.

Holroyd, S., & Duryee, J. (1997). Substance use disorders in a geriatric psychiatry outpatient clinic: Prevalence and epidemiologic characteristics. *Journal of Nervous & Mental Disease, 185*(10), 627–632.

Hylek, E. M., Heiman, H., Skates, S. J., et al. (1998). Acetaminophen and other risk factors for excessive warfarin anticoagulation. *Journal of the American Medical Association, 279*(9), 657–662.

Ikels, C. (1991). Aging and disability in China: Cultural issues in measurement and interpretation. *Social Science Medicine, 32*(6), 649–665.

Jinks, M. J., & Raschko, R. (1990). A profile of alcohol and prescription drug abuse in a high-risk community-based elderly population. *Drug Intelligence Clinical Pharmacology, 24*(10), 971–975.

Kirchner, J. E., Zubritsky, C., Marisue, C., et al. (2007). Alcohol consumption among older adults in primary care. *Journal of General Internal Medicine, 22*(1), 92–97.

Koenig, H. G., George, L. K., & Schneider, R. (1994). Mental health care for older adults in the year 2020: A dangerous and avoided topic. *Gerontologist, 34*(5), 674–679.

Korrapati, M. R., Loi, C. M., & Vestal, R. E. (1992). Adverse drug reactions in the elderly. *Drug Therapy, 22*(7), 21–30.

Lassila, H. C., Stoehr, G. P., Ganguli, M., Seaberg, E. C., Gilby, J. E., Belle, S. H., & Echement, D. A. (1996). Use of prescription medications in an elderly rural population: The MoVIES project. *Annals of Pharmacotherapy, 30*(6), 589–595.

Lemke, S., & Moos, R. H. (2003). Treatment and outcomes of older patients with alcohol use disorders in community residential programs. *Journal of Studies on Alcohol, 64*(2), 219–226.

Loi, C. M., & Vestal, R. E. (1988). Drug metabolism in the elderly. *Pharmacological Therapy, 36*(1), 131–149.

McBride, D. C., Inciardi, J. A., Chitwood, D. D., McCoy, C. B., and TNAR Consortium. (1992). Crack use and correlates of use in a national population of stress heroin users. *Journal of Psychoactive Drugs, 24*(4), 411–416.

Monane, M., Monane, S., & Semla, T. (1997). Optimal medication use in elders: Key to successful aging. *Western Journal of Medicine, 167*(4), 233–237 (comment, 238–239).

Montamat, S. C., & Cusack, B. (1992). Overcoming problems with polypharmacy and drug misuse in the elderly. *Clinics in Geriatric Medicine, 8*(1), 143–158.

Moore, A. A., Gould, R., Reuben, D. B., et al. (2005). Longitudinal patterns and predictors of alcohol consumption in the United States. *American Journal of Public Health, 95*(3), 458-465.

Moore, A. A., Whiteman, E. J., Ward, K. T. (2007). Risks of combined alcohol/medication use in older adults. *American Journal of Geriatric Pharmacotherapy, 5*(1), 64–74.

National Institute on Alcohol Abuse and Alcoholism. (1995) Diagnostic criteria for alcohol abuse. *Alcohol Alert, 30*(PH 359), 1–6. Available from http://pubs.niaaa.nih.gov/.

Onder, G., Pedone, C., Landi, F., et al. (2002). Adverse drug reactions as cause of hospital admissions: Results from the Italian Group of Pharmacoepidemiology in the Elderly (GIFA). *Journal of the American Geriatrics Society, 50*(12), 1962–1968.

Oslin, D. W., Pettinati, H.M., & Volpicelli, J. R. (2002). Alcoholism treatment adherence: Older age predicts better adherence and drinking outcomes. *American Journal of Geriatric Psychiatry, 10,* 740–747.

Oslin, D. W., Streim, J. E., Parmelee, P., et al. (1997). Alcohol abuse: A source of reversible functional disability among residents of a VA nursing home. *International Journal of Geriatric Psychiatry, 12*(8), 825–832.

Rimm, E. B., Giovannucci, E. L., Willett, W. C., et al. (1991). Prospective study of alcohol consumption and risk of coronary disease in men. *Lancet, 338*(8765), 464–468.

Rizack, M. A., & Hillman, C. D. M. (1987). *The Medical Letter handbook of adverse drug interactions.* New York: Medical Letter.

Rummans, T. A., Evans, J. M., Krahn, L. E., & Fleming, K. C. (1995). Delirium in elderly patients: Evaluation and management. *Mayo Clinic Proceedings, 70*(10), 989–998.

Satre, D. D., Mertens, J. R., Arean, P. A., & Weisner, C. (2004). Five-year alcohol and drug treatment outcomes of older adults versus middle-aged and younger adults in a managed care program. *Addiction, 99,* 1286–1297.

Schonfeld, L., Dupree, L. W., et al. (2000). Cognitive-behavioral treatment of older veterans with substance abuse problems. *Journal of Geriatric Psychiatry and Neurology, 13*(3), 124–129.

Simon, G., et al. (1996). Predictors of chronic benzodiazepine use in a health maintenance organization sample. *Journal of Clinical Epidemiology, 49*(9), 1067–1073.

Simoni-Wastila, L., & Yank, H. K. (2006). Psychoactive drug abuse in older adults. *American Journal of Geriatric Pharmacotherapy, 4*(4), 380–394.

Sorock, G. S., Chen, L. H., Gonzalgo, S. R., & Baker, S. P. (2006). Alcohol-drinking history and fatal injury in older adults. *Alcohol, 40*(3), 193–199.

Spencer G. (1989). *Projections of the population of the United States, by age, sex, and race: 1988 to 2080.* Current Population Reports, series P-25, no. 1018, U.S. Bureau of the Census. Washington, D.C.: U.S. Government Printing Office.

Stein, B. E. (1994). Avoiding drug reactions: Seven steps in writing prescriptions. *Geriatrics, 49*(9), 28–30, 33–36.

Stoehr, G. P., Ganguli, M., Seaberg, E. C., Echement, D. A., & Belle, S. (1997). Over-the-counter medication use in an older rural communtity: The MoVIES project. *Journal of the American Geriatrics Society, 45*(2), 158–165.

Substance Abuse and Mental Health Services Administration (SAMHSA). (2007). *Results from the 2006 National Survey on Drug Use and Health: National findings.* NSDUH Series H-32, DHHS Publication No. SMA 07-4293. Rockville, MD: SAMHSA, Office of Applied Studies.

Vestal, R. E., & Cusack, B. J. (1996). Pharmacology and aging. In E. L. Schneider & J. W. Rowe (Eds.), *Handbook of the biology of aging* (4th ed.). San Diego: Academic Press.

Widlitz, M., & Marin, D. (2002). Substance abuse in older adults, an overview. *Geriatrics, 57*(12), 29–34.

Madhu R. Korrapati
Robert E. Vestal
Revised by James T. McDonough Jr. (2001)
Shahrzad Mavandadi (2009)

AGONIST.

An agonist is a drug or an endogenous substance that binds to a receptor (it has affinity for the receptor binding site) and produces a biological response (it possesses intrinsic activity). The binding of a drug agonist to the receptor produces an effect that mimics the physiological response observed when an endogenous substance (e.g., hormone, neurotransmitter) binds to the same receptor. In many cases, the biological response is directly related to the concentration of the agonist available to bind to the receptor. As more agonist is added, the number of receptors occupied increases, as does the magnitude of the response. The potency (strength) of the agonist for producing the physiological response (how much drug is needed to produce the effect) is related to the strength of binding (the affinity) for the receptor and to its intrinsic activity. Most drugs bind to more than one receptor; they have multiple receptor interactions.

See also **Agonist-Antagonist (Mixed); Antagonist.**

BIBLIOGRAPHY

Ross, E. M. (1990). Pharmacodynamics: Mechanisms of drug action and the relationship between drug concentration and effect. In A. G. Gilman et al. (Eds.), *Goodman and Gilman's the pharmacological basis of therapeutics*, 8th ed. New York: Pergamon. (2005, 11th ed. New York: McGraw-Hill Medical.)

Nick E. Goeders

AGONIST-ANTAGONIST (MIXED).

A mixed agonist-antagonist is a drug or receptor ligand that possesses pharmacological properties similar to both agonists and antagonists for certain receptor sites. Well-known mixed agonist-antagonists are drugs that interact with opioid (morphine-like) receptors. Pentazocine, nalbuphine, butorphanol, and buprenorphine are all mixed agonist-antagonists for opioid receptors. These drugs bind to the μ (mu) opioid receptor to compete with other substances (e.g., morphine) for this binding site; they either block the binding of other drugs to the μ receptor (i.e., competitive antagonists) or produce a much smaller effect than that of "full" agonists (i.e., they are only partial agonists). Therefore, these drugs block the effects of high doses of morphine-like drugs at μ opioid receptors, while producing partial agonist effects at κ (kappa) and/or δ (delta) opioid receptors. Some of the mixed opioid agonist-antagonists probably produce analgesia (pain reduction) and other morphine-like effects in the central nervous system by binding as agonists to κ opioid receptors.

In many cases, however, there is an upper limit (ceiling) to some of the central nervous system effects of these drugs (e.g., respiratory depression). Furthermore, in people physically addicted to morphine-like drugs, the administration of a mixed opioid agonist-antagonist can produce an absti-nence (withdrawal) syndrome by blocking the μ opioid receptor and preventing the effects of any μ agonists (i.e., morphine) that may be in the body. Pretreatment with these drugs can also reduce or prevent the euphoria (high) associated with subse-quent morphine use, since the μ opioid receptors are competitively antagonized. Therefore, the mixed opioid agonist-antagonists are believed to have less abuse liability than full or partial opioid receptor agonists.

As more and more subtypes of receptors are discovered in other neurotransmitter systems (there are now more than five serotonin receptor subtypes and five dopamine receptor subtypes), it is quite likely that mixed agonist-antagonist drugs will be identified that act on these receptors as well.

See also **Agonist; Antagonist.**

BIBLIOGRAPHY

Gilman, A. G., et al., Eds. (1990). *Goodman and Gilman's the pharmacological basis of therapeutics*, 8th ed. New York: Pergamon. (2005, 11th ed. New York: McGraw-Hill Medical.)

Kenakin, T. (2003). *A pharmacology primer: Theory, appli-cation and methods*. New York: Academic Press.

NICK E. GOEDERS

AIDS (ACQUIRED IMMUNE DEFI-CIENCY SYNDROME). *See* Alcohol and AIDS; Injecting Drug Users and HIV; Needle and Syringe Exchanges and HIV/AIDS; Prisons and Jails: Drug Use and HIV/AIDS in; Substance Abuse and AIDS.

AL-ANON. Al-Anon is a fellowship very similar to Alcoholics Anonymous (AA), but it is for family members and friends of alcoholics rather than alco-holics themselves. Although formally separate from the fellowship of AA, it has incorporated into its groups the AA Twelve Steps and Twelve Traditions, as well as AA's beliefs and organizational philosophy. These tools and beliefs are directed toward helping families of alcoholics cope with the baffling and dis-turbing experiences of living in close interaction with

an active alcoholic. In this sense, as noted by Rudy (1986), it is a satellite organization of AA.

Proselytizing organizations such as AA, of necessity, attempt to reduce or eliminate the ties of newcomers with other significant persons and groups who are not members. Rather than attempt to sever those bonds for prospective AA members, Al-Anon evolved as a way to include families in a parallel organization, and thus initiate them into the beliefs and practices of AA. In addition, as AA expanded and more alcoholics went into recovery, close relatives became aware that their own per-sonal problems could be reduced by applying AA principles to themselves and working through the Twelve-Step program, even though they were not alcoholic. In 1980 there were 16,500 Al-Anon groups worldwide, including 2,300 Alateen groups of children of alcoholics (Maxwell, 1982).

A BRIEF HISTORY

Early in the 1940s, women married to alcoholic men started attending AA meetings, and they soon began to meet together informally. By the late 1940s there were so many family members at AA affairs that the AA Board of Trustees had to decide how to manage this valuable but perplexing influx. Since relatives of AA members had already begun to hold their own meetings, the board recom-mended that AA meetings be limited to alcoholics, and that these family groups should be listed at the AA General Service office as a resource for family members of alcoholics. Several spouses of alco-holics began their own clearinghouse committee to coordinate the approximately 90 groups already in existence, and there was soon a separate network distinct from AA. In order to maintain the connec-tion to AA, the founders shortened the first two letters of "alcoholic," and the first four letters of "anonymous" and called the organization Al-Anon, a name that has persisted.

In 1950, Bill W., a founder of AA, persuaded his wife Lois to get involved with the fledgling Al-Anon. The rapidly accumulating lists in the General Service office were turned over to her and to an associate, Anne B., who contacted those on the list, "and soon they had more work than they could handle" (Wing, 1992, p. 136). For two years, the two conducted their activities at Stepping Stones, the suburban home of Bill W. and Lois. In 1952, they moved to New York City, where volunteer workers could more easily be recruited.

AL-ANON MEMBERSHIP AND MEETING CHARACTERISTICS

The 2006 Al-Anon/Alateen Member Survey indicated that a majority of members are Caucasian (88%), married (57%), and female (85%). In 2008 there were 24,000 Al-Anon Family Groups worldwide, with a majority of these groups in the United States. Using estimates provided by Cermak (1989) on the average size of Al-Anon meetings (which range from 12 to 15 participants), it is estimated that roughly 324,000 people attend Al-Anon each week. According to the 2006 survey, the average age of Al-Anon members is 55, and about 53 percent of members are retired or hold professional or managerial positions. About 59 percent of Al-Anon members have been, or continue to be, married to an alcoholic. Al-Anon members tend, as a rule, to be relatively well educated. About 24 percent of the membership reported having completed some college, 26 percent reported having earned a college degree, and 24 percent reported having completed some postgraduate education. In general, 30 percent of Al-Anon members are relatively new to Al-Anon (less than 2 years as members), although about one in four members (23%) report long-term affiliation (over 20 years). Typically, Al-Anon members attend five to seven meetings each month, and approximately 59 percent of Al-Anon members have a sponsor or a mentor who aids a member through the prescribed twelve steps of Al-Anon.

AL-ANON'S STRATEGY

Al-Anon strives to direct its members' attention away from the active alcoholic with whom they attempt to interrelate, and toward their own behavior and emotions. This strategy is based on the impression that, in many ways, the family members of alcoholics have personalities that resemble those of alcoholics. That is, they repeatedly attempt to control the feelings and behaviors of the alcoholics in their midst by simple force of personal will, much as alcoholics attempt to control their drinking by the sheer force of their individual will. In both instances, a denial syndrome emerges that protects their compulsive drive toward continued control. In sum, family members often become codependent, so that they become as obsessed with the alcoholic's behavior as he or she is with the bottle (Huppert, 1976).

For example, an alcoholic's spouse or partner may often vainly attempt to control the alcoholic's drinking. Except for brief periods, however, most pleas are rejected and most promises are not kept. In such a case, while the alcoholic continues to drink and enjoy the brief emotional payoffs of intoxication, the spouse or other caretaker must try to cope for both of them by running the household, rearing the children, and working steadily to earn a living. If the alcoholic then shows signs of improvement in a treatment center, the spouse or life partner may resent it deeply, for strangers have done more in a short period than all the partner's efforts over the years. It thus appears to the alcoholic's partner and relatives as though they have not been wise enough, or determined enough, or superhuman enough to get the alcoholic in their life to stop drinking.

Al-Anon attempts to introduce the Twelve Steps of AA into the lives of family members in order to reduce the resentments and controlling behavior they typically display. Al-Anon emphasizes an adaptation of AA's first step: "We admit we are powerless to control an alcoholic relative, that we are not self-sufficient." Such a step is an admission that it is a waste of time to try to control what is beyond their capacities. Using this strategy, it is no longer necessary for the family members to deny that their control efforts are powerless, and this relieves them of the enormous sense of accumulated burden and guilt. In addition, it allows acceptance of outside treatment and its possible success.

RESEARCH ON AL-ANON

Only a few studies have investigated the effectiveness of Al-Anon, and nearly all of these studies have done so in the context of randomized clinical trials intended to both help the significant other of a substance abuser and to engage the substance abuser in formal treatment. Barber and Gilbertson (1996), for example, randomized concerned significant others (CSOs) into one of three interventions, and a fourth group of CSOs were referred to Al-Anon. CSOs assigned to individual counseling and Al-Anon reported significant gains in personal functioning, but—unlike in the formal interventions—none of the affected family members of the CSOs in the Al-Anon group entered substance abuse treatment. In a similar study, Miller and colleagues (1999) reported that the frequency of Al-Anon meeting attendance could be significantly increased when CSOs were assigned to an individualized Al-Anon facilitation therapy relative to interventions with a cognitive behavioral or intervention focus. Significant gains in CSO personal functioning—including reduced depression, increased relationship happiness, and reduced state-trait anger—were reported in all conditions including the Al-Anon group. However, similar to the findings by Barber and Gilbertson (1996), rates of treatment engagement for the substance abusers were lowest in the Al-Anon facilitation group. Thus, consistent with the expressed strategy of the Al-Anon program, evidence suggests that psychosocial improvement may occur over time for Al-Anon participants. Problem drinkers and illicit drug abusers appear to derive less benefit when CSOs become actively engaged in Al-Anon, relative to other interventions for CSOs.

See also **Adult Children of Alcoholics (ACOA); Codependence; Families and Drug Use; Treatment, Behavioral Approaches to: Twelve-Step and Disease Model Approaches.**

BIBLIOGRAPHY

Al-Anon Family Group Headquarters. (1984). *Al-Anon faces alcoholism* (2nd ed.). New York: Author.

Barber, J. G., & Gilbertson, R. (1996). An experimental study of brief unilateral intervention for the partners of heavy drinkers. *Research on Social Work Practice, 6*(3), 325–336.

Cermak, T. (1989). Al-Anon and recovery. In M. Galanter (Ed.), *Recent developments in alcoholism: Vol. 7* (pp. 91–104). New York: Plenum Press.

Huppert, S. (1976). The role of Al-Anon groups in the treatment program of a V.A. alcoholism unit. *Hospital and Community Psychiatry, 27*(10), 693–697.

Maxwell, M. (1982). Alcoholics Anonymous. In E. Gomberg, H. R. White, & J. Carpenter (Eds.), *Alcohol, science, and society revisited* (pp. 295–305). Ann Arbor: University of Michigan Press.

Miller, W. R., Meyers, R. J., & Tonigan, J. S. (1999). Engaging the unmotivated in treatment for alcohol problems: A comparison of three strategies for intervention through family members. *Journal of Consulting and Clinical Psychology, 67*(5), 688–697.

Rudy, D. R. (1986). *Becoming alcoholic: Alcoholics Anonymous and the reality of alcoholism.* Carbondale: Southern Illinois University Press.

Wing, N. (1992). *Grateful to have been there: My 42 years with Bill and Lois, and the evolution of Alcoholics Anonymous.* Park Ridge, IL: Parkside Publishing.

HARRISON M. TRICE
REVISED BY J. SCOTT TONIGAN (2009)

ALATEEN. Alateen is a division of the Al-Anon Family Group. Its members typically are teenagers whose lives have been impacted by someone else's problem drinking. Roughly, 59 percent are age 14 or younger, while 26 percent are ages 15 to 16 and 15 percent are age 17 or more. The problem drinkers in their lives are predominantly one or both parents, but brothers and sisters are not uncommon.

The prevailing story about the origin of Alateen is quite straightforward. Legend has it that in 1957 a 17-year-old in California was attending Alcoholics Anonymous (AA) and Al-Anon meetings with his parents. His father had just gotten sober in AA and his mother was an active member of Al-Anon. Although the teenager decided that the Twelve Steps of AA were helping him, his mother suggested that instead of attending AA meetings he start a teenaged group and pattern it after Al-Anon. The young man found five other teenaged children of alcoholic parents and, while the adult groups met upstairs, he got them together downstairs.

As other teenagers came forward from Al-Anon groups, the idea spread and it is estimated that as of 2008 about 3,500 Alateen groups meet worldwide. In formal terms, however, these groups are an important and an integral part of Al-Anon Family Groups. They are coordinated from the Al-Anon Family Group Headquarters in New York City and tied closely to their public-information programs. Thus, Alateen uses AA's Twelve Steps, but alters step twelve to simply read "carry the message to others," rather than "to other alcoholics." Alateen groups meet in churches and schoolrooms, often in the same building as Al-Anon, but in a different room.

Although there are a few exceptions, an active, adult member of Al-Anon usually serves as a sponsor. Also, members of Alateen can choose a personal sponsor from other Alateen members or from Al-Anon members.

Alateen enables its members to openly share their experiences and to devise ways of coping with the problem of living closely with a relative who has a drinking problem. The strategy is to change their own thinking about the problem-drinking relative. Alateen teaches that alcoholism is like diabetes—it cannot be cured, but it can be arrested. Members learn that they did not cause it, and they cannot control it or cure it. Scolding, tears, or persuasion, for example, are useless. Rather, "they learn to take care of themselves whether the alcoholic stops or not" (Al-Anon Family Groups, 1991). They apply the Twelve Steps to themselves—to combat their often obsessive thinking about controlling alcoholic relatives and to help them stop denying those relatives' alcoholism. In addition, they adapt and apply AA's Twelve Traditions to the conduct of their groups. For example, they practice anonymity, defining it not as secrecy, but as privacy and the lowering of competitiveness among members. A 1990 survey of Alateen members indicated an increase in the number of black, Hispanic, and other minority members.

In essence, Alateen uses the strategy of AA itself to learn how to deal with obsession, anger, feelings of guilt, and denials. Newcomers, like newcomers in AA, gain hope when they bond with other teenagers to help one another cope with alcoholic parents and other relatives with drinking problems (Al-Anon Family Groups, 2003).

See also **Adult Children of Alcoholics (ACOA); Codependence; Families and Drug Use; Treatment, Behavioral Approaches to: Twelve-Step and Disease Model Approaches.**

BIBLIOGRAPHY

Al-Anon/Alateen (2008). Available from http://www.al-anon.alateen.org.

Al-Anon Family Groups (2003). *Alateen—hope for children of alcoholics.* New York: Author.

Al-Anon Family Groups (1991). *Youth and the alcoholic parent.* New York: Author.

Paton, A., & Touquet, R. (2005). *ABC of alcohol,* 4th ed. Oxford, U.K.: Blackwell Publishing.

HARRISON M. TRICE

ALCOHOL

This entry includes the following essays:
CHEMISTRY AND PHARMACOLOGY
HISTORY OF DRINKING (INTERNATIONAL)
HISTORY OF DRINKING IN THE UNITED STATES
PSYCHOLOGICAL CONSEQUENCES OF CHRONIC ABUSE

CHEMISTRY AND PHARMACOLOGY

Alcohol is produced by a chemical process known as fermentation, in which microorganisms (bacteria or yeast) transform the sugars found naturally in fruits, vegetables, and grains into alcohol, carbon dioxide, and energy. Alcohol production can be expedited by providing optimal environmental conditions for these microbes. Five basic molecular forms of alcohol have been discovered. These forms vary only in the number of carbon atoms in each molecule, but this small difference results in substantial differences in their characteristics. Methanol (CH_3OH), for example, is an extremely dangerous form of alcohol that can cause death shortly after ingestion.

The form of alcohol produced intentionally for oral consumption is ethyl alcohol, also called ethanol. Ethanol has a very simple molecular structure: It is composed of only two carbon atoms, six hydrogen atoms, and one oxygen atom (C_2H_5OH). Ethanol is said to be hydrophilic (water-loving) because its chemical structure is similar to water, and the two compounds readily mix together. In addition, both ethanol and water are polar; that is, each molecule has a positive charge on one end and a negative charge on the other end. The polar structures of both alcohol and water cause the molecules to arrange themselves head to tail, with the positive end of one molecule attracting the negative end of another molecule. This is an important property, for it underlies their ability to be mixed together, and ethanol is not consumed in its pure form, but is generally diluted to some degree.

Most drinks with alcoholic content do not exceed an 8 percent concentration (beer is a good example). Wines do not usually exceed 15 percent, and most liquors are still below 50 percent, or 100 proof by weight or volume. The hydrophilic nature of ethanol also allows it to be readily absorbed following ingestion. Ethanol is not an especially potent compound compared to other drugs of abuse, but because it can be easily consumed in large quantities and is readily absorbed, pharmacologically active blood levels can be reached quickly.

EFFECTS ON THE BODY AND THERAPEUTIC USES

Ethanol is a general central nervous system depressant, producing sedation and even sleep as the dose increases. The degree of this depression is proportional to its concentration in the blood, although this relationship is more predictable when ethanol levels are rising than it is three or four hours later, when blood levels are falling. This variance occurs because during the first 15 or 20 minutes after an ethanol dose, the peripheral venous blood is losing ethanol to the tissues, while the brain has reached equilibrium with the arterial blood supply. Thus, brain alcohol levels are initially higher than venous blood alcohol levels, but since all blood samples for ethanol determinations are taken from a peripheral vein, the venous blood ethanol concentrations are appreciably lower immediately after ingestion than they are a few hours later, when the entire system has achieved equilibrium.

The reticular activating system of the brain stem is the area most sensitive to ethanol's effects, which accounts for the loss of integrative control of the brain's higher functions. Anecdotal reports of a stimulating effect, especially at low doses, are likely due to the depression of the mechanisms that normally control speech and other behaviors that evolved from training or prior experiences. However, there may be a genetic basis for this initial stimulating effect, since rodents that differ genetically show differences in the degree of initial stimulation or excitement. Upon drinking a moderate amount of ethanol, humans may quickly pass through the "stimulating" phase. Memory, the ability to concentrate, and insight are affected next, whereas confidence often increases as moods swing from one extreme to another. If the dose is increased, neuromuscular coordination becomes impaired. It is at this point that drinkers may be the most dangerous, because they are still able to move about but their reaction times and judgment are impaired and sleepiness must be fought. The ability to drive an automobile or operate machinery is therefore compromised. With higher doses, general (sleep) or surgical (unconsciousness) anesthesia may develop, with respiration dangerously depressed.

Ethanol is believed by many to have a number of medicinal, or therapeutic, uses—most of which are based on anecdotal reports, and few have substantiated claims. One well-known but misguided use of ethanol is to treat hypothermia (exposure to freezing conditions). Ethanol dilates blood vessels, bringing warmth from the core of the body to the skin. Although this initial effect of the alcoholic beverage appears to "warm" the patient, essential body heat is actually lost, causing a dangerous drop in core temperature. Another example is ethanol's effects on sleep. It is believed that a "nightcap" relaxes one and puts one to sleep. Indeed, acute administration of ethanol may decrease sleep latency (the time it takes to fall asleep), but this effect dissipates after a few nights. In addition, waking time during the latter part of the night is increased, and there is a pronounced rebound insomnia that occurs once the ethanol use is discontinued.

Some beneficial uses of ethanol have been identified. For pregnant women, ethanol reduces uterine contractions and is used as an emergency treatment to delay premature delivery. It also is used to treat poisoning from methanol and ethylene glycol. Most of ethanol's therapeutic benefits are derived from applying it to the skin, since it is an excellent skin disinfectant. Ethanol can lessen the severity of dermatitis, reduce sweating, cool the skin during a fever, and, when added to ointments, help other drugs penetrate the skin. These therapeutic uses are for acute problems only. Until recently, it was felt that the chronic drinking of ethanol led only to organ damage. Evidence now suggests that low or moderate intake of ethanol (1–2 drinks per day) can indirectly reduce the risk of a heart attack. However, the doses must be low enough to avoid liver or other organ damage. This beneficial effect is thought to be due to the elevation of high-density lipoprotein cholesterol (HDL-C) in the blood, which, in turn, slows the development of arteriosclerosis and, presumably, a heart attack. This relationship has not been proven but has been culled from the results of several epidemiological studies.

Several mechanisms have been proposed to explain how oral ethanol exerts its effects. Originally, the effects of alcohol were thought to be nonspecific; that is, it was believed that alcohol generally altered the fluidity of cell membranes (particularly neurons). This disturbance alters ion channels in the membrane, resulting in a reduction in the propagation of neuronal transmission. The anesthetic gases share this property with ethanol. Furthermore, it has been shown that the degree of membrane disordering is directly proportional to the drug's lipid solubility. It has also been argued that such membrane effects occur only at very high doses. Scientists now increasingly believe that the effects of alcohol are more specific—that ethanol binds with and alters the function of a group of proteins called ligand-gated ion channels (LGICs). Specifically, ethanol has been found to augment the activity of the neurotransmitter gamma-aminobutyric acid (GABA) by its actions on an LGIC receptor site close to the GABA receptor. The effect of this action is to increase the movement of chloride across biological membranes. Again, this effect would alter the degree to which neuronal transmission is maintained.

Other LGIC neurotransmitter receptors that have been shown to be modulated by ethanol include those that bind glutamate (the NMDA type), glycine, acetylcholine (the nicotinic type), and serotonin (the 5-HT$_3$ type). Interestingly, some of these receptors are triggered by ethanol while others are inhibited by it, suggesting that the influence is likely nonspecific. Other pathways susceptible to ethanol involve the voltage-dependent calcium channels. These pathways play a major role in neurotransmitter release, hormone secretion, and the regulation of gene expression.

PHARMACOKINETICS AND DISTRIBUTION

Ethanol is quickly and rapidly absorbed, with 20 percent absorbed from the stomach and the rest from the first section of the small intestines (called the duodenum). Thus, the onset of action is related in part to how fast it passes through the stomach. Having food in the stomach can slow absorption because the stomach does not empty its contents into the small intestines when it is full. However, drinking on an empty stomach leads to almost instant intoxication because the ethanol not absorbed in the stomach passes directly to the small intestine. Maximal blood levels are achieved about 30–90 minutes after ingestion. As mentioned earlier, ethanol mixes with water quite well, and once

it enters the body it travels to all fluids and tissues, including the placenta in a pregnant woman. After the 20 to 30 minutes required for equilibration, blood alcohol levels are a good estimate of brain alcohol levels. Ethanol freely enters all blood vessels, including those in the small air sacs of the lungs. Once in the lungs, ethanol exchanges freely with the air, making a breath sample a good estimate of the amount of ethanol in the body. A breathalyzer device is often used by police officers to detect the presence of ethanol in an individual.

Between 90 and 98 percent of the ethanol dose is metabolized. The amount of ethanol that can be metabolized per unit of time is roughly proportional to the individual's body weight (and probably the weight of the liver). Adults can metabolize about 120 milligrams per kilogram per hour, which translates to about 30 milliliters (one ounce) of pure ethanol in about three hours. Women generally achieve higher blood alcohol concentrations than men, even after the same unit dose of ethanol per weight, because women have a lower percentage of total body water, and because they may have less activity of alcohol-metabolizing enzymes in the wall of the stomach. The enzymes responsible for ethanol and acetaldehyde metabolism—alcohol dehydrogenase and aldehyde dehydrogenase, respectively—are under genetic control. Genetic differences in the activity of these enzymes account for the fact that different racial groups metabolize ethanol and acetaldehyde at different rates. The best-known example is that certain Asian groups have a less active variant of the aldehyde dehydrogenase enzyme. Thus, when they consume alcohol, they accumulate higher levels of acetaldehyde than other groups, such as Caucasians, which causes a characteristic response called "flushing." This is actually a type of hot flash, with reddening of the face and neck. Some experts believe that the relatively low levels of alcoholism in such Asian groups may be due to this genetically based aversive effect.

TOXIC EFFECTS

Chronic consumption of excessive amounts of ethanol can lead to a number of neurological disorders, including altered brain size, permanent memory loss, sleep disturbances, seizures, and psychoses. Some of these neuropsychiatric syndromes, such as Wernicke's encephalopathy, which causes permanent brain damage, and Korsakoff's psychosis, a neurologic syndrome resulting from this brain damage, can be debilitating. Other, less obvious, problems also occur during chronic ethanol consumption. The chronic drinker usually fails to meet basic nutritional needs and is often deficient in a number of essential vitamins, which can lead to brain and nerve damage. Chronic drinking also causes damage to a number of major organs.

By far, one of the most important causes of death in alcoholics (other than by accidents) is liver damage. The liver is the organ that metabolizes ingested and body toxins, and it is essential for natural detoxification. Alcohol damage to the liver ranges from acute fatty liver to hepatitis, necrosis, and cirrhosis. Single doses of ethanol can deposit droplets of lipids, or fat, in the liver cells (called hepatocytes). With an accumulation of such lipids, the liver's ability to metabolize other body toxins is reduced. A weekend drinking binge can produce measurable increases in liver fat. In fact, liver fats can double after only two days of drinking even when blood ethanol levels range between twenty and eighty milligrams per deciliter (mg/dL), suggesting that one need not be drunk to experience liver damage.

Alcohol-induced hepatitis is an inflammatory condition of the liver. The symptoms are anorexia, fever, and jaundice. The size of the liver increases, and its ability to cleanse the blood of other toxins is reduced. Cirrhosis is the terminal and most dangerous type of liver damage. Cirrhosis occurs after many years of intermittent bouts with hepatitis or other liver damage, resulting in the death of liver cells and the formation of scar tissue in their place. Fibrosis of the blood vessels leading to the liver can result in elevated blood pressure in the veins around the esophagus, which may rupture and cause massive bleeding. Ultimately, the cirrhotic liver fails to function and is a major cause of death among alcoholics. Although only a small percentage of drinkers develop cirrhosis, it appears that a continuous drinking pattern results in greater risk than does intermittent drinking, and an immunological factor may be involved.

The role of poor nutrition in the development of some of these disorders is well recognized but not very well understood. Ethanol provides 7.1 kilocalories of energy per gram. Thus, a pint of whiskey provides around 1,300 kilocalories, a substantial amount of raw energy that is devoid of any essential nutrients. Even when food intake is high, nutritional disturbances can exist, because ethanol can impair the absorption of vitamins B_1, B_{12}, and folic acid. Ethanol-related nutritional problems are also associated with magnesium, zinc, and copper deficiencies. A chronic state of malnutrition can produce symptoms that are indistinguishable from chronic ethanol abuse.

Fetal alcohol syndrome (FAS) was recognized and described in the 1980s. Children of chronic drinkers are born deformed, and the abnormality is characterized by reduced brain function—as evidenced by a low intelligence, smaller than usual brain size, slower than normal growth rates, characteristic facial abnormalities (widely spaced eyes and flattened nasal area), other minor malformations, and developmental and behavioral problems. Fetal malnutrition caused by ethanol-induced damage to the placenta can also occur, and fetal immune function appears to be weakened, resulting in the child's greater susceptibility to infectious disease. Depending on the population studied, the rate of FAS ranges from 1 in 300 to 1 in 2,000 live births; however, the incidence is 1 in 3 infants born to alcoholic mothers. A safe lower limit of ethanol consumption for pregnant women that avoids the risk of having a child with FAS has not been established. The lowest reported level of ethanol that resulted in FAS was about 75 ml (2.5 oz.) per day during pregnancy. Among alcoholic mothers, if drinking during pregnancy is reduced, then the severity of the resulting syndrome is reduced.

TOLERANCE, DEPENDENCE, AND ABUSE

Tolerance, a feature of many different drugs, develops rather quickly to many of ethanol's effects after frequent exposure. When tolerance develops, the dose must be increased to achieve the original effect. Ethanol is subject to two types of tolerance: tissue (or functional) tolerance and metabolic (or dispositional) tolerance. Metabolic tolerance is due to alterations in the body's capacity to metabolize ethanol, which is achieved primarily by a greater activity of enzymes in the liver. Metabolic tolerance only accounts for 30 to 50 percent of the total response to alcohol in experimental conditions. Tissue tolerance, however, decreases the brain's sensitivity to ethanol and may be quite extensive. The development of tolerance can take just a few weeks, or it may take years, depending on the amount and pattern of ethanol intake. As with other central nervous system depressants, when the dose of ethanol is increased to achieve the desired effects (e.g., sleep), the margin of safety actually decreases, as the dose comes closer to producing toxicity and the brain's control of breathing becomes depressed.

Like tolerance, dependence on ethanol can develop after only a few weeks of consistent intake. The degree of dependence can be assessed only by measuring the severity of the withdrawal signs and symptoms observed when ethanol intake is terminated. Victor and Adams (1953) provided perhaps one of the best descriptions of the clinical aspects of ethanol dependence. Patients typically arrive at the hospital with the "shakes," sometimes so severe that they cannot perform simple tasks without assistance. During the next 24 hours, an alcoholic might experience hallucinations, which typically are not too distressing. Convulsions, however, which resemble those in people with epilepsy, may occur in susceptible individuals about a day after the last drink. Convulsions usually occur only in those who have been drinking extremely large amounts of ethanol. If the convulsions are severe and unattended to medically, the individual may die. Many somatic effects, such as nausea, vomiting, diarrhea, fever, and profuse sweating are also part of alcohol withdrawal. Some 60 to 84 hours after the last dose, there may be confusion and disorientation, and more vivid hallucinations may begin to appear. This phase of withdrawal is often called the delirium tremens, or DTs. Before the days of effective treatment, a mortality rate of 5 to 15 percent was common among alcoholics whose withdrawal was severe enough to cause DTs. The presence of other medical problems, which is commonly the case among alcohol-dependent individuals, has been shown to increase the risk of death during delirium tremens.

TREATMENT FOR ALCOHOL DEPENDENCE

The first step in treating alcoholics is to remove the ethanol from the system, a process called detoxification. Since rapid termination of ethanol (or any other central nervous system depressant) can be life threatening, people who have been using high doses should be slowly weaned from the ethanol by taking a less toxic substitute depressant. Ethanol itself cannot be used safely because it is eliminated from the body too rapidly, making it difficult to control the treatment. Although barbiturates were once employed in this capacity, the safer benzodiazepines have become the drugs of choice. Not only do they prevent the development of potentially fatal convulsions, but they reduce anxiety and help promote sleep during the withdrawal phase. New medications are constantly tested for their ability to aid in the treatment of alcohol withdrawal. Once a person has become abstinent, various methods can be used to maintain abstinence and encourage sobriety. Some of these are pharmacologic and others involve social support networks or formal psychological therapies.

One pharmacologic therapy involves making drinking an adverse toxic event for the individual. This is done by giving a drug such as disulfiram (Antabuse) or citrated calcium carbimide, which inhibit the metabolism of acetaldehyde (a toxic by-product of alcohol metabolism). When ethanol is ingested by someone on disulfiram, the acetaldehyde levels rise very high and very quickly. Increased acetaldehyde concentrations result in facial flushing, nausea, and rapid heartbeat; in rare cases, severe reactions have resulted in death due to cardiovascular collapse. Disulfiram has not been successful in maintaining abstinence in all patients, however, and it may be most effective if its daily ingestion is supervised by someone other than the patient (e.g., a spouse).

Another drug, naltrexone (Revia, Vivitrol), an opiate antagonist first introduced for the treatment of opiate dependence, is also used for the treatment of alcohol dependence. Naltrexone has a high affinity for the μ-opiate receptor, part of a reward pathway that has been implicated in the development of alcohol dependence. The exact mechanism by which naltrexone reduces craving for alcohol is not known, but studies suggest that naltrexone blocks natural opiates released by alcohol, making alcohol consumption less rewarding. The precise mechanism of action of another medication used to maintain abstinence, acamprosate (Campral), is not completely understood. The drug is believed to work on the GABA and glutamate systems. Research suggests that chronic alcohol abuse may disturb the balance in the brain between glutamate-mediated excitation and GABA-mediated inhibition, and that acamprosate may help to restore the normal balance.

Many support groups are available to help people remain abstinent. Alcoholics Anonymous (AA) is one of the most widely known and available. The AA program is structured around a self-help philosophy and emphasizes total avoidance of alcohol and any dependence-producing medications. Instead it relies on a "sponsor" system, providing support partners who are personally experienced with alcoholism and alcoholism recovery. A number of other types of psychological and behavioral approaches to treatment are also widely used.

See also **Accidents and Injuries from Alcohol; Alcoholics Anonymous (AA); Alcoholism: Origin of the Term; Blood Alcohol Concentration; Blood Alcohol Concentration, Measures of; Breathalyzer; Complications; Delirium Tremens (DTs); Driving, Alcohol, and Drugs; Driving Under the Influence (DUI); Epidemiology of Alcohol Use Disorders; Fetal Alcohol Syndrome; Gamma-Aminobutyric Acid (GABA); Naltrexone; Social Costs of Alcohol and Drug Abuse; Treatment, Pharmacological Approaches to: Disulfiram; Treatment, Pharmacological Approaches to: Naltrexone; Withdrawal: Alcohol; Withdrawal: Benzodiazepines.**

BIBLIOGRAPHY

Brunton, L. L., Lazo, J., & Parker, K. (Eds.). (2006). *Goodman and Gilman's the pharmacological basis of therapeutics* (11th ed.). New York: McGraw-Hill.

Davies, M. (2003). The role of GABA$_A$ receptors in mediating the effects of alcohol in the central nervous system. *Journal of Psychiatry & Neuroscience, 28*(4), 263–274.

Goldstein, A., Aronow, L., & Kalman, S. M. (1974). *Principles of drug action: The basis of pharmacology* (2nd ed.). New York: Wiley.

Goldstein, D. B. (1983). *Pharmacology of alcohol.* New York: Oxford University Press.

Victor, M., & Adams, R. D. (1953). The effect of alcohol on the nervous system. *Research Publications: Association for Research in Nervous and Mental Disease, 32,* 526–573.

West, L. J. (Ed.). (1984). *Alcoholism and related problems: Issues for the American public.* Englewood Cliffs, NJ: Prentice-Hall.

Winger, G., Woods, J. H., & Hoffman, F. G. (2004). *A handbook on drug and alcohol abuse: The biomedical aspects* (4th ed.). New York: Oxford University Press.

SCOTT E. LUKAS
REVISED BY LEAH R. ZINDEL (2009)

HISTORY OF DRINKING (INTERNATIONAL)

Anthropologists view myth as the belief system of a given people or culture. Regarding the first human consumption of alcohol, they may not be able to know for certain, but they conjecture that it may have occurred when individuals tasted overripe fruit or soured grain. The taste, or the feeling that resulted, or both, may have been pleasant enough to prompt repetition and then experimentation. This experience would have occurred various times and at a number of different places.

Alcohol is significant historically. This simple substance, presumably present since bacteria first consumed some plant cells nearly 1.5 billion years ago, became so deeply embedded in human societies that it affected their religion, economics, politics, and innumerable social and ritual activities. Alcohol played different roles from one culture to the next but even within a given culture over time. This single chemical compound, used (or sometimes emphatically avoided), shaped a diverse array of customs, attitudes, beliefs, values, and effects. A brief review of the history of this relationship illustrates both unity and diversity in the ways people have thought about and treated alcohol. (Special attention is paid in this entry to the United States.)

THE ORIGIN OF ALCOHOL

Ethanol, the form of alcohol used to produce favorable effects, is created naturally in the fermentation of exposed fruits, vegetables, and grains that have become overripe and through the intervention of people who accelerate the process by controlling the conditions of fermentation. Drinks that produce various favorable effects, as well as alcohol-related problems, are labeled *alcoholic*, and labels (like other definitions) are cultural constructs. Wine is thought of as a basic component of meals in much of France and Italy; beer is considered a basic component of meals in Scandinavia and Germany. Additionally, some fruit juices, candies, and desserts may have high levels of alcohol but are not labeled as alcohol. Thus many cultural beliefs people have about alcohol relate more to their social habits and expectations than to the actual pharmacological or biochemical substance and its effect on the human body.

According to the Bible, one of the first tasks Noah performed after the great flood was to plant a vineyard (Genesis 9:21). According to the predynastic Egyptians, the great god Osiris taught people to make beer, a substance that served both religious and nutritional purposes for them. Similarly, early Greeks credited the god Dionysus with bringing them wine, which they drank mainly as a form of worship. In Roman times, the god Bacchus was thought to be both the originator of wine and always present within it. It was a goddess, Mayahuel, with 400 breasts, who supposedly taught the Aztecs how to make *pulque* from the sap of the maguey plant, a mild beer still important in the diet of many Indians in Mexico, where it is often referred to as *the milk of our Mother*. In each of these cultures, alcohol was associated with the supernatural.

PREHISTORY AND ARCHEOLOGY

Archeologists have discovered alcoholic residues in pots dating from 3500 BCE, which proves that wine was made from grapes in Mesopotamia (in the area of modern Iran). This discovery makes alcohol use almost as old as farming, and, in fact, beer and bread were first produced at the same place at about the same time and from the same ingredients. Little is known about the gradual process by which people learned to control fermentation, to blend drinks, or to store and ship them in ways that kept them from souring, but the distribution of local styles of wine vessels serves as a guide to the flow of commerce in antiquity.

Early wines and beers were not similar to modern varieties of these beverages, but historically, the distinction existed between the two: wine is and was generally derived from fruits or berries, whereas beers and ales are and were derived from grain or a grain-based bread. Until as recently as AD 1700, both were often relatively dark, dense with sediments, and extremely uneven in quality. Homemade wines tended to have relatively little in the way of vitamins or minerals but could last a long time if adequately sealed. However, home-brewed beers tended to be highly nutritious but to last only a few days before going sour (i.e., before the fermenting sugars and alcohol were depleted and liquid turned to vinegar).

In Egypt between 2700 and 1200 BCE, beer was an important part of the daily diet, and it was buried in royal tombs and offered to the deities.

Many frescos and carvings in Egyptian tombs depict brewing and drinking; early papyri include commercial accounts of beer, a father's warning to his student son about the danger of drinking too much, praises to the god who brought beer to earth, and other indications of its importance and known effects. In fact, the earliest written code of laws, from Hammurabi's reign in Babylon around 2000 BCE, devoted considerable attention to the production and sale of beer and wine, including regulations about standard measures, consumer protection, and the responsibilities of servers.

During the rise of Ancient Greece and the Roman Empire (roughly 800 BCE–AD 400), grapes were grown to the north and westward in Europe, and wine was important for medicinal and religious purposes, although it was not yet a commonplace item in the diet of poor people. The much-touted sobriety of the Greeks is presumably based on their custom of diluting wine with water and drinking only after meals, in contrast to neighboring populations who often sought drunkenness through beer as a transcendental state of altered consciousness. Certainly heavy drinking was an integral part of Greek religious orgies that, in commemorating their deities, later came to be called *Dionysiac* (or, in the case of the Romans, *Bacchic*). Notably, Alexander the Great, who came from the area of Macedonia, or north of Greece, was reported to have used alcohol to drunkenness.

Romans saw their alcohol use as relative temperance by contrast to the boisterous heavy drinking of their tribal neighbors in all directions, whom they devalued as the bearded ones, *barbarians*, meaning those who were other than Roman. The geographic spread of Latin-based languages and grape cultivation coincided with the spread of the Roman Empire through Europe and the accompanying diffusion of the Mediterranean diet—rich in carbohydrates and low in fats and protein—with wine as the usual beverage. In striking contrast were non-Latin speakers, who were less reliant on bread and pasta and without olive oil; they drank beers and meads, and presumably drunkenness was more common. Plato considered wine an important adjunct to philosophical discussion, and St. Paul is said to have recommended it as an aid to digestion.

The Hebrews established a new pattern around the time of their return from the Babylonian exile and the construction of the Second Temple (c. 500 BCE). Religious practice in family rituals included periodic sacred drinking of wine, accompanied by a pervasive ethic of temperance, a pattern that persisted into modern times and distinguished religious Jews from their gentile neighbors. Early Christians (many of whom had been Jews) praised the healthful and social benefits of wine while condemning drunkenness. Many biblical references to drinking are favorable, and the Gospel report that Jesus chose wine to symbolize his blood was perpetuated in the rite of the Eucharist, a Christian sacrament.

From the Iron Age in France (c. 600 BCE), distinctive drinking vessels found in tombs strongly suggest that political leadership involved redistribution of goods to one's followers, with wine an important symbol of wealth. Archeologists have learned so much about the style and composition of pots made in any given area that they can often trace routes and times of trade, military expansion, or migrations by noting where fragments of drink containers are found. Although less is known about Africa at that time, the assumption is that mild fermented home brews (such as banana beer) were commonplace, as they were in Latin America. In Asia, most is known about China, where as early as 2000 BCE grain-based beer and wine were used in ceremony, offered to the gods, and included in royal burials. Indigenous peoples in most of North America and Oceania, curiously, appear not to have had alcoholic beverages until contact with white Europeans.

Alcohol in classical times served as a disinfectant and was thought to strengthen the blood, stimulate nursing mothers, and relieve various ills. It was also used as an offering to both gods and ancestral spirits. Obviously, alcohol and its consumption had highly positive meanings for early peoples, as they do in modern times for many non-Western societies.

FROM 1000 TO 1500

The Middle Ages was marked by a rapid spread of both Christianity and Islam. Large-scale political and economic integration spread with them to many areas that had previously seen only local warring factions, and sharp social stratification between nobles and commoners was evident at courts and manors, where food and drink became more elaborate. National groups began to appear, with cultural differences (including preferred drinks and ways of drinking), increasingly noted by travelers, of whom there were growing numbers. Excessive drinking by poor people was often criticized but may well have been limited to festive occasions. With population increases, towns and villages proliferated, and taverns became important social centers, often condemned by the wealthy as subverting religion, political stability, and the family. But for many peasants and craftspeople, the household remained the primary economic unit, with home-brewed beer being a major part of the diet.

During this period, the use of *hops* (dried leaves of the hop plant used to give beer its distinctive bitter taste), which enhanced both the flavor and durability of beer, was introduced. In Italy and France, wine became even more popular, both in the diet and in commerce. Distillation had been known to the Arabs since about 800, but among Europeans, a small group of clergy, physicians, and alchemists monopolized that technology until about 1200, producing spirits as beverages for a limited luxury market and for broader use as a medicine. Gradual overpopulation was halted by the Black Death (a pandemic of bubonic plague), and schisms in the Catholic Church resulted in unrest and political struggles later in this period.

Across northern Africa and much of Asia, populations, among whom drinking and drunkenness had been lavishly and poetically praised as valuable ways of altering consciousness, became temperate and sometimes abstinent, in keeping with the tenets of Islam and the teachings of Buddha and of Confucius. China and India both had episodes of prohibition, but neither country was consistently so. Among Hindus, some castes drank liquor as a sacrament, whereas others scorned it, vivid proof that a culture, in the anthropological sense of a set of beliefs and practices that guide group members, can include various behaviors and views.

As the Middle Ages gave way to the Renaissance, both population and economy expanded throughout most of Europe. Because the Arabs (who had ruled from 711 to 1492) had been expelled from Spain and Portugal, they cut off overland trade routes to Asia; European maritime exploration therefore resulted in increasing commerce all around the coasts of Africa. The so-called Age of Exploration led to the startling encounter with high civilizations and other tribal peoples who had long occupied the Americas. Alcoholic beverages appear to have been totally unknown north of Mexico, although a vast variety of beers, chichas, pulques, and other fermented brews were important in Mexico as foods, as offerings to the gods and to ancestral spirits, and as shortcuts to religious ecstasy. Throughout sub-Saharan Africa, home-brewed beers were plentiful, nutritious, and symbolically important, as they came to be described in later years.

During the Middle Ages, drinking was commonplace, little different from eating, and drunkenness appears to have been infrequent, tolerated in association with occasional religious festivals, and of little concern in terms of health or social welfare. Alcoholic beverages were thought to be invigorating to humans, appreciated by spirits, and important to sociability.

FROM 1500 TO 1800

Wealth and extravagance were manifest in the rapidly growing cities of Europe, but so were poverty and misery, as class differences became even more exaggerated. The Protestant Reformation, which set out to separate sacred from secular realms of life, seemed to justify an austere morality that included injunctions against celebratory drunkenness. If the body was the vessel of the spirit, which itself was divine, one should not desecrate it with alcohol. Puritans viewed intoxication as a moral offense, although they drank beer as a regular beverage and appreciated liquor for its supposed warming, social, and curative properties.

Public drinking establishments evolved, sometimes as important town-meeting places and sometimes as the workers' equivalent of social clubs, with better heat and lighting than homes, with news and gossip, games and companionship. Coffee, tea, and chocolate were also introduced to Europe at this time, and each became popular enough to be the focus of specialized shops. But each was also suspect for a time, while physicians debated whether they were dangerous to the health; clergy debated their effects on morality; and political and business leaders feared that retail outlets would become breeding places of crime, labor unrest, and civil disobedience. Brandies (*brantwijns*, liquor distilled from wines to be shipped as concentrates) spread among the aristocracy, and champagne was introduced as a luxury wine, as were various cordials and liqueurs. Brewing and winemaking grew from cottage industries to major commercial ventures, incorporating many technical innovations, quality controls, and other changes.

The gin epidemic in mid-eighteenth-century London is sometimes cited as showing how urban crowding, cheap liquor, severe unemployment, and dismal working conditions combined to produce widespread drinking and dissolution, but the vivid engravings by William Hogarth may exaggerate the problem. At the same time, the artist extolled beer as healthful, soothing, and economically sound. In France, even peasants began to drink wine regularly. In 1760, Catherine the Great set up a state monopoly to profit from Russia's prodigious thirst, and Sweden did similarly soon after.

Throughout the islands of the Pacific, local populations reacted differently to the introduction of alcohol, sometimes embracing it enthusiastically and sometimes rejecting it. Eskimos were generally quick to adopt it, as were Australian Aborigines, to the extent that some interpret their heavy drinking as an attempt to escape the stresses of losing their valued traditional ways of life. Detailed information about the patterns of belief and behavior associated with drinking among the diverse populations of Asia and Africa vividly illustrates that alcohol resulted in many kinds of comportment, depending more on sociocultural expectations than any qualities inherent in the substance.

Throughout Latin America and parts of North America, the Spanish and Portuguese conquistadors found that indigenous peoples already had home brews that were important to them for sacred, medicinal, and dietary purposes. The Aztecs of Mexico derived a significant portion of their nutritional intake from pulque but reserved drunkenness as the prerogative of priests and old men. Cultures throughout the rest of the area similarly used *chicha* (beer made from maize, manioc, or other materials). The Yaqui (in the area of modern Arizona) made a wine from cactus as part of their rain ceremony, and specially prepared chicha was used as a royal gift by the Inca of Peru. Religious and political leaders from the colonial powers were ambivalent about what they perceived as the risks of public drunkenness and the profits to be gained from producing and taxing alcoholic beverages. A series of inconsistent laws and regulations, including sometime prohibition for Indians, were probably short-lived experiments, affected by such factors as local revolts and different opinions among religious orders.

As merchants from various countries competed to gain commercial advantage in trading with the various Native American groups of North America, liquor quickly became an important item. Indeed, the British colonial government recognized the importance of alcohol among American Indians, insuring a steady supply of alcohol when negotiating treaties with the tribes. At the Treaty of Easton, in 1758, alcohol was said to have flowed freely throughout the bargaining process, an effort by colonial negotiators to extract more lands from the Lenape and Shawnee. For many but not all American Indian tribes in the eighteenth and nineteenth centuries, alcohol was a *deadly medicine* introduced by European settlers. As Pequot author William Apess wrote in 1833, "My sufferings were through the white man's measure, for they most certainly brought spirituous liquors first among my people" (Apess, 1992, p. 121).

A common belief is that Native Americans are genetically vulnerable to alcohol, but some tribes (such as Hopi and Zuni) never accepted it, and others drank with moderation. Indeed, a hereditary mechanism responsible for certain tribes' propensity for drink remains elusive. The Seneca in New York State are an interesting case study because they went from having no contact with alcohol through a series of stages, culminating in a religious ban. When brandy first arrived, friends would save it for an unmarried young man, who would drink it ceremoniously to help in his required ritual quest for a vision of the animal that would become his guardian spirit. In later years, drinking became secular; anyone could drink, and boisterous brawling was a frequent outcome. In 1799, when a tribal leader who was already alcoholic had a very different kind of vision, he promptly preached abstention from alcohol, an end to warfare, and devotion to farming, all of which remain important in modern times in the religion that is named after him, Handsome Lake.

Clearly, alcohol plays many roles in the history of any people, and changes in attitudes can be abrupt, illustrating again the importance that social constructions of reality have in relation to alcohol and its uses.

THE NINETEENTH CENTURY

The large-scale commercialization of beer, wine, and distilled liquor spread rapidly in Europe as many businesses and industries became international in scope. Large portions of the European proletariat were no longer tied to the land for subsistence, and new means of transportation facilitated vast migrations. The industrial revolution was not an event but a process, in which, for many people, work became separated from home. The arbitrary pace imposed by wage work contrasted markedly with the seasonal pace of traditional agrarianism.

In Europe, political boundaries were approximately those of the twentieth century; trains and steamships changed the face of trade; and old ideas about social inequality were increasingly challenged. Alcohol lost much of its religious importance as ascetic Protestant groups, and even fervent Catholic priests in Ireland, associated crime, family disruption, unemployment, and a host of other social ills with it, and taxation and other restrictions were broadly imposed. In Russia, the czar ordered prohibition, but only briefly as popular opposition mounted and government revenues plummeted. Those who paid special attention to physical and mental illnesses were quick to link disease with long-term heavy drinking, although liquor remained an important part of medicine for various curative purposes. In Britain, Europe, and Australia a few institutions sprang up late in the nineteenth century to accommodate so-called inebriates, individuals said to suffer from the disease of inebriety. Although there was little consensus about how or why drinking created problems for some people but not for others, heredity, bad company, and iatrogenic (used to describe a symptom of a disease) causes were cited frequently as leading drinkers into dangerous consumption patterns.

THE TWENTIETH CENTURY

While alcohol remained valued and continually used, cultures began to reassess its role as research and experience provided more understanding about its effects. World War I prompted many countries to enact national austerity programs curbing the alteration of foodstuffs into alcoholic beverages. Absinthe was thought to be so harmful to one's health that it was prohibited in several European countries. Sweden experimented with rationing alcohol, and Iceland banned beer, but not wine or liquor. Furthermore, the Russian czar again attempted to impose prohibition. Due to excessive rates of heavy alcohol consumption and the resulting societal ills, such as violence, Scandinavian countries implemented a variety of regulations, including state monopolies, increased taxation, and restrictions on the location and times of sale. After employing various regulations and statues, these countries turned to large-scale social research in order to understand and influence excessive alcohol consumption.

While several Western countries were expanding their spheres of influence in sub-Saharan Africa, they agreed briefly on a multinational treaty that outlawed the sale of alcoholic beverages there, although they did nothing to curtail production of domestic drinks by various tribal populations. A flurry of scientific analyses of indigenous drinks surprised many by demonstrating their significant nutritional value, and more detailed ethnographic studies showed how important they were in terms of ideology, for vows, communicating with supernatural beings, honoring ancestors, and otherwise building social and symbolic credit—among native societies not only in Africa but also in Latin America and Asia. Closer attention to the social dynamics of drinking and other aspects of culture showed that the impact of contact with Western cultures is not always negative and that for many peoples the role of alcohol remained diverse and vital.

The worldwide economic depression of the 1930s slowed the growth of alcohol consumption; however, the economic boom that followed World War II caused a rapid rise in drinking. Subsequently, some observed a new temperance movement emerging, which placed greater emphasis on total avoidance of alcohol. A phenomenon that grew out of Scandinavian social research, this movement used a public health approach to address the societal issues associated with alcohol, employing such tactics as increased taxes, warning labels for all alcoholic beverages sold, and banning or restricting alcohol

advertising. Prevention strategies such as these, which were already employed throughout the United States, grew in popularity throughout Europe and other countries. In addition, the World Health Organization (WHO) of the United Nations called for a 25 percent worldwide reduction of alcohol consumption between 1985 and 2000. Furthermore, the WHO recommended that member countries adopt similar policies. New assumptions about the role of the state in support of public health and social welfare shaped people's expectations about drinking and its outcomes. Mass media and international conglomerates actively engaged in the expansion of markets, especially into developing countries.

GLOBAL CONSUMPTION OF ALCOHOL IN THE EARLY 2000S

The World Health Organization (WHO) estimated that approximately 2 billion people consumed alcohol beverages worldwide (WHO, 2004). However, the consequences associated with alcohol consumption were not equivalent across all nations. For example, drinking was the leading risk factor for disease burden for low-mortality developing countries and is third-largest among developed countries (Rehm & Eschmann, 2002). In comparing the overall alcohol consumption among 189 member states between the years of 1961 and 2001, the WHO documented a general increase in average alcohol consumption from 1961 to 1980 among adults (individuals 15 years of age or older). Afterwards, global alcohol consumption levels decreased slightly and remained stable at approximately 5.1 liters of pure alcohol (including beer, wine, and spirits) per adult capita. Of that total, 1.9 liters was represented by beer consumption, spirits account for 1.7 liters, and wine accounts for 1.3 liters (WHO, 2004).

However, when examining these trends by region, one gets a much clearer representation of global alcohol consumption. Regions included in the WHO analysis are categorized as follows: African region, region of the Americas, South-East Asia region, European region, Eastern Mediterranean region, and Western Pacific region. The population mean of adult per capita alcohol consumption was highest among the European region. Moreover, the European region's average alcohol consumption (approximately 10.5 liters) was four liters greater than the next highest region, the Americas (approximately 6.5 liters). In general, regions with the highest mean alcohol consumption (European, African, and the Americas) were decreasing, while regions with the lowest consumption (Southeast Asian and Western Pacific) were increasing. However, the Eastern Mediterranean region exhibited a consistently low level of alcohol consumption, which was perhaps due to the Muslim influence prevalent among the majority of the countries included in that region (WHO, 2004).

See also **Advertising and the Alcohol Industry; Chocolate; Coffee; Tea.**

BIBLIOGRAPHY

Abel, E. L. (2001). The gin epidemic: Much ado about what? *Alcohol and Alcoholism, 36*(5), 401–405.

Apess, W. (1992). *On our own ground: The complete writings of William Apess, a Pequot.* O'Connell, B. (Ed.). Amherst: University of Massachusetts Press.

Badri, M. B. (1976). *Islam and alcoholism.* Indianapolis, IN: American Trust.

Edenberg, H. J. (2007). The genetics of alcohol metabolism: Role of alcohol dehydrogenase and aldehyde dehydrogenase variants. *Alcohol Research & Health, 30*(1), 5–13.

Garriott, J. C. (2003). Pharmacology and toxicology of ethyl alcohol. In J. C. Garriott (Ed.), *Medical-legal aspects of alcohol* (pp. 23–38). Tuscon, AZ: Lawyers & Judges.

Hattox, R. S. (1985). *Coffee and coffeehouses: The origins of a social beverage in the medieval Near East* (University of Washington Near Eastern Studies 3). Seattle: University of Washington Press.

Horowitz, M., Maddox, A., Bochner, M., Wishart, J., Bratasiuk, R., Collins, P., et al. (1989). Relationships between gastric emptying of solid and caloric liquid meals and alcohol absorption. *American Journal of Physiology: Gastrointestinal and Liver Physiology, 257,* G291–298.

Lieber, C. S. (1997). Gender differences in alcohol metabolism and susceptibility. In R. W. Wilsnack & S. C. Wilsnack (Eds.), *Gender and alcohol* (pp. 77–89). New Brunswick, NJ: Rutgers Center of Alcohol Studies.

McGovern, P. (1996). *The origins and ancient history of wine.* New York: Gordon & Breach.

National Institute on Alcohol Abuse and Alcoholism. (2001). *Cognitive impairment and recovery from alcoholism* (Alcohol Alert, 53). Available from http://www.niaaa.nih.gov/publications/.

National Institute on Alcohol Abuse and Alcoholism. (2004). *Alcohol's damaging effects on the brain* (Alcohol Alert, 63). Available from http://www.niaaa.nih.gov/.

O'Brien, J. M., & Alexander, T. W. (1992). *Alexander the Great: The invisible enemy.* New York: Routledge.

Oscar-Berman, M., Shagrin, B., Evert, D. L., & Epstein, C. (1997). Impairments of brain and behavior: The neurological effects of alcohol. *Alcohol Health & Research World, 21*(1), 65–75.

Partanen, J. (1991). *Sociability and intoxication: Alcohol and drinking in Kenya, Africa, and the modern world.* Helsinki: Finnish Foundation for Alcohol Studies.

Rehm, J., & Eschmann, S. (2002). Global monitoring of average volume of alcohol consumption. *Sozialund Präventivmedizin, 47*(1), 48–58.

Shultz, J., Weiner, H., & Westcott, J. (1980). Retardation of ethanol absorption by food in the stomach. *Journal of Studies on Alcohol, 41,* 861–870.

Vallee, B. L. (1994). Alcohol in human history. In B. Jansson, H. Jornvall, U. Rydberg, & L. Terenius (Eds.), *Toward a molecular basis of alcohol use and abuse* (pp. 1–8). Basel, Switzerland: Birkhauser Verlag.

World Health Organization. (2004). *WHO global status report on alcohol 2004.* Geneva, Switzerland: Author.

DWIGHT B. HEATH
REVISED BY ADAM E. BARRY (2009)
SARAH W. TRACY (2009)

HISTORY OF DRINKING IN THE UNITED STATES

When the *Arbella* departed England for Boston's shores in 1630, its Puritan voyagers had stowed away three times as much beer as water, plus some 10,000 gallons of wine. Colonial Americans regarded alcohol as the *Good Creature of God* and early settlers, like their European and British forbears, drew a strong distinction between drinking and drunkenness, the latter being the work of the devil. Whether rum distilled from West Indian sugar, home-brewed beer, or imported wines, alcohol was a staple of colonial life. America's first rum distillery opened in 1700 in Boston, and other coastal New England cities followed in short order, opening their own distilleries and pushing the alcohol preferences of the colonials away from beer and cider toward spirits.

In what is now the United States, colonial drinking patterns and those of the young republic generally reflected the alcohol habits of the countries from which immigrants had come. Beer was a staple of colonial life and the earliest settlers took to brewing a variety of agricultural products. Connecticut governor John Winthrop, Jr. was said to have brewed a fine beer made from Indian corn, whereas Benjamin Franklin developed a spruce beer. Hard cider was also popular, and colonials began to distill applejack from their cider as well. Rum (distilled from West Indies sugar production) became an important item in international trade, following routes dictated by the economic rules of the British Empire. In the infamous Triangle Trade, captive black Africans were shipped to the West Indies for sale as slaves. Many worked on plantations there, producing not only refined sugar, a sweet and valuable new faddish food, but also molasses, much of which was shipped to New England. Distillers there turned it into rum, which was in turn shipped to West Africa, where it could be traded for more slaves.

Geography also played a role in shaping colonial America's drinking habits. Rum was not easy to transport far inland, so as the settlers pushed further west, grain whiskey became increasingly popular. Farmers in the western settlements produced a surplus of grain, and one bushel of corn could yield 3 gallons of liquor, which not only kept longer than the corn, but also was easier to transport. The arrival of the whiskey-drinking Scotch-Irish on the western frontier pushed rum still further from the alcoholic mainstream. The Scotch-Irish brought their distilling skills with them and improved the quality of American grain whiskey.

The American Revolution (1775/6–1783) interrupted the triangular trade, pushing rum to the periphery, as more North Americans shifted to whiskey. After the war, when the first federal excise tax was imposed (on whiskey) in 1790, to help cut the debt of the new United States, producers' anger about a tax increase was expressed in the Whiskey Rebellion of 1794. To quell the uprising, federal troops (militia) were used for the first time.

Although the first temperance reformers may have been Native Americans seeking to end the damage colonials wrought on their people through alcohol, the American temperance movement is generally said to have begun with Benjamin Rush, a noted physician and signer of the Declaration of Independence. Rush's concerns about the health of the young republic led him to publish *An Inquiry into the Effects of Ardent Spirits upon the Human Body and Mind* in 1784. Fearing that the health of his new nation might be jeopardized by intoxicated voters, Rush could not bear the prospect of drunkards shaping the new republic's destiny. Rush could make a strong case, for elections often featured heavy drinking, and the annual per capita consumption of absolute alcohol figured between 4 and 6 gallons (about twice the rate in 2000). Rush was the first to articulate a disease concept of intemperance; he also distinguished between healthful fermented beverages such as beer and cider, and the more potent and dangerous distilled spirits.

DEVELOPMENTS IN THE NINETEENTH CENTURY

Alcohol flowed freely in a variety of contexts within the United States during the first half of the nineteenth century: Neighbors still drank while helping each other—for example, in barn-raising or reciprocal labor exchange during the harvest. But for the urban masses, leisure and a middle class emerged as new phenomena. Drinking, which was increasingly forbidden in the workplace as dangerous or inefficient, gradually became a recreational activity, often timed to mark the transition between the workday and home life. Within American cities, the saloon, with its whiskey, beer, warm cheap meals, and camaraderie, became an urban fixture—one that social reformers would seize on as the nineteenth century wore on. As markets grew, foods became diverse, so that beers and ciders (usually hard) lost their special value as nourishing and energizing. The rugged individualism of the frontier, touted by presidential candidates such as Andrew Jackson and embodied in the image of the lumberjack, the cowboy, and the miner, seemed to encourage drinking as a sign of virility and patriotism. Per capita alcohol consumption rose precipitously between 1790 and 1830, from an average of 5.8 gallons annually to 7.1 gallons in 1810; this per capita level held relatively steady until the 1830s.

A wave of mounting religious concern that has been called the Second Great Awakening swept over the United States early in the 1800s, however, and by 1850 a dozen states had enacted prohibition. Neo-republicans fearful for the fate of the young nation and Protestant clergy concerned for the moral health of the republic led the campaign. Lyman Beecher, a Yale-educated Calvinist minister and neo-republican, embodied this reform impulse. Beecher led an evangelical life preaching throughout the United States between 1800 and 1850, urging temperance on his congregations as they built what he believed to be a divinely inspired republic where civil and religious liberty held the day. Temperance, however, was not the only reform pressed on the American people during the Second Great Awakening: Peace, abolition, bans on profanity and Sabbath breaking, women's rights, common school education, and humane treatment of the mentally ill were all championed in the era of reform that preceded the Civil War.

Evangelical Protestant clergymen established the American Society for the Promotion of Temperance in 1826. By 1836 this group had changed its name to the American Temperance Society and adopted a platform of total abstinence (rather than the elimination of only distilled beverages). In the early 1840s Americans rallied in the name of temperance, *taking the pledge* for sobriety and lobbying in record numbers to end the licensing of saloons. The Washingtonian Movement, a grassroots total abstinence movement, held parades and public talks, offered new recruits financial help and moral support, and established institutions for inebriates—Washingtonian Homes—that relied on moral suasion to keep their residents on the water wagon. Late antebellum America also witnessed renewed middle-class campaigns for local and state prohibition. The prohibition laws that were enacted, however, were cast aside as the Civil War loomed. In the years leading up to the War Between the States, however, the Good Creature of God became *demon rum.*

In the Reconstruction period, another wave of sentiment against alcohol arose, as large numbers of immigrants (many of them Catholic and hailing from so-called wet cultures) were seen by Protestant Yankees as trouble: competing for jobs, changing the political climate, and challenging old values. Alcohol, drunkenness, and the saloon were linked to poverty, political corruption, prostitution, and workplace inefficiency; in short, degeneration at the societal and individual levels. Frances Willard's Woman's Christian Temperance Union (WCTU) redefined temperance, along with a host of other social purity reforms as a women's issue involving home protection. At the WCTU's prompting, Congress mandated the inclusion of *scientific temperance* education in all high-school physiology textbooks.

At approximately the same time as the WCTU picked up the temperance torch, a group of physicians, clergy, and social reformers established the American Association for the Cure of Inebriates (AACI), to promote a new specialty of medicine that would manage those whose alcohol consumption had run amuck. Members of the AACI established a network of private institutions to treat habitual drunkards, offering restorative medical, moral, and vocational assistance. California, Iowa, Massachusetts, and New York followed suit, establishing state and municipal inebriate asylums. In this age of industrial capitalism, all institutions endeavored to restore the inebriate's breadwinning potential as well as his sobriety. The AACI faded as the drive for national prohibition grew. By 1920 most of the inebriate institutions had closed their doors and chronic drunkenness was again viewed as a primarily moral, political, and legal issue.

Ultimately, the church-based Anti-Saloon League (ASL), founded in 1895 and supported by such industrial magnates as Henry Ford and Pierre du Pont, spearheaded the drive for prohibition. Under Superintendent Wayne Wheeler, the ASL pursued an innovative bipartisan lobbying strategy that secured prohibitory state legislation and, in 1919, ratification of the Eighteenth Amendment, establishing the United States as a dry nation. Anti-German sentiment and a reaction against German American-owned breweries accompanied World War I and assisted in ending the commercial sale of alcohol.

Native American populations, in the meantime, suffered various degrees of displacement, exploitation, and annihilation, sometimes as a result of deliberate national policy and sometimes as a result of local tensions. The stereotype of the drunken Indian became embedded in novels, news accounts, and the public mind, although the image applied to only a small segment of life among several hundred Native populations. Some Native Americans remained abstinent and some returned to abstinence as part of a deliberate espousal of indigenous values—for example, in the Native American Church, using peyote as a sacrament, or in the sun dance or sweat lodge, using asceticism as a combined religious and intellectually cleansing precept.

From Asia, Africa, and Oceania, explorers, traders, missionaries, and others brought back increasingly detailed descriptions of non-Western drinking practices and their outcomes. It is from such ethnographic reports, often sensationalized, that we can guess about the earlier distribution of native drinks and can recognize new alcoholic beverages as major commodities in the commercial exploitation of populations. Although some of the sacramental associations of traditional beverages were transferred to new ones, the increasing separation of brewing from the home, the expansion of a money-based economy, and the apparent prestige value of Western drinks all tended to diminish the significance of home brews. In African mines, Latin American plantations, and even some U.S. factories prior to Prohibition, liquor became an integral part of the wage system, with workers required to accept alcohol in place of some of their cash earnings. In some societies where drinking had been unknown before Western colonization, the rapid spread of alcohol appears to have been an integral part of a complex process that eroded traditional values and authority

LEGACY OF THE TWENTIETH CENTURY

It has been said that the average person's life in 1900 was more like that of ancestors thousands of years earlier than like that of most people today. The assertion certainly applies to the consumption of liquor. Pasteurization, mass production, commercial canning and bottling, and rapid transport all transformed the public's view of beer and wine in the twentieth century. The spread of ideas about individualism and secular humanism loosened the hold of traditional religions on the moral precepts of large segments of the population. New assumptions about the role of the state in support of public health and social welfare color society's expectations of drinking and its outcomes. Mass media and international conglomerates are actively engaged in the expansion of markets, especially into developing countries.

World War I prompted national austerity programs in many countries that curtailed the diversion of foodstuffs to alcoholic beverages but did not quite reach the full prohibition for which the United States became famous. Often called *the noble experiment*, the Eighteenth Amendment to the Constitution was the first amendment to deal with the workday behavior of people who have no important public roles. It forbade commercial transaction of alcohol but said nothing about drinking or possession. Most authorities agree that, during the early years of Prohibition, there was relatively little production of alcoholic beverages and not much smuggling or home production. It was not long, however, before illegal sources sprang up. Moonshiners distilled liquor illegally, and bootleggers smuggled it within the United States or from abroad. Speakeasies sprang up as clandestine bars or cocktail lounges, and a popular counterculture developed in which drinking was even more fashionable than before. Some entrepreneurs became immensely wealthy and brashly confident and seemed beyond the reach of the law, whether because of superior firepower, corruption, or perhaps both.

With Prohibition, the U.S. government had suffered from the loss of excise taxes on alcohol, which accounted for a large part of the annual federal budget. The stock-market crash, massive unemployment, the crisis in agriculture, and worldwide economic depression aggravated an already difficult situation, and civil disturbances spread throughout the country. Some of the same influential people who had pressed strongest for prohibition reversed their stands, and the Twenty-first Amendment, the first and only repeal to affect the U.S. Constitution, did away with the federal prohibition of alcohol in 1933. Although the national government retained close control over manufacturing and distribution to maximize tax collection, specific regulations about retail sales were left up to the states. An odd patchwork of laws emerged, with many states remaining officially dry, others allowing a local option by counties or towns, some imposing a state monopoly, some requiring that drinks be served with food, and others expressly prohibiting it, some insisting that bars be visible from the street, and others demanding the opposite, and so on. The last state to vote itself wet was Mississippi, in 1966, and many communities remain officially dry in the early twenty-first century. The older federal law prohibiting the sale of alcohol to Native Americans was not repealed until

1953, and many Indian reservations and Alaskan Native communities remain dry by local choice.

The experience of failed prohibition in the United States is famous, but a similar combination of problems involving lawlessness, corruption, and related issues led to repeal, after shorter experiments, in Iceland, Finland, India, Russia, and parts of Canada, demonstrating again that such drastic measures seem not to work except where supported by consensus and religious conviction (e.g., as in Saudi Arabia, Iran, and Ethiopia). It is ironic that some Native American reservations with prohibition have more alcohol-related deaths than those without. A more salutary factor is the growth of culturally sensitive programs for prevention and treatment that are being developed, often by the communities themselves, for Native and other minority populations.

In the mid-twentieth century a number of alcoholics formed a mutual-help group, modeled in part on the earlier Washingtonians and taking inspiration from the Oxford Group, whose core principles included absolute honesty, absolute purity, absolute unselfishness, and absolute love: Alcoholics Anonymous (AA). AA has grown to be an international fellowship of individuals whose primary purpose is to keep from drinking. At about the same time, scientists from a range of disciplines started to study various aspects of alcohol and alcoholism, and society's knowledge has grown rapidly in the decades since. Because of the large constituency of recovering alcoholics, the subject has become politically acceptable, and the disease concept has overcome much of the moral stigma that was formerly associated with alcoholism. Establishment of a National Institute on Alcohol Abuse and Alcoholism in 1970 signaled a major government commitment to the field, and its incorporation among the National Institutes of Health in 1992 indicates that concerns about wellness have largely displaced theological preoccupations.

Consumption of all alcoholic beverages increased gradually in the United States from repeal until the early 1980s, with a marked increase following World War II, although it never reached more than one-third of what is estimated for the corresponding period a century earlier. Around 1980 sales of spirits started dropping and have continued to do so. A few years later, wine sales leveled off and gradually declined until the late 1990s, when they began to climb again, perhaps in association with the finding that red wine confers some cardiovascular benefit. Beer sales also appear to have passed their peak; they continue to slowly decline. In 2005 Americans consumed, on average, 2.24 gallons of absolute alcohol per year, representing a slight increase from the previous few years, but significantly less than a decade ago. These overall reductions occurred despite increased advertising. They took place along with the return of a new clean living movement that emphasizes physical exercise, the consumption of less-processed foods, and concern for health, especially the prevention of chronic diseases of middle age: obesity, diabetes, cardiovascular disease, and cancer. America's baby boomer generation has also hit midlife, and it seems that this large demographic segment is shaping the nation's drinking habits.

Linked with the reduction in drinking, what some observers call a new temperance movement has emerged, in which individuals not only drink less but also call for others to do the same. The decline would be enforced by laws and regulations that increase taxes, index liquor prices to inflation, diminish numbers and hours of sales outlets, require warning labels, ban or restrict advertising, and otherwise reduce the availability of alcohol. Mothers Against Drunk Driving (MADD), founded in 1980; Students Against Driving Drunk (SADD), established in 1981; and campaigns against fetal alcohol syndrome (FAS), fetal alcohol effect (FAE), and domestic violence associated with alcohol consumption have all increased public awareness of the social destruction drinking may cause apart from the harms that can occur to the drinker. Such a harm reduction approach is by no means limited to the United States. Its popularity is growing throughout Europe and among groups elsewhere, even as alcohol consumption continues to rise in Asia and many developing countries.

See also **Prohibition of Alcohol; Temperance Movement; Woman's Christian Temperance Union.**

BIBLIOGRAPHY

Austin, G. A. (1985). *Alcohol in Western society from antiquity to 1800: A chronological history.* Santa Barbara, CA: ABC-Clio Information Services.

Barrows, S., & Room, R. (Eds.). (1987). *The social history of alcohol: drinking and culture in modern society.* Berkeley, CA: Alcohol Research Group, Medical Research Institute of San Francisco.

Barrows, S., & Room, R. (Eds.). (1991). *Drinking: Behavior and belief in modern history.* Berkeley: University of California Press.

Blocker, J. S. (1980). *American temperance movements: Cycles of reform* (2nd ed.). Boston: Twayne.

Blum, R. H. (1974). *Society and drugs I. Social and cultural observations.* San Francisco: Jossey-Bass.

Chang, K. C. (Ed.). (1977). *Food in Chinese cultures: Anthropological and historical perspectives.* New Haven, CT: Yale University Press.

Courtwright, D. T. (2001). *Forces of habit: Drugs and the making of the modern world.* Cambridge, MA: Harvard University Press.

Eames, A. (1993). *Blood, sweat, and beer.* Berkeley, CA: Milk and Honey Press.

Edwards, G. (2003). *Alcohol: The world's favorite drug.* New York: St. Martin's Griffin.

Gomberg, E. L., White, H. R., & Carpenter, J. A. (Eds.). (1982). *Alcohol, science, and society revisited.* Ann Arbor: University of Michigan Press.

Goodman, J., Lovejoy, P. E., & Sheratt, A. (Eds.). (1995). *Consuming habits: Drugs in history and anthropology.* London: Routledge.

Gusfield, J. (1986). *Symbolic crusade: Status politics and the American temperance movement* (2nd ed.). Urbana: University of Illinois Press.

Hamer, J., & Steinbring, J. (Eds.). (1980). *Alcohol and native peoples of the North.* Lanham, MD: University Press of America.

Heath, D. B. (1994). *International handbook on alcohol and culture.* Westport, CT: Greenwood.

Heath, D. B., & Cooper, A. M. (1981). *Alcohol use in world cultures: A comprehensive bibliography of anthropological sources.* Toronto: Addiction Research Foundation.

Lender, M., & Martin, J. (1987). *Drinking in America: A social-historical explanation* (Rev. ed.). New York: Free Press.

MacAndrew, C., & Edgerton, R. B. (1969). *Drunken comportment: A social explanation.* Chicago: Aldine.

Mail, P. D., & McDonald, D. R. (1980). *Tulapai to Tokay: A bibliography of alcohol use and abuse among Native Americans of North America.* New Haven, CT: Human Relations Area Files Press.

Marshall, M. (1979). *Beliefs, behaviors, and alcoholic beverages: A cross-cultural survey.* Ann Arbor: University of Michigan Press.

Murdoch, C. G. (1998). *Domesticating drink: Women, men, and alcohol in America, 1870–1940.* Baltimore: Johns Hopkins University Press.

Musto, D. (1989). *The American disease: Origins of narcotic control* (Rev. ed.). New York: Oxford University Press.

Pan, L. (1975). *Alcohol in colonial Africa.* Helsinki: Finnish Foundation for Alcohol Studies.

Parsons, E. F. (2003). *Manhood lost: Fallen drunkards and redeeming women in the nineteenth-century United States.* Baltimore: Johns Hopkins University Press.

Pinney, T. (2005). *A history of wine in America: From Prohibition to the present.* Berkeley: University of California Press.

Rorabaugh, W. (1987). *The alcoholic republic: An American tradition.* New York: Oxford University Press.

Rotskoff, L. (2001). *Love on the rocks: Men, women, and alcohol in post-World War II America.* Chapel Hill: University of North Carolina Press.

Rouché, B. (1960). *Alcohol: The neutral spirit.* Boston: Little, Brown.

Royce, J. E. (1989). *Alcohol problems and alcoholism: A comprehensive survey* (2nd ed.). New York: Free Press.

Segal, B. M. (1987). *Russian drinking: Use and abuse of alcohol in pre-revolutionary Russia.* New Brunswick, NJ: Rutgers Center of Alcohol Studies.

Segal, B. M. (1990). *The drunken society: Alcohol abuse and alcoholism in the Soviet Union.* New York: Hippocrene.

Siegel, R. K. (1989). *Intoxication: Life in pursuit of artificial paradise.* New York: Dutton.

Snyder, C. R. (1958). *Alcohol and the Jews: A cultural study of drinking and sobriety.* Glencoe, IL: Free Press.

Tracy, S. W. (2005). *Alcoholism in America from Reconstruction to Prohibition.* Baltimore: Johns Hopkins University Press.

Tracy, S. W., & Acker, C. J. (2004). *Altering American consciousness: The history of alcohol and drugs in the United States, 1800–2000.* Amherst: University of Massachusetts Press.

Waddell, J. O., & Everett, M. W. (Eds.). (1980). *Drinking behavior among southwestern Indians: An anthropological perspective.* Tucson: University of Arizona Press.

Wallace, F. C. (1970). *The death and rebirth of the Seneca.* New York: Knopf.

Weil, A. (1986). *The natural mind: A new way of looking at drugs and the higher consciousness* (Rev. ed.). Boston: Houghton Mifflin.

White, W. L. (1998). *Slaying the dragon: The history of addiction treatment and recovery in America.* Bloomington, IL: Lighthouse Press.

DWIGHT B. HEATH
REVISED BY SARAH W. TRACY (2009)

PSYCHOLOGICAL CONSEQUENCES OF CHRONIC ABUSE

Chronic alcohol abuse (heavy drinking over a long period) can lead to numerous adverse effects—to direct effects such as impaired attention, increased anxiety, depression, and increased risk-taking behaviors—and to indirect effects such as impaired cognitive abilities, which may be linked to nutritional deficiencies from long-term heavy drinking.

A major difficulty in describing the effects of chronic alcohol abuse is that many factors interact with such consumption, resulting in marked individual variability in the psychological consequences. In addition, defining what constitutes chronic and abusive drinking in relation to resulting behavioral problems is not simply a function of frequency and quantity of alcohol consumption. For some individuals, drinking three to four drinks per day for a few months can result in severe consequences, whereas for others, six drinks per day for years may not have any observable effects. One reason for this variability is related to genetic differences in the effects of alcohol upon individuals. Though not all of the variability can be linked to genetic predispositions, it has been demonstrated that the interactions between individual genetic characteristics and environmental factors are important in determining the effects of chronic alcohol consumption.

Other factors to consider when assessing the effects of chronic drinking are connected to the age and sex of the drinker. In the United States, heavy chronic drinking occurs with the greatest frequency in white men, ages nineteen to twenty-five. For the majority of individuals in this group, heavy drinking declines after age twenty-five to more moderate levels and then decreases to even lower levels after age fifty. As might be expected, the type and extent of psychological consequences depend on the age of the chronic drinker. Research has indicated that younger problem drinkers are more likely to perform poorly in school, have more arrests, and be more emotionally disturbed than older alcoholics. Also, younger drinkers have more traffic accidents, which may result from a combination of their heavy drinking and increased risk-taking behavior. Many of the more serious consequences of chronic alcohol use occur more frequently in older drinkers—individuals in their thirties and forties; these include increased cognitive and mental impairments, divorce,

absenteeism from work, and suicide. Chronic drinking in women tends to occur more frequently during the late twenties and continues into the forties, but the onset of alcohol-related problems appears to develop more rapidly in women than in men. In a study of Alcoholics Anonymous members, women experienced serious problems only seven years after beginning heavy drinking, as compared to an average of more than eleven years for men, a phenomenon that has been called *telescoping* of the adverse effects in women.

Black and Hispanic men in the United States tend to show prolonged chronic drinking beyond the white male's reduction period during his late twenties. Thus, for many of the effects of chronic drinking discussed below, age, sex, and duration of drinking are important factors that mediate psychological consequences.

NEGATIVE CONSEQUENCES

In the early 1990s, it was estimated that between 7 and 10 percent of all individuals drinking alcoholic beverages experience some degree of negative consequences as a result of their drinking pattern. Most people believe that chronic excessive drinking results in a variety of behavioral consequences, including poor work/school performance and inappropriate social behavior. These two behavioral criteria are used in most diagnostic protocols aimed at determining if a drinking problem exists. Several surveys have found that heavy chronic drinking does produce a variety of school- and job-related problems. A survey of personnel in the U.S. armed services found that for individuals considered heavy drinkers, 22 percent showed job-performance problems. Health professionals may also show high rates of alcohol problems, with a late 1980s British survey indicating that physicians experience such problems at a rate of 3.8 times that of the general population. A variety of surveys have consistently shown that chronic excessive drinking leads to loss of support by moderate-drinking family and friends.

Among couples in which only one member drinks, the incidence of divorce is estimated to be over 50 percent. Often the interpersonal problems that surround a problem drinker can lead to family violence; a study published in 2001 found that 30 to 40 percent of men and 27 to 34 percent of women who commit domestic violence were inebriated at the time of the crime. Other survey data indicate that people who drink alcohol frequently are more likely to become involved with others who share their drinking patterns—particularly those who do not express concern about the individual's excessive and altered behavior that results from drinking. The increased association with fellow heavy drinkers as one's main social-support network can itself result in increased alcohol use.

The interaction between the social setting and the individual, the current level of alcohol intoxication, and past drinking history all play a role in the psychological consequences of chronic heavy drinking. It is impossible to determine which changes in behavior result only from the use of alcohol.

Depression. One major psychological consequence resulting from chronic heavy drinking for a subpopulation of alcohol abusers (predominantly women) is the feeling of loss of control over one's life, commonly manifested as depression. (While not conclusive, some studies suggest that the menstrual cycle may be an additional factor for this population.) In many cases, increased drinking occurs as the depression becomes more intense. It has been postulated that increased drinking is an attempt to alleviate depression.

Unfortunately, since this so-called cure usually has little success, a vicious drinking cycle ensues. While no specific causality can be assumed, research on suicide has indicated that chronic alcohol abuse is involved in 20 to 36 percent of reported cases. The level of suicide in depressed individuals with no alcohol abuse is substantially lower—about 10 percent. It is not clear if the chronic drinking results in depression or if the depression is a preexisting psychopathology, which is exacerbated by the drinking behavior. The rapid improvement of depressive symptoms seen in the majority of alcoholics within a few weeks of detoxification (withdrawal) suggests that, for many, depressive symptoms are reflective of toxic effects of alcohol. In one study, for example, 67 percent of patients acutely hospitalized for alcohol dependence were found to have high levels of depressive symptoms. Following detoxification from alcohol, only 13 percent continued to be depressed. Regardless of the cause, it appears that the combination of depression and drinking can be a potent determinant for increasing the potential to commit suicide.

Aggression. For one subpopulation of chronic alcohol abusers (mainly young men), an increase in overall aggressive behaviors has been reported. A number of studies indicate that many of these individuals have an underlying antisocial personality disorder or an aggressive predisposition, which is exacerbated by chronic alcoholic drinking. In a study of men and women between the ages of twenty-one and thirty-five, subjects were randomly assigned to drink either an alcoholic or nonalcoholic beverage. The subjects were then engaged in a competitive task in which they could respond in an aggressive manner. The researchers found that among these individuals—both male and female—those with an aggressive predisposition were more likely to be aggressive in this competitive situation. For male subjects, however, the single greatest predictor of aggressive behavior was elevated blood alcohol concentration in conjunction with an aggressive predisposition.

Sex Drive. Although it is often assumed that alcohol increases sexual behavior, chronic excessive use has been found to decrease the level of sexual motivation in men. In some gay male populations, in which high alcohol consumption is also associated with increased high-risk sexual activity, this decrease in sex drive does not appear to result; however, for many chronic male drinkers, a long-term consequence of heavy drinking is reduced sexual arousal and drive. This may be the combined result of the decreased hormone levels produced by the heavy drinking and the decline of social situations in which sexual opportunities exist.

Cognitive Changes. Perhaps the best-documented changes in psychological function resulting from chronic excessive alcohol use are impaired cognitive functioning. While no evidence exists for any overall change in basic intelligence, specific cognitive abilities become impaired by chronic alcohol consumption. These most often include visuo-spatial deficits, language (verbal) impairments, and in more severe cases, memory impairments (alcoholic amnestic syndrome). A specific form of dementia, alcoholic dementia, has been described as occurring in a small fraction of chronic alcohol abusers. The pattern and nature of the cognitive effects, as measured on neuropsychological assessment batteries in chronic alcohol abusers, exhibit a wide variety of individual patterns. Also, up to 25 percent of chronic alcoholics tested show no detectable cognitive deficits. Although excessive alcohol use has been clearly implicated in such deficits, a variety of co-existing lifestyle behaviors might be responsible for the cognitive impairments observed. For example, poor eating habits leading to vitamin deficiencies result in cognitive deficits similar to those observed in some alcohol abusers. Head trauma from accidents, falls, and fights (frequent experiences for heavy drinkers) may also produce similar cognitive deficits.

Therefore, it is extremely difficult to determine the extent to which the direct toxic effects of heavy drinking are responsible for the impairments—or if they are a result of the many alterations in behaviors that become part of the heavy-drinker lifestyle.

The specific psychological consequences of chronic drinking are complex and variable, but there is clear evidence that chronic abuse of alcohol results in frequent and often disastrous psychological and behavioral problems for drinkers and for those close to them.

See also **Aggression and Drugs: Research Issues.**

BIBLIOGRAPHY

Akers, R. (1985). *Deviant behavior: A social learning approach*. Belmont, CA: Wadsworth.

Caetano, R., Schafer, J., & Cunradi, C. B. (2001). Alcohol-related intimate partner violence among white, black and Hispanic couples in the United States. *Alcohol Research & Health, 25*, 58–65.

Cahalan, D. (1970). *Problem drinkers: A national survey*. San Francisco: Jossey-Bass.

Davidson, K. M. (1995). Diagnosis of depression in alcohol dependence: Changes in prevalence with drinking status. *British Journal of Psychiatry, 166*, 199–204.

Fishburne, P., Abelson, H. I., & Cisin, I. (1980). *National survey on drug abuse: Main findings*. Washington, DC: U.S. Government Printing Office.

Giancola P. R. (2006). Influence of subjective intoxication, breath alcohol concentration, and expectancies on the alcohol-aggression relation. *Alcoholism: Clinical and Experimental Research, 30*, 844–850.

Royce, J. E. (1989). *Alcohol problems and alcoholism* (rev. ed.). New York: Free Press.

Vaillant, G. (1983). *The natural history of alcoholism*. Cambridge, MA: Harvard University Press.

HERMAN H. SAMPSON
NANCY L. SUTHERLAND
REVISED BY ANDREW J. HOMBURG (2001)
LEAH R. ZINDEL (2009)

ALCOHOL AND AIDS.

Alcohol plays a role in virtually every aspect of HIV. Its use is connected with behaviors that lead to infection, makes infection more likely biologically, hastens disease progression, and interferes with adherence to treatment regimens and access to health care. Damage to the liver is often aggravated by infection with hepatitis B or C as well as effects of antiretroviral medication. The importance of these relationships led to the establishment of an AIDS research program at the National Institute on Alcohol Abuse and Alcoholism (NIAAA) in 1987 (Auerbach et al., 1994). This entry presents evidence for the role of alcohol in each of these domains.

SEXUAL RISK BEHAVIOR

An ongoing debate regarding the relationship between alcohol use and sexual risk behavior is the difficulty—impossibility, even—of establishing a causal connection. Numerous studies have documented correlations between alcohol use in connection with sex and riskier sexual behavior. In one approach, overall drinking patterns are correlated with risky sex; information on typically significant relationships is obtained (reviewed in Cooper, 1992; Halpern-Felsher et al., 1996). Another commonly used strategy is to assess whether alcohol has been used in connection with sex and to correlate this with sexual risk. Again, information on significant relationships is generally obtained. Such correlations fail to establish causality; more convincing would be evidence that risky sex takes place only when alcohol is consumed, and not when it is not (see Leigh & Stall, 1993). In fact, even were these results to be obtained it would be impossible to rule out the explanation that people drink in order to feel relaxed enough to approach another person for sex.

Event-level studies take the approach of eliciting qualitative narratives regarding recent episodes of sex—usually both safe and risky—and analyzing the narrative for elements reflecting causal relationships (reviewed in Leigh, 2002; Weinhardt & Carey, 2000). Findings from these studies generally show that individuals who are safe when they are sober are also safe when they are intoxicated, with the exception that drinking at first intercourse was associated with decreased condom use.

More convincing regarding causality are experiments in which exposure to alcohol is systematically manipulated. Some investigators have sought to determine whether alcohol itself, or people's expectations of alcohol's effects, is responsible for risky behavior. These studies initially used a *balanced placebo* factorial design that enables separation of the effects of alcohol itself from expectancies regarding alcohol (reviewed in Hull & Bond, 1986; Leigh, 1989). Thus, if individuals have the expectation that alcohol will increase their sex drive or make them more socially relaxed, then they are likely to feel these effects. The literature relating alcohol expectancies to sex-related factors is limited. However, one interesting study randomly assigned 60 men to one of three arms: alcohol, placebo (belief that alcohol had been consumed), or sober (Gordon, Carey, & Carey, 1997). While alcohol itself impaired the men's ability to negotiate condom use during role plays relative to sober men, men in the placebo condition who had strong sex-related alcohol expectancies voiced more negative attitudes toward condoms.

Some experimental laboratory-based studies have compared the *disinhibition theory* of alcohol's effects with the *alcohol-induced myopia theory* (introduced by Steele & Josephs, 1990). Disinhibition theory asserts that alcohol releases one's more primal instincts that otherwise would be held in check by social propriety. Alcohol myopia theory predicts that because alcohol restricts the cognitive range of an individual, that person is likely to focus on salient elements in the environment, irrespective of their effects on socialized behavior; in this case, on whether they promote safe or unsafe behavior. In one article (MacDonald et al., 2000), four ingenious experiments were reported that were designed to pit these theories against each other. Results supported the alcohol myopia theory:

Intoxicated participants in the impelling cue condition (toward risky sex) expressed significantly stronger intentions to have sex than those in the inhibiting condition, while no difference based on cue condition was observed for sober or (also sober) placebo participants.

In summary, evidence that alcohol is causally related to sexual behavior is strongest in the experimental studies. The last experiment described suggests, however, that, depending on which cues are most salient, alcohol use can lead either to risky or safe behavior, although the salient items in most sexual situations are likely to be more impelling than inhibitory. Among HIV-infected individuals, preventing risk behavior that may transmit the virus to others is made challenging by excessive use of alcohol (e.g., Purcell et al., 2005). This situation represents a significant public health problem.

IMMUNE FUNCTION

The deleterious effects of heavy and chronic use of alcohol on immune function in healthy individuals are well documented (reviewed in Cook, 1998; Isaki & Kresina, 2000). In HIV disease, heavy chronic use of alcohol is associated with a variety of immune deficits. Studies using animal models of HIV infection and human studies can be reviewed regarding this association.

Animal Studies. Much of the work on chronic alcohol abuse and rate of progression of HIV disease has been conducted in murine (mouse) or simian (higher primate) models. In these studies, animals are typically infected with an HIV-like retrovirus, given alcohol, and then challenged by exposure to another pathogen (infectious agent), often with assessment of immune indices. Such studies in murine models have demonstrated effects of acute alcohol consumption to reduce the synthesis and release of tumor cell necrosis factor (Nelson et al., 1990) and concomitant increased proliferation (rapid growth in number) of pneumonia-causing bacteria in the lungs (Nelson et al., 1990; Shahbazian et al., 1992).

Chronic alcohol consumption has also been shown to decrease host resistance to secondary infection and to impair immune function in a variety of ways in mice (reviewed in Dingle and Oei, 1997). Chronic alcohol administration resulted in decreased CD8+/interferon-gamma+T lymphocytes, a fivefold increase in viremia (viral levels in the blood), and double the number of monocyte/macrophages in the brain (Potula et al., 2007). This cell type is the primary route of entry for HIV into the nervous system. Greater inflammation was observed in the brains of the alcohol-fed mice. In rhesus macaques infected with simian immunodeficiency virus (SIV), chronic alcohol consumption increased rates of viral replication (Poonia et al., 2006). These investigators obtained evidence that this effect may have been partially mediated by differential distributions of lymphocyte subsets in the intestine (Poonia et al., 2006). Monkeys chronically fed alcohol also exhibited more rapid disease progression (Bagby et al., 2006). In another SIV study, decreased caloric intake and metabolic dysregulation were observed along with depressed immune function (Molina et al., 2006).

Human Studies. Human studies are more difficult to conduct because many confounding factors can influence results, which may explain the much-greater number of animal studies. However, some approaches have been used to study effects of alcohol, both in vitro (in the test tube) and in vivo (in the live individual), on immune function among HIV-infected humans. Alcohol increases vulnerability to HIV infection in vitro. Lymphocyte proliferation following exposure to HIV peptides is reduced in the presence of alcohol (Nair et al., 1990), as is natural killer cell activity (Nair et al., 1994). A similar study, but in which blood was drawn prior to and following heavy drinking of participants, was reported by Bagasra and colleagues (1990). In another study using this model, HIV viral replication was enhanced in the presence of alcohol (Basgara et al., 1996). Interestingly, some of the immunologic effects of alcohol can be inhibited by administration of naltrexone, an opioid receptor antagonist frequently used in the treatment of alcoholism (Wang et al., 2006), suggesting its potential use as an adjunctive therapy for HIV-infected alcoholics.

In vivo, heavy substance use has been shown to be associated with increased viral load and lower CD4 counts (Lucas et al., 2002). While a strength of this study is that medication adherence was adjusted in the model (see following section on alcohol's effects on adherence), effects of alcohol use were not distinguished from those of other substances of abuse. A null effect of heavy drinking on cytokine (signaling proteins that are released by immune cells and that serve to communicate among cells) production was reported for patients co-infected with HIV and hepatitis C virus (HCV) (Graham et al., 2007). A study of HIV-infected patients initiating antiretroviral therapy found an inferior virologic response to treatment among those with a mood, anxiety, or substance use disorder; results for alcohol abuse or dependence (as indicated by *DSM-IV* criteria) were significant both for virologic rebound and virologic failure (Pence et al., 2007). Alcohol's effects on immune function in HIV disease may also increase the biological likelihood of transmission. A study of women showed that recent moderate-to-high levels of alcohol consumption (2 or more drinks the day before study participation) were associated with increased vaginal shedding of HIV-1 (Theall et al., 2008).

Researchers have wondered if the alterations in immunity caused by alcohol translate into more rapid disease progression. One study, taking into account alcohol's effects on adherence (see below) as well as immune function, modeled a simulation of HIV disease and estimated that hazardous drinkers (those who consumed five or more drinks at a sitting) lost three years of survival if they drank once per week, and 6.4 years if consumption was daily (Braithewaite et al., 2007). Another study followed 595 HIV-infected persons with alcohol problems (as specified by NIAAA; greater than 14 drinks per week or 5 or more drinks on a single occasion for men under 66 years; more than 7 drinks per week or four or more drinks on a single occasion for older men and all women) prospectively for seven years, assessing CD4 counts and viral load levels, controlling for confounders such as depression and medication adherence (Samet et al., 2007). They found that among patients not receiving antiretroviral therapy, heavy alcohol consumption was associated with a lower CD4 count but not higher viral load compared with abstinent subjects. For patients on antiretroviral therapy, heavy alcohol consumption was not associated with different levels of either marker.

Thus, results using animal models show consistently that alcohol consumption is associated with depressed immunity. The results for humans are less consistent, and more research, particularly research to identify mechanisms for effects, will be helpful.

Adherence to Treatment. In the mid-1990s, highly active antiretroviral treatment (HAART) became available and changed the lives of many people with HIV from living with a death sentence to living with a manageable chronic disease. Adherence to these treatments is vital both to prolong patients' lives and to prevent mutation of the virus to become resistant to the drugs. As treatment regimens have gotten simpler—HAART medications can be taken as a single pill as of 2008—adherence has become easier, but non-adherence is still common. Alcohol use and abuse have proven to be a barrier to medication adherence across a variety of studies. Non-adherent (operationalized as less than perfectly adherent) men and women in one study were distinguished only by alcohol-related factors such as greater number of drinks (Parsons et al., 2007). One longitudinal study that followed 3,761 men and women for five years found hazardous alcohol use (defined by NIAAA as in the study above) to be independently (of many sociodemographic factors) associated with decreased ART utilization, 2-week adherence, and viral suppression (Chander et al., 2006). Another large longitudinal study followed cohorts of men and women receiving treatment (Lazo et al., 2007). Participants were followed for five years and underwent assessment of psychosocial factors, including drinking, and adherence every six months. Adherence was predicted by the presence of depression in men, and the occurrence of binge drinking in women. This study is unique in that it identified some sex-specific barriers to adherence. Another multi-faceted study used backward regression analysis to identify a parsimonious model of adherence (Holstad et al., 2006). The final model included abstinence from alcohol.

Physical and psychological trauma and alcohol abuse proved to be a barrier to adherence in another study (Mugavero et al., 2006). Correlates of non-adherence, defined as having missed any doses over the prior seven days, was predicted by the number of categories of lifetime traumatic events, the Addiction Severity Index alcohol score, and being uninsured. While psychological depression was not assessed in this study, the results point to the *nexus*

of risk (O'Leary, 2001) that characterizes the lives of many people who become infected with HIV. Indeed, depressive symptoms and major depressive disorder were extremely prevalent in a study of HIV patients with substance use disorders (Berger-Greenstein et al., 2007). Depression and alcohol use are well known to be linked (Dorus et al., 1987), and depression predicts relapse after drinking cessation (Kodl et al., 2008). Trauma, mental health problems, addiction, and sexual risk are so often intertwined in these individuals' lives that it is difficult to establish a single factor as causative of infection or failure of adherence.

An intervention study was designed to improve adherence and reduce drinking among 143 hazardous drinkers in New York (Parsons et al., 2007). At a three-month follow-up, adherence was significantly higher, and viral load and CD4 count had improved. However, no significant effects on drinking were observed, and at a six-month follow-up none of the outcomes was statistically significant.

Misuse of alcohol has a substantial impact on HIV-infected patients' ability to adhere to their medical regimens. One intervention study showed somewhat promising effects; more work to reduce or eliminate alcohol use among HIV patients is needed.

ORGAN DAMAGE

The organs most vulnerable to alcohol-induced damage, the liver and the brain, are also challenged by HIV disease and treatment. Further, many individuals with HIV are co-infected with hepatitis C or B (HCV; HBV) due to previous needle-sharing or sexual behavior. Among HIV-infected persons, HCV is considerably more common than HBV. Both of these viral infections often lead to fibrosis, cirrhosis, and death. HIV itself hastens progression to end-stage liver disease among HCV-infected patients (Graham et al., 2001). In patients co-infected with HIV and HCV, heavy alcohol use is associated with more rapid progression of liver disease (Benhamou et al., 2001; Castellares et al., 2008; Cooper & Cameron, 2005; Pol et al., 1998) and mortality related to liver disease (Salmon-Ceron et al., 2005). However, many studies designed to identify predictors of liver disease in co-infected patients have not assessed alcohol use, and it is unknown as of 2008 how frequently their healthcare providers assess and/or intervene to reduce their drinking. It is interesting to note that HIV-positive individuals who learn that they are co-infected with hepatitis reduce their drinking, possibly because their providers have counseled them to do so (Tsui et al., 2007). It has been recommended that co-infected patients abstain from alcohol altogether (Conigliaro et al., 2006).

Alcohol affects the nervous system in healthy individuals, particularly in the context of chronic alcoholism. The most commonly observed deficits are in abstract thinking ability, complex perceptual-motor skills, and learning and recall (for a review, see Grant, 1987). HIV crosses the blood-brain barrier (Nottet et al., 1996), and since most therapies do not, viral replication takes place there relatively unchecked (Ellis et al., 2007). Prior to the advent of HAART, about 30 percent of AIDS patients developed AIDS dementia complex, accompanied by the loss of up to 40 percent of neurons (Dickson, 1986; for recent reviews see Anthony & Bell, 2008; Hult et al., 2008). In HIV-infected patients, alcoholism is associated with altered brain morphology (Pfefferbaum et al., 2006) and works synergistically (having a multiplying effect) with HIV infection to damage white matter in the brain (Pfefferbaum et al., 2007). Alcohol and an envelope protein of HIV (gp120) act in concert to increase the permeability of the blood-brain barrier, induce stress fiber formation, and inhibit the formation of reactive oxygen species (ROS) (Shiu et al., 2007). ROS prevents oxidative damage that can lead to cognitive dysfunction. Alcoholism and HIV infection can produce neurocognitive deficits that neither does alone (Sassoon et al., 2007).

Chronic abuse of alcohol is damaging to the liver and the central nervous system. In some cases, alcohol potentiates (causes a multiplying effect on) the negative effects of HIV infection in both organs.

SUMMARY

This review has provided evidence that alcohol negatively influences many aspects of HIV. It is associated with elevated sexual risk behavior, which may lead to infection or transmission. It produces negative effects on immune function and disease

course. It is associated with reduced adherence to medical regimens, giving rise to elevated viral loads and the potential for the virus to develop resistance to medications. Finally, it shortens the time to liver damage and mortality among patients co-infected with hepatitis. It also worsens neurocognitive dysfunction. Given all of these negative consequences, and recommendations that drinking be reduced or eliminated for HIV-positive persons, the paucity of interventions designed as of 2008 to reduce alcohol use in this population is surprising. Care providers should be encouraged to assess alcohol problems, which can be done easily with the approach described in the online NIAAA Clinician's Guide, and to intervene in the step-by-step manner presented in the Clinician's Guide four-item CAGE (Samet et al., 2004). Providers should be encouraged to identify and intervene with alcohol problems in their patients, and educated on how to do so. More attention to alcohol abuse should be paid by providers, and improved interventions to reduce or eliminate drinking by HIV-infected patients should also be developed, tested, and disseminated.

See also **HIV Risk Assessment Battery (RAB); Substance Abuse and AIDS.**

BIBLIOGRAPHY

Aharonovich, E., Hatzenbuehler, M. L., Johnston, B., O'Leary, A., Morgenstern, J., Wainberg, M. L., et al. (2006). A low-cost, sustainable intervention for drinking reduction in the HIV primary care setting. *AIDS Care, 18,* 561–568.

Anthony, I. C., & Bell, J. E. (2008). The neuropathology of HIV/AIDS. *International Review of Psychiatry, 20,* 15–24.

Auerbach, J. D., Wypijewska, C., Brodie, H., & Hammond, K. (Eds.). (1994). *AIDS and behavior: An integrated approach.* Washington, DE: National Academy of Sciences, Institute of Medicine: National Academy Press.

Bagasra, O., Kajdacsy-Balla, A., Lischner, H. W., & Pomerantz, R. J. (1996). Alcohol intake increases human immunodeficiency virus type 1 replication in peripheral human peripheral blood mononuclear cells. *Journal of Infectious Diseases, 167,* 789–797.

Bagasra, O., Whittle, P., Kajdacsy-Balla, A., & Lischner, H. W. (1990). Effects of alcohol ingestion in in vitro susceptibility of peripheral blood mononuclear cells to infection with HIV-1 and on CD4 and CD8 lymphocytes. *Alcoholism: Clinical and Experimental Research, 14,* 351–358.

Bagby, G. J., Zhang, P., Purcell, J. E., Didier, P. J., & Nelson, S. (2006). Chronic binge alcohol consumption accelerates progression of simian immunodeficiency disease. *Alcoholism: Clinical and Experimental Research, 30,* 1781–1790.

Benhamou, Y., Di Martino, V., Bochet, M., Colombet, G., Thibault, V., Liou, A., Katlama, C., & Poynard, T. for the MultivirC Group. (2001). Factors affecting liver fibrosis in Human Immunodeficiency Virus- and Hepatitis C Virus-coinfected patients: Impact of protease inhibitor therapy. *Hepatology, 34,* 283–287.

Berger-Greenstein, J. A., Cuevas, C. A., Brady, S. M., Trezza, G., Richardson, M. A., & Keane, T. M. (2007). Major depression in patients with HIV/AIDS and substance abuse. *AIDS Patient Care and STDs, 21,* 942–955.

Braithewaite, R. S., Conigliaro, J., Roberts, M. S., Shechter, S., Schaefer, A., McGinnis, K., et al. (2007). Estimating the impact of alcohol consumption on survival for HIV+ individuals. *AIDS Care, 19,* 459–466.

Castellares, C., Barreiro, P., Martin-Carbonero, L., Labarga, P., Vispo, M. E., Casado, R., et al. (2008). Liver cirrhosis in HIV-infected patients: Prevalence, aetiology, and clinical outcome. *Journal of Viral Hepatitis, 15,* 165–172.

Chander, G., Lau, B., & Moore, R. D. (2006). Hazardous alcohol use: A risk factor for non-adherence and lack of suppression of HIV infection. *Journal of Acquired Immune Deficiency Syndrome, 43,* 411–417.

Conigliaro, J., Justice, A., Gordon, A. J., & Bryant, K., for the VACS Alcohol and Behavior Change Research Group. (2006). Role of alcohol in determining Human Immunodeficiency Virus outcomes: A conceptual model to guide the implementation of evidence-based interventions into practice. *Medical Care, 44* (Suppl. 2), S1–S6.

Cook, R. T. (1998). Alcohol abuse, alcoholism, and damage to the immune system: A review. *Alcoholism: Clinical and Experimental Research, 22,* 1927–1942.

Cooper, M. L. (1992). Alcohol and increased behavioral risk for AIDS. *Alcohol Health and Research World, 16,* 64–72.

Cooper, M. L., & Cameron, D. W. (2005). Effect of alcohol use and highly active antiretroviral therapy on plasma levels of hepatitis C virus (HCV) in patients coinfected with HIV and HCV. *Clinical Infectious Diseases, 41*(Suppl. 1), S105–S109.

Dickson, D. W. (1986). Multinucleated giant cells in acquired immune deficiency syndrome: Origin from endogenous microglia? *Archives of Pathology and Laboratory Medicine, 110,* 967–968.

Dingle, G. A., & Oei, T. P. S. (1997). Is alcohol a cofactor in HIV and AIDS? Evidence from immunological and behavioral studies. *Psychological Bulletin, 122,* 56–71.

Dorus, W., Kennedy, J., Gibbons, R. D., & Ravi, S. D. (1987). Symptoms and diagnosis of depression in alcoholics. *Alcoholism: Clinical and Experimental Research, 11,* 150–154.

Ellis, R., Langford, D., & Masliah, E. (2007). HIV and antiretroviral therapy in the brain: Neuronal injury and repair. *Nature Reviews Neuroscience, 8,* 33–44.

Gordon, C. M., Carey, M. P., & Carey, K. B. (1997). Effects of a drinking event on behavioral skills and condom attitudes in men: Implications for HIV risk from a controlled experiment. *Health Psychology, 16,* 490–495.

Graham, C. S., Baden, L. R., Yu, E., Mrus, J. M., Carnie, J., Heeron, T., et al. (2001). Influence of Human Immunodeficiency Virus infection on the course of Hepatitis C Virus infection: A meta-analysis. *Clinical Infectious Diseases, 33,* 562–569.

Graham, C. S., Wells, A., Edwards, E. M., Herren, T., Tumilty, S., Stuver, S. O., et al. (2007). Effect of exposure to injection drugs or alcohol on antigen-specific immune responses in HIV and Hepatitis C coinfection. *Journal of Infectious Diseases, 195,* 847–856.

Grant, I. (1987). Alcohol and the brain: Neuropsychological correlates. *Journal of Consulting and Clinical Psychology, 55,* 310–324.

Halpern-Felsher, B. L., Millstein, S. G., & Ellen, J. M. (1996). Relationship of alcohol use and risky sexual behavior: A review and analysis of findings. *Journal of Adolescent Health, 19,* 331–336.

Holstad, M. K., Pace, J. C., De, A. K., & Ura, D. R. (2006). Factors associated with adherence to antiretroviral therapy. *Journal of the Association of Nurses in AIDS Care, 17,* 4–15.

Hull, J. G., & Bond, C. F. (1986). Social and behavioral consequences of alcohol consumption and expectancy: A meta-analysis. *Psychological Bulletin, 99,* 347–360.

Hult, B., Chana, G., Masliah, T., & Everall, I. (2008). Neurobiology of HIV. *International Review of Psychiatry, 20,* 3–13.

Isaki, L., & Kresina, T. F. (2000). Directions for biomedical research in alcohol and HIV: Where are we now and where can we go? *AIDS Research and Human Retroviruses, 16,* 1197–1207.

Justice, A. C., Lasky, E., McGinnis, K. A., Skanderson, M., Conigliaro, J., Fultz, S. L., et al., for the VACS 3 Project Team. (2006). Medical disease and alcohol use among veterans with Human Immunodeficiency Infection. *Medical Care, 44*(Suppl. 2), S52–S60.

Kodl, M. M., Fu, S. S., Willenbring, M. L., Gravely, A., Nelson, D. B., & Joseph, A. M. (2008). The impact of depressive symptoms on alcohol and cigarette consumption following treatment for alcohol and nicotine dependence. *Alcoholism: Clinical and Experimental Research, 32,* 92–99.

Lazo, M., Gange, S. J., Wilson, T. E., Anastos, K., Ostrow, D. G., Witt, M. D., et al. (2007). Patterns and predictors of changes in adherence to highly active antiretroviral therapy: Longitudinal study of men and women. *Clinical Infectious Diseases, 45,* 1377–1385.

Leigh, B. C. (1989). In search of the seven dwarves: Issues of measurement and meaning in alcohol expectancy research. *Psychological Bulletin, 105,* 361–373.

Leigh, B. C. (2002). Alcohol and condom use: A meta-analysis of event-level studies. *Sexually Transmitted Diseases, 29,* 476–482.

Leigh, B. C., & Stall, R. (1993). Substance use and risky sexual behavior for exposure to HIV: Issues in methodology, interpretation, and intervention. *American Psychologist, 48,* 1035–1045.

Lucas, G. M., Gebo, K. A., Chaisson, R. E., & Moore, R. D. (2002). Longitudinal assessment of the effects of drug and alcohol abuse on HIV-1 treatment outcomes in an urban clinic. *AIDS, 16,* 767–774.

MacDonald, T. K., Fong, G T., Zanna, M. P., & Martineau, A. M. (2000). Alcohol myopia and condom use: Can alcohol intoxication be associated with more prudent behavior? *Journal of Personality and Social Psychology, 78,* 605–619.

Molina, P. E., McNurlan, M., Rathmacher, J., Lang, C. H., Zambell, K. L., Purcell, J., et al. (2006). Chronic alcohol accentuates nutritional, metabolic, and immune alterations during asymptomatic simian immunodeficiency syndrome. *Alcoholism: Clinical and Experimental Research, 30,* 2065–2078.

Mugavero, M., Ostermann, J., Whetten, K., Leserman, J., Swartz, M., Stangl, D., et al. (2006). Barriers to antiretroviral adherence: The importance of depression, abuse, and other traumatic events. *AIDS Patient Care and STDs, 20,* 418–428.

Nair, M. P. N., Kumar, N. M., Kronfol, Z. A., Saravdatz, L. A., Pottathil, R., Greden, J. F., et al. (1994). Selective effect of alcohol on cellular immune responses of lymphocytes from AIDS patients. *Alcohol, 11,* 85–90.

Nair, M. P. N., Schwartz, S. A., Kronfol, Z. A., Heimer, E. P., Pottathil, R., & Greden, J. F. (1990). Immunoregulatory effects of alcohol on lymphocyte responses to human immunodeficiency virus proteins. *Alcoholism: Clinical and Experimental Research, 14,* 221–230.

Nelson, S., Bagby, G. J., & Summer, W. R. (1990). Alcohol-induced suppression of tumor cell necrosis factor: A potential risk factor for secondary infection in the acquired immune deficiency syndrome. *Alcoholism: Clinical and Experimental Research, 14,* 211–220.

Nottet, H. S. L. M., Persidsky, Y., Sasseville, V. G., Nukuna, A. N., Bock, P., Zhai, Q. H., et al. (1996). Mechanism for the transendothelial migration of HIV-infected monocytes into brain. *Journal of Immunology, 156,* 1284–1295.

O'Leary, A. (2001). Substance use and HIV: Disentangling the nexus of risk. Introduction to special issue. *Journal of Substance Abuse, 13,* 1–3.

Parsons, J. T., Golub, S. A., Rosof, E., & Holder, C. (2007). Motivational interviewing and cognitive-behavioral intervention to improve HIV medication adherence among hazardous drinkers: A randomized, controlled trial. *Journal of Acquired Immune Deficiency Syndromes, 46,* 443–450.

Parsons, J. T., Rosof, E., & Mustanski, B. (2007). Patient-related factors predicting HIV medication adherence among men and women with alcohol problems. *Journal of Health Psychology, 12,* 357–370.

Pence, B. W., Miller, W. C., Gaynes, B. N., & Eron, J. J. (2007). Psychiatric illness and virologic response in patients initiating highly active antiretroviral therapy. *Journal of Acquired Immune Deficiency Syndromes, 44,* 159–166.

Pfefferbaum, A., Rosenbloom, M. J., Adalsteinsson, E., & Sullivan, E. V. (2007). Diffusion tensor imaging with quantitative fiber tracking in HIV infection and alcoholism comorbidity: Synergistic white matter damage. *Brain, 130,* 48–64.

Pfefferbaum, A., Rosenbloom, M. J., Rohlfing, T., Adalsteinsson, E., Kemper, C. A., Deresinski, S., et al. (2006). Contribution of alcoholism to brain dysmorphology in HIV infection: Effects on the ventricles and corpus callosum. *Neuroimage, 33,* 239–251.

Pol, S., Lamorthe, B., Thi, N. T., Thiers, V., Carnot, F., Zylberberg, P. B., et al. (1998). Retrospective analysis of the impact of HIV infection and alcohol use on chronic hepatitis C in a large cohort of drug users. *Journal of Hepatology, 28,* 945–950.

Poonia, B., Nelson, S., Bagby, G. J., & Veazey, R. S. (2006). Intestinal lymphocyte subsets and turnover are affected by chronic alcohol consumption: Implications for SIV/HIV infection. *Journal of Acquired Immune Deficiency Symdromes, 41,* 537–547.

Poonia, B., Nelson, S., Bagby, G. J., Zhang, P., Quniton, L., & Veazey, R. S. (2006). Chronic alcohol consumption results in higher simian immunodeficiency virus replication in mucosally inoculated rhesus macaques. *AIDS Research and Human Retroviruses, 22,* 589–594.

Potula, R., Jaorah, J., Knipe, B., Leibhart, J., Chrastil, J., Heilman, D., et al. (2007). Alcohol abuse enhances neuroinflammation and impairs immune responses in an animal model of Human Immunodeficiency Virus-1 encephalitis. *American Journal of Pathology, 168,* 1335–1344.

Purcell, D. W., Moss, S., Remien, R. H., Parsons, J. T., Woods, W. J., & the SUMIT Team. (2005). Illicit substance use and sexual risk behavior among HIV-seropositive gay and bisexual men. *AIDS, 19*(Suppl. 1), S37–S47.

Salmon-Ceron, D., Lewden, C., Morlat, P., Bevilacqua, S., Jougla, E., Bonnet, F., et al., & the Mortality 2000 Study Group. (2005). Liver disease as a major cause of death among HIV infected patients: Role of hepatitis B and C and alcohol. *Journal of Hepatology, 42,* 799–805.

Samet, J. H., Cheng, D. M., Libman, H., Nunes, D. P., Alperen, J. K., & Saitz, R. (2007). Alcohol consumption and HIV disease progression. *Journal of Acquired Immune Deficiency, 46,* 194–199.

Samet, J. H., Phillips, S. J., Horton, N. J., Traphagen, E. T., & Freedberg, K. A. (2004). Detecting alcohol problems in HIV-infected patients: Use of the CAGE questionnaire. *AIDS Research and Human Retroviruses, 20,* 151–155.

Sassoon, S. A., Fama, R., Rosenbloom, M. J., O'Reilly, A., Pfefferbaum, A., & Sullivan, E. V. (2007). Component cognitive and motor processes of the digit symbol test: Differential deficits in alcoholism, HIV infection, and their comorbidity. *Alcoholism: Clinical and Experimental Research, 31,* 1315–1324.

Shahbazian, L. M., Darban, H. R., Darban, J. R., Stazzone, A. M., & Watson, R. R. (1992). Influence of the level of dietary ethanol in mice with murine AIDS on resistance to Streptococcus pneumoniae. *Alcohol and Alcoholism, 27,* 345–352.

Shiu, C., Barbier, E., Di Cello, F., Choi, H. J., & Stins, M. (2007). HIV-1 gp120 as well as alcohol affect blood-brain barrier permeability and stress fiber formation: Involvement of reactive oxygen species. *Alcoholism: Clinical and Experimental Research, 31,* 130–137.

Steele, C. M., & Josephs, R. A. (1990). Alcohol myopia: Its prized and dangerous effects. *American Psychologist, 45,* 921–933.

Theall, K. P., Amedee, A., Clark, R. A., Dumestre, J., & Kissinger, P. (2008). Alcohol consumption and HIV-1 vaginal RNA shedding among women. *Journal of Studies on Alcohol and Drugs, 69,* 454–458.

Tsui, J. I., Saitz, R., Cheng, D. M., Nunes, D., Libman, H., Alperen, J. K., et al. (2007). Awareness of hepatitis C diagnosis is associated with less alcohol use among persons co-infected with HIV. *Journal of General Internal Medicine, 22,* 822–825.

Wang, X., Douglas, S. D., Peng, J-S., Metzger, D. S., O'Brien, C. P., Zhang, T., et al. (2006). Naltrexone inhibits alcohol-mediated enhancement of HIV infection of T lymphocytes. *Journal of Leukocyte Biology, 79,* 1166–1172.

Weinhardt, L. S., & Carey, M. P. (2000). Does alcohol lead to risk behavior? Findings from event-level research. *Annual Review of Sex Research, 11,* 125–157.

ANN O'LEARY
MARK HATZENBUEHLER

ALCOHOL- AND DRUG-EXPOSED INFANTS.

Since the 1970s, increasing recognition of the use of alcohol and drugs by women during pregnancy has led to concern for possible deleterious effects to the developing fetus. With the greater societal acceptance of drug use that began in the 1970s and the development of smokable forms of drugs that were formerly only used by injection, women of childbearing age and pregnant women dramatically increased their use of alcohol and other substances.

SUBSTANCES USED BY PREGNANT WOMEN

Tobacco and alcohol are the most commonly used drugs during pregnancy. In the United States, tobacco exposure complicates 25 percent of all pregnancies, and alcohol, although widely recognized as causing harm to the fetus, is consumed by about 20 percent of pregnant women. Illicit drug use occurs in about 5.5 percent of all pregnancies, a figure that may be an underestimate as national surveys are based on self-report. Based on these data, about 450,000 pregnancies annually are complicated by drug exposure and approximately 820,000 by alcohol exposure in the United States. Among illicit drugs, marijuana is most frequently used, followed by cocaine. Crack use, cocaine in its smokable form, became an epidemic in the 1990s among poor, urban women. Heroin, methamphetamine, methylenedioxymethamphetamine (MDMA, Ecstasy) are also used during pregnancy, as well as phencyclidine (PCP), ketamine, and LSD, but to a lesser extent.

Additionally, legal drugs, such as methadone and buprenorphine, may be prescribed for treatment of heroin addiction during pregnancy, and the burgeoning use of antidepressants during pregnancy has resulted in identification of SSRIs (selective serotonin reuptake inhibitors) as potentially harmful to fetal development. Anti-epileptic drugs are also medically prescribed during pregnancy when necessary. Nicotine-replacement therapy is often recommended during pregnancy, though concerns exist about the injurious fetal effects of the drug.

FETAL IMPACT OF MATERNAL USE

The majority of alcohol dependent and drug-addicted women use multiple substances. Since all drugs are carried across the placenta from mother to fetus, the newborn (neonate) is frequently exposed to a multiple-drug cocktail. The clinical condition of the newborn and infant long-term development depend on the type of drugs used, the frequency, amount, duration, trimester of use, and the time since last use. Since embryonic and fetal development unfolds in an orderly fashion, first trimester exposure may affect physical and organ development, whereas third trimester exposure may affect brain processes while leaving physical development unaffected. Thus functional impairment may exist with normal anatomic development.

Newborns recently exposed to heavy alcohol, heroin, methadone, or other opioids during pregnancy may experience withdrawal, or neonatal abstinence syndrome. Alcohol withdrawal symptoms occur generally within twelve hours of birth; opiate withdrawal symptoms may be delayed up to a week but tend to occur within forty-eight hours. Methadone withdrawal symptoms may not occur for as long as two weeks.

The Finnegan Scale, created by Loretta Finnegan, was devised to measure symptoms of withdrawal, which include irritability, tremor, and increased muscle tone. Other symptoms include jitteriness, high-pitched cry, poor feeding, seizures, vomiting, diarrhea, apnea (suspension of breathing), sweating, frequent yawning, sneezing, symptoms of fever, and sleeping difficulties. Drug-exposed newborns frequently present with prematurity, low birth weight, or intrauterine growth retardation (IUGR), drug or alcohol related birth defects, or facial dysmorphism that signal the need to monitor for withdrawal symptoms. For heroin or opioid exposed infants, withdrawal occurs in 55 to 94 percent of

infants. Heroin exposure withdrawal symptoms can persist for about ten days postnatally whereas those associated with methadone can last up to eight weeks.

MANAGEMENT

A thorough alcohol and drug use history should be obtained from the expectant mother and should be corroborated by testing the urine of both mother and newborn for alcohol and other drugs. Drug assessment of infant meconium can detect drug use during the last two trimesters of pregnancy, in contrast to the twelve-hour to two-week window apparent through urine screening. Newborns should be closely monitored for signs of withdrawal for a minimum of forty-eight to seventy-two hours and longer when the mother has been on methadone maintenance treatment. Since symptoms of withdrawal are nonspecific and may be confused with a variety of infections or metabolic disturbances, a search for concurrent illness to explain symptoms is also mandatory.

Most hospital nurseries use a standardized neonatal abstinence syndrome scoring system such as the Finnegan Scale. The hospital monitors the neonate's sleep habits, temperature, and weight. The earliest withdrawal symptoms are treated by intravenous fluids, swaddling, holding, rocking, a low-stimulation environment, and small feedings of hyper-caloric formula for weight gain. If symptoms continue or increase, medication may be initiated. Common medications include camphorated tincture of opium (Paregoric) or phenobarbital for opioid withdrawal, Phenobarbital or Diazepam for alcohol withdrawal. Diazepam is also used to help with cocaine hyperexcitability.

Interviewing the exposed mother is essential in evaluating the anticipated home environment and the extent of maternal addiction or dependence. Unfortunately, infants exposed to drugs and alcohol in utero are often at high risk for abuse and/or neglect. Normal maternal-infant bonding is difficult in the case of an irritable, poorly responsive neonate and a mother dealing with guilt, low self-esteem, poverty, inadequate housing, and an abusive or absent partner or parent, all of which often accompany her own drug addiction. A referral to child protection services may therefore be indicated.

Women who use drugs or alcohol during pregnancy are also highly likely (50%) to have significant mental health problems, especially depression and anxiety requiring referral, and a history of sexual abuse. Domestic violence is often present, especially with illicit drug use that involves criminal activity. The Drug Abuse Screening Test (DAST) or the Michigan Alcohol Screening Test (MAST) can be useful in establishing the extent of drug and/or alcohol dependence. The TWEAK alcohol screening test—an acronym for Tolerance, Worried, Eye-opener, Amnesia, and Kut down (as in "cut down consumption")—consists of five questions and was developed to screen pregnant women for harmful drinking habits. The involvement of social services for follow-up is paramount to ensure the health of both mother and infant. Breastfeeding is contraindicated as drugs and alcohol pass readily to the infant through breast milk. A significant percentage of drug-exposed or heavily alcohol-exposed infants need foster care placement. Infants whose parents are addicted to tobacco, crack-cocaine, marijuana, or methamphetamine are at risk for continued drug exposure in the home environment.

Alcohol and substance abuse during pregnancy are related to a higher risk for medical or obstetric complications, including high blood pressure, poor nutrition, sexually transmitted diseases, and preterm birth. Risk of human immunodeficiency virus (HIV)/AIDS is also high. Lack of, or inadequate, prenatal care and mental health problems are common. Obstetric management is complex, and substance abuse treatment, mental health, and social services coordinated with prenatal care are necessary.

OUTCOME
Research studies beginning in the 1970s with the identification of Fetal Alcohol Syndrome (FAS) and cresting in the 1990s with the crack-cocaine epidemic resulted in a growing body of literature on the negative effects of alcohol and drugs on child developmental outcomes.

Alcohol is the most widely used human teratogen, the leading cause of birth defects, and one of the leading causes of mental retardation. FAS, characterized by growth deficiency, mental retardation, and facial dysmorphology, affects two thousand to twelve thousand U.S. children a year. Many more prenatally alcohol-exposed children have varying degrees of learning disabilities and motor, behavioral, or physical problems, categorized broadly as Fetal Alcohol Spectrum Disorders (FASD).

There is no known safe dose of alcohol exposure during pregnancy. Low-to-moderate prenatal exposure has been associated with Attention-Deficit Hyperactivity Disorder (ADHD), visual-motor problems, learning and memory impairment, poorer information processing speed, and IQ decrements at school age. Adolescents and adults prenatally exposed continue to demonstrate these problems as well as social behavioral deficits. The amount and duration of prenatal exposure are related generally to the severity of problems seen. By 2008 imaging studies had begun to document reductions and alterations in specific brain areas associated with prenatal alcohol exposure and the impairments found in alcohol-exposed offspring.

Tobacco accounts for more cases of Sudden Infant Death Syndrome (SIDS) than all other abused substances, and is the major environmental cause of low birth weight. Maternal smoking during pregnancy does not appear to be related to infant malformations but has been related to long-lasting deficits in child cognitive function. Prenatal tobacco exposure has been related to infant visual and hearing impairments, childhood ADHD, and delinquent behaviors and poor educational attainment in adolescence and adulthood. Continued exposure to passive smoke in the household should be considered an additional risk factor affecting child behavior.

Marijuana is the most commonly used illegal drug during pregnancy. Two prospective cohort studies in Pittsburgh and Ottawa looked at the relationship between heavy marijuana exposure and outcome. As with alcohol and tobacco, marijuana exposure was related to attentional and behavioral problems, including delinquency. Short-term memory and visual reasoning problems were seen in the preschool years, and poor ability to organize and integrate cognitive information and poorer visual-perceptual skills were evident by nine to twelve years. Attentional problems appeared to resolve by adolescence. Depressive symptoms were also found to increase at school age.

The majority of cocaine-exposed infants are exposed to multiple substances, primarily alcohol, tobacco, and marijuana, so research has attempted to differentiate cocaine effects from those of other drugs through large prospective cohort studies. No cocaine syndrome with consistent dysmorphology had been identified as of 2008. Cocaine exposure has been related to behavioral problems, jitteriness, sleep dysregulation, excitability, poor feeding, and poor visual attention in the neonatal period. Greater risks of infectious diseases, SIDS and, for very low birth-weight preterm infants, a higher incidence of vascular hemorrhage have been found.

Long-term follow up studies to school age cocaine-exposed children reveal persistent language and attentional problems, identifiable as early as one year of age. Visual-motor and visual-reasoning deficits to school age have been linked to the extent of exposure. Studies of behavioral outcome have been inconsistent but have suggested increased aggressive and delinquent behavior. Although specific deficits have been noted related to the severity of prenatal cocaine exposure, the early alarmist and media reports in the 1990s of the hopelessly damaged crack baby have proved to be erroneous.

Heroin and methadone are the most commonly used opiates during pregnancy, affecting about ten thousand infants annually in the United States. Opiate exposure does not appear to be related to structural abnormalities among offspring, although neurobehavioral abnormalities may last up to six months postnatally. Follow-up of small samples of children prenatally exposed to heroin or methadone at school age indicate a higher rate of conduct disorder and lower school achievement than non-exposed children.

Methamphetamine is the most widely used stimulant drug in the world. A Swedish study that followed methamphetamine-exposed children to fourteen years found them to have delayed math and language development, peer behavioral problems, and poorer physical fitness compared to norms. Exposure to methamphetamine fumes in the home is also a concern for developmental toxicity.

There are no long-term studies, as of 2008, on PCP or MDMA, although studies were under way. The caretaking environment of the drug- or alcohol-exposed child is often not optimal, because of maternal addiction, also contributing to poorer child outcomes. Screening and treatment for substance use and mental health disorders among pregnant women are paramount in order to reduce the morbidity associated with prenatal drug and alcohol exposure.

See also **Fetal Alcohol Syndrome; Fetus, Effects of Drugs on the; Pregnancy and Drug Dependence.**

BIBLIOGRAPHY

Cernerud, L. (1996). Amphetamine addiction during pregnancy: 14-year follow-up of growth and school performance. *Acta Paediatrica, 85,* 204–208.

Huizink, A., et al. (2006). Maternal smoking, drinking or cannabis use during pregnancy and neurobehavioral and cognitive functioning in human offspring. *Neuroscience and Biobehavioral Reviews, 30,* 24–41.

Lewis, B. A., et al. (2007). Cocaine and tobacco effects on children's language trajectories. *Pediatrics, 120,* e78–e85.

Singer, L. T., et al. (2004). The home environment and cognitive outcomes of cocaine exposed, preschool children. *Journal of the American Medical Association, 291,* 2448–2456.

Slikker, W., et al. (1998). *Handbook of Developmental Neurotoxicology.* New York: Academic Press.

Smeriglio, V. L., et al. (1999). Prenatal drug exposure and child outcome. *Clinics in Perinatology, 26,* 1–16.

Substance Abuse and Mental Health Services Administration. (2004). Results from the 2004 National Survey on Drug Use and Health; National Findings.

U.S. Department of Health and Human Services. (1996). Behavioral studies of drug-exposed offspring: Methodological issues in human and animal research (NIDA Monograph 164). Washington, DC: Author.

JOYCE F. SCHNEIDERMAN
REVISED BY LYNN TWAROG SINGER (2009)

ALCOHOL- AND DRUG-FREE HOUSING. Alcohol- and drug-free (ADF) housing, also called sober housing, sober-living environments, or alcohol-free living centers, provides accommodation for people who choose to live free of alcohol and/or drugs. ADF housing is ordinary housing located in residentially zoned areas, in architecture that includes single-family housing, multi-family housing, apartment complexes, and shared housing (co-housing).

DEFINITIONS AND PRINCIPALS

ADF housing provides domestic settings to support residents' day-to-day efforts to maintain sobriety. Nearly all residents in ADF housing are recovering from alcohol/drug problems. The residents come from myriad social and economic backgrounds. Most attend AA or NA meetings; many are participants and clients in the community's health, education, and social services; some residents are involved in the justice system. The house might include a few residents who prefer sober living for reasons not related to personal alcohol/drug problems.

The house itself is the service that supports sobriety. The house is managed in whole or in part by the residents, and no clinical or counseling services are provided on-site. Although residents often attend these services off-site, providing them on-site could seriously defeat the purpose of ADF housing in two ways. First, the housing would lose the protection of Fair Housing Amendments Act of 1988 (FHAA) regarding rights to live in any residentially zoned area and personal privacy under the Fourth Amendment. Second, the housing would lose its efficacy to support personal choices to maintain sobriety.

The FHAA prohibits housing discrimination by allowing people with disabilities to live together for a shared purpose such as mutually assisted recovery and maintenance of an abstinent lifestyle. The act expands protections of family housing to include people in recovery not related by blood or marriage. Practically speaking, this means state and local jurisdictions cannot establish limits on numbers of persons occupying the house or upon lengths of stay that do not apply to all residences in the community. Additionally, state or local jurisdictions cannot impose licensure or certification requirements that do not apply equally to all residential land-uses in the community (American Planning Association).

FHAA protections are likely to be lost if formal counseling, education, or other non-residential services are provided on-site. Limited services can be provided that would reasonably be provided in any residence, such as visiting nurse services or in-home tutoring. The test is whether a local or state jurisdiction could insist the facility be zoned and licensed consistent with state and local standards for the delivery of such services. Without protection under the Fair Housing Amendments Act, experience shows that local communities exclude ADF residences from safe and economically stable areas most conducive to recovery. In California, for example, as of 2008 the state and several cities were pursuing legislation to restrict numbers of residents, restrict locations, and impose intrusive inspection and drug-testing requirements on sober-living facilities (Sober Living Network).

Equally important to protection of basic housing rights is protection of ADF housing as a setting for recovery and sober living. The capacity of the house to support day-to-day alcohol-free living, including oversight by management and occasional house-calls, would be compromised if non-residential services were provided on the premises, just as the quality of private family life would be infringed by having to accommodate non-family uses in a private family home. Service providers, referral sources, and benefactors who rely on ADF housing usually understand this separation and respect the primary rules under which every sober-living house operates: (1) residents remain sober at all times (no drinking or drug use); (2) residents pay their rent on time; and (3) residents participate in house rules relating to daily living, such as housekeeping, clean-up, guest policies, curfews, and participation in house meetings. (Kaskutas, 1999).

Increasing numbers of research studies indicate that such ADF residences extend residents' sobriety, improve their income, and reduce service utilization (McCarty et al., 1993). Studies also find that ADF housing benefits a variety of residents from many backgrounds, including people who have been in jail (Polcin, 2006). As of 2008, work was under way to investigate the utility of various ADF housing forms to meet the needs of various groups and determine which groups do well in which settings (Kaskutas & McLellan, 1998). Answers to these questions can calibrate housing design and operations. Answers can also help strengthen quality standards so the most promising examples can expand reliably, which is important in order to meet the rising demand for ADF housing.

FEATURES OF ADF HOUSING

ADF housing first appeared with the temperance movement in the 1830s, and the architecture of sober housing has operated within national patterns of residential accommodation for low-income renters since that time. As the U.S. urbanized, communities provided sober accommodation in rooming houses and hotels whose proprietors did not permit their boarders or renters to drink on the premises. As suburbs developed and single-family homes became the norm, architecture for ADF residences included houses originally designed to accommodate families or individuals living independently. Current forms of sober housing include single-room occupancy (SRO) hotels, rooming houses, single-family houses, and multi-family housing. These forms of sober housing have emerged alongside the growth of the twelve step recovery movement, which started in the late 1930s. Although the AA does not own or operate sober housing, most operators are highly sympathetic to AA (some require attendance at AA meetings), and many AA members depend upon sober housing as part of their daily recovery regimen.

Freestanding, independent sober residences were able to function quietly in large cities until redevelopment turned toward city centers in the 1960s and 1970s, destroying large amounts of low-income housing. SROs were particularly devastated. The independent recovery community lost access to low-income housing and to new housing opportunities. Only independently owned ADF facilities already in operation were able to continue.

ADF Service Models and Supporting Organizations.
Starting in the 1970s and 1980s, recovery-oriented ADF housing differentiated into three basic models, each with its own association: resident-run housing; peer-based entrepreneurial sober housing networks; and program-affiliated sober housing. Healthy competition has developed among these models.

Oxford Houses are resident-run housing established by middle-class professionals in recovery who seek large resident-run single-family facilities in the suburbs and other desirable residential areas. Oxford Houses operate according to a charter drawn up by a few founding Oxford House residents in the mid-1980s (Oxford House, 1988). Having benefited from federal legislation providing small start-up grants, Oxford Houses were estimated as of 2008 to include about one thousand facilities in the United States and Europe.

In the peer-based entrepreneurial model, ADF housing relies on property managers/owners of ADF housing, many of them in recovery themselves, to create their own organization. This organization sets its own standards and provides its own governance to assure close adherence to ADF housing principles. For example, the Sober Living Network in Los Angeles has about 250 member-houses, according to its Web site.

Program-affiliated ADF facilities operate according to a step-wise progression of accommodation, rules, and expectations designed to promote successful movement into recovery. Some of these programs function as several sober residences linked together by central management (Beacon House, San Pedro; Sun Street Center) or loosely linked by geography in proximity to recovery services and neighborhood social centers (Los Angeles neighborhood recovery centers). Other programs operate sober residences in connection with other off-site program activities that provide counseling, vocational, and health/social services (Escondido program, VOA, Salvation Army). In California approximately one hundred ADF houses, called Sober Living Environments or SLEs, belong to a statewide association that advocates their interests with the state alcohol/drug agency and the state legislature (California Association of Addiction Recovery Resources, 2008).

Operational Configuration.
Recovery-oriented ADF facilities operate with great flexibility through a system of interconnected axes (Wittman, 1993). This system lets ADF housing follow basic principles consistent with community resources of housing stock, the recovery population seeking ADF housing, and relationship to public agencies providing AOD-related professional services.

ADF facilities may vary in size from a few people living in a single-family home to more than one hundred rooms in a residential hotel that has been converted into a sober living facility. Thanks to FHAA protections, ADF facilities may be located in any residentially zoned area where affordable, accessible housing is available. The architectural design emphasizes domestic qualities that help people relax and relate to each other in comfortable, informal, and natural settings.

Occupancy may be open to a variety of people in recovery and to abstainers or may focus on particular groups of people in recovery, such as employees, professional people, participants in a multi-component recovery program, people involved with the criminal justice system, or people grouped by age and gender. Also, house rules range from mandatory directives for all parts of life in the facility that all residents must follow to a framework with relatively few general rules designed to provide latitude for individual resident schedules and preferences.

ADF house management styles ranges from democratic, resident-run houses (Oxford Houses) to management by a founder and hand-picked successors (Sober Living Network) to managers selected by executives of the program operating the residence. Also, some ADF residences are free-standing business entities operating as a private corporation, either for profit or not-for-profit. Other residences are tied to AOD treatment/recovery programs, to other health and social service providers, and to other organizations that provide ADF accommodation for their members, such as colleges with sober-housing dormitories. Additionally, some ADF housing occupies the entire facility, such as a single-family house dedicated to sober living. Other ADF housing shares facilities with compatible uses, for example, ADF housing upstairs with nonalcohol commercial activities on a ground level.

CHALLENGES

The following ADF housing challenges appear and re-appear in various forms over the years.

Demonstration of effectiveness. Well-run ADF facilities have functioned well on face validity as residents and ADF housing managers conscientiously support recovery (maintain sobriety) and operate with great sensitivity to neighborhood concerns. However, as federal support for community alcohol and drug programs in the early 2000s requires evidence-based results and accountability, state alcohol and drug program agencies are beginning to ask for formal evaluations of ADF facility operations. Pathbreaking qualitative research done in the 1990s to describe the utility of sober residence operations in terms of resident experiences (Kaskutas & McLellan, 1998) was in the early 2000s being supplemented with quantitative analysis that calibrates the performance of ADF settings (Polcin, 2006). These findings are being used to help set clearer standards for quality operation.

Capacity to Accommodate New Groups. The recovery movement attracts groups with a variety of drinking/drug problems, including those with mental disabilities, nonviolent offenders, and general population groups such as college students and employees. In practice, ADF housing operators have long accommodated residents from these groups on an individual basis as circumstances permit. However, as residential facilities to serve the mentally ill evaporated, as prisons became overcrowded, and as affordable housing for low-income people withered, pressures mounted on ADF settings to provide accommodation for special-needs residents.

The demands of dual-need and multi-need groups test the limits of ADF housing. Sponsoring agencies that provide services to the dual-diagnosed mentally ill, for example, do not share ADF housing requirements for strict sobriety and use of off-site services. Many agencies providing services for chronic inebriates with mental health problems prefer a harm reduction approach using supportive housing rather than an abstinence model (CSH references). Supportive housing allows residents occasional slips and provides on-site services. Similarly, drug-testing and reporting requirements introduce complications for accommodation of parolees and offenders under court supervision. Although these circumstances contradict basic house policies regarding sobriety and on-site services, some ADF residences go part way to accommodate some residents with special needs. A few ADF residences follow a so-called damp policy that does not allow drinking on the premises but permits off-site drinking within limits.

Despite differences in philosophy, supportive housing and sober housing have similar residential architecture requirements, as noted below. Thus it is possible for some cities to experiment with so-called wet housing under a harm reduction approach that allows chronic homeless inebriates in a high-density urban area to drink in their rooms and to obtain counseling and health services on-site (Downtown Emergency Service Center). This housing first approach provides a safe environment for someone who would otherwise continue a long history of high service utilization and nuisance behavior. This approach is a community-level (municipal) response to the dearth of federal- and state-supported action to meet housing needs of such groups with high service needs, including offenders being released from prison and young people graduating from the foster care system (Pearson et al., 2007).

Economic Viability. The basic economic model for ADF house operation, as for any ordinary residence, depends on payment of rent or a mortgage. Financial operation of ADF housing is based nominally on standard housing market factors. However, ADF residents in recovery usually are below-average earners who are not able to pay full market rents.

One problem is how to make ADF housing economically viable for ADF residents who cannot afford standard market rates. In the Oxford House model, residents share the cost of renting the house to create affordable accommodation in a market-rate environment at a modest per-person cost. Otherwise, answers depend on making a case to win support from public and foundation/personal supporters that find the investment attractive. Public support for ADF housing must compete with other public-housing alternatives such as conventional low-income housing and supportive housing. Public funding also invites public oversight that may challenge the very foundations of ADF housing. Foundation and personal giving approaches target foundations and individuals (such as house alumni) who are especially attracted by ADF housing values and able to give back in appreciation for the help they received personally.

Community Resistance. Neighborhood resistance (Not In My Back Yard, or NIMBYism) remains a continuing challenge for ADF housing to be met in two ways. While firmly insisting that local authorities uphold recovering people's rights to housing, ADF operators further recognize the importance of outreach and responsiveness to neighborhood concerns. This responsiveness includes being accessible and participating in neighborhood activities (neighborhood clean-ups, block parties, neighborhood safety

campaigns, holiday celebrations). Outreach to engage neighbors provides opportunities to debunk concerns based on fears, misperceptions, ignorance, rumors, and incorrect information. There is no evidence to show that ADF housing increases crime or decreases property values; sometimes the opposite occurs in distressed neighborhoods. Neighborhood disturbances and confrontations rarely occur at well-run houses. The antidote to NIMBY concerns is outreach and contact with the neighbors rather than increased surveillance by law enforcement or more inspections by public officials.

Architectural Quality. Architecture for ADF facilities (design and use of settings to help people jointly maintain their sobriety day by day) is critical to program and financial success. Design features deeply influence how residents feel about themselves, how they perceive each other, and their attitudes toward living sober. These feelings, perceptions, and attitudes translate into personal behavior and group expectations. These features can be measured and evaluated, and researchers and ADF operators could do more to explore effects for recovery experiences and outcomes. The following are some suggestions:

Location of the facility needs to be in a safe area, accessible to public transportation.

The facility perimeter needs to be secure and entry needs to be controlled to manage the occupancy of the house and to discourage contraband.

The circulation system needs to bring people together in socially spontaneous ways (socio-petal) rather than to keep them apart in ways that encourage isolation (socio-fugal).

The house needs a room large enough for all residents to gather for regular house meetings.

Residents need their defined sleeping space, including lockable storage, that provides some privacy and separation (protection) from other residents.

Outdoor areas, views, and plants are vital to support human needs for contact with the rhythms of daylight and the passage of time and contact with sunlight.

Quality fixtures and furnishings are vital to effective operation, how residents feel about themselves, and how they view each other.

The house should be fully maintained and kept clean, and all equipment should be safe and in good repair as a matter of respect and functionality. Fire safety and building codes need to be met, or an upgrade plan needs to be in place.

Well-maintained and attractive houses help create support among neighbors.

Certification. High standards, followed with great fidelity by each facility, are critical to successful ADF housing. Traditionally certification has been experiential and word-of-mouth, residing within the personal integrity of well-known housing managers operating houses in close-knit local communities.

As ADF housing operations expand from the personal to an organizational basis, it is necessary to assure high-quality operation for each house. The challenge for the traditional craft of ADF management is responding to rising demands for accountability, organizational complexity, and new electronic operating technologies. In California, two perspectives are contending with each other. The tradition of owner/manager responsibility for the house is being expanded to peer-based oversight in which an association of residents (Oxford House) and/or on-site managers (SLN owner/operators) hold their members accountable for high-quality operation. Alternatively, a modern professional-technical perspective seeks to create statewide licensing standards, with input from residents and house-managers, to be overseen by public agencies at the state and local level (California State Department of Alcohol and Drug Programs; California Association of Addiction Recovery Resources, 2008).

These two approaches head in opposite directions. Either ADF housing operators create a peer-based certification system recognized by the state, or the state certifies ADF housing with input from the ADF housing community to help write standards and licensing procedures. The former approach supports the experiential foundation of the recovery-based sober housing movement and falls under the Fair Housing Amendments Act. The latter approach supports the notion that the state is responsible for operating standards to protect the public and ADF housing residents. Advocates for peer-based certification vigorously object that requirements for public agency oversight will create a special class of licensed housing that loses protection under the FHAA, resulting in restrictive local zoning controls and intrusive inspections. They also argue there is no reason to believe that state controls on ADF residences will achieve better results than resident-run or peer-managed houses, and there are concerns that state controls will suppress self-supervision and innovation, replacing them with a cumbersome, nonresponsive and ineffectual state bureaucracy.

ADF housing may find itself a niche as its full value comes to be appreciated, which was happening in the early 2000s as new populations sought out ADF housing in the absence of other appropriate residential accommodation. As demand for ADF housing grows, two forces were expected to shape its movement in positive ways. Growing research and evaluation was anticipated to provide useful feedback, and organizational growth was anticipated to expand the traditional focus on operation of individual houses to include shared operating standards.

As of 2008, however, the ominous question of who would control ADF housing remained unanswered. It might continue to be resident-run/peer-managed, with primary focus on the identify and quality of the individual house, or control might shift to public agency supervision by state and local agencies with primary focus on operation of a certification system, The answer goes to the heart of ADF concepts and their political expression at the community level. A number of observers, including many ADF housing providers, believe that state supervision would abridge FHAA protections leading to loss of locations and housing stock and to imposition of unworkable restrictions. As the battle for controlled continued, peer-entrepreneur ADF housing operators considered taking legal action to maintain protection under the Fair Housing Amendments Act.

See also **Treatment: A History of Treatment in the United States.**

BIBLIOGRAPHY

American Planning Association. (1997, September). Policy guide on community residences. Available from http://www.planning.org/.

California Association of Addiction Recovery Resources (CAARR). (2008). See especially Sober Housing tab, and the HEARTH Newsletter, December 2008, "Sober living environments in California" and "Update on news for residential programs about fair housing laws." Available from http://www.caarr.org.

Downtown Emergency Services Center, Supportive Housing for Chronic Homeless Alcoholics at 1811 Eastlake. Available from http://www.desc.org/.

Kaskutas, L. A. (1999). The social model approach to substance abuse recovery: A program of research and evaluation. Center for Substance Abuse Treatment, Department of Health and Human Services.

Kaskutas, L. A., & McLellan, A. T. (1998). Special issue: The social model approach to substance abuse recovery. *Journal of Substance Abuse Treatment, 15*(1), 5–74.

McCarty, D., Argeriou, M., Vallely, J., & Christian, C. (1993). Development of alcohol and drug-free housing. *Contemporary Drug Problems, 20*(3), 521–540

Molloy, J. P. (1990). *Self-run, self-supported houses for more effective recovery from alcohol and drug addiction.* DHHS Publication No. ADM 90-1678. Rockville, MD: Office of Treatment Improvement.

Oxford House. (1988). *The Oxford House manual.* Great Falls, VA: Author.

Pearson, C. L., Locke, G., Montgomery, A. E., & Buron, L. (2007). *The applicability of housing first models to homeless persons with serious mental illness: Final report.* Prepared for U.S. Department of Housing and Urban Development Office of Policy Development and Research. Prepared by Walter R. McDonald & Associates, Inc., Rockville, MD and Abt Associates Inc., Cambridge, MA.

Polcin, D. L. (2006). What about sober living for parolees? *Criminal Justice Studies, 19*(3), 291–300.

Sober Living Network. (2008). Available from http://www.soberhousing.net.

Wittman, F. D. (1993). Affordable housing for people with alcohol and other drug problems. *Contemporary Drug Problems, 20,* 541–609.

Wittman, F. D., & Madden, P. (1988). *Alcohol recovery programs for homeless people.* Rockville, MD: National Institute on Alcohol Abuse and Alcoholism.

FRIEDNER D. WITTMAN
JIM BAUMOHL
REVISED BY FRIEDNER D. WITTMAN (2009)

ALCOHOL, SMOKING AND SUBSTANCE INVOLVEMENT SCREENING TEST (ASSIST).

The Alcohol, Smoking and Substance Involvement Screening Test (ASSIST) was developed under the auspices of the World Health Organization (WHO) by an international group of specialist addiction researchers and clinicians in response to the public health burden associated with problematic substance use worldwide. The ASSIST was designed to screen for problem or risky use of tobacco, alcohol, cannabis, cocaine, amphetamine-type stimulants (ATS), sedatives, hallucinogens, inhalants, opioids and "other drugs." A risk score is obtained for each substance and falls into either a "low," "moderate," or "high" risk category. This determines the type of intervention, "none," "brief intervention," or "brief intervention plus referral."

See also **Diagnosis of Substance Use Disorders: Diagnostic Criteria; Treatment, Stages/Phases of: Screening and Brief Intervention.**

BIBLIOGRAPHY

WHO ASSIST Working Group. (2002). The Alcohol, Smoking and Substance Involvement Screening Test (ASSIST): Development, reliability and feasibility. *Addiction, 97* (9): 1183–1194.

THOMAS BABOR

ALCOHOL USE DISORDER AND ASSOCIATED DISABILITIES INTERVIEW SCHEDULE. *See* AUDADIS.

ALCOHOL USE DISORDERS IDENTIFICATION TEST (AUDIT).

Originally developed as the result of a World Health Organization (WHO) collaborative project among six countries—Australia, Bulgaria, Kenya, Mexico, Norway, and the United States—the Alcohol Use Disorders Identification Test (AUDIT) is a screening instrument designed to assess hazardous or harmful alcohol consumption (Saunders, Aasland, Babor, De La Fuente, & Grant, 1993). Due to the cross-national study from which it originated, the AUDIT holds the distinction of being the first alcohol screening instrument specifically designed for international use (Babor, Higgins-Biddle, Saunders, & Monteiro, 2001). Screening refers to the administration of a questionnaire to estimate the

Response scale & scoring					
Item 1	Never	Monthly or less	2–4 times/month	2–3 times/week	4 or more times/week
Item 2	1 or 2	3 or 4	5 or 6	7–9	10 or more
Items 3–8	Never	Less than monthly	Monthly	Weekly	Daily or almost daily
Items 9–10	No		Yes, but not in the last year		Yes, during the last year
	0 Points	1 Point	2 Points	3 Points	4 Points

Table 1. Response scale for each of the 10 AUDIT items and designation of the point value associated with each response. (Adapted from Saunders, Aasland, Babor, De La Fuente, & Grant, 1993.) ILLUSTRATION BY GGS INFORMATION SERVICES. GALE, CENGAGE LEARNING

probability that a specific condition exists among members of a population. While screenings are intended to provide insight into the people who are likely to have a disorder, these instruments do not establish a definitive diagnosis (Stewart & Connors, 2004; 2005).

INSTRUMENT CONSTRUCTS AND CONTENT

The AUDIT represents an early intervention tool. More specifically, the AUDIT is intended to identify a broad spectrum of problem drinking before significant harm or dependence may develop. Overall, three constructs are examined by this 10-item instrument: hazardous alcohol use, alcohol dependence symptoms, and harmful alcohol use.

Hazardous Alcohol Use. The first three questions of the AUDIT assess the domain of hazardous alcohol use. One's drinking behavior is considered hazardous when the *risk* of harmful physical and/or psychological consequences is increased (Babor, Higgins-Biddle, Saunders, & Monteiro, 2001). Overall, this section measures one's alcohol consumption behaviors by assessing the frequency of drinking alcohol (Question 1), the typical quantity of alcohol consumed daily (Question 2), and the frequency of heavy drinking (Question 3). It is important to note that the AUDIT determines heavy drinking to be the consumption of six or more drinks, as based upon European standard drink sizes. The U.S. equivalent to this standard for heavy drinking would be five or more drinks. Consuming five or more drinks in one sitting is often referred to as binge drinking (Wechsler, Davenport, Dowdall, Moeykens & Castillo, 1994). Accordingly, a heavy drinking cut-off of four or more drinks should be utilized to determine heavy drinking among women (Wechsler, Dowdall, Davenport & Rimm, 1995).

Alcohol Dependence Symptoms. AUDIT items 4 through 6 examine adverse reactions as a result of one's personal drinking behaviors/practices. More specifically, these items assess impaired control over drinking behaviors; that is, inability to cease drinking once started (Question 4), failure to perform normal expectations due to drinking (Question 5), and alcohol consumption the morning following a heavy drinking session (Question 6).

Harmful Alcohol Use. The final four items of the AUDIT examine harmful alcohol use. *Harmful* drinking is defined by the *presence* of physical and/or psychological consequences (Babor, Higgins-Biddle, Saunders, & Monteiro, 2001). Therefore, this section assesses alcohol-related problems by exploring feelings of guilt or remorse after drinking within the past year (Question 7), blackouts (the inability to remember all events that transpired during the previous drinking session) experienced within the past year (Question 8), injuries to oneself or others as a result of drinking (Question 9), and whether others—friends, relatives, health professionals—express concern about one's drinking (Question 10).

SCORING AND INTERPRETATION

Each of the 10 items of the AUDIT is scored from 0 to 4, depending upon the respective response. Therefore, possible total scores range from 0 to 40 (Saunders, Aasland, Babor, De La Fuente, & Grant, 1993). The following table outlines the response scale for each of the 10 items and also designates the point value associated with each response.

Total AUDIT score typically denotes one's alcohol-related risk. Consequently, a higher total score corresponds to increased likelihood of hazardous and harmful drinking behavior. In general, total scores of 8 or greater are indicative of hazardous and harmful alcohol use and may represent potential alcohol dependence. Due to individual characteristics, such as gender and body size, that influence the effects of alcohol, using a cut-off score of 7 is recommended to increase AUDIT sensitivity among populations of women and men older than 65 years of age. Conversely, using a criterion score of 10 increases the survey's specificity, and yet causes a loss of sensitivity (Babor, Higgins-Biddle, Saunders, & Monteiro, 2001). In comparing AUDIT scores to diagnostic data relating to alcohol dependence, medium-level alcohol problems are represented by scores ranging from 8 to 15, whereas high-level alcohol problems are represented by scores of 16 or more (Miller, Zweben, DiClemente, & Rychtarik, 1992). Moreover, tentative guidelines suggest that scores between 8 and 15 typically require professionals to provide guidance addressing the reduction of hazardous drinking, while scores between 16 and 19 mandate brief counseling and further observation. AUDIT scores of 20 or greater merit further, in-depth alcohol dependence evaluation and may require referral to a specialist (Babor, Higgins-Biddle, Saunders, & Monteiro, 2001).

See also **Addiction: Concepts and Definitions; Alcoholism: Origin of the Term; Australia; Kenya; Mexico; Nordic Countries (Denmark, Finland, Iceland, Norway and Sweden); Research: Clinical Research.**

BIBLIOGRAPHY

Babor, T. F., Higgins-Biddle, J. C., Saunders, J. B., & Monteiro, M. G. (2001). *AUDIT: The Alcohol Use Disorders Identification Test: Guidelines for use in primary care.* (2nd ed.). Geneva, Switzerland: World Health Organization.

Miller, W. R., Zweben, A., DiClemente, C. C., & Rychtarik, R. G. (1992). *Motivational enhancement therapy manual: A clinical research guide for therapists treating individuals with alcohol abuse and dependence.* (Project MATCH Monograph Series, Vol. 2). Rockville, MD: National Institute of Alcohol Abuse and Alcoholism.

Saunders, J. B., Aasland, O. G., Babor, T. F., De La Fuente, J. R., & Grant, M. (1993). Development of the Alcohol Use Disorders Identification Test (AUDIT): WHO collaboration project on early detection of persons with harmful alcohol consumption II. *Addiction, 88,* 791–804.

Wechsler, H., Davenport, A., Dowdall, G., Moeykens, B., & Castillo, S. (1994). Health and behavioral consequences of binge drinking in college: A national survey of students at 140 campuses. *Journal of the American Medical Association, 272*(21), 1672–1677.

Wechsler, H., Dowdall, G. W., Davenport, A., & Rimm, E. B. (1995). A gender-specific measure of binge drinking among college students. *American Journal of Public Health, 85*(7), 982–985.

ADAM E. BARRY

ALCOHOLICS ANONYMOUS.

Addiction to alcohol and other substances is arguably the greatest public health problem in the developed world. Societies have developed myriad ways to try to combat this complex problem. One of these ways, created by those who have personally experienced addiction, is an organization called Alcoholics Anonymous (AA). This entry provides an overview of AA, beginning with a definition of the organization, followed by a description of how it came into being and how it has evolved over the years. The core philosophy of AA is summarized, coupled with a description of the membership process and how affiliation works to promote recovery. Finally, scientific findings are brought to bear on the efficacy of AA compared to other treatments.

DEFINITION

AA is a mutual-help organization. Mutual-help organizations consist of persons voluntarily coming together with a shared problem and seeking solutions through the collective expression of their personal narratives (Humphreys, 2004). In the case of AA, that shared problem is addiction to alcohol. AA is self-directed and self-governed and does not rely on the expertise of any outside group or individual. The individual members themselves are in charge of the organization and provide expertise derived from their own lived experiences. Every member is both a provider and a recipient of help. This culture of reciprocal helping is at the very heart of AA and reflects the philosophy that even the most troubled people have the capacity to help others and that to help others is to help oneself (Maton, 1988). Other important features of AA include the absence of fees, the ubiquity of meetings, and a well-delineated program for change.

The absence of fees in AA is a practice that reduces potential barriers to participation. Individuals with a broad spectrum of financial resources and levels of personal organization are involved (Humphreys & Tucker, 2002). The only criterion for attending an AA meeting is the desire to stop drinking alcohol. To pay for expenses such as coffee, room rental, and organizational literature, participants voluntarily contribute small amounts of money during meeting time.

The sheer number and ubiquity of AA meetings, found at all times of the day, all over the world, also greatly facilitates participation. Attendance need not be predicated on a specific time of day or location. Participation need not be discontinued if a member relocates to a new town. By breaking down financial and logistical barriers, AA provides a worldwide community that transcends time or place, offering nearly universal access to individuals who find themselves in chaos due to their alcoholism.

AA, unlike some other mutual-help organizations, has a developed philosophy and program of change outlined in a book titled *Alcoholics Anonymous*. The book was published in 1939 and is known universally by its members as *The Big Book* because of the thick paper on which it was originally printed (Humphreys, 2004). AA is not affiliated with any specific religion but does espouse the importance of spirituality and a Higher Power in the process of transformative healing.

ORIGINS AND DEVELOPMENT

AA was founded in 1935. Its origins can be traced to a 1920s American evangelical movement called the Oxford Group (Humphreys, 2004). The Oxford Group preached overcoming alcoholism through a spiritual transformation. Members of the Oxford Group who were struggling with alcoholism reached out to William Griffith Wilson (known as Bill W., the cofounder of AA). Wilson was an alcoholic who had tried repeatedly to stay sober. Members of the Oxford Group were ultimately able to convince Wilson that a spiritual transformation was indeed a key component of recovery. Wilson described his transformation, which occurred during yet another emergency detoxification, as follows: "the result was instant, electric, beyond description. The place lit up, blinding white .... Blazing came the tremendous thought: You are a free man" (W. 1949, p. 372).

In May 1935, through his Oxford Group connections, Wilson met with Dr. Robert Holbrook Smith (subsequently known as AA cofounder Dr. Bob), who also suffered from alcoholism for many years. The two men met and talked for several hours, and the first AA meeting was born. They both experienced a profound sense of healing in sharing their stories, and both came to believe that for alcoholics to recover, they need to meet and talk with other alcoholics. As Wilson wrote, "to talk with another alcoholic, even though I failed with him, was better than to do nothing" (Trice & Staudenmeier, 1989, p. 17). Smith was, in effect, Wilson's first sponsor.

Soon after, the two began working together with other alcoholics. By August 1936, AA meetings within an Oxford Group context were being held both in Akron, Ohio, and New York City. Both men decided to sever their relationship with the Oxford Group, primarily to move the organization out of a strictly Protestant religious framework that limited the appeal of AA to many alcoholics. The small AA groups were then on their own. By 1940, their newly formed board of trustees listed twenty-two cities in which groups were well established and holding weekly meetings. When the first edition of *The Big Book* was distributed (1939), AA had several hundred members. When Smith died in 1950, AA had 50,000 members. After 1950 AA steadily expanded and inspired similar organizations such as Narcotics Anonymous, Gamblers Anonymous, and Overeaters Anonymous. In the early twenty-first century, AA could be found in one hundred nations in addition to the United States and had perhaps five to six million members worldwide (Humphreys, 2004).

The incredible expansion of AA has necessitated a flexible organizational structure to provide cohesion and communication, without sacrificing the important AA precepts of autonomy and self-governance. Two coordinating groups have acted to link together the thousands of AA local groups in the United States and abroad. In the first year of AA, the founders, along with members of the first New York City group, formed a tax-free charitable trust with a board of trustees composed of both alcoholic and nonalcoholic members. It acted as a mechanism for the collection and management of

An Alcoholics Anonymous meeting. HANK MORGAN/PHOTO RESEARCHERS, INC.

voluntary contributions and as a general repository of the collective experience of all AA groups.

As of the early twenty-first century the board of trustees consists of fourteen alcoholic and seven nonalcoholic members who meet quarterly. At an annual conference, specific regions elect the alcoholic board members for four-year terms. The board appoints the nonalcoholic members for a maximum of three terms of three years each. An annual conference was established in 1955 at the Twentieth Anniversary Convention of AA. It expresses to the trustees the opinions and experiences of AA groups throughout the movement. Individuals in the General Service Office (GSO) in New York City interpret and implement the deliberations of these two groups on a daily basis.

PHILOSOPHY AND PROGRAM OF ALCOHOLICS ANONYMOUS

In AA, alcoholism is viewed as a disease with physical, moral, and spiritual components. The disease is conceptualized as a chronic one, from which one is never cured, but from which one can be in recovery by practicing the principles of AA. The core principles of AA are known as the *Twelve Steps*, and practicing them is called *working the program*. Full sobriety is achieved when the individual is abstinent from alcohol and working the program, which loosely summarized consists of living out the ideals of honesty, humility, selflessness, and mindfulness, in relationship with a Higher Power and others in one's community. Although the achievement of abstinence alone is considered important, it is not considered complete recovery in itself (Humphreys, 2004).

The idea of a spiritual transformation is a core feature of the early origins of AA, as well as a cornerstone of its philosophy. The Higher Power of AA is conceptualized or defined individually by group participants. Members may subscribe to any of various characterizations of God as a power beyond themselves, for example, a personal figure such as Jesus Christ, the Christian concept of God, the ineffable mystery of the universe, or the awe-inspiring support and acceptance experienced through the community of AA fellowship. What is essential to the AA philosophy is not how members conceptualize the Higher Power, but rather that they are willing to give themselves over to that Higher Power, no longer relying exclusively on personal resources or ego for the answer to problems.

The spiritual aspect of AA can present an obstacle to participation for some would-be members. The use of the word *God* and *Higher Power* throughout the AA literature can be alienating for some persons who do not identify with such religious concepts. For these individuals, in particular, it is essential to point out that how one defines a power that lies beyond the self is individual and private, and it is not imposed by the organization. For this reason, the group emphasis on a power beyond the self need not prevent nonreligious individuals from becoming members (Humphreys, 2004).

AA asserts that in the disease of alcoholism, stopping drinking altogether, that is, total abstinence, is the core feature of recovery and that there is no place for drinking in moderation if one is an alcoholic. In the scientific literature, the outcome of abstinence versus moderate drinking not surprisingly appears to depend on the severity of physical dependence (Rosenberg, 1993). Having made the claim for abstinence, AA asserts that stopping the consumption of alcohol is necessary but not sufficient for full recovery. A *dry drunk* is an individual who is not drinking but who continues the behaviors typical of an alcoholic. Such individuals do not typically practice the steps that would lead to a spiritual transformation, and thus the chronic problems in their lives continue even though consumption of alcohol has ceased.

The AA program or path to sobriety is the Twelve Steps. They are as follows:

1. We admitted we were powerless over alcohol—that our lives had become unmanageable.

2. Came to believe that a Power greater than ourselves could restore us to sanity.

3. Made a decision to turn our will and our lives over to the care of God as we understood Him.

4. Made a searching and fearless moral inventory of ourselves.

5. Admitted to God, to ourselves, and to another human being the exact nature of our wrongs.

6. Were entirely ready to have God remove all these defects of character.

7. Humbly asked Him to remove our shortcomings.

8. Made a list of all persons we had harmed, and became willing to make amends to them all.

9. Made direct amends to such people wherever possible, except when to do so would injure them or others.

10. Continued to take personal inventory and when we were wrong promptly admitted it.

11. Sought through prayer and meditation to improve our conscious contact with God as we understood Him, praying only for knowledge of His will for us and power to carry that out.

12. Having had a spiritual awakening as the result of these steps, we tried to carry this message to alcoholics and to practice these principles in all our affairs.

PROCESS OF AFFILIATION

Affiliation is a process, not a single event within AA. Its elements and phases act to select and make ready certain alcoholics and problem drinkers for affiliation, leaving behind others with less readiness. The process begins before the problem drinker ever goes to a meeting (Trice, 1957). If the person has heard favorable reports about AA; if long-time drinking friendships have faded; if no will-power models of self-quitting have existed in the immediate background; and if the drinker has formed a habit of often sharing troubles with others, the stage is set for affiliation. It is further enhanced if, upon first attending meetings, the person has had experiences leading to the decision that the troubles associated with drinking far outweigh the pleasures of drinking (which is called *hitting bottom*). Typically, this means that affiliates, by contrasted with nonaffiliates, have had a longer and more severe history of alcoholism, and those with more severe alcohol problems are more likely to make consistent efforts to affiliate than are those with less severe problems (Emrick et al., 1993; Trice & Wahl, 1958).

Five other specific phases follow from those forces that make for commitment to the AA program: (1) first-stepping, (2) making a commitment, (3) accepting one's problem, (4) telling one's story, and (5) doing twelfth-step work (Rudy, 1986). First-stepping involves the initial contact with AA; it often entails orientation meetings that dwell on the group's notions of alcoholism as a disease and on step one in the twelve-step program: "We admitted we were powerless over alcohol...that our lives had become unmanageable." The newcomer in time may become associated with an experienced AA member, who may become the newcomer's sponsor. Quick action by the AA group—closeness of initial contact—to include the newcomer increases the likelihood of affiliation (Sonnenstuhl & Trice, 1987). Obviously interested newcomers are urged to take on the challenge of attending ninety meetings in ninety days. In effect, the receiving group seeks to keep a close watch over the newcomer, gently guiding the person to forego other commitments and increase commitments to the AA program.

Decisive third and fourth phases involve the willingness to tell one's own drinking story, with the beginning phrase, for example, "I'm Chris and I'm an alcoholic." Throughout the initial weeks and months, newcomers are gently and sometimes bluntly pressed to realize that they are alcoholics. They are encouraged to go public and tell their stories before the entire group at an open meeting. In numerous instances, newcomers may already have decided that they are alcoholic. In other cases, this realization may require a lengthy process of self-examination before it occurs. In still others, it may never occur, making them less likely to become authentic AA members. The public telling of one's story is an act of self-disclosure and ownership that conveys an inner conversion and acceptance of the precepts of AA. Members counsel newcomers on the appropriate first time to tell their stories, and their narrations are cause for many congratulations. Much applause typically attends this open act of commitment.

A final phase involves the literal execution of the program's twelfth step: "Having had a spiritual awakening as a result of these Steps, we tried to carry this message to alcoholics, and to practice these principles in all our affairs." In essence, doing twelfth-step work exemplifies a basic belief in AA, namely, one is never recovered from the disease; one is only recovering. As a consequence, a member can maintain sobriety only by remaining active in AA and by steadily engaging in carrying the program to those who are still active alcoholics. In short, by doing twelfth-step work, members reinforce their membership and the new definition of self.

Throughout this affiliation process, another dynamic can also be at work—slipping—a relapse into drinking by a recovering AA member. After reviewing six relevant studies, plus a summary of his own fieldwork with AA, Rudy reported that among both newly committed and longer-term members "slipping is a common occurrence, but it is possible that it serves a function in Alcoholics Anonymous.... [It is] a deviant behavior and the function of this deviance is boundary maintenance" (Rudy, 1980, p. 728). The response of most AA members to another's slipping is sympathy and understanding, sentiments that in turn enhance group solidarity. In essence, "their abstinence is dependent on interaction with those who slip" (Rudy, 1980, p. 731).

WHO AFFILIATES

What are the characteristics of people with drinking problems who undergo the affiliation process, contrasted with those who do not, even though exposed to the opportunity? Research in North America has consistently found no relationship between AA affiliation and demographic variables such as age, social class, race, employment status, and parental socio-economic status (Emrick et al., 1993; Trice & Roman, 1970). The fact that AA appeals to an extremely broad range of cultural, religious, and ethnic populations has been demonstrated by its adoption in cultures as diverse as Egypt, Brazil, Canada, India, Cameroon, Trinidad, and Japan, to cite only seven of more than one hundred nations in which the fellowship has taken hold (Humphreys, 2004).

Although it was once believed that AA affiliates have certain personality traits in common (Ogborne, 1989), this premise has not been demonstrated empirically. All that can be said confidently of research in this area is that sociability and comfort with group activities usually predict greater AA affiliation, and discomfort with spiritual/religious topics usually predicts less affiliation. Yet even these generalities deserve qualification, as Internet-based meetings as of 2008 offered AA affiliation without group meetings, and many self-proclaimed atheists are AA (Mäkelä et al., 1996; Winzelberg & Humphreys, 1999).

In contrast, alcohol-problem characteristics have fairly consistently been shown to predict AA participation. In general, participation in AA is more likely when an individual's drinking problem is severe, as indexed by symptoms of physical dependence, intense anxiety about and loss of control over consumption, and high volume bingeing (Emrick et al., 1993). Greater problem severity predicts help-seeking of all forms (i.e., not just AA, but also treatment). A heavy drinker is more likely to recognize the existence of a problem, and other people are more likely to express worry and urge the drinker to take steps to change. But AA also tends to appeal to more seriously alcoholic individuals because that is the population its approach and philosophy are designed to help. The common AA stories of compulsive drinking, physical dependence, and hitting bottom heard in meetings and found in *The Big Book* reflect the experiences of the organization's founders and make its fellowship a particularly good fit for individuals whose lives have been negatively shaped by alcohol use. In contrast, some less severe problem drinkers find that the AA emphasis on loss of control, life calamities caused by drinking, and the need for lifelong abstinence are alien and off-putting (Klaw & Humphreys, 2000).

THERAPEUTIC MECHANISM

AA provides a new orientation, toward alcohol, toward oneself, and toward others. "One of A.A.'s great strengths lies in the quality of its social environment: the empathetic understanding, the acceptance and concern which alcoholics experience there which, along with other qualities, make it easier to internalize new ways of feeling, thinking, and doing" (Maxwell, 1982). Even brief exposure to AA introduces the alcoholic to the idea that self-regulation seems to be rarely achieved solely by self-reliance and willpower. Its basic premise describes the compelling sense of ego powerlessness, but it immediately offers the potent substitute of a viable community that provides individual attention,

an explanation of alcoholism, and simple prescriptions for sobriety. "In a community that shares the same distresses and losses, accepts its members' vulnerabilities and applauds and rewards successes, A.A. provides a stabilizing, sustaining, and ultimately, transforming group experience" (Khantzian & Mack, 1989, p. 76).

Within the AA community, there are group-based specific therapeutic strategies unlikely to exist in professionally directed psychotherapy. Examples include (1) empirically based hope; (2) direct attack on denials; (3) practical guidelines for achieving sobriety; and (4) one-to-one sponsorship. When problem drinkers first attend meetings they are immediately aware of others who have confronted the same problem, and they hear these people speak about dramatic improvements in their lives through participation in AA and application of the twelve steps. Moreover, the AA program consistently reminds them that denial of the realities surrounding their drinking is a major barrier to any change. Telling one's story, either in open or closed sessions, helps to dissolve the entrenched denial that prevents positive change.

The twelve steps provide an organized approach for change and growing self-awareness. When members reach twelfth-step work, they see how much they have changed and how different they are from what they once had been, and this change reinforces their need to work the program. In addition, simple, practical guidelines are repeated in group-tested sayings that help people avoid using alcohol, such as first things first, one day at a time, and easy does it.

AA typically arranges for the informal sponsorship of newcomers, who often identify with and closely relate to their sponsors. Sponsors are recovering alcoholics who make themselves available at all hours of the day and night for phone or in-person discussion. Valuable treatment strategies are voluntary, free of charge, and occur between peers. Drinkers who drop out or who reject active membership in AA may nevertheless be helped by its unique therapeutic mechanisms. (Several organizations in the alcohol or drug recovery field use similar approaches.)

CRITICAL EVALUATIONS

AA existed for many years prior to much modern alcohol treatment research. As a result, it enjoyed a large membership and significant popular and professional respect long before it was subjected to rigorous scientific evaluation. Some critics noted the lack of scientific demonstrations of AA's effectiveness as recently as the 1980s (Peele, 1989). However, in subsequent years, a number of longitudinal studies confirmed what AA members had long believed: AA involvement is a potent predictor of achieving and maintaining abstinence from alcohol (Emrick et al., 1993; Humphreys, 2004). AA participation also predicts improved psychological and social functioning (Humphreys, 2004).

Timko and her colleagues (2006), for example, randomized 345 substance abuse treatment outpatients to receive either a routine referral to AA and Narcotics Anonymous or an intensive referral in which clinical staff and peers actively facilitated involvement in the fellowship (Timko et al., 2006). At six-month follow-up, rates of twelve-step group involvement were substantially higher in the intensive referral condition, and improvement in drug and alcohol problems was 60 percent greater as well. This does not imply that AA alone is sufficient for all individuals with alcohol problems. In a well-known clinical trial, Walsh and colleagues (1991) showed that while assignment to AA alone produced significant reductions in drinking and related problems, even greater improvement was experienced by individuals who received AA supplemented by professional treatment (Walsh et al., 1991). As of the early twenty-first century, AA was extremely well respected in the addictions field by a wide range of treatment professionals.

One aspect of AA that continued as of 2008 to generate skepticism from some potential members and helping professionals is its spiritual emphasis. This issue has been a particularly sore one in the U.S. court system. Although AA is not a religion, it has sufficient spiritual content to convince a number of judges that mandating AA participation (for example, for drinking and driving offenders) violates the separation of church and state (Humphreys et al., 2004). Discomfort with AA's spiritual aspect has also led some individuals to create alternative organizations with different philosophies, including Smart Recovery and Secular Organization for Sobriety. For most members, however, AA's spiritual focus is sufficiently flexible and subjective that it accommodates personal beliefs, regardless of religious orientation or lack thereof.

AA is a mutual-help group for the alleviation of human suffering related to alcoholism and is potentially distinct from other treatments for alcoholism in that it relies on peer alcoholics helping each other through a specified program of change. AA meetings are free, occur at all times of the day, all over the world, and are open to anyone who has a genuine desire to stop drinking and heal their disease. AA began in the 1930s when two alcoholics (Bill W. and Dr. Bob) met and shared their personal narratives and through that encounter helped each other begin a process of recovery from their own addiction to alcohol. The two then resolved to go out and help other alcoholics in a similar way. From the 1930s into the twenty-first century, AA evolved into a worldwide organization with five to six million members. AA is not a religion, but it does espouse the importance of a spiritual transformation in the process of recovery. The exact mechanism through which AA helps alcoholics is not fully understood, but most certainly it includes the creation of a new social milieu, acceptance by people who have been there, constant reinforcement to work the program, not the least of which is seeing among beginning members how one's life used to look, and direct attack on denials by a group sophisticated in the many guises denial can take. Studies show that people from varied backgrounds have joined and benefited from membership in AA but that AA may ultimately be more accessible to individuals with more severe alcohol dependence. Longitudinal studies have confirmed the clear benefit of involvement in AA for achieving and maintaining abstinence, as well as improved social and psychological functioning.

See also **Alcoholism: Abstinence versus Controlled Drinking; Alcoholism: Origin of the Term; Gambling; Treatment: An Overview of Alcohol Abuse/ Dependence.**

BIBLIOGRAPHY

Emrick, C. D., Tonigan, J. S., Montgomery, H., & Little, L. (1993). Alcoholics anonymous: What is currently known? In B. S. Mccrady & W. R. Miller (Eds.), *Research on Alcoholics Anonymous: Opportunities and alternatives* (pp. 41–78). New Brunswick, NJ: Rutgers Center for Alcohol Studies.

Humphreys, K. (2004). *Circles of Recovery: Self-Help Organizations for Addictions*. Cambridge, UK: Cambridge University Press.

Humphreys, K., & Tucker, J. A. (2002). Toward more responsive and effective intervention systems for alcohol-related problems. *Addiction, 97*, 126–132.

Humphreys, K., Wing, S., Mccarty, D., Chappel, J., Gallant, L., Haberle, B., et al. (2004). Self-help organizations for alcohol and drug problems: toward evidence-based practice and policy. *Journal of Substance Abuse Treatment, 26*, 151–158; discussion 159–165.

Khantzian, E. J., & Mack, J. E. (1989). Alcoholics Anonymous and contemporary psychodynamic theory. In Galanter (Ed.), *Recent developments in alcoholism: Treatment research*. New York: Plenum.

Klaw, E., & Humphreys, K. (2000). Life stories of Moderation Management mutual help group members. *Contemporary Drug Problems, 27*, 779–803.

Mäkelä, K., Arminen, I., Bloomfield, K., Eisenbach-Stangl, I., Helmersson Bergmark, K., Mariolini, N., et al. (1996). *Alcoholics Anonymous as a mutual help movement: A study in eight societies.* Madison: University of Wisconsin Press.

Maton, K. I. (1988). Social support, organizational characteristics, psychological well-being, and group appraisal in three self-help group populations. *American Journal of Community Psychology, 16*, 53–77.

Maxwell, M. (1982). Alcoholics Anonymous. In E. Gomberg, H. R. White, & A. Carpenter (Eds.), Alcohol, science and society revisited. Ann Arbor: University of Michigan Press.

Ogborne, A. C. (1989). Some limitations of Alcoholics Anonymous. In M. Galanter (Ed.), *Recent developments in alcoholism: Treatment research, volume 7* (pp. 55–66). New York: Plenum.

Peele, S. (1989). *Diseasing of America: Addiction treatment out of control.* Lexington, MA: Lexington Books.

Rosenberg, H. (1993). Prediction of controlled drinking by alcoholics and problem drinkers. *Psychological Bulletin, 113*, 129–139.

Rudy, D. R. (1980). Slipping and sobriety: The functions of drinking in A.A. *Quarterly Journal of Studies on Alcohol, 41*, 727–732.

Rudy, D. R. (1986). *Becoming alcoholic: Alcoholics Anonymous and the reality of alcoholism.* Carbondale: Southern Illinois University Press.

Sonnenstuhl, W. J., & Trice, H. M. (1987). The social construction of alcohol problems in a union's peer counseling program. *Journal of Drug Issues, 17*, 223–254.

Timko, C., Debenedetti, A., & Billow, R. (2006). Intensive referral to 12–Step self-help groups and 6-month substance use disorder outcomes. *Addiction, 101*, 678–688.

Trice, H. M. (1957). A study of the process of affiliation with A.A. *Quarterly Journal of Studies on Alcohol, 18*, 38–54.

Trice, H. M., & Roman, P. M. (1970). Sociopsychological predictors of affiliation with Alcoholics Anonymous: A longitudinal study of "treatment success." *Social Psychiatry, 5*, 51–59.

Trice, H. M., & Staudenmeier, W. J., Jr. (1989). A sociocultural history of Alcoholics Anonymous. In M. Galanter (Ed.), *Recent developments in alcoholism: Treatment research, Volume 7* (pp. 11–36). New York: Plenum.

Trice, H. M., & Wahl, R. (1958). A rank order analysis of the symptoms of alcoholism. *Quarterly Journal of Studies on Alcohol, 19*, 636–648.

W., W. (1949). The society of Alcoholics Anonymous. *American Journal of Psychiatry, 106*, 370–376.

Walsh, D. C., Hingson, R. W., Merrigan, D. M., Levenson, S. M., Cupples, L. A., Heeren, T., et al. (1991). A randomized trial of treatment options for alcohol-abusing workers. *New England Journal of Medicine, 325*, 775–782.

Winzelberg, A., & Humphreys, K. (1999). Should patients' religious beliefs and practices influence clinicians' referral to 12-step self-help groups? Evidence from a study of 3,018 male substance abuse patients. *Journal of Consulting and Clinical Psychology, 67*, 790–794.

HARRISON M. TRICE
REVISED BY ANNA LEMBKE (2009)
KEITH N. HUMPHREYS (2009)

ALCOHOLISM: ABSTINENCE VERSUS CONTROLLED DRINKING.

Until the 1970s therapists and researchers in the alcohol field accepted full and continuous abstinence as the only treatment goal for alcohol dependence. Every form of reduced use at the end of treatment was seen as complete failure and any renewed use after abstinence periods as a full relapse. This position became controversial when two young scientists published the results of a randomized clinical trial (Sobell & Sobell, 1973a, b) in which controlled drinking (CD) was not only observed but even supported as a treatment goal superior to traditional abstinence (not drinking [ND]). Amazingly, after 15 years of heavy debate and intensive research, the scientific community lost interest in this topic. Publications between 1985 and the early 2000s that attempted to clarify the mysteries of the debate were quite rare. Only a few empirical papers (e.g., Kavanagh et al., 1996; Heather et al., 2000; Dawson et al., 2005), some reviews and special journal issues (e.g., Sobell & Sobell, 1995), and a series of commentaries; a detailed review by Klingemann and colleagues (2004) and a special issue in *Addiction Research & Theory* with contributions by Coldwell and Heather (2006) and others have targeted CD in those years.

This entry reviews the early studies and discusses relevant terms and concepts for CD as well as the scientific evidence. A final section offers conclusions for healthcare practice and research. According to modern classification (*DSM-IV-TR*, American Psychiatric Association, 2003) the entry uses *alcohol use disorder* (AUD) as a generic term for *alcohol abuse* and *alcohol dependence*, and *alcohol use problems* will cover a broader range, including also hazardous alcohol use (e.g., daily use of more than recommended quantities).

BACKGROUND AND HISTORY

The heated debate over this partly invidious controversy is hard to understand for those who did not experience this research period beginning in about 1985. At that time patients were mostly severe alcohol dependents, and abstinence was the only accepted treatment goal. In addition, and contrary to views held in Europe, the philosophy of Alcoholics Anonymous (AA) was the major theoretical backdrop for this treatment concept in the United States as well as the dominant political power determining the allocation of research funding, which hindered studies that questioned the traditional belief system.

After initial remarks in an earlier publication (Davies, Myers, & Sheperd, 1956), Davies (1962) published results of a follow-up study with treated alcohol dependents, between seven and eleven years after discharge. He found that seven out of 93 showed a normal alcohol use pattern. This paper caused an intensive European debate in journals (e.g., commentaries in the *Quarterly Journal Studies of Alcohol* in 1962) and conferences (for a description see Glatt, 1995). The heavy but controlled debate spilled over the other side of the Atlantic when two treatment studies were published from Australia (Lovibond & Caddy, 1970) and the United States (Sobell & Sobell, 1973a, 1973b, 1976). For the first time, controlled drinking was recognized as a preferred treatment goal, accompanied by a specific program to support this

goal called *Individualized Behavior Therapy* (IBT). Components of IBT were, among others: functional analysis of the patients' drinking behavior (e.g., cues and reinforcement schedules), stress coping training, video confrontation with one's own (repulsive) behavior under the influence of alcohol and aversion therapy (in a bar situation, unwanted drinking behavior was punished by light electric stimulation). It is an irony that the Davies publication in 1962, which originally stimulated the debate on CD, was based on incorrect data about the drinking behavior of the seven patients (Edwards, 1985, 1994).

The design included two steps of treatment allocation (Sobell & Sobell, 1973a): 70 diagnosed male gamma-alcohol dependents according to the classification of Jellinek (1960), who had admitted themselves to treatment, were first assigned by the staff to either ND or CD. Patients were assigned on the basis of previous experiences with ND or CD, their personal preference, their belief in AA or CD principles, and the attitudes of their social support system. Then 50 percent of each group were randomly assigned to either an experimental or control condition. Each group received conventional state-hospital inpatient treatment: group discussions, participation in AA meetings, physiotherapy, and occupational therapy. The two experimental groups (ND- and CD-experimental) participated in 17 additional IBT sessions that took place in a bar and a living room-like laboratory setting (to establish real life conditions), with CD as goal in the CD groups and ND in the ND groups (Sobell & Sobell, 1973a). There is an inconsistency in the design description: According to Sobell and Sobell (1973b), the experimental groups did not receive the conventional treatment, in addition to IBT.

Follow-ups by the research group after one and two years analyzed the following: days of controlled alcohol use (maximum of six standard drinks daily), of full abstinence or relapse and days of "functioning well" (days of abstinence or CD), as well as a range of other outcome criteria (e.g., occupational, marital and driver's licence status, general outcome indices). A third year follow-up study was conducted by independent researchers who had no knowledge of the patients' treatment allocation (Caddy, Addington, & Perkins, 1978). The following results were found:

1. Subjects with the IBT program in the CD-setting (CD-E) had significantly more days of controlled alcohol use ("functioning well") than the controls (CD-C; 95% compared to 75% of the entire third year follow-up period);

2. CD-E had significantly fewer "drunk days" than CD-C, no differences were found for abstinent and CD days;

3. the "General Index of Outcome" was significantly better for CD-E than CD-C;

4. the IBT conditions (CD-E and ND-E) showed better outcomes in the vocational status than the controls. All reported significant differences between the CD groups that were not found between the two ND groups.

The results were quite stable over time and can be interpreted as follows:

1. IBT improves the combined rate of days with abstinence or controlled use ("functioning well") for patients with less severe alcohol use problems (CD conditions) compared to traditional treatment.

2. Patients with more severe problems (ND conditions) show a lower rate of "functioning well" days of alcohol use. This rate was not improved by IBT in comparison to traditional intervention.

Critics followed three lines of argumentation:

1. Based on the observation that the patients of the CD groups showed less severe alcohol use problems, the successful cases of CD were not seen as real *alcoholics*.

2. Others criticized the publication of the study because it might initiate an epidemic of relapse. The third critique by Pendery, Maltzman, and West (1982) accused the authors of having committed fraud, based on some questionable follow-up findings. This accusation heated up the controversy on the whole concept and conclusions, but was disproved later on by an independent committee (Dickens et al., 1982).

The background for the clash between the new concept and the dominant treatment philosophy at that time was a controversy about the degree of irreversibility of the problem behavior. "Loss of control" (Jellinek, 1960) was seen as the core symptom and as an unchangeable, biologically based incapacity of the alcohol dependent.

This viewpoint was supported by the AA movement and the treatment professionals. But it was questioned by two young psychologists who argued that alcohol dependence should not be seen as an irreversible disease state, but as a learned negative behavior pattern that could be relearned with application of behavior therapy techniques just like any other human behavior. (For a discussion of the resulting scientific and popular controversy, see Marlatt, 1983). The controversy played out on several levels: between traditional concepts and new models for the understanding of AUD, between longstanding experience and new scientific evidence, between psychiatrists/counsellors and psychologists, between old and young.

PARALLEL AND SUBSEQUENT SCIENTIFIC DEVELOPMENTS

CD began to lose its explosive force around 1985. Emerging scientific evidence fundamentally changed major views on the alcohol problem and its treatment:

1. Progress in epidemiology: Increasing epidemiological research since 1970 and a better observation and measurement of alcohol use have shown that a wide range of patterns and intensities of alcohol use problems and different relapse patterns exist (Miller, 1996).

2. Development of a public health view: The increasing knowledge on the amount and range of AUD in the general population has stimulated a broader public health view on alcohol problems and the question of how to reduce the alcohol-related burden of a country. It became obvious for preventive purposes to also reach the much larger group of problem drinkers who did not show signs of physical dependence (tolerance and withdrawal). Therefore further CD research concentrated on this new group, combining the CD treatment goal with new interventions such as cognitive behavior therapy (CBT), motivational interviewing (MI), and brief interventions (stimulated by first papers from Orford, Oppenheimer, & Edwards, 1976, and Miller & Joyce, 1979; for an overview see Bien, Miller, & Tonigan, 1993; Miller, Wilbourne, & Hettema, 2003).

3. Refinement of treatment designs and outcome measures: Progress in better controlled

experimental designs (e.g., Project Match, 1993), better classification of patients (e.g., *DSM-IV*), and better questionnaires for the full range of alcohol-related problems (e.g., the AUDIT-Alcohol Use Disorder Identification Test, Saunders et al., 1993) reduced the critique on methodological weaknesses of the early treatment studies.

SCIENTIFIC EVIDENCE FOR CD

Later data from the U.S. National Epidemiologic Survey on Alcohol and Related Conditions (NESARC, Dawson et al., 2005) reported 17.7 percent "low risk drinkers," and Vaillant (2003) found figures between 4 percent and 17 percent for "controlled drinking" (depending on the type of subcohort) in his 60-year longitudinal study. Treatment follow-up studies reported figures for CD in groups of "alcoholics" around 34 percent and in problem drinkers around 63 percent (Vogler, Weissbach, & Compton, 1977), 17 percent in groups with more or less severity of alcohol dependence (Heather et al., 2000), and 12 percent in alcohol dependents with ND treatments (Bottlender & Soyka, 2005; Polich, Armor, & Braiker, 1981). Altogether positive CD figures vary extremely between 5 percent and 90 percent (Körkel, 2002)!

Rosenberg (2004) summarized the patient and disorder characteristics that are found to be correlated with stable controlled drinking, either in ND or CD programs.

Severity of the dependence syndrome: One of the ongoing problems (Stockwell, 1986) and a topic of highly controversial debates remains the question if severity of AUD matters or not (Saunders et al., 1993). Both sides have some empirical support. Walters (2000) found in a meta-analysis of 17 CD trials that outcome is neither related to the severity of alcohol disorders nor to the type of *DSM* diagnosis. Miller and colleagues (1992) in a long-term follow-up study, Miller and Hester (1986) in a review, and Rosenberg (2004) concluded the contrary that dimensional measures of severity and dependence "reliably separated successful abstainers from successful asymptomatic drinkers" (Miller, 1992). Sanchez-Craig and Lei (1986) found that

in a group of behavior problem drinkers, CD is superior to the AB treatment goal. There is some evidence that patients with less severe symptoms have a higher probability for successful CD. But there is no evidence-based cut-off point available as of 2008 for the allocation of patients to either CD or AB.

Self-concept/self-efficacy and alcohol belief system: Subjects who reject "being an alcoholic," which is probably related to less experience of tolerance, withdrawal, and other severe negative consequences, who have a positive attitude towards CD (Orford & Keddie, 1986) or a high self-concept to control alcohol use (Kavanagh, Sitharthan, & Sayer, 1996) tend to have a better outcome in CD.

Drinker's choice of the treatment goal: Several studies have shown that positive CD outcomes can be increased by following the problem drinkers' choice of treatment and treatment target (Booth et al., 1992). If more severe alcohol dependents are involved, the majority tends to choose ND at the beginning of treatment or change later on to ND (Öjehagen & Berglund, 1989; Hodgins et al., 1997).

Social support: The degree of positive social support, such as the drinker's social network or family attitudes and willingness to support, are also correlated with better outcome (e.g., Moos, Finney & Cronkite, 1990).

One might expect, that after 45 years of research into CD, specific treatment components would have been developed and tested improving the rate of successfully treated patients with CD. But there is consensus among most of the researches involved in the field, and supported by many studies, reviews, and meta-analyses (e.g., Walters, 2000; Heather et al., 2000), that there is no specific intervention and no specific treatment target that leads to a significantly higher rate of CD.

REFLECTING ON THE CONTROLLED DRINKING CONTROVERSY

In an invited editorial for the journal *Addiction*, Sobell and Sobell (1995) drew three conclusions

Dimensions of CD	Characteristics of ideal CD	Examples of positive CD outcome
(1) Low risk amount of daily use	Abstinence or < 20 g pure alcohol/day/(f.) < 30 g pure alcohol/day/(m.)	Continuous abstinence or ≤ 4 days/month with higher use than 20/30 g.
(2) No binge drinking	Less than 4 (f) or 5 (m) drinks in a drinking situation	≤ 4 binges/month
(3) Situational full abstinence • traffic • workplace • hazardous sport • pregnancy/breast feeding • certain diseases • use of certain medication	Abstinence in all critical situations	≤ 4 occasions of alcohol use/month in critical situations
(4) No functional use • for sedation and stress reduction • to overcome social inhibition	No functional use in critical situations Alternative behavioral repertoire	Functional use in <10% of critical situations/month Alternative coping skills

Table 1. Dimensions of and criteria for ideal CD for subjects with AUD and examples of criteria for positive outcome. ILLUSTRATION BY GGS INFORMATION SERVICES. GALE, CENGAGE LEARNING

from the research in the previous 25 years which remain valid in the early 2000s:

1. Recovery of severe alcohol dependents involves predominantly ND.

2. Recovery of problem drinkers involves predominantly CD (they called it "reduced drinking").

3. The prevalence and pattern of CD seem to be independent of the selected treatment program content and goal.

After 40 years of research on CD the following key lessons have been learned (for recent overviews, see also Booth, 2006; Heather, 2006). First, contrary to AA and early scientific belief CD does occur, even in the groups of alcohol dependents, but more prevalent in alcohol abusers, with or without formal intervention and with CD or ND as treatment goal. Second, CD figures cannot be increased systematically, either by specific intervention components, the type of treatment goal (ND or CD), or by treatment allocation guidelines, based on patient or disorder characteristics. These conclusions are an intriguing challenge to researchers' understanding of the core components and mechanisms of dependence, but quite disappointing for clinical practice. The difficulty of handling CD in clinical practice might partly explain large

differences in the acceptance of CD: According to Rosenberg (2004), support for this treatment concept is widespread in Australia, Great Britain, and Scandinavia, whereas ND is the dominant approach in Northern America and Central and Western Europe.

CLARIFYING TERMS AND CONCEPTS FOR CONTROLLED DRINKING

Normal drinking, social drinking, non-problem drinking, controlled drinking, reduced drinking, light and moderate drinking are terms used to describe unproblematic alcohol use patterns beyond total abstinence (for details see Sobell & Sobell, 2004). This confusion is probably caused by a lack of clarity in defining and separating topics such as diagnoses (Babor & Caetano, 2008), treatment goals, treatment outcome criteria, or outcome measurement. Therefore, a core standard concept for CD is needed: From a public health view a pattern of low-risk use in terms of amount, pattern, situation, and drinking function should be the overall target for the whole (alcohol using) adult population, and also for CD of subjects with AUD. More specifically, this outcome would mean the following:

1. Less than about 30 g (m) resp. 20 g (f) pure alcohol/day (British Medical Association, 1995),

2. no binge drinking,

3. no alcohol use in critical situations like: workplace, dangerous sports, traffic, pregnancy, certain illnesses and use of certain medication,

4. no functional use to cope with stress, mood problems, or social deficits.

For historic and practical reasons researchers continue to use the term CD, but in the understanding and meaning of a low-risk alcohol use pattern. Table 1 depicts on the left side the mentioned dimensions of CD, in the center criteria for an ideal CD behavior, and on the right side examples for the definition of successful CD behavior in patient or population cohort studies. Such a concept could help to clarify CD behavior, and it enhances comparisons between different studies and allows comparable ratings of clinically relevant treatment progress.

IMPLICATIONS OF CONTROLLED DRINKING FOR CLINICAL PRACTICE

No sound evidence-based patient or disorders characteristics of successful CD have been detected as of 2008. Who is a candidate for CD? Clinical decisions should be guided by answers to the following questions:

1. Does the patient have a CD treatment goal preference and does he or she clearly believe in his or her abilities to cope with the demands of CD?

2. If yes,

3. Do patient and disorder characteristics enhance the probability for CD?

4. Do the somatic status and social/professional conditions allow CD?

5. Does a social support and control system exist for CD?

6. If all yes,

7. Do I as a therapist accept and support CD, and am I able to treat the patient adequately?

To be more on the safe side in therapeutic decision-making, it is recommended that only those patients be selected who have a higher chance for stable CD. Doing so would exclude patients with a more severe load of symptoms, more negative social conditions, a history of continued relapse, individuals with alcohol-related somatic disorders, and any patient with specific professional conditions that require full abstinence (e.g., pilots).

The decision process becomes even more complicated for deprived patients with longstanding and severe AUD, where abstinence is the only reasonable treatment choice, but is not accepted as a goal by patients. In these cases, is controlled use less harmful than uncontrolled use? There is no evidence as of 2008 for correct procedures, but an ethical requirement to also help those patients. Pros and cons have to be weighed carefully. Therapists have to base their decisions on personal experience and probably on a *stepped-care* procedure (Sobell & Sobell, 2000).

Heather (2006) distinguishes three target groups for CD:

1. Non-treatment seeking subjects with alcohol use problems: This group covers the hazardous/harmful alcohol users and those with *DSM-IV* abuse. They are either targeted by population-based preventive guidelines to control their drinking pattern or by early screening in the general medical services.

2. Subjects with alcohol use disorders seeking treatment: This group of patients can be found in outpatient and inpatient treatment centers and usually have at least a dependence diagnosis, with signs of a more severe state of dependence.

3. Subjects with severe alcohol use disorders and high comorbidity not motivated for treatment: This group is characterized by severe patterns of alcohol dependence, long history, high comorbidity, and a high level of social problems (homeless, unemployed, living in an alcohol positive environment). In many cases it is highly unrealistic to attempt to motivate these patients for abstinence treatment, and any improvement in the amount and pattern of abuse might be helpful for their survival.

As of 2008, much remained unexplained about the controlled drinking controversy. A cooperative effort involving addiction research, experimental psychology, and cognitive neuroscience is urgently needed to shed light on this 40-year-old mystery.

See also **Alcohol.**

BIBLIOGRAPHY

American Psychiatric Association. (2003). *Diagnostisches und Statistisches Manual Psychischer Störungen. DSM-IV-TR*. Deutsche Bearbeitung und Einführung von H.

Saß, H.-U. Wittchen, M. Zaudig und I. Houben. Göttingen: Hogrefe.

Babor, T. F., & Caetano, R. (2008). The trouble with alcohol abuse: What are we trying to measure, diagnose, count and prevent? *Addiction, 103*(7), 1057–1059.

Bechara, A., Noel, X., & Crone, E. A. (2006). Loss of will-power: Abnormal neural mechanisms of impulse control and decision making in addiction. In R. E. Wiers & A. W. Stacy (Eds.), *Handbook of implicit cognition and addiction* (pp. 215–232). Thousands Oaks, CA: Sage.

Bien, T. H., Miller, W. R., & Tonigan, J. S. (1993). Brief interventions for alcohol problems: A review. *Addiction, 88*(3), 315–335.

Booth, P. G. (2006). Idiosyncratic patterns of drinking in long-term successful controlled drinkers. *Addiction Research & Theory, 14*(1), 25–33.

Booth, P. G., Dale, B., Slade, P. D., & Dewey, M. E. (1992). A follow-up study of problem drinkers offered a goal choice option. *Journal of Studies on Alcohol, 53*(6), 594–600.

Bottlender, M., & Soyka, M. (2005). Outpatient alcoholism treatment: Predictors of outcome after 3 years. *Drug and Alcohol Dependence, 80*(1), 83–89.

British Medical Association. (1995). *Alcohol: Guidelines on sensible drinking.* London: Wiley.

Bühringer, G. (2006). Allocating treatment options to patient profiles: Clinical art or science? *Addiction, 101*(5), 646–652.

Bühringer, G., Wittchen, H.-U., Gottlebe, K., Kufeld, C., & Goschke, T. (2008). Why people change? The role of cognitive-control processes in the onset and cessation of substance abuse disorders. *International Journal of Methods in Psychiatric Research, 17*(Suppl. 1), S4–S15.

Caddy, G. R., Addington, H. J., Jr., & Perkins, D. (1978). Individualized behavior therapy for alcoholics: A third year independent double-blind follow-up. *Behavior Research and Therapy, 16*(5), 345–362.

Coldwell, B., & Heather, N. (2006). Introduction to the special issue. *Addiction Research & Theory, 14*(1), 1–5.

Davies, D. L. (1962). Normal drinking in recovered alcohol addicts. *Quarterly Journal of Studies on Alcohol, 23,* 94–104.

Davies, D. L., Myers, M., & Sheperd, M. (1956). The two-years' prognosis of 50 alcohol addicts after treatment in hospital. *Quarterly Journal of Studies on Alcohol, 17*(3), 485–502.

Dawson, D. A., Grant, B. F., Stinson, F. S., Chou, P. S., Huang, B., & Ruan, W. J. (2005). Recovery from *DSM-IV* alcohol dependence: United States, 2001–2002. *Addiction, 100*(3), 281–292.

Dickens, B. M., Doob, A. N., Warwick, O. H., & Winegrad, W. C. (1982). *Report of the Committee of Enquiry into Allegations Concerning Drs. Linda and Mark Sobell.* Toronto: Addiction Research Foundation.

Edwards, G. (1985). A later follow-up of a classic case series: D. L. Davies's 1962 report and its significance for the present. *Journal of Studies on Alcohol, 46*(3), 181–190.

Edwards, G. (1994). D. L. Davies and 'Normal drinking in recovered alcohol addicts': The genesis of a paper. *Drug and Alcohol Dependence, 35*(3), 249–259.

Glatt, M. M. (1995). Controlled drinking after a third of a century. *Addiction, 90*(9), 1157–1160.

Goschke, T. (2003). Voluntary action and cognitive control from a cognitive neuroscience perspective. In S. Maasen, W. Prinz, & G. Roth (Eds.), *Voluntary action: An issue at the interface of nature and culture* (pp. 49–85). Oxford: Oxford University Press.

Heather, N. (2006). Controlled drinking, harm reduction, and their roles in the response to alcohol-related problems. *Addiction Research & Theory, 14*(1), 7–18.

Heather, N., Brodie, J., Wale, S., Wilkinson, G., Luce, A., Webb, E. et al. (2000). A randomized controlled trial of moderation-oriented cue exposure. *Journal of Studies on Alcohol, 61*(4), 561–570.

Hodgins, D. C., Leigh, G., Milne, R., & Gerrish, R. (1997). Drinking goal selection in behavioral self-management treatment of chronic alcoholics. *Addictive Behaviors, 22*(2), 247–255.

Jellinek, E. M. (1960). *The disease concept of alcoholism.* New Brunswick, N.J.: Hillhouse.

Kavanagh, D. J., Sitharthan, T., & Sayer, G. P. (1996). Prediction of results from correspondence treatment for controlled drinking. *Addiction, 91*(10), 1539–1545.

Klingemann, H., Room, R., Rosenberg, H., Schatzmann, S., Sobell, L., & Sobell, M. (2004). *Kontrolliertes Trinken als Behandlungsziel— Bestandesaufnahme des aktuellen Wissens* [Controlled drinking as treatment goal—Appraisal of the current knowledge]. Bern: Hochschule für Sozialarbeit HSA. Zugriff am 02.05.2008. Verfügbar unter http://www.soziale-arbeit.bfh.ch/.

Körkel, J. (2002). Kontrolliertes trinken: Eine Übersicht. *Suchttherapie, 3*(2), 87–96.

Lovibond, S. H., & Caddy, G. R. (1970). Discriminated aversive control of alcoholics' drinking behavior. *Behavior Therapy, 1,* 437–444.

Marlatt, G. A. (1983). The controlled-drinking controversy. A commentary. *American Psychologist, 38*(10), 1097–1110.

Miller, W. R. (1992). Building bridges over troubled waters: A response to "Alcoholism, politics, and bureaucracy: The consensus against controlled-drinking therapy in America." *Addictive Behaviors, 17*(1), 79–81.

Miller, W. R. (1996). What is a relapse? Fifty ways to leave the wagon. *Addiction, 91*(Suppl. 12), S15–S27.

Miller, W. R., & Hester, R. K. (1986). The effectiveness of alcoholism treatment: What research reveals. In W. R. Miller & N. Heather (Eds.), *Treating addictive behaviors: processes of change* (pp. 121–174). New York: Plenum.

Miller, W. R., & Joyce, M. A. (1979). Prediction of abstinence, controlled drinking, and heavy drinking outcomes following behavioral self-control training. *Journal of Consulting and Clinical Psychology, 47*(4), 773–775.

Miller, W. R., Leckmann, A. L., Delaney, H. D., & Tinkcom, M. (1992). Long-term follow-up of behavioral self-control-training. *Journal of Studies on Alcohol, 53,* 249–261.

Miller, W. R., Wilbourne, P. L., & Hettema, J. E. (2003). What works? A summary of alcohol treatment outcome research. In R. K. Hester & W. R. Miller (Eds.), *Handbook of alcoholism treatment approaches: Effective alternatives* (3rd ed., pp. 13–63). Boston: Allyn and Bacon.

Moos, R. H., Finney, J. W., & Cronkite, R. C. (1990). *Alcoholism treatment: Context, process and outcome.* New York: Oxford University Press.

Öjehagen, A., & Berglund, M. (1989). Changes of drinking goals in a two-year out-patient alcoholic treatment program. *Addictive Behaviors, 14*(1), 1–9.

Orford, J., & Keddie, A. (1986). Abstinence or controlled drinking in clinical practice: A test of the dependence and persuasion hypotheses. *Addiction, 81*(4), 495–504.

Orford, J., Oppenheimer, E., & Edwards, G. (1976). Abstinence or control: The outcome for excessive drinkers two years after consultation. *Behavior Research and Therapy, 14*(6), 409–418.

Pendery, M. L., Maltzman, I. M., & West, L. J. (1982). Controlled drinking by alcoholics? New findings and a reevaluation of a major affirmative study. *Science, 217,* 169–175.

Polich, J. M., Armor, D. J., & Braiker, H. B. (1981). *The course of alcoholism: Four years after treatment.* New York: Wiley.

Project Match Research Group. (1993). Project MATCH: Rationale and methods for a multisite clinical trial matching patients to alcoholism treatment. *Alcoholism: Clinical and Experimental Research, 17,* 1130–1145.

Rosenberg, H. (1993). Prediction of controlled drinking by alcoholics and problem drinkers. *Psychological Bulletin, 113*(1), 129–139.

Rosenberg, H. (2004). International research: Target groups. In H. Klingemann, R. Room, H. Rosenberg, S. Schatzmann, L. Sobell, & M. Sobell (Eds.), *Kontrolliertes Trinken als Behandlungsziel—Bestandesaufnahme des aktuellen Wissens* [Controlled drinking as treatment goal—appraisal of the current knowledge] (pp. 69–79). Bern: Hochschule für Sozialarbeit HSA. Zugriff am 30.06.2008 unter http://www.soziale-arbeit.bfh.ch/.

Sanchez-Craig, M., & Lei, H. (1986). Disadvantages to imposing the goal of abstinence on problem drinkers: An empirical study. *Addiction, 81*(4), 505–12.

Saunders, J. B., Aasland, O. G., Babor, T. F., de, la Fuente, Jr., & Grant, M. (1993). Development of the Alcohol Use Disorders Identification Test (AUDIT): WHO Collaborative Project on Early Detection of Persons with Harmful Alcohol Consumption--II. *Addiction, 88*(6), 791–804.

Sobell, M. B., & Sobell, L. C. (1973 a). Individualized behavior therapy for alcoholics. *Behavior Therapy, 4*(1), 49–72.

Sobell, M. B., & Sobell, L. C. (1973 b). Alcoholics treated by individualized behavior therapy: One year treatment outcome. *Behavior Research and Therapy, 11*(4), 599–618.

Sobell, M. B., & Sobell, L. C. (1976). Second year treatment outcome of alcoholics treated by individualized behavior therapy: Results. *Behavior Research and Therapy, 14*(3), 195–215.

Sobell, M. B., & Sobell, L. C. (1995). Controlled drinking after 25 years: How important was the great debate? *Addiction, 90*(9), 1149–1153.

Sobell, M. B., & Sobell, L. C. (2000). Stepped care as a heuristic approach to the treatment of alcohol problems. *Journal of Consulting and Clinical Psychology, 68*(4), 573–579.

Sobell, M. B., & Sobell, L. C. (2004). Semantics and definitions. In H. Klingemann, R. Room, H. Rosenberg, S. Schatzmann, L. Sobell, & M. Sobell (Eds.), *Kontrolliertes Trinken als Behandlungsziel— Bestandesaufnahme des aktuellen Wissens* [Controlled drinking as treatment goal—appraisal of the current knowledge] (pp. 35–40). Bern: Hochschule für Sozialarbeit HSA. Zugriff am 30.06.2008 unter http://www.soziale-arbeit.bfh.ch/.

Stockwell, T. (1986). Cracking an old chestnut: Is controlled drinking possible for the person who has been severely alcohol dependent? *British Journal of Addiction, 81*(4), 455–456.

Vaillant, G. E. (2003). A 60-year follow-up of alcoholic men. *Addiction, 98*(8), 1043–1051.

Verdejo-Garcia, A., Bechara, A., Recknor, E. C., & Perez-Garcia, M. (2006). Executive dysfunction in substance dependent individuals during drug use and abstinence: An examination of the behavioral, cognitive and emotional correlates of addiction. *Journal of the International Neuropsychological Society, 12*(3), 405–415.

Vogler, R. E., Weissbach, T. A., & Compton, J. V. (1977). Learning techniques for alcohol abuse. *Behavior Research and Therapy, 15*(1), 31–38.

Walters, G. D. (2000). Behavioral self-control training for problem drinkers: A meta-analysis of randomized control studies. *Behavior Therapy, 31,* 135–149.

GERHARD BÜHRINGER

ALCOHOLISM: ORIGIN OF THE TERM.
The term *alcoholism* is of relatively recent date; knowledge of the adverse effects of heavy alcohol

(ethanol) consumption is not. A proverb describes alcohol as "both mankind's oldest friend and oldest enemy." Alcohol occurs in nature, and humans have long known how to ferment plants to create it; both its moderate and excessive use have therefore occurred since prehistory. The Bible cautions: "Do not look at wine when it is red, when it sparkles in the cup and goes down smoothly. At the end it bites like a serpent and stings like an adder" (Proverbs 23:31–32). A drunken Noah (Genesis 9:20–28) is one of a long line of such literary descriptions. In the Greco-Roman era drunks appeared in the *Character Sketches* of Theophrastus, in the *Satyricon* of Petronius Arbiter, and in the *Epistles* of Seneca. Shakespeare's porter in *Macbeth* (Act II, Scene 3) was another.

EARLY HISTORY

Viewing the long-term adverse effects of alcohol as a disease predates the term *alcoholism*. Benjamin Rush (1745–1813) and Thomas Trotter (1760–1832), both physicians, wrote extensively in this vein, using words such as *drunkenness*. Their elder contemporary Benjamin Franklin (1706–1790) produced a glossary of 228 synonyms in use in 1737 for "being under the influence of alcohol." It was not until 1849 that the Swedish physician and temperance advocate Magnus Huss (1807–1890) first used the word *alcoholism* in his book *Alcoholismus Chronicus (The Chronic Alcohol-disease)*. Huss's term, used originally in a descriptive sense to denote the consequences of the prolonged consumption of large quantities of alcohol, has come to connote a disease, believed by some to result in such consumption.

Huss meant by the term *chronic alcoholism* "those pathologic symptoms which develop in such persons who over a long period of time continually use wine or other alcoholic beverages in large quantities" and stated that it "corresponds with chronic poisoning." His book is filled with detailed case histories illustrating the various symptoms that might occur. Sweden was at that time ranked highest in the list of countries that consumed liquors, and Huss, as attending physician to the Serafim Clinic in Stockholm, had ample opportunity to observe cases. The London *Daily News* of December 8, 1869, carried a story on "the deaths of two persons from alcoholism," which according to the *Oxford English Dictionary* was the first popular use of the word in English. From that time on, its use in both the professional and the popular literature greatly expanded.

TEMPERANCE MOVEMENT

In the United States during this period, the term *drunkness* was commonly used to refer to excessive use of alcohol. The Temperance Movement during the nineteenth and early twentieth centuries in America arose in response to increasing social and physiological difficulties attributed to drunkenness. With the growing use of distilled drinks in America, increased awareness was drawn to their effects when used to excess (domestic violence, decreased work performance, etc.). As a result, groups inspired by religious leaders advocating moderation in (temperance) or abstention from alcohol use came together in the Temperance Movement. Temperance Associations, many of them based in the New England states, formed in increasing numbers. At the zenith of the movement (1830s), there were more than 6,000 local Temperance organizations across the United States.

The Temperance movement was international. One of the first U. S. groups to cross the ocean was the Order of the Good Templars, formed in Utica, New York, in 1851. Among the most popular Temperance Groups in America were the Women's Christian Temperance Union (created in 1874) and the Anti-Saloon League (founded in 1895). Among the more well-known Temperance advocates were Carrie Nation, Susan B. Anthony, and Frances E. Willard. Some of the lasting effects of the women's temperance movement were the passage of legislation requiring government regulation of the import, manufacture, and sale of alcohol; impetus toward research on the long-term and chronic effects of alcohol use; and a mandate that alcohol education become part of the national academic curriculum for primary and secondary students.

As these factions gained in membership and power in America, they essentially became political activist groups and effectively lobbied for governmental control of liquor throughout the country. They were successful in the creation and passage of numerous pieces of legislation, one of which was the 18th Amendment authorizing prohibition.

PROHIBITION

During the period of national prohibition in the United States (1919–1933) little attention was paid to the consequences of alcohol consumption. Because consumption was illegal—permanently, it was assumed—it was thought that there would be few consequences. Indeed, such consequences as cirrhosis of the liver did decline abruptly during this period. But as enthusiasm for prohibition waned, and especially after it was repealed, a need to promote treatment became increasingly evident. One group involved in this promotion used *alcoholism* as the key word in their efforts, and accordingly were called the *alcoholism movement* by sociologists who subsequently studied their work. In an early statement of this movement, Dwight Anderson (1942) predicted that "When the dissemination of these ideas is begun through the existing media of public information, press, radio, and platform, which will consider them as news, a new public attitude can be shaped." It was also felt that the term, together with the disease connotations attached to it, would encourage the involvement of physicians in its study and treatment. The medical profession was viewed as critical to the success of the effort to increase the nation's concern about the consequences of alcohol consumption. The formation in 1944 of the National Council on Alcoholism, the largest public interest group in this area, was a project of the same movement. Their successful efforts may be the reason that the term *alcoholism* developed and sustained a degree of popularity in the United States beyond that which it achieved in Europe or even in Scandinavia, where it was first used.

CENTER OF ALCOHOL STUDIES

During the late 1930s and 1940s, the Center of Alcohol Studies, the first interdisciplinary research center devoted exclusively to alcohol-related problems and issues, was developed. Initially located at Yale University, it was directed by physician Dr. Edward W. Haggard (Yale University Laboratory of Applied Physiology and Biodynamics) and also physiologist and biostatistician E. M. Jellinek. Jellinek headed the Section on Alcohol Studies, which focused on the effects of alcohol on the body. Dr. Haggard was also the founder in 1940 of the seminal publication titled the *Quarterly Journal of Studies on Alcohol*. The *Quarterly Journal of Studies on Alcohol* has evolved into the highly respected, juried *Journal of Studies on Alcohol*.

With the concept of alcoholism growing through Prohibition, there was an increased need for studying the subject, resulting in the creation of Yale's Summer School of Alcohol Studies in 1943. In 1944 Yale founded the Yale Pain Clinics, the first outpatient alcoholism treatment facilities in the nation.

The Yale Center of Alcohol Studies was at the forefront of the medical and sociocultural movement dedicated to the recognition of alcoholism as a major public health issue. As a result, in the 1950s the American Medical Association formally accepted alcoholism as a diagnosable and treatable illness.

In 1962 the Center relocated from Yale to Rutgers University. Subject matter experts from the Center are frequently called upon by the World Health Organization, the National States' Conference on Alcoholism, the Cooperative Commission on the Study of Alcoholism, and by the National Council on Alcoholism Blue Ribbon Panels. The Center is largely responsible for federal legislation that created the National Alcohol Research Center Program.

UNDERSTANDING OF ALCOHOLISM BROADENED

As the term *alcoholism* became widely used, its meaning broadened. In a 1941 review of treatment, ten definitions of chronic alcoholism and sixteen definitions of alcohol addiction were collected from the international literature. Originally used by Huss to refer to a disease that consisted of the *consequences* of alcohol consumption, *alcoholism* came in time to represent a disease that *caused* high levels of alcohol consumption (Jellinek, 1960). A variant theory attempts to preserve the original meaning: High levels of alcohol consumption resulted in damage to the central nervous system, which in turn caused the high levels of consumption to continue (Vaillant, 1983). That is, the term *alcoholism* evolved over time from a primarily descriptive term to a largely explanatory concept. An example of a definition of *alcoholism* with clear explanatory intent is one that Robert Rinaldi and colleagues produced in 1988 through an elaborate consensus exercise (a Delphi process) among eighty American experts, who defined the term as "a chronic, progressive, and potentially fatal biogenetic and psychosocial disease characterized by tolerance and physical dependence manifested by a loss of control, as well as diverse personality changes and social consequences" (Rinaldi et al., 1988). As a counterpoint to this development, a growing and increasingly influential literature holds that problems developing in the context of alcohol consumption do not constitute a disease at all (Fingarette, 1988).

The greater interest taken in alcohol consumption and its consequences as a result of the popularization of the term *alcoholism* has been both useful and problematic. For example, in a review of alternative definitions, Thomas Babor and Ronald Kadden (1985) concluded: "Clearly, the past and present lack of consensus concerning the definition of alcoholism and the criteria for its diagnosis does not provide a solid conceptual basis to design screening procedures for early detection or casefinding." Because of its imprecise meaning, the term *alcoholism* was now dropped from the two major official systems of diagnosis of diseases—the International Classification of Diseases of the World Health Organization and the *Diagnostic and Statistical Manual of Mental Disorders* (*DSM-IV-TR*) of the American Psychiatric Association—where it has been replaced by a variety of alcohol-use, alcohol-related, and alcohol-induced disorder terminologies. A recent comprehensive study of treatment deliberately avoided the use of the word *alcoholism*, but suggested that the word was not incompatible with the phrase that it chose to use—*alcohol problems*—to refer to any problem occurring in the context of alcohol consumption (Institute of Medicine, 1990, pp. 30–31).

COMPLEX PROBLEMS

Recent attempts to be precise represent a return to the more straightforward, descriptive use of *alcoholism* by its originator, Huss. Two major realities contributed to this change of direction. One is that the problems people experience from alcohol use are complex. Although alcohol may be a factor in some such problems—even an important factor—it is not often the full explanation for them. Multiple factors, including heredity, early environment, cultural factors, personality factors, situational factors, and others, contribute to the development of human problems and must be considered in their resolution. This formulation does not minimize the important role of alcohol in such problems or say that reducing or eliminating alcohol consumption may not be a critical factor in resolving them. Secondly, an extremely broad spectrum of problems arises in the context of alcohol consumption. Although a substantial proportion of these problems arise from those who drink too much over a long period of time and who usually have multiple problems (those to whom the term *alcoholism* is applied), an even greater burden of problems arises from those who drink too much over *short* periods

of time and who have only a *few* problems. The simple reason is that there are more of the latter than of the former (Institute of Medicine, 1990, chapter 9). Effectively reducing the burden upon society requires dealing with both populations. An exclusive concentration on *alcoholism* may overlook this reality.

The term *alcoholism* retains its place in general, nontechnical speech as an indicator of serious problems that are the consequences of prolonged heavy alcohol consumption. Its continued popularity has some advantages, for the public-health consequences of such alcohol consumption are enormous. The presence of a convenient shorthand term for this fact in the public consciousness—*alcoholism*—serves as a continuing reminder of this major unfinished item on the public-health agenda. Certainly, there is a legitimate place in society for the use of alcohol. With equal certainty, too many individuals fail to use alcohol wisely or well.

COSTLY CONSEQUENCES

The ravages that prolonged exposure to alcohol produces in the human body are manifold, as Huss well understood. They include, but are not limited to, neurological problems (damage to the central and peripheral nervous systems), cirrhosis (fibrosis and shrinking) and other diseases of the liver, hypertension (high blood pressure), heart disease, psychological disorders, and many forms of cancer, particularly of the digestive tract. Added to these, consequences of short-term but intense exposure to alcohol also include the common behavioral effects of intoxication as well as a high proportion of all accidents, burns, violence, suicide, and especially automobile crashes.

The National Survey on Drug Use and Health (NSDUH) asks persons who are 12 or more years of age a variety of questions about alcohol use, abuse, and dependence during the past year, using *DSM-IV*-specified criteria such as symptoms of withdrawal, increased tolerance, use in dangerous situations, interactions with law enforcement and the legal system, and interference with major obligations and responsibilities such as school, job, or family. According to averages gleaned from surveys conducted in 2002, 2003, and 2004; 7.6 percent, or 18.2 million people, age 12 or older met clinical criteria for alcohol abuse or dependence. Broken out by age group, this corresponds to 5.9 percent of those aged 12 to 17, 17.4 percent of those 18 to 25, 11.1 percent of 26 to 34 year olds, 7.5 percent aged 35 to 49, and 3.0 percent among those 50 or more years of age.

When looked at in terms of ethnicity, Native Americans or Alaskan Natives had the highest incidence of alcohol abuse or dependence (14.0%), followed by Native Hawaiians or Pacific Islanders (8.5%), Hispanics (8.2%), Caucasians (7.9%), African-Americans (6.5%), and Asians (4.3%). Poverty and alcohol abuse or dependence are statistically linked: 9.4 percent of persons with family incomes of less than 125 percent of the federal poverty threshold met abuse or dependence criteria. This decreased to 7.7 percent of those with family incomes between 125 percent and 199 percent of federal poverty threshold, fell to 7.2 percent of those with family incomes between 200 percent and 399 percent of the federal poverty threshold, and remained at 7.2 percent of those living at 400 percent or more of the federal poverty threshold. Individuals who met criteria for alcohol abuse or dependence were also more likely to have been treated at an emergency medical facility (ER or Urgent Care facility) than their non-alcohol abusing or dependent peers (34.2% and 27.9%, respectively).

The difficulties that alcohol abuse or dependence create are legion—and its remediation would be a remarkable step forward.

See also **Alcohol: History of Drinking in the United States; National Survey on Drug Use and Health (NSDUH); Prohibition of Alcohol; Temperance Movement; Woman's Christian Temperance Union.**

BIBLIOGRAPHY

American Psychiatric Association. (2000, with revision 2004, October). *DSM-IV-TR: Diagnostic and statistical manual of mental disorders.* (4th ed.). Washington, DC: American Psychiatric Association.

Anderson, D. (1942). Alcohol and public opinion. *Quarterly Journal of Studies on Alcohol, 3,* 376.

Babor, T. F., & Kadden, R. (1985). Screening for alcohol problems: Conceptual issues and practical considerations. In N. C. Chong & H. M. Cho (Eds.), *Early identification of alcohol abuse* (pp. 1–30). Washington, DC: U.S. Government Printing Office.

Bynum, W. F. (1968). Chronic alcoholism in the first half of the 19th century. *Bulletin of the History of Medicine, 42,* 160–185.

Chen, C. M. & Yi, H. (2006, August). *Surveillance Report #77: Trends in alcohol-related morbidity among short-stay community hospital discharges, United States, 1979–2004.* Bethesda, MD: National Institute on Alcohol Abuse and Alcoholism, Division of Epidemiology and Prevention Research, Alcohol Epidemiologic Data System.

Fingarette, H. (1988). *Heavy drinking: The myth of alcoholism as a disease.* Berkeley: University of California Press.

Huss, M. (1852). *Chronische alkoholskrankheit oder alcoholismus chronicus* [Alcoholismus chronicus or the chronic alcohol disease]. (G. van dem Busch, Trans., into German from the Swedish, with revisions by the author). Stockholm and Leipzig: C. E. Fritze. (Original work published 1849).

Institute of Medicine. (1990). *Broadening the base of treatment for alcohol problems.* Washington, DC: National Academy Press.

Institute of Medicine. (1987) *Causes and consequences of alcohol problems: An agenda for research.* Washington, DC: National Academy Press.

Jellinek, E. M. (1960). *The disease concept of alcoholism.* Highland Park, NJ: Hillhouse Press.

Lakins, N. E., Williams, G. D. & Yi, H. (2006, August). *Surveillance report #78: Apparent per capita alcohol consumption: National, state, and regional trends, 1977–2004.* Bethesda, MD: National Institute on Alcohol Abuse and Alcoholism, Division of Epidemiology and Prevention Research, Alcohol Epidemiologic Data System.

National Institute on Alcohol Abuse and Alcoholism. (2000, June). *10th special report to the U.S. Congress on alcohol and health.* (NIH Publication No. 00-1583). Rockville, MD: U.S. Department of Health and Human Services, National Institutes of Health.

Newes-Adeyi, G., Chen, C. M., Williams, G. D. & Faden, V. B. (2005, October). *Surveillance report #74: Trends in underage drinking in the United States, 1991–2003.* Bethesda, MD: National Institute on Alcohol Abuse and Alcoholism, Division of Epidemiology and Prevention Research, Alcohol Epidemiologic Data System.

Rehm, J., Gmel, G., Sempos, C. T., & Trevisan, M. (2003). Alcohol-related morbidity and mortality. *Alcohol Research & Health, 27*(1), 39–51.

Rinaldi, R. C., Steindler, E. M., Wilford, B. B., & Goodwin, D. (1988). Clarification and standardization of substance abuse terminology. *Journal of the American Medical Association, 259,* 555–557.

Substance Abuse and Mental Health Services Administration, Office of Applied Studies. (2005). *Results from the 2004 National Survey on Drug Use and Health: National findings.* (DHHS Publication No. SMA 05-4062, NSDUH Series H-28). Rockville, MD: Author.

Substance Abuse and Mental Health Services Administration, Office of Applied Studies. (2004). *Results from the 2003 National Survey on Drug Use and Health:*

National findings. (DHHS Publication No. SMA 04-3964, NSDUH Series H-25). Rockville, MD: Author.

Substance Abuse and Mental Health Services Administration, Office of Applied Studies. (2003). *Results from the 2002 National Survey on Drug Use and Health: National findings.* (DHHS Publication No. SMA 03-3836, NSDUH Series H-22). Rockville, MD: Author.

Turner, T. B., Borkenstein, R. F., Jones, R. K., & Santora, P. B. (Eds.). (1985). *Alcohol and highway safety.* (Supplement no. 10 to the *Journal of Studies on Alcohol*). New Brunswick, NJ: Rutgers University Center of Alcohol Studies.

U.S. Alcohol Epidemiologic Data Reference Manual. (1994, July). *County alcohol problem indicators, 1986–1990.* (4th ed.). (Vol. 3). (NIH Publication No. 94-3747). Rockville, MD: U.S. Department of Health and Human Services.

U.S. Alcohol Epidemiologic Data Reference Manual. (1996 September). *State trends in alcohol-related mortality, 1979–92.* (1st ed.). (Vol. 5). (NIH Publication No. 96-4174). Rockville, MD: U.S. Department of Health and Human Services.

U.S. Alcohol Epidemiologic Data Reference Manual. (1998, November). *Drinking in the United States: Main findings from the 1992 National Longitudinal Alcohol Epidemiologic Survey (NLAES).* (1st ed.). (Vol. 6). (NIH Publication No. 99-3519). Rockville, MD: U.S. Department of Health and Human Services.

U.S. Alcohol Epidemiologic Data Reference Manual. (2003, June). *State trends in drinking behaviors, 1984–2001.* (Vol. 7). (NIH Publication No. 02-5213). Rockville, MD: U.S. Department of Health and Human Services.

U.S. Alcohol Epidemiologic Data Reference Manual. (2004, June). *U.S. apparent consumption of alcoholic beverages based on state sales, taxation, or receipt data.* (4th ed.). (Vol. 1). (NIH Publication No. 04-5563). Rockville, MD: U.S. Department of Health and Human Services.

U.S. Alcohol Epidemiologic Data Reference Manual. (2006, January). *Alcohol use and alcohol use disorders in the United States: Main findings from the 2001–2002 National Epidemiologic Survey on Alcohol and Related Conditions (NESARC).* (Vol. 8). (NIH Publication No. 05-5737). Rockville, MD: U.S. Department of Health and Human Services.

Vaillant, G. E. (1983). *The natural history of alcoholism: Causes, patterns, and paths to recovery.* Cambridge, MA: Harvard University Press.

World Health Organization. (2004). *Global status report on alcohol 2004.* (WM 274 [NLM Classification]). Geneva, Switzerland: World Health Organization, Department of Mental Health and Substance Use.

Yi, H., Chen, C. M., & Williams, G. D. (2006, August). *Surveillance report #76: Trends in alcohol-related fatal traffic crashes, United States, 1977–2004.* Bethesda, MD: National Institute on Alcohol Abuse and Alcoholism, Division of Epidemiology and Prevention Research, Alcohol Epidemiologic Data System.

Yoon, Y. & Yi, H. (2006, August). *Surveillance report #75: Liver cirrhosis mortality in the United States, 1970–2003.* Bethesda, MD: National Institute on Alcohol Abuse and Alcoholism, Division of Epidemiology and Prevention Research, Alcohol Epidemiologic Data System.

FREDERICK B. GLASER
REVISED BY PAMELA V. MICHAELS (2009)

ALKALOIDS. This is the general term for any number of complex organic bases that are found in nature in seed-bearing plants. These substances are usually colorless but bitter to the taste. Alkaloids often contain nitrogen and oxygen and possess important physiological properties.

Examples of alkaloids include not only quinine, atropine, and strychnine but also caffeine, nicotine, morphine, codeine, and cocaine. Therefore, many drugs that are used by humans for both medical and nonmedical purposes are produced in nature in the form of alkaloids. Naturally occurring receptors for many alkaloids have also been identified in humans and other animals, suggesting an evolutionary role for the alkaloids in physiological processes.

See also **Caffeine; Cocaine; Codeine; Morphine; Nicotine.**

BIBLIOGRAPHY

Fattorusso, E., & Taglialatela-Scafati, O., Eds. (2007). *Modern alkaloids: Structure, isolation, synthesis and biology.* Weinheim, Germany: Wiley-VCH.

Hesse, M. (2002). *Alkaloids.* Weinheim, Germany: Wiley-VCH.

NICK E. GOEDERS

ALLERGIES TO ALCOHOL AND DRUGS. In addition to alcohol, opiates, and barbiturates, some street drugs have been reported to induce allergic reactions. These allergic phenomena are most frequently mediated by reactions of the immune system known as immediate hypersensitivity and delayed hypersensitivity. Immediate hypersensitivity is mediated by the serum protein immunoglobulin E (IgE), whereas delayed hypersensitivity is mediated by thymus-derived lymphocytes (the white blood cells called T cells).

IMMEDIATE HYPERSENSITIVITY

The symptoms and signs associated with IgE-mediated immune reactions are urticaria (hives); bronchospasm that produces wheezing; angioedema (swelling) of face and lips, or full-blown anaphylaxis (a combination of all the above symptoms and lowering of blood pressure). Abdominal pain and cardiac arrhythmias (irregular heartbeat) may also occur with anaphylaxis. Any or all of these symptoms occur when IgE, which has previously been synthesized by a sensitized lymphocyte, fixes to mast cells or basophils in the skin, bronchial mucosa, and intestinal mucosa. This cell-fixed IgE then binds the antigen that triggers the release of the following: histamine, slow-reacting substance of anaphylaxis (SRSA), bradykinin, and other mediators that induce these symptoms. Examples of this type of allergic reaction are the allergic responses to either bee stings or to penicillin.

Similar symptoms may also occur when mediators are released by mast cells in response to chemical or physical stimuli, which is called an anaphylactoid reaction. In this instance, the mast cell or basophil is directly activated by the chemical to release mediators without having to bind to IgE. Examples of this type of reaction are responses to intravenous contrast material, such as dye injected for diagnostic imaging procedures, or the hives induced by exposure to cold.

DELAYED HYPERSENSITIVITY

Reactions occur when antigenic chemicals stimulate T lymphocytes and induce their proliferation. T effector cells are then recruited into the tissue site. These effector cells bind the antigen and subsequently release effector molecules, such as interleukins, chemotactic factors, and enzymes. These effector molecules induce an inflammatory response in the area and may also induce formation of a granuloma (a mass of inflamed tissue) by macrophages and inflammatory cells. Symptoms of delayed hypersensitivity reactions are skin rashes, which may be red, pruritic (itchy), or bullous (blistered) in nature. Granulomas can cause lymph node enlargement and nodules in the skin or in organs. Examples of this response are poison ivy, cosmetic allergies, erythema nodosum, and sarcoidosis.

ALLERGIC RESPONSE TO ALCOHOL

True anaphylactic or anaphylactoid reactions to alcohol (ethanol) are rare. More commonly, people who report hives, facial flushing, nausea, tachycardia, or other reactions to alcohol are actually experiencing the so-called alcohol flushing reaction.

This reaction occurs most commonly in individuals who lack an active form of an enzyme, acetaldehyde dehydrogenase, which is essential to the metabolism of alcohol. People who have this condition complete the first step of alcohol metabolism, conversion of alcohol to acetaldehyde, a toxic intermediary, but are slow to complete the second step, conversion of acetaldehyde to acetate, a common waste product. The acetaldehyde builds up rapidly, causing the flushing reaction. The alcohol flushing reaction occurs most commonly among Asians; up to 40 percent carry the gene encoding the inactive enzyme, though the gene also occurs in other ethnic groups. Not unexpectedly, this genetic variation is associated with a decreased risk of alcoholism. It is a less severe reaction than that occurring when an individual ingests alcohol after having been treated with the medication disulfiram (Antabuse), which irreversibly blocks the enzyme acetaldehyde dehydrogenase. Symptoms of the disulfiram-ethanol reaction may include flushing, nausea, vomiting, shortness of breath, sweating, dizziness, blurred vision, and confusion.

Most true allergic reactions to ingested alcoholic beverages are actually secondary to other chemicals in the beverage such as yeasts, metabisulfite preservatives, papain, or dyes. However, there are reports of true allergic reactions in which the offending agent was shown to be ethanol itself. Symptoms of anaphylaxis have been reported to occur in several subjects following ingestion of beer and/or wine, and these symptoms were reproduced in one patient by administration of 95 percent ethanol. Hives have been reported with ethanol ingestion, and hives on contact with ethanol have been reported for some Asian patients. Bronchospasm was precipitated in some asthmatic patients by administration of ethanol, and contact hypersensitivity to 50 percent ethanol solution was produced in 6 percent of subjects tested.

ALLERGIES TO OPIATES, BARBITURATES, AND STREET DRUGS

There have been reports of morphine-induced hives in some people, and studies show that morphine can cause histamine release directly from cells without binding to specific receptors on cells. Anaphylaxis may also occur with either morphine or codeine, and IgE antibodies against morphine and codeine have been found in patients experiencing anaphylaxis. Thus, the opiates can mediate allergic reaction by either mechanism, and the antagonist drug naloxone will not reverse these reactions. There are also reports of heroin causing bronchospasm.

Some instances of anaphylaxis associated with the medical administration of opiates or local anesthesia during surgery are due to the often-included preservative methylparaben, rather than to the opiate itself. Anaphylaxis may occur with more than one local anesthetic and/or analgesic compound in the same patient because of the methylparaben preservative. Numerous reports exist for anaphylactoid reactions following the use of barbiturates for the induction of anesthesia. The drugs themselves may induce histamine release. This may also be mediated through a true allergic IgE mediated response in some patients. Skin rashes also occur frequently following barbiturate usage, which may be a hypersensitivity reaction or a pseudo-allergic reaction.

Street drugs have been reported to induce asthma and/or anaphylaxis. Bronchospasm may occur in patients smoking cocaine or in those injecting heroin. This response may occur more often in patients who have a previous history of asthma. The asthma may persist after the subjects have stopped smoking cocaine. Pulmonary edema (fluid in the lungs) may also occur with freebasing cocaine.

These side effects are not likely to be mediated by the immune system. However, a hypersensitivity pneumonitis to cocaine has been described and is associated with elevated levels of IgE. Marijuana does not appear to increase the incidence of either asthma or anaphylaxis.

BIBLIOGRAPHY

Ettinger, N. A., & Albin, R. J. (1989). A review of the respiratory effects of smoking cocaine. *American Journal of Medicine, 87,* 664–668.

Fakuda, T., & Dohi, S. (1986). Anaphylactic reaction to fentanyl or preservative. *Canadian Anesthetists' Society Journal, 33,* 826–827.

Hicks, R. (1968). Ethanol, a possible allergen. *Annals of Allergy, 26,* 641.

Karvoren, J., & Hannuksel, A. M. (1976). Urticaria from alcoholic beverages. *Acta Allergan, 31,* 167.

Kelso, J., et al. (1990). Anaphylactoid reaction to ethanol. *Annals of Allergy, 64,* 452.

McLelland, J. (1986). The mechanism of morphine induced urticaria. *Archives of Dermatology, 122,* 138.

Przybilla, B., & Ring, J. (1983). Anaphylaxis to ethanol and sensitization to acetic acid. *Lancet, 1,* 483.

Rebhun, J. (1988). Association of asthma and freebase smoking. *Annals of Allergy, 60,* 339.

Rilbet, A., Hunziker, N., & Braun, R. (1980) Alcohol contact urticaria syndrome. *Dermatologica, 161,* 361.

Rubin, R., & Neugarten, J. (1990). Codeine associated asthma. *American Journal of Medicine, 88,* 438.

Seto, A., Tricomi, S., Goodwin, D. W., Kolodney, R., Sullivan, T. (1978). Biochemical correlates of ethanol-induced flushing in Orientals. *Journal of Studies on Alcohol, 39,* 1–11.

Shaikh, W. A. (1970). Allergy to heroin. *Allergy, 45,* 555.

Shanahan, E. C., Marshall, A. G., & Garrett, C. P. U. (1983). Adverse reactions to intravenous codeine phosphate in children. A report of three cases. *Anesthesia, 38,* 40.

Ting, S., et al. (1988). Ethanol induced urticaria: A case report. *Annals of Allergy, 60,* 527.

Wilkins, J. K., & Fortner, G. (1985). Ethnic contact urticaria to alcohol. *Contact Dermatology, 12,* 118.

MARLENE ALDO-BENSON
REVISED BY LEAH R. ZINDEL (2009)

AMANTADINE. Amantadine is a medication (Symmetrel) that is believed to be an indirect dopamine agonist; this means that it releases the neurotransmitter dopamine from nerve terminals in the brain. Since some of the symptoms of cocaine withdrawal and cocaine dependence are thought to be related to abnormalities in the dopamine systems of the brain, and these are thought to contribute to relapse, amantadine has been examined as a treatment possibility.

After chronic cocaine use, many patients' dopamine systems either fail to release sufficient dopamine or are insensitive to the dopamine that is released. This relative dopamine deficit is believed to be responsible for the dysphoria of cocaine withdrawal. It was hoped that amantadine would relieve their dysphoria and reduce relapse back to cocaine abuse by increasing the release of dopamine in the brains of cocaine-dependent patients. Amantadine has been effective in reducing depressive symptoms in patients with neurological disorders such as Parkinson's disease, which is due to the death of dopamine-producing cells in the brain; however, no solid evidence exists that it is helpful in preventing continued cocaine use or relapse to cocaine use after detoxification.

See also **Cocaine; Treatment, Stages/Phases of: Medical Detoxification; Withdrawal: Cocaine.**

BIBLIOGRAPHY

Kampman, K. M., et al. (2000). Amantadine in the treatment of cocaine-dependent patients with severe withdrawal symptoms. *American Journal of Psychiatry, 159*, 2052–2054.

THOMAS R. KOSTEN

AMERICAN SOCIETY OF ADDICTION MEDICINE (ASAM).

The American Society of Addiction Medicine (4601 North Park Avenue, Arcade Suite 101, Chevy Chase, MD 20815; http://www.asam.org) is a not-for-profit organization of physicians in all medical specialties and subspecialties who devote a significant part of their practice to treating patients addicted to, or having problems with, alcohol, nicotine, and other drugs. The society strives to have addiction recognized as a medical disorder by health insurance and managed care providers, and the medical community at large. Many of its members are actively involved in medical education, research, and public policy issues concerning the treatment and prevention of addiction.

The roots of ASAM can be traced to the early 1950s, when Dr. Ruth Fox organized regular meetings at the New York Academy of Medicine with other physicians interested in alcoholism and its treatment. These meetings led to the establishment, in 1954, of the New York City Medical Society on Alcoholism, which eventually became the American Medical Society on Alcoholism (AMSA). Another state medical society devoted to addiction as a subspecialty, the California Society for the Treatment of Alcoholism and Other Drug

Dependencies, was established in the 1970s. By 1982, the American Academy of Addictionology was incorporated, and all these groups united within AMSA the following year. Because the organization was concerned with all drugs of addiction, not only alcohol, and was interested in establishing addiction medicine as part of mainstream medical practice, the organization was renamed the American Society on Alcoholism and Other Drug Dependencies, which in 1989 was changed to the American Society of Addiction Medicine (ASAM). In 1988, the American Medical Association (AMA) House of Delegates admitted ASAM as a voting member, and in 1990, the AMA recognized addiction medicine as a medical specialty. In the late 1990s, ASAM and the American Managed Behavioral Healthcare Association (AMBHA) began an ongoing collaboration to publish statements of consensus on various issues such as the effective treatment of addictive disorders and credentialing of clinical professionals, among others. The stated mission and goals of ASAM are to increase access to and improve the quality of addictions treatment; educate physicians, medical students, and the public; promote research and prevention; and establish addiction medicine as a specialty recognized by the American Board of Medical Specialties.

By the early 2000s, membership in the society exceeded 2,500, with chapters in all fifty states, as well as overseas. Membership consists of private- and group-practice physicians, corporate medical directors, residents, and medical students, as well as retired physicians. ASAM-certified members with at least five years of active participation in the society, as well as involvement in related organizations and activities, may become Fellows.

Educational activities of the society are conducted through publications, courses, and clinical and scientific conferences. Publications include, among others, a bimonthly newsletter, *ASAM News*; the *Journal of Addictive Diseases*, published quarterly; the *ASAM Principles of Addiction Medicine*, a comprehensive reference guide; and the *Patient Placement Criteria for the Treatment of Substance–Related Disorders*, a clinical guide for matching adult and adolescent patients to appropriate levels of care. Courses include the Ruth Fox Course for Physicians; Medical Review Officer

(MRO) certification training; and in-depth studies of addiction medicine. An annual medical–scientific conference includes scientific symposia, clinically oriented courses and workshops, and presentations of submitted papers.

In April 2001, ASAM revised its Patient Placement Criteria for the Treatment of Substance-Related Disorders to make consistent diagnostic terminology with language within the American Psychiatric Association's *Diagnostic and Statistical Manual of Mental Disorders* (*DSM–IV*). This revised edition was borne of numerous requests to ASAM for criteria that more effectively meet the needs of patients suffering from both mental and substance-related afflictions. In addition to reiterating and updating its guide for adult and adolescent levels of care, the revised edition addresses the concept of the *unbundling* of clinical services, which takes into account the needs of individual patients as opposed to the limitations of a particular treatment setting.

In its continued effort to establish the legitimacy of addiction medicine as a subspecialty within medicine, ASAM administers a six-hour certification examination, is a primary sponsor of medical postgraduate fellowships in alcoholism and drug abuse, and has developed guidelines for the training of physicians in this area of medical practice.

ASAM aggressively lobbies Congress on various mental health and substance-related health issues. After the U.S. Senate passed similar legislation in 2007, eighteen ASAM representatives visited members of Congress in support of HR 1424, also known as the *parity bill*, which would expand 1996 mental health legislation. HR 1424 would require group health plans to provide mental and/or substance abuse benefits at a level equal to medical and surgical benefits. A vote of the House of Representatives was expected in 2008. In addition to its personal lobbying efforts, the ASAM Web site offers a parity "War Room," instructing ASAM members on talking points, sample letters, and other strategies for influencing Congress, as well as distributing e-newsletters and other information to members.

BIBLIOGRAPHY

Hermos, J. A. (2008). Early age-of-onset drinking predicts prescription drug misuse among teenagers and young adults: A national survey. *Journal of Addiction Medicine, 2*(1), 22–30.

Mee-Lee, D. (Ed.). (2001). *Patient placement criteria for the treatment of substance-related disorders.* Philadelphia: Lippincott, Williams, & Wilkins.

Stanley, H. W., & Niemi, R. G. (2007). Vital statistics on American politics 2007–2008. Washington, DC: Congressional Quarterly Press.

MARC GALANTER
JEROME H. JAFFE
REVISED BY NANCY FAERBER (2001)
MATTHEW MAY (2009)

AMOBARBITAL. Amobarbital (Amytal) is one of the many different members of the barbiturate family of central nervous system depressants used to produce relaxation, sleep, anesthesia, and anticonvulsant effects. In terms of the duration of its effects, it is considered an intermediate-acting barbiturate. When taken by mouth, its sedating effects take about 1 hour to develop and last about 6 to 8 hours, although it takes considerably longer for all the drug to leave the body.

In addition to its use as a sedative, amobarbital is occasionally used in psychiatric evaluation in so-called Amytal interviews, to relax patients in order to help them recall memories or information that has been repressed due to trauma. This technique was sometimes called *narcoanalysis* or *narcotherapy.*

DOSAGE AND ADMINISTRATION

Amobarbital may be given orally, intramuscularly, or intravenously for the treatment of insomnia or anxiety. The adult dosage for sedation is 15 to 50 milligrams but 65 to 200 milligrams for sleep. For treating convulsions, the adult dose is 65 to 200 milligrams, with a maximum dose of 500 milligrams.

Amobarbital should not be given to patients with a history of addiction; personal or family history of porphyria; severe kidney, liver, or lung disease; or hypersensitivity to barbiturates.

Amobarbital is incompatible with a number of medications, including dimenhydrinate, phenytoin, hydrocortisone, insulin, morphine, cimetidine, pancuronium, streptomycin, tetracycline, vancomycin, and penicillin G. It may decrease the effectiveness of birth control pills containing estrogen. It has also been shown to increase the risk of birth defects if taken during pregnancy.

PSYCHIATRIC USE

The use of amobarbital in "Amytal interviews" has declined since the mid-1990s because of its relatively low success rate. One medical text published in the mid-1990s noted that the amount of clinically useful information obtained by this method is quite limited. Amobarbital interviews appear to be useful primarily in distinguishing between psychosis and delirium. Psychotic patients usually improve with amobarbital, whereas delirious patients get worse.

DEPENDENCY AND ABUSE

Amobarbital has been largely replaced by benzodiazepine medications as a sedative because of the high risk of abuse. It has been dropped from the 1999 edition of the *Physicians' Desk Reference*, which implies that it is no longer manufactured in the United States. As of 2000, it is still available in Canada. Although amobarbital has been less popular with addicted patients than the more rapidly acting barbiturates (secobarbital and pentobarbital), it is still sold on the street as "blues" or "rainbows" (combinations of amobarbital and secobarbital). A daily dose of 500 to 600 milligrams is considered sufficient to produce dependence. The time necessary to produce dependence is estimated at 30 days. It has often been noted that the symptoms of barbiturate dependence resemble those of chronic alcoholism, though barbiturate withdrawl is more often associated with life-threatening complications than alcohol withdrawl.

EMERGENCY TREATMENT

Overdose. Although the toxic dose of amobarbital varies according to height, weight, and other factors, 1 gram taken by mouth usually produces serious poisoning in an adult. Two to 10 grams are usually a fatal dose. Emergency treatment is supportive, including oxygen administration if necessary, fluid therapy and other standard treatment for shock, and forced diuresis if the patient has normal kidney function. This procedure speeds the excretion of the barbiturate in the urine.

Withdrawal. The symptoms of withdrawal from amobarbital or any barbiturate may be severe or even fatal if the patient has been taking the drug in large doses (800 mg/day). The barbiturate withdrawal syndrome is similar to delirium tremens. Within 12 to 20 hours after withdrawal, the patient becomes restless and weak. During the second and third days, 75 percent of patients develop convulsions, which may progress to status epilepticus and death. From the third to the fifth day, untreated withdrawal syndrome is marked by delirium, hallucinations, insomnia, fever, and dehydration. To prevent withdrawal syndrome, patients are treated with a dose of phenobarbital equivalent to one-third of the daily dose of amobarbital on which they are dependent. This initial dose of phenobarbital is decreased by 30 milligrams per day until the patient's system is clear of drugs.

See also **Barbiturates.**

BIBLIOGRAPHY

Beers, M. H., & Berkow, R., Eds. (1999). *The Merck manual of diagnosis and therapy*, 17th ed. Whitehouse Station, NJ: Merck Research Laboratories. (M. H. Beers, R. S. Porter, and T. V. Jones [2006]. 18th ed.)

Brophy, J. J. (1994). Psychiatric disorders. In L. M. Tierney et al. (Eds.), *Current medical diagnosis & treatment*, 33rd ed. Norwalk, CT: Appleton & Lange. (S. J. McPhee et al. [2007]. 47th ed. New York: McGraw-Hill Medical.)

Hardman, J. G., & Limbird, L. E., Eds. (1996). *Goodman and Gilman's the pharmacological basis of therapeutics*, 9th ed. New York: McGraw-Hill Medical. (2005, 11th ed.)

Medical Economics Company (1999). *Physicians' desk reference*, (PDR), 53rd ed. Montvale, NJ: Thomson. (2008, 62nd ed.)

Wilson, B. A., Shannon, M. T., & Stang, C. L., Eds. (1995). *Nurse's drug guide*, 3rd ed. Norwalk, CT: Appleton & Lange.

SCOTT E. LUKAS
REVISED BY REBECCA J. FREY (2001)

AMOTIVATIONAL SYNDROME.

The term *amotivational syndrome* is often used interchangeably with *apathy syndrome*. Both terms refer to a set of characteristics that have been associated with the use of marijuana, cocaine, and inhalants.

Based on experiments conducted in the 1960s and 1970s, amotivational syndrome is characterized by a broad range of symptoms, including general apathy, lethargy, severe reduction in activities, difficulty in carrying out long-term plans, depression, and an inability to concentrate. The condition has long been associated with chronic marijuana use. Two studies conducted in the absence of controlled conditions linked amotivational syndrome to preexisting or coexisting mood disorders (i.e. anxiety, depression). In an early study (Kupfer et al., 1973), researchers suggested that amotivational syndrome might be a manifestation of pre-existing mood disorders, making individuals more susceptible to the syndrome. Specifically, they found that individuals who used marijuana frequently (i.e. three or more times a week) had discernible characteristics such as depression and lower energy levels. In a more recent study, R. E. Musty and L. Kaback (1995) investigated symptoms of depression among chronic heavy users (medians: daily use for six years) and light users (medians: several times per month for 4.5 years). They concluded that amotivational symptoms observed among chronic heavy marijuana users in this clinical sample were primarily caused by coexisting depression. Experiments conducted under controlled laboratory conditions, meanwhile, have offered mixed results regarding the amotivational effects of marijuana (Foltin et al., 1990; Kagel et al., 1980). A 2002 study by D. R. Cherek and colleagues aroused the suspicion that one factor that may contribute to the mixed results of other studies is the lack of operationally defined motivation. By defining motivation in precise behavioral terms, Cherek and colleagues found acute amotivational symptoms following marijuana smoking among occasional users (one to four times per month).

Apathy refers to a set of symptoms that includes anhedonia (an inability to experience pleasure from normally pleasurable events), reduced initiative, and decreased spontaneous activity. In the neurological literature, apathy is generally considered the result of decreased function in the subcortical regions, particularly a reduction in dopamine, a brain chemical associated with pleasure and motivation. Apathy is also exhibited in individuals diagnosed with frontal-subcortical disorders such as Parkinson's disease and HIV dementia. In a 2006 study examining prefrontal cortex

function, Antonio Verdejo-García and colleagues found that substance-dependent individuals exhibited greater behavioral problems across different areas—including apathy, disinhibition, and executive dysfunction—than healthy individuals. In addition, Ari Kalechstein and colleagues (2002) suggested that, independent of depression, apathy was exhibited during the initial phases of abstinence for some cocaine-dependent individuals. In a 2005 study, Thomas Newton and colleagues found that following acute administration of a high dose of cocaine, apathy predicted hedonic (self-reported "High") but not craving response to cocaine. Patients with high apathy reported increased hedonic response. Similar to Kalechstein and colleagues' findings (2002), the reported effects were not due to depression.

Neither the amotivational syndrome nor the apathy syndrome is included in the fourth edition of the *Diagnostic and Statistical Manual of Mental Disorders* (1994), and future research is needed to illuminate the role these conditions play in drug addiction and recovery. These findings have the potential to warrant dopamine-enhancing treatment for substance-dependent individuals.

See also **Cocaine; Depression; Dopamine; Marijuana (Cannabis).**

BIBLIOGRAPHY

American Psychiatric Association. (1994). *Diagnostic and statistical manual of mental disorders* (4th rev. ed., *DSM-IV-R*), Washington, DC: Author.

Cherek, D. R., Lane, S. D., & Dougherty, D. M. (2002). Possible amotivational effects following marijuana smoking under laboratory conditions. *Experimental and Clinical Psychopharmacology, 10*(1), 26–38.

Foltin, R. W., Fischman, M. W., Brady, J. V., Bernstein, D. J., Capriotti, R. M., Nellis, M. J., et al. (1990). Motivational effects of smoked marijuana: Behavioral contingencies and low-probability activities. *Journal of the Experimental Analysis of Behavior, 53*(1), 5–19.

Kagel, J. H., Battalio, R. C. & Miles, C. G. (1980). Marijuana and work performance: Results from an experiment. *Journal of Human Resources, 15*(3), 373–395.

Kalechstein, A. D., Newton, T. F., & Leavengood, A. H. (2002). Apathy syndrome in cocaine dependence. *Psychiatry Research, 109*(1), 97–100.

Kupfer, D. J., Detre, T., Koral, J., & Fajan, P. (1973). A comment on the "amotivational syndrome" in marijuana smokers. *American Journal of Psychiatry, 130*(12), 1319–1322.

Levy, M. L., Cummings, J. L., Fairbanks, L. A., Masterman, D., Miller, B. L., Craig, A. H., et al. (1998). Apathy is not depression. *Journal of Neuropsychiatry and Clinical Neuroscience, 10*(3), 314–319.

Marin, R. S. (1996). Apathy: concept, syndrome, neural mechanisms, and treatment. *Seminars in Clinical Neuropsychiatry, 1*(4), 304–314.

Musty, R. E. & Kaback, L. (1995). Relationships between motivation and depression in chronic marijuana users. *Life Science, 56,* 2151–2158.

National Institute on Drug Abuse. (2004). *NIDA InfoFacts: Inhalants.* Washington, DC: Author. Available from http://www.nida.nih.gov/.

Newton, T. F., Kalechstein, A. D., Garza, R. D. L., Cutting, D. J., & Ling, W. (2005). Apathy predicts hedonic but not craving response to cocaine. *Pharmacology, Biochemistry and Behavior, 82*(1), 236–240.

Verdejo-García, A., Bechara, A., Recknor, E. C., & Pérez-García, M. (2006). Executive dysfunction in substance dependent individuals during drug use and abstinence: An examination of the behavioral, cognitive, and emotional correlates of addiction. *Journal of the International Neuropsychological Society, 12*(3), 405–415.

Wang, G. J., Chang L., Volkow, N. D., Telang, F., Logan, J., Ernst, T., & Fowler, J. S. (2004). Decreased brain dopaminergic transporters in HIV-associated dementia patients. *Brain, 127*(11), 2452–2458.

SHARON HSIN HSU
G. ALAN MARLATT

AMPHETAMINE. Amphetamine was first synthesized in 1887, but its central nervous system (CNS) stimulant effects were not noted at that time. After rediscovery, in the early 1930s, its use as a respiratory stimulant was established and its properties as a central nervous system stimulant were described. Reports of abuse soon followed. As had occurred with cocaine products when they were first introduced in the 1880s, amphetamine was promoted as being an effective cure for a wide range of ills without any risk of addiction. The medical profession enthusiastically explored the potentials of amphetamine, recommending it as a cure for everything from alcohol hangover and depression to the vomiting of pregnancy and weight reduction. These claims that it was a miracle drug contributed to public interest in the amphetamines, and they rapidly became the stimulant of choice—since they were inexpensive, readily available, and had a long duration of action.

Derivatives of amphetamine, such as methamphetamine, were soon developed and both oral and intravenous preparations became available for therapeutic uses. Despite early reports of an occasional adverse reaction, enormous quantities were consumed in the 1940s and 1950s, and their liability for abuse was not recognized. During World War II, the amphetamines, including methamphetamine, were widely used as stimulants by the military in the United States, Great Britain, Germany, and Japan, to counteract fatigue, to increase alertness during battle and night watches, to increase endurance, and to elevate mood. It has been estimated that approximately 200 million Benzedrine (amphetamine) tablets were dispensed to the U.S. armed forces during World War II. In fact, much of the research on performance effects of the amphetamines was carried out on enlisted personnel during this period, as the various countries sought ways of maintaining an alert and productive armed force. Although amphetamine was found to increase alertness, little data were collected supporting its ability to enhance performance.

Since 1945, use of the amphetamines and cocaine appears to have alternated in popularity, with several stimulant epidemics occurring in the United States. There was a major epidemic of amphetamine and methamphetamine abuse (both oral and intravenous) in Japan right after the war. The epidemic was reported to have involved, at its peak, some half-million users and was related to the release with minimal regulatory controls of huge quantities of surplus amphetamines that had been made for use by the Japanese military. Despite this experience, there were special regulations governing their manufacture, sale, or prescription in the United States until 1964 (Hall et al., 1991).

The first major amphetamine epidemic in the United States peaked in the mid-1960s, with approximately 13.5 percent of the university population estimated, in 1969, to have used amphetamines at least once. By 1978, use of the amphetamines had declined substantially, contrasting with the increase of cocaine use by that time. The major amphetamine of concern in the United States in

Homemade amphetamine sulfate. DAVID HOFFMAN PHOTO LIBRARY/ALAMY.

the 1990s is methamphetamine, with pockets of "ice" (smoked methamphetamine) abuse.

Amphetamines are now controlled under Schedule II of the Controlled Substances Act. Substances classified within this schedule are found to have a high potential for abuse as well as currently accepted medical use within the United States. Amphetamine, methamphetamine, cocaine, methylphenidate, and phenmetrazine are all stimulants included in this schedule.

MEDICAL UTILITY

Amphetamines are frequently prescribed for the treatment of narcolepsy, obesity, and for childhood attention deficit disorder. They are clearly efficacious in the treatment of narcolepsy, one of the first conditions to be successfully treated with these drugs. Although patients with this disorder can require large doses of amphetamine for prolonged periods of time, attacks of sleep can generally be prevented. Interestingly, tolerance does not seem

to develop to the therapeutic effects of these drugs, and most patients can be maintained on the same dose for years.

Although the amphetamines have been used extensively in the treatment of obesity, considerable evidence exists for a rapid development of tolerance to the anorectic (appetite loss) effects of this drug, with continued use having little therapeutic effect. These drugs are extremely effective appetite suppressants, but after several weeks of use the dose must be increased to achieve the same appetite-suppressant effect. People remaining on the amphetamines for prolonged periods of time to decrease food intake can reach substantial doses, resulting in toxic side effects (e.g., insomnia, irritability, increased heart rate and blood pressure, and tremulousness). Therefore, these drugs should only be taken for relatively short periods of time (4–6 weeks). In addition, long-term follow-up studies of patients who were prescribed amphetamines for weight loss have not found any advantage in using this medication to maintain weight loss. Data indicate that weight lost under amphetamine maintenance is rapidly gained when amphetamine use is discontinued. In addition to the lack of long-term efficacy, the dependence-producing effects of amphetamines make them a poor choice of maintenance medication for this problem.

The use of amphetamines in the treatment of attention deficit disorders in children, remains extremely controversial. It has been found that the amphetamines have a dramatic effect in reducing restlessness and distractibility as well as lengthening attention span, but there are side effects. These include reports of growth impairment in children, insomnia, and increases in heart rate. Those promoting their use point to their potential benefits and they advocate care in limiting treatment dose and duration. Opponents of their use, while agreeing that they provide some short-term benefits, conclude that these do not outweigh their disadvantages. Amphetamine therapy has also been attempted, but with little success, in the treatment of Parkinson's disease, and both amphetamine and cocaine have been suggested for the treatment of depression, although the evidence to support their efficacy does not meet current standards demanded by the U.S. Food and Drug Administration.

PHARMACOLOGY

The amphetamines act by increasing concentrations of the neurotransmitters dopamine and norepinephrine at the neuronal synapse, thereby augmenting release and blocking uptake. It is the augmentation of release that differentiates amphetamines from cocaine, which also blocks uptake of these transmitters. Humans given a single moderate dose of amphetamine generally show an increase in activity and talkativeness, and they report euphoria, a general sense of well-being, and a decrease in both food intake and fatigue. At higher doses repetitive motor activity (i.e., stereotyped behavior) is often seen, and further increases in dose can lead to convulsions, coma, and death. This class of drugs increases heart rate, respiration, diastolic and systolic blood pressure, and high doses can cause cardiac arrhythmias. In addition, the amphetamines have a suppressant effect on both rapid eye movement sleep (REM)—the stage of sleep associated with dreaming—and total sleep. The half-life of amphetamine is about ten hours, quite long when compared to a stimulant like

cocaine, which has a half-life of approximately one hour, or even methamphetamine which has a half-life of about five hours.

The amphetamine molecule has two isomers: the d-$(+)$ and l-$(-)$ isomers. There is marked stereo-selectivity in their biological actions, with the d-isomer (dextroamphetamine) considerably more potent. For example, it is more potent as a locomotor stimulant, in inducing stereotyped behavior patterns, and in eliciting central nervous system excitatory effects. The isomers appear to be equipotent as cardiovascular stimulants. The basic amphetamine molecule has been modified in a number of ways to accentuate various of its actions. For example, in an effort to obtain appetite suppressants with reduced cardiovascular and central nervous system effects, structural modifications yielded such medications as diethylproprion and fenfluramine, while other structural modifications have enhanced the central nervous system stimulant effects and reduced the cardiovascular and anorectic actions, yielding medications such as methylphenidate and phenmetrazine. These substances share, to a greater or lesser degree, the properties of amphetamine.

TOXICITY

A major toxic effect of amphetamine in humans is the development of a schizophrenia-like psychosis after repeated long-term use. The first report of an amphetamine psychosis occurred in 1938, but the condition was considered rare. Administration of amphetamine to normal volunteers with no histories of psychosis (Griffith et al., 1970) resulted in a clear-cut paranoid psychosis in five of the six subjects who received d-amphetamine for one to five days (120–220 mg/day), which cleared when the drug was discontinued. Unless the user continues to take the drug, the psychosis usually clears within a week, although the possibility exists for prolonged symptomology. This amphetamine psychosis has been thought to represent a reasonably accurate model of schizophrenia, including symptoms of persecution, hyperactivity and excitation, visual and auditory hallucinations, and changes in body image. In addition, it has been suggested that there is sensitization to the development of a stimulant psychosis—once an individual has experienced this toxic effect, it is readily reinitiated, sometimes at lower doses and even following long drug-free periods.

Amphetamine abusers taking repeated doses of the drug can develop repetitive behavior patterns which persist for hours at a time. These can take the form of cleaning, the repeated dismantling of small appliances, or the endless picking at wounds on the extremities. Such repetitive stereotyped patterns of behavior are also seen in nonhumans administered repeated doses of amphetamines and other stimulant drugs, and they appear to be related to dopaminergic facilitation. Cessation of amphetamine use after high-dose chronic intake is generally accompanied by lethargy, depression, and abnormal sleep patterns. This pattern of behavior, opposite to the direct effects of amphetamine, does not appear to be a classical abstinence syndrome. The symptoms may be related to the long-term lack of sleep and food intake that accompany chronic stimulant use as well as to the catecholamine depletion that occurs as a result of chronic use.

Animals given unlimited access to amphetamine will self-administer it reliably, alternating days of high intake with days of low intake. They become restless, tremulous, and ataxic, eating and sleeping little. If allowed to continue self-administering the drug, most will take it until they die. Animals maintained on high doses of amphetamines develop tolerance to many of the physically and behaviorally debilitating effects, but they also develop irreversible damage in some parts of the brain, including long-lasting depletion of dopamine. It has been suggested that the prolonged anhedonia seen after long-term human amphetamine use may be related to this, although the evidence for this is not very strong.

BEHAVIORAL EFFECTS

Nonhumans. As with all psychomotor stimulant drugs, at low doses animals are active and alert, showing increases in responding maintained by other reinforcers, but often decreasing food intake. Higher doses produce species-specific repetitive behavior patterns (stereotyped behavior), and further increases in dose are followed, as in humans, by convulsions, hyperthermia, and death. Tolerance (loss of response to a certain dose) develops to many of amphetamine's central effects, and cross-tolerance among the stimulants has been demonstrated in rats. Thus, for example, animals tolerant to the anorectic effects of amphetamine

also show tolerance to cocaine's anorectic effects. Although there is tolerance development to many of amphetamine's effects, sensitization develops to amphetamine's effects on locomotor activity. Thus, with repeated administration, doses of amphetamine that initially did not result in hyperactivity or stereotypy can, with repeated use, begin to induce those behaviors when injected daily for several weeks. In addition, there is cross-sensitization to this effect, such that administration of one stimulant can induce sensitization to another one. In contrast to cocaine, however (in which an increased sensitivity to its convulsant effects develops with repeated use), amphetamines have an anticonvulsive effect.

Learned behaviors, typically generated by operant schedules of reinforcement, are generally affected by the amphetamines in a rate-dependent fashion. Thus, behaviors that occur at relatively low rates in the absence of the drug tend to be increased at low-to-moderate doses of amphetamine, while behaviors occurring at relatively high frequencies tend to be suppressed by those doses of amphetamine. In addition, with high doses most behaviors tend to be suppressed. As is seen with other stimulants, such as cocaine, environmental variables and behavioral context can play a role in modulating these effects. For example, behavior under strong stimulus control shows tolerance to repeated amphetamine administration much more rapidly than does behavior under weak stimulus control. In addition, if the amphetamine-induced behavioral disruption has the effect of interfering with reinforcement delivery, tolerance to that effect develops rapidly. Tolerance does not develop to the amphetamine-induced disruptions when reinforcement density is increased or remains the same.

Amphetamines can serve as reinforcers in nonhumans and, as described above, can produce severely toxic consequences when available in an unlimited fashion. However, when available for a few hours a day, animals will take them in a regular fashion, showing little or no tolerance to their reinforcing effects.

Humans. A substantial number of studies have been carried out evaluating the effects of amphetamines on learning, cognition, and other aspects of performance. The data indicate that under most conditions the amphetamines are not general performance enhancers. When there is improvement in performance associated with amphetamine administration, it can usually be attributed to a reduction in the deterioration of performance due to fatigue or boredom. Attention lapses that impair performance after sleep deprivation appear to be reduced by amphetamine administration; however, as sleep deprivation is prolonged, this effect is reduced. A careful review of the literature in this area (Laties & Weiss, 1981) concluded that improvement is more obvious with complex, as compared with simple, tasks.

In addition, in trained athletes, whose behavior shows little variability, only very small improvements can be seen. Laties and Weiss have argued persuasively, however, that the small changes in performance induced by amphetamines can result in the 1 to 2 percent improvement that may make the difference in a close athletic competition. Although the facilitation in performance after amphetamine does not appear to be substantial, it is sufficient to "spell the difference between a gold medal" and any other. Unfortunately, such data have led athletes to take stimulants prior to athletic events, particularly those in which strenuous activity is required over prolonged periods (e.g., bicycle racing), leading to hyperthermia, collapse, and even death in some cases.

The mood-elevating effects of the amphetamines are generally believed to be related to their abuse. Their use is accompanied by reports of increased self-confidence, elation, frequently euphoria, friendliness, and positive mood. When amphetamine is administered repeatedly, tolerance develops rapidly to many of its subjective effects (such that the same dose no longer exerts much of an effect). This means that the user must take increasingly larger amounts of amphetamine to achieve the same effect. As with nonhuman research subjects, there is however, little or no evidence for the development of tolerance to amphetamine's reinforcing effects.

Experienced stimulant users, given a variety of stimulant drugs, often cannot differentiate among cocaine, amphetamine, methamphetamine, and methlyphenidate—all of which appear to have similar profiles of action. Since these drugs have different durations of action, however, it becomes easier to make this differentiation over time.

ABUSE

In the United States in the 1950s, nonmedical amphetamine use was prevalent among college students, athletes, truck drivers, and housewives.

The drug was widely publicized by the media when very little evidence of amphetamine toxicity was available. Pills were the first form to be widely abused. Use of the drug expanded as production of amphetamine and methamphetamine increased significantly, and abusers began to inject it. An extensive black market in amphetamines developed, and it has been estimated that 50 to 90 percent of the quantity commercially produced was diverted into illicit channels. In the 1970s, manufacture of amphetamines was substantially curtailed, amphetamines were placed in Schedule II of the Controlled Substances Act, and abuse of these substances was substantially reduced. Perhaps only by coincidence, as amphetamine use declined, cocaine use increased.

The amphetamines, as with other stimulants, are generally abused in multiple-dose cycles (i.e., binges), in which people take the drug repeatedly for some period of time, followed by a period in which they take no drug. Amphetamines are often taken every three or four hours for periods as long as three or four days, and dosage can escalate dramatically as tolerance develops. Like cocaine binges, these amphetamine-taking occasions are followed by a "crash" period in which the user sleeps, eats, and does not use the drug. Abrupt cessation from amphetamine use is usually accompanied by depression. Mood generally returns to normal within a week, although craving for the drug can last for months.

There is little evidence for the development of physical dependence to the amphetamines. Although some experts view the "crash" (with lethargy, depression, exhaustion, and increased appetite) that can follow a few days of moderate-to-high dose use as meeting the criteria for a withdrawal syndrome, others believe that the symptoms can also be related to the effects of chronic stimulant use. When using stimulants people do not eat or sleep very much and, as well, catecholamine depletion may well be contributing to these behavioral changes.

TREATMENT

As of the mid-1990s, little information is available about the treatment of amphetamine abusers, and no reports of successful pharmacological interventions exist in the treatment literature. As with cocaine abuse, the most promising non-pharmacological approaches include behavioral therapy, relapse prevention, rehabilitation (e.g., vocational, educational, and social-skills training), and supportive psychotherapy. Unlike cocaine, however, minimal clinical trials with potential treatment medications for amphetamine abuse have been carried out. The few that have been attempted report no success in reducing a return to amphetamine use.

See also **Amphetamine Epidemics, International; Pharmacokinetics: General; Treatment: An Overview.**

BIBLIOGRAPHY

Ali, S. F., Ed. (2000). *The neurochemistry of drugs of abuse: Cocaine, ibogaine, and substituted amphetamines.* New York: New York Academy of Sciences.

Angrist, B., & Sudilovsky, A. (1978). Central nervous system stimulants: Historical aspects and clinical effects. In L. L. Iversen, S. D. Iverson, & S. H. Snyder (Eds.), *Handbook of psychopharmacology.* New York: Plenum.

Griffith, J. D., et al. (1970). Experimental psychosis induced by the administration of *d*-amphetamine. In E. Costa and S. Garattini (Eds.), *Amphetamines and related compounds.* New York: Raven Press.

Grilly, D. M. (1989). *Drugs and human behavior.* Needham, MA: Allyn & Bacon. (2005, 5th ed.)

Hall, J. N., & Broderick, P. M. (1991). Community networks for response to abuse outbreaks of methamphetamine and its analogs. *Methamphetamine Abuse: Epidemiologic Issues and Implications.* M. A. Miller & N. J. Kozel, (Eds.), *Research Monograph Series, 115.* National Institute on Drug Abuse.

Iversen, L. (2008). *Speed, ecstacy, ritalin: The science of amphetamines.* New York: Oxford University Press USA.

Laties, V. G., & Weiss, B. (1981). *Federation proceedings, 40,* 2689–2692.

MARIAN W. FISCHMAN

AMPHETAMINE EPIDEMICS, INTERNATIONAL.

The history and epidemiology of amphetamines illustrate particularly well the way in which the medical use and nonmedical use (or "abuse") of drugs can be intimately linked, both in terms of supply and other factors that drive demand. Amphetamines were introduced as medicines in the late 1930s and 1940s, leading to an epidemic of pharmaceutical overuse, frank abuse, and addiction by the 1950s in much of the developed world. In certain nations the drugs were controlled quite early,

but medical recognition of the widespread excessive consumption and deleterious effects of amphetamines was, in general, belated. Their licit use was only curtailed internationally after 1970, promoting a global shift to nonmedical use of illicitly manufactured amphetamines and, where available, cocaine. Amphetamine use has since remained endemic throughout much of the world.

The years since approximately 1990 have seen an expansion in the illicit supply of methamphetamine in particular, and surges in the nonmedical use of (and addiction to) amphetamine-type stimulants in several nations and regions. Not all of these surges can be described as "epidemics," if the term is used to denote a conversion of nonusers to users, in a strict analogy to infectious disease. However, switching to amphetamines from other drugs, or the intensification of use among less frequent users of amphetamines, both have important public health consequences, so it might be counterproductive to observe the analogy too strictly.

This period of increase in nonmedical amphetamine usage has also seen a parallel resurgence in the medical consumption and supply of amphetamines and related stimulants in some nations, especially for attention deficit/hyperactivity disorder (ADHD). The use of hallucinogenic amphetamines of the "Ecstasy" variety has similarly tracked the recent rises in medical and nonmedical amphetamine use. These drugs are treated elsewhere in this encyclopedia.

THE INTRODUCTION OF AMPHETAMINES IN THE 1930S AND 1940S

Pharmacologically, the amphetamines are best regarded as synthetic analogs of adrenaline and ephedrine, both of which provided the impetus for their discovery. Like adrenaline (and noradrenaline), they promote wakefulness and stimulate certain functions in the central nervous system, as well as peripheral functions mediated by sympathetic nerves—hence their characterization as "sympathomimetics." Credit for the first discovery of the amphetamines as drugs belongs to the Japanese pharmacologist Nagai Nagayoshi (1844–1929), who in the 1890s produced methamphetamine in his research on ephedrine, which he had previously identified as the active ingredient in the medicinal herb ephedra. Though ephedrine was taken up in

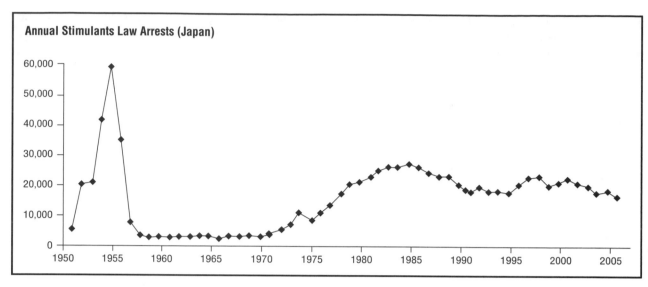

Figure 1. Annual stimulant law violations, Japan. The initial outbreak of methamphetamine injection, and gradual expansion of endemic nonmedical usage patterns, as traced by arrests after 1949, when pharmaceutical methamphetamine was made a controlled substance in Japan. (Adapted from Brill and Hirose, 1969; United Nations, 2007.) ILLUSTRATION BY GGS INFORMATION SERVICES. GALE, CENGAGE LEARNING

Japanese medicine, methamphetamine was not, and this work appears to have gone unnoticed in the West. In the 1920s, ephedrine was independently "discovered" and introduced into Western medicine, where it quickly became popular as a decongestant and an asthma remedy, for which it was more convenient than adrenaline because of its oral availability.

In 1929 the independent California biochemist Gordon Alles synthesized amphetamine in a pursuit of a better oral anti-asthmatic, and his animal experiments and self-experimentation revealed both its sympathomimetic and central stimulant actions, including euphoria. In 1932 Alles received a patent on the orally available salts of amphetamine for use as medicines. Shortly thereafter, the Smith, Kline and French (SKF) drug firm acquired Alles's patent, having taken their own patent on the medical use of the oily base form of amphetamine in 1933.

By 1934, SKF had introduced the Benzedrine Inhaler, a tube containing over 300 milligrams of oily amphetamine base, as an inexpensive over-the-counter congestion remedy throughout North America. Not long afterwards they introduced the inhaler in Latin America and Europe. From 1935 SFK sponsored clinical research to explore various possible uses for their Benzedrine Sulfate oral amphetamine product, including multiple sclerosis; dysmenhorrea, or painful menstruation; and bed-

wetting. By late 1937 the firm had settled on, and received American Medical Association (AMA) approval for, three initial indications: narcolepsy, post-encephalytic Parkinsonism, and minor depression. For the next decade these indications, and especially depression, would represent the drug's main official uses and the focus of SKF's marketing. At the onset of the Second World War, amphetamine's use as an antidepressant was becoming established in North America and much of Europe, while in Germany at least two drug firms had begun marketing methamphetamine, an old drug lacking patent protection, along the same lines.

During the Second World War, amphetamines were distributed by the military on all sides to maintain wakefulness and for the purported improvement of performance under fatigue. In the Blitzkrieg of late 1939 and early 1940, the German military consumed something on the order of 10 million tablets of methamphetamine monthly. By late 1940, German military consumption dropped an order of magnitude, after perfunctory early studies that showed improved scores on certain tests of mental and hand-eye performance were not borne out by more careful research. In addition, experience with the drug in combat pointed to problems with impaired judgment, post-drug exhaustion, and abuse. Usage dropped still further in 1941, when Germany placed both

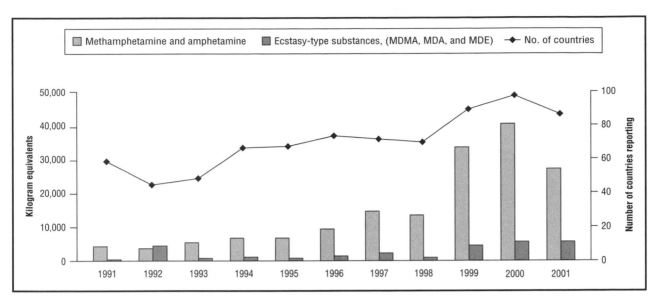

Figure 2. Reported global seizures of amphetamine-type stimulants, 1999–2001. Global drug seizure data indicate increased illicit supplies of amphetamines, largely from East Asia. (Source: United Nations, 2003.) ILLUSTRATION BY GGS INFORMATION SERVICES. GALE, CENGAGE LEARNING

methamphetamine and amphetamine under narcotics regulation, and again in 1942, with the official recognition that these amphetamines were dangerously addictive. The Japanese military appears to have used oral methamphetamine throughout the war, while both the British and American militaries used amphetamine, even though they were aware of the German change of policy. However, in contrast to American military consumption, British military usage seems to have become more cautious later in the war, following experiences similar to Germany's: Amphetamine's apparent performance-enhancing effects were not consistently demonstrable in careful lab experimentation, and mainly reflected optimism and distorted self-perception due to the drug's subjective effects.

In Japan, the immediate postwar years saw an epidemic of nonmedical methamphetamine use, promoted by the familiarity of the population with the drug from military usage, by austerity and social dislocation caused by the war, and by the easy availability of the drug. In 1946 the injection abuse of the drug was already becoming common, and in 1949 the government sharply reduced pharmaceutical supplies and made illicit amphetamine possession and sale illegal under special stimulant control legislation. In 1954 the Japanese methamphetamine epidemic reached its peak at an estimated 2 million abusers in a population not

much higher than 80 million. Usage declined sharply thereafter, but this was followed by a serious increase in heroin use, largely driven by the easy switch from amphetamine injection.

Widespread wartime use of amphetamine may have similarly begun a postwar epidemic of nonmedical amphetamine use in the United States, albeit one less visible because it lacked the stigma associated with injection. A landmark 1945 study of military personnel imprisoned for mainly minor infractions found not only that oral consumption of high doses of amphetamine base from Benzedrine Inhalers was widespread and that many had begun abusing the inhalers in military service before imprisonment, but that military exposure to Benzedrine (mainly in tablet form provided by a medical officer) was more than five times more common among abusers than non-abusers. Thus, official military use of amphetamine appears to have significantly increased the incidence of amphetamine abuse among American servicemen. Such abuse also grew among young American civilians in the 1940s, as documented by Beatnik writers and jazz musicians. Although the high abuse potential of amphetamine inhalers was known to North American law enforcement by the end of the Second World War, the products were not entirely removed from over-the-counter sale until the early 1960s.

THE POSTWAR PANDEMIC OF
AMPHETAMINE USE

The medical use of amphetamine also began to grow dramatically in the war years. Its magnitude in the United States at the end of the war is revealed by a patent lawsuit between SKF and a smaller firm named Clark & Clark, which had been producing both imitation Benzedrine Sulfate and colorful pills for use, still unapproved, in weight loss. In late 1945 the two firms together were selling approximately 30 million tablets a month for civilian use in the United States, of which perhaps half was for depression and related psychiatric indications. Assuming that all these tablets were taken on the typical two tablets per day schedule, there were at least half a million Americans using oral amphetamines medically in 1945. These are conservative figures that disregard the production by other firms of amphetamine and (unpatented) methamphetamine, as well as the fact that amphetamine was probably consumed, on average, less frequently than twice daily. After winning the legal dispute and keeping its patent monopoly on amphetamine, and then achieving approval to market the drug for weight loss in 1947, SKF's sales of Benzedrine tablets and Dexedrine brand dextroamphetamine tablets more than tripled between 1945 and 1949. Medical amphetamine use similarly flourished in other developed countries during the immediate postwar period, and the drug became widely accepted as an everyday "antidepressant" (a term that first appears in late 1940s Benzedrine advertising).

The United States was the postwar world's leading producer and consumer of amphetamines. According to voluntary production surveys by the U.S. Food and Drug Administration (FDA), annual production of oral amphetamines by U.S. firms increased nearly fourfold between 1949, when SKF's key patent expired and competitors entered the market, and 1953. In 1962 the FDA's estimate of national production (and consumption) had reached about 8 billion 10-milligram tablets of amphetamine and methamphetamine salts. This translates into more than 40 tablets per American per year, and FDA estimates would grow only slightly by the end of the 1960s. Thus, by the beginning of the 1960s, the American market was essentially saturated with amphetamines, leading to significant iatrogenic addiction problems—although it would take another decade for significant alarm at this situation to emerge. In the early 1960s the large-scale diversion of pharmaceutical amphetamines to black-market channels for nonmedical use was also well-established.

The best evidence regarding the European countries in which medical amphetamine use flourished during the postwar period comes from the United Kingdom. A study of retail prescriptions filled in the Newcastle area during 1960 found that about 3 percent were for oral amphetamines, consistent both with U.K. national prescribing figures at the time and with contemporary prescribing in the United States. The most popular preparation was SKF's Dexamyl (or Drinamyl), a blend of dextroamphetamine and the barbiturate amobarbital. One third of amphetamine prescriptions were for weight loss, a third for clear-cut psychiatric disorders (e.g., depression, anxiety), and the remaining third for ambiguous, mostly psychiatric and psychosomatic complaints. The typical amphetamine patient was between 36 and 45 years old and female. Indeed, based on the Newcastle data, it seems that in 1960, females were twice as likely as males to receive amphetamine for psychiatric adjustment per doctor visit. Furthermore, between 2 percent and 3 percent of the total population of Newcastle must have received amphetamine prescriptions in the course of a year and, shockingly, 6.7 percent to 10 percent of these were judged by their doctors to be dependent to some degree.

With such large quantities of amphetamines being consumed medically and nonmedically in the 1950s and 1960s, the negative effects of the drugs naturally became more apparent. Amphetamine psychosis was first observed in the 1930s among long-term narcoleptic users of the drug, and individual case reports mounted during the 1940s and early 1950s, both among those prescribed tablets and those abusing inhalers. Initially, psychotic episodes were attributed to latent schizophrenia "unmasked" by the drug, or to another psychiatric defect in the victim. The definitive 1958 study of the condition by psychiatrist Philip Connell made this view untenable. A typical set of paranoid symptoms (e.g., sinister voices emanating from toilet bowls, cars or helicopters following one's every move) were uniform across a wide variety of personality types, arguing against any shared predisposing feature of mentality or neurology. In addition, the psychosis generally took time to develop, suggesting a cumulative effect. Although almost all of the 40 patients described by the British psychiatrist had engaged in some high-dose nonmedical use before their crises, a large proportion had first taken amphetamines by prescription. They could not, therefore, be stigmatized as deviant thrill-seekers. Finally, patients recovered fully a week or two after they ceased amphetamine use, proving they were never schizophrenics. Amphetamine psychosis clearly could happen to any individual, and eventually it would, given enough use of the drug.

Nevertheless, amphetamines for both weight loss and everyday psychological distress retained many medical defenders, who tended to argue that even if amphetamines caused psychosis when excessively consumed, character defects were responsible for the excessive consumption of amphetamines. Thus these drugs could still safely be prescribed to most people. This reasoning overlooked the fact that amphetamines are addictive, and indeed they were not recognized as such by pharmacologists when the drugs were initially introduced. However, new definitions of drug dependency promulgated by the World Health Organization and other expert bodies since the late 1950s moved the concept away from an older opiate-based model, in which physical withdrawal was definitive, to one centered on compulsive drug use and an erosion of psychosocial function. As this new concept of drug dependency took hold in the 1960s, it became clearer that amphetamine-type stimulants were seriously dependency-producing, and that they could therefore no longer be defended as "merely habituating," like caffeine.

REACTIONS TO THE FIRST EPIDEMIC IN THE 1960S

The realization that amphetamine pharmaceuticals presented a major abuse and dependency hazard came earlier to some countries. As noted, Nazi Germany had declared both amphetamine and methamphetamine to be addictive narcotics early in the Second World War, and in 1944, neutral Sweden followed suit when significant oral abuse first emerged. Swedish medical use of these amphetamines remained low thereafter, though pharmaceutical smuggling from neighboring countries maintained supply on the black market. However, when supposedly safer new amphetamines

were introduced in the later 1950s—phenmetrazine (trade name Preludin, for dieting) and methylphenidate (Ritalin, for depression)—they were widely prescribed, and their injection abuse soon exploded. These pharmaceuticals were taken off the medical market in 1965 and 1968, respectively. Still, in 1970 the number of addicted stimulant injectors in Stockholm was estimated at about 0.5 percent of the population (said to be comparable to heroin addiction prevalence in New York City at the time), and these abusers were primarily supplied with smuggled pharmaceutical amphetamine.

During the 1960s the overlapping problems of nonmedical amphetamine use, overmedication, and iatrogenic addiction began raising alarms in the United Kingdom and, eventually, the United States. Apart from the medical addiction explored by the Newcastle studies, purely recreational oral abuse of pharmaceutical amphetamines became widespread in London's Soho district and other areas associated with youth subcultures in the middle of the decade (among whom Drinamyl was especially popular and known as "Purple Heart"). Legislation making it illegal to possess the pills without a prescription was enacted, without any dramatic impact. Family practitioners organized their own prescribing moratoria, and these voluntary measures began to reduce amphetamine supplies in the United Kingdom to some extent by the end of the decade.

In the United States, amphetamines figured prominently in a series of scandals and Congressional hearings throughout the 1960s in connection with topics such as the role of truckers in trafficking diverted pharmaceuticals, the overmedication of women for weight loss, and polydrug abuse and addiction in Vietnam (where servicemen were supplied by the military with large quantities of dextroamphetamine). Nonmedical drug use generally became an increasingly important public issue, as the social changes of the 1960s moved the phenomenon from the social margins to the spotlight. Thus, an amphetamine injection outbreak in the San Francisco "hippie" enclave of Haight-Ashbury in 1967 and 1968 garnered enormous national press and political attention. "Speed freaks," as the amphetamine injectors were known within the hippie counterculture, engaged in a distinctive pattern of collective and frequent injection to multiply the initial "rush" experience, which they continued until total exhaustion and collapse ensued. American "speed freaks" of the late 1960s seemed to prefer methamphetamine, and much of this was supplied from small-scale illicit labs, although the great majority of amphetamines sold on the street at the time were oral pharmaceutical preparations. Thus, pharmaceutical oversupply remained the greatest source of nonmedical amphetamine problems through the end of the 1960s.

While defenders of pharmaceutical industry interests attempted to keep the issues separate, the frightening but relatively rare problem of injection abuse and the much larger problem of prescription drug overuse were associated politically as well as epidemiologically. At the end of the 1960s, the same type of scandal that had arisen regarding the overmedication of women with minor tranquilizers emerged around amphetamines, particularly as dispensed in diet pill form. One of the first modern drug use surveys measured strictly medical past-year amphetamine use in 1970 at 5 percent of American adults, while a more thorough survey of both medical and nonmedical amphetamine use in New York State found that 6.5 percent of the state's 13.8 million residents over 14 years of age had used amphetamines in the past 6 months, and of these, 39 percent had used them nonmedically. Virtually all the nonmedical users were taking pharmaceutical amphetamines, and legitimately prescribed amphetamines accounted for much of the nonmedical use. As in Newcastle, the typical user was middle-aged. Extrapolating to the United States as a whole, the New York prevalence figures would indicate that, in 1970, about 10 million Americans used amphetamines either medically or nonmedically (or both).

Accepting the medical dependency rates derived from the Newcastle studies, a conservative measure as applied to an American population containing many nonmedical users more freely supplied with amphetamines, the United States in 1970 must have contained around a million people suffering amphetamine dependency to some extent, as well as over 300,000 addicted or amphetamine-dependent individuals, strictly defined. The vast majority of these dependent individuals were supplied by the pharmaceutical industry, and many, perhaps most, obtained at least some of their amphetamines by prescription. However, unlike their counterparts in Britain and some other countries, the American medical profession resisted limits on the drugs even after such facts

became known. The AMA did not officially caution that dependency could develop from prescribed amphetamines until 1978.

LEGISLATION AND CONVENTION ON PSYCHOTROPIC SUBSTANCES, 1971

At the beginning of the 1970s a United Nations drug control treaty was instituted, expanding long-standing international opiate controls to cannabis and synthetic drugs of abuse, including the amphetamines. The 1971 Convention on Psychotropic Substances established the modern system of controlled substance "schedules" and required signatory nations to institute internal legal controls on designated drugs. Due to pharmaceutical industry lobbying, the initial U.S. legislation along these lines, the 1970 Comprehensive Drug Abuse Prevention and Control Act, included only a handful of rarely prescribed injectable methamphetamine products in Schedule II, leaving some 6,000 oral amphetamine and methamphetamine products in the much less restricted Schedule III. However, in 1971, U.S. narcotics authorities employed powers gained under the act to move all oral amphetamines, including methylphenidate and phenmetrazine, to Schedule II, where their prescriptions would be nonrefillable and subject to strict record keeping. Their production would also be limited to a quota adequate for medical demand. Prescription rates briefly soared when the changes were announced, but they fell to less than half their original levels when the changes came into effect.

Given the drop in prescriptions, narcotics authorities set 1972 U.S. amphetamine production quotas at one-fifth those of 1971 (one tenth officially reported medical production for 1969, and around one twentieth actual 1969 production), the equivalent of 400 million 10-milligram doses of amphetamine and methamphetamine salts. This was accomplished with the cooperation of the U.S. Federal Drug Administration, which was reevaluating the amphetamines as antidepressants and obesity drugs and would soon declare them of limited value for their most popular indications, leaving only narcolepsy and the then-rare pediatric condition now known as attention deficit hyperactivity disorder (ADHD).

Nonmedical amphetamine use was quickly overshadowed by rising cocaine use. Although nonmedical amphetamine use remained endemic in the United States and elsewhere after 1971, it can still be said that the first global amphetamine epidemic was brought under some control through aggressive restrictions on pharmaceutical supplies of the drugs (along with law enforcement measures against illicit distributors), much like the Japanese methamphetamine outbreak of the early 1950s.

AMPHETAMINE'S RESURGENCE

While there has been much public discussion and alarm over a methamphetamine (or "meth") epidemic in the United States, Japan, Australia, and elsewhere since the 1990s, solid quantitative evidence does not unequivocally support a dramatic general upswing in the nonmedical use of amphetamines. Instead, it may be better to picture a fairly constant endemic "background" of amphetamine and methamphetamine use, punctuated locally by outbreaks or transitory intensifications of usage and increased addiction rates triggered by increased supply or social changes. To be sure, since the late 1990s there has been a general increase in global supplies, particularly of methamphetamine produced in China and Myanmar (Burma), which recently dislodged Holland from its longstanding position as the world's leading source of illicit amphetamines. This increase in supply has been associated with localized surges in amphetamine abuse and its public health impacts. For instance, high-purity crystalline methamphetamine (sometimes known as "ice") from such

Asian sources was responsible for a sudden and destructive upsurge in methamphetamine use in Hawaii during the late 1980s.

In the mainland United States, increased supply—signaled by a rise in seizures of methamphetamine—has correlated with a distinct rise in emergency room mentions of amphetamines, especially since 2000. Usage was relatively higher in smaller cities and rural areas than in large cities, marking the importance of small-scale local manufacture along with Asian imports. A similar pattern holds for Australia, another nation with a longstanding amphetamine abuse tradition (and the second highest prevalence of nonmedical use in the world in the early 2000s; see Figure 3). In Thailand, which was leading the world in prevalence of nonmedical amphetamine use in the mid-2000s, the severe abuse and addiction problems are clearly tied to increases in large-scale illicit methamphetamine manufacture in the region.

On the other hand, in Japan, where amphetamines have long been the leading illicit drug of abuse, a dramatic increase in amphetamine-class drug seizures from 1999 to 2001—associated with the increase in large-scale East Asian methamphetamine manufacture—saw no increase in amphetamine abuse or related arrests in the general population. Thus, an increase in methamphetamine supply is not the only determinant of nonmedical amphetamine-use trends. It may be that Japan's longstanding familiarity with methamphetamine

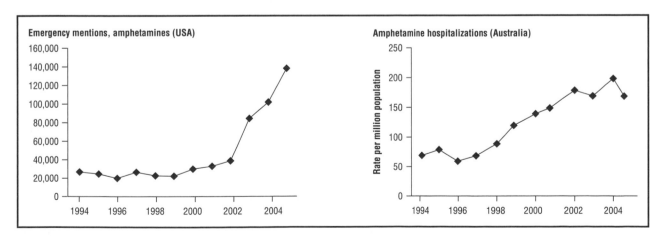

Figure 3. Trends in amphetamines-related hospitalization 1994–2005: (a) United States emergency room mentions of amphetamine-type stimulants (2003–2005 figures not directly comparable to pre-2003); (b) Australia amphetamine–related hospital separations. (Sources: Drug Abuse Warning Network and Roxburgh & Degenhardt.) ILLUSTRATION BY GGS INFORMATION SERVICES. GALE, CENGAGE LEARNING

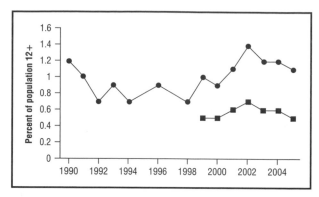

Figure 4. Nonmedical use of meth/amphetamines (USA). Past-year nonmedical use of amphetamine-type stimulants of all kinds (top) and of methamphetamine (bottom), 1990–2005. (Source: Substance Abuse and Mental Health Services Administration, National Survey on Household Drug Use Data.) ILLUSTRATION BY GGS INFORMATION SERVICES. GALE, CENGAGE LEARNING

means that there are no potential user groups unfamiliar with the drug that might take it up when supplies become easier or cheaper to obtain.

Moreover, in some nations, methamphetamine is not the only major amphetamine-type drug of abuse. While amphetamine-related emergency room mentions in the United States increased over 40 percent between 1994 and 2002, the proportion attributed specifically to methamphetamine showed a consistent decline, from over 60 percent to barely 40 percent of the total. Prevalence data from U.S. household drug use surveys tell a similar story: At least since 1999, methamphetamine has only accounted for about half of the past-year nonmedical use of amphetamine-type stimulants— which overall saw a gentle decline during the early 1990s—followed by a recent rise back to former levels (see Figure 4).

As in the original epidemic, pharmaceutical amphetamines account for a large part of American amphetamine abuse in the first decade of the 21st century. Detailed analysis of U.S. survey data shows that approximately half of the 3 million past-year nonmedical users of amphetamines in 2002 through 2004 used only non-methamphetamine drugs, particularly methylphenidate and amphetamine medications for attention deficit disorder. Further, one-quarter of them had only used ADHD stimulants in their entire lives. Past-year nonmedical users strictly of pharmaceuticals for ADHD also accounted for half of the amphetamine-abusing

Americans meeting some criteria for dependency, and for almost a third of the 300,000 who were dependent according to *DSM-IV* criteria.

Thus, the rise in nonmedical stimulant use in the United States during the late 1990s and early 2000s may owe much to the parallel, dramatic increase in methylphenidate and amphetamine prescribing for attention deficit disorder in the nation. The medical consumption of these two drugs grew 20-fold and 35-fold, respectively, between 1990 and 2005, and they have increasingly been prescribed for adolescents and adults. The relationship between ADHD medication prescribing and amphetamine abuse may involve both supply and the cultural determinants of demand. Widespread prescribing releases large supplies of amphetamines into the population, and thus increases the chance of misuse by those with prescriptions, and of resale to those without other access to the drugs. Both of these trends are well documented, especially at universities and high schools. (A similar leakage of supply occurred in the 1960s, with widespread prescribing of amphetamine antidepressants and diet pills.)

In addition, there is evidence that some current nonmedical users of amphetamines consume the drugs for essentially the same effects as those who take the drugs by prescription; namely, for a short-term improvement of working concentration. If so, then the medicalization of distractability, under the banner of attention deficit disorder (or attention deficit hyperactivity disorder), creates a demand that promotes amphetamine abuse. Finally, the return to normalization of the amphetamines as ADHD medications, after two decades of successful control through medical usage restrictions, inevitably undermines control efforts dependent on instilling a sense of danger around the drugs.

Evidently, even if methamphetamine supplies were somehow cut off completely, the longstanding endemic pattern of mostly oral nonmedical use of other amphetamines would, in many countries, continue. For stimulant addiction and its sequelae (such as amphetamine psychosis) to be fully controlled, licit amphetamine-type pharmaceuticals would also have to be entirely eliminated from circulation, because these represent a significant source of supply and a cultural priming factor for amphetamine abuse. Nevertheless, the rise in the world supply of methamphetamine raises special concerns because, in many populations of users, the dominant form of administration is intravenous, and because the use of the drug is still associated with frequent, and collective injection (as was the case among the "speed freaks" of the late 1960s); multiple sexual partners; and risky sexual practices. For example in Russia, which has serious local outbreaks of both amphetamine abuse and AIDS, amphetamine use is associated with higher rates of HIV infection than heroin use without amphetamines. Thus, syringe-exchange programs and similar harm-reduction measures that have proved effective in reducing blood-borne infectious disease in the case of heroin may also be important in minimizing the public health threat presented by outbreaks or transitory intensifications of amphetamine abuse.

See also **Epidemics of Drug Abuse in the United States; International Drug Supply Systems.**

BIBLIOGRAPHY

American Medical Association Council on Scientific Affairs. (1978). Clinical aspects of amphetamine abuse. *Journal of the American Medical Association, 240*(21), 2317–2319.

Brandon, S., & Smith, D. (1962). Amphetamines in general practice. *Journal of the College of General Practitioners, 5*(4), 603–606.

Brill, H., & Hirose, T. (1969). The rise and fall of a methamphetamine epidemic: Japan 1945–1955. *Seminars in Psychiatry, 1*, 179–194.

Cho, A. (1990). Ice: A new dosage form of an old drug. *Science, 249*(4969), 631–634.

Connell, P. H. (1958). *Amphetamine psychosis.* Oxford: Oxford University Press.

Connell, P. H. (1965). Adolescent drug taking. *Proceedings of the Royal Society of Medicine, 58*, 409–412.

Drug Abuse Warning Network (DAWN). (2003). Trends in drug-related emergency department visits, 1994–2002 at a glance. *The DAWN Report, November 2003.* Washington, DC: U.S. Department of Health and Human Services. Available from http://dawninfo.samhsa.gov/old_dawn/.

Drug Abuse Warning Network. (2008). National estimates of drug-related emergency department visits. *DAWN* Series: D-26 (2004), D-28 (2006), and D-279. Washington, DC: U.S. Department of Health and Human Services. Available from http://dawninfo.samhsa.gov/.

Gfoerer, J., & Brodsky, M. (1992). The incidence of illicit drug use in the United States, 1962–1989. *British Journal of Addiction, 87*(9), 1345–1351.

Inciardi, J., & Chambers, C. (1972). The epidemiology of amphetamine use in the general population. *Canadian Journal of Criminology and Corrections, 14*, 166–172.

Jackson, C. O. (1971). The amphetamine inhaler: A case study of medical abuse. *Journal of the History of Medicine and Allied Sciences, 26*(2), 187–196.

Jackson, C. O. (1976). Before the drug culture: Amphetamine/barbiturate abuse in American society. *Clio Medica, 11*, 47–58.

Kiloh, L. G., & Brandon, S. (1962). Habituation and addiction to amphetamines. *British Medical Journal, 2*(5296), 40–43.

Kozlov, A. P., Shaboltas, A. V., Toussova, O. V., Verevochkin, S. V., Masse, B. R., Perdue, T., et al. (2006). HIV incidence and factors associated with HIV acquisition among injection drug users in St Petersburg, Russia. *AIDS, 20*(6), 901–906.

Kramer, J., Fischman, V., & Litlefield, D. (1967). Amphetamine abuse: Patterns and effects of high doses taken intravenously. *Journal of the American Medical Association 201*(5), 305–309.

Kroutil, L. A., VanBrunt, D. L., Herman-Stahl, M. A., Heller, D. C., Bray, R. M., & Penne, M. A. (2006). Nonmedical use of prescription stimulants in the United States. *Drug Alcohol Dependence, 84*(2), 135–143.

Molitor, F., Ruiz, J. D., Flynn, N., Mikanda, J. N., Sun, R. K., & Anderson, R. (1999). Methamphetamine use and sexual and injection risk behaviors among out-of-treatment injection drug users. *American Journal of Drug and Alcohol Abuse, 25*(3), 475–493.

Monroe R., & Drell, H. (1947). Oral use of stimulants obtained from inhalers. *Journal of the American Medical Association, 135*, 909–915.

Parry, H., Balter, M. B., Mellinger, G. D., Cisin, I. H., & Manheimer, D. I. (1973). National patterns of psychotherapeutic drug use. *Archives of General Psychiatry, 28*(6), 769–783.

Perman, E. (1970). Speed in Sweden. *New England Journal of Medicine, 283*, 760–761.

Piness, G., Miller, H., & Alles, G. (1930). Clinical observations on phenylethanolamine sulfate. *Journal of the American Medical Association, 94*, 790–791.

Rasmussen, N. (2008). America's first amphetamine epidemic, 1929–1971: A quantitative and qualitative retrospective with implications for the present. *American Journal of Public Health*, 98(6), 974–985.

Rasmussen, N. (2008). *On speed: The many lives of amphetamine.* New York: New York University Press.

Rawlin, J. W. (1968). Street level abusage of amphetamines. In J. R. Russo (Ed.), *Amphetamine abuse*. Springfield, IL: Charles Thomas.

Roxburgh, A., & Degenhardt, L. (2006). *Drug-related hospital stays in Australia, 1993–2005*. Syndey, Australia: National Drug and Alcohol Research Centre.

Scott, P. D., & Willcox, D. R. C. (1965). Delinquency and the amphetamines. *British Journal of Psychiatry, 111,* 865–875.

Shepherd, J. (1968). The cruel chemical world of speed. *Look Magazine*, March 5, 53–59.

Smith, D. E. (1969). Speed freaks vs. acid heads: Conflict between drug subcultures. *Clinical Pediatrics, 8*(4), 185–188.

Steinkamp, P. (2006). Pervitin testing, use, and misuse in the German Wehrmacht. In W. Eckart (Ed.), *Man, medicine, and the state: The human body as an object of government sponsored medical research in the 20th century* (pp. 61–71). Stuttgart: Franz Steiner Verlag.

United Nations Office on Drugs and Crime. (2003). *Ecstasy and amphetamines: Global survey 2003*. New York: United Nations.

United Nations Office on Drugs and Crime. (2007). *World Drug Report 2007*. New York: United Nations.

Wells, F. (1980). The effects of a voluntary ban on amphetamine prescribing by doctors on abuse patterns: Experience in the United Kingdom. In J. Caldwell (Ed.), *Amphetamines and related stimulants: Chemical, biological, clinical and social aspects* (pp. 189–192). Boca Raton, CRC Press.

World Health Organization Expert Committee on Addiction-Producing Drugs. (1957). Seventh report. *World Health Organization technical report, 116*. Available from http://whqlibdoc.who.int/.

NICOLAS RASMUSSEN

AMYGDALA. The amygdala, a region of the brain, is part of the limbic system. The limbic system is a group of similar brain structures related functionally. They provide the basis for emotion and motivated behaviors including reward-related events. The amygdala is located in the temporal lobe and consists of several different parts. It plays a role in various brain functions including epilepsy, emotion, learning and memory, and drug abuse.

In particular, the role of the extended amygdala has become an area of recent investigation. The extended amygdala refers to a group of brain structures that extend from the amygdala to the nucleus accumbens; these brain regions are believed to participate in the general reward circuitry of the brain. The mesolimbic dopamine system sends projections to the amygdala; these axons arise from the dopamine cells in the ventral tegmental area.

The amygdala has long been established as an important area mediating stimulus-reward associations. This behavior is believed to play an important role in the seeking and using of drugs of abuse, especially cocaine. An informative way to study drug abuse in animal models is through the self-administration of drugs that are abused by humans. Rats can be trained to self-administer cocaine, and then the experimenter can interfere with the neurochemical transmission in the amygdala in particular, modulating dopamine receptors and concentrations. The result of this manipulation is that the animals will increase or decrease their rate of administration of drugs. Thus, the amygdala makes a significant contribution to the study of cocaine-taking behavior.

The amygdala also contributes to the rewarding properties of ethanol. Studies have examined the effect of altering neurotransmission in the amygdala on ethanol self-administration. Similar to the findings reported for cocaine, modulation of the amygdala causes animals to change their rate of ethanol administration.

The amygdala is also involved in the effects of chronic drug exposure on the brain. Small changes in neurochemicals in the extended amygdala suggest that it may be mediating chronic drug action. These studies indicate that changes in the amygdala after long-term drug exposure may contribute to relapse.

Together, the amygdala and nucleus accumbens may be the main brain regions that underlie the brain changes associated with drug (particularly cocaine) addiction.

See also **Brain Structures and Drugs; Cocaine; Dopamine.**

BIBLIOGRAPHY

Aggleton, J. (2000). *The amygdala: A functional analysis,* 2nd ed. New York: Oxford University Press USA.

Lautin, A. (2001). *The limbic brain.* New York: Springer.

STEPHANIE DALLVECCHIA-ADAMS

ANABOLIC STEROIDS. Anabolic steroids are synthetic versions of the naturally occurring male sex hormone, testosterone. They are more properly called anabolic-androgenic steroids (AASs), because they have both bodybuilding (anabolic) effects and masculinizing (androgenic) effects. The masculinizing effects of testosterone cause male characteristics to appear during puberty in boys, such as enlargement of the penis, hair growth on the face and pubic area, muscular development, and deepened voice. Females also produce natural testosterone, but ordinarily in much smaller amounts than males.

AASs are sometimes referred to simply as steroids. Steroid means only that a substance either resembles cholesterol in its chemical structure or is made from cholesterol in the body. Thus, AASs are one kind of steroid. (They are not to be confused with an entirely different group of steroids called corticosteroids—of which prednisone and cortisone are examples—which are commonly used to treat illnesses such as arthritis, colitis, and asthma. In contrast to anabolic steroids, corticosteroids can cause muscle tissue to be wasted.) AASs are also referred to as ergogenic drugs, which means performance-enhancing. Street or slang terms for AASs include "roids" and "juice."

Soon after testosterone was first isolated and synthesized in the laboratory in 1935, a number of synthetics were created to be used as medicines. The synthetic forms were developed because natural testosterone did not work very long when given as a pill or injection (it is subject to rapid breakdown in the body). Bodybuilders may have begun using AASs to build muscle size and strength as early as the 1940s. Olympic athletes started to use these drugs in the 1950s. Most of this use went undetected, however, because the technology of drug testing did not allow reliable detection of AASs in the urine until the 1976 Olympic Games. Even so, anabolic steroids did not become a household word until Canadian sprinter Ben Johnson tested positive for AASs at the Seoul Olympic Games in 1988. In the same year, a study reported that 6.6 percent of American male high school seniors had tried AASs. This study made it clear that elite athletes were not the only ones taking these drugs. By 1991, AASs were added by federal law to the list of Schedule III of the Controlled Substances Act. Schedule III

Generic name	Representative brand names
Injectable testosterone esters[a]	
Testosterone cypionate	Depo-Testosterone (Slang name: Depo-T), Virlon IM
Testosterone enanthate	Delatestryl
Testosterone propionate	Testex, Oreton propionate
Other injectables	
Nandrolone decanoate	Deca-Durabolin (Slang names: Deca, Deca-D)
Nandrolone phenpropionate	Durabolin
Methenolone enanthate	Primobolan Depot
Veterinary injectables used by humans	
Trenbolone acetate	Finaject (Finajet) 30, Parabolan
Boldenone undecylenate	Equipoise
Stanozolol	Winstrol V
Pills (17-alkylated AASs)[b]	
Ethylestrenol	Maxibolan
Fluoxymesterone	Halotestin
Methandroslenolene	Dianabol (Slang names: D-bol, D-ball)
Methenolone	Primobolan
Methyltestosterone	Android (10 & 25), Metandren, Oreton Methyl, Testred, Virilon
Oxandrolone	Anavar
Oxymetholone	Adroyd, Anadrol-50
Oxymesterone	Oranabol
Stanozolol	Winstrol

[a]Least toxic to liver and cholesterol levels; cause estrogen levels to increase.
[b]Most toxic to liver and cholesterol levels.

Table 1. Anabolic steroids used by bodybuilders. ILLUSTRATION BY GGS INFORMATION SERVICES. GALE, CENGAGE LEARNING

Controlled Substances are recognized to have value as prescribed medicines, but also have a potential for abuse that may lead to either low to moderate physical dependence or high psychological dependence. Table 1 lists the names of some AASs that bodybuilders have used. Hundreds of AASs have been synthesized, and more comprehensive lists exist (Wright & Cowart, 1990; Yesalis, 2000).

Two naturally occurring steroids, dehydroepiandrosterone (DHEA) and androstenedione, are used by the body to make testosterone and estrogen (Corrigan, 1999). The benefits and adverse effects of synthetic DHEA and androstenedione are mostly unknown, but they are commonly believed to have anabolic and androgenic effects. Unlike other AASs, DHEA and androstenedione are neither regulated by the Food and Drug Administration nor listed as controlled substances in the United States. DHEA has been sold over-the-counter as a nutritional supplement in the United States since 1994, even though the International Olympic Committee,

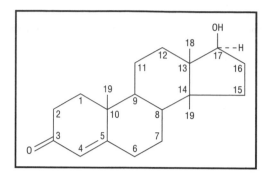

Figure 1. Testosterone molecule. The numbers refer to carbon atoms, and the hydrogen and hydroxyl groups are at carbon 17. ILLUSTRATION BY GGS INFORMATION SERVICES. GALE, CENGAGE LEARNING

many U.S. sports organizations, and some countries such as Australia ban it.

GENERAL CHEMICAL STRUCTURE

Testosterone has a four-ring structure composed of nineteen carbon atoms. Accordingly, the carbon atoms are labeled by number from one to nineteen (see Figure 1). Many synthetic forms of testosterone are made by adding either an alkyl group or an ester to the seventeen-carbon atom. An alkyl group is a chain of carbon and hydrogen atoms. An ester is formed by reacting an acidic chain of carbon and hydrogen atoms to the −OH group on the seventeen-carbon atom. In general, when an alkyl group is added to the seventeen-carbon atom, the resulting drug can be taken as a pill; however, these so-called seventeen-alkylated AASs are relatively toxic to the liver and are more likely to cause negative effects on cholesterol levels. By contrast, when an ester is formed at the seventeen-carbon atom, an injectable form of testosterone is created that is less toxic to the liver and cholesterol levels. Other AASs are created by making modifications at other carbon atoms.

MEDICAL AND NONMEDICAL USES

AASs are prescribed by physicians to treat a variety of medical conditions (Bagatell & Bremner, 1996). The most accepted use is for treating boys and men unable to produce normal levels of their own testosterone, a condition known as testosterone deficiency or hypogonadism. AASs are also used to treat a rare skin condition called hereditary

angioedema, certain forms of anemia (deficiency of red blood cells), advanced breast cancer, and endometriosis (a painful condition in females in which tissue usually found only in the uterus develops in other body parts). AASs are also combined with female hormones to treat distressing symptoms that can accompany menopause. Experimentally, AASs have been used to treat a condition in which bone loss occurs (osteoporosis), to treat impotency and low sexual desire, and as a male birth control pill. In addition, AASs have been used in the treatment of Acquired Immune Deficiency Syndrome (AIDS) to stimulate appetite, weight gain, strength, and improvements in mood. Most of these medical uses are uncommon, either because the conditions are rare (such as angioedema) or because other treatments are preferred (such as erythropoeitin for anemia). Nevertheless, AASs are important medicines to have available.

Nonmedically, AASs are used to enhance athletic performance, physical appearance, and fighting ability. Since society endows people who look physically fit and attractive with many benefits and recognition, some individuals see AASs as a means to those benefits. Three groups of AAS users have been described:

1. The athlete group aims to win at any cost. The athlete also believes, sometimes correctly, that the competition is using AASs. The anticipated rewards to the athlete are the glory of victory, social recognition and popularity, and financial incentives (college scholarships, major league contracts).

2. The aesthete group aims to create a beautiful body, as if to make the body into a work of art. Aesthetes may be competitive bodybuilders, or aspiring models, actors, or dancers. They put their bodies on display to obtain admiration and financial rewards.

3. This group of AAS users seeks to enhance their ability to fight or intimidate. They include body guards, security guards, prison guards, police, soldiers, bouncers, and gang members. These people depend on fighting for their very survival.

Whether AASs actually work to improve performance and appearance has been debated.

Invariably, users believe AASs do work, but some scientific studies have failed to show an effect. However, there are serious limitations to how these studies were done and what they could show. In general, most researchers agree that AASs can work in some individuals to enhance muscle size and strength when combined with a proper exercise program and diet (Bagatell & Bremner, 1996; Bhasin et al., 1996). By contrast, AASs probably do not improve performance of aerobic or endurance activities (Yesalis, 2000).

CONSEQUENCES OF USE

AASs have been associated with a variety of undesirable effects. The most severe consequence attributed to their use is death. One study of mice given AASs revealed a shortened life span (National Institute on Drug Abuse, 2000). In humans, the distinction between fatalities that occur among relatively healthy athletes who use AASs and patients with illnesses (such as anemia) who are prescribed AASs is important, because ill patients are already at a higher risk for an early death. Nevertheless, reported deaths in nonmedical steroid users (such as athletes and aesthetes) have occurred from liver disease, cancer, heart attacks, strokes, and suicide (Yesalis, 2000; Pope & Brower, 2000). Clearly, anyone using AASs should have their health monitored by a physician.

Psychiatric Effects. Another serious, life-threatening consequence has been violent aggression toward other people. Both the medical literature and newspapers contain reports of previously mild-mannered individuals who committed murder and lesser assaults while taking AASs (Thiblin et al. 1997). Although reports of severe violence generate both alarm and widespread attention, the total number of such reports is small. Moreover, the effects of AASs on violent behavior vary widely depending on the social circumstances and the characteristics of the individual. Nevertheless, most but not all studies in humans have found that high doses of AASs increase feelings and thoughts of aggressiveness (Yesalis & Cowart, 1998). Although an increase in feelings and thoughts of violence does not always lead to violent behavior, it can be very distressing to the individual and to those around him or her. "Roid rage" is a slang expression used to describe the aggressive feelings, thoughts, and behaviors of AAS users.

Other psychiatric effects of AASs include mood swings and psychosis (Pope & Brower, 2000). AAS users commonly report that they feel energetic, confident, and even euphoric during a cycle of use. They may have a decreased need for sleep or find it difficult to sleep because of their high energy level. Such feelings may give way to feeling down, depressed, irritable, and tired between cycles of use. With continued use of high AAS doses, moods may shift suddenly, so that the user feels on top of the world one moment, irritable and aggressive the next, and then depressed or nervous. The appetite may also swing widely with cycles of use (Wright & Cowart, 1990). During a cycle on AASs, huge quantities of food may be consumed to support the body's requirements for muscle growth and energy. During the "off cycles," appetite may diminish.

The term *psychosis* means that a person cannot distinguish between what is real and what is not. For example, a person may believe that other people intend harm when no real threat exists; or a person may believe that an impossible, life-threatening stunt can be performed with no problem. Such false beliefs are called *delusions*. The psychotic person may also experience hallucinations, such as hearing a voice that is not there. Fortunately, most psychiatric effects of AASs tend to disappear soon after AASs are stopped, although a depressed mood may last for several months. Obviously, when suicides, homicides, or legal consequences from assault have occurred, they cannot be reversed simply by stopping one's use of AASs.

Effects on the Liver. AASs can affect the liver in various ways, but the seventeen-alkylated AASs are more toxic to the liver than other AASs. Most commonly, AASs cause the liver to release extra amounts of enzymes into the bloodstream that can be easily measured by a blood test. The liver enzymes usually return to normal levels when AASs are stopped. The liver also releases a substance called bilirubin, which in high amounts can cause the skin and eyes to turn yellow (a condition called jaundice). As many as 17 percent of patients treated with the seventeen-alkylated AASs develop jaundice (Yesalis, 2000). Nonmedical AAS users can also develop jaundice. Although untreated jaundice can be dangerous and even fatal, jaundice usually disappears within several weeks of stopping AASs. Jaundice can also signal other dangerous conditions of the liver, such as hepatitis, so a physician should always treat it. Another condition that occurs among patients treated with AASs is peliosis hepatis, in which little sacs of blood form in the liver. Death can occur from bleeding if one of the sacs ruptures. Finally, liver tumors may occur in 1 to 3 percent of individuals (including athletes) using high doses of the seventeen-alkylated AASs for more than two years (Yesalis, 2000). Rare cases of liver tumors have been reported with other types of AASs as well. Some of the tumors are cancerous, and although more than half of the tumors disappeared when AASs were stopped, others resulted in death.

Potential to Affect the Heart. AASs can cause changes in cholesterol levels (Yesalis, 2000). Low amounts of a certain kind of cholesterol (high-density lipoprotein cholesterol) in the blood are known to increase the risk of heart attacks. AASs, especially the seventeen-alkylated ones, cause a lowering of this so-called good form of cholesterol. When AASs are stopped, however, cholesterol levels return to normal. Another risk factor for heart attacks and strokes is high blood pressure. Studies have shown that AASs can cause small increases in blood pressure, which return to normal when AASs are stopped. As a result of strenuous exercise, many athletes develop an enlarged heart that is not harmful. Some, but not all studies, suggest that AAS users can develop a harmful enlargement of the heart. As noted previously, heart attacks and strokes have been reported in AAS users, but studies are needed to determine if AAS users have a higher risk of heart attacks and strokes than non-users (Yesalis, 2000).

Sexual Side Effects. AASs can alter the levels of several sex-related hormones in the body, resulting in many adverse effects (Wright & Cowart, 1990; Yesalis & Cowart, 1998). In males, the prostate gland can enlarge, making it difficult to urinate; the testes shrink; and sterility can occur. The effects on the prostate, the testes, and sterility reverse when AASs are stopped; however, at least one case of prostate cancer has been reported, an exception to reversibility. Males can also develop enlarged breast tissue from taking AASs, an effect medically

termed *gynecomastia* (it is referred to by male users as "bitch tits"). Gynecomastia occurs because testosterone is chemically changed in the body to the female hormone, estrogen. Thus, the male user experiences higher amounts of estrogen than normal. Painful lumps in the male breast may persist after stopping AASs, and they sometimes require surgical removal. Females, however, may undergo shrinkage of their breasts, as a response to higher amounts of male hormone than normal. Menstrual periods become irregular and sterility can occur in females as well. Deepened voice and an enlarged clitoris are effects in females, which do not always reverse after stopping AASs. Women may also develop excessive hair growth in typically masculine patterns, such as on the chest and face. Finally, both males and females may experience increases and decreases in their desire for sex.

Other Effects. In children of both sexes before the onset of puberty, AASs can initiate the characteristics of male puberty and cause the bones to stop growing prematurely. The latter effect can result in shorter adult heights than would otherwise occur. AASs can cause premature baldness in some individuals, and it can cause acne. The acne is reversible with cessation of AASs. Other possible effects include small increases in the number of red blood cells, worsening of a condition called sleep apnea (in which afflicted persons stop breathing for short intervals during sleep), and worsening of muscle twitches (known as tics) in those who are predisposed.

Patterns of Illicit Use. AASs are commonly smuggled from countries where they are obtained over-the-counter without a prescription, and then sold illegally in the United States. Dealers and users typically connect in weight-lifting gyms. Users report that AASs are relatively easy to obtain.

Steroids are taken as pills, through skin patches, and by injection (Bagatell & Bremner, 1996). Injection occurs into large muscle groups (buttocks, thigh, or shoulder) or under the skin, but not into veins. Cases of acquired immune deficiency syndrome (AIDS) have been reported in steroid users due to needle sharing. Steroids are often taken in cycles of six to twelve weeks on the drugs, followed by six to twelve weeks off. At the beginning of a cycle, small doses are taken with the intent to build to larger doses, which are then tapered at the end of a cycle. Illicit users typically consume ten to one hundred times the amounts ordinarily prescribed for medical purposes, requiring them to combine or "stack" multiple steroid drugs. The actual dose cannot always be determined, however, because illicit steroids may contain both falsely labeled and veterinary preparations. (Drugs purchased on the illicit market do not always contain what the labels indicate, and law-enforcement officials have confiscated vials contaminated with bacteria.)

Steroid users commonly take other drugs, each with their own risks, to manage the unpleasant side effects of steroids, to increase the body-building effects, and/or to avoid detection by urine testing (Wright & Cowart, 1990). For example, estrogen blockers, such as tamoxifen or clomiphene, are taken to prevent breast enlargement. Water pills (diuretics) are taken both to dilute the urine prior to drug testing and to eliminate fluid retention so that muscles will look more defined. Human chorionic gonadotropin (HCG) is an injectable, nonsteroidal hormone that stimulates the testicles to produce more testosterone and to prevent them from shrinking. Human growth hormone is another nonsteroidal hormone that is taken to increase muscle and body size.

Addictive Potential. As with other drugs of abuse, dependence on AASs occurs when a user reports several of the following symptoms: Inability to stop or cut down use, taking more drugs than intended, continued use despite having negative effects, tolerance, and withdrawal. "Tolerance" refers to needing more of a drug to get the same effect that was previously obtained with smaller doses, or of having diminished effects with the same dose. In terms of the anabolic effects, tolerance was demonstrated in animals in the 1950s. In recent studies, 12 to 18 percent of nonmedical AAS users reported tolerance (Yesalis, 2000; Copeland et al., 2000). Whether tolerance develops to the mood-altering effects of AASs is unknown. *Withdrawal* refers to the uncomfortable effects users experience when they stop taking AASs. As noted previously, many of the undesirable effects reverse when AASs are stopped, however, others can begin—such as depressed mood, fatigue, loss of appetite, difficulty sleeping, restlessness, decreased sex drive, headaches, muscle aches, and a desire for more

AASs (Copeland et al., 2000). The depression can become so severe that suicidal thoughts occur. The risk of suicide described previously is thought to be highest during the withdrawal period.

Studies indicate that between 14 and 57 percent of nonmedical AAS users develop dependence on AASs (Yesalis, 2000), and rare cases have been reported in women (Copeland et al., 2000). These studies support the addition of AASs to the list of Schedule III controlled substances. Nevertheless, AASs may differ from other drugs of abuse in several ways. First, neither physical nor psychological dependence on AASs has been reported to occur when AASs are prescribed for treating medical conditions. This differentiates the AASs from the opioid pain killers and the sedative-hypnotics. Second, dependence may develop primarily to the muscle-altering effects of AASs, rather than the mood-altering effects. Some researchers have questioned whether AASs produce dependence at all, because most definitions of dependence require that drugs be taken primarily for their mood-altering effects. Third, AAS users appear more preoccupied with their bodies and how they look than do users of other drugs of dependence.

ANABOLIC STEROIDS: SUMMARY
The anabolic-androgenic steroids are related to the male sex hormone, testosterone. They have both masculinizing and bodybuilding effects. AASs are useful to treat a variety of mostly uncommon medical conditions. They are sometimes used for the nonmedical purposes of enhancing athletic performance and physical appearance. Most researchers agree with users that AASs can increase muscle size and strength in some individuals when combined with a proper exercise program and diet. Many are also concerned about the potential for harmful effects with AASs, especially when the patterns of illicit use are considered. Drugs obtained on the illicit market may be contaminated, falsely labeled, or may contain substances not approved for human use. Multiple steroid and nonsteroidal drugs are combined, and AAS doses may exceed therapeutic doses by ten to one hundred times. Although the seventeen-alkylated AASs are commonly used because pills are more convenient than injections, they are more toxic to the liver and cholesterol levels than the injectable testosterone esters. Nevertheless, injections carry their own risks

from improper injection techniques to dirty and shared needles.

The most serious side effects of AASs seem relatively uncommon, such as deaths or near-deaths from liver disease, heart attacks, strokes, cancer, suicide, and homicidal aggression. Most other side effects appear to be reversible when AASs are stopped, such as altered cholesterol levels, some liver effects, most psychiatric effects, testicular shrinkage, sterility, high blood pressure, and acne. Exceptions to reversibility include lumps in the male breast, deepened voice and enlarged clitoris in females, and cessation of bone growth in children. Moreover, some individuals may develop dependence on AASs, making it difficult for them to stop using. Stopping use can also produce distressing withdrawal symptoms, the worst of which is suicidal depression. Finally, studies of the long-term effects of using AASs are lacking, so safety cannot be assumed with the high-dose use of these drugs.

See also **Sport, Drugs in International.**

BIBLIOGRAPHY

Bagatell, C. J., & Bremner, W. J. (1996). Drug therapy: Androgens in men—uses and abuses. *New England Journal of Medicine, 334,* 707–714.

Bhasin, S., et al. (1996). The effects of supraphysiological doses of testosterone on muscle size and strength in normal men. *New England Journal of Medicine, 335,* 1–7.

Bronson, F. H., & Matherne, C. M. (1997). Exposure to anabolic-androgenic steroids shortens life span of male mice. *Medicine and Science in Sports and Exercise, 29,* 615–619.

Copeland, J., Peters, R., & Dillon, P. (2000). Anabolic-androgenic steroid use disorders among a sample of Australian competitive and recreational users. *Drug and Alcohol Dependence, 60,* 91–96.

Corrigan, A. B. (1999). Dehydroepiandrosterone and sport. *Medical Journal of Australia, 171,* 4, 206–208.

National Institute on Drug Abuse. (2000). Research Report: *Anabolic Steroid Abuse.*

Pope, Jr., H. G., & Brower, K. J. (2000). Anabolic-androgenic steroid abuse. In B. J. Sadock & V. A. Sadock (Eds.), *Comprehensive textbook of psychiatry.* Philadelphia: Lippincott Williams & Wilkins. (2004, 8th ed.)

Taylor, W. (2002). *Anabolic steroids and the athlete.* Jefferson, NC: Human McFarland.

Thiblin, I., Kristiansson, M., & Rajs, J. (1997). Anabolic androgenic steroids and behavioural patterns among violent offenders. *Journal of Forensic Psychiatry, 8,* 299–310.

Wright, J. E., & Cowart, V. S. (1990). *Anabolic steroids: Altered states.* Carmel, IN: Benchmark Press.

Yesalis, C. E., Ed. (2000). *Anabolic steroids in sport and exercise.* Champaign, IL: Human Kinetics.

Yesalis, C. E., & Cowart, V. S. (1998). *The steroids game.* Champaign, IL: Human Kinetics.

KIRK J. BROWER

ANALGESIC. Analgesics are drugs used to control pain without producing anesthesia or loss of consciousness. Analgesics vary in terms of their class, chemical composition, and strength. Mild analgesics, such as aspirin (e.g., Bayer, Bufferin), acetominophen (e.g., Tylenol), and ibuprofen (e.g., Advil), work throughout the body. More potent agents, including the opiates codeine and morphine, work within the central nervous system (the brain and spinal cord). The availability of the more potent analgesics is more carefully regulated than that of aspirin and other similar analgesic/anti-inflammatory agents that are sold in drugstores over-the-counter. The more potent opiate agents typically require prescriptions to be filled by pharmacists.

An important aspect of analgesics is that they work selectively on pain, but not on other types of sensation, such as touch. In this regard, they are easily distinguished from anesthetics that block all sensation. Local anesthetics, such as those used in dental work, make an area completely numb for several hours. General anesthetics typically are used to render patients unconscious for surgery.

See also **Pain, Drugs Used for.**

BIBLIOGRAPHY

Hardman, J. G., et al., Eds. (1996). *The pharmacological basis of therapeutics,* 9th ed. New York: McGraw-Hill Medical. (2005, 11th ed.)

GAVRIL W. PASTERNAK

ANHEDONIA. Anhedonia is the inability to derive pleasure from ordinary activities. Generally, certain stimuli (e.g., food, water, the company of friends) serve as positive reinforcers in normal individuals. (*Positive reinforcement* is a descriptive term used by behavioral scientists to denote an increase in the probability of a behavior occurring in response to the presentation of a stimulus, such as food.)

Anhedonia may be idiopathic (of unknown cause), it may occur as a side effect of certain drugs (for example, the antipsychotic medications) that act as dopamine-receptor antagonists, or it may be an aspect of certain psychiatric disorders. Anecdotally associated with schizophrenia and post-psychotic depression, anhedonia is also associated with chronic unipolar depression, according to the *Diagnostic and Statistical Manual of Mental Disorders* (1994). It is also associated with drug dependence, a core symptom of which is the depression that occurs when the drug is no longer self-administered (Koob & Le Moal, 1997). The presence of anhedonia in chronic drug users is of considerable theoretical interest because it may give insight into the biological mechanisms that underlie drug dependence.

The acute administration of drugs of abuse elevates dopamine and serotonin levels in the nucleus accumbens, a brain structure that has been implicated in reinforcement. After the termination of drug use, dopamine and serotonin levels in the nucleus accumbens decrease below baseline levels, suggesting that this is the neurochemical basis for the associated anhedonia.

The hypothalamic-pituitary-adrenal (HPA) axis is another system that has been implicated in the anhedonia associated with drug withdrawal. The neuropeptide corticotropin-releasing factor (CRF) helps to regulate the HPA axis. CRF induces behavioral and physiological responses resembling those observed during exposure to stress, which includes the release of corticosteroids such as cortisol from the adrenal glands. Withdrawal from drugs of abuse such as cocaine, amphetamine, alcohol, and cannabinoids induces a strong activation of brain CRF systems, and antagonism of brain CRF receptors alleviates the negative affective symptoms associated with drug withdrawal (Koob, 1999). Chronic activation of the HPA axis may also lead to the development of anhedonia. This may explain why major depression is the most common comorbid psychiatric disorder in patients with Cushing's disease, which results from elevated systemic glucocorticoid levels.

See also **Brain Structures and Drugs; Depression; Dopamine; Physical Dependence; Reinforcement; Withdrawal.**

BIBLIOGRAPHY

American Psychiatric Association. (1994). *Diagnostic and statistical manual of mental disorders* (4th ed.). Washington, DC: Author.

Koob, G. F. (1999). Stress, corticotropin-releasing factor, and drug addiction. *Annals of the New York Academy of Sciences, 897,* 27–45.

Koob, G. F., & Le Moal, M. (1997). Drug abuse: Hedonic homeostatic dysregulation. *Science, 278* (5335), 52–58.

Rossetti, Z. L., Hmaidan, Y., & Gessa, G. L. (1992). Marked inhibition of mesolimbic dopamine release: A common feature of ethanol, morphine, cocaine, and amphetamine abstinence in rats. *European Journal of Pharmacology, 221* (2-3), 227–234.

Sonino, N., & Fava, G. A. (2001). Psychiatric disorders associated with Cushing's syndrome: Epidemiology, pathophysiology, and treatment. *CNS Drugs,* 15 (5), 361–373.

Spanagel, R., & Weiss, F. (1999). The dopamine hypothesis of reward: Past and current status. *Trends in Neuroscience,* 22 (11), 521–527.

ANTHONY PHILLIPS
REVISED BY MAHLON HALE (2009)

ANORECTIC. This term derives from Greek (*a + oregein*, meaning "not to reach for"; later, *anorektos*) and it refers to a substance that reduces food intake. It came into use in English about 1900. Anorectic agents (also referred to as anorexics, anorexegenics, or appetite suppressants) fall into a number of categories according to the brain neurotransmitter system through which they work.

Central nervous system (CNS) stimulants that act through the noradrenergic and dopaminergic systems include cocaine, amphetamine-like compounds, mazindol, and phenylpropanalamine. Serotonergic compounds include fenfluramine, fluoxetine, and sertraline. Several endogenous peptides (within the body) also have anorectic actions, in that they inhibit food intake—these include cholecystokinin, glucagon, and the bombesin-like peptides.

Not *all* agents that can suppress appetite are medically approved for such use. For example, cocaine is approved *only* as a local anesthetic.

See also **Amphetamine.**

BIBLIOGRAPHY

Colman, E. (2005). Anorectics on trial: A half century of federal regulation of prescription appetite suppressants. *Annals of Internal Medicine, 143*, 5, 380–385.

TIMOTHY H. MORAN

ANOREXIA. *Anorexia* literally means "loss of appetite" and may be accompanied by moderate to extreme weight loss. People suffering from anorexia have little desire to eat, usually as a consequence of serious illness. It is often a symptom of depression and an accompaniment of alcohol and drug abuse, especially the abuse of cocaine and amphetamines. Anorexia should not be confused with anorexia nervosa, which is a mental illness with physical side effects akin to anorexia.

See also **Anorexia Nervosa; Bulimia Nervosa; Overeating and Other Excessive Behaviors.**

SERENA C. IACONO
WILLIAM G. IACONO

ANOREXIA NERVOSA. Anorexia nervosa is a mental illness that is often accompanied by severe physical complications. Although the prevalence of anorexia nervosa among men may be rising, females are ten times more likely to receive this diagnosis than males. About 0.5 percent of young women are affected, with onset in late adolescence typical.

Anorectics frequently deny their illness, and many may otherwise appear well. Anorexia nervosa is characterized by deliberate weight loss, which is not explainable by disease or illness, and a refusal to maintain a healthy weight. It is accompanied by a distorted sense of body image and a fear of becoming fat regardless of current size or weight. Anorectics with the restricting subtype severely limit their diet by eating little food and/or food with low caloric content. Excessive exercise is also common. People with the bingeing and purging subtype may eat excessive amounts of food and engage in compensatory behavior, such as self-induced vomiting or misuse of diuretics and laxatives to alter the consequences of their perceived binge.

Including the term *anorexia* as part of the label for those with this disorder is somewhat misleading because those with anorexia nervosa purposefully deny themselves food in a misguided attempt to lose weight. Appetite is only lost after significant physical wasting occurs (i.e., muscles have degenerated).

Anorectics may develop a state of starvation that affects every major organ system in the body, especially the cardiac and electrolyte systems. People with this disorder also have thin, pale, inelastic skin; experience low blood pressure; feel cold all the time; lose hair on their head and sometimes grow body hair (lanugo) to conserve heat. The reproductive system is also affected with many women going through stages of amenorrhea (loss of three consecutive menstrual periods). As the most fatal of recognized mental illnesses, deaths occur in more than 10 percent of the anorectic population. Starvation, suicide, and electrolyte imbalance are among the leading causes of death for people with anorexia nervosa.

While the causes of anorexia nervosa are generally unknown, there are a few repeated patterns in the occurrence of the disorder. For example, anorexia is most commonly found in young women from industrialized countries, many of which promote unattainable standards of thinness through various kinds of media. In addition, the development of anorexia nervosa is genetically influenced, with altered neurobiology characteristic of both active and remitted phases of disorder. In general, anorectics tend to be perfectionistic, over-achievers of average or higher intelligence. They are also prone to depression and anxiety disorders. The bingeing and purging subtype tends to be impulsive and often has concurrent problems with alcohol and drug abuse, risky sexual behavior, and suicidal ideation and attempts.

Treatment for this disorder is twofold. The first objective is to restore weight and save life, which can require hospitalization. The second objective is to address the psychological issues contributing to weight loss and the fixation on physical appearance as a basis for self-esteem.

See also **Anorexia; Bulimia Nervosa; Overeating and Other Excessive Behaviors.**

BIBLIOGRAPHY

Hoek, H. W. (2006). Incidence, prevalence and mortality of anorexia nervosa and other eating disorders. *Current Opinion in Psychiatry, 19*(4), 389–394.

Morris, J., & Twaddle, S. (2007). Anorexia nervosa. *British Medical Journal, 334*(7599), 894–898.

National Institute of Mental Health. (2007). *Eating disorders* (NIH Publication No. 07–4901). Bethesda, MD: Author.

SERENA C. IACONO
WILLIAM G. IACONO

ANSLINGER, HARRY JACOB, AND U.S. DRUG POLICY.

For almost a third of a century, one man, Harry Jacob Anslinger (1892–1975), played the dominant role in shaping and enforcing U.S. drug policy. From 1930 to 1962, Anslinger served as Commissioner of the Federal Bureau of Narcotics (FBN, later Drug Enforcement Administration), which was housed in the U.S. Treasury Department. Only J. Edgar Hoover served a longer term in a federal appointed position. Anslinger also served as chief U.S. delegate to international drug agencies, including the United Nations, until 1970. He saw three major pieces of drug legislation through Congress, and much of his legacy remained current as of 2008. Therefore, to understand the evolution and state of federal drug policy, one must examine Anslinger's life and work.

Anslinger was born in Altoona, Pennsylvania, on May 20, 1892, the eighth of nine children in a Swiss immigrant family. In his book *The Murderers*, Anslinger wrote about an incident early in his life that shaped his ideas about narcotic drugs. At the age of twelve, he was sent to the drugstore by a neighbor to pick up a package of morphine for the neighbor's wife who was screaming in pain. Anslinger wrote: "I recall driving those horses, lashing at them, convinced that the woman would die if I did not get back in time. When I returned with the package—it was morphine—the man

hurried upstairs to give the woman the dosage. In a little while, her screams stopped and a hush came over the house. I never forgot those screams. Nor did I forget that the morphine she had required was sold to a twelve-year-old boy, no questions asked" (Anslinger & Oursler, 1961).

About a decade after this incident, Congress passed the Harrison Narcotics Act of 1914, the first federal law against selling or using narcotics. Prior to that, narcotics were inexpensive, and many people used them as legal painkillers. Some people became addicted, often without realizing it, maintaining a steady dosage of cheap drugs that enabled them to manage their pain and continue to function satisfactorily at work and at home.

At age fourteen, Anslinger started working for the Pennsylvania Railroad while taking high school courses in his free hours. Without a high school diploma, he entered Pennsylvania State College in 1913 and completed a two-year program in engineering and business management. He continued to work part-time and summers for the railroad and played the piano for silent movies.

During summer break from Penn State, a very young Anslinger was exposed to a second incident that would shape his life—this one involved a fellow Pennsylvania Railroad worker, an immigrant named Giovanni, whom Anslinger found shot and beaten alongside the railroad tracks. Anslinger suspected that the hard-working, humble Giovanni was the victim of an extortionist working for the so-called Black Hand (*Mano Nero* in Italian). Giovanni survived the attack, and Anslinger questioned him while he was recovering in the hospital. After guaranteeing Giovanni that his family would be safe, Anslinger learned that Big Mouth Sam was the perpetrator. Anslinger found Big Mouth Sam and greeted him with "I'm Giovanni's boss and friend." In *The Murderers*, Anslinger wrote: "I told him I knew he was the one who pumped all that le[a]d into Giovanni's body and dumped him in the ditch. 'If Giovanni dies,' I warned him, 'I'm going to see to it that you hang. Do you understand that?' Big Mouth started to object again but I cut him short. 'And if he lives and you ever bother him again, or any of my men, or try to shake any of them down any more, I'll kill you with my own hands.'" Anslinger concluded, "Such was my first direct encounter with this transplanted

Anslinger helped create the 1931 Narcotics Limitations Convention, which regulated the production of drugs for medical uses. AP IMAGES brotherhood of plunder, extortion, thievery and murder" (Anslinger & Oursler, 1961, p. 10). Throughout his career, Anslinger kept a sharp eye on underworld-type characters, effecting many of their arrests because of drug smuggling.

In 1917, Anslinger volunteered to help the American effort in World War I and worked for the U.S. Army as assistant to the chief of inspection of equipment. In 1918, Anslinger entered the U.S diplomatic service. He spoke fluent Dutch and German, and his first post, which lasted three years, was the Netherlands, where he was assigned as liaison to the entourage of deposed Kaiser Wilhelm. In summer 1921, he was sent to Hamburg, Germany, and in 1923, he was reassigned from Germany to Venezuela for a frustratingly dull three-year tour as U.S. vice consul in LaGuaira, the port for the capital city of Caracas.

FEDERAL BUREAU OF NARCOTICS

In 1920, the Prohibition Amendment made importing, manufacturing, or selling alcoholic beverages illegal throughout the United States and its possessions. People with sacramental or medicinal needs could possess a small amount of alcohol. History clearly shows that illegal liquor became an instant success. In 1926, Anslinger became U.S. consul in Nassau in the British Bahamas, at the time a principal source from which illegal alcohol was smuggled into the United States. Consul Anslinger was quickly recognized for his effective work in persuading the British authorities to cooperate in curbing the flow of alcohol. The Volstead Act (1919) and the Harrison Act (1914), which were aimed respectively at enforcing Prohibition and controlling the distribution of narcotic drugs, were both tax measures under the jurisdiction of the Treasury Department. The U.S. Treasury soon borrowed Anslinger from the Department of State to serve in its Prohibition Unit, which then enforced both acts. The Narcotics Division of the Prohibition Unit was headed from 1920 to 1930 by Colonel Levi G. Nutt. However, Nutt was fired in 1930 after a 1929 investigation revealed misconduct in his office, which he denied. On July 1, 1930, three years before Prohibition ended, the drug-regulation functions were shifted to a new Federal Bureau of Narcotics (FBN), and on September 23, 1930, President Herbert C. Hoover appointed Anslinger its first Commissioner.

Immediately, Anslinger began what would be an important part of his legacy: He espoused the notion that the threat of punitive measures would deter drug traffickers and users. So for thirty-plus years, Anslinger claimed that higher fines and longer prison terms were the best corrective action for the increasing narcotic drug-use problem in the United States.

Because the Harrison Act was passed as a revenue measure, individual states had to legislate prohibition and penalties. So through the 1920s, almost every state created narcotic control laws. However, by 1930, some leaders in government, medicine, and pharmaceuticals began to urge passage of a federal law for a few reasons: The states' laws were very uneven, states did not have the support and resources to effectively curb drug trafficking, and the media were beginning to report on drug addiction, planting the seed for ensuing hysteria around drug addicts.

Anslinger and the FBN promoted passage of the Uniform State Narcotic Drug Act, mostly because it kept out of their jurisdiction the so-called nuisance drug marijuana. A voracious reader, Anslinger probably was aware of the National Wholesale Druggists' Association's position that cannabis should not be included in any federal legislation because it "was not what might be called a habit-forming drug" (Musto, 1987, p. 217). Anslinger knew that cramming the courts with marijuana cases would cast an unfavorable judicial light on the Bureau, so he instructed his agents to police more lethal drugs, cocaine, and opiates. Yet during his tenure as commissioner, Anslinger dominated the enactment of U.S. narcotics laws.

MARIJUANA TAX ACT OF 1937

Supporting the Uniform State Narcotic Drug Act, Anslinger almost never mentioned marijuana during the first half of the 1930s. However, in 1936, F. W. Russe, secretary of Mallinckrodt Chemical Works, wrote to Anslinger asking whether the news he had heard about a bill titled the Secret Service Reorganization Act was accurate. The act would collapse a number of federal bureaus into one, and the FBN was among them. Thus, Anslinger could have been forced out of his position, and the FBN diluted.

At that moment, Anslinger found the argument that he would pull out every time he wanted stronger narcotics-abuse penalties: the threat of marijuana corrupting the nation's youth. At that time, marijuana (*Cannabis sativa*) had limited favor among a few Caribbean Blacks, Hispanic Americans, and jazz musicians. A number of responsible studies of the effects of marijuana (such as one by the Hemp Commission in British India in 1985) and its more potent form, hashish, had pronounced the drug relatively harmless. Evidence in Anslinger's personal files shows that he was aware of such studies (Anslinger Papers). However, to promote the so-called marijuana-menace scare, Anslinger related shocking accounts of heinous crimes induced by marijuana, and he introduced the theory that smoking marijuana was a dangerous gateway to other more serious addictions. His cause received a boost from the originally church-sponsored-now-cult film *Reefer Madness*, a morality tale that popularized Anslinger's visions of the hazards of drug use. As a result, the Reorganization Act was abandoned. Anslinger's Bureau was saved.

Yet Anslinger's campaign to save the Bureau brought the topic of marijuana much more into the media, and because many groups clamored for protection against dope fiends, Anslinger agreed to help draft the Marijuana Tax Act, placing marijuana in the same highly restricted category as heroin and cocaine. President Franklin Delano Roosevelt signed the bill on August 2, 1927. Research on its toxic properties was stifled because the FBN would not license its use by researchers outside of government. Although its therapeutic value in alleviating nausea due to chemotherapy for cancer patients or for treating glaucoma came to be generally recognized, the drug remained a Schedule One narcotic.

BOGGS ACT OF 1951

In the late 1940s, Anslinger claimed that the drug problem was caused by judges imposing lenient sentences on drug offenders. Anslinger's supporters in Congress picked up the argument, and the resulting legislation, the Boggs Act of 1951, increased the ten-year maximum sentence for drug offenders to a two-to-five-year sentence for first offenders, a mandatory five-to-ten-year sentence for second offenders, and a mandatory

twenty-year sentence for third offenders; second and third offenders had no chance of probation or parole. When the act passed through Congress with almost no debate and no objection, Senator Estes Kefauver quoted Anslinger, referring to the increased penalties, saying, "I think it would just about dry up the traffic" (Congressional Record, October 20, 1951, 82nd Congress, 1st Session, 97: 13675). Narcotics traffic did not "dry up."

NARCOTICS CONTROL ACT

On November 3, 1951, the *New York Times* reported that President Truman had signed the Boggs Act and that the Veterans of Foreign Wars voted to "urge stronger state narcotics laws, with stiffer penalties for offenders," including "the death penalty for persons selling narcotics to teenagers." Thus, the quest for even stronger penalties was to continue.

The November 23, 1953, the *Washington Post* ran this headline: "Anslinger Asks Senate Action on Addict Bill; Hospitalization Law Still Needed, He Says; Drug Use Declines." And his hometown newspaper, which reported on him regularly, ran this headline: "Anslinger Calls for Stiffer Penalties on Dope Peddlers to Protect Youth of Nation." Both articles reported on Anslinger's testimony before the Senate Juvenile Delinquency Subcommittee, during which he called for stiffer state and federal penalties against drug peddlers to help break up the rings of racketeers preying on the nation's youth.

Anslinger never wavered from this position, despite the expert opinion of, among others, sociologist Alfred R. Lindesmith, who claimed that the prohibition control technique and the "complete removal of the control issue from the medical domain" were the causes of the country's addiction problems (Lindesmith, 1956). Lindesmith narrowed the problem to "non-addicted lords of the underworld" as the "focal point of the new infection." He added, "These men [the non-addicted bosses] are rarely apprehended or punished; it is the user, exploited by the system, who suffers the major portion of the heavy penalties that are imposed." And he pointed out that "police suppression, by increasing the danger of distribution and reducing supplies, keeps up prices and profits," thus keeping the illicit market alive, drug lords safe, and addicts facing prison.

The *New York Times* covered Anslinger's testimony in a June 3, 1955, article, quoting him as claiming that the nation's failure to curb drug addiction lay primarily with "the legislators and other officials" who had been lax in creating and enforcing stringent narcotics laws. Congresspersons reacted to Anslinger's testimony with a groundswell of bills for narcotics legislation with even stiffer penalties.

On April 30, 1956, the Daniel subcommittee presented findings and recommendations that Anslinger himself could have written. It drafted Senate Bill 3760, and on May 15, 1956, the Senate Judiciary Committee unanimously approved the bill. When President Eisenhower signed the Narcotic Control Act on July 18, 1956, he put into place the heaviest penalties for U.S. narcotics law violations to that date.

Three months later, probably not coincidentally, Senator Price Daniel announced his bid for governor of Texas (and received praise from the *New York Times* for his work on the Senate Juvenile Delinquency Subcommittee, saying that its early completion was "unusual . . . in the run of Congressional investigations").

This rash of bills introduced in Congress demonstrates one of the more evident results of Anslinger's tenure: Elected officials rallied behind him and his notion of demon drug addicts corrupting the nation's young people. Protecting the nation's youth was a sure ticket to re-election. This worked well for Anslinger, despite an even more extensive study performed by a joint committee of the American Bar Association and the American Medical Association on which Rufus King served—King, the original author of this entry—as it gave Anslinger strong support in Congress (King 1974).

INTERNATIONAL DRUG POLICIES

By 1930, when Anslinger became commissioner, the patterns of international controls had also been largely set, with the United States urging stringent repression and most of the rest of the world remaining indifferent or resistant. (The basic Hague Convention of 1912 would not have been ratified by more than a few nations had not the United States insisted upon its inclusion in the Paris peace treaties, which created the League of Nations in 1921.) Although the United States never joined the League of Nations, U.S. representatives were given a voice in drug matters, and Anslinger dominated international deliberations, leading the U.S. delegations first to the drug-control agencies of the League of Nations and then to those of the United Nations even after his resignation as FBN commissioner.

Anslinger participated in drafting the 1931 Narcotics Limitation Convention, which imposed controls on the production of drugs for legitimate medical uses; he pressed for the 1936 Convention for Suppression of Illicit Traffic, which sought to persuade other nations to impose criminal sanctions on domestic distribution and consumption. When World War II isolated Geneva and ended most of the functions of the League of Nations based there, he arranged for moving the international drug agencies to New York City, where they continued to operate. After the war, he was the leading proponent of a Single Convention, finally approved in 1961, after ten years of drafting. It incorporated much of the U.S. law-enforcement orientations, including obligations upon members to control crops and production, to standardize identification and packaging, and to impose severe criminal penalties on drug offenders. But lacking enforcement sanctions, the Single Convention had little effect.

AFTER FBN: ANSLINGER'S LEGACY

Some reports say that Anslinger was forced out of the FBN by the Kennedy administration. More reliable evidence says he was not. In fact, he offered his resignation on his seventieth birthday, May 20, 1962, but the Kennedy administration asked him to remain as acting commissioner until a successor could be found. He did so and was pleased when his closest aide, Deputy Commissioner Henry L. Giordano, was appointed by President Kennedy as the new commissioner and promised that he would make no changes in policies established by Anslinger. And he did not. In fact, in 1967, Giordano was still presenting exaggerated marijuana claims in his testimony before the U.S. Congress, reminiscent of Anslinger's 1930's testimony (Treasury-Post Office Departments and Executive Office Appropriations, Hearings, before a subcommittee of the Committee on Appropriations, 90th Cong., 1st sess., 1967, 404–485).

Kennedy also permitted Anslinger to remain as U.S. representative to the United Nations, a post he held until 1970. Anslinger, for his part, praised Attorney General Robert Kennedy, the president's younger brother, for pursuing top figures in the Mafia, not merely jailing addicts. After the Kennedy assassination in 1963, President Lyndon B. Johnson moved much of the federal drug-control apparatus from the Treasury Department to the Department of Justice.

Anslinger retired to his home in Altoona, Pennsylvania, and died in 1975. He donated his papers to Pattee Library (later Paterno Library) at the Pennsylvania State University (PSU), University Park, Pennsylvania. The thirteen boxes are housed in the Historical Collections and Labor Archives (Accession 1959-0006H).

Anslinger's legacy lives on. Presidents Nixon (1969–1974), Reagan (1981–1989), and George H. W. Bush (1989–1993) intensified the drug war, justifying such efforts with arguments initially developed by Anslinger. Congress, too, continued to be influenced by Anslinger's views. Congressional speeches and penal statutes continue to be extreme and racially biased. Marijuana is still a Schedule One narcotic, grouped with heroin and cocaine.

In hindsight, a three-pronged approach to narcotics—punishment for importing and selling drugs, medical treatment for addicts, and honest education about the facts of drug use—sounds like sensible drug policy that could have benefited the United States since the 1930s. Anslinger's detractors call him evil, which is probably too strong. However, he was overzealous and a product of his upbringing. He had seen the pain that addiction caused his neighbor's wife. He had seen the evil of organized crime. He had seen decisive American military force in World War I destroy the empires of Germany and Austria-Hungary. He had seen the Allies fight crime and exact severe punishment. He wanted to fight the evil of drug addiction. The solution seemed simple: make everything connected with narcotics—sale, use, importation, manufacture—illegal. Lock up everyone involved in any way with any drug for as long as possible. He seems not to have realized that his extreme criminalization

policies created a niche for international criminals to fill and little-to-no recourse for medical doctors and addicts to legally attempt to cure reliance on narcotic drugs. The punitive over medical approach, Anslinger's greatest legacy, continues.

See also **Prohibition of Alcohol.**

BIBLIOGRAPHY

Anslinger, H. J., & Gregory, J. D. (1963). *The protectors: The heroic story of the narcotics agents, citizens, and officials in their unending, unsung battles against organized crime in America and abroad.* New York: Farrar, Straus.

Anslinger, H. J., & Oursler, W. (1961). *The murderers: The story of the narcotics gangs.* New York: Farrar, Straus and Cudahy.

Anslinger, H. J., & Thompkins, W. F. (1953). *The traffic in narcotics.* New York: Funk and Wagnalls.

Brecher, E. M., and the Editors of *Consumer Reports Magazine.* (1972). *Licit and illicit drugs: The Consumers Union Report on narcotics, stimulants, depressants, inhalants, hallucinogens, and marijuana—including caffeine, nicotine, and alcohol.* Boston: Little, Brown.

Carroll, R. (2004). *Harry Anslinger's role in shaping America's drug policy: Federal drug control.* Binghamton, NY: Pharmaceutical Products Press.

Carroll, R. (2004). *The Narcotics Control Act triggers the great nondebate: Treatment loses to punishment: Federal drug control.* Binghamton, NY: Pharmaceutical Products Press.

Harry J. Anslinger Papers, 1835–1970 (bulk 1918–1963). Accession 1959–0006H, Historical Collections and Labor Archives, Special Collections Library, University Libraries, Pennsylvania State University.

Keys, D. P., & Galliher, J. F. (2000). *Confronting the drug control establishment: Alfred Lindesmith as a public intellectual.* Albany: State University of New York Press.

King, Rufus. (1974). *The drug hang-up: America's fifty-year folly* (2nd ed.). Springfield, IL: Charles C. Thomas.

Lindesmith, A. R. (1965). *The addict and the law.* Bloomington: Indiana University Press.

Lindesmith, A. R. (1956). Traffic in dope, medical problem. *Nation,* 339.

McWilliams, J. (1990). *The protectors.* Newark: University of Delaware Press.

Musto, D. F. (1987). *The American disease: Origins of narcotic control.* New York: Oxford University Press. (Original work published in 1973)

Walker III, W. O. (Ed.). (1996). *Drugs in the Western Hemisphere: An odyssey of cultures in conflict.* Wilmington: Scholarly Resources, Jaguar Books on Latin America, No. 12.

RUFUS KING
REVISED BY JAMES T. MCDONOUGH JR. (2001)
REBECCA CARROLL (2009)

ANTAGONIST. An antagonist is a drug that binds to a receptor (i.e., it has affinity for the receptor binding site) but does not activate the receptor to produce a biological response (i.e., it possesses no intrinsic activity). Antagonists are also called receptor "blockers" because they block the effect of agonists. The pharmacological effects of an antagonist therefore result in preventing agonists (e.g., drugs, hormones, neurotransmitters) from binding to and activating the receptor. A competitive antagonist competes with an agonist for binding to the receptor. As the concentration of antagonist is increased, the binding of the agonist is progressively inhibited, resulting in a decrease in the physiological response. High antagonist concentrations can completely inhibit the response. This inhibition can be reversed, however, by increasing the concentration of the agonist, since the agonist and antagonist compete for binding to the receptor. A competitive antagonist, therefore, shifts the dose-response relationship for the agonist to the right, so that an increased concentration of the agonist in the presence of a competitive antagonist is required to produce the same biological response observed in the absence of the antagonist.

A second type of receptor antagonist is an irreversible antagonist. In this case, the binding of the antagonist to the receptor (its affinity) may be so strong that the receptor is unavailable for binding by the agonist. Other irreversible antagonists actually form chemical bonds (e.g., covalent bonds) with the receptor. In either case, if the concentration of the irreversible antagonist is high enough, the number of receptors remaining that are available for agonist binding may be so low that a maximum biological response cannot be achieved even in the presence of high concentrations of the agonist.

See also **Agonist; Agonist-Antagonist (Mixed); Antagonists of Alcohol and Drugs; Naloxone; Naltrexone.**

BIBLIOGRAPHY

Ross, E. M. (1990). Pharmacodynamics: Mechanisms of drug action and the relationship between drug concentration and effect. In A. G. Gilman et al. (Eds.), *Goodman and Gilman's the pharmacological basis of therapeutics,* New York: Pergamon. (2005, 11th ed. New York: McGraw-Hill Medical.)

NICK E. GOEDERS

ANTAGONISTS OF ALCOHOL AND DRUGS. Pharmacologic antagonists are medications designed to counteract the effects of another drug. Most drugs of abuse exert their effect on the central nervous system (CNS) by binding to a specific chemical receptor in the brain where they mimic the actions of endogenous (natural) neurotransmitters. Therefore, they are pharmacologic agonists (i.e., they mimic the action) at that particular neuronal receptor or binding site. Pharmacologic antagonists work against the agonist by preventing the drug effect.

Generally, the antagonist is chemically similar enough to the agonist to fit into the receptor site but dissimilar enough to exert little or no pharmacologic action. Instead, the antagonist occupies the receptor site, preventing the agonist drug from binding to the site and exerting its action, which is called a *competitive antagonism*. In addition to pharmacologic antagonists, another group of drugs useful in the treatment of addiction are the *partial agonists*, which act as weak agonists at the receptor site while blocking the effects of the drug of abuse. One way to understand this phenomenon is to think of the receptor site as a lock and the endogenous neurotransmitter as the master key. The agonist drug acts as a duplicate key, similar enough to the master key to open the lock, whereas the antagonist key is similar enough to the master key to fit into the lock but dissimilar enough not to open the lock but instead to jam it. The partial agonist can open the lock with some effort, but often, the key will stick.

Pharmacologic antagonists can be used to treat both the immediate and long-term effects of drugs of abuse. For example, overdose, either intentional, as in a suicide attempt, or unintentional, as occurs when a street drug of unknown potency is used, is one of the most serious consequences of drug abuse. In addition to the usual supportive emergency care that is given to patients when they are brought into the hospital, pharmacologic antagonists of drugs of abuse can be administered to counteract directly the dangerous effects of these drugs. Pharmacologic antagonists may also be used preventively, to decrease craving and prevent relapse in individuals who are addicted to an agonist drug. This entry reviews the most commonly used pharmacologic antagonists of alcohol and other drugs of abuse.

NALOXONE

Naloxone (Narcan) is an injectable opiate antagonist used to reverse the severe respiratory depression induced by an opiate overdose, such as heroin can cause. It is also used in certain therapeutic situations such as when the effect of a narcotic given for legitimate medical reasons must be reversed (e.g., following surgery during which opiates are used during anesthesia). Sometimes naloxone is given in an emergency situation in order to confirm a suspected opiate overdose. Naloxone can also be employed to diagnose chronic opiate abuse, but in most cases narcotics can be detected by standard laboratory testing without the risk of inducing sudden withdrawal symptoms, as occurs when an opiate-dependent person is administered an opiate antagonist. In the event of an opiate overdose, naloxone should be used in the context of other supportive medical care, including the administration of CPR, oxygen, and mechanical ventilation, as may be required given the severity of the overdose. The abrupt return to consciousness that naloxone induces in overdose patients can be jarring, causing tremor and hyperventilation. Naloxone administered too rapidly or in too high a dose can precipitate withdrawal symptoms, including nausea, vomiting, tachycardia (rapid heartbeat), and sweating. Since the half-life of naloxone is generally less than two hours and that of many opiates considerably longer, the drug must be given by continuous intravenous infusion for a least a day following the acute overdose.

FLUMAZENIL

Flumazenil (Romazicon) was developed as an aid to the management of benzodiazepine (e.g., Valium) overdose. It also reverses the effects of benzodiazepines used for the induction and maintenance of anesthesia. Flumazenil works at the benzodiazepine receptor site in the brain, also known as the GABA/benzodiazepine receptor complex, where it displaces the benzodiazepine from the binding site. Flumazenil works quickly; when injected, its effects can be seen within one to two minutes. However, since the half-life of the drug is only about one hour and that of many benzodiazepines is considerably longer, multiple injections may need to be given. In an overdose situation, flumazenil is considered to be an adjunct to, rather than a replacement for, conventional supportive care. In clinical studies, 80 percent of patients admitted to the hospital with a benzodiazepine overdose responded to flumazenil with an improvement in their level of consciousness.

There is considerable controversy over the use of flumazenil in a patient who has overdosed, either intentionally or not. Benzodiazepine overdose alone is rarely fatal. If the patient has taken only a benzodiazepine, chances are good that he or she will wake up once the drug wears off, with or without an antagonist. In the case of a mixed overdose, such as when a patient takes amphetamines or certain kinds of antidepressants along with the benzodiazepine, the benzodiazepine could actually have the therapeutic effect of preventing seizures in these individuals. Administering flumazenil could actually induce dangerous seizures in this situation. Reversing the sedating effects of the benzodiazepine rapidly can also cause agitation or anxiety. In clinical studies, up to 3 percent of patients treated with flumazenil required treatment for anxiety or agitation. Flumazenil may be best used in situations when benzodiazepines are taken in combination with other depressants (i.e., downers) such as alcohol because the combination of multiple central nervous system (CNS) depressants can be fatal. Flumazenil can also be useful in some cases as a diagnostic tool: If the antagonist revives an unresponsive patient, the likelihood that other CNS depressants are present is lower.

NALTREXONE

Naltrexone (Revia, Vivitrol), an opiate antagonist, was first introduced for the treatment of opiate dependence, but it is used most often for the treatment of alcohol dependence. Although chemically similar to naloxone, naltrexone was synthesized to be an effective opiate antagonist that could be administered orally. (In contrast, naloxone is destroyed in the gastrointestinal tract when taken by mouth.)

Naltrexone has a high affinity for the μ opiate receptor, which has been implicated in the development of alcohol dependence. The exact mechanism by which naltrexone reduces the risk of heavy drinking is not known, but studies suggest that alcohol stimulates the release of endogenous opiate agonists and that naltrexone then blocks these natural opiates, making alcohol consumption less rewarding.

Naltrexone was originally available only in tablet form, but in 2006 a long-acting injection formulation (Vivitrol) was introduced. This extended release suspension is injected once a month into the gluteal muscle of the buttock. The drug is then released slowly from this site over the course of a month. Long-acting naltrexone has an important advantage over oral naltrexone: For each month that the patient receives an injection, there is no risk of the patient either forgetting a dose or choosing not to take a dose. Naltrexone is not approved by the Food and Drug Administration for the treatment of patients who are actively drinking, but rather for the prevention of relapse and as an adjunct to psychotherapy in individuals who have already demonstrated an ability to abstain from alcohol outside an institutional setting. The most common side effects associated with naltrexone are nausea and headache; patients who receive the long-acting formulation often experience discomfort at the site of the injection. Although liver toxicity has not been reported at the approved dosage, naltrexone has been reported to cause liver damage at five times the therapeutic dose. This adverse effect is an important consideration for alcohol-dependent patients, however, since some may already have alcohol-related liver disease.

BUPRENORPHINE AND NALOXONE

Buprenorphine (Suboxone, Subutex) is a partial μ opiate receptor agonist and a K opiate receptor antagonist that is used both for the treatment of pain and for the treatment of opiate dependence.

Buprenorphine is chemically similar to other opiates such as morphine, codeine, and heroin, but it produces less euphoria (drug high) than these agents. When used for the treatment of opiate dependence, buprenorphine is initially given in a sublingual fixed-dose combination tablet with the opiate antagonist naloxone (Suboxone). The presence of the naloxone in the tablet is intended to prevent abuse of the buprenorphine; when the medication is taken correctly (dissolved under the tongue), the buprenorphine is absorbed directly into the bloodstream, avoiding metabolism by the liver while the naloxone is only minimally absorbed by this route and thus exerts only a minimal pharmacologic effect. If the patient attempts to abuse the medication by dissolving the tablets and injecting them into the bloodstream, the naloxone will have full pharmacologic effect and induce withdrawal symptoms. A second formulation of buprenorphine (Subutex) does not include naloxone.

Buprenorphine, like methadone, is used for the treatment of opiate dependence, but unlike methadone, use of buprenorphine is not limited to being dispensed in a clinic. The Drug Addiction Treatment Act (DATA) of 2000 allows physicians who meet certain requirements to treat a limited number of dependent patients with buprenorphine in their office practice. In a study of 326 opiate-addicted persons treated in a physician's office, 18 percent of subjects assigned to treatment with buprenorphine, and 21 percent of subjects assigned to treatment with buprenorphine and naloxone achieved a *clean* urine compared with only 6 percent of those randomized to placebo. The dependent patient is first treated at the doctor's office with buprenorphine alone (Subutex), titrated (measured for strength) to an effective dose over a period of two days, and then transferred to the combination product (Suboxone). Pharmacists filling prescriptions for buprenorphine and naloxone tablets are required by law to verify both that the physician is certified to write for the medication and that the prescription is legitimate (i.e., not a forgery). The most common adverse effects of buprenorphine are sedation, nausea, hypotension (decreased blood pressure), respiratory depression, and diaphoresis (sweating). Patients may also become physically or psychologically dependent on buprenorphine, but the intensity of this dependence is less severe than with other opiates.

VARENICLINE

Varenicline (Chantix), an aid to smoking cessation, was introduced in 2006. It is a partial agonist of the α4β2 nicotinic receptor, which is believed to mediate the addicting effects of nicotine. Varenicline both blocks the effects of nicotine and acts as a mild agonist; that is, it stimulates the nicotine receptor, but at a much lower level than nicotine. Varenicline is taken orally and is intended to be used in combination with psychosocial support. The dose of the drug is titrated upward over a period of eight days and then given over a 12-week period. Patients who are able to stop smoking should continue the medication for another 12 weeks to decrease the likelihood of relapse. Not everyone who takes varenicline is able to quit smoking, but in clinical trials, varenicline was significantly more effective than bupropion (Zyban), another non-nicotine drug used to treat nicotine addiction. In one study, 44 percent of patients assigned to varenicline were able to stop smoking, compared to 30 percent of those assigned to bupropion and only 17 percent of those assigned to placebo (an inactive medication).

The most common side effects with varenicline are nausea, vomiting, sleep disturbance (vivid or abnormal dreams), constipation, and flatulence (gas). Varenicline can also cause serious psychiatric effects, most significantly depression and even suicide. Although these effects are not common, given their severity, physicians are advised to monitor all patients taking varenicline for changes in behavior and mood. Patients are also advised to contact their physician if they experience agitation, depressed mood, behavior changes, or suicidal thoughts.

See also Treatment: An Overview of Alcohol Abuse/ Dependence; Treatment, Pharmacological Approaches to: Methadone; Treatment, Pharmacological Approaches to: Naltrexone.

BIBLIOGRAPHY

Fudala, P. J., Bridge, T. B., Herbert, S., Williford, W. O., Chiang, C. N., Jones, K., et al. (2003). Office-based treatment of opiate addiction with a sublingual-tablet formulation of buprenorphine and naloxone. New England Journal of Medicine, 349(10), 949–958.

McEvoy, G. K. (Ed.). (2003). American Hospital Formulary Service (AHFS) drug information. Bethesda, MD: American Society of Health-System Pharmacists.

Minozzi, S., Amato, L., Vecchi, S., Davoli, M., Kirchmayer, U., & Verster, A. (2006). Oral naltrexone maintenance treatment for opiate dependence. Cochrane Database of Systematic Reviews, 1. Art. No.: CD001333. DOI: 10.1002/14651858.CD001333.pub2.

Potts, L. A., & Garwood, C. L. (2007). Varenicline: The newest agent for smoking cessation: Clinical review. American Journal of Health-System Pharmacy, 64(13), 1381–1384.

U.S. Food and Drug Administration. (2008, February 1). FDA issues public health advisory on Chantix (Press release). www.fda.gov/.

LEAH R. ZINDEL

ANTIDEPRESSANTS. See Treatment, Pharmacological Approaches to: Antidepressants.

ANTIDOTE. A medication or treatment that counteracts a poison or its effects. An antidote may work by reducing or blocking the absorption of a poison from the stomach. It might counteract its effects directly, as in taking something to neutralize an acid. Or an antidote might work by blocking a poison at its receptor site. For example, a medication called *naloxone* will block opiates such as heroin at its receptors and prevent deaths that occur because of heroin overdose. In a sense, drug antagonists can all be antidotes under some circumstances, but not all antidotes are drug antagonists.

Many cities have a telephone "poison hot line," where information on antidotes is given. In case of drug overdose or poisoning, it is advisable to call for expert medical help immediately.

See also Antagonist; Poison.

BIBLIOGRAPHY

Klaassen, C. D. (1990). Principles of toxicology. In A. G. Gilman et al. (Eds.), Goodman and Gilman's the pharmacological basis of therapeutics, 8th ed. New York: Pergamon. (2005, 11th ed.). New York: McGraw-Hill Medical.

MICHAEL J. KUHAR

ANTISOCIAL PERSONALITY DISORDER.

Antisocial personality disorder (ASPD) is particularly germane to alcohol and drug use disorders (A/DUD) because it co-occurs in a large proportion of those with A/DUD, and it confounds the diagnosis of, influences the course of, and is an independent risk factor for the development of A/DUD. ASPD when comorbid with an A/DUD may also be more heritable than ASPD alone.

DSM-IV DIAGNOSIS WITH CONDUCT DISORDER

Using the diagnostic criteria of the *DSM-IV*, the diagnostic classification system published by the American Psychiatric Association and in widespread use, ASPD is defined as a disorder characterized by general disregard for and violation of the rights of others that begins in childhood or early adolescence and continues into adulthood. To receive a diagnosis of ASPD, the individual must be at least eighteen years old and have a history of conduct disorder.

The diagnosis of conduct disorder requires that at least three of the following behaviors must have occurred in any twelve-month period of time before the age of fifteen (or age thirteen for some behaviors): running away from home overnight at least twice (or once without returning); staying out late contrary to parental rules (beginning before age thirteen); repeated truancy (beginning before age thirteen); initiating physical fights; using weapons; cruelty to animals or to people; forcing someone into sexual activity; frequent bullying; robbing, or mugging someone; arson; vandalism; frequent lying to obtain favors or goods; breaking into someone's house or car; and stealing.

In addition, three of the following behaviors must have occurred since the age of fifteen: consistent irresponsibility; failure to conform to social norms; irritability and aggressiveness; deceitfulness; reckless disregard for safety of oneself or of others; impulsivity or failure to plan ahead; and lack of remorse for hurtful or manipulative behaviors. *DSM-IV* acknowledges but does not recognize as a full disorder a syndrome of adult antisocial behavior without the childhood component (Adult Antisocial Behavior Syndrome, AABS). Individuals with AABS are similar to their ASPD counterparts on adult antisocial behavior, drinking and drug use history, and other psychiatric comorbidity.

ICD-10 WITHOUT CONDUCT DISORDER

Conceptualization of ASPD differs in the diagnostic classification system formulated and published by the World Health Organization, the *International Classification of Diseases* (*ICD-10*). In that system, ASPD is termed *dissocial personality disorder* (DPD) and does not require the presence of conduct disorder, although some of the dissocial behaviors must have occurred early in life. To meet criteria for DPD, an individual must have three of the following persistent behaviors: callous unconcern for the feeling of others; gross irresponsibility and disregard for social norms; incapacity to maintain enduring relationships; incapacity to experience guilt and benefit from experience; low tolerance for frustration and low threshold for aggression; and marked proneness to blame others for the dissocial behavior. The *ICD-10* diagnosis of DPD is, therefore, more severe than the *DSM-IV* diagnosis of ASPD.

A large percentage of those with A/DUD meet criteria for ASPD. Data from a 2001–2002 survey of 43,000 adults eighteen or older in the U.S. general population showed that among those with a lifetime history of any *DSM-IV* alcohol use disorder (AUD), 10.4 percent of men and 6.6 percent of women (compared with 5.5 percent of men and 1.9 percent of women overall) had a diagnosis of ASPD, and, combining ASPD and AABS, 39.4 percent of men and 34.0 percent of women had any antisocial behavior syndrome (ASB). Among those with drug use disorders (DUD), the prevalence estimates were even greater: 20.7 percent of men and 14.1 percent of women had ASPD, and 44.0 percent of men and 39.0 percent of women had AABS.

The reverse associations are also true. Three times as many men with ASPD as without meet lifetime criteria for AUD, and five times as many men with ASPD as without meet criteria for DUD. The associations are even stronger among women, with twelve times as many women with ASPD as without meeting criteria for AUD and thirteen times as many meeting criteria for DUD.

THERAPIES AND TREATMENT

ASPD affects the course of A/DUD. Individuals with A/DUD complicated by ASPD have a more chronic and severe course, including an earlier age of alcohol/drug initiation, greater quantity and frequency of use, and higher number of lifetime substance use problems. Furthermore, evidence indicates that although ASPD alcoholics are more likely to enter treatment than alcoholics without ASPD, they have a poorer response to treatment, relapsing much earlier than alcoholics without ASPD, and may respond only to certain therapies. For instance, psychotherapies designed to increase motivation (e.g., motivational enhancement therapy; MET) or to link behaviors and misperceptions to consequences (e.g., cognitive behavioral therapy; CBT) have been shown to have only modest efficacy. Twelve-step facilitation (TSF) has also been only somewhat helpful. Studies have not been consistent, however, in determining which treatment option is particularly efficacious for those with A/DUD comorbid with ASPD. Evidence from studies performed in the 1990s and early part of this century is equivocal regarding the efficacy of certain medications on outcomes in those with A/DUD and ASPD, and has not supported a preferred treatment modality for those with both disorders, thus precluding definitive recommendations for clinicians. No medications are approved for treatment of ASPD; however, medications may be used to treat specific symptoms (e.g., aggression or anger).

Antisocial behavior beginning in childhood has been identified as an independent risk factor in the development of A/DUD; the presence of such childhood behaviors carries a sixfold odds of future development of a substance use disorder. Lee Robins (1966), in her landmark follow-up study of child guidance clinic patients, was one of the first to document this association, which has since been replicated in numerous studies in clinical and general population samples.

CAUSATION

The consistently strong association between ASPD and A/DUD raises questions as to the cause: Does engaging in antisocial behaviors lead to problematic substance use? Or do substance use disorders lead to engagement in aggression and antisocial acts? Research seems to favor the hypothesis that A/DUD is a secondary condition of ASPD. A third possible explanation to account for the association is that there is a shared predisposition or vulnerability underlying both disorders. Several studies using genetically informative samples of both adolescents and adults suggest that alcohol dependence, drug abuse and dependence, and ASPD (as well as childhood antisocial behaviors) share a common genetic vulnerability characterized by a general tendency to externalizing behaviors. This result is consistent with data that suggest A/DUD with ASPD is more heritable than A/DUD alone, as was suggested in the classic Stockholm Adoption Study (1981) indicating that adopted-out sons of fathers with ASPD-like alcoholism had a risk of alcoholism nine times that of adopted-out sons of other fathers.

Evidence from neuropharmacological studies has established some intriguing possibilities. Associations of various behaviors with certain neurotransmitters and their respective enzymes and receptors have been observed, such as serotonin (aggression, impulsivity, low socialization), dopamine (novelty seeking), and monoamine oxidase (depression, aggression, impulsivity). Further, the activity of the autonomic nervous system, which regulates an individual's stress response, appears to be lower in aggressive and antisocial individuals. The interactions among neurotransmitters have led researchers to postulate the existence of multiple neurotransmitter dysfunctions leading to loss of impulse control and an increased appetite for novel experiences.

ASPD is a common concomitant of alcohol and drug use disorders that is associated with accelerated course and poorer outcomes for individuals with these disorders. Although its etiology remained unknown as of 2008, evidence from neuropharmacologic and genetic studies provided some leads. Although symptoms may be managed, as with many personality disorders, there is no proven treatment for ASPD, and findings as of 2008 were equivocal regarding the efficacy of treatment matching using ASPD as an indicator. It is an important disorder to consider in individuals with an A/DUD.

See also **Addictive Personality and Psychological Tests; Childhood Behavior and Later Substance Use; Conduct Disorder and Drug Use; Dopamine; Serotonin.**

BIBLIOGRAPHY

Alpert, J., Fromke, S. Maysles, A., Jarecki, E., Davis, K., Heilbroner, D. et al. (2007). *Addiction* [HBO documentary]. HBO, National Institute of Drug Abuse, National Institute of Alcohol Abuse and Alcoholism, the Robert Wood Johnson Foundation.

American Psychiatric Association. (1994). *Diagnostic and statistical manual of mental disorders* (4th ed.). Washington, DC: Author.

Cloninger, R. C., Bohman, M., & Sigvardsson, S. (1981). Inheritance of alcohol abuse: Cross-fostering analysis of adopted men. *Archives of General Psychiatry, 38,* 861–868.

Dick, D. M., Aliev, F., Wang, J. C., Grucza, R. A., Schuckit, M., Kuperman, S. et al. (2008). Using dimensional models of externalizing psychopathology to aid in gene identification. *Archives of General Psychiatry, 65,* 310–318.

Grant, B. F., Hasin, D. S., Stinson, F. S., Dawson, D. A., Chou, S. P., Ruan, W. J., et al. (2004). Prevalence, correlates, and disability of personality disorders in the United States: Results from the National Epidemiologic Survey on Alcohol and Related Conditions. *Journal of Clinical Psychiatry, 65,* 948–958.

Goldstein, R. B., Compton, W. M., Pulay, A. J., Ruan, W. J., Pickering, R. P., Stinson, F. S., et al. (2007). Antisocial behavioral syndromes and *DSM-IV* drug use disorders in the United States: Results from the National Epidemiologic Survey on Alcohol and Related Conditions. *Drug and Alcohol Dependence, 90,* 145–158.

Goldstein, R. B., Dawson, D. A., Saha, T. D., Ruan, W. J., Compton, W. M., Grant, B. F., et al. (2007). Antisocial behavioral syndromes and *DSM-IV* alcohol use disorders: Results from the National Epidemiologic Survey on Alcohol and Related Conditions. *Alcoholism: Clinical and Experimental Research, 31,* 814–828.

Hesselbrock, V. M., Meyer, R., & Hesselbrock, M. (1992). Psychopathology and addictive disorders: The specific case of antisocial personality disorder. In C. P. O'Brien & J. H. Jaffe (Eds.), *Addictive States* (pp. 179–191). New York: Raven Press.

Project MATCH Research Group. (1997). Project MATCH secondary a priori hypotheses. *Addiction, 92,* 1671–1698.

Robins, L. N. (1966). *Deviant children grown up*. Baltimore: Wilkins.

van Goozen, S. H. M., & Fairchild, F. (2006). Neuroendocrine and neurotransmitter correlates in children with antisocial behavior. *Hormones and Behavior, 50,* 647–654.

Waldman, I. D., & Slutske, W. S. (2000). Antisocial behavior and alcoholism: A behavioral genetic perspective on comorbidity. *Clinical Psychology Review, 20,* 255–287.

Yoshino, A., Fukuhara, T., & Kato, M. (2000). Pre-morbid risk factors for alcohol dependence in antisocial personality disorder. *Alcohol in Clinical Experimental Research, 24,* 35–38.

KATHLEEN K. BUCHOLZ
REVISED BY REBECCA J. FREY (2001)
ELLEN LOCKARD EDENS (2009)
KATHLEEN K. BUCHOLZ (2009)

ANXIETY. Anxiety refers to an unpleasant emotional state, a response to anticipated threat or to specific psychiatric disorders. In anxiety, the anticipated threat is often imagined. Anxiety consists of physiological and psychological features. The physiological symptoms can include breathing difficulties (hyperventilation, shortness of breath), palpitations, sweating, light-headedness, diarrhea, trembling, frequent urination, and numbness and tingling sensations. The anxious person is usually hypervigilant and startles easily. The subjective psychological experience of anxiety is characterized by feelings of apprehension or fear of losing control, depersonalization and derealization, and difficulties in concentration. Strains around the performance of social roles (e.g., spouse, parent, wage earner) and certain life situations (e.g., separating from parents when starting school or leaving home, illness) can generate anxiety symptoms. Other factors can contribute to the etiology of anxiety, such as use of alcohol, caffeine and other stimulant drugs (e.g., amphetamine), a family history of anxiety symptoms, or a biological predisposition. In certain cases, recurrent anxiety symptoms will lead an individual to avoid certain situations, places, or things (phobias). In many cases, an anxious emotional state can motivate positive coping behaviors (e.g., anxiety that leads to studying for an exam). When the anxiety becomes excessive and impairs functioning, it can lead to the development of psychiatric illness. Individuals differ in their predisposition to anxiety.

Different constellations of anxious mood, physical symptoms, thoughts, and behaviors, when maladaptive, constitute various anxiety disorders. Panic disorder is characterized by brief, recurrent, anxiety attacks during which individuals fear death or losing their mind and experience intense physical symptoms. People with obsessive compulsive disorder experience persistent thoughts that they perceive as being senseless and distressing (obsessions) and that they attempt to neutralize by performing repetitive, stereotyped behaviors (compulsions). The essential feature of phobic disorders (e.g., agoraphobia, social phobia, simple phobia) is a persistent fear of one or more situations or objects that leads the individual to either avoid the situations or objects or endure exposure to them with great anxiety. Generalized anxiety disorder is diagnosed in individuals who persistently and excessively worry about several of their life circumstances and experience motor tension and physiologic arousal. Anxiety disorders are the psychiatric illness most frequently found in the general population.

Anxiety states can result from underlying medical conditions, and therefore these conditions should always be looked for when evaluating problematic anxiety. When anxiety develops into a psychiatric illness, various forms of treatment are available to reduce it. The choice of treatment often depends on the specific disorder. Medications may be used, including anxiolytics (e.g., benzodiazepines, buspirone) and antidepressants (e.g., imipramine, fluoxetine). Psychotherapies offered generally consist of cognitive-behavioral interventions (e.g., exposure therapy), but they can include psychotherapy of a supportive nature or more psychodynamically oriented approaches. Some people with severe anxiety may turn to alcohol or nonprescribed sedative-hypnotics for symptom relief, and this in turn may exacerbate the underlying condition.

See also **Prescription Drug Abuse; Risk Factors for Substance Use, Abuse, and Dependence: An Overview.**

BIBLIOGRAPHY

American Psychiatric Association (2000). *Diagnostic and statistical manual of mental disorders*, 4th ed. Washington, DC: American Psychiatric Press.

Brawman-Mintzer, O., & Lydiard, R. B. (1997). Generalized anxiety disorder. In A. Tasman, G. Kay, and J. A. Lieberman (Eds.), *Psychiatry*, 1st ed. (1100–1118). Philadelphia, PA: W. B. Saunders Company.

Peurifoy, R. Z. (2005). *Anxiety, phobias, and panic.* New York: Grand Central Publishing.

Shear, M. K. (1997). Panic disorder with and without agoraphobia. In A. Tasman, G. Kay, and J. A. Lieberman (Eds.), *Psychiatry*, 1st ed. (1020–1036). Philadelphia, PA: W. B. Saunders Company.

MYROSLAVA ROMACH
KAREN PARKER

APHRODISIAC. An aphrodisiac is a food, drink, drug, scent, or device that purportedly increases sexual desire or arousal. Even though there is a 5,000-year-old tradition of pursuing sexual enhancement through the use of plants, drugs, and magic, the U.S. Food and Drug Administration (FDA) declared in 1989 that there is no scientific proof that any over-the-counter aphrodisiac works to increase libido and that the only available evidence of aphrodisiacs is, at best, anecdotal and subjective. Double-blind, placebo-controlled studies designed to test the effectiveness of these putative aphrodisiacs are lacking, primarily due to cultural taboos associated with this type of research. Another problem with proving the effectiveness of aphrodisiacs is that many of these substances affect mood but do not have specific sexual effects. Alcohol, for example, has been thought to increase sexual receptiveness. But alcohol is a depressant, and although drinking may decrease inhibitions and thereby lead to increased social contact, it can actually decrease sexual performance.

In the 1990s sildenafil, a phosphodiesterase type 5 (PDE-5) inhibitor, was developed by Pfizer, Inc., to treat angina pectoris (chest pain caused by constriction of coronary arteries). Although Phase I clinical trials yielded disappointing results for the management of angina, scientists discovered that sildenafil could induce marked penile erections. Pfizer therefore decided to market sildenafil for erectile dysfunction, rather than for angina. The drug was patented in 1996 and approved for use in erectile dysfunction by the FDA on March 27, 1998. The first pill approved to treat erectile dysfunction in the United States, it was offered for sale under the brand name Viagra Since the introduction of sildenafil, two other PDE-5 inhibitors have been marketed: vardenafil (Levitra, Bayer AG) and tadalafil (Cialis, Eli Lilly and Company). PDEs participate in the metabolism of the intracellular second messengers, cyclic adenosine monophosphate (cAMP) and cyclic guanosine monophosphate (cGMP), which are involved in signaling pathways in cavernous smooth muscle. Accumulation of cGMP in the cavernous smooth muscle activates an intracellular cascade that induces a loss of contractile tone of penile blood vessels, thus engorging the tissue with blood and producing an erection. The inhibition of PDE-5 by sildenafil, vardenafil, and tadalafil promotes an erection by inhibiting the degradation of cGMP. Nitric oxide (NO), in turn, increases the production of cGMP to contribute to penile erections. Ultimately, however, even though these compounds make sexual activity possible in men with erectile dysfunction, they do not increase sexual desire, and any potential utility in women has yet to be determined. It is unlikely that PDE-5 inhibitors will have any effect on libido in females either, but these compounds could cause the blood vessels in the vagina (and other genital tissue, including the clitoris) to become engorged with blood, which helps the vagina become properly lubricated in preparation for intercourse. Finally, many botanical medicinal herbs—and drugs derived from these herbs and touted as putative aphrodisiacs—have been shown to have effects on the NO-signaling pathway. For example, the saponins from ginseng (ginsenosides) have been shown to relax the corpus cavernosum, which may aid in the treatment of men suffering from erectile dysfunction. Many plant extracts or purified drugs derived from Chinese medicinal herbs also affect NO pathways.

See also **Ginseng.**

BIBLIOGRAPHY

Achike, F. I., & Kwan, C. Y. (2003). Nitric oxide, human diseases and the herbal products that affect the nitric oxide signalling pathway. *Clinical and Experimental Pharmacology and Physiology, 30*(9), 605–615.

Briganti, A., Salonia, A., Gallina, A., Saccà, A., Montorsi, P., Rigatti, P., et al. (2005). Drug insight: Oral phosphodiesterase type 5 inhibitors for erectile dysfunction. *Nature Clinical Practice Urology, 2*(5), 239–247.

Kim, N., Azadzoi, K. M., Goldstein, I., & Saenz de Tejada, I. (1991). A nitric-oxide like factor mediates nonadrenergic noncholinergic neurogenic relaxation of penile corpus cavernosum smooth muscle. *Journal of Clinical Investigation, 88,* 112–118.

Mayer, M., Stief, C. G., Truss, M. C., & Uckert, S. (2005). Phosphodiesterase inhibitors in female sexual dysfunction. *World Journal of Urology, 23*(6), 393–397.

Murphy, L. L., & Lee, T. J. (2002). Ginseng, sex behavior, and nitric oxide. *Annals of the New York Academy of Sciences, 962,* 372–377.

Saenz de Tejada, I. (2002). Molecular mechanisms for the regulation of penile smooth muscle contractility. *International Journal of Impotence Research, 14* (Suppl. 1), S6–S10.

Sandroni, P. (2001). Aphrodisiacs past and present: A historical review. *Clinical Autonomic Research, 11*(5), 303–307.

NICHOLAS E. GOEDERS

ARCOS. *See* **Automation of Reports and Consolidated Orders System (ARCOS).**

ARGOT. *See* **Slang Terms in U.S. Drug Cultures.**

ARRESTEE DRUG ABUSE MONITORING (ADAM AND ADAM II).

The Arrestee Drug Abuse Monitoring (ADAM) program was a data collection system that evolved from the landmark Drug Use Forecasting (DUF) program of the National Institute of Justice (NIJ). DUF collected data from 1987 to 1997 in 23 cities across the United States. It was originally designed to collect interview and bioassay (urine) data from persons within 48 hours of arrest. In a brief interview the program collected information on each arrestee's drug use, including drug-use history and arrests. DUF was, however, a convenience sample of arrestees and consequently represented an unknown profile of persons arrested and an unknown segment of arrestees who use drugs.

In 1997 NIJ and Abt Associates redesigned the DUF program to place the data collection effort on a more scientifically defensible basis, renaming it ADAM. The redesign defined each catchment area as a primary city (i.e., Chicago) and its home or surrounding county (Cook County), developed a probability-based sampling plan for each county, sampled booking facilities within each county, and sampled arrestees within each booking facility. ADAM also redesigned the interview instrument to include a number of questions on alcohol use; treatment, health issues, and drug market activity, and expanded the number of sites. All original sites were reconstituted and retrained on the new protocols from 1998 to 1999. New instrumentation and sampling procedures began in January 2000, marking the beginning of a new trend line for the series.

In its revised form, ADAM had several goals:

- Establish prevalence estimates of numbers of arrestees using drugs in each of the sentinel sites.

- Develop estimates of the number of heavy or chronic drug users in each area.

- Understand the nature and activity of different drug markets over time.

- Understand the characteristics of drug-using offenders (crimes committed, treatment needs, drug careers).

- Understand the relationship between accessing treatment and participating in drug markets in each county annually.

- Work closely with local law enforcement and treatment groups to use ADAM data locally.

The ADAM protocol called for the collection of face-to-face interviews lasting approximately 25 minutes from a probability-based sample of arrestees from sampled booking facilities for 14 consecutive days each quarter. In ADAM the data collection shift is based on the 6- to 8-hour period of a day in each booking facility sampled in which the highest flow of arrestees occurs. The sampling protocol divides each 24-hour period into that heavy period ("flow") and the remaining portion of the 24-hour period when cases have accumulated and interviewers are not present (the "stock" period). Arrestees are sampled proportionately from the stock cases and at timed intervals throughout the flow period, resulting in a representation of the 24-hour period of arrests.

Because individuals are released throughout the day and night before they can be interviewed, each case is weighted to represent its probability of selection. Cases are weighted using the data of all persons arrested during the 14-day window by assigning the probability of being selected using variables that impact such a selection—charge, time of day, day of the week, race or ethnicity, and age. Eligible arrestees are sampled from the total

number of persons booked in each facility. All arrestees who have been held no more than 48 hours since arrest are male, and are physically able to respond to questions are eligible to participate. Although data collection for female arrestees continued in many sites after 2000, sampling protocols and case weighting were done only with the male population.

All interviews and specimen provision are voluntary; all interviews and test results are confidential, and no individual-identifying data are collected. Urine specimens are collected at the time of interview, mailed nightly to an external laboratory, and then tested for the presence of each of nine substances. In ADAM a local team collected data at each site directed by a nearby research group working in collaboration with, and trained, funded, and monitored by, a national contractor. Approximately 200 to 250 cases were generated each data collection cycle at each site, although larger, higher-volume sights produced a somewhat greater number of cases

ADAM began as 23 former DUF sites and expanded to a total of 39 sites by 2003. Approximately 20,000 interviews were collected each year. Data continued to show that over half of all arrestees test positive for some illegal substance in their system at the time of arrest, predominantly marijuana. However, like DUF, ADAM provided timely data on the movement of methamphetamine use from its earliest pockets in Southern California to areas such as Des Moines, Iowa; Las Vegas, Nevada; Portland, Oregon; Omaha, Nebraska; and Oklahoma City, Oklahoma, where the number of positive tests increased each year. As was true in its original DUF form, ADAM remained a bellwether for detecting the earliest (and often the heaviest) changes in illegal drug use.

NIJ discontinued ADAM in 2003, citing a lack of funds. Seeing the need for the data ADAM had compiled, the Office of National Drug Control Policy (ONDCP) in 2007 reinstituted collection with Abt Associates in 10 former ADAM sites, renaming the program ADAM II. Ten ADAM II sites were selected, with the focus on sites east of the Mississippi to continue examining any movement of methamphetamine use eastward. The ten sites chosen were New York (Borough of Manhattan), Washington, D.C., Atlanta, Georgia (Fulton

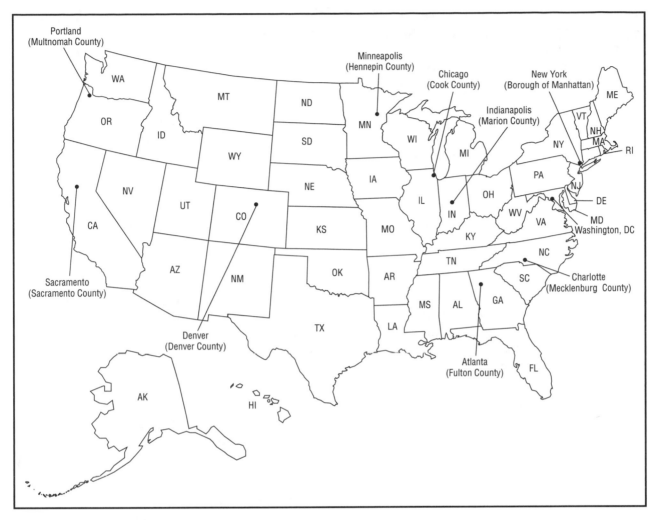

Figure 1. ADAM II sites. ILLUSTRATION BY GGS INFORMATION SERVICES. GALE, CENGAGE LEARNING

County), Charlotte, North Carolina (Mecklenburg County), Indianapolis, Indiana (Marion County), Minneapolis, Minnesota (Hennepin County), Chicago (Cook County), Denver, Colorado (Denver County), Portland, Oregon (Multnomah County), and Sacramento, California (Sacramento County).

For ADAM II all protocols, instruments, and sampling remain the same as in ADAM, so trend lines can be developed for each drug at each site. There have been, however, a few important changes from the original ADAM model. Additional questions regarding methamphetamine manufacture were also developed and included in the instruments drug market section and a test for oxycodone was added to the drug test panel. In addition, the national contractor's local field staff now collects data in cooperation with local site directors

who maintain working relationships with each booking facility. In ADAM II data are collected in two back-to-back quarters each year (as opposed to each quarter) and annualized to represent the year.

BIBLIOGRAPHY

DuPont, R. L., & Wish, E. D. (1992). Operation tripwire revisited. *Annals of the American Academy of Political and Social Science, 521* (1), 91–111.

Office of National Drug Control Policy (in press). *Arrestee Drug Abuse Monitoring Program 2007*, Executive Office of the President.

United States Department of Justice, Office of Justice Programs. (2003). *Arrestee Drug Abuse Monitoring Annual Report 2000*, April, NCJ 193913.

DANA E. HUNT

ASSESSMENT OF SUBSTANCE ABUSE. *See* **Alcohol, Smoking and Substance Involvement Screening Test (ASSIST); AUDADIS; Drug Abuse Screening Test (DAST); HIV Risk Assessment Battery (RAB); Michigan Alcoholism Screening Test (MAST); Semi-Structured Assessment for Drug Dependence and Alcoholism (SSADDA); Semi-Structured Assessment for the Genetics of Alcoholism (SSAGA); T-ACE.**

ASSET FORFEITURE. Asset forfeiture is the involuntary relinquishment of money or property without compensation as a consequence of a commission of a crime. Forfeiture laws authorize prosecutors to file civil lawsuits asking a court for permission to take property from a criminal defendant that was either used in the crime or was the fruit of a criminal act. Since the 1970s, federal asset forfeiture laws have been used against drug dealers. By 2000, however, there were many in Congress and the legal community who urged reform of these forfeiture laws, as they have often resulted in harsh and unfair outcomes for innocent third parties. Congress responded by passing the Civil Asset Forfeiture Reform Act of 2000.

FORFEITURE ACT

In 1970, Congress enacted the Comprehensive Drug Abuse Prevention and Control Act, also known as the Forfeiture Act. The Forfeiture Act authorized federal prosecutors to bring civil forfeiture actions against certain properties owned by persons convicted of federal drug crimes. The act was not used much because it limited forfeiture to the property of persons convicted of participating in continuing criminal enterprises. In 1978, Congress amended the law to allow forfeiture of anything of value used or intended to be used by a person to purchase illegal drugs. This amendment expanded the act to allow the forfeiture of all proceeds and property traceable to the purchase of illegal drugs. The amended law authorized the federal government to proceed *in rem* against property. *In rem* forfeiture proceedings are actions taken against the property, not the owner of the property, which allows the government to remove property from persons suspected of a crime without ever charging them with a crime.

Congress amended the Forfeiture Act again in 1984 as part of the Comprehensive Crime Control Act. The amendment authorized the federal government to pursue *in rem* forfeitures of land and buildings. Federal authorities may seize any real property purchased, used, or intended to be used to facilitate narcotics trafficking. Although Congress appears to have intended the law to apply only to drug manufacturing or storage facilities, federal courts have interpreted the law to allow the seizure of any real property, including fraternity houses, hotels, ranches, and private residences. In addition, courts have allowed forfeitures regardless of whether the property was used to store or manufacture drugs.

THE PROCESS OF SEIZING PROPERTY

The process of seizing property under the Forfeiture Act is straightforward. Forfeiture begins with the constructive or actual seizure of property after a warrant has been issued by a federal district court. This warrant must be based on the reasonable belief that the property was used in a crime subject to forfeiture, but this belief can be based on hearsay and circumstantial evidence. After the property is seized, the court holds it until the case is resolved.

In a civil forfeiture proceeding, the government must prove that the property is subject to forfeiture because there is a substantial connection between the property and the crime. If the defendant fails to rebut this proof with sufficient evidence, the government is allowed to keep the property. At the trial, the government's standard of proof is by a preponderance of the evidence, a lesser burden of proof than the criminal standard of a reasonable doubt.

DISTRIBUTION OF PROCEEDS

The Forfeiture Act permits law enforcement agencies to receive a part of the proceeds from property forfeiture. Prior to the 1984 amendments, all revenue derived from a federal asset forfeiture was deposited in the U.S. Treasury general fund. The 1984 law allowed federal law enforcement agencies to keep all proceeds from confiscated property and to use the proceeds to support asset-seizure programs. State and local law enforcement agencies that turned over their seizure cases to federal authorities received up to 80 percent of the profit after the property had been sold. Many legal scholars criticized this feature of the law, arguing that it detracts from the traditional police function of fighting crime and created incentives for police to pursue forfeitures that lacked probable cause. Proponents of this budgetary scheme argue that drug activity is the source of much violent crime and that the proceeds benefit community programs and increase the capacity to fight violent crime.

Most states also have forfeiture laws upon conviction of certain crimes. These laws often mandate forfeiture of prohibited drugs; property used to contain, protect, or secure prohibited drugs; firearms; and vehicles. In contrast to the federal law, many states require that profits from the sale of forfeited property be deposited in the state's general treasury fund.

DEFENSES TO FORFEITURE

Defendants have employed several defenses to forfeiture, and some have proved successful. If notice and a hearing before a court do not precede the initial seizure, a defendant may argue that forfeiture violates the Due Process Clause of the Fifth and Fourteenth Amendments. If a forfeiture is disproportionate to the offense that gave rise to it, it may be found to violate the Eighth Amendment's Excessive Fines Clause.

Congress has also responded to criticism by enacting the so-called innocent owner defense in civil drug forfeiture cases. These are cases in which forfeiture is sought without prosecution of the owner. A defendant in a civil forfeiture case may invoke this defense if the property was connected with illegal drugs without the owner's knowledge or consent. For example, if the owner of an automobile innocently allows another person to borrow the car and that person commits a drug offense in the car, the owner can offer this defense and retain the car.

As state and federal prosecutors intensified their use of asset forfeiture laws, public dissatisfaction grew. By the early 1990s, the federal government was prosecuting only 20 percent of the individuals from whom it seized property through forfeiture. According to Department of Justice statistics, over 28,000 properties were seized in 1996, with a combined value of $1.264 billion. Critics have argued that the government routinely violates the Fifth Amendment's ban against taking property without due process of law, largely because it sees forfeiture as an easy way to collect funds. Supporters have countered that forfeiture has helped in the war on drugs by stripping criminals of their resources.

CIVIL ASSET FORFEITURE REFORM ACT OF 2000

Congress intervened by passing the Civil Asset Forfeiture Reform Act of 2000, which requires federal prosecutors to show a substantial connection between the property and the crime. In addition, it allows the property to be released by the district court pending final disposition of the case when the owner can demonstrate that possession by the government causes a hardship to the owner. Moreover, the law allows owners of property to sue the government for any damage to the property if the victim of the seizure prevails in a civil forfeiture action.

Though the 2000 act promised more safeguards for an innocent owner's interest in property and placed the burden of proof on the government to establish a preponderance of evidence that the property is subject to forfeiture, the law has not reduced the amount of seized and forfeited property. Although relying solely on the dollar amount of property seized per year to measure the effect of the act is misleading, as the forfeiture of several large assets can raise the yearly amount, the amounts have continued to move upward. In 2006 the Assets Forfeiture Fund/Seized Asset Deposit Fund increased from $659 million in 2005 to $1.25 billion. The 2006 report by the government concluded that there would be a "strong current and future potential stream of assets flowing" into the fund.

BIBLIOGRAPHY

Assets Forfeiture Fund and Seized Asset Deposit Fund Annual Financial Statement Fiscal Year 2006. (2006). Washington, DC: Office of the Inspector General, Audit Division, U.S. Dept. of Justice.

O'Meara, K. (2000, August 7). When feds say seize and desist. *Insight on the News.*

West's Encyclopedia of American Law. (1997). St. Paul, MN: Westgroup.

FREDERICK K. GRITTNER

ASSIST. *See* **Alcohol, Smoking and Substance Involvement Screening Test (ASSIST).**

ASSOCIATION FOR MEDICAL EDUCATION AND RESEARCH IN SUBSTANCE ABUSE (AMERSA). The Association for Medical Education and Research in Substance Abuse (AMERSA) is a national organization of more than 300 medical and allied faculty, which was founded in 1976 for the promotion of education and research in the field of substance abuse. The organization was derived from an informal coalition of U.S. Federal Career Teachers in alcoholism and drug abuse; these career teachers, one on the faculty of each of fifty-five medical schools, were funded by the National Institute on Drug Abuse (NIDA) and the National Institute on Alcohol Abuse and Alcoholism (NIAAA) to promote enhanced teaching at their respective medical campuses. The Career Teachers Program, established in 1972, was regarded as a highly successful vehicle for highlighting an issue of considerable importance in the medical curriculum. As the program wound down (it came to an end in 1981), the participants felt it important to secure the continuation of their mission and established AMERSA as a national membership organization open to all medical faculty and faculty in allied health programs.

In the year of its establishment, AMERSA held its first national meeting, which was followed by meetings of increasing attendance in each succeeding year. The national meetings have been the focus of federal participation in teaching programs and have focused on curriculum techniques and new research findings.

AMERSA established a quarterly publication, *Substance Abuse*, in 1979, presenting educational and research findings; it serves as a vehicle for broadening the base of teaching in the members' fields. In addition, a variety of curricula were established by members, with coordination through the AMERSA national headquarters (located in Providence, Rhode Island) and augmented by the Center for Medical Fellowships in Alcoholism and Drug Abuse, located at New York University.

Full membership is available for all persons holding faculty appointments in health-professional schools and/or to those involved in substance abuse education or research. Membership benefits include a free subscription to *Substance Abuse*; reduced rates at the annual conference; and a national voice that supports academic programs in universities, professional schools, and organizations that promote substance abuse education and research.

The organization's members work in a variety of ways to effect their educational ends. Much effort is invested in developing curriculum and curriculum outlines for courses directed at a variety of disciplines and various educational levels. In addition, most members work actively within their respective departments to develop subspecialty expertise—as in psychiatry and internal medicine. Efforts are also directed at schoolwide initiatives—as with programs organized through the deans of medical schools.

See also **Alcohol; Models of Alcoholism and Drug Abuse.**

BIBLIOGRAPHY

Association for Medical Education and Research in Substance Abuse (AMERSA). Available from http://www.amersa.org.

National Institute on Drug Abuse (NIDA) (2007). *Drugs, brains, and behavior: The science of addiction.* Bethesda, MD: National Institute on Drug Abuse.

MARC GALANTER

ATROPINE. *See* **Scopolamine and Atropine.**

ATTENTION DEFICIT HYPERACTIVITY DISORDER. The *DSM-IV* taxonomy (American Psychiatric Association 1994) denotes three variants of attention deficit hyperactivity disorder (ADHD): (1) inattentive, (2) hyperactive-impulsive, and (3) attention-hyperactive with impulsivity. The percentage of affected individuals in each ADHD category is respectively estimated at 20 to 30 percent, below 15 percent, and 50 to 70 percent. Females are overrepresented in the inattentive subtype (which has fewer coexisting emotional and behavioral disorders), whereas boys are more frequently diagnosed with the other two types (which are featured by more severe psychosocial disturbances). The relative absence of behavioral disturbance in the inattentive type may impede treatment initiation (Spencer et al., 2007; Staller & Faraone, 2006). However, symptoms of inattention are more likely to continue into adulthood compared to hyperactive and impulsive symptoms (Hart et al., 1995; Biederman et al., 2000), indicating that this disorder may have the most serious lasting adverse effects on adjustment.

To qualify for diagnosis according to *DSM-IV* criteria, at least six of nine symptoms must be present. Commonly, another diagnosis is also present, particularly conduct disorder or oppositional defiant disorder. Girls with ADHD demonstrate less severe aggression, disruptive behaviors, and hyperactivity as well as a lower prevalence of conduct disorder and oppositional defiant disorder than boys (Staller & Faraone, 2006). Approximately 25 percent of children with ADHD develop antisocial personality disorder (Weiss & Hechtman, 1993; Wender et al., 2001). Mood disorders, anxiety disorders, and substance use disorders are overrepresented in adults who had childhood ADHD (Fayyad et al., 2007).

EPIDEMIOLOGY

A meta-analysis of 102 epidemiological studies concluded that the prevalence of ADHD is 5.29 percent in children and adolescents and 4.4 percent in adults. Boys have 2.45 times greater likelihood of an ADHD diagnosis than girls (Polanczyk & Rohde, 2007). The disorder persists into adulthood in about 30 percent of cases (Polanczyk & Rohde, 2007; Fayyad et al., 2007).

ETIOLOGY

Genetic Factors. Heritability in the range of 0.80 for males and females has been reported in family (Staller & Faraone, 2006) and twin studies (Spencer et al., 2007). Molecular genetic studies strongly implicate the dopaminergic system in the etiology of ADHD (Spencer et al., 2007).

Non-Genetic Factors. Acute brain injury, particularly in the anterior region, frequently results in attentional disturbance and behavioral overactivity.

Malnutrition, exposure to alcohol and tobacco additives, and medical illness in the mother during development of the fetus also augment risk for ADHD. Perinatal events, especially hypoxia, also amplify risk for ADHD. There is no compelling evidence as of 2008 indicating that parenting behavior, exposure to food additives, or television cause ADHD.

Neurobiology. Imaging studies have shown morphological abnormalities in the frontal cortex, cerebellum, and subcortical structures; however, the clinical significance of these findings remains uncertain. Functional magnetic resonance imaging (fMRI) studies point to a frontal cortical disturbance that may account for the impairment in executive cognitive capacities along with behavioral undercontrol and poor emotional regulation.

RELATION BETWEEN ADHD AND DRUG ABUSE

Substance use initiation occurs at a younger age and accelerates more rapidly in youths with ADHD (Biederman et al., 1998; Wilens et al., 1998; Molina & Pelham, 2003; Staller & Faraone, 2006). The association between substance use and ADHD is stronger in girls than in boys (Disney et al., 1999; Staller & Faraone, 2006). An association between childhood ADHD and risk for substance use disorder, especially when there is co-occurring childhood conduct disorder (CD), has been documented in many studies (Fayyad et al., 2007). Genetic factors and neurobiological systems are common to both ADHD and the early age onset variant of substance use disorder.

TREATMENT

An 80 percent improvement rate has been reported using psychostimulants in children and adolescents (Markowitz et al., 2003) and 60 percent in adults (Wender et al., 2001). Prognosis following pharmacological treatment is the same for both genders (Pelham et al., 1989). Youths receiving only medication for fourteen months have been reported in one large-scale study to have the same prognosis as youths receiving combined medication management and behavior modification (MTA Cooperative Group, 1999). Disorders co-occurring with ADHD are responsive to behavioral treatments; hence, interventions need to be tailored to the child's particular pattern of disturbance. Because ADHD in childhood amplifies risk for substance use and substance use disorder, effective treatment may prevent these outcomes.

See also **Amphetamine; Methylphenidate; Pemoline; Psychomotor Stimulant; Risk Factors for Substance Use, Abuse, and Dependence.**

BIBLIOGRAPHY

American Psychiatric Association. (1994). *Diagnostic and statistical manual of mental disorders* (4th ed.). Washington, DC: Author.

Biederman, J., Mick, E., & Faraone, S. V. (2000). Age-dependent decline of symptoms of attention deficit hyperactivity disorder: Impact of remission definition and symptom type. *American Journal of Psychiatry, 157*, 816–818.

Biederman, J., Wilens, T., & Mick, E., & Spencer, T. (1998). Does attention-deficit hyperactivity disorder impact the developmental course of drug and alcohol abuse and dependence? *Biological Psychiatry, 44,* 269–273.

Disney, E. R., Elkins, I. J., McGue, M., & Iacono, W. G. (1999). Effects of ADHD, conduct disorder, and gender on substance use and abuse in adolescence. *American Journal of Psychiatry, 156*, 1515–1521.

Fayyad, J., De Graaf, R., Kessler, R., Alonso, J., Angermeyer, M., Demyttenaere, K., et al. (2007). Cross-national prevalence and correlates of adult attention-deficit hyperactivity disorder. *British Journal of Psychiatry, 190*, 402–409.

Hart, E., Lahey, B., Loeber, R., Applegate, B., & Frick, P. J. (1995). Developmental change in attention-deficit hyperactivity disorder in boys: A four-year longitudinal study. *Journal of Abnormal Child Psychology, 23, 729–749.

Markowitz, J. S., Straughn, A. B., & Patrick, K. S. (2003). Advances in the pharmacotherapy of attention-deficit-hyperactivity disorder: Focus on methylphenidate formulations. *Pharmacotherapy, 23,* 1281–1299.

Molina, B. S., & Pelham, W. E. (2003). Childhood predictors of adolescent substance use in a longitudinal study of children with ADHD. *Journal of Abnormal Psychology, 112,* 497–507.

MTA Cooperative Group. Multimodal Treatment Study of Children with ADHD (1999). A 14-month randomized clinical trial of treatment strategies for attention-deficit/hyperactivity disorder. *Archives of General Psychiatry, 56,* 1073–1086.

Pelham, W. E., Walker, J. L., Jason, L., Sturges, J., & Hoza, J. (1989). Comparative effects of methylphenidate on ADD girls and ADD boys. *Journal of the American Academy of Child and Adolescent Psychiatry, 28, 773–776.

Polanczyk, G., & Rohde, L. A. (2007). Epidemiology of attention-deficit/hyperactivity disorder across the lifespan. *Current Opinion in Psychiatry, 20,* 386–392.

Spencer, T. J., Biederman, J., & Mick, E. (2007). Attention-deficit/hyperactivity disorder: Diagnosis, lifespan, comorbidities, and neurobiology. *Journal of Pediatric Psychology, 32,* 631–642.

Staller, J., & Faraone, S. V. (2006). Attention-deficit hyperactivity disorder in girls. *Epidemiology and Management: Therapy in Practice, 20,* 107–123.

Weiss, G., & Hechtman, L. T. (1993). *Hyperactive children grown up: ADHD in children, adolescents, and adults.* New York: Guilford.

Wender, P. H., Wolf, L. E., & Wasserstein, J. (2001). Adults with ADHD: An overview. *Annals of the New York Academy of Sciences, 931,* 1–16.

Wilens, T. E., Biederman, J., & Mick, E. (1998). Does ADHD affect the course of substance abuse? Findings from a sample of adults with and without ADHD. *American Journal of Addictions, 7,* 156–163.

RALPH TARTER

AUDADIS. The Alcohol Use Disorder and Associated Disabilities Interview Schedule (AUDADIS) (Grant et al., 1995) is an interview used to assess alcohol and drug use, abuse, and dependence, and many other potentially associated conditions, including medical and psychiatric disorders. The AUDADIS was designed for lay interviewers in large-scale surveys. It is fully structured, meaning that all questions are read to respondents exactly as written.

The AUDADIS was initially developed for the National Longitudinal Alcohol Epidemiologic Survey (NLAES), a survey that was conducted in 1991 and 1992 with 42,862 participants. The AUDADIS was updated into the AUDADIS-IV for the National Epidemiologic Survey on Alcohol and Related Conditions (NESARC; Grant et al., 2004), conducted with 43,086 participants in 2001 and 2002 (http://niaaa.census.gov/), with a three-year follow up interview to evaluate changes over time. The AUDADIS and AUDADIS-IV were developed by researchers at the Laboratory on Epidemiology and Biometry at the National Institute on Alcohol Abuse and Alcoholism (NIAAA). The

AUDADIS has also been used in a longitudinal general population study of at-risk drinkers (e.g., Hasin et al., 2007).

The AUDADIS-IV was designed to assess alcohol, drug, and psychiatric disorders according to DSM-IV criteria. Alcohol and drug use is covered in detail, substance by substance, as are DSM-IV alcohol and drug abuse and dependence. The psychiatric coverage of the AUDADIS-IV includes mood disorders, including DSM-IV primary major depressive disorder (MDD), bipolar I, bipolar II, and dysthymia. AUDADIS-IV anxiety disorders include DSM-IV primary panic disorder with and without agoraphobia, social and specific phobias, and generalized anxiety disorder. Personality disorders (PDs), assessed on a lifetime basis, included DSM-IV avoidant, borderline, dependent, narcissistic, obsessive-compulsive, paranoid, schizoid, schizotypal, and antisocial personality disorders (APD). Nicotine use and dependence are also covered, but not abuse, as DSM-IV does not include a category for nicotine abuse. All but one of the DSM-IV disorders were assessed by asking about all symptoms and diagnostic criteria for each disorder. Schizophrenia/psychotic disorders were assessed by asking if a doctor had evaluated the participant as having this disorder, since previous studies found that asking the specific symptoms of psychosis in a survey interview took a lot of time in an interview and the results were not reliable or valid. Most DSM-IV disorders are covered in two main time periods: the last 12 months (considered current) and prior to the past 12 months (past). Together, these two periods cover the lifetime history. Personality disorders were asked about on a lifetime basis only, with an explanation to participants that the questions were meant to cover lifelong, stable patterns of thoughts and behaviors.

In addition, in the psychiatric sections, age at onset of each condition was asked, as was number of episodes and duration of longest episode for conditions that could occur more than once. In addition, treatment for all above disorders was covered. Finally, family history of alcohol use disorders, drug use disorders, depression, and antisocial personality disorders were assessed for relatives, including parents, siblings, children, and also more distant relatives.

Medical disorders in the AUDADIS and AUDADIS-IV included those with a hypothesized relationship to alcohol consumption. Disability was assessed for physical and emotional disability. A number of risk factors for and consequences of alcohol use, drug use, and psychiatric disorders were covered, including stigma due to race, gender, religion, weight, disability, and sexual orientation, childhood abuse, neglect and positive family factors, current stresses and social support, and partner violence as perpetrator and victim. Socioeconomic and demographic information is also collected.

The AUDADIS-IV has been used in a computer-assisted format in some studies. In this form, a computer program is designed so that after each question and answer, the computer checks the answer for consistency with some previous answers and presents the next question to the interviewer that needs to be asked. A computer-assisted interview is easier for interviewers when complex branching patterns of questions and answers occur, such as in the AUDADIS. Thus, this type of computerization saves time and reduces errors. DSM-IV diagnoses are produced from the interview data on a group basis by computer program, to be used for research purposes.

The reliability of the AUDADIS and AUDADIS-IV was studied in test-retest reliability studies. In these studies, a series of participants were interviewed once with the interview being tested and then re-interviewed by a second interviewer who did not know the results of the first interview. Reliability for disorders or other conditions was computed by determining the level of agreement of the pairs of interviewers over the level that would be expected by chance (e.g., a coin flip), given how common the disorders are. Examples of test-retest reliability studies of the AUDADIS are those in general population samples (Grant et al. 1995, 2003; Ruan et al. 2008), in a clinical sample of substance abusers (Hasin et al., 1997), and in Puerto Rican primary care patients (Canino et al., 1999). The reliability of alcohol and drug use and dependence is generally excellent. The reliability of the psychiatric sections of the AUDADIS-IV is all in the fair-to-excellent range, similar to or better than the reliability of other interviews that have been used in surveys.

Validity research is more complex than reliability research. Validity studies usually involve testing whether diagnoses obtained from a given assessment procedure agree with other measures or variables in theoretically predicted ways. For an interview such as the AUDADIS, designed for non-clinician interviewers, such testing can include agreement with clinician assessments, with other assessment procedures in widespread use, or other variables such as clinical correlates or longitudinal course. Convergent, discriminative, and construct validities of AUDADIS-IV alcohol use disorder criteria and diagnoses were good to excellent, including when administered to a sample of heavier-than-average drinkers in the United States and in an eleven-country World Health Organization study (Ustün et al. 1997). In addition, clinician reappraisals agreed well with AUDADIS diagnoses of alcohol dependence and major depression in a study conducted in Puerto Rico (Canino et al. 1997).

Controversy exists on whether diagnoses that result from fully structured interviews are the same that experienced, well-trained clinicians would make. The study involving clinical reappraisals in Puerto Rico suggested that the AUDADIS-IV is valid relative to clinician diagnoses, but more studies in different types of samples are needed to ensure that this is a generally applicable result.

See also **Diagnosis of Substance Use Disorders: Diagnostic Criteria; Diagnostic and Statistical Manual (DSM).**

BIBLIOGRAPHY

Canino, G., Bravo, M., Ramírez, R., Febo, V. E., Rubio-Stipec, M., Fernandez, R. L., et al. (1999). The Spanish Alcohol Use Disorder and Associated Disabilities Interview Schedule (AUDADIS): Reliability and concordance with clinical diagnoses in a Hispanic population. *Journal of Studies on Alcohol, 60*(6), 790–799.

Chatterji, S., Saunders. J. B., Vrasti, R., Grant, B. F., Hasin, D., & Mager, D. (1997). Reliability of the alcohol and drug modules of the Alcohol Use Disorder and Associated Disabilities Interview Schedule—Alcohol/Drug-Revised (AUDADIS-ADR): An international comparison. *Drug and Alcohol Dependence, 47*(3), 171–185.

Grant, B. F., Dawson, D. A., Stinson, F. S., Chou, P. S., Kay, W., & Pickering, R. (2003). The Alcohol Use Disorder and Associated Disabilities Interview Schedule-IV (AUDADIS-IV): Reliability of alcohol consumption, tobacco use, family history of depression, and psychiatric diagnostic modules in a general population sample. *Drug and Alcohol Dependence, 71*(1), 7–16.

Grant, B. F., Harford, T. C., Dawson, D. A., Chou, P. S., & Pickering, R. P. (1995). The Alcohol Use Disorder and Associated Disabilities Interview schedule (AUDADIS): Reliability of alcohol and drug modules in a general population sample. *Drug and Alcohol Dependence, 39* (1), 37–44.

Grant, B. F., Stinson, F. S., Dawson, D. A., Chou, S. P., Dufour, M. C., Compton, W., et al. (2004) Prevalence and co-occurrence of substance use disorders and independent mood and anxiety disorders: Results from the National Epidemiologic Survey on Alcohol and Related Conditions. *Archives of General Psychiatry, 61* (8), 807–816.

Hasin, D., Carpenter, K. M.., McCloud, S., Smith, M., & Grant, B. F. (1997). The alcohol use disorder and associated disabilities interview schedule (AUDADIS): Reliability of alcohol and drug modules in a clinical sample. *Drug and Alcohol Dependence, 44* (2–3), 133–141.

Hasin, D. S., Keyes, K. M, Hatzenbuehler, M. L., Aharonovich, E. A., & Alderson, D. (2007). Alcohol consumption and posttraumatic stress after exposure to terrorism: Effects of proximity, loss, and psychiatric history. *American Journal of Public Health, 97* (12), 2268–2275.

Ruan, W. J., Goldstein, R. B., Chou, S. P., Smith, S. M., Saha, T. D., Pickering, R. P., et al. (2008). The Alcohol Use Disorder And Associated Disabilities Interview Schedule-IV (AUDADIS-IV): Reliability of new psychiatric diagnostic modules and risk factors in a general population sample. *Drug and Alcohol Dependence, 92* (1–3), 27–36.

Ustün, B., Compton, W., Mager, D., Babor, T., Baiyewu, O., Chatterji, S., et al. (1997). WHO study on the reliability and validity of the alcohol and drug use disorder instruments: Overview of methods and results. *Drug and Alcohol Dependence, 47* (3), 161–169.

DEBORAH HASIN

AUDIT. *See* **Alcohol Use Disorders Identification Test (AUDIT).**

AUSTRALIA. Australia is an Anglophone, predominantly European, nation that occupies an island the size of the continental United States. In

1788 the British turned the island into a penal colony, and since then its indigenous population has been supplanted by an English-speaking society of predominantly Anglo-Celtic origin. This population was supplemented by European immigrants after World War II, and a smaller population of Asian immigrants began arriving in the early 1970s. Australia's indigenous people, Aborigines and Torres Strait Islanders, now comprise 2 percent of the population of 20,000,000.

TOBACCO IN AUSTRALIA

Tobacco smoking causes more than 80 percent of all drug-related deaths in Australia, and it was responsible for 8 percent of the burden of disease in 2003, compared to 2 percent from alcohol and 2 percent from illicit drugs. Prior to European settlement, Aboriginal Australians obtained nicotine by chewing the leaves of *Duboisia hopwoodii*, which they call *pituri*, but widespread smoking did not begin in the indigenous population until after the British colonization.

In the early nineteenth century, most of the white male population smoked pipes. This remained the dominant form of tobacco use until the 1900s, when cigarettes gained popularity. Smoking increased among men during and after World War I and among women in the 1950s and 1960s.

Smoking began to decline among Australian men in the 1950s and among women in the 1980s. Daily smoking declined by 40 percent between 1985 (29% of the population) and 2007 (17%), as shown in Figure 1. Australia now has one of the lowest rates of adult smoking in the OECD. Indigenous Australians still have high smoking rates, however: 53 percent of Aboriginal and Torres Strait Islander people were smokers in 2004–2005.

Tobacco Policies. The low contemporary rates of smoking among Australians reflect the effects of the extensive tobacco control measures introduced since the 1970s (see Table 1). The introduction of these policies reflects the success of public health and tobacco control advocates in persuading governments to actively work to reduce smoking prevalence by substantially increasing the price of tobacco, banning its promotion, and reducing opportunities for smoking in the workplace, bars, and public places.

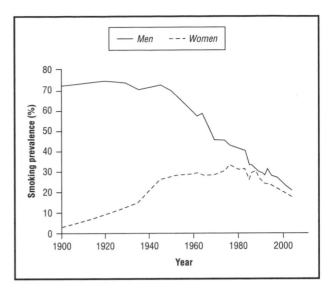

Figure 1. Australian smoking prevalence, 1900–2000. (Sources: Adapted from Tyrrell, 1999 and AIHW, 2007.) ILLUSTRATION BY GGS INFORMATION SERVICES. GALE, CENGAGE LEARNING

Tobacco-related Harm. Tobacco-related harm accounted for an estimated 15,511 deaths in Australia in 2003, while tobacco-related disease was responsible for the loss of 204,788 disability-adjusted life years (DALY). The major causes of both death and disability were lung cancer, chronic obstructive pulmonary disease, and ischemic heart disease. Tobacco-related death and disease has been declining along with the steeply declining prevalence of smoking, although the decline began later in women because of their later uptake of smoking.

ALCOHOL USE

Young working-class males dominated the Australian population from early settlement until the middle of the nineteenth century, leading to a high per capita alcohol consumption during this period. Consumption halved between the Gold Rush in the 1850s and the end of the nineteenth century, as Australia became a settled, urbanized, and family-oriented society, with better education and greater opportunities for recreations other than drinking. Spirits drinking dominated the colonial period but declined with the emergence of a local brewing industry in the late nineteenth century.

A temperance movement in the latter part of the nineteenth century moderated consumption. This movement did not achieve legislated prohibition,

Advertising	• Direct media advertising phased out 1973–1976. • Bans on advertisements that promote smoking 1992. • Advertising at sports events prohibited.
Health warnings	• Mandatory warning labels on cigarette packets 1972. • Graphic health warning on cigarette packs 2006.
Age restrictions Taxation	• Bans on sale of tobacco products to persons under 18. • Federal excise tax on tobacco since 1901. • Taxation on cigarettes changed to a 'per stick' basis 1999. • Excise per stick raised 6 monthly in line with the CPI.
Public smoking Restrictions	• Smoking banned in enclosed public places and workplaces. • 7/8 jurisdictions ban smoking in licensed premises.
Licensing of tobacco retailers	• Licence required to sell tobacco products in 5/8 jurisdictions.
Smoking in cars	• South Australia banned smoking in cars with children under 16 in 2007.
Sales bans	• Sale of smokeless tobacco banned in 1991.

Table 1. Tobacco control measures in Australia. ILLUSTRATION BY GGS INFORMATION SERVICES. GALE, CENGAGE LEARNING

but it succeeded in closing hotels at 6:00 p.m. during World War I, a restriction that lasted until the mid-twentieth century, despite the development of a black market in alcohol, colloquially known as "sly-grogging." Alcohol consumption steadily declined from the early 1900s to reach a low in the early 1930s.

Consumption increased between the late 1930s and late 1970s as a result of the nation's growing affluence and the incorporation of alcohol into everyday life in the late 1960s and early 1970s. Alcohol has been heavily promoted via industry sponsorship of sports such as cricket, rugby league football, and horse racing. Wine drinking emerged in the late 1960s, encouraged by European postwar migration, increased travel by Australians to Europe, and the introduction of a sales tax in the early 1970s that favored wine over other forms of alcohol. Alcohol consumption steadily increased during the postwar period, peaking in the late 1970s before declining during the 1980s. It remained relatively steady during the 1990s and 2000s.

In 2003 Australia's per capita alcohol consumption was 7.2 liters per capita, putting it 27th in the world. This was lower than in wine-drinking societies such as France (9.3 liters) and Spain (10.0) and the beer-drinking United Kingdom (9.6), and only marginally higher than New Zealand (6.8), Canada (7.0) and the United States (6.8).

According to the Australian Institute of Health and Welfare (AIHW), in 2006 around 16 percent of Australians abstained from drinking alcohol (20% of women and 13% of men). Of these, 7 percent were ex-drinkers and 9 percent had never consumed a full alcoholic drink. Of the drinkers, 9 percent drank daily, 41 percent drank weekly, and 34 percent drank less than weekly. Women were found to be much more likely to drink less weekly than men were (39% versus 28%). Over half of the drinkers reported that they usually consumed one to two standard drinks (about 10 grams, or 0.6 fluid ounces, of alcohol) per occasion (75% of women and 50% of men). Among men, 59 percent reported either abstaining (13%) or drinking at a low-risk level (46%) and the remainder drank at levels that placed them at risk of short-term (40%) or long-term (10%) harms to their health. Among women, the comparable percentages were: 68 percent abstaining or drinking at low risk; 39 percent at high risk for short-term harms and 10 percent at high risk for long-term harms (AIHW, 2007).

Of the different types of beverages, 47 percent of alcohol is consumed as beer, compared with 32 percent for wine, and 21 percent for spirits. Males are much more likely to consume light and full-strength beer than women, who are much more likely to drink wine. Young men are overrepresented among the substantial minority of drinkers who drink most days of the week and are at risk of short-term harm. The typical quantity consumed and the frequency of drinking among young women has grown closer to that of men, however, reflecting the greater participation of women in paid work, increasing incomes for women, and a weakening of taboos against drinking among women. With the conspicuous exception of Aboriginal alcohol use, ethnic differences in alcohol use have not been investigated.

Alcohol Policy. During the 1970s, state governments liberalized controls on alcohol while increasing treatment for alcohol dependence and introducing random breath testing to reduce alcohol-related motor vehicle crashes. Australia was one of the first countries to introduce compulsory blood testing for persons involved in automobile accidents. It also reduced the blood alcohol level defined as intoxication from 0.08 percent to 0.05 percent. This policy has had strong public support because of its success in reducing road fatalities. Alcohol was also included as part of the National Campaign Against Drug Abuse, which was launched in 1985, and a National Health Policy on Alcohol was produced in 1989 and updated in 2005.

Alcohol-related Harms. In 2003, alcohol use accounted for an estimated 2 percent of the burden of disease in Australia and averted an estimated 1 percent of disease burden through reduction of cardiovascular disease. It accounted for 1,100 premature deaths and 61,000 DALYs. The major contributors to premature death were alcohol abuse, suicide and self-inflicted injuries, road traffic accidents, and cancers of the oral cavity, esophagus, and the breast (AIHW, 2007).

ILLICIT DRUGS
Cannabis, heroin, amphetamines, cocaine, and MDMA (methylenedioxymethamphetamine, or "Ecstasy") have been the major illicit drugs used in Australia (see Figure 2). Cannabis is illegally grown and amphetamines are produced in the country, while opiates and cocaine are imported. The 2004 National Drug Strategy Household Survey found that cannabis was used by 34 percent of persons over the age of 14 years at some time in their lives, while 11 percent reported having used it in the past year. Lifetime cannabis use increased between 1973 and 1998 but has declined since (AIHW, 2007).

At the same time, around 2 percent of persons over 14 had injected heroin at least once, and just under 0.5 percent reported that they had used heroin in the past year. There were estimated to be 74,000 dependent heroin users in 1997–1998. Heroin use increased during the middle 1990s, but it declined steeply after the onset of a heroin shortage at the beginning of 2001. Amphetamine derivates had been used by 9 percent of Australian adults, and 11 percent of those 20 to 29 years of age reported using these substances in the previous year. Males are more likely than females to have used amphetamines, and they typically do so in their late teens. The use of the amphetamine analogue MDMA increased from 2 percent in 1995 to 8 percent in 2004, with 3 percent reporting use in the previous year. Lifetime use of cocaine is 5 percent of adults, with 1 percent using in the previous year.

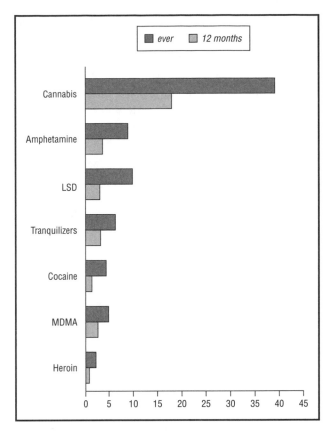

Figure 2. Prevalence of illicit drug use among Australian adults in 2004. (Adapted from AIHW, 2007.) ILLUSTRATION BY GGS INFORMATION SERVICES. GALE, CENGAGE LEARNING

Australia has a higher rate of lifetime cannabis use (34%) than the United States (33%), the United Kingdom (22%) and the Netherlands (18%). The prevalence of heroin dependence in Australia is similar to that in the European Union and the United Kingdom, and it is a little higher than in the United States, which has a much higher rate of cocaine use (10%) than Australia (3%).

Illicit-drug Policy. The aim of the 1986 National Campaign Against Drug Abuse was to "minimize the harmful effects of drugs on Australian society" by increasing public education and expanding treatment for opioid and other drug dependence. Australia's harm-minimization approach was exemplified by its response to the HIV epidemic in the early 1980s. This effort involved frank public education campaigns, the introduction of needle and syringe exchange programs, the diversion of drug offenders into treatment, the expansion of methadone maintenance and drug-free treatment programs, and not enforcing laws against the possession of injecting equipment.

Bipartisan support for harm-minimization weakened in 1997 when the Prime Minister, John Howard, and the cabinet vetoed a proposed trial of prescribing heroin for opioid dependent persons, a program that had been approved by a majority of state and federal health and law enforcement ministers. The federal government subsequently allocated more than $A500 million to education, treatment, and law enforcement to reduce opioid overdose deaths and illicit-drug-related crime. The prime minister also directly funded abstinence-oriented NGO (nongovernmental organization) treatment services, and he created the Australian National Council on Drugs, whose chair, Brian Watters, opposed harm minimization.

Harm minimization was retained in 1998 in a compromise national policy but broadened to include "abstinence-oriented strategies." Until the election of a Labor government in December 2007 national drug policy used the rhetoric of being "tough on drugs" to cover a strong budgetary emphasis on law enforcement and interdiction, together with increased funding for abstinence-oriented and methadone treatment and programs that divert drug users into treatment.

Illicit Drug-Related Harm. Illicit drug use in Australia accounts for around 2 percent of the burden of disease. This is primarily attributable to heroin overdose deaths and deaths and illness from Hepatitis C infections. The number of fatal overdoses rose from 6 in 1964 to over 1,000 in 1999, before declining by 40 percent in 2001. Australia has low rates of HIV infection among injecting drug users (IDUs), with fewer than 8 percent of new cases being IDUs and 3 percent of IDUs infected with HIV. This low rate of infection reflects Australia's geographic isolation, the low numbers of visitors and immigrants, and the early introduction of needle and syringe exchange programs. Among IDUs, 50 percent are infected with Hepatitis C, and the rate of new Hepatitis C infections is estimated to be 15 percent per year.

See also **Alcohol; Amphetamine; Amphetamine Epidemics, International; Cannabis, International Overview; Foreign Policy and Drugs, United States; Harm Reduction; Hepatitis C Infection; Heroin; International Drug Supply Systems; Tobacco.**

BIBLIOGRAPHY

Australian Institute of Health and Welfare. (2007). *Statistics on drug use in Australia, 2006.* Canberra: Author. Available from http://www.aihw.gov.au/.

Lewis, M. (1992). *A rum state: Alcohol and state policy in Australia.* Canberra: Australian Government Publishing Service.

Manderson, D. (1993). *From Mr. Sin to Mr. Big: A history of Australian drug laws.* Melbourne: Oxford University Press.

Room, R. (1988). "The dialectic of drinking in Australian life: From the Rum Corps to the wine column." *Australian Drug and Alcohol Review, 7,* 413–437.

Tyrrell, I. (1999). *Deadly enemies: Tobacco and its opponents in Australia.* Kensington: University of New South Wales Press.

WAYNE HALL
CORAL GARTNER

AUTOMATION OF REPORTS AND CONSOLIDATED ORDERS SYSTEM (ARCOS).

The Controlled Substances Act of 1970 requires all manufacturers and distributors of controlled substances to report their activities to the attorney general of the United States, via the Drug Enforcement Administration (DEA), on a regular basis (quarterly or monthly). The DEA uses the Automation of Reports and Consolidated Orders System (ARCOS) to collect and track this information, and it reports on a statistically valid sampling of all information received.

CLASSIFICATION OF CONTROLLED SUBSTANCES

The substances covered by the Controlled Substances Act include legal prescription and over-the-counter pharmaceuticals as well as potentially addictive or abusable illegal drugs. The U.S. government classifies drugs into five schedules (categories), based on potential for abuse and addiction, potential harmfulness, and medical utility.

The drugs classified into Schedule I have no accepted medical utility in the United States but have tremendous potential for abuse and addiction. Some Schedule I drugs are methamphetamine, MDMA (street name: Ecstasy), PCP, heroin, LSD, marijuana, and crack. Schedule II drugs have high potential for abuse, dependence, or addiction but may have accepted medical uses in the United States. Drugs in this category are many of the prescription stimulants, depressants, and narcotics. Some Schedule II drugs are codeine, morphine, cocaine, and Ritalin. Prescribers of Schedule II drugs must use special forms and cannot indicate refills. These prescriptions must be hand-delivered to the pharmacy, except under specific emergency circumstances. Drugs in Schedules III, IV, and V are progressively less addictive or prone to abuse or dependence. These drugs may be similar to those in Schedule II but with lower narcotic concentrations. Some Schedule III drugs are sedatives, "crank," anabolic steroids and other body-building drugs, Tylenol with codeine, and some milder sedatives and barbiturates. Schedule IV contains many of the milder antianxiety, antidepressant, appetite suppressant, stimulant, and sleep-inducing drugs, such as Valium, Librium, Ativan, Meridia, Ambien, Halcion, and Cylert, as well as Rohypnol. Schedule V drugs pose the lowest risk of abuse and dependence; they include nonprescription substances such as commercial cough medicines and antidiarrheals.

ARCOS PROGRAM DESCRIPTION

The DEA requires registration and regulatory compliance by all manufacturers of controlled substances; all health care providers licensed or certified to prescribe, dispense, or administer them; and all pharmacies permitted to fill prescriptions. The DEA is also tasked with monitoring the flow of controlled substances across national borders.

ARCOS functions as a comprehensive tracking system for controlled substances, extending from the point of manufacture to distribution for retail use in dispensing facilities such as hospitals, medical offices, clinics, other in- or outpatient settings, and commercial sales through pharmacies or other registered retailers, such as chain stores with pharmacy departments. Manufacturers, distributors, and retailers must track and report all Schedule II through Schedule V activities on a regular basis. ARCOS synthesizes the data from approximately 1,100 data sources into a report form submitted to the DEA. By comparing manufacture and distribution reports, the government regulating agencies are better able to determine the means by which drugs are moved from legal to illegal venues,

which is called *drug diversion*. Among the most common ways in which controlled substances are illegally diverted are by physicians (most frequent) or other health care practitioners who prescribe medication for abusing/dependent individuals or who write prescriptions to known drug dealers; pharmacists who falsify records (second most frequent) and then sell their controlled substance inventory illegally; staff at dispensing facilities who steal and then traffic drugs; commercial theft (such as burglary); and forgery of prescriptions, either by theft of prescription pads or by changing quantity, dose, or refill amounts on legitimately written prescriptions.

The DEA has an Office of Diversion Control (ODC) designed to investigate, track, and trend drug-diversion activities. The office is multidisciplinary and uses the expertise of chemists, pharmacologists, information technology experts, field operations investigators, and special agents. The ODC's work is simplified as a result of the data collected and reported by ARCOS.

Since 2005, ARCOS has employed an electronic data interchange (EDI) reporting system, which has dramatically increased the efficiency of the former paper-based reporting mechanism. DEA registrants using this system log onto the ODC Web site's secured portal and upload their required reports instantly.

Only pharmaceutical manufacturers and distributors report to ARCOS. Manufacturers of controlled substances are required to report their inventories, acquisitions and dispositions of all substances contained in Schedule I as well as narcotic and gamma-hydroxybutyric acid (GHB) substances in Schedule III. They must also report all synthesizing activities involving Schedules I and II, narcotics, and GHB as well as some specific controlled psychotropic drugs contained in Schedules III and IV. Distributors of controlled substances are mandated to report their inventories, acquisitions, and dispositions of all substances contained in Schedules I and II as well as narcotic and gamma-hydroxybutyric acid (GHB) substances in Schedule III. As of 2008, approximately 1,100 manufacturers and distributors report to ARCOS; this is a very small number in comparison to the more than one million registrants contained in the Drug Enforcement Administration's (DEA) Controlled Substances Act database.

For each annual data-reporting period, myriad reports are generated, depending on the needs and requirements of the DEA as well as the reporting states and other entities. The summary data is synthesized into six major reports:

- *Retail Drug Distribution by Zip Code for Each State* reports drug amounts, in grams, distributed to each retail registrant, sorted by state and zip code.

- *Retail Drug Distribution by Drug Code for Total U.S.* is a quarterly tally of the total drug quantities distributed to each registrant, sorted by state.

- *Quarterly Distribution in Grams per 100K Population* indicates quarterly drug consumption, sorted by state, by number of grams per 100,000 population.

- *Cumulative Distribution in Grams per 100K Population* is similar to the report above, with a cumulative yearly tally. Every state is ranked in ascending order by each drug.

- *Statistical Summary for Retail Drug Purchases* sorts average purchase for each drug by business activity and state.

- *U. S. Summary of Retail Drug Purchases* presents a cumulative picture of the average purchase of each drug, by business activity, for the entire United States.

See also **Controlled Substances Act of 1970; Controls: Scheduled Drugs/Drug Schedules, U.S.**

BIBLIOGRAPHY

Drug Enforcement Administration. (2008). Automation of reports and consolidated orders system (ARCOS). Available from http://www.deadiversion.usdoj.gov/.

Drug Enforcement Administration. Automation of reports and consolidated orders system (ARCOS). (1997). *ARCOS registrant handbook* (Rev. ed.). Available from http://www.deadiversion.usdoj.gov/.

Drug Enforcement Administration. Office of Diversion Control. (2006). ARCOS retail drug summary reports. Available from http://www.deadiversion.usdoj.gov/.

Drug Enforcement Administration. Automation of reports and consolidated orders system (ARCOS). *National drug code dictionary.* Available from http://www.deadiversion.usdoj.gov/.

PAMELA V. MICHAELS

AYAHUASCA. The use of naturally psychoactive products is a feature of shamanic practices across the globe, but the peoples of the Americas seem to have been blessed with an extraordinary variety. Archeological evidence of the use of psychoactive preparations in the Americas dates back thousands of years, and the same archeological record shows the high importance placed on these substances in the religious and cultural life of the Americas prior to European contact. Upon the conquest of the Americas, the use of these preparations was suppressed by the Christian Church, which rightly saw the use of these drugs as a threat to its religious hegemony over the peoples of the New World. In spite of this, and in spite of continued threats of suppression as a part of various national and international drug prohibition regimes, the use of psychoactive drugs in the spiritual life of native and mestizo peoples in the Americas has continued to the early twenty-first century. In recent decades the acceptance of these drugs in cultural settings outside of their traditional homes has slowly seeped into more Westernized elements of society in both Europe and the Americas. Among the most notable of these psychoactive plant-based churches are those that center their ritual existences around the hallucinogenic preparation ayahuasca. Two churches, the Santo Daime and Uniao do Vegetal (UDV), which had their origins among the mestizo populations of the Brazilian interior in the mid-twentieth century, have spread the ritual use of ayahuasca from Amazonia first, then via the influx of people from the Amazon backcountry, to the great cities of Brazil. From the cities of Brazil, these churches have spread in recent years to the cosmopolitan cities of the developed world.

Moving from the other cultural direction have been both scientists and "ayahuasca tourists." Among the early members of the latter class are the Beat writers Allen Ginsberg and William S. Burroughs, whose *The Yage Letters* remains a common entry point for curious Westerners to the literature and experience of ayahuasca. Combining the roles of scientist, shaman, and tourist/adventurer is perhaps the most important figure in the cross-cultural journey of ayahuasca in recent years, Terrence McKenna, who with his brother Dennis has perhaps done more than any other individual to promulgate the study and use of natural hallucinogens, or to use his own term, *entheogens,* outside of their traditional context in the Amazon and elsewhere. Terrence, who died in 2000, was the adventurer and shaman of the pair, writing numerous books such as *The Invisible Landscape* and *The Archaic Revival*. Both chronicle his experiences with traditional and pharmacological psychedelic drugs and his hypothesis that psychedelic drug use was a source of both religious belief and the evolution of human intelligence. Dennis was the scientist of the pair, and he produced a number of contributions to our understanding of the pharmacology of psychoactive ethnobotanical preparations such as ayahuasca.

Ayahuasca is an Amazonian herbal preparation that has most likely been used for religious and shamanic purposes in the Amazon basin for thousands of years, although the first definitive reports of its use by outside explorers may be traced to the mid-nineteenth century. Ayahuasca, which is variously known as *Caapi, Natema, Mihi, Yage, La Purga,* or *Santo Daime* depending on the cultural context in which it is encountered, is a Quechua word meaning "spirit vine," which roughly encapsulates its traditional purpose and use in the cultures of the Amazon and their more recent global offshoots. Ayahuasca is a brew of various plants, usually slow-boiled to concentrate the plant extracts, which is drunk by the user to obtain its effects. It is prepared in a variety of ways comparable to the large number of cultures in which it is important, but it always contains the vine *Banisteriopsis caapi* and typically a plant containing dimethyltryptamine (DMT), most often *Psychotria viridis*. Usually consumed under the guidance of a shaman, who often uses chants and a low-light environment to guide the experience, the combination produces several hours of profound hallucinatory experiences that, in the context of the compound's use, allow contact with the spirit world and permit spiritual physical and psychological healing to occur. The content of the hallucinations often contains consistent elements across users, with visions of serpents and spiritual beings of various sorts being quite common. Visions of death can also occur with some frequency, as can reactions of intense fear in some users, properties—in addition to the nausea it produces—that make ayahuasca unlikely to be used at all outside of a ritual or therapeutic setting.

The compound nature of ayahuasca makes it one of the most advanced and potent products of any traditional pharmacopoeia in the world. To understand the pharmacological sophistication of the prehistoric shamans who created ayahuasca, it is necessary to understand the psychoactive constituents of the two plants from which it is made. *Banisteriopsis caapi* contains significant amounts of the β-carbolines harmaline and harmine, both of which are potent inhibitors of the enzyme monoamine oxidase (MAO), as well as the source of a number of other significant effects on the nervous system. *Psychotria viridis* is rich in the powerful hallucinogen DMT. DMT, however, is broken down rapidly in the gut and blood by MAO, rendering it inactive when ingested alone. However, when extracts of the two plants are combined, the MAO inhibition provided by the alkaloids in *Banisteriopsis caapi* permits DMT to enter first the bloodstream and then the brain where it exerts its effects on consciousness and perception. Interestingly, both DMT and β-carbolines are present endogenously in the human body. DMT has been implicated in the production of dreams and β-carbolines in anxiety and depression. As mentioned above, a number of preparations of ayahuasca exist: Some contain other psychoactive plants such as tobacco or cocoa leaves, and others like *pharmahuasca* are merely purified DMT and harmine in pill form, seen sometimes in the developed world.

With regard to human psychological health, the few studies of the psychological traits of those who use ayahuasca in a ritual setting on a regular basis have shown reduced levels of panic and hopelessness, and a generally improved outlook. Physically, besides the acute nausea the drug often produces, there is little evidence of negative effects. What research has been done on ayahuasca and its major constituents, DMT and the harmala alkaloids, suggests that its beneficial effects on the psyche are dependent on the set and setting of an individual's encounter with the drug. Whereas those who use ayahuasca in its traditional cultural milieu may often gain from the experience, those who approach it as tourists or thrill seekers are more likely to have neutral or negative psychological outcomes in the absence of an experienced shaman to guide the *journey*, as the ayahuasca experience is often called. In traditional contexts and in the newer ayahuasca-using churches, ayahuasca seems to actually be beneficial in reducing the abuse of other substances. For these reasons, ayahuasca seems unlikely to become an abused drug (indeed, no reliable reports of ayahuasca abuse are available), although its use might become more common as the culture of the developed world becomes more accustomed to the ancient spiritual technology ayahuasca represents in its traditional Amazonian context.

See also **Hallucinogenic Plants; Hallucinogens; Plants, Drugs From.**

BIBLIOGRAPHY

Metzner, R. (Ed.). (2006). *Sacred vine of spirits: Ayahuasca.* Rochester, VT: Park Street Press.

Rätsch, C., & Hofmann, A. (Eds.). (2005). *Encyclopedia of psychoactive plants: Ethnopharmacology and its applications.* Rochester, VT: Park Street Press.

RICHARD G. HUNTER

BARBITURATES. Barbiturates refer to a class of general central nervous system depressants that are derived from barbituric acid, a chemical discovered in 1863 by the Nobel Prize winner in chemistry (1905) Adolf von Baeyer (1835–1917). Barbituric acid itself is devoid of central depressant activity; however, German scientists Emil Hermann Fischer and Joseph von Mering made some modifications to its structure and synthesized barbital, which was found to possess depressant properties. Scientists had been looking for a drug to treat anxiety and nervousness but without the dependence-producing effects of opiate drugs such as opium, codeine, and morphine. Other drugs such as bromide salts, chloral hydrate, and paraldehyde were useful sedatives, but they all had problems such as toxicity or they left such a bad taste in patients' mouths that they preferred not to take them. Fischer and von Mering noted that barbital produced sleep in both humans and animals. It was introduced into chemical medicine in 1903 and was soon in widespread use.

By 1913, the second barbiturate, phenobarbital, was introduced into medical practice. Since that time, more than 2,000 similar chemicals have been synthesized but only about 50 of these have been marketed. Although the barbiturates were quickly used to treat a number of disorders effectively, their side effects were becoming apparent. The chief problem, an overdose, can result in respiratory depression, which can be fatal. By the mid-1950s, more than 70 percent of admissions to a poison-control center in Copenhagen, Denmark, involved

barbiturates. Additionally, it became apparent that the barbiturates were subject to abuse, which could lead to dependence, and that a serious withdrawal syndrome could ensue when the drugs were abruptly discontinued. In the 1960s, the introduction of a safer class of hypnotic drugs, the benzodiazepines reduced the need for barbiturates.

Barbiturates are dispensed in distinctly colored capsules making them very easy to identify by the lay public. In fact, users within the drug culture often refer to the various barbiturates by names associated with their physical appearance. Examples of these names include blue birds, blue clouds, yellow jackets, red devils, sleepers, pink ladies, and Christmas trees. The term *goofball* is often used to describe barbiturates in general. All barbiturates are chemically similar to barbital, the structure of which is shown in Figure 1.

All barbiturates are general central nervous system depressants. This means that sedation, sleep, and even anesthesia will develop as the dose is increased. Some barbiturates also are useful in reducing seizure activity and so have been used to treat some forms of epilepsy. The various barbiturates differ primarily in their onset and duration of action, ability to enter the brain, and the rate at which they are metabolized. These differences are achieved principally by adding or subtracting atoms to the two branches on position #5 in Figure 1. The barbiturates are classified on the basis of their duration of action, which ranges from ultrashort-acting to long-acting. The onset of action of the ultrashort-acting barbiturates occurs in seconds

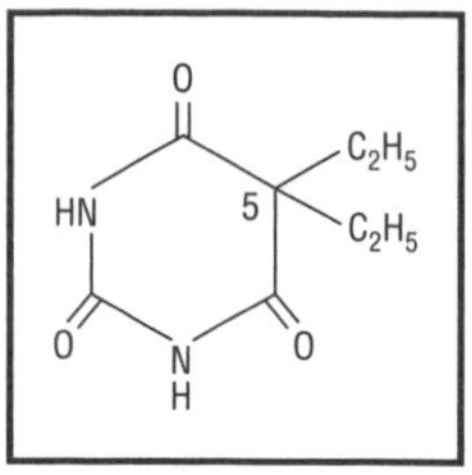

Figure 1. Chemical structure of barbital. ILLUSTRATION BY GGS INFORMATION SERVICES. GALE, CENGAGE LEARNING

Drug class and generic names	Trade names	Routes of administration*	Half-life (in hours)
Ultrashort-acting:			
methohexital sodium	Brevital	IV	3.5–6**
thiamylal sodium	Surital	IV	†
thiopental sodium	Pentothal	IV	3–8**
Short-acting:			
butalbital	‡	PO	35
hexobarbital	Sombulex	PO; IV	3–7
pentobarbital	Nembutal	PO; IM	15–48
secobarbital	Seconal	PO; IM	15–40
Intermediate-acting:			
amobarbital	Amytal	PO; IM	8–42
aprobarbital	Alurate	PO	14–34
butabarbital	Butisol	PO	34–42
talbutal	Lotusate	PO	†
Long-acting:			
phenobarbital	Luminal	PO; IV	24–96
mephobarbital	Mebaral	PO	11–67

*IV = intravenous; IM = intramuscular; PO = oral.
**Values are for whole body, half-life in the brain is less than 30 minutes.
†Half-life data not available for human subjects.
‡Various preparations in combination with acetaminophen.

Table 1. Classification of barbiturates on the basis of duration of action. (Source: Rall, 1990, Csáky, 1979.) ILLUSTRATION BY GGS INFORMATION SERVICES. GALE, CENGAGE LEARNING

and lasts a few minutes. The short-acting compounds take effect within a few minutes and can last four to eight hours, while the intermediate- and long-acting barbiturates can take almost an hour to take effect but last six to twelve hours. Table 1 lists the common barbiturates, their trade names, typical route of administration, and plasma half-life. The plasma half-life is a measure of how long the drug remains in the blood, but not how long the effects last, although it does provide a general indication of when to expect the effects to wane (a half-life of five hours means that one-half of the drug will be removed from the system in five hours; one-half of the remaining drug will be removed during the next five hours, etc.).

EFFECTS ON THE BODY AND THERAPEUTIC USES

Barbiturates affect all excitable tissues in the body. However, neurons are more sensitive to their effects than other tissues. The depth of central nervous system depression ranges from mild sedation to coma and depends on many factors including which drug is used, its dose, the route of administration, and the level of excitability present just before the barbiturate was taken. The most common uses for the barbiturates are still to promote sleep and to induce anesthesia. Barbiturate-induced sleep resembles normal sleep in many ways, but there are a few important differences. Barbiturates reduce the amount of time spent in rapid eye movement or REM sleep—a very important phase of sleep. Prolonged use of barbiturates causes restlessness during the late stages of sleep. Since the barbiturates remain in our bodies for some time after we awaken, there can be residual drowsiness that can impair judgment and distort moods for some time after the obvious sedative effects have disappeared. Curiously, some people are actually excited by barbiturates, and the

individual may even appear inebriated. This paradoxical reaction often occurs in the elderly and is more common after taking phenobarbital.

The general use of barbiturates as hypnotics (sleeping pills) has decreased significantly, since they have been replaced by the safer benzodiazepines. Phenobarbital and butabarbital are still available, however, as sedatives in a number of combination medications used to treat a variety of inflammatory disorders. These two drugs also are used occasionally to antagonize the unwanted overstimulation produced by ephedrine, amphetamine, and theophylline.

Since epilepsy is a condition of abnormally increased neuronal excitation, any of the barbiturates can be used to treat convulsions when given in anesthetic doses; however, phenobarbital has a selective anticonvulsant effect that makes it particularly useful in treating grand mal seizures. This selective effect is shared with mephobarbital and metharbital. Thus, phenobarbital is often used in hospital emergency rooms to treat convulsions such as those that develop during tetanus, eclampsia, status epilepticus, cerebral hemorrhage, and poisoning by convulsant drugs.

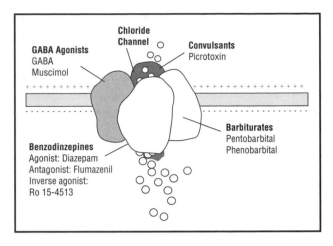

Figure 2. Barbiturates. ILLUSTRATION BY GGS INFORMATION SERVICES. GALE, CENGAGE LEARNING

The benzodiazepines are, however, gradually replacing the barbiturates in this setting as well.

It is not completely understood how barbiturates work but, in general, they act to enhance the activity of GABA on GABA-sensitive neurons by acting at the same receptor on which GABA exerts its effects (see Figure 2). GABA is a neurotransmitter that normally acts to reduce the electrical activity of the brain; its action is like a brake. Thus, barbiturates enhance the braking effects of GABA to promote sedation. There is an area in the brain called the reticular activating system, which is responsible for maintaining wakefulness. Since this area has many interconnecting or polysynaptic neurons, it is the first to succumb to the barbiturates, and that is why an individual becomes tired and falls asleep after taking a barbiturate.

PHARMACOKINETICS AND DISTRIBUTION

The ultrashort-acting barbiturates differ from the other members of this class mainly by the means by which they are inactivated. Methohexital and its relatives are very soluble in lipids (i.e., fatty tissue). The brain is composed of a great deal of lipid; when the ultrashort-acting barbiturates are given intravenously, they proceed directly to the brain to produce anesthesia and unconsciousness. After only a few minutes, however, these drugs are redistributed to the fats in the rest of the body so their concentration is reduced in the brain. Thus, recovery from IV barbiturate anesthesia can be very fast. For this reason, drugs such as methohexital and thiopental are used primarily as intravenous anesthetic agents and not as sedatives.

The other longer-acting barbiturates must be metabolized by the liver into inactive compounds before the effects wane. Since these metabolites are more soluble in water, they are excreted through the kidneys and into the urine. As is the case with most drugs, metabolism and excretion is much quicker in young adults than in the elderly and infants. Plasma half-lives are also increased in pregnant women because the blood volume is expanded due to the development of the placenta and fetus.

TOLERANCE, DEPENDENCE, AND ABUSE

Repeated administration of any number of drugs results in eventual compensatory changes in the body. These changes are usually in the opposite direction of those initially produced by the drug such that more and more drug is needed to achieve the initial desired effect. This process is called tolerance. There are two basic mechanisms for tolerance development: tissue tolerance and metabolic or pharmacokinetic tolerance. Tissue tolerance refers to the changes that occur on the tissue or cell that is affected by the drug. Metabolic tolerance refers to the increase in the processes that metabolize or break down the drug. This process generally occurs in the liver. Barbiturates are subject to both types of tolerance development.

Tolerance does not develop equally in all effects produced by barbiturates. Barbiturate-induced respiratory depression is one example. Barbiturates reduce the drive to breathe and the processes necessary for maintaining a normal breathing rhythm. Thus, while tolerance is quickly developing to the desired sedative effects, the toxic doses change to a lesser extent. As a result, when the dose is increased to achieve the desired effects (e.g., sleep), the margin of safety actually decreases as the dose comes closer to producing toxicity. A complete cessation of breathing is often the cause of death in barbiturate poisoning (Rall, 1990).

If tolerance develops and the amount of drug taken continues to increase, then physical dependence can develop. This means that if the drug is suddenly stopped, the tissues' compensatory effects become unbalanced and withdrawal signs appear. In the case of barbiturates, mild signs of withdrawal include apprehension, insomnia, excitability, mild tremors, and loss of appetite. If the dose was very high, more severe signs of withdrawal can occur, such as weakness, vomiting, decrease in blood pressure regulatory mechanisms (so that pressure drops when a person rises from a lying position, called orthostatic hypotension), increased pulse and respiratory rates, and grand mal (epileptic) seizures or convulsions. Delirium with fever, disorientation, and hallucinations may also occur. Unlike withdrawal from the opioids, withdrawal from central nervous system depressants such as barbiturates can be life threatening. The proper treatment of a barbiturate-dependent individual always includes a slow reduction in the dose to avoid the dangers of rapid detoxification.

Few, if any, illegal laboratories manufacture barbiturates. Diversion of licit production from pharmaceutical companies is the primary source for the illicit market. Almost all barbiturate users take it by mouth. Some try to dissolve the capsules and inject the liquid under their skin (called skin-popping) but the toxic effects of the alcohols used to dissolve the drug and the strong alkaline nature of the solutions can cause lesions of the skin. Intravenous administration is a rare practice among barbiturate abusers.

Many barbiturate users become dependent to some degree during the course of treatment for insomnia. This type of problem is called iatrogenic, because it is initiated by a physician. In some instances the problem will be limited to continued use at gradually increasing doses at night, to prevent insomnia that is in turn due to withdrawal. However, some individuals who are susceptible to the euphoric effects of barbiturates may develop a pattern of taking increasingly larger doses to become intoxicated, rather than for the intended therapeutic effects (for example, to promote sleepiness). To achieve these aims, the person may obtain prescriptions from a number of physicians and take them to a number of pharmacists—or secure their needs from illicit distributors (dealers). If the supply is sufficient, the barbiturate abuser can rapidly increase the dose within a matter of weeks. The upper daily limit is about 1,500 to 3,000 milligrams; however, many can titrate their daily dose to the 800 to 1,000 milligram range such that the degree of impairment is not obvious to others. The pattern of abuse resembles that of ethyl (drinking) alcohol, in that it can be daily or during binges that last from a day to many weeks at a time. This pattern of using barbiturates for intoxication is more typically seen in those who, from the beginning, obtain barbiturates from illicit sources rather than those who began by seeking help for insomnia.

Barbiturates are sometimes used along with other drugs. Often, the barbiturate is used to potentiate, or boost, the effects of another drug upon which a person is physically dependent. Alcohol and heroin are commonly taken together in this way. Since barbiturates are "downers," they also are used to counteract the unwanted overstimulation associated with stimulant-induced intoxication. It is not uncommon for stimulant abusers (on cocaine or amphetamines) to use barbiturates to combat the continued "high" and the associated motor disturbances associated with heavy and continued cocaine use. Also, barbiturates are used to ward off the early signs of withdrawal from alcohol.

Treatment for barbiturate dependence is often conducted under carefully controlled conditions, because of the potential for severe developments, such as seizures. Under all conditions, a program of supervised withdrawal is needed. Many years ago, pentobarbital was used for this purpose and the dose was gradually decreased until no drug was given. More recently, phenobarbital or the benzodiazepines—chlordiazepoxide and diazepam—have been used for their greater margin of safety. The reason that the benzodiazepines sometimes work is because the general central nervous system depressants—barbiturates, alcohol, and benzodiazepines—develop cross-dependence to one another. Thus a patient's barbiturate or alcohol withdrawal signs are reduced or even eliminated by diazepam.

See also **Withdrawal.**

BIBLIOGRAPHY

Csáky, T. Z. (1979). *Cutting's handbook of pharmacology: The actions and uses of drugs*, 6th ed. New York: Appleton-Century Crofts.

Gilman, A. G., et al., Eds. (2005). *Goodman and Gilman's the pharmacological basis of therapeutics*, 11th ed. New York: McGraw-Hill Medical.

Henn, D., & DeEugenio, D. (2007). *Barbiturates*. New York: Chelsea House Publications.

Henningfield, J. E., & Ator, N. A. (1986). Barbiturates: Sleeping potion or intoxicant? In *The encyclopedia of psychoactive drugs*. New York: Chelsea House.

Mendelson, J. H., & Mello, N. K. (1992). *Medical diagnosis and treatment of alcoholism*. New York: McGraw-Hill.

Rall, T. W. (1990). Hypnotics and sedatives. In A. G. Gilman et al. (Eds.), *Goodman and Gilman's the pharmacological basis of therapeutics*, 8th ed. New York: Pergamon. (2005, 11th ed. New York: McGraw-Hill Medical.)

Winger, G., Hoffman, F. G., & Woods, J. H. (1992). *A handbook of drugs and alcohol abuse: The biomedical aspects*, 3rd ed. New York: Oxford University Press. (2004, 4th ed.)

Scott E. Lukas

BARBITURATES: COMPLICATIONS.

Barbiturates are central nervous system (CNS) depressants (downers). These drugs produce sedative, hypnotic, and anesthetic effects. Depending on the dose used, any single drug in this class may produce sedation (decreased responsiveness), hypnosis (sleep), and anesthesia (loss of sensation). A small dose will produce sedation and relieve anxiety and tension; a somewhat larger dose taken in a quiet setting will usually produce sleep; an even larger dose will produce unconsciousness. The sleep produced by barbiturates, however, is not identical with normal sleep. Normal sleep consists of several phases, including slow-wave sleep, or deep sleep, and rapid-eye-movement (REM) sleep. In the REM sleep phase, skeletal muscles relax, eyes move rapidly and frequently, and dreaming occurs. Dreaming is believed to play an important role in learning and memory. Barbiturates decrease REM (or dreaming) sleep, which may explain why the sleep associated with barbiturates is less restorative than natural sleep.

As is true for most drugs that act on the CNS, the effects of these drugs are also influenced markedly by the user's previous drug experience, the circumstances in which the drug is taken, and the route of administration of the drug. For example, a dose taken at bedtime may produce sleep, whereas the same dose taken during the daytime may produce a feeling of euphoria, incoordination, and emotional response. This, in many ways, is what happens with alcohol intoxication. In fact, the behavioral effects of this class of drugs is very similar to those observed after drinking alcohol, and the user may experience impairment of skills and judgment not unlike that experienced with alcohol. It is therefore not surprising that the effects of barbiturates are enhanced when taken in combination with alcohol, anti-anxiety drugs (benzodiazepines), and

other CNS depressants such as opioids, antihistamines, and over-the-counter cough and cold medications containing these drugs. Barbiturates, however, differ from some other sedative-hypnotic drugs in that they do not elevate the pain threshold. In fact, patients experiencing severe pain may become agitated and delirious if they are given barbiturates without also receiving analgesics (pain killers).

Barbiturates are generally classified as being long, intermediate, short, and ultra-short acting on the basis of their duration of effect. The long-acting barbiturates, such as phenobarbital, which were at one time mainly employed as daytime sedatives for the treatment of anxiety, produce sedation that lasts from twelve to twenty-four hours. Although no longer prescribed widely for that purpose, phenobarbital is one of the drugs used for the treatment of grand mal epilepsy. The short- and intermediate-acting drugs such as pentobarbital and secobarbital, which were once mainly employed as hypnotics, produce CNS depression that lasts for three to twelve hours, depending on the compound used. The ultra-short-acting barbiturates (e.g., thiopental) are used for the induction of anesthesia because of the ease and rapidity with which they induce sleep when given intravenously. The effects of barbiturates on judgment and other mental as well as motor skills, however, may persist much longer than the duration of the hypnotic effect. For this and other reasons, for the treatment of anxiety or insomnia, barbiturates have largely been replaced by the generally safer group of drugs called benzodiazepines.

The respiratory system is significantly depressed by the administration of barbiturate doses that are larger than those usually prescribed. Furthermore, there is a synergistic effect (i.e., one that is greater than simply adding the drugs' effects) when barbiturates are combined with alcohol and other central nervous system depressants—often with a fatal outcome. Barbiturates are frequently used for suicides. For this reason, too, barbiturates have been displaced by less toxic benzodiazepines. The symptoms of acute barbiturate toxicity resemble the effects observed after excessive alcohol ingestion. Although repeated administration of barbiturates results in CNS tolerance, thus producing less intoxication, tolerance does not appear to develop to the same extent for the respiratory depressant and lethal effects of the barbiturates; the person addicted to barbiturates may therefore be at a greater risk of respiratory toxicity because of less pronounced CNS euphoric effects with higher doses, which may lead the individual to increase the dosage, resulting in respiratory depression. Tolerance to barbiturates also affects metabolism; the administration of these drugs speeds up not only their own metabolism (i.e., shortens their effectiveness) but also the metabolism of a large number of other drugs. This property has been of use in some special cases (as in jaundice of the newborn), but it can be hazardous in others when it decreases the effectiveness of another drug (e.g., an anticoagulant used to treat blood clots).

Long-term users experience withdrawal symptoms when the barbiturate is stopped abruptly. Abrupt cessation also leads to an increase in the amount and intensity of REM sleep (REM rebound). The intensity of the withdrawal symptoms varies with the degree of abuse and may range from sleeplessness and tremor in mild cases to delirium and convulsions in severe cases. Fatalities have occurred as a result of barbiturate withdrawal; this is more likely to occur with short-acting barbiturates. In some individuals, barbiturates may produce CNS excitement rather than CNS depression. This type of idiosyncratic reaction occurs most frequently in elderly people. Among the side effects sometimes seen, there may be rashes and muscle and body aches.

See also **Expectancies; Sleep, Dreaming, and Drugs.**

BIBLIOGRAPHY

Charney, D. S., Mihic, S. J., & Harris, R. A. (2005). Hypnotics and sedatives. In L. Brunton, J. Lazo, & K. Parker (Eds), *The pharmacological basis of therapeutics* (11th ed.). New York: McGraw-Hill.

Kalant, H., & Roschlau, W. H. E. (1989). *Principles of medical pharmacology*, 5th ed. Toronto: B. C. Decker.

JAT M. KHANNA
REVISED BY LEAH R. ZINDEL (2009)

BEERS AND BREWS.

Beers and brews are beverages produced by yeast-induced fermentation of malted cereal grains, usually barley malt, to which hops and water have been added. They generally contain 2 to 9 percent ethyl alcohol, although some may contain as much as 15 percent. Various types and flavors are created by adding different combinations

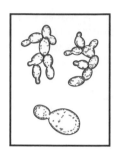

Figure 1. Yeast. ILLUSTRATION BY GGS INFORMATION SERVICES. GALE, CENGAGE LEARNING

of malts and cereals and allowing the process to continue for varying lengths of time.

BREWING HISTORY

The origin of beer is unknown, but it was an important food to the people of the Near East, probably from Neolithic times, some 10,000 years ago. The making of beer and of bread developed at the same time. In Mesopotamia (the ancient *land between the rivers* as the Greeks called it), an early record from about 5,000 years ago describing the recipe of the "wine of the grain" was found written in Sumerian cuneiform on a clay tablet. In ancient Egypt, at about the same time, barley beer was brewed and consumed as a regular part of the diet. It was known as *hek* and tasted like a sweet ale, since there were no hops in Egypt. Egyptians continued to drink it for centuries, although the name was changed to *hemki*. More than 3,200 years ago, the Chinese made a beer called *kiu* that was most likely made from two parts millet and one part rice. With water added, the concoction was heated in clay pots; flour and various plants were added to provide the yeast and flavors, respectively.

The ancient Greeks, however, preferred wine and considered beer to be a drink of barbarians. Beer was drunk on special occasions in ancient Rome; Plutarch wrote of a feast in which Julius Caesar served his officers beer as a special reward after they had crossed the Rubicon river. Once the art of brewing reached England, beers and ales became the preferred drink of the rich and poor alike. King Henry VIII of England was said to consume large quantities during breakfast. It was soon discovered that sailors who drank beer avoided scurvy, a disease caused by a lack of adequate amounts of Vitamin C. Thus, beer was added to each ship's provisions and was even

Figure 2. Barley. ILLUSTRATION BY GGS INFORMATION SERVICES. GALE, CENGAGE LEARNING

Figure 3. Hops. ILLUSTRATION BY GGS INFORMATION SERVICES. GALE, CENGAGE LEARNING

carried on the *Mayflower* during the crossing of the Atlantic Ocean in 1620. American colonists quickly learned to make their beer with Indian corn (maize), and much U.S. beer is still made with corn, although rice and wheat are also used in the mix with barley malt.

MAKING BEER

The first step in making beer is to allow barley to sprout (germinate) in water, a process that releases an important enzyme, amylase. Germinated barley seeds are called malt. Once the malt is crushed and suspended in water, the amylase breaks down the complex starch into more basic sugars. The reaction is stopped by boiling, and the concoction is filtered. This clear solution is mixed with hops (to provide the bitter flavor) and a starter culture of yeast (to begin the alcoholic fermentation process). Carbon dioxide gas (the fizz or bubbles) is produced, along with ethyl alcohol (ethanol or drinking alcohol). The malt and hops are then removed (and generally sold for cattle feed) while the yeast is skimmed off as fermentation proceeds. After the desired effect is achieved, the beer is filtered and bottled, or it is stored in kegs for aging. During the aging process (2 to 24 weeks) proteins settle to the bottom or are digested by enzymes. The carbonation (fizz) that occurred during fermentation is then drawn off and forced back in during the bottling process.

BEER TYPES

There are two major types of beers: top-fermenting and bottom-fermenting. Top fermentation occurs at room temperature 59° to 68°F (15°–20°C) and is so named because the yeast rises to the top of the vessel during fermentation. This older process produces beers that have a natural fruitiness and

include the wheat beers, true ales, stouts, and porters. Their flavor is most completely expressed when served at moderate (i.e., room) temperatures. The development of yeasts that sank during this process resulted in brews that were more stable between different batches. Most of the major brewers have switched to the bottom yeasts and cold storage (lagering). The significance of using yeast that sinks during fermentation is that airborne yeasts cannot mix with the special yeast and contaminate the process.

The most popular type of beer in the United States is lager, a pale, medium-hop-flavored beer. It is mellowed several months at 33°F (0.5°C) to produce its distinctive flavor. Lager beers average 3.3 to 3.4 percent ethyl alcohol by weight and are usually heavily carbonated. Pilsner is a European lager (that originated in medieval Pilsen, now the Czech city of Plzen) that is stored longer than other lagers and has a higher alcohol content and a rich taste of hops. Dark beers are popular in Europe but are not generally produced in the United States. The dark color is achieved by roasting the malt; dark beer has a heavier and richer taste than lager beer. British beers are many and varied, both pale and dark; some have a number of unique additives, including powdered eggshell, crab claws or oyster shells, tartar salts, wormwood seeds, and horehound juice. Porter, popular in England, is another dark beer—originally called porter's beer, it was a mixture of ale and beer. The porters of today are a sweet malty brew and contain 6 to 7 percent alcohol. Malt liquors are beers that are made using a higher percentage of fermentable sugars, resulting in a beverage with 5 to 9 percent alcohol content; the mild fruity flavor has a spicy taste and lacks the bitterness of hops. Low-calorie (sometimes called "light" or "lite")

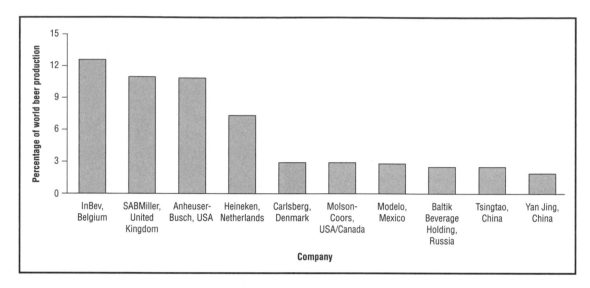

Figure 4. Top 10 brewing companies, 2005. (Adapted from Barth Report, 2005/2006, Barth Haas Group.) ILLUSTRATION BY GGS INFORMATION SERVICES. GALE, CENGAGE LEARNING

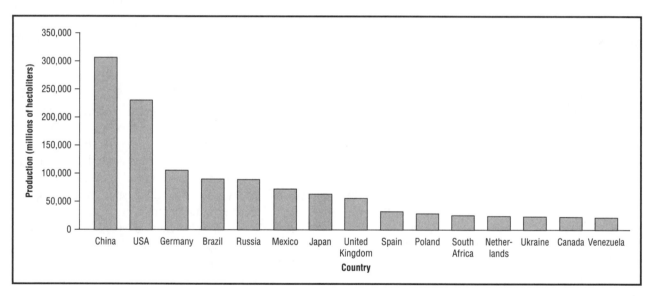

Figure 5. Top 15 beer-producing nations, 2005. (Adapted from Barth Report, 2005/2006, Barth Haas Group.) ILLUSTRATION BY GGS INFORMATION SERVICES. GALE, CENGAGE LEARNING

beers are produced by decreasing the amount of grain used in the initial brew (using more water per unit of volume) or by adding an enzyme that reduces the amount of starch in the beer. These light beers contain only about 2.5 to 2.7 percent alcohol.

Brewing is subject to national laws concerning allowable ingredients in commercial products. Although chemical additives are allowed by some countries (e.g., the United States), German and Czech purity laws consider beers and brews a natural historical resource and disallow anything that

was not part of the original (medieval) brewing tradition. Individuals sensitive to U.S. or Canadian beers are often able to drink pure beers.

See also **Alcohol: History of Drinking.**

BIBLIOGRAPHY

Able, B. (1976). *The book of beer.* Chicago: Henry Regnery.

Alcoweb (1996a). Beer production by country (1995–1997). *Alcohol, Health: Beer production* (Cited August 22, 2000). Available from http://www.alcoweb.com.

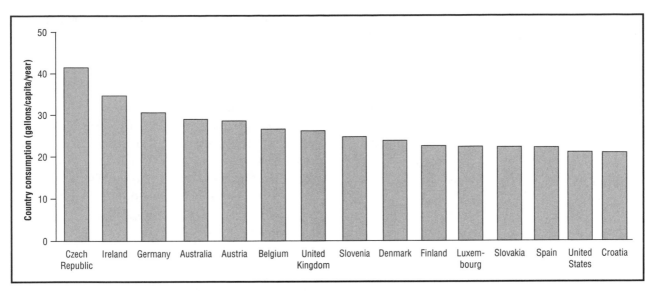

Figure 6. Top 15 beer-consuming nations, 2003. (Adapted from Kirin Holdings Company, Ltd.) ILLUSTRATION BY GGS INFORMATION SERVICES. GALE, CENGAGE LEARNING

Alcoweb (1996b). Consumption of beer by country between 1995 and 1998. *Alcohol, Health: Evolution of beer consumption* (Cited August 22, 2000). Available from http://www.alcoweb.com.

Bamforth, C. W. (2004). *Beer: Health and nutrition.* New York: Wiley-Blackwell.

Beer: Global Industry Guide. (2006). Research and Markets. Available from http://www.researchandmarkets.com.

Beverage World International (1999). First annual top 10 global brewers report. May–June, 24.

Heath, D. B. (2000). *Drinking occasions: Comparative perspectives on alcohol & culture.* London: Routledge.

Jackson, M. (1988). *The New World guide to beer.* Philadelphia: Running Press.

Prepared Foods (1999). Beer-bellied yanks. (Beer consumption increases in the U.S., Spain, UK, and Germany.) Aug, 37.

SCOTT E. LUKAS
REVISED BY NANCY FAERBER (2001)

BEHAVIORAL ECONOMICS. *Drug dependence* can be conceptualized as a "syndrome in which the use of a drug is given a much higher priority than other behaviors that once had higher value" (Jaffe, 1990). Thus, understanding drug dependence requires understanding how drugs of dependence are valued and how the valuation of drugs changes in relation to other reinforcers. For example, individuals as they progress to addiction will engage in actions that jeopardize their employment, families, and health in pursuit of drugs.

This change in valuation can be understood through the field of inquiry referred to as behavioral economics. Indeed, the value of behavioral economics derives from its unique ability to quantify the valuation of qualitatively different reinforcers (Bickel et al., 1992; Bickel et al., 1995; Bickel & Vuchinich, 2000; Hursh, 1980, 1991) through the use of two conceptual and methodological approaches.

DEMAND

The first concept from behavioral economics to address this important issue is demand. The demand law refers to the observation that total consumption decreases as price increases, all else being equal (Allison, 1979). Price can be any number of manipulations (e.g., response requirement, monetary price, delay, changes in the amount of the commodity while holding the monetary or work price constant) that decreases the availability of a commodity. Indeed, drug self-administration studies that vary price (response requirement) report results consistent with the demand law; that is, drug consumption decreases as the response requirement increases (Griffiths et al., 1980; Young & Herling, 1986).

However, behavioral economics does more than simply restate this observation with a different terminology; it adds to it by quantitatively characterizing the relation between price and consumption via the economic measure of own-price elasticity (Bickel & DeGrandpre, 1996; Hursh & Bauman, 1987; Samuelson & Nordhaus, 1985). Own-price elasticity measures the proportional change in consumption across price conditions. If consumption of a particular reinforcer decreases proportionally to a large extent as price increases, then the consumption is referred to as elastic. If consumption decreases proportionally to a limited extent as price increases, then the consumption is referred to as inelastic. Elastic and inelastic consumption are quantified by elasticity coefficients greater than 1.0 and less than 1.0, respectively (Hursh, 1980). When examined across a broad range of prices, elasticity of demand for many reinforcers is often mixed: inelastic at low prices and elastic at higher prices.

With this method, then, qualitatively different reinforcers can be compared and distinguished in drug-dependent populations. For example, in one study, money and cigarettes were compared among cigarette-deprived subjects on progressive ratio schedules (Bickel & Madden, 1999; Bickel et al., 2000a). Response requirements were increased across sessions and the same response requirement was imposed separately for both commodities. At the lowest response requirements, money was self-administered to a greater extent than cigarettes (a greater intensity of demand). As response requirement increased, money was shown to be more sensitive to price than cigarettes. The own-price elasticities of money and cigarettes were 2.1 and 0.9, respectively, with money being 2.3-fold more sensitive to price. Such efforts can be meaningfully extended to clinical settings via simulation technology (Petry & Bickel, 1998; Jacobs & Bickel, 1999).

Jacobs and Bickel used questionnaires to assess the reported consumption of cigarettes and heroin separately and concurrently across a range of prices ($0.01 to $1,120) in opioid-dependent smokers undergoing treatment for heroin addiction. Across conditions in which cigarettes and heroin were available alone, or concurrently, demand for heroin was less elastic than for cigarettes. For example,

heroin consumption was defended to a greater extent across increases in price than cigarettes. Taken together, these studies indicate that individuals with drug dependence value the primary drug of dependence more than other commodities. These observations also appear to have clinical utility. For example, in one study, MacKillop and Murphy (2007) used a hypothetical alcohol purchase task among college students who were consuming a high quantity of alcohol. These individuals received a brief intervention to reduce their alcohol consumption and those that demonstrated less sensitivity to price reported greater alcohol consumption six months after the intervention.

DELAY DISCOUNTING

A second concept from behavioral economics is delay discounting. Delay discounting measures the subjective value of a smaller immediate reinforcer versus a larger later reinforcer as a function of the delay (Rachlin et al., 1991). Delay discounting produces a quantitative value useful for assessing behavioral impulsivity: the inability to forgo immediate reinforcement in favor of a self-controlled option (Rachlin & Green, 1972). When applied to the field of drug dependence, delay discounting has been useful for identifying characteristics of drug abusers (Bickel & Marsch, 2001).

A typical delay discounting procedure asks a participant to make a series of judgments between two choices: an immediately available reinforcer or a larger delayed reinforcer. For example, participants are asked if they would rather be given $100 immediately or $1,000 after a 6-month delay. The value-immediate reinforcer is adjusted after each judgment until the participant is indifferent between the immediate and delayed reinforcer (Rachlin et al., 1991; Kowal et al., 2007). The process is then repeated for the same value of reinforcement at several delays: one day, one week, one month, one year, and so forth until a series of indifference points are generated. The measure can be administered orally using a series of cards (Rachlin et al., 1991), by pen and paper, or through a computer program (Johnson & Bickel, 2002).

The indifference points decrease in value as a proportion of the delay. Indifference points for each delay are used to fit a function that predicts choice behavior. The standard fit for a discounting measure is Mazur's 1987 hyperbolic discount function:

$$v = \frac{V}{(1+k[D])}$$

In the Mazur function the discounted value (the value at which the individual is indifferent between immediate and delayed) is v, the undiscounted value (the value of the amount offered after the delay) is V, and D is the delay. Fitting the data to the function empirically derives the constant k; it represents the rate of discounting. Higher k values produce steeper discounting functions; that is, the higher the k the more likely an individual is to switch to the immediate reinforcer at a lower value. Thus, individuals who are more impulsive produce higher k values.

Delay discounting rates for delay to money reinforcers have been used to describe differences between a variety of forms of substance abusers and non-abusers. Individuals who use drugs make impulsive choices based on immediate reinforcement. A substance abuser forgoes long-term health, social, and economic benefits in favor of a short-term high. Steeper rates of discounting have been found between current smokers and never smokers (Bickel et al., 1999; Mitchell, 1999; Reynolds et al., 2004), light smokers and never smokers (Johnson et al., 2007), between abusers of alcohol and non-abusers (Petry, 2001; Richards et al., 1999; Vuchinich & Simpson, 1998;), between cocaine dependent and non-abusers (Coffey et al., 2003; Heil et al., 2006), and between opiate-dependent and non-abusing controls (Madden et al., 1999; Kirby et al., 1999; Madden et al., 1997).

Delay discounting rates are consistent with demand for specific commodities. Smokers, when offered the choice between a cigarette immediately and a number of cigarettes equivalent to larger sums of money later, discount cigarettes more steeply than money (Bickel et al., 1999; Baker et al., 2003). Heroin addicts discount heroin gains more steeply than money (Madden et al., 1997; Odum et al., 2000); alcohol abusers discount alcohol more steeply than money (Petry, 2001), and cocaine users discount cocaine gains more steeply than money (Coffey et al., 2003). When offered

their preferred commodity, substance abusers show more difficulty choosing the self-controlled option, even when such choices are purely hypothetical. They almost singularly prefer a small amount of their preferred drug immediately to larger amounts available after a short delay.

This approach to studying delay discounting may have several important implications. First, rates of discounting may reflect and summarize the progression of addiction. Discounting rate increases when comparing controls to recently abstinent alcoholics to active alcoholics. Among smokers, the amount of nicotine consumed correlates directly with discounting rates (Ohmura et al., 2005; Johnson et al., 2007). Moreover, no difference in discount rates was found between ex-smokers (abstinent 1 year or longer) and never smokers (Bickel et al., 1999). Future work may address the relation of delay discounting and progression of addiction.

Secondly, delay discounting may have clinical utility similar to demand; that is, rate of discounting may predict relapse of a substance abuser seeking treatment. Yoon and colleagues (2007) measured discounting rates of women who spontaneously quit smoking while pregnant. Steep delay discounting rates predicted the likelihood that the woman would return to smoking in the post-partum session of the experiment. Similarly, among adolescent smokers attempting to quit, a similar measure of delay discounting using real money predicted successful abstinence in a contingency management program (Krishnan-Sarin et al., 2007). Additional research may expand this finding to all substance abuse disorders: steeper discounting rates coincide with poorer treatment outcomes. Collectively, these behavioral economic approaches provide a coherent and novel way to understand and measure drug dependence. Although more research is necessary, findings as of 2008 support the robustness and utility of this approach.

See also **Impulsivity and Addiction.**

BIBLIOGRAPHY

Allison, J. (1979). Demand economics and experimental psychology. *Behavioral Sciences, 24,* 403–415.

Baker, F., Johnson, M. W., & Bickel, W. K. (2003). Delay discounting in current and never-before cigarette smokers: Similarities and differences across commodity, sign, and magnitude. *Journal of Abnormal Psychology, 112,* 382–392.

Bickel, W. K., Hughes, J. R., DeGrandpre, R. J., Higgins, S. T., & Rizzuto, P. (1992). Behavioral economics of drug self-administration. IV. The effects of response requirement on consumption of and interaction between concurrently available coffee and cigarettes. *Psychopharmacology, 107,* 211–216.

Bickel, W. K., DeGrandpre, R. J., & Higgins, S. T. (1995). The behavioral economics of concurrent drug rein-forcers: A review and reanalysis of drug self-adminis-tration research. *Psychopharmacology, 118,* 250–259.

Bickel, W. K., & DeGrandpre, R. J. (1996). Psychological science speaks to drug policy: The clinical relevance and policy implications of basic behavioral principles. In W. K. Bickel & R. J. DeGrandpre (Eds.), *Drug policy and human nature: Psychological perspectives on the control, prevention and treatment of illicit drug use* (pp. 31–52). New York: Plenum.

Bickel, W. K., & Madden, G.J. (1999a). A comparison of measures of relative reinforcing efficacy and behavioral economics: Cigarettes and money in smokers. *Behavioral Pharmacology, 10,* 627–637.

Bickel, W. K., Odum, A. L., & Madden, G. L. (1999b). Impulsivity and cigarette smoking: Delay discounting in current, never, and ex-smokers. *Psychopharmacology, 146,* 447–454.

Bickel, W. K., Marsch, L. A., & Carroll, M. E. (2000a). Deconstructing relative reinforcer efficacy and situating the measures of pharmacological reinforcement with behavioral economics: A theoretical proposal. *Psychopharmacology, 153,* 44–56.

Bickel, W. K., & Vuchinich, R. E. (2000b). *Reframing health behavior change with behavioral economics.* Mahwah, NJ: Erlbaum.

Bickel, W. K., & Marsch, L. A. (2001). Toward a behavioral economic understanding of drug dependence: Delay discounting processes. *Addiction, 96,* 73–86.

Coffey, S. F., Gudleski, G. D., Saladin, M. E., & Brady, K. T. (2003). Impulsivity and rapid discounting of delayed hypothetical rewards in cocaine-dependent individuals. *Experimental and Clinical Psychopharmacology, 11,* 18–25.

Griffiths, R. R., Bigelow, G. E., & Henningfield, J. E. (1980). Similarities in animal and human drug taking behavior. In N. K. Mello (Ed.), *Advances in substance abuse* (Vol. 1). Greenwich, CT: JAI Press, pp. 1–90.

Heil, S. H., Johnson, M. W., Higgins, S. T., & Bickel, W. K. (2006). Delay discounting in currently using and currently abstinent cocaine-dependent outpatients and non-drug-using matched controls. *Addictive Behavior, 31,* 1290–1294.

Hursh, S. R. (1980). Economic concepts for the analysis of behavior. *Journal of the Experimental Analysis of Behavior, 34,* 219–238.

Hursh, S. R. (1991). Behavioral economics of drug self-administration and drug abuse policy. *Journal of the Experimental Analysis of Behavior, 56,* 377–393.

Hursh, S. R., & Bauman, R. A. (1987). The behavioral analysis of demand. In L. Green & J. H. Kagel (Eds.), *Advances in behavioral economics* (Vol. 1, pp. 117–165). Norwood, NJ: Ablex.

Jacobs, E. A., & Bickel, W. K. (1999). Modeling drug consumption in the clinic via simulation procedures: Demand for heroin and cigarettes in opioid-dependent outpatients. *Experimental and Clinical Psychopharmacology, 7,* 412–426.

Jaffe, J. H. (1990). Drug addiction and drug abuse. In A. G. Goodman, T. W. Rall, A. S. Niles & P. Taylor (Eds.), The pharmacological basis of therapeutics, 8th ed., pp. 522–573). New York: Pergamon Press.

Johnson, M. W., & Bickel, W. K. (2002). Within-subject comparison of real and hypothetical money rewards in delay discounting. *Journal of the Experimental Analysis of Behavior, 77,* 129–146.

Johnson, M. W., Bickel, W. K., & Baker, F. (2007). Moderate drug use and delay discounting: A comparison of heavy, light, and never smokers. *Experimental and Clinical Psychopharmacology, 15,* 187–194.

Kirby, K. N., Petry, N. M., & Bickel, W. K. (1999). Heroin addicts have higher discount rates for delayed rewards than non-drug-using controls. *Journal of Experimental Psychology: General, 128,* 78–87.

Kowal, B. P., Yi, R., Erisman, A. C., & Bickel, W. K. (2007). A comparison of two algorithms in computerized temporal discounting procedures. *Behavioural Processes, 75,* 231–236.

Krishnan-Sarin, S., Reynolds, B., Duhig, A. M., Smith, A., Liss, T., McFetridge, A., et al. (2007). Behavioral impulsivity predicts treatment outcome in a smoking cessation program for adolescent smokers. *Drug and Alcohol Dependence, 88,* 79–82.

MacKillop, J., & Murphy, J. G. (2007). A behavioral economic measure of demand for alcohol predicts brief intervention outcomes. *Drug and Alcohol Dependence, 89,* 227–233.

Madden, G. J., Bickel, W. K., & Jacobs, E. A. (1999). Discounting of delayed rewards in opioid-dependent outpatients: Exponential or hyperbolic discounting functions? *Experimental and Clinical Psychopharmacology, 7,* 284–293.

Madden, G. J., Petry, N., Badger, G. J., & Bickel, W. K. (1997). Impulsive and self-control choices in opioid-dependent patients and non-drug-using control participants: Drug and monetary rewards. *Experimental Clinical Psychopharmacology, 5,* 256–262.

Mazur, J. E. (1987). An adjusting procedure for studying delayed reinforcement. In M. L. Commons, J. E. Mazur, J. A. Nevin, & H. Rachlin (Eds.), *Quantitative analysis of behavior, Vol. 5. The effects of delay and of intervening events on reinforcement value* (pp. 55–73). Mahwah, NJ: Erlbaum.

Mitchell, S. H. (1999). Measures of impulsivity in cigarette smokers and non-smokers. *Psychopharmacology, 146,* 455–464.

Odum, A. L., Madden, G. J., & Gary, J. (2000). Needle sharing in opioid-dependent outpatients: Psychological processes underlying risk. *Drug and Alcohol Dependence, 60,* 259–266.

Ohmura, Y., Takahashi, T., & Kitamura, N. (2005). Discounting delayed and probabilistic monetary gains and losses by smokers of cigarettes. *Psychopharmacology, 82,* 508–515.

Petry, N. M. (2001). Delay discounting of money and alcohol in actively using alcoholics, currently abstinent alcoholics, and controls. *Psychopharmacology, 154*(3), 243–250.

Petry, N. M., & Bickel, W. K. (1998). Can simulations substitute for reality? *Addiction, 93,* 605–606.

Rachlin, H., & Green, L. (1972). Commitment, choice, and self-control. *Journal of the Experimental Analysis of Behavior, 17,* 15–22.

Rachlin, H., Raineri, A., & Cross, D. (1991). Subjective probability: A judgment of representativeness. *Cognitive Psychology, 3,* 430–454.

Reynolds, B., Richards, J. B., Horn, K., & Karraker, K. (2004). Delay discounting and probability discounting as related to cigarette smoking status in adults. *Behavioural Processes, 65,* 35–42.

Richards, B., Zhang, L., Mitchell, H., & de Wit, H. (1999). Delay or probability discounting in a model of impulsive behavior: Effect of alcohol. *Journal of the Experimental Analysis of Behavior, 71,* 121–143.

Samuelson, P. A., & Nordhaus, W. D. (1985). *Economics* (12th ed.). New York: McGraw-Hill.

Vuchinich, R. E., & Simpson, C. A. (1998). Hyperbolic temporal discounting in social drinkers and problem drinkers. *Experimental and Clinical Psychopharmacology, 6,* 292–305.

Yoon, J. H., Higgins, S. T., Heil, S. H., Sugarbaker, R., Thomas, C. S., & Badger, G. J. (2007). Delay discounting predicts postpartum relapse to cigarette smoking among pregnant women. *Experimental and Clinical Psychopharmacology, 15,* 176–186.

Young, A. M., & Herling, S. (1986). Drugs as reinforcers: Studies in laboratory animals. In S. R Goldberg & I. P. Stolerman (Eds.), *Behavioral analysis of drug dependence* (pp. 9–67). Orlando, FL: Academic Press.

WARREN K. BICKEL
LOUIS A. GIORDANO
REVISED BY WARREN K. BICKEL (2009)
BRYAN A. JONES (2009)

BEHAVIORAL TOLERANCE.

In everyday language, tolerance implies the ability to withstand something. In pharmacology, the term *tolerance* is close to this meaning. To understand the technical meaning of the word, however, requires an understanding of the concept of the *potency* of a drug. A drug's potency is expressed in terms of the amount (the dose) of the drug needed to produce a certain effect. To illustrate, drugs may be compared with respect to potency. For example, relief from headache may be achieved with 650 milligrams of aspirin or with 325 milligrams of ibuprofen; in this case ibuprofen is said to be more potent, because less drug is needed to produce a particular effect (relief of headache). Tolerance is said to occur when a drug becomes *less potent* as a result of prior exposure to that drug. That is, following exposure (usually repeated or continuous administrations) to a drug, it may take more of the drug to get the same effect as originally produced.

The expression *behavioral tolerance* often is used simply to refer to a drug's decreased potency in affecting a specified behavior after repeated or continuous exposure to the drug. In other contexts, however, the expression has taken on a more restricted and special meaning; it is employed only when behavioral factors have been shown experimentally to have contributed to the development of tolerance.

This special meaning is applied when either of two sets of circumstances are encountered. In the first, drug tolerance is shown to be specific to the context in which the drug is administered; in the second, drug tolerance is shown to occur only if drug administration precedes particular behavioral circumstances. Examples of each may help clarify the distinctions between them and between "simple" tolerance and behavioral tolerance.

Context-specific tolerance has been researched extensively by Siegel and his colleagues (see Siegel, 1989, for an overview). In a typical experiment two groups of subjects are compared; subjects in both groups receive the same number of repeated exposures to the drug (e.g., morphine) and then are tested for their response to the drug (e.g., alleviation of pain). For one group, the test occurs in the environment where drugging took place; for the other the test occurs in a novel environment. Typically, only those from the group tested in the familiar environment show tolerance. Siegel's theory is that subjects develop, via the principles of Pavlovian conditioning, a conditioned compensatory response that is elicited by the drug-administration context—and that this response counteracts the effect of the drug (see Baker & Tiffany, 1985, for a different view). The phenomenon of context-specific tolerance helps explain why many overdoses of abused drugs occur when the drug is taken in a novel situation—the new context does not elicit compensatory responses that counteract the effects of the drug.

The importance of the temporal relationship between drug administration and behavior is illustrated by the phenomenon of "contingent" tolerance. The basic technique for identifying contingent tolerance was pioneered by Chen (1968), and a clear example is provided by Carlton and Wolgin (1971). Three groups of rats had the opportunity to drink milk for 30 minutes each day. For each group, injections of a drug or just a saline vehicle were made twice each day: For Group 1, each session was preceded by an injection of 2 milligrams per kilogram of amphetamine, followed by an injection of just the saline vehicle; for Group 2, the order of injections was reversed: saline before drinking, amphetamine after; Group 3 (the control group) received saline both before and after each session.

For Group 1 the drug initially decreased drinking, but during the course of several administrations, drinking recovered to control levels (i.e., tolerance developed). For Group 2, no effect on drinking was observed as a function of receiving the drug after sessions, so after several days (by which time subjects in Group 1 were tolerant) these subjects were given amphetamine before (rather than after) and saline after sessions (i.e., the conditions for Group 1 were implemented). Even though these subjects had received amphetamine just as frequently as the subjects in Group 1, when it was given before the session, drinking was suppressed just as much as it had been for Group 1 initially. Following repeated precession exposure to amphetamine the subjects in Group 2 became tolerant. These findings and many others like them show that, in many cases, for tolerance to develop to a drug's behavioral effects, mere repeated exposure to the drug is not enough. In addition, the drug must be active while the behavior of interest is occurring. (See Goudie & Demellweek, 1986, and Wolgin, 1989, for reviews.)

Contingent tolerance is sometimes called *learned* tolerance because it appears that it is a manifestation of learning to behave accurately while under the influence of a drug. An influential theory about the origin of contingent tolerance is the "reinforcement loss" theory of C. R. Schuster, W. S. Dockens and J. H. Woods (1966; for a review see Corfield-Sumner & Stolerman, 1978). Loosely stated, the theory is that contingent tolerance will emerge in situations where the initial effect of the drug is to produce a loss of reinforcement (e.g., result in a failure to meet the demands of the task). Although there are limits to the generality of the theory (Genovese et al. 1988), it has an excellent predictive record.

See also **Addiction: Concepts and Definitions; Reinforcement; Tolerance and Physical Dependence; Wikler's Conditioning Theory of Drug Addiction.**

BIBLIOGRAPHY

Baker, T. B., & Tiffany, S. T. (1985). Morphine tolerance as habituation. *Psychology Review, 92*, 78–108.

Carlton, P. L., & Wolgin, D. L. (1971). Contingent tolerance to the anorexigenic effects of amphetamine. *Physiology of Behavior, 7*, 221–223.

Chen, C. S. (1968). A study of the alcohol-tolerance effect and an introduction of a new behavioral technique. *Psychopharmacologia, 12*, 433–440.

Corfield-Sumner, P. K., & Stolerman, I. P. (1978). Behavioral tolerance. In D. E. Blackman & D. J. Sanger (Eds.), *Contemporary research in behavioral pharmacology*. New York: Plenum.

Genovese, R. F., Elsmore, T. R., & Witkin, J. M. (1988). Environmental influences on the development of tolerance to the effects of physostigmine on schedule-controlled behavior. *Psychopharmacology, 96,* 462–467.

Goudie, A. J., & Demellweek, C. (1986). Conditioning factors in drug tolerance. In S. R. Goldberg & I. P. Stolerman (Eds.), *Behavioral analysis of drug dependence.* New York: Academic.

Koob, G. F., & Le Moal, M. (2005). *Neurobiology of addiction.* New York: Academic Press.

McKim, W. (2006). *Drugs and behavior: An introduction to behavioral pharmacology,* 6th ed. Upper Saddle River, NJ: Prentice Hall.

Schuster, C. R., Dockens, W. S., & Woods, J. H. (1966). Behavioral variables affecting the development of amphetamine tolerance. *Psychopharmacologia, 9,* 170–182.

Siegel, S. (1989). Pharmacological conditioning and drug effects. In A. J. Goudie & M. W. Emmett-Oglesby (Eds.), *Psychoactive drugs: Tolerance and sensitization.* Clifton, NJ: Humana.

Wolgin, D. L. (1989). The role of instrumental learning in behavioral tolerance to drugs. In A. J. Goudie & M. W. Emmett-Oglesby (Eds.), *Psychoactive drugs: Tolerance and sensitization.* Clifton, NJ: Humana.

MARC N. BRANCH

BENZODIAZEPINES.

The benzodiazepines were introduced into clinical practice in the 1960s for the treatment of anxiety and sleep disorders. Members of this class of drug were classified initially as *minor tranquilizers* although this term has fallen into disfavor. These agents have proven to be safe and effective alternatives to older sedative-hypnotic agents such as barbiturates, chloral hydrate, glutethimide, and carbamates. Benzodiazepines are widely prescribed drugs, with 8.3 percent of the U.S. population reporting medical use of these agents in 1990.

BASIC PHARMACOLOGY

All benzodiazepines produce similar pharmacologic effects, although the potency for each effect may vary with individual agents. They decrease or abolish anxiety, produce sedation, induce and maintain sleep, control certain types of seizures, and relax skeletal muscles. The basic chemical structure is shown in Figure 1.

Dissimilarity in the effects of different benzodiazepines tend to be more quantitative than qualitative in nature. Many of these differences are attributable to how benzodiazepines are absorbed, distributed, and metabolized in the body. A few benzodiazepines—clorazepate for example—are pro-drugs; that is, they become active only after undergoing chemical transformation in the body. The extent to which a benzodiazepine is soluble in fatlike substances—that is, the degree to which it is lipophilic—determines the rate at which it crosses the tissue barriers that protect the brain. Drugs that are highly lipophilic such as diazepam (Valium) rapidly enter and then leave the brain. Benzodiazepines are metabolized in the body in a number of ways (see Table 1). Many benzodiazepines are transformed in the liver into compounds that possess pharmacologic activity similar to that of the originally administered drug. Diazepam, prazepam, and halazepam are all converted to the active metabolite desmethyldiazepam, which is eliminated from the plasma at a very slow rate. Oxazepam (Serax) and lorazepam (Ativan), in contrast, are conjugated with glucuronide, a substance formed in the liver, to form inactive metabolites that are readily excreted into the urine.

Most of the effects that result from the administration of benzodiazepines are a consequence of the

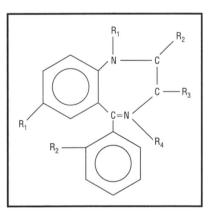

Figure 1. Outline of the basic structure of the benzodiazepines. R denotes substituent groups such as -H, -O, -OH, $-NO_2$, and -Cl that are attached to the core benzodiazepine structure. These groups determine the precise physiochemical and pharmacologic properties of each benzodiazepine. (Adapted from Rall, T.W. (1990). *Hypnotics and Sedatives: Ethanol.*) ILLUSTRATION BY GGS INFORMATION SERVICES. GALE, CENGAGE LEARNING

Anxiolytics					
Generic name	Trade name	Usual dose (mg/day)	Half-life (hours)	Transformation pathway	Metabolites (half-life, hours)
Alprazolam	Xanax	0.75–4	8–15	Oxidation	Alphahydroxyalprazolam Benzophenone
Bromazepam			20–30	Oxidation	
Chlordiazepoxide	Librium	15–100	5–30		Desmethylchlordiazepoxide Demoxepam Desmethyldiazepam (36–96)
Clonazepam	Klonopin	1.5–20	18–50	Nitroreduction	Inactive 7-amino or 7-acetyl amino derivatives
Clobazam	Frisium	20–30	18	Oxidation	Desmethylclobazam (up to 77)
Clorazepate	Tranxene	15–60	30–100	Oxidation	Desmethyldiazepam (36–96)
Diazepam	Valium	4–40	20–70	Oxidation	Desmethyldiazepam (36–96)
Halazepam	Paxipam	60–160	14	Oxidation	Desmethyldiazepam (36–96) 3-hydroxyhalazepam
Lorazepam	Ativan	2–4	10–120	Conjugation	Inactive glucuronide conjugate
Oxazolam				Oxidation	Desmethyldiazepam (36–96)
Oxazepam[a]	Serax	30–120	5–15	Conjugation	Inactive glucuronide conjugate
Prazepam	Centrax	20–60	30–100	Oxidation	Desmethyldiazepam (36–96)
Hypnotics					
Brotizolam			4–7	Oxidation	
Estazolam	ProSom	1–2	8–24	Oxidation	
Flunitrazepam			10–40	Oxidation nitro-reduction	Desmethylflunitrazepam
Flurazepam	Dalmane	15–30	.5–3.0	Oxidation	Desalkylflurazepam (36–120) Hydroxyethyl flurazepam (1–4) Flurazepam aldehyde (2–8)
Lormetazepam			8–20	Conjugation	
Nitrazepam	Mogadon	2.5–10	20–30	Nitroreduction	
Quazepam	Doral	7.5–15	20–40	Oxidation	Oxoquazepam (25–35) Desalkylflurazepam (36–120)
Temazepam	Restoril	15–30	8–20	Conjugation	
Triazolam	Halcion	.125–.5	2–6	Oxidation	
Perioperative hypnotic					
Midazolam	Versed	1–2.5 mg/ml	1–4	Oxidation	Hydroxymethylmidazolam

Note: The half-life of a compound is the amount of time that must pass for the level of that agent in the plasma to be reduced by half.
[a]Oxazepam is also a metabolite of diazepam, clorazepate, prazepam, halazepam, and temazepam.

Table 1. Benzodiazepines available in the United States. (Adapted from *Drug Facts and Comparisons* (1994). St. Louis, MO: Facts and Comparisons. Greenblatt, D.J. (1991), Benzodiazepine hypnotics: Sorting the pharmacokinetic facts. *Journal of Clinical Psychiatry*, 52 (Suppl. 9), 4–10. Greenblatt, D.J., & Shader, R.I. (1987). Pharmacokinetics of antianxiety drugs. In H.Y. Meltzer (Ed.), *Psychopharmacology: The Third Generation of Progress*. NY: Raven Press.) ILLUSTRATION BY GGS INFORMATION SERVICES. GALE, CENGAGE LEARNING

direct action of these agents on the central nervous system. Benzodiazepines interact directly with proteins that form the benzodiazepine receptor. Benzodiazepine receptors exist as part of a larger receptor complex (Figure 2). The interaction of the neurotransmitter gamma-amino butyric acid (GABA) with this complex leads to the enhanced flow of chloride ions into neurons (Kardos, 1993). This complex is referred to as the GABA$_A$ receptor-chloride ion channel complex. Much of the available evidence indicates that the action of benzodiazepines involves a facilitation of the effects of GABA and similarly acting substances on the GABA$_A$ receptor complex, thus leading to an increased movement of chloride ions into nerve cells. Entry of chloride ions into neurons tends to diminish their responsiveness to stimulation by other nerve cells, and consequently substances that produce an increase in chloride flow into cells depress the activity of the central nervous system. This depressant effect becomes manifested as either sedation or sleep. Agents that increase chloride ion inflow include not only the benzodiazepines but also other central nervous system depressant agents such as ethanol (alcohol) and the barbiturates. Benzodiazepines differ from barbiturates in that they require the release of GABA to affect the movement of chloride, whereas at higher doses barbiturates, through their own direct effects, can act to increase chloride inflow into cells.

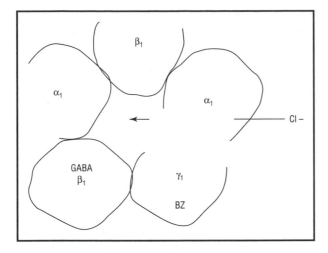

Figure 2. Schematic of one possible form of the GABA$_A$, receptor-chloride ion channel complex. Chloride ions enter through the center channel formed by alpha (α), beta (β), and gamma (γ) subunits. GABA receptors on β subunits regulate the flow of chloride ions through the channel. The activity of GABA receptors can be modulated by benzodiazepine receptors located on the γ subunit. (Figure created by Rebecca Bulotsky.) ILLUSTRATION BY GGS INFORMATION SERVICES. GALE, CENGAGE LEARNING

The GABA$_A$ receptor complex is composed of alpha, beta, and gamma subunits (Zorumski & Isenberg, 1991). Each subunit consists of a chain of twenty to thirty amino acids. Multiple subtypes of the alpha, beta, and gamma subunits have been shown to exist, and the types of subunits that form a single receptor complex appear to vary in different areas of the central nervous system. Some researchers have proposed that different drugs selectively interact with benzodiazepine receptors composed of a particular kind of α subunit, thereby leading to differences in drug effects. Although there is little evidence to support this hypothesis, future research should clarify the issue.

New compounds, such as the imidazopyridines, have been developed that act at the benzodiazepine receptor but are chemically distinct from the benzodiazepines. Zolpidem is an imidazopyridine used in clinical practice as a hypnotic agent. Other new drugs have been synthesized that can stimulate the benzodiazepine receptor but do not produce the maximal effects that result from the administration of higher doses of benzodiazepines. These drugs are classified as partial agonists. The drug abecarnil, which belongs to the beta-carboline class of compounds, is an example of such an agent that has been used experimentally to treat anxiety.

Flumazenil is a benzodiazepine derivative that has no activity of its own but acts to antagonize the actions of benzodiazepines at the benzodiazepine receptor. It is used to reverse the effects of these drugs during anesthesia or in benzodiazepine overdoses. Other compounds, including some of the beta-carbolines such as methyl-beta-carboline-3-carboxylate, act on the benzodiazepine receptor to produce effects that are opposite to those of benzodiazepines (Kardos, 1993; Zorumski & Isenberg, 1991). Administration of these inverse agonists can lead to the appearance of anxiety and convulsions.

THERAPEUTIC USE

Benzodiazepines are used for a variety of therapeutic purposes. Anxiety is the experience of fear that occurs in a situation where no clear threat exists. Numerous studies have demonstrated that anxiety disorders, including generalized anxiety disorder and many phobias, can be treated effectively with benzodiazepines. Panic disorder is a psychiatric illness in which patients experience intense sporadic attacks of anxiety often accompanied by the avoidance of open spaces and other places or objects that are associated with panic. High-potency benzodiazepines such as alprazolam (Xanax) or clonazepam (Klonopin) can prevent the occurrence of panic attacks in patients suffering from panic disorder. Flurazepam (Dalmane), triazolam (Halcion), and the other benzodiazepines listed in Table 1 are used in the treatment of insomnia and other sleep disorders. All rapidly acting benzodiazepines marketed in the United States have hypnotic effects. Classification of a benzodiazepine as a hypnotic is often more a marketing strategy than it is a decision based on pharmacologic differences among the class of drugs.

Status epilepticus is a seizure or a series of seizures that occurs over an extended period of time. This condition can lead to irreversible brain damage and is often successfully managed by the intravenous infusion of diazepam. Clonazepam is used either alone or in combination with other anticonvulsant medications to treat absence seizure and other types of seizure disorders. Clorazepate is used to control some types of partial seizures—that is, seizures that occur in a limited area of the brain. The increase in central nervous system excitability, seizures, and anxiety that may appear during alcohol withdrawal can be treated with any benzodiazepine. Midazolam (Versed) is a benzodiazepine that is rapidly metabolized in the body and is used to help induce anesthesia during surgical procedures. The skeletal-relaxant properties of benzodiazepines make them useful for the treatment of back pain due to muscle spasms.

ADVERSE EFFECTS

Benzodiazepines have proven to be exceptionally safe agents. The dose at which these agents are lethal tends to be exceedingly high. Fatalities are more apt to occur when these drugs are taken in combination with other central nervous system depressant agents such as ethanol. Sedation is a common adverse effect associated with benzodiazepine use. Light-headedness, confusion, and loss of motor coordination may all result following the administration of benzodiazepines. Memory impairment may be detected in individuals treated with benzodiazepines, and this effect may prove to be particularly troublesome to elderly patients who are experiencing memory-related problems. Psychomotor impairment can be hazardous to individuals when they are driving. This problem can be exacerbated in individuals who consume ethanol while they are being treated with benzodiazepines. Hypnotic agents that are converted into active metabolites that are slowly eliminated from the body, such as flurazepam, may produce residual daytime effects that can impair tasks such as driving. The adverse effects of benzodiazepines on performance tend to be more of a problem in elderly people than in younger individuals. Patients with cirrhosis, a liver degenerative disease, are also more likely to experience benzodiazepine toxicity than are those with normal liver function. The appearance of the adverse effects associated with benzodiazepine administration in both elderly people and in cirrhotic patients can be minimized by treating them with agents such as oxazepam and lorazepam, which tend not to accumulate in the blood because they are excreted rapidly into the urine as glucuronide conjugates.

A small number of patients may exhibit paradoxical reactions when they are treated with benzodiazepines (Rall, 1990). These may include low-level anxiety, restlessness, depression, paranoia, hostility, and rage. Sleep patterns may be disrupted by benzodiazepine administration, and nightmares may increase in frequency. Benzodiazepines suppress two stages of the sleep cycle—the stage of deepest sleep, stage IV, and the rapid eye movement (REM) stage in which dreaming occurs.

TOLERANCE AND PHYSICAL DEPENDENCE

Tolerance to a drug involves either a decrease in the effect of a given dose of a drug during the course of repeated administration of the agent or the need to increase the dose of a drug to produce a given effect when it is administered repeatedly. Chronic treatment of animals with benzodiazepines leads to a reduction in potency of these agents as enhancers of chloride ion uptake. These effects at the cellular level are paralleled by the appearance of tolerance to the sedative effects of benzodiazepines. Tolerance also develops to the impairment of motor coordination that is produced by these drugs. Limited evidence suggests that the antianxiety effects of benzodiazepines may not diminish with time, or at the very least that benzodiazepines retain their effectiveness as antianxiety agents for several months.

Physical dependence results from adaptive changes in the nervous system that may be related to the development of tolerance. Dependence of this sort can be detected by the appearance of a characteristic abstinence or withdrawal syndrome when chronic administration of a drug is either abruptly discontinued or after the administration of an antagonist to the drug that has been taken for a prolonged period of time (Ciraulo & Greenblatt, 1995). Individuals who are treated chronically with benzodiazepines may exhibit signs and symptoms of withdrawal when the administration of these drugs is discontinued. Minor symptoms of withdrawal include anxiety, insomnia, and nightmares. Less common and more serious symptoms include psychosis, death, and generalized seizures. Signs of withdrawal may become evident twenty-four hours after the discontinuation of a benzodiazepine that is rapidly eliminated from the blood. Peak abstinence symptoms may not appear until two weeks after discontinuation of a benzodiazepine that is removed from the body slowly. Some of the symptoms that appear after benzodiazepine treatment is discontinued may be due to the recurrence of the anxiety disorder for which the drug had been originally prescribed.

In animals, the severity of withdrawal can be directly related to the dose and length of time of administration of a benzodiazepine. This kind of relationship has been harder to demonstrate in clinical studies. Many patients who are treated with benzodiazepines for prolonged periods of time may experience at least some symptoms of withdrawal, but most of these individuals should not be viewed as benzodiazepine "addicts" because they have relied on their medications for medical reasons, have taken the medications as directed by their physicians, and will not continue to compulsively seek out benzodiazepines once their prescribed course of treatment with these medications has been discontinued. The intensity of abstinence symptoms that may be seen in patients who are physically dependent on benzodiazepines can be markedly reduced if patients are allowed to gradually taper off their medications. There may be a risk of physical withdrawal from benzodiazepines in some patients who abruptly stop the medication following as few as four weeks after treatment. Patients who discontinue taking rapidly metabolized hypnotic drugs such as triazolam may be at risk for experiencing rebound insomnia, even if they have been under treatment for a few days to one week. Serious problems associated with benzodiazepine withdrawal are more likely to be a problem for patients who have been treated with high doses of these medications for four or more months.

ABUSE AND DEPENDENCE

Although no consensus exists as to the definition of drug addiction, diagnostic criteria for drug abuse and dependence have been developed by both the American Psychiatric Association and the World Health Organization. Drug abuse can be viewed as the use of a pharmacological substance in a manner that is not consistent with existing medical, social, or legal standards and practice. Alternatively, drug abuse has been defined in the Diagnostic and Statistical Manual of Mental Disorders of the APA as involving a "maladaptive pattern of substance use manifested by recurrent and significant adverse consequences related to repeated use" (American Psychiatric Association, 2000). Abuse of drugs may involve the use of drugs for recreational purposes—that is, drugs are administered to experience their mood-elevating (euphoric) effects. For some individuals, self-administration of drugs for these purposes may lead to compulsive drug-seeking behavior and other extreme forms of

drug-controlled behavior. These behavior patterns may become further reinforced by the effects of withdrawal symptoms that dependent individuals attempt to reduce by the administration of the abused agent. The APA specifies that individuals can be classified as being drug dependent if they exhibit signs of drug tolerance, symptoms of withdrawal, cannot control their drug use, feel compelled to use a drug, and/or continue to use a substance even if the consequences of this use may prove harmful to them (American Psychiatric Association, 2000).

Abuse of drugs may sometimes represent self-medication. Cocaine and amphetamine users sometimes rely on benzodiazepines to relieve the jitteriness that may result from the administration of psychomotor stimulants. Some abusers of benzodiazepines may be medicating themselves with these agents to treat preexisting conditions of anxiety and depression.

The abuse liability of benzodiazepines—that is, the likelihood that they will be misused—has been assessed in studies of the tendency of either human beings or animals to administer these agents to themselves and studies of the subjective effects that result from the administration of different benzodiazepines. When provided access to cocaine and other psychomotor stimulants, animals will consistently self-administer these agents at high rates over time. Primates will intravenously self-administer benzodiazepines at moderate rates that are below those observed for the administration of barbiturates or cocaine. This finding and the results of a number of additional animal studies indicate that the benzodiazepines have a lower abuse liability than do the barbiturates or the psychomotor stimulants (Ciraulo & Greenblatt, 1995).

Individuals with a history of sedative-hypnotic abuse will self-administer triazolam and diazepam (Roache & Griffiths, 1989). In contrast, normal volunteers do not prefer diazepam to placebo. Subjective responses to drugs can be assessed through the use of instruments such as the Addiction Research Center Inventory-Morphine Benzedrine Group Scale and the Profile of Moods States that help to standardize the reports of subjects concerning their drug-induced experiences. Investigations in which subjective responses of normal subjects to benzodiazepine administration have been assessed indicate that these agents tend not to produce mood elevations in normal populations. On the other hand, individuals with a history of either alcoholism or sedative-hypnotic abuse are more likely to experience euphoria after the administration of a single dose of either diazepam or other benzodiazepines. Adult children of alcoholics experience mood elevation after the ingestion of either alprazolam or diazepam, thus suggesting that these individuals may have a predisposition to benzodiazepine abuse.

Studies suggest that benzodiazepines are less likely to be abused than the barbiturates, opiates, or psychomotor stimulants, but that they carry more risk for abuse than do medications such as the antianxiety agent buspirone or drugs that have sedating effects such as the antihistamine diphenhydramine (Preston et al., 1992). There also may be differences among the benzodiazepines themselves. Some authorities believe that diazepam has greater abuse liability than halazepam, oxazepam, chlordiazepoxide, or clorazepate, although others believe that there is little difference among them. Diazepam, lorazepam, alprazolam, and triazolam all produce mood effects that are similar to those of known drugs of abuse. The rate at which these drugs reach the brain after administration may be a major determining factor in the onset of euphoria or pleasant effects associated with abuse. Inferences about abuse potential are made on the basis of subjective effects and self-administration in drug abusers and alcoholics. Many experts question the applicability of these findings to the general population.

Studies that accurately reflect the extent of benzodiazepine abuse in the United States are not available. A survey of American households produced by the National Institute on Drug Abuse suggested that the nonmedical use of tranquilizers was not a major health problem (Ciraulo & Greenblatt, 1995). Only 2.4 percent of individuals between the ages of 18 and 24 and 1.3 percent of survey respondents who were older than 26 reported using tranquilizers for nonmedical purposes. This type of survey does not take into account benzodiazepine usage among groups such as homeless people, prisoners, and migrant workers, and so it cannot convey a complete picture of how benzodiazepines are misused at the nationwide level (Cole & Chiarello, 1990).

Benzodiazepines are frequently used by individuals who abuse other drugs, but they are rarely used as either initial or primary drugs of abuse. Benzodiazepine abusers often take these drugs in combination with other agents. In Scotland, drug abusers have often injected temazepam in combination with the opioid drug buprenorphine (Ruben & Morrison, 1992). Large percentages of methadone-clinic patients have urine tests that are positive for benzodiazepines. Methadone-maintenance patients have indicated that diazepam, lorazepam, and alprazolam can produce desirable pleasurable effects (Sellers et al., 1993). Whether methadone patients use benzodiazepines to increase the effects of methadone or as self-medication for anxiety is not clear.

The percentage of alcoholics admitted for treatment who also concurrently use benzodiazepines ranges between 12 to 23 percent. High rates of benzodiazepine abuse have been found in alcoholics who have experienced failure in treatment programs for alcohol abuse. Clinical experience suggests that benzodiazepine abuse occurs with the greatest frequency in alcoholics with severe dependence and in alcoholics who abuse multiple types of drugs.

Individuals with a history of either alcohol abuse or alcohol dependence often have anxiety disorders. The issue of treating alcoholics with benzodiazepines is complex because some of these patients can take the medications without abusing them or relapsing to alcohol use whereas others take them in higher than prescribed doses and find that their desire to drink alcohol is increased.

BENZODIAZEPINES: SUMMARY

A large number of benzodiazepines are available for clinical use. These agents all share a set of pharmacologic properties that result from enhanced chloride flux at the $GABA_A$-receptor complex, which in turn results in the inhibition of neuronal activity in many regions of the central nervous system. Differences in activity among the benzodiazepines appear to be related primarily to differences in rates of absorption and metabolism, although recent research has suggested that intrinsic activity at benzodiazepine receptor subtypes also may influence drug effects. These drugs have been used extensively to treat anxiety, insomnia, seizures, and other disorders. They are safe and effective and their use has rarely been associated with irreversible adverse effects. Both physical and psychological dependence may be problematic for some individuals who are treated on a long-term basis with these agents or who have abused alcohol or other drugs.

See also **Benzodiazepines: Complications; Sleep, Dreaming, and Drugs; Withdrawal: Benzodiazepines.**

BIBLIOGRAPHY

American Psychiatric Association. (2000). *Diagnostic and statistical manual of mental disorders*, 4th ed. Washington, DC: American Psychiatric Press.

Brinkerhoff, S. (2003). *Drug therapy and anxiety disorders.* Broomall, PA: Mason Crest Publishers.

Ciraulo, D. A., & Greenblatt, D. J. (1995). Sedative-, hypnotic-, or anxiolytic-related disorders. In B. J. Sadock et al. (Eds.), *Comprehensive textbook of psychiatry*, 6th ed. Baltimore: Lippincott Williams & Wilkins (2000, 7th ed.)

Cole, J. O., & Chiarello, R. J. (1990). The benzodiazepines as drugs of abuse. *Journal of Psychiatric Research, 24*, (Suppl. 2), 135–144.

Kardos, J. (1993). The GABA-A receptor channel mediated chloride ion translocation through the plasma membrane: New insights from 36 Cl-ion flux measurements. *Synapse, 13*, 74–93.

Preston, K. L., et al. (1992). Subjective and behavioral effects of diphenhydramine, lorazepam and methocarbamol: Evaluation of abuse liability. *Journal of Pharmacology and Experimental Therapeutics, 262 2*, 707–720.

Rall, T. W. (1990). Hypnotics and sedatives: Ethanol. In A. G. Gilman et al. (Eds.), *Goodman and Gilman's the pharmacological basis of therapeutics*, 8th ed. New York: Pergamon. (2005, 11th ed. New York: McGraw-Hill Medical.)

Roache, J. D., & Griffiths, R. R. (1989). Diazepam and triazolam self-administration in sedative abusers: Concordance of subject ratings, performance and drug self-administration. *Psychopharmacology, 99*, 309–315.

Ruben, S. M., & Morrison, C. L. (1992). Temazepam misuse in a group of injecting drug users. *British Journal of Addiction 87*, 1387–1392.

Sellers, E. M., et al. (1993). Alprazolam and benzodiazepine dependence. *Journal of Clinical Psychiatry, 54*, (Suppl. 10), 64–75.

Trimble, M. (2001). *Benzodiazepines.* New York: Routledge.

Zorumski, C. F., & Isenberg, K. E. (1991). Insights into the structure and function of GABA-Benzodiazepine receptors: Ion channels and psychiatry. *American Journal of Psychiatry, 148*, 162–173.

DOMENIC A. CIRAULO
CLIFFORD KNAPP

BENZODIAZEPINES: COMPLICATIONS.

Benzodiazepines have been widely used to allay anxiety and to induce sleep. Until the 1990s, they were believed to be both effective and extremely safe, but problems with these drugs started to become evident in the early 1980s. Since then, the medical profession in many countries has tried to inculcate a cautious attitude toward their prescription and use. Lay people and the media have also become increasingly critical of the widespread use of these medicines for apparently trivial indications. To understand these problems, some knowledge of various aspects of the different types and effects of these medicines is essential.

THERAPEUTIC USE OF BENZODIAZEPINES

Benzodiazepines are primarily used to lessen a patient's anxiety or to induce sleep. They also have other important uses, including the treatment of seizure disorders and skeletal muscle spasticity (e.g., cerebral palsy), as well as the management of alcohol withdrawal. They are also used with other drugs for the induction and maintenance of anesthesia during minor surgical procedures. Benzodiazepines include such drugs as chlordiazepoxide (Librium), diazepam (Valium), lorazepam (Ativan), and oxazepam (Serax). The term *benzodiazepine* describes a basic chemical structure common to all these medicines. Essentially, all these drugs work the same way and are differentiated mainly by their dose and duration of action. Some, like diazepam, are long acting and can be taken once daily; others, like lorazepam and alprazolam (Xanax), need to be taken more often. Many sleeping tablets (hypnotics) are benzodiazepines, and these include short-acting drugs such as triazolam (Halcion) and medium-acting drugs such as temazepam (Restoril).

An international survey done in the early 1980s showed that tranquilizers and sedatives of any type had been used at some time during the previous year by 12.9 percent of adults in the United States, 11.2 percent in the United Kingdom, 7.4 percent in the Netherlands, and 15.9 percent in France. Persistent long-term users comprised 1.8 percent of all adults in the United States, 3.1 percent in the United Kingdom, 1.7 percent in the Netherlands, and 5.0 percent in France. In a study conducted on elderly adults living in the United States in 1996, 7.5

percent were found to be taking anti-anxiety agents and 4.8 percent were using sedative-hypnotics (primarily benzodiazepines) (Aparasu, Mort, & Brandt, 2003). In another study of elderly adults living in the United States, 16 percent of new users of benzodiazepines continued to take the medication for up to 4 years (Gray et al., 2003). Generally, people starting tranquilizers have at least a 10 percent chance of going on to long-term use (more than 6 months). Some of these chronic users have chronic medical or social problems, and the tranquilizer blunts the unpleasant feelings of tension, anxiety, insomnia, and, to a lesser extent, depression.

UNWANTED (SIDE) EFFECTS

Side effects are reactions to drugs that are not therapeutic or helpful, and they are therefore unwanted. The most common side effects from taking benzodiazepines are drowsiness and tiredness, and these effects are most marked within the first few hours after large doses. Other complaints produced by benzodiazepines include dizziness, headache, blurred vision, and feelings of unsteadiness. The elderly are particularly sensitive to tranquilizers because of age-related changes in the way that the drugs are metabolized and excreted. These individuals may become unsteady on their feet or even mentally confused. The feelings of drowsiness are, of course, useful for inducing sleep.

With the longer-acting benzodiazepines, and with higher doses of medium-duration or short-acting drugs, drowsiness can still be present the morning after taking a sleeping tablet, and the drowsiness may even persist into the afternoon. Elderly persons are more likely to experience such residual, or "hang-over," effects. In those elderly individuals with cognitive deterioration or dementia (e.g. Alzheimer's Disease) a benzodiazepine may worsen symptoms of cognition and dementia. Older patients taking benzodiazepine sedatives are especially at risk of falls resulting in hip fractures, and they also are at an increased risk of being involved in a motor vehicle accident.

In addition to sedation, special testing in a psychology laboratory indicates that alertness, coordination, performance at skilled work, mental activities, and memory can all be impaired by benzodiazepines. Patients should be warned about these risks and advised not to drive or operate machinery, at least initially, until the effects of the benzodiazepine can be assessed and the dosage adjusted if necessary. If driving is essential to the patient's livelihood, small doses should be taken at first and the amount built up gradually under medical supervision. Judgment and memory are often impaired early in treatment, so important decisions should be deferred.

As with many drugs affecting the brain, benzodiazepines can interact with other drugs, especially alcohol. People taking tranquilizers or hypnotics should avoid drinking alcoholic beverages because the additive effects of these two central nervous system depressants can be dangerous. Other drugs whose effects may be enhanced include antihistamines (e.g., for hay fever), painkillers, and antidepressants. Cigarette smoking may lessen the effect of some benzodiazepines by promoting their more rapid breakdown by the liver.

Patients taking benzodiazepines may also show so-called paradoxical responses—or effects that are the opposite of those intended. For example, feelings of anxiety may be heightened rather than lessened, and insomnia may be intensified. Even more disturbing, patients may feel hostile and aggressive. They may engage in uncharacteristic criminal activities, sexual improprieties, or offenses such as soliciting sex or self-exposure, or they may show excessive emotional responses such as uncontrollable bouts of weeping or giggling. All of these are signs of the release of inhibitions, and they are also characteristic of alcohol effects in some people. Although these paradoxical effects may not last long, they necessitate stopping use of the benzodiazepine.

Benzodiazepines can affect breathing in individuals who already have breathing problems, such as those associated with bronchitis. Other side effects that may be occasionally encountered include excessive weight gain, rash, impairment of sexual functioning, and irregularities of menstruation. Benzodiazepines should be avoided during pregnancy whenever possible, as there may be a risk of congenital malformations to the fetus. When given during childbirth, benzodiazepines pass into the unborn infant and may depress the baby's breathing after birth. They also pass into the mother's milk and may sedate the suckling baby too much.

Many people have taken an overdose of a tranquilizer as a suicide attempt or gesture. Fortunately, these drugs are usually quite safe when taken alone, and the person generally wakes up unharmed after a few hours' sleep. However, if the benzodiazepine is combined with alcohol or another central nervous system depressant, the outcome could be serious or even fatal.

There are more subtle side effects of benzodiazepines that can interfere in various ways with the treatment of the anxiety or sleep disorder for which they are used. These drugs lessen the symptoms of these problems, but they do not alter the underlying problem, whether it be an unhappy marriage, a precarious job, or some other situation. Indeed, by lessening the symptoms, the individual being treated may lose his or her motivation to identify, confront, and tackle the basic problems. Giving a benzodiazepine medicalizes the problem by making the nervous or sad person into a patient, implying that there is something physically wrong. Finally, some events like bereavement need "working through"—typically by grieving—but benzodiazepines can stop this normal process and actually prevent the bereaved individual from coming to terms with loss.

LONG-TERM EFFECTS OF BENZODIAZEPINES

It is not clear whether benzodiazepines and hypnotics continue to be effective after months or years of daily use. Undoubtedly, many patients believe that they continue to benefit by being less anxious or by sleeping better. After prolonged use, however, the effect of the drugs may be more to stop the anxiety or insomnia that stems from withdrawal than to combat any continuing, original anxiety. Most of the side effects lessen over time, a process known as *tolerance*. Some impairments, however, such as memory disturbances, may persist indefinitely, although patients usually come to terms with this, perhaps by resorting to written reminders.

A process called *rebound* occurs when stopping the drug makes the underlying condition worse. For a patient with insomnia, for example, benzodiazepines may improve sleep by inducing it more rapidly, making it sounder, and prolonging it. When the medication is stopped, rebound may occur on the following night or two, with the insomnia being worse than ever. Eventually, the rebound insomnia subsides, but the patient may have become distressed enough to resume the medication, thereby running the risk of indefinite use. The risk of rebound is greatest with short-acting benzodiazepines, especially in higher dose.

A similar problem follows stopping a daytime tranquilizer, particularly the benzodiazepine lorazepam.

Anxiety and tension rebound to levels higher than those experienced on treatment, and often higher than the initial complaints. Tapering off the tranquilizer over a week or two lessens or avoids this complication. Rebound may even be seen in the daytime between doses of the tranquilizer. The patient, increasingly anxious as the effect of the earlier dose wears off, watches the clock until his or her next dose is due. Rebound may also occur later in the day after taking a short-acting sleeping tablet the night before.

ABUSE POTENTIAL

Only a few patients prescribed benzodiazepines push the dose up above recommended levels. If this happens, the user may become intoxicated, have slurred speech, and experience a lack of coordination. Some people with alcohol problems also abuse benzodiazepines. Intravenous (IV) injection of benzodiazepines and hypnotics has become an increasing problem and has led to controls on the manufacture and prescription of these drugs in various countries, including the United States and the United Kingdom. Some addicts abuse benzodiazepines alone; others combine it with heroin-type drugs. The injection of benzodiazepines can result in clotting of the veins. It also carries the risk of infectious diseases, such as hepatitis and HIV/AIDS, from sharing dirty syringes.

WITHDRAWAL

In withdrawal, symptoms occur that the patient has not previously experienced. These symptoms come on a day or two after stopping alprazolam or lorazepam, and a week or so after stopping diazepam or chlordiazepoxide. The symptoms rise to a crescendo and then usually subside over two to four weeks. In an unfortunate few, the symptoms seem to persist for months on end—a condition sometimes called *post-withdrawal syndrome*. The existence of this condition is disputed by some doctors, who ascribe the symptoms to a return of the original anxiety for which the drug was given.

Patients undergoing withdrawal commonly experience bodily symptoms of anxiety such as tremor, palpitations, dry mouth, or hot and cold feelings. Insomnia is usually marked, and some patients complain of unpleasant feelings of being out of touch with reality or with their own bodies. Severe headaches and muscle aches and pains can occur, sleep is greatly disturbed, and there is a loss of appetite, leading to the loss of several pounds of weight. Disturbances of perception are characteristic of benzodiazepine withdrawal and include intolerance to loud noises or bright lights, numbness or a "pins and needles" sensation, unsteadiness, a feeling of being in motion (as on a ship at sea), and the experience of strange smells and tastes. Some people become quite depressed, and on rare occasions a patient may experience epileptic fits (seizures) or a paranoid psychosis (with feelings of persecution and loss of contact with reality).

Withdrawal symptoms are evidence of physical dependence; they show that the body has become so used to the effects of the drug that it cannot manage without it. When the drugs are discontinued, approximately one-third of long-term benzodiazepine users experience withdrawal, even when the tranquilizer or hypnotic is tapered off. Some users have tried to stop the medication and have encountered problems. Many others have never tried to stop and so are unaware that they are dependent. Because these people continue to take the doses prescribed by their doctors, it took the medical profession a long time to admit the scale of the problem. In addition, the similarity between some withdrawal symptoms and features of the original anxiety has led to confusion in the mind of both the patient and the doctor. True withdrawal symptoms, however, arise at a predictable time after stopping the benzodiazepine and are new experiences for the patient, while the old anxiety and insomnia symptoms are familiar to the patient and may return at any time, depending on external stresses.

Essentially, before discontinuing benzodiazepines, the patient must be prepared for withdrawal by being told what to expect. He or she should be taught other ways of combating anxiety, and withdrawal should be accomplished by gradually tapering off the dose over six to twelve weeks, or occasionally longer. Many people experience little or no upset, but a few undergo much distress. Sometimes substituting the long-acting diazepam in place of the short-acting lorazepam or alprazolam helps. Antidepressants may be needed if the patient becomes very depressed, but by and large, other drugs are unhelpful. Family and social support is essential. Usually, the family doctor can supervise the withdrawal quite safely, but occasionally specialist advice should be sought. A self-help group may also provide useful continued advice and support. It is important that benzodiazepines are never stopped abruptly, for there is a greatly increased risk of severe complications such as seizures or convulsions if this is done.

When they were first introduced, benzodiazepines were considered to be safe drugs, and they were prescribed widely and for long periods of time. They have now been shown to be potentially problematic medicines with undoubted benefits but definite risks. For short-term treatment in the severely anxious and sleepless, they are still useful—although other drugs are beginning to supplement and even supplant them. For the bulk of anxious people, though, nondrug treatments are increasingly popular.

See also **Addiction: Concepts and Definitions; Iatrogenic Addiction; Sleep, Dreaming, and Drugs; Tolerance and Physical Dependence.**

BIBLIOGRAPHY

American Psychiatric Association. (1990). *Benzodiazepine dependence, toxicity, and abuse: A task force report.* Washington, DC: Author.

Aparasu, R. R., Mort, J. R., & Brandt, H. (2003). Psychotropic prescription use by community-dwelling elderly in the United States. *Journal of the American Geriatrics Society 51*(5), 671–677.

Curran, H. V., & Golombok, S. G. (1985). *Pill popping: How to get clear.* Boston: Faber & Faber.

Gray, S. L., Eggen, A. E., Blough, D., Buchner, D., & LaCroix, A. Z. (2003). Benzodiazepine use in older adults enrolled in a health maintenance organization. *American Journal of Geriatric Psychiatry 11*(5), 568–576.

McEvoy, G. K. (Ed.). (2003). *American Hospital Formulary Service (AHFS) drug information.* Bethesda, MD: American Society of Health-System Pharmacists.

Woods, J. H., Katz, J. L., & Winger, G. (1987). Abuse liability of benzodiazepines. *Pharmacological Reviews, 39*(4), 251–419.

MALCOLM H. LADER
REVISED BY LEAH R. ZINDEL (2009)

BENZOYLECOGNINE. Cocaine is metabolized by plasma and liver enzymes (cholinesterases) to water-soluble metabolites that are excreted in the urine. The two major metabolites are benzoylecognine and ecognine methyl ester, with only benzoylecognine reported to have behavioral activity. Since cocaine has a relatively short half-life and may only

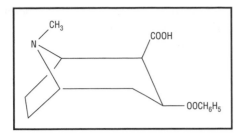

Chemical structure of benzoylecognine. ILLUSTRATION BY GGS INFORMATION SERVICES. GALE, CENGAGE LEARNING

Betel palm and betel nut. ILLUSTRATION BY GGS INFORMATION SERVICES. GALE, CENGAGE LEARNING

be present in the urine for twenty-four to thirty-six hours, benzoylecognine levels in urine are useful markers of cocaine use, because its levels are present for a longer time in urine, two to four days, depending on the quantity of cocaine ingested. Assays for this metabolite are frequently employed in treatment programs, to evaluate compliance with the program, and in workplace drug testing to indicate cocaine use. Under these conditions, it is important to keep in mind that benzoylecognine in the urine is an indication of prior cocaine use, but reflects neither current use nor impairment.

See also **Cocaethylene: Immunologic, Hepatic, and Cardiac Effects; Cocaine; Drug Testing Methods and Clinical Interpretations of Test Results.**

BIBLIOGRAPHY

Jufer, R. A., et al. (2000). Elimination of cocaine and metabolites in plasma, saliva, and urine following repeated oral administration to human volunteers. *Journal of Analytical Toxicology, 24,* 7, 467–477.

Kolbrich, E. A., et al. (2006). Major and minor metabolites of cocaine in human plasma following controlled subcutaneous cocaine administration. *Journal of Analytical Toxicology, 30,* 8, 501–510.

MARIAN W. FISCHMAN

BETEL NUT. The betel or areca nut is the nut of the betel palm, *Areca catechu,* cultivated from eastern Africa to the South Pacific. Betel and its effects have been known throughout south and Southeast Asia at least since the time of Herodotus (fourth century BCE) as the palm is described in his work as well as in later writings in Pali and Sanskrit. Betel is thought to be the fourth most

commonly used psychoactive substance in the world (after caffeine, nicotine, and alcohol), with the number of users estimated to be well into the hundreds of millions. Betel use is endemic, especially among aboriginal populations, from the Indian Ocean to the South Pacific. It is also commonly found in immigrant communities in the West. Betel is typically chewed like a chewing tobacco and the pigments in the nut color the saliva bright red. In a habitual user, these pigments may also dye the teeth red or black.

CHEMICAL INTERACTIONS

The betel nut is commonly used in the form of a *quid,* which usually contains the nut itself, betel leaf, and slaked lime to extract the active alkaloids from the plant constituents of the quid. Betel leaf comes from the betel plant, *Piper betle,* which is distinct from the betel palm that produces the nut. Depending on the cultural context, other plants may be added, tobacco being the most common additive. Pharmacologically, the areca nut is the most important constituent of the quid, and the major psychoactive constituent is arecoline, an alkaloid with mild stimulant properties similar to those of nicotine in that it interacts with receptors for the neurotransmitter acetylcholine, although in a less specific fashion than nicotine. The immediate effects of betel chewing are euphoria, increased alertness, a sensation of warmth in the body, as well as increased salivation and sweating. The usual dose is a half nut. Two or more nuts are enough to produce severe side effects or death. Like tobacco, and especially in combination with it (as in the south Asian gutka), areca chewing is addictive, although this remains a subject of some controversy. Also like tobacco, its use is associated with substantial health risks. Most habitual users will develop oral submucous fibrosis (OSF) within as little as five years. OSF involves a *bald tongue*, white lesions in the mouth, and an intolerance of spicy foods. Roughly 8 percent of those who develop OSF will go on to develop cancer. Betel chewing is implicated as a carcinogenic practice by the observation that as many as half of all malignant cancers in betel-chewing communities are oral cancers, most often oral squamous cell carcinomas.

CANCER RISKS

Although the association of cancer risk with tobacco use has received worldwide attention, those risks associated with betel preparations have not. This is particularly important to note, as it is evident that the likelihood of developing areca-associated cancers is higher than those associated with tobacco. Areca use, particularly in combination with tobacco, also seems to produce cancers much earlier than tobacco alone, which has led to a significant increase in the incidence of cancers in those under 50 in areas where the use of gutka-like betel preparations has become common. Gutka is a ready-made preparation of dried chopped betel nuts, various spices, and tobacco. It appears that gutka is particularly carcinogenic because of the addition of tobacco, which adds to both the carcinogenicity and to the addictive properties of the chew. Gutka is sold in stores and groceries throughout south Asia and in south Asian immigrant communities in other countries, most notably the United Kingdom. It is often packaged in bright containers with attractive labels and marketed to children as young as five years of age, all of which make gutka a particularly pernicious public health problem in those areas where it is in common use. In terms of positive effects, betel leaves and betel nut are used in a number of traditional medical systems, but scientific evidence of medicinal uses for the areca nut or its chemical constituents is minimal.

CULTURAL SIGNIFICANCE AND USES

As might be expected of a substance that has been used across such a large geographic area for thousands of years, its patterns of use and cultural significance are widely varied. In the Indian traditional medical systems of Ayurveda and Unani, betel has a number of uses in the treatment of digestive disorders and as a tonic, and similar uses are recorded in a number of other traditional systems. Betel has a number of cultural and ritual uses beyond its use as a stimulant. In Vietnam, the ceremonies surrounding marriage are referred to as "matters of betel and areca," and this association with marriage is also seen in India, Indonesia, and the Solomon Islands. In Malaysia and Melanesia, betel nuts are used for ritual purposes by magicians, both in love magic and as a poison. In India, the betel has many ritual uses and the palm itself is associated with Ganesha, lord of beginnings and remover of obstacles, which points to the cultural importance of betel in initiating and facilitating social interactions, much like the offer of a cigarette provides a point of entry for social interaction in other parts of the world.

The diversity of geographic and cultural milieus in which betel is used has not only led to a wide variety of cultural associations and uses of the nut and the palm itself, but has also spawned a wide variety of preparations of the betel for consumption. Betel wine is made in some regions, but betel is typically chewed. In most regions, the betel quid is the preferred form, although the nuts may also be raw, roasted, or fermented. In many cases, the quid is adulterated with other substances to enhance its flavor or effects. In south Asia, cardamom, cloves, and sandalwood are often added. The nut is also consumed chopped without betel leaf as paan masala, which is widely available in ready-made pouches in stores in south Asia and beyond. When tobacco is added to paan masala, it is referred to as gutka.

The cultural patterns of betel use are also complex and changing in response to the effects of immigration and the encroachment of a global culture. Among many aboriginal cultures of Southeast Asia and Oceania (e.g., Taiwan, and Malaysia and Papua New Guinea), betel use is associated with the maintenance of local tradition against the influx of immigrants and outside influence. In many of these situations, use by youth is increasing as a means of self-definition. In India and Taiwan, the use of betel by children has been on the rise in recent years. In most countries, however, where modern culture is viewed as more attractive, betel chewing is more the province of the old. Similar dichotomies exist in the gender of users; in some cultures betel chewing is largely the province of women, as is the case in Cambodia, where women are more than 30 times more likely to be betel users than men. In other countries, such as Taiwan, it is principally a male habit.

The cultural trend that is the cause for greatest concern is the rise of widespread gutka use in south Asian communities. Most disturbing is the widespread use of gutka by children and adolescents, who are particularly vulnerable to tobacco addiction and more than likely vulnerable to the habit-forming properties of betel as well. In some parts of India, as many as 50 percent of children have a betel-chewing habit, a statistic that is likely to have an enormous impact on the health system of that nation as they develop OSF and cancer. This is also likely to be a problem in those Western countries with large numbers of south Asian immigrants, as areca nut use is totally unregulated and doctors and public health authorities are unfamiliar with the diseases it is likely to produce. Furthermore, the rate of betel use among immigrant communities may actually be higher than the rate in their home country, as one study found that as many as 80 percent of adult Bangladeshis living in London were regular betel users, as compared to a rate of 20 to 40 percent across the south Asian region (Gupta & Ray, 2004). In the Indian state of Kerala, authorities have gone so far as to ban the sale of smokeless tobacco, and similar proposals have been made at the national level. However, the use of betel without tobacco is likely to remain deeply ingrained in those cultures where it has been used for millennia, and with that use a heightened level of oral cancers will persist.

The future of betel use is likely to show complex patterns, not unlike those of tobacco use, which is declining in the West but rising in countries like China. In many regions of Asia, betel use seems destined to decline over the foreseeable future, as public health authorities become more vocal about the risks and populations discard the traditions associated with betel use for the attractions of modern global culture. The possibility exists that betel use might spread to cultures unfamiliar with its use and even less familiar with its risks, but the hope is that regulations against its use by children and adolescents may be promulgated to minimize potential harm in both new and old populations of betel users.

See also **Plants, Drugs From.**

BIBLIOGRAPHY

Gupta, P. C., & Ray, C. S. (2004). Epidemiology of betel quid usage. *Annals of the Academy of Medicine of Singapore, 33*(4 Suppl.), 31–36.

Rätsch, C., & Hofmann, A. (Eds.). (2005). *Encyclopedia of psychoactive plants: Ethnopharmacology and its applications.* Rochester, VT: Park Street Press.

RICHARD G. HUNTER

BHANG. This is one of the many names given to the hemp plant, *Cannabis sativa*, and its products. Bhang is of Hindi origin (from *bhāg*, which came into English about 1563) and refers to the leaves and flowering tops of uncultivated hemp plants. In 1895, the Indian Hemp Commission took the position that bhang was not a major health hazard. Bhang is taken in a beverage in India called *thandaii*, may be served in sweetmeats, or is used in making ice cream. It is often served at weddings or religious festivals and is freely available from sidewalk stands in the major cities. Generally, in India, the use of bhang and other cannabis products has been considered lower class. Probably as a result of continuing British-based influence, the upper-class drugs are alcohol and opium.

See also **Cannabis Sativa; Marijuana (Cannabis); Plants, Drugs From; Slang Terms in U.S. Drug Cultures.**

BIBLIOGRAPHY

Booth, M. (2005). *Cannabis: A history.* New York: MacMillan.

LEO E. HOLLISTER

BLOOD ALCOHOL CONCENTRATION. The consumption of alcoholic beverages results in the absorption into the bloodstream of alcohol (ethanol, also called ethyl alcohol) from the stomach and small intestine. The amount of alcohol distributed in the blood is termed blood alcohol concentration (BAC) and is proportional to the quantity of ethanol consumed. It is expressed as the weight of alcohol in a fixed volume of blood, for example, grams per liter (g/l) or milligrams per deciliter (mg/dl). The measurement of blood alcohol concentrations has both clinical and legal applications.

The most important factors that determine BAC are the presence of food in the stomach, the concentration of alcohol consumed, the rate and volume of alcohol consumed, and gender. Consuming food with alcohol generally decreases the volume of alcohol that can be quickly absorbed into the bloodstream. This is more evident for small volumes of more concentrated alcohol such as hard liquor than for larger volumes such as beer, a lower concentrated form of alcohol. Consuming more than one drink per hour causes the BAC to increase rapidly because it typically exceeds the rate at which the body can metabolize alcohol. The percentage of body fat that contributes to a person's total weight also affects BAC. A larger proportion of fat provides less body water into which the alcohol can distribute, thus increasing BAC. For this reason, women generally have a higher BAC for a given number of drinks when compared to men, even when accounting for the difference in body weight associated with sex.

See also **Alcohol**.

BIBLIOGRAPHY

Fisher, H., Simpson, R., & Kapur, B. (1987). Calculation of blood alcohol concentration (BAC) by sex, weight, number of drinks and time. *Canadian Journal of Public Health, 78,* 300–304.

MYROSLAVA ROMACH
KAREN PARKER
REVISED BY GEORGE A. KENNA (2009)

BLOOD ALCOHOL CONCENTRATION, MEASURES OF.

The first analytical methods for measuring alcohol (ethanol) in blood and other body fluids were developed in the nineteenth century. Although by modern standards these pioneer efforts were fairly crude, they were sufficiently reliable to establish a quantitative relationship between blood-alcohol concentration (BAC) and the various signs and symptoms of inebriation. A significant advance in methodology came in 1922 when Erik M. P. Widmark published his micro-method for analyzing ethanol in specimens of capillary blood.

WIDMARK METHOD

In Widmark's day the small amounts (aliquots) of blood needed for each analysis could be measured more accurately by weight than by volume, since constriction pipettes were not yet available. Widmark therefore weighed the amount of blood required to the nearest milligram (0.001 g) with the aid of a torsion balance. He then reported the results of ethanol determinations in terms of mass per mass units, actually milligram of ethanol per gram of whole blood (mg/g), sometimes referred to as *per mille* (meaning, *parts per thousand*). This way of reporting BAC survives today in Scandinavian countries where Widmark's method became widely used for legal purposes.

LATER BAC METHODS

Modern methods of ethanol analysis (such as gas chromatography) plus the availability of modern clinical laboratory equipment made it more convenient to dispense the aliquots of blood needed for analysis by volume rather than by weight. Micropipettes and more recently diluter-dispenser devices are now widely used for dilution of blood prior to the analysis. The term *concentration* has little meaning when used alone, because it can be expressed in many different ways. The choice of units for reporting BAC differs among countries: for example, milligrams per hundred milliliters (mg/100 ml) in Great Britain (unfortunately often appearing as the ambiguous

Concentration unit	Country	Legal limit	g/100ml
Percent weight/ volume (% w/v)	United States*	80mg /100 ml	0.08 g/100 ml
Milligrams per 100 milliliter (mg/dl)	Britain	80 mg/100 ml	0.08 g/100 ml
Milligrams per milliliter (mg/ml)	Netherlands	0.50 mg/ml	0.05g/100ml
Milligrams per gram (mg/g)***	Sweden**	0.20 mg/g	0.02g/100ml
Milligrams per gram (mg/g)	Norway**	0.50 mg/g	0.05g/100ml

*The Uniform Vehicle Code of the National Committee on Uniform Traffic Laws and Ordinances recommends 0.08 grams per 100 milliliters of blood or per 210 liters of breath; all U.S. states have adopted this recommendation.
**1 milliliter whole blood weighs 1.055 grams.
***Conversion of weight/weight measurement is approximate

Table 1. Concentrations of alcohol (ethanol) in whole blood for legal purposes. ILLUSTRATION BY GGS INFORMATION SERVICES. GALE, CENGAGE LEARNING

State	BAC defined as illegal per se (mg/dl)	Administrative license suspension 1st offense	Restore driving privileges during suspension?	Do penalties include interlock/ forfeiture?*	DUI related fatalities in 2006
Alabama	0.08	90 days	No	No/No	475
Alaska	0.08	90 days	After 30 days	Yes/Yes	23
Arizona	0.08	90 days	After 30 days	Yes/Yes	585
Arkansas	0.08	120 days	Yes	Yes/Yes	254
California	0.08	6 months	After 30 days	Yes/Yes	1,779
Colorado	0.08	3 months	After 30 days	Yes/No	226
Connecticut	0.08	90 days	Yes	No/No	129
Delaware	0.08	3 months	No	Yes/No	57
District of Columbia	0.08	2–90 days	Yes	Yes/No	18
Florida	0.08	6 months	After 30 days	Yes/Yes	1,376
Georgia	0.08	1 year	After 30 days	Yes/Yes	604
Hawaii	0.08	3 months–1 year	After 30 days	No/Yes	84
Idaho	0.08	90 days	After 30 days	Yes/No	106
Illinois	0.08	3 months	After 30 days	Yes/Yes	594
Indiana	0.08	180 days	After 30 days	Yes/Yes	319
Iowa	0.08	180 days	After 90 days	Yes/No	148
Kansas	0.08	30 days	No	Yes/No	170
Kentucky	0.08	—	—	Yes/No	272
Louisiana	0.08	90 days	After 30 days	Yes/Yes	475
Maine	0.08	90 days	Yes	Yes/Yes	74
Maryland	0.08	45 days	Yes	Yes/No	268
Massachusetts	0.08	90 days	No	Yes/No	174
Michigan	0.08	—	—	Yes/Yes	440
Minnesota	0.08	90 days	After 15 days	Yes/Yes	183
Mississippi	0.08	90 days	After 90 days	Yes/Yes	375
Missouri	0.08	30 days	No	Yes/Ycs	500
Montana	0.08	—	—	Yes/Yes	126
Nebraska	0.08	90 days	After 30 days	Yes/No	89
Nevada	0.08	90 days	After 45 days	Yes/No	186
New Hampshire	0.08	6 months	No	Yes/No	52
New Jersey	0.08	—	—	Yes/No	341
New Mexico	0.08	90 days	After 30 days	Yes/No	186
New York	0.08	Variable	Yes	Yes/Yes	558
North Carolina	0.08	30 days	After 10 days	Yes/Yes	554
North Dakota	0.08	91 days	after 30 days	Yes/Yes	50
Ohio	0.08	90 days	after 15 days	Yes/Yes	488
Oklahoma	0.08	180 days	Yes	Yes/Yes	263
Oregon	0.08	90 days	After 30 days	Yes/Yes	196
Pennsylvania	0.08	—	—	Yes/Yes	600
Rhode Island	0.08	—	—	Yes/Yes	42
South Carolina	0.08	30 days	Yes	Yes/Yes	523
South Dakota	0.08	—	—	No/No	80
Tennessee	0.08	—	—	Yes/Yes	509
Texas	0.08	90 days	No	Yes/Yes	1,677
Utah	0.08	90 days	No	Yes/No	69
Vermont	0.08	90 days	No	No/Yes	29
Virginia	0.08	7 days	No	Yes/Yes	379
Washington	0.08	90 days	After 30 days	Yes/Yes	294
West Virginia	0.08	6 months	After 30 days	Yes/No	161
Wisconsin	0.08	6 months	Yes	Yes/Yes	364
Wyoming	0.08	90 days	Yes	No/No	80
Puerto Rico	0.08	—	—	—	215

*A multiple offender's vehicle may be seized and disposed.

Table 2. States legal limits for blood alcohol concentration (BAC) level. (Source: Traffic Safety Facts, 2006. National Highway Traffic Safety Administration, U.S. Department of Transportation.) ILLUSTRATION BY GGS INFORMATION SERVICES. GALE, CENGAGE LEARNING

mg%), gram percent weight per volume (g% w/v) in the United States, and milligrams per milliliter (mg/ml) in many European countries. Other ways of reporting BAC in clinical medicine are milligrams per deciliter (mg/dl), grams per liter (g/liter), or micrograms per liter (μg/liter). When countries outside Scandinavia enacted legal limits for ethanol in the blood of motorists, the concentrations were defined in units of mass of ethanol per unit volume; whether it was grams, milligrams, or micrograms of ethanol in a volume of milliliters, deciliters, or liters seems chosen arbitrarily.

BAL (mg/dl)	(BAC)	Effects
50	(0.05%)	There may be no observable effects on behavior, but thought, judgment, and restraint may be more lax and vision is affected. Significantly more errors in tasks that require divided attention; more steering errors; and increased likelihood of causing an accident.
80	(0.08%)	Reaction time for deciding and acting increases. Motor skills are impaired. The likelihood of a crash increases to three to four times the likelihood when sober.
100	(0.10%)	Six times as likely to be involved in a crash. Reaction time to sights and sounds increases. Physical and mental coordinations are impaired: Movement becomes noticeably clumsy.
150	(0.15%)	Twenty-five times as likely to be involved in a crash. Reaction time increases significantly, especially in tasks that require divided attention. Difficulty performing simple motor skills. Physical difficulty in driving.
200	(0.20%)	One hundred times as likely to be involved in a crash. Motor areas of brain significantly depressed, and all perception and judgment distorted. Difficulty standing, walking, and talking; driving erratic.
300	(0.30%)	Confusion and stupor; inability to track a moving object with the eyes. Passing out is likely.
400	(0.40%)	Coma is likely.
450–500	(0.45%–0.50%)	Death is likely.

Table 3. Effects of blood alcohol levels. (Source: Adapted from Mothers Against Drunk Driving (MADD) and the National Safety Council.) ILLUSTRATION BY GGS INFORMATION SERVICES. GALE, CENGAGE LEARNING

Because the specific gravity of whole blood is greater than water (on average, 1 ml of whole blood weighs 1.055 g), BAC expressed in terms of mass per mass (w/w) is not the same as mass per volume (w/v). In fact, a concentration of 0.10 percent w/v equals 0.095 percent w/v. This difference of about 5.5 percent could mean punishment or acquittal in borderline cases of driving while under the influence of alcohol. With the *per se* ethanol limits in U.S. states, great care is needed to ascertain whether w/v or w/w units were intended by the legislature when the statute was drafted. Table 1 gives examples of the statutory limits of breath-ethanol concentrations commonly used to report BAC for legal purposes in several countries.

If ethanol were determined in plasma or serum, the concentration would be about 10 to 15 percent higher than for the same volume of whole blood, because there is more water in the sample after the erythrocytes (red blood cells) are removed.

SI MEASUREMENTS

In clinical chemistry laboratories, the Système International d'Unités (SI) has gained worldwide acceptance. According to the SI system, the amount of substance implies *mole* rather than mass. The mole, or a submultiple thereof, replaces mass units such as grams or milligrams. Accordingly, the concentration of a substance of known molecular weight might appear as mole/liter or millimole per liter (mmol/l) or micromole per liter (μmol/liter). Note that liter is the preferred unit of volume when reporting concentrations of a substance in solution in the SI system. The molecular weight of ethanol is 46.06, and therefore a concentration of 1.0 mol/l corresponds to 46.06 g of ethanol in 1 liter of solution. Likewise 1.0 mmol/l contains 46.06 mg; 1.0 μmol/l contains 46.06 μg, and so on. Publications in the field of biomedical alcohol research often report BAC in this way. It follows that 0.1 g percent w/v or 100 mg/dl is the same as 21.7 mmol/l.

CONVERSION OF BREATH TO BLOOD ETHANOL

Statutory limits of BAC existed in several countries before methods of analyzing the breath were developed. It therefore became a standard practice to convert the concentration of ethanol measured in the breath (BrAC) into the presumed concentration in the blood. For this purpose, a conversion factor, usually 2,100:1 was used. Presumably, it was less troublesome to make this conversion than to rewrite the statute to include both BAC and BrAC as evidence of impairment. Accordingly, breath-ethanol analyzers were calibrated in such a way that the readout was obtained directly in terms of the presumed BAC. This conversion of breath to blood ethanol created the dilemma of a constant blood/breath ratio existing for all subjects under all conditions of testing. In the United States and elsewhere, a blood/breath factor of 2,100:1 was approved for legal purposes with the understanding that this gives a margin of safety (about 10%) to the accused. Indeed, more recent research suggests that the blood/breath factor should be 2,300:1 for closer agreement between direct BAC and the result derived from BrAC. In the Netherlands and Great Britain, 2,300:1 was chosen as the legal limit of BrAC when evidential breath-ethanol analyzers were introduced.

Both the prescribed BAC or BrAC limits for motorists and the units of concentration differed among countries and even within regions of the same country. The notion of reaching an international agreement about one common BAC or BrAC limit for motorists is an attractive one, but hardly attainable.

BIBLIOGRAPHY

Jones, A. W. (1989). Measurement of alcohol in blood and breath for legal purposes. In K. E. Crow & R. D. Batt (Eds.), *Human metabolism of alcohol* (Vol. I). Boca Raton, FL: CRC Press.

Widmark, E. M. P. (1922). Eine Mikromethode zur Bestimmung von Äthylalkohol im Blut. *Biochemical Zeitschrift, 131*, 473.

A. W. JONES
REVISED BY GEORGE A. KENNA (2009)

BOLIVIA. Bolivia is a landlocked nation situated in the central part of South America. Bolivia's 424,165 square miles has an estimated population of 9,247,816 as of July 2008. The ethnic breakdown of the population becomes crucial for understanding the political dynamics and the role of the coca/cocaine trade in the region: white, 15 percent; Aymara Indians, 25 percent; Quechua Indians, 30 percent; and mestizos (mixed white and Amerindian), 30 percent. Bolivia is rich in mineral resources, having deposits of petroleum, natural gas, tin, lead, zinc, copper, silver, and gold. Since the early sixteenth-century Spanish Conquest of South America, the resources have been in the hands of a European elite, with indigenous peoples largely becoming landless peasantry. Approximately 70 percent of the population lives in the Altiplano

region, where the climate is less harsh than in the higher mountains. The other 30 percent, primarily Inca descendants, reside in the Yungas, Chapare, and Beni regions where coca plants (Erythroxylum coca) are cultivated.

The conquest and colonial rule were traumatic experiences for the Inca. Easily susceptible to European diseases, the native populations succumbed to tuberculosis, smallpox, and influenza. Combined with the harsh colonial systems of rule, the population decreased significantly following Spanish Conquest. The Inca populations also diminished due to the introduction of the mita obligations. *Mita* is a Quecha word meaning *turn* or *time*; the word was used to describe a forced-labor draft imposed by the Spanish on indigenous people. Native men were forced to labor for one year out of every six for Spanish rulers. Among the Inca, there had been a mita system that was reciprocal in the sense that in return for labor, the leader provided appropriate remuneration, land to grow food, acceptable working conditions, and health care. However, under Francisco de Toledo (c. 1515–1584), a Spanish viceroy of the area (1569–1581), the Mita system was both exploitive and racist. The Incas were worked to exhaustion in the mines with no ability to effectively challenge the conditions. A new form of slavery arose in which the Spanish set impossible work quotas to ensure that the workers remained forever in debt. Effectively, generations of young men were worked to death. The Spanish forced indigenous servitude in the mining industry. The local populations resorted to substance use as one way to cope with their deteriorating conditions.

Between 1556 and 1780, Potosi, located in south-central Bolivia, became one of the largest and richest cities in the world. In addition to the riches pooled from mining, the Catholic Church levied a 10 percent tax on coca leaves, and the income ensured the building of churches and Catholic schools. Thus in industry and through the imposition of the Catholic Church, local peoples were impoverished and decimated.

HISTORY OF COCA

The coca plant is integral to the Bolivian economy and was used by native inhabitants prior to the Spanish Conquest. The Spanish focused first on local mineral wealth. Initially they had little understanding of coca as there was no equivalent plant in the Old World. Within a year following the rediscovery of silver at Potosi (the Incas had already known of the deposits) and the Spanish exploitation of indigenous labor, approximately seven thousand Incas were working local mines. As mines went deeper the Incas relied increasingly on chewing coca leaves. By 1548 the miners were chewing over a million kilos per year.

The capital city La Paz arose in response to the coca and silver trade. Coca was brought there to be auctioned, and silver merchants rested there before embarking on their journey to the coast and on to Spain. Thus, the coca and mining industries were linked. In 1552 the Catholic Church petitioned Charles I of Spain (also known as Charles V, Holy Roman Emperor). This petition was resolved at the First Council of Lima, where for the first time coca chewing was perceived as ruining the health of the Inca people. The Church emphasized the plant's intoxicating effect, but no concern was expressed regarding the mortality rates in the silver mines. The Church likened the opiate effects to demonic possession as it sought to supplant perceived pagan beliefs with Catholic ones. Coca was linked to a pre-Christian past. But coca suppression became a political problem for the colonists when the Incas refused to work in the mines without the drug. To make matters more complicated, the Incas were used to being paid in coca leaves. In the end, the Spanish authorities decided not to suppress the coca industry for economic reasons.

The discovery of mercury at Huancavelica in 1571 entailed the extension of the mita system to the mercury mines. Mercury was used in extracting silver from ore and increased the yield but was extremely toxic for workers. A far higher death rate occurred at Huancavelica than at Potosi. Few Incas completed the one year of labor conscription. Those miners who were sustained by coca chewing were thus exploited both by the colonial monopoly of the drug and the slave system of forced mining labor.

The mita system lasted until the early nineteenth-century Bolivarian Revolution, which transformed South America from European colonialism to independent states. The revolutionary Simón Bolívar (1783–1830) wished to establish liberty based upon the progressive ideas of the United States, but this vision was thwarted by internal divisions. The large landowners perceived an opportunity to establish states based upon their own interests. Therefore, the legacy of the revolution left the land in question largely untouched. The soldiers who had been provided with land bonds sold them to landowners, which created a greater concentration of land in the hands of a few European families until the land reforms in the 1950s. The society stratified economically and racially was reduced to white European and Creole families controlling the large estates and various Inca tribes providing the labor necessary to maintain them.

Wealth accumulated in the hands of a few. By 1900 José María Gamarra, the so-called coca king, dominated the Bolivian market; he owned 32 percent of all the haciendas in the Yungas region. The owners of the cocaine-producing haciendas formed the Sociedad de Propietarios de Yungus e Inquivisi (Society of Yungas and Inquivisi) (SPY) in 1830. The primary aim of the society was to ensure the hacienda coca growers had a voice in Bolivian politics. They also wanted to promote the use of coca in the urban centers. When the second opium convention took place in Geneva in 1925 cocaine was included as part of the League of Nations debate on narcotics. The plant was seen by Bolivians as integral to the national psyche and this was the argument put forward by the Bolivian representative.

The Bolivian government's official position was influenced by SPY. Prior to the 1949 UN conference on illicit drugs, SPY'S strategy was to highlight the nutritional value of coca chewing as well as its medicinal qualities. The United Nations Report of 1950, following an investigation of the conditions in Bolivia, concluded coca chewing did not have any nutritional value. The authors also noted coca chewing was extensive among the malnourished native populations, who were not eating properly because they were spending their income on coca chewing. The 1950 UNODC report undermined the various SPY arguments that coca chewing helped with altitude sickness and had nutritional and medicinal value. Instead, the report highlighted Indian populations that chewed coca to combat the physical and psychological effects of poverty.

GOVERNMENTAL FACTORS
AND THE COCAINE INDUSTRY

Land reform, which occurred in 1952 following the victory of the National Revolutionary Movement (MNR), resulted in many large haciendas being subdivided and the land being given to the peasants. Land reform initially reduced reliance on coca for many people. Following land distribution the peasants had the ability to grow crops for food. Coca plantations were replaced with coffee as a cash crop as Bolivia entered the international market. Some people believe that with the alleviation of poverty and stress in the 1950s and 60s, coca chewing declined. However, political unrest contributed to cocaine once again becoming important in the national economy. A military junta replaced the National Revolutionary Movement (MNR) in 1964. The junta ruled until 1969 when elections were allowed and a leftist, Juan José Torres, was elected president. As he aligned Bolivia with Chile and Cuba, Bolivia became increasingly unstable and cocaine rose in importance.

In 1971 Hugo Bánzer, supported by the CIA, forcibly ousted President Torres in a coup. Bánzer employed Klaus Barbie (1913–1991), the former Nazi head of the Gestapo in Lyons, known as the Butcher of Lyons, who assisted the fledgling junta by using terror to silence opposition. He also orchestrated the cocaine trade through his shipping company Transmaritania. This activity marked a significant change in Bolivia as the government was now officially involved in cocaine production and distribution. Bánzer had encouraged landowners to grow cotton as a cash crop to sustain the Bolivian economy, but the price of cotton collapsed. As Bolivian cocaine production increased, the price fell from $1,500 per gram to $200 per gram in the United States.

Hugo Bánzer left office in 1978 after his wife was caught smuggling cocaine into the United States. In 1979 Barbie and Roberto Suárez, a cocaine smuggler, orchestrated another army coup. Union leaders were shot, universities were closed, printing presses were firebombed, and mass executions were carried out in the La Paz football stadium. Barbie and Delle Chiaie, an Italian far-right paramilitary man, were given the respective tasks of securing internal security and gaining international recognition. In 1980 they initiated an antidrugs campaign, which resulted in the elimination of Suárez's cocaine rivals and the suppression of other resistance to the regime. In 1981, U.S. support was rescinded, and the regime collapsed.

The economic and political developments in the 1970s, coupled with U.S. cocaine demand, drove peasants to replant coca in the Yungas region. Following the collapse of tin and Bolivian mines closing in the 1980s, many peasants migrated to the Chapare region to cultivate coca. Although the cocaine economy was marked by violence, the Chapare region farmers built their own organizational structures, the *sindicatos*, to mediate conflict, thereby creating their own forms of democracy. The coca of the Chapare region is rich in alkaloids, making it ideal for processing into cocaine rather than being chewed. The population in Chapare doubled in the 1980s. In 1987 coca was generating $3 billion per year—over one-fourth of Bolivia's gross national product.

In 1986 the United States in its war on drugs instigated Operation Blast Furnace. A force under the control of the Drug Enforcement Administration (DEA), which included six Black Hawk helicopters and two hundred personnel, attempted to stop drug trafficking in the Beni province. Resistance from local farmers halted the operation after four months, and the squad was disbanded.

The U.S.-backed Agroyungas project attempted to limit production through providing aid to farmers. The aim was to entice farmers to grow other cash crops. Villagers received improved electricity and water supplies. Initially the plan was a success, but as the farmers switched from coca to coffee, they were exposed to the vagaries of the international market. When international coffee prices dropped and fertilizer prices became prohibitive, peasants abandoned their crops. In addition, the coffee plants used in the area were susceptible to insects that devoured the coffee seeds, decimating the local coffee production. As a result, many peasants returned to coca cultivation for its guaranteed income. Other forms of crop substitution provided some initial gains but were abandoned. Lobbyists for financially strapped U.S. farmers argued that subsidies for anti-drug crop substitution projects were undermining their ability to compete. The Agroyungas project was concluded in 1990.

In 1988 the Bolivian government, urged by the United States, passed the Ley 1008, which decreed harsh penalties for drug trafficking and attempted to regulate coca production. It regulated licit supplies in the traditional Yungas region and attempted to eradicate illicit coca in the Chapare region by compensating peasants and to eradicate coca in other regions, such as Beni, without compensation. This decree resulted in the destruction of 990 acres of coca plantations in the Yungas and 790 acres in Chapare. Growers were provided with $2,000 for destroying their coca crops. Money corrupted this plan: Planters paid inspectors for a drug free certificate, poor farmers were targeted by the narcotic police who needed to meet crop eradication goals, and wealthier people bribed the police. Prisons filled with poor farmers who waited up to four years for a trial.

The issue of drug eradication foundered. There are several examples. In 1991 President Jaime Paz Zamora named Faustino Rico Toro as head of antinarcotics operations. Toro had a history of cocaine trafficking and exploited his position to solidify his cocaine operation. He was eventually exposed as a trafficker and was sentenced to Cochambamba Prison as Paz Zamora's regime collapsed with drug trafficking allegations in 1994. Cocaine cultivation declined in the later 1990s as production switched to Columbia. Bolivia tried to eliminate the drug altogether as it sought international aid.

In 1998 President Hugo Bánzer signed the *Plan Dignidad* (Dignity Plan) with the United States. This plan sought total eradication of cocaine cultivation by 2002, but it ran into serious opposition from indigenous coca growers who staged a series of protests seeking to bring down the government. The army quelled the discontent but several peasants died. The peasants then began to target the police and a surrogate war erupted.

The tensions resulted in the eventual victory of the Movimiento al Socialismo (MAS) Party, headed by Evo Morales, who was elected president in 2005. The United States brought new pressure to Bolivia to eradicate coca plantations with its emphasis on zero tolerance. The United States wanted Bolivia to implement the Dignity Plan, but the plan was perceived by the new regime as an outside imposition on Bolivian national identity. Moreover, suppression in one country entails increased production in another as the demand outstrips supply. Morales stated that he wants to preserve the legal market for coca leaves and promote the export of legal coca products. As of 2008, the government maintained that coca leaves are part of Bolivian culture, whereas cocaine should be suppressed because it is chemically manufactured and a product of the colonialists. This tolerance of coca identified Morales as opposing the U.S. zero tolerance policy.

TOBACCO

The one major Bolivian tobacco producer, Cia Industrial de Tabaco SA (Citsa), produces 12 brands, some home produced, others manufactured under license from Phillip Morris USA. This monopoly is constantly challenged by a thriving illicit market that undercuts the price through evading taxes. An estimated 50 percent of the market is contraband.

Laws passed in 2007 prohibited the sale of single cigarettes and packs of ten to curb the demand for contraband. These measures were also an attempt to set health standards and stem the high incidence of smoking among the urban poor.

ALCOHOL

The traditional alcoholic drink of Bolivia, *chicha*, is a pale sour beverage derived from corn and drunk from a gourd that has a rounded bottom so it has to be constantly held. The drinking ritual requires that a small amount of the liquid be thrown on the ground to bless the Inca goddess Pachamama, the goddess of the earth. Bolivia has its own brands of liquor, Singani, which is made from grapes and usually combined with a soft drink mixer to make a chuflay. It also produces its own beers such as Paceña and the high-end brand Huari. Prior to the Spanish Conquest, the Incas had consumed alcohol only during religious ceremonies. Post conquest, alcohol use rose significantly as the Inca populations coped with imposed social changes that eroded their culture.

See also **Coca Plant.**

BIBLIOGRAPHY

Cockburn, A., & St. Clair, J. (1999). *Whiteout: The CIA, drugs, and the press.* London: Verso.

Scott, P. D., & Marshall, J. (1998). *Cocaine politics: Drugs, armies, and the CIA in Central America.* Berkeley: University of California Press.

Streatfield, D. (2001). *Cocaine: An unauthorized biography.* New York: Picador.

Thoumi, F. (2003). *Illegal drugs, economy and society in the Andes.* Baltimore: Johns Hopkins University Press.

DEAN WHITTINGTON

BORDER MANAGEMENT.

The effective management of U.S. borders has become a priority for the U.S. government as it attempts to control illegal immigration, fight terrorism, and prevent the importation of illegal narcotics. Although most of the focus has been placed on the U.S.-Mexico border, increasing drug traffic and illegal immigration, coupled with national security concerns, have led to more surveillance of the U.S.-Canada border as well. The effectiveness of border management has historically been difficult because many federal agencies had some jurisdiction in this area. The failure to coordinate and consolidate border operations limited the ability of the government to meet its objectives. However, in the aftermath of the September 11, 2001, terrorist attacks on the World Trade Center and the Pentagon, the federal government has increased the funding of border management and moved agencies into the new Department of Homeland Security. In addition, public discontent over the continued influx of illegal aliens from Mexico has made border policies part of the national political debate.

ODAP REVIEW AND RECOMMENDATIONS
In 1977, a U.S. government interagency team led by the Office of Drug Abuse Policy (ODAP) conducted a comprehensive review of border control and recommended consolidation of the principal border control functions into a single border management agency. Executive departments failed to agree on distribution of resources and organizational placement of the new agency, however, and so the border management agency never materialized.

Border control in the United States was described in the ODAP review as an extremely complex problem involving vast distances, many modes of transportation, millions of arrivals and departures, and millions of tons of cargo. Laws to be enforced involved illegal drugs and other contraband, terrorists, public health threats, agricultural pests and diseases, endangered species, entry visas, duties, and so forth. Nine federal agencies shared border-control responsibilities, contributing to overlap, duplication of effort, and duplicated management systems.

The ODAP report recommended consolidating the inspection and patrolling functions, including operational and administrative support. The potential for improved effectiveness in a consolidated border

management agency was widely recognized. A similar report by the U.S. Government Accountability Office (GAO) also recommended single-agency management and responsibility for border control. Controversy over which activities to include and which executive department should control the new agency was, however, effective in blocking further action.

DEFINING HIDTA
The Anti-Drug Abuse Act of 1988 and the U.S. Office of National Drug Control Policy Reauthorization Act of 1998 authorized the director of the Office of National Drug Control Policy (ONDCP) to designate areas within the United States that exhibit serious drug trafficking problems and harmfully affect other areas of the nation as High Intensity Drug Trafficking Areas (HIDTA). The HIDTA Program provides additional federal resources to those areas to help eliminate or reduce drug trafficking and its harmful consequences. Law enforcement organizations within HIDTA assess drug trafficking problems and design specific initiatives to reduce or eliminate the production, manufacture, transportation, distribution, and chronic use of illegal drugs and money laundering.

When designating a new HIDTA, the ONDCP director consults with the attorney general, the secretary of the treasury, the secretary of homeland security, heads of the national drug control program agencies, and the appropriate governors. Each HIDTA is governed by its own executive board of approximately 16 members—eight federal members and eight state or local members. These boards facilitate interagency drug control efforts to eliminate or reduce drug threats. The executive boards ensure that threat-specific strategies and initiatives are developed, employed, supported, and evaluated. HIDTA-designated counties include approximately 14 percent of U.S. counties; they are present in 45 states, Puerto Rico, the U.S. Virgin Islands, and the District of Columbia. The Southwest Border HIDTA (California, Arizona, New Mexico, and Texas) was established in 1990. It is subdivided into five regions, encompassing 47 counties in the four Southwest border states.

CONGRESS PASSES IIRIRA
Major change came when Congress passed the Illegal Immigration Reform and Immigrant Responsibility

Act of 1996 (IIRIRA). The IIRIRA is a tough, enforcement-oriented law that seeks to restrict the passage of undocumented aliens across the U.S. borders. The IIRIRA mandated increasing the number of U.S. Border Patrol agents by 5,000. The law also mandated that the additional Border Patrol agents be deployed in sectors along the border in proportion to the number of illegal crossings at each sector. The legislation, however, requires that the attorney general coordinate with and act in conjunction with state and local law enforcement agencies to ensure that deployment of resources to the border does not degrade or compromise the capabilities of interior Border Patrol stations.

Even before the passage of the IIRIRA, the Border Patrol had begun to implement new enforcement strategies. A 1998 GAO report noted that the Immigration and Naturalization Service (INS) had made progress in implementing some, but not all, aspects of the necessary strategy to curtail illegal entry in the Southwest. The strategy, begun in 1994, called for the Border Patrol to (1) allocate additional resources in a four-phased approach, starting with the areas of highest-known illegal activity; (2) make maximum use of physical barriers; (3) increase the proportion of time Border Patrol agents spend on border enforcement activities; and (4) identify the appropriate mix of technology, equipment, and personnel needed for the Border Patrol. At ports of entry along the Southwest border, the strategy called for the inspection program to increase inspector staff and use additional technology to increase the deterrence and detection of illegal entry and to improve management of legal traffic and commerce.

In addition to the increases in personnel, the IIRIRA required the construction of new barriers along the border and authorized the purchase of new equipment. The law directed the attorney general to have additional barriers installed to deter illegal crossings, especially in areas of high numbers of illegal entries. The legislation mandated the construction of fencing and road improvements in the 14-mile border area near San Diego, starting at the Pacific Ocean and extending eastward. In particular, the law mandated the construction of second and third fences, in addition to the existing reinforced fence, as well as roads between the fences.

CUSTOMS AND BORDER PROTECTION ESTABLISHED

Border management became an even more pressing issue following the September 11, 2001, terrorist attacks. In 2003 Congress established the Department of Homeland Security, which contains federal agencies once housed in other departments. U.S. Customs and Border Protection (CBP) is an agency that is charged with regulating and facilitating international trade, collecting import duties, and enforcing U.S. trade laws. Its other primary mission is to prevent terrorists and terrorist weapons from entering the United States. CBP is also responsible for apprehending individuals attempting to enter the United States illegally and for stemming the flow of illegal drugs and other contraband. Former agencies subsumed under CBP include the U.S. Customs Service, the Border Patrol, and the Immigration and Naturalization Service. The Office of Intelligence and Operations Coordination (OIOC) is a new agency that coordinates antiterrorism efforts.

One of CBP's major efforts in curtailing illegal immigration and the importation of illegal narcotics is the Secure Borders Initiative, popularly known as SBInet. SBInet is an attempt at an integrated solution for border management, using the best mix of personnel, infrastructure, and technology to detect and respond to breaches of the borders with Mexico and Canada. What makes this initiative different from past efforts is the hiring of a private corporation (Boeing) to develop the suite of technological tools that CBP will use to coordinate border security. The goal of SBInet is to cover the entire 6,000 miles of international border; its first stage is 28 miles in the Tucson, Arizona, sector. This sector is the most heavily trafficked area of the border, making the pilot project a good test for the new system. The pilot project will examine the usefulness and reliability of technology that may include sensors, thermal imagery, remote cameras, and improved communications. Infrastructure changes may include roads, bridges, fences, and improved lighting. Under SBInet, Boeing is required to provide a solution that not only advises an agency of an entry but also identifies the entry, classifies the entry as to threat, supplies a means to efficiently respond to an entry, and brings the entry to the appropriate law enforcement agency for resolution.

Despite efforts such as SBInet, border management under the CBP has continued to draw criticism. A 2007 report by the GAO estimated that 21,000 people who should not have been allowed to enter the U.S. came through official border crossing points between October 1, 2005, and September 30, 2006. Staffing problems and poor management were cited as reasons that persons were able to enter the country improperly. Another 2007 GAO report also found that the terrorist watch list was not being used consistently throughout the border management system.

As for policing illegal narcotic shipments, CBP has employed technology to assist its agents. For example, giant X-ray machines have been installed at ports of entry. Trucks and their cargo are examined in this unobtrusive way to detect cocaine vapors. Other high-tech equipment, such as night-vision goggles, motion sensors, and low-light TV cameras, are now being used on the border.

See also **Drug Interdiction; Operation Intercept; U.S. Government Agencies: U.S. Customs and Border Protection (CBP).**

BIBLIOGRAPHY

Andreas, P. (2000, April). U.S.-Mexico drug control in the age of free trade. *Borderlines, 8*(4), 1–4.

Havemann, J. (1978). Carter's reorganization plans: Scrambling for turf. *National Journal, 10*(20), 788–794.

Osuna, J. P. (1999, January). Update on selected enforcement provisions of the illegal immigration reform and immigrant responsibility act of 1996. 99-1 *Immigration Briefings.*

U.S. Government Accountability Office. (2007, November). *Border security: Despite progress, weaknesses in traveler inspections exist at our nation's ports of entry* (GAO-08-329 T). Washington, DC: U.S. Government Printing Office.

U.S. Government Accountability Office. (2007). Terrorist watch list screening: Opportunities exist to enhance management oversight, reduce vulnerabilities in agency screening processes, and expand use of the list. (GAO-08-110). Washington, DC: U.S. Government Printing Office.

U.S. Office of National Drug Control Policy. Retrieved May 28, 2008, from http://www.whitehousedrugpolicy. gov.

RICHARD L. WILLIAMS
REVISED BY FREDERICK K. GRITTNER (2009)

BRAIN STRUCTURES AND DRUGS.

Psychoactive or behaviorally active drugs are substances that alter internal and external behavioral processes, including activity levels, emotions, and cognitive ability. As a result of these effects, using some of these substances can lead to compulsive drug use and drug addiction, while using others can manage neuropsychological disorders. In both cases these drugs modify existing neuronal systems and their function. To understand the actions of drugs on the brain, it is necessary to understand the molecules that these drugs interact with and how these interactions affect the brain circuits and systems that regulate normal, adaptive behavior. This entry contains information intended to assist readers in understanding the biological basis of drug actions on the brain and particularly the actions of commonly abused drugs. First, the general classification of brain cells is discussed and then brain structures and circuits as they relate to normal, adaptive function and drug action. The classification of brain cells based on the chemical nature of communication between cells is then discussed as it relates to the actions of abused drugs.

CLASSIFICATION OF BRAIN CELLS

The brain is a complex structure that has many different types of cells. Brain cells are subdivided into two general categories based on a number of criteria, including (1) neurons (nerve cells) that rapidly (in the space of milliseconds) receive and transmit information through specialized structures termed synapses (points of communication between neurons containing specialized structures to release, receive, and eliminate neurotransmitters), or (2) glia, which maintain a homeostatic, balanced environment that allows for efficient communication between neurons. Neurons are further subdivided according to (a) shape or size; (b) their connections; (c) the distance over which they transmit information; and (d) which chemicals are released to transmit information to other cells. Although a role for glia is becoming more appreciated, most of the effects produced by psychoactive drugs that are well understood result from actions on neurons that process or transmit information through synapses. However, in general, actions of drugs on the brain are complex and seldom involve only one type of brain cell. Neurons in one brain region send inputs to and receive outputs from other regions. These factors have made the identification of specific cells in the brain responsible for a given drug effect difficult to distinguish. This fact applies even to the simplest behaviors, which involve complex interactions among millions of cells. For these reasons, the understanding of the processes underlying addiction is incomplete; however, as explained below, significant progress was made in this area between 1985 and the early twenty-first century.

ORGANIZATION OF THE BRAIN: BRAIN REGIONS

The Cerebral Cortex. A number of experimental approaches have been developed to study the neural basis of behavior. One of these approaches involved studying the role of specific brain regions in behavior. The brain is composed of distinct substructures. The most general categorization scheme separates the brain into segments called lobes. From front to back these include the frontal, parietal, and occipital lobes, and the cerebellum. The temporal lobe is on the lateral surface of the brain. The outermost surface of the brain is called the cortex; this part of the brain rapidly evolved over the last 5 million years and is responsible for the generally improved cognitive abilities found in humans relative to other organisms.

Areas of the cortex are organized in two general functions: (1) primary sensory cortex where specific information arrives through vision, audition, taste, proprioception (the unconscious perception of movement) and smell, and (2) association cortex where the primary sensory information is integrated to form a unified perception of the external world. It is the evolutionary expansion of association cortex that allows humans to create complex perceptions of the world, deduce information beyond immediate sensory experience, and to make decisions based upon this information. In particular, association in frontal cortex subserves higher cognitive functions and allows complex planning and decision making to guide adaptive behavior. Therefore, to guide adaptive behavior, the brain must integrate sensory information, emotional perceptions, and previous experiences (memories) into a predictive model of the external world and then initiate the appropriate behavioral response.

The Thalamus. Information processing includes sensory information that comes in from sense organs (e.g., eyes, ears, tongue) to the brain through the spinal cord or directly through cranial nerves (nerve cells connected directly to the brain). This incoming information from sense organs goes to a central relay station called the thalamus. The thalamus is specialized, much like the cerebral cortex, in that defined areas receive input that is specific to a sensory modality. For example, input from the eyes through the optic nerve goes to a region of the thalamus called the dorsal lateral geniculate nucleus. This area of the thalamus, in turn, sends the information transmitted from sense organs to the appropriate primary sensory area of the cortex. For example, the lateral geniculate sends visual information to the area of the cortex specialized for vision, which is located in the occipital lobe. Similarly, the cerebral cortex sends commands to the effector systems (usually muscles) that act on the environment through a parallel thalamic relay system. Obviously, the thalamus is a very important structure for the coordination of inputs and outputs from the brain. Thus, degenerative diseases of this structure are highly debilitating, as are drugs that specifically alter the function of this structure.

The Brain Stem. Other areas of the brain are responsible for life processes of which we are not usually aware. These processes are generally controlled by the part of the brain called the brain stem, which is located between the spinal cord and the cerebral hemispheres of the brain. The brain stem is evolutionarily the most primitive portion of the brain and contains the cell bodies that maintain critical life functions, such as heart rate, blood pressure, breathing, and other involuntary or unconscious life-sustaining processes. A number of psychoactive agents have actions on neurons located in the brain stem. For example, opiates such as morphine or heroin have a direct inhibitory effect on the brain stem respiration (breathing) centers, which explains why heroin overdoses are often fatal—the breathing centers stop working. A significant part of the reticular formation is also located in the brain stem. This system sends outputs into the brain and down the spinal cord. It regulates arousal by increasing or decreasing the brain's responses to environmental events. The brain stem is also important in the control of pain and contains the cell bodies for some important nerve cells involved in the euphoric (pleasurable) and depressant actions of drugs.

BRAIN SYSTEMS

The Limbic System. Another important anatomical brain system through which abused drugs act is the limbic system. This system is a collection of structures that lie between the brain stem and the cerebral cortex. It includes the olfactory bulb, prefrontal and cingulate cortices, nucleus accumbens, amygdala, hypothalamus, hippocampus and septum, all of which have direct connections with one another. Parts of the brain stem are also included in the limbic system because of their strong connections to the other brain regions in the limbic system. In particular, the dopamine cells in the ventral tegmental area send strong projections to the rest of the limbic system. The limbic system is involved in the control of motivated behaviors, such as eating, drinking, and sexual behaviors, and in the expression of emotional behaviors, including anxiety and aggression. Tumors or lesions of these structures often lead to abnormal emotional expression. Drugs that directly affect this system can produce changes in goal-directed behaviors, mood (euphoria-dysphoria), and emotions. Importantly, drugs of abuse directly or indirectly modulate the dopamine projections within the limbic system to reinforce drug-seeking behavior.

The Motor System. Motor function (movement) involves a number of brain structures that include the caudate nucleus-putamen, which sits above and in front of the thalamus, the premotor cortex, and the motor cortex as previously described. This system is particularly important in generating repetitive behaviors, such as those involved in the conduct of daily tasks that are habitual (such as riding a bike or typing a letter). The fact that the use of addictive drugs becomes habitual is thought to strongly involve the habit circuitry in motor systems.

NEUROTRANSMITTER SUBSTANCES

Besides categorizing the parts of the brain by structure, the brain can also be separated into systems based on the distribution of the chemicals that nerve cells use to communicate with one another. Thus, cell bodies for some important nerve cells are localized in specific brain nuclei (collections of nerve cell bodies). Some drugs of abuse have specific actions on subsets

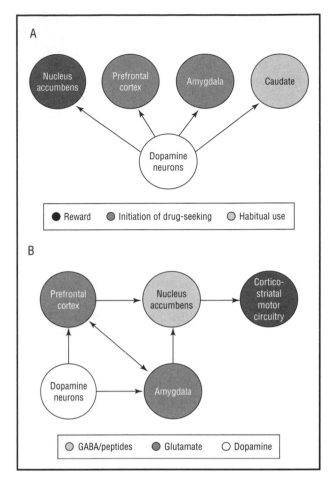

Figure 1. Neuronal circuit involved learning addictive behavior and relapse. (A) The major components of the system for learning drug-seeking behaviors are the same as learning normal reward seeking, and include the dopamine pathways from the ventral tegmental area to the nucleus accumbens caudate, amygdala, and frontal cortex. The role of these regions in reward learning can be simplified as indicated in the legend. (B) The circuitry underlying relapse involves the same structures involved in learning and is precipitated by dopamine release into or sensory activation of the prefrontal cortex and amygdala followed by involvement of the nucleus accumbens and caudate (corticostriatal) habit pathways. ILLUSTRATION BY GGS INFORMATION SERVICES. GALE, CENGAGE LEARNING

of cells that use or release a specific chemical to communicate with other cells. For example, alcohol (ethanol) is believed to act on at least four systems in the brain: the ones containing the nerve cells that release dopamine, serotonin, glutamate, and gamma-aminobutyric acid (GABA). The cell bodies of dopamine- and serotonin-releasing nerve cells are localized to specific brain stem regions and project widely to the limbic system, while glutamate-releasing and GABA-releasing cells are distributed widely throughout the brain.

Readers may wonder where the different actions of drugs of abuse occur in the brain. The simple answer is that drugs act directly or indirectly on dopamine neurons to increase dopamine release into the limbic system. Thus, while the drug itself may not directly affect dopamine release, through actions on nerve cells adjacent to the dopamine system, the drug does release dopamine. Next is a brief description of how different classes of drugs of abuse act to release dopamine. Stimulant drugs (e.g., amphetamine, cocaine, methamphetamine) produce overall effects on the brain resulting in increased activity, faster speech and thought patterns, and euphoria. This overall effect results from an ability to increase brain dopamine levels by preventing the elimination of dopamine from the brain. Alcohol is thought to activate dopamine systems by inhibiting the GABA neurons that normally inhibit dopamine cells, thereby releasing the dopamine system from inhibitory control. Nicotine also stimulates dopamine cells, in part by acting directly on dopamine cells and in part by releasing glutamate onto dopamine cells to indirectly excite them. Opioids (e.g., heroin, morphine, oxycodone) do not act directly on dopamine cells, but on the GABA neurons regulating dopamine cells. Thus, by inhibiting GABA cells, the opioids activate the dopamine cells.

BIOLOGICAL BASIS OF ADDICTION

Activation of Reward Learning. The capacity to learn behavioral strategies to obtain rewarding stimuli such as food and sex is central to human survival and adaptation to the environment. The brain circuitry mediating this essential function is outlined in Figure 1 and shows that the mesocorticolimbic dopamine system is a central component of it (Berridge & Robinson, 1998). A common effect of all drugs of abuse is to stimulate reward learning by activating dopamine transmission. New rewarding situations stimulate dopamine release to facilitate the development of behaviors designed to obtain the reward. Addictive drugs pharmacologically stimulate dopamine release, thereby mimicking this reward learning neurochemical situation and promoting the development of behaviors to obtain the drug in the future. This process is often called the reinforcement of behavior, and most addictive drugs release far more dopamine than can be physiologically achieved by natural rewarding stimuli. Accordingly, addictive drugs strongly reinforce drug-seeking

behavioral strategies, ultimately to the exclusion or diminution of behavioral strategies designed to obtain natural rewards, such as friendship, social cooperation, and even food and sex. Indeed, well-learned drug-seeking strategies become largely unconscious and proceed as a procedural memory, akin to riding a bike, where once the task is well learned the bicyclist no longer consciously thinks about how to ride the bike (Kelley, 2004).

Addiction as a Compulsive Drug-Seeking Behavior. Once drug-seeking behaviors are well learned, the release of dopamine is not required for an addict to seek the drug and relapse to using it. Rather, as a learned behavior, the motivation to obtain the drug relies predominantly on cortical and allocortical drive into motor circuits in the brain, including the nucleus accumbens and caudate. Thus, as shown in Figure 1, brain areas such as the prefrontal cortex, amygdala, and hippocampus send glutamatergic projections into the basal ganglia motor circuit. In particular, glutamatergic projections to the nucleus accumbens are thought to be strongly modified by chronic drug use, making it increasingly difficult for an addict to control his or her behavior and making the addict increasingly vulnerable to relapse. Using animal models, some studies have catalogued many enduring changes in these projections that are associated with chronic drug use and contribute to relapse vulnerability (Kalivas & O'Brien, 2008). This includes molecular changes that result in poor regulation of glutamate release and changes in how the neurons interpret both glutamate and dopamine signals. This loss of synaptic homeostasis parallels the loss of behavioral homeostasis that characterizes addiction (Koob & Le Moal, 2001). Importantly, the loss of homeostasis, or allostasis, is progressive and typically worsens as more of the drug is used. A goal of research in this area in the early twenty-first century is to identify the molecular changes produced by chronic drug use and to reverse them in order to restore synaptic homeostasis and thereby permit an addict to achieve greater control over the motivation to seek the drug and relapse to using it.

Addiction as a Disease of Adolescence. The vast majority of drug addicts begin drug use in adolescence (Volkow & Li, 2005). This fact is thought to be explained by the neurobiological development of the brain that takes place during adolescence. The adolescent brain has a larger number of synapses in the prefrontal cortex than the brain of an adult. Likewise, dopamine concentrations are elevated in adolescence. Thus, normal adolescent brain development involves the gradual pruning back of synapses in the prefrontal cortex. The greater number of synapses and dopamine content is thought to contribute to the high level of exploratory behavior and risk taking in adolescents as compared to adults. This exploratory activity has obvious evolutionary advantages by allowing adolescents to discover and interpret their environment in order to develop the adaptive, enduring behavior patterns that increase the probability of becoming stable and nurturing adults. Thus, the capacity of the environment to influence and change an adolescent is much greater than for an adult, and the repeated exposure to addictive drugs has a more profound shaping influence on the adolescent brain. Included in this shaping is the reward learning of behaviors that maximize obtaining drug reward, making the adolescent particularly prone to developing addictive behaviors.

USING NEUROBIOLOGY TO TREAT ADDICTION

This is a simplified description of complex neuronal networks that are believed to play a major role in the development of drug addiction as a compulsive relapsing disorder. In some ways knowledge is fairly complete, such as to which molecules a drug binds in the brain, but knowledge of how this initial drug action changes behavior and comes to dominate a person's life is as of 2008 yet to be clarified. The key to this understanding is the emerging knowledge of how the brain works both in terms of its circuitry and at the molecular level to interpret the world as context and to establish new behaviors. Addictive drugs usurp this process and produce pathological changes in this brain machinery. Reversing these changes promises to determine the future in treating and ultimately curing addictive disorders. To accomplish this goal, pharmacological therapies need to be coupled with psychosocial interventions. Pharmacologically restoring normal brain functions can permit the resolution of addiction, but psychosocial interventions are necessary to help addicts rebuild their lives.

See also **Alcohol: Chemistry and Pharmacology; Dopamine; Neurotransmitters; Opiates/Opioids; Overdose, Drug (OD).**

BIBLIOGRAPHY

Berridge, K. C., & Robinson, T. E. (1998). What is the role of dopamine in reward: Hedonic impact, reward learning, or incentive salience. *Brain Research Reviews, 28,* 309–369.

Kalivas, P. W., & O'Brien, C. (2008). Drug addiction as a pathology of staged neuroplasticity. *Neuropsychopharmacology Reviews, 33,* 166–180.

Kelley, A. E. (2004). Memory and addiction: Shared neural circuitry and molecular mechanisms. *Neuron, 44,* 161–179.

Koob, G. G., & Le Moal, M. (2001). Drug addiction, dysregulation of reward, and allostasis. *Neurospychopharmacology, 24,* 97–129.

Volkow, N. D., & Li, T. K. (2005). Drugs and alcohol: Treating and preventing abuse, addiction, and their medical consequences. *Pharmacology and Therapeutics, 108,* 3–17.

JAMES E. SMITH
REVISED BY STEVEN I. DWORKIN (2001)
PETER W. KALIVAS (2009)

BREATHALYZER. Breath-analysis machines detect and measure the alcohol present in deep lung air and convert this to an estimate of blood alcohol concentration (BAC). This calculation is based on the small but constant proportion of alcohol that the body excretes through the lungs. Regardless of interpersonal variations in metabolism, for legal purposes in most countries, the BAC is a ratio of breath to blood of 1:2100, although research indicates that the ratio of 1:2400 is more accurate (Swift, 2003). Breath analysis machines use methods such as thermal conductivity and infrared absorption to detect alcohol in lung air. Because breath alcohol analysis is quick and non-invasive, it is a useful tool in a variety of situations. The breathalyzer has traditionally been associated with law enforcement agencies for monitoring drinking and driving. However, it is increasingly being used in clinical settings. A number of models—both portable and fixed ones—are available.

Breathalyzer is the trade name of the model manufactured by Smith and Wesson, but the name has become synonymous with breath test machines. Breath-analysis machines have emerged as a powerful tool for law enforcement officers in policing motorists who may be operating motor vehicles while under the influence of illegal levels of alcohol.

Officers routinely conduct field sobriety tests on motorists they suspect of driving while intoxicated. An officer first requests that the motorist suspected of intoxication perform certain physical tests, such as walking a straight line, putting a finger to the nose, or balancing on one foot, in order to corroborate the officer's suspicion of intoxication of the motorist based on objective findings. If the officer concludes that the motorist has failed one or more of these tests, the officer requests that the motorist submit to a breathalyzer test. The results of the test either bolster innocence or corroborate police opinion testimony of intoxication, or in those states that set presumptive blood alcohol intoxication levels, to demonstrate that the motorist's blood alcohol level exceeded the permissible level.

If a motorist refuses to take a breathalyzer test, the police cannot compel the person to take the test. However, states have enacted implied consent laws that are civil, rather than criminal, in nature. Under these laws, if a motorist refuses to take the breathalyzer test, the motorist's driver's license is automatically suspended for a set period of time. Thus, motorists who are confronted with the alternatives must balance the criminal sanctions that follow a high alcohol reading from the breathalyzer against the immediate suspension of their driving privileges. However, in the late 1990s, some states, including New York and California, enacted laws that made refusing a breathalyzer test a crime. In these and several other states, legislators concluded that a license suspension was not a severe enough penalty for drunk drivers.

Because breathalyzer test results serve as powerful incriminating evidence, defendants and their lawyers often seek to challenge the reliability of the tests. This has produced a group of experts that routinely testify as to the way the test was administered and the reliability of the breathalyzer machine itself. The breathalyzer must be calibrated periodically. Calibration is a procedure performed by laboratory personnel to ensure the accuracy and reliability of the instrument. Routine maintenance is also performed to ensure the continued accuracy and proper function of the breathalyzer. Once calibrated, a certificate of calibration is completed by the laboratory and a certified copy provided to the law enforcement agency using that breathalyzer. Failure to follow maintenance schedules can raise a reasonable doubt about the machine's results and lead to an acquittal. Apart from the alleged technical defects of a breathalyzer, experts often testify that the officer failed to follow the proper protocol for operating the machine or that the defendant's blood alcohol level was incorrectly inflated due to biological factors.

Breathalyzers are also being used as preventive devices. In some states, courts order persons convicted of repeat offenses for driving while under the influence of alcohol, to install a breathalyzer interlock on their cars. The driver must breathe into the machine before starting the car. If the alcohol level is too high, the car will not start. After the car has started, the driver must periodically breathe into the device for a retest. If the driver fails the test, the car honks its horn and flashes its lights. Safety measures have also been developed to prevent circumvention of the protective device by using special driver recognition methods to prevent an unauthorized person from giving a breath sample.

Disposable home alcohol breathalyzer tests are widely available and come in handy to do a quick test. The test consists of a disposable tube that contains yellow crystals, which turn green in the presence of alcohol. As breath passes through the tube, the length of the green color change indicates whether one is above or below the legal driving limit. Any green color change indicates the presence of alcohol in a person's breath. The product is not to be used in a court of law. Additionally, the manufacturer, suppliers, agents, distributors, and retailers assume no responsibility for consequences when persons who test negative with this device are later discovered to be under the influence of alcohol or to have their judgment impaired by alcohol.

See also **Driving Under the Influence (DUI).**

BIBLIOGRAPHY

Giles, H. G., & Kapur, B. M. (1990). *Alcohol and the identification of alcoholics.* Lexington, KY: D. C. Heath.

Swift, R. M. (2003). Direct measurement of alcohol and its metabolites. *Addiction, 98* (Suppl. 2), 73–80.

MYROSLAVA ROMACH
KAREN PARKER
REVISED BY FREDERICK K. GRITTNER (2001)
GEORGE A. KENNA (2009)

BRITAIN. The legal use of what are now termed *illicit drugs* was widespread in 19th-century Britain. Opiates in various forms were used at all levels of society, both for self-medication and for what is now called "recreational use." At that time, the differentiation between medical and nonmedical usage was not clearly established, and concepts such as "addiction" were not widely accepted. The story of drug use in Britain since the late 19th century is the story of how and why drugs came to be defined as a social problem. A number of factors led to the establishment of certain forms of drug-control policy although they often had little relationship to the objective dangers of the drugs concerned.

EARLY EFFORTS AT CONTROL

In the early 20th century, there was limited involvement by either doctors or the state in the control of drug use and addiction. The supply of opiates and other drugs in Britain was controlled by the pharmaceutical chemist. As dispensers and sellers of drugs over the counter, they were the de facto agents of control. A rudimentary medical system of treatment operated via the Inebriates Acts (codified in the 1890s), whereby some inebriates could be committed to a form of compulsory institutional treatment. Legislation covered only liquids that were drunk (e.g., laudanum), and not injectables. Users of hypodermic morphine or cocaine were therefore not included under this system.

Drug addiction was not perceived as a pressing social problem in early 20th-century Britain, nor, indeed, was it one. During this period, the number of addicts decreased and overall consumption declined. No specific figures are available, but various indicators, such as poisoning mortality statistics, confirm this conclusion. Nevertheless, the 20th century brought increased controls and the classification of opiates and other drugs as "dangerous."

Drugs classified in this way were regulated through a penal system of control rather than through the mechanisms of health policy.

Two factors brought about regulation. The first was Britain's involvement in an international system of drug control; the second was the impact of World War I (1914–1918) and its aftermath. U.S. pressure on the international scene pushed an initially unwilling Britain into a system of control that rapidly expanded from the regulations discussed at the 1909 Shanghai Convention to the worldwide system envisaged at the Hague Opium Convention of 1911–1912.

Prior to World War I, however, only the United States, by way of the Harrison Narcotics Act of 1914, had put this system of drug control into operation. Britain favored a simple extension of the existing Pharmacy Acts. The influence of emergency wartime conditions, however, brought a differently located and more stringent form of control. The fear of a cocaine epidemic among British soldiers patronizing prostitutes in the West End of London—a fear that, on later investigation, proved to have been largely illusory—allowed the passage of drug regulations in 1916 under the Defence of the Realm Act. International drug control, in turn, became part of the postwar peace settlement at Versailles. The 1920 Dangerous Drugs Act therefore enshrined a primarily penal approach, and drug control was located in the Home Office rather than in the Ministry of Health, which was established in 1919.

TWO APPROACHES

British drug policy was henceforward marked by a tension between rival conceptualizations of the drug-addiction issue—drugs as a penal issue versus drugs as a health matter. The 1920s saw this conflict at its height. Britain seemed likely to follow a penal course similar to that of the United States, and British legislation was consciously modeled on the Harrison Narcotics Act. British doctors soon reasserted their professional control, however. In 1926, Britain's Rolleston Report legitimated a medical approach that could entail medical "maintenance prescribing" of opiates to a patient who would otherwise be unable to function. The Rolleston Report established what became known as the British System of drug control. This was a liberal, medically based system, albeit one that operated under Home Office control.

This system remained in operation for nearly forty years, until the rapid changes of the 1960s forced a reassessment. During the 1920s, 1930s, and 1940s, the number of addicts were small and there were few nonmedical users (less than 500). It is generally recognized that the British System of medical control operated because of this situation, rather than as the cause of it. This equilibrium began to break down after World War II (1939–1945), when a more extensive recreational, or nonmedical, use of drugs (such as heroin and cocaine) began to spread. There were a variety of reasons for this spread, including the spread of cannabis (marijuana) from the new immigrant population to the white population, the overprescribing of heroin by a number of London doctors, thefts from pharmacies, and the arrival of Canadian heroin addicts. Other drugs, particularly amphetamines, also became recreationally popular.

A GROWING PROBLEM

The official number of heroin addicts rose rapidly—from 94 persons in 1960 to 175 in 1962. The number of cocaine users, meanwhile, increased from 30 in 1959 to 211 in 1964. Nearly all of these were nonmedical consumers. The average age of new addicts also dropped sharply. Initial government reaction, in the 1961 report of the first Brain Committee, was muted. The second report, however, which came out in 1965 after the committee had been hastily reconvened, had an air of urgency. Controls were introduced on amphetamines in 1964. The report's proposals (implemented in the Dangerous Drugs Act of 1967) took the prescribing of heroin and cocaine out of the hands of general practitioners and placed it in those of specialist hospital doctors working in drug-dependence units. A formal system was established that notified the Home Office about addicts.

The clinic system established in 1968 did not operate as originally intended. In the 1970s, as the rise in the number of addicts appeared to stabilize, clinic doctors moved toward a more active concept of treatment, substituting orally administered methadone for injected heroin, and often insisting on short-term treatment contracts rather than on maintenance prescribing. These clinic policies aided

the emergence of a black market for drugs in Britain in the late 1970s. An influx of Iranian refugees from the Islamic Revolution of 1979, who brought financial assets in the form of heroin, also stimulated the market.

The British elections of 1979 returned a Conservative government with a renewed emphasis on a penal response to illicit drugs. Britain participated enthusiastically in the U.S.-led international "War on Drugs," but there were also strong forces inside Britain arguing for a more health-focused approach. In 1985 the discovery of acquired immunodeficiency syndrome (AIDS) among injecting drug users in Edinburgh, Scotland, was the trigger for policies that emphasized the reduction of harm from drug use rather than a prohibitionist approach. Nevertheless, in the early 1990s the tension between penal and health concepts and the interdependence of the two approaches to policy still remained unresolved.

THE PROBLEM WORSENS

The use of drugs within British society continued to expand in the 1990s and 2000s. Amphetamines are still second only to cannabis as the most widely used drugs in the United Kingdom, but few users are in contact with drug treatment services or seek any medical help. Services are oriented toward opiate users, and black-market amphetamine is not expensive, so there is a lower likelihood that financial problems will force users into treatment. Heroin use has also increased. During the 1980s this growth emerged in a large number of communities around the country, and it did so in a pattern different from that of the 1960s. This new pattern of use mainly involved adolescents and young adults, and the heroin was taken by a new method called "chasing the dragon"—a process in which the heroin is heated on tin foil, with the vapors being inhaled through a tube. But there was great regional variation, with injecting still popular in some areas. Overall, however, heroin use continued to grow: the number of known addicts rose from about 5,000 in 1980 to approximately 50,000 in the late 1990s, and by the mid-2000s it easily exceeded 100,000.

Cocaine use has also increased. In 1996, just over 1 percent of the population from 16 to 24 years of age reported ever having used cocaine. By

2003–2004, however, almost 5 percent of this age group reported cocaine use. Yet the speed and penetration of crack cocaine into the country has not been as rapid or as substantial as U.S. commentators had predicted. In the early 2000s only a fraction of a percent of persons 16 to 59 years of age told researchers that they had used crack. Indeed, in 2003–2004, heroin was still identified as the main problem drug for two-thirds of individuals entering drug treatment. The use of Ecstasy (MDMA, or methylenedioxymethamphetamine) received wide media publicity during the late 1990s and early 2000s, but surveys suggest it is used less frequently than other "dance drugs" such as amphetamine. The use of hallucinogens such as LSD has decreased considerably, although, in contrast, psilocybin, or "magic," mushrooms have become more popular.

NATIONAL STRATEGIES

For most of the 1990s, the British government has continued to publish national strategies on drugs, the first of which appeared in the 1980s. In 1995, *Tackling Drugs Together: A Strategy for England, 1995–1998* was published, and strategies for Scotland and Wales followed. The strategy committed the government to take effective action through law enforcement, accessible treatment, and a new emphasis on education and prevention to increase community safety and reduce drug-related crime. The strategy also attempted to reduce both young people's drug use and the health risks and damage associated with drug use. In 1998 the new Labour government published *Tackling Drugs Together to Build a Better Britain: The Government's Ten Year Strategy for Tackling Drug Misuse*, which reiterated these main themes. That same year, a former chief constable, Keith Hellawell, was appointed "drug czar," or national coordinator; his deputy had a background in rehabilitation services. Hellawell resigned in 2002, partly in protest over the reclassification of cannabis as a Class C drug, and he was not replaced.

In the 2000s, the relationship between penal and health responses in drug policy has remained central. A series of interventions have been developed that are designed to get drug users out of crime and into treatment. These include arrest referral schemes and drug treatment and testing orders, which provide an alternative to custody for drug-using offenders who agree to undergo treatment. A drug court system, similar to those in the United States, is being piloted in London and Leeds. At the same time, treatment services in prisons have expanded since the incorporation of the prison health service into the National Health Service, and new treatment programs and a through-care service for drug-using prisoners have been set up. However, mandatory urine testing in prisons and the testing of individuals for drugs upon arrest, rather than after being charged with an offense, have proved controversial.

Some policy analysts have argued that U.K. policy is moving to a harsher stance—in effect, toward coercive or compulsory treatment, with a greater emphasis on criminal justice initiatives. Despite this, there have been a series of other developments that continue to emphasize the health aspects of drug use. In 2001 the government established the National Treatment Agency (NTA), which has a remit to improve the availability and effectiveness of drug treatment services. Drug treatment, and particularly methadone maintenance, is regarded as a way of reducing drug-related crime. The new criminal justice measures on drugs have also brought more drug users into treatment instead of sending them to prison. Thus, the duality of policy approaches clearly continues.

See also **Anslinger, Harry Jacob, and U.S. Drug Policy; Britain: Alcohol Use and Policy; Britain: Tobacco Use and Policy; Canada, Drug and Alcohol Use in; China; Eastern Europe; France; Germany; International Control Policies; Ireland, Republic of; Italy; Netherlands; Opiates/Opioids; Opioid Dependence: Course of the Disorder Over Time; Opium: International Overview; South Africa; Treatment.**

BIBLIOGRAPHY

Berridge, V. (1993). "AIDS and British drug policy: Continuity or change?" In V. Berridge and P. Strong (Eds.), *AIDS and contemporary history*. Cambridge: Cambridge University Press.

Berridge, V. (1999). *Opium and the people: Opiate use and drug control policy in nineteenth and early twentieth century England* (Rev. ed.). London: Free Association Books.

Chivite-Matthews, N., Richardson, A., O'Shea, J., Becker, J., Owen, N., Roe, S., et al. (2005). *Drug Misuse Declared: Findings From the 2003/04 British Crime Survey*. Home Office Statistical Bulletin. London: Home Office. Available from http://www.homeoffice.gov.uk/rds/pdfs05/hosb0405.pdf

Royal College of Psychiatrists and Royal College of Physicians. (2000). *Drugs: Dilemmas and choices.* London: Gaskell.

VIRGINIA BERRIDGE
REVISED BY ALEX MOLD (2009)

BRITAIN: ALCOHOL USE AND POLICY.

The place of alcohol in British society, and the state's policy toward it, have long been hotly contested topics. Images and perceptions of alcohol in Britain have varied dramatically from one generation to another and the discourse relating to alcohol has been constantly shifting. Through the nineteenth and twentieth centuries, alcohol control was debated and shaped successively in terms of the free market (1820–1830s), of moralistic individual behavior (1840s–1860s), of social reform (1870s–1914), of national efficiency (First World War) of leisure (1920s–1930s), of health (1950s–1980s), of competition policy (1990s), and as a public order issue (early 2000s). In the early twenty-first century official attitudes toward alcohol are complex, with government agencies or departments having various attitudes. On the one hand, there are worries about health implications of excess consumption and issues of late night disturbances, but at the same time there have been moves to liberalize sales of alcohol in the interests of promoting tourism and the booming British *night time economy*.

PATTERNS OF CONSUMPTION

One characteristic of British consumption has been the propensity, alongside normal drinking, for sections of the community to indulge in periodic bouts of excessive alcohol consumption. The excesses of the *gin age* in the eighteenth century, the weekend drinking of Victorian industrial workers to the detriment of Monday work performance, the excesses of the highly paid shipyard and munitions workers of World War I, and the early 2000s *binge drinking* by young people in town centers and entertainment spots are all examples of this.

In the preindustrial age alcohol use and customs pervaded all areas of social life, with beer and spirits the preferred beverages, although whisky was dominant in Scotland. The inns and alehouses were indeed centers of community life and varied greatly in character. However, from 1850, the range of social activities carried out in the public house began to contract and the *pub* became more a leisure center for the working class, with the middling and upper social groups preferring to drink at home or in clubs, although public houses and off licenses also catered for a flourishing trade in alcohol fetched from the bar and consumed at home. Pubs came in all sorts and sizes, ranging from old inns, to city gin palaces, to sleepy rural establishments to decrepit and unsanitary beer houses. By the end of the nineteenth century the vast majority of pubs were owned by regional or national brewers on a tied house system, which strictly limited the range of beverages available to the consumer.

Per capita consumption of alcohol steadily dropped from its peak in the 1880s and 1890s to a trough in the 1950s. Large numbers of smaller and less salubrious pubs were swept away, and the larger brewers pursued a policy of providing larger improved houses with far more comfortable and better leisure facilities. These appealed to the middle classes and to women drinkers. The period from 1980 into the early 2000s, however, saw a dramatic shift in British drinking habits. The alcoholic beverages industry came to be dominated by large multinational companies, and the pubs largely owned by leisure companies rather than brewers. The number of pubs sharply declined, with those that remained specializing in themes and in providing catering and entertainment. The drinks industry set out to appeal to the youth market by advertising and promoting exotic drinks, especially those with fruit flavors or served with mixers. There was also something of a feminization of alcohol, again promoted by advertising, and rates of female drinking among the young rivalled those of men. There was a marked shift in consumption patterns. Beer sales, especially traditional ales, declined, in contrast to spirits and to wine. Although sales in public houses declined, there was a shift in sales to supermarkets and off licenses. The price of alcohol, particularly of wine, fell significantly after the 1960s in real terms, under the influence of competition regulations from the European Union. The result was a sharp rise in per capita consumption levels, back to those of a hundred years earlier; alcohol became more embedded in the leisure culture, entertainment industries, and social mores, appealing across the generations.

REGULATION OF ALCOHOL SALES

Governments in Britain were concerned about the dangers of intoxicants as far back as Tudor and Stuart times, largely on account of their potential for stirring up sedition or criminality. Accordingly, alcohol came to only be sold with an excise license and with permission from the local justices of the peace. The Home Office was the government department that had overall responsibility for licensing and alcohol issues. Although a free trade in beer in special beerhouses was allowed between 1830 and 1869, the Victorians systematized and tightened the licensing laws. However, this control and regulation was minimal and in no sense expressed a policy of promoting temperance. Although after 1860 elite politicians became concerned about the social evils of drinking, they were wary about regulating for the working class in advance of public opinion.

Restrictions on Sunday hours of sale were the only notable exceptions. Inspired by U.S. examples, many people in the temperance movement argued passionately for the local veto, a device whereby local communities could vote to be drink free. However, they showed scant interest in building coalitions for more general reform of liquor licensing, for example, schemes for a broader local control by elected boards or councils as part of local government reform, even though there was considerable support for such local solutions among politicians. Another problem was the way in which the drink issue became polarized in party political terms with the majority of the drink *trade* (businesses) throwing its weight behind the Conservative Party and the prohibitionists supporting the radical wing of the Liberal Party, making the building of consensus difficult.

The First World War saw something of a moral panic about the supposedly adverse effects of alcohol upon the war effort, and a Central Control Board was set up to impose restrictions and in some limited areas run the whole trade itself along disinterested management lines. The Board set about a positive program of improving pubs and encouraging catering and counterattractions. The Board itself was abolished soon after the war, but its legacy lived on in the form of higher taxation on alcohol, as well as restricted opening hours of public houses. Latenight opening was prohibited and an *afternoon gap* introduced, which remained a feature of British alcohol laws for the next fifty years. Eighteen was settled as the minimum age when alcohol might be purchased. During the mid-twentieth century the political salience of the alcohol issue declined, and the issue was less polarized between political parties. The drinks industry henceforth astutely developed a network of lobbyists in Whitehall, the seat of executive power.

The period between 1970 and the early 2000s was characterized by policies of marked liberalization of sales. This pattern in part reflects the libertarian political culture of modern Britain, the importance of tourism in the economy, the impact of the European Union, and the extent to which alcohol has become entwined with the broader leisure industries. Liberalization took the following forms: a) widespread sales from supermarkets with minimum restrictions on hours of sale and accompanied by promotional offers; b) efforts to ensure free competition and the play of market forces; and c) an effective end to restrictions upon the hours of sale. The afternoon gap was abolished in England and Wales in 1988 (a decade earlier in Scotland) and in November 2005 a flexible pattern of evening closing was permitted, effectively allowing late-night opening. At the same time the responsibility for licensing was transferred from the local magistrates to elected local councils, although their remit and powers were very heavily constrained by guidelines from the central government.

OPPOSITION TO ALCOHOL CONSUMPTION AND ABUSE

The prevalence of cheap gin during the eighteenth century and the subsequent excesses aroused a great deal of critical attention. In this period William Hogarth (1697–1764) published many striking engravings depicting the devastating effects of cheap spirits and alcohol upon the lower classes, such as *Gin Lane* and *Beer Street*. The 1830 English Beer Act, which was an attempt to promote free trade principles and undermine monopolistic brewers in the interests of providing a purer product, also attracted an outcry on the grounds that it encouraged drunkenness and disorder. However, such criticisms tended to be episodic, and it was only after 1830 that a more organized temperance movement began to challenge the role of alcohol.

This temperance movement received strong support across the classes, particularly among nonconformist churches and some of the major manufacturers. After 1860 prohibitionists dominated the movement up till the 1890s, but temperance sentiment of a more moderate kind flourished at the turn of the century, and elite opinion became more sympathetic seeing intemperance as a component of broader social problems.

After 1890, however, the temperance forces were weakened by internecine warfare between the orthodox prohibitionists and the supporters of Scandinavian disinterested management, a schism which lasted until the 1930s. The Society for the Study of Addiction, by contrast, provided a basis for those challenging the moralistic assumptions of the temperance movement and who saw the issue in terms of individual addiction, a medical problem. The temperance movement sharply declined in the twentieth century, and after 1945 the chief pressure on the government came from those in the medical and psychiatric professions who promoted the disease concept of alcohol. Gradually in the 1960s and 1970s the emphasis shifted toward a concern with excessive social drinking in general. Partly this change reflected shifts in medical fashion and also the increased attention paid to preventative health. In the early twenty-first century an alcohol control lobby emerged comprising policy sponsors from psychiatry, professions such as clinical psychology, social work, and sections of the medical world interested in preventative medicine, along with social care workers and joined by the remnants of the old temperance organizations and various voluntary organizations in the social field. The body, Alcohol Concern, which had an advisory function for government, provided a focus for these groupings in the 1980s and 1990s, although in subsequent years the Royal College of Physicians played a more important coordinating role.

SHIFTING APPROACHES TO ALCOHOL

In the period following 1945 alcohol policy fragmented, with a number of different government departments having their own bureaucratic viewpoint or interest. In the 1950s and 1960s the issue was predominantly seen as one of health, but no proactive policy was pursued. The liquor licensing and law and order issues remained under the control of the Home Office. The ministries of agriculture, employment and trade, and industry were stalwart supporters of liberalization and a range of pressure

groups, notably the British Tourist Authority also favored this, as well as the powerful players in the drinks industry. Against this liberalization the alcohol control lobby stressed the health risks of drinking more than safe limits.

In the early 2000s, however, a good deal of media spotlight has fallen upon the antisocial effects of *binge drinking* (as used in popular parlance to denote drunken sprees) upon late-night behavior, and casualty departments of National Health Service hospitals. In 2004 the government produced an Alcohol Harm Reduction Strategy for England, stressing the gravity of alcohol problems. However, critics pointed out the lack of funding to be allocated to it and to the extent to which the strategy rested upon partnership with the drinks industry. In view of these concerns, and increasing media attention to *Britain's drink problem*, it may seem paradoxical that the government should have pressed ahead to extend drinking hours. In part the move was justified as an attempt to *civilize* drinking by encouraging a French-style café culture without the pressure of last orders at 11 p.m. closing time and the act introduced better policing and more effective local authority control. However, it also demonstrates the degree to which Tony Blair's *New Labour* government prioritized economic development and the promotion of the leisure industries. Symptomatic of this has been the shift of alcohol licensing policy from the Home Office (concerned with law and order) to the Department of Culture, Media, and Sport, whose focus is leisure activities.

The attention paid to public order issues and binge drinking has somewhat eclipsed the concern about increased levels of regular consumption among the middle-aged as a result of the fall in price in real terms. It is a paradox that the sale of alcohol between 1975 and 2005 in Britain has been subject to a liberalization of policy at a time when the reverse process has happened with smoking. Thus, although it is as of 2008 possible to find a pub to drink in at almost any hour of the day, it is illegal to smoke inside it. This situation reflects the fact that tobacco control policy has been entirely confined within a discourse of health policy (including harm to others through passive smoking), whereas with alcohol the framing of the question remains contested between health, leisure, public order, and economic spheres.

See also Alcohol: History of Drinking (International); Britain; Britain: Tobacco Use and Policy; Foreign Policy and Drugs, United States; International Drug Supply Systems.

BIBLIOGRAPHY

Baggott, R. (1990). *Alcohol, politics, and social policy.* Aldershot, Hampshire, England: Gower.

Greenaway, J. (2003). *Drink and British politics since 1830: A study in policy making.* New York: Palgrave Macmillan.

Harrison, B. (1994). *Drink and the Victorians: The temperance question in England 1815–1872* (2nd ed.). Keele, Staffordshire, England: Keele University Press.

Jennings, P. A. (2007). *The local: A history of the English pub.* Stroud, Gloucestershire, England: Tempus.

Plant, M., & Plant, M. (2006). *Binge Britain: Alcohol and the national response.* Oxford: Oxford University Press.

Thom, B. (1999). *Dealing with drink: Alcohol and social policy from treatment to management.* London: Free Association Press.

Wilson, G. B. (1940). *Alcohol and the nation.* London: Nicholson and Watson.

JOHN GREENAWAY

BRITAIN: TOBACCO USE AND POLICY.

The growth of tobacco production and consumption in Britain has been dependent on developments in agriculture, the technology of production, the way that industry was organized, and the availability of safety matches. In the 19th century, tobacco was consumed through pipes or, in the case of the middle class, cigars. This usage had implications for the debate about tobacco and health.

EARLY HEALTH CONCERNS

An analysis of the *Lancet*, a British medical journal founded in 1823, indicates that, beginning about 1850, the main concerns were with the alleged links between tobacco and such general complaints as "dyspeptic derangement," insanity, paralysis, hysteria, rickets, impotence, and loss of memory. The one specific issue linked to pipe smoking was cancer of the lip. Nevertheless these concerns were never pursued systematically. Instead, tobacco continued to be linked in a random way with "muscular debility," jaundice, cancer of the tongue, "weakness of the extremities," trembling hands, and "tottering knee."

In fact, one of the main concerns was over the adulteration of tobacco with substances such as sugar, alum, lime, flour, rhubarb leaves, starch, treacle, burdock leaves, endive leaves, and red and black dye.

At this time, tobacco was also seen as having health benefits. It was noted, for example, that smokers rarely suffered from tuberculosis, and its effects in alleviating stress among such groups as laborers and soldiers were well known. As early as 1872, it was reported that nicotine, cyanide, ammonia, and sulphide were constituents of tobacco smoke, and insurance companies suggested that separate mortality records should be kept of smokers and nonsmokers. Pipes began to incorporate filters at this time, and perforations were made in the bottom of the bowl, which allegedly kept the lower layer of tobacco dry and reduced the amount of oil in the smoke. Nevertheless, the principal emphasis of the *Lancet* in this period was in favor of moderation. Lung cancer was still rare, and only a minority of doctors believed that moderate smoking was harmful to adults.

It is surprising how little this debate was affected by the advent of cigarette smoking in the 1880s. It was only with the invention of the Bonsack machine in 1883—and its adoption by the W.D. and H.O. Wills tobacco manufacturer—that the mass production of cigarettes became possible. Thereafter, expenditures on advertising increased rapidly, as did consumption. Some doctors began to experiment with filters, while others warned against the practice of inhaling smoke directly into the lungs. In the same way that the growth of the tobacco industry was dependent on economic and technological trends, the development of the cigarette marks the convergence of corporate capitalism, technology, mass marketing, and advertising. However as with pipe smoking, the *Lancet* approved of smoking cigarettes in moderation, and concerns were again centered on adulteration.

In many ways, then, the stance of the *Lancet* was purity, not abolition, and its articles focused on abuse, not use. Indeed, manufacturers submitted cigarettes to the journal for medical approval. Nonetheless there were a large number of antismoking organizations, including the British Anti-Tobacco Society, the Anti-Tobacco Legion, and the Scottish Anti-Tobacco Society. In France, the Société contre l'abus du tabac (Society against the Abuse of Tobacco) was founded, also to encourage moderation and oppose smoking among children. The *Lancet*, meanwhile, regarded these organizations as exaggerating the danger of smoking, and most of them were unsuccessful at mobilizing mass support.

Children and Smoking. The antismoking organizations founded in the early 1900s specifically to oppose smoking by children enjoyed more success. These included the British Lads Anti-Smoking Union, the International Anti-Cigarette League, and the Hygienic League and Union for the Suppression of Cigarette Smoking by Juveniles. The campaign against juvenile smoking conveys the cultural context for the relationship between smoking and health in the early 1900s. The 1904 Inter-Departmental Committee on Physical Deterioration recommended that legislation be passed to prohibit the sale of tobacco to children and its sale in sweetshops, suggestions that ultimately passed into law in the 1908 Children's Act. However, this legislation had only indirect links with the earlier anti-tobacco movements, while it had much closer connections with related debates about child labor and "national fitness."

The actual effects of smoking on the health of children were always ambiguous. More significant from the point of view of the middle-class social reformer was the way the cigarette became a badge of identity for working-class youth. Smoking was linked with the vices of adulthood—swearing, gambling, and hooliganism—and the solution that was encouraged by boys clubs was the playing of games. Most organizations that opposed smoking by children were established through churches and Sunday schools, and they had an essentially moral purpose in the context of wider debates about urbanization and physical degeneracy. Thus, opponents of juvenile smoking employed medical evidence in rather an opportunistic way, and they were essentially concerned with morality and citizenship.

SMOKING IN THE MID-20TH CENTURY

If the 19th century was the era of the pipe and the cigar, the 1950s were the heyday of the cigarette. In the 1930s, statisticians employed by insurance companies had begun to link smoking to reduced life expectancy and cancer. By the end of the Second World War, concerns about lung cancer had intensified. Changes in mortality were investigated by the epidemiologists Richard Doll and Austin Bradford Hill, whose famous article establishing the link

between cigarette smoking and lung cancer was published in the *British Medical Journal* in 1950.

Nevertheless, cigarette smoking remained a widespread social activity in the 1950s, and the health dangers were only slowly communicated to the general public. Figures for Britain indicate that 64 percent of men and 37 percent of women smoked cigarettes by 1953. Criticisms of the original article by Doll and Bradford Hill were only gradually allayed by their later cohort study. In Britain, the important, and influential, first report of the Royal College of Physicians, *Smoking and Health* (1962) clarified the arguments by stating that heavy smokers were 30 times more likely to contract lung cancer than non-smokers. Sir George Godber, the nation's deputy chief medical officer, played a key role in the genesis of this report, but it also fit in with the "modernizing" agenda of the Royal College. Public health was increasingly oriented around the concept of "risk," targeting real behavior. However, real action on the ground once again followed gradually. In Britain, cigarette advertising on television was not banned until 1967, while health warnings on cigarette packets appeared in 1971.

THE GOVERNMENT RESPONSE TO HEALTH CONCERNS

The response in the 1950s and 1960s by the Ministry of Health and such bodies as the Central Council for Health Education was certainly limited. Despite the research by Doll and Bradford Hill, the Ministry of Health took little action until a report by the Medical Research Council appeared in 1957. This report declared that the link between smoking and lung cancer was one of direct cause and effect. Even so, responsibility for health education antismoking efforts was delegated to the local authorities, the most demoralized branch of the National Health Service. The posters and use of vans by the Central Council, in hindsight, appears naïve and woefully inadequate, partly because of a failure to appreciate the scale of the behavioral problem involved. Overall, scientific caution, bureaucratic inertia, commercial pressure, and anxiety about government intervention all played a part. Governments concentrated on attempting to change individual habits rather than directly controlling the industry, and the resources allocated to health education antismoking efforts were very limited. Thus, it appears that both government and the tobacco industry wanted to keep people smoking because of the wealth that cigarettes create, with the former being made even more sensitive because of the perceived electoral implications of policy changes. In this sense, the relationship between government and industry in this area is similar to what has occurred in the food, alcohol, and pharmaceutical industries.

Politicians from the Labour Party emerge from this story with more credit than their political opponents. Despite a lack of action at the government level, Labour MPs (members of Parliament) were engaged in antismoking activities in the mid-1960s, and they were influential in the decision to ban cigarette advertising on television. Nevertheless, an examination of the ways that the health dangers of smoking were conveyed to the British public— through newspapers, radio, and television—during this period demonstrates that the way that these health messages were received were influenced in important ways by the medium through which they were conveyed. For example, while the *Guardian* newspaper reported the issues in a thorough and serious manner, the *Daily Express* argued that smokers should be allowed to make up their own minds, while the *Times* opposed government intervention. Overall, popular magazines, newspapers, advertisements, and radio broadcasts interpreted, accepted, rejected, or constructed their own views of the smoking and health controversy in fundamentally different ways.

MOUNTING EFFORTS

By the 1970s, the case against smoking had been proven and was accepted within the medical establishment, although rejected by pressure groups such as the Freedom Organisation for the Right to Enjoy Smoking Tobacco (FOREST). A second report followed from the Royal College of Physicians, *Smoking and Health Now* (1971), and this period also saw the establishment of the antismoking group Action on Smoking and Health (ASH). New developments were limited, but they were significant in two areas. The first was the recognition of the dangers of passive, or second-hand, smoking, a development that has had a significant impact on attitudes toward the risks of tobacco use. A key paper on lung cancer rates among the nonsmoking wives of heavy smokers was published in the *British Medical Journal* in 1981. Along with HIV/AIDS, this brought environmental concerns back into public health.

The second major development was the belated recognition that tobacco was an addictive substance, and that nicotine was the real cause of physical dependence.

Acknowledged in the 1960s, but not assuming policy significance until the 1990s, this increasingly called into question the idea that smoking was an essentially voluntary activity. The emphasis on addiction showed the power of pharmaceutical interests to define a new public health, in which treatment and "magic bullets" became part of the armory of prevention.

SMOKING PATTERNS

The effect of these efforts on the tobacco companies themselves was considerable, with evidence emerging from the United States that in the postwar period these companies had marketed cigarettes despite knowing full well the harmful effects of tobacco on health. At the same time, comparatively large numbers of people continued to smoke in the face of the acknowledged scientific evidence. Indeed, smoking has remained central to an individual and group identity firmly rooted in a specific liberal notion of the self. Children continue to smoke for the reasons they always have done: because cigarettes symbolize a rite of passage into an adult world. Adults, too, remain locked into a cult of individuality that opposes the standardizing tendencies of policy. In fact, there are signs of a backlash against antismoking policies, illustrating how the act of smoking continues to have a romantic status in popular culture. Nevertheless cigarette smoking is also increasingly stratified by education, social class, and ethnicity. It is also closely associated with social deprivation, and it is particularly prevalent among working-class women. Thus, the emphasis on individual responsibility runs the risk of denying that some social groups are more susceptible to behavioral risks, and of ignoring the fact that behavior is not merely a matter of choice.

Progress in some areas has been matched by delay in others. While the White Paper *Smoking Kills* (1998) noted that 120,000 people were dying each year from illnesses directly related to smoking, it was accompanied by a failure to curb cigarette advertising through motor racing. The most striking shift in tobacco use and policy in Britain has been the gradual acceptance of the argument that all workplaces and public spaces should be smoke free, which has led to the banning of smoking in pubs and restaurants. This policy trend began in workplaces in the Republic of Ireland in March 2004, and it was subsequently introduced in Scotland (March 2007), Wales (April 2007), and finally in England (July 2007). Anecdotal evidence for Ireland indicates almost total compliance, and the picture for England is similar. Overall, smoking illustrates important trends in the focus and discourse of public health in Britain since the mid-nineteenth century.

See also **Britain; Britain: Alcohol Use and Policy; Foreign Policy and Drugs; International Drug Supply Systems; Tobacco: A History of Tobacco; Tobacco: An International Overview; Withdrawal: Nicotine (Tobacco).**

BIBLIOGRAPHY

Berridge, V. (2007). *Marketing health: Smoking and the discourse of public health in Britain, 1945–2000.* Oxford, UK: Oxford University Press.

Doll, R., & Bradford Hill, A. (1950). Smoking and carcinoma of the lung. *British Medical Journal, 2,* 739–748.

Hilton, M. (2000). *Smoking in British popular culture 1800–2000.* Manchester, UK: Manchester University Press.

Hirayama, T. (1981). Non-smoking wives of heavy smokers have a higher risk of lung cancer: A study from Japan. *British Medical Journal, 282,* 183–185.

Lock, S., Reynolds, L .A., & Tansey, E. M., (Eds.). (1998). *Ashes to ashes: The history of smoking and health.* Amsterdam: Rodopi.

Royal College of Physicians. (1962). *Smoking and health.* London: Pitman.

Royal College of Physicians. (1971). *Smoking and health now.* London: Pitman.

Secretary of State for Health, and Secretaries of State for Scotland, Wales and Northern Ireland. (1998). *Smoking kills: A white paper on tobacco.* Available from http://www. arc hive.official-documents.co.uk/document/cm41/4177/4177.htm

JOHN WELSHMAN

BULIMIA NERVOSA. Bulimia nervosa is a mental disorder defined by recurrent episodes of eating unusually large quantities of food (a binge) followed by compensatory behaviors, such as vomiting, laxative abuse, and excessive exercise or fasting. Bulimia nervosa is associated with a persistent concern over body weight and shape that may include fear of gaining weight and a desperate need to lose weight. Bulimia is divided into two categories: purging type and non-purging type. Purging bulimics, who make up the vast majority of the bulimic population, use compensatory behaviors such as self-induced vomiting or inappropriate use of laxatives, whereas non-purging bulimics compensate their binges with behaviors such as excessive exercise or fasting.

Binge eating can be, and often is, triggered by environmental and psychological factors, which in turn lead to an irresistible craving for food. During a binge, a person feels out of control and consumes more calories than most people would eat in the same situation (excluding common events such as holidays or celebrations). Binges typically occur in secret and the food one rapidly consumes during a binge is typically calorie dense and nutritionally void. An episode of bingeing can result in the consumption of thousands of calories and can last anywhere from a few minutes to several hours, perhaps occurring several times a day.

EFFECTS

Binges followed by repeated use of compensatory behaviors can cause severe fluid and electrolyte imbalances. Abuse of diuretics can lead to kidney problems and severe dehydration. Purging type bulimics suffer more from these problems than the non-purging type. The electrolyte imbalances that result from these abuses can lead to seizures, cardiac arrhythmias, muscular weakness, and even sudden death. Bulimics who use purging compensatory behaviors often develop tooth decay and loss from excessive self-induced vomiting or a laxative dependency from inappropriate and prolonged usage. Furthermore, those who purge through means of self-induced vomiting can do permanent and severe damage to their esophagus and may develop gastroesophageal reflux disorder.

Although people suffering from anorexia nervosa may have emaciated figures, it is more difficult to identify people who suffer from bulimia because, by definition, their weight is in the normal or overweight range. In fact, if a bingeing and purging individual weighs less then 85 percent of what is considered to be their minimally healthy weight, the appropriate diagnosis becomes anorexia nervosa. However, despite the absence of easily observable physical features, bulimics often show detectable signs of the disorder. Bulimics may eat large amounts of food with no weight change, frequently take trips to the bathroom after meals, make kitchen visits at night, and rigidly adhere to exercise routines. Unlike anorectics who typically lack insight into their problems, bulimics are often distressed by their symptoms and ashamed of their behaviors. In addition, people suffering from bulimia are traditionally more prone to impulsive behavior, which can be manifested through abuse of drugs and alcohol or risk-taking behaviors. The comorbidity of bulimia with other psychiatric conditions is pronounced and includes anxiety disorders, major depression, dysthymia, substance use disorders, and personality disorders.

The age of onset for bulimia tends to correspond to late adolescence or early adulthood, slightly later in life than the onset of anorexia nervosa, which sometimes precedes the development of bulimia. In both clinical settings and general population studies, about 90 percent of identified bulimics are female. Among females in the general population, the prevalence of bulimia ranges from 1 percent to 3 percent, with even higher rates reported for college women. In westernized cultures, people of all backgrounds and ethnicities are affected by bulimia.

ONSET AND CAUSATION

The etiology of bulimia nervosa is multi-factorial, reflecting a combination of genetic, biological, and dispositional traits interacting with environmental risk factors to influence its development. Bulimia runs in families, and twin studies indicate a significant genetic contribution. Low self esteem, feelings of inadequacy, and a sense of lack of control over one's life may be contributing factors. Stressful life events, such as parental divorce and past sexual abuse, also confer increased risk for the development of bulimia. Cultural factors are also likely to be important, especially for women who embrace the images of ideal body types that are portrayed by modern media. These media messages glorify thinness and perpetuate narrow conceptions of beauty that include only women with certain body weights and shapes. The importance of such portrayals is borne out by studies that show that the prevalence of eating disorders is much higher in cultures in which the media play a large part in people's daily lives than in those cultures in which citizens are not exposed to many media forms. In addition, in less developed societies in which media influence has grown with modernization, the prevalence of eating disorders has increased.

TREATMENT

There are several different methods of treatment for bulimia nervosa, with preferred treatment involving a combination of therapies adjusted to meet the needs of the individual. Psychological treatment is likely to include cognitive behavioral therapy, with an additional emphasis placed on nutritional guidance and body image adjustment. Pharmacological treatment often involves antidepressants, particularly selective serotonin reuptake inhibitors (SSRIs). In addition to being particularly helpful for bulimics with comorbid major depression or anxiety disorders, these medications also appear to reduce bingeing and purging, diminish the chances of relapse, and improve eating attitudes. The overlap of bulimia with substance abuse plus the compulsive nature of disordered eating has given rise to addiction models of eating disorders and twelve step treatment programs modeled after those developed for the treatment of substance dependence. However, these addiction models have proliferated in the absence of solid empirical support.

See also **Anorexia Nervosa; Overeating and Other Excessive Behaviors.**

BIBLIOGRAPHY

Klump, K. L., Burt, S. A., McGue, M., & Iacono, W. G. (2007). Changes in genetic and environmental influences on disordered eating across adolescence: A longitudinal twin study. *Archives of General Psychiatry, 64* (12), 1409–1415.

Makino, M., Tsuboi, K., & Dennerstein, L. (2004). Prevalence of eating disorders: A comparison of Western and non-Western countries. *Medscape General Medicine* (online), *6* (3).

Phillips, E. L., & Pratt, H. D. (2005). Eating disorders in college. *Pediatric Clinics of North America, 52* (1), 85–96.

Wilson, G. T., Grilo, C. M., & Vitousek, K. M. (2007). Psychological treatment of eating disorders. *American Psychologist, 62* (3), 199–216.

MARION OLMSTED
DAVID GOLDBLOOM
MIROSLAVA ROMACH
KAREN PARKER
REVISED BY SERENA C. IACONO (2009)
WILLIAM G. IACONO (2009)

CAFFEINE. In the early twenty-first century, caffeine continues to be the most widely used psychoactive substance in the world. It can be found in a variety of dietary sources and medications, including coffee, tea, candy, soft drinks, and over-the-counter analgesics (pain medications) and cold remedies (Ogawa & Ueki, 2007). As a legal stimulant, caffeine is consumed daily by approximately 80 percent of the world's population, and it is available to both children and adults. Studies have shown caffeine consumption to be on the increase among children and adolescents in the United States. Average levels of daily caffeine consumption vary widely from country to country, with estimates for citizens of the United States and Canada averaging from 210 to 238 milligrams (mg)/person/day as compared to more than 400 mg/person/day for residents of Sweden and Finland. These daily dose levels are significantly higher than those shown to affect human behavior. For example, positive effects of caffeine on mood have been found at doses as low as 40 to 60 milligrams and positive effects on cognitive performance have been reported at a dose of 75 milligrams. Given that an 8 ounce serving of brewed coffee contains 135 milligrams of caffeine, an 8 ounce serving of green tea contains 30 milligrams of caffeine, a 1.5 ounce milk chocolate bar contains 10 milligrams of caffeine, and a 12-ounce cola drink contains 46 milligrams of caffeine, it is clear that people all over the world are consuming behaviorally active doses of caffeine on a daily basis.

CAFFEINE ABUSE/DEPENDENCE

The *Diagnostic and Statistical Manual of Mental Disorders* (4th ed., *DSM-IV*) of the American Psychiatric Association does not list diagnoses of caffeine abuse or dependence, stating that insufficient clinical and research data were available in 1994 to support their inclusion among other substance use disorders. In the fifteen years since then, a number of reports were published demonstrating that a subset of the general adult population demonstrates clinical symptoms of caffeine abuse or dependence that are similar to those associated with other psychoactive substances such as alcohol and cocaine. For example, one survey-based study found that 44 percent of caffeine users endorsed at least three symptoms of caffeine dependence (Hughes et al., 1998).

A *DSM-IV* diagnosis of substance dependence requires that an individual meet at least three of the following seven criteria: (1) tolerance; (2) withdrawal; (3) intake of the substance in larger amounts or over a longer period of time than intended; (4) persistent desire or unsuccessful efforts to reduce intake or control use; (5) a great deal of time spent on the activities needed to obtain, use, or recover from the effects of the substance; (6) important social, occupational, or recreational activities are stopped or reduced because of substance use; and (7) continued use despite knowledge of a persistent or recurrent physical or psychological problem likely to have been caused or exacerbated by the substance. The following sections consider these criteria in relation to caffeine.

Tolerance. In clinical studies of caffeine, one of the most frequently reported symptoms of dependence is tolerance. That is, regular caffeine users often report that the stimulant effects they initially experienced from a single cup of coffee now required consuming two or more cups of coffee to achieve the same effect. In addition to such anecdotal case reports, both human and non-human research studies have shown evidence of tolerance to the effects of caffeine. In animals, chronic caffeine administration has been shown to produce partial tolerance to various effects of caffeine and can produce complete tolerance to caffeine's stimulating effect on locomotor activity (involving movement from place to place) in rats. In humans, initial doses of 250 milligrams of caffeine can increase systolic and diastolic blood pressure. Tolerance to these effects develops quickly, however, often within four days. Less is known about tolerance to the central nervous system stimulant effects of caffeine. Indirectly, however, studies have shown that 300 milligrams of caffeine will often elicit self-reports of jitteriness in people who normally abstain from caffeine but will not elicit such statements from regular caffeine users.

Withdrawal. Another dependence criterion is the appearance of a withdrawal syndrome following abrupt termination of daily caffeine. Although there have been relatively few demonstrations of caffeine withdrawal in non-humans, abrupt termination of chronic daily caffeine has been shown clearly to decrease locomotor behavior in rats. Considerably more research on caffeine withdrawal has been done in humans. Anecdotal reports of caffeine withdrawal date back to the 1800s, with more systematic survey findings originating in the 1930s and continuing into the early twenty-first century. The cardinal symptom associated with caffeine withdrawal is a headache, which seems to develop gradually and can be throbbing and severe. Other caffeine withdrawal symptoms are fatigue (e.g., sleepiness, lethargy, drowsiness), depressed mood, and trouble concentrating. Some studies have also linked symptoms of anxiety to caffeine withdrawal.

Individual differences in the severity of caffeine withdrawal symptoms are considerable, ranging from mild to severe and such symptoms have been observed in persons consuming as little as 100 milligrams of caffeine per day. While withdrawal symptoms generally show a dose effect (e.g., more severe symptoms with higher levels of baseline use), variability is clearly present. In research with persons who were unaware they were experiencing caffeine withdrawal, some individuals experienced symptoms they reported as incapacitating (e.g., inability to go to work or care for children). In humans, caffeine withdrawal typically begins 12 to 24 hours after the last intake of caffeine, peaks at 20 to 48 hours, and can last from two to seven days. As with other drugs, caffeine suppresses caffeine withdrawal symptoms in a dose-dependent manner, so that the magnitude of suppression increases as the caffeine dose is increased.

The other dependence criteria often endorsed by regular caffeine users include a persistent desire or unsuccessful efforts to cut down or control use and continued use despite knowledge of a persistent or recurrent physical or psychological problem that is likely to be caused or exacerbated by continued use. In one study of caffeine use in pregnant women, more than half (57%) met *DSM-IV* criteria for dependence on caffeine (lifetime) and 45 percent reported a persistent desire or unsuccessful efforts to cut down or control use (Svikis et al., 1998). Another study with adolescents found that nearly one-fourth (21%) endorsed at least three of the seven *DSM-IV* criteria for dependence (Bernstein et al., 1998). Less frequently endorsed criteria for dependence on caffeine include considerable time spent on activities needed to obtain, use, or recover from its effects and giving up important social, occupational, or recreational activities to use caffeine. Clearly, these latter symptoms are more applicable to illicit drugs of abuse.

In one review of caffeine abuse and dependence, researchers indicated that despite its absence from *DSM-IV*, it is important for clinicians and practitioners to recognize that their patients may be dependent on caffeine and that some may experience distress as a function of being unable to control or stop their use. The authors advocate for practitioners to educate patients about possible sources of caffeine and how it may contribute to their medical or psychological problems. They also recommend that companies that sell or market products containing caffeine should indicate clearly the caffeine content of their products; warn about

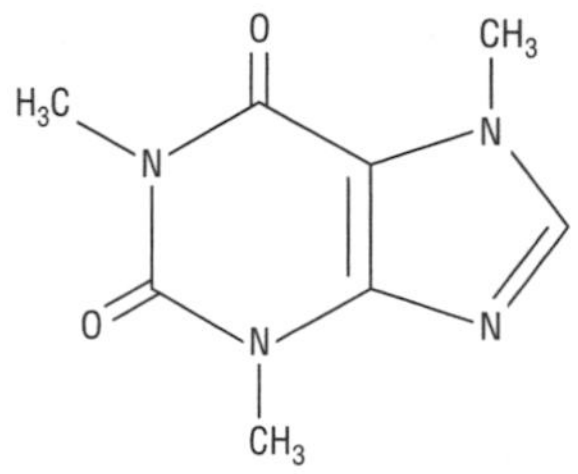

Figure 1. The caffeine molecule. ILLUSTRATION BY GGS INFORMATION SERVICES. GALE, CENGAGE LEARNING

Source	Standard value (in milligrams)	Minimum (in milligrams)	Maximum (in milligrams)
Coffee (6 oz/180 ml)			
ground roasted	102	77	186
instant	72	35	211
decaffeinated	4	2	10
Tea (6 oz/180 ml)			
leaf or bag	48	34	58
instant	36	29	37
Cola soft drink (12 oz/360 ml)	43	2	58
Energy drink (Jolt, 12 oz; Red Bull, 8.3 oz)	100	67	100
Chocolate milk (6 oz/180 ml)	4	2	5
Chocolate bar (1.45–1.75 oz/ 40–50 g)	7	5	31
Caffeine-containing over-the-counter medications			
analgesics and cold preparations	32	15	100
appetite suppressants and stimulants	100	50	350

Table 1. Caffeine content in common dietary and medicinal sources. ILLUSTRATION BY GGS INFORMATION SERVICES. GALE, CENGAGE LEARNING

limiting consumption by infants and children; and affirm that long-term consumption of large quantities of caffeine can lead to medical problems.

CLASS AND CHEMICAL STRUCTURE

Caffeine is an alkaloid that is often classified as a central nervous system stimulant. Caffeine is structurally related to xanthine, a purine molecule with two oxygen atoms (see Figure 1). Several important compounds, including caffeine, consist of the xanthine molecule with methyl groups attached. A methyl group consists of a carbon atom and three hydrogen atoms. These methylated xanthines, called methylxanthines, are differentiated by the number and location of methyl groups attached to the xanthine molecule. Caffeine is a 1, 3, 7-trimethylxanthine. The *tri* refers to the fact that caffeine has three methyl groups. The *1, 3, 7* refers to the position of the methyl groups on the purine molecule. Other important methylxanthines are theophylline, theobromine, and paraxanthine. All of these methylxanthines are metabolites of caffeine. In addition, theophylline and theobromine are ingested directly in some foods and medications.

Sources. Coffee and tea are the world's primary dietary sources of caffeine. In North America, approximately three-fourths of dietary caffeine comes from coffee. Elsewhere, tea is the most widely consumed beverage (after water), with black tea use more prevalent in Europe, North America, and North Africa, and green tea use more prevalent in Asia. Other sources of caffeine are cocoa products, cola beverages and so-called energy drinks. Caffeine is found in more than sixty species of plants. Coffee is derived from the beans (seeds) of several species of Coffea plants, and the leaves of Camellia sinensis plants are used in caffeine-

containing teas. Chocolate comes from the seeds or beans of the caffeine-containing cocoa pods of Theobroma cacao trees. Table 1 shows the amounts of caffeine found in common dietary and medicinal sources. As shown in the table, the range of values for each shows how substantially caffeine content can vary depending on such factors as method of preparation or commercial brand.

Effects on Mood and Performance. A substantive literature exists reporting the positive effects of caffeine at doses of 30 to 60 milligrams (see Smith 2005 for review). In particular, research has shown that caffeine use is correlated with improved performance on tasks that require sustained attention and effort. Although less robust, other studies have shown that low doses of caffeine (less than 200 mg) have a positive effect on speed of response and increase the person's positive sense of self-worth, with better concentration as well as higher levels of energy, self-confidence, alertness, and motivation. Interestingly, much of the research has focused on caffeine in coffee. Fewer studies have focused on caffeine in tea, although research as of 2008 has yielded generally similar findings. Higher doses of caffeine have been shown to improve or disrupt performance of complex tasks and increase physical endurance, work output, hand tremor, and reports of nervousness, jitteriness, restlessness, and anxiousness. Caffeine has also been associated with increased production of cortisol and epinephrine, adrenal hormones that are secreted in response to stress. Consequently, it is suggested that caffeine intake may lead to exaggerated responses to the stressful events of normal daily life and, thus, contribute to an increased risk for cardiovascular disease.

DISCOVERY

Caffeine, derived from natural caffeine-containing plants, has been consumed for centuries by various cultures. Consumption of tea was first documented in China in 350 CE, although there is some evidence that the Chinese first consumed tea as early as the third century BCE. Coffee cultivation began around 600 CE, probably in what later became Ethiopia.

Caffeine was first chemically isolated from coffee beans in 1820 in Germany. By 1865, caffeine had been identified in tea, maté (a drink made from the leaves of a South American holly), and kola nuts (the chestnut-sized seed of an African tree).

THERAPEUTIC USES

Caffeine can be found in a variety of over-the-counter preparations marketed as analgesics, stimulants, cold remedies, decongestants, and menstrual-pain relievers. As an ingredient in analgesics, caffeine is used widely in the treatment of ordinary types of headaches, although evidence for caffeine's analgesic effects is limited. That is, caffeine may only diminish headaches caused by caffeine withdrawal. It should be noted, however, that caffeine has been combined with an ergot alkaloid in the treatment of migraines. In addition, there is some evidence to suggest that caffeine contributes to the constriction of cerebral blood vessels (Cornelis & El-Sohemy, 2007). Because of various effects of caffeine on the respiratory system, caffeine has historically also been used to treat asthma, chronic obstructive pulmonary disease, and neonatal apnea (transient cessation of breathing in newborns). Later, other agents such as theophylline were usually preferred for the treatment of asthma and chronic obstructive pulmonary disease.

ABUSE

Strain and colleagues (1994) presented a number of case reports describing individuals who consume large amounts of caffeine—exceeding one gram per day (1,000 mg). While infrequent, such excessive intake, observed more frequently among psychiatric patients, drug and alcohol abusers, and anorectic patients, can produce a range of symptoms ranging from muscle twitching, anxiety, restlessness, nervousness, insomnia, rambling speech, tachycardia (rapid heartbeat), and cardiac arrhythmia (irregular heartbeat), as well as psychomotor agitation and sensory disturbances such as ringing in the ears and flashes of light. The disorder characterized by excessive caffeine intake has been referred to as *caffeinism*. There is some suggestion that excessive caffeine consumption can be linked to psychoses and anxiety disorders. Substantial amounts of caffeine are also used by a small percentage of competitive athletes, despite specific sanctions against such use.

ETIOLOGY

Twin study research has shown that caffeine use begins at an earlier age than nicotine, alcohol, or other substance use. It appears that at age nine, monozygotic (MZ; identical twin) and dizygotic (DZ; fraternal twin) correlations for caffeine use are quite similar, suggesting family environment contributes substantively to patterns of use. Starting at age ten, however, MZ and DZ correlations diverge and then from age 20 to age 35, MZ twin correlations (0.45) substantially exceed those of DZ twins (0.25). This pattern supports genetic factors influencing patterns of caffeine consumption, since MZ twins have 100 percent of their genes in common; whereas DZ twins have, on average, only 50 percent of their genes in common. Other studies have shown that genetic factors play a role in problematic caffeine use as well (e.g., heavy use, tolerance, and withdrawal). Further, as of 2008 emerging evidence suggests a common genetic link between caffeine dependence, substance use disorders, and psychiatric comorbidities (Kendler et al., 2008).

SELF-ADMINISTRATION STUDIES

Abused drugs are reliably self-administered under a range of environmental circumstances by humans and most are also self-administered by laboratory animals. Caffeine has been self-injected by laboratory non-human primates and self-administered orally and intravenously by rats, but there has been considerable variability across subjects and across studies (Griffiths & Woodson, 1988). Human self-administration of

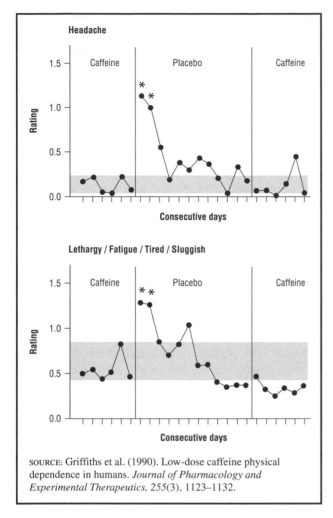

Headache

Lethargy / Fatigue / Tired / Sluggish

SOURCE: Griffiths et al. (1990). Low-dose caffeine physical dependence in humans. *Journal of Pharmacology and Experimental Therapeutics*, 255(3), 1123–1132.

Figure 2. Caffeine withdrawal. The termination effects of daily caffeine consumption. ILLUSTRATION BY GGS INFORMATION SERVICES. GALE, CENGAGE LEARNING

1989). Subjects tend to show less caffeine preference as the caffeine dose increases from 100 to 600 milligrams, and some subjects reliably avoid caffeine doses of 400 to 600 milligrams.

The nature of and time course of effects of terminating daily caffeine consumption are summarized in Figure 2 and summarize findings from seven adult subjects. All followed a caffeine-free diet throughout the study and received identically appearing capsules daily. Prior to the study, subjects had received 100 milligrams of caffeine daily for more than 100 days. Placebo capsules were substituted for caffeine without the subjects' knowledge, and subjects continued to receive placebo capsules for twelve days, after which caffeine administration was resumed. The top panel of the figure shows that substitution of placebo for caffeine produced statistically significant increases (asterisks) in the average ratings of headache during the first two days of placebo substitution. Headache ratings gradually decreased over the next twelve days and continued at low levels during the final caffeine condition. The bottom panel of the figure shows that the substitution of placebo for caffeine produced similar time-limited increases in subjects' ratings of lethargy/fatigue/tired/sluggish.

ORGAN SYSTEMS

Caffeine affects the cardiovascular, respiratory, gastrointestinal and central nervous systems. Most notably, caffeine stimulates cardiac muscles, relaxes smooth muscles, produces diuresis (urine production) by acting on the kidney, and stimulates the central nervous system. The potential of dietary doses of caffeine to stimulate the central nervous system is primarily inferred from caffeine's behavioral effects. Low-to-moderate caffeine doses can produce changes in mood (e.g., increased alertness) and performance (e.g., improvements in vigilance and reaction time), even in light, nondependent caffeine users. Higher doses produce reports of nervousness and anxiousness, measurable disturbances in sleep, and increases in tremor. Very high doses can produce convulsions.

Consumption. Caffeine's cardiovascular effects are variable and depend on dose, route of administration, rate of administration, and history of caffeine consumption. Caffeine doses between 250

caffeine has been variable, as well; however, it is clear that human subjects will self-administer caffeine, either in capsules or in coffee, and even when they are not informed that caffeine is the drug under study. For example, heavy coffee drinkers given repeated choices between capsules containing 100 milligrams of caffeine or placebo under double-blind conditions (in which neither the subject nor the experimenter knows which capsules contain the active drug) showed clear preference for the caffeine capsules and, on average, consumed between 500 and 1,300 milligrams of caffeine per day. Experimental studies with low-to-moderate caffeine consumers have found that between 30 and 60 percent of those subjects reliably choose caffeine over placebo in blind-choice tests (Griffiths Bigelow, & Liebson, and 350 milligrams can produce small increases in blood pressure in caffeine-abstinent adults. Historically, it was thought that daily caffeine administration produced tolerance to these cardiovascular effects within several days, not affecting the blood pressure of regular caffeine users consuming comparable daily caffeine doses. However, later evidence suggests that blood pressure remains reactive to the pressor (blood pressure increasing) effects of caffeine in the diet and that caffeine use may substantially contribute to cardiovascular morbidity and mortality (Vlachopoulos et al., 2005). Chronic caffeine consumption has also been associated with increased aortic stiffness and wave reflections, which may further heighten the risk of cardiovascular disease. Additionally, a study involving a genetic marker of caffeine metabolism provided strong evidence that caffeine can contribute to the risk of coronary heart disease and myocardial infarction (Cornelis et al., 2006).

High caffeine doses can produce a rapid heartbeat (tachycardia) and in rare cases irregularities in heartbeat (cardiac arrhythmia). Caffeine's effects on peripheral blood flow and vascular resistance are variable. In contrast, caffeine appears to increase cerebrovascular resistance and decrease cerebral blood flow.

Moderate doses of caffeine can increase respiratory rate in caffeine-abstinent adults. Caffeine also relaxes the smooth muscles of the bronchi. Because of the effects of caffeine on respiration, it has been used to treat asthma, chronic obstructive pulmonary disease, and neonatal apnea (transient cessation of breathing in newborns).

Moderate doses of caffeine can act on the kidney to produce diuretic effects that diminish after chronic dosing. Caffeine has a variety of effects on the gastrointestinal system, particularly the stimulation of acid secretion. These effects can contribute to digestive upset and to ulcers of the gastrointestinal system. In addition, caffeine increases the concentration of free fatty acids in plasma and increases the basal metabolic rate.

TOXICITY

High doses of caffeine, typically doses above 300 milligrams, can produce restlessness, depression, anxiousness, nervousness, excitement, flushed face, diuresis, gastrointestinal problems, and headache.

Psychiatric symptoms may also be exacerbated by caffeine use in individuals with schizophrenia. Doses above 1,000 milligrams can produce rambling speech, muscle twitching, irregular heartbeat, rapid heartbeat, sleeping difficulties, ringing in the ears, motor disturbances, anxiety, vomiting, and convulsions. Psychosis has also been noted in normal individuals who consume toxic doses of caffeine. Adverse effects of high doses of caffeine have been referred to as caffeine intoxication, a condition recognized by the American Psychiatric Association. Extremely high doses of caffeine—between 5,000 and 10,000 milligrams—can produce convulsions and death.

Extremely high doses of caffeine, well above dietary amounts, have been shown to produce teratogenic effects (birth defects) in mammals (Griffiths & Woodson, 1988). Although there is some evidence to the contrary, dietary doses of caffeine do not appear to affect the incidence of malformations or of low-birth-weight offspring. Although there has been some suggestion that caffeine consumption increases the incidence of benign fibrocystic disease of the breast and cancer of the pancreas, kidney, lower urinary tract, and breast, associations have not been clearly established between caffeine intake and any of these conditions.

Controversies continue over the medical risks of caffeine. Although research has not definitively resolved all the controversies, health-care professionals must make recommendations regarding safe and appropriate use of caffeine. In one survey of physician specialists, more than 65 percent recommended reductions in caffeine in patients with arrhythmias, palpitations, tachycardia, esophagitis/hiatal hernia, fibrocystic disease, or ulcers, as well as in patients who are pregnant (Hughes, Amori, & Hatsukami, 1988).

Prenatal Caffeine Use. Historically, caffeine use during pregnancy has been associated with a variety of adverse consequences, most notably miscarriage and low birth weight. The U.S. Food and Drug Administration recommended that "Women who are pregnant or planning to get pregnant should speak with their doctor about using caffeine." In general, the literature suggested that practitioners advocate that pregnant women limit their caffeine use to less than 300 milligrams per day. One study with 1,063 women, however, yielded inconsistent findings, noting that as little as 200 milligrams per day was associated with increased risk of miscarriageng (Weng, Odouli, & Li, 2008). Compared to nonusers, women who consumed up to 200 milligrams of caffeine daily had an increased risk of miscarriage (15% vs. 12%), and the risk doubled for women consuming more than 200 milligrams daily (25%), even after controlling for potential confounders. Clearly, the safest advice a practitioner can give a pregnant woman is to abstain from caffeine use during pregnancy, particularly in the first trimester.

PHARMACOKINETICS

Absorption and Distribution. Caffeine can be effectively administered orally, rectally, intramuscularly, or intravenously; however, it is usually administered orally. Orally consumed caffeine is rapidly and completely absorbed into the bloodstream through the gastrointestinal tract, producing effects in as little as fifteen minutes and reaching peak plasma levels within an hour. Food reduces the rate of absorption. Caffeine readily moves through all cells and tissue, largely by simple diffusion, and thus is distributed to all body organs, quickly reaching equilibrium between blood and all tissues, including brain. Caffeine crosses the placenta, and it passes into breast milk. Many drugs interact with caffeine and since most individuals use multiple substances, this is important to recognize.

Metabolism and Excretion. The bloodstream delivers caffeine to the liver, where it is converted to a variety of metabolites. Most of an ingested dose of caffeine is converted to paraxanthine and then to several other metabolites. A smaller proportion of caffeine is converted to theophylline and theobromine; both of those compounds are also further metabolized. Some of these metabolites may contribute to caffeine's physiologic and behavioral effects.

The amount of time required for the body of an adult to remove half of an ingested dose of caffeine (i.e., the half-life) is three to seven hours. On average, about 95 percent of a dose of caffeine is excreted within 15 to 35 hours. Cigarette smoking produces a twofold increase in the rate at which caffeine is eliminated from the body. There is a twofold decrease in the caffeine elimination rate in women using oral contraceptive steroids and during the later stages of pregnancy. Newborn infants eliminate caffeine at markedly slower rates, requiring over 10 days to eliminate about 95 percent of a dose of caffeine. By one year of age, a child's caffeine elimination rates increase substantially, exceeding those of adults; school-aged children eliminated caffeine twice as fast as adults.

MECHANISMS OF ACTION

Three mechanisms by which caffeine might exert its behavioral and physiological effects have been proposed: (1) blockade of receptors for adenosine; (2) inhibition of the activity of phosphodiesterase (an enzyme) resulting in the accumulation of cyclic nucleotides; and (3) translocation of intracellular calcium (Griffiths & Woodson, 1988). Only one of these, however, the blockade of adenosine receptors, occurs at caffeine concentrations in plasma produced by dietary consumption of caffeine. Adenosine (an autacoid, or cell-activity modifier), found throughout the body, has a variety of effects that are often opposite to caffeine's effects. Because caffeine is structurally very similar to adenosine, it can bind to the receptor sites normally occupied by adenosine, thereby blocking adenosine binding and preventing adenosine's normal activity. Thus, caffeine's ability to stimulate the central nervous system and increase urine output and gastric secretions may be due to the blockade of adenosine's normal tendency to depress the central nervous system and decrease urine output and gastric secretions. The methylxanthine metabolites of caffeine (including paraxanthine, theophylline, and theobromine) are also structurally similar to adenosine and block adenosine binding.

See also **Addiction: Concepts and Definitions; Chocolate; Coffee; Tolerance and Physical Dependence.**

BIBLIOGRAPHY

American Psychiatric Association. (1994). *Diagnostic and statistical manual of mental disorders* (4th ed.). Washington, DC: Author.

Bernstein, G. A., Carroll, M. E., Thuras, R. D., Cosgrove, K. P., & Roth, M. E. (1998). Caffeine dependence in teenagers. *Drug and Alcohol Dependence, 52,* 99–107.

Childs, E., & DeWit, H. (2006). Subjective, behavioral, and physiological effects of acute caffeine in light, nondependent caffeine users. *Psychopharmacology, 185*(4), 514–523.

Cornelis, M. C., & El-Sohemy, A. (2007). Coffee, caffeine and coronary heart disease. *Current Opinion in Clinical Nutrition and Metabolic Care, 10,* 745–751.

Cornelis, M. C., El-Sohemy, A., Kabagambe, E. K., & Campos, H. (2006). Coffee, CYP1A2 genotype and risk of myocardial infarction. *Journal of American Medical Association, 295,* 1135–1141.

Dews, P. B. (Ed.). (1984). *Caffeine.* New York: Springer-Verlag.

Food and Drug Administration. (2007). Medicines in my home: Caffeine and your body. *FDA & You, 14* (Fall). Available from http://www.fda.gov/.

Graham, D. M. (1978). Caffeine: Its identity, dietary sources, intake, and biological effects. *Nutrition Reviews, 36,* 97–102.

Griffiths, R. R., Bigelow, G. F., & Liebson, I. A. (1989). Reinforcing effects of caffeine in coffee and capsules. *Journal of Experimental Analysis of Behavior, 52*(2), 127–140.

Griffiths, R. R., Evans, S. M., Heishman, S. J., Preston, K. L., Sannerud, C. A., Wolf, B., et al. (1990). Low-dose caffeine physical dependence in humans. *Journal of Pharmacological and Experimental Therapy, 255,* 1123–1132.

Griffiths, R. R., & Woodson, P. P. (1988). Caffeine physical dependence: A review of human and laboratory animal studies. *Psychopharmacology, 94,* 437–451.

Hughes, J. R., Amori, G., & Hatsukami, K. D. (1988). A survey of physician advice about caffeine. *Journal of Substance Abuse, 1,* 67–70.

Hughes, J. R., Oliveto, A. H., Helzer, J. E., Higgins, S. T., & Bickel, W. K. (1992). Should caffeine abuse, dependence or withdrawal be added to *DSM-IV* and *ICD-10? American Journal of Psychiatry, 149,* 33–40.

Hughes, J. R., Oliveto, A. H., Liguori, A., Carpenter, J., & Howard, T. (1998). Endorsement of *DSM-IV* dependence criteria among caffeine users. *Drug and Alcohol Dependence, 42,* 99–107.

James, J. E. (2004). Critical review of dietary caffeine and blood pressure: A relationship that should be taken more seriously. *Psychosomatic Medicine, 66*(1), 63–71.

Jones, H. E., & Griffiths, R. R. (2003). Oral caffeine maintenance potentiates the reinforcing and stimulant subjective effects of intravenous nicotine in cigarette smokers. *Psychopharmacology, 165,* 280–290.

Juliano, L. M., & Griffiths, R. R. (2004) A critical review of caffeine withdrawal: Empirical validation of symptoms and signs, incidence, severity, and associated features. *Psychopharmacology, 176*(1), 1–29.

Kendler, K. S., Myers, J., & Gardner, C. O. (2006). Caffeine intake, toxicity, and dependence and lifetime risk for psychiatric and substance use disorders: An epidemiologic and co-twin control analysis. *Psychological Medicine, 36*(12), 1717–1725.

Kendler, K. S., & Prescott, C. A. (1999). Caffeine intake, tolerance, and withdrawal in women: A population-based twin study. *American Journal of Psychiatry, 156*(2), 223–228.

Kendler, K. S., Schmitt, E., Aggen, S. H., & Prescott, C. A. (2008). Genetic and environmental influences on alcohol, caffeine, cannabis, and nicotine use from early adolescence to middle adulthood. *Archives of General Psychiatry, 65,* 674–682.

Lane, J. D., Pieper, C. F., Phillips-Bute, B. G., Bryant, J. E., & Kuhn, C. M. (2002). Caffeine affects cardiovascular and neuroendocrine activation at work and home. *Psychosomatic Medicine, 64*(4), 595–603.

Ogawa, N., & Ueki, H. (2007). Clinical importance of caffeine dependence and abuse. *Psychiatry and Clinical Neurosciences, 61,* 263–268.

Rall, T. W. (1990). Drugs used in the treatment of asthma. In A. G. Gilman, T. W. Rall, A. S. Nies, & P. Taylor, (Eds.), *The pharmacological basis of therapeutics* (8th ed.) New York: Pergamon.

Smith, A. (2002). Effects of caffeine on human behavior. *Food and Chemical Toxicology, 40*(9), 1243–1255.

Spiller, G. A. (Ed.) (1984). *The methylxanthine beverages and foods: Chemistry, consumption, and health effects.* New York: Alan R. Liss.

Strain E. C., Mumford, G. K., Silverman, K., & Griffiths, R. R. (1994). Caffeine dependence syndrome: Evidence from case histories and experimental evaluation. *Journal of the American Medical Association, 272,* 1043–1048.

Svikis, D. S., Berger, N., Haug, N. A., & Griffiths, R. R. (2005). Caffeine dependence in combination with a family history of alcoholism as a predictor of continued use of caffeine during pregnancy. *American Journal of Psychiatry, 162,* 2344–2351.

Vlachopoulos, C., Panagiotakos, D., Ioakeimidis, N., Dima, I., & Stefanadis, C. (2005). Chronic coffee consumption has a detrimental effect on aortic stiffness and wave reflections. *American Journal of Clinical Nutrition, 81*(6), 1307–1312.

Weiss, B., & Laties, V. G. (1962). Enhancement of human performance by caffeine and the amphetamines. *Pharmacological Review, 14,* 1–36.

Weng, X., Odouli, R., & Li, D. (2008). Maternal caffeine consumption during pregnancy and the risk of miscarriage: A prospective cohort study. *American Journal of Obstetrics and Gynecology, 198,* 279e1–279e8.

KENNETH SILVERMAN
ROLAND R. GRIFFITHS
REVISED BY DACE S. SVIKIS (2009)
LORI KEYSER-MARCUS (2009)

CALCIUM CARBIMIDE.

CALCIUM CARBIMIDE. Citrated calcium carbimide is a mixture of two parts citric acid to one part calcium carbimide; it slows the metabolism of alcohol (ethanol) from acetaldehyde to acetate, so it is used in the treatment of alcoholism. It is also known as calcium cyanamide. As an antidipsotropic—an antialcohol or alcohol-sensitizing medication, it has been used for treatment in Canada, the United Kingdom, and Europe since its introduction for clinical use in 1956. Its only therapeutic use is for the treatment of alcoholism. In Canada it is sold under the brand name Temposil. As of 2000, however, calcium carbimide is still not approved for use in the United States.

PHARMACOLOGY

The pharmacokinetic data on the absorption metabolism and elimination of carbimide in humans are incomplete. Since nausea, headache, and vomiting occur because of the rapid absorption of carbimide, for treatment purposes it is formulated as a slow-release tablet. Peak plasma concentrations of carbimide following oral administration in experimental animals occur at 60 minutes; the drug is then metabolized at a relatively rapid rate so that half disappears about every 90 minutes (i.e., an apparent elimination half-life of 92.4 minutes). In humans, an alcohol challenge reaction will occur on an average of 12 to 24 hours after drinking.

Alcohol (ethanol) is normally metabolized first to acetaldehyde, which is then quickly metabolized further so that levels of acetaldehyde are ordinarily quite low in the body (acetaldehyde is toxic). Carbimide produces competitive inhibition of hepatic (liver) aldehyde-NAD oxidoreductase dehydrogenase (ALDH), the enzyme from the liver responsible for oxidation of acetaldehyde into acetate and water. Within two hours of taking carbimide by mouth, ALDH inhibition occurs. If alcohol is then ingested, blood acetaldehyde levels are increased; also mild facial flushing, rapid heartbeat, shortness of breath, and nausea occur with just one drink. As more is drunk, the severity of the reaction increases, with rising discomfort and apprehension. Severe reactions can pose a serious medical risk that requires immediate attention.

DOSAGE AND ADMINISTRATION

In Canada, Temposil is available as round, white 50-mg tablets engraved with the letters "LL" and "U13." The usual dosage is 50 or 100 mg every twelve hours. The drug should never be given to an intoxicated patient and preferably no sooner than 36 hours after the last drink.

Calcium carbimide should be used with caution in patients with asthma, coronary artery disease, or myocardial disease.

In the event of an overdose, the patient should be given pure (100%) oxygen by mask or antihistamines administered intravenously.

SIDE EFFECTS

Unlike disulfiram, carbimide does not have the potential side effect of liver damage. Carbimide, however, exerts antithyroid activity, which can be clinically significant in patients with preexisting hypothyroid disease. According to a 1999 Canadian monograph, other side effects of calcium carbimide include fatigue, skin rashes, ringing in the ears, mild depression, a need to urinate frequently, and impotence. The clinical significance of transient white blood cell increases remains unclear.

USE IN TREATMENT

The rationale for use of carbimide in alcoholism treatment is similar to that of disulfiram. The threat of an unpleasant reaction, which one may expect following drinking, is sufficient to deter drinking. For alcoholics in treatment who take a drink, the ensuing reaction is unpleasant enough to strengthen their overall conditioned aversion to alcohol. Their reduction of alcohol consumption during carbimide treatment is expected to result in general bodily improvement. A second approach involves the use of carbimide as part of a relapse-prevention treatment, whereby an individual might take it in anticipation of a high-risk situation. As of 2000, scientific evidence supporting the efficacy of carbimide in alcoholism treatment is inconclusive because of a lack of well-controlled clinical trials. No multicenter clinical trials have yet been performed.

See also **Risk Factors for Substance Use, Abuse, and Dependence: Learning; Treatment, Pharmacological Approaches to: Aversion Therapy; Treatment, Pharmacological Approaches to: Disulfiram.**

BIBLIOGRAPHY

Medical Economics Company. (1999). *Physicians' desk reference*, (PDR), (53rd ed.). Montvale, NJ: Thomson. (2008, 62nd ed.)

Miller, W. R., & Wilbourne, P. L. (2002). Mesa Grande: A methodological analysis of clinical trials of treatments for alcohol use disorders. *Addiction, 97,* 3, 265–277.

Peachey, J. E., & Annis, H. (1985). New strategies for using the alcohol-sensitizing drugs. In C. A. Naranjo & E. M. Sellers (Eds.), *Research advances in new psychopharmacological treatments for alcoholism* (pp. 199–218). New York: Excerpta Medica.

Peachey, J. E., et al. (1989a). Calcium carbimide in alcoholism treatment. Part 1: A placebo-controlled, double-blind clinical trial of short-term efficacy. *British Journal of Addiction, 84,* 877–887.

Peachey, J. E., et al. (1989b). Calcium carbimide in alcoholism treatment. Part 2: Medical findings of a short-term, placebo-controlled, double-blind clinical trial. *British Journal of Addiction, 84,* 1359–1366.

JOHN E. PEACHEY
REVISED BY REBECCA J. FREY (2001)

CANADA. From the founding of the nation onward, alcohol and drugs have been vexing problems in Canada. Despite difficulties, important strides have been made in dealing with such problems. Persistent, sometimes brilliant, efforts at prevention, treatment, and legal controls have made all the difference. Fortunately, Canada has a long history of research on alcohol and drug abuse and methods for controlling it.

HISTORY OF USE

When explorers and settlers came to Canada in the 1600s, they found small, scattered populations of Indians and Inuit. These peoples had no indigenous psychoactive drugs, and they had not discovered alcohol. Some groups smoked various grasses, but they had little nicotine or other drugs. Many, but not all, native Canadians took easily to alcohol, and it quickly became a problem. Alcohol was often used as barter in the fur trade with native groups to get better prices. Many native groups had a tradition of "eat it all" feasts because food could not be preserved. For some this soon became "drink it all" feasts with drunkenness and wild behavior. Earlier settlers also drank heavily as many social events had free alcohol, and pubs were often the first buildings put up in new settlements.

Temperance movements held down alcohol consumption in the 1800s, especially for Methodist and Presbyterian settlers. Prohibition during the 1930s also controlled alcohol problems. Prohibition in Canada, however, was enacted at the provincial level, never by the federal government, and did not last very long in most places. Alcohol and tobacco consumption increased greatly in the years after World War II.

Drugs such as coca and opiates were available in many over-the-counter preparations in the early 1900s, but legislation soon did away with them. Heroin, other opiates, and cannabis were largely unknown in Canada before the 1960s, and cocaine became popular only in the 1980s.

PATTERNS AND TRENDS

In Canada alcohol, tobacco, cannabis, and cocaine are the most prevalently used and abused drugs. A 2004 national survey found that 79.3 percent of adults were drinkers, 7.2 percent were lifetime abstainers, and 13.5 percent were former drinkers. Since 1989 the proportion of drinkers has increased slightly (from 77.7 to 79.3%). About seven percent usually drank five or more drinks per occasion in 2004; 14.8 percent found that alcohol had adversely affected their health; 8.1 percent, their marriages or home life; and 6.9 percent, their finances. All these harmful results had increased between 1989 and 2004 for adults. However, students' alcohol use declined between 1999 and 2007, along with some alcohol problems.

About 20 percent of adults in Canada smoked cigarettes in 2004, but the rate declined slightly in the following few years. Among students, very large declines occurred between 1999 and 2007 in the numbers who smoked tobacco (28.4 to 11.99%).

In 2004 about 44.5 percent of adults reported some illicit drug use in their lifetime, but no trend data are available. In that 2004 survey, 14.1 percent reported using cannabis in the past year; 1.9 percent, cocaine or crack; and less than 1 percent, LSD, speed, or heroin. 1.19 percent had used Ecstasy (MDMA, or methylenedioxymethamphetamine). About 10.1 percent reported harm to their physical health from illicit drug use in the past year, and 5.1 percent reported harm to their home life. Among students aged 14 to 18, drug use declined between 1999 and 2007 for virtually all illicit drugs except cannabis. Cannabis use continued to increase among students—about 26 percent used it at least once in 2008. Also, more students reported cannabis use and driving than reported drinking and driving. Use of solvents and binge drinking has shown no decline among students. Use of Oxy-Contin is becoming a problem for some students; this drug is often found in parents' prescriptions, which students use illicitly.

Traditionally Canada was an importer of illicit drugs, but now it is also a producer. Many cannabis-growing operations were found from 2003 to 2008. In addition, numerous labs for making Ecstasy were closed by police. In 2006 some 5.2 million Canadian-made Ecstasy pills were seized. Canada now exports cannabis and ecstasy to the United States, Asia, and Europe, according to police reports.

CONSEQUENCES

Although some declines have been seen, serious physical and social consequences from drug and alcohol use remain a problem in Canada. These consequences include death, injuries, admissions to treatment, and impaired driving.

Statistics Canada estimates yearly deaths due to alcohol to be 6,507, with 1,146 due to motor vehicle accidents, 1,037 due to liver cirrhosis, and 9,555 due to suicide. In addition 82,100 admissions to hospitals occurred because of alcohol. There were 34,728 deaths attributed to tobacco, with 12,151 for lung cancer, 6,671 for chronic obstructive pulmonary disease, and the remainder for other diseases. There were 194,000 estimated admissions for tobacco-related cases. Finally, there were only 805 deaths due to illicit drugs, with 329 for suicide, 160 for poisonings, and 61 for AIDS. Only 6,940 admissions to hospitals were attributed to illicit drugs. Clearly smoking creates a far greater health burden for society than does alcohol or other drugs. It should be noted, too, that alcohol reduces some death rates from heart disease and hence creates some benefits that tobacco and illicit drugs lack.

Research has shown that in Ontario, the largest province, rates of both alcohol and drug problems declined in the period 1975 to 1990. For example, heavy alcohol consumption, liver cirrhosis, hospital admissions, and impaired driving all declined substantially, with liver cirrhosis rates declining by 32

percent and drinking and driving mortality by 57 percent. These reductions have been attributed to greatly increased prevention and treatment efforts. This includes a tripling of numbers of alcoholics treated, a doubling of the numbers in Alcoholics Anonymous, more alcohol education, and more health prevention programs for workers. However, in the early twenty-first century, alcohol consumption increased again, whereas impaired driving charges remained stable or increased somewhat. Canada experienced a long wave of heavy consumption after World War II, then a long wave of decreased consumption, followed by a shorter wave of stability in alcohol consumption. Whether the future portends another long wave of heavy consumption is unclear, but there are a few unsettling signs.

The trend in impaired driving in Canada has been going downward for many years. In 2008 there were about 30,000 convictions for impaired driving in Canada. The peak years for impaired driving were in the late 1970s; convictions have declined by more than 50 percent since that time. The decline was largely due to the passage of a law in Canada that made 0.08 the legal limit for blood alcohol concentration and mandated a variety of other prevention and legally based programs for impaired drivers. The 0.08 law was well-publicized, and for the first time police had a portable breath tester. Other measures include longer jail terms and larger fines for impaired drivers. Reductions in alcohol-related deaths and injuries on the road in Canada represent a real success for both public health and the law.

Similar successes have been found with tobacco smoking. During the 1950s about half of Canadian adults smoked cigarettes. However, the 2008 rate is around 20 percent, and most smokers smoke fewer cigarettes. Death rates from lung cancer have fallen dramatically since the 1980s and 1990s. Much of this decline is due to government health warnings about smoking, the restrictions on smoking in public places such as restaurants and theaters, and large tax increases on tobacco products. The cost of cigarettes has more than tripled since the late 1980s. There is, however, a large black market in cigarettes. Canadian tobacco companies a few years ago sold cigarettes at low prices through native reservations, but the government stopped this. Some Indian reservations make "native" cigarettes and sell them at about half the price of regular cigarettes. They represent a significant problem in reducing levels of smoking in Canada.

An important consequence of alcohol and drug use is that people need treatment for their addictions. Good estimates of how many people were recently treated for addiction in Canada are difficult to obtain. The number of treatment agencies and clinics is large; there is no set definition of treatment, or of addiction. Actual counts were made for Ontario in 1992, when about 50,000 people were treated for alcohol problems. By 2007 that number had increased somewhat. About 5.2 percent of adults in Ontario met the criteria for alcohol addiction. Also, in the 2007 Ontario school survey, 19 percent of students met the criteria for hazardous drinking, and 15 percent had a drug problem. About 1.5 percent of students reported being treated for an alcohol or drug problem at some time during the past year.

Most Canadians can obtain treatment for alcohol and drug problems, except those in isolated small communities. The national health care system means most medical treatment is free. Also, many employee-based assistance programs provide access to care for addicted employees. Most addiction treatment in Canada is done on an outpatient basis (about 80%). Several Canadian studies have shown that outpatient and inpatient treatment achieve similar improvement rates. Inpatient treatment for addiction can be difficult to obtain except in large centers with specialized inpatient care.

ALCOHOL AND DRUG REGULATIONS

Canada has a complex federal system of government. There are 10 provinces, plus northern territories, and the federal government in Ottawa. The federal government is responsible for legislation on illicit drugs, most of the laws on impaired driving, and some of those on smoking. Provincial governments make all legislation on the sale and distribution of consumer products, such as alcohol and tobacco; hence, multiple regulations govern the sale of alcoholic beverages and nicotine in all forms. The federal government has overall control over the national health plan, which is universal and prepaid. However, health care is delivered by provincial health systems through hospitals, clinics, and private professionals. This system makes it difficult to create a national picture of what is happening in the area of addictions. For example, it is impossible to have a national view of how many alcoholics or drug addicts are in treatment or what treatment they are receiving.

Traditionally, regulation in the addictions area can be summarized as hard on drugs, but easy on alcohol and tobacco. Canada entered the drug wars of the 1970s and 1980s by arresting and criminalizing many drug users, but few importers and dealers. Access to alcohol was constantly made easier by lowering age limits, reducing prices, and many other aspects of alcohol control. However, in the 1990s to 2008, alcohol liberalization slowed, and controls on tobacco purchasing increased, along with prices for tobacco products. Also cannabis legislation was modified to reduce criminal penalties for possession and to allow discharges for convictions. Cannabis growing and importing, however, remain serious crimes. The use of cannabis for medical purposes is now allowed, albeit under strict regulation.

NATIONAL AND INTERNATIONAL PERSPECTIVES

Canada has often been at the forefront of efforts to prevent, control, and treat the consequences of drug and alcohol use. One of the first international drug treaties was organized by Bishop Brent, a Canadian clergyman. The Shanghai Opium Convention was the first to get international control over narcotics; Brent and others were the main organizers for this convention. Since that time Canada has supported and signed all major drug control treaties. Canadian policy makers and scientists have often participated in legal and health commissions and organizations concerned with alcohol and drug problems. The first head of the World Health Organization was a Canadian physician and Canadian experts have often been involved in WHO planning and its work at the international and country levels.

The future prospects for controlling alcohol and drug abuse nationally are difficult to discern at present. There are many hopeful portents; for example, there is a long-term decline in alcohol consumption and related problems. Smoking rates are also down substantially. Drug use among youth is on a long-term downward trend. However, cannabis use has not declined among students, and cannabis and driving is now more common than drinking and driving. Also, use of OxyContin has increased as students take their parents' prescription drugs from the medicine chest. Continued vigilance and action will be needed to make sure that cannabis and OxyContin do not become larger problems.

See also **Foreign Policy and Drugs, United States; International Drug Supply Systems.**

BIBLIOGRAPHY

Centre for Addiction and Mental Health. (2007). The 2007 Ontario Student Drug Use Survey (OSDUS) drug report: Executive summary, Toronto.

Smart, R. G., & Ogborne, A. C. (1996). Northern spirits: A social history of alcohol in Canada. Toronto: Addiction Research Foundation.

Statistics Canada. (2005). Canadian addiction survey (CAS) 2004: Ottawa. Available from http://www.statcan.ca/.

REGINALD G. SMART

CANCER, DRUGS, AND ALCOHOL.

DISEASE BURDEN ATTRIBUTABLE TO ALCOHOL

The World Health Organization's 2000 Comparative Risk Assessment Study (see Ezzati et al., 2004; Lopez et al., 2006; Rehm et al., 2004), found alcohol to be one of the most important risk factors for the global burden of disease, with alcohol ranking fifth, just behind tobacco (the alcohol-attributable burden was 4.0% of the global burden, compared to 4.1% for tobacco). Only underweight resulting from malnutrition and underfeeding, unsafe sex, and high blood pressure (which ranked first, second, and third, respectively) had more impact on the burden of disease than tobacco and alcohol (World Health Organization, 2002).

In 2002, 3.7 percent of all deaths worldwide were attributable to alcohol (6.1% for men; 1.1% for women). In addition, 4.4 percent of all disability-adjusted life years (7.1% for men; 1.4% for women) were attributable to alcohol (Rehm et al., 2006). (These percentages are net numbers that take into account the cardioprotective effect of alcohol.)

CARCINOGENESIS

In studies in which water containing ethanol is administered to laboratory animals, a dose-related increase has been noted in hepatocellular adenomas and carcinomas (U.S. National Toxicology Program, 2004); in head and neck carcinomas, fore-stomach carcinomas, testicular interstitial-cell adenomas, and osteosarcomas of the head and neck (Soffritti et al., 2002); and in mammary adenocarcinomas in female rats (Watabiki et al., 2000). The carcinogenic effect also increased when the ethanol was co-administered with known carcinogens.

The conversion of alcohol (ethanol) to acetaldehyde (the major metabolite of alcohol) in the liver requires the enzyme alcohol dehydrogenase, and acetaldehyde is transformed to acetic acid by the enzyme aldehyde dehydrogenase. Deficiencies in aldehyde dehydrogenase (which is most common among those of Asian descent) result in high levels of accumulated acetaldehyde in the body, which contribute to the development of malignant esophageal tumors (Baan et al., 2007; International Agency for Research on Cancer, 2007).

ALCOHOL AND CANCER

Comparative risk analyses and calculations on the alcohol-attributable burden of disease have revealed that cancer deaths worldwide are the third largest category of deaths caused by alcohol consumption (after unintentional injuries, at 25.9%, and cardiovascular disease, at 23.3%), accounting for 18.7 percent of alcohol-attributable deaths among men in 2002 (Rehm et al., 2006). Among women, the single largest category of alcohol-attributable deaths was cancer deaths, which accounted for 25.0 percent of deaths caused by alcohol consumption.

In February 2007, the Working Group of the International Agency for Research on Cancer (IARC), which comprises 26 scientists from 15 countries, confirmed that research evidence has shown that alcoholic beverages are carcinogenic to humans. Specifically, the group confirmed the causality between alcohol consumption and the occurrence of the following malignant neoplasms: oral cavity, pharynx, larynx, esophagus, liver, colorectum, and female breast cancer (Baan et al., 2007; International

Malignant neoplasms	ICD-10	Reference to meta-analyses and reviews	Effect	Causality
Lip & oropharyngeal cancer	C00-C14	English et al. (1995); Single et al. (1996, 1999); Sjögren et al. (2000); Gutjahr et al. (2001); Ridolfo & Stevenson (2001) *There are enough data to calculate relative risk for subcategories of disease, e.g. Bagnardi et al. (2001); Corrao et al. (2004)*	Detrimental	Confirmed
Esophageal cancer	C15	English et al. (1995); Single et al. (1996, 1999); Sjögren et al. (2000); Gutjahr et al. (2001); Ridolfo & Stevenson (2001); Rehm et al. (2004); Corrao et al. (2004)	Detrimental	Confirmed
Stomach cancer	C16	Bagnardi et al. (2001) *It was concluded that inconsistencies in research provide inadequate evidence that alcohol causes stomach cancer (English et al., 1995; Baan et al., 2007; IARC, 2007).*	Detrimental	Unclear (inconsistent results)
Cancer of small intestine	C17	Baganardi et al. (2001)	Detrimental	Not confirmed
Colon cancer	C18	Bagnardi et al. (2001); Corrao et al. (2004); Cho et al. (2004); Moskal et al. (2007); Bofetta & Hashiba (2006). *The IARC identified colorectal cancer as causally related to alcohol drinking in its meeting in February 2007 (Baan et al., 2007; IARC, 2007).*	Detrimental	Confirmed
Rectal cancer	C20	Bagnardi et al. (2001); Corrao et al. (2004); Cho et al. (2004); Moskal et al. (2007); Bofetta & Hashiba (2006). *The IARC identified colorectal cancer as causally related to alcohol drinking in its meeting in February 2007 (Baan et al., 2007; IARC, 2007).*	Detrimental	Confirmed
Liver cancer	C22	English et al. (1995); Single et al. (1996, 1999); Sjögren et al. (2000); Bagnardi et al. (2001); Gutjahr et al. (2001); Ridolfo & Stevenson (2001); Rehm et al. (2004); Corrao et al. (2004)	Detrimental	Confirmed
Gallbladder cancer	C23	Baganardi et al. (2001)	Detrimental	Not confirmed
Pancreatic cancer	C25	Baganardi et al. (2001)	Detrimental	Not confirmed
Laryngeal cancer	C32	English et al. (1995); Single et al. (1996, 1999); Sjögren et al. (2000); Gutjahr et al. (2001); Ridolfo & Stevenson (2001); Rehm et al. (2004); Bagnardi et al. (2001), Corrao et al. (2004), Altieri et al. (2005)	Detrimental	Confirmed
Lung cancer	C34	*This was excluded from the list of diseases causally related to alcohol. This decision has not been revised through any further meta-analysis. Meta-analyses on alcohol and lung cancer found only a borderline significant result (Bagnardi et al. 2001; Freudenheim et al., 2005) and the last substantive reviews found no sufficient support for a causal relationship (Bandera et al., 2001; Wakai et al., 2007).*	Detrimental	Unclear (inconsistent results)
Female breast cancer	C50	Single et al. (1996, 1999); Sjögren et al. (2000); Bagnardi et al. (2001); Gutjahr et al. (2001); Ridolfo & Stevenson (2001); Rehm et al. (2004); Singletary (2003); Hamajima et al. (2002); Corrao et al. (2004); Key et al. (2006); Singletary & Gapstur (2001); Ellison et al. (2001); Smith-Warner et al. (1998). *English et al. (1995) concluded that there was only limited evidence for causality; although they found a consistent relationship, subsequent studies using the same criteria have concluded that there is sufficient evidence of a relationship (Baan et al., 2007; IARC, 2007).*	Detrimental	Confirmed
Ovarian cancer	C56	Bagnardi et al. (2001) *English et al. (1995), consistent with IARC (1988), have concluded inadequate evidence that alcohol causes ovarian cancer*	Detrimental	Not confirmed
Prostate cancer	C61	Bagnardi et al. (2001)	Detrimental	Not confirmed
Kidney cancer	C64	Hu et al. (2003); Hsu et al. (2007)	Beneficial	Lack of carcinogenicity (Inverse trend)
Bladder cancer	C67	Bagnardi et al. (2001b)	Detrimental	Not confirmed
Non-Hodgkin's lymphoma	C82-C83	Morton et al. (2005); Besson et al. (2006)	Mainly beneficial or no effect	Lack of carcinogenicity (Inverse association or no association)

Table 1. Association between alcohol consumption and cancer as identified by various meta-analyses and reviews. ILLUSTRATION BY GGS INFORMATION SERVICES. GALE, CENGAGE LEARNING

Agency for Research on Cancer, 2007). Furthermore, lack of carcinogenicity was confirmed for renal-cell cancer and non-Hodgkin's lymphoma. Evidence on causality between alcohol consumption and risks of other types of cancer was sparse or inconsistent. (These results are summarized in Table 1.) In addition, the working group concluded that there is "sufficient evidence" for the carcinogenicity of ethanol in animals, and it classified the ethanol in alcoholic beverages as carcinogenic to humans

Cancer of the Upper Digestive Tract (Oral Cavity, Pharynx, Larynx, and Esophagus). Causality for these cancers was confirmed during the first IARC Monographs meeting on the evaluation of carcinogenic risks of alcohol to humans (IARC, 1988). Studies showed that daily consumption of approximately 50 grams of ethanol increases the risk for these cancers two to three times, compared with the risk for abstainers. The effects of drinking and smoking were found to be multiplicative.

Liver Cancer. Causality for liver cancer was also confirmed during the first IARC Monographs meeting. The evidence suggests that the consumption of alcohol is an independent risk factor for primary liver cancer.

Breast Cancer in Women. Causality for breast cancer was also confirmed. Based on several epidemiological studies, each additional 10 grams (less than one standard drink) of alcohol per day is associated with an increase of 7.1 percent in the relative risk (RR) of breast cancer (Hamajima et al., 2002), though this risk is possibly higher (Key et al. estimated it at 10% in 2006). Even for regular consumption of about 18 grams of alcohol per day, the increase in RR is statistically significant. Hamajima et al. reported that about 4 percent of the female breast cancer cases in developed countries may be attributable to alcohol consumption. The mechanism of association between alcohol and breast cancer may involve increased levels of estrogen (Boffetta & Hashibe, 2006; Foster & Marriott, 2006) or increased levels of plasma insulin-like growth factor (IGF) produced by the liver due to moderate consumption of alcohol (Yu & Berkel, 1999).

Colorectal Cancer. A causal relation between alcohol and colorectal cancer has been established

by the IARC (Baan et al., 2007). Research studies provide evidence for an increased relative risk of about 1.4 percent for colorectal cancer with regular consumption of about 50 grams of alcohol per day, compared with abstainers. This association is similar for both colon cancer and rectal cancer (Cho et al., 2004; Moskal et al., 2007).

Moskal and colleagues (2007) estimated a 15 percent increase in the risk of colon or rectal cancer for an increase of 100 grams (about 7 standard drinks) of alcohol per week. Low folate intake increases the risk of colorectal cancer, and alcohol could act through folate metabolism or synergistically with low folate intake to increase the risk, however the effects may be moderate (Boffetta & Hashibe, 2006). Moskal and associates also suggested a genotoxic effect of acetaldehyde, a metabolite of alcohol, and genetic polymorphism in subjects as factors for enhancing the risk of colorectal cancer.

Kidney Cancer. Evidence shows no increase in risk for renal-cell cancer with increasing alcohol consumption. Several studies have reported that increased alcohol consumption was associated with a significantly lower risk for renal-cell cancer for both men and women (Hu et al., 2003; Hsu et al., 2007).

Non-Hodgkin's Lymphoma. Several studies have demonstrated an inverse association or no association between alcohol consumption and non-Hodgkin's lymphoma. The majority of the studies show a lower risk in drinkers than in abstainers (Morton et al., 2005; Besson et al., 2006).

Lung Cancer. As evidence for a possible biological mechanism was not conclusive, and residual confounding from smoking could not be excluded, it was decided to exclude lung cancer from the list of diseases influenced by alcohol.

Stomach Cancer. The association of stomach cancer with the consumption of alcoholic beverages is not confirmed. Epidemiological studies show inconsistent results and the interpretation of the findings is not clear.

TOBACCO AND CANCER
The role of tobacco as a carcinogen is well established and described elsewhere.

Malignant neoplasms	ICD-10	Reference to meta-analyses and reviews	Effect	Causality
Oropharyngeal cancer	C00-C14, D00.0	English et al. (1995)	Detrimental	Confirmed
Esophageal cancer	C15, D00.1	English et al. (1995)	Detrimental	Confirmed
Stomach cancer	C16, D00.2	Tredaniel et al. (1997)	Detrimental	Confirmed
Pancreas cancer	C25, D01.9	English et al. (1995)	Detrimental	Confirmed
Laryngeal cancer	C32, D02.0	English et al. (1995)	Detrimental	Confirmed
Trachea, bronchus and lung cancers	C33-C34	Simonato et al. (2001)	Detrimental	Confirmed
Cervical cancer	C53, D06	Plummer et al. (2003)	Detrimental	Confirmed
Urinary tract cancer	C64-C68	Zeegers et al. (2000)	Detrimental	Confirmed
Renal cell carcinoma	C64	Hunt (2005)	Detrimental	Confirmed
Bladder cancer	C67, D09.0	Brennan et al. (2000; 2001)	Detrimental	Confirmed
Acute myeloid leukemia	C92.0	Brownson et al. (1993)	Detrimental	Confirmed

Table 2. Association between tobacco and cancer as identified by various meta-analyses and reviews. ILLUSTRATION BY GGS INFORMATION SERVICES. GALE, CENGAGE LEARNING

In 2004, the U.S. Surgeon General added the following diseases to the list of those for which evidence is sufficient to conclude a causal relationship between smoking and disease: stomach cancer, renal cell carcinoma, uterine cervical cancer, and pancreatic cancer. (For the full list of the malignant neoplasms casually associated with tobacco, see Table 2.)

ILLEGAL DRUGS (MARIJUANA) AND CANCER
In many countries, marijuana is the second most commonly smoked substance (after tobacco), and it is considered to be the least risky among the various illegal drugs. However, there is a concern that smoking marijuana may be a risk factor for tobacco-related cancers, because the smoke of marijuana, like that of tobacco, contains a number of the same carcinogens. However, smoking marijuana may actually be more harmful than smoking tobacco, since more tar is inhaled and retained when smoking marijuana.

Several studies support the biological plausibility of an association of marijuana smoking with lung cancer on the basis of molecular, cellular, and histopathologic findings. However, the role of marijuana as a risk factor for lung cancer is difficult to assess because most marijuana smokers are also tobacco smokers. The epidemiologic evidence that marijuana smoking may lead to lung cancer is limited and inconsistent (Mehra et al., 2006; Hashibe et al., 2005, 2006).

An IARC study reviewed several epidemiological studies that assessed the association of marijuana use and cancer risk including lung, head and neck, colorectal, non-Hodgkin's lymphoma, prostate, cervical cancers, and glioma (Hashibe et al., 2005). Due to methodological limitations in the existing studies—including selection bias, possible underreporting where marijuana use is illegal, small sample sizes, limited generalizability, and too few heavy marijuana users in the study samples—the authors concluded that the reviewed studies are not adequate to evaluate the impact of marijuana use on cancer risk. In view of the growing interest in medicinal marijuana, further epidemiologic studies are needed to clarify the true risks of regular marijuana smoking on cancer and other health conditions.

See also **Alcohol: Chemistry and Pharmacology; Cannabis Sativa; Complications: Immunologic; Complications: Liver (Clinical); Epidemiology of Alcohol Use Disorders; Epidemiology of Drug Abuse; Tobacco: Medical Complications.**

BIBLIOGRAPHY

Altieri, A., Garavello, W., Boseti, C., Gallus, S., & La Vecchia, C. (2005). Alcohol consumption and risk of laryngeal cancer. *Oral Oncology 41*(10), 956–965.

Baan, R., Straif, K., Grosse, Y., Secretan, B., El Ghissassi, F., Bouvard, V., et al. (2007). Carcinogenicity of alcoholic beverages. *The Lancet Oncology, 8*(4), 292–293.

Bagnardi, V., Blangiardo, M., La Vecchia, C., & Corrao, G. (2001). Alcohol consumption and the risk of cancer. *Alcohol Research & Health, 25*(4), 236–270.

Bandera, E.V., Freudenheim, J. L., & Vena, J. E. (2001). Alcohol and lung cancer: A review of the epidemiologic evidence. *Cancer Epidemiology, Biomarkers & Prevention 10*(8), 813–821.

Besson, H., Brennan, P., Becker, N., Nieters, A., De San-jose, S., Font, R., et al. (2006). Tobacco smoking, alcohol drinking and non-Hodgkin's lymphoma: A European multicenter case-control study (Epilymph). *International Journal of Cancer,* 119(4), 901–908.

Boffetta, P. & Hashibe, M. (2006). Alcohol and cancer. *Lancet Oncology 7,* 149–156.

Brennan, P., Bogillot, O., Cordier, S., Greiser, E., Schill W., Vineis, P., et al. (2000). Cigarette smoking and bladder cancer in men: A pooled analysis of 11 case-control studies. *International Journal of Cancer,* 86(2), 289–294.

Brennan, P., Bogillot, O., Greiser, E., Chang-Claude, J., Wahrendorf, J., Cordier, S., et al. (2001). The contribution of cigarette smoking to bladder cancer in women (pooled European data). *Cancer Causes & Control,* 12(5), 411–417.

Brownson, R. C., Novotny, T. E., & Perry, M. C. (1993). Cigarette smoking and adult leukemia: A meta-analysis. *Archives of Internal Medicine,* 153(4), 469–475.

Cho, E., Smith-Warner, S. A., Ritz, J., van den Brandt, P. A., Colditz, G. A., Folsom, A. R., et al. (2004). Alcohol intake and colorectal cancer: A pooled analysis of 8 cohort studies. *Annals of Internal Medicine,* 140(8), 603–613.

Corrao, G., Bagnardi, V., Zambon, A. & Vecchia, C. L. (2004). A meta-analysis of alcohol consumption and the risk of 15 diseases. *Preventive Medicine 38*(5), 613–619.

Efird, J. T., Friedman, G. D., Sidney, S., Klatsky, A., Habel, L. A., Udaltsova, N. V., et al. (2004). The risk for malignant primary adult-onset glioma in a large, multi-ethnic, managed-care cohort: Cigarette smoking and other lifestyle behaviors. *Journal of Neurooncology,* 68(1), 57–69.

English, D. R., Holman, C. D. J., Milne, E., Winter, M. J., Hulse, G. K., Codde, G., et al. (1995). *The quantification of drug caused morbidity and mortality in Australia 1995.* Canberra, Australia: Commonwealth Department of Human Services and Health.

Ezzati, M., Lopez, A. D., Rodgers, A., & Murray, C. (2004). *Comparative quantification of health risks: Global and regional burden of disease attributable to selected major risk factors.* Geneva: World Health Organization.

Foster, R. K. & Marriott, H. E. (2006). Alcohol consumption in the new millennium: Weighing up risks and benefits for our youth. *Nutrition Bulletin 31,* 286–331.

Gutjahr, E., Gmel, G., & Rehm, J. (2001). Relation between average alcohol consumption and disease: An overview. *European Addiction Research,* 7(3), 117–127.

Freudenheim, J. L., Ritz, J., Smith-Warner, S. A., Albanes, D., Bandera, E. V., Brandt, P. A., et al. (2005) Alcohol consumption and risk of lung cancer: A pooled analysis of cohort studies. *American Journal of Clinical Nutrition 82*(3), 657–667.

Hamajima, N., Hirose, K., Tajima, K., Rohan, T., Calle, E. E., Heath, C. W., et al. (2002). Alcohol, tobacco and breast cancer: Collaborative reanalysis of individual data from 53 epidemiological studies, including 58,515 women with breast cancer and 95,067 women without the disease. *British Journal of Cancer, 87*(11), 1234–1245.

Hashibe, M., Morgenstern, H., Cui, Y., Tashkin, D. P., Zhang, Z. F., Cozen, W., Mack, T. M., & Greenland, S. (2006). Marijuana use and the risk of lung and upper aerodigestive tract cancers: Results of a population-based case-control study. *Cancer Epidemiology Biomarkers & Prevention,* 15(10), 1829–1834.

Hashibe, M., Straif, K., Tashkin, D. P., Morgenstern, H., Greenland, S., & Zhang, Z. F. (2005). Epidemiologic review of marijuana use and cancer risk. *Alcohol,* 35(3), 265–275.

Holly, E. A., Lele, C., Bracci, P. M., & McGrath, M. S. (1999). Case-control study of non-Hodgkin's lymphoma among women and heterosexual men in the San Francisco Bay Area, California. *American Journal of Epidemiology,* 150(4), 375–389.

Hsairi, M., Achour, N., Zouari, B., Ben Romdhane, H., Achour, A., Maalej, M., & Nacef, T. (1993). Etiologic factors in primary bronchial carcinoma in Tunisia. *Tunisie Medicale 71,* 265–268.

Hsu, C. C., Chow, W. H., Boffetta, P., Moore, L., Zaridze, D., Moukeria A., et al. (2007). Dietary risk factors of kidney cancer in eastern and central Europe. *American Journal of Epidemiology,* 166(1), 62–70.

Hu, J., Mao, Y., & White, K. (2003). Diet and vitamin or mineral supplements and risk of renal cell carcinoma in Canada. *Cancer Causes & Control,* 14(8), 705–714.

Hunt, J. D., van der Hel, O. L., McMillan, G. P., Boffetta, P., & Brennan, P. (2005). Renal cell carcinoma in relation to cigarette smoking: Meta-analysis of 24 studies. *International Journal of Cancer,* 114(1),101–108.

International Agency for Research on Cancer (IARC). (1988). *IARC monographs on the evaluation of carcinogenic risks to humans: Vol. 44. Alcohol drinking.* Lyon: IARC Monographs Working Group. http://monographs.iarc.fr/.

International Agency for Research on Cancer (IARC). (2006). *Preamble to the IARC monographs on the evaluation of carcinogenic risks to humans.* Lyon: Available from http://monographs.iarc.fr/.

International Agency for Research on Cancer (IARC). (2007). *IARC monographs on the evaluation of carcinogenic risks to humans: Vol. 96. Alcoholic beverage consumption and ethyl carbamate (urethane).* Lyon: Author.

Key, J., Hodgson, S., Omar, R. Z., Jensen, T. K., Thomson, S. G., Boobis, A. R., et al. (2006). Meta-analysis of studies of alcohol and breast cancer with consideration of the methodological issues. *Cancer Causes and Control 17*(6), 759–770.

Lopez, A. D., Mathers, C. D., Ezzati, M., Jamison, D.T., & Murray, C. J. (2006). *Global burden of disease and risk factors.* New York & Washington: Oxford University Press and The World Bank.

Mehra, R., Moore, B. A., Crothers, K., Tetrault, J., & Fiellin, D. A. (2006). The association between marijuana smoking and lung cancer: A systematic review. *Archives of Internal Medicine, 166*(13), 1359–1367.

Morton, L. M., Zheng, T., Holford, T. R., Holly, E. A., Chiu, B. C., Constantini, A. S., et al. (2005). Alcohol consumption and risk of non-Hodgkin lymphoma: A pooled analysis. *The Lancet of Oncology, 6*(7), 469–476.

Moskal, A., Norat, T., Ferrari, P., & Riboli, E. (2007). Alcohol intake and colorectal cancer risk: A dose-response meta-analysis of published cohort studies. *International Journal of Cancer 120*(3), 664–671.

Plummer, M., Herrero, R., Franceschi, S., Meijer, C. J., Snijders, P., Bosch, F. X., et al. (2003). Smoking and cervical cancer: Pooled analysis of the IARC multicentric case-control study. *Cancer Causes & Control 14*(9), 805–814.

Rehm, J., Patra, J., Baliunas, D., Popova, S., Roerecke, M., & Taylor, B. (2006). *Alcohol consumption and the global burden of disease 2002.* Geneva: World Health Organization, Department of Mental Health and Substance Abuse, Management of Substance Abuse (Internal document for the meeting of the WHO Technical Advisory Group on Alcohol Epidemiology).

Rehm, J., Room, R., Monteiro, M., Gmel, G., Graham, K., Rehn, N., et al. (2004). Alcohol use. In M. Ezzati, A. Lopez, A. Rodgers, & C. Murray, (Eds.), *Comparative quantification of health risks: Global and regional burden of disease attributable to selected major risk factors* (Vol. 1, pp. 959–1108). Geneva: World Health Organization.

Ridolfo, B. & Stevenson, C. (2001). *The quantification of drug-caused mortality and morbidity in Australia 1998.* Canberra, Australia: Australian Institute of Health and Welfare.

Sidney, S., Quesenberry, C. P., Jr., Friedman, G. D., & Tekawa, I. S. (1997). Marijuana use and cancer incidence (California, United States). *Cancer Causes & Control 8*(5), 722–728.

Simonato, L., Agudo, A., Ahrens, W., Benhamou, E., Benhamou, S., Boffetta, P., et al. (2001). Lung cancer and cigarette smoking in Europe: An update of risk estimates and an assessment of inter-country heterogeneity. *International Journal of Cancer 91*(6), 876–887.

Single, E., Robson, L., Rehm, J., & Xie, X. (1999). Morbidity and mortality attributable to alcohol, tobacco, and illicit drug use in Canada. *American Journal of Public Health, 89*(3), 385–390.

Single, E., Robson, L., Xie, X., & Rehm, J. (1996). *The cost of substance abuse in Canada.* Ottawa, Ontario: Canadian Centre on Substance Abuse.

Singletary, K. W. & Gapstur, S. M. (2001). Alcohol and breast cancer: Review of epidemiologic and experimental evidence and potential mechanisms. *Journal of the American Medical Association 286*(17), 2143–2151.

Sjögren, H., Eriksson, A., Brostrom, G., & Ahlm, K. (2000). Quantification of alcohol-related mortality in Sweden. *Alcohol and Alcoholism, 35*(6), 601–611.

Soffritti, M., Belpoggi, F., Cevolani, D., Guarino, M., Padovani, M., Maltoni, C., et al. (2002). Results of long-term experimental studies on the carcinogenicity of methyl alcohol and ethylalcohol in rats. *Annals of the New York Academy of Sciences, 982,* 46–69.

Tredaniel, J., Boffetta P., Buiatti, E., Saracci, R., & Hirsch, A. (1997). Tobacco smoking and gastric cancer: Review and meta-analysis. *International Journal of Cancer, 72*(4), 565–573.

U.S. Department of Health and Human Services. (2004). *The health consequences of smoking: A report of the Surgeon General.* Atlanta, GA: Author.

U.S. National Toxicology Program. (2004). *Toxicology and Carcinogenesis Studies of Urethane + Ethanol (CAS Nos. 51-79-6 & 64-17-5) in F344/N rats and B6C3F1 mice (drinking-water studies).* NTP Technical Report No. 510. Bethesda, MD: National Institutes of Health.

Wakai, K., Nagata, C., Mizoue, T., Tanaka, K., Nishino, Y., Tsuji, I., et al. (2007). Alcohol drinking and lung cancer risk: An evaluation based on a systematic review of epidemiological evidence among the Japanese population. *Japanese Journal of Clinical Oncology 37*(3), 168–174.

Watabiki, T., Okii, Y., Tokiyasu, T., Yoshimura, S., Yoshida, M., Akane, A., et al. (2000). Long-term ethanol consumption in ICR mice causes mammary tumor in females and liver fibrosis in males. *Alcoholism: Clinical & Experimental Research, 24*(Suppl. 4), 117S–122S.

World Health Organization. (2002). *World health report: Reducing risks, promoting healthy life.* Geneva: Author.

Yu, H. & Berkel, H. (1999). Do insulin-like growth factors mediate the effect of alcohol on breast cancer risk? *Medical Hypotheses 52*(6), 491–496.

Zeegers, M. P., Tan, F. E., Dorant, E., & van Den Brandt, P. A. (2000). The impact of characteristics of cigarette smoking on urinary tract cancer risk: A meta-analysis of epidemiologic studies. Review. *Cancer, 89*(3), 630–639.

Zhang, Z.-F., Morgenstern, H., Spitz, M. R., Tashkin, D. P., Yu, G.-P., Marshall, J. R., et al. (1999). Marijuana use and increased risk of squamous cell carcinoma of the head and neck. *Cancer Epidemiology Biomarkers & Prevention 8*(12), 1071–1078.

SVETLANA POPOVA
JÜRGEN REHM

CANNABINOIDS.

Cannabis or marijuana has been used for thousands of years for medicinal, religious, and recreational purposes (Mechoulam et al., 1991). Extracts of this plant material were first introduced to Western Europe from India for medicinal purposes in the middle of the nineteenth century by William O'Shaughnessy, a British physician.

Marijuana is the most widely used illegal drug in the United States (Johnston et al., 2007) and many individuals believe that it should be legalized for medicinal purposes. Its primary psychoactive constituent, δ^9-tetrahydrocannabinol (δ^9-THC), has already been approved by the U.S. Food and Drug Administration as a synthetic oral formulation (called dronabinol) to treat nausea and vomiting related to the chemotherapy administered to cancer patients and as an appetite stimulant for AIDS patients.

δ^9-THC belongs to a class of drugs called cannabinoids, which despite great structural diversity (Figure 1), produce pharmacological effects similar to those of marijuana. In addition to the 60 to 70 cannabinoids that have been identified in marijuana, chemists have synthesized hundreds of cannabinoid analogs that vary greatly in their pharmacological potency including the highly potent compounds WIN55,212-2 and CP-55,940. Another major cannabinoid present in marijuana, cannabidiol (CBD), is structurally similar to δ^9-THC, though it lacks psychoactivity (Figure 1). An oromucosal (mouth) spray containing equal parts of δ^9-THC and CBD, known as Sativex, has been approved in Canada to treat pain and spasticity in multiple sclerosis patients.

In humans, cannabinoids produce a constellation of pharmacological and psychological effects including increased heart rate, reddened conjunctivae (the clear membranes covering the white part of the eye), impaired short-term memory, increased appetite, mild euphoria, perceptual alterations, time distortion, and intensified sensory experiences. Similarly, in laboratory animals, cannabinoids reliably produce a variety of effects including hypomotility (decreased activity of the gut), catalepsy (muscular rigidity), decreased pain sensitivity, hypothermia (decreased body temperature), memory impairment, and increased heart rate.

ENDOGENOUS CANNABINOID SYSTEM

Beginning in the early 1990s a series of discoveries revealed the existence of a naturally occurring cannabinoid system in humans and animals known as the endogenous cannabinoid (endocannabinoid) system. This system is comprised of two different receptors that have been identified and cloned, endogenous ligands (chemicals that bind to the receptors and activate them) and enzymes regulating the biosynthesis and degradation of these ligands (Ahn et al., 2008). CB_1 cannabinoid receptors are expressed throughout the central nervous system in brain regions regulating learning and memory, feeding, pleasure, emotionality, pain, and motor behavior, as well as in the periphery (Herkenham et al., 1991). These receptors are predominantly located presynaptically where their stimulation generally inhibits the release of neurotransmitters including GABA, glutamate, and acetylcholine throughout the central nervous system. In contrast, CB_2 cannabinoid receptors are primarily located in peripheral tissues, though these receptors are also present on microglial cells in the brain and are also expressed at low levels in brainstem neurons. While CB_1 cannabinoid receptors are responsible for the central nervous system (CNS) effects of cannabinoids, CB_2 cannabinoid receptors are associated with immune responses and their stimulation generally elicits anti-inflammatory effects. The availability of CB_1 (e.g., rimonabant) and CB_2 (e.g., SR144528) receptor antagonists has been useful in determining the receptor mechanism of action of different cannabinoids (Figure 1). Of note, rimonabant (Acomplia) has been medically approved in Europe and Mexico as a weight-loss drug for obese patients.

The two best characterized endocannabinoids that bind to and activate both cannabinoid receptors are n-arachidonoyl ethanolamine (anandamide), which is translated from the word "eternal bliss" in Sanskrit, and 2-arachidonoyl glycerol (2-AG), both of which vary greatly in structure from other cannabinoids (Figure 1). In contrast to classical neurotransmitters, which are stored in synaptic vesicles and released from the presynaptic neuron following an action potential, these lipid signaling molecules are enzymatically produced in the postsynaptic neuron upon demand through a calcium-dependent process and travel retrogradely (in a reverse direction) to the presynaptic neuron where they inhibit neurotransmitter release (Ahn et al., 2008). Following their

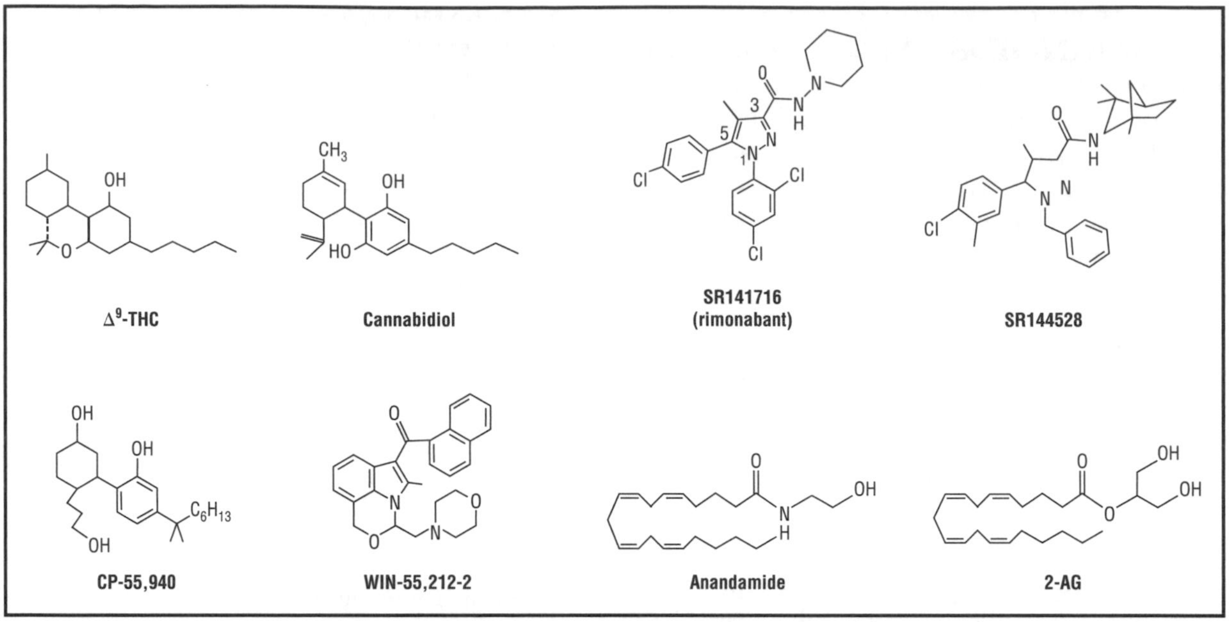

Figure 1. Structures of naturally occurring cannabinoids (Δ^9-THC and cannabindiol), synthetic cannabinoid analogs (CP-55,940 and WIN-55,212-2), the selective CB_1 antagonist rimonabant, the selective CB_2 receptor antagonist SR144528, and endogenous cannabinoids (anandamide and 2-AG). ILLUSTRATION BY GGS INFORMATION SERVICES. GALE, CENGAGE LEARNING

release, both anandamide and 2-AG are rapidly broken down. Anandamide degradation is regulated primarily by fatty acid amide hydrolase (FAAH), while monoacylglycerol lipase (MGL) and, to a lesser extent, α/β-hydrolase 6 and α/β-hydrolase 12, are responsible for 2-AG catabolism. Two sn-1-specific diacylglycerol lipases (DAGL$_\alpha$ and DAGL$_\beta$) have been identified that can produce 2-AG. Initially the sequential actions of an N-acyl phosphatidyl ethanol-amine-producing transacylase and a phospholipase D were hypothesized to regulate anandamide biosynthesis. However, genetically modified mice lacking this enzyme displayed normal endocannabinoid levels thus ruling out a direct role of these enzymes in anandamide biosynthesis. Alternative enzymatic pathways for anandamide biosynthesis are currently under investigation.

PHYSIOLOGICAL FUNCTION

Through the use of genetically altered mice and specific drugs that either disrupt or augment endocannabinoid signaling, accumulating evidence indicates that the endogenous cannabinoid system modulates a wide range of physiological processes (Pacher et al., 2006) including feeding, regulation of body weight, learning and memory, neuroprotective mechanisms from excitotoxic insults and traumatic brain injury, pain and inflammation, and substance abuse. CB_1 knockout mice as well as wild type mice that are treated with CB_1 receptor antagonists display decreases in food intake and lipogenesis (the synthesis of fatty acids) through distinct central and peripheral mechanisms. Drugs blocking CB_1 receptors also reduce behavioral effects of a variety of drugs including opioids (e.g., morphine), nicotine, and alcohol in laboratory animals. Additionally, endogenous cannabinoids are produced and released on demand to dampen the damage caused by brain injury or seizures in animal models. Drugs preventing the breakdown of the endocannabinoids reduce pain and inflammation as well as elicit antidepressant-like and anti-anxiety-like effects in laboratory animals. Finally, the endogenous cannabinoid system appears to modulate a specific type of learning called extinction in which learned behavior is suppressed when reinforcement is withheld (Lutz, 2007). Specifically, disruption of CB_1 receptor signaling disrupts the ability of mice to extinguish behaviors that are associated with aversive, but not positive, memories.

POTENTIAL

Cannabinoids are a diverse class of drugs that produce effects similar to those produced by marijuana.

The endogenous cannabinoid system modulates a wide variety of behaviors and physiological processes. A great deal of research is focused on elucidating the function of the endogenous cannabinoid system, and exploring its potential as a target for new pharmacotherapies.

See also **Cannabis; Cannabis Sativa; Marijuana (Cannabis).**

BIBLIOGRAPHY

Ahn, K., McKinney, M. K., & Cravatt, B. F. (2008). Enzymatic pathways that regulate endocannabinoid signaling in the nervous system. *Chemical Reviews, 108,* 1687–1707.

Herkenham, M., Lynn, A. B., Johnson, M. R., Melvin, L. S., de Costa, B. R., & Rice, K. C. (1991). Characterization and localization of cannabinoid receptors in rat brain: A quantitative in vitro autoradiographic study. *Journal of Neuroscience, 11,* 563–583.

Johnston, L. D., O'Malley, P. M., Bachman, J. G., & Schulenberg, J. E. (2007). *Monitoring the future national survey results on drug use, 1975–2006. Volume II: College students and adults ages 19-45* (NIH Publication No. 07-6206). Bethesda: National Institute on Drug Abuse.

Lutz, B. (2007). The endocannabinoid system and extinction learning. *Molecular Neurobiology, 36,* 92–101.

Mechoulam, R., Devane, W. A., Breuer, A., & Zahalka, J. (1991). A random walk through a cannabis field. *Pharmacology Biochemistry and Behavior, 40,* 461–464.

Pacher, P., Batkai, S., & Kunos, G. (2006). The endocannabinoid system as an emerging target of pharmacotherapy. *Pharmacological Reviews, 58,* 389–462.

ARON H. LICHTMAN

CANNABIS, INTERNATIONAL OVERVIEW.

The marijuana plant Cannabis sativa contains a bewildering array of organic chemicals, with representatives of almost all chemical classes present, including mono- and sesquiterpenes, carbohydrates, aromatics, and a variety of nitrogenous compounds. Interest in the study of this plant has largely focused on the resinous matter, as it is this material that is invested with the pharmacological activity peculiar to the plant. This resin is secreted by the female plant as a protective agent during seed ripening, although it can be found as a microscopic exudate through the aerial portions of plants of either sex. The pure resin, hashish or charas, is the most potent part of the plant and has served as the source material for most chemical studies. The family of chemicals isolated from this source has been referred to as the cannabinoid group.

The production of cannabinoids and their associated terpenes in cannabis is subject to environmental factors as well as hereditary determinants. Their biosynthesis occurs in specialized glands populating the surface of all aerial structures of the plant. These compounds apparently serve as defensive agents in a variety of antidessication, antimicrobial, antifeedant, and UV-B pigmentation roles. In addition, the more intense ambient UV-B of the tropics, in combination with the UV-B lability of cannabidiol, may have influenced the evolution of an alternative biogenetic route from cannabigerol to tetrahydrocannabinol in some varieties. Delta-9-tetrahydrocannabinol (THC) is the cannabinoid responsible for the main psychoactive effects of most cannabis drug preparations. THC is thought to be produced by the plant from cannabidiol (CBD) that, in turn, is derived from cannabigerol (CBG) generated from noncannabinoid precursors. It was isolated in 1964 by Raphael Mechoulam, Yechiel Gaoni, and Habib Edery of the Weizmann Institute in Rehovot, Israel. The pharmacological actions of THC result from its binding to the cannabinoid receptor CB1 located in the brain. These specialized receptors in the brain are for endogenous cannabinoids manufactured by the body such as anandamide, 2-arachidonyl glyceride (2-AG), and other related compounds. These cannabinoids have a natural role in pain modulation, control of movement, and memory. The natural role of cannabinoids in immune systems remains unclear. The brain develops tolerance to cannabinoids and animal research demonstrates the potential for dependence, but this potential is observed under a narrower range of conditions than exist for benzodiazepines, opiates, cocaine, or nicotine.

MEDICAL USE AND SIDE EFFECTS

As bewildering as the array of organic chemicals is the variety of claims made for cannabis and cannabinoids. THC may be an effective anticancer treatment, with studies from 1975 and 2007 showing tumor reduction in mice. A two-year study in which rats and mice were force-fed tetra-hydrocannabinol dissolved in corn oil showed reduced body mass, enhanced survival rates, and decreased tumor incidences in several sites, mainly organs under hormonal control. It also caused testicular atrophy and uterine and ovarian hypoplasia, as well as hyperactivity and convulsions immediately after administration. In mice, low doses of THC reduce the progression of atherosclerosis. A U.K.-based company, GW Pharmaceuticals, has developed Sativex, a cannabinoid pharmaceutical product, that is administered as an oral spray to be absorbed by the patient's mouth. In April 2005 the company received regulatory approval for the sale of this product in Canada for the symptomatic relief of neuropathic pain in multiple sclerosis and as an adjunctive analgesic treatment in patients with advanced cancer who experience moderate to severe pain during the highest tolerated dose of strong opioid therapy for persistent background pain.

On the other end of the spectrum, in 2007 *The Lancet* published a study indicating that cannabis users have, on average, a 41 percent greater risk of developing psychosis than nonusers. The risk was most pronounced in cases with an existing risk of psychotic disorder and was said to increase to 200 percent for the most frequent users. Some early-twenty-first-century research has also shown a correlation between cannabis use and increased cognitive function in schizophrenic patients.

EARLIER USE AND EFFORTS TO CONTROL

Although considerable debate surrounds the medical benefits and health risks of using cannabis products, there is no doubting their potential as a recreational drug. Details of cannabis' use in premodern Asian, African, and Arabic societies are difficult to rely on for various reasons, including, for example, the confusion between the terms *hashish* (cannabis), *afyūn* (opium), and *banj* (drugs) in medieval Islamic law. However, by the time Europeans began to observe consumption in these regions in the nineteenth century, it was clear that cannabis substances were varied and enjoyed multiple roles as medicines, tonics, and intoxicants. Local attitudes toward cannabis preparations were similarly varied, so that on the one hand they were embraced in marriage rituals

and religious festivals, and on the other they were featured in cautionary rhymes, such as the following from Sind, a poet from an historic area now within the borders of Pakistan:

> It is not charas but a curse.
> It burns the chest and heart to its worse.
> It brings on dimness of the eyes.
> To phlegm and cough it must give rise.
> To blind the eyes it never fails.
> Or cripple limbs that once were hale.
> In what but death, ends its sad tale?

Premodern governments adopted a variety of positions toward cannabis-consuming societies. Mughal administrators in eighteenth-century India sought to raise revenue by taxing trade in its preparations, while at one point in Egypt a prohibition was enforced whereby users of cannabis faced having their teeth pulled out as punishment for indulgence in the drug. Western governments first confronted the task of governing cannabis-consuming societies in the eighteenth century as parts of Asia and Africa became incorporated within European empires. Yet little consistency emerged as imperial administrators tended to adopt and adapt policies put in place by their predecessors. This led to a contradiction within the British Empire, for example, where officials in India remained content to allow locals to consume cannabis after paying a duty on it, while their counterparts in Egypt insisted on a complete ban. At one point, smugglers bought cannabis from the British in Bombay only to smuggle it into Egypt past the British officers of the Coastguard Camel Corps.

The international drug regulatory system that binds together all members of the United Nations (UN) within a common legal framework on intoxicating substances, including cannabis, had its origins in the politics of empire. Cannabis was first included in these regulations as a result of the 1925 meeting of the League of Nations in Geneva to discuss new opium controls. The substance had been scarcely featured in discussions about drugs before World War I in Shanghai or the Hague, and had been rarely mentioned in debates under the auspices of the League of Nations before 1925. However, at the 1925 meeting, the Egyptian delegate, Mohamed El Guindy, described cannabis as a "scourge which reduces man to the level of the brute and deprives him of health and reason, self-control and honour." Cannabis was not on the agenda for the League's second opium convention but a number of countries rallied to the Egyptian cause, particularly the United States. That country's delegation had little interest in the subject of cannabis, which was not viewed as a problem at home in the 1920s, but instead sought allies for its controversial proposals on opium. The United States may also have been attracted to the Egyptian agenda: to embarrass the capitulary powers, the European states that exercised colonial control over Egypt. Despite the opposition of the United Kingdom and the British administration in India, which derived a sizable revenue from taxing cannabis consumption there, the International Opium Convention (the 1925 Geneva Convention) included the first international controls on cannabis thanks to Egypt's intervention.

These events in 1925 created the international control regime for cannabis under particularly curious circumstances. A body controlled largely by Western government officials decided to impose controls on substances mainly consumed by Asians, Africans, and some South Americans, most of whom were not consulted about this major policy move, and despite the fact that there was little evidence presented or informed discussion. Indeed, the decisions of 1925 also meant that Western governments found themselves formulating laws and designing control mechanisms for cannabis before a domestic market even existed for it. One can thus argue that control options were therefore severely limited when consumers did eventually materialize in the West.

The growth in Western markets for cannabis products began in the 1930s in the United States. There in the Southern states, Mexican migrant workers brought their cannabis-using habits with them, and they soon spread across the nation via out-of-work Americans traveling the country in search of employment during the Great Depression. Cannabis was cheap and readily available; it easily grew in the warm environment of the South and proved an attractive option to the poor who could not afford alcohol as a recreational drug. In the United Kingdom in the 1950s, migrant workers from the country's Asian and African colonies brought their cannabis use with them as they arrived to meet the demand for labor in the postwar economy. Again, the poorer members of the indigenous community took to the migrant's intoxicant during a period of domestic austerity.

MODERN USE AND EFFORTS TO CONTROL

The picture changed in the 1960s when cannabis was adopted as an emblem of the counterculture in Western countries. As the drug was an intoxicant most associated with Asians, Africans, and South Americans, it served as a ready symbol of the rejection of the orthodoxies of Western society by middle-class white youth. In the decades since, domestic markets for cannabis have increased in Western societies, although this has less to do with its place in the short-lived counterculture movements of the 1960s and more to do with the nature of the hybridized youth cultures that have developed in urban centers and attached meanings to customs perceived to be "black" or "African" in origin. One recent study indicated that in the United Kingdom about 20 percent of 16- to 24-year-olds had used cannabis in the last year, compared with approximately 9 percent of the general population. In the United States, almost 7 percent of the 12 to 17 age group had used cannabis in the last month, and across the population 6 percent indulged during that same timeframe, representing about 14.8 million people.

Regulatory responses to these consumers have been framed within an international drug control system that became more restricted after World War II. The 1950s were a decade in which the reputation of cannabis sank to a new low, with the World Health Organization stating in 1954 that "there is no justification for the medical use of cannabis preparations" (WHO, 1954, p. 10). The 1961 UN Single Convention on Narcotic Drugs had as its basic principle the notion that nonmedical consumption of drugs should be prohibited, and it aimed to control cannabis more tightly by closer definition of the various preparations of the drug.

The UN has continued to take a hard line on cannabis since then; it has sought to maintain a consensus on the drug when faced with independent actions by individual states. For example, in 2003 the United Kingdom decided to reclassify cannabis and Philip Emafo, then the head of the International Narcotics Control Board, responded by arguing that "no government should take unilateral measures without considering the impact of its actions and ultimately the consequences for an entire system that took governments almost a century to establish" (BBC News, 2003). However, it is clear that most governments have moved away from severe sentences for possession of the smallest amounts of cannabis, which marked the 1960s.

Broadly speaking, the pattern in most Western countries is to limit the punishment for possession of small amounts of the drug that are most likely for personal consumption to warnings or small fines. More severe penalties are aimed at suppliers and traffickers of the drug. Possession usually remains an offense in these circumstances and, in effect, cannabis policy moves within the orbit of the police and the judiciary rather than politicians and legislators, as it is the discretion of the former that decides how cannabis users are treated. Since the 1960s a range of groups have emerged to represent all shades of cannabis consumers, from those who seek more ready access to the drug for medical reasons to those who seek to repeal all laws related to cannabis. As most Western governments have moved to a legal system where personal use rarely carries severe sentences, and as ongoing research into cannabis continues to reveal that its use may involve hazards as well as benefits, it is unlikely that groups campaigning for legalization will enjoy success in the near future.

See also **Cannabinoids; Cannabis Sativa; Epidemics of Drug Abuse in the United States; Hashish; International Drug Supply Systems; Marijuana (Cannabis); Tetrahydrocannabinol (THC).**

BIBLIOGRAPHY

Bock, A. W. (2000). *Waiting to inhale*. Santa Ana, CA: Seven Locks Press.

Bonnie, R. J. and Whitebread, C. H. (1974). *The marijuana conviction: The history of marijuana prohibition in the United States*. New York: The Lindesmith Center.

Booth, M. (2003). *Cannabis: A history*. New York: St. Martin's Press.

Cannabis law sends 'wrong signal' (February 26, 2003). BBC News. Available from http://news.bbc.co.uk/.

Courtwright, D. (2001). *Forces of habit: Drugs and the making of the modern world*. Cambridge, MA: Harvard University Press.

Grinspoon, L. & Bakalar J. B. (1979). *Psychedelic drugs reconsidered*. New York: The Lindesmith Center.

World Health Organization. (1954). Expert Committee on Drugs Liable to Produce Addiction. Fourth Report. Geneva.

JAMES MILLS

CANNABIS SATIVA.

CANNABIS SATIVA. This is the botanical name for the hemp plant that originated in Asia. It is the basis of the hemp industry as well as the source of the widely used intoxicant tetrahydrocannabinol (THC), the active agent in marijuana, hashish, ganja, and bhang.

HISTORY

The use of *Cannabis sativa* has been recorded for thousands of years, beginning in Asia. It was known to the ancient Greeks and later to the Arabs, who, during their spread of Islam from the seventh to the fifteenth centuries, also spread its use across the Levant and North Africa. Some 200–300 million people are estimated to use cannabis in some form worldwide. Thus, it is not only one of the oldest known but also one of the most widely used mind-altering drugs.

Since the 1960s, the rise in its use in the United States has been enormous and associated with the youth movement and countercultural revolution. Although the drug was in use before that time, it was popular only in some ethnic and specialized groups (e.g., jazz musicians). By the 1990s, some 30–40 million Americans are estimated to have used it and a substantial number use it regularly—although since 1979 the number of youngsters initiated into its use has been declining after a steep rise with an increasingly lower age of first use.

BOTANY

Cannabis sativa grows in the tropical, subtropical, and temperate regions. It is generally considered a single species of the mulberry family (Moraceae) with multiple morphological variants (e.g., *Cannabis indica* or *Cannabis americana*). It is an herb of varying size; some are quite bushy and attain a height of 10 to 15 feet (3 to 4.6 m). Due to genetic differences, some plants produce strong fibers (but little THC) and others produce a substantial quantity of THC but weak fibers. The fiber-producer is grown commercially for cloth, rope, roofing materials, and floor coverings; this was cultivated as a cash crop in colonial America for such purposes (Hart, 1980). During World War II, when it appeared that the United States might be cut off from Southeast Asian hemp, necessary to

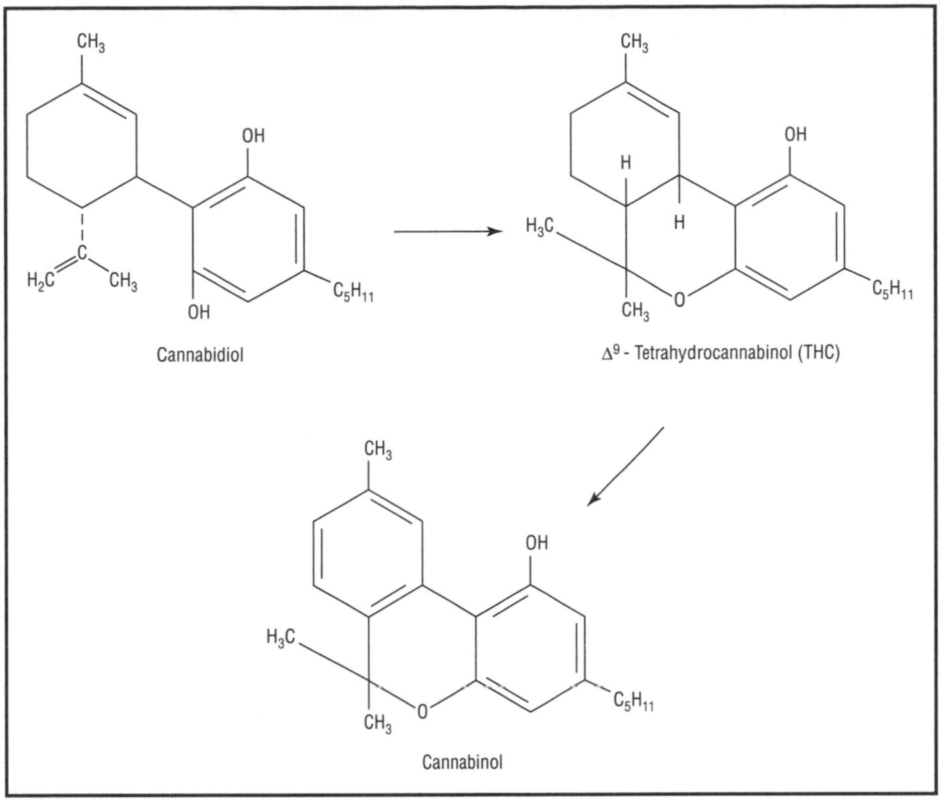

Figure 1. Biosynthetic pathway of cannabinoids. ILLUSTRATION BY GGS INFORMATION SERVICES. GALE, CENGAGE LEARNING

the war effort, the plants were cultivated in the mid-western states. Some of them continue to grow wild today, but since they are of the fiber-producing variety, they contain little drug content.

The drug-producing variety is widely cultivated in societies where its use is condoned. Illegal crops are also planted, some in the United States. The choice parts are the fresh top leaves and flowers of the female plant. The leaves have a characteristic configuration of five deeply cut serrated lobes. When they are harvested, they often resemble lawn cuttings—which accounts for the slang term "grass."

CHEMISTRY

The collective name given to the terpenes found in cannabis is *cannabinoids*. Most of the naturally occurring cannabinoids have now been identified, and three are the most abundant—cannabidiol (CBD), tetrahydrocannabinol (THC), and cannabinol (CBN). The steps from CBD to THC to CBN represent the biosynthetic pathway in the

plant. THC is an optically active resinous material that is very lipid-soluble but water-insoluble; these physical properties make pharmacological investigations difficult, since various nonpolar solvents must be used. Although many other materials have been found in this plant, the cannabinoids are unique to it and THC is the only one with appreciable mental affects. THC is believed to be largely, if not solely, responsible for the effects desired by those who use cannabis socially. Virtually all the effects produced by smoking or eating some of the whole plant can be attained by using THC alone.

USE AS A SOCIAL DRUG

Cannabis grows so easily that it is called a weed. In the United States, where it remains illegal, it is possible for those who wish to use it as a social drug to grow their own supply. The ease of cultivation keeps the price of imported illicit marijuana down, which helps account for some of its widespread use. Such cultivation is, however, as illegal as possession of the drug obtained from illicit "street" sources.

See also **Anslinger, Harry Jacob, and U.S. Drug Policy; Marijuana (Cannabis); Monitoring the Future; Tetrahydrocannabinol (THC).**

BIBLIOGRAPHY

Booth, M. (2005). *Cannabis: A history.* New York: MacMillan.

Earleywine, M. (2005). *Understanding marijuana: A new look at the scientific evidence.* New York: Oxford University Press USA.

Grotenhermen, F. (2002). *Cannabis and cannabinoids: Pharmacology, toxicology, and therapeutic potential.* London: Routledge.

Hart, R. H. (1980). *Bitter grass: The cruel truth about marihuana.* Shawnee Mission, KS: Psychoneurologia Press.

Razdan, R. K. (1986). Structure-activity relationships in cannabinoids. *Pharmacology Review, 38,* 75–148.

LEO E. HOLLISTER

CARIBBEAN, ILLICIT DRUGS IN.
Although the purview of this encyclopedia is all drugs, including alcohol and tobacco, the focus here is on marijuana, cocaine, and heroin, which are illegal substances that present a wide variety of societal and national security dangers for Caribbean countries. The dangers posed by these illicit substances threaten the stability and sovereignty of many of the nations in the region.

DIMENSIONS OF THE PROBLEM
Of the three substances mentioned above—marijuana, cocaine, and heroin—marijuana is the only substance produced in the Caribbean. The cultivation of marijuana varies among the region's countries. Belize, Guyana, Jamaica, St. Vincent and the Grenadines, and Trinidad and Tobago are among the countries with the highest levels of production. For decades, Jamaica had one of the highest levels of production and export, with the product being the nation's largest cash crop at times. *Ganja*, as marijuana is popularly called there and elsewhere in the Caribbean, is traditionally harvested after two main annual seasons of five- to six-month cycles. However, the *indica* variety matures in three or four months, making four harvests possible per year.

Economic conditions, the profitability of the drug market, geography, and the balloon effect of countermeasures in Belize, Jamaica, and Latin America (in which successful eradication efforts in one area only lead to increased production in another area, just as squeezing a balloon causes it to expand elsewhere) are among reasons that other Caribbean countries have taken to significant marijuana production and export, mainly to the United States. In the case of Guyana, for example, two principal features are conducive to myriad clandestine activities: physical geography and population density (with four people per square kilometer, Guyana has one of the lowest population densities in the world). It is therefore surprising that major marijuana cultivation did not begin there before the late 1980s.

Most of the marijuana cultivation in Trinidad and Tobago is done in the forested northern and central ranges and along the coast. As in Guyana and elsewhere, joint police-army operations, with notable support from the United States, are at the center of eradication and confiscation countermeasures. Elsewhere in the region, marijuana is cultivated in significant amounts in the Dominican Republic, French Guiana, Puerto Rico, St. Kitts-Nevis, and Suriname. As one might expect, there is variation in the size of plots cultivated—in some places production is primarily for domestic use, but in many areas the product is also grown for export.

The problem of narcotics consumption and abuse in the Caribbean involves mainly marijuana and cocaine, with heroin also being problematic in some places. Drug consumption and abuse in the region are not limited to any single social class or economic or ethnic group, although the consumption of certain drugs is higher in certain groups. Marijuana, for example, is predominantly the working-class drug of choice. Crack cocaine is widespread among the lower and middle classes because it has the attributes of being "hard" and a "status" drug, while also being inexpensive. Heroin, on the other hand, is a rich man's drug. Apart from the cost factor, the impact of heroin abuse in the region has been mitigated by a fear of using needles.

Like production, drug use differs from place to place. The greatest concern is in Jamaica, the Bahamas, the Dominican Republic, Guyana, Trinidad and Tobago, and in parts of the eastern Caribbean. While marijuana is abused in many places, it has a long history of accepted socioreligious use dating back to the introduction of indentured workers from India following the abolition of slavery. Indeed, the word *ganja* is a Hindi word. Marijuana's socioreligious use patterns have changed over the years. This use is now associated primarily with the Rastafarians, Afrocentric social-religious sects that identify with the late Ethiopian emperor Haile Selassie (1892–1975). Hence, socioreligious usage is found in places with significant numbers of Rastafarians, including Jamaica, the eastern Caribbean, Guyana, and Trinidad and Tobago.

Cocaine abuse in the Caribbean is a result of the spillover from the illicit cocaine trade. Crack cocaine is readily available in many places, particularly in the principal transit states: the Bahamas, Jamaica, Belize, the Dominican Republic, Guyana, Puerto Rico, and Trinidad and Tobago. Needless to say, cocaine addiction can lead to singularly devastating acts, as in the 1994 case in Guyana in which a 30-year-old deranged crack addict murdered six people, including his own mother, in a machete attack in a village along the Atlantic Coast.

Apart from trading their own ganja in the United States, Canada, and Europe, some Caribbean countries are important transshipment centers for South American cocaine, heroin, and ganja bound for Europe and North America. For more than two decades, the Bahamas, Belize, and Jamaica dominated this business, but in the first decade of the twenty-first century the Dominican Republic, Guyana, Haiti, Trinidad and Tobago, and eastern Caribbean countries have featured more prominently, as the 2008 edition of the U.S. State Department's *International Narcotics Control Strategy Report* shows. For instance, the geography of the Bahamian archipelago makes it an excellent candidate for drug transshipment, given its 700 islands and strategic location in the airline flight path between Colombia and southern Florida.

The geography and topography of Belize also make that country ideal for drug smuggling. There are large jungle areas, sparse settlements, and about 140 isolated airstrips that facilitate stops on flights from South America to North America. Moreover, there is virtually no radar coverage beyond the 30-mile radius of the international airport at Belize City. There has been an increasing use of maritime routes in and out of Belize, however. Crack has also been featured more prominently in the country's trade. Several features of the Dominican Republic make that country a prime trafficking candidate as well, including proximity to Colombia, the Bahamas, Puerto Rico, and the southern United States; a long, often desolate, 193-mile-long border with Haiti; a coastline of nearly 1,000 miles; and poorly equipped police and military authorities. As for Jamaica, it has long been important to the drug trade, given its long coastline; proximity to the United States; its many ports, harbors, and beaches; and its closeness to the Yucatan and Windward passages. Trafficking takes place by both air and sea in Jamaica.

DRUGS AND SECURITY

Thus, what generally is called "the drug problem" in the Caribbean is really a multidimensional phenomenon with considerable societal and national security implications. However, the phenomenon does not present a security challenge merely because of its production, trafficking, and other dimensions. It does so essentially because of the following reasons: (1) these aspects of the drug trade have multiple consequences and implications, such as marked increases in crime, systemic and institutionalized corruption, and arms trafficking, among other factors; (2) drug operations and their consequences have increased in scope and gravity since the 1980s; (3) drug smuggling has a dramatic impact on agents and agencies of national security and good governance, in military, political, and economic ways; and (4) the sovereignty of many countries is subject to infringement, by both state and non-state actors, because of drugs.

In the 1980s, most Caribbean leaders found it impolitic to accept that their countries faced a drug threat. Over the years, however, the scope and severity of the threat increased and became patently obvious to observers within and outside of the region. Leaders could, therefore, no longer deny it. In June 2000, at a multinational high-level meeting on criminal justice in Trinidad and Tobago, that country's attorney general made the following declaration on behalf of the Caribbean:

There is a direct nexus between illegal drugs and crimes of violence, sex crimes, domestic violence, maltreatment of children by parents and other evils.... Our citizens suffer from drug addiction, drug-related violence, and drug-related corruption of law enforcement and public officials. The drug lords have become a law unto themselves.... Aside from the very visible decimation of our societies caused by drug addiction and drug-related violence, there is another insidious evil: money laundering.... It changes democratic institutions, erodes the rule of law, and destroys civic order with impunity.

This statement by Attorney General Ramesh Lawrence Maharaj remains accurate and points clearly to the nexus between drugs and crime.

There is a local-global nexus in the region's drug-related crime, reflected in the fact that the crime is not all ad hoc, local crime; rather, some of it is transnational and organized, extending to North America, Europe, and elsewhere. Violent crime dramatizes the quotidian experiences of individual and corporate citizens in the Caribbean, reaching almost pandemic proportions in parts of the region. Indeed, a 2007 report by United Nations Office on Drugs and Crime (UNODC) and the World Bank indicated that murder rates in the Caribbean—at 30 per 100,000 population annually—were higher than in any other region of the world and had risen in recent years for many Caribbean countries. That study offers evidence of the wide-ranging economic, social, and other negative impact crime is having on the societies and nations in the region. In fact, as reported in an article titled "Crime Hurting Jamaica Tourism," in addressing the 47th Annual General Meeting of the Jamaica Hotel and Tourist Association in June 2008, Jamaica's Tourism Minister Edmund Bartlett averred dramatically, "Crime, in my mind, is the single most debilitating factor, the one area that is worrying to me beyond anything else, and I must tell you that the fuel crisis is not as worrying to me as crime. The turmoil in the aviation industry is not as worrying to me as crime."

Several aspects of drug-related crime are noteworthy. First, murder, fraud, theft, and assault are precisely the crimes likely to be associated with drugs. The experiences of the Bahamas, the U.S. Virgin Islands, Haiti, Guyana, Jamaica, Puerto Rico, Haiti, the Dominican Republic, and Trinidad and Tobago offer evidence of this. Clearly, then,

drugs and crime are among the clear and present dangers facing the region. This was highlighted at the highest levels of the Caribbean Community (CARICOM) in April 2008, when the CARICOM leaders convened for a special security summit in Trinidad. Drug-related crime is even more important because it affects tourism, a national economic enterprise. Caribbean observers have known for some time what the *New York Times* declared in April 1994: Drug-related crime has transformed the "paradise" character of the U.S. Virgin Islands and other Caribbean vacation spots, driving fear into locals and tourists alike and depressing tourism (Rohter, 1994).

MULTIPLE RESPONSES

A range of measures are being adopted by states in the Caribbean to fight this problem. These measures are multidimensional, multilevel (national, regional, and international), and multi-actor. They need to be multidimensional because drug operations and their impact occur on many different dimensions. They need to be multilevel because drug operations and many of the problems they precipitate are both national and transnational. Moreover, they have to be multi-actor for the above reason and because Caribbean governments lack the necessary financial and other resources to meet the threats and challenges facing their nations. Hence, antidrug efforts require the involvement not only of governments but also of corporate bodies, nongovernmental organization (NGOs), and regional and international agencies such as the Regional Security System (RSS), the Organization of American States (OAS), the Inter-American Drug Abuse Control Commission (CICAD), and the U.N. Office on Drugs and Crime (UNODC).

The kind and impact of efforts introduced and maintained depend on three main factors: perceptions of the nature and scope of the predicament, national capacity, and foreign support. National efforts are wide-ranging in scope, if not sufficiently substantive in character. They include law enforcement, education, interdiction, demand reduction, rehabilitation, crop substitution, improved port management, better regulation of financial services, and legislation. Circumstances are such that measures cannot be undertaken only sequentially, however. Education, rehabilitation, interdiction, and the other measures have to be applied at the same time. Indeed, in many places a misperception of the situation led to a failure to adopt simultaneous measures, which contributed to a worsening of the problem.

Foreign support is vital. Such assistance is not only bilateral, but multilateral as well, coming from the Europe Union, the OAS, and the UNODC, among other places. Most Caribbean countries have national drug councils that are supposed to set policy. They usually are composed of officials from various government agencies as well as NGOs and the private sector. The National Council on Drug Abuse (NCDA) of Jamaica, Programa para la prevención del uso indebido de drogas (PROPUID) of the Dominican Republic, the National Council for Drug Abuse Prevention (NaCoDAP) of the Netherlands Antilles, and the National Drug Council (NDC) of the Bahamas are a few examples of these bodies. Understandably, structures and operational efficiency vary from country to country.

In conclusion, it must be noted that all the Caribbean countries have joined the relevant international regimes, including the 1961 United Nations Single Convention on Narcotic Drugs; the 1971 Convention on Psychotropic Substances; and the 1988 Convention Against Illicit Traffic in Narcotic Drugs and Psychotropic Substances. Indeed, the Bahamas has the distinction of being the first country to ratify the 1988 convention, which it did on January 30, 1989. This convention includes provisions on drug trafficking, money laundering, organized crime, and arms trafficking, and it requires states to strengthen laws concerning financial reporting, extradition, asset forfeiture, and other subjects. It also urges adherents to improve cooperation in intelligence, interdiction, eradication, and other areas.

In terms of bilateral agreements, most Caribbean states have Mutual Legal Assistance Treaties (MLATs) with the United States. MLATs provide for training, joint interdiction, asset sharing, extradition, intelligence sharing, and material and technical support. Some countries, such as the Bahamas and Jamaica, have long had several complementary agreements with the United States. Bilateral treaties also exist with countries other than the United States. For instance, Belize has agreements with Mexico for intelligence sharing between the two, and for Mexican assistance with demand reduction

and rehabilitation. Bilateral agreements also exist between Suriname and Colombia, Suriname and Guyana, Cuba and Guyana, Venezuela and Guyana, Jamaica and Mexico, Suriname and the Netherlands Antilles, Trinidad and Tobago and Venezuela, Cuba and Panama, and other sets of countries.

See also **Cocaine; Colombia; Drug Interdiction; Foreign Policy and Drugs, United States; Heroin; International Control Policies; International Drug Supply Systems; Marijuana (Cannabis); Mexico; U.S. Government: Agencies in Drug Law Enforcement and Supply Control.**

BIBLIOGRAPHY

Crime hurting Jamaica tourism. (2008). *Caribbean360.com*, June 11. Available from http://www.caribbean360.com.

Griffith, I. L. (1997). *Drugs and security in the Caribbean: Sovereignty under siege.* University Park: Pennsylvania State University Press.

Griffith, I. L. (Ed.). (2000). *The political economy of drugs in the Caribbean.* London: Macmillan.

Griffith, I. L. (2006). Drugs, arms, and human security in the Caribbean. In S. Basdeo & H. Nicol (Eds.), *Caribbean integration and cooperation in the Americas* (pp. 108–133). Port of Spain, Trinidad and Tobago: Lexicon Books.

Griffith, I. L., & Munroe, T. (1995). Drugs and democracy in the Caribbean. *Journal of Commonwealth & Comparative Politics, 33*(3), 357–376.

Klein, A., Day, M., & Harriott, A. (Eds.). (2004). *Caribbean drugs: From criminalization to harm reduction.* London: Zed Books.

Maharaj, R. L. (2000). Remarks of Maharaj, the attorney general and minister of legal affairs of the Republic of Trinidad and Tobago at the opening of the Caribbean-United-States-European-Canadian Ministerial (Criminal Justice and Law Enforcement) Conference, Port of Spain, Trinidad, June 12–13, 2000.

Rodriquez-Beruff, J., & Cordero, G. (2004). The Caribbean: "The third border" and the war on drugs. In C. Youngers and E. Rosen (Eds.), *Drugs and democracy in Latin America: The impact of U.S. policy.* Boulder, CO: Lynne Rienner.

Rohter, L. (1994). Slaying in St. Thomas stains image of an "American paradise." *New York Times*, April 19.

United Nations Office on Drugs & Crime. (2007). *Crime, violence, and development: Trends, costs, and policy options in the Caribbean.* (Report No. 37820; A Joint Report by the United Nations Office on Drugs and Crime and the Latin American and the Caribbean Region of the World Bank.) New York: Author.

U.S. Department of State. (2008) *International narcotics control strategy report.* Washington, DC: Author.

IVELAW LLOYD GRIFFITH

CATECHOLAMINES. The catecholamines are a series of structurally similar amines (e.g., dopamine, epinephrine, norepinephrine that function as hormones, as neurotransmitters, or both. Catecholamines are produced by the enzymatic conversion of tyrosine, sharing the chemical root of 3, 4-dihydroxyphenylethanolamine. The three major catecholamines (mentioned above) derive from sequential enzymatic reactions—tyrosine is converted to dihydroxyphenylacetic acid (dopa); dopa, which is not an end product but a common intermediate (and the medication of choice for Parkinson's disease), is converted to dopamine; dopamine is converted to noradrenaline (also called norepinephrine); and noradrenaline is converted to adrenaline (also called epinephrine). These substances are the neurotransmitters for the sympathetic neurons (nerve cells) of the autonomic nervous system, as well as for three separate broad sets of brain neuropathways.

See also **Dopamine; Neurotransmitters; Norepinephrine.**

BIBLIOGRAPHY

Sadock, B. J., & Sadock, V. A. (2007). *Kaplan and Sadock's synopsis of psychiatry: Behavioral sciences/clinical psychiatry* (10th ed.). Philadelphia, PA: Lippincott, Williams & Wilkins.

FLOYD BLOOM

CAUSES OF SUBSTANCE ABUSE.
See **Risk Factors for Substance Use, Abuse, and Dependence.**

CHEMISTRY AND PHARMACOLOGY OF ALCOHOL. *See* **Alcohol: Chemistry and Pharmacology.**

CHILD ABUSE AND DRUGS. To provide perspective on the issues discussed in this entry, a description of the extent of child abuse and neglect and drug abuse follows. Some of the ways in which child abuse and drugs may be related are then discussed. For example, exposure to alcohol and other drugs (AOD) may have an impact on the child pre- or postnatally. Parental substance abuse may affect parenting and increase the risk of child abuse. Having a history of child abuse may increase a person's risk of having a substance-abuse problem. And children of substance-abusing parents may engage in some form of abuse or neglect of their own offspring.

Child-abusing parents and substance-abusing parents share certain risk factors, such as poor parenting skills, family disorganization, involvement in criminal activity, and a disproportionately high incidence of mental and physical illnesses. Thus, children growing up in such households may be at risk of adverse developmental, social, behavioral, and health consequences. However, not all children exposed will manifest negative consequences. Some of these children will manage to cope effectively with such adversities and others will be helped by positive interventions.

EXTENT OF CHILD ABUSE AND NEGLECT
In 2006, according to information collected as part of the National Child Abuse and Neglect Data System overseen by the U.S. Department of Health and Human Services, state and local child protective service agencies investigated 3,573,000 million referrals for children reported to be abused or neglected. Of these, about 905,000 were determined to be victims of abuse or neglect, representing 1,210 per 100,000 children in the United States. Three-quarters of these children had no history of prior victimization. Approximately 64 percent of the children experienced neglect, 16 percent were victims of physical abuse, 9 percent were victims of sexual abuse, and 7 percent were victims of emotional or psychological maltreatment. During 2006 an estimated 1,530 children from 0 to 17 years old died as a result of abuse or neglect at a rate of 2.04 children per 100,000 in the national population.

These statistics represent only the reported cases. Research suggests that the number of victims of child abuse and neglect in the United States is much higher, with estimates varying depending on definitions of maltreatment and the age of the groups surveyed. In one national population-based survey of children's self-reports and caregiver reports, Finkelhor, Ormrod, Turner, and Hamby (2005) estimated that a total of 14 percent of children in the United States had experienced some form of child maltreatment; 75 percent were victims of emotional abuse, 48 percent physical abuse, 22 percent neglect, and 8 percent sexual abuse.

EXTENT OF DRUG ABUSE

According to the Substance Abuse and Mental Health Services Administration (SAMHSA, 2004), an estimated 21.6 million (9.1%) of people in the United States were considered to have a substance use disorder (SUD) in 2003. Of these, approximately 15 million had alcohol dependence, 4 million had drug dependence, and about 3 million had both alcohol and drug dependence disorders. Using data from the National Household Survey on Drug Abuse, SAMHSA (2003) estimated that 6 million children (9%) lived with at least one parent who abused or was dependent on alcohol or an illicit drug during the past year. Findings from the National Longitudinal Alcohol Epidemiologic Survey indicated that approximately 15 percent of children were living in households with one or more adults who currently abused or were dependent on alcohol, and 43 percent of children lived with one or more adults who had abused or been dependent on alcohol at some time in their lives (Grant, 2000). Based on this data, Grant estimated that approximately one-fourth of children are exposed to alcohol abuse or dependence in their families. In 2002 and 2003, 4.3 percent of pregnant women reported the use of illicit drugs during the past month and 4.1 percent reported binge alcohol use (SAMHSA, 2005). In one study of 36 hospitals, mainly in urban areas, Freier, Griffith, and Chasnoff (1991) reported prenatal exposure to illegal drugs in approximately 11 percent of all births each year. In sum, a substantial number of children are being exposed to substances and parental substance-abuse problems one way or another in the United States.

IMPACT OF DRUG EXPOSURE ON CHILDREN

A number of states legally define in utero exposure to alcohol and other drugs as child abuse. All 50 states require mandated reporting of suspected child abuse. Although the states differ in terms of who is identified as a mandatory reporter, in most states medical or social services personnel are mandated to report such cases to protective services workers (Liss, 1994). Because of concerns about the consequences of being reported, these mandatory reporting laws can result in the avoidance of prenatal care by substance-abusing pregnant women. For this reason, social services employees may hesitate to notify authorities. In addition, the notification of authorities may appear to be racially biased and discriminatory if more poor women of color are referred. Although researchers continue to debate the value of mandatory reporting laws (Margolin et al., 2005), the effectiveness of these laws is not known.

Alcohol may have teratogenic effects (resulting in abnormalities in the fetus) leading to fetal alcohol syndrome (FAS), alcohol-related neurodevelopmental disorder (ARND), or alcohol-related birth defects (ARBD). The effects of other drugs have also been studied, such as cocaine, methamphetamine, marijuana, opiates, and phencyclidine (PCP). Although some children who have been exposed to these drugs or alcohol may manifest immediate problems, including drug withdrawal and developmental delays, with good postnatal environments many of them can overcome their exposure in utero if systemic damage is not severe. The major effects of most drugs at birth are preterm deliveries of low-birth-weight infants, indicative of growth retardation that may affect both mental and physical development.

The quality of an infant's postnatal environment as actively constructed by the mother or caregiver appears to be the most significant factor in determining the impact of drugs on the drug-exposed or non-drug-exposed infant. Studies find that children born to drug-abusing mothers can look normal or be resilient to their in utero (prenatal) exposure to drugs if they are provided with a nurturing environment that includes responsiveness to their needs, stimulation, and early childhood education.

Few longitudinal studies have tracked the impact of drug exposure on children. The longest follow-up study is of prenatal opiate-exposed children evaluated at 10 years of age. Moreover, it is very difficult to separate the impact of a poor postnatal environment from prenatal drug exposure (unless the children are adopted). The few longitudinal studies conducted of prenatal drug-exposed infants have determined that almost no long-term developmental problems are directly related to their drug exposure. A few cross-sectional studies of children of drug abusers have found clinically significant negative impacts on their emotional, academic, and behavioral status. These studies suggest that the greater the degree of maternal drug abuse, the greater the negative impact on the child's mental and behavioral status as measured by standardized clinical measures. One study, conducted by Adger (2000), found that children of alcoholics (COAs) are between four and nine times as likely to develop an alcohol use disorder as other children. These children are also at risk for other mental health problems, including internalizing problems such as depression and anxiety, as well as externalizing disorders such as attention deficit hyperactivity disorder, conduct disorder, and oppositional defiant disorder (Clark et al., 1997). Children of illicit drug abusers are more likely than other children to demonstrate immature, impulsive, or irresponsible behavior, and to have lower IQ scores and poorer school attendance. All these characteristics have been found to increase the risk of substance abuse.

Living with a parent who is actively abusing alcohol or other drugs causes stress for all family members, including very young children. Substance-abusing parents are often unable to be consistently available, either because of their own use or their concerns about their partner's use (Zucker, Ellis, Bingham, et al., 1996). The shame and stigma associated with substance-abuse problems makes their identification difficult, and often requires skillful screening, interviewing, and assessment of direct and indirect indicators.

Children can also be hurt by ingesting or inhaling alcohol and other drugs. Four major ways exist for children to become intoxicated: passive inhalation, accidental self-ingestion, being given drugs by a minor, and deliberate poisoning by an adult. In addition, infants can ingest alcohol, nicotine, and other drugs through breast milk. Passive inhalation of crack (freebase cocaine), PCP, marijuana, or hashish has negative effects.

The increase in methamphetamine abuse during the last decade, particularly among women of child-bearing age, has led to reports of children being physically and emotionally neglected and exposed to serious environmental hazards, such as dirty needles and toxic materials. Children living with parents who manufacture synthetic designer drugs in their homes, such as methamphetamine, are exposed to hazardous toxic chemicals. Some substance-abusing parents allow their children to drink alcohol or use the drugs they find lying around the house. Some parents deliberately give their children alcohol or other drugs (i.e., tincture of opium) to reduce their crying, sedate them, or induce intoxication to amuse the parents. Any relatively healthy child with unexplained neurological symptoms, seizures, or death may have been exposed to drugs.

SUBSTANCE ABUSE AND RISK OF CHILD ABUSE

Child welfare authorities consider parental substance abuse to be a major risk factor for child abuse. An estimated 40 to 80 percent of the 3 million children who come to the attention of the child welfare system live in families with AOD problems (Young, Gardner, & Dennis, 1998). In addition, a 1997 Child Welfare League of America (CWLA) study of state child welfare agencies estimated that 67 percent of parents in the child welfare system required substance-abuse treatment services.

Under the influence of alcohol and other drugs, adults are less inhibited and have reduced judgment and emotional control. Uppers (stimulants such as cocaine, methamphetamine, PCP, and amphetamines) can cause anxiety, irritability, paranoia, and aggressiveness. Downers (depressants such as alcohol, opiates, sedatives, and barbiturates) have also been related to depression, irritability, and loss of control while disciplining children. It has been suggested that organic brain damage, hypoglycemia, and sleep disturbances caused by alcohol exacerbates child abuse by alcoholics. Substance-abusing parents are often irritable and angry because of neurochemical imbalances caused by persistent drug abuse.

Children of substance abusers are frequently more difficult to parent because of the increased prevalence of attention deficit disorder (ADD), hyperactivity, conduct disorders, and learning disorders. Some so-called difficult temperament characteristics are caused by in utero exposure to drugs, some by genetic inheritance, and others by lack of nurturing and inconsistent parenting. However, these characteristics in children may place them at risk for being abused.

Psychosocial risk factors for child abuse include the following:

- *Poverty and Stress.* Many children of drug-abusing parents or caretakers are raised in poverty. Money that would normally be available for food, clothing, transportation, medical and dental care, and to provide social and educational opportunities for the children is often diverted to purchases of alcohol and drugs. Crack-addicted parents sometimes use food stamps and welfare checks to purchase crack. Lack of money to handle daily crises elevates the usual level of life stressors and increases parental anger and irritability. Unemployment, which frequently results in low self-esteem, can lead to increased child abuse.

- *Poor Parenting Skills.* Drug-abusing parents or caretakers have been found to have less adequate parenting skills, spend less time with their children, have unrealistic developmental expectations that can lead to excessive punishment, and lax or inconsistent discipline. Verbal abuse in the form of threatening, chastising, belittling, and criticizing are common.

- *Family Violence and Conflict.* High levels of family conflict found in drug-abusing families can lead to family violence, and drug abusers often belong to subcultures where violence is commonplace. The absence of empathy and support among family members in the home environment increases the risk of child abuse and family violence.

- *Mental Disorders.* Approximately 90 percent of drug abusers have other mental disorders, such as depression, bipolar-affective disorder, narcissism, antisocial personality, organic brain disease, and psychosis. Mental disorders of this nature can have a severe impact on a person's ability to parent and may lead to child abuse. Depression, bipolar disorder, and psychosis can cause parents to become angry, irrational, and abusive, whereas parents with personality disorders may be impulsive.

- *Physical Illness and Handicaps.* Physical illness and physical handicaps can reduce the patience parents need to handle the stress inherent in dealing with children. Physical illness is more common in substance-abusing families because of their lifestyle and lack of preventive health care. Intravenous drug abusers and their children have higher rates of common infections, as well as increased exposure to diseases transmitted through the blood (HIV/AIDS and hepatitis), sexually transmitted diseases (syphilis, gonorrhea, and herpes), and tuberculosis.

- *Criminal Involvement.* Drug-abusing parents are at high risk for criminal involvement by nature of their use alone or by the need to obtain considerable sums of money to support their habit. Prostitution, theft, and drug dealing are reported in about half of all drug-abusing parents. Arrest and incarceration may increase the stress on the family and can reduce inhibitions against sexual abuse upon reunification of the family.

Alcohol and drug use and abuse have also been directly implicated as risk factors for becoming abusive or neglectful. For example, some studies have reported a relationship between parental alcohol abuse and parental perpetration of physical child abuse (Chaffin, Kelleher, & Hollenberg, 1996; Kelleher, Chaffin, Hollenberg, et al., 1994; Kotch, Browne, Dufort, et al., 1999). Others have not found such an association, or the associations that were found were limited to certain subgroups of alcohol-using parents (Miller, Maguin, & Downs, 1997). In one 18-year longitudinal study of a New Zealand birth cohort, Woodward and Fergusson (2002) found that young people reared by mothers with a history of alcohol or drug problems and depression tended to report higher levels of their mother's use of physical punishment and child maltreatment during childhood (birth to age 16).

High rates of physical abuse have been reported in alcoholic and opiate-addicted families. In one study, conducted by Miller and co-workers (1997), mothers with histories of alcohol problems were more likely to report using harsh punishment on their children compared to women without such histories. Studies have also reported that parental drinking or a family history of alcoholism was a risk factor for childhood sexual abuse. Miller and her colleagues also speculated that parental alcohol abuse may increase a child's vulnerability to sexual abuse by interfering with the parents' ability to provide a supportive, nurturing, and protective environment. Other research (Fleming, Mullen, & Bammer, 1997) has found several factors associated with a girl's risk of being sexually abused, including experiencing physical abuse; having a mother who is mentally ill; being socially isolated; and not having someone in whom to confide. In addition, whereas an alcoholic father was found to be a risk factor for childhood sexual abuse by a family member, an alcoholic mother was a risk factor for childhood sexual abuse by a person outside the family.

Child molesters are often intoxicated when the abuse occurs. Alcohol's influence on the brain allows a disinhibition of socially proscribed behaviors, including incest and the sexual molestation of children. A 1988 study found 48 percent of fathers who had committed incest were alcoholic but that 63 percent of fathers were drinking at the time of the abuse. However, further research is needed about the extent and nature of the connection between parental AOD and subsequent child abuse.

CHILD ABUSE AS A RISK FACTOR FOR SUBSTANCE ABUSE

A high percentage of drug abusers, particularly those in inpatient and residential treatment programs, report having been sexually abused as children (Dansky, Saladin, Brady, et al., 1995; Moran, Vuchinich, & Hall, 2004; Navajits, Weiss, & Shaw, 1997; Schiff, El-Bassel, Engstrom, et al., 2002; Wallen & Berman, 1992). However, few prospective longitudinal studies have been conducted to determine whether abused and neglected children are more likely to develop AOD problems when they grow up, compared to similar but nonabused children. Of the existing studies, the most consistent finding is that childhood abuse and neglect may increase the risk for alcohol and drug problems, particularly among women. Widom and colleagues followed a large group of children with documented cases of physical and sexual abuse and neglect, and assessed the extent to which they developed alcohol and other drug problems in adulthood. At the approximate age of 29, women

(but not men) with documented histories of childhood abuse and/or neglect were at increased risk for alcohol abuse (but not drug abuse) (Widom, Ireland, & Glynn, 1995; Widom, Weiler, & Cottler, 1999). In a further follow-up, abused or neglected women (but not men) remained at risk for alcohol problems (Widom, White, Czaja, et al., 2007), compared to nonabused and non-neglected participants; but at age 40, they also reported the use of illicit drugs (marijuana, cocaine, heroin, and psychedelics) (Widom, Marmorstein, & White, 2006).

In sum, there are a number of ways in which child abuse and drugs may be related. Unfortunately, it is difficult to draw firm policy conclusions from the existing empirical research because of a number of methodological limitations and challenges inherent in research in this area. Ambiguous definitions of child abuse and neglect, varying age ranges defining childhood, varying definitions of alcohol and substance-abuse problems, reliance on retrospective self-reports, use of specialized treatment samples, and lack of control groups threaten the validity and generalizability of findings. Although there is strong justification to expect several levels of association between child abuse and drug abuse, convincing and consistent evidence does not yet exist.

PROPOSED RESPONSES

Reasonable evidence exists to suggest that children who are raised by substance-abusing parents are at increased risk for a number of adversities in childhood, including being abused or neglected; witnessing domestic violence; and being exposed to parents with problems associated with substance abuse (high rates of mental illness, criminal behavior, suicide attempts, etc.). Although more research is needed on the long-term effects of having substance-abusing parents, alcohol and substance-abuse treatment agencies should routinely ask their clients if they have been or are being physically or sexually abused. It is also important that child welfare agencies determine whether caregiver or family member substance abuse is present. In these cases, prevention will depend on advances in the identification and treatment of substance-abusing parents, particularly in primary care settings. The school setting is another primary site for the provision of services to children affected by parental substance abuse through a variety of programs targeting children of different ages.

Because it is not possible to remove all children from risky family environments, additional research is needed on ways to protect children. Caregivers and professionals can help maltreated children develop coping strategies that do not involve alcohol and/or drugs and help them become more resilient so as to avoid future alcohol and drug abuse. Some children are resilient to negative outcomes, even though they were exposed to drugs in utero or lived with drug-abusing parents. Some of these children might have been sheltered by a caring adult who addressed their needs. The emerging literature on resiliency processes and mechanisms should be reviewed (Rutter, 1990) and used to inform research with children of drug abusers to make preventive interventions more effective.

Children of drug-addicted mothers may be resilient to their high-risk environments if their mothers realize the negative impact of their chaotic lives on their infants and work to improve their parenting skills. Improvement may include finding external supports to learn parenting skills, such as parent-and-family-skills training programs; locating good early childhood education for the child and outside child care; and possibly even considering foster care or adoption. Research has shown more positive outcomes for drug-exposed infants when the mothers were willing to use external social supports when necessary to provide the best opportunities for learning and emotional growth for the child.

See also **Attention Deficit Hyperactivity Disorder; Coping and Drug Use; Families and Drug Use; Fetal Alcohol Syndrome; U.S. Government Agencies: National Institute on Alcohol Abuse and Alcoholism (NIAAA); U.S. Government Agencies: National Institute on Drug Abuse (NIDA).**

BIBLIOGRAPHY

Adger, H. (2000). Children in alcoholic families: Family dynamics and treatment issues. In S. Abbott (Ed.), *Children of alcoholics: Selected readings*, Volume II (pp. 385–395). Rockville, MD: National Association of Children of Alcoholics.

Chaffin, M., Kelleher, K., & Hollenberg, G. J. (1996). Onset of physical abuse and neglect: Psychiatric, substance abuse, and social risk factors from prospective community data. *Child Abuse and Neglect, 20*(3), 191–203.

Child Welfare League of America (CWLA) (1997). *Alcohol and other drug survey of state child welfare agencies.* Available from http://www.cwla.org/.

Clark, D. B., Moss, H. B., Kirisci, L., Mezzich, A. C., Miles, R., & Ott, P. (1997). Psychopathology in pre-adolescent sons of fathers with substance use disorders. *Journal of the American Academy of Child and Adolescent Psychiatry, 36*(4), 495–502.

Dansky, B. S., Saladin, M. E., Brady, K. T., Kilpatrick, D. G., & Resnick, H. S. (1995). Prevalence of victimization and posttraumatic stress disorder among women with substance use disorders: Comparison of telephone and in-person assessment samples. *Substance Use & Misuse, 30*, 1079–1099.

Finkelhor, D., Ormrod, R., Turner, H., & Hamby, S. L. (2005). The victimization of children and youth: A comprehensive national survey. *Child Maltreatment, 10*, 5–25.

Fleming, J., Mullen, P., & Bammer, G. (1997). A study of potential risk factors for sexual abuse in childhood. *Child Abuse & Neglect, 21*(1), 49–58.

Freier, M. C., Griffith, D. R., & Chasnoff, I. J. (1991). In utero drug exposure: Developmental follow-up and maternal-infant interaction. *Seminars in Perinatology, 15*, 310–316.

Grant, B. (2000). Estimates of U.S. children exposed to alcohol abuse and dependence in the family. *American Journal of Public Health, 90*, 112–114.

Kelleher, K., Chaffin, M., Hollenberg, J., & Fischer, E. (1994). Alcohol and drug disorders among physically abusive and neglectful parents in a community-based sample. *American Journal of Public Health, 84*(10), 1586–1590.

Kotch, J. B., Browne, D., Dufort, V., Winsor, J., & Catellier, D. (1999). Predicting child maltreatment in the first four years of life from characteristics assessed in the neonatal period. *Child Abuse & Neglect, 23*, 305–319.

Liss, M. (1994). Child abuse: Is there a mandate for researchers to report? *Ethics & Behavior, 4*, 133–146.

Margolin, G.., Chien, D., Duman, S. E., Fauchier, A., Gordis, E. B., Oliver, P. H., et al. (2005). Ethical issues in couple and family research. *Journal of Family Psychology, 19*, 157–167.

May, P. A., & Gossage, J. P. (2001). Estimating the prevalence of fetal alcohol syndrome: A summary. *Alcohol Research & Health, 25*(3), 159–167.

Miller, B. A., Maguin, E., & Downs, W. R. (1997). Alcohol, drugs, and violence in children's lives. In M. Galanter (Ed.), *Recent developments in alcoholism, Volume 13: Alcohol and violence: Epidemiology, neurobiology, psychology, family issues* (pp. 357–385). New York: Plenum Press.

Moran, P. B., Vuchinich, S., & Hall, N. K. (2004). Associations between types of maltreatment and substance use during adolescence. *Child Abuse & Neglect, 28,* 565–574.

Najavist, L. M., Weiss, R. D., & Shaw, S. R. (1997). The link between substance abuse and posttraumatic stress disorder in women: A research review. *American Journal on Addictions, 6,* 273–283.

National Institute on Drug Abuse (1996). *National Pregnancy and Health Survey: Drug use among women delivering live births: 1992.* Rockville, MD: Author.

Rutter, M. (1990). Psychosocial resilience and protective mechanisms. In J. E. Rolf et al. (Eds.), *Risk and protective factors in the development of psychopathology.* New York: Cambridge University Press.

Schiff, M., El-Bassel, N., Engstrom, M., & Gilbert, L. (2002). Psychological distress and intimate physical and sexual abuse among women in methadone maintenance treatment programs. *Social Service Review, 76,* 302–320.

Straussner, S. L. A., & Fewell, C. H. (Eds.). (2006). *Impact of substance abuse on children and families: Research and practice implications.* Philadelphia: Haworth Press.

Streissguth, A. P. (1994). A long-term perspective of FAS. *Alcohol Health and Research World, 18,* 74–81.

Substance Abuse and Mental Health Services Administration. (2003). *Children living with substance-abusing or substance-dependent parents.* National Household Survey on Drug Abuse. Rockville, MD: Author.

Substance Abuse and Mental Health Services Administration. (2004). *Overview of findings from the 2003 National Survey on Drug Use and Health.* Office of Applied Studies, NSDUH Series H-24, DHHS Publication No. SMA 04-3963. Rockville, MD: Author.

Substance Abuse and Mental Health Services Administration. (2005). *Substance use during pregnancy: 2002 and 2003 update.* National Survey on Drug Use and Mental Health. Rockville, MD: Author.

U.S. Department of Health and Human Services, Administration for Children, Youth and Families. (2007). *Child maltreatment 2006.* Washington, D.C.: U.S. Government Printing Office. Available from http://www.acf.hhs.gov/.

Wall, A. E., & Kohl, P. L. (2007). Substance use in maltreated youth: Findings from the National Survey of Child and Adolescent Well-Being. *Child Maltreatment, 12*(1), 20–30.

Wallen, J., & Berman, K. (1992). Possible indicators of childhood sexual abuse for individuals in substance abuse treatment. *Journal of Child Sexual Abuse, 1,* 63–74.

Widom, C. S., & Hiller-Strumhofel, S. (2001). Alcohol abuse as a risk factor for and consequence of child abuse. *Alcohol Research and Health, 25*(1), 52–57.

Widom, C. S., Ireland, T., & Glynn, P. J. (1995). Alcohol abuse in abused and neglected children followed-up: Are they at increased risk? *Journal of Studies on Alcohol, 56,* 207–217.

Widom, C. S., Marmorstein, N. R., & White, H. R. (2006). Childhood victimization and illicit drug use in middle adulthood. *Psychology of Addictive Behaviors, 20*(4), 394–403.

Widom, C. S., Weiler, B. L., & Cottler, L. B. (1999). Childhood victimization and drug abuse: A comparison of prospective and retrospective findings. *Journal of Consulting and Clinical Psychology, 67*(6), 867–880.

Widom, C. S., White, H. R., Czaja, S. J., & Marmorstein, N. R. (2007). Long-term effects of child abuse and neglect on alcohol use and excessive drinking in middle adulthood. *Journal of Studies on Alcohol and Drugs, 68*(3), 317–326.

Woodward, L. J., & Fergusson, D. M. (2002). Parent, child, and contextual predictors of childhood physical punishment. *Infant and Child Development, 11*(3), 213–235.

Young, N., Gardner, S., & Dennis, K. (1998). *Responding to alcohol and other drug problems in child welfare.* Washington, DC: CWLA Press.

Zucker, R. A., Ellis, D. A., Bingham, C. R., & Fitzgerald, H. E. (1996). The development of alcoholic subtypes: Risk variations among alcoholic families during the childhood years. *Alcohol, Health and Research World, 20*(1), 46–54.

KAROL L. KUMPFER
JAN BAYS
REVISED BY CATHY SPATZ WIDOM (2009)

CHILDHOOD BEHAVIOR AND LATER SUBSTANCE USE.

A wealth of research has investigated connections between early childhood behavior and later substance use. Studies have examined a range of constructs in isolating predictors of later substance use and misuse. This review provides an overview of key findings and theoretical constructs, including temperamental factors, social learning theory, primary socialization theory, and genetic influences. Although most children and adolescents who experiment with substances do not go on to develop a substance use disorder, most adults with substance use disorders began using substances as youths (Substance Abuse and Mental Health Services Administration, 2005). Thus, understanding the nature of childhood substance use is crucial to understanding the trajectory toward abuse and dependence.

PERSONALITY FACTORS AFFECTING DRUG USE

Longitudinal personality research has isolated early temperamental predictors of later substance use. Factors of childhood personality have been strongly related to adolescent personality, which is in turn related to adolescent and young adult substance use (Brook et al., 1995). A now-classic study by Jack Block, Jean Block, and Susan Keyes (1988) found personality factors such as poor impulse control, uninhibited emotional expression, and decreased emotional adaptability predicted later marijuana and hard-drug use. Thomas A. Wills and colleagues (2000) showed that high physical activity level, negative emotionality, and inflexibility were risk factors for later substance use. Protective factors against later substance use included the capacity to focus and the ability to experience and express positive emotions (Wills et al., 2000). The environment plays a strong role in the expression and modulation of heritable (capable of being inherited) temperamental traits. For example, life stressors and deviant peer networks have predicted lower impulse control, which increases the risk for later drug use (Wills et al., 2000). Conversely, children who display high levels of impulse control and the capacity to delay reward have demonstrated less vulnerability in response to external stressors (Wills et al., 2000). In summary, certain temperamental traits are predictive of later substance use, but a complex relationship exists between innate traits and the mediating influence of environment in the expression of those traits.

SOCIAL LEARNING THEORY

Social learning theory suggests that parental and peer modeling of substance use influences both the substance-related behaviors of children and children's expectations about the consequences of use. Social learning theory posits three sequential stages of action: (a) observation and imitation, (b) social encouragement and support, and (c) positive expectations toward future substance use (Peratritis et al., 1995). Albert Bandura, the first proponent of social learning theory, emphasized a strong cognitive component, focusing on the shaping of expectancies and pointing out that observation can equip adolescents with the skills either to acquire and use or to reject substances (Peratritis et al., 1995). Accordingly, greater parental use, peer use, and more substance offers have been associated with greater risk of adolescent substance use (Castro et al., 2006; Li et al., 2002). Conversely, parental non-use has demonstrated a buffering effect on the powerful influence of peer use (Li et al., 2002).

PRIMARY SOCIALIZATION THEORY

Primary socialization theory postulates that the socialization process shapes the nature and strength of attitudes and social behaviors, including norms related to drug use. Strong positive affiliations with socialization groups such as families, school systems, and religious groups are more likely to result in the transmission of conventional norms and result in pro-social behavior. Adolescents with higher religiosity have a lower incidence of substance use disorders (Miller et al., 2000), a relationship that extends into adulthood (Kendler et al., 1997). Weak bonds with socialization groups are more likely to result in affiliation with deviant peer clusters, which may ultimately result in deviant behaviors such as substance use (Oetting & Donnermeyer, 1998a). Weak bonds with family are commonly associated with lack of effective parental monitoring, which in turn relates to substance use initiation, escalation, and advancement to abuse (Chilcoat et al., 1996; Reifman et al., 1998; Getz and Bray, 2005). Association with substance-using peers has a well-documented relationship with adolescent experimental substance use (e.g. Petraitis et al., 1995; Getz & Bray, 2005; Mason et al., 2007). Recent work suggests a reciprocal relationship wherein association with substance-using peers directly encourages use, while adolescents who use are more likely to select friends who use substances (Simons-Morton, 2007). Additionally, certain traits such as anger, aggression, and sensation seeking and psychopathologies such as attention deficit hyperactivity disorder, conduct disorder, oppositional defiant disorder, and antisocial personality disorder interfere with the primary socialization process and make substance use more likely (Oetting et al., 1998b).

GENETIC INFLUENCES

Genetic factors, widely studied in differentiating pathways of substance use, are likely instrumental in the transition from use in childhood to dependency in adulthood (Hasin et al., 2006; Rose & Dick, 2004–2005). Laura Jean Bierut et al. (1998) found genetic risks for substance use disorders to be both common (i.e., one predisposing factor for all substance use disorders) and substance-specific (i.e., distinct genetic factors for alcohol, marijuana, cocaine, and nicotine). Kenneth S. Kendler and colleagues (2003) found only common genetic risks for substance abuse and dependency. A later twin study identified substance-specific factors for both licit and illicit drugs and even further specificity for nicotine and caffeine dependence (Kendler, 2007). Howard J. Edenberg et al. (2004) found a gene that significantly predicts alcohol dependence, a relationship that may be influenced by a neural response to alcohol. Generally speaking, genetic studies have been most conclusive regarding alcohol, demonstrating a heritability of 50–60 percent (Hasin et al., 2006).

CONCLUSION

Early experimental substance use predicts later substance use disorders, and both are related to a variety of intrapersonal, social/contextual, and biological factors. Certain childhood personality traits are associated with adolescent traits, which later relate to experimental substance use. The power of these traits is strengthened or limited through complex environmental interactions. Social learning theory provides a useful framework for understanding how parental and peer modeling of behavior and shaping of expectancies can profoundly influence substance use behavior. Primary socialization theory highlights the important role of social networks in the transmission of behavioral norms about substance use. Naturalistic studies have demonstrated the profound influence parental substance use and quality of child supervision have upon risk for or protection against child substance use. Likewise, having friends who use substances is implicated in both the development and escalation of substance use. While genetic studies have demonstrated a heritable risk for alcohol dependence, it is unclear whether dependence risks are substance-specific or general.

An understanding of these complex and various forces is crucial in more skillfully approaching substance use disorders at the public health level. Current research is focusing on the relative influence of individual variables and their interactions within multi-factorial models. One recent study of a biosocial model, for example, found that intrapersonal influences on substance use behavior become more powerful in more harmful contexts (Foshee et al., 2007). Powerful integrative models provide hope for greater adaptability of research across contexts and effectiveness in translating this work into viable treatment and prevention programs.

See also **Child Abuse and Drugs; Conduct Disorder and Drug Use; Coping and Drug Use; Families and Drug Use; Intimate Partner Violence and Alcohol/ Substance Use.**

BIBLIOGRAPHY

Bierut, L. J., Dinwiddie, S. H., Begleiter, H., Crowe, R. R., Hesselbrock, V., Nurnberger, J. I., Jr., et al. (1998). Familial transmission of substance dependence: Alcohol, marijuana, cocaine, and habitual smoking: A report from the collaborative study on the genetics of alcoholism. *Archives of General Psychiatry, 55*(11), 982–988.

Block, J., Block, J. H., & Keyes, S. (1988). Longitudinally foretelling drug usage in adolescence: Early childhood personality and environmental precursors. *Child Development, 59*(2), 336–355.

Brook, J. S., Whiteman, M., Cohen, P., & Shapiro, J. (1995). Longitudinally predicting late adolescent and young adult drug use: Childhood and adolescent precursors. *Journal of the American Academy of Child & Adolescent Psychiatry, 34*(9), 1230–1238.

Castro, F. G., Brook, J. S., Brook, D. W., & Rubenstone, E. (2006). Paternal, perceived maternal, and youth risk factors as predictors of youth stage of substance use: A longitudinal study. *Journal of Addictive Diseases, 25*(2), 65–75.

Chilcoat, H. D., & Anthony, J. C. (1996). Impact of parent monitoring on initiation of drug use through late childhood. *Journal of the American Academy of Child & Adolescent Psychiatry, 35*(1), 91–100.

Edenberg, H. J., Dick, D. M., Xuei, X., Tian, H., Almasy, L., Bauer, L., et al. (2004). Variations in GABRA2, encoding the alpha 2 subunit of the GABA(A) receptor, are associated with alcohol dependence and with brain oscillations. *American Journal of Human Genetics, 74,* 705–714.

Foshee, V. A., Ennett, S. T., Bauman, K. E., Granger, D. A., Benefield, T., Suchindran, C., et al. (2007). A test of biosocial models of adolescent cigarette and alcohol involvement. *Journal of Early Adolescence, 27*(1), 4–39.

Getz, J. G., & Bray, J. H. (2005). Predicting heavy alcohol use among adolescents. *American Journal of Orthopsychiatry, 75*(1), 102–116.

Hasin, D., Hatzenbuehler, M., & Waxman, R. (2006) Genetics of substance use disorders. In W. R. Miller & H. M. Carroll (Eds.), *Rethinking substance abuse: What the science shows and what we should do about it.* New York: Guilford.

Kendler, K. S., Gardner, C. O., & Prescott, C. A. (1997). Religion, psychopathology, and substance use and abuse: A multimeasure, genetic-epidemiologic study. *American Journal of Psychiatry, 154*(3), 322–329.

Kendler, K. S., Jacobson, K. C., Prescott, C. A., & Neale, M. C. (2003). Specificity of genetic and environmental risk factors for use and abuse/dependence of cannabis, cocaine, hallucinogens, sedatives, stimulants, and opiates in male twins. *American Journal of Psychiatry, 160*(4), 687–696.

Kendler, K. S., Myers, J., & Prescott, C. A. (2007). Specificity of genetic and environmental risk factors for symptoms of cannabis, cocaine, alcohol, caffeine, and nicotine dependence. *Archives of General Psychiatry, 64*(11), 1313–1320.

Li, C., Pentz, M. A., & Chou, C. (2002). Parental substance use as a modifier of adolescent substance use risk. *Addiction, 97*(12), 1537–1550.

Mason, W. A., Hitchings, J. E., McMahon, R. J., & Spoth, R. L. (2007). A test of three alternative hypotheses regarding the effects of early delinquency on adolescent psychosocial functioning and substance involvement. *Journal of Abnormal Child Psychology, 35*(5), 831–843.

Miller, L., Davies, M., & Greenwald, S. (2000). Religiosity and substance use and abuse among adolescents in the National Comorbidity Survey. *Journal of the American Academy of Child & Adolescent Psychiatry, 39*(9), 1190–1197.

Substance Abuse and Mental Health Services Administration (SAMHSA), Office of Applied Studies. (2005). *Overview of findings from the 2004 National Survey on Drug Use and Health.* Rockville, MD: U.S. Department of Health and Human Services.

Oetting, E. R., & Donnermeyer, J. F. (1998a). Primary socialization theory: The etiology of drug use and deviance. (Part I). *Substance Use & Misuse, 33*(4), 995–1026.

Oetting, E. R., Deffenbacher, J. L., & Donnermeyer, J. F. (1998b). Primary socialization theory: The role played by personal traits in the etiology of drug use and deviance: II. *Substance Use & Misuse, 33*(6), 1337–1366.

Petraitis, J., Flay, B. R., & Miller, T. Q. (1995). Reviewing theories of adolescent substance use: Organizing pieces in the puzzle. *Psychological Bulletin, 117*(1), 67–86.

Reifman, A., Barnes, G. M., Dintcheff, B. A., Farrell, M. P., & Uhteg, L. (1998). Parental and peer influences on the onset of heavier drinking among adolescents. *Journal of Studies on Alcohol, 59*(3), 311–317.

Rose, R. J., & Dick, D. M. (2004–2005). Gene-environment interplay in adolescent drinking behavior. *Alcohol Research & Health, 28*(4), 222–229.

Simons-Morton, B. (2007). Social influences on adolescent substance use. *American Journal of Health Behavior, 31*(6), 672–684.

Wills, T. A., Sandy, J. M., & Yaeger, A. (2000). Temperament and adolescent substance use: An epigenetic approach to risk and protection. *Journal of Personality. Special Issue: Personality Processes and Problem Behavior, 68*(6), 1127–1151.

GREG COHEN

ANNA LEMBKE

CHINA. Ancient China was a golden age for alcohol, although during much of this early period mineral powders were also taken as *immortality drugs,* often in conjunction with wine. The most popular of these substances was called "cold eating powder" (*hanshisan*), used in alchemy with cinnabar and consumed with copious amounts of alcohol between the Latter Han (25 BCE–220 CE) and Tang periods (618–907).

A tea revolution marked the Tang, permanently relegating alcohol to a lesser position among the culturally privileged intoxicants. New processing techniques and advances in cultivation methods combined with the widespread promotion of tea as a suitable substitute for alcohol by monastic Buddhism. Medical writers also acknowledged its medicinal and therapeutic qualities, recommending tea to nurture the stomach, clear inflammations in the throat, and aid digestion.

SPREAD OF SMOKING OPIUM AND TOBACCO
Opium use also appeared during the Tang, and was imported from the Middle East by sea and overland by caravan. By the Ming period (1368–1644), it occupied an important position within traditional medicine and was recommended as a general panacea against a wide variety of ailments, from cholera, plague, heat stroke, headache, inflammations, fever, vomiting, and diarrhea to stomach pains.

At first, however, opium was eaten, and its spread from the eighteenth century onward depended on the discovery of an entirely novel mode of delivery, namely smoking, which began with tobacco. Tobacco was first introduced in China by European traders in the late sixteenth century. The tobacco plant rapidly became a popular crop, particularly in the tropical south where many medicinal virtues were attributed to it. In the hot, humid summers of the south, tobacco fumes were thought useful in fighting off miasmic diseases such as malaria; in the provinces of the north, smoking was used against the effects of cold and hunger.

Opium blended with tobacco, a combination called *madak*, was responsible for the spread of smoked opium. The mixture was prepared by the owners of smoking houses and fetched prices significantly higher than for pure tobacco. Only by the end of the eighteenth century was the tobacco content eliminated, allowing the smoking of pure opium to become a marker of social status: In a period marked by increased social mobility and conspicuous consumption, large amounts of money could be spent in one evening on pure opium. Wealth and status could be displayed far more effectively by smoking many pipes of pure opium than by drinking expensive tea or alcohol.

The shift away from madak toward pure opium was facilitated by changes in the quality of opium produced in India: Malwa—shipped from India by Portuguese traders—not only varied in quality, it was also fiery and irritating when smoked pure, whereas high-quality Patna—produced in India under British control—was mild and pleasant to the palate. The quality of Patna further improved after poppy cultivation in Bengal was monopolized by the East India Company in 1793, the paste being bought and transported to the rest of Asia by independent traders.

THE OPIUM WAR
Between 1797 and 1820 high-quality opium percolated through the coastline in south China following well-established contacts among local merchants, official intermediaries, and contraband traders. Smuggling was undertaken by British, Parsi, Jewish, Dutch, Portuguese, Danish, and American traders as well as local pirates. The sheer amount of illegally imported opium was blamed by some officials for reducing the

empire's silver holdings, and a small number of officials in favor of prohibition managed to convince the Daoguang emperor (r. 1820–1850) that war with foreign powers was the only solution. The reasons for the abrupt change in favor of a policy of opium prohibition in the 1830s were also related to internal court politics and not only the consequence of the actions pursued by the British government in support of free trade: Chinese scholars turned opium prohibition into a political agenda, enabling them for the first time since the Manchu conquest in 1644 to challenge the dominant position of the court aristocracy.

As part of a new prohibition policy, the imperial administration dispatched Lin Zexu (1785–1850) in 1839 as commissioner to Guangdong in order to bring all opium imports to a halt. Opium stocks were confiscated, the movement of foreigners was further restricted, and in a highly symbolic act of purification, 20,000 chests of imported opium were burnt in public. The retaliatory action by British forces provided the spark for the first Sino-British War (1839–1842), later remembered as the Opium War. As a consequence of the war, several treaty ports were opened to foreign trade.

POPULARITY OF OPIUM
As the poppy was increasingly cultivated in China, smoking progressed down the social scale during the second half of the nineteenth century and it gradually became a popular marker of male sociability. Either in opium houses or at home, opium would be smoked by friends while enjoying leisurely conversations or in groups where a pipe was passed around. Even among the less privileged, the example of a "lonely smoker" was generally eschewed: Smoking was a collective experience, an occasion for social intercourse, a highly ritualized event including strict parameters for the consumption of opium. During the socioeconomic changes experienced in the second half of the nineteenth century, opium- and teahouses as well as alcohol-serving inns provided spaces of social comfort where even the poor could socialize.

Besides the complex social rituals involved in opium smoking, the medicinal virtues of the paste were a major reason for its spread in the nineteenth century. Opium was primarily a painkiller, and self-medication—before modern synthetic medications became available—was the chief motive for smoking: to reduce pain, fight fevers, stop diarrhea, and suppress coughs. The lowering of the cost of opium allowed ordinary people to relieve the symptoms of endemic diseases such as dysentery, cholera, and malaria and to cope with fatigue, hunger, and cold. The spread of affordable opium used in small quantities thanks to the sophisticated mechanism of the opium pipe allowed even the most dispossessed to benefit occasionally from the panacea in the nineteenth century.

RISE OF PROHIBITION
If opium was medicine as much as recreation, the transition from a tolerated opium culture to a system of prohibition attempted by China's late imperial and republican governments from 1906 to 1949 produced a cure that was far worse than the disease. After the Boxer Rebellion in 1900 the Qing concluded a number of bilateral treaties, including a commercial treaty with Great Britain in September 1902, an opium treaty with Germany in October 1903, and one regulating the opium trade with Portugal. In 1906 the Qing formally declared a 10-year opium suppression plan with the support of the United States. The foreign powers were so impressed with the achievements during the initial test period that the 10-year agreement was renewed in 1911, the very year that the last dynasty was overthrown: China thus waged the world's first war on drugs, becoming the initial link in a chain of antidrug campaigns that would gradually span the globe in the twentieth century.

Efforts to curb opium use continued in republican China (1911–1949), and a series of opium suppression laws were passed from 1929 to 1934, while the government launched a Six-Year Opium Suppression Plan that not only criminalized the trafficking of illegal drugs but also threatened habitual users who relapsed after treatment with punishments ranging from imprisonment to summary execution. Tens of thousands of ordinary people were imprisoned and died from epidemics in crowded cells, while those deemed beyond any hope of redemption were simply executed. Opium smokers also died in detoxification centers either because the medical authorities failed effectively to treat the ailments for which opium was taken in the first place or because replacement treatments were poorly conceived and badly administered.

MORPHINE AND HEROIN
Official attempts to police the bloodstream of the nation engendered corruption, a black market, and a criminal underclass. They also accelerated the spread of morphine and heroin. Both were widely smoked in the first decades of the twentieth century, although some of the heroin pills taken for recreational purposes contained only a very small proportion of alkaloids and were often based on lactose or caffeine. Morphine and heroin had few concrete drawbacks, and a number of practical advantages that persuaded many opium smokers to switch under prohibition. Pills were convenient to transport, relatively cheap, odorless and thus almost undetectable in police searches, and easy to use because they no longer required the complicated paraphernalia and time-consuming rituals of opium smoking.

Heroin pills, red pills in particular, enabled consumers to replicate the smoking culture created around opium while avoiding most of the problems produced by anti-opium legislation: They allowed narcotic culture to be reproduced in a different legal context. Although some heroin pills were weak in opiate content, semisynthetics were also increasingly injected by the poor. The dirty needles were often shared and sometimes caused lethal septicemia and transmitted a range of infectious diseases.

SUBSTANCE USE UNDER COMMUNISM
The Chinese Communist Party actively participated in the illegal opium trade during its fight against the government in the 1930s and 1940s. Opium was one of the most important financial resources of the party, allowing it to overcome a number of fiscal difficulties and build an alternative state in the hinterland. After the Communist takeover of the country in 1949, however, it took the party a mere three years to eliminate all illegal substances: A dense network of police institutions, resident committees, and mass organizations were used to crush drug offenders, some even being denounced by their own family members. Public trials and mass executions dealt a final blow to the narcotics culture, while tens of thousands of offenders were sent to labor camps, often for life.

Although it is often believed that the Communists successfully eliminated the so-called drug plague, medical and social variables were as important in the long-term erosion of the narcotics culture as political factors. Penicillin appeared in the 1940s as the first antibiotic that could successfully treat a whole range of diseases that had been managed previously with opium: Antibiotics took over the medical functions of opiates. On the other hand, the social status of opium was already on the decline in the 1930s, abstinence being seen as a mark of pride and a badge of modernity among social elites, very much as the rising middle classes elsewhere started to free themselves from morally reprehensible "drugs."

CIGARETTES

With opium use on the wane, the cigarette was seen as fashionable and modern. Despite the spread of morphine and heroin as alternatives to opium, the commodity that most benefited from prohibition was the ready-made cigarette. It was light and palatable, easy to store and handy to use, capable of delivering nicotine straight to the lungs in short spans of time: perfectly attuned to the faster pace of city life. British American Tobacco thrived in republican China, selling half a billion cigarettes a month in a number of provinces in the 1930s, and under Mao Tse-tung in 1952 its sophisticated system of mass distribution and production was transferred to the authority of the Chinese government.

Tobacco cultivation and cigarette production were vigorously promoted by the Communist Party, as the cigarette was allowed to take over the everyday rituals and social roles of opium within a thriving smoking culture that appeared impervious to the deleterious effects of nicotine. Cigarettes evoked power and prestige, and were promoted by the top leadership. Deng Xiaoping even expressed his gratitude to the cigarette as the reason for his longevity. By the end of the twentieth century China emerged as the largest market for cigarettes and the world's leading tobacco producer. China, for example, produced over 2,000 million kilograms of leaf tobacco in 2000, representing more than a third of the world's production. However, the country is also huge market for foreign leaf tobacco, as over 320 million Chinese are smokers—about a quarter of all smokers around the world. The China National Tobacco Corporation, a government-owned monopoly, annually produces 1.7 trillion cigarettes per year, while those who can afford it prefer to smoke imported cigarettes. The vast majority of China's smokers are male adults, with only 4 to 7 percent women. The tobacco industry contributes about 10 percent of state revenue and has been the state's top revenue generator for over a decade. In the early twenty-first century there are few signs that smoking in China is on the decline.

See also **Britain; Foreign Policy and Drugs, United States; International Drug Supply Systems; Opium: International Overview; Tobacco: An International Overview.**

BIBLIOGRAPHY

Dikötter, F., Laamann, L., & Xun, Z. (2004). *Narcotic culture: A history of drugs in China*. Chicago: University of Chicago Press.

Lee, P. (1999). *The big smoke: The Chinese art and craft of opium*. Bangkok: Lamplight Books.

Newman, R. K. (October 1995). Opium smoking in late imperial China: A reconsideration. *Modern Asian Studies, 29*, 765–794.

Poo, M. -C. (May 1999). The use and abuse of wine in ancient China. *Journal of the Economic and Social History of the Orient, 42* (2), 123–151.

Slack, E. R. (2000). *Opium, state, and society: China's narco-economy and the Guomindang, 1924–1937*. Honolulu: University of Hawaii Press.

Traver, H. (1992). Opium to heroin: Restrictive legislation and the rise of heroin consumption in Hong Kong. *Journal of Policy History, 4* (3), 307–324.

FRANK DIKÖTTER

CHINESE AMERICANS, ALCOHOL AND DRUG USE AMONG.

According to the 2000 U.S. Census report, the largest subpopulation of Asian and Pacific Islanders (AAPIs) is Chinese American (23%). A total of 2.7 million people reported their ethnicity as Chinese alone or in combination with other Asian groups or races. The Chinese American ethnic community consists of people from many countries: the People's Republic of China, the Republic of China (Taiwan), and various countries in Southeast Asia, Latin America, and the Caribbean. The U.S. Department of Commerce (2004) indicated that 69 percent of Chinese Americans are foreign born, and 83 percent speak a Chinese language/dialect at home.

Given that AAPIs are among the fastest growing minority group in the United States (Chen, 1996) and that Chinese Americans constitute a significant portion of AAPIs, it is important to understand substance use behavior in the Chinese American population. The discussion that follows presents research evidence for alcohol use, cigarette smoking, and overall substance use among Chinese Americans.

ALCOHOL USE

In China, historically, alcohol was sanctioned for religious ceremonies, especially ancestor worship. Today, in China and among Chinese immigrants, alcohol is commonly served at celebrations and banquets, and some people consume alcohol at meals—beer, wine, brandy, or whiskey. Drinking-centered institutions, however, are absent (Hsu, 1955; Singer, 1972; Wang, 1968). In Chinese tradition, moderate drinking is believed to have medicinal effects, but excessive use is believed to bring on "nine-fold harm" (Yu & Liu, 1986–1987) and is condemned in folk culture as one of the four vices. Examples of the nine-fold harm include impairment of intellect and predisposition to physical illness.

Chinese cultural beliefs regarding the religious and medicinal benefits of moderate drinking and the harm associated with excessive use may control drinking patterns in China, but when people move into a new cultural setting, their alcohol use may be influenced by the extent to which they learn the customs, attitudes, and behavioral characteristics of the surrounding culture. This process is defined as *acculturation* (Austin & Lee, 1989; Zane & Mak, 2003). David Sue (1987) hypothesized that alcohol abuse is more congruent with American, rather than Chinese values, since Chinese values are antithetical to alcohol abuse. Recent research evidence has provided some support for this hypothesis: Acculturation seems to serve as a risk factor for Chinese Americans' drinking behavior (Hahm et al., 2003, 2004; Hendershot et al., 2005, 2008).

Two earlier studies investigated alcohol use among Chinese and other AAPIs. Harry H. L. Kitano and Iris Chi (1986–1987) found differences in alcohol consumption patterns among respondents from Chinese, Japanese, Korean, and Filipino adults. The lowest prevalence of heavy drinking was reported by Chinese Americans (14% male, 0% female). Most of the Chinese male heavy drinkers were in the age category 26–35.

Subsequently, Chi and colleagues (1988) found that among Chinese American males in their Los Angeles sample, those most likely to drink at any level were under the age of 45 and of relatively high social and educational backgrounds. They found that parental drinking, going to or giving parties, and having friends who drank were the important variables distinguishing drinkers from abstainers among their Chinese adult male sample. Furthermore, results of recent research suggested that parental drinking and male gender were significantly associated with a greater likelihood of lifetime and current alcohol use among Chinese and Korean Americans (Hendershot et al., 2005).

Genetic factors that may influence alcohol use among Chinese Americans have been investigated. An ethanol sensitivity, also known as the "flushing syndrome," is caused by deficiency of the aldehyde dehydrogenase isozyme (ALDH2) genotype, which leads to impairment in metabolizing alcohol. Seldom found in whites, ALDH2 deficiency is most commonly observed among people of northeast Asian descent: Chinese, Japanese, and Koreans (Crabb et al., 1995; Wolff, 1973). Possession of ALDH2*2 alleles has been found to be a protective factor against alcohol dependence (Luczak et al., 2006). A group of researchers at University of California, San Diego, have studied extensively the role of ALDH2 in drinking behavior among Chinese American and Korean American college students (Doran et al., 2007; Hendershot et al., 2005; Luczak et al., 2003; Wall et al., 2001). For example, Luczak and colleagues (2003) found that binge drinking (i.e., heavy episodic drinking) was negatively associated with religious service attendance among Korean American college students and Chinese American college students with Western religious affiliation. In addition, this protective effect of religious service attendance was stronger among those who were not protected by an ALDH2*2 allele.

CIGARETTE SMOKING

Smoking among Chinese Americans is a serious public health problem (Hu et al., 2006). Although Chinese Americans seem to smoke less than whites and other AAPIs (Price et al., 2002), smoking prevalence within the Chinese American population is high. The smoking prevalence among men has been significantly higher than that among women (Centers for Disease Control, 1992; Fu et al., 2003; Thridandam et al., 1998). In the first population-based study of

Chinese Americans' smoking behavior, Yu and colleagues (2002) found that the prevalence of smoking was 2 percent for females and 34 percent for males. Particularly, male prevalence of smoking is far above the Healthy People 2010 target goal, initiated by the U.S. Department of Health and Human Services.

In addition to gender, research evidence has suggested that the prevalence of smoking among Chinese Americans varies depending on a number of factors including English proficiency, healthcare utilization, cultural beliefs, and education level. Yu and associates (2002) found that low education level was significantly associated with smoking among men. This relationship is consistent with research findings in China (Chen, 1995).

In terms of healthcare utilization, Yu and colleagues (2002) found that smoking among men was significantly linked to utilization of non-Western healthcare resources and lack of knowledge of early cancer warning signs. Similarly, in a sample of Chinese American males, Kent K. Hu and colleagues (2006) found that current smokers had less knowledge about the health effects of tobacco compared to non-smokers. Compared to former smokers, current smokers were less likely to have a regular doctor.

In terms of English proficiency, Hu and colleagues (2006) found that current smokers were less likely to be proficient in English than those who had never smoked. Yu and colleagues (2002) suggested that English proficiency may be a factor that is closely linked to age. Men with lower English proficiency tended to be older and foreign-born and reported significantly higher rates of current smoking compared to a sample of younger participants with higher English proficiency, which reported lower rates of current smoking. In addition, researchers (Fu et al., 2003) found that less English-proficient Chinese American male smokers are not as likely to receive advice on quitting smoking from a physician.

Cultural beliefs related to cigarette smoking have played an important role in Chinese Americans' smoking behavior (Hu et al., 2006; Tu et al., 2000). In Shin-Ping Tu and colleagues' study (2000), they found several culturally bound themes for cigarette use and smoking cessation. For instance, based on the concept of *yin* and *yang*, some participants believed that physical exercise may "balance" the negative consequences of cigarettes. Individuals also reported that smoking is a culturally accepted behavior, such that refusing to accept cigarettes offered in social situations is perceived as impolite and disrespectful. In Hu and colleagues' study (2006), they found that male smokers were more likely to have these traditional cultural beliefs about smoking than non-smoking males. Overall, the researchers suggested that these traditional beliefs, which indicated more favorable attitudes toward smoking, may pose challenges for smoking cessation among Chinese American men.

Recent research has also examined the link between depression and smoking among the Chinese American population. Janice Y. Tsoh and associates (2003) found that the level of depressive symptoms among Chinese American smokers is analogous to those observed in white populations in the United States. Higher levels of depressive symptoms were more common among female participants and those who were not employed. These symptoms were also associated with significant nicotine withdrawal and high temptation to smoke when experiencing negative emotional situations.

Given the important role of culture in smoking behavior, culturally appropriate smoking cessation programs have been developed for both Chinese American youth and adults (Fang et al., 2006; Ma et al., 2004). Both studies achieved positive results. Particularly, 38 percent of adult smokers (Chinese and Korean Americans) reported quitting smoking three months after receiving intervention in Fang and colleagues' study. The results of these studies provide promising steps toward developing efficacious smoking cessation programs for Chinese Americans.

OVERALL SUBSTANCE USE

Increased efforts have been made to examine the within-group difference in substance use behavior among AAPIs. Based on two earlier studies in San Francisco, Tooru Nemoto and colleagues (1993, 1999) found that drug use patterns vary depending upon ethnicity, gender, immigrant status, and age group. For example, compared to other Asian ethnic groups, Chinese Americans were more likely to take sedatives orally and less likely to inject drugs. Most Chinese Americans used marijuana as their first illicit drug, and social pressure from friends was noted as the most common reason to begin using drugs. The Chinese immigrants did not begin using drugs until immigrating to the United States. This may be due to low accessibility of illicit drugs in their native country.

Studies based on large samples of AAPI youth in Hawaii and California have consistently reported that Chinese American adolescents have the lowest rates of substance use compared to white, Filipino, Japanese, and Pacific Islander/Hawaiian adolescents (Pearson, 2002; Wong et al., 2004). In a California statewide sample of 4,300 Asian American high school students, Teresa A. Otsuki (2003) found that for Chinese American females, alcohol, marijuana, and cigarette use were significantly related to depression. Smoking had an inverse relationship with self-esteem.

Rumi Kato Price and colleagues (2002) examined data from large national surveys and found that rates of substance use and abuse among Chinese Americans were significantly lower than Japanese Americans. For example, Chinese American adults had significantly lower rates of any alcohol use and cigarette smoking in a 12-month period than those of Japanese American adults. Chinese American youth had significantly lower rates of any alcohol use and cigarette smoking in a 12-month period than those of Japanese American youth. Authors also noted higher rates of smoking and drinking among Korean American youth than those among Chinese American youth. In addition, researchers found that mixed-heritage Chinese American youth were 4.3 times as likely to use substances as those who had unmixed-heritage. The results of this study highlighted the potential need for reclassifying ethnicity to estimate substance use and abuse among Chinese American adolescents.

In a study to examine etiology and prevention of substance use among AAPI youth, Tracy W. Harachi and colleagues (2001) reviewed three studies and indicated several factors related to substance use among Chinese American youth. For example, parents' and peers' disapproval for substance use were negatively related to lifetime use of cigarettes, alcohol, and marijuana. Family discord and greater level of acculturation were positively related to alcohol use. Harachi et al. (2001) recommended that more research is needed to examine risk factors for substance use among Chinese Americans and other AAPIs.

GOALS FOR TWENTY-FIRST-CENTURY RESEARCH

In earlier studies, much of the research on substance use was based on grouping all AAPIs together. Researchers made significant efforts in examining the ethnic difference in substance use among AAPIs from the 1990s to the early twenty-first century. This step enabled them to compare substance use patterns between Chinese Americans and other ethnicities. Although Chinese Americans overall exhibit lower rates for alcohol and other drug use, smoking remains a serious health issue for Chinese Americans (Hu et al., 2006). While research evidence has indicated a few important social, environmental, and cognitive factors that influence substance use among Chinese Americans, more research is still needed to enhance the understanding of smoking behavior among Chinese Americans.

See also **Risk Factors for Substance Use, Abuse, and Dependence: Race/Ethnicity.**

BIBLIOGRAPHY

Austin, G., & Lee, H. (1989). Substance abuse among Asian-American youth (Prevention Research Update 5, Winter). Portland, OR: Western Center for Drug-Free Schools and Communities.

Centers for Disease Control. (1992). Cigarette smoking among Chinese, Vietnamese, and Hispanics—California, 1989–1991. *Morbidity Mortality Weekly Report, 41,* 362–367.

Chen, A. (1996). Demographic characteristics of Asian and Pacific Islander Americans: Health implications. *Asian American Pacific Islander Journal of Health, 4*(1–3), 40–49.

Chen, M. Z. (1995). Smoking in China. *World Health Forum, 16,* 10–11.

Chi, I., Kitano, H. H. L., & Lubben, J. E. (1988). Male Chinese drinking behavior in Los Angeles. *Journal of Studies on Alcohol, 49*(1), 21–25.

Crabb, D. W., Edenberg, H. J., Thomasson, H. R., & Li, T. K. (1995). Genetic factors that reduce risk for developing alcoholism in animals and humans. In: H. Begleiter & B. Kissin (Eds.), *The genetics of alcoholism* (pp. 202–220). New York: Oxford University Press.

Doran, N., Myers, M. G., Luczak, S. E., Carr, L. G., & Wall, T. L. (2007). Stability of heavy episodic drinking in Chinese- and Korean-American college students: Effects of ALDH2 gene status and behavioral undercontrol. *Journal of Studies on Alcohol and Drugs, 68*(6), 789–797.

Fang, C. Y., Ma, G. X., Miller, L. L., Tan, Y., Su, X., & Shives, S. (2006). A brief smoking cessation intervention for Chinese and Korean American smokers. *Preventive Medicine, 43,* 321–324.

Fu, S. S., Ma, G. X., Tu, X. M., Siu, P. T., & Metlay, J. P. (2003). Cigarette smoking among Chinese Americans and the influence of linguistic acculturation. *Nicotine & Tobacco Research, 5*(6), 803–811.

Hahm, H. C., Lahiff, M., & Guterman, N. B. (2003). Acculturation and parental attachment in Asian-American adolescents' alcohol use. *Journal of Adolescent Health, 33,* 119–129.

Hahm, H. C., Lahiff, M., & Guterman, N. B. (2004). Asian American adolescents' acculturation, binge drinking, and alcohol- and tobacco-using peers. *Journal of Community Psychology, 32,* 295–308.

Harachi, T. W., Catalano, R. F., Kim, S., & Choi, Y. (2001). Etiology and prevention of substance use among Asian American youth. *Prevention Science, 2*(1), 57–65.

Hendershot, C. S., Dillworth, T. M., Neighbors, C., & George, W. H. (2008). Differential effects of acculturation on drinking behavior in Chinese- and Korean-American college students. *Journal of Studies on Alcohol and Drugs, 69,* 121–128.

Hendershot, C. S., Macpherson, L., Myers, M. G., Carr, L. G., & Wall, T. L. (2005). Psychosocial, cultural, and genetic influences on alcohol use in Asian American youth. *Journal of Studies on Alcohol, 66,* 185–195.

Hsu, F. L. K. (1955). *American and Chinese.* London: Cresset Press.

Hu, K. U., Woodall, E. D., Do, H. H., Tu, S., Thompson, B., Li, E. A. L., et al. (2006). Tobacco knowledge and beliefs in Chinese American men. *Asian Pacific Journal of Cancer Prevention, 7,* 434–438.

Kitano, H. H. L., & Chi, I. (1986–1987). Asian-Americans and alcohol use. *Alcohol Health and Research World, 11*(2), 42–47.

Luczak, S. E., Corbett, K., Oh, C., Carr, L. G., & Wall, T. L. (2003). Religious influences on heavy episodic drinking in Chinese-American and Korean-American college students. *Journal of Studies on Alcohol, 64*(4), 467–471.

Luczak, S. E., Glatt, S. J., & Wall, T. L. (2006). Meta-analyses of ALDH2 and ADH1B with alcohol dependence in Asians. *Psychological Bulletin, 132,* 607–621.

Ma, G. X., Shive, S. E., Tan, Y., Thomas, P., & Man, V. L. (2004). Development of a culturally appropriate smoking cessation program for Chinese-American youth. *Journal of Adolescent Health, 35,* 206–216.

Mizruchi, E. H., & Perrucci, R. (1962). Norm qualities and differential effects of deviant behavior: An exploratory analysis. *American Sociological Review, 27,* 391–399.

Nemoto, T., Aoki, B., Huang, K., Morris, A., Nguyen, H., & Wong, W. (1999). Drug use behaviors among Asian drug users in San Francisco. *Addictive Behaviors, 24*(6): 823–838.

Nemoto, T., Guydish, J., Young, M., & Clark, W. (1993). Drug use behaviors among Asian Americans in San Francisco. In L. Harris (Ed.), *Problems of drug dependence, proceedings of the 54th annual scientific meeting, The College on Problems of Drug Dependence, Inc.* (NIDA Research Monograph Series 132, p. 199). Washington, DC: U.S. Department of Health and Human Services.

Otsuki, T. A. (2003). Substance use, self-esteem, and depression among Asian American adolescents. *Journal of Drug Education, 33*(4): 369–390.

Pearson, R. S. (2002). The 2002 Hawai'i student alcohol, tobacco, and other drug use study: Hawai'i adolescent prevention and treatment needs assessment. Honolulu: Hawai'i Department of Health, Alcohol, and Drug Abuse Division.

Price, R. K., Risk, N. K., Wong, M. M., & Klingle, R. S. (2002). Substance use and abuse by Asian Americans and Pacific Islanders: Preliminary results from four national epidemiologic studies. *Public Health Reports, 117,* 539–550.

Singer, K. (1972). Drinking patterns and alcoholism in the Chinese. *British Journal of Addiction, 67,* 3–14.

Sue, D. (1987). Use and abuse of alcohol by Asian Americans. *Journal of Psychoactive Drugs, 19*(1), 57–66.

Thridandam, M., Fong, W., Jang, M., Louie, L., & Forst, M. (1998). A tobacco and alcohol use profile of San Francisco's Chinese community. *Journal of Drug Education, 28,* 377–393.

Tsoh, J. Y., Lam, J. M., Delucchi, K. L., & Hall, S. (2003). Smoking and depression in Chinese Americans. *The American Journal of the Medical Sciences, 326*(4), 187–191.

Tu, S. P., Walsh, M., Tseng, B., & Thompson, B. (2000). Tobacco use by Chinese American men: An exploratory study of the factors associated with cigarette use and smoking cessation. *Asian American Pacific Islander Journal of Health, 8,* 46–57.

U.S. Census Bureau. (July 7, 2001). Census 2000 redistricting data. Washington, DC: Author. Available from http://www.census.gov.

U.S. Department of Commerce (2004). We the people—Asians in the United States: Census 2000 special reports. Washington DC: U.S. Department of Commerce.

Wall, T. L., Shea, S. H., Chan, K. K., & Carr, L. G. (2001). A genetic association with the development of alcohol and other substance use behavior in Asian Americans. *Journal of Abnormal Psychology, 110*(1), 173–178.

Wang, R. P. (1968). A study of alcoholism in Chinatown. *International Journal of Social Psychiatry, 14,* 260–267.

Wolff, P. (1973). Vasomotor sensitivity to ethanol in diverse Mongoloid populations. *American Journal of Human Genetics, 25,* 193–199.

Wong, M. M., Klingle, R. S., & Price, R. K. (2004). Alcohol, tobacco, and other drug use among Asian American and Pacific Islander adolescents in California and Hawaii. *Addictive Behaviors, 29,* 127–141.

Yu, E. S. H., Chen, E. H., Kim, K. K., & Abdulrahim, S. (2002). Smoking among Chinese Americans: Behavior, knowledge, and beliefs. *American Journal of Public Health, 92*(6), 1007–1013.

Yu, E. S. H., & Liu, W. T. (1986–1987). Alcohol use and abuse among Chinese-Americans. *Alcohol Health and Research World, 11*(2), 14–17.

Zane, N., & Mak, W. (2003). Major approaches to the measurement of acculturation among ethnic minority populations: A content analysis and an alternative empirical strategy. In K. M Chun, P. B. Organista, & G. Marin (Eds.), *Acculturation: Advances in Theory, Measurement, and Applied Research* (pp. 39–60). Washington, DC: American Psychological Association.

RICHARD F. CATALANO
TRACY W. HARACHI
REVISED BY SHARON HSU (2009)
G. ALAN MARLATT (2009)

CHLORAL HYDRATE.

Chloral hydrate is one of the oldest sedative agents still in use. It was made by the German chemist Liebig in 1832 and introduced into general use in 1869 as a substitute for laudanum, an alcoholic solution of opium. Chloral hydrate differs from the barbiturates in that it is a simple molecule composed of two carbon atoms, three hydrogen atoms, two oxygen atoms, and three chloride atoms. It is the famous (or infamous) substance added to alcohol to make a *Mickey Finn*, a drink known to cause those who drink it to become unconscious. Because it shares many effects of other central nervous system depressants, it can be used to treat the alcohol withdrawal syndrome. Chloral hydrate was a popular sedative for elderly patients because its effects occur quickly, last only a short time, and leave no nagging hangover effect. However, it is inconvenient to use (up to 2 grams must be taken by mouth) and, after the introduction of the benzodiazepines, its use has decreased.

See also **Benzodiazepines; Opiates/Opioids; Sedative.**

BIBLIOGRAPHY

Harvey, S. C. (1980). Hypnotics and sedatives. In A. G. Gilman et al. (Eds.), *Goodman and Gilman's the pharmacological basis of therapeutics* (6th ed.). New York: Macmillan. (2005, 11th ed. New York: McGraw-Hill Medical).

SCOTT E. LUKAS

CHLORDIAZEPOXIDE.

Chlordiazepoxide (brand name Librium) is a member of the benzodiazepine family of drugs currently used to treat insomnia, anxiety, muscle spasms, and some forms of epilepsy. It was the first benzodiazepine to be used in clinical practice in the 1960s, as an alternative to phenobarbital or meprobamate, in treating psychoneuroses, anxiety, and tension. Its advantage over barbiturates and other central nervous system depressants is that it is less toxic, especially after an overdose.

In addition to the previously mentioned uses, chlordiazepoxide is frequently used to treat the seizures or delirium tremens (DTs) that appear during alcohol withdrawal. In the late 1990s, Dr. Michael Mayo-Smith conducted a meta-analysis to determine if benzodiazepines effectively prevent delirium in patients experiencing DTs. Although benzodiazepines were shown to be effective, this study was not conclusive since chlordiazepoxide was the only benzodiazepine tested, and further testing is needed on other benzodiazepines before an overall claim can be made (Johnson et al., 1997).

See also **Barbiturates; Benzodiazepines; Delirium Tremens (DTs); Meprobamate; Phenobarbital.**

BIBLIOGRAPHY

Johnson, J. R., et al. (1997). Pharmacologic treatment of alcohol withdrawal. *JAMA, The Journal of the American Medical Association, 278,* 1317–1319.

United States Pharmacopeial Convention (1999). Chlordiazepoxide and clidinium. In *Advice for the patient: Drug information in lay language* (19th ed.). Montvale, NJ: Thomson Healthcare. (2005, 25th ed.)

SCOTT E. LUKAS
REVISED BY PUBLISHER (2001)

CHOCOLATE.

CHOCOLATE. An ingredient of many popular treats—candies, sweets, baked goods, soft drinks, hot drinks, ice cream, and other frozen desserts. It is prepared, often as a paste, from the roasted crushed seeds (called cocoa beans) of the small South American cacao tree called *Theobroma cacao* (this is not the shrub known as the coca plant, which produces cocaine, *Erythroxylon coca*).

The cacao tree has small yellowish flowers, followed by fleshy yellow pods with many seeds. The dried, partly fermented fatty seeds are used to make the paste, which is mixed with sugar to produce the chocolate flavor loved throughout the world. Cocoa butter and cocoa powder are other important extracts from the bean. Cocoa beans were introduced to Europe by the Spanish, who brought them back from the New World in the sixteenth century. They had first been used by the civilizations of the New World—Mexicans, Aztecs, and Mayan royalty—in a ceremonial unsweetened drink and as a spice in special festive foods, such as molé. They were first used in Europe by the privileged classes to create a hot, sweet drink. By the seventeenth century, cocoa shops and coffee shops (cafés) became part of European life, serving free tobacco with drinks and thereby increasing trade with the New World colonies.

Chocolate produces a mild stimulating effect caused by the theobromine and caffeine it contains. Both are alkaloids of the chemical class called xanthines. Theobromine in high doses has many effects on the body, and it is possible to become addicted to some xanthines, such as caffeine. Nevertheless, some people are so attracted to the flavor that compulsive or obsessive use has resulted in the newly coined term *chocoholic*. Some scientists are researching the phenylethylamine in chocolate as the factor that encourages compulsive chocolate ingestion.

See also **Alkaloids; Caffeine; Theobromine.**

BIBLIOGRAPHY

Nehlig, A. (2004). *Coffee, tea, chocolate, and the brain.* London: CRC Press.

Serafin, W. E. (1996). Drugs used in the treatment of asthma. In A. G. Gilman et al. (Eds.), *Goodman and Gilman's the pharmacological basis of therapeutics* (9th ed.). New York: McGraw-Hill Medical. (2005, 11th ed.)

MICHAEL J. KUHAR

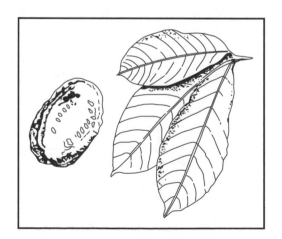

Figure 1. Cacao leaves and pod. ILLUSTRATION BY GGS INFORMATION SERVICES. GALE, CENGAGE LEARNING

CHROMOSOME.

CHROMOSOME. Chromosomes are structures in the nucleus of the cell that contain the DNA or hereditary material which form genes. Genes are the commonly known units of heredity, and some may contribute to a tendency toward addiction in ways that are not yet understood. Each chromosome is an elongated structure that is clearly visible during cell division. Humans possess twenty-three pairs including the sex chromosomes. A male has an X and a Y sex chromosome, whereas a female has two X sex chromosomes. One of each pair comes from each parent.

See also **Gene.**

BIBLIOGRAPHY

Lima-de-Faria, A. (2003). *One hundred years of chromosome research and what remains to be learned.* New York: Springer.

Miller, O. J., & Therman, E. (2000). *Human chromosomes.* New York: Springer.

MICHAEL J. KUHAR

CHRONIC PAIN.

CHRONIC PAIN. Chronic or persistent pain is defined as pain that lasts for longer than six months. Chronic pain can stem from cancer, illness, injury, or postsurgical changes. Often, persons with chronic pain suffer from syndromes that cannot be confirmed by laboratory tests. These chronic pain syndromes include central pain syndromes, fibromyalgia, headache, lower back pain, myofascial pain syndrome, neuropathic pain, and phantom limb pain. Frequent locations of chronic pain include the back, head, joints, chest, abdomen, and extremities. Chronic pain is common and its sufferers are more likely to have anxiety or depression, have poor perception of their health, decreases in their quality of life, and experience a disruption of their livelihood than those who are not in pain.

In most cases, there is no cure for the chronic pain so treatment is aimed at pain control and rehabilitation. Unfortunately, chronic pain is often ineffectively treated because physicians can be reluctant to prescribe strong, potentially addictive medications. The ineffective pain treatment is compounded by commonly associated conditions such as depression, insomnia, fatigue, and a decrease in general physical functioning. Therefore, treating the pain alone is not sufficient.

The optimal approach to the chronic pain sufferer is an interdisciplinary team that may be comprised of a pain management physician, nurse specialist, psychologist, physical therapist, pharmacist, and vocational counsellor. The physician conducts a thorough assessment of the patient and determines the appropriate medical interventions. The psychologist conducts a thorough psychological assessment, educates the patient on techniques to reduce pain, and tends to any associated mental health illnesses. The nurse specialist acts as a case manager and educator. The physical therapist ascertains the patient's physical endurance, flexibility, and strength and conducts the physical rehabilitation process. The vocational counsellor identifies and devises strategies to allow the patient to return to work. In addition to dispensing medications, the pharmacist will review past and present use of medicinal agents and educate the patient on the proper use of medications.

PHARMACOLOGICAL MANAGEMENT OF CHRONIC PAIN

In the treatment of chronic pain, drugs (analgesics) are usually administered in a stepwise fashion beginning with mild, relatively safe agents and progressing to stronger agents as necessary. In 1986, the World Health Organization (WHO) proposed a stepwise plan, frequently called the analgesic ladder, for the oral treatment of cancer pain. This plan provides adequate pain relief for up to 90 percent of cancer patients but may have limited success for other chronic pain patients. Step one of the ladder is recommended for patients with mild pain and consists of nonopioid analgesics, step two is for moderate pain and consists of mild opioids, and step three is for severe pain and consists of strong opioids. More than one analgesic may be used at a time for an added effect, a procedure called adjuvant therapy.

Nonopioid analgesics consist of acetaminophen and nonsteroidal anti-inflammatory drugs (NSAIDs). Acetaminophen is an effective analgesic that has a minimal side effect profile. Nonsteroidal anti-inflammatory drugs have both analgesic and anti-inflammatory properties. Examples of nonsteroidal anti-inflammatory drugs are aspirin, ibuprofen, naproxen, meclofenamate, piroxicam, and more recently celebrex and vioxx. Major side effects associated with the use of nonsteroidal anti-inflammatory drugs include kidney toxicity, bleeding disorders, and stomach disorders.

Opioid analgesics are available in different strengths. Examples of opioid analgesics are morphine, fentanyl, methadone, and meperidine. The side effects of opioids may be much more serious than those seen with nonopioid analgesics. Side effects include respiratory depression, alterations in consciousness (e.g. drowsiness, sedation, confusion), nausea, vomiting, constipation, urinary retention, and itching.

Other medications used in the treatment of chronic pain include antidepressants and anticonvulsants. Nerve blocks, injection of anesthetics into trigger points, or injection of steroids into the epidural space of the spinal cord may also be utilized. Implantable methods are utilized as treatments of last resort. These methods involve implanting drug delivery systems or electrodes into specific areas of the spinal cord.

TOLERANCE, DEPENDENCE, AND ADDICTION

The continued use of opioids leads to tolerance, in which increasingly higher doses of drug must be used to obtain the original level of pain relief. Tolerance develops slowly, occurring over a period of months to years. Cross-tolerance to other opioids develops, although to a lesser extent. Tolerance can be differentiated from physical dependence and addiction.

Physical dependence is a characteristic of opioid use because of the mode of action. It reflects a state of neurological adaptation to the drug. With physical dependency, discontinuation of opioid use leads to withdrawal symptoms (e.g. sweating, tearing, rapid heart rate, nasal discharge, abdominal cramps, nausea, and vomiting). To prevent withdrawal symptoms, patients on long term opioid use are gradually weaned off the medication. Physical dependence on opioids does not lead to addiction, although it may compel the patient to seek opioids to relieve symptoms of withdrawal.

For chronic pain patients taking opioids, tolerance and physical dependence are not indicators of addiction. Addiction is not a characteristic of opioid use, rather, it is dependent upon the user. In fact, the medical use of opioids is only very rarely associated with addiction. The agonist-antagonist class of opioids (buprenorphine, butorphanol, nalbuphine, pentazocine, and dezocine) has a low abuse potential.

Any patient taking opioids to treat chronic pain can meet the criteria for addiction set forth by the American Psychiatric Association in the *Diagnostic and statistical manual of mental disorders: DSM-IV.* Therefore, it is very difficult to diagnose addiction in chronic pain patients who are taking opioids. Chronic pain patients who are being ineffectively treated could display the drug-seeking behavior that is characteristic of addiction, a phenomenon called *pseudoaddiction.* Alternatively, the patient receiving effective pain treatment may take extreme measures to insure an adequate supply of medication. This behavior is termed *therapeutic dependence.*

Suggestive signs of addiction within the context of opioid therapy for chronic pain include:

- Loss of control over opioid use;
- Preoccupation with the use of opioids despite adequate pain control; and
- Continued use of opioids even with their adverse consequences.

See also **Analgesic; Opiates/Opioids.**

BIBLIOGRAPHY

Ashburn, M. A., & Rice, L. J. (1998). *The management of pain.* New York: Churchill Livingstone.

Ashburn, M. A., & Staats, P. S. (1999). Management of chronic pain. *Lancet, 353,* 1865–1869.

Gallagher, R. M., Ed. (1999). *The medical clinics of North America: Chronic pain.* Philadelphia, PA: W. B. Saunders Company.

Mayo Clinic. (2002). *Mayo Clinic on chronic pain* (2nd ed.). Rochester, MN: Mayo Clinic.

Thorn, B. E. (2004). *Cognitive therapy for chronic pain: A step-by-step guide.* New York: The Guilford Press.

BELINDA ROWLAND

CIVIL COMMITMENT. The term used for compulsory or mandatory drug abuse treatment is *civil commitment.* Civil commitment is a community alternative to prison that can include temporary court-ordered treatment confinement for chronic drug abusers, particularly narcotic addicts responsible for a large number of crimes. Civil commitment is a strategy for diverting drug abusers, who would not seek treatment voluntarily. In early studies civil commitment decreased daily narcotic use and criminal involvement and in later studies had similar outcomes to voluntary community treatment (Leukefeld & Tims, 1988; Leukefeld, Tims & Farabee, 2002).

Currently the criminal justice system is crowded with drug abusers. For example, more than 700,000 U.S. prisoners have re-entered the community every year since 2000 (Glaze & Bonczar, 2006). A high number of these prisoners are drug abusers. For example, 83 percent of state prisoners reported drug use, and 32 percent reported drug use at the time of their offense (Mumola & Karberg, 2006). About half of jail inmates meet dependence criteria (Karberg & James, 2005), and two-thirds of arrestees in major U.S. cities drug tested positive (NIJ, 2003). Almost 70 percent of probationers reported using drugs or alcohol (Mumola, 1998; Leukefeld, Tims, & Farabee, 2002).

Since the early 1980s the justice system has focused on determinate sentencing and long prison terms, which increase the number of incarcerated drug abusers. Prison-based treatment improves outcomes (Prendergast, Hall, Wexler, Melnick, & Cao, 2004; Wexler, 2003) as does aftercare and continued care (Inciardi, Surratt, Martin, & Hopper,

2002; McCollister, French, Inciardi, Butzin, Martin, & Hopper, 2003), which are similar to civil commitment but cost less. In addition, the popularity of prison diversion in an increasing number of drug courts (Belenko, 2001; Wilson, Mitchell, & Mackenzie, 2006) is, like civil commitment, a way of keeping drug users in the community rather than in prison.

HISTORICAL CONTEXT

The first United States compulsory treatment facility was established in 1935 as the U.S. Public Health Service Hospital for the treatment of narcotic addicts in Lexington, Kentucky, and was called a *farm* then. Three years later, a second hospital was established in Fort Worth, Texas, to provide treatment after detoxification. Early follow-up studies in the 1940s reported that narcotic addicts treated under legal coercion with post-hospital supervision had better outcomes than voluntary patients (Maddux, 1988). However, later studies did not generally support these early positive findings. Consequently, federal treatment staff recommended the enactment of a federal civil commitment law for narcotic addicts.

In 1962 President John F. Kennedy convened the White House Conference on Narcotic and Drug Abuse, which recommended that a federal civil commitment program for narcotic addicts be developed to treat narcotic addicts—mostly heroin addicts. Civil commitment was advocated to protect society by reducing crime and to rehabilitate drug abusers; this resulted in the federal Narcotic Addict Rehabilitation Act (NARA) of 1966. At that time almost twenty-five states had their own civil commitment laws (Inciardi, 1988). For example, California began the first civil commitment program, called the Civil Addict Program (CAP). Because of its relative success, the New York Narcotic Addiction Control Commission (NACC) established the largest and costliest civil commitment program in 1966, called the New York State Civil Commitment Program.

BACKGROUND

In 1962 the U.S. Supreme Court upheld the case of *Robinson v. California* (370 U.S. 660) and ruled that a state could establish a program of compulsory treatment or civil commitment for narcotic addiction and

that such treatment could involve periods of involuntary confinement, with penal sanctions for failure to comply. Consequently, the California Civil Addict Program (CAP) was initiated with clear correctional department commitment procedures. Narcotic addicts convicted of a felony or misdemeanor were committed for seven years and then returned to court for disposition of their original charge, or their time served was credited toward their sentence. Addiction was determined by two court-appointed physicians, and patients underwent a sixty-day evaluation period (McGlothlin, Anglin, & Wilson, 1977). Both inpatient and outpatient phases were used for treatment, which incorporated modified therapeutic community principles. During the 1970s infrequent drug use was tolerated by the California Civil Commitment Program if the narcotic addict's overall behavioral pattern was acceptable (Anglin, 1988). This resulted in an overall finding that participants exhibited sustained reductions in drug use, fewer multiple relapses, and relapses that were of shorter duration separated by longer periods of non addiction (Anglin, 1988). However, by 1990, the length of the California commitment period was reduced from seven years to about three years, the community treatment phase was less organized, ancillary services were dramatically cut, and no treatment service was available beyond a minimal, 120-hour Civil Commitment Education Program (Wexler, 1990).

ALTERNATE TO INCARCERATION

The federal NARA, the California CAP, and the New York civil commitment programs were developed to control and to rehabilitate compulsive drug abusers by providing treatment as an alternative to incarceration in correctional facilities. Eligible addicts convicted of a crime could be committed by the court or could choose commitment rather than incarceration. Narcotic addicts not involved in criminal proceedings could commit themselves voluntarily or could be involuntarily institutionalized with a petition from another individual (McGlothlin, Anglin, & Wilson, 1977). Supervised aftercare with drug testing was a major part of civil commitment, which ranged from three years to seven years. Although most studies reported that federal civil commitment was generally not successful, the federal funding for community follow-up treatment in the NARA legislation provided seed money for establishing drug-treatment programs in major U.S. urban areas (Maddux, 1988). Although the New York State Civil Commitment Program failed (Inciardi, 1988), which was partly attributable to its administration by a social welfare agency with little experience with narcotic addicts, the California program was moderately effective in modifying behavior by using experienced and trained addictions treatment personnel (Anglin, 1988). Specifically, California follow-up studies found that participants reduced their daily heroin use as well as their property crime and antisocial activities. Although many became re-addicted, their relapses were typically shorter and less frequent than individuals not involved in civil commitment treatment (Anglin, 1988). The general conclusion drawn from these studies was that civil commitment, when adequately implemented, might be effective in reducing narcotic addiction. However, repeated interventions were typically required because drug dependence is a chronic condition marked by relapses (Leukefeld & Tims, 1988) or as commonly depicted in the early twenty-first century—drug addiction is a chronic and relapsing disorder.

EVALUATION OF CIVIL COMMITMENT

Civil commitment helped narcotic addicts enter treatment and proved successful for some. Outcome studies generally show that successful treatment is associated with the amount of time spent in treatment and that long-term community supervision with drug testing is important for compulsory treatment. In addition, civil commitment can make treatment available before a crime is committed, and it provides clear treatment goals rather than only punishment. However, civil commitment has limitations. It is costly and can overwhelm facilities without adequate funding and staff. Many addicts are also unwilling or unsuited for participation. Although external coercion such as civil commitment can bring drug users into treatment, it cannot assure that drug abusers will be motivated to engage in treatment. Finally, civil commitment is controversial, because it restricts an individual's constitutional rights of free choice.

See also **Civil Remedies; Coerced Treatment for Substance Offenders; Conduct Disorder and Drug Use; Criminal Justice System, Treatment in the; Drug Courts; Drug Interdiction; Narcotic Addict**

Rehabilitation Act (NARA); New York State Civil Commitment Program; Prisons and Jails; Prisons and Jails, Drug Treatment in; Rockefeller Drug Laws; Treatment, Specialty Approaches to: Therapeutic Communities; Treatment, Stages/Phases of: Aftercare; Treatment Accountability for Safer Communities (TASC); Treatment: Outpatient versus Inpatient Setting; U.S. Government Agencies: U.S. Public Health Service Hospitals.

BIBLIOGRAPHY

Anglin, D. (1988). The efficacy of civil commitment in treating narcotic addiction. In C. G. Leukefeld & F. M. Tims (Eds.), *Compulsory treatment of drug abuse: Research and clinical practice* (NIDA Research Monograph 86) (pp. 8–34). Rockville, MD: U.S. Department of Health and Human Services.

Belenko, S. (2001). *Research on drug courts: A critical review 2001 update.* Alexandria, VA: National Drug Court Institute.

Glaze, L. E., & Bonczar, T. P. (2006). *Probation and parole in the United States, 2005.* (Bureau of Justice Statistics Bulletin NCJ215091). Washington, DC: U.S. Department of Justice.

Inciardi, J. A. (1988). Compulsory treatment in New York: A brief narrative history of misjudgment, mismanagement, and misrepresentation. *The Journal of Drug Issues, 18*(4), 547–560.

Inciardi, J. A., Surratt, H. L., Martin, S. S., & Hopper, R. M. (2002). The importance of aftercare in a corrections-based treatment continuum. In C. G. Leukefeld, F. M. Tims, & D. Farabee (Eds.), *Treatment of Drug Offenders: Policies and Issues* (pp. 204–206). New York: Springer Publishing Company.

Karberg, J. C. & James, D. J. (2005). *Substance dependence, abuse, and treatment of jail inmates, 2002.* Washington, DC: U.S. Department of Justice, Office of Justice Programs, Bureau of Justice Statistics.

Leukefeld, C. G., & Tims, F. M. (1988). *Compulsory treatment of drug abuse: Research and clinical practice* (NIDA Research Monograph 86). Rockville, MD: U.S. Department of Health and Human Services.

Leukefeld, C. G., Tims, F. M. & Farabee, D. (Eds.). (2002). *Treatment of Drug Offenders: Policies and Issues.* New York: Springer Publishing Company.

Maddux, J. F. (1988). Clinical experience with civil commitment. In C. G. Leukefeld & F. M. Tims (Eds.), *Compulsory treatment of drug abuse: Research and clinical practice* (NIDA Research Monograph 86). Rockville, MD: U.S. Department of Health and Human Services.

McCollister, K. E., French, M. T., Inciardi, J. A., Butzin, C. A., Martin, S. S., & Hooper, R. M. (2003). Post-release substance abuse treatment for criminal offenders: A cost-effectiveness analysis. *Journal of Quantitative Criminology, 19*, 389–407.

McGlothlin, W. H., Anglin, M. D., & Wilson, B. D. (1977). *An evaluation of the California Civil Addict Program* (Services Research Monograph Series). Rockville, MD: U.S. Department of Health, Education, and Welfare.

Mumola, C. (1998) *Substance abuse and treatment, state and federal prisoners, 1997.* (NCJ Publication No. 172871). Washington, DC: Department of Justice.

Mumola, C. J., & Karberg, J. C. (2006). *Drug use and dependence, state and federal prisoners, 2004.* (Bureau of Justice Statistics Special Report NCJ213530). Washington, DC: U.S. Department of Justice.

National Institute of Justice (2003). *Arrestee Drug Abuse Monitoring; Annual Report* (pp. 135–136). Washington, DC: U.S. Department of Justice, Office of Justice Programs, 2003.

Prendergast, M. L., Hall, E. A., Wexler, H. K., Melnick, G., & Cao, Y. (2004). Amity prison-based therapeutic community: 5-year outcomes. *Prison Journal, 84*, 36–60.

Wexler, H. K. (1990). Summary of findings and recommendations of the second invited review of California Department of Corrections substance abuse treatment efforts (Unpublished manuscript). New York: Narcotics and Drug Research.

Wexler, H. K. (2003). The promise of prison-based treatment for dually diagnosed inmates. *Journal of Substance Abuse Treatment, 25*, 223–231.

Wilson, D. B., Mitchell, O., & Mackenzie, D. L. (2006). A systematic review of drug court effects on recidivism. *Journal of Experimental Criminology, 2*, 459–487.

HARRY K. WEXLER
REVISED BY CARL LEUKEFELD (2009)

CIVIL REMEDIES. Civil remedies are defined as procedures and sanctions, specified by civil statutes and regulations, used to prevent or reduce criminal problems and incivilities (Mazerolle & Roehl, 1998). Drug control is a primary application of many civil remedy programs. Police departments, city prosecutors, and community members use civil remedies in an effort to disrupt illegal activities at drug-selling locations. This approach to drug control typically targets non-offending third parties (e.g., landlords, property owners) and utilizes nuisance and drug abatement statutes. These types of abatement statutes include repair requirements, fines, padlocks/closing, and property forfeiture and seek to make owners and landlords maintain drug- and nuisance-free properties. Police often work with teams of city agency representatives to inspect drug nuisance properties, coerce landowners to clean up blighted properties, post "no trespassing" signs, enforce civil law codes and municipal regulatory rules, and initiate court proceedings against property owners who fail to comply with civil law citations.

Growth in the use of civil remedies as a crime control or crime prevention tactic is attributable to several factors. First, the accessibility of civil remedy tools provides frustrated and disadvantaged communities with alternative avenues to reverse the spiral of decline. Second, the increasing use of civil remedies comes at a time when communities and law enforcement officials recognize that many criminal remedies are neither effective nor desirable for a wide range of problems. Third, growth in civil remedy approaches to crime control coincides with increasing societal emphasis on prevention.

Many civil remedy actions seek to reduce signs of physical (e.g., broken windows, graffiti, trash) and social (e.g., public drinking, loitering, public urination) incivilities in the hope that cleaned-up places will break the cycle of neighborhood decline and subsequently decrease victimization, fear of crime, and alienation. Code enforcement, drug nuisance abatement, neighborhood cleanup and beautification, and Crime Prevention through Environmental Design (CPTED) interventions are civil remedy actions that are typically used to control drug problems. Youth curfews, gang injunctions, ordinances controlling public behavior, and restraining orders are other examples of civil remedies that seek to alter criminal opportunities and prevent drug-selling problems from escalating.

Pressures on property owners and managers often result in corrections of health and safety violations, enforced cleanup and upkeep efforts, evictions of problem tenants, and improved property management. Bans on drug paraphernalia, alcohol-related billboard advertising, spray paint, and cigarette machines in high crime areas are used in an attempt to disrupt the illegal activities at drug-selling locations. Injunctions against gangs, youth curfews, and domestic violence restraining orders are used to prevent and deter potential perpetrators from engaging in criminal behavior. When useful civil statutes are absent, community groups, legislators, and policy makers often work together to enact new legislation.

Unlike traditional criminal sanctions, civil remedies attempt to resolve underlying problems (e.g., the motel's poor management, the absentee owner's neglect). The use of civil remedies tends to be proactive and oriented toward prevention; it aims to enhance quality of life and eliminate opportunities for problems to occur or reappear.

Police use existing public health and controlled substances acts to send warning letters to property owners informing them that complaints of problem activities (e.g., drug dealing) have been reported on their property, advise them of steps to take in preventing or minimizing the problems, and offer assistance in resolving the problem. The letters serve as an official notice of drug activity. Fines and other civil penalties may occur if violations are not corrected, and there are fees for reinspections to cover city costs. If owners do not correct the problem, there are penalties that include fines, closure of the property for up to one year, and sale of the property to satisfy city costs. The city attorney's office can file suit against owners who do not take responsibility for their property.

Civil remedies offer an attractive alternative to criminal remedies since they are relatively inexpensive and easy to implement. Citizens can make a difference by documenting problems, urging police and prosecutors to take appropriate civil action, or spearheading drives to establish useful local ordinances. A group of neighbors can pursue a nuisance abatement action in small claims court without the assistance of police or public prosecutors (Roehl, Wong, & Andrews, 1997). Moreover, civil laws require a lower burden of proof than criminal actions and do not involve the requirements of criminal due process, making them easier to apply yet open to concerns about fairness and equity (Cheh, 1991).

A nonprofit organization, Safe Streets Now! (SSN), has developed a civil remedies program that is based on filing small claims court actions against property owners who fail to address known problems on their property. However, in the thirty-five programs around the United States that have adopted this approach as of 2008, the vast majority of problems are corrected before the filing of a court action. The program seeks to empower neighborhood groups and enhance community organizing. In a 2000 study the SSN approach was lauded as an excellent one for reducing or eliminating issues with problem properties. However, the study also revealed that successful programs were dependent on effective program directors.

The use of civil remedies to solve crime and disorder problems continues to grow in popularity. Police regularly use civil laws, local city regulations, and ordinances to control drug, disorder, and other crime problems. Community groups often work with policy makers to instigate civil remedy action to solve intractable neighborhood problems. The civil remedy approach appears to be an effective and relatively cost-effective approach to control drug problems (Mazerolle, Price, & Roehl, 2000).

BIBLIOGRAPHY

Mazerolle, L. G., Price, J., & Roehl, J. (2000). Civil remedies and drug control: A randomized field trial in Oakland, CA. *Evaluation Review, 24* (2), 211–239.

Mazerolle, L. G., & Roehl, J. (1998). Civil remedies and crime prevention: An introduction. In L. G. Mazerolle & J. Roehl (Eds.), *Civil remedies and crime prevention: Crime prevention studies* (Vol. 9, pp. 1–20). Monsey, NY: Criminal Justice Press.

Mazerolle, L. G., Soole, D., & Rombouts, S. (2006). Street-level drug law enforcement: A meta-analytical review. *Journal of Experimental Criminology, 2,* 409–435.

Roehl, J., & Guertin, K. (2002). *An evaluation of the Safe Streets Now! approach: Civil remedies for drugs, crime, and nuisance problems, final report.* Available from http://www.ncjrs.gov/.

Roehl, J., Wong, H., & Andrews, C. (1997). *The use of civil remedies by community organizations for neighborhood crime and drug abatement.* Pacific Grove, CA: Institute for Social Analysis.

LORRAINE GREEN MAZEROLLE
REVISED BY FREDERICK K. GRITTNER (2009)

CLINICAL TRIALS NETWORK. The National Institute on Drug Abuse (NIDA) established the National Drug Abuse Treatment Clinical Trials Network (CTN) to accelerate the translation of science-based addiction treatments into community-based practice.

The mission of the CTN is to improve the quality of addiction treatment throughout the nation, using science as the vehicle. The network brings together practitioners from community-based drug abuse treatment programs and scientists from university-based research centers in an alliance that fosters communication and collaboration. This alliance facilitates the development and implementation of evidence-based treatments in community practice settings. Two key principles guide the activities of the CTN:

1. Addiction treatment services will improve as evidence-based treatments are broadly implemented in community-based treatment programs.
2. Randomized controlled clinical trials are the gold standard for generating evidence-based treatments.

The CTN has completed more than 20 clinical trials and enrolled more than 9,000 trial participants. These trials have tested pharmacological, behavioral, and integrated treatment interventions for adolescents and adults with a variety of substance use disorders. Some of the CTN's findings have been packaged into comprehensive training and treatment tools for use by practitioners.

INFRASTRUCTURE AND PROCESS
The CTN actively engages community practitioners in the research enterprise through a formal infrastructure. The network started in 1999 with six university-based research centers and about 40 community treatment programs. It is now a collaboration of 16 research centers and more than 150 treatment programs working cooperatively with NIDA. Scientists and practitioners from a variety of medical and behavioral treatment specialties are represented. CTN researchers are internationally prominent experts in substance abuse, and many of the network's treatment programs are acknowledged as leading programs in patient care. A clinical coordinating center (CCC) and a data and statistics center (DSC) provide research operations and advisory support. By-laws guide the CTN and stipulate that researchers and practitioners have equal influence in the network's

activities. NIDA administers the CTN's affairs through its Center for the Clinical Trials Network (CCTN).

The CTN infrastructure provides the foundation for sound planning and ensures the quality, reliability, and utility of the results of its research. The policies and procedures of the CTN support the mission and infrastructure, guide the research, and ensure process integrity. The following steps in the research life cycle outline this approach:

1. In consultation with NIDA, CTN researchers and practitioners propose and select research topics and identify a research team to lead each study.
2. An independent review board (Data and Safety Monitoring Board) initially and periodically assesses each research study for its public health significance, scientific integrity, and design adequacy, as well as participant safety and ethical considerations.
3. Compliance with federal regulations for research conduct and human subjects protection is required. It includes those protections required by the Office for Human Research Protections (OHRP, http://www.hhs.gov/ohrp/), the Food and Drug Administration (FDA, http://www.fda.gov/), and local institutional review boards.
4. The DSC and CCC monitor data management, protocol adherence, and regulatory compliance.
5. The NIDA CCTN oversees investigator performance and trial progress.

ACCOMPLISHMENTS AND FUTURE DIRECTIONS
The primary focus of the CTN's first 20 clinical trials has been to test pharmacological, behavioral, and integrated treatment approaches for substance use disorders. CTN trials have also addressed topics ranging from the treatment of substance use disorders in special patient populations, including adolescents, pregnant women, patients with co-occurring mental health disorders, and Spanish speakers, to the integration into substance abuse treatment programs of interventions aimed at the prevention of infection with HIV and sexually transmitted diseases. In addition to these large multisite

clinical trials, more than 30 smaller studies have used the CTN infrastructure to investigate the cost-effectiveness of treatment interventions, pharmacogenetics, drug use epidemics in underserved populations, and many other issues. The network's diverse research activities have been and will continue to be a fertile training ground for university- and community-based clinician-investigators and research staff, including international research fellows. For more details on the CTN program and specific CTN research studies, see the network's Web site at http://www.drugabuse. gov/CTN/.

The CTN has engaged in the following dissemination initiatives to ensure that its research results are widely accessible and that its findings are efficiently communicated to treatment providers:

- NIDA has joined with the Substance Abuse and Mental Health Services Administration (SAMHSA) to form the Blending Initiative (http://www.drugabuse.gov/), which seeks to make evidence-based addiction treatments available and readily accessible. Through this mechanism, findings from CTN studies are incorporated into tools that treatment providers can use in their practices.

- The CTN's Dissemination Library (http:// ctndisseminationlibrary.org/) is the public repository of its scientific publications, treatment manuals, presentations, study brochures, and other materials.

- Data sets (http://www.ctndatashare.org/) for completed CTN trials are made available to the public to permit the wider research community to use the data and derive the greatest possible benefit from the network's resources.

The CTN's position at the intersection of the research and clinical provider communities will continue to allow the network to address urgent challenges in drug abuse treatment. Areas for future study may include the integration of primary care and substance abuse treatment systems, the development and delivery of effective chronic care models for addiction treatment, and the assessment of holistic approaches to the treatment of patients with co-occurring substance use and mental health and somatic disorders.

See also **U.S. Government Agencies: National Institute on Drug Abuse (NIDA); U.S. Government Agencies: Substance Abuse and Mental Health Services Administration (SAMHSA).**

BIBLIOGRAPHY

Bennett, R. J., Sackett, D. L., Haynes, R. B., & Neufeld, V. R. (1996). Evidenced-based medicine: What it is and what it isn't. *BMJ (British Medical Journal), 312,* 71–72.

Centre for Evidence-Based Medicine Web site. Available from http://www.cebm.net.

McCarty, D., Fuller, B., Kaskutas, L. A., Wendt, W. W., Nunes, E. V., & Miller, M. (2008). Treatment programs in the National Drug Abuse Treatment Clinical Trials Network. *Drug and Alcohol Dependence, 92,* 200–207.

BETTY TAI

CLONE, CLONING.

Cloning has multiple definitions in the scientific world. In molecular biology, *cloning* refers to the isolation or amplification of an exact replica of a DNA sequence. DNA clones are typically manipulated by making small code changes and/or splicing multiple pieces together prior to use in experiments. Cell clones are exact copies of individual cells and are typically used for experiments that involve multiple replications under different conditions or for producing mass quantities of a cellular product. Animal clones are derived from a single cell and are genetically identical to the donor animal.

Cloning is an essential technique in drug addiction research, particularly in the generation of genetically engineered mice. In the early twenty-first century mice were becoming the organism of choice for drug addiction research because their neural circuitry and neurochemistry are similar to humans, and they readily partake in and respond to drugs of abuse. Moreover, the ability to remove or overproduce single genes in mice allows researchers to study the influence of particular genes on the neurochemical and behavioral effects of addictive drugs. To genetically engineer mice, the DNA of stem cells is altered in the laboratory using molecular cloning. These manipulated cells are then used to create two lines of mice that are genetically identical with the exception of a single gene; one line possesses a normal copy of the gene, whereas the other line has a mutated copy. By comparing the drug-induced changes in the brains and behavior of the two mouse lines, researchers have been able to selectively assess the contribution of single genes to drug addiction.

One example of the use of cloning in drug addiction research is the generation and characterization of dopamine transporter (DAT) knockout mice. The DAT gene was of great interest because it codes for the protein that clears dopamine from the synapse and is a target for cocaine. The blockade of DAT by cocaine and the resulting increase in synaptic dopamine is thought to underlie many of cocaine's euphoric and addictive properties. Embryonic stem (ES) cells derived from a normal mouse were amplified using cellular cloning, meaning that scientists started with a few ES cells and let them divide over multiple generations to produce millions of identical clones. Then, molecular cloning techniques were used to delete essential DNA sequences specifically in the section of the genome that codes for the DAT. These altered ES cells were used to generate mice that are identical to normal mice except for their inability to produce any DAT. By characterizing the neurochemistry and behavior of these mice at baseline and following cocaine administration, scientists have learned a great deal about the DAT-dependent and DAT-independent effects of cocaine and their relationship to drug addiction, as well as other behaviors mediated by dopamine.

See also **Dopamine.**

BIBLIOGRAPHY

Capecchi, M. R. (1989). The new mouse genetics: Altering the genome by gene targeting. *Trends in Genetics,* 5(3), 70–76.

Giros, B., Jaber, M., Jones, S. R., Wightman, R. M., & Caron, M. G. (1996, February 15) Hyperlocomotion and indifference to cocaine and amphetamine in mice lacking the dopamine transporter. *Nature, 379*(6566), 606–612.

Palmiter, R. D., and Brinster, R. L. (1985, June). Transgenic mice. *Cell, 41*(2), 343–345.

Sora I., Wichems C., Takahashi N., Li X. F., Zeng Z., Revay R., et al. (1998, June 23). Cocaine reward models: Conditioned place preference can be established in dopamine- and in serotonin-transporter knockout mice. *Proceedings of the National Academy of Sciences of the United States of America, 95* (13), 7699–7704.

Stephens, D. N., Mead, A. N., & Ripley, T. L. (2002, September 13). Studying the neurobiology of stimulant and alcohol abuse and dependence in genetically manipulated mice. *Behavioral Pharmacology, 13*(5–6), 327–345.

DAVID WEINSHENKER

CLUB DRUGS. The term *club drugs* is neither a pharmacological nor medical classification, but rather a cultural one referring to a chemically and psychoactively diverse group of drugs used and abused on the club and rave scenes of the late twentieth and early twenty-first centuries. Due to the ever-changing and novelty seeking nature of the youth-culture that spawned the term, no list of *club drugs* is likely to be complete, though most lists include MDMA, GHB, ketamine, rohypnol, methamphetamine, and LSD. One might add that changes in the youth culture may also render the club drugs obsolete as a useful grouping, as the cultural moment that brought them to the fore has largely passed. Further, use of the drug most commonly identified with the club drug class, MDMA, declined substantially in the late 1990s and early twenty-first century. Nonetheless, these drugs, together or apart, continue to be used and abused, particularly by young people with an experimental attitude towards drug use. A more useful name for the class might be *novelty drugs* owing to the fact that most users are attracted to these drugs by their actual or relative novelty compared to other drugs with more established reputations.

Whether the time of club drugs as cultural phenomena has passed or not, it is important that the cultural memory of their impact is not lost. Many young people faced with the choice to use drugs in 2008 were old enough to recall the cocaine epidemic of the 1980s, which in itself was in part a product of the loss of cultural memory of the cocaine epidemic of the 1930s. Like cocaine in its heyday, many club drug users took to these drugs because they seemed more benign than cocaine or heroin, the dangers of which were well known both to clinicians and the wider public. Lacking direct experience of the negative consequences of the use of these drugs led to a much more casual approach to their use than would have been the case with a hard drug such as heroin.

MDMA was not used recreationally until the 1980s, so information on the clinical consequences of its use and abuse was lacking both publicly and within the research community. Two decades later, due to research and clinical experience, the adverse consequences of MDMA use and abuse were more widely known. The lesson here is that experimenting with drugs is precisely that, an experiment, and often one whose result is more negative than anticipated.

MDMA is a psychoactive drug that emerged as a recreational drug in the mid-1980s, though it was first synthesized decades earlier. It is an amphetamine-derived hallucinogen, sometimes described as an empathogen or entactogen due to the enhanced feelings of emotional and physical closeness to others it generates in many users. Although it had a reputation as a benign so-called love drug, MDMA contributed to hundreds of deaths in its short time as an abused drug. It has been linked to seizures as well as kidney and cardiovascular failure. MDMA has produced long-term neurotoxicity in animals and a number of frequent human users have exhibited long lasting cognitive and emotional deficits.

Both rohypnol and GHB gained notoriety as *date-rape drugs* due to their criminally abused propensity for impairing memory and inducing unconsciousness. Again, both were fairly new to the world of recreational drug use, although rohypnol belongs to the same class of drugs, the benzodiazepines, as Valium, a drug with a well-known history of abuse. GHB, by contrast, is produced naturally in the human brain at low concentrations and may be involved in the regulation of sleep architecture. These drugs are especially dangerous when used with alcohol, which exacerbates their depressant effects often leading to stupor, respiratory depression, and in some cases coma and death. Like alcohol, GHB and rohypnol seem to cause an increase in violent behavior in some users. Another similarity to alcohol is the relative ease with which use of these drugs can result in overdose, dependency, and severe withdrawal syndromes. These drugs have been linked to such a disproportionate number of negative events that as of 2008 many countries had opted to increase restrictions on their use.

Methamphetamine has a long and well-documented history of abuse and toxic effects. Its appearance on the club scene seems to be linked to its low cost and the negative perception of cocaine as an alternative psychostimulant. Methamphetamine is substantially more toxic to the brain and liver than cocaine but it shares some of cocaine's potentially lethal effects on the cardiovascular system. Amphetamine use has also been linked to toxic psychosis.

Ketamine is a dissociative anesthetic formerly used in humans but subsequently largely restricted to veterinary use. Ketamine shares its major site of action with phencyclidine (PCP) and, like the latter drug, can produce many of the symptoms of psychosis in humans, including hallucinations and indifference to pain or death. Given that chronic PCP use has been associated with the development of long-term psychosis, it seems likely that this may prove to be a risk with ketamine as well. Ketamine is thought to have few other toxic effects, and some studies have demonstrated its potential as an acute antidepressant when used in low doses.

LSD is another drug with a well-known history of misuse and abuse. Its dangers lie in its hallucinogenic properties, which may cause users to physically harm themselves or others. LSD also seems to aggravate depression and psychosis. Outside its intense psychological effects LSD has few, if any, physiological side effects even when taken at doses well in excess of those used recreationally.

Club drugs are hardly risk-free, as has been made abundantly clear by many hospital admissions as well as basic and clinical research. A particularly risky and difficult-to-analyze aspect of the club drug phenomena is that most club drug users use several of these drugs as well as tobacco and alcohol. With such a variety of drugs being abused by individual users, toxic and other dangerous results are far more likely to occur and be less predictable in terms of long-term consequences.

See also **Amphetamine; Hallucinogens; Lysergic Acid Diethylamide (LSD) and Psychedelics; MDMA; Methamphetamine; Phencyclidine (PCP); Psychomotor Stimulant.**

BIBLIOGRAPHY

Club Drugs. National Institute on Drug Abuse (NIDA). Available from http://www.nida.nih.gov/.

Fritz, J. (1999). *Rave culture, an insider's overview*. Victoria, BC: Smallfry Press.

Knowles, C. R. (2001). *Up all night: A closer look at club drugs and rave culture.* North Springfield, VT: Red House Press.

RICHARD G. HUNTER

COCA PASTE. Coca paste is the first crude extraction product of coca leaves from the coca plant; it is obtained in the process of extracting cocaine from these leaves. The leaves are mashed with alkali and kerosene and then sulfuric acid (and sometimes also potassium permanganate). The result is an off-white or light-brown paste containing 40 to 70 percent cocaine, as well as other alkaloids, benzoic acid, kerosene residue, and sulfuric acid (ElSohly, Brenneisen, & Jones, 1991). Peruvian and Bolivian paste is illegally exported to Ecuador or Colombia, where it is purified into cocaine hydrochloride and then illicitly shipped to markets throughout the world. Although cocaine is the major component of coca paste, the paste is chemically complex, reflecting additives used by the clandestine laboratories performing the extraction from the coca leaves.

Coca paste, also called cocaine paste or pasta, is smoked, primarily in Latin American countries, by mixing about 0.2 ounces (0.5 g) of it with tobacco (called "tabacazo") or with marijuana (called "mixto") in a cigarette. When this dab of coca paste is smoked with tobacco, only 6 percent of the cocaine reaches the smoker—but because most of the paste samples contain significant amounts of manganese as well as several gasoline residues, the inhaled condensate is an extremely toxic substance. Despite the low bioavailability of cocaine from coca paste when it is smoked, use of this illegal substance by the smoking route reached epidemic proportions in Latin America in the late 1970s. More recently, coca paste smoking has been reported in the Netherlands, the Antilles, Panama, and the United States, although the level of use remains very low.

The effects of coca-paste smoking have been reported to be as toxic as those seen after intravenous or smoked cocaine (i.e., crack) in the United States. In fact, coca-paste smokers can achieve cocaine blood levels comparable to those seen in users injecting or smoking cocaine (Paly et al., 1980). Smoking the paste leads to an almost immediate euphoric response, and users smoke it repeatedly. As with smoking cocaine (freebasing), large quantities of the paste are taken repeatedly within a single smoking session, which is terminated only when the drug supply is depleted. Users report a dysphoric response (unease, illness) within about thirty minutes after smoking, so more paste is generally smoked at this time if available.

Substantial toxicity has been reported for chronic use of the coca-paste—tobacco combination, with users smoking it repeatedly, and progressing from stimulant-related effects and euphoria to hallucinations and paranoid psychoses. In fact, studies carried out in Peru defined a mental disorder of coca-paste smoking, made up of four distinct phases—euphoria, dysphoria, hallucinosis, and paranoid psychosis (Jeri et al., 1980). Since substantial amounts of paste are smoked at one time, the paranoid psychosis seen after chronic stimulant use has also been reported for paste use. As with cocaine abusers, experienced users of coca paste usually turn to criminal activities to support their illicit drug use.

See also **Bolivia; Crime and Drugs; Pharmacokinetics: General; Psychomotor Stimulant.**

BIBLIOGRAPHY

ElSohly, M. A., Brenneisen, R., & Jones, A. B. (1991). Coca paste: Chemical analysis and smoking experiments. *Journal of Forensic Sciences, 36,* 93–103.

Jeri, F. R., et al. (1980). Further experience with the syndromes produced by coca paste smoking. In F. R. Jeri (Ed.), *Cocaine 1980.* Lima: Pacific Press.

Karch, S. B. (2006). A brief history of cocaine. *JAMA, The Journal of the American Medical Association, 295,* 22, 2665–2666.

Paly, D., et al. (1980). Cocaine: Plasma levels after cocaine paste smoking. In F. R. Jeri (Ed.), *Cocaine 1980.* Lima: Pacific Press.

Van Dyck, C., & Byck, R. (1982). Cocaine. *Scientific American, 246,* 128–141.

MARIAN W. FISCHMAN

COCA PLANT. The coca plant is a cultivated shrub, generally found in the Andean Highlands and the northwestern areas of the Amazon in South America. The plant, however, can be grown in many parts of the world and in the early part of the twentieth century much of the cocaine used in medicine was obtained from plants grown in Asia. Of the more than 200 species of the genus *Erythroxylon*, only *E. coca* variety *ipadu*, *E. novogranatense*, and *E. novogranatense* variety *truxillense* contain significant amounts of cocaine, ranging from 0.6 to 0.8 percent. In addition to cocaine, the leaves of the coca plant contain eleven other alkaloids, although no others are extracted for their euphorogenic effects.

Coca plants have long histories of use for both their medicinal and stimulant effects. Coca leaves are believed to have been used for well over a millenium, since archeological evidence from Peruvian burial sites of the 6th century CE suggests coca use. In fact, ancient Indian legends describe its origin and supernatural powers. The Inca called the coca plant a "gift of the Sun God," and attributed to it many magical functions. The Inca and the other civilizations of the Andes used coca leaves for social ceremonies, religious rites, and medicinal purposes. Because of their energizing property, coca leaves were also used by soldiers during military campaigns or by messengers who traveled long distances in the mountains. Under the Spanish conquest of the sixteenth century, coca plants were systematically cultivated and the custom of chewing coca leaves or drinking coca tea was widely adopted as part of the Indian's daily life in South America. Use of coca leaves as both a medicinal and a psychoactive substance continues to be an integral part of the daily life of the Indians living in the Andean highlands. Substantial societal controls have existed concerning the use of these leaves, and minimal problematic behavior related to use of the coca leaves has been reported.

In the highland areas of Peru and Bolivia, and less frequently, in Ecuador and Colombia, the dried leaves are mixed with lime or ash (called "tocra") and both chewed and sucked. A wad containing 0.4 to 1 ounce (10 to 30 g) of leaf is formed, and daily consumption by coca-leaf chewers is between 1 and 2 ounces (30 and 60 g). The Indian populations in the Amazonian areas, however, crush the dried leaves, mix the powder with an alkaline substance, and chew it. Coca leaves are chewed today in much the same way that they were chewed hundreds of years ago.

Substantial cocaine plasma levels can be attained when coca leaves are chewed along with an alkaline

Figure 1. Coca leaf. ILLUSTRATION BY GGS INFORMATION SERVICES. GALE, CENGAGE LEARNING

substance, which increases the bioavailability of the drug by changing its pH. Volunteers allowed to chew either the leaf or the powdered form of coca mixed with an alkaline substance reported numbing in the mouth and a generally stimulating effect which lasted an average of approximately an hour after the coca chewing was begun (Holmstedt et al., 1979). This time-course corresponded to the ascending limb of the cocaine plasma-level curve, suggesting that the effect was cocaine-induced. Absorption of cocaine occurs from the buccal mucosa (inner cheek wall) as well as from the gastrointestinal tract after saliva-containing coca juice is swallowed. In fact, plasma concentrations in coca chewers are about what would be predicted if a dose of cocaine equivalent to that in the leaves was administered in a capsule (Paly et al., 1980).

See also **Bolivia; Coca Paste; Colombia.**

BIBLIOGRAPHY

Holmstedt, B., et al. (1979). Cocaine in the blood of coca chewers. *Journal of Ethnopharmacology, 1*, 69–78.

Karch, S. B. (2006). A brief history of cocaine. *JAMA, The Journal of the American Medical Association, 295*, 22, 2665–2666.

Mortimer, W. G. (2000). *History of coca: The divine plant of the Incas.* Honolulu, Hawaii: University Press of the Pacific

Paly, D., et al. (1980). Plasma levels of cocaine in native Peruvian coca chewers. In F. R. Jeri (Ed.), *Cocaine 1980.* Lima: Pacific Press.

MARIAN W. FISCHMAN

COCA/COCAINE, INTERNATIONAL.

When Amerigo Vespucci landed on the coast of what is now Venezuela in 1499, the first thing he saw was a group of native peoples chewing coca leaf. The captain and most of his crew thought the practice disgusting, but it did not take Spanish colonists long to discover that chewing small amounts of coca leaf gave them more energy. In 1559, the Spanish herbalist and physician Nicholas Monardes, who practiced in the port city of Seville, heard stories about coca and saw the plants collected by those returning from the New World, making him one of the first Europeans to learn about coca. He wrote, "Surely it is a thyung of greate consideration, to see how the Indians are so desirous to be deprived of their wittes, and be without understanding" (Monardes, 1925). The fact that no one became seriously ill from chewing too many of the leaves suggested that other components of the leaves caused nausea, and indeed those who chewed the plant developed unpleasant side effects long before they had ingested enough to become ill. It is now known that plasma levels never reach very great heights in leaf chewers, or in coca tea drinkers, which explains why few other cocaine-induced effects occurred among the Indians—and why reports of cocaine-related deaths among Indian coca chewers and tea drinkers have remained rare until the present day.

EARLY CULTIVATION OF COCA

Spanish settlers started arriving in Peru even before Francisco Pizarro's army completely subjugated the Incas in the 1530s. Immigrants were given tracts of land and an allotment of slave laborers. Initially, the occupiers paid relatively little attention to coca, but when they realized how much coca leaf the Indians were chewing, and how badly they wanted cocaine, it didn't take long for coca to become a cash crop. In fact, coca growing became so profitable that the immigrant farmers stopped growing their normal staple crops and devoted all of their acreage to coca cultivation. The situation reached crisis proportions when the colonial government was unable to procure enough hay to feed the horses it had also imported (Gagliano, 1994).

Food shortages became severe, and the second Spanish viceroy was forced to pass legislation requiring crop substitution and prohibiting farmers from devoting more than 10 percent of their land to coca growing. The prohibition was largely ignored, however. In 1545, silver was discovered high in the mountains, at Potosi. The Indian slaves refused to work in the abysmal conditions of the mines without their ration of coca. King Phillip badly needed the cash that the silver would bring, and so coca was supplied to the workers. Attempts at crop substitution were abandoned at this time, and the government decided instead to tax coca production. There was so much money to be made selling coca, however, that the taxes proved little disincentive to the growers. This arrangement came to an end when the Spanish lost control of the New World, which more or less freed the indigenous peoples from slavery.

Cocaine abuse did not become an issue for Europeans until the late 1800s. For one thing, supplies of coca leaf were scarce. For another, coca travels poorly, and it took up a great amount of room in ships' holds. So, after they had shipped home all the plundered gold and silver, the Spanish made sugar, rather than coca, their export of choice. The exportation of coca leaf to Europe simply made no economic sense, at least not when there were more profitable alternatives, and sugar was in great demand in Europe. Markets evolve, however, and the near simultaneous occurrence of three important technical advances turned the export market on its head and made the exportation of coca into an attractive proposition.

COCA COMES TO EUROPE

All during the time that the Spanish occupied the New World, they took great pains not to let the rest of Europe know what was going on in the New World, and all knowledge of the place was strictly embargoed. When the Spanish embargo ended, coca growers found better ways to preserve coca leaves during transit, and the French discovered a way to make a wine from the coca leaves. The wine proved to be an immensely popular product, and it was soon for sale worldwide. In spite of the wine's popularity, there was never a case of toxicity reported from its use. This was because the natural properties of the coca leaf prevented it from being abused. The process for isolating pure cocaine from coca was not discovered until 1860, but French pharmacists discovered a way to partly extract cocaine from coca, leaving most of the waxes and tannins behind. They added coca leaves to average Bordeaux wines (the Dutch preferred Malaga wine)—in a ratio of roughly ten parts wine to one part dried, ground, coca leaves—let the mixture steep for a few days, and then removed the leaves, thereby creating "coca wine."

An average glass of this wine contained only 6 milligrams of cocaine, but this was enough, when combined with the wine, to provide a pleasurable experience. Attempts at raising the cocaine concentration by adding more leaves were doomed to failure, because when too many leaves were added, or if the leaves were allowed to steep too long, the final product contained tannins and wax in far greater concentrations than were contained in the handful of leaves chewed by the Indians, which would have made it undrinkable. Still, even with its low cocaine content, coca wines became extremely popular as relatively harmless stimulant tonics.

THE EUROPEAN COCA INDUSTRY

As the New World opened up to explorers, contract botanists working for the Royal Botanical Gardens at Kew, outside of London, began to send coca seeds back to England. Although many more exist in the wild, there are only four cultivated variations of *Erythroxylum taxa*: *E. coca* var. *coca*, *E. novogranatense* var. *novogranatense*, *E. coca* var. *ipadu*, and *E. novogranatense* var. *truxillense* (Johnson et al., 2005). Some of the species contain a good deal more cocaine than others, however. Seeds from the most popular commercial variety of coca arrived at the Kew Botanical Gardens in 1869. They were collected from the area south of Cuzco, in Peru. Plants from these seeds were continuously cultivated at Kew for 40 years, and they were also sent to other botanical gardens administered by Kew. At one time there were British-owned coca plantations operating in Africa, India (where Darjeeling tea is now grown), and Malaysia. Fortunately for the Dutch planters in Java, their government was not enthused about the prospects of growing coca, for they already had a substantial problem with opium cultivation and addiction. As a consequence of this delay, the Dutch botanical gardens, located outside of Jakarta, entered the cocaine market only after the Kew plants had become widely disseminated to British dependencies. However, the coca plants obtained by the

Dutch growers contained more than twice as much cocaine as the commercial varieties grown in South America, which no doubt explains why, in the early 1900s, sales from Java eclipsed those from South America (Reens, 2003). Unfortunately, not much is known about the origin of the root stock used by the Dutch. The original seedlings were purchased from a Brussels trading company, Herman Linden and Sons, but how that company obtained the plants, or where they obtained the plants, is not known.

MEDICAL USES OF COCAINE

In 1860 Albert Von Niemann (1834–1861), a doctoral student at the University of Göttingen, devised a method for extracting cocaine hydrochloride from coca leaves, and experimentation with medical uses for the new substance soon began. During the 1870s, the work of Dr. Alexander Hughes Bennett in Edinburgh stimulated further investigation. (In their book *Opium and the People* [1987] Virginia Berridge and Griffith Edwards discuss the competition among British doctors to report on the sustaining properties of the coca leaf during exertion.)

Shortly after Von Neiman's discovery, the German company Merck of Darmstadt began producing minute quantities of cocaine (less than a few ounces a year). Because it was so expensive, there was no commercial market for purified cocaine at the time, and no one in the medical community yet had a clear idea of the benefits of cocaine. Nonetheless, Merck continued to produce small amounts of the drug every year, if for no other reason than to prove they were the world's greatest pharmaceutical chemists. In 1884, however, the company was rewarded for its perseverance. In that year Sigmund Freud (1856–1939) published his famous paper "Über Coca," in which he recommended the use of cocaine for the treatment of a variety of unrelated medical conditions—including the treatment of morphine addiction.

Much more important than Freud's discovery was the one made by Carl Koller (1857–1944), Freud's roommate in the dormitory at Vienna General Hospital. Freud and Koller had experimented with cocaine by taking it themselves and observing the effects they experienced. On a weekend visit with his fiancée Martha Bernays (1861–1951),

Freud demonstrated the drug's marvelous effects to her. At the same time, Koller was busy discovering that cocaine was a local anesthetic. Acting on a hunch, he put some drops of cocaine into a guinea pig's eye and discovered that the eye became insensitive to pain. Koller then tried it on himself and confirmed that his discovery was valid (Oeppen, 2003).

Before he made his great discovery, Koller was living in poverty and had to convince a friend (an eye surgeon) to go to the upcoming meeting of the Heidelberg Ophthalmologic Society and present a paper describing his findings. The paper was read on September 19,1884. An American named Henry Noyes was in the audience, and he mailed an account of the meeting back to the editors of the *New York Medical Record*. Noyes's account was published on October 11, 1884, less than one month after the discovery was announced (Noyes, 1884). The discovery of cocaine's local anesthetic properties led to an explosive increase in the demand for the drug, as well as a huge increase in its price. In 1883, Merck had produced only a few ounces of cocaine in the entire year, but the following year the company's production was measured in tons.

The demand for cocaine was more than adequately met by the venture capitalists and pharmaceutical houses of the day. Coca plantations sprang up all over the world, and there was soon a predictable glut of cocaine. As a result, prices began to drop and competition for customers began to increase. The Parke-Davis Company and Merck found themselves in a battle for world dominance of the cocaine market. The Parke-Davis product was thought to be of better quality at a lower price, and the company built on that reputation by providing Freud with samples and an honorarium.

ADDICTS, DOCTORS, AND QUACKS

The first American to experiment with cocaine anesthesia was Dr. William Stewart Halsted (1852–1922), a visiting surgeon at Bellevue Hospital in New York City. Within a week after reading of Koller's discovery, Halsted and his associates Richard Hall and Frank Hartley had experimented on themselves, on their surgical colleagues, and on an occasional patient. Halsted built upon Koller's initial work, and he observed that when cocaine was injected into nerves, it blocked the perception of pain within the area supplied by those nerves. Halsted and his group published their first paper on cocaine-induced nerve blocks just six weeks after Koller's announcement. Unfortunately, Koller also became addicted to cocaine, and he remained addicted to the drug even after he was appointed professor of surgery at Johns Hopkins Medical School. His friend, the famous physician William Osler, was a professor of medicine at the same school, and he eventually cured Halsted of his addiction—but only by addicting him to morphine instead. Halsted remained addicted to morphine until his death in 1922 (Colp, 1984).

Surplus cocaine at cheap prices meant that winemakers no longer had to bother soaking coca leaves in wine. Instead, they just added a pound or so of cocaine to a vat of cheap red wine. The final product contained anywhere from 60 to 120 milligrams of cocaine per glass, a considerable increase over the benign 6 milligrams in the old French versions. The practice of spiking inferior product with purified cocaine was not just limited to winemakers, however. The producers of patent medicines, the "snake oil" remedies so popular in the early twentieth century, began adding enormous amounts of cocaine to their wares. Predictably, reports of death and injury soon became a regular feature of medical journals all around the world (Adams, 1905).

In the early 1900s there were literally thousands of these remedies for sale. Their chief ingredient was alcohol, but cocaine and opium were almost always part of the formula. Dr. Fahrney's Teething Syrup, which contained heroin, surely must have been a very effective agent with which to console teething children, while Casebeer's Coca Calisaya was advertised as an "agreeable and efficient tonic," capable of "sustaining the strength under extreme physical exertion," not to mention curing those "enfeebled by sickness or disability." This product was composed mainly of alcohol and cocaine, with some cherry flavoring added. Perhaps the most outrageous of the products was Coca-Bola chewing gum. The makers of the gum recommended it be used "at occasional intervals throughout the day," even though each stick of gum contained 710 milligrams of cocaine (Adams, 1905). In order to put this amount in perspective, a modern "line" of cocaine weighs in at 50–70 milligrams, and a piece of rock cocaine, or "crack," contains even less. Chewing one stick of the gum would have amounted to "snorting" 10 lines of cocaine at one time. The predictable result was toxicity and addiction.

The end of World War I brought an end to the legitimate German cocaine industry, which comprised a cartel of drug makers who produced cocaine in addition to their other products. Article 295 of the Versailles Peace Treaty incorporated within it all of the previous provisions of the Hague Convention of 1912, which Germany had refused to sign. Manufacturers were prohibited from selling cocaine except for explicitly medical purposes. The clandestine laboratory had yet to be invented, and the antidrug legislation was thus intended to rein in legitimate drug makers. Nonetheless, low-level cocaine consumption continued among the wealthy of Berlin and Paris.

COCAINE GOES UNDERGROUND

By the 1920s nearly everyone in the civilized world knew someone whose life had been adversely affected by cocaine, and very few were particularly anxious to repeat the experience. This is clearly reflected in the literature of the time. The most famous writer to cash in on the problem of the cocaine craze was Arthur Conan Doyle (1859–1930). Doyle had trained as an ophthalmologist at the Vienna General Hospital, which was home to Freud and Koller, so it is hardly surprising that his fictional character Sherlock Holmes knew all about the properties of cocaine (Musto, 1989).

In 1919 Sax Rohmer (born Arthur Henry Ward, 1883–1959), the creator of the Fu Manchu stories, wrote a novel titled *Dope: A Story of Chinatown and the Drug Traffic*. The book was a thinly veiled retelling of the events surrounding the cocaine-related death of an East End actress named Billie Carleton (nee Florence Stewart, 1896–1918). In 1926 another British novelist, Aleister Crowley (1875–1947) wrote *Diary of a Drug Fiend*, in which the hero, Peter Pendragon, is introduced to cocaine and heroin by his girlfriend. The story was set in London's Mayfair district and it, too, seemed to be based on the Billie Carleton story.

In less than 50 years from the time it was first purified in 1860, cocaine had gone from a wonder drug to a scourge. Cocaine users were looked upon as deviant losers, although cocaine abuse continued in Europe at a low level until the beginning of World War II. Most of the cocaine sold in Europe came from sources in Southeast Asia and traveled via supply lines that remained intact for much longer than those that served the United States. At the time, cultivation in South America was in decline, which affected the U.S. market, but production in Southeast Asia persisted unabated until the war in the Pacific finally disrupted that supply.

One of the lesser-known chapters of history involves Japan's adventures in the cocaine trade. Japan bought much of Indonesia's coca output and maintained its own coca plantations in Taiwan (then the Japanese possession called Formosa) and Iwo Jima. Coca leaves were shipped to Tokyo for refining, and the cocaine was sold on the black market, both by drug smugglers and by the Japanese government itself. The government had a competitive advantage because it owned a major interest in Japan's major shipping line. In fact, Japan partly financed the occupation of China by selling cocaine and heroin to the Chinese (Karch, 1998). At the Tokyo War Crimes Trials that followed World War II, Japan was charged with crimes against humanity not only for the Nanking Massacre, but also for drug dealing. One of the exhibits used at the trials was a copy of a Japanese war bond, for which payment was guaranteed by sales of narcotics in occupied China.

COCAINE'S RESURGENCE

Cocaine reemerged as a major drug of abuse and an illegal commodity on world markets in the mid-1970s. This could never have occurred were it not for a waning of both individual and social memories of the negative effects of cocaine. Readers of the popular press in the early 1980s would never have guessed that cocaine was toxic, or that there had ever been any previous problems with the drug. At the time, cocaine had almost disappeared from world markets, and prices were so high that only the very rich, and particularly entertainment and fashion celebrities, could afford the drug. In his autobiography, the great jazz musician Miles Davis (1926–1991) wrote that in 1972 he was earning more than half a million dollars a year, and that he was spending most of this money on cocaine.

In November 1983, the British medical journal the *Lancet* editorialized about cocaine, writing that it "may thus be reasonably safe when used in a socially well-integrated fashion by people living in a stable community," and at the same time insisting that "its dangers must be overrated." This view confirmed the opinions espoused by many experts in the United States. That the *Lancet* could make such a statement in 1983 indicates that: (1) the authors of the editorial had had little exposure to chronic cocaine users, (2) they knew even less about the history of the drug, and (3) not much cocaine was available in the country at that time.

In 1989, the Reuters News Service reported, with some concern, that cocaine seizures in the United Kingdom had reached 227 kilograms in that year, amounting to an increase of 27 percent from the previous year (*Philadelphia Inquirer*, January 19, 1989). As late as May 2008, the British press still considered the seizure of a mere 140 kilograms of cocaine as worthy of mention. By way of comparison, at roughly the same time, the U.S. Coast Guard reported it had interdicted 21 tons of cocaine sitting in plain sight on the deck of a tramp steamer (*Washington Post*, March 21, 2007).

Even though the extraction process used today is not very different from the process used in the 1870s, the coca plants grown in the early twenty-first century are somewhat different from those of the nineteenth century. For one thing, they contain more cocaine, though whether this is a result of old-fashioned cross breeding or genetic engineering is hard to say. DNA analysis done in the early twenty-first century showed that modern coca leaves contain far more cocaine than those from the first decade of the twenty-first century (Johnson, 2003).

In addition, the production and sale of cocaine increased dramatically in the 1970s. In the mid-1970s, sales of cocaine by the Medellin cartel of Colombia amounted to, at most, 40 kilograms of cocaine a week. By the end of the 1970s, however, that amount had grown to several hundred kilograms, and by the early 1980s the cartel's output was measured in tons per week. By the start of the 1990s, Boeing 727s containing 5 to 7 tons of cocaine made weekly trips across Mexico to the United States. Further, as had been the case 100 years earlier, cocaine prices began to fall. In

Medellin in 1982, one kilogram of pure cocaine sold for $20,000, but by early 1984 the wholesale delivery price had dropped to only $4,000 per kilogram. This occurred partly because Bolivia had also gone into the cocaine refining business, and partly because production had expanded in all of Colombia's neighboring countries as well (Office of National Drug Control Policy, 1996).

CRACK COCAINE
The technical advance that really drove the new wave of cocaine abuse was the advent of crack. This was, in fact, exactly the same drug that had been responsible for so much misery a century earlier, but it was now in a different, more dangerous, form. The first crack smokers began to appear at psychiatric clinics in 1986 in the Bahamas, which in the mid-1980s was an important part of the trans-shipment route for cocaine from South America. Smoking crack enables more cocaine to get into the body more quickly, thereby achieving higher blood concentrations—and thus higher "highs." In the process, all the natural safeguards provided by using coca leaf, either by chewing or by drinking coca-wine, were bypassed. Crack was an irresistible force, and with so much cocaine available, the only difference between 1884 and 1984 was the magnitude of the problem.

When crack made its debut in Europe, it was considered just one of many drugs being abused, and it was therefore accorded no special status. Yet the press, both in the United Kingdom and the United States, had unfairly conflated the "desperate state of America's inner cities, whose problems crack had worsened but not created" with the effects of the drug itself (Royal College of Psychiatrists, 2000). A study of South London drug addicts published in the *British Journal of Addiction* in 1990 found that only 1 percent of the study subjects smoked cocaine in the absence of other drugs, while the majority of other attendees combined their crack with methadone or heroin (Strang, Griffiths, & Gossop, 1990). The study also found that the number of crack smokers had increased from 13 percent to 29 percent in just over a decade.

COCAINE IN THE TWENTY-FIRST CENTURY
Traditionally, coca is grown high in the Andes. In 2008, however, drug and plant seizures suggested

that coca cultivators had managed to hybridize (or perhaps even genetically engineer) a new strain of coca that grows very well in the Amazon jungle (Carroll, 2008). In spite of intense efforts and great expenditures on the part of the United States, coca supplies do not appear to have decreased significantly during the first years of the twenty-first century. According to the United Nations, in 2005, slight production decreases in Bolivia and Peru were more than offset by increases in Colombia. In 2006, meanwhile, just the reverse occurred, with decreased Colombia production offset by increases elsewhere in the Andes (United Nations Office on Drugs and Crime, 2008).

The most recent data suggest that, if anything, the situation has deteriorated further. On June 18, 2008, the United Nations Office on Drug and Crime (UNDOC) released its yearly Andean coca production survey, showing a marked increase in coca cultivation. According to the most recent data, the total area of land under coca cultivation in Bolivia, Columbia, and Peru in 2007 was thought to be 181,600 hectares, amounting to a 16 percent increase over 2006 and the highest level since 2001. The increase was driven by a 27 percent rise in Columbia (for a total of 99,000 hectares), and smaller increases of 5 and 4 percent, respectively, in Bolivia and Peru.

Surprisingly, even though coca cultivation has increased, the actual amount of cocaine produced was unchanged. In 2007, global potential production of cocaine was estimated at 994 metric tons, essentially the same as the 984 tons reported in the 2006 survey. The UNODC coca survey shows that almost half of Columbia's cocaine production, 288 tons, and one-third of the cultivation (35,000 hectares) came from just 10 of Columbia's 195 municipalities (5%).

The head of UNODC Costa was quoted as saying "Just like in Afghanistan, where most opium is grown in provinces with a heavy Taliban presence, in Columbia most coca is grown in areas controlled by insurgents." Even so, Columbian cocaine production remained almost unchanged in 2007 at 600 tons.

Citizens of the United States continue to be the world's main cocaine consumers, but the amount consumed elsewhere in the world is rising steadily. In the early twenty-first century, 90 percent of the cocaine smuggled into the United States originated in Colombia and passed through the Mexico-Central America corridor. Drug trafficking in all of North America during this period has been controlled by powerful, well-funded criminal organizations. These organizations have waged war against the Mexican authorities in an attempt to keep Mexico the main transit route for cocaine shipments to the United States. Criminal organizations in Mexico have also continued to profit from the sale of heroin, methamphetamine, and cannabis in the United States (International Narcotics Control Board, 2008).

Europe is the second largest market for cocaine, and seizures have risen significantly in Finland, Germany, Ireland, Portugal, Spain, and Switzerland. Outside of the United States, the highest rates of cocaine abuse are in Spain, the United Kingdom, and Italy. In 2004 in the United Kingdom, 5.2 percent of 16- to 19-year-olds and 14.1 percent of 20- to 24-year-olds reported having cocaine in the previous year (Reuter & Stevens, 2007). Interpol estimates that 200 to 300 tons of cocaine make their way into Europe every year. Just five years ago most British cocaine seizures were measured in kilograms. Now they are measured in tons (Bureau for International Narcotics and Law Enforcement Affairs, 1999).

John Walters, the head of the White House Office of Narcotics and Drug Control Program, said at a 2007 press conference in Haiti that cocaine production had risen to 1,400 metric tons in that year (Schneider, 2008). If correct, this figure represents a 40 percent increase over yearly production for each of the previous five years of "Plan Colombia," a multibillion dollar aid package designed to eradicate coca production in South America. (According to the International Narcotics Control Board [2008] South American production stood at 1,008 metric tons in 2004, 980 metric tons in 2005, and 984 metric tons in 2006.) The supply side of the cocaine market has proven to be adaptable and resistant to eradication efforts, in spite of the vast tracts of land that have been deforested. Instead, the use of fertilizers and pesticides, as well as better production technologies, has improved coca yields.

U.S. demand is easily met by a fraction of the amount that is actually produced in South America, and the remainder is now being diverted to the United Kingdom and Europe, via the coast of Portugal and Africa. In its 2008 annual report, the International Narcotics Control Board drew attention to the fact that West Africa is rapidly developing into a major smuggling route for cocaine from Latin America on its way to Europe. (The African country of Guinea Bissau may now be the world's first true narco-state, where all government officials are the employ of various Colombian cartels, and the only reliable source of income is drug trafficking.) One troubling side effect of this phenomenon is that in the countries of western Africa, cocaine use has also increased by the people who live there—and who now derive much of their income from cocaine sales. Rising levels of seizures in Africa, especially along the Gulf of Guinea and off the coast of Cape Verde, show that Africa's role as a transshipment point is rapidly increasing.

Efforts at interdiction appear to have been more successful than eradication. The United Nations believes that as much as 42 percent of all the cocaine produced in 2006 was interdicted, largely as a result of improved cooperation among law enforcement bodies around the world. Nearly 60 percent of all global cocaine seizures in 2005 took place in South America, the Caribbean, and Central America, while North America accounted for 28 percent, and Europe for about 14 percent.

The only remaining legitimate use of cocaine is for head and neck surgery. Unlike any other local anesthetic, cocaine causes blood vessels to contract. By injecting an area with cocaine, the surgeon not only eliminates the pain of surgery, but also greatly reduces blood loss, a goal in all surgical procedures. At the end of World War II, a League of Nations committee estimated that total, worldwide medical consumption amounted to less than 10 tons per year (Atzenwiler, 1944). In 2007, estimated production approached 1,000 tons per year (National Drug Intelligence Center, 2007). However, the amount needed for legitimate medicinal cocaine use remains at only 10 tons.

See also **Cocaine; Freud and Cocaine; International Drug Supply Systems.**

BIBLIOGRAPHY

Adams, S. (1905). The great American fraud. *Colliers,* October 7, pp. 14–15.

Anonymous. (1983, November 26). Images of Cocaine. *Lancet, 322*(8361), 1231–1232.

Antonil. (1978). *Mama Coca.* London: Hassle Free Press.

Atzenwiler, L. (1944). *Prewar production and distribution of narcotic drugs and their raw materials.* Geneva: League of Nations Permanent Central Opium Board.

Barnett, G., Hawks, R., & Resnick, R. (1981). Cocaine pharmacokinetics in humans. *Journal of Ethnopharmacology, 3*(2–3), 353–366.

Berridge, V., & Edwards, G. (1987). *Opium and the people: Opiate use in nineteenth-century England.* New Haven, CT: Yale University Press.

Bromley, L., & Hayward, A. (1988). Cocaine absorption from the nasal mucosa. *Anaesthesia, 43*(5), 356–358.

Bureau for International Narcotics and Law Enforcement Affairs. (1999). 1998 International Narcotics Control Strategy Report. Washington, DC: U.S. Department of State.

Carroll, R. (2008). First coca crop found in Brazilian rainforest. *The Guardian,* March 19. Available from http://www.guardian.co.uk/.

Colp, R., Jr. (1984). Notes on Dr. William S. Halsted. *Bulletin of the New York Academy of Medicine, 60*(9), 876–887.

Davis, M. (1990). *Miles, The Autobiography.* New York: Touchstone.

Drug Enforcement Administration. (1980). DEA History Book, 1975–1980. Washington, DC: DEA. Available from http://www.dea.gov/.

Freud, S. (1884). Über Coca. *Wein Centralblatt fur die ges Therapie, 2,* 289–314.

Gagliano, J. (1994). *Coca prohibition in Peru: The historical debates.* Tucson: University of Arizona Press.

Hatsukami, D. K., & Fischman, M. W. (1996). Crack cocaine and cocaine hydrochloride: Are the differences myth or reality? *Journal of the American Medical Association, 276*(19), 1580–1588.

Hirschmüller, A., (1995). E. Merck and cocaine: On Sigmund Freud's cocaine studies and their relation to the Darmstadt industry. *Gesnerus, 52*(1–2), 116–132.

Homstedt, B., Lindgren, J. E., Rivier, L., Plowman, T. (1979). Cocaine in blood of coca chewers. *Journal of Ethnopharmacology, 1*(1), 69–78.

International Narcotics Control Board. (2007). *Precursors and chemicals frequently used in the illicit manufacture of narcotic drugs and psychotropic substances: Report of the INCB for 2007 on the implementation of Article 12 of the United Nations Convention against Illicit Traffic in Narcotic Drugs and Psychotropic Substances of 1988.* Vienna: Author.

International Narcotics Control Board. (2008). Report of the International Narcotics Control Board for 2007. Vienna: Author.

Jekel, J. F., Allen, D. F., Podlewski, H., Clarke, N., Dean-Patterson, S., & Cartwright, P. (1986). Epidemic free-base cocaine abuse: Case study from the Bahamas. *Lancet, 1*(8479), 459–462.

Johnson, E. L., Saunders, J. A., Mischke, S., Helling, C. S., & Emche, S. D. (2003). Identification of *Erythroxylum taxa* by AFLP DNA analysis. *Phytochemistry, 64*(1), 187–197.

Johnson, E. L., Zhang, D., & Emche, S. D. 2005. Inter- and intra-specific variation among five Erythroxylum taxa assessed by AFLP. *Annals of Botany, 95*(4), 601–608.

Karch, S. (1998). *A brief history of cocaine.* Boca Raton, FL: CRC Press.

Karch, S. (2003). *A history of cocaine: The mystery of coca java and the Kew plant.* London: Royal Society of Medicine Press.

Kloner, R. A., Hale, S., Alker, K., & Rezkalla, S. (1992). The effects of acute and chronic cocaine use on the heart. *Circulation, 85*(2), 407–419.

Mariani, A. (1890). *Coca and its therapeutic applications.* Paris: Jaros Press.

Mazor, S. S., Mycyk, M. B., Wills, B. K., Brace, L. D., Gussow, L., Erickson, T. (2006). Coca tea consumption causes positive urine cocaine assay. *European Journal of Emergency Medicine, 13*(6), 340–341.

Monardes, N. (1925). *Joyfull Newes Out of the Newe Founde Worlde.* (Introduction by Stephen Gaselee). London: Constable and Company. (Original work published in Spanish in 1574; first English translation by John Frampton in 1577.)

Mortimer, W. G. (1974). *History of coca: "The divine plant" of the Incas.* Fitzhugh Ludlow Memorial Library Edition. San Francisco: And/Or Press. (Original work published 1901.)

Musto, D. F. (1989). Why did Sherlock Holmes use cocaine? *Pharmacy in History, 31*(2), 78–80.

National Drug Intelligence Center. (2007). *National threat assessment 2006.* (Document 2006-20Q17-001). Washington, DC: U.S. Department of Justice.

Niemann, A. (1860). Über eine neue organische Base in Cocablättern. Göttingen, E. A. Huth.

Noyes, H. (1884). Murate of cocaine as a local anesthetic to the cornea: The Opthalmological Congress in Heidelberg. Med Rec, 417–418.

Oeppen, R. S. (2003). Discovery of the first local anaesthetic—Carl Koller (1857–1944). *British Journal of Oral Maxillofacial Surgery, 41*(4), 243.

Office of National Drug Control Policy, Executive Office of the President. (1996). *National Drug Control Strategy: 1996.* Washington, DC: Author. Available from http://www.ncjrs.gov/.

Parke, Davis & Company (1974). Coca Erythroxylon and its derivatives. (Promotional Brochure 1885). Translated and reprinted in R. Byck (Ed.), Cocaine Papers of Sigmund Freud. Stonehill Publishers: New York.

Peoples, L. L., Kravitz, A.V., & Guillem, K. (2007). The role of accumbal hypoactivity in cocaine addiction. *Scientific World Journal, 7,* 22–45.

Reens, E. (2003). La coca de Java. In S. Karch (Ed.), *A history of cocaine: The mystery of coca java and the Kew plant.* London: Royal Society of Medicine Press. (Original work published in Paris, 1919.)

Reuter P., & Stevens, A. (2007). *An analysis of UK drug policy.* London: UK Drug Policy Commission.

Royal College of Psychiatrists, and Royal College of Physicians. (2000). Drugs: Dilemmas and Choices. London: Gaskell.

Scherzer, Karl Von. (1861–1863). *Narrative of the circumnavigation of the globe by the Austrian frigate Novara, (Commodore B. von Wulleerstorf-Urbair) undertaken by order of the Imperial government in the years 1857, 1858, & 1859.* London: Saunders & Otley.

Schneider, M. L. (2008). Rethink the fight against cocaine. *Christian Science Monitor*, May 23. Available from http://www.csmonitor.com/.

Sieveking, E. H. (1874). Coca and its therapeutic use. *British Medical Journal.*

Strang, J., Griffiths, P., & Gossop, M. (1990). Crack and cocaine use in South London drug addicts: 1987–1989. *British Journal of Addiction 85*(2) 193–196.

United Nations Office on Drugs and Crime. (2008). *Coca cultivation in the Andean Region: A survey of Bolivia, Colombia, and Peru.* Vienna: Author. Available from http://www.unodc.org/.

STEVEN B. KARCH

COCAETHYLENE: IMMUNOLOGIC, HEPATIC, AND CARDIAC EFFECTS.

Cocaethylene, a compound synthesized by the body when cocaine is used concurrently with alcohol, was first identified in 1979. Because the half-life (the time required for the body to break down and eliminate half of the substance) of cocaethylene is three to five times that of cocaine, it extends the euphoric sensation of cocaine and lessens the dysphoria (unpleasantness or discomfort) associated with its cessation. In 2006, according to the National Survey on Drug Use and Health, 33 percent of the nation's 17 million heavy drinkers also abused illicit drugs, including cocaine. Use patterns for the combination of alcohol and cocaine appear to differ according to the form of cocaine that is abused (Gossop et al., 2006). Users of powder cocaine appear to increase both alcohol and cocaine consumption when the two agents are used concurrently whereas users of crack cocaine decrease their consumption of alcohol during high-dose episodes. Crack cocaine users are also likely to reserve alcohol for use at the end of crack-using sessions (Gossop et al., 2006).

Cocaethylene, also known as ethylcocaine, ethylbenzoylecgonine, and benzoylecgonine ethyl ester, is reported to be more damaging to both the heart and brain than cocaine. Although the mechanism by which the combination of cocaine and ethanol may be particularly harmful to the cardiovascular system is unknown, two hypotheses have been proposed to explain this phenomenon:

1. It may significantly increase the myocardial oxygen demand and simultaneously diminish supply, leading to a marked supply and demand imbalance. In human volunteers, the use of both drugs produces a greater increase in heart rate than either substance alone;

2. The concomitant ingestion of cocaine and ethanol can lead to the production of a metabolite (breakdown product) that induces marked constriction of the coronary arteries, leading to myocardial ischemia (impaired function due to inadequate oxygen), infarction (cell death), and/or sudden death of the individual.

Laboratory models for the formation of cocaethylene have been difficult to develop. In one study, dogs failed to produce cocaethylene following the administration of cocaine intravenously. However, when the ability of human and dog liver cells to produce cocaethylene was compared, cocaethylene formation was greater in the dog. The investigators concluded that the route of cocaine administration might be an important factor in the formation of cocaethylene. In a study of primates, the effects of intravenously administered cocaine on extracellular dopamine, cocaethylene, and cocaine were equal in their ability to increase extracellular dopamine in the caudate nucleus. Similar to cocaine, cocaethylene inhibits the dopamine

transporter, thereby blocking the reuptake of dopamine from the synapse. Further studies appear warranted in species that more closely resemble humans to determine the pathways and significance of the cocaine and ethanol combination.

Animal studies suggest that the toxicity that results from combined cocaine and ethanol use is not due to enhanced sensitivity to alcohol in cocaine abusers. In rats, cocaethylene exposure during the fetal brain growth spurt period slows brain growth. Cocaethylene is also a neuroteratogen (adversely affecting the development of the nervous system) as indicated by altered concentrations of catecholamine (such as norepinephrine) and indoleamine (such as serotonin) neurotransmitters in developing brains, with a region-specific alteration in neurotransmitter levels following six days of cocaethylene exposure. It also appears that cocaethylene is more similar to ethanol than cocaine in terms of adverse effects on neural development.

Cocaethylene is now recognized as playing a significantly damaging role in brain development and function and as a cardiovascular risk factor. Because cocaine and alcohol are frequently used concurrently, the negative effects of cocaethylene have substantial public health implications. However, much remains to be learned regarding the reinforcing (rewarding) effects of cocaethylene and its mechanism of adverse effects.

See also **Alcohol; Benzoylecognine; Cocaine; Complications: Cardiovascular System (Alcohol and Cocaine); Complications: Immunologic; Complications: Liver (Clinical); Drug Interactions and Alcohol; Fetus, Effects of Drugs on the; Reward Pathways and Drugs.**

BIBLIOGRAPHY

Chen, W. J. A., & West, J. R. (1997). Cocaethylene exposure during the brain growth spurt period: Brain growth restrictions and neurochemisty studies. *Developmental Brain Research, 10,* 220–229.

Gossop, M., Manning, V., & Ridge, G. (2006). Concurrent use and order of use of cocaine and alcohol: Behavioural differences between users of crack cocaine and cocaine powder. *Addiction, 101*(9), 1292–1298.

Pirozhkov, S. V., & Watson, R. R. P. (1993). Immunomodulating and hepatotoxic effects of cocaine and cocaethylene: Enhancement by simultaneous ethanol administration. *Alcologia, 5,* 113–116.

Song, N., Parker, R. B., & Laizure, C. S. (1999). Coca-ethylene formation in rat, dog, and human hepatic microsomes. *Life Sciences, 64,* 2101–2108.

Substance Abuse and Mental Health Services Administration. (2007). *Results from the 2006 National Survey on Drug Use and Health: National findings* (Office of Applied Studies, NSDUH Series H-32, DHHS Publication No. SMA 07-4293). Rockville, MD: Author.

ALBERT D. ARVALLO
RONALD ROSS WATSON
REVISED BY LEAH R. ZINDEL (2009)

COCAINE. The abuse of cocaine has become a major public-health problem in the United States since the 1970s. During that period it emerged from relative obscurity, when it was described by experts as a harmless recreational drug with minimal toxicity. By the mid-1980s cocaine use had increased substantially, and led to drug taking at levels that caused severe medical and psychological problems. Cocaine (also known as *coke, snow, lady, crack,* and *ready rock*), is an alkaloid with both local anesthetic and psychomotor stimulant properties. Users generally take it in binge cycles, using it repeatedly within hours or days, alternating with periods of non-use. Many users are recalcitrant to treatment, and the substantial criminal penalties for possession and sale have not yet reduced its heavy use. In fact, information in 2007 from the Community Epidemiologic Work Group (CEWG, 2007) showed an increase in cocaine/crack use in several regions of the United States.

HISTORY

Cocaine is extracted from the coca plant (*Erythroxylon coca*), a shrub now found mainly in the Andean highlands and the northwestern parts of the Amazon in South America. The history of coca plant use by the cultures and civilizations that lived in these areas (including the Inca) goes back more than a thousand years, with archeological evidence of coca use found in their burial sites. The Inca called the plant a "gift of the Sun god" and believed that the leaf had supernatural powers. They used the leaves much as the highland Indians of South America do today. A wad of leaves, along with some ash, is placed in the mouth and both chewed and sucked. The ash helps extract cocaine from the coca leaf, and the cocaine is efficiently absorbed through the mucous membranes of the mouth.

During the height of the Inca Empire (eleventh through fifteenth centuries) coca leaves were reserved for the nobility and for religious ceremonies, since it was believed that coca was of divine origin. With the conquest of the Inca Empire by the Spanish in the 1500s, coca use was banned. The Conquistadors soon discovered, however, that coca was an aid to working in the high mountain air and served as an incentive for the Indians, so in 1569 King Philip II (1527–1598) declared that coca was not devilish and could be used.

Although glowing reports of the stimulant effects of coca reached Europe, coca use did not achieve popularity. This may have been because coca plants could not be grown in Europe, and the active ingredient in coca leaves did not survive the long ocean voyage from South America. After the German chemist Albert Niemann (1880–1921) isolated cocaine from coca leaves in 1860 and the drug was subsequently purified, it became more popular. Commercial endeavors aided its popularity by combining cocaine with wine (e.g., Vin de Coca), products that were enthusiastically and uncritically endorsed by notables of the time.

Both interest in and use of cocaine spread to the United States, where extracts of coca leaves were added to many patent medicines. Physicians began prescribing it for a variety of ills including dyspepsia, gastrointestinal disorders, headache, neuralgia, toothache, and more, and its use increased dramatically. By the beginning of the twentieth century, the harmful effects of cocaine were noted, and its utility was reassessed. As part of a broader regulatory effort, the U.S. government controlled its manufacture and sale. In 1914 the Harrison Narcotics Act forbade use of cocaine in over-the-counter medications and required the registration of those involved in the importation, manufacture, and sale of either coca or opium products. This substantially reduced cocaine use in the United States, and use remained relatively low until the late 1960s, when it moved into the spotlight once again.

MEDICAL UTILITY

Cocaine is a drug with both anesthetic and stimulant properties. Its local anesthetic and vasoconstriction effects remain its major medical use. Carl Koller (1857–1944) established its local anesthetic effect in the mid-1880s in experiments on the eye, but because it causes sloughing of the cornea, it is no longer used in eye surgery. Because it is the only local anesthetic capable of causing intense vasoconstriction, cocaine is beneficial in surgeries where shrinking of the mucous membranes and the associated increased visualization and decreased bleeding are necessary. Therefore, it remains useful for topical administration in the upper respiratory tract. When used in clinically appropriate doses and with medical safeguards in place, cocaine appears to be a useful and safe local anesthetic.

PHARMACOKINETICS

Cocaine can be taken by a number of routes of administration—oral, intranasal, intravenous, and smoking. Although the effects of cocaine are similar no matter what the route, some routes clearly contribute to the likelihood that the drug will be abused. The likelihood that cocaine will be taken for nonmedical purposes is related to the rate of increase in cocaine brain level (as measured by blood levels); routes that provide the largest and most rapid changes in brain level are associated with greater self-administration. The oral route, not used by cocaine abusers, is characterized by relatively slow absorption, and peak levels do not appear until approximately an hour after ingestion. Cocaine, however, is quickly absorbed when it is inhaled into the nose as a powder (cocaine hydrochloride). Because of its local anesthetic properties, cocaine numbs or "freezes" the mucous membranes; drug purchasers on the street use this to test for purity. When cocaine is used intranasally (*snorting*), cocaine blood levels, as well as subjective and physiological effects, peak at about 20 to 30 minutes, but reports of a "rush" are not as strong as when the drug is smoked or administered intravenously. Intranasal users report that they are ready to take a second dose of the drug within 30 to 40 minutes after the first dose. Although this was the most common way to use cocaine in the mid-1980s, it declined in popularity relative to smoked cocaine after the advent of crack mid-decade. Snorting cocaine powder appears to have risen slightly in the last 10 years, while smoking and injecting have decreased (DASIS, 2007).

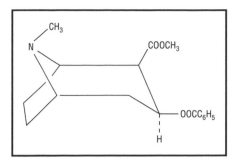

Figure 1. Chemical structure of cocaine. ILLUSTRATION BY GGS INFORMATION SERVICES. GALE, CENGAGE LEARNING

When taken intravenously, venous blood levels peak virtually immediately, and subjects report a substantial rush. This route was, until the mid-1980s, traditionally the choice of the experienced user, since it provided a rapid increase in brain levels of cocaine with a parallel increase in subjective effects. The amount of cocaine in blood and brain drop in parallel with the stimulating effects of cocaine, and cocaine users report that they are ready for another intravenous dose within about 30 to 40 minutes. Users of intravenous cocaine are also more likely to combine their cocaine with heroin (i.e., a *speedball*) than are users by other routes.

In the mid-1980s smoking cocaine began to achieve popularity. Freebase, or *crack*, is cocaine base that is not destroyed at temperatures required to volatilize it. As with intravenous cocaine, blood levels peak almost immediately, and a substantial rush ensues after smoking it. Users can prepare their own freebase from the powdered form they purchase on the street, or they can purchase it in the form of crack, or *ready rock*. The development of a smokable form of cocaine provided a more socially acceptable route of drug administration (both nicotine and marijuana cigarettes provided the model for smoking cocaine), resulting in a drug that was both easy to use and highly toxic, since this route allowed for frequent repeated dosing with a readily available and relatively inexpensive drug. The use of intravenous cocaine, in contrast, was limited to those able to acquire the paraphernalia and willing to put a needle in a vein. The toxicity of the smoked route of administration is related, in part, to the fact that a potent dose of cocaine is available to anyone who can afford it.

Cocaine is frequently taken with other drugs such as alcohol, marijuana, or opiates. In 2006 in the United States, many cocaine deaths involved more than one drug. When taken with alcohol, a metabolite (cocaethylene) forms that appears to be only slightly less potent than cocaine in its behavioral effects. It is possible that some of the toxicity reported after relatively low doses of cocaine might well be due to the combination of cocaine and alcohol.

Cocaine is broken down rapidly by enzymes (esterases) in the blood and liver. The major metabolites of this action (all relatively inactive) are benzoylecgonine, ecgonine, and ecgonine methyl ester, all of which are excreted in the urine. People with deficient plasma cholinesterase activity—fetuses, infants, pregnant women, patients with liver disease, and the elderly—are all likely to be sensitive to cocaine and therefore at higher risk for adverse effects than are others.

PHARMACOLOGY

Research has focused on the neurochemical and neuro-anatomical substrates that mediate cocaine's reinforcing effects. Although a number of neurotransmitter systems are involved, there is growing evidence that cocaine's effects on dopaminergic neurons in the mesolimbic and/or mesocortical neuronal systems of the brain are most closely associated with its reinforcing (i.e., pleasurable) and other behavioral effects. The initial site of the pleasurable effects may be the dopamine transporter of mesolimbocortical neurons. Cocaine action at the dopamine transporter inhibits dopamine reuptake, resulting in higher levels of dopamine at the synapse. These pathways may mediate the reinforcing effects of other stimulants and opiates as well. A substantial body of evidence suggests that dopamine plays a major role in mediating cocaine's reinforcing effects, although it is clear that cocaine affects not only the dopamine but also the serotonin and norepinephrine systems.

TOXICITY

In addition to blocking the reuptake of several neurotransmitters, cocaine use results in central nervous system stimulation and local anesthesia. This latter effect may be responsible for the neural and myocardial depression seen after taking large doses. Cocaine use has been implicated in a broad range of medical complications covering virtually every one of the body's organ systems. At low doses cocaine causes increases in heart rate, blood pressure, respiration, and body temperature. There have been suggestions that cocaine's physiologic effects can interact with ongoing behavior, resulting in increased toxicity, such as the additive effects on elevated body temperature of cocaine itself and the increased exertion caused by cocaine. Cocaine intoxication has been associated with cardiovascular toxicity, including heart attacks, stroke, vasospasm, and cardiac arrhythmias.

Cocaine users generally binge, repeatedly, for several hours or days, then follow this with a period in which none is taken. When cocaine is taken repeatedly, chronic intoxication can cause a psychosis, characterized by paranoia, anxiety, a stereotyped repetitive behavior pattern, and vivid visual, auditory, and tactile hallucinations. Less severe behavioral reactions to repeated cocaine use include irritability, hypervigilance (a state of increased sensory awareness of potential threats), suspiciousness, hyperactivity, and eating and sleep disturbances. In addition, when a cocaine binge ceases, users experience a crash, characterized by depression, fatigue, and eating and sleep disturbances. Initially, little cocaine craving accompanies the crash, but as time increases since the last dose of cocaine, users think of little else but the next dose.

Several studies have shown that although initially cocaine increases the neurotransmitters dopamine, serotonin, and norepinephrine, chronic cocaine use reduces function of these neurotransmitters. Positron emission tomography (PET) studies in human cocaine users show a reduction in dopamine release and dopamine receptor availability. These changes are seen for weeks after cocaine use is discontinued, showing that chronic cocaine use can produce long-lasting changes. It is possible that some of the cognitive deficits seen in chronic cocaine users (described in detail below) are related at least in part to these long-lasting changes in neurotransmitter function.

In addition to functional imaging studies in cocaine users, structural imaging studies have also shown evidence of potential neurotoxicity of chronic cocaine use. Magnetic resonance imaging (MRI) studies comparing volumes of specific brain regions between cocaine users and non-drug-using controls have shown that cocaine users have reduced volumes of the prefrontal cortex and increased volumes of caudate and putamen. More recently, studies using diffusion tensor imaging (DTI) have shown evidence of subtle white matter pathology in cocaine users compared to non-drug using controls. These subtle changes in white matter structure were associated with an increase in a measure of impulsivity, implying that the impulsive behaviors seen in cocaine users may be related to changes in brain structure produced by chronic cocaine use.

BEHAVIORAL EFFECTS

Nonhuman Research Subjects. One of cocaine's characteristics, as a psychomotor stimulant, is its ability to increase the motor behavior of animals. Single low doses produce increases in exploration, locomotion, and grooming. With increasing doses, locomotor activity decreases, and stereotyped behavior patterns (continuous repetitious chains of behavior) emerge. When administered repeatedly, cocaine produces increased levels of locomotor activity, increases in stereotyped behavior, and increases in susceptibility to drug-induced seizures (i.e., *kindling*). This sensitization occurs in a number of different species and has been suggested as a model for psychosis or schizophrenia in humans. Although sensitization to cocaine's unconditioned behavioral effects generally occurs, such effects are related to dose, environmental context, and schedule of cocaine administration. For example, sensitization occurs more readily when dosing is intermittent rather than continuous and when dosing occurs in the same environment as testing.

Learned behaviors, in which animals make responses that have consequences (e.g., press a lever to get food), generally show a rate-dependent effect of cocaine. As with amphetamine, cocaine increases low rates of responding and decreases high rates of responding. Environmental variables and behavioral context can modify this effect. For example, responding maintained by food delivery was decreased by doses of cocaine that either had no effect or increased comparable rates of responding maintained by shock avoidance. Cocaine's effects can also be modified by drug history. Although repeated administration can result in sensitization to cocaine's effects on unlearned behaviors, it generally results in tolerance to cocaine's effects on schedule-controlled responding. This may parallel the tolerance to the pleasurable effects of cocaine seen in humans. This decrease in effect after repeated dosing is influenced by behavioral as well as pharmacological factors.

Human Research Subjects. A major behavioral effect of cocaine in humans is its mood-altering effect, generally believed to be related to its potential for abuse. Traditionally, subjective effects have provided the basis for classifying a substance as having abuse potential, and the subjective effects of cocaine are similar to stimulant drugs of abuse, such as reports of *high*, *liking*, and *euphoria*; increased vigor, friendliness, and stimulation scores; and decreased sedation scores. Subjective effects correlate well with single intravenous or smoked doses of cocaine, peaking soon after administration and dissipating with decreasing plasma concentrations. When cocaine is administered repeatedly, tolerance develops rapidly, so the same dose no longer exerts much of an effect. Users must take increasingly larger amounts of cocaine to achieve the same effect. Tolerance to the cardiovascular effects of cocaine is less complete; there is a potential for the cocaine user to take doses of cocaine that lead to cardiovascular toxicity to try to achieve the euphoric effects of the drug.

Although users claim that their performance is improved by cocaine use, the data do not support their assertions. In general, cocaine has little effect on performance unless performance has deteriorated because of fatigue. Under those conditions cocaine can bring it back to non-fatigue levels. This effect, however, is relatively short-lived, since cocaine has a half-life of less than one hour.

Researchers have studied behavioral effects of chronic cocaine use through a variety of measures, including questionnaires and behavioral laboratory tasks. Using these measures, cocaine dependent individuals demonstrate higher impulsivity and poorer decision-making than non-drug-using control subjects. Some studies have found a correlation between brain imaging findings and behavioral measures in cocaine users, proving that the behavioral changes seen in cocaine-dependent individuals are related to structural or functional changes in their brains. Impulsivity and poor decision-making explain why cocaine dependence is difficult to treat.

TREATMENT

Despite substantial efforts directed toward treatment, cocaine dependence continues to be challenging for clinicians. As of 2008 the U. S. Food and Drug Administration (FDA) had approved no medications for the treatment of cocaine dependence. However, substantial advances have been made toward improved treatments for this disorder since the late 1990s. At present the mainstay of treatment continues to be non-drug-related. The most effective treatment for reducing cocaine use is a form of behavioral therapy known as contingency management (CM). In CM, patients are given positive reinforcement (such as gift certificates, merchandise, etc.) for providing cocaine-negative urine samples. The main drawback with CM is the difficulty in successfully integrating CM into treatment programs outside research settings, largely due to the cost of the rewards. Another psychological or behavioral treatment that reduces cocaine use is cognitive-behavioral therapy, or CBT; it is often combined with drug therapy in outpatient treatment studies. In CBT, therapists work with the cocaine user to identify and avoid situations and other cues associated with cocaine use.

A number of medications for cocaine dependence were initially successful in open-label trials, but later showed no difference from placebos in controlled trials. Because animal studies show that the rewarding effects of cocaine are mediated by dopamine, several dopamine antagonists have been studied in an attempt to block the rewarding effects of cocaine. Unfortunately, these medications have not proven to be efficacious in placebo-controlled trials. As mentioned above, PET studies demonstrate that chronic cocaine users have lower dopamine release and receptor binding. Consistent with this finding, medications that enhance dopamine function have had more promising results.

A medication that has consistently reduced cocaine use in placebo-controlled trials is disulfiram (Antabuse). Disulfiram is FDA approved for the treatment of alcohol dependence, where it blocks the breakdown of acetaldehye, a noxious alcohol metabolite. Disulfiram also blocks other enzymes that metabolize a range of molecules, including dopamine. Disulfiram's success may be mediated by its effect at inhibiting dopamine beta-hydroxylase, thereby increasing dopamine and reducing norepinephrine concentrations in the brain. Other drugs, such as dextroamphetamine, that worked in at least some placebo-controlled trials also increase dopamine function either directly or indirectly. However, dextroamphetamine can be abused. The wakefulness-promoting medication, modafinil, has a lower abuse potential than dextroamphetamine and has also been effective at reducing cocaine use, possibly by indirectly affecting dopamine through the glutamate system. Other medications that worked in at least one placebo-controlled trial include topiramate and propranolol. Several medications can reduce cocaine use when combined with the behavioral therapy CM, including citalopram, L-dopa, desipramine, and buproprion. The latter three were not effective in clinical trials that did not incorporate CM. Several novel treatments will be studied over the next few years. These include a vaccine that blocks cocaine from getting into the brain as well as pharmacologic agents, such as selective dopamine beta-hydroxylase inhibitors and adenosine antagonists.

In spite of the substantial progress that has been made in development of treatments for cocaine dependence, as yet none have proven effective in the large-scale trials necessary to receive FDA approval. It may well be that different medications will be effective for the various target populations and that variations in dosages and durations of treatment might be required, depending on a variety of patient characteristics. In addition, it is likely that any drug therapy for cocaine dependence will need to be combined with a behavioral intervention to show the greatest efficacy.

See also **Coca/Cocaine, International; Epidemics of Drug Abuse in the United States; Epidemiology of Drug Abuse; Freebasing; Freud and Cocaine; National Survey on Drug Use and Health (NSDUH).**

BIBLIOGRAPHY

Bock, G., & Whelan, J. (1992). *Cocaine: Scientific and social dimensions.* (Ciba Foundation Symposium 166). Chichester, UK: Wiley.

Community Epidemiology Work Group. (2007). *Epidemiologic trends in drug abuse: Highlights and executive summary* (Vol. I). Bethesda, MD: National Institutes on Drug Abuse, 1998, pp. 59–66.

DASIS Report: Cocaine route of administration trends: 1995–2005. (2007). Rockville, MD: Substance Abuse and Mental Health Services Administration, Office of Applied Studies. Available from http://www.oas.samhsa.gov/.

Johanson, C. E., & Fischman, M. W. (1989). Pharmacology of cocaine related to its abuse. *Pharmacological Reviews, 41,* 3–52.

Kleber, H. D. (1989). Treatment of drug dependence: What works. *International Review of Psychiatry, 1,* 81–100.

Kleber H. D., Weiss, R. D., Anton, R. F., George, T. P., Greenfield, S. F., Kosten, T. R., et al. (2007, April). Work Group on Substance Use Disorders; American Psychiatric Association; Steering Committee on Practice Guidelines: Treatment of patients with substance use disorders. (2nd ed.). American Psychiatric Association. *American Journal of Psychiatry, 164*(4 Suppl.), 5–123.

Landry, D. W., Zhao, K., Yang, G. X., Glickman, M., & Georgiadis, T. M. (1993). Antibody-catalyzed degradation of cocaine. *Science, 259*, 1899–1901.

Volkow, N. D., & Li, T. K. (2004, Dec. 5) Drug addiction: The neurobiology of behaviour gone awry. *Nature Reviews Neuroscience, 5*(12), 963–70.

MARIAN W. FISCHMAN
REVISED BY F. GERARD MOELLER (2009)

CODEINE. Codeine is a natural product found in the opium poppy (*Papaver somniferum*). An alkaloid of opium, codeine can be separated from the other opium alkaloids, purified, and used alone as an analgesic (painkiller). It is however most often used along with mild nonopioid analgesics, such as aspirin, acetaminophen, and ibuprofen. These combinations are particularly effective; the presence of the mild analgesics permits far lower codeine doses. Using lower doses of codeine has the advantage of reducing side effects, such as constipation. Codeine is one of the most widely used analgesics for mild to moderate pain.

Structurally, codeine is very similar to morphine, differing only by the presence of a methoxy ($-OCH_3$) group at position 3, instead of morphine's hydroxy ($-OH$) group. The major advantage of codeine is its excellent activity when taken by mouth, unlike many opioid analgesics. Codeine

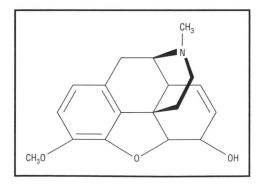

Figure 1. Chemical structure of codeine. ILLUSTRATION BY GGS INFORMATION SERVICES. GALE, CENGAGE LEARNING

itself has very low affinity for opioid receptors, yet it has significant analgesic potency. In the body, it is metabolized into morphine, and it is believed that the morphine generated from codeine is actually the active agent. Codeine has also been widely used as a cough suppressant. Codeine can be abused, and problems of abuse have often been linked to codeine-containing cough medicines, since they were once easily obtained over the counter. Chronic dosing with high codeine doses will produce tolerance and physical dependence, much like morphine.

See also **Controls: Scheduled Drugs/Drug Schedules, U.S.; Papaver Somniferum.**

BIBLIOGRAPHY

Reisine, T., & Pasternak, G. (1996). Opioid analgesics and antagonists. In A. G. Gilman et al. (Eds.), *Goodman and Gilman's the pharmacological basis of therapeutics* (9th ed.). New York: McGraw-Hill Medical. (2005, 11th ed.)

Smith, H. S. (1996). *Opioid therapy in the 21st century.* New York: Oxford University Press USA.

GAVRIL W. PASTERNAK

CODEPENDENCE. The term *codependence* replaced an earlier term, *coalcoholism*, in the early 1970s and achieved widespread acceptance among the general public during the 1980s. Both terms point to problematic beliefs and behaviors that family members of individuals with substance use disorders tend to have in common, and the term *codependence* has been applied to every possible type of addiction.

A rather large non-scientific literature has developed on the topic of codependence. Self-help books addressing codependency (e.g., *Codependent No More*; Beattie, 1987) have sold more than a million copies. Much of the literature is couched in terms of the need to deal with injuries to emotions sustained during childhood—that is, to heal the wounds of the *inner child*, a term popularized by John Bradshaw.

DEFINITION AND CONSTRUCT VALIDITY
Despite the popularity of the concept of codependence in both the general public and among some clinicians, there is a dearth of empirical research on the construct validity of codependence. Furthermore,

a variety of definitions of the construct exist. As noted by Gotham and Sher (1996), codependency has been described as an addiction, a personality disorder, a so-called psychosocial condition, and an interpersonal style.

Potter-Efron and Potter-Efron (1989) define a codependent person as "someone who has been significantly affected in specific ways by current or past involvement in an alcoholic, chemically dependent or other long-term highly stressful family environment" (p. 37). Potter-Efron and Potter-Efron include characteristics of codependency related to both basic personality traits (such as neuroticism) and psychological symptoms (such as anxiety). They described codependents as being affected by involvement with highly stressful family environments. The effects include fear, shame/guilt, prolonged despair, anger, denial, rigidity, impaired identity development, and confusion.

Using Potter-Efron and Potter-Efron's Codependency Assessment Questionnaire (CAQ), Gotham and Sher (1996) assessed the construct validity of codependency. The researchers found that this measure of codependency showed reliability and exhibited a one-dimensional factor structure. However, most of the relation between codependency and family history of alcoholism resulted from general negative affectivity or neuroticism, and there was little in the way of unique information afforded by this measure beyond what one would obtain with more traditional measures of personality.

CHARACTERISTICS

As noted above, codependency has been described in a number of ways. Cermak (1986) described codependency as a personality disorder. Cermak's codependent personality disorder included a number of purported characteristics of codependent individuals. Codependents are thought to have a continued investment of self-esteem in the ability to control both oneself and others in the face of serious adverse consequences. They are thought to exclude their own needs to meet the needs of others. They also are said to experience anxiety and boundary distortions around intimacy and separation. They are enmeshed in relationships with people with psychological disorders, such as personality disorders or substance use disorders. Furthermore, under Cermak's description, codependents have three or more

of the following: reliance on denial, constriction of emotions, depression, hypervigilance, compulsions, anxiety, substance abuse, experience of physical or sexual abuse, stress-related medical illnesses, or persistence in a primary relationship with an active substance abuser for at least two years without seeking outside help.

EMPERICAL EVIDENCE OF CODEPENDENCY

Stafford (2001) reviewed proposed definitions of codependency, issues related to the construct validity of codependency, and instruments used to measure codependency. She noted that the myriad definitions and the lack of an operational definition of codependency has been a major impediment to evaluating the utility of codependency as a construct. Furthermore, the author noted that capricious and vague criteria are often included in instruments used to assess codependency and concluded that there is a lack of robust normative data on these instruments. Based on her review, the author advised that professionals should maintain a high degree of skepticism before accepting codependency as a meaningful concept. Other reviewers (Harter, 2000; Sher, 1991) have concluded that there is little empirical evidence for specific syndromes attributed to being a family member of an alcoholic in the literature on adult children of alcoholics (ACOA) and codependence.

However, in 2008, it may be premature to discount the concept of codependence entirely. Lyon and Greenberg (1991) tested the theory that women with an alcoholic parent would be more helpful and more attracted to a man who was portrayed as exploitive than to a man who was portrayed in a more socially desirable manner. Codependent participants (defined as female children of at least one alcoholic parent) and control participants were led to believe that a male experimenter was either nurturant or exploitive. Results suggested that female offspring of an alcoholic parent offered more help to an experimenter presented as exploitive compared to an experimenter presented as nurturant. Furthermore, on self-reported measure of attitudes towards parents, codependents rated their alcoholic fathers more favorably than their mothers and more favorably than the control group rated their nonalcoholic fathers. Thus, according to the authors, codependents appear to maintain positive regard for their alcoholic parent and are seemingly willing to help exploitive others outside the family environment. However, it is important to note that the codependent group evinced greater self-reported depression than the control group, and thus depression was confounded with codependency to some extent.

Although codependence and related concepts appear to have been embraced by a number of people in the general public and the addiction treatment community, there is little consensus as to what is meant by the term and limited support for various measures purported to assess key components of the concept. Clearly, the family members of alcoholics and other addicted individuals are exposed to a wide range of stressors both inside and outside the home. Moreover, they are likely to experience a range of behavioral problems likely owing to both a problematic home environment as well as genetic liabilities shared with the addicted relative (in the case of children and other biological relatives; Sher 1991). Thus, skepticism over the concept of codependence should not be equated with skepticism over the very real difficulties of individuals who grow up in or live in alcoholic homes. However, it may be better to frame these difficulties within established psychiatric nomenclature (e.g., adjustment disorders, mood disorders, substance use disorders, personality disorders) rather than positing a unique type of disorder that is specific to growing up with or living with an addict.

See also **Adult Children of Alcoholics (ACOA); Al-Anon; Alateen; Families and Drug Use.**

BIBLIOGRAPHY

Beattie, M. (1987). *Codependent no more.* San Francisco: Harper & Row.

Bradshaw, J. J. (1988). *Healing the shame that binds you.* Deerfield Beach, FL: Health Communications.

Cermak, T. L. (1986). *Diagnosing and treating co-dependence.* Center City, MN: Hazelden.

Gotham, H. J., & Sher, K. J. (1996). Do codependent traits involve more than basic dimensions of personality and psychopathology? *Journal of Studies on Alcohol, 1,* 34–39.

Harter, S. L. (2000). Psychosocial adjustment of adult children of alcoholics: A review of the recent empirical literature. *Clinical Psychology Review, 20,* 311–337.

Lyon, D., & Greenberg, J. (1991). Evidence of codependency in women with an alcoholic parent: Helping out Mr. Wrong. *Journal of Personality and Social Psychology, 61,* 435–439.

Potter-Efron, R. T., & Potter-Efron, P. S. (1989). Assessment of codependency with individuals from alcoholic and chemically dependent families. *Alcoholism Treatment Quarterly, 6,* 37–57.

Sher, K. J. (1991). *Children of alcoholics: A critical appraisal of theory and research.* Chicago: University of Chicago Press.

Stafford, L. L. (2001). Is codependency a meaningful concept? *Issues in Mental Health Nursing, 22,* 273–286.

KENNETH J. SHER
ANDREW K. LITTLEFIELD

COERCED TREATMENT FOR SUBSTANCE OFFENDERS.

The issue of mandating or coercing offenders into treatment has been controversial in the past, but as of 2008 is becoming less contentious as evidence accumulates that demonstrates its effectiveness. Originally, treatment advocates maintained that it was an abuse of civil rights to force anyone, even a convicted felon, into unwanted treatment. While this claim might be true for the ordinary citizen, proponents of coercion maintained that those with a history of interrelated substance abuse and criminal activity had lost their right to such considerations. More to the point, some suggested that linkages between criminal and substance abusing behavior paved the way for serious re-consideration of whether offenders had already forfeited their civil rights by violating laws that resulted in the loss of freedom (through imprisonment) or the imposition of constraints while in the community. Others maintained that the state had both a duty and a right to insist that offenders take measures to reduce the likelihood that such behavior would recur in the future.

HISTORY OF COERCION INTO TREATMENT

Coercion of offenders into treatment began in the 1930s with the construction of two federal *farms* in Lexington, Kentucky, and Fort Worth, Texas. The farms were later called *hospitals* and were developed primarily for federal prisoners in need of drug abuse treatment. Volunteers into treatment were also accepted. However, most volunteers left without community follow-up after withdrawal from drugs. Perhaps not surprisingly, relapse was high. As of 2008 most treatment professionals distinguish between withdrawal from drugs or alcohol, and actual treatment. Treatment for withdrawal (lasting a few days) is not viewed as treatment for substance abuse, which typically lasts from weeks to months and in some cases, especially with offenders, for years.

The coerced treatment of substance abusers resulted from frustration over the fact that substance abusers had limited (or no) incentive to seek treatment, which frequently resulted in criminal behavior. Coercion into treatment was seen as a means of reducing arrests, crime, and drug use. From the criminal justice perspective, drug use was—and is—forbidden, although from a public health harm reduction perspective, reduced drug use was viewed as a positive achievement. Although coerced treatment for substance abuse was traditionally associated with community treatment, it eventually became an important component of the justice system and its approach to offenders with a substance abuse history.

NARCOTIC ADDICT REHABILITATION ACT

In 1966, the Narcotic Addict Rehabilitation Act (NARA), based on New York and California civil commitment coerced treatment models, was enacted by Congress as a federal civil commitment program to reduce drug use. Court-ordered treatment was initially provided at the Lexington and Fort Worth hospitals. Subsequently, in-patient treatment facilities were opened in several cities and served as the foundation for community-based drug abuse treatment. When NARA was phased out, the U.S. Public Health Service facilities were transferred to the Federal Bureau of Prisons in the mid-seventies (Leukefeld & Tims, 1988, pp. 236–251).

TREATMENT ACCOUNTABILITY FOR SAFER COMMUNITIES (TASC)

In the 1970s, prison-based programs such as Cornerstone in Oregon and Stay 'n' Out in New York State gained a reputation for successful treatment of inmate substance abusers. Another well-known program associated with coerced substance abuse treatment was the Treatment Alternatives to Street Crime (TASC) program, later called Treatment Accountability for Safer Communities. TASC was based originally in New York City and Washington, DC, although as of 2008 the association had established more than two hundred programs throughout the United States. TASC made a critical contribution to the justice and treatment delivery systems by emphasizing the importance of strengthening linkages between the two systems. Previously, criminal justice practitioners tended to view treatment as too soft an approach for criminals, while treatment professionals viewed the justice system as too rigid. In addition, for years treatment advocates maintained that substance abusers needed to hit bottom and want treatment, in order for treatment to be successful. The justice system, by contrast, felt that society at large could not afford to wait until substance abusers hit bottom or wanted to be treated. Eventually, however, the two systems learned to collaborate, with rewarding and impressive results.

Although effectiveness of treatment could be measured in several ways, in the context of treatment for substance abusing offenders, many agreed that appropriate goals were reductions in criminal and substance abuse behaviors following treatment. Thus, it was important to study the post-treatment outcomes of such offenders to determine whether they refrained from future crime or substance abuse.

Beginning in the mid-eighties, evidence began to mount which suggested that, in fact, coerced treatment for offenders with a history of substance abuse was associated with reductions in both drug/alcohol use and criminal activity (Wexler et al., 1992, pp. 156–175).

In the late nineties, researchers conducted coordinated studies at three prison-based substance abuse treatment programs in California, Delaware, and Texas, to test the effectiveness of adding an aftercare component to their programs. Although these three programs were located in different geographical regions, in different states and with different (though comparable) populations, research findings were virtually the same: The aftercare component increased the effectiveness of the three treatment programs. Simply put, those offenders who had completed treatment did better (in terms of drug use or criminal arrests after release from prison and treatment) than those who had not received treatment. In addition, those who had completed treatment and received aftercare did better than those who completed treatment but did not receive aftercare (Knight et al., 1999, pp. 337–351; Martin et al., 1999, pp. 294–320; Wexler et al., 1999, pp. 321–336).

These studies appeared to confirm the cost effectiveness of both treatment and aftercare, confirming findings of earlier research (CALDATA, 1994, p. 89) that reported that for every dollar spent on treatment, the state benefited sevenfold. By the beginning of the new millennium, additional research suggested that treatment for substance offenders was cost effective (Aos et al., 2001; McCollister et al., 2003). These findings were important in responding to questions raised by those who wondered whether treatment for offenders was ultimately cost effective. But researchers warned that findings should be interpreted with caution because offenders might have entered treatment voluntarily rather than because it was mandated. However, imprisoned offenders have very few choices, and to that extent they are already in a state of coercion.

MOTIVATIONAL READINESS FOR TREATMENT

The issue of motivational readiness for treatment has been cited as a problem for those mandated to treatment. Clearly, whether offenders are motivated to seek treatment has implications for how receptive they may be to such treatment. Clinicians have developed training to address this issue. Motivational training for treatment has gained recognition as a method for facilitating entry into treatment for substance abuse by those who may otherwise resist such treatment.

DRUG TREATMENT ALTERNATIVE-TO-PRISON (DTAP)

In 2003, a White Paper published by the National Center on Addiction and Substance Abuse at Columbia University (CASA) reported findings from its evaluation of the Drug Treatment Alternative-to-Prison (DTAP) program based in Brooklyn, New York. Although the DTAP program was originally a kind of diversion program for prisoners charged with drug crimes, the program was changed to a deferred sentencing model. This meant that participants who pled guilty to a felony might enter treatment as an alternative to prison but that program violations would immediately result in punishment and imprisonment.

The CASA evaluation found that DTAP graduates had re-arrest rates that were 33 percent less than those of the matched comparison group two years following treatment; reconviction rates were 45 percent less. In addition, DTAP graduates were three and one-half times more likely to be employed than they were prior to incarceration. (Ninety-two percent were employed following graduation from DTAP, compared to only 26 percent who were employed prior to incarceration.) Findings for non-graduate participants in the program were more impressive also than for non-participants.

CASA calculations were that DTAP costs were substantially less than the costs for ordinary imprisonment ($64,338); the average cost of residential drug treatment, vocational training, and support services for a DTAP participant was $32,975, barely more than half the cost of imprisonment.

See also **Prisons and Jails, Drug Treatment in; Shock Incarceration and Boot-Camp Prisons; Treatment, Stages/Phases of: Aftercare.**

BIBLIOGRAPHY

Aos, S., Phipps, P., Barnoski, R. & Lieb, R. (2001). The comparative costs and benefits of programs to reduce crime, version 4.0. Olympia, WA: Washington State Institute for Public Policy. Document No. 01-05-1201, May 2001.

Arrestee drug abuse monitoring program annual report. (1998). Washington, DC: U.S. Government Printing Office.

Blankenship, J., Dansereau, D., & Simpson, D. (1999). Cognitive enhancements of readiness for corrections-based treatment for drug abuse. *Prison Journal 79*(4), 431–445.

Bureau of Justice Statistics. (1999). *Substance abuse and treatment, state and federal prisoners, 1997.* Washington, DC: U.S. Government Printing Office.

Bureau of Justice Statistics. (2007). *Prisoners in 2006.* Washington, DC: U.S. Government Printing Office.

California Department of Alcohol and Drug Programs. (1994). Evaluating recovery services: The California Drug and Alcohol Treatment Assessment (CALDATA). National Opinion Research Center at the University of Chicago and Lewin-VHI, Inc., Fairfax, VA.

Drug abuse treatment in prisons and jails. (1992). (NIDA Monograph No. 118), pp. 156–175.

Field, G. (1985). The cornerstone program: A client outcome study. *Federal Probation 49*, 50–55.

Hiller, M. L., Knight, K., Rao, S. R., & Simpson, D. D. (2002). Assessing and evaluating mandated correctional substance-abuse treatment: Policies and issues. In C. G. Leukefeld, F. Tims, & D. Farabee (Eds.), *Assessing and evaluating mandated correctional substance-abuse treatment* (pp. 41–56). New York: Springer.

Knight, D., Simpson, D., & Hiller, M. (1999). Three-year reincarceration outcomes for in-prison therapeutic community treatment in Texas. *Prison Journal 79*(3), 337–351.

Leukefeld, C. G. (1988). *Compulsory treatment for drug abuse: Research and clinical practice.* (NIDA Research Monograph No. 86, pp. 236–251).

Martin, S. S., Butzin, C. A., Saum, C. A., & Inciardi, J. A. (1999). Three-year outcomes of therapeutic community treatment for drug-involved offenders in Delaware: From prison to work release to aftercare. *Prison Journal 79*(3), 294–320.

McCaffrey, B. R. (2000). *Drug abuse and the criminal justice system: Saving lives and preventing crime through treatment, pp. 1–2.* Washington, DC: Connection: A newsletter linking the users and producers of drug abuse services research, Academy for Health Services Research and Health Policy, August 2000.

McCollister, K. E., French, M. T., Inciardi, J. A., Butzin, C. A., Martin, S. S., & Hooper, R. M. (2003). Post-release substance abuse treatment for criminal offenders: A Cost-effectiveness analysis. *Journal of Quantitative Criminology, 19*(4), 389–407.

National Center on Addiction and Substance Abuse at Columbia University (CASA). (2003). *Crossing the bridge: An evaluation of the Drug Treatment Alternative-to-Prison (DTAP) Program: A CASA white paper.* (Funded by National Institute on Drug Abuse.)

Pearson, F. S., & Lipton, D. S. (1999). A meta-analytic review of the effectiveness of corrections-based treatments for drug abuse. *Prison Journal 79*(4), 384–410.

Treatment Episode Data Set. (2006). *Treatment Episode Data Set (TEDS) 1994–2004: National admissions to substance abuse treatment services.* Rockville, MD: Department of Health and Human Services, Substance Abuse and Mental Health Services Administration, Office of Applied Studies.

Treatment Episode Data Set. (2006). *Treatment Episode Data Set (TEDS) 2004: Discharges from substance abuse treatment services.* Rockville, MD: Department of Health and Human Services Administration, Office of Applied Studies.

Wexler, H. K., Falkin, G. P., Lipton, D. S., & Rosenblum, A. B. (1992). Outcome evaluation of a prison therapeutic community for substance abuse treatment. In C. G. Leukefeld, F. Tims, & D. Farabee (Eds.), *Drug abuse treatment in prisons and jails, NIDA research monograph 118 t* (pp. 156–175)

Wexler, H. K., Melnick, G., Lowe, L., & Peters, J. (1999). Three-year reincarceration outcomes for amity in-prison therapeutic community and aftercare in California. *Prison Journal 79*(3), 321–336.

MARIE F. RAGGHIANTI

COFFEE. Coffee is the world's most common source of caffeine, providing a little more than half of all caffeine consumed daily. In the United States, coffee is usually a beverage made by percolation or infusion from the roasted and ground or pounded seeds of the coffee tree (genus *Coffea*), a large evergreen shrub or small tree, which was native to Africa but now is grown widely in warm regions for commercial crops. Caffeine from coffee accounts for an estimated 125 milligrams of the 211 milligrams of U.S. caffeine consumed per capita per day. Recent estimates suggest that more than 50 percent of the adolescents and adults in the United States consume some type of coffee beverage. Coffee is one of the main natural commodities in international trade, ranking second only to petroleum in dollar value. Approximately fifty countries export coffee and virtually all of those countries rely on it as a major source of foreign exchange. An estimated 25 million people make their living in the production and distribution of coffee products.

In addition to caffeine, roasted coffee contains at least 610 other chemical substances, which may contribute to its smell, taste, and physiological effects.

Figure 1. Coffee plant. ILLUSTRATION BY GGS INFORMATION SERVICES. GALE, CENGAGE LEARNING

Nevertheless, coffee's primary psychoactive ingredient is caffeine. The amount of caffeine in an individual cup of coffee varies considerably, depending on the type and amount of coffee used, the form of the final coffee product (e.g., ground roasted or instant), and the method and length of brewing. On average, a 6-ounce (177 milliliters) cup of ground roasted coffee contains about 100 milligrams caffeine; the same amount of instant coffee typically contains about 70 milligrams caffeine. However, the caffeine content of any given 6-ounce cup of coffee can vary considerably and can reach as much as 210 milligrams. Drip coffee typically contains more caffeine than percolated; decaffeinated coffee contains a small amount of caffeine, approximately 4 milligrams in a 6-ounce cup. Individual servings of caffeinated coffee contain amounts of caffeine that have been shown experimentally to produce a range of effects in humans including the alteration of mood and performance and the development of physical dependence with chronic daily use.

Coffee cultivation probably began around 600 CE in Ethiopia, but the drink was spread into the Middle East and Europe. Today, much of the world's coffee is grown in South and Central America, particularly Brazil and Colombia, and in several African countries. Coffee beverages derive primarily from the seeds of two species of *Coffea* plants, *Coffea arabica* and *Coffea canephora* var. *robusta*. Robusta coffees contain approximately twice as much caffeine as Arabicas. Arabica beans are used in the majority of the coffee consumed today, particularly in the higher quality coffees. Since processing for instant and decaffeinated coffee extracts flavor components from the bean, the stronger flavored beans, typically Robusta beans, are used for these coffee products. Caffeine extracted in the decaffeination process is sold for use in soft drinks and medications.

The coffee bean, covered with several layers of skin and pulp, occupies the center of the coffee berry. During the first part of coffee production, the outer layers of the coffee berry are removed, leaving a green coffee bean. The beans are then roasted, removing between 14 and 20 percent of their water and changing their color from green to various shades of brown; generally, the beans get darker as more water is extracted. The beans are then ground and ready for use. To produce instant coffee, roasted and ground coffee is percolated to produce an aqueous coffee extract. That extract is dehydrated by spray or freeze-drying to produce water-soluble coffee extract solids. Since this process removes flavor and aroma from the coffee, compounds are added to the extracts at the completion of the process to restore the lost characteristics.

See also **Caffeine; Colombia.**

BIBLIOGRAPHY

Barone, J. J., & Roberts, H. (1984). Human consumption of caffeine. In P. B. Dews (Ed.), *Caffeine*. New York: Springer-Verlag.

Smith, B. D. (2006). *Caffeine and activation theory: Effects on health and behavior.* London: CRC Press.

Spiller, G. A. (Ed.). (1984). *The methylxanthine beverages and foods: Chemistry, consumption, and health effects.* New York: Alan R. Liss.

KENNETH SILVERMAN
ROLAND R. GRIFFITHS

COLA/COLA DRINKS. Cola drinks are carbonated soft drinks that contain some extract of the kola nut in their syrup. Kola nuts are the chestnut-sized and -colored seeds of the African kola tree (*Cola nitida* or *Cola acuminata*). For the soft-drink industry, the trees are, as of 2008, grown on plantations throughout the tropics. Historically, kola nuts were valued highly among African societies for their stimulating properties. Kola nuts were cracked into small pieces and chewed for the effect, which increased energy and elevated mood in extremes of heat, hunger, exhaustion, and the like. European colonists in Africa learned of the effect and some chewed the nuts. In the 1800s, Europeans brought kola nuts to various strenuous endeavors in Africa and in other regions, and they began to increase the areas under cultivation. Kola nuts were soon finely powdered and made into syrups for ease of use, with no loss of effect, it was claimed.

The active ingredient responsible for these stimulatory properties is caffeine, a powerful brain stimulant, which is also present in other plants such as coffee, cocoa, tea, and maté. Besides reversing drowsiness and fatigue, a heightened awareness of stimuli and surroundings may occur. Studies have shown that less energy may be expended by the

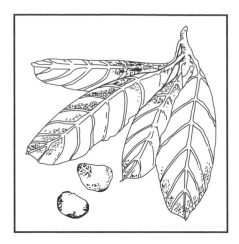

Figure 1. Kola leaf. ILLUSTRATION BY GGS INFORMATION SERVICES. GALE, CENGAGE LEARNING

musculature with equal or greater results—in animals as well as humans—but excess use causes tolerance and dependence, often unrealized until deprivation results in severe headaches. Large doses can cause nervous irritation, shaking, sleep disturbances, insomnia, and aggravation of stomach ulcers or high blood pressure.

In the late 1800s, in the United States, cola drinks came onto the market with other carbonated or phosphated (fizzy) drinks. Coca-Cola, one of the first and most popular, contained extracts of both the coca plant (cocaine) and the kola nut (caffeine), but by the early 1900s, with the realization of its dangers, cocaine was removed and replaced by additional caffeine and a decocainized extract. Drinking cola is common in the United States and emulated worldwide, with many brands competing for a huge and growing consumer market. As of 2008, colas were available with sugar or artificial sweeteners, with or without caffeine, with or without caramel coloring (clear), thus indicating that people seem to like the flavor regardless of the specific ingredients or the effect.

David Courtwright's historical study of the origins of the worldwide use of kola points out that the makers of Coca-Cola faced litigation in the United States as early as 1911 on the grounds that the caffeine in the drink was habit-forming and an unlabeled additive in a product advertised to children and adults alike. The result of the trial forced Coca-Cola to reduce caffeine amounts by half, but by then the product was available throughout the United States. During World War II, American soldiers introduced Coke to Europe and Japan, and dozens of bottling plants were built immediately after the war ended. By 1991, Coke was available in 155 nations.

Despite the truthful claims by soft-drink companies of responsible improvements to their products by removing kola extract, caffeine remains the key psychoactive ingredient of these soft drinks. Courtwright argues that products such as Coca-Cola are not only stimulating drugs, but cultural and political symbols that never would have become so in the absence of caffeine or a like stimulant.

Several medical studies conducted in the late-twentieth century linked the consumption of cola drinks by physically active adolescent girls to increased bone fractures as compared to those who abstained from colas. A Harvard University School of Public Health study could not determine the exact cause, but speculated that phosphoric acid contained in cola drinks adversely affects calcium metabolism and bone mass. Coupled with the belief that many teens replace milk with soda in their diets increased the likelihood of a decrease in bone density. In addition, research indicates that adolescents who consume excessive amounts of colas (1.5 liters per day or eleven liters per week) or other caffeinated beverages experience daily or near–daily headaches. Public health officials have also noted a dramatic increase in calorie consumption among adolescent cola drinkers.

Phosphoric acid in cola has also been linked to weakened bone density in older women. A 2006 Tufts University study found that regular consumers of cola drinks were likelier to experience decreased bone mineral density in the hip. Such a decrease could lead to osteoporosis and, ultimately, fractures of the hip that are often debilitating or even fatal among older women. However, critics of the 2006 study noted that while the corollaries between phosphoric acid in cola and bone deterioration are quite plausible, research comparing bone loss over time between cola drinkers and non-cola drinkers is necessary to confirm a connection.

See also **Caffeine; Coca Paste; Coca Plant.**

BIBLIOGRAPHY

Courtwright, D. T. (2002). *Forces of habit: Drugs and the making of the modern world*. Cambridge, MA: Harvard University Press.

Fitzpatrick, L. (2001). Secondary causes of osteoporosis. *Mayo Clinic Proceedings, 77,* 453–468.

Graham, D. M. (1978). Caffeine: Its identity, dietary sources, intake and biological effects. *Nutritional Review, 36,* 97–102.

Hering-Hanit, R., & Gadoth, N. (2004). Caffeine-induced headache in children and adolescents. *Cephalagia, 23,* 332–335.

Lewin, L. (1964). *Phantastica: Narcotic and stimulating drugs, their use and abuse.* New York: Dutton.

Tucker, K. L. (2006). Colas, but not other carbonated beverages, are associated with low bone mineral density in older women: The Framingham Osteoporosis Study. *American Journal of Clinical Nutrition, 84,* 936–942.

Wyshak, G. (2000). Teenaged girls, carbonated beverage consumption, and bone fractures. *Archives of Pediatrics and Adolescent Medicine, 154,* 610–613.

MICHAEL J. KUHAR
REVISED BY MATTHEW MAY (2009)

COLLEGE ON PROBLEMS OF DRUG DEPENDENCE (CPDD), INC.

The College on Problems of Drug Dependence (Martin W. Adler, Ph.D., Executive Officer, CPDD, Department of Pharmacology, 3420 N. Broad Street, Philadelphia, PA 19140; http://views. vcu.edu/cpdd/) is the nation's oldest organization devoted to the problem of drug use and addiction. It is an incorporated, not-for-profit, scientific organization that acts independently of both the U.S. government and the pharmaceutical industry while fostering an exchange of knowledge and resources across the academic, medical, governmental, and business communities. The CPDD is known internationally as a World Health Organization Collaborating Center for research and training in the field of drug dependence. The CPDD also offers consulting services and, along with the National Institute on Drug Abuse, supports drug-dependence testing and research at several select U.S. universities.

Among the goals of the CPDD are the following:

1. to support, promote, and carry out abuse-liability research and testing, both at the preclinical and clinical levels;

2. to serve as advisor to both the public and private sectors, nationally and internationally;

3. to sponsor an annual scientific meeting in fields related to drug abuse and chemical dependence.

The annual scientific meeting of the CPDD has become one of the few forums where scientists from diverse disciplines can discuss problems of drug abuse and drug dependence at a rigorous academic and scientific level.

A primary goal of the CPDD is the publication of data on the physical-dependence potential and abuse liability of opioids, stimulants, and depressants, as well as the development of a new methodology for drug evaluation. These data provide an independent scientific evaluation of drugs that might have abuse liability. A number of scientists from various medical schools work collaboratively to assess these drugs. The data are collated in the Laboratory of Medicinal Chemistry, National Institute of Diabetes, Digestive and Kidney Diseases (NIDDK), National Institutes of Health (NIH), Bethesda, MD. They are discussed by the Drug Evaluation Committee of the CPDD before publication. Government agencies can use the data to help determine whether a medically useful drug should be scheduled under the Controlled Substances Act to restrict access and thus reduce possible abuse.

The contemporary CPDD originated in 1913, as the Committee on Drug Addiction of the Bureau of Social Hygiene in New York City. In 1928, the Bureau of Social Hygiene provided funds to the Division of Medical Sciences, National Research Council (NRC), of the National Academy of Sciences (NAS), for the support of a chemical, pharmacological, and clinical investigation of narcotic drugs by the Committee on Drug Addiction, NRC, NAS. This research continued until World War II. From 1939 to 1947, the Committee on Drug Addiction served as an advisory group to the U.S. Public Health Service (Eddy, 1973).

The Committee on Drug Addiction was reestablished in 1947 as the Committee on Drug Addiction and Narcotics (CDAN), in the Division of Medical Sciences of the NRC, NAS. In 1965, CDAN's name was changed to the Committee on Problems of Drug Dependence (CPDD). The CPDD remained as an NRC, NAS committee until 1976, when it became an independent scientific organization, the Committee on Problems of Drug Dependence (CPDD), Inc. It was guided by a

Board of Directors with the sponsorship of nine major scientific organizations (May & Jacobson, 1989). In 1991, the CPDD underwent its most recent reorganization and its name was modified to reflect its contemporary role. Now known as the College on Problems of Drug Dependence, Inc., the CPDD has become a scientific membership organization that enables its members to have a voice on issues relating to drug abuse. Sixteen institutions and professional and scientific societies are affiliated with or have liaison representation with the CPDD, including such diverse groups as the American Chemical Society, the American Medical Association, and the Food and Drug Administration.

The members of the CPDD are involved in all the aspects of the effects of drugs subject to abuse—encompassing the enormous range from social, economic, and political issues through basic research in molecular biology and the study of the interaction of these drugs with specific receptors in the central nervous system. Membership is divided into four categories: Fellows, Regular Members, Associate Members, and Student Members. In addition, corporations with an interest in the field may join as Corporate Members. The CPDD sponsors the publication of the monthly journal, *Drug and Alcohol Dependence*, an international journal covering the scientific, epidemiological, sociological, economic, and political aspects of substance abuse.

See also **Drug Types; World Health Organization Expert Committee on Drug Dependence.**

BIBLIOGRAPHY

College on Problems of Drug Dependence (CPDD). Available from http://www.cpdd.vcu.edu.

Eddy, N. B. (1973). *The National Research Council involvement in the opiate problem, 1928–1971.* Washington, D.C.: National Academy of Sciences.

May, E. L., & Jacobson, A. E. (1989). The Committee on Problems of Drug Dependence: A legacy of the National Academy of Sciences. A historical account. *Drug and Alcohol Dependence, 23,* 183–218.

ARTHUR E. JACOBSON
REVISED BY NANCY FAERBER (2001)

COLOMBIA. Colombia's role in illicit drug production and trafficking has evolved over the past several decades. Colombia is the only country where three plant-based illegal drugs—marijuana, cocaine, and heroin—are produced. Drug trafficking has played a major role in Colombia's history for the past 30 years, profoundly impacting Colombian democratic institutions, the ongoing civil conflict, and its environment. Definitively explaining why Colombia's illicit economies have played such a central role is impossible. Many analysts point to Colombian geography; the country has both Atlantic and Pacific coastlines, large jungle areas with little or no state presence, and relatively unpoliced borders. Black markets also have deep roots in Colombian political culture and institutions, and the country has a long history of smuggling, contraband, and corruption. Drug production and trafficking methods have evolved in response to changing counternarcotics policies, primarily programs established and funded by the U.S. government. Colombia does not have a major tradition of indigenous ritual drug consumption, with only a few small indigenous groups (making up less than 2% of the total population) regularly using coca and hallucinogenic plants for religious and medicinal reasons. Nonindigenous Colombians have historically low rates of illicit consumption.

Determining the full extent of drug production and trafficking is impossible, given the serious problems with existing data and statistics, which are often estimates driven by political agendas. In part, these difficulties are the result of the nature of illicit economies; because these activities are illegal, they are hidden and thus inherently difficult to quantify. In addition, many of the statistics describing the illicit drug trade are methodologically unsound and ideologically driven (Thoumi, 2005). The United Nations and various U.S. drug enforcement agencies often produce varying statistics, in part because of the technological and methodological differences in their measurement, for example, in estimating Colombian coca cultivation (including overflights versus satellite photography, and the degree of small-scale sampling). There have been significant disagreements over the estimates of the role of illegal armed groups in the drug trade (see below). Figures about the Colombian drug trade vary widely depending on the source. During the 1980s and 1990s the drug trade was widely described as contributing significantly to Colombia's economic stability during the era's debt crisis; this was later disputed by some Colombian economists, who estimated that the amount of money entering the national economy was less than originally believed. The illicit economy did indisputably impact regional economies, such as the cities of Medellin and Cali and other smaller periodic hubs of drug production and trafficking. These areas have clearly experienced boom-bust cycles, with drug trade profits fueling construction and other economic activity. Such economic activity has not, however, led to longer-term financial stability in these areas. These boom-bust cycles distort local economies rather than provide the basis for long-term investment. The state is unable to capture resources through taxation to invest in infrastructure and public services. Some scholars argue that although the illicit economy has played a smaller role in Colombia's overall economy since the 1990s, the damage done by the black market has increased because of its long-term impact and the role drug trafficking has assumed in sustaining illegal armed groups (Thoumi, 2003).

Colombian counternarcotics policies are profoundly influenced by U.S. policies; the United States provides significant funding for these programs. Since 1989 the U.S. government has defined drug trafficking as a national security threat, so its counternarcotics programs abroad aim to lower the amount of illicit drugs entering the United States. In Colombia, such programs have additional objectives as part of counterinsurgency and, since 9/11, counterterrorism programs, as the U.S. and Colombian governments intend to deny insurgent groups resources derived from the illicit drug trade.

Counternarcotics efforts include legal restrictions on precursor chemicals to prevent drug manufacturing, financial laws to limit money laundering, eradication (the destruction of plant crops), and interdiction to interrupt trafficking routes. Eradication to destroy marijuana, coca, and opium poppy plants can be voluntary, usually done by hand by farmers themselves, often in exchange for social services and technical support for transitioning to legal agricultural crops, known as alternative development or crop substitution programs. Forced eradication can involve manual eradication carried out by military or police forces, or through fumigation, the aerial spraying of chemical herbicides. Fumigation first began in Colombia in the 1970s, targeting

marijuana plants. Large-scale fumigation operations began to target coca crops in southern Colombia in the late 1990s. Peasant farmers in these areas allege that spraying causes health problems, and destroys legal crops and livestock, as well as negatively impacting the watershed and ecological diversity; government officials claim that coca cultivation itself is more ecologically damaging and that no definitive health effects have been proven.

In the 1970s a boom in marijuana cultivation along Colombia's Atlantic coast created a class of newly rich traffickers supplying the U.S. market. Large maritime vessels carried bulk shipments of marijuana to prearranged points off the U.S. coast. Law enforcement efforts spearheaded by the U.S. Drug Enforcement Administration (DEA) shut down these trafficking routes.

Colombia first became significantly involved in the cocaine trade as a site for refining and trafficking beginning in the late 1970s, when coca paste produced in Peru and Bolivia was brought there for processing and then shipped to the United States. In the early twenty-first century the cultivation of coca has expanded enormously in Colombia. Unlike in Peru and Bolivia, where peasants have for centuries grown and chewed the coca leaf (a mild stimulant, compared with its processed form, cocaine), in Colombia this practice is limited to a very few, small indigenous groups.

Colombia's well-publicized cartels, first in Medellin and then Cali, expanded from marijuana to the processing and export of cocaine. A small number of powerful drug kingpins, including Carlos Lehder-Rivas, Jorge Ochoa, Pablo Escobar, Griselda Blanco, Jose Rodriguez-Gacha, and the Herrera brothers, came to control a billion-dollar cocaine industry that processed coca grown primarily in Bolivia and Peru. As cocaine and then crack became more popular within the United States, the cartels developed new forms of trafficking, including the use of mules (individuals paid to transport drugs by ingesting them; this practice is extremely dangerous because of possibility of detection as well as death if the protective sealant ruptures). Air-dropping involves parachuting waterproof containers of drugs into the ocean from low-flying planes off the coast of Florida. These containers are then picked up by boats and brought ashore as a means of escaping radar detection. Traffickers also frequently smuggle narcotics within legal shipments of commercial goods, relying on high profit margins to offset the small percentage of such shipments that are confiscated by customs officials. Each new innovation requires law enforcement officials to develop new detection methods.

Colombia first began producing opium poppies for heroin in 1986; by 2003 there were approximately 4,000 hectares in production supplying consumers in the eastern United States and Europe. Poppies are grown in higher altitudes, primarily the southwestern mountains, making eradication efforts more difficult.

IMPACT ON DEMOCRACY

The power and violence of the drug industry have had a profound impact on Colombia's democratic institutions, as signified by the expression *plata o plomo*—silver or lead—meaning "take the bribe or take a bullet." Drug lords achieved significant political influence through threats, bribery, and political contributions. In the early 1980s Pablo Escobar was elected as a congressional alternate, this being the most visible effort of drug traffickers to co-opt the electoral process. Later in the same decade the Medellin cartel waged war on the Colombian government, killing hundreds of judges, police investigators, journalists, and public figures. The killing of a major public figure became known as *magnicidio* (from the word for murder, *homicidio*); those assassinated by drug traffickers included Minister of Justice Rodrigo Lara Bonilla (in 1984) and presidential frontrunner Luis Carlos Galan (in 1989).

Some U.S. officials were led to refer to Colombia as a "narcostate" during the administration of President Ernesto Samper (1994–1998) when the DEA released evidence that his campaign had accepted contributions from the Cali cartel, resulting in a large investigation implicating a number of politicians and generating an ongoing crisis for his administration. Gunmen linked to the drug trade regularly attacked judicial investigators, judges, and prosecutors, contributing to the weakening of the Colombian legal system and a larger crisis in the rule of law. In 2008 the so-called *para-politica* scandal erupted when investigative journalists uncovered relationships between drug-trafficking paramilitaries and hundreds of public officials, including members of Congress, governors, mayors, and other local politicians.

DRUGS AND CONFLICT

Although the vast majority of Colombian violence is attributed to common crime, much of this violence is believed to be related to the drug trade. During the 1980s and 1990s Colombia had one of the highest homicide rates in the world. Colombia is also home to the longest-running internal conflict in the hemisphere, the partisan political conflict of the 1950s that was reborn as the Marxist guerrilla insurgencies of the 1960s and 1970s. Scholars and politicians continue to debate the role of the illicit narcotics trade in the conflict; throughout the 1980s and 1990s many insisted that the primary reason for the conflict was political and ideological. Following his election as president in 1998, Alvaro Uribe (2002–2010) refused to acknowledge Colombia as a country in conflict, instead insisting that "if Colombia would not have drugs, it would not have terrorists." All analysts agree that the profits from the illegal drug trade have shifted the dynamic of violent conflict, allowing armed groups to become self-financing, limit their reliance on public support, and expand their military strength into new areas.

Guerrilla groups active in areas of coca cultivation, primarily the Revolutionary Armed Forces of Colombia (Fuerzas Armadas Revolucionarias de Colombia or FARC), have increasingly financed their activities by taxing coca crops and by protecting drug processing labs and other illicit installations. While coca cultivation declined in the 1990s in Peru and Bolivia due in part to U.S.-financed eradication programs, cultivation in Colombia increased, leaving overall Andean coca production constant. Although coca production in Colombia in 1991 accounted for approximately 13 percent of the world's total production, by the end of the 1990s that number had increased to 75 percent. The dramatic increase in coca cultivation in southern Colombia, a FARC stronghold since the 1960s, coincided with the organization's strategic effort to increase its military capabilities in the mid-1990s. U.S. State Department officials have used the arrests of individuals allegedly linked with FARC in Mexico and Brazil to bolster their claims that FARC members are "narcoguerrillas" and that Colombia's drug cartels and guerrillas are completely integrated. The United States did extradite two senior FARC leaders for their role in drug trafficking, but these trials resulted in initial verdicts of not guilty. Many scholars argue that historically FARC has been involved only minimally in the illicit industry's most lucrative stages: transshipment and sale of drugs on the international market. Evidence of the group's growing criminalization continues to increase, however.

Right-wing paramilitary groups reached the height of their power in the middle of the first decade of the twenty-first century. In the 1980s, money from the drug trade allowed paramilitary death squads to grow from small groups linked to local military commanders to private armies. The fusion of counterinsurgency ideology and illegal narcotics revenue produced one of the most lethal fighting forces in Latin America. As the owners of vast haciendas (the result of money laundering and efforts to buy their way into the landed gentry, known as *reverse agrarian reform*), drug traffickers needed protection from guerrilla kidnapping and extortion. Paramilitary groups linked to drug cartels (particularly the Medellin cartel) worked closely with Colombian military officers to eliminate suspected guerrilla sympathizers, while at the same time they attacked Colombian authorities who were attempting to investigate drug trafficking. In 1997 paramilitary spokesmen announced the creation of a national coordinating body of paramilitary groups, the United Self-Defense Forces of Colombia (Autodefensas Unidas de Colombia or AUC). Newly created mobile squads carried out numerous massacres as paramilitary forces moved to control new areas of the country. In 2003 the government began a demobilization program targeting these groups; critics of the process have demonstrated that many groups remain significantly involved in drug trafficking. Dozens of paramilitary leaders have been extradited to the United States to face drug trafficking charges.

COUNTERNARCOTICS POLICIES IN COLOMBIA

Beginning in 1989 with the so-called Andean strategy, U.S. funds, equipment, and logistical support, and personnel from the DEA, the CIA, and other agencies have played a leading role in counternarcotics operations in Colombia. U.S.-assisted operations resulted in the killing of Pablo Escobar in 1993 and the jailing of the heads of the Cali cartel in 1994. However, the breakup of the two largest cartels did not lead to a long-term decline in Colombian drug trafficking. These drug syndicates have since been replaced by smaller, more vertically integrated trafficking organizations—often called *baby cartels*—whose nimble, independent traffickers are much more difficult to detect and infiltrate. These traffickers employ new and constantly changing shipping routes through Central America, Mexico, and the Caribbean and increasingly through Africa, for moving cocaine and, increasingly, heroin.

First passed by Congress in 2000, the U.S. assistance package known as Plan Colombia shifted the bulk of counternarcotics assistance to the Colombian Army. Although Colombian President Andrés Pastrana's original Plan Colombia (1998) presented a four-pronged strategy to support efforts for peace, development, political reform, and citizen security, U.S. assistance has been massively skewed toward militarized counternarcotics operations. Described as an "emergency" supplemental package, President Bill Clinton's $1.3 billion program made Colombia the third largest recipient of U.S. security assistance in the world at that time. The centerpiece of the proposal was $600 million to support Colombian Army operations in the FARC stronghold of southern Colombia. This funding trained and equipped new Colombian Army counternarcotics battalions by providing them with helicopters, transport, and intelligence assistance. The package also devoted significant resources to development, rule of law, and human rights programs. Since then subsequent yearly appropriations have maintained funding levels between $700 million and $1 billion; in 2008 the funding appropriation shifted to increase the balance between military and nonmilitary spending.

The drug trade in Colombia continues to evolve. FARC has been hard hit by government counterinsurgency programs, with a number of high-profile desertions and commanders killed in combat. Analysts predict that many regional fronts may deepen their involvement in criminal activities, including illicit drug production and trafficking. Despite the official demobilization of AUC, paramilitary control structures persist in many areas of the country and analysts believe that their central role in drug trafficking will continue as well. Coca cultivation in Colombia has spread from its southern jungles to other regions throughout the nation: along the Venezuelan border and Pacific coast, and in the southern Magdalena Valley region.

See also **Crop Control Policies; Drug Interdiction; Foreign Policy and Drugs, United States; International Drug Supply Systems.**

BIBLIOGRAPHY

Crandall, R. (2008). *Driven by drugs: U.S. policy toward Colombia*. Boulder, CO: Lynne Reinner.

International Crisis Group. (January 27, 2005). *War and drugs in Colombia*. Latin American Report No. 11. Washington, DC: Author.

Kenney, M. (2007). *From Pablo to Osama: Trafficking and terrorist network, government bureaucracies, and competitive adaptation*. University Park: Penn State Press.

Thoumi, F. (2003). *Illegal drugs, economy and society in the Andes*. Washington, DC: Woodrow Wilson Press.

Thoumi, F. (2005). Let's all guess the size of the illegal drug industry. *The Journal of Drug Issues, 35*(11), 185–200.

WINIFRED TATE

COMPLICATIONS

This entry includes the following essays:

MEDICAL AND BEHAVIORAL TOXICITY OVERVIEW
CARDIOVASCULAR SYSTEM (ALCOHOL AND COCAINE)
COGNITION
ENDOCRINE AND REPRODUCTIVE SYSTEMS
IMMUNOLOGIC
LIVER (CLINICAL)
LIVER (METABOLIC)
MENTAL DISORDERS
NEUROLOGICAL
NUTRITIONAL
ROUTE OF ADMINISTRATION

MEDICAL AND BEHAVIORAL TOXICITY OVERVIEW

Alcohol and other drugs of abuse cause considerable adverse health effects. Both legal and illegal drugs (substances) of abuse are taken to modify mood, feeling, thinking, and perception. As with most drugs (medications), both acute and chronic toxicities occur. In general, the term *acute* refers to the short period of time when the drug is present in the body, exerting its main effects. The term *chronic* refers to a longer period, usually years. Acute toxicity results in the impairment of behavior leading to other complications (e.g., trauma), and in the case of some drugs, high doses can decrease breathing (respiratory depression) or change the rhythm of the heart, leading to accidental or intentional death. Chronic use can result in organ damage, which may lead to chronic illness or death (as with alcoholic cirrhosis of the liver). Persistent use of many classes of drugs also leads to *tolerance* (so

that an increased amount of the drug is required to produce the same effects) and physiologic (physical) dependence, so that a withdrawal syndrome is associated with sudden cessation of drug use. Drug users who use hypodermic needles and syringes (injecting drug users [IDUs]) are at risk for blood-borne diseases associated with the use of contaminated equipment, such as Hepatitis B and C and human immunodeficiency virus (HIV 1 and 2, the viruses responsible for acquired immunodeficiency syndrome [AIDS]).

This entry focuses on alcohol as the representative drug, but other drugs of abuse are mentioned when appropriate. In North America, the diagnosis of alcohol and other psychoactive substance abuse/dependence is usually made according to the *Diagnostic and Statistical Manual of Mental Disorders* (*DSM*) of the American Psychiatric Association (APA). The fourth edition, text revision, referred to as *DSM-IV-TR*, defines psychoactive substance dependence as the presence of at least three of the following (within the same 12-month period):

1. tolerance, as defined by either of the following: (a) need for markedly increased amounts of the substance to achieve intoxication or desired effect; (b) markedly diminished effect with continued use of the same amount of the substance

2. withdrawal, as manifested by either of the following: (a) the characteristic withdrawal syndrome for the substance (b) the same (or closely related) substance taken to relieve or avoid withdrawal symptoms

3. the substance is often taken in larger amounts or over a longer period than was intended

4. a persistent desire for or unsuccessful efforts to cut down or control substance use

5. a great deal of time is spent in activities necessary to obtain the substance (e.g., visiting multiple doctors or driving long distances), use the substance (e.g., chain smoking), or recover from its effects

6. important social, occupational, or recreational activities are given up or reduced because of substance use

7. continued substance use despite knowledge of having had a persistent or recurrent physical or psychological problem that was likely to have been caused or exacerbated (worsened) by the

substance (e.g., recurrent cocaine use despite recognition of cocaine-induced depression; continued drinking despite recognition that an ulcer was made worse by alcohol consumption)

The diagnosis of alcohol and other substance abuse (as opposed to dependence) relies on the following:

A maladaptive pattern of substance use leading to clinically significant impairment or distress as manifested by one or more of the following occurring at any time during the same 12-month period:

1. recurrent substance use resulting in a failure to fulfill major obligations at work, school, or home (e.g., repeated absences or poor work performance related to substance use; substance-related absences, suspensions, or expulsions from school; neglect of children or household)

2. recurrent use in situations in which it is physically hazardous (e.g., driving an automobile or operating a machine when impaired by substance use)

3. recurrent substance-related legal problems (e.g., multiple arrests for substance-related disorderly conduct)

4. continued substance use despite having persistent or recurrent social or interpersonal problems caused or exacerbated by the effects of the substance (e.g., arguments with family members about consequences of intoxication; physical fights)

Alternatively, the symptoms have never met criteria for substance dependence for this class of substance.

These criteria continue to evolve, as can be tracked at the Web site maintained by the American Psychiatric Association, and are likely to be changed in the future (progress was under way as of 2008 for the publication of *DSM-V*, which was expected to be published in 2012). Clearly the lack of one of the above diagnoses does not preclude a given person from being at risk for complications of alcohol or drug use (e.g., trauma as a result of intoxication).

ACUTE EFFECTS OF ALCOHOL

At the level of the cell, very high doses of alcohol (ethanol) seem to act by disrupting fat (lipid) structure in the central nervous system (anesthetic effect). Lower doses are thought to interact with various proteins and neurotransmitter receptors, such as glutamate, gamma-amino butyric acid (GABA), glycine, serotonin (e.g., 5HT3), and neuronal nicotinic receptors. Other actions may involve modulation of membrane ion (e.g., calcium) channels. The reinforcing (rewarding) effects of alcohol may be mediated via dopamine (a neurotransmitter) in specific brain regions; dopamine acts as an intermediary compound in the reinforcement process. The reinforcement of responses to other drugs of abuse, such as cocaine, is also thought to be mediated via dopamine.

The acute effects of alcohol are well known. In low doses, it causes blood vessels to dilate, and the skin to become flushed and warm. The individual under the influence of alcohol experiences a feeling of relaxation and mild sedation but may become talkative with loss of inhibitory control of emotions. Small doses (one to two drinks) do not impair complex intellectual ability; however, as the dose increases (two or more drinks or as the blood alcohol concentration approaches and exceeds the legal limit) impairment at multiple levels of the nervous system occurs. All types of motor performance are eventually affected, including maintenance of posture, control of speech, and eye movements. Movement becomes slower and more inaccurate. Mental functioning decreases, such that there is impairment in attention and concentration and a diminishing ability to make mental associations. Concurrently, the ability to attend to incoming sensory information is decreased. Night and color vision are impaired. Judgment and discrimination and the ability to think and reason clearly are adversely affected. Further increased doses result in a stuporous condition associated with sleeping, with vomiting, and little appreciation of surroundings. This level is followed by coma and sometimes death from decreases in the functioning of the brain centers that control respiration.

ACUTE EFFECTS OF OTHER DRUGS OF ABUSE

Other drugs of abuse can be classified into stimulants, depressants, opioids, and drugs that alter perception (including hallucinogens). The effect of any drug depends on the dose taken at any one time, the previous drug experience of the user, the circumstances in which the drug is taken, and the manner (route of administration) in which the drug is taken.

Stimulants such as cocaine and amphetamine produce euphoria, increased confidence, increased sensory awareness, increased anxiety and suspiciousness, decreased appetite, and a decreased need for sleep. Physiological effects include increases in heart rate, blood pressure, and pupil size, and decreases in skin temperature.

Depressants such as the minor tranquillizers (including the benzodiazepines, barbiturates, and other sedative-hypnotics) produce acute effects of a similar nature to alcohol, which is also a depressant. Actual effects vary according to drug, so that benzodiazepines (such as diazepam [Valium]) produce less drunkenness compared to alcohol or barbiturates. The term *opioid* refers to both drugs derived from opium (opiates) and other synthetic drugs with similar actions, those acting on the same receptor system. The term *narcotic* is usually synonymous with opioid, but it can technically also include other drugs listed in the Harrison Narcotics Act (e.g., cocaine). Opioids produce euphoria, sedation (to which rapid tolerance develops), itching, increased talkativeness, increased or decreased activity, a sensation of stomach turning, nausea, and vomiting. There are minor changes in blood pressure, and the pupils become constricted (smaller). Drugs that alter perception include those above as well as marijuana, phencyclidine (PCP), and lysergic acid diethylamide (LSD). In general, most drugs of abuse can cause hallucinations under some circumstances. The drugs that more specifically affect perception (hallucinogens) produce a combination of depersonalization, altered time perception, body-image distortion, perceptual distortions (usually visual), and sometimes feelings of insight. Physiological effects such as changes in heart rate and blood pressure may also occur.

HARMFUL EFFECTS

This section reviews the harmful effects of alcohol and drugs. Alcohol and drugs contribute not only to the ill health of the individual, but directly to reckless behaviors that result in injury. For example, the impact of alcohol and drug abuse on the rate of motor vehicle accidents is well-known, but individuals under the influence of alcohol or drugs also engage in other dangerous behaviors at a high rate. They are more likely than others to harm themselves accidentally, as in falls or intentionally, as in suicide. They are also more likely to harm others, as when they engage in violent activities and/or in criminal behaviors.

Accidents. Alcohol is a significant factor in accident-related deaths. The main causes are motor-vehicle accidents, falls, drownings, and fires and burns. Approximately 50 percent of motor vehicle fatalities (driver, pedestrian, or cyclist) in the United States are alcohol-related, with the incidence having decreased slightly in the 1990s and early years of the twenty-first century. These alcohol-related accidents are more common at nights and on weekends. Falls are the most frequent cause of nonfatal accidents and the second most frequent cause of fatal accidents. Various studies indicate that alcohol is a factor in 17 to 53 percent of fatal falls and 21 to 77 percent of nonfatal falls (Hingson & Howland, 1987; Kool et al., 2008). Fatal falls occur at the highest rate among young males (Ramstedt, 2008). The higher the blood alcohol content (BAC), the higher is the risk for falls. The third leading cause of accidental death in the United States is drowning. About half (47–65%) of adult deaths by drowning are alcohol-related (U.S. Department of Health and Human Services, 2000). Fires and burns are the fourth leading cause of accidental death in the United States. Studies on burn victims show that alcohol intoxication is common. Cigarette smoking while drinking is a common cause of fires and burn injuries, with estimates of the rate of intoxication ranging from 37 to 64 percent. Users of other drugs of abuse (e.g., cocaine and opioids) also have higher rates of accidents than the non-drug-abusing population. The combination of cocaine and alcohol has been reported to be commonly associated with motor-vehicle deaths. Between 1984 and 1987 in New York City, 18 percent of motor-vehicle deaths showed evidence of cocaine use at autopsy. Cigarette smokers have higher rates of accidents than do nonsmokers. In an Australian study of fatally injured drivers, those drivers who tested positive for any psychoactive substance were significantly more likely than drug-free drivers to have been the individual responsible for the accident (Drummer et al., 2004). Drugs that alter perception, such as PCP, are also associated with accidents mostly related to an impaired sense of judgment.

Crime. Associations between criminal activity and alcohol use have been established; however, a clear causal relationship between alcohol use and crime has not been established as of 2008. The strongest association between crime and alcohol use occurs in young males. Other forms of drug abuse (e.g., heroin and cocaine) have much higher associations with criminality. For example, the majority of persons enrolled in methadone programs have extensive criminal careers. Those involved in drug dealing are at a high risk of being either a perpetrator or a victim of homicide.

Family Violence. Several studies show an association between alcohol use/abuse and spousal abuse; however, the nature of this interaction was not well understood as of 2008. Intoxication is associated with negative behaviors among episodic drinkers, which are less common among steady drinkers, suggesting that drinking may be a short-term solution to problems for regular drinkers. Clearly, alcohol use is associated with physical violence in some families, and there also appears to be a link between alcohol and child abuse. Female caregivers with a diagnosis of alcohol abuse, alcohol dependence, recurrent depression, or antisocial personality are more likely to report physical abuse of their children than those without these diagnoses (Bland & Orn, 1986).

Suicide. Alcohol dependence is a risk factor for suicide; the lifetime risk of an alcohol-dependent individual committing suicide ranges from 2 to 18 percent. From 20 to 36 percent of suicide victims have a history of alcohol abuse or had been drinking prior to death. Alcohol use is linked more often to impulsive than to premeditated suicides and to the use of firearms rather than to other modes of killing. Death from overdose of illicit drugs is common; most of these are thought to be accidental but some are intentional.

Trauma or Severe Injuries. A history of trauma has been found to be a marker for (sign of) alcohol abuse. Emergency room trauma victims have high rates of intoxication. Furthermore, heavy alcohol use both interferes with recovery from serious injuries and increases rates of mortality for a given injury. Users of illicit drugs have a higher age-adjusted rate of mortality than do non-users. Many of these deaths result from trauma.

Effects in Pregnancy. Alcohol is firmly established as a teratogen (an agent that produces defects in the developing fetus) and is considered the most common known cause of mental retardation. Fetal alcohol syndrome (FAS) defects range from specific structural bodily changes to growth retardation and subtle cognitive-behavioral abnormalities. The diagnostic criteria for fetal alcohol syndrome include: prenatal (before birth) and postnatal (after birth) growth retardation; characteristic craniofacial defects; central nervous system (CNS) dysfunction; and organ system malformations. When only some of these criteria are met, the diagnosis is termed fetal alcohol effects (U.S. Department of Health and Human Services, 2000). The abnormalities in physical appearance seem to decrease with age, whereas the cognitive deficiencies tend to persist. There is no clear dose-response relationship between alcohol use and abnormalities. The safe amount of drinking during pregnancy (if it exists at all) is unknown. The peak level of blood (or brain) alcohol attained and the timing in relation to gestation (and particular organ development) are probably more important than the total amount of alcohol consumed during pregnancy. Genetic and maternal variables also seem to be important. Native American and African American children seem to be at high risk. While the public is generally aware of the relationship between alcohol consumption and fetal abnormality, surveys reveal that there is a need for greater public education in this area.

Use of other substances of abuse can also result in negative pregnancy outcomes. Smoking is associated with low birth weight. Cocaine use in pregnancy has been associated with complications (e.g., placental separation and in utero bleeding), and it appears to be associated with congenital abnormalities. Heroin use in pregnancy is associated with premature delivery and low birth weight; often there is a withdrawal syndrome in the baby at birth. Methadone (a long-acting opioid) usually reduces rates of prematurity and low birth weight but still causes as much or more opioid withdrawal in the newborn.

Cancer. Epidemiologic evidence exists for an increased risk of certain types of cancer in association with alcohol consumption. These include cancer of the esophagus, oropharynx (mouth and throat), and liver. Other cancers possibly associated with alcohol consumption include cancer of the breast, stomach, prostate, and colon (Geokas, 1984). Alcohol plays a synergistic (multiplicative) role with smoking tobacco in the development of cancer, particularly with respect to the head, neck, and esophagus. There are several possible mechanisms through which alcohol enhances the onset of cancer. Alcohol appears to modify the immune response to cancers, facilitate delivery of carcinogens (substances which enhance cancer onset), and impair protective responses. Overall, alcohol is considered to act as a co-carcinogen; for example, it increases the likelihood of certain smoking-induced cancers.

Smoking is, of course, well established as a cause of lung as well as other cancers. Smoking is responsible for 85 percent of lung cancers and has been associated with cancers of the mouth, pharynx, larynx, esophagus, stomach, pancreas, uterine cervix, kidney, ureter, and bladder (Bartecchi et al., 1994). Chewing tobacco (smokeless tobacco) is associated with mouth cancer. The chewing of betel nuts with lime is common in Asia and results in the absorption of arecoline (a mild stimulant). This practice also causes cancer of the mouth. It has been suggested that marijuana smoking also causes lung cancer, since high tar levels are present in the smoked products.

ALCOHOL USE AND ABUSE AMONG ADOLESCENTS

Alcohol use among adolescents is a serious worldwide problem. Surveys indicate that up to 54 percent of eighth graders, and up to 84 percent of twelfth graders report having consumed alcohol (O'Malley et al., 1998). There is little doubt that parents' attitudes and habits concerning drinking are important influences on adolescent drinking (Ary et al., 1993). However, there is also evidence that adolescents who abuse alcohol often have coexisting psychopathology such as conduct disorder and bouts of depression and anxiety (Clark & Bukstein, 1998).

Another significant reason for concern about alcohol ingestion by adolescents is the close association of alcohol abuse with the use of other drugs. There is considerable evidence that alcohol use tends to precede the use of illicit drugs, and

some researchers argue that, based on long-term studies, alcohol serves as a *gateway* to the use of illicit substances. Alcohol users were found to have a significantly higher prevalence of cigarette smoking, marijuana use, and cocaine use than non-users of alcohol, as early as the eighth grade. This difference persists through grade 12 and thereafter (Kandel & Yamaguchi, 1993). In one twin study, early use of alcohol by male adolescents (before age 17) was positively correlated with adult alcohol use and dependence and to the use of other drugs of abuse (Grant et al., 2006).

EFFECTS OF ALCOHOL AND OTHER DRUGS ON BODILY SYSTEMS

The toxic effects of alcohol on organ systems are pervasive, largely because alcohol mixes easily with water, and is thus distributed widely throughout the body. While alcohol is itself toxic, its effects are also mediated by acetaldehyde, a toxic metabolite. Tobacco also has pervasive toxic effects; when inhaled as cigarette smoke, its components escape metabolism by the liver and are introduced directly and rapidly into the bloodstream. Also like alcohol, the toxic effects of tobacco are due to more than one substance, chief among them nicotine, which is responsible for the cardiotoxic effects of tobacco, and tar, which has its greatest noxious effects on the lungs and mucus membranes. The toxic effects of other drugs of abuse on organ systems are more limited but still not insignificant.

Neurologic Effects. Acute alcohol consumption causes impairment as described above. Alcohol potentiates the action of many drugs that produce acute effects on the brain. High blood-alcohol levels can result in blackouts. This condition is the acute loss of memory associated with intoxication, although the person usually behaves in apparently normal fashion during this period. Blackouts are also seen with the ingestion of other CNS depressants, such as barbiturates and benzodiazepines.

The main adverse neural consequences of chronic alcohol consumption are the following: brain damage (manifested by dementia and alcohol amnestic syndrome); complications of the withdrawal syndrome (seizures, hallucinations); and peripheral neuropathy. Chronic alcohol consumption results in tolerance, followed by an increased long-term consumption that likely leads to tissue damage. Physical dependence may also develop, manifested by a withdrawal syndrome on sudden cessation of drinking. The brain damage, when severe, is usually classified as one of two main disorders. The first is a type of global (general) dementia. It is estimated that 20 percent of those individuals admitted to state mental hospitals suffer from alcohol-induced dementia (Freund & Ballinger, 1988). The second is an alcohol-induced amnestic (memory-loss) syndrome, more commonly known as Wernicke-Korsakoff syndrome. This is related to thiamine (Vitamin B$_1$) deficiency. The *Wernicke* component refers to the acute neurologic signs, which consist of ocular (eye) problems such as a sixth cranial nerve palsy (disturbed lateral gaze), and ataxia (gross incoordination of muscle movements); the *Korsakoff* component refers to the memory impairment, which tends to be selective for short-term memory and is usually not amenable to treatment once it has become manifest.

Milder forms of these disorders are also detectable with neuropsychologic testing or brain imaging techniques (computed tomography [CT scans]; magnetic resonance imaging [MRI]). Studies of detoxified alcoholics (without other evidence of organic brain damage) reveal that 50 to 70 percent have impairments in neuropsychologic assessment (Eckardt & Martin, 1986). In most of these cases there is reversibility with abstinence from alcohol. Severe liver disease (e.g., acute hepatitis, advanced cirrhosis) may also contribute to this neurologic impairment. CT scans reveal that many alcoholics have cerebral atrophy, which consists of decreased brain weight, an increase in spaces (sulci) between various regions of the brain, and an increase in size of ventricles (spaces filled with cerebrospinal fluid). In a minority of cases, these structural changes are reversible with abstinence. Seizures are associated with heavy alcohol consumption and usually occur in association with alcohol withdrawal. Abstinence from alcohol is usually the only treatment needed for this type of seizure. The hallucinations that are mostly associated with alcohol withdrawal are usually treated with drugs: benzodiazepines and antipsychotics. *Peripheral neuropathy* is damage to peripheral nerves and is associated with chronic alcoholism. Direct toxic effects of alcohol and concurrent nutritional deficiencies cause this damage.

The neuropathy results in changes in sensation and occasionally motor function, usually in the legs. Sometimes this condition can occur acutely with intoxication. For example, the abnormal posture in association with a drunken stupor can result in radial nerve (so-called Saturday night) palsy (paralysis of a body part that may be accompanied by loss of feeling and uncontrolled body movements). Alcoholics are also at increased risk of subdural hematomas (blood clots due to ruptured intracranial veins secondary to trauma) and of stroke. The neurologic complications associated with the acute use of other drugs of abuse (e.g., cocaine) include seizures (convulsions) and strokes.

Other drugs can also produce neurologic symptoms. High doses of some opioids, such as propoxyphene (Darvon) or meperidine (Demerol) cause seizures. Substances that can cause delirium (reversible disorientation and agitation) include cannabis (marijuana), phencyclidine (PCP), lysergic acid diethylamide (LSD), and atropine. Sudden cessation of use of CNS depressants (benzodiazepines, barbiturates, and alcohol) can result in seizures and hallucinations. Chronic use of other substances of abuse can also result in neurologic complications. Tobacco use is associated with increased rates of stroke (but it appears to be associated with lower rates of Parkinson's disease, a progressive disorder affecting control of movement). Solvent abuse (via inhalation) can cause damage to the cerebellum (the part of the brain controlling movement) and to peripheral nerves. A form of *synthetic heroin* (MPTP, 1-methyl-4-phenyl-1,2,5,6-tetrahydropyridine), an analog of meperidine (Demerol), has been demonstrated to cause a severe form of Parkinson's disease.

Psychiatric Effects. Alcohol-related diagnoses are common among psychiatric patients. For example, one study (Moore et al., 1989) showed that 30 percent of those admitted to a psychiatric unit had a concurrent alcohol-related diagnosis. Alcohol alone may produce symptoms and signs that mimic psychiatric disorders. Examples include depression, anxiety disorder, psychosis, and antisocial personality disorder. Alternatively, an alcohol-related disorder may coexist with one of these or may aggravate the psychiatric disorder. Alcohol as a CNS depressant tends to cause low mood states (hypophoria) with chronic use. It may cause or worsen clinical depression. If alcohol is the primary cause of a depressed mood state, then abstinence from alcohol, as the sole treatment, rapidly improves the disorder. Hallucinations may occur during alcohol withdrawal, mimicking a psychotic disorder. Similarly, the anxiety associated with alcohol withdrawal may mimic an anxiety disorder. Anxiety and hallucinations may also be seen during withdrawal from sedative-hypnotics. Aggressive, illegal or irresponsible behavior associated with alcoholism may lead to an erroneous diagnosis of antisocial personality disorder.

When alcohol is used for self-medication in some psychiatric conditions, such as anxiety disorders, it tends only to be of short-term help and leads to more long-term problems. Other drugs of abuse, such as the stimulants cocaine and amphetamine, also produce anxiety and occasionally may produce a psychotic state during acute intoxication. This usually disappears rapidly as the drug effects wear off. Withdrawal following chronic use of stimulants may be associated with depression, excessive fatigue, and somnolence (a *crash*). Tobacco smoking also appears to be associated with depression. (Individuals with a history of depression are more likely to smoke and may develop depression when they try to stop.) Although the nature of the relationship is unclear, patients with psychiatric diagnoses (e.g., schizophrenia) have higher rates of smoking than the general population. Hallucinogens (such as LSD and PCP) commonly cause an acute psychotic disorder that typically disappears as drug effects wear off; however, in some cases there may be longer lasting effects. Antisocial personality disorder is a common pre-existing diagnosis in those who abuse alcohol and drugs.

Endocrine and Reproductive Effects. Alcohol produces both acute and chronic effects on virtually all endocrine organs (hormone-producing glands). Acutely, alcohol raises plasma catecholamines, which are chemicals released from nerve endings that are responsible for certain emotional reactions: the so-called fear, flight, and fight. Epinephrine (adrenaline) is released from the inside (medulla) of the adrenal gland and norepinephrine (noradrenaline) from sympathetic neurons (nerve cells) and the adrenal glands. Alcohol also causes release of cortisol from the outside (cortex) of the adrenal gland both acutely and chronically.

Cortisol is a hormone (chemical messenger) responsible for multiple effects on the body, including changes in the immune response, glucose regulation, fat breakdown, blood pressure, and mood. Alcohol-induced cortisol excess can mimic Cushing's disease (a condition associated with excess cortisol production, often caused by a tumor on the adrenals) and is known as pseudo-Cushing's disease. Alcohol affects the hypothalamus (an area of the brain), where it modifies chemical-releasing factors, which in turn control release of hormones from the pituitary (a gland in the brain linked to the hypothalamus by a special blood supply), which in turn affect endocrine organs throughout the body. Acutely, alcohol also inhibits the release of antidiuretic hormone (ADH) from the posterior pituitary, which results in increased urine production. The best documented chronic endocrine effect of alcohol is male hypogonadism, a condition resulting from low sex-hormone function. Signs of the condition are small testes and decreased body hair. Symptoms include loss of libido (sex drive) and impotence. Hypogonadism can result from alcohol lowering testosterone levels both by direct effects on the testes and indirectly via the hypothalamus.

Alcoholic liver disease may also produce feminization in men, as a result of impaired metabolism (breakdown) of female sex hormones such as estrogen. Signs of such feminization in men include gynecomastia (enlarged breasts) and female fat distribution. In women who drink alcohol excessively, there is a high prevalence of gynecologic disorders (missed periods and problems in functioning of ovaries) and a possibly earlier onset of menopause than in nondrinkers. In women alcohol is metabolized at different rates according to the particular phase of the menstrual cycle. Other hormonal effects have been described in association with acute alcohol ingestion, including the impaired release of growth hormone and increased release of prolactin, a hormone involved in milk production. Thyroid function, which controls the body's rate of metabolism, can be indirectly affected as a result of alcoholic liver disease. This effect occurs from impaired conversion of T4 (a form of thyroid hormone) to T3 (a more active form of thyroid hormone). Furthermore, in alcoholism, there are abnormalities in the proteins to which thyroid hormone binds, making thyroid function tests difficult to interpret. Overall thyroid function is usually normal despite mild abnormalities in the tests.

Other drugs, particularly the opioids, also have multiple effects on the endocrine system. Opioids produce a degree of hypogonadism as a result of lowered testosterone in males and disturbed menstrual function in females. This effect results from opioid inhibition of gonadotropin releasing hormone (GRH) in the hypothalamus, which in turn inhibits release of lutenizing hormone (LH) and follicle stimulating hormone (FSH) from the pituitary. Opioids also inhibit corticotropin releasing factor (CRF), which results in decreased adrenocorticotrophic hormone (ACTH) and decreased cortisol release. Nicotine causes release of epinephrine and norepinephrine, which in turn increase blood pressure and heart rate. Nicotine also enhances the release of ADH from the pituitary, which decreases urine output (i.e., it counteracts alcohol's effects).

Cardiovascular Effects. Alcohol has direct effects on both cardiac muscle and cardiac electrophysiology (electrical functioning). These effects are also dependent on the prior history of alcohol use (i.e., whether there have been underlying cardiac changes due to chronic use) and whether there is any evidence of underlying heart disease. Acutely, alcohol is a myocardial depressant (decreases heart muscle function), and chronically, it may cause a degeneration of cardiac muscle (known as cardiomyopathy), which can lead to heart failure (a condition in which excess body fluids and inadequate pumping function of the heart are present). Abstinence from alcohol leads to improvement in function in some cases. Both acute alcohol intoxication and acute withdrawal can lead to cardiac arrhythmias (abnormal heart rhythms). The most frequent association is with atrial fibrillation (frequent uneven and uncoordinated contraction of the atria, the blood collection chambers of the heart). This condition is usually not life threatening and mostly disappears without specific treatment. Multiple epidemiologic studies have established a relationship between alcohol and high blood pressure (hypertension). Between 5 and 24 percent of hypertension is considered to be alcohol related (Klatsky, 1987). The relationship seems to hold most strongly for white males over the age of 55, consuming at least 3 standard drinks per day on a chronic basis. Many cases resolve with abstinence.

Acute alcohol withdrawal is often associated with hypertension, but this condition usually lasts for only a few days.

High levels of alcohol consumption are associated with increased rates of coronary heart disease (disease of the blood vessels that supply heart muscle), while low levels of consumption (in comparison to complete abstinence) may be associated with a mild protective effect. Evidence for an inverse relationship between moderate alcohol consumption and coronary heart disease is derived from epidemiological and clinical case-control and cohort studies. Early investigators, impressed by the relatively low incidence of coronary heart disease in France despite an intake of saturated fats at least three times that of the United States (the so-called French paradox), focused their studies on the potential cardioprotective properties of red wine (Klatsky et al., 2003). Other studies, however, indicate that all alcoholic beverages—wine, beer, and liquor—when consumed in moderation, are associated with a lower coronary artery disease risk (Rimm et al., 1996). In dose-range studies, the equivalent of two alcoholic drinks per day was associated with a decreased incidence of coronary heart disease compared with no drinks, whereas higher doses result in an increased risk of infarction as well as the well-known problems produced by alcohol excess. Scientists describe this relationship between alcohol intake and coronary heart disease-when shown graphically—as a J-shaped or U-shaped curve, with the greatest benefit accruing at moderate doses, which correlate with the lowest point on the curve. Individuals may find themselves caught in a dilemma between the oft-preached dangers of drinking and these acclaimed benefits. Because most American households already are exposed to alcohol (Thun et al., 1997), advice as to the benefits of moderation may be offered without reserve. However, low levels of consumption are not recommended specifically as a preventive measure against coronary heart disease. In the case of abstainers, the risks of initiating alcohol consumption may outweigh its potential benefits. This reservation is especially applicable in families that include adolescents.

Chronic tobacco use is the most important of the preventable causes of coronary heart disease, and cigarette smoking is a much greater risk factor than is alcoholism. It should be noted, however, that in some studies, 80 to 90 percent of alcoholics are also cigarette smokers, though this high a prevalence of smoking is not universal. Acutely, nicotine results in constriction (narrowing) of blood vessels and an increase in heart rate. The coronary arteries supply the heart muscle. Long-term tobacco use results in an increase in atherosclerosis (build up of fat and other products inside the walls of blood vessels) in most of the arteries throughout the body and increases coagulation (clotting). This has important adverse effects on the coronary arteries (causing angina [chest pain] and infarction [heart attack]); the aorta (causing aneurysms, a ballooning effect on the arterial wall, which can be fatal); the carotid arteries (which can cause strokes); the femoral arteries (causing intermittent claudication, or pain on walking); and the renal arteries (causing kidney failure and some hypertension).

The acute use of cocaine (a stimulant) results in increases in heart rate and blood pressure and causes narrowing of peripheral and coronary arteries. Repeated use of cocaine has been associated with abnormal heart beats, myocardial infarction (heart attack), and possibly myocardial fibrosis (an increase of scar tissue within the heart). Acute use of opioids has minor effects on blood pressure. There are no important chronic adverse effects of opioids on the cardiovascular system. Marijuana acutely causes increases in heart rate and blood flow.

Respiratory System Effects. Acutely, alcohol does not usually interfere with lung function; however, a decrease in cough reflexes and a predisposition to reflux (regurgitate) stomach fluids into the lungs can result in the impairment of bacterial clearance in the respiratory tract after intoxication. Chronic alcohol consumption is associated with several pulmonary infectious diseases; these include pneumonia, lung abscess, and tuberculosis. Aspiration pneumonia occurs in association with high levels of alcohol intoxication; it is thought to be caused by the inhalation of bacteria caused by the impairment of the usual reflexes, such as coughing. For some persons with asthma, alcoholic beverages can induce bronchospasm (airway narrowing). This condition is thought to be related to non-alcoholic components in the beverage. Acute alcohol consumption also has a direct depressant effect on the respiratory center located in the brainstem. Accordingly, an overdose (intentional or unintentional) can result in death from respiratory failure (decreased ability to breathe). Alcohol also contributes to respiratory depression when taken with other central nervous system depressants such as barbiturates and benzodiazepines (minor tranquillizers). Acute alcohol intake worsens sleep apnea, a condition in which breathing ceases for periods of time during sleep. Pancreatitis and alcoholic cirrhosis are associated with pulmonary effusions (buildup of fluid around the lung).

Cigarette smoking causes emphysema, chronic bronchitis, and lung cancer. The smoking of marijuana on a frequent long-term basis may also increase the likelihood of these disorders, though this correlation has not been definitively proven. Acutely, the intravenous injection of opiate drugs may cause pulmonary edema (accumulation of fluid in the lungs), which can be life-threatening. Chronic use of intravenous drugs may cause pulmonary fibrosis (scar tissue in the lung). This effect is probably related to impurities, such as talc, associated with the cutting of the drug (diluting the dose with fillers) prior to its sale and eventual injection.

Effects on the Gastrointestinal Tract and Pancreas. Acutely, alcohol alters motor function of the esophagus. Chronic use of alcohol increases gastroesophageal reflux. Alcohol alone does not appear to cause peptic ulcers (as smoking cigarettes does), but alcohol interferes with healing. Alcohol disrupts the mucosal barrier in the stomach and causes gastritis (inflammation of the stomach), which can lead to hemorrhage, especially when combined with aspirin. Alcohol also interferes with the cellular junctions within the small intestine, which can result in the disturbance of fluid and nutrient absorption, producing diarrhea and malabsorption. Any resulting nutritional deficiencies can further aggravate this process.

Heavy drinking interferes significantly with pancreatic structure and function. Alcohol abuse and gallstone disease are the major causes of pancreatitis, and alcoholism alone is responsible for most cases of chronic pancreatitis. Alcohol changes cellular membranes, disrupting transport mechanisms and the movement of vital ions and nutrients essential for normal cellular function. Acetaldehyde, a breakdown product of alcohol (and also present in cigarette smoke), is toxic to cells and has been proposed as a causative agent in the development of this disorder (Geokas, 1984). Acute pancreatitis is life threatening; patients have abdominal pain, nausea, and vomiting. Increased levels of pancreatic enzymes, such as amylase and lipase, accompany this disorder. Treatment is usually by conservative measures, such as replacement of fluids and pain relief. Chronic pancreatitis may occur without symptoms, or it can become evident due to the occurrence of chronic abdominal pain and evidence of malabsorption (weight loss, fatty stools, and nutritional deficiencies) or, uncommonly, with the appearance of diabetes mellitus resulting from the destruction of the endocrine as well as the exocrine function of the pancreas.

Liver Effects. Alcoholic liver disease is a major cause of morbidity and mortality in the United States; in 2004 chronic liver disease and cirrhosis of the liver was the twelfth leading cause of death. Alcohol causes three progressive pathological (abnormal) changes in the liver: fatty liver, alcoholic hepatitis, and cirrhosis. These changes are useful in a prognostic sense but can only be diagnosed with a liver biopsy (in which a needle is inserted in the liver to obtain a small amount of tissue for study), which is not always feasible or practical. More than one pathological condition may exist at any one time in a given patient. Fatty liver, the most benign of the three conditions, is usually completely reversible with abstinence from alcohol; it occurs at a lower threshold of drinking than do alcoholic hepatitis and cirrhosis. Alcoholic hepatitis ranges in severity from no symptoms at all to severe liver failure with a fatal outcome; it can be followed by complete recovery, chronic hepatitis, or cirrhosis. Treatment is primarily supportive.

Similarly, the symptoms and signs of cirrhosis range from none at all to coma and death. Cirrhosis consists of irreversible changes in liver structure resulting from an increase in scar tissue. A consequence of this condition is an abnormal flow of blood through the liver (shunts), which can result in bleeding and the presentation of toxic substances (e.g., ammonia) to the brain. This, in turn, may result in effects ranging from impaired thinking to coma and death. Abstinence from alcohol can prevent progression of cirrhosis and reduces mortality and morbidity (illness) from this condition.

Medications may also help to reduce mortality from alcoholic liver disease. One medication, propothiouracil (an antithyroid drug), is thought to work by reducing oxygen requirements, though its efficacy has yet to be proved. The efficacy of another medication, prednisone (a steroid), which reduces inflammation, appears to be limited. One promising new approach under investigation involves agents that work against tumor necrosis factor, a pro-inflammatory cytokine (chemical messenger) implicated in the pathophysiology of alcoholic liver disease. Women appear to be at higher risk for liver damage than are men.

Opioid use alone has not been associated with liver disease, but some opioids such as morphine can cause spasm of the bile duct, which results in acute abdominal pain. Tobacco use is associated with a more rapid metabolism (breakdown) of certain drugs in the liver, which means that sometimes higher or more frequent dosing of medications is required for smokers. This effect is thought to relate to the tars in tobacco rather than to the nicotine. High doses of cocaine have been associated with acute liver failure.

Acute and chronic viral hepatitis (types B, C, and D) is common in users of intravenous drugs. It is not the drug itself that causes hepatitis (inflammation of the liver) but rather the introduction of the viruses associated with the sharing of needles or other drug paraphernalia. Viruses and bacteria introduced by injecting drugs cause other problems, such as HIV infection and AIDS, endocarditis (infection of heart valves), cellulitis (skin infection), and abscesses.

Immune System Effects. Alcohol affects the immune system both directly and indirectly. It is often difficult to discern the direct effects of alcohol from concurrent conditions, such as malnutrition and liver disease. Alcohol affects host defense factors in a general way; it also seems to predispose those who drink heavily to specific types of infection. With respect to host factors, alcohol alone can reduce both the number and function of white blood cells (both polymorphonuclear leucocytes and lymphocytes). This effect predisposes toward infection while it interferes with the ability to counteract infection. Mechanical factors are also important. For example, alcohol intoxication resulting in a depressed level of consciousness (and depressed cough reflex) predispose toward aspiration pneumonia. Specific infections for which alcoholics are at higher risk, compared to the population at large, include pneumococcal pneumonia (the most common form of pneumonia), other lung infections (e.g., Hemophilus influenzae, Klebsiella), abscesses (anaerobic infections), and pulmonary tuberculosis. Alcoholics with liver disease are at increased risk of spontaneous bacterial peritonitis (inflammation of the lining of the abdominal cavity). Other infections possibly associated with alcoholism include bacterial endocarditis (infection of the heart valves), bacterial meningitis (infection of the covering of the brain), pancreatitic abscess, and diphtheria (an infectious disease). HIV-infected drug abusers are at increased risk of tuberculosis as well as a multitude of other infections. As mentioned above, injecting drug users are also susceptible to a variety of infections associated with the use of non-sterile equipment. Changes in immune function have been reported to occur in users of other drugs of abuse, including heroin, cocaine, and marijuana. The precise relationship of the immune function change to the drug of abuse is not understood as of the early twenty-first century. Lifestyle factors such as poor nutrition are also likely to contribute to this connection.

Nutritional Effects. In heavy alcohol consumers, malnutrition is common and results from several conditions. Alcohol abusers often have poor dietary habits, resulting from the irritating effects of alcohol on the stomach lining. Alcohol also provides a significant number of calories per serving (7.1 kcal/gm), depressing appetite further. In some cases, alcoholics will subsist on alcohol alone without eating food over extended periods of time. In women, heavy alcohol consumption is associated with lower than usual body weight to a degree similar to that also associated with tobacco smoking; there is less weight-lowering effect in men. Specific nutritional disorders associated with alcoholism include anemia (due to iron or folate deficiency); thiamine (Vitamin B_1) deficiency, causing beriberi or Wernicke's encephalopathy or neuropathy; malabsorption; and defective immune and hormonal responses. Alcohol also interferes with the absorption of vitamins (such as pyridoxine and Vitamin A), minerals (such as zinc), and other nutrients (such as glucose and amino acids) (Mezey, 1985).

Abuse of other drugs also can lead to malnutrition, though specific syndromes have not been identified as of the early twenty-first century. Tobacco use is associated with depressed appetite as well depletion of Vitamins A and C. Amphetamines and cocaine are stimulants and have the effect of suppressing appetite. Drug-seeking behavior may also result in a general indifference toward food.

Metabolic Effects. Alcohol is metabolized (broken down) in the liver to acetaldehyde and hydrogen and then to carbon dioxide and water. Acetaldehyde is toxic to many different cellular functions. Alcohol affects carbohydrate, lipid (fat), and protein metabolism. Alcohol can cause low blood glucose (hypoglycemia) due to inhibition of glycogen (liver stores of carbohydrate) metabolism. Alcohol also raises blood sugar and acids (alcoholic ketacidosis). By interfering with the elimination of uric acid, alcohol may precipitate acute attacks of gout. Increased urinary excretion of magnesium can result in muscle weakness. Alcohol causes disturbances in blood lipids, mostly increases in triglycerides and high density lipoprotein (HDL) cholesterol.

Acute alcohol consumption can decrease, whereas chronic consumption can increase, the metabolism of certain drugs. Tobacco smoking also increases the metabolism of some drugs, such as theophylline and caffeine. This response results from the increased activity of various liver enzymes as discussed above.

Hematologic (Blood) Effects. The effects of alcohol on the hematologic system can either be direct, or it can be indirect (as a result of liver disease or nutritional deficiencies). Uncommonly, acute consumption of a very large dose of alcohol in a short time has direct effects on the bone marrow, resulting in decreased production of red cells, white cells, and platelets. Anemia is a common problem in alcoholics and may be due to a variety of factors. The most frequent effect seen in alcoholics following chronic consumption is an increase in the size of the red blood cells (macrocytosis). This increase is mainly due to direct toxic effects on the red cell membrane but may also be due to a deficiency of folate, a vitamin found in green vegetables. Folate deficiency in alcoholics is caused mainly by impaired intake and absorption of folate.

Iron deficiency anemia is also seen because of impaired intake of iron and because of frequent bleeding (due to a variety of factors, such as coagulation defects, gastritis, and the impaired healing of peptic ulcer). Iron-overload syndromes are also diagnosed in alcoholics and are due to multiple causes. Chronic alcohol consumption can also lead to hemolytic (excess breakdown of red blood cells) anemia, which is mainly seen in association with liver disease. Platelet production and function can be suppressed by alcohol, resulting in prolonged bleeding times. Other drugs also exert hematologic effects. Experimental addiction to opioids results in a reversible anemia and a reversible increase in erythrocyte sedimentation rate (a nonspecific indicator of the presence of a disease process). Smoking allows carbon monoxide to enter the body and bind to hemoglobin (carboxyhemoglobinemia), which consequently causes an increase in red cell production (erythrocytosis). The hematocrit value (the proportion of blood attributable to red blood cells) and the plasma fibronogen (a clotting factor) rise and increase blood viscosity; platelets (sticky constituents of blood important in wound healing) aggregate more in smokers. These thickening factors, together with damage to the insides of blood vessels, increase the probability of both stroke and heart attack (myocardial infarction) in smokers. White cells are also at increased levels in smokers (leucocytosis).

Skeletal Muscle Effects. Chronic alcohol consumption can result in muscle cell necrosis (death). Two main patterns are seen: (1) An acute alcoholic myopathy (disturbance of muscle function) occurs in the setting of binge drinking, sometimes associated with stupor and immobilization. This condition results in severe muscle pain, swelling, elevated creatine kinase (a muscle enzyme), and myoglobinuria (muscle protein in the urine which can cause kidney failure). (2) This pattern consists of a more slowly evolving syndrome of proximal muscle (those closest to the trunk) weakness and atrophy (decreased size). Milder degrees of muscle injury are quite common and consist of elevated levels of the muscle enzyme creatine kinase. Cocaine use can also cause muscle damage (rhabdomyolysis), resulting in abnormalities of creatine kinase. Most drugs of abuse (especially depressants) may indirectly cause muscle damage as a result of prolonged abnormal posture, for example, sleeping in an intoxicated state on a hard surface.

Renal Effects. Alcohol abuse causes a variety of electrolyte and acid-base (blood chemistry) disorders, which include decreases in the levels of phosphate, magnesium, calcium, and potassium. These abnormalities relate to disorders within the functioning kidney tubules (involved in secretion and reabsorption of minerals). The abnormalities usually disappear with abstinence from alcohol.

Heroin use has been associated with a form of kidney failure known as heroin nephropathy. Its precise relationship to heroin use is unclear and may be due, instead, to adulterants used to dilute the drug or to viral diseases such as hepatitis C or HIV that are spread through intravenous drug use. Secondary effects on the kidneys from drug and alcohol abuse also occur (for example, from the effects of trauma or muscle damage as described above).

See also **Crime and Alcohol; Crime and Drugs; Inhalants; Intimate Partner Violence and Alcohol/Substance Use; Social Costs of Alcohol and Drug Abuse; Substance Abuse and AIDS; Tobacco: Medical Complications.**

BIBLIOGRAPHY

American Psychiatric Association. (2000). *Diagnostic and statistical manual of mental disorders*, (4th ed.), text revision. Washington, DC.: Author.

Ary D. V., Tildesley, E., Hops, H., & Andrews, J. (1993). The influence of parent, sibling, and peer modeling and attitudes on adolescent use of alcohol. *International Journal of Addiction, 28,* 859–880.

Bartecchi, C. E., Mackenzie, T. D., & Schrier, R. W. (1994). The human costs of tobacco use. *New England Journal of Medicine, 330,* 907–912.

Bland, R., & Orn, H. (1986). Family violence and psychiatric disorder. *Canadian Journal of Psychiatry, 31,* 129–137.

Brick, J. (2008). Handbook of the medical consequences of alcohol and drug abuse, 2nd ed. New York: Haworth.

Clark D. B., & Bukstein O. G. (1998). Psychopathology in adolescent alcohol abuse and dependence. *Alcohol Health & Research World 22,* 117–126.

Day, C. P. (2007). Treatment of alcoholic liver disease. *Liver Transplantation, 13*(S2), S69–S75.

Drummer, O. H., Gerostamoulos, J., Batziris, H., Chu, M., Caplehorn, J., Robertson, M. D., & Swann, P. (2004). The involvement of drugs in drivers of motor vehicles killed in Australian road traffic crashes. *Accident Analysis and Prevention* 36(2), 239–248.

Eckardt, M. J., & Martin, P. R. (1986). Clinical assessment of cognition in alcoholism. *Alcoholism (NY), 10*(2), 123–127.

Freund, G., & Ballinger, W. E. (1988). Loss of cholinergic muscarinic receptors in the frontal cortex of alcohol abusers. *Alcoholism (NY), 12*(5), 630–638.

Geokas, M. C. (Vol. Ed.). (1984). Ethyl alcohol and disease. *Medical Clinics of North America, 68*(1), 1–246.

Grant, J. D., Scherrer, J. F., Lynskey, M. T., Lyons, M. J., Eisen, S. A., Tsuang, M. T., et al. (2006). Adolescent alcohol use is a risk factor for adult alcohol and drug dependence: Evidence from a twin design. *Psychological Medicine, 36*(1), 109–118.

Heron, M. P. (2007). Deaths: Leading causes for 2004. *National Vital Statistics Reports, 56*(5), 12.

Hingson, R., & Howland, J. (1987). Alcohol as a risk factor for injury or death resulting from accidental falls: A review of the literature. *Journal of Studies in Alcohol, 48*, 212–219.

Kandel D. B., & Yamaguchi, K. (1993). From beer to crack: Developmental patterns of drug involvement. *American Journal of Public Health, 83*, 851–855.

Klatsky, A. L. (1987). The cardiovascular effects of alcohol. *Alcohol and Alcoholism, 22*(Suppl. 1), 117–124.

Klatsky A. L., Friedman, G. D., Armstrong, M. A., & Kipp, H. (2003). Wine, liquor, beer, and mortality. *American Journal of Epidemiology, 158*, 585–595.

Kool, B., Ameratunga, S., Robinson, E., Crengle, S., & Jackson, R. (2008). The contribution of alcohol to falls at home among working-aged adults. *Alcohol, 42*(5), 383–388.

Mezey, E. (1985). Effect of ethanol on intestinal morphology, metabolism, and function. In H. K. Seitz & B. Kommerell (Eds.), *Alcohol related diseases in gastroenterology* (pp. 342–360). Berlin: Springer-Verlag.

Moore, R. D., Bone, L. R., Geller, G., Mamon, J. A., Stokes, E. J., & Levine, D. M. (1989). Prevalence, detection, and treatment of alcoholism in hospitalized patients. *Journal of the American Medical Association, 261*, 403–407.

O'Malley, P. M., Johnston, L. D., & Bachman, J. G. (1998). Alcohol use among adolescents. *Alcohol Health & Research World, 22*, 85–93.

Ramstedt, M. (2008). Alcohol and fatal accidents in the United States—A time series analysis for 1950–2002. *Accident Analysis & Prevention, 40*(4), 1273–1281.

Rimm, E. B., Klatsky A., Grobbee D., & Stampfer, M. J. (1996). Review of moderate alcohol consumption and reduced risk of coronary heart disease: Is the effect due to beer, wine, or spirits? *British Medical Journal, 312*, 731–736.

Sher, L. (2006). Alcohol consumption and suicide. *QJM Advance Access, 99*, 57–61.

Thun, M. J., Peto, R., Lopez, A. D., Monaco, J. H., Henley, S., Heath, C. W., et al. (1997). Alcohol consumption and mortality among middle-aged and elderly U.S. adults. *New England Journal of Medicine, 337*, 1705–1714.

U.S. Department of Health and Human Services. (2000). *Tenth special report to the U.S. Congress on alcohol and health.* Washington, DC: U.S. Government Printing Office.

Vong, S., & Bell, B. P. (2004). Chronic liver disease mortality in the United States, 1990–1998. *Hepatology, 39*(2), 476–483.

JOHN T. SULLIVAN
REVISED BY RALPH MYERSON (2001)
LEAH R. ZINDEL (2009)

CARDIOVASCULAR SYSTEM (ALCOHOL AND COCAINE)

Alcohol remains the most commonly used drug of abuse in the United States. Between 5 and 10 percent of the male population may be considered alcohol abusers with upwards of 21 percent of hospital admissions having an alcohol-related diagnosis. At least 500,000 deaths per year can be attributed to alcohol abuse. Excessive alcohol consumption increases mortality but also causes preventable illness. Alcohol abuse increases morbidity among hospitalized patients and plays a major role in admissions and mortality of patients in ICUs. Ethanol-related disorders consume as much as 20 percent of total health-care expenditures in the United States.

What constitutes excessive ingestion of alcohol has been determined. A standard serving (14 g of ethanol) of alcohol translates into 12 ounces (340 ml) of beer (5% alcohol v/v); 5 ounces (142 ml) of wine (12.5% alcohol v/v); and 1.5 fluid ounces (43 ml) of 80-proof spirits (40% alcohol v/v). *National Institute on Alcoholism and Alcohol Abuse Guidelines* recommends that men consume no more than 14 drinks per week and no more than four drinks per day. For women the amounts are lower, with no more than seven drinks per week and one to two drinks per day. These estimates are higher than those considered *moderate drinking* by many health providers, which recommend one and two drinks a day for women and men, respectively. Beneficial or adverse effects of drinking on the body are related to the amount consumed. Many Americans routinely consume more than the recommended serving and number of drinks.

PROTECTIVE EFFECTS OF ETHANOL INGESTION

Light-to-moderate drinking has beneficial effects on cardiovascular health through increases in high-density lipoprotein cholesterol, attenuation of inflammatory responses, and/or changes in blood clot formation. One to two glasses of red wine per day reduces the risk of cardiovascular disease, particularly coronary artery disease, suggesting that drinking red wine overcomes risks for coronary artery disease posed by high serum cholesterol concentrations (referred to as the *French Paradox*). A positive association exists between moderate alcohol use and survival in heart attack patients wherein both heavy drinkers and abstainers have poorer prognoses. Risk of blockage reforming in coronary arteries is lowered after stent implantation in patients consuming moderate amounts of alcohol. Light and moderate alcohol consumption raises blood concentrations of high-density lipoprotein (HDL), the so-called good cholesterol. About one-half of the protection afforded by moderate ethanol consumption is ascribed to an increased HDL cholesterol concentration in the blood. However, this protection vanishes if ethanol consumption is high enough to induce severe liver disease. Light to moderate alcohol drinking elevates plasma apolipoproteins, the plasma proteins that transport cholesterol in the blood, which also seems to afford a certain degree of protection.

Ethanol protects against clot formation by inhibiting platelet activation and platelet thrombus formation by interfering with the precursor of protaglandins, arachidonic acid, mobilization and subsequent inhibition of thromboxane A2 synthesis. Thromboxane A2 promotes platelet aggregation and contributes to clot formation with corresponding narrowing of coronary arteries. Reducing thromboxane A2 following ethanol ingestion decreases clot formation thereby preventing reductions in coronary blood flow. Ethanol may maintain coronary vessel blood flow through dilatation of coronary arteries and other mechanisms that protect the heart from injury. Moderate alcohol ingestion improves post-heart attack functions and increases nitric oxide production (a potent vasodilator) by the coronary arteries.

All of these mechanisms promote coronary blood flow, preventing reductions in oxygen delivery to jeopardized heart muscle at risk for ischemic injury. Active metabolites including polyphenolics, such as resveratrol within alcoholic beverages but primarily red wine, may prevent cardiovascular disease. Red wine enhances the dilation of blood vessels in patients with elevated cholesterol levels. Dealcoholized red wine, red wine, or resveratrol prevent cholesterol-induced reductions in coronary blood flow. Thus several mechanisms may account for the original description of the beneficial effects of moderate red wine drinking on cardiovascular function.

ACUTE DETRIMENTAL EFFECTS OF BINGE DRINKING ON THE DEVELOPMENT OF ARRHYTHMIAS

The *holiday heart syndrome* occurs as a result of alcohol-induced arrhythmias (abnormal heart rhythms), in otherwise healthy individuals. The chief arrhythmia is atrial fibrillation, which is described as rapid, irregular twitching of the atrial muscle. The syndrome was first described in heavy drinkers, who typically presented with symptoms of irregular heart rhythm on weekends or after holidays, but it may also occur after binge drinking in patients who usually drink little or no alcohol. The rhythm disorders usually convert to normal sinus rhythm within 24 hours of cessation of ethanol consumption. The association between alcoholic beverage ingestion and atrial fibrillation has been questioned when analysis is done using large (presumably, unbiased) populations of individuals.

Ethanol enhances sympathetic activation and increases norepinephrine release. Norepinephrine activates cardiac adrenergic receptors and initiates a cascade of events that result in increased heart rate and strength of contraction of the heart muscle. Higher doses initiate arrhythmias characteristic of holiday heart syndrome. Ethanol may also reduce parasympathetic activity and decrease heart rate variability, factors known to predispose the myocardium to arrhythmias. Although acute alcohol abuse most commonly causes atrial arrhythmias, it can also increase the risk of ventricular arrhythmias, a prime factor leading to sudden cardiac death in people who consume large quantities of alcohol. Ethanol-induced inhibition of cardiac sodium movement across cardiac muscle membranes via specific channels provides one potential mechanism for triggering supraventricular and ventricular arrhythmias. Following cessation of alcohol consumption, both low blood potassium and magnesium increase the risk for development of arrhythmias secondary to altered plasma electrolyte imbalances. In addition to possible electrophysiological derangements, repeated doses of ethanol depress left ventricular ejection fraction at blood alcohol concentrations seen with moderate to severe alcohol intoxication.

ADVERSE CARDIOVASCULAR EFFECTS OF HEAVY DRINKING

Heavy drinking is detrimental to the heart, leading to increased mortality that appears independent of coronary arterial disease. Alcoholics generally present with greater left ventricular dysfunction but exhibit a lower incidence and less severe narrowing of coronary arteries than patients complaining of chest pain. Excessive ethanol consumption can result in a syndrome termed *alcoholic heart muscle disease* (AHMD). AHMD is rarely produced by short-term ethanol administration. In general, alcoholic patients consuming more than 90 grams of alcohol per day (approximately seven to eight standard drinks per day) for more than 5 years are at risk for the development of asymptomatic AHMD. Those alcoholics who continue to drink develop symptoms associated with defects in the ability of the heart to pump blood. With continued heavy drinking, AHMD progresses with the development of an alcoholic cardiomyopathy with the signs and symptoms of heart failure. Long-term heavy alcohol consumption is the leading cause of a non-ischemic, dilated cardiomyopathy, herein referred to as *alcoholic cardiomyopathy*. Patients with an alcoholic cardiomyopathy have a worse outcome than patients with an idiopathic dilated cardiomyopathy if drinking is not abated or severely arrested.

Alcohol-induced cardiac muscle injury produces an initial decline in cardiac pumping capacity. Following this initial decline, a variety of compensatory mechanisms are activated, including the adrenergic nervous system, the rennin-angiotensin system, and the cytokine response. Some of these compensatory changes have been detected in alcoholic patients. In the short term, these compensatory systems restore cardiovascular function to within a normal range so that the alcoholic patient remains asymptomatic. However, with time, the sustained activation of these systems can lead to secondary damage to the ventricle, activating and accelerating the subsequent decompensation of the heart's pumping function, resulting in the transition from asymptomatic to symptomatic heart failure.

Chronic heavy drinking (more than 90 grams per day for more than 5 years) is the initial insult that modifies myocardial function in humans, eventually producing derangements in myofibrillar architecture, including disarray of the contractile elements and cardiac function resulting in reduced cardiac output. The degree of dysfunction is dependent upon the duration of alcohol drinking and amount of ethanol consumed. Because of difficulties in obtaining serial measurements in humans, various rodent models have been used to mimic the pattern of human alcohol consumption. The thickness of the left ventricular wall does not diminish in hearts from rats with short-term exposure to a diet containing alcohol. However, prolonged alcohol exposure leads to decreases in myocardial protein followed by a decrease in left ventricle mass, ventricular wall thickness and posterior wall thickness. The structural abnormalities are followed by a decrease in cardiac output secondary to reduced stroke volume rather than changes in heart rate. With extended alcohol exposure, signs of progressive heart disease appear with evidence of further myocardial derangements associated with the evolution of the myocardium to a dilated cardiomyopathy. This was exemplified in rodents through alcohol-induced increases in end-diastolic diameter, end-systolic diameter, and left ventricular mass. In addition, the left ventricle pressure-volume relationship was shifted down and to the right, characteristic of a dilated ventricle cardiomyopathy. Hence a slow, progressive, left ventricular dilation and wall thinning continues until there are symptomatic signs of heart failure with systolic dysfunction observed with continued heavy drinking.

Ethanol decreases cardiac function via 1) changes in the myocardial handling of calcium ion fluxes that are necessary for proper contraction and relaxation of the heart, 2) the abundance of proteins (actin and myosin) that serve to physically contract the muscle, and 3) the covalent binding of reactive molecules to proteins. Ethanol depresses cardiac contractile function by decreasing the rate and extent of pressure development and slowing the rate of relaxation in whole heart or depression of the development of tension in isolated cardiomyocytes.

Sex Differences in Response to Chronic Alcoholism. Men and women are adversely affected by heavy drinking. The acute response to binge drinking does not differ by sex. However, with long-term drinking sex-dependent differences appear. Women report lower lifetime cumulative levels of drinking than men. Females respond to chronic alcohol abuse in a fashion distinct from males. Initially women may be protected from detrimental effects of alcohol in that there is a lower degree of cardiac dysfunction and loss of the contractile proteins, actin and alpha myosin. As the duration of alcohol abuse increases females exhibit more severe declines in cardiac muscle contractility leading to severe reductions in ejection fraction in dilated cardiomyopathies.

ADVERSE EFFECTS OF COCAINE ON THE HEART

Cocaine is the second most commonly used illicit drug in the United States. In 2005, there were 448,481 cocaine-related visits to emergency departments in the United States with an over representation of 35 to 44 year olds. The frequency of cocaine-related medical emergencies has increased concomitant with the rise in drug use. Chest discomfort was reported in 40 percent of patients who presented to the emergency department after cocaine use; however, the cause of the chest pain remained obscure as of 2008. Cocaine use accounts for one-fourth of all non-fatal heart attacks in young patients.

The cardiovascular complications of cocaine abuse are adrenergic and include cocaine-associated acute coronary syndromes, myocardial ischemia and infarction, aortic dissection, and sudden cardiac death. Cocaine increases heart rate, elevates blood pressure, and enhances vasomotor tone, which are worsened by alcohol ingestion. Cocaine blocks the reuptake of norepinephrine and dopamine at the presynaptic adrenergic terminals, causing an accumulation of catecholamines at the postsynaptic receptor, thus acting as a powerful sympathomimetic agent. In addition, the ability of the vasculature to deliver oxygen is compromised by cocaine's ability to increase platelet aggregation

and may produce a narrowing of coronary vessels following vasoconstriction of large epicardial and small coronary resistance vessels. Delayed or recurrent constriction of the coronary arteries may occur hours after the serum cocaine concentration has declined and appears to be caused by cocaine's major metabolites (breakdown products). The cocaine-induced surge in catecholamine concentrations elevates shear-stress forces, increasing the risk of a tear in vessel walls and aortic dissection. The net effect is that cocaine leads to enhanced myocardial demand by increasing heart rate, blood pressure, and contractility, and lowers oxygen delivery through vasoconstriction of coronary vessels.

Cocaine directly blocks the sodium channels in heart muscle cells and may produce or worsen cardiac arrhythmias. Cocaine increases the risk of ventricular fibrillation. It is speculated that the increase in left ventricular mass (associated with long-term cocaine use) and the development of fibrotic areas serve as the underlying anatomic substrate, increasing the propensity for ischemia and arrhythmias.

Cocaine abuse induces acute or chronic deterioration of left ventricular performance. Acute left ventricular systolic and diastolic dysfunction has been attributed to the effects of cocaine or its metabolites on the handling of calcium by heart muscle cells. In addition, intravenous administration of cocaine can lead to infective endocarditis with subsequent damage to heart valves and deterioration of heart function. The use of cocaine appears to be a greater independent risk factor than the use of other drugs for the development of endocarditis. One possible explanation is that the elevation of the heart rate and systemic arterial pressure that accompanies cocaine use may induce valvular and vascular injury predisposing cocaine users to bacterial invasion. Cocaine use may also increase the risk of infection by lowering an individual's immune response to bacteria. Cocaine addiction induces protracted decreases in innate immune mechanisms lowering the host's ability to combat microbial invasion. With intravenous use, the adulterants or non-cocaine processing ingredients that are often present in cocaine may cause endocarditis with the ensuing cardiovascular complications associated with valvular heart disease.

The effects of ethanol on the mammalian heart are complex and are dependent upon both the amount and duration of alcohol consumption. Low or moderate ethanol consumption provides protection from cardiovascular disease. Excessive drinking is associated not only with increased mortality, but also with premature death and preventable ill health. Binge drinking increases the potential for arrhythmias that generally rectify themselves following abstinence from further drinking. Alcoholic patients consuming approximately seven to eight standard drinks per day for more than ten years are at risk to develop asymptomatic alcoholic heart muscle disease. Individuals who continue to drink may develop the signs and symptoms of overt heart failure. The point at which changes in normal physiological function culminate in intrinsic cell dysfunction is incompletely understood as of 2008.

The biggest public health challenge is to identify patients who are at risk but not yet symptomatic of alcohol-induced cardiac muscle disease and to develop strategies to prevent the transition to a symptomatic disease stage. Unfortunately, the general population is not routinely screened for asymptomatic alcoholic heart muscle disease. Pronounced left ventricular dilation, wall thinning, systolic dysfunction, and signs and symptoms of overt heart failure characterize symptomatic alcoholic heart muscle disease. Treatment involves complete abstinence or a severe reduction in ethanol consumption coupled with treatment of the heart failure.

Cocaine addiction gives rise to a separate set of problems and often culminates in cardiac arrhythmia. The combination of alcohol and cocaine may be even more dangerous than cocaine alone. In the presence of alcohol (ethanol), in humans, cocaine is metabolized to the compound cocaethylene. This chemical renders the combination of cocaine and alcohol more lethal than either alone.

See also **Alcohol: History of Drinking (International); Cocaine; Overdose, Drug (OD); Prevention, Education and.**

BIBLIOGRAPHY

Abou-Agag, L. H., Khoo, N. K., Binsack R., White, C. R., Darley-Usmar, V., Grenett, H. E., et al. (2005) Evidence of cardiovascular protection by moderate alcohol: Role of nitric oxide. *Free Radical Biology and Medicine, 39,* 540–548.

Adams, M. A., Bobik, A., & Korner, P. I. (1989). Differential development of vascular and cardiac hypertrophy in genetic hypertension: Relation to sympathetic function. *Hypertension, 14,* 191–202.

Adams, M. A., & Hirst, M. (1986). The influence of adrenal medullectomy on the development of ethanol-induced cardiac hypertrophy. *Canadian Journal of Physiology and Pharmacology, 64,* 592–596.

Adams, M. A., & Hirst, M. (1990). Metoprolol suppresses the development of ethanol-induced cardiac hypertrophy in the rat. *Canadian Journal of Physiology and Pharmacology, 68,* 562–567.

Askanas, A., Udoshi, M., & Sadjadi, S. A. (1980). The heart in chronic alcoholism: A noninvasive study. *American Heart Journal, 99,* 9–16.

Benjamin, E. J., Levy, D., Vaziri, S. M., D'Agostino, R. B., Belanger, A. J., & Wolf, P. A. Independent risk factors for atrial fibrillation in a population-based cohort: The Framingham Heart Study. *Journal of the American Medical Association, 271,* 840–844.

Brody, S. L., Slovis, C. M., & Wrenn, K. D. (1990). Cocaine-related medical problems: Consecutive series of 233 patients. *American Journal of Medicine, 88,* 325–331.

Brugger-Andersen, T., Ponitz, V., Snapinn, S., & Dickstein, K. (2008). Moderate alcohol consumption is associated with reduced long-term cardiovascular risk in patients following a complicated acute myocardial infarction. *International Journal of Cardiology,* In press, 2008.

Caetano, R., Ramisetty-Mikler, S., Floyd, L. R., & McGrath, C. (2006). The epidemiology of drinking among women of child-bearing age. *Alcoholism: Clinical and Experimental Research, 30,* 1023–1030.

Coimbra, S. R., Lage, S. H., Brandizzi, L., Yoshida, V., & da Luz, P. L. (2005). The action of red wine and purple grape juice on vascular reactivity is independent of plasma lipids in hypercholesterolemic patients. *Brazilian Journal of Medical and Biological Research, 38,* 1339–1347.

Delgado-Rodriguez, M., Gomez-Ortega, A., Mariscal-Ortiz, M., Palma-Perez S., & Sillero-Arenas, M. (2003). Alcohol drinking as a predictor of intensive care and hospital mortality in general surgery: A prospective study. *Addiction, 98,* 611–616.

Eichhorn, E. J., & Bristow, M. R. (1996). Medical therapy can improve the biological properties of the chronically failing heart: A new era in the treatment of heart failure. *Circulation, 94,* 2285–2296.

Eisenhofer, G., Lambie, D. G., & Johnson, R. H. (1983). Effects of ethanol on plasma catecholamines and norepinephrine clearance. *Clinical Pharmacology & Therapeutics, 34,* 143–147.

Ellison, R. C., Zhang, Y., Hopkins, P. N., Knox, S., Djousse, L., & Carr, J. J. (2006). Is alcohol consumption associated with calcified atherosclerotic plaque in the coronary arteries and aorta? *American Heart Journal, 152,* 177–182.

Ettinger, P. O., Wu, C. F., De La Cruz, C., Jr., Weisse, A. B., Ahmed, S. S., & Regan, T. J. (1978). Arrhythmias and the "holiday heart": Alcohol-associated cardiac rhythm disorders. *American Heart Journal, 95,* 555–562.

Faris, R. F., Henein, M. Y., & Coats, A. J. (2003). Influence of gender and reported alcohol intake on mortality in non-ischemic dilated cardiomyopathy. *Heart Disease, 5,* 89–94.

Fenelon, G., Balbao, C. E., Fernandes, R., Arfelli, E., Landim, P., Ayres, O., et al. (2007). Characterization of the acute cardiac electrophysiologic effects of ethanol in dogs. *Alcoholism: Clinical and Experimental Research, 31,* 1574–1580.

Fernandez-Sola, J., Estruch, R., Nicolas, J. M., Pare, J. C., Sacanella, E., Antunez, E., et al. (1997). Comparison of alcoholic cardiomyopathy in women versus men. *American Journal of Cardiology, 80,* 481–485.

Foltin, R. W., & Fischman, M. W. (1988). Ethanol and cocaine interactions in humans: Cardiovascular consequences. *Pharmacology, Biochemistry, and Behavior, 31,* 877–883.

Frost, L., & Vestergaard, P. (2004). Alcohol and risk of atrial fibrillation or flutter: A cohort study. *Archives of Internal Medicine, 164,* 1993–1998.

Gazzieri, D., Trevisani, M., Tarantini, F., Bechi, P., Masotti, G., Gensini, G. F., et al. (2006). Ethanol dilates coronary arteries and increases coronary flow via transient receptor potential vanilloid 1 and calcitonin gene-related peptide. *Cardiovascular Research, 70,* 589–599.

Grant, B. F., Harford, T. C., Muthen, B. O., Yi, H-Y., Hasin, D. S., & Stinson, F. S. (2007). *DSM-IV* alcohol dependence and abuse: Further evidence of validity in the general population. *Drug and Alcohol Dependence, 86,* 154–156.

Guarnieri, T., & Lakatta, E. G. (1990). Mechanism of myocardial contractile depression by clinical concentrations of ethanol: A study in ferret papillary muscles. *Journal of Clinical Investigation, 85,* 179–184.

Halsted, C. (1980). Alcoholism and malnutrition. *American Journal of Clinical Nutrition, 33,* 2705–2270.

Hirota, Y., Bing, O. H., & Abelmann, W. H. (1976). Effect of ethanol on contraction and relaxation of isolated rat ventricular muscle. *Journal of Molecular and Cellular Cardiology, 8,* 727–732.

Kennedy, J. M., Stewart, C., Light, K. E., & Wyeth, R. P. (2002). Effects of gender on the cardiac toxicity elicited by chronic ethanol intake in rats. *Toxicology and Applied Pharmacology, 179,* 111–118.

Kim, S. D., Beck, J., Bieniarz, T., Schumacher, A., & Piano, M. R. (2001). A rodent model of alcoholic heart muscle disease and its evaluation by echocardiography. *Alcoholism: Clinical and Experimental Research, 25,* 457–463.

Klatsky, A. L. (1994). Epidemiology of coronary heart disease: Influence of alcohol. *Alcoholism: Clinical and Experimental Research, 18,* 164–171.

Klatsky, A. L. (2008). Alcohol, wine, and vascular diseases: An abundance of paradoxes. *American Journal of Physiology: Heart and Circulatory Physiology, 294,* H582–H583.

Klatsky, A. L., Friedman, G. D., Armstrong, M. A., & Kipp, H. (2003). Wine, liquor, beer, and mortality. *American Journal of Epidemiology, 158,* 585–595.

Klein, G., Gardiwal, A., Schaefer, A., Panning, B., & Breitmeier, D. (2007). Effect of ethanol on cardiac single sodium channel gating. *Forensic Science International, 171,* 131–135.

Kochanek, K. D., & Smith, B. L. (2004). Death: Preliminary data for 2002. *National Vital Satatistics Reports, 52,* 1–47.

Kokolis, S., Marmur, J. D., Clark, L. T., Kassotis, J., Kokolis, R., Cavusoglu, E., et al. (2006). Effects of alcoholism on coronary artery disease and left ventricular dysfunction in male veterans. *Journal of Invasive Cardiology, 18,* 304–307.

Kupari, M., Koskinen, P., Suokas, A., & Ventilä, M. (1990). Left ventricular filling impairment in asymptomatic chronic alcoholics. *American Journal of Cardiology, 66,* 1473–1477.

Lang, C. H., Frost, R. A., Sumner, A. D., & Vary, T. C. (2005). Molecular mechanisms responsible for alcohol-induced myopathy in skeletal muscle and heart. *International Journal of Biochemical and Cellular Biology, 37,* 2180–2195.

Lazarević, A. M., Nakatani, S., Nesković, A. N., Marinković, J., Yasumura, Y., Stojicić, D., et al. (2000). Early changes in left ventricular function in chronic asymptomatic alcoholics: Relation to the duration of heavy drinking. *Journal of the American College Cardiology, 35,* 1599–1606.

Lochner, A., Cowley, R., & Brink, A. J. (1969). Effects of ethanol on metabolism and function of perfused hearts. *American Heart Journal, 78,* 770–780.

Malyutina, S., Bobak, M., Kurilovitch, S., Gafarov, V., Simonova, G., Nikitin, Y., et al. (2002). Relation between heavy and binge drinking and all-cause and cardiovascular mortality in Novosibirsk, Russia: A prospective cohort study. *Lancet, 360,* 1448–1458.

Mathews, E. J., Gardin, J. M., Henry, W. L., Del Negro, A. A., Fletcher, R. D., Snow, J. A., et al. (1981). Echocardiographic abnormalities in chronic alcoholics with and without overt congestive heart failure. *American Journal of Cardiology, 47,* 570–578.

Minor, R. L. J., Scott, B. D., Brown, D. D., & Winniford, M.D. (1991). Cocaine-induced myocardial infarction in patients with normal coronary arteries. *Annals of Internal Medicine, 115,* 797–806.

Morelli, S., De Marzio, P., Suppa, M., Gnecchi, M., Giordano, M., Aguglia, F., et al. (1989). Holiday heart syndrome: Spontaneous reversibility of the electrocardiographic and echocardiographic alterations. *Cardiologia, 34,* 721–724.

Mostafa, S. M., & Murthy, B. V. (2002) Alcohol-associated admissions to an adult intensive care unit: An audit. *European Journal of Anaethesia, 19,* 193–196.

Niroomand, F., Hauer, O., Tiefenbacher, C. P., Katus, H. A., & Kuebler, W. (2004). Influence of alcohol consumption on restenosis rate after percutaneous transluminal coronary angioplasty and stent implantation. *Heart, 90,* 1189–1193.

Piano, M. R. (2002). Alcoholic cardiomyopathy: Incidence, clinical characteristics and pathophysiology. *Chest, 212,* 1638–1650.

Piano, M. R., Geenen, D. L., Schwertz, D. W., Chowdhury, S. A., & Yuzhakova, M. (2007). Long-term effects of alcohol consumption in male and female rats. *Cardiovascular Toxicology, 7,* 247–254.

Rosenqvist, M. (1998). Alcohol and cardiac arrhythmias. *Alcoholism: Clinical and Experimental Research, 22,* 318S–322S.

Segel, L. D. (1988). The development of alcohol-induced cardiac dysfunction in the rat. *Alcohol and Alcoholism, 23,* 391–401.

Silberbauer, K., Juhasz, M., Ohrenberger, G., & Hess, C. (1988). Noninvasive assessment of left ventricular diastolic function by pulsed Doppler echocardiography in young alcoholics. *Cardiology, 75,* 431–439.

Smothers, B. A., Yahr, H. T., & Ruhl, C. E. (2004). Detection of alcohol use disorders in general hospital admissions in United States. *Archives of Internal Medicine, 164,* 749–756.

Sofuoglu, M., Nelson, D., Babb, D. A., & Hatsukami, D. K. (2001). Intravenous cocaine increases plasma epinephrine and norepinephrine in humans. *Pharmacology and Biochemical Behavior, 68,* 455–459.

Spies, C. D., Sander, M., Stangl, K., Renadez-Sola, J., Preedy, V. R., Rubin, E., et al. (2001). Effects of alcohol on the heart. *Current Opinion in Critical Care, 7,* 337–343.

Stewart, S., Hart, C. L., Hole, D. J., & McMurray, J. V. (2001). Population prevalence, incidence, and predictors of atrial fibrillation in the Renfrew/Paisley study. *Heart, 86,* 516–521.

Urbano-Marquez, A., Estruch, R., Fernandez-Smith, J., Nicolas, J. M., Carlos, J., & Rubin, E. (1995). The greater risk of alcoholic cardiomyopathy and myopathy in women compared with men. *Journal of the American Medical Association, 274,* 149–154.

U.S. Department of Health and Human Services, Public Health Service, National Institute of Health, National Institute on Alcohol Abuse and Alcoholism. (1997). Epidemiology of alcohol use and alcohol-related consequences. In *Ninth Special Report to the U.S. Congress on Alcohol and Health* (pp. 1–31). Bethesda, MD: Author.

Vaillant, G. E. (2003). A 60-year follow-up of alcoholic men. *Addiction, 98,* 1043–1051.

Vary, T. C., & Deiter, G. (2004). Chronic alcohol administration inhibits synthesis of both myofibrillar and sarcoplasmic proteins in heart. *Metabolism Clinical and Experimental,* 54, 212–219.

Vary, T. C., Kimball, S. R., & Sumner, A. (2007). Sex-dependent differences in the regulation of myocardial protein synthesis following long-term ethanol consumption. *American Journal of Physiology Regulatory Integrative and Comparative Physiology, 292,* R778–R787.

Wang, Z., Zou, J., Cao, K., Hsieh, T. C., Huang, Y., & Wu, J. M. (2005). Dealcoholized red wine containing known amounts of resveratrol suppresses atherosclerosis in hypercholesterolemic rabbits without affecting plasma lipid levels. *International Journal of Molecular Medicine, 16,* 533–540.

Wu, C. F., Sudhaker, M., Ghazanfar, J., Ahmed, S. S., & Regan, T. J. (1976). Preclinical cardiomyopathy in chronic alcoholics: A sex difference. *American Heart Journal, 91,* 281–286.

Yamashita, S. (1971). Effect of alcohol on normal rat heart. *Japanese Heart Journal, 12,* 242–250.

THOMAS C. VARY

COGNITION

Psychoactive drugs of abuse are used for their perceived mind-altering effects; however, the drug user may not be aware of additional cognitive effects produced by the drugs. A cognitive effect is an impact on mental functions such as the processes of learning, perceiving, imagining, remembering, feeling, thinking, reasoning, knowing, and judging.

Psychoactive drugs produce cognitive effects by causing chemical changes in the brain. These effects are frequently short-lived and correspond to the duration and intensity of the chemical changes in the brain. However, cognitive effects can persist after the drug has been eliminated from the body, and some can be irreversible.

ALCOHOL

Ethanol (also called ethyl alcohol) is the consumable alcohol content in beer, wine, distilled spirits, or medicinal compounds; it acts by depressing or reducing cognitions. Initially, alcohol reduces inhibitions, which results in more spontaneity or impulsivity and a feeling of relaxation. As the amount of alcohol acting on the brain increases, the ability to perceive, remember, reason, and judge is progressively impaired. Executive functioning, including planning and working memory, may also become impaired, even with a moderate dose of alcohol. Further increases in the amount of alcohol can depress the brain and cognitions to the point of loss of consciousness. Because of the cognitive impairment the person may not perceive the impairment (e.g., "I'm not drunk") and may take undue risks (e.g., drunk driving and other indiscretions).

Alcoholic blackouts are impairments of the memory of events that occurred while conscious but under the influence of alcohol. Such blackouts are not limited to chronic alcoholics. Long-term use of alcohol can lead to subtle impairment of perceiving, responding, and remembering that may not be detectable without formal neuropsychological testing. As many as two-thirds of abstinent alcoholics in treatment have some impairment in learning, memory, problem solving, and perceptual motor skills. Overall intelligence and language skills are typically spared. There is considerable evidence that cognitive recovery begins about two weeks following detoxification and can continue for several years in alcoholics who remain abstinent. The aging brain is more susceptible to the effects of alcohol than is the brain of a younger alcohol abuser. Consequently, the probability of making a full recovery decreases with age. Alcohol dementia is the most severe form of alcohol-related cognitive impairment and includes profound amnesia. Moreover, deficits can persist throughout a person's life even if they stop drinking.

Paranoid states of unfounded suspicion or jealousy may manifest or be aggravated under the influence of alcohol. In alcoholic hallucinations, people can have vivid but unreal perceptions while conscious; these typically occur as a result of neurochemical changes in the brain when alcohol use is abruptly discontinued after periods of excessive drinking.

TRANQUILIZERS, SEDATIVES, AND HYPNOTICS

These drugs are often collectively referred to as *downers*. People taking them are at risk for the same cognitive impairments produced by the consumption of alcohol. The elderly are particularly at risk for confusion.

STIMULANTS

Stimulant drugs have effects that are the reverse of depressant drugs: They arouse the nervous system. These drugs include cocaine, amphetamines (speed), and caffeine. In low doses perception is heightened, attention is increased, and thought processes are accelerated, resulting in a feeling of greater alertness. Memory, however, can be affected resulting in impaired recall of material learned while under the influence of stimulants. Higher doses intensify the above effects and lead to restlessness and rapidity of thoughts, which reduce attention. Vulnerable people can become paranoid or even psychotic. Higher effective doses of stimulants can occur via intravenous administration or inhalation of cocaine, rapidly affecting the brain and resulting in an abrupt *rush* or *high*. These effects are typically short-lived but are so intensely pleasurable that individuals often repeat doses. Discontinuation of stimulants after a long period of use often leads to a temporary period of depression. Heavy amphetamine use has been linked to paranoid psychotic episodes and vivid hallucinations. However, amphetamine use itself does not appear to lead to long-term cognitive impairment. Long-term cocaine users can develop cognitive problems, particularly memory and concentration deficits, and impaired executive functioning.

MARIJUANA

Marijuana (cannabis) is often used for the subjective effects of relaxation and a decreased potential for conflicts. It is also known to distort perception of time and to reduce responsiveness. Long-term use of marijuana has been associated with apathy, under-achievement, and lack of motivation. However, in general the evidence linking marijuana use to permanent cognitive changes is inconclusive.

HALLUCINOGENS

Hallucinogenic drugs distort perceptions and cause hallucinations. They include lysergic acid diethylamide (LSD), phencyclidine (PCP), mescaline, psilocybin mushrooms, and several newer drugs with hallucinatory and stimulant effects called *designer drugs*, (e.g., Ecstasy). In addition to profound effects on perceptions, hallucinogenic drugs affect responsiveness, learning, and judgment. Some users experience flashbacks, which are spontaneous vivid recollections of experiences that occurred while under the influence of hallucinogens. Flashbacks can occur long after the last use of the hallucinogen. Hallucinogen Persisting Perception Disorder is identified by the *Diagnostic and Statistical Manual of Mental Disorders, Fourth edition (DSM-IV)* as the transient recurrence of disturbances in perception that are reminiscent of those experienced during one or more earlier hallucinogen intoxication. To meet criteria for the disorder these symptoms must not be due to current intoxication, they must cause clinically significant distress or impairment in social, occupational, or other important areas of functioning, and they cannot be due to a general medical condition.

USE DURING PREGNANCY

Psychoactive drugs used during pregnancy affect the developing fetus. Prenatal exposure, particularly to alcohol but possibly to marijuana or stimulants, has been associated with cognitive impairments detectable early in the child's life and eventually resulting in developmental problems as well as school, social, and occupational difficulties.

See also **Imaging Techniques: Visualizing the Living Brain.**

BIBLIOGRAPHY

Kaplan, R. F. (2004). Neuropsychology of alcoholism: Effects of premorbid and comorbid disorders. In H. R. Kranzler & J. A. Tinsley (Eds.), *Dual diagnosis and treatment: Substance abuse and comorbid disorders* (2nd ed., pp. 461–486). New York: Marcel Dekker.

Lezak, M. D., Howieson, D. B., & Loring, D. W. (2004). *Neuropsychological assessment* (4th ed.). New York: Oxford University Press.

Martin, P. R., & Hubbard, J. R. (2000). Substance abuse and related disorders. In M. H. Ebert, P. T. Loosen, & B. Nurcombe (Eds.), *Current diagnosis & treatment in psychiatry* (pp. 233–259). New York: Lange Medical Books/McGraw-Hill.

Martin, P. R., Lovinger, D. M., & Breese, G. R. (1995). Alcohol and other abused substances. In P. Munson & R. A. Mueller (Eds.), *Principles of pharmacology: Basic concepts and clinical applications* (pp. 417–452). New York: Chapman & Hall.

PETER MARTIN
GEORGE MATHEWS

ENDOCRINE AND REPRODUCTIVE SYSTEMS

Many fundamental challenges remain in understanding the impact of alcohol and drugs on endocrine and reproductive function. Many factors can influence the degree to which drug or alcohol abuse can cause an abnormality of endocrine or reproductive function. These factors include (a) the amount and duration of consumption, (b) the route of illegal drug administration, (c) whether there is preexisting or concurrent damage to an endocrine/reproductive organ, (d) concurrent use of another drug, and (e) genetic risk for an endocrine disorder. Often our knowledge about these factors and how they interact with one another is more limited than what is known about the range of endocrine and reproductive dysfunction associated with the chronic consumption of alcohol and the abuse of illicit drugs.

Knowledge is also limited because some endocrine or reproductive consequences may become evident only when a laboratory (biochemical) test indicates an abnormal result. The absence of a physical sign or a clinical symptom may lead to the false impression that there is no endocrine or reproductive consequence. In addition, there are challenges in ascertaining whether the alcohol- or drug-abuse related endocrine or reproductive dysfunction is due to the drug itself or to the social context in which the drug is used. Finally, endocrine or reproductive disturbances may also occur from the consequences of withdrawal syndromes that occur when the ingestion of the drug or alcohol is stopped or reduced.

HYPOTHALAMUS/PITUITARY GLAND

The brain directly or indirectly influences most endocrine and reproductive function—specifically by the functional interactions of the brain's hypothalamus and pituitary gland with the target endocrine organs. The hypothalamus produces pituitary-regulating hormones; all are peptides except one (dopamine). In response to each of these hypothalamic hormones, the pituitary releases a hormone, which influences the function of an endocrine or reproductive organ.

Alcohol. The anecdotal reports of changes in sexual function following alcohol consumption provided the stimulus for much of the research targeting hypothalamic-pituitary relationships because impairments here can often result in sexual dysfunction. Although acute alcohol use has been reported in public surveys to be associated with increased sexual drive and functioning, clinical and animal research has revealed major hormonal dysfunctions in chronic or heavy alcohol users.

Heavy alcohol use increases prolactin (PRL), the pituitary hormone associated with the preparation during pregnancy for breast milk secretion; however, chronic alcohol use inhibits the pituitary release of luteinizing hormone (LH) and follicle-stimulating hormone (FSH). Both LH and FSH are important in regulating the sex hormones produced by the testes in males and the ovaries in females. Yet, the acute administration of alcohol does not produce significant changes in PRL, LH, or FSH serum levels.

Heavy alcohol consumption is associated with an increase in pituitary-secreted adrenocorticotropic hormone (ACTH), partly explaining the *pseudo*-Cushing's syndrome (moon-faced appearance, central obesity, muscle weakness) and the increased release of melanocyte-stimulating hormone (MSH), which possibly leads to increased skin pigmentation. Although there is no consistent effect of heavy alcohol use on the pituitary's release of thyroid-stimulating hormone (TSH) or growth hormone (GH), a rise in the blood alcohol level is associated with the inhibition of antidiuretic hormone (ADH) release from the posterior pituitary, resulting in increased urination.

Drugs. Complaints of derangements of libido (sex drive) and sexual functioning in opioid (heroin) addicts were among the first lines of clinical evidence to suggest the possible role of such narcotics in altering hypothalamic-pituitary functioning. Although most of what is known about drug-abuse related hypothalamic-pituitary abnormalities focuses on heroin use, the epidemic proportions of cocaine abuse and dependence in the 1980s have brought renewed scientific interest to this area.

Studies have shown that opioid use is associated with increased serum PRL without producing disturbances in serum GH or TSH levels, and cocaine use has been associated with both high and low PRL levels. The contradictory findings in the case of cocaine use might be attributable to the variations in patterns of cocaine use. Animal studies have shown that gonadotropin-releasing hormone (GnRH), released from the hypothalamus, did not stimulate PRL following acute cocaine administration, and it did not prevent acute cocaine-associated PRL suppression. Elevated levels of dopamine have been observed during acute cocaine administration, but chronic cocaine use may deplete dopamine.

Some investigators have reported a normal rise in TSH released by the pituitary in response to stimulation by the hypothalamic hormone called thyrotropin-releasing hormone (TRH) in patients receiving methadone therapy for opioid addiction. Others have observed a blunted TSH and PRL response following TRH administration in active heroin users.

Although normal basal LH secretion has been observed in cocaine abuse, opiate use is associated with decreased basal FSH and LH levels in males. In female heroin addicts, these low levels of the pituitary gonadotropins result in a consistently normal FSH response and a variable LH response following a GnRH challenge.

Some researchers have demonstrated normal functioning of the hypothalamic-pituitary-adrenal (HPA) axis in former heroin addicts who were maintained on methadone both long-term and only for a number of months. However, there is also evidence suggesting that methadone alters the normal biological rhythm of hormonal secretion.

SEX HORMONES
Diminished sexual drive and performance in opioid users have raised questions about the relationship between such narcotic drug use and disturbances in the levels of sex hormones. Although some reports

show no significant differences in serum testosterone levels between heroin addicts, methadone-maintained patients, and normal controls, other studies have not confirmed these results. Some researchers have reported that plasma levels of testosterone are consistently lower in active heroin addicts and in addicts who self-administer heroin in controlled research settings, and to be within the normal range in long-term methadone-maintained patients. Additionally, some evidence shows that plasma testosterone levels that are depressed under circumstances of heroin administration followed by methadone maintenance and then withdrawal gradually returned to preheroin-use levels. Alcohol consumption and cocaine use in excessive amounts are also associated with low testosterone levels.

Opioid effects on the estrogens produced by both men and women may be responsible for the clinical observations of sexual dysfunction. In the male heroin addicts studied, the plasma estradiol concentrations were either low or within normal ranges; in women, the plasma estrogens are low. A clear explanation of these observed derangements in plasma testosterone and estrogens is unknown. Female heroin addicts frequently experience cessation of or irregular menses. However, most regain normal menstrual function when stabilized on methadone and under these circumstances fertility seems unaffected. The anecdotal reports and, in limited cases, experimental evidence of the influence of marijuana on sexual function and sex-hormone levels are also inconsistent and confusing in humans.

The illicit drug-related disturbances discussed above suggest that the narcotic-related depressions in sex-hormone production of the ovaries and testes can occur because they reduce the pituitary's stimulation of these sex organs. However, this has not been a consistent finding.

REPRODUCTION AND PREGNANCY

Impotence, atrophy of the testes, infertility, and decreased libido are common complaints in male alcoholics. These observations are thought to be secondary to the direct effects of alcohol on testicular tissue, to an alcohol-associated decrease in sperm motility, and to an alcohol-related decrease in vitamin A and zinc. Both vitamin A and zinc are important in maintaining testicular tissue growth.

In young women, alcohol abuse is associated with amenorrhea (loss of menses) and anovulation (lack of ovulation), and in chronic users, with early menopause. There is evidence that vaginal blood flow decreases as the blood alcohol level increases. There is evidence that alcohol is a protective factor against cardiovascular disease in postmenopausal women, by increasing estradiol production that normally decreases after menopause.

Despite these clinical observations, when rigorously investigated, there were no consistent changes in progesterone or testosterone. Consequently, it is difficult to determine whether these observations were due to alcohol-related liver disease, malnutrition, or the direct toxic effects of chronic alcohol use.

During pregnancy, alcoholism is associated with increased risk of spontaneous abortion (miscarriage), and the development of fetal alcohol syndrome (FAS) has been associated with drinking during pregnancy. FAS is a characteristic pattern of skin or facial abnormalities with growth and developmental impairments, which are believed to be related to alcohol's suppression of the sex hormone progesterone. The features of FAS may vary whereas fetal abnormalities associated with alcohol can be divided into the following four categories: (a) growth deficiency, (b) central nervous system dysfunction, (c) head and facial abnormalities, and (d) other major and minor malformations. In addition, abnormal development of the mammary gland was found to be associated with drinking before and during pregnancy. In animal studies, alcohol has been shown to decrease progesterone, which is important during mammary gland maturation, resulting in its decreased weight. The composition of milk produced is also affected in those that consume or have consumed alcohol. In animal studies milk production is decreased and it contains less protein and lactose with an increase in lipids.

ADRENAL GLANDS

Our understanding of the relationship between opioid drug use and the functioning of the adrenal gland is based on incomplete and often contradictory information. Some scientists have published reports of normal plasma levels of cortisol (a hormone released from the adrenals) during heroin use and withdrawal, under research conditions of heroin self-administration, and during methadone-maintenance treatment. In other studies, researchers have found low plasma cortisol and ACTH levels in heroin users. In methadone-treated patients, ACTH produced by the pituitary stimulates the adrenal gland to produce cortisol. In another study, there was a decreased plasma cortisol response to stimulation with intravenous cosyntropin (an ACTH-like substance) in methadone-treated patients. There are also reports of low normal or subnormal plasma cortisol levels in heroin users and disturbances in the daytime cortisol secretion from the adrenal gland in methadone-maintained patients.

The variable findings from these studies may be attributed to differences in the types of drugs used, in the state of stress-associated drug withdrawal, in patterns of drug use, in study design, or to a combination of these and other as yet unknown factors. There is also the well-known problem of inaccurate ACTH measurement, often resulting in falsely low values.

CARBOHYDRATE METABOLISM

The opioids are virtually the only class of *illegal* drugs for which there is information about the pharmacologic effects on serum glucose levels. There are long-standing reports of opiate-associated hyperglycemia (elevated blood sugar concentration), but the mechanisms explaining these findings are not fully understood. In association with chronic opioid use, there are reports of both low levels of serum glucose and high levels of insulin. The conflicting results of some investigations may be due, in part, to differences in study design (e.g., the nutritional state of the research subjects, the amount of glucose used in clinical studies, or the time(s) of glucose administration).

To briefly review the regulation of glucose control: The pancreas, an endocrine organ located in the upper abdomen, plays a central role by secreting glucagon to raise serum glucose levels and by secreting insulin to lower serum glucose levels. After the discovery of endogenous opioid peptides in the human pancreas, subsequent research provided information that one such endogenous opioid, beta-endorphin, stimulates the secretion of glucagon and a biphasic rise in insulin concentration. This may, in part, explain

the observations of both elevated and reduced serum glucose levels in heroin users. Whatever the nature of the mechanism, glucose metabolism is deranged in both heroin and methadone users by a direct or indirect parameter of serum glucose regulation.

The alcohol-related aberrations of carbohydrate metabolism are also quite complex. Some investigators have demonstrated that acutely administered alcohol may result in a reversible and mild resistance to the glucose-lowering effects of insulin, perhaps explaining the observations of a rise in glucose following alcohol use. Increased alcohol consumption decreases glucose production by creating more triglycerides and lactic acid in the body during alcohol metabolism. In individuals who are fasting, alcohol administration can lead to a severe depression of serum glucose, primarily by reducing its production in the liver. Serum glucose levels are also lower in chronic alcohol users with concurrent alcohol-related liver disease. Nevertheless, serum levels are elevated in alcoholics with concurrent alcohol-related destruction of the pancreas. Even without other concurrent diseases, alcohol consumption may result in either no changes or in minimal to mild elevations or reductions in serum glucose. There also appears to be a difference in alcohol's effects on glucose according to the sex. In animal studies, it appears that females tend to be affected more by alcohol and, with chronic ingestion, produce less glucose.

THE THYROID GLAND

Located in the anterior aspect of the neck, the thyroid gland secretes thyroxine (T_4) and other hormones whose principal purpose is to regulate the metabolism of other tissues in the body. TSH, which is produced by the pituitary, controls the thyroid production of T_4. Therefore alterations in thyroid function can be the result of problems directly involving the gland or disruptions in the TSH-mediated control of the thyroid gland.

Despite the frequency, duration, or amount of use, it appears that there are no clinical signs or symptoms of thyroid dysfunction in chronic heroin or alcohol users. Disturbances in biochemical indices (laboratory tests) of thyroid function are, however, not uncommon in opiate or alcohol use. In heavy drinkers, the total T_4 is decreased while the amount of biologically available T_4 (free T_4) and other indices of thyroid function are normal. An increase in thyroid volume has been observed in both women and men with the increase of alcohol consumption.

In active heroin users or during heroin withdrawal, total T_4 levels are increased in association with normal, subnormal, or high levels of other parameters of thyroid function. In addition T_3 (triiodothyronine) levels have been found to be elevated in heroin users. In methadone-maintained people, there are reports of normal and slight-to-significant increases in total T_4 in conjunction with increased levels of thyroxine-binding globulin (TBG), a protein that binds thyroid hormones in blood. Interestingly, methadone maintenance is associated with a correction of these biochemical disturbances.

There are a number of possible explanations for the biochemical derangements observed during opiate use. The total T_4 is increased whenever there is an increase in TBG, to maintain an adequate range of biologically active T_4. Perhaps the increase in total T_4 is the result of a direct opiate-induced elevation of TBG. It is also possible that the altered liver function seen in chronic heroin and alcohol users is responsible for TBG abnormalities leading to disturbances in T_4 levels. Finally, it is possible that opiate-related or alcohol-related disturbances are due to a combination of the above mechanisms as well as to some other still undefined processes.

BONE METABOLISM

The observations of increased fractures sustained by alcoholics have prompted investigations about the role that alcohol may play in disturbances of the structure and the mechanical properties of bone. Some studies have shown reduced bone mass in alcoholics, while others have reported decreases in compact and trabecular bone mass—a condition called osteoporosis. Some of these disturbances in new bone formation may be mediated by alcohol's impairment of calcium and Vitamin D metabolism, both of which are crucial to bone metabolism. In a human study, lower calcium blood levels were found in individuals that consumed alcohol, resulting from a greater excretion of calcium from their bodies. In addition, alcohol impairs bone formation by inhibiting osteoblasts, the cells responsible for such formation.

Nevertheless, there does remain considerable doubt as to whether the bone complications are because of alcohol itself or because of alcohol-related liver disease, of malnutrition, or of a host of other potential factors. Chronic liver disease unrelated to alcohol has also been a cause of osteoporosis and other bone diseases.

IMPORTANCE TO PUBLIC HEALTH

The endocrine and reproductive consequences of drug and alcohol abuse are extensive and profound. Both drug and alcohol abuse result in clinically significant derangements in many different endocrine systems. Although knowledge about the dimensions of such disturbances to endocrine and reproductive function slowly increases, the scientific mechanisms accounting for these observations remain to be elucidated. Given the role of alcohol and drugs in society, however, the spectrum of related endocrine and reproductive complications can be expected to expand and, thereby, increase in public-health significance.

See also **Alcohol: History of Drinking (International); Alcohol: History of Drinking in the United States; Alcoholism: Abstinence versus Controlled Drinking; Cocaine; Complications: Liver (Clinical); Dopamine; Heroin; Methadone Maintenance Programs; Opiates/Opioids; Opioid Complications and Withdrawal; Risk Factors for Substance Use, Abuse, and Dependence: Drug Effects and Biological Responses; Sexuality and Substance Abuse.**

BIBLIOGRAPHY

Bikle, D. D., Stesin, A., Halloran, B., Steibach, L., & Recker, R. (1993). Alcohol-induced bone disease: Relationship to age and parathyroid hormone levels. *Alcoholism: Clinical and Experimental Research, 17*(3), 690–695.

Cooper, O. B., Brown, T. T., & Dobs, A. S. (2003). Opiate drug use: A potential contributor to the endocrine and metabolic complications in human immunodeficiency virus disease. *CID, 37*(Suppl. 2), S132–S136.

Felig, P., Baxter, J. D., Broadus, A. E, & Frohman, W. L. (1987). *Endocrinology and metabolism.* (2nd ed.). New York: McGraw-Hill.

Gordon, G. G., Southren, R. L., Vittek, J., & Lieber, C. S. (1979). Effect of alcohol ingestion on hepatic aromatase activity and plasma activity and plasma steroid hormones in the rat. *Metabolism, 28*(1), 20–24.

Hadi H. A., Hill, J. A., Castillo, R. A. (1987). Alcohol and reproductive function: A review. *Obstetrical and Gynecological Survey, 42*(2), 69–74.

Heil, S. H., & Subramanian, M. G. (1998). Alcohol and the hormonal control of lactation. *Alcohol Health Research World, 22*(3), 178–184.

Jaouhari, J., Schiele, F., Pirollet, P., Lecomte, E., Paille, F., & Artur, Y. (1993). Effect of a three-week withdrawal therapy. *Bone and Mineral, 21*(3), 171–178.

Latinen, K., Lamberg-Allardt, C., Tunninen, R., Karonen, S. L., Tahetla, R., Ylikahri, R., et al. (1991). Transient hypoparathyroidism during acute alcohol intoxications. *New England Journal of Medicine, 324*(11), 721–727.

Latinen, K., & Valimaki, M. (1993). Bone and the "Comforts of Life." *Annals of Medicine, 25*(4), 412–425.

Pepersack, T., Fuss, M., Otero, J., Bergmann, P, Valsamis, J., & Corvilain, J. (1992). Longitudinal study of bone metabolism after ethanol withdrawal in alcoholic patients. *Journal of Bone and Mineral Research, 7*(4), 383–387.

Rasheed, A., & Tareen, I. A. (1995). Effects of heroin on thyroid function, cortisol and testosterone level in addicts. *Polish Journal of Pharmacology 47*(5), 441–444.

Sampson, H. W. (1998). Alcohol's harmful effects on bone. *Alcohol Health and Research World, 22*(3), 190–194.

Smith, C. G., & Asch, R. H. (1987). Drug abuse and reproduction: Fertility and sterility. *The American Fertility Society, 48*(3), 355–373.

Stampfer, M. J., Colditz, G. A., Willett, W. C., Speizer, F. E., & Hennekens, C. H. (1988). A prospective study of moderate alcohol consumption and the risk of coronary disease and stroke in women. *New England Journal of Medicine, 319*, 267–273.

Sumida, K. D., Cogger, A. A., & Matveyenko, A. V. (2007). Alcohol-induced suppression of gluconeogenesis is greater in ethanol fed female rat hepatocytes than males. *Alcohol, 41*, 67–75.

Swift, R., & Davidson, D. (1998). Alcohol hangover. *Alcohol Health and Research World, 22*(1), 54–60.

Valeix, P., Faure, P., Bertrais, S., Verganaud, A. C., Dauchet, L., & Hereberg, S. (2008). Effects of light to moderate alcohol consumption on thyroid volume and thyroid function. *Clinical Endocrinology, 68*, 988–995.

Zitzmann, M. & Nieschlag, E. (2001). Testosterone levels in healthy men and the relation to behavioural and physical characteristics: Facts and constructs. *European Journal of Endocrinology, 144*, 183–197.

LAWRENCE S. BROWN JR.
REVISED BY RALPH MYERSON (2001)
FELINA MARIE CORDOVA (2009)
RONALD ROSS WATSON (2009)

IMMUNOLOGIC

This article describes the basic and clinical immunologic aspects of alcohol and drug abuse.

ALCOHOL

The physiological characteristics of alcohol (ethanol) allow it to interfere with the functions of immune cells. Alcohol is able to completely mix with water and, to some degree, is fat soluble. It crosses membranes by diffusion across a concentration gradient, going from high to low concentrations. Historically, alcohol has been associated with lower host resistance and increased infectious diseases. For example, alcoholism has been closely associated with lung abscesses, bacteria being found in the blood, abdomen infection, and tuberculosis. Although these infections might be a result of malnutrition or poor living conditions, prolonged consumption of alcohol also results in alterations of immune responses, seriously impairing the body's normal host defense not only to invading microbes but also to its defense against cancer cells.

These disruptions are the combined result of direct toxic effects on the immune system and indirect effects such as malnutrition, oxidative stress, endocrine changes and the complications of liver disease. The alcoholic's predisposition to extracellular and intracellular infection indicates the effects of alcohol consumption at the local, humoral immunity (includes antibodies and B cells), and cellular levels, inhibiting immune response and host defense. Some evidence suggests that disrupted regulation of the neuroimmune-endocrine networks may be a major risk factor for the development of alcohol-induced immunosupression, leading to the collapse of host defense. Bidirectional communication can occur between the immune and neuroendocrine systems. Accordingly, stimulated lymphoid cells send signals mediated by soluble mediators (termed *cytokines*) and other immune products to inform the central nervous system about the activity of the immune system. Neuroendocrine molecules, in turn, may complete a feedback loop by modulating neural output. Thus, effective feedback communications between the endocrine and the immune systems may be crucial to the host's response.

Clinical and experimental studies indicate a relationship between excessive alcohol use and compromised immune responses (Szabo, 1997). Human studies have shown that chronic alcohol ingestion is associated with abnormalities of both humoral and cellular immunity (Diaz et al., 2002; Szabo, 1997). These abnormalities include a depression of serum bactericidal (body's ability to kill bacteria) activity, alterations of immunoglobulin production, leucopenia (abnormally low number of leukocytes), defects in Chemotaxis (movement based on a chemical, can be attractant or repellent), decreased antigen trapping and processing, and decreased T-cell mitogenesis (mitosis). The clear association between alcoholism and infections such as tuberculosis and listeriosis (has a wide range of effects from being sick to Meningitis and is caused by L. Monocytogenes and is usually acquired from food) indicates defective functioning of cell-mediated immunity. A study has linked alcohol abuse and deficient T-cell responsiveness (Szabo, 1997). Skin-test reactivity using purified protein derivative and dinitrochlorobenzene has also demonstrated poor responses in alcoholics with liver disease. Natural killer (or NK) cell activity is impaired in acute alcohol intoxication and in chronic alcoholic liver disease. NK cells are programmed to recognize and destroy abnormal cells, such as virus-infected or tumor cells. Some researchers have speculated that decreased NK cell activity may be intimately involved in the increased incidence of tumors in alcoholics.

Having animals ingest alcohol also has a profound effect on decreasing the weight of their peripheral lymphoid organs as measured by a decreased number of thymocytes and splenocytes (T cells in the thymus and spleen). In mice, alcohol use produces thymic and splenic atrophy and alterations in the circulating lymphocytes and lymphocyte subpopulations, as well as alterations in cellular and humoral immunity and impaired cytokine production. Also impaired by dietary alcohol are antibody-dependent cellular toxicity, lymphocyte proliferation, B-lymphocyte functions, and cytokine production by lymphoid cells (in the lymph and lymph nodes). Thus, alcohol-induced immunosuppression may render alcoholics more susceptible to tumorigenesis (tumor development) and infection.

Alcoholics are susceptible to infections by bacteria such as Listeria monocytogenes, Vibrio vulnificus, Pasteurella multocida, Aeromonas hydrophilia, Klebsiella pneumoniaeand legionalla pneumophila and Mycobacterium tuberculosi. The severity of these infections has raised the possibility of a

neutrophil (white blood cell) and macrophage (cells in the innate immune system that kill pathogens by phagocytosis/swallowing them) abnormality in these patients. The proper functioning of neutrophils is critical for host defense against microorganisms. Neutrophils are the chief phagocytic (kill by swallowing) leukocyte of the blood; they are short-lived cells having a life span of approximately four days. Their production is a tightly regulated process centered in the bone marrow. Chronic alcoholics have often been noted to be leukopenic (low levels of leukocytes). The toxic effect of alcohol is now believed to be caused by the depression of the T-cell-derived colony-stimulating factor rather than to direct suppression of myeloid (bone marrow) precursors secondary to bone marrow toxicity.

Neutrophils (cells of the innate immune system that use phagocytosis) must recognize the invading pathogens, engulf them, and destroy them using a number of killing mechanisms, which include adherence, chemotaxis, locomotion, phagocytosis, and intracellular killing. Several functions of neutrophils are affected by alcohol in vitro, including impairment of chemotaxis, decreased migration of neutrophils within vessels, altered adherence to nylon fibers in vitro, impaired phagocytosis, and decreased intracellular killing of bacteria. In humans with advanced cirrhosis from chronic (prolonged and excessive) ingestion of ethanol and impaired phagocytic capacity, decreased metabolic activity was observed in the liver's reticuloendothelial system; there also were impairments of neutrophil chemotaxis, bacterial phagocytosis and killing, and alterations of neutrophil-antigen expression. Neutrophil dysfunction is therefore responsible for aggravating the susceptibility to secondary infections seen in alcoholics.

The balance of the cellular and humoral immune system response to antigens is controlled by communication between immunocompetent (healthy cells of the immune system) cells. They are regulated to a great extent by cytokines produced mostly by T-helper cells and macrophages. Cytokines and biologically active polypeptide intercellular messengers regulate the growth, mobility, and differentiation of leukocytes. Thus, cytokines have extremely important roles in the communication network that links inducer and effector cells to immune and inflammatory cells.

Given that any perturbation in the tightly controlled cytokine regulatory system can result in immune alterations modifying host resistance to infectious disease and cancer, the influence of alcohol consumption on cytokine secretion has been investigated considerably. Several studies have indicated a correlation between circulating levels of macrophage-derived cytokines and disease progression during chronic alcohol consumption (Szabo, 1997). Increased plasma concentrations of tumor necrosis factor have been observed in cases of alcoholic liver disease and, interestingly, related significantly to decreased long-term survival. Plasma interleukin-I (also a cytokine) is also significantly increased in these patients (relative to healthy controls) but does not correlate with increased mortality. Additionally, higher levels of the cytokines interleukin-6, interleukin-8, and interleukin-10 have been found in chronic heavy drinkers, with a reverse in levels possible after the cessation of drinking.

In alcohol-fed mice, researchers found that, compared to controls, production of all cytokines was suppressed by chronic alcohol consumption, suggesting general immunosupression. The elevated levels of cytokines in some animals with murine (mouse) AIDS were, however, increased further by alcohol ingestion as compared to controls, which reflected the alcohol-induced aggravation of some AIDS symptoms. Similarly, those cytokines suppressed by murine AIDS were further suppressed by alcohol. Thus, alcohol exacerbated their immune dysfunction. In simians (higher primates), animals with HIV infection had increased virus replication when exposed to alcohol. There was increased proliferation of cells isolated from humans with HIV, when they were treated with alcohol in vitro. Several pathways may be involved in mediating the interaction between the endocrine system and the immune system. Some findings indicate that the pituitary peptide hormones can directly influence immune response. In addition, when a neurotransmitter is released in lymphoid tissues, it may locally modify the functional properties of lymphocytes and the release of cytokines.

In human studies on the effects of alcohol, hormone levels and immune responses to monitor changes of immune response and neurotransmitters are usually detected in serum. Since the serum levels of these parameters cannot accurately reflect the local situation in the lymphoid organs or tissues, some results from these studies, therefore, could be misleading. No animal model for alcohol studies can mimic the complications of alcoholic liver diseases often observed in humans. Furthermore, because individual animals differ in their hormonal status, even within the same strain of animal, and it is difficult to define the hormone status of animals, some results from animal studies may also be misleading. Therefore, further research is needed as of 2008 on the mechanism of alcohol's effects on the neurological system at the cellular and systemic levels. Similarly, research on the interaction between the endocrine and immune systems should continue to enhance the understanding of the complex changes caused by the direct and indirect effects of alcohol consumption.

COCAINE

Cocaine acts directly on lymphoid cells (the lymph and lymph nodes) and indirectly modulates the immune response by affecting the level of neuroendocrine hormones. The first studies about the impact of cocaine use on the immune response were initiated because epidemiological data demonstrated a high prevalence of acquired immunodeficiency syndrome (AIDS) in polydrug users. Depending on the different administration routes, the plasma levels of cocaine in humans appear to be in the range of 0.1 to 1 micrograms per milliliter (µg/ml). Such concentrations last only for thirty to sixty minutes and then decline because of cocaine's short biological half-life (about 1 hour). Consequently, the direct effects of cocaine and its metabolites on immune cells should occur only during a short time, except in heavy cocaine users who use the drug several times a day every day. Besides the direct effects on immune cells, cocaine could indirectly affect the immune response via its impact on the neuroendocrine system, and both have been shown (Pellegrino, 1998; Watzl, 1990).

Short-term exposure of mice to cocaine by daily intraperitoneal (within the abdominal cavity) injection for fourteen days reduced body, spleen, and thymus weight in the animal. Cocaine increased the responsiveness of lymphocytes to mitogens (cell proliferation initiators) and the delayed hypersensitivity responsiveness, but it suppressed the antibody response. Many animal studies, however, suggest that the immune system requires continuous exposure to cocaine to demonstrate its suppressing or stimulating effects and may also be dependent on the dose (Pellegrino, 1998). After a single dose of cocaine (0.6 mg/kg), non-habitual cocaine users showed a significant stimulation of natural killer cell activity, which is vital to defend against cancers. The level of natural killer cells was also increased, but the levels of T-helper and suppressor cytotoxic cells, B cells, and monocytes were not elevated. In contrast, T cell levels were found to be decreased in newborns that were exposed to cocaine through maternal use during gestation.

Cocaine causes neuroendocrine-mediated effects on the immune response. It stimulates the brain's hypothalamus to increase secretion of beta-endorphin. As a result of cocaine administration, beta-endophin binds to opioid receptors on monocytes and lymphocytes and exerts multiple stimulating and suppressing effects on these cells, including secretion of immunoregulatory cytokines. The net outcome of the reactions related to the immune response of the host is difficult to assess because of other possible determinants of these interactions (such as the psychological and social state of the cocaine user).

There are other mechanisms that might operate to mediate cocaine-induced Immunomodulation (T cells secreting cytokines and enhancing or decreasing this activity), including nutritional deficiencies and their impact on lymphoid cells. As early as 1870, the French physician Charles Gazeau suggested that coca leaves might be used to suppress the appetite. With food deprivation, which is common in circumstances of habitual drug use, the self-administration of cocaine by rats increased. Although data indicate a poor nutritional status for cocaine users, no study has as of 2008 assessed the nutritional status of drug users as it contributes to a compromised immune competence. Cocaine clearly modifies hormones with immunoregulatory properties via neurological effects. In addition, malnutrition could be a factor in cocaine use, resulting in altered disease and tumor resistance. Intravenous use of drugs, including cocaine, is associated with the transmission of human immunodeficiency virus (HIV), and ultimately the development of AIDS. Immunomodulation by cocaine after HIV infection could accelerate disease development as well as decrease overall resistance to a variety of pathogens found frequently in intravenous drug users. One of the proposed mechanisms for this lowering of the immune response occurs through the high levels of TGF-β (a cytokine) found in cocaine users with HIV, which will decrease the immune system's ability to respond and allow virus replication.

TOBACCO

Although it is well known that the use of tobacco is a major health hazard, millions of Americans continue to smoke and the popularity of smokeless tobacco is on the rise. Tobacco use is the chief cause of lung cancer in smokers of tobacco and is strongly linked with the oral cancers of those who use chewing tobacco or snuff.

The pulmonary alveolar macrophage (PAM) is the cellular component of the immune system comprising the first line defense of the lung, offering protection against inhaled particles, including irritants and microbial invaders. Because PAM has exposure to both the bloodstream and the atmosphere, it is uniquely suited to perform its protective functions, which include clearance of foreign material, immune modulation, and modulation of surrounding tissue. There is general agreement that the number of PAMs in smokers' lungs is increased two to twenty times above that found in the lungs of nonsmokers. It also appears that there is a difference in the morphology and certain aspects of the function of alveolar macrophages between the two groups. In general, PAMs from smokers are larger, contain more lysosomes and lysosomal enzymes, and are more metabolically active than those from nonsmokers, suggesting that they may be in a chronically stimulated, more active state. These enlarged PAMs might lead to the inference that there would be greater phagocytotic capacity in the lungs of smokers, resulting in increased clearance of foreign matter. However, the responsiveness of smokers' macrophages to foreign bodies or bacteria was equal to or less than that of non-smokers, leading researchers to conclude that chronic stimulation of PAMs by cigarette smoke may be harmful rather than beneficial to the immunocompetence of the lung.

There is some disagreement as to whether smoking affects the phagocytotic and bactericidal activity of PAMs. The question of whether tobacco smoke alters the tumoricidal (tumor killing) ability of PAMs has not yet been answered. Thus, the relationship between cigarette smoking, neutrophil accumulation in the lung, and lung destruction continues to be researched. It is known that particles from cigarette smoke are present in the PAMs of smokers, and researchers have found that the PAMs of cigarette smokers release a potent chemotactic factor for neutrophils (chemotactic factor: chemicals that can recruit or keep away the neutrophils), whereas those of nonsmokers did not. Therefore, cigarette smokers had an increased number of neutrophils in the lavage fluid (cells taken through needle aspiration, can be cells from the breast/milk duct in the ductal lavage, or can be broncheoalveolar cells [King et al., 2003; Wang et al., 2005]) in the lung biopsy tissue as compared to nonsmokers. Neutrophils store and release elastase, an enzyme that can break down connective tissue, a process that is implicated in the development of certain lung diseases. Smokers' lungs are exposed to a large chronic burden of elastase from neutrophils, which may predispose them to lung destruction.

A number of animal and human studies comparing blood samples of smokers and non-smokers have indicated that smokers have altered immunoglobulin levels (Prescott, 2008). Elevated levels of immunoglobulin E (IgE) were present in a high proportion of the smoke-exposed animals but in none of the control animals. Studies on human subjects have also revealed that IgE levels were higher in smokers than in nonsmokers. A study of coal workers showed that both mining and non-mining smokers had depressed serum IgA and IgM levels as compared with similar groups of nonsmokers. A disturbing finding in relationship to increased immunoglobulin levels in smokers is the effect that maternal smoking may have on the fetus. In newborn infants of mothers who smoked during pregnancy, IgE was elevated three-fold. Tobacco smoke affects fetal immunoglobulin synthesis, stresses the fetal immune system, and can predispose the infant to subsequent sensitization. It has been estimated that maternal smoking causes 34 percent of the reported asthma in childhood.

Natural killer cells, thought to serve important anti-tumor and antiviral functions in the body, have been found to be decreased in adult smokers as well as in cord blood from infants whose mothers either smoked during pregnancy or inhaled second-hand smoke (Watson & Witten, 2001). Studies of the white blood cells called basophils in the peripheral blood indicated that there are alterations linked to tobacco smoking as well.

Smoking has also been found to be associated with autoimmune diseases. Tobacco use and rheumatoid arthritis have been linked, with a higher risk associated with those with greater tobacco consumption. Smoking can accelerate disease progression as TNF-α (Tumor Necrosis Factor) (a cytokine) levels are elevated in smokers with rheumatoid arthritis. Smoking also increases the odds for developing the autoimmune disease systemic lupus erythematosus (SLE). One plausible way that this can occur is by smoking, causing DNA damage and creating anti-dsDNA antibodies, levels of which can help to identify active disease in patients with SLE.

In considering the effect that tobacco use has on immunocompetence, other confounding variables must also be accounted for, including genetic factors, pre-existing disease, and nutritional status. Smoking has been observed to cause deficiencies of Vitamin C, beta-carotene (Vitamin A), and other nutrients that have important functions in protecting immunity.

Tobacco smoking causes deleterious effects on the pulmonary and systemic immune systems of experimental animals and humans. Aspects of both cell-mediated and humoral immunity are affected. It is often difficult to compare studies directly because of the variability in smoking behaviors and the differences among tobacco products. Although it is expected that heavy smoking causes the most amount of immune system damage, that does not mean light to moderate smoking is safe. Thus, if some alterations due to smoking are reversible, it is not yet known whether long-term smoking may cause the impairment of the immune system to become permanent. Further, simultaneous exposure to other air contaminants or air pollution may exert damaging synergistic effects on local or systemic immune defenses.

MORPHINE AND OTHER OPIOIDS

Several studies have revealed a parallel between morphine abuse and immune inhibition (Wang et al., 2005). In vitro studies have shown that polymorphonuclear cells and monocytes from patients subjected to morphine treatment were severely depressed in their phagocytic and killing properties as well as in their ability to generate superoxide. Opioid addiction also caused alterations in the frequencies of T-cells and null lymphocytes in human peripheral blood.

There is convincing evidence of the presence of opioid receptors on various types of human immune cells. The presence of opioid receptors on immune cells may allow for modulation of specific immune functions in the presence of exogenous (not a natural part of the body, from an outside source) opiates. Various administration schedules for opioids were shown to potentiate infection by *Klebsiella pneumoniae*, *Streptococus pneumoniae*, and *Candida albicans*. The increased susceptibility was partly due to decreased reticuloendothelial-system activity as well as a reduction in the number of phagocytes, not by a direct cytotoxic effect of the opioid. In addition, susceptibility to HIV and tuberculosis has been associated with opioid use.

Chronic administration of morphine has also inhibited a primary antibody response of mice as B cell levels have been found to be depressed when the mice were exposed to morphine. These effects were worsened by naloxone (a non-addictive analog of morphine that blocks opiate receptors), indicating that morphine inhibits the immune system in a specific manner—via its interaction with opioid receptors. Other studies in animals such as rats and monkeys have shown that morphine can decrease NK cell activity, perhaps reducing resistance to tumors.

Such changes, which can also include morphine suppression of spleen and body weight, show evidence of a significant reduction in immune function.

MARIJUANA

Several approaches have been used to study the effects of marijuana or its active component, tetrahydrocannabinol (THC), on the human immune system. These include using cells isolated from chronic marijuana smokers, from volunteers who have been exposed only to marijuana smoke or from non-exposed donors whose cells are exposed to THC in the laboratory. A survey of chronic marijuana smokers showed a depressed response of their cells to stimulation with mitogens (substances that cause cell division).

Several studies have shown that marijuana smoking and THC is immunosuppressive (Klein et al., 1997; Klein et al., 2000; Tashkin et al., 2002). Immune alterations have been associated with marijuana or THC, including significantly reduced serum IgG levels in chronic smokers; inhibition of natural killer cell activity; inhibition of phagocytic activity through altered macrophages; elevation of serum IgD levels; increased neutrophils; and reduced T-cell numbers. THC also inhibited DNA-, RNA-, and protein synthesis in stimulated human lymphocytes.

Studies performed in animals have produced more consistent findings than those in humans. In most cases, THC is associated with suppression of various immune parameters. Mice that have been exposed to THC are more susceptible to infections through *Legionella pneumophila* and *Candida albicans*. The greater the consistency observed in animal studies probably reflects the influence of genetic factors, consistent dosage levels, diet, and other conditions that can readily be controlled in animal studies.

Animal studies have thus provided strong evidence of the immunosuppressive effects of THC. Such effects have been clearly demonstrated by animals, who when exposed to THC, were more susceptible to infections than non-exposed animals (Cabral & Pettit 1998). In mice and guinea pigs, THC has also exacerbated viral infection and reduced resistance to bacterial pathogens.

See also **Alcohol and AIDS; Alcohol: Chemistry and Pharmacology; Cocaine; Marijuana (Cannabis); Opiates/Opioids; Tobacco: Medical Complications; Tobacco: Smokeless.**

BIBLIOGRAPHY

Baldwin, G. C., Roth, M. D., & Tashkin, D. P. (1998). Acute and chronic effects of cocaine on the immune system and the possible link to AIDS. *Journal of Neuroimmunology, 83,* 133–138.

Baldwin, G. C., Tashkin, D. P., Buckley, D. M., Park, A. N., Dubinett, S. M., & Roth, M. D. (1997). Marijuana and cocaine impair alveolar macrophage function and cytokine production. *American Journal of Respiratory and Critical Care Medicine, 156*(5), 1606–1613.

Cabral, G. A., & Dove Pettit, D. A. (1998). Drugs and immunity: Cannabinoids and their role in decreased resistance to infectious disease. *Journal of Neuroimmunology, 83,* 116–123.

Costenbader, K. H., & Karlson, E. W. (2006). Cigarette smoking and autoimmune disease: What can we learn from epidemiology? *Lupus.* 15, 737–745.

Diaz, L. E, Montero A., Gonzaels-Gross, M., Vallejo, A. I., Romeo, J., & Marcos, A. (2002). Influence of alcohol consumption on immunological status: A review. *European Journal of Clinical Nutrition, 56*(Suppl. 3), S50–S53.

Hutchinson, D., Shepstone, L., Moots, R., Lear, J. T., and Lynch, M. P. (2001). Heavy cigarette smoking is strongly associated with rheumatoid arthritis (RA), particularly in patients without a family history of RA. *Annals of Rheumatic Disease,* 60, 223–227.

Janeway, C. A., Travers, P., Walport, M., & Shlomchik, M. (2001). *Immunobiology: The immune system in health and disease.* New York, NY: Inside North America-Garland Publishing.

Johnson, T. R., Knisely, J. S., Christmas, J. T., Schnoll, S. H., & Ruddy, S. (1996). Changes in immunologic cell surface markers during cocaine withdrawal in pregnant women. *Brain, Behavior, and Immunity, 10*(4), 324–336.

Karlix, J. L., Behnke, M., Davis-Eyler, F., Wobie, K., Adams, V., et al. (1998). Cocaine suppresses fetal immune system. *Pediatric Research, 44*(1), 43–46.

King, B. L., Tsai, S. C., Gyrga, M. E. (2003). Detection of chromosomal instability on paired breast surgery and ductal lavage specimens by interphase fluorescence in situ hybridization. *Clinical Cancer Research, 9,* 1509–1516.

Klein, T. W, Friedman, H., & Specter, S. (1997). Marijuana, immunity and infection. *Journal of Neuroimmunology, 83,* 102–115.

Klein, T. W., Lane, B., Newton, C. A., & Friedman, H. (2000). The cannabinoid system and cytokine network. *Experimental Biology and Medicine, 225,* 1–8.

Kumar, R., Perez-Casanova, A. E., Tirado, G., Noel, R. J., Torres, C., Rodriguez, I., et al. (2005). Increased viral replication in Simian Immunodeficiency Virus/Simian-HIV-infected Macaques with self-administering model of chronic alcohol consumption. *Journal of Acquired Immune Deficiency Syndrome, 39*(4), 386–390.

MacGregor, R. R. (1986). Alcohol and immune defense. *Journal of the American Medical Association, 256,* 1474–1479.

Madigan, M. T., Martinko J. M., & Parker, J. (2003). *Brock Biology of Microorganisms.* Upper Saddle River, NJ: Prentice Hall.

Pellegrino, T., & Bayer, B. M. (1998). In vivo effects of cocaine of immune function. *Journal of Neuroimmunology, 83,* 139–147.

Prescott, S. L. (2008). Effects of early cigarette smoke exposure on early immune development and respiratory disease. *Pediatric Respiratory Reviews, 9,* 3–10.

Roy, S., Wang, J., Kelschenbach, J., Koodie, L., & Martin, J. (2006). Modulation of immune function by morphine: Implications for susceptibility to infection. *Journal of Neuroimmune Pharmacology, 1,* 77–89.

Szabo, G. (1997). Alcohol's contribution to compromised immunity. *Alcohol Health & Research World, 21*(1), 30–38.

Tashkin, D. P., Baldwin, G. C., Sarafian, T., Dubinett, S., & Roth, M. D. (2002). Respiratory and immunologic consequences of marijuana smoking. *Journal of Clinical Pharmacology, 42,* 71S-81S.

Wallace, C. L., & Watson, R. R. (1990). Immunomodulation by tobacco. In R. R. Watson (Ed.), *Drugs of abuse and immune function.* Boca Raton, FL: CRC Press.

Wang, J., Barke, R. A., Charboneau, R., & Roy, S. (2005). Morphine impairs host immune response and increases susceptibility to Streptococcus pneumoniae lung infection. *Journal of Immunology, 174,* 426–434.

Watson, R. R., & Witten, M. (2001). *Environmental tobacco smoke.* Boca Raton, FL: CRC Press.

Watzl, B., & Watson, R. R. (1990). Immunomodulation by cocaine: A neuroendocrine mediated response. *Life Sciences, 46,* 1319–1329.

Yahya, M. D., & Watson, R. R. (1987). Minireview: Immunomodulation by morphine and marijuana. *Life Sciences, 41,* 2503–2510.

RONALD R. WATSON
FELINA MARIE CORDOVA

LIVER (CLINICAL)

The liver is the largest internal organ of the human body, normally weighing about 3.3 pounds (1.5 kg). It occupies the right upper quadrant of the abdominal cavity just below the diaphragm. As befitting its anatomical prominence, its function is essential to maintain life. Surgical removal of the entire liver from any animal (including humans) would result in the animal's falling into a coma shortly thereafter and then dying. The absence of a certain critical mass of functioning liver tissue is incompatible with life. While the human liver has a remarkable resilience and regenerative capacity after injury or illness, this is true only up to a certain point. If illness damages the liver beyond the point of no return, the person dies.

The liver has a multitude of complex functions and is justly called the laboratory of the human body. It secretes a digestive juice called *bile* into the intestine, called bile; it produces a number of essential proteins, clotting factors, and fatty substances; it stores and conserves energy-producing sugars; it detoxifies both internally produced and external toxins and drugs that would otherwise be poisonous to the human organism—just to name some of its important functions.

What can seriously jeopardize this very important organ and consequently the well-being and survival of the individual? For one, there are diseases—both congenital and acquired—over which a person has little or no control, such as some genetically determined and developmental abnormalities, circulatory liver problems, certain tumors, and infections. A very large part of *hepatology* (the technical term to describe the study and treatment of liver diseases) is, however, devoted to liver problems created by a peculiar human behavior—the abuse of alcohol and drugs. Whereas discussions as to whether alcoholism and drug abuse are truly self-inflicted problems elicit a variety of opinions, the liver disease that results from substance abuse in a given individual could have been avoided if the substance-abusing behavior had not occurred. Beyond the psychosocial consequences of substance abuse, diseases of the liver (and brain) represent the major complications of alcohol and drugs. The morbidity (disease incidence) and mortality (death incidence) from alcoholic and drug-induced liver injury are very high. In the scientific literature, it is well established that the mortality from alcoholic liver disease is correlated with per capita alcohol consumption; in fact, the prevalence of alcoholism in a given society has been calculated from liver mortality statistics. While alcohol is a direct liver toxin, most of the other commonly abused psychoactive substances are generally not known to affect the liver directly to a great extent. Their major contribution to liver morbidity and mortality is via exposing people to viral hepatitis, a potentially fatal disease.

ALCOHOLIC LIVER DISEASES

This section discusses the range of alcoholic liver diseases. The interrelationship between them is illustrated in Figure 1.

Alcoholic Fatty Liver. Fat accumulation in the liver is an almost universal response to excessive

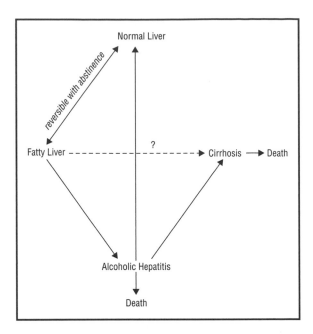

Figure 1. Interrelationships between various forms of alcoholic liver disease. ILLUSTRATION BY GGS INFORMATION SERVICES. GALE, CENGAGE LEARNING

alcohol consumption. It occurs in the majority of heavy drinkers. How and why fat accumulates in liver cells is complicated and not completely understood; however, its presence may be observed. If a piece of biopsied liver tissue from an alcoholic is examined under the microscope, the observer will see that many liver cells are loaded with big bubbles consisting of fat, almost totally occupying the cell. In most cases, this fatty change does not matter much as far as the patient's health is concerned. It is an almost invariable response to too much alcohol consumption and an early warning. The person who has nothing worse than an alcoholic fatty liver may not feel sick at all, and only if a biopsy is done can the fatty liver be diagnosed. The doctor may feel an enlarged liver by palpation (pushing on the abdomen to feel the internal organs), which may be a bit tender. The laboratory test may show a slight elevation in the blood of some liver enzymes, best known by their initials: SGOT (or AST) and SGPT (or ALT). These enzymes are elevated because some of them tend to leak out of the fatty liver cells into the blood.

If a person stops drinking, the fat disappears from the liver cells, the swelling subsides, and the AST and ALT levels become normal. The two-way arrow in the diagram of Figure 1 indicates that fatty liver is reversible with abstinence, and the condition may fluctuate back and forth between normal and fatty liver with abstinence and drinking, respectively. Thus, fatty liver in itself is not likely a serious situation; it is an early warning that the liver does not respond well to alcohol and that its condition may worsen. There was a time when fatty liver was regarded as a precursor of the end-stage liver disease called cirrhosis (indicated by the broken arrow and question mark on Figure 1), but most physicians do not now believe that this direct connection exists.

Alcoholic Hepatitis. Alcoholic hepatitis is a potentially more serious form of alcoholic liver disease. A certain proportion of alcoholics, in addition to accumulating fats in their livers when drinking, will develop inflammation (hepatitis means liver inflammation) consisting of an accumulation of white blood cells, the death (necrosis) of some of the liver cells, and the presence of some very characteristic material called *Mallory bodies*. Again, all these changes can be seen under the microscope in a biopsied piece of tissue.

The clinical picture of alcoholic hepatitis varies. At one extreme is the person who feels perfectly well and only the biopsy could indicate that something is wrong. At the other extreme is the dying patient with a swollen and painful liver, jaundice (a yellowing of the entire body from bile pigment leaking into the blood), fever, and disturbed consciousness. Between these extremes are people with varying degrees of illness; for example, with or without some jaundice, with or without pain and fever. The white blood cell count is usually elevated. The bilirubin (bile pigment) level may be elevated in patients who have turned yellow (a pale to deep mustard). The liver enzymes are higher than normal in the blood because they leak out of the inflamed liver cells. However, these values are not as high as in viral hepatitis. In alcoholic hepatitis AST (SGOT) is higher than ALT (SGPT). This finding helps to distinguish alcoholic hepatitis from viral hepatitis, which is difficult to do at times. In viral hepatitis not only are the absolute enzyme values higher, but the ratio is reversed: ALT is higher than AST.

Thus, the outcome of alcoholic hepatitis can be death (worst scenario) or recovery (best scenario), as shown on Figure 1. Even if the patient does not die in a given episode, repeated episodes of drinking and alcoholic hepatitis can lead to the last stage of alcoholic liver disease: cirrhosis.

Alcoholic Cirrhosis. In terms of histology (tissue damage) alcoholic cirrhosis is an end-stage disease: a cirrhotic liver cannot become normal. In Figure 1, there is no arrow between cirrhosis and normal liver. Clinically, cirrhosis is a serious disease, potentially fatal, but not inevitably so. Alcoholism, while not its only cause, is by far the most common. Under the microscope a cirrhotic liver shows a disorganized architecture: the dead (necrotic) liver cells have been replaced by scar tissue. The liver tries to repair itself. In a somewhat haphazard fashion it attempts to produce new liver tissue in the form of nodules, which are separated from each other by scar tissue. These newly formed liver nodules may indeed sustain liver function and thus life for a time, but at a price: the liver's blood circulation is mechanically compressed. Thus, pressure increases in the blood vessels leading to the liver. Some of these overloaded blood vessels, especially those on the border of the stomach and esophagus (called esophageal varices), can rupture at any time, causing a major hemorrhage.

Patients in the cirrhotic stage of alcoholic liver disease present their symptoms in various ways. Some of them look quite normal; only the biopsy will reveal the presence of cirrhosis. Others are jaundiced, the yellow color from bile pigment leaking out of the damaged liver into the blood, thus staining the skin and the whites of the eyes. Still others have large fluid accumulations in their extremities (edema) or in their abdominal cavity (ascites). The latter may make these patients— men or women—look like they are nine months pregnant. Some may vomit blood because of the hemorrhaging. In most advanced cases, there is just not enough functioning liver tissue left; the liver no longer can perform its laboratory function, and the person slips into a coma and may die. When cirrhotic patients are examined by doctors, their livers do not feel smooth but bumpy from the nodules that have formed. At first the liver may be swollen and enlarged, but in the later stages it shrinks. The ultrasound picture suggests a patchy, disorganized liver architecture. The spleen may enlarge from the increased pressure in the blood vessels. The liver enzymes (AST and ALT) may be moderately

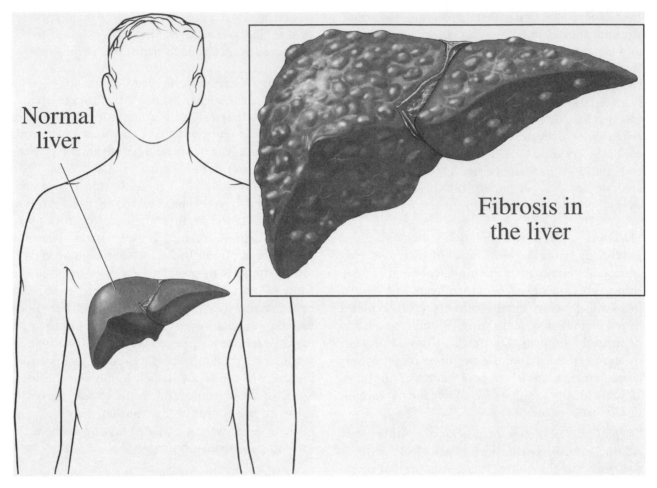

Normal liver

Fibrosis in the liver

Cirrhosis of the liver. NUCLEUS MEDICAL ART/PHOTOTAKE

elevated as in other forms of alcoholic liver disease, but this elevation has no prognostic importance. More ominous signs pointing toward severely compromised liver functions are the following: a decrease in blood level of albumin (an important protein manufactured by the liver), deficiency in blood-clotting factors that are also made in the liver, and the presence of anemia (low hemoglobin and red blood cell count).

Causes of Death in Cirrhosis. Ascites (fluid accumulation in the abdomen) is very uncomfortable and unsightly but by itself usually does not kill, unless infection develops, which is always a threat. Generally, cirrhosis compromises the immune system, rendering cirrhotic alcoholics susceptible to all sorts of potentially overwhelming infections. Portal hypertension is also a serious complication of the cirrhotic fibrosis. The obstruction to portal vein flow through the liver results in the development of other vein channels to accommodate the return of blood from the abdominal organs, which ordinarily flows through the portal vein. The result is the development of varices (enlarged, engorged veins) in the stomach and esophagus. These enlarged, thin-walled veins are prone to rupture, leading to one of the most serious complications of cirrhosis of the liver—bleeding varices. This constitutes an emergency and calls for immediate intervention in the form of measures to control the bleeding. A variety of therapies are available, all of which have been employed with a varying degree of success that depends on the severity of the hemorrhage and the skill and experience of the physician. Once the bleeding has been controlled, the patient should be considered for an appropriate permanent venous shunt procedure whereby venous blood bypasses the liver. Finally, total decompensation of liver cell function may cause coma and death.

The good news is that even when there is irreversible cirrhosis at the tissue level, death may not be inevitable. Survival depends mainly on two factors: luck and alcohol abstinence. Abstaining alcoholics with cirrhosis can stabilize and survive on what's left of their liver tissue without necessarily and relentlessly progressing to one of the fatal outcomes.

Risk Factors for Alcoholic Liver Disease. There are no certain answers to the question of who is likely to get alcoholic liver disease. Fatty liver is an almost universally predictable response to heavy alcohol consumption, but this by itself is seldom a serious problem. A smaller number of people develop alcoholic hepatitis and still fewer (variously estimated in different populations between 5 percent and 25 percent of alcoholics) end up with cirrhosis. Considering the large number of alcoholics in the general population, the minority who develop cirrhosis still represent large numbers; cirrhosis is one of the leading causes of all deaths.

Still, why do some alcoholics develop alcoholic hepatitis and cirrhosis, while others who drink equally heavily do not? The amount of alcohol consumption and the length of time of heavy drinking is certainly one risk factor. Gender may be another: women's livers generally are more vulnerable to the effects of alcohol than those of men, given equal alcohol exposures. Chronic viral infection, especially chronic Hepatitis C infection, has been shown to be another risk factor. Finally, there may be a genetically determined but still unclarified individual susceptibility, which may explain why some people never get cirrhosis; why some do after many years of alcoholism; and why still others get cirrhosis at a young age or after a relatively short drinking career.

Prognosis and Treatment. The issues of prognosis and treatment cannot be separated. The cornerstone of treatment is complete abstinence from alcohol. Achieving abstinence can arrest the progression of liver disease, even in established cirrhosis; continued drinking leads to deterioration and death.

One therapeutic issue relating to alcoholism is relevant to liver disease. The drug disulfiram (Antabuse) is sometimes prescribed to reinforce abstinence. Its unpleasant, sometimes severe interaction with alcohol is a deterrent against drinking. Since disulfiram (as so many other drugs) has been occasionally reported to produce liver toxicity of its own, the presence of alcoholic liver disease is sometimes regarded as a relative contraindication against prescribing disulfiram. Some clinicians believe, however, that liver toxicity caused by alcohol far outweighs any risk that may be caused by disulfiram. Another drug used to treat alcohol dependence, naltrexone (Revia, Vivitrol), can also cause liver injury when given in excessive doses. Its use in patients with active liver disease requires careful consideration by the prescribing physician. Another drug for the maintenance of abstinence, acamprosate (Campral), does not have the disadvantage of the other two agents. Its elimination is dependent on the kidney, rather than the liver, and can be used to reinforce abstinence even in individuals with mild-to-moderate liver impairment.

Other treatment techniques beyond abstinence have been proposed to aid in recovery from alcoholic liver damage. In the late 1980s, a Toronto research group reported the beneficial effect of propylthiouracil (PTU). PTU is a drug normally used for the treatment of thyroid disease, but by reducing oxygen demand in the body (including in the liver), it might help to repair the damage caused by alcohol. The early results were promising but have not been confirmed by other researchers. Other drugs, such as corticosteroids (to decrease inflammation) or colchicine (to decrease scar formation) have dubious value.

There are relatively effective treatments available for some of the complications of alcoholic liver disease that enable patients to survive and thus begin their abstinence program. Fluid accumulation in the extremities (edema) or in the abdomen (ascites) can he helped by diet modifications (salt restriction), water-removing drugs (diuretics), albumin infusion, or tapping the abdomen with a needle to withdraw fluid.

Infections can be treated with antibiotics. The brain syndrome associated with liver failure (so-called hepatic encephalopathy or, in severe cases, hepatic coma) can improve with dietary means (protein restriction) or some drugs (e.g., neomycin, lactulose). Potentially or actually bleeding esophageal varicose veins can be obliterated by sclerotherapy, a procedure in which certain injections are delivered through a gastroscope (a tube inserted through the mouth that makes it possible to visualize the stomach). Risk of bleeding can be lessened by beta-blocking (heart-rate slowing) drugs or some surgical procedures to decrease pressure.

Finally, there is the possibility of liver transplantation. If all else fails, a successful liver transplant cures alcoholic liver disease. Apart from the general problems of donor matching and supply, some people have raised objections to offering transplantation for alcoholic liver disease on ethical grounds, claiming that the condition is self-inflicted. This is not an acceptable objection and goes against medical ethics. Well-motivated recovering alcoholics are entitled as much as anybody else to a life-saving procedure. In fact, studies have shown that the dramatic and heroic nature of this operation may be an extremely powerful motivator for future abstinence by liver recipients. Numerous successful transplants have been carried out on alcoholics.

DRUGS AND THE LIVER
Although many drugs in medicinal use may be toxic to the liver, most of the psychoactive drugs that people tend to abuse are not known to be particularly harmful. Occasional liver damage has been reported with solvent sniffing and cocaine use, but this is not a common problem. Narcotics (opioids), anti-anxiety, and other sedative drugs (such as barbiturates), marijuana, and hallucinogens do not usually cause liver injury.

There are, however, several relevant secondary issues concerning drug abuse and the liver. For one, a damaged liver (for example, from alcohol or hepatitis) results in poor tolerance of sedatives, because good liver function is necessary to eliminate sedatives properly. Impaired liver function can therefore result in an exaggerated sedative effect. Conversely, some sedatives, notably barbiturates (which were often abused in the past and sometimes still are), actually stimulate (induce) certain liver enzymes, which can result in increased elimination (i.e., decreased effect) of another therapeutically necessary drug. For example, a barbiturate user (or abuser) may have poor effect from a clotting preventative (anti-coagulant) drug that is necessary in heart disease or after a stroke. Some drugs do the

opposite: they inhibit liver enzymes. For example, the anti-ulcer drug cimetidine (Tagamet), which has no psychoactive effect per se, can cause such enzyme inhibition. If a person at the same time also happens to use or abuse a sedative, the sedative can have an exaggerated effect. Generally speaking, the normal liver transforms or inactivates drugs to less active or harmless forms. A notable and important exception is acetaminophen, one of the most commonly used medications against pain and fever (e.g., the various Tylenol preparations). The liver can transform acetaminophen into a toxic metabolite that can cause a potentially lethal liver injury. Generally, this does not happen at ordinary therapeutic acetaminophen dose levels. In the case of an acetaminophen overdose, however, such severe liver toxicity can occur that a person will die within days. Most of such overdoses are, of course, suicide attempts.

Acetaminophen itself does not have any psychoactive (mind-altering) properties; thus people do not abuse it to induce euphoria. Many combination narcotic prescription painkillers, however, contain acetaminophen. People seeking narcotic *highs* from such preparations might inadvertently ingest acetaminophen in large enough quantities to subject themselves to potentially severe liver injury. The person who is overdosing with suicidal intent is more likely to be discovered and brought to quick medical attention than an unintentionally overdosing drug abuser. Unfortunately, the antidote against acetaminophen poisoning, acetylcysteine, is effective only if it is given within a few hours (less than a day) after the ingestion of the drug. By the time acetaminophen poisoning has been suspected, the opportunity for treatment with the antidote may have already passed. An additional issue with acetaminophen is strong evidence of increased risk when alcohol and acetaminophen are combined. In alcoholics, relatively low doses of acetaminophen can cause severe and potentially fatal liver damage.

Viral Hepatitis in Drug Abusers. The major cause of liver damage in those individuals who abuse drugs is not direct toxicity from the drug, but rather from the transmission of viruses from person to person through contaminated needles and syringes. The problem of viral hepatitis, then, is largely that of injecting drug users (IDUs). At least five types of disease-causing hepatitis viruses have been identified, designated by the letters A to E. Of the five, Hepatitis A and E are not particularly associated with injecting drug abuse; but the other three are, and they will be discussed in some detail.

Hepatitis B. Hepatitis B (which used to be called serum hepatitis) is endemic to some parts of the world, such as Southeast Asia, where as many as 10 percent of the population may be infected. In the Western world, IDUs represent the greatest reservoir for Hepatitis B virus. It is transmitted through a direct blood-borne route, such as the following:

1. Contaminated needles and syringes (which drug addicts notoriously did not sterilize in the past).

2. From an infected mother across the placenta and through the umbilical cord of a developing fetus.

3. From accidental needle-stick injuries involving contaminated blood in health care workers.

4. From any blood-to-blood contact occurring during sexual intercourse. At one time blood transfusions were a common source of infection, but screening tests can now identify infected donors.

The symptoms of Hepatitis B infection vary. In its severest form, it can cause general malaise, fever, jaundice, coma, and death. The majority of patients, even with marked jaundice and fever, do not die. Many infected people do not even have an overt illness; they may not feel sick at all or may just have transient, flu-like symptoms. There may be a tender enlargement of the liver. If such people are tested in the laboratory, they have elevated liver enzymes, such as AST (also known as SGOT) and ALT (also known as SGPT), which are usually much higher than the values found in alcoholic liver disease. The bilirubin (bile pigment) level will be high if the person has yellow jaundice. The diagnosis is confirmed when serologic tests are positive for a viral particle called Hepatitis B antigen. Those who recover from the illness and clear the virus from their bodies will develop a protective antibody that will prevent them from becoming infected again. The antibody can be detected in a laboratory test.

The majority of people who get infected with Hepatitis B recover and acquire protective antibodies.

A sizable minority of those who survive, however, perhaps 10 percent, will continue to carry the virus, remaining *antigen positive*. Some of these individuals will have a chronic liver inflammation that will develop into cirrhosis. The cirrhosis caused by Hepatitis B is essentially similar to alcoholic cirrhosis, with the same consequences and potential complications described above. Moreover, Hepatitis B has the potential to cause liver cancer in some of those who develop cirrhosis. Not only is Hepatitis B in such chronically infected individuals a threat to their own survival, but it is also a source of infection to others, particularly to their needle-sharing partners, to their sexual partners, and to their developing fetuses and newborn babies.

A vaccine to prevent Hepatitis B has been available in the United States since 1982; however, it was not until the introduction of a recombinant form of the vaccine in the early 1990s that universal immunization for all newborns and adolescents became feasible. While most individuals born in the 1990s and many born in the 1980s are now immunized, millions of Americans remain unvaccinated. The Advisory Committee on Immunization Practices (ACIP) recommends that all IDUs be immunized against Hepatitis B infection. Other individuals for whom immunization is strongly recommended include sexually active heterosexuals with more than one sex partner within a six-month period or those who have contracted a sexually transmitted disease; men who have sex with men; persons at occupational risk of infection (e.g., health care professionals); hemodialysis patients; household or close contacts of persons with chronic Hepatitis B viral infection; residents and staff of institutions for the developmentally disabled; persons with chronic liver disease or human immunodeficiency virus (HIV) infection; and international travelers to areas of the world where Hepatitis B is endemic.

Hepatitis C. Until about 1990, Hepatitis C was called non-A-non-B Hepatitis, because there were viral hepatitis cases that were caused by neither of the two identifiable viruses, A and B. An antibody test can now identify this virus, which is called Hepatitis C. The antibody detected is not a protective antibody, but it is similar to the AIDS (HIV) antibody in that it indicates the presence of the virus. Many cases of viral hepatitis caused by blood transfusions in the past were due to Hepatitis C infection. The antibody test can eliminate this source of transmission, as it is used to screen the donor blood supply.

Injecting drug users, however, remain a major reservoir and source for the spread of this virus. Hepatitis C is transmitted similarly to Hepatitis B—and, for that matter, to HIV—primarily through direct blood-to-blood contact (by contaminated injection paraphernalia) and to a lesser extent, but still possibly, via sex and from mother to fetus. The primary infection very often goes unnoticed. The laboratory tests, in addition to Hepatitis C antibodies, will show elevated ALT and AST levels. Because Hepatitis C is a newly identified virus, its natural history is not yet clear. A fair amount of evidence suggests that chronic hepatitis, eventual cirrhosis, and liver cancer may be an even greater risk with Hepatitis C than it is with Hepatitis B. Some studies in the medical literature indicate that 50 to 80 percent of intravenous drug addicts may be infected with Hepatitis C.

Hepatitis D. Hepatitis D is a very unusual virus, which was originally called delta agent and later renamed Hepatitis D. It is an incomplete virus that can exist only in the presence of Hepatitis B. When the two organisms combine, the outcome is a particularly nasty, potentially lethal hepatitis, both in terms of acute mortality and chronic consequences. Discovered in Italy about 1990, in North America Hepatitis D is known to be primarily harbored by the IDU population.

PREVENTION AND TREATMENT OF VIRAL HEPATITIS

Obviously, the best prevention for injection drug users would be to stop injecting drugs. Other, often more realistic prophylactic measures—as with HIV—are the use of sterile (or at least bleached) needles and syringes, needle exchange programs, and condoms for sexual activities.

Immediately after a known or suspected exposure to Hepatitis B, the injection of an antibody preparation known as Hepatitis B immune globulin can prevent illness. A more permanent prophylaxis in high-risk populations is provided by the Hepatitis B vaccine, which gives long-term immunity in previously uninfected individuals. IDUs certainly represent

one of these high-risk populations, although the widespread use of the Hepatitis B vaccine in this group raises some obvious logistic dilemmas. As of 2008, there is no passive or active immunization available for Hepatitis C.

During the first decade of the twenty-first century, a number of new agents were introduced for the treatment of chronic Hepatitis B and C infections. Hepatitis C infection can be treated with the combination of two antiviral drugs: pegylated interferon (PegIntron, Pegasys) and ribavirin (Rebetol, Copegus). Pegylated interferon must be injected once weekly and can cause severe side effects, including flu-like symptoms, fatigue, irritability and depression. Ribavirin is better tolerated but is ineffective alone and must be used in combination with the interferon. The treatment is given over a period of months; some patients are still not able to clear the virus after a year's therapy. Treatment success depends on a number of factors, including the strain of virus being treated and the patient's ability to tolerate the interferon side effects. Hepatitis B can also be treated with a form of interferon (Intron A), which is successful in eliminating the virus in about half of all patients treated. Two oral agents are also used: lamivudine (Epivir HBV) and adefovir (Hepsera). These drugs can sometimes eliminate the Hepatitis B virus; but even if they do not, when taken long term they can suppress viral replication, potentially preventing liver damage. Finally, as mentioned under alcoholic liver disease, the most radical form of therapy in the end stages is liver transplantation.

See also **Needle and Syringe Exchanges and HIV/AIDS; Risk Factors for Substance Use, Abuse, and Dependence: An Overview; Social Costs of Alcohol and Drug Abuse.**

BIBLIOGRAPHY

Gold, M. S. (1991). *The Good News about Drugs and Alcohol.* New York: Villard.

Lieber, C. S. (1992). *Medical disorders of alcoholism.* New York: Plenum.

Mast, E. E., Weinbaum C. M., Fiore, A. E., Alter, M. J., Bell, B. P., Finelli, L., et al. (2006). A comprehensive immunization strategy to eliminate transmission of hepatitis B virus infection in the United States: recommendations of the Advisory Committee on Immunization Practices (ACIP) Part II: Immunization

of Adults. *Morbidity and Mortality Weekly Report, 55,*
1–25.

Mezey, E. (1982). Alcoholic liver disease. In H. Popper &
F. Shaffner (Eds.), *Progress in liver diseases* (pp. 555–
572). New York: Grune & Stratton.

Shapiro, C. N. (1994). Transmission of hepatitis viruses.
Annals of Internal Medicine, 120, 82–84.

Woolf, G. M., & Levy, G. A. (1988). Chronic viral hepatitis. *Medicine in North America, 21,* 3379.

PAUL DEVENYI
REVISED BY RALPH MYERSON (2001)
LEAH R. ZINDEL (2009)

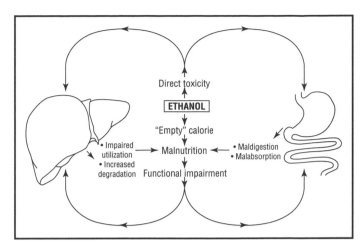

Figure 1. Interaction of direct toxicity of ethanol on liver and gut with malnutrition secondary to dietary deficiencies, maldigestion and malabsorption. (Adapted from Lieber, C. S. (1991a). *Alcohol, liver, and nutrition.* Journal of the American College of Nutrition, 10 *602–632.*) ILLUSTRATION BY GGS INFORMATION SERVICES. GALE, CENGAGE LEARNING

LIVER (METABOLIC)

Worldwide, alcohol (also called ethanol or ethyl alcohol) is one of the most commonly used mood-altering drugs. Alcohol, in different quantities for different people, is also a toxic drug: When used to excess, it taxes the body's economy, produces pathological changes in liver and other tissues, and can cause disease and death. In urban areas of the United States, just one of the complications—scarring or cirrhosis of the liver—is the fourth or fifth most frequent cause of death for people between the ages of twenty-five and sixty-five. Understanding how the sequential steps in the metabolism of alcohol correspond to specific changes in liver and other tissues promises to improve prospects that rational methods can be developed to prevent and treat alcohol abuse.

PATHOLOGY OF ALCOHOL ABUSE

Alcohol abuse affects all organs of the body (Lieber, 1992a). It atrophies many tissues, including the brain and endocrine glands. Indeed, altered hepatic (liver) metabolism plays a key role in a variety of endocrinological imbalances, such as gonadal (sex organ) dysfunctions and reproductive problems. Alcohol also exerts toxic effects on the bone marrow; it alters hematological status, causing macrocytic anemias (in which red blood cells are larger and less functional than normal), and it scars the heart and other muscles. This entry focuses mainly on the liver and gastrointestinal tract, as these are the sites where alcohol enters the body and has some of its most serious effects; this focus also provides examples of the insights and possible benefits that can be derived from the application of information from biochemistry, pathology, and molecular biology.

Liver disease, one of the most devastating complications of alcoholism, was formerly attributed exclusively to the malnutrition associated with alcoholism. Indeed, nutritional deficiencies are common in the alcoholic for various reasons, some socioeconomic, but these deficiencies also occur because alcohol is a unique compound. Alcohol is a psychoactive drug; but unlike other drugs that have negligible energy value, alcohol has a high energy (calorie) content—each gram of alcohol contributes 7.1 kilocalories, which means that a cocktail or a glass of wine provides 100 to 150 kilocalories. Thus, alcoholic beverages are similar to food in energy terms; but unlike food, they are virtually devoid of vitamins, protein, and other nutrients; they provide empty calories.

As shown in Figure 1, because of its large energy load, alcohol decreases the appetite for food and displaces other nutrients in the diet, thereby promoting primary malnutrition (Lieber, 1991a). Nutrition is also impaired because alcohol affects the gastrointestinal tract. Alcohol-induced intestinal lesions, including pancreatitis (inflammation of the pancreas), are associated with maldigestion and malabsorption, causing secondary malnutrition. Moreover, malnutrition itself creates functional impairment of the gut. Finally, alcohol (ethanol or its metabolite acetaldehyde) also adversely affects nutritional status by altering the hepatic activation or degradation of essential nutrients. Indeed, in experimental animals, malnutrition may produce a variety of liver alterations, including fatty liver and fibrosis; however, the relative contribution of malnutrition to the development of liver disease in the alcoholic cannot be clearly quantified as of 2008.

Furthermore, studies have shown that either the initial liver lesion (the fatty liver) or the ultimate stage of cirrhosis can be produced by excess alcohol, even in the absence of dietary deficiencies (Lieber & DeCarli, 1991), because ethanol (via its metabolism and/or its metabolite acetaldehyde) exerts direct hepatotoxic (toxic to the liver) effects. Thus, malnutrition plays a permissive but not a necessary role in alcohol-related somatic pathology.

METABOLISM OF ETHANOL AND SOME INTERACTIONS

Ethanol is readily absorbed from the gastrointestinal tract. Only 2 percent to 10 percent of that absorbed is eliminated through the kidneys and lungs; the rest is oxidized (metabolized) in the body, principally in the liver. Except for the stomach, extrahepatic (outside the liver) metabolism of ethanol is small. This relative organ specificity probably explains why, despite the existence of intracellular mechanisms to maintain homeostasis (equilibrium), ethanol disposal produces striking metabolic imbalances in the liver (Lieber, 1991b). These effects are aggravated by the lack of a feedback mechanism to adjust the rate of ethanol oxidation to the metabolic state of the hepatocyte (liver cell) and the inability of ethanol, unlike other major sources of calories, to be stored in the liver or to be metabolized or stored to a significant degree in peripheral tissues. As summarized here, the displacement by ethanol of the liver's normal substrates (targets of metabolism) and the metabolic disturbance produced by the oxidation of ethanol and its products explain many of the hepatic and metabolic complications of alcoholism.

A major pathway for ethanol metabolism involves alcohol dehydrogenase (ADH), an enzyme found in the cytoplasm of cells that catalyzes the conversion of ethanol to acetaldehyde. Liver ADH exists in multiple molecular forms (isozymes) that arise from various permutations of different types of subunits. Extrahepatic tissues contain isozymes of ADH with a much lower affinity for ethanol

than the hepatic isozymes; as a consequence, at the levels of ethanol achieved in the blood, these extrahepatic enzymes are inactive; therefore, extrahepatic metabolism of ethanol is negligible, with the exception of gastric (in the stomach) metabolism. Because of the extraordinarily high gastric ethanol concentration after alcohol consumption, even the gastric ADH with low affinity for ethanol becomes active, and significant gastric ethanol metabolism ensues. This action decreases the bioavailability of ethanol and represents a kind of protective barrier against systemic effects, at least when ethanol is consumed in small amounts. This gastric barrier disappears after the stomach is removed (gastrectomy; Caballeria et al., 1989) and may be lost, in part, in the alcoholic, because of a decrease in gastric ADH (Di Padova el al., 1987).

Similar effects may also result from gastric ADH inhibition by some commonly used drugs. For example, aspirin and certain drugs used to treat ulcers (histamine H2-blockers; Di Padova et al., 1992) inhibit gastric ADH activity and result in increased blood levels of ethanol when alcohol is consumed in amounts equivalent to social drinking. Furthermore, women have a lower gastric ADH activity than do men (Frezza et al., 1990); as a consequence, women's blood ethanol levels are higher for a given intake, an increase that is compounded by their body composition (more fat, less water than men) and on average, a lower body weight. Their higher blood ethanol levels in turn may contribute to women's greater susceptibility to alcohol.

Alcohol dehydrogenase converts ethanol to acetaldehyde and hydrogen. Hydrogen is a form of fuel that can be burned (oxidized). Normally, the liver burns fat to produce the energy required for its own functioning; but when alcohol is present, its hydrogen displaces fat as the preferred fuel. When the liver stops burning fat and instead burns the hydrogen from the ethanol, however, fat accumulates and a fatty liver develops, which is the first stage of alcoholic liver disease (Lieber, 1992a). Once a fatty liver has developed, fat accumulation does not increase indefinitely, even though alcohol consumption may continue (Salaspuro et al., 1981). Fat deposition is offset at least in part by the secretion of fat in the form of lipoprotein, resulting in hyperlipemia (elevated amounts of fat in blood).

Hyperlipemia of a moderate degree is commonly associated with early stages of alcoholic liver injury but wanes with the progression of liver disease (Lieber & Pignon, 1989). In some individuals, marked hyperlipemia may develop, sometimes associated with Zieve's syndrome—hemolytic anemia, fatty liver, and jaundice.

This metabolic condition represents the potentiation by alcohol of an underlying abnormality in the metabolism of either lipids (essential hyperlipemia) or carbohydrates (prediabetes, pancreatitis). In addition, the degree of hyperlipemia is also influenced by the duration of alcohol intake. The capacity for a hyperlipemic response develops progressively and is accompanied by an increased activity of enzymes of the endoplasmic reticulum (within the living cells) engaged in lipoprotein production. This hyperlipemia involves all lipoprotein classes, including high-density lipoproteins (HDL), which have been said to be involved in protection against atherosclerosis and in the lesser incidence of coronary complications in moderate drinkers compared to total abstainers. However, factors other than alcohol may also contribute to this apparent protection. The ability of the liver to respond with hyperlipemia reflects the integrity of the hepatocytes; its capacity decreases with the development of more severe liver injury.

The chemical reaction associated with ethanol oxidation in the liver is known as hepatic redox, a contraction of reduction/oxidation. Elucidation of the hepatic redox reaction via the alcohol dehydrogenase pathway has furthered understanding of associated disorders in carbohydrate, purine, and protein metabolism, including hypoglycemia (low blood sugar), hyperlactacidemia (excessive levels of lactic acid in the blood), and acidosis as well as hyperuricemia (elevated uric acid levels in blood) (Lieber, 1992a). In addition to the enzyme ADH, alcohol is also oxidized in the liver by the enzyme system referred to as the microsomal ethanol-oxidizing system (MEOS), which involves a specific cytochrome P-450 (P450IIE1) (Lieber, 1987). Contrary to ADH, this pathway is inducible by chronic alcohol consumption. In rat livers (Lieber et al., 1988) and in liver biopsies of heavy drinkers (Tsutsumi et al., 1989), a five- to tenfold increase of this alcohol-inducible form was found. This induction represents one of the most striking biochemical differences between heavy drinkers and normal subjects and provides an explanation for the metabolic tolerance to ethanol—a more rapid metabolism—that develops after alcohol abuse. The induction spills over to microsomal systems that metabolize other substrates, resulting in cross-tolerance to other drugs—not only sedatives and tranquilizers but also many commonly used medications such as anticoagulants and hypoglycemic agents. Thus, heavy drinkers require an increased dosage of many commonly used medications, at least at the initial stage, prior to the development of severe liver disease. When severe liver disease develops it will offset the enzyme induction, at which time drug dosage may have to be decreased.

What complicates the treatment of heavy drinkers even further is the fact that the microsomal enzymes (especially P450IIE1) also activate many xenobiotic agents (substances from outside the body) to become highly toxic compounds. This reaction explains the increased vulnerability of heavy drinkers to the hepatotoxic effects of industrial solvents, anesthetics, analgesics (painkillers), and chemical carcinogens. The latter contribute to the increased incidence of various cancers in the alcoholic. Alcohol has a major impact on gastrointestinal cancers, with a significant increase in the incidence of neoplasms (tumors) of the oropharynx, the esophagus, the stomach, the liver, and the colon (Garro & Lieber, 1990). Alcohol also plays a role in the activation of commonly used drugs and even over-the-counter analgesics such as acetaminophen (Tylenol, also known as paracetamol) to toxic metabolites (Sato et al., 1981). Additionally, in the heavy drinker, both the breakdown and hepatic depletion of vitamin A are increased (Leo & Lieber, 1982), with adverse consequences. Also, alcohol increases the toxicity of vitamin A (Leo et al., 1982), complicating supplementation with the vitamin in the presence of alcohol abuse. Alcohol abuse additionally promotes the microsomal breakdown of testosterone and its conversion to estrogens, which, together with testicular toxicity and decreased testosterone production, results in hypoandrogenism (loss of masculinity) (Lieber, 1992a).

In addition to environmental factors, individual differences in rates of ethanol metabolism appear to be genetically controlled. The role of heredity in the development of alcoholism in humans is still under investigation as of 2008. The induction of the previously mentioned MEOS pathway also leads to increased conversion of alcohol to acetaldehyde, a highly reactive and thus potentially toxic compound.

TOXICITY OF ACETALDEHYDE

Acetaldehyde (an intermediate metabolite of alcohol) causes injury through the formation of adducts (bonds) with proteins, resulting in antibody formation, inactivation of many key enzymes, decreased deoxyribonucleic acid (DNA) repair, and alterations in cell structures such as microtubules, mitochondria, and plasma membranes (Lieber, 1988, 1992a). Acetaldehyde also promotes synthesis of hepatic collagen, the key protein of scar tissue. Furthermore, it causes glutathione depletion, thereby worsening the toxicity mediated by free radicals, which results in lipid peroxidation and other tissue damage (Lieber, 1991b). Because of the far-reaching toxicity of this metabolite of ethanol, some of the liver cells die. Their death attracts inflammatory cells, which results in the more severe stage of alcoholic hepatitis, one of the precursors to the ultimate scarring or cirrhosis.

Once cirrhosis develops, a number of complications ensue, including obstruction of blood flow, with portal hypertension (elevated pressure in the veins leading from the intestine to the liver) and life-threatening internal bleeding from distended veins, called varices. There is also a buildup of water in the abdominal cavity, called ascites (Lieber, 1992a).

Acetaldehyde is particularly elevated if drinking occurs in pregnancy; it crosses the placenta (Karl et al., 1988) and has been incriminated in the pathogenesis of the fetal alcohol syndrome (FAS), the most common preventable cause of congenital abnormalities.

The bulk of acetaldehyde is oxidized to acetate by an acetaldehyde dehydrogenase produced by the liver mitochondria. Lack of the active form of the enzyme in some Asians explains their high blood acetaldehyde and flushing reaction after alcohol intake. Disulfiram (Antabuse, a drug used to treat alcohol intake dependence) is an inhibitor of acetaldehyde dehydrogenase. It raises the acetaldehyde levels after drinking and thereby causes flushing and several adverse effects that can be utilized in an effort to sustain abstinence in patients motivated to take the compound.

TREATMENT

Alcoholics suffer commonly from malnutrition. Therefore, nutritional deficiencies when present should be corrected, although such efforts were found to be ineffective in fully preventing liver disease due to the intrinsic toxicity of ethanol (Lieber, 1991b; Lieber & DeCarli, 1991). Although progress is being made at offsetting the direct toxicity of ethanol through chemical means (Lieber, 1992b), as of 2008 the single fully effective way of preventing somatic alcoholic injury remains control of the toxic agent ethanol through control of consumption. Complete abstinence is required in those who are genetically (or otherwise) prone to develop craving or to exhibit dependence, or those who are predisposed to develop the major somatic complication with chronic use of alcohol. For the others, moderation is recommended. What is considered *moderate* or *excessive* has been the subject of debate. One view is that on the average, moderate drinking represents no more than one drink a day in women and no more than two drinks a day in men, with a drink being 12 ounces of regular beer, 5 ounces of wine, or 1.5 ounces of distilled spirits (80 proof) (Dietary Guidelines, 2005). It is important, however, that *excess* be defined individually, taking into account not only gender, but also heredity and personal idiosyncrasies.

See also **Addiction: Concepts and Definitions; Cancer, Drugs, and Alcohol; Naltrexone; Social Costs of Alcohol and Drug Abuse.**

BIBLIOGRAPHY

Caballeria, J., Frezza, M., Hernández-Muñoz, R., DiPadova, C., Korsten, M. A., Baraona, E. et al. (1989). The gastric origin of the first pass metabolism of ethanol in man: Effect of gastrectomy. *Gastroenterology, 97,* 1205–1209.

Dietary Guidelines. (2005). *Nutrition and your health: Dietary guidelines for Americans 2005.* Washington, DC: U.S. Department of Agriculture. Available from www.health.gov/.

DiPadova, C., Roine, R., Frezza, M., Gentry, R. T., Baraona, E., & Lieber, C. S. (1992). Effects of ranitidine on blood alcohol levels after ethanol ingestion: Comparison with other H2-receptor antagonists. *Journal of the American Medical Association, 267,* 83–86.

DiPadova, C., Worner, T. M., Julkunen, C. S., & Lieber, C. S. (1987). Effects of fasting and chronic alcohol consumption on the first pass metabolism of ethanol. *Gastroenterology, 92,* 1169–1173.

Frezza, M., DiPadova, C., Pozzato, G., Terpin, M., Baraona, E., & Lieber, C. S. (1990). High blood alcohol levels in women: Role of decreased gastric alcohol dehydrogenase activity and first pass metabolism. *New England Journal of Medicine, 322,* 95–99.

Garro, A. J., & Lieber, C. S. (1990). Alcohol and cancer. *Annual Review of Pharmacology and Toxicology, 30,* 219–249.

Karl, P. I., Gordon, B. H., Lieber, C. S., & Fisher, S. E. (1988). Acetaldehyde production and transfer by the perfused human placental cotyledon. *Science, 242,* 273–275.

Leo, M. A., Arai, M., Sato, M., & Lieber, C. S. (1982). Hepatotoxicity of vitamin A and ethanol in the rat. *Gastroenterology, 82,* 194–205.

Leo, M. A., & Lieber, C. S. (1982). Hepatic vitamin: A depletion in alcoholic liver injury. *New England Journal of Medicine, 307,* 597–601.

Lieber, C. S. (1987). Microsomal ethanol oxidizing system (MEOS). *Enzyme, 37,* 45–56.

Lieber, C. S. (1988). Metabolic effects of acetaldehyde. *Biochemical Society Transactions, 16,* 241–247.

Lieber, C. S. (1991a). Alcohol, liver, and nutrition. *Journal of the American College of Nutrition, 10,* 602–632.

Lieber, C. S. (1991b). Hepatic, metabolic, and toxic effects of ethanol: 1991 update. *Alcoholism: Clinical and Experimental Research, 15,* 573–592.

Lieber, C. S. (Ed.). (1992a). *Medical and nutritional complications of alcoholism: Mechanisms and management.* New York: Plenum Press.

Lieber, C. S. (1992b). Hepatotoxicity of alcohol and implications for the therapy of alcoholic liver disease. In J. Rodes & V. Arroyo (Eds.), *Therapy in liver disease* (pp. 348–367). Barcelona: Ediciones Doyma.

Lieber, C. S., & Decarll, L. M. (1991). Hepatotoxicity of ethanol. *Journal of Hepatology, 12,* 394–401.

Lieber, C. S., & Pignon, J.-P. (1989). Ethanol and lipids. In J. C. Fruchart & J. Shepherd (Eds.), *Human plasma lipoproteins: Chemistry, physiology and pathology* (pp. 245–280). New York: Walter DeGruyter.

Lieber, C. S., Lasker, J. M., DeCarli, L. M., Saeli, J., & Wojtowicz, T. (1988). Role of acetone, dietary fat, and total energy intake ininduction of hepatic microsomal ethanol oxidizing system. *Journal of Pharmacology and Experiment Therapeutics, 247,* 791–795.

Salaspuro, M. P., et al. (1981). Attenuation of the ethanol induced hepatic redox change after chronic alcohol consumption in baboons: Metabolic consequences in vivo and in vitro. *Hepatology, 1,* 33–38.

Sato, C., Matsuda, Y., & Lieber, C. S. (1981). Increased hepatotoxicity of acetaminophen after chronic ethanol consumption in the rat. *Gastroenterology,80,* 140–148.

Tsutsumi, R., Lasker, J. M., Shimizu, M., Rosman, A. S., & Lieber, C. S. (1989). The intralobular distribution of ethanol-inducible P450IIE1 in rat and human liver. *Hepatology, 10,* 437–446.

CHARLES S. LIEBER
REVISED BY RALPH MYERSON (2001)
LEAH R. ZINDEL (2009)

MENTAL DISORDERS

The terms *comorbidity* and *dual diagnosis* describe the co-occurrence of two or more distinct psychiatric disorders. A range of psychiatric disorders, including affective disorders, anxiety disorders, and personality disorders, are often comorbid with substance use and substance use disorders (SUDs), which include alcohol and drug abuse and dependence. The association and interaction between specific SUDs and psychiatric disorders, the underlying reasons for their frequent co-occurrence, and the most effective treatments for SUD and co-occurring psychiatric diagnoses are important research areas that have been the subject of numerous studies and still require extensive future investigation.

The literature on the treatment of co-occurring psychiatric and substance use disorders is quite limited, with a particular paucity of studies evaluating non-pharmacologic interventions. The most extensively studied treatments are those for SUDs that are co-occurring with mood and anxiety symptoms and disorders. Although some studies show efficacy for specific interventions, many do not. Further, of the studies that show better outcomes for treatments that target co-occurring psychiatric symptoms, many fail to show an improvement in SUD outcomes (Nunes & Levin, 2004).

An important aspect of identifying and understanding common associations between SUDs and other psychiatric disorders involves knowing the time course of the disorders. Knowledge of which disorder is primary and which is secondary in time, or whether they developed simultaneously, provides researchers and clinicians with an improved understanding of the causation of these disorders; their general characteristics, development, and outcome; and the optimal treatment approaches. One explanation for comorbid SUD and psychiatric disorders is the *self-medication* hypothesis, in which substance use develops after the onset of the other psychiatric disorder as a means of coping with psychiatric symptoms. Another possibility is that substance use and SUDs precede the psychiatric disorder and induce neurochemical, biological and psychological changes that increase vulnerability to other psychiatric disorders. A third possibility is that SUDs and comorbid psychiatric disorders arise from a shared vulnerability; this vulnerability could involve genetic, familial, and/or environmental risk factors and stressors. Generally the presence of an SUD increases the risk of developing other psychiatric disorders and vice versa. Additionally, psychiatric disorders are often more strongly and consistently associated with substance dependence than with substance abuse alone.

SAMPLES AND STUDY DESIGNS

General Population Samples. Between the 1980s and the early twenty-first century, four large-scale epidemiologic surveys collected data on SUDs and comorbid disorders in the general U.S. population. These surveys have all used structured interviews conducted by non-clinician interviewers. They are, however, dissimilar in other respects, such as their diagnostic criteria, instruments, sampling techniques, definition of what constitutes a *current diagnosis*, and the types of disorders and other variables they investigated.

The first of these surveys, the Epidemiologic Catchment Area Survey (ECA), was conducted at five sites and used the Diagnostic Interview Schedule to investigate prevalence and comorbidity of *DSM-III* SUDs and affective, anxiety, and psychotic disorders. The second was the National Comorbidity Survey (NCS), which used the Michigan version of the Composite International Diagnostic Interview (UM-CIDI) to collect data on SUDs, affective, anxiety, and psychotic disorders based on *DSM-III-R* criteria. The third survey, conducted in 1992, was the National Longitudinal Epidemiologic Survey (NLAES), which drew from a larger sample than the previous studies and focused on SUDs and depressive disorders; the NLAES used the Alcohol Use Disorders and Associated Disabilities Interview Schedule (AUDADIS), which gathered sufficient data for later *DSM-IV* diagnoses of SUDs and other psychiatric disorders.

The fourth survey, which is large-scale, is the National Epidemiologic Survey on Alcohol and Related Conditions (NESARC). Wave 1 of the NESARC collected data on SUDs, affective, anxiety, and personality disorders, various sociodemographic variables, and family history from 43,093 respondents ages 18 and older. The NESARC achieved a response rate of 81 percent and collected data from respondents that were excluded from the NLAES, such as college students who live in group quarters; blacks, Hispanics, and young adults were oversampled. The NESARC implemented the *DSM-IV* version of the AUDADIS (AUDADIS-IV). Because of the size and scope of its sample, the NESARC is capable of providing precise and accurate information on SUD and psychiatric disorder risk by ethnic group.

Clinical Samples. Clinical studies include only patients in treatment for SUDs and/or other psychiatric disorders. Factors that influence rates of prevalence and comorbidity in clinical samples include diagnostic definitions, treatment admission policies, the study's exclusion and inclusion criteria, and sample size, which may be small. Treatment samples are susceptible to selection biases, which may result in overestimates of comorbidity and prevalence; individuals with more than one disorder are more likely to enroll in treatment. Studies, however, that draw on clinical samples may contribute to the understanding of how one disorder affects the course and outcome of another.

SUBSTANCE USE DISORDERS AND AFFECTIVE DISORDERS

Depression and Substance Use Disorders. Data from the ECA, NCS, and NLAES indicate strong associations between major depression and current and lifetime SUDs, with odds ratios (ORs) ranging from 1.9 to 7.2 depending on the survey. NESARC data on alcohol use disorders showed a significant association between major depressive disorder (MDD) and lifetime alcohol dependence (OR = 1.4), with the odds ratio adjusted for various sociodemographic characteristics and the presence of other psychiatric disorders; current (past 12-month) alcohol dependence showed a significant association with MDD when the odds ratio were adjusted for sociodemographic characteristics only (Hasin et al., 2007a). By contrast, both lifetime and current alcohol abuse were not significantly associated with MDD. In an analysis of NESARC data on current and lifetime drug use disorders, both current and lifetime drug dependence were significantly associated with MDD

(OR= 2.2 and OR 1.5, respectively) and dysthymia (OR = 2.8 and 1.7, respectively); lifetime but not current abuse showed significant associations with MDD (Compton et al., 2007). Among NESARC respondents with MDD, rates of any alcohol use disorder were 14.1 percent and 40.3 percent for 12-month and lifetime timeframes, respectively (Hasin et al., 2005); drug use disorder prevalence was 4.6 percent and 17.2 percent for 12-month and lifetime timeframes.

The strength of associations between SUDs and MDD may vary with ethnicity. In the NESARC sample, odds ratios for the association between current alcohol use disorders and MDD were significantly greater in blacks than in whites; for drug use disorders, the odds ratios were significantly greater in both blacks and Native Americans (Huang et al., 2006a). Differences may also be observed when comparing individuals with substance-induced depressive episodes and independent depressive episodes, as was done in a sample from the Collaborative Study on the Genetics of Alcoholism (COGA). Although the depressive symptoms experienced by both groups were similar, those with substance-induced depression were more likely to have greater maximum drinking levels, SUD or antisocial personality disorder diagnoses, and to be male, not white, and less educated. Compared to individuals without depression, those with substance-induced depression also reported a significantly more extensive family history of alcoholism (Schuckit et al., 2007).

Data from a study of male twins (n = 3372) suggests reciprocal causation between MDD and alcohol dependence, in which MDD increases the risk of alcohol dependence and alcohol dependence increases the risk of MDD (Lyons et al., 2006). The presence of alcohol dependence in one twin was associated with an increased risk of alcohol dependence only or combined dependence and MDD in the other twin, though not MDD only; and when one twin had MDD only, it was associated with an elevated risk of MDD only or combined MDD and alcohol dependence in the other twin, but not dependence only. In addition to a mechanism of reciprocal causation, the results could be explained by the presence of correlated genetic and environmental influences on alcohol dependence and MDD. A sibling-pair analysis identified linkage on chromosome 1 for alcoholism and depression

phenotypes (Nurnberger et al., 2001). In a COGA sample, a number of single nucleotide polymorphisms (SNPs) in the CHRM2 gene on chromosome 7 were associated with alcohol dependence, depression, or a combined phenotype (Wang et al., 2004), findings that were replicated by Luo and colleagues (2005). Both SUDs and depressive disorders also have strong familial components.

Comorbid affective disorders and SUDs are often highly prevalent in clinical settings. In the Sequential Treatment Alternative to Relieve Depression (Star*D) sample, one-third of the 4,010 patients with MDD experienced concurrent SUD. In this sample, individuals with concurrent MDD and SUD were more likely to be male, younger, divorced or never married, and/or not Hispanic. They also tended to exhibit greater functional impairment than individuals without SUD comorbidity and were more likely to experience an earlier onset of depression, a larger number of depression symptoms, more frequent comorbid anxiety disorders, greater mood variation, higher rates of suicidal ideation, and poorer self-outlook (Davis et al., 2008). Few studies have investigated treatments for dual diagnosis MDD and SUD patients, though evidence suggests that concomitant depression may predict a worse outcome for SUDs, including higher relapse rates and that remission from substance dependence is linked to a decreased risk of depression. One study showed that primary care patients with comorbid SUDs and MDD who received a better standard of care for the treatment of their depression, including better quality psychotherapy and antidepressant regimens, showed similar improvement to MDD patients without comorbid SUDs and significantly lower risk of depression at a 12-month follow-up than MDD/SUD patients who did not receive improved care (Watkins et al., 2006); the improved outcome may also be attributed, in part, to the referrals to substance abuse treatment programs that the MDD/SUD patients in quality care received, which reduced their substance use levels.

Bipolar Disorder and Substance Use Disorders. Individuals experiencing manic episodes tend also to exhibit increased drinking. The use of illegal drugs, particularly stimulants, is common among individuals with bipolar disorder. In the NESARC sample, both current and lifetime drug dependence and alcohol dependence were significantly associated with bipolar I disorder (Hasin et al., 2007a; Compton et al., 2007); current and lifetime alcohol dependence and lifetime drug dependence were also significantly associated with bipolar II disorder. Lifetime prevalence of concomitant SUDs and bipolar I was 58 percent for alcohol use disorders and 37.5 percent for drug use disorders in the NESARC sample (Grant et al., 2005).

Among patients with bipolar I and II disorders, concurrent SUDs worsened the outcome of bipolar disorder, reduced compliance to treatments, and increased the risk of suicidal behavior (Cerullo & Strakowski, 2006); some findings suggest that drug abuse may lead to an earlier onset of bipolar I disorder in families that also have a history of mania (Winokur et al., 1998). One placebo-controlled trial has suggested that for individuals with bipolar disorder and alcohol dependence, a regimen of valproate and lithium significantly reduces drinking but does not impact other psychiatric outcomes (Salloum et al., 2005).

Posttraumatic Stress Disorder (PTSD) and Substance Use Disorders.

Lifetime prevalence of SUDs in general population samples of individuals with PTSD ranges from 21 to 43 percent (Jacobsen et al., 2001). In a review of clinical samples of SUDs, lifetime PTSD has ranged from 26 to 52 percent, and current PTSD from 15 to 41 percent (Schafer & Najavits, 2007). Rates of PTSD/SUD comorbidity may vary with specific substances as well. In a sample drawn from the Australian general population (Mills et al., 2006), alcohol use disorders were the most common SUDs among individuals with PTSD, with a prevalence of 24.1 percent. Among individuals with SUDs, PTSD was most prevalent among those with opioid use disorders (33.2%) and sedative use disorders (28.5%), compared to 5.4 percent of individuals with alcohol use disorders and 5.2 percent with cannabis use disorders.

Several mechanisms may explain the association between PTSD and SUDs. One is the self-medication hypothesis, which posits that individuals use substances to cope with posttraumatic symptoms. A second is the *high-risk* hypothesis, in which substance use and associated high risk behaviors increase the chances of an individual experiencing a traumatic event and subsequently developing PTSD. A third, the *susceptibility* hypothesis, asserts that the risk of PTSD increases due to the vulnerability in the brain and body brought about by heavy substance use or SUDs. Lastly, PTSD and SUDs may be affected by a third variable, such as general poor coping skills (Schafer & Najavits, 2007).

Certain environmental cues exert a particular influence on substance use in individuals with PTSD. Human laboratory studies have shown that, compared to neutral cues, exposure to trauma-related cues increases craving for substances in individuals with PTSD. PTSD/SUD patients who have recently become abstinent after SUD treatment were more likely to report substance use relapse in response to negative emotions than to substance-related cues; generally, situations involving negative emotions, conflict, high stress, and bodily discomfort are linked to greater substance use in these dual diagnosis patients.

PTSD/SUD patients generally report poorer health and functioning, increased psychiatric comorbidity, and earlier onset of substance abuse than patients presenting with either diagnosis alone. PTSD may also interfere with SUD treatment by decreasing treatment adherence and increasing the chances of relapse. Among dual diagnosis individuals, the seeking safety model—a psychotherapy that teaches coping skills in multiple domains—appears across several studies to be an effective treatment for comorbid PTSD and SUDs. More research is needed to explore effective pharmacological treatments for dual PTSD and SUD diagnoses.

Even in the absence of PTSD, substance use has been associated with exposure to traumatic events. In studies conducted among Israeli high school students, proximity to terrorist attacks was associated with greater subsequent use of alcohol and cannabis, even after depressive and posttraumatic symptoms were controlled for (Schiff et al., 2007). Following the 9/11 attacks on the World Trade Center, alcohol consumption (Wu et al., 2006; Vlahov et al., 2004) and cigarette and cannabis use (Vlahov et al., 2004) increased among New York City residents. Proximity to the 9/11 attack and past alcohol dependence also predicted higher levels of drinking after the attack in a sample of adults from northern New Jersey (Hasin et al., 2007b).

SUBSTANCE USE DISORDERS AND OTHER ANXIETY DISORDERS

Substance Use Disorders and Panic Disorders.

A close relationship exists between alcohol use disorders and panic disorders (Cosci et al., 2007). The self-medication hypothesis may apply to panic disorders and alcohol use disorders and so might the possibility that panic symptoms arise from neuro-chemical changes associated with heavy alcohol use, dependence, and withdrawal and to an increased sensitivity to carbon dioxide, which may increase the risk of panic symptoms. Alcohol use disorders and panic disorders may also stem from a strong familial component; family history studies have shown a relationship between alcohol use disorders and panic disorders, as in one study in which the risk of panic disorder was significantly greater (OR = 1.9) in 8,296 relatives of alcoholic probands compared to 1,654 controls (Nurnberger et al., 2004).

ECA and NCS data suggest that panic disorder increases the risk for both alcohol and drug dependence (Regier et al., 1990; Kessler et al., 1997). When the odds ratios were adjusted for various sociodemographic variables and other psychiatric disorders, lifetime alcohol dependence in the NESARC sample was significantly associated with panic disorder without agoraphobia (OR = 1.3) and lifetime drug dependence was associated with panic disorder with and without agoraphobia (OR = 2.4 and 1.6, respectively) (Hasin et al., 2007a; Compton et al., 2007). In the NESARC sample, associations between any panic disorder and alcohol use disorders were significantly stronger in Asians than in whites, blacks, and Native Americans; among Hispanics, the association was significantly stronger than in whites.

Substance Use Disorders and Other Anxiety Disorders. As with panic disorders, other anxiety disorders are commonly comorbid with SUDs. NESARC findings, with odds ratios adjusted for sociodemographic variables and other psychiatric disorders, show significant associations between current and lifetime drug dependence and generalized anxiety disorder (ORs = 2.5 and 1.6, respectively), lifetime alcohol dependence and specific phobia (OR = 1.4), and any lifetime alcohol use disorder and social phobia (OR = 1.2).

For alcohol use and anxiety disorders, comorbidity could arise in part from an interaction of anxiolytic and anxiogenic processes (Kushner et al., 2000). Drinking could provide short-term relief from anxiety but also lead to the expectation that anxiety will return once drinking is stopped; this expectation could in turn lead to more drinking and the emergence of a feed-forward cycle in which overall levels of drinking and anxiety increase. The risk of anxiety disorders and SUDs may also be transmitted through the family, as shown in family history studies in which relatives of alcoholic probands exhibit significantly higher rates of anxiety symptoms and disorders.

SUBSTANCE USE DISORDERS AND PERSONALITY DISORDERS

Borderline Personality Disorder. SUDs are highly prevalent among individuals with Borderline Personality Disorder (BPD), across community, inpatient and outpatient samples (Trull et al., 2000). Across BPD samples, rates of SUDs range from 22.7 to 86 percent. For studies of BPD and SUD comorbidity it may be difficult for patients to describe traits associated with their BPD alone, as substance use is associated with and contributes to impulsivity, interpersonal problems, and emotional dysregulation and instability. Some findings point to an association between alcohol sensitivity, alcohol use and impulsivity/disinhibition, a central trait of BPD. Impulsivity may lead to a number of risky behaviors, including the heavy use of alcohol and drugs. The development of comorbid BPD and SUDs may stem from personality traits such as impulsivity and poor emotional regulation that are central to both disorders.

Antisocial Personality Disorder. SUDs and antisocial behavior frequently co-occur. Current and lifetime alcohol dependence, drug dependence, and drug abuse are significantly associated with antisocial personality disorder in the NESARC samples (Hasin et al., 2007a; Compton et al., 2007). Twin and family studies have shown that drug abuse and dependence, alcohol dependence, childhood conduct disorder, and adult antisocial behavior share an underlying genetic liability (Kendler et al., 2003), a key reason why they so frequently co-occur. Substance dependence, childhood conduct disorder, and antisocial personality disorder appear to fall on a single underlying spectrum of externalizing psychopathology. Analyses of COGA data have provided evidence for an association between the GABRA2 gene, located on chromosome 4, and alcohol dependence; significant association has also been found between GABRA2 and drug dependence (for marijuana and other illegal drugs), childhood conduct disorder, and antisocial personality disorder (Dick, 2007). Another

COGA study tested the association between SNPs in the CHRM2 gene and a general externalizing factor comprised of alcohol and drug dependence, antisocial personality disorder, conduct disorder, and the personality traits of novelty seeking and sensation seeking; the association was tested for the factor as a whole and for the individual components. One SNP was related to alcohol dependence, another to drug dependence, and two each to novelty seeking and sensation seeking. The general factor was significantly associated with 6 SNPs, a larger number than any of its individual components; however, the single SNP related to alcohol dependence was not related to the general factor as a whole (Dick et al., 2008).

GENERAL ISSUES

Studies focusing on two types of disorders when investigating comorbidity frequently fail to control for other disorders. This pattern is especially true in cases of SUDs, affective, and anxiety disorders, which commonly co-occur. When other psychiatric disorders are controlled for, often there will be a decrease in the magnitude of the association between the two disorders studied. The understanding of treatment and functioning might also significantly improve with proper control for comorbidity, suggesting that in some dual diagnosis cases the more severe clinical presentation might result from a general burden of psychiatric comorbidity rather than a specific relationship between the two disorders studied.

More research is needed on integrated treatment for individuals with comorbid SUDs and other psychiatric disorders. Treatments tailored to only one disorder also tend to work for patients with dual diagnoses. For example, a substance use intervention will reduce substance use both in patients with SUDs only and in patients with comorbid SUDs and another psychiatric disorder. However, there are mixed findings as to whether the improvement in one disorder will carry over to the other disorder in comorbid patients (Nunes & Levin, 2004). For a large number of disorders it was unclear as of 2008 which integrated treatments would be more efficacious than treatments tailored to a single disorder. As of 2008, many studies of integrated treatments for SUD and comorbid disorder had not been replicated, perhaps due to the fact that they suffered from small sample sizes and high attrition rates. Further, these studies are not randomized or well-controlled, do not verify patient reports of symptoms, and/or do not measure key treatment outcomes and effects (Tiet & Mausbach, 2007); across studies diagnostic definitions may also be inconsistent.

Often these studies also fail to examine the interaction of the effects of medications with substance use and psychiatric symptoms. Prescription medications are also liable to be improperly used. NESARC data on non-medical prescription drug disorders show that these disorders are strongly associated with a number of Axis I and II psychiatric disorders (Huang et al., 2006b; Agrawal et al., 2006). Among mood disorders the strongest association with non-medical prescription drug use disorders is with bipolar I disorder, among anxiety disorders the strongest association is with panic disorder with agoraphobia; and among personality disorders the strongest association is with antisocial personality disorder (Huang et al., 2006b).

See also **Conduct Disorder and Drug Use; Epidemiology of Alcohol Use Disorders; Epidemiology of Drug Abuse; Research: Measuring Effects of Drugs on Mood; Risk Factors for Substance Use, Abuse, and Dependence; Social Costs of Alcohol and Drug Abuse; Structured Clinical Interview for DSM-IV (SCID).**

BIBLIOGRAPHY

Agrawal, A., Lynskey, M. T., Madden, P. A. F., Bucholz, K. K., Heath, A. C., et al. (2006). A latent class analysis of illicit drug abuse/dependence: Results from the National Epidemiologic Survey on Alcohol and Related Conditions. *Addiction, 102,* 94–104.

Cerullo, M. A., & Strakowski, S. M. (2006). Substance use disorders in bipolar disorder: An Update. *Current Psychosis and Therapeutics Reports, 4,* 171–175.

Compton, W. M., Thomas, Y. F., Stinson, F. S., & Grant, B. F. (2007). Prevalence, correlates, disability, and comorbidity of DSM-IV drug abuse and dependence in the United States: Results from the national epidemiologic survey on alcohol and related conditions. *Archives of General Psychiatry, 64*(5), 566–576.

Cosci, F., Schruers, K. R. J., Abrams, K., & Griez, E. J. L. (2007). Alcohol use disorders and panic disorder: A review of the evidence of a direct relationship. *Journal of Clinical Psychiatry, 68,* 874–880.

Davis, L., Uezato, A., Newell, J. M., & Frazier, E. (2008). Major depression and comorbid substance use disorders. *Current Opinion in Psychiatry, 21,* 14–18.

Dick, D. M. (2007). Identification of genes influencing a spectrum of externalizing psychopathology. *Current Directions in Psychological Science, 16,* 331–335.

Dick, D. M., Aliev, F., Wang, J. C., Grucza, R. A., Schuckit, M., Kuperman, S., et al. (2008). Using dimensional models of externalizing psychopathology to aid in gene identification. *Archives of General Psychiatry, 65,* 310–318.

Grant, B. F., Stinson, F. S., Hasin, D. S., Dawson, D. A., Chou, P. S., Ruan, W. J., et al. (2005). Prevalence, correlates, and comorbidity of bipolar I disorder and axis I and II disorders: Results from the National Epidemiologic Survey on Alcohol and Related Conditions. *Journal of Clinical Psychiatry, 66,* 1205–1215.

Hasin, D. S., Goodwin, R. D., Stinson, F. S., & Grant, B. F. (2005). Epidemiology of major depressive disorder. *Archives of General Psychiatry, 62,* 1097–1106.

Hasin, D. S., Keyes, K. M., Hatzenbuehler, M. L., Aharonovich, E. A., & Alderson, D. (2007b). Alcohol consumption and posttraumatic stress after exposure to terrorism: Effects of proximity, loss, and psychiatric history. *American Journal of Public Health, 97,* 2268–2275.

Hasin, D. S., Stinson, F. S., Ogburn, E., & Grant, B. F. (2007a). Prevalence, correlates, disability, and comorbidity of DSM-IV alcohol abuse and dependence in the United States: Results from the National Epidemiologic Survey on Alcohol and Related Conditions. *Archives of General Psychiatry, 64,* 830–842.

Huang, B., Dawson, D. A., Stinson, F. S., Hasin, D. S., Ruan, W. J., Saha, T. D., et al. (2006b). Prevalence, correlates, and comorbidity of nonmedical prescription drug use and drug use disorders in the United States: Results of the National Epidemiologic Survey on Alcohol and Related Conditions. *Journal of Clinical Psychiatry, 67,* 1062–1073.

Huang, B., Grant, B. F., Dawson, D. A., Stinson, F. S., Chou, S. P., Saha, T. D., et al. (2006a). Race-ethnicity and the prevalence and co-occurrence of *Diagnostic and Statistical Manual of Mental Disorders, Fourth Edition,* alcohol and drug use disorders and Axis I and II disorders: United States, 2001 to 2002. *Comprehensive Psychiatry, 47,* 252–257.

Jacobsen, L. K., Southwick, S. M., & Kosten, T. R. (2001). Substance use disorders in patients with posttraumatic stress disorder: A review of the literature. *American Journal of Psychiatry, 158,* 1184–1190.

Kessler, R. C., Crum, R. M., Warner, L. A., Nelson, C. B., Schulenberg, J., & Anthony, J. C. (1997). Lifetime co-occurrence of *DSM-III-R* alcohol abuse and dependence with other psychiatric disorders in the National Comorbidity Survey. *Archives of General Psychiatry, 54,* 313–321.

Kushner, M. G., Abrams, K., & Borchardt, C. (2000). The relationship between anxiety disorders and alcohol use disorders: A review of major perspectives and findings. *Clinical Psychology Review, 20,* 149–171.

Luo, X., Kranzler, H. R., Zuo, L., Blumburg, H., Wang, S., & Gelernter, J. (2005). CHRM2 gene predisposes to alcohol dependence, drug dependence, and affective disorders: Results from an extended case-control structured association study. *Human Molecular Genetics, 14,* 2421–2434.

Lyons, M. J., Schultz, M., Neale, M., Brady, K., Eisen, S., Toomey, R., et al. (2006). Specificity of familial vulnerability for alcoholism versus major depression in men. *Journal of Nervous and Mental Disease, 194,* 809–817.

Mills, K. L., Teesson, M., Ross, J., & Peters, L. (2006). Trauma, PTSD, and substance use disorders: Findings from the Australian National Survey of Mental Health and Well-Being. *American Journal of Psychiatry, 163,* 652–658.

Nunes, E. V., & Levin F. R. (2004). Treatment of depression in patients with alcohol or other drug dependence: A meta-analysis. *Journal of the American Medical Association, 291,* 1887–1896.

Nurnberger, J. I., Jr., Foroud, T., Flury, L., Su, J., Meyer, E. T., Hu, K., et al. (2001). Evidence for a locus on chromosome 1 that influences vulnerability to alcoholism and affective disorder. *American Journal of Psychiatry, 158,* 718–724.

Nurnberger, J. I., Jr., Wiegand, R., Bucholz, K., O'Connor, S., Meyer, E. T., Reich, T., et al. (2004). A family study of alcohol dependence: Coaggregation of multiple disorders in relatives of alcohol-dependent probands. *Archives of General Psychiatry, 61,* 1246–1256.

Regier, D. A., Farmer, M. E., Rae, D. S., Locke, B. Z., Keith, S. J., Judd, L. L., et al. (1990). Comorbidity of mental disorders with alcohol and other drug abuse: Results from the Epidemiologic Catchment Area (ECA) Study. *Journal of the American Medical Association, 264,* 2511–2518.

Salloum, I. M., Cornelius, J. R., Daley, D. C., Kirisci, L., Himmelhoch, J. M., & Thase, M. E. (2005). Efficacy of Valproate maintenance in patients with bipolar disorder and alcoholism: A double-blind, placebo-controlled study. *Archives of General Psychiatry, 62,* 37–45.

Schafer, I., & Najavits, L. M. (2007). Clinical challenges in the treatment of patients with posttraumatic stress disorder and substance abuse. *Current Opinion in Psychiatry, 20,* 614–618.

Schiff, M. Z., Hillah, H., Rami, B., & Hasin, D. S. (2007). Exposure to terrorism and Israeli youths' cigarette, alcohol, and cannabis use. *American Journal of Public Health, 97,* 1852–1858.

Schuckit, M. A., Smith, T. L., Danko, G. P., Pierson, J., Trim, R. Nurnberger, J. I., et al. (2007). A comparison of factors associated with substance-induced versus independent depressions. *Journal of Studies on Alcohol and Drugs, 68,* 805–812.

Tiet, Q. Q., & Mausbach, B. (2007). Treatments for patients with dual diagnoses: A review. *Alcoholism: Clinical and Experimental Research, 31,* 513–536.

Trull, T. J., Sher, K. J., Minks-Brown, C., Durbin, J., & Burr, R. (2000). Borderline personality disorder and substance use disorders: A review and integration. *Clinical Psychology Review, 20,* 235–253.

Vlahov, D., Galea, S., Ahern, J., Resnick, H., Boscarino, J. A., Gold, J., et al. (2004). Consumption of cigarettes, alcohol, and marijuana among New York City residents six months after the September 11 terrorist attacks. *American Journal of Drug and Alcohol Abuse, 30,* 385–407.

Wang, J. C., Hinrichs, A. L., Stock, H., Budde, J., Allen, R., Bertelsen, S., et al. (2004). Evidence of common and specific genetic effects: Association of the muscarinic acetylcholine receptor M2 (CHRM2) gene with alcohol dependence and major depressive syndrome. *Human Molecular Genetics, 13,* 1903–1911.

Watkins, K. E., Paddock, S. M., Zhang, L., & Wells, K. B. (2006). Improving care for depression in patients with comorbid substance misuse. *American Journal of Psychiatry, 163,* 125–132.

Winokur, G., Turvey, C., Akiskal, H., Coryell, W., Solomon, D., Leon, A., et al. (1998). Alcoholism and drug abuse in three groups—bipolar I, unipolars, and their acquaintances. *Journal of Affective Disorders, 50,* 81–89.

Wu, P., Duarte, C. S., Mandell, D. J., Fan, B., Liu, X., Fuller, J., et al. (2006). Exposure to the World Trade Center Attack and the use of cigarettes and alcohol among New York City public high-school students. *American Journal of Public Health, 96,* 804–807.

BRIAN L. COOK
GEORGE WINOKAUR
REVISED BY DANIEL P. HAYES (2001)
DEBORAH S. HASIN (2009)
HILA E. KATZ (2009)

NEUROLOGICAL

Alcohol and other psychotropic drugs affect the central nervous system (CNS) and its activity, thereby altering cognitive functioning. The specific substance or combination of substances consumed, the quantity in which they are used, and the duration of their use are factors influencing the effects of substances on CNS structural and functional integrity. This entry reviews the acute and chronic effects of alcohol and other psychotropic drugs on the CNS and on cognitive functioning. The studies reviewed have used a variety of methodologies, including neuropsychological tests, magnetic resonance imaging (MRI), functional magnetic resonance imaging (fMRI), and positron-emission tomography (PET), to assess neurocognitive alterations and attempt to link those alterations to specific structures and systems in the CNS.

ALCOHOL

Alcohol is a CNS depressant, and acute alcohol intoxication typically results in impaired judgment, slurred speech, and uncoordinated motor movements. Other cognitive functions such as selective attention, decision-making, and hand-eye coordination may also suffer impairment during intoxication. Diminished inhibitory control, coupled with an intoxicated individual's inability to evaluate the consequences of his or her actions, can increase risk-taking, aggressive, or dangerous behaviors. Alcohol intoxication is often linked to traumatic injuries, including traumatic brain injuries. Binge drinking, in which a large quantity of alcohol is consumed within a relatively short amount of time, can lead to memory lapses and alcoholic blackouts; when experiencing a blackout, an individual cannot recall events that took place during the period of intoxication. Extremely high doses of alcohol depress consciousness, leading to sleepiness, coma, respiratory depression, and death. The effects of acute intoxication are dose dependent, although the specific doses of alcohol needed to experience these effects are influenced by factors such as body weight and tolerance.

Across studies that administer neuropsychological tests to long-term, heavy drinkers and/or individuals with alcohol use disorders, the most consistent cognitive deficits appear to be in the domains of attention, memory (including declarative memory and short-term memory), visuospatial learning and functioning, postural stability, and a set of executive functions that includes decision-making, problem-solving, working memory, and response inhibition (Crews et al., 2005; Sullivan et al., 2002; Sullivan et al., 2000). These impairments may worsen in direct proportion to the duration and frequency of drinking (Parsons, 1998; Beatty et al., 2000) or may be detectable only after a minimum of several years of heavy drinking (Eckardt et al., 1998). The impairments may also result from traumatic brain injuries suffered during intoxication and from the direct effects of alcohol itself.

Heavy and long-term drinkers suffer from neuronal damage and decreased brain volume. MRI studies have shown that the damage and loss of volume in heavy drinkers tend to be most severe in the frontal lobes, temporal lobes, anterior hippocampus, and cerebellum (Pfeifferbaum et al., 1995; Rourke & Loberg, 1996), areas linked to executive cognitive functions, memory, and motor movements. However, cell loss is not restricted to these brain regions only and may be widespread throughout a number of cortical and subcortical areas. Autopsy studies have shown that the brains of alcoholics are smaller and weigh less than the brains of non-alcoholic controls. The brains of chronic heavy drinkers also evince enlarged sulci (the cortex's furrows and fissures) and ventricles, further evidence of volume loss; however, research on the correlation between enlarged ventricles and poorer performance on neuropsychological measures has yielded inconsistent findings (Bates et al., 2002). Alcohol has a direct toxic effect on neurons and is also linked to a loss of neurogenesis (the formation of neurons), particularly in the hippocampus, a region associated with the encoding and formation of new memories. Damage to these areas may underlie the cognitive deficits seen in heavy long-term drinkers and the increased loss of control and compulsive drinking associated with alcohol dependence. PET studies have also revealed a drop in glucose metabolism in the frontal lobes among individuals with alcohol use disorders (Johnson-Greene et al., 1997); the metabolic decrease is associated with poor performance on neuropsychological tests, particularly executive function tasks, even in the absence of cortical atrophy.

Alcohol also alters the CNS by directly interacting with neurotransmitters and modifying their activity. Alcohol enhances the activity of gamma-aminobutyric acid (GABA), the main inhibitory neurotransmitter in the CNS. Chronic alcohol use reduces the efficiency of GABA receptors, a reduction linked to an increased risk during alcohol withdrawal of excitotoxic neuronal damage which results from abnormally increased activity and transmission of excitatory neurotransmitters such as glutamate. GABA(A) receptors mediate tolerance, anxiolysis, motor coordination impairment, and several other important alcohol effects. GABRA2, a gene located on chromosome 4, encodes the alpha-2 subunit of the GABA(A) receptor. The gene has been associated with alcohol dependence (Covault et al., 2004; Edenberg et al., 2004) and with brain wave oscillations in the beta frequency range (Porjesz et al.,

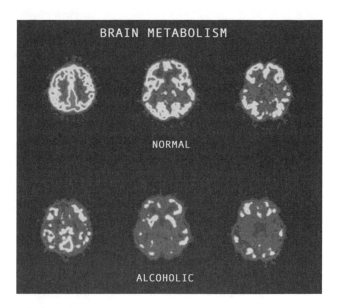

A PET scan compares a normal brain with that of alcoholic. ISM/PHOTOTAKE

2002), an endophenotype related to alcohol dependence. Another neurotransmitter associated with drinking behavior is serotonin, which has also been implicated in mood regulation, sleep, and impulsive and aggressive behaviors. The serotonin transport protein (5-HTT), which takes released serotonin back up into the presynaptic neuron, controls the extracellular concentration of serotonin. Some evidence suggests that 5-HTTLPR, a promoter region polymorphism in SLC6A4, the gene encoding the 5-HTT, interacts with child abuse and maltreatment in predicting early drinking among children from low-income families (Kaufman et al., 2007). Acute alcohol intoxication has also been shown to inhibit glutamate, a neurotransmitter involved in learning and memory. It is possible that this inhibition plays a role in alcohol-related blackouts (Bates et al., 2002).

There is evidence of partial recovery of neurocognitive functioning and brain mass after a period of abstinence from heavy, chronic drinking. Neuroimaging studies show decreases in ventricular size and increases in the volume of gray and white matter after abstinence (Pfefferbaum et al., 1995; O'Neill et al., 2001; Sullivan et al., 2000). There is also evidence of renewed neurogenesis in the hippocampus, as seen in the appearance of new dentate gyrus cells (Bartels et al., 2007); this neurogenesis contributes to learning, memory and the regulation of mood. However, other studies among heavy drinkers show that decreased blood flow in the cerebellum may persist even after months of abstinence and that the cognitive abilities most vulnerable to alcohol—such as memory, problem-solving, abstraction, and selective and divided attention—may also take months or years before recovery is evident. Some evidence suggests that former heavy drinkers who are currently abstinent do not rely on the same neural systems they once used for the performance of various cognitive tasks (Pfefferbaum et al., 2001; De Rosa et al., 2004). However, these individuals may use new and more widely spread areas, resulting in decreased cognitive efficiency; an example of this is a study of verbal working memory, in which chronic drinkers used larger areas of frontal cortex than controls (Desmond et al., 2003). Cortical recovery following long-term heavy drinking may also involve a reorganization of neurocognitive processing and strategies (Crews et al., 2005).

CANNABIS

Cannabis is the most widely used illegal drug world-wide. Acute intoxication results in disruptions of attention, memory, and perceptual-motor functioning. As with alcohol, cannabis also impairs decision-making abilities and complex visual and motor functioning, so that an intoxicated individual cannot safely drive or operate heavy machinery.

Studies administering various neuropsychological tests to chronic cannabis users have shown that, compared to controls, chronic users tend to demonstrate poorer performance on tasks related to attention, memory, and executive function; cannabis users also experience a loss of self-control and behavioral inhibitions (Hall et al., 1999; Fletcher et al., 1996; Roger & Robbins, 2001). Frequency and duration of use, as well as effects of cumulative dosage, have all been associated with these cognitive impairments (Bolla et al., 2002; Solowij et al., 2002). However, a meta-analytic review of neuropsychological studies among cannabis users did not show significant impairments in various domains; the most prominent effect was a subtle memory deficit (Grant et al., 2003).

Neuroimaging studies, including those using PET and fMRI, have linked impairments in attention, verbal and working memory, and decision-making to alterations in activation, tissue volume and density, and blood flow particularly in the prefrontal cortex, basal ganglia, anterior cingulate, and hippocampus regions (Mathew et al., 1997). Heavy users also show decreased cerebellar metabolism (Volkow et al., 1996). Some research has shown reductions of up to 12 percent of the hippocampus volume and 7.1 percent of the amygdala in long-term heavy cannabis users. Dense concentrations of cannabinoid receptors are typically found in areas of the cerebral cortex, hippocampus, and basal ganglia; there are speculations that cannabinoids interfere with activity between these regions, which in part may account for the disruptions in attention and memory seen in heavy users.

Compared to non-users of cannabis, different patterns of blood flow and brain activation have been observed in chronic users when confronted with the same cognitive tasks (Lundqvist, 2005). In performing spatial working memory tasks, long-term heavy users appear to experience greater and more widespread brain activity than controls, suggesting that they have decreased cognitive efficiency and subtle widespread impairments in neurocognitive performance. In tasks of verbal recall, heavy users have shown decreased blood flow in the prefrontal cortex. Cognitive deficits may be reversible, at least in part, after a period of abstinence, though further research is required as of 2008 to determine the duration of the impairments.

OPIATES

Opiates lead to a generalized depression of cognition and intoxication may result in impaired perception, memory, learning, and reasoning, which are accompanied by changes in mood and drowsiness.

Chronic heroin use has been associated with deficits in impulse control (Pau et al., 2002; Davis et al., 2002; Lee & Pau, 2002). Heroin and other opiate users also perform poorly on reward-based decision tasks (Madden et al., 1997). Although some evidence suggests that current heroin users may show deficits in a number of cognitive domains such as attention and memory before detoxification (Guerra et al., 1987; Lee & Pau, 2002), other evidence indicates that there are no significant or long-lasting deficits in attention or cognitive tasks requiring mental flexibility (Pau et al., 2002; Davis et al., 2002). Long-term heroin users also appear to be vulnerable to lesions in the frontal and temporal lobes (Ornstein et al., 2000).

In neuroimaging scans, individuals with opiate dependence show decreased gray matter in the fusiform gyrus, prefrontal, and superior temporal cortex; there may also be a widening of the ventricles, which indicates a loss of brain volume. A reduced concentration of the neuronal marker N-acetylaspartate (NAA) and glutamate/glutamine may also be found among opiate addicts. For cognitive tasks, opiate dependent individuals have shown increased frontoparietal and cerebellar activation compared to non-user controls, indicating a decrease in cognitive efficiency. Opiate dependent individuals show particularly poor performance in tasks of spatial planning, paired association learning, and visual pattern recognition; these impairments have also been noted in currently abstinent individuals (with an average duration of abstinence of 8 years) compared to individuals with no history of opiate use (Ersche et al., 2006). However, in some tasks such as the Category Test of the Halstead Battery, which measures abstract reasoning, opiate users do not tend to show increased impairment relative to non-users, suggesting that the associated regions in the frontal lobes may be spared. By contrast, in the Tapping Test and the Tactual Performance Test for spatial memory, they do show impairment (Hill et al., 1979).

METHAMPHETAMINE AND COCAINE

Methamphetamines and cocaine act as CNS stimulants; they increase CNS arousal and psychomotor activity. The increased arousal during acute intoxication may result in a dysfunction in higher-order control processes used to monitor or inhibit ongoing behavior, such that there is a corresponding increase in errors, impulsivity, and hyperactivity. More severe consequences of even a single dose of cocaine may include seizures, strokes, and intracerebral hemorrhages.

During cognitive tasks methamphetamine users experience difficulty filtering out information irrelevant to the task; there is also evidence that they experience deficiencies in processing speed and delayed recall of information (Salo et al., 2002). Neuroimaging provides evidence that chronic methamphetamine users experience abnormal changes in frontal lobe, temporal lobe, and subcortical brain metabolism, which may result from neuronal damage to areas of the basal ganglia and frontal cortex and a decreased density of dopaminergic neurons in the putamen and caudate. Chronic methamphetamine use may lead to a decrease in dopamine transporters in the dorsolateral prefrontal cortex; an increase in these transporters after a period of abstinence has not, however, been associated with a corresponding improvement in cognitive tasks. Even after a period of abstinence lasting months, there may be lower levels of the neuronal marker NAA in the basal ganglia. Methamphetamine users also tend to show deficits in decision-making tasks that are linked to regions in the frontal cortex, particularly the ventromedial frontal cortex.

Chronic cocaine use, defined both in terms of frequency and duration, is associated with poorer performance on a number of cognitive tasks relative to non-cocaine-using controls. These tasks call on executive control, manual dexterity, psychomotor speed, verbal learning and recall, and visuospatial skills; cocaine-dependent individuals users administered the Wisconsin Card Sorting Test show poorer short-term memory as well (Rosselli & Ardila, 1996). Performance on neuropsychological tests appears to be correlated to the amount of drug used over an individual's lifetime. Cocaine use constricts cerebral blood vessels and in doing so may disrupt blood flow to various parts of the brain. There is also evidence that chronic use adversely impacts white matter maturation experienced as individuals grow older (Bartzokis et al., 2000). Reduction in brain volume and impairments on cognitive tasks may persist years after abstinence. In one study (Fein et al., 2002) a group of abstinent crack-cocaine dependent individuals showed a significant amount of reduction in prefrontal gray matter volume compared to healthy, non-user controls.

ECSTASY

MDMA use is associated with serotonergic dysfunction (Yucel et al., 2008; Montoya et al., 2002). The impairments in visual and verbal memory seen in MDMA users are linked to serotonin function and levels of 5-HIAAA (a metabolite of serotonin) in the cerebrospinal fluid, and animal studies have shown neurotoxic effects of MDMA on serotonin and dopamine neurons (Lundqvist, 2005). Chronic, repeat users also show impairments in response inhibition, attention, and coding of information to long-term memory. Among adolescent users, abnormal functioning of the hippocampus is associated to poorer performance on tasks of working memory, an important executive function. In fMRI studies of MDMA users, abnormal activation patterns and functioning have also been observed in frontotemporal and parietal regions during working memory tests (e.g., Daumann et al., 2003). MDMA users who also consume other drugs suffer from decreased gray matter across various areas of the cortex, cerebellum, and brainstem (Cowan et al., 2003).

Neurocognitive deficits may remain for longer than six months after the period of abstinence commences. Impairments to memory and other cognitive faculties may be reversible, although the extent of recovery depends on the dosage and duration of drug use.

GENERAL ISSUES

A number of issues need to be addressed in future studies of neurocognitive impairments and neurobiological alterations in alcohol and drug users. One area of exploration is the similarities and differences in cognitive impairments when comparing different substances. Although many of the substances negatively impact similar cognitive domains, such as different aspects of memory and executive functioning, it is important to recognize the differences between substances. Doing so improves understanding of the impact of individual substances on the underlying neurobiological makeup and allows professionals to tailor more effective treatments to individuals with specific substance use disorders. For example, a comparison of heroin abusers and amphetamine abusers on measures of the Wisconsin Card Sorting Test showed that amphetamine abusers tend to perform more poorly on the measure of extra-dimensional shift but that both categories of users performed the pattern recognition measure with a similar deficits (Ornstein et al., 2000). Cognitive deficits may undermine treatment in substance using individuals even after they enter a period of abstinence; each substance may have its own negative impact on treatment strategies, which often require focus, attention, memory, and the ability to communicate, make decisions, and organize thought.

Another important issue to consider is that a number of alcohol and drug users frequently use multiple substances. A particularly frequent drug pairing, for example, is found in cannabis users who also drink. Additional research is needed on how multiple drugs interact to impact brain structure, neurotransmitter systems, and neurocognitive functioning and how the effects of polydrug use differ from the use of a single substance. One of the weaknesses in the research as of 2008 is a frequent failure to account for polydrug use in study subject populations. For example, studies have shown that drinking may be a significant confounding factor in the cognitive impairments seen in individuals with cocaine abuse (Bolla et al., 2000). Some research also suggests that cannabis may act as a confounding factor in the neuropsychological measures of ecstasy users (Croft et al., 2001).

Further investigation is needed on pre-existing neurocognitive vulnerabilities to substance use. While substance use itself exacerbates qualities such as impulsivity, lack of attention, and poor decision-making skills, there is strong evidence that these traits may also precede initial substance use. For example, individuals with attention deficit hyperactivity disorder (ADHD), conduct disorder, and/or antisocial personality disorder, as well as individuals who score high on ratings of sensation-seeking and novelty-seeking, have been shown to have a significantly higher risk of initiating substance use and developing substance use disorders than individuals without those traits or disorders (Kuperman et al., 2001; Kendler et al., 2003; Martin et al., 2002; Cloninger et al., 1995). Additionally, when substance use begins during late childhood or adolescence, when the brain has greater plasticity and is undergoing rapid developmental changes, the effects of the substance may become incorporated into brain development; for instance adolescent binge drinkers may experience more extensive damage to the frontal association cortex than later-onset binge drinkers. Substance use disorders are also highly comorbid with other psychiatric disorders, such as affective and anxiety disorders, which themselves contribute to alterations in brain structure and function and may negatively impact performance on neuropsychological tests. As of 2008 future studies were need to take better account of psychiatric comorbidity in study samples of substance users.

See also **Accidents and Injuries from Alcohol; Imaging Techniques: Visualizing the Living Brain.**

BIBLIOGRAPHY

Bartels, C., Kunert, H. J., Stawicki, S., Kroner-Herwig, B., Ehrenreich, H., & Krampe, H. (2007). Recovery of hippocampus-related functions in chronic alcoholics during monitored long-term abstinence. *Alcohol and Alcoholism, 42*(2), 92–102.

Bartzokis, G., Beckson, M., Lu, P. H., Edwards, N., Rapoport, R., Wiseman, E., et al. (2000). Age-related brain volume reductions in amphetamine and cocaine addicts and normal controls: Implications for addiction research. *Psychiatry Research, 98,* 93–102.

Bates, M. E., Bowden, S. C., & Barry, D. (2002). Neurocognitive impairment associated with alcohol use disorders: Implications for treatment. *Experimental and Clinical Psychopharmacology, 10*(3), 193–212.

Beatty, W. W., Tivis, R., Stott, H. D., Nixon, S. J., & Parsons, O. A. (2000). Neuropsychological deficits in sober alcoholics: Influences of chronicity and recent alcohol consumption. *Alcoholism: Clinical and Experimental Research, 24*(2), 149–154.

Block, R. I., O'Leary, D. S., Hichwa, R. D., Augustinack, J. C., Boles Ponto, L. L., & Ghoneim, M. M. (2002). Effects of frequent marijuana use on memory-related regional cerebral blood flow. *Pharmacology and Biochemical Behavior, 72*(1–2), 237–250.

Bolla, K. I., Brown, K., Eldreth, D., Tate, K., & Cadet, J. L. (2002). Dose-related neurocognitive effects of marijuana use. *Neurology, 59,* 1337–1343.

Bolla, K. I., Funderburk, F. R., & Cadet, J. L. (2000). Differential effects of cocaine and cocaine alcohol on neurocognitive performance. *Neurology, 54,* 2285–2292.

Cloninger, C. R., Sigvardsson, S., Pryzbeck, T. R., & Syrakic, D. M. (1995). Personality antecedents of alcoholism in a national area probability sample. *European Archives of Psychiatry and Clinical Neuroscience, 245*(4–5), 239–244.

Covault, J., Gelernter, J., Hesselbrock, V., Nellissery, M., & Kranzler, H. R. (2004). Allelic and haplotypic associated of GABRA2 with alcohol dependence. *American Journal of Medical Genetics, Part B: Neuropsychiatric Genetics, 129B,* 104–109.

Cowan, R. L., Lyoo, I. K., Sung, S. M., Ahn, K. H., Kim, M. J., Hwang, J., et al. (2003). Reduced cortical gray matter density in human MDMA (ecstasy) users: A voxel-based morphometry study. *Drug and Alcohol Dependence, 72,* 225–235.

Crews, F. T., Buckley, T., Dodd, P. R., Ende, G., Foley, N., Harper, C., et al. (2005). Alcoholic neurobiology: Changes in dependence and recovery. *Alcoholism: Clinical and Experimental Research, 29*(8), 1504–1513.

Croft, R. J., Mackay, A. J., Mills, A. T., & Gruzekuer, G. H. (2001). The relative contributions of ecstasy and cannabis to cognitive impairment. *Psychopharmacology (Berlin), 153,* 373–379.

Daumann, J., Fimm, B., Willmes, K., Thron, A., & Gouzoulis-Mayfrank, E. (2003). Cerebral activation in abstinent ecstasy (MDMA) users during a working memory task: A functional magnetic resonance imaging (fMRI) study. *Brain Research and Cognitive Brain Research, 16,* 479–487.

Davis, P. E., Liddiard, H., & McMillan, T. M. (2002). Neuropsychological deficits and opiate abuse. *Drug and Alcohol Dependence, 67,* 105–108.

De Rosa, E., Desmond, J. E., Anderson A. K., Pfefferbaum, A., & Sullivan, E. V. (2004). The human basal forebrain integrates the old and new. *Neurobiology, 41*(5), 825–837.

Desmond, J. E., Chen, S. H., DeRosa, E., Pryor, M. R., Pfefferbaum, A., & Sullivan, E. V. (2003). Increased fronto-cerebellar activation in alcoholics during verbal working memory: An fMRI study. *Neuroimage, 19,* 1510–1520.

Eckardt, M. J., File, S. E., Gessa, G. L., Grant, K. A., Guerri, C., Hoffman, P. L., et al. (1998). Effects of moderate alcohol consumption on the central nervous system. *Alcoholism: Clinical and Experimental Research, 22*(5), 998–1040.

Edenberg, H. J., Dick, D. M., Xuei, X., Tian, H., Almasy, L., Bauer, L. O., et al. (2004). Variations in GABRA2, encoding the α2 subunit of the GABAA receptor, are associated with alcohol dependence and with brain oscillations. *American Journal of Human Genetics, 74,* 704–714.

Ersche, K. D., Clark, L., London, M., Robbins, T. W., & Sahakian, B. J. (2006). Profile of executive and memory function associated with amphetamine and opiate dependence. *Neuropsychopharmacology, 31,* 1036–1047.

Fein, G., Di Sclafani, V., & Meyerhoff, D. J. (2002). Prefrontal cortical volume reduction associated with frontal cortex function deficit in 6-week abstinent crack-cocaine dependent men. *Drug and Alcohol Dependence, 68,* 87–93.

Fletcher, J. M., Page, J. B., Francis, D. J., Copeland, K., Naus, M. J., Davis, C. M., et al. (1996). Cognitive correlates of long-term cannabis use in Costa Rican men. *Archives of General Psychiatry, 53*(11), 1051–1057.

Grant, I., Gonzalez, R., Carey, C. L., Natarajan, L., & Wolfson, T. (2003). Non-acute (residual) neurocognitive effects of cannabis use: A meta-analytic study. *Journal of the International Neuropsychological Society, 9,* 679–689.

Guerra, D., Sole, A., Cami, J., & Tobena, A. (1987). Neuropsychological performance in opiate addicts after rapid detoxification. *Drug and Alcohol Dependence, 20,* 261–270.

Hill, R. C., Roemer, D., & Buescher, H. H. (1979). The preclinical testing of drugs for opiate-like dependence-producing properties. *Pharmacological Therapy, 5*(1–3), 505–509.

Johnson-Greene, D., Adams, K. M., Oilman, S., Koeppe, R. A., Junck, L., Kluin, K. J., et al. (1997). Effects of abstinence and relapse upon neuropsychological function and cerebral glucose metabolism in severe chronic alcoholism. *Journal of Clinical and Experimental Neuropsychology, 19*(3), 378–385.

Kaufman, J., Yang, B., Douglas-Palumberi, H., Crouse-Artus, M., Lipschitz, D., Krystal, J. H., et al. (2007). Genetic and environmental predictors of early alcohol use. *Biological Psychiatry, 61,* 1228–1223.

Kendler, K., Prescott, C. A., Myers, J., & Neale, M. C. (2003). The structure of genetic and environmental risk factors for common psychiatric and substance use disorders in men and women. *Archives of General Psychiatry, 60,* 929–937.

Kuperman, S., Schlosser, S. S., Kramer, J. R., Bucholz, K., Hesselbrock, V., Reich, T., et al. (2001). Developmental sequence from disruptive behavior diagnosis to adolescent alcohol dependence. *American Journal of Psychiatry, 158,* 2022–2026.

Lee, T. M., & Pau, C. W. (2002). Impulse control differences between abstinent heroin users and matched controls. *Brain Injury, 16*(10), 885–889.

Lundqvist, T. (2005). Cognitive consequences of cannabis use: Comparison with abuse of stimulants and heroin with regard to attention, memory and executive functions. *Pharmacology and Biochemical Behavior, 81,* 319–330.

Madden, G. J., Petry, N. M., Badger, G. J., & Bickel, W. K. (1997). Impulsive and self-control choices in opiod-dependent patients and non-drug-using control participants: Drug and monetary rewards. *Experimental and Clinical Psychopharmacology, 5*(3), 256–262.

Martin, C. A., Kelly, T. H., Rayens, M. K., Broqli, B. R., Brenzel, A., Smith, W. J., et al. (2002). Sensation seeking, puberty, and nicotine, alcohol, and marijuana use in adolescence. *Journal of the American Academy of Child and Adolescent Psychiatry, 41*(12), 1495–1502.

Mathew, R. J., Wilson, W. H., Coleman, R. E., Turkington, T. G., & DeGrado, T. R. (1997). Marijuana intoxication and brain activation in marijuana smokers. *Life Science, 60*(23), 2075–2089.

Montoya, A. G., Sorrentino, R., Lukas, S. E., & Price, B. H. (2002) Long-term neuropsychiatric consequences of "ecstasy" (MDMA): A review. *Harvard Review of Psychiatry, 10(4),* 212–220.

O'Neill, J., Cardenas, V. A., & Meyerhoff, D. J. (2001). Effects of abstinence on the brain: Quantitative magnetic resonance imaging and magnetic resonance spectroscopic imaging in chronic alcohol abuse. *Alcoholism: Clinical and Experimental Research 25*(11), 1673–1682.

Ornstein, T. J., Iddon, J. L., Balacchino, A. M., Sahakian, B. J., London, M., Everitt, B. J., et al. (2000). Profiles of cognitive dysfunction in chronic amphetamine and heroin abusers. *Neuropsychopharmacology, 23,* 113–1126.

Parsons, O. A. (1998). Neurocognitive deficits in alcoholics and social drinkers: A continuum? *Alcoholism: Clinical and Experimental Research 22*(4), 954–961.

Pau, C. W., Lee, T. M., & Chan, S. F. (2002). The impact of heroin on frontal executive functions. *Archives in Clinical Neuropsychology, 17*(7), 663–770.

Pfefferbaum, A., Desmond, J. E, Galloway, C., Menon, V., Glover, G. H., & Sullivan, E. V. (2001). Reorganization of frontal systems used by alcoholics for spatial working memory: An fMRI study. *Neuroimage, 14,* 7–20.

Pfefferbaum, A., Sullivan, E. V., Mathalon, D. H., Shear, P. K., Rosenbloom M. J., & Lim, K. O. (1995). Longitudinal changes in magnetic resonance imaging brain volumes in abstinent and relapsed alcoholics. *Alcoholism: Clinical and Experimental Research, 19*(5), 1177–1191.

Porjesz, B., Begleiter, H., Wang, K., Almasy, L., Chorlian, D. B, Stimus, A. T., et al. (2002). Linkage and linkage disequilibrium mapping of ERP and EEG phenotypes. *Biological Psychology, 61,* 229–248.

Rogers, R. D. & Robbins, T. W. (2001). Investigating the neurocognitive deficits associated with chronic drug misuse. *Current Opinions in Neurobiology, 11,* 250–257.

Rosselli, M., & Ardila, A. (1996). Cognitive effects of cocaine and polydrug abuse. *Journal of Clinical and Experimental Neuropsychology, 18*(1), 122–135.

Salo, R., Nordahl, T. E., Possin K., Leamon, M., Gibson, D. R., Galloway, G. P., et al. (2002). Preliminary evidence of reduced cognitive inhibition in methamphetamine-dependent individuals. *Psychiatry Research, 111,* 65–74.

Solowij, N., Stephens, R. S., Roffman R. A., Babor, T., Kadden, R., Miller, M., et al. (2002). Cognitive functioning of long-term heavy cannabis users seeking treatment. *Journal of the American Medical Association, 287*(9), 1123–1131.

Sullivan, E. V., Harding, A. J., Pentney, R., Dlugos, C., Martin P. R., Parks, M. H., et al. (2003). Disruption of frontocerebellar circuitry and function in alcoholism. *Alcoholism: Clinical and Experimental Research, 27*(2), 301–309.

Sullivan, E. V., Rosenbloom, M. J., & Pfefferbaum, A. (2000). Pattern of motor cognitive deficits in detoxified alcoholic men. *Alcoholism: Clinical and Experimental Research, 24*(5), 611–621.

Volkow, N. D., Gillespie, H., Mullani, N., Tancredi, L., Grant, C., Valentine, A., et al. (1996). Brain glucose metabolism in chronic marijuana users at baseline and during marijuana intoxication. *Psychiatry Research 67*(1), 29–38.

Peter L. Carlen
Mary Pat McAndrews
Revised by Mary Carvlin (2001)
Efrat Aharonovich (2009)

NUTRITIONAL

Malnutrition is a common problem among abusers of alcohol and other addictive substances, contributing significantly to their deleterious effects. Nutritional problems among alcohol and substance abusers begin with inadequate or poorly selected food intake and continue with incomplete absorption or metabolism of nutrients. The effects are often insidious, and may take many years to manifest themselves. This entry not only describes the various nutritional deficits associated with substance abuse but also explains the biologic mechanisms by which they occur.

ALCOHOL

Alcoholic beverages were long used as a source of nourishment for the sick, as a means of promoting appetite, and as a treatment for pain and infection. Traditionally, wine and beer were considered foods. They were used ceremonially, including as a part of ceremonial healing for ailing (and pregnant) persons who refused or could not tolerate a solid diet. Eventually, alcoholic beverages moved from use in purely ceremonial occasions to being a reason for social occasions in some cultures, among some classes, and for some individuals. However, alcoholic beverages have a habit-forming, or addictive, element, and for some people this can become a life-threatening or fatal addiction.

The Use of Alcohol in Medicine: Recent History. In 1900, Wilbur Atwater and Francis Benedict reported on experiments they conducted at Wesleyan University, in which they attempted to define whether alcohol could actually be considered a food. They showed that alcohol is oxidized in the body and that the energy so derived can indeed be used as a fuel for metabolic purposes. Before that, in 1877, Francis E. Anstie had written his treatise *On the Uses of Wine in Health and Disease.* In fact, the long tradition of using alcoholic beverages within the medical profession persisted into the twentieth century. Sir Robert Hutchison, a noted British physician, wrote in 1905 that there was reason to believe (not that there was evidence) that alcohol increases disease resistance. Alcohol was actually used to treat serious infectious disease, such as typhus, into the late 1920s—until it was shown that patients treated with milk and beef tea had better survival rates.

The use of alcohol to treat disease was based on the belief that it would somehow overcome disability and renew strength. Other than this use, the major indication for alcohol was for analgesia (pain suppression). The basic analgesic properties of alcohol and alcoholic beverages were utilized for hundreds of years in the management of the injured and those requiring surgery. Prior to the time of anesthetics, for example, patients were offered brandy to reduce the agonizing pain of amputations. The decline and cessation of these medical uses of alcohol came about with the development of inhalation anesthetics and more efficient analgesics.

Alcohol, Obesity, and Wasting. In nonalcoholics, calories from alcohol are utilized as efficiently as calories from carbohydrates or fats, and alcohol provides more calories per gram than carbohydrates. Indeed, while carbohydrates yield 4 kilocalories per gram (kcal/gm) on combustion, when alcohol is combusted in a bomb calorimeter it yields 7.1 kcal/gm. This suggests that when alcohol is consumed in addition to a diet that maintains body weight, weight gain occurs. Fictitious characters such as Shakespeare's Sir John Falstaff suggest that obesity was already considered a characteristic of heavy drinkers in the 1600s.

The realization came about gradually that in fact chronic heavy drinking leads not to obesity but to weight loss and an inability to sustain adequate nutritional status, a condition known as "wasting." Wasted alcoholics were first portrayed by British artists such as William Hogarth (1697–1764), who were intent on showing both the social and medical evils of drinking gin—a recent import to Britain from Holland that became a fad. All ages and classes of British society indulged in the new drink. In eighteenth- and nineteenth-century England, when artists were portraying the physical deterioration associated with heavy gin drinking, it was assumed that drinking eventually led to wasting only because the drunkard was disinterested in food. This idea persisted into the twentieth century. By the 1940s, it was also well recognized that chronic alcoholics are malnourished because of an impaired utilization of nutrients.

While obesity may occur in heavy eaters who consume alcohol, it is now well-known that chronic alcoholics are undernourished. Furthermore, studies have shown that long-term, heavy consumption of alcohol, in addition to food consumption, is not associated with the gain in body weight that would be expected from the calorie intake (Lieber, 1991). In addition, if dietary carbohydrate is replaced by alcohol, weight loss does occur (as in the so-called Drinking Man's Diet of the 1960s and 1970s). This energy deficit has been attributed to induction of the microsomal ethanol oxidizing system that metabolizes alcohol. Induction of this metabolic pathway results in increased sympathetic tone, generating heat. Charles S. Lieber, in reviewing current knowledge of the question in the early 1990s, noted that this does not explain the fact that there is little or no weight deficit when alcohol is consumed with a very low-fat diet.

Alcohol and Malnutrition. Diet-related causes of malnutrition in alcoholics include a low dietary intake of calories and nutrients. This low intake occurs because of poor appetite (which may result from the irritating effects of alcohol on the stomach lining), inebriation, and a diversion of food dollars into support of the alcohol habit. In addition, malnutrition may be caused by the impaired absorption of nutrients, poor nutrient utilization, and increased nutrient losses in body wastes. In 1940 it was suggested that alcoholism was the major cause of malnutrition in the industrialized world (Jolliffe, 1940). The impaired absorption of nutrients may result from the reduced absorptive capacity of the alcohol-damaged gut. Nutrients that are poorly absorbed by alcoholics include the B vitamins, particularly folic acid, thiamin (Vitamin B_1), and riboflavin (Vitamin B_2). Folic acid deficiency, which causes megaloblastic anemia, is particularly common in heavy drinkers.

Multiple nutritional deficiencies, including deficiencies of water- and fat-soluble vitamins, are also common in alcoholics who have pancreatic and liver disease. Chronic alcoholic pancreatitis (inflammation of the pancreas) is common in people who consume 150 grams (5.25 fl. oz) or more of alcohol per day for at least 10 years and also eat a high-fat diet. In these individuals the digestive functions of the pancreas become impaired, and therefore food is not broken down into nutrients that can be absorbed. This type of pancreatitis is a major cause of malabsorption of nutrients in alcoholics.

Alcoholic cirrhosis is a condition in which the liver cells responsible for the biotransformation of nutrients to metabolically active forms are replaced by fibrous tissue. Cirrhosis develops slowly in heavy drinkers and presents a special risk in those who consume about 35 percent or more of their total caloric intake as alcohol. Cirrhosis is the chief cause of impaired nutrient utilization in such individuals (Morgan, 1982). However, cirrhosis is caused not by a nutritional deficiency but by the toxic effects of alcohol on the liver (Lieber, 1988). Deficiencies of minerals and trace elements, particularly zinc, are common in alcoholics. Contributory causes are low intake and increased losses in the urine.

Alcohol, Nutrition, and Brain Damage. When they go on drinking sprees during which they do not eat food, alcoholics put themselves at risk for brain damage. Evidence exists for this condition only in Caucasians who are genetically predisposed, however. An acute confusional state known as Wernicke's encephalopathy may occur in those who engage in these bouts of drinking. This condition can be rapidly reversed, however, if the patient is given massive doses of intravenous thiamin within a period of 48 hours from the onset of the symptoms. If this acute condition is not treated with thiamin, a chronic state of irreversible brain damage, known as Korsakoff's syndrome, or Korsakoff's pychosis, develops, in which there is moderate-to-severe dementia (Victor et al., 1971).

Alcohol and Heart Disease. In the 1990s, evidence indicated that while moderate drinking may reduce the risk of heart disease, alcohol abuse increased the risk of heart disease. Alcohol has the effect of increasing blood (plasma) levels of high-density lipoproteins (HDL), and an elevation of these blood lipids is associated with a lower risk of heart disease. In a 1992 British study, it was shown that women who consume a moderate amount of alcohol (1–20 g/day) have lower triglyceride (fat) levels and higher HDL levels in their blood (Razay et al., 1992). This was interpreted by the authors of the study as strong evidence for supporting a lower risk of heart disease. It is important to note, however, that in this study the women who were the moderate drinkers were also slimmer than the nondrinking group, and lower body weight is also known to reduce the risk of heart disease. Since then, studies that have controlled for this and other potential confounding factors have shown that moderate alcohol consumption does have a cardioprotective effect. Heart disease in alcoholics, in addition to resulting from the nutritional imbalance associated with chronic heavy drinking, can also result from the direct toxic effects of alcohol on the heart muscle (Brigden & Robinson, 1964).

Alcohol and Osteoporosis. As with heart disease, the effects of alcohol on bone formation can be positive or negative, depending on the demographic group studied and the amount of alcohol consumed. Data from the Framingham Heart Study, for example, suggest that consumption of at least 7 ounces of alcohol per week can improve bone mineral densities in older postmenopausal women. This effect is not fully understood, but it may be due to an augmentation of estrogen levels (Felson et al., 1995). The formation of new bone tissue in heavy drinkers, by contrast, is reduced in both men and women. This causes a marked decrease in bone mass and strength, leading to severe osteoporosis. Alcohol has a direct effect on bone formation, and there are also metabolic effects, including deleterious effects on Vitamin D metabolism, parathyroid hormone, and calcitonin (Sampson, 1997). Because inebriation is also associated with a high risk of falls, alcoholics who have osteoporosis are at particular risk to sustain hip fractures. While many of these effects are metabolic in nature and not directly linked to poor nutritional status, an inadequate intake of foods rich in calcium in favor of "empty" alcohol calories is an additional risk factor for osteoporosis in alcoholics (Bikle et al., 1985).

Methods for Assessing Nutritional Status in Alcoholics. One method used to assess caloric and nutrient intake in actively drinking alcoholics is direct observation, which is seldom feasible outside a treatment facility. Another method, which is also feasible only in the detoxification section of a rehabilitation facility, hospital, or nursing home, involves weighing food served.

When alcoholics are asked to recount what they have eaten, however, they may not report accurately. For example, when asked leading questions, they may provide answers that the question indicates are correct or ideal. They may provide the questioner with an account of a make-believe diet, or they may exaggerate the amounts of food they have eaten. These responses, which are worthless for the purpose of assessing the amount of calories consumed from food or for assessing the nutrients consumed, may be given by alcoholics who do not remember what they have eaten, or the purpose may be to please the dietitian, physician, or nurse seeking the information. Alcoholics may also exaggerate the amount they eat, reporting what has been served to them rather than what was actually consumed. (This type of over-reporting of food intake is also frequently found in people consuming other drugs that suppress the appetite.)

The presence of malnutrition is assessed in alcoholics (as well as non-alcoholics) by using anthropometric (body) measurements—including weight-for-height measurements, calculation of the body mass index (BMI, a person's body weight divided by the square of his or her height), or the circumference of the upper arm and the thickness of the fat on the back of the arm. Alcoholics show muscle wasting in the upper arms, which may suggest malnutrition even when body weight is not markedly decreased. Although alcoholics with advanced liver disease are frequently wasted, weight loss may not register in numerical terms because of fluid retention within the abdominal cavity (ascites).

Biochemical measurements are valuable for assessing the nutritional status of alcoholics. The measurement of plasma albumin levels is particularly important, for a value of less than 3.5 grams per 100 milliliters of plasma indicates that protein-energy malnutrition exists.

Nutrient Intolerance in Alcoholics with Liver Disease. Alcoholics with liver disease are very intolerant of high-protein diets. If high-protein diets are provided during periods of nutritional rehabilitation, alcoholics may develop signs of liver failure. Such alcoholics are also intolerant of Vitamin A if this vitamin is taken in amounts that exceed 10,000 international units (IU) per day. Continued intake of Vitamin A at a high daily dosage can worsen liver damage and precipitate liver failure (Roe, 1992).

Nutritional Rehabilitation of Alcoholics. The nutritional rehabilitation of alcoholics can be carried out successfully only when abstinence is enforced or the alcoholic voluntarily stops drinking. If an alcoholic has advanced liver disease or impairment of pancreatic function such that digestion and absorption of nutrients are impaired, optimal nutritional status cannot be maintained. The goal of nutritional rehabilitation is the treatment of existing protein-energy malnutrition by increasing caloric intake from carbohydrates and the treatment of existing vitamin, mineral, and trace-element deficiencies. The appetite will return after alcohol withdrawal symptoms have abated, but the efficient absorption of vitamins may not be recovered until 10 to 14 days after drinking ceases. Intolerance of milk and other dairy foods is common during rehabilitation, because alcohol inhibits lactase, an enzyme involved in the digestion of milk sugars. Because of the resulting lactose intolerance, as well as the protein intolerance mentioned earlier, extreme caution should be exercised in diet prescription (Roe, 1979).

TOBACCO

Smoking diminishes the appetite, so that, on average, smokers have lower body weights than nonsmokers. Nevertheless, on average, smokers have greater waist-to-hip circumference ratios than nonsmokers. This suggests that smoking may have an effect on body-fat distribution. Central (torso) adiposity, reflected by this change in circumferential measurements, has been shown to increase the risk of cardiovascular disease. The cessation of smoking is usually associated with moderate weight gain, at least in part because of increased food intake (Troisi et al., 1991). Smoking is also associated with the depletion of systemic antioxidants, including vitamins A and C. The depletion of these vitamins may be partly responsible for some of the deleterious effects of smoking (Yanbaeva, 2007).

MULTIPLE SUBSTANCE ABUSE AND NUTRITION

The effects of multiple-drug use on nutrition depend on the properties and toxic characteristics of the drugs used, as well as the dose, frequency, and duration of use, as well as the time in life when the drugs are used. Narcotic drugs, such as heroin, impair appetite, so food intake is often diminished. If the drug is injected intravenously, malnutrition may be secondary to blood-borne bacterial infection or acquired immunodeficiency syndrome (AIDS). Amphetamine ("speed") is the stimulant drug that most inhibits appetite. If taken in large doses, amphetamines also prevent sleep and stimulate activity, so energy expenditure may be high and weight loss is common.

Cocaine and crack are also stimulants. They reduce appetite and may induce gastrointestinal symptoms such as nausea, which further lessens food intake (Brody et al., 1990). In general, unlike tobacco or alcohol abuse, the abuse of narcotic and stimulant drugs is not associated with the depletion of specific micronutrients. Rather, their use results in a general apathy toward food, characterized by a lack of appetite and, in many cases, a lack of interest in the quality of the food.

In a 1995 study of 140 cocaine- and heroin-addicted persons (without organic pathology) admitted to a hospital for detoxification, 92 percent weighed under the mean for the population and 30 percent weighed less than 80 percent of the mean for the population. Eighteen percent of the patients were considered to be severely malnourished. The majority (66%) of the patients were anorexic upon admission, with an average caloric intake of 978 kcal/day for females and 1265 kcal/day for males. Among an additional 18 patients admitted with both drug addiction and acute organic pathology, nutritional status was universally poor. The investigators noted that malnutrition in this addicted population was most closely related to female sex, degree of addiction, anorexia with poor caloric and fluid intake, and disturbed family and social support (Santolaria-Fernández et al., 1995).

SUBSTANCE ABUSE AND NUTRITION IN PREGNANCY

Relationships between substance abuse of pregnant women and impaired nutrition of their fetuses and newborns were summarized in a 1990 report by the U.S. Institute of Medicine, a branch of the National Academy of Sciences, titled *Nutrition during Pregnancy.*

Alcohol use during pregnancy can lead to poor birth outcomes. One condition in infants with specific defects in neuronal and cranial development is designated "fetal alcohol syndrome." Even the daily consumption of more than two glasses of wine or a daily mixed drink can lead to fetal alcohol syndrome, but this condition is most common among the offspring of mothers who are chronic heavy drinkers or binge drinkers. Alcohol use during pregnancy is also known to be associated with prenatal and postnatal growth retardation. After birth, infants of heavy drinkers may fail to suck, either because of the presence of withdrawal symptoms or because of cleft palate (which may be part of the fetal alcohol syndrome).

Cigarette smoking during pregnancy can affect both maternal and fetal nutrition (Werler et al., 1985). Effects are due to an increased metabolic rate in smokers and to toxic effects from tobacco that impair the mother's utilization of certain nutrients, including iron, Vitamin C, folic acid, and zinc. Low-birth-weight infants are more likely to be the offspring of smokers than of nonsmokers. Scientists originally thought that this was because smokers consumed fewer calories than nonsmokers, and because the transfer of nutrients from the mother to the fetus via the placenta was reduced in smokers. While research continues to show that smoking has a negative impact on birth weight, scientists are now questioning whether this is due to poor nutrition or some other toxic effect of smoking (Matthews et al., 1999).

Cocaine and amphetamine use in pregnancy also lead to increased numbers of low-birth-weight infants. This may be caused by low food intake by the mother, for these drugs do reduce appetite. The risk of malnutrition in the newborns of women who have used cocaine during pregnancy is caused by the abnormal development of the infant's small intestine. These intestinal disorders in the infant may be extremely severe and may be associated with enterocolitis or bowel perforation, which can be fatal. If these infants survive, special methods of feeding via a vein (parenteral nutrition) are required. Although drugs other than cocaine are known to cause a constriction of blood vessels in pregnant women, only cocaine has been shown to produce these bowel disorders in infants (Telsey et al., 1988; Spinazzola et al., 1992).

See also **Alcohol: Chemistry and Pharmacology; Alcohol: History of Drinking; Complications: Liver (Clinical); Overeating and Other Excessive Behaviors.**

BIBLIOGRAPHY

Anstie, F. E. (1877). *On the uses of wine in health and disease.* London: Macmillan.

Atwater, W. O., & Benedict, F. B. Experiments on the metabolism of matter and energy in the human body. DOA Bulletin No. 69. Washington, DC: U.S. Department of Agriculture.

Bikle, D. D., Genant, H. K., Cann, C., Recker, R. R., Halloran, B. P., & Strewler, G. J. (1985). Bone disease in alcohol abuse. *Annals of Internal Medicine, 103,* 42–48.

Brigden, W., & Robinson, J. (1964). Alcoholic heart disease. *British Medical Journal, 2*(5420), 1283–1289.

Brody, S. L., Slovis, C. M., & Wrenn, K. D. (1990). Cocaine-related medical problems: Consecutive series of 233 patients. *American Journal of Medicine, 88*(4), 325–330.

Felson, D. T., Zhang, Y., Hannan, M. T., Kannel, W. B., & Kiel, D. P. (1995). Alcohol intake and bone mineral density in elderly men and women: The Framingham Study. *American Journal of Epidemiology, 142*(5), 485–492.

Hutchison, R. (1905). *Food and the principles of dietetics.* New York: W. Wood.

Jolliffe, N. (1940). The influence of alcohol on the adequacy of B vitamins in the American diet. *Quarterly Journal of the Study of Alcohol, 1,* 74–84.

Lieber, C. S. (1988). The influence of alcohol on nutritional status. *Nutrition Review, 46*(7), 241–251.

Lieber, C. S. (1991). Perspectives: Do alcohol calories count? *American Journal of Clinical Nutrition, 54*(6), 976–982.

Matthews, F., Yudkin, P., & Neil, A. (1999). Influence of maternal nutrition on outcome of pregnancy: Prospective cohort study. *British Medical Journal, 319*(7206), 339–343.

Morgan, M. Y. (1982). Alcohol and nutrition. *British Medical Bulletin, 38,* 21–29.

Razay, G., Heaton, K. W., Bolton, C. H., & Hughes, A. O. (1992). Alcohol consumption and its relation to cardiovascular risk factors in British women. *British Medical Journal, 304,* 80–83.

Roe, D. A. (1979). *Alcohol and the diet.* Westport, CT: AVI.

Roe, D. A. (1992). *Geriatric nutrition.* Englewood Cliffs, NJ: Prentice Hall.

Sampson, H. W. (1997). Alcohol, osteoporosis and bone regulating hormones. *Alcoholism Clinical and Experimental Research, 21*(3), 400–403.

Santolaria-Fernández, F. J., Gomez-Sirvent, J. L., Gonzales-Reimers, C. E., Batista-Lopez, J. N., Jorge-Hernandez, J. A., Rodriguez-Moreno, F., et al. (1995). Nutritional assessment of drug addicts. *Drug and Alcohol Dependence, 38*(1), 11–18.

Spinazzola, R., Kenigsberg, K., Usmani, S. S., & Harper, R. G. (1992). Neonatal gastrointestinal complications of maternal cocaine abuse. *New York State Journal of Medicine, 92*(1), 22–23.

Telsey, A. M., Merrit, A., & Dixon, S. D. (1988). Cocaine exposure in a term neonate: Necrotizing enterocolitis as a complication. *Clinical Pediatrics, 27*(11), 547–550.

Troisi, R. J., Heinold, J. W., Vokonas, P. S., & Weiss, S. T. (1991). Cigarette smoking, dietary intake and physical activity: Effects on body fat distribution—the Normative Aging Study. *American Journal of Clinical Nutrition, 53*(5), 1104–1111.

U.S. Institute of Medicine. (1990). *Nutrition during pregnancy.* Washington, DC: National Academy Press.

Victor, M., Adams, R. D., & Collins, G. H. (1971). *The Wernicke-Korsakoff syndrome: A clinical and pathological study of 245 patients, 82 with post-mortem examination.* Philadelphia: F. A. Davis.

Werler, M. M., Pober, B. R., & Holmes, L. B. (1985). Smoking and pregnancy. *Teratology, 32*(3), 473–481.

Yanbaeva, D. G., Dentener, M. A., & Creutzberg, E. C., et al. (2007). Systemic effects of smoking. *Chest,* 131, 1557–1566.

DAPHNE ROE
REVISED BY MARY CARVLIN (2001)
LEAH R. ZINDEL (2009)

ROUTE OF ADMINISTRATION

The mode of drug administration—ingestion (by mouth), nasal insufflation (snorting), inhalation (smoking), or injection (intravenous, subcutaneous, or intramuscular)—can be responsible for a number of medical complications to alcohol and other drug use. These complications are discussed as direct and indirect results of the various modes (route) of administration.

COMPLICATIONS DUE TO INGESTION

Ingestion is the way alcohol, liquid medicines, pills, and capsules are usually taken. Ingested drugs enter the gastrointestinal (GI) system, undergo some digestive processing, and enter the bloodstream through the walls of the stomach and intestines. Most medical complications from drug ingestion are a result of the corrosive and irritant effects of the drugs on the GI system. Alcohol and a variety of medicines, including aspirin, can cause intense, localized irritation to the GI mucous membranes, leading to ulceration and GI bleeding. Pharmaceutical manufacturers attempt to decrease the danger of GI irritation by adding buffers to their pills and capsules. Buffers are inert or non-active ingredients that cushion the corrosive effect of the active ingredients. However, if drug users attempt to dissolve pills intended for oral use and inject them, these buffers will often cause problems, such as abscesses or embolisms.

COMPLICATIONS DUE TO NASAL INSUFFLATION (SNORTING)

Medical complications from nasal insufflation (snorting) are usually caused by stimulant drugs, such as the amphetamines or cocaine. These drugs are breathed into the nose and absorbed into the bloodstream through the capillaries in the nasal mucous membrane. While these drugs cause a certain amount of surface irritation, the major damage is caused by their action as vasoconstrictors—they reduce the diameter of blood vessels and with chronic use can severely limit the delivery of blood through the capillaries to the inner membranes of the nose. The result of this is that tissue damaged by contact with the drugs is unable to repair itself, and progressive necrosis (tissue death) follows. With chronic cocaine use, this process can result in actual holes through the septum (the dividing tissue) between the nostrils. When tobacco is insufflated as snuff, the risk of cancer of the nasal passages is increased.

The nasal insufflation of drugs—especially heroin—can trigger asthmatic attacks serious enough to require treatment in a hospital intensive care unit (ICU). In one inner-city hospital, 56 percent of patients admitted to the ICU for severe asthma reported snorting heroin. Attacks were reported more frequently, but not exclusively, when the heroin was cut (combined) with adulterants such as Vitamin B_{12} or diphenhydramine, an antihistamine. None of the patients reported heroin as an asthma trigger following initial insufflation, suggesting that the attacks stem not from a direct irritant effect, but rather from a gradual allergic sensitization to the drug.

Complications Due to Smoking (Inhaling). The fastest delivery of large amounts of drug directly to the brain is through smoking (inhaling). Drugs taken in this way go directly to the lungs and are absorbed along with oxygen directly into the blood heading for the brain. The two terms, smoking and inhaling, as a means of drug intake, are clearly differentiated when, on the one hand, material is actually burned and the resulting smoke is taken into the lungs—as with tobacco or marijuana—or on the other hand, when fumes from volatile substances are inhaled, such as glue or gasoline. They may be confused or used interchangeably, however, when material is vaporized through heat and the vapor is inhaled—as with cocaine freebase (crack).

Smoking. Smoke from any material will act as an irritant to the lungs and bronchial system, eventually causing problems that can range from chronic bronchitis to emphysema or cancer of the mouth, throat, and/or lungs. Both tobacco and marijuana contain a number of tars and potential carcinogens (cancer-triggering substances), and both produce potentially toxic concentrations of carbon monoxide. Though it has been argued that tobacco is the worst danger because it is smoked very frequently, it has also been pointed out that the mode of using marijuana is worse—holding the smoke in the lungs for a long time. Epidemiologic studies have yet to prove conclusively that marijuana smoke causes severe lung disease or cancer, though its use has been linked to chronic bronchitis and emphysema. As a vasoconstrictor, nicotine in tobacco promotes mouth ulceration and gum disease. It can be said that people who smoke lose their teeth, while those who don't, don't. Besides its irritant effects, the smoking of tobacco may also promote respiratory disease by weakening the immune system and by paralyzing the cilia (the tiny hairlike organs) in the cells of the lungs that push out foreign matter.

Inhalation (Sniffing). The inhalation (sniffing) of volatile hydrocarbons, such as solvents, can cause death by asphyxiation or suffocation, can impair judgment, and may produce irrational, reckless behavior. Abnormalities also have occurred in liver and kidney functions, and bone-marrow damage has occurred. These may be due to hypersensitivity to the substances or chronic heavy exposure. Chromosome damage and blood abnormalities have been reported, and solvents have been cited as a cause of gastritis (inflammation of the stomach), hepatitis (inflammation of the liver), jaundice, and peptic ulcers; however, such effects are due more to the actions of the drugs than to the route of administration. Chronic users have developed slow-healing ulcers around the mouth and nose, loss of appetite, weight loss, and nutritional disorders. Irreversible brain damage has been reported, too. Many deaths attributed to solvent inhalants are caused by suffocation when users pass out with the plastic bags containing the substance still covering their noses and mouths. There is also a very real danger of death from acute solvent poisoning or aerosol inhalation. The mere provision of adequate ventilation and the avoidance of sticking one's head in a plastic bag are by no means sufficient safeguards against aerosol dangers.

Other hazards may include freezing the larynx or other parts of the airway when refrigerants are inhaled and potential spasms as these areas defrost. Blockage of the pulmonary membrane, through which oxygen is absorbed into the lungs, can also occur. Death may also result from the ingestion of toxic ingredients along with the aerosol substance. The possibility is made more likely by the fact that commercial products not produced for human consumption are not required to list their ingredients on the label. Individual substances may produce a spectrum of toxic reactions depending on their contents. These have included gastric pain, headaches, drowsiness, irritability, nausea, mucous-membrane irritation, confusion, tremors, nerve paralysis, optic-nerve damage, vomiting, lead poisoning, and anemia. The inhaling of aerosol fluorocarbons can cause sudden-sniffing death (SSD), wherein the heart is hypersensitized to the body's own hormone epinephrine (adrenaline), leading to a very erratic heartbeat, increased pulse rate, and cardiac arrest.

The inhaling of amyl, butyl, or isobutyl nitrites can cause intense headaches, an abrupt drop in blood pressure, and loss of consciousness through orthostatic hypotension (increased heart rate and palpitations), with a threat of myocardial infarction (heart attack).

COMPLICATIONS DUE TO INJECTION

The injection of drugs generally involves the use of the hypodermic needle, first invented in the early nineteenth century and used initially for the medical delivery of the opiate painkiller morphine, for the rapid control of intense pain. This combination was first used extensively for battlefield wounds during the Crimean War (1853–1856) and the American Civil War (1861–1865). As its name implies, the hypodermic needle pierces the skin—the dermis. Hypodermic injections may be subcutaneous, directly beneath the skin surface; intramuscular, into the muscle tissue; or intravenous, into a vein. (A number of injection-related medical complications are directly skin-related.)

While the hypodermic needle is the primary means of drug injection, drug addicts who do not have access to hypodermics have made use of a number of ingenious, and often very dangerous, substitutes. Nonhypodermic-needle means of injection may involve such paraphernalia as lancets or scalpels, or any small sharp blade to make an opening, and the insertion of an eyedropper, tubing and bulb, or any means of squirting the drug into the resultant wound. In extremes, addicts have used such implements as a pencil, ballpoint or fountain pen, or the sharpened end of a spoon.

Intra-arterial Injection. Injections are never made intentionally into arteries. Accidental intra-arterial injection will produce intense pain, swelling, cyanosis (blueness), and coldness of the body extremity injected. Intra-arterial injection resulting in these symptoms is a medical emergency and, if untreated, may produce gangrene of the fingers, hands, toes, or feet and result in possible required amputation of these parts.

Transmittal of Disease through Injection. The greatest number and variety of medical complications of drug use caused by the mode of administration occur as a result of injection. Among the highest risk, and that with the most frequent fatal and disabling consequences, is the transmittal of disease through the use of non-sterile needles and the sharing of such needles.

Human Immunodeficiency Virus (HIV). Needle-using drug abusers comprise one of the primary high-risk populations for contracting human immunodeficiency virus (HIV). The primary recognized routes of transmission for HIV are (1) sexual contact through unprotected anal or vaginal intercourse—particularly if there are damaged tissues or sores present that provide direct access to the bloodstream; (2) contact with infected blood through needle sharing or through transfusions of blood or blood products; and (3) in utero or at-birth transmission from a mother to her baby. Acquired immunodeficiency syndrome (AIDS), the most severe and life-threatening result of HIV infection, involves the destruction of the infected person's immune system and the development of cancers and infections that the body can no longer fight off.

The incidence of HIV infection among needle-using drug abusers is closely related to local use traditions, habits, and the prevalence of HIV infection among other addicts. The highest incidence is in areas such as New York City, where there is a tradition of needle sharing or where *shooting galleries*—places where users can rent or share *works*—are commonly used and where there is a high prevalence of HIV among the homosexual population. Users in other geographical locations, such as San Francisco, seem to be more conservative in their social-usage patterns, and when they do share needles, tend to keep the same *shooting partners* over a longer period of time. HIV-prevention efforts in some areas have focused on needle and syringe exchange, while others, particularly where needle exchange is not legalized, have community-outreach workers teaching users how to sterilize their needles between each use with household bleach. The gist of both campaigns is that users who share their needles or who use dirty needles are at risk for contracting HIV through their drug use. Those who use sterile needles are not. Both approaches are considered stopgap, however, and are apt to be condemned as encouraging of drug abuse.

All needle-using drug abusers are considered at extremely high risk for HIV infection, and HIV screening is performed routinely at most drug-treatment centers. The virus has a long incubation period and may be present for seven or more years before active symptoms of opportunistic disease appear. Early symptoms may include: a persistent rash or lesion; unexplained weight loss; persistent night sweats or low-grade fever; persistent diarrhea or fatigue; swollen lymph glands, depression or states of mental confusion.

Hepatitis and Other Liver Disorders. Hepatitis B and Hepatitis C, often referred to as serum (fluid-related) hepatitis, are the most common medical complication of needle drug use. Like HIV, hepatitis can spread in other ways than needle use, such as sexual intercourse or other direct sharing of blood and bodily fluids. Several strains, however, can be spread by contaminated foods, particularly shellfish, or by unhygienic practices in food handling. Research in the 2000s indicates that some forms of hepatitis spread via an anal/oral progression, so it is recommended that hands are washed thoroughly after all bowel movements or any other anal-area or fecal-matter handling, as a means of prophylaxis.

Unlike AIDS, hepatitis is often not fatal if it is detected and treated at an early stage. Symptoms of all forms of hepatitis include fatigue, loss of appetite, pain in the upper abdomen, jaundice (yellow skin and a yellowish-to-chartreuse tinge to the sclerae [white of the eye]), general itching, dark urine reaching the color of cola drinks with light-tan to cream-colored feces, and mental depression. Gamma globulin injection can provide short-term immunity to all forms of hepatitis and can reduce the symptoms of serum hepatitis if it is given during the gestation period. Treatment includes bed rest, nutritional support, and avoidance of alcohol or any other substance that may further irritate the liver. Caregivers should wear rubber gloves while handling patients. Patients with any form of hepatitis should avoid preparing food for others and use separate towels, bed linens, and eating utensils until symptoms disappear. Toilet seats and any spilled bedpan matter should be disinfected and hands should then be washed thoroughly with soap. Condoms should be used for any genital contact.

Hepatitis can cause hepatic fibrosis—development of fibrous tissue in the liver. It can also cause or exacerbate cirrhosis (scarring of the liver), although this is most often a result of chronic alcohol abuse. Symptoms of cirrhosis include jaundice (yellowish skin and eye whites), fatigue, ankle swelling, enlargement of the abdomen, and a full feeling in the right upper abdomen.

Tetanus and Malaria. According to Senay and Raynes, the first case of tetanus associated with needle-using substance abuse was reported in England in 1886. By the 1990s, between 70 and 90 percent of tetanus cases occurred to drug abusers. As a medical complication to drug injection, tetanus most often occurs from *skin-popping*, which is cutaneous injection. A majority of cases occur in women, and this is attributed to less-substantial venous development than in men and a smaller population with tetanus immunization.

Malaria (caused by the Plasmodium parasite) was first reported among drug users in the United States in 1926. It affects intravenous drug abusers and was brought to the United States by needle-sharing sailors who had been exposed to malaria in Africa. The initial outbreak in New Orleans spread to New York City in the 1930s and resulted in several hundred deaths from tertian malaria among drug abusers. A second outbreak occurred in the 1970s, as a result of malaria-infected U.S. veterans returning to the States from Vietnam.

The spread of both these diseases among needle-sharing drug abusers has been kept somewhat in check, particularly on the East Coast and in Chicago, by the inclusion of 15 to 30 percent quinine (a natural antimalarial), as filler, to stretch profits in illicit opioid drug mixtures in those areas. Quinine (an alkaloid from chinchona bark) is a protoplasmic poison that prevents the germination of the fastidious tetanus anaerobe, Clostridium tetani, under the skin and in adjacent muscle tissue. Although the quinine amount is not sufficient to eradicate malaria once it has taken hold in the body, it does help prevent the disease by killing the malarial parasites in the hypodermic syringe.

COMPLICATIONS TO HEART AND BLOOD VESSELS

Drug abuse is related to a number of heart and blood vessel medical complications. Some of these, such as alcoholic cardiomyopathy, are a direct result of the drug's toxic effects. Others are at least partially related to needle use.

Endocarditis, an infection of the tissues in the heart, usually a heart valve, is a progressive disease characterized by frequent embolization (fragments that break off from the inflamed area and travel in the bloodstream, where they can obstruct blood vessels) and severe heart-valve destruction that can be fatal if not treated. This disease can result from repeated injection of the infective agents into the blood system, usually from nonsterile needles and/or unusual methods of injection. Infective endocarditis is highly prevalent among drug abusers and should be suspected in any needle-using abuser who shows such symptoms as the following: fever of unknown origin; heart murmur; pneumonia; embolic phenomena; or blood cultures that are positive for Candida, Staphylococcus aureus, or enterococcus, or Gram-negative organisms.

MISCELLANEOUS COMPLICATIONS

Blood-vessel changes caused by necrotizing angiitis (polyarteritis—the inflammation of a number of arteries) or a swelling that leads to tissue loss have been demonstrated in intravenous amphetamine abusers, resulting in cerebrovascular occlusion (blockage in brain blood vessels) and intracranial hemorrhage or stroke.

Problems in the lungs often develop from inert materials that are included as cutting agents or as buffers and binding agents in drugs that come in pill form but are liquified and injected. These substances do not dissolve, so their particles may become lodged in the lungs, causing chronic pulmonary fibrosis and foreign-body granulomas. These same buffers and binding agents may also become lodged in various capillary systems, including the tiny blood vessels in the eye.

Finally, injection-induced infections reaching the skeleton can be responsible for such bone diseases as septic arthritis and osteomyelitis. Gangrene can develop from cutting off circulation to the extremities and may necessitate amputation or be fatal.

See also **Inhalants: Extent of Use and Complications; Needle and Syringe Exchanges and HIV/AIDS.**

BIBLIOGRAPHY

Cohen, S., & Gallant, D. M. (1981). *Diagnosis of drug and alcohol abuse.* Brooklyn, NY: Career Teacher Center, State University of New York.

Henry, J. A. (2003). Comparing cannabis with tobacco. *British Medical Journal, 326,* 942–943.

Krantz, A. J., Hershow, R. C., Prachand, N., et. al. (2003). Heroin insufflation as a trigger for patients with life-threatening asthma. *Chest, 123,* 510–517.

Senay, E. C., & Raynes, A. E. (1977). *Treatment of the drug abusing patient for treatment staff physicians.* Arlington, VA: National Drug Abuse Center.

Seymour, R. B., & Smith, D. E. (1987). *The physician's guide to psychoactive drugs.* New York: Haworth.

Seymour, R. B., & Smith, D. E. (1990). Identifying and responding to drug abuse in the workplace. *Journal of Psychoactive Drugs, 22*(4), 383–406.

Wilford, B. B. (1981). *Drug abuse: A guide for the primary care physician.* Chicago: American Medical Association.

DAVID E. SMITH
RICHARD B. SEYMOUR
REVISED BY RALPH MYERSON (2001)
LEAH R. ZINDEL (2009)

COMPULSIONS. Historically, compulsions have been described as difficult to resist behaviors, regardless of the motivation. In psychiatry, the term has been used classically to describe repetitive behaviors that are performed with the goal of reducing or preventing anxiety or distress. These uncomfortable feelings have historically been referred to as "ego-dystonic." These behaviors contrast with ones motivated by the seeking of pleasure or gratification, behaviors that have been termed hedonic or "ego-syntonic." Within this context, the term "compulsion" has been applied in particular to obsessive-compulsive disorder (OCD). In OCD, compulsive behaviors are considered unwanted or distressing, and these behaviors contrast with pleasurable or hedonic ones seen in other disorders; for example, sensation- or euphoria-seeking aspects of drug addiction. In the early twenty-first century, a greater appreciation of the alterations in motivation underlying behaviors in addiction influenced the conceptualization of compulsive behaviors in addiction. Compulsions may be conceptualized as behaviors that are performed in the absence of reinforcement. As such, drug-seeking and drug-taking behaviors in drug addiction typically become more habitual or compulsive over time. Investigations of habit formation in preclinical models implicate an important role for the brain region called the dorsal striatum, and investigations of drug dependent individuals also implicate this brain region. These and other data support the notion that as behaviors move from being impulsive to compulsive in nature, there is progressive involvement of dorsal as compared to ventral portions of the striatum in the decision-making processes governing engagement in motivated behaviors.

See also **Addiction: Concepts and Definitions.**

BIBLIOGRAPHY

Belin, D., & Everitt, B. J. (2008). Cocaine seeking habits depend upon dopamine-dependent serial connectivity linking the ventral with the dorsal striatum. *Neuron, 57,* 432–441.

Brewer, J. A., & Potenza, M. N. (2008). The neurobiology and genetics of impulse control disorders: Relationships to drug addictions. *Biochemical Pharmacolology, 75,* 63–75.

Everitt, B. J., & Robbins, T. W. (2005). Neural systems of reinforcement for drug addiction: From actions to habits to compulsion. *Nature Neuroscience, 8,* 1481–1489.

Grant, J. E., & Potenza, M. N. (2006). Compulsive aspects of impulse control disorders. *Psychiatric Clinics of North America, 29,* 539–551.

Yin, H. H., & Knowlton, B. J. (2006). The role of the basal ganglia in habit formation. *Nature Reviews Neuroscience, 7,* 464–476.

MARC N. POTENZA

COMPUTERIZED DIAGNOSTIC INTERVIEW SCHEDULE FOR DSM-IV (C DIS-IV). Developed in the late 1970s for use in the first epidemiological multisite study of the prevalence and incidence of psychiatric disorders in the United States, the Diagnostic Interview Schedule (DIS) continues to hold a prominent place in the psychiatric assessment armamentarium. Now administered in a computerized format, it has been updated to reflect changes in the *DSM*. This highly structured psychiatric interview carefully operationalizes the fourth edition (*DSM-IV*) criteria into specific questions, so when administered by an interviewer, it may be used to create diagnoses according to the *DSM-IV*. The C DIS-IV has maintained most of the unique properties of the original DIS, including the hallmark infrastructure known as the PFC (Probe Flow Chart), as well as age of onset of criteria and demographic, social, and psychiatric risk factors. The computerized version expands on the original version with the addition of impairment, remission, ages of onset, and offset of risk factors. The C DIS-IV, with skip instructions built in, minimizes administration errors, making it ideal for both clinicians and trained nonclinicians.

The PFC elicits information used to determine whether a symptom is clinically significant. Only if it meets the threshold for clinical significance is the symptom probed further to explore potential causality. The PFC classifies the endorsed symptom as always attributable to medication, drugs, or alcohol; physical conditions or injuries; or possibly psychiatric in nature. For example, in the depression module, it is important to know whether the loss of appetite was ever due to a physical illness or injury, or to medication, drugs, or alcohol. If it was due to hypothyroidism and only experienced with this condition, a special code signifies physical illness or injury as the cause of the symptom. For disorders that are conditional on an exposure, such as pathological gambling, post-traumatic stress disorder (PTSD), or substance use disorders, the PFC is not necessary.

The substance use disorder module of the C DIS-IV is a comprehensive assessment of consequences of alcohol use, tobacco products, and other substances, including marijuana, stimulants, sedatives, cocaine, heroin, other opiates, hallucinogens, phencyclidine (PCP), and inhalants. Only users who meet a threshold of having used the substance more than five times in their lifetime will continue to answer questions about that substance. The route of administration of a substance is elicited, as is age of onset and offset for each drug used. Specifically, each abuse and dependence criterion is operationalized independently; quantity-frequency data for each drug are also collected. For each criterion, the number of questions created varies. Further, unlike some other diagnostic assessments, the C DIS-IV does not make a generic diagnosis of "drug abuse and/or dependence." Instead, it makes individual abuse/dependence diagnoses. The problem with the former is that there are numerous types of drugs to assess independently (such as opiates, cocaine and other stimulants, sedatives, and cannabis), and when they are lumped together, individual criteria become blurred. Also, unlike other assessments, the C DIS-IV does not use abuse questions to screen for dependence.

The complexity of the C DIS-IV can be appreciated by simply observing the number of questions used to make a diagnosis; each criterion is not necessarily assessed by only one question. For example, the alcohol module includes 32 questions for abuse and dependence; alcohol abuse is assessed with 7 questions. Nicotine dependence requires 35 questions. The drug modules all follow a similar pattern, but the specific withdrawal syndrome varies, depending on the substance. Although a withdrawal syndrome is not required for some drugs, it is assessed, for surveillance purposes. In addition to alcohol and drug use disorders, the C DIS-IV yields data needed to diagnose somatization/pain, specific phobia/social phobia/agoraphobia/panic, generalized anxiety disorder, post-traumatic stress disorder, depression/dysthymia, mania/hypomania, schizophrenia/schizophreniform/schizoaffective, obsessive-compulsive disorder, anorexia nervosa/bulimia, attention deficit disorder, separation anxiety, oppositional disorder, conduct disorder, antisocial personality, pathological gambling, and dementia.

The DIS algorithms have been extensively tested (Robins & Cottler, 2004). The C DIS-IV encompasses all the essentials of good diagnostic interviews: It accurately represents the diagnostic criterion; it captures the ill, while not incorrectly asking the unaffected; it does not double-count symptoms; it is educationally and culturally acceptable; it does not depend on medical record review; and it has standardized questions. It is an excellent choice for investigators conducting comorbidity research (i.e., on the co-occurrence of disorders), as well as nosological research (i.e., on the classification of disorders).

See also **Addiction: Concepts and Definitions; Diagnosis of Substance Use Disorders: Diagnostic Criteria; Diagnostic and Statistical Manual (DSM); Models of Alcoholism and Drug Abuse.**

BIBLIOGRAPHY

Regier, D. A., et al. (1984). The NIMH Epidemiologic Catchment Area (ECA) program: Historical context, major objectives and study population characteristics. *Archives of General Psychiatry, 41*, 934–941.

Robins, L. N., & Cottler, L. B. (2004). Making a structured psychiatric diagnostic interview faithful to the nomenclature. *American Journal of Epidemiology, 60*, 808–813.

LINDA B. COTTLER
ARBI BEN ABDALLAH
CATHARINE MENNES

CONDITIONED TOLERANCE. *Tolerance* refers to the diminishment or the loss of a drug effect over the course of repeated administrations. Some researchers have postulated that an important factor in the development of tolerance is Pavlovian conditioning of drug-compensatory responses. The administration of a drug may be viewed as a Pavlovian conditioning trial. The stimuli present at the time of drug administration are the conditional stimulus (CS), while the effect produced by the drug is the unconditional stimulus (UCS). Many drug effects involve disruption of the homeostatic level of physiological systems (e.g., alcohol lowers body temperature), and these disruptions elicit compensatory responses that tend to restore functioning to normal levels. The compensatory, restorative response to a drug effect is the unconditional response (UCR). Repeated administrations of a drug in the context of the same set of stimuli can result in the usual pre-drug cues coming to elicit as a conditional response (CR) the compensatory, restorative response. The conditional drug-compensatory CR would tend to reduce the drug effect when the drug is administered with the usual pre-drug

cues—thus accounting for tolerance, or at least some aspects of tolerance.

One test of the Pavlovian conditioning model of tolerance is whether conditional drug-compensatory responses are elicited by pre-drug cues. In one experiment with rats (Crowell, Hinson, & Siegel, 1981), injections of alcohol in the context of one set of stimuli were alternated with injections of saline solution in the context of a different set of stimuli for several days. Each day, the rats' body temperatures were measured. Alcohol lowered body temperatures the first time it was given, but this effect diminished over the course of the repeated alcohol administrations—that is, tolerance developed to the hypothermic effect of alcohol. To determine if a drug-compensatory CR was elicited by the usual pre-drug cues, the rats were given a placebo CR test. In a placebo CR test, saline solution is administered instead of the drug. The placebo CR test was given to some rats under conditions where they were expecting alcohol; that is, saline was administered with the usual pre-drug cues. For the remaining rats, the placebo CR test was given under conditions where there should have been no expectancy of alcohol; that is, saline was administered with cues that had previously signaled only saline. Rats given saline with the usual pre-drug cues had elevated body temperatures, while rats given saline without the usual pre-drug cues showed little temperature change. Thus, it was possible to directly observe the drug-compensatory CR, in this case hyperthermia opposed to the hypothermic effect of alcohol. Other experiments similar to the one just described have found drug-compensatory CRs following the development of tolerance to various effects of opiates, barbiturates, and benzodiazepines (Siegel, 1983).

Conditioned responses occur only when the conditional stimulus is presented. If drug-compensatory CRs contribute to tolerance, then tolerance should only be evident in the presence of the usual pre-drug cues that are the CS. This expectation was tested in the experiment by Crowell, Hinson, and Siegel (1981), involving tolerance to the hypothermic effect of alcohol. After all rats had developed tolerance to the hypothermic effect of alcohol, a test was given in which some rats received alcohol with the usual pre-drug cues, while other rats received alcohol when the usual pre-drug cues were not present. Although all rats had displayed tolerance prior to the test, only those rats given alcohol in the presence of the usual pre-drug cues (i.e., with the CS) showed tolerance during the test. The explanation of this "situational specificity" of tolerance is that when alcohol is given with the usual pre-drug cues, the drug-compensatory CR occurs and reduces the drug effect—but when alcohol is given without the usual pre-drug cues, the drug-compensatory CR does not occur and the drug effect is not reduced. Other research has demonstrated situational specificity with regard to tolerance to opiates, barbiturates, and benzodiazepines (for a complete review see Siegel, 1983).

In order to eliminate a CR, it is necessary to present the CS not followed by the UCS, a procedure termed *extinction*. Research indicates that the loss of tolerance occurs as a result of extinction of drug-compensatory CRs. Again referring to the experiment of Crowell, Hinson, and Siegel (1981), rats were given alcohol in the presence of a consistent set of cues until tolerance developed. Then, all drug injections were stopped for several days. During this period some animals were given extinction trials, in which the usual pre-drug cues were presented but only saline was injected. The other animals did not receive extinction trials and were left undisturbed during this time. Subsequently, all animals were given a test in which the drug was given with the usual pre-drug cues. The animals that had received extinction trials were no longer tolerant, whereas animals that had not been given extinction trials retained their tolerance. Similar results—in which tolerance is retained unless extinction trials are given—occur for tolerance to opiates, barbiturates, and benzodiazepines (Siegel, 1983).

The drug-compensatory CRs that contribute to tolerance may also be involved in withdrawal-like symptoms that occur in detoxified drug addicts. Detoxified addicts often report experiencing withdrawal-like symptoms when they return to places where they formerly used drugs, although they are now drug free. The places where the addict formerly used drugs act as CSs and still elicit drug-compensatory CRs; even when the addict is drug free, the drug-compensatory CRs achieve expression. Thus, it is postulated that the drug-compensatory CRs elicited by the usual pre-drug cues in the drug-free post-addict result in a withdrawal-like syndrome (Hinson & Siegel, 1980). This conditional post-detoxification withdrawal syndrome may motivate the post-addict to resume drug taking (to alleviate the symptoms).

See also **Addiction: Concepts and Definitions; Risk Factors for Substance Use, Abuse, and Dependence: Learning; Tolerance and Physical Dependence; Wikler's Conditioning Theory of Drug Addiction.**

BIBLIOGRAPHY

Crowell, C., Hinson, R. E., & Siegel, S. (1981). The role of conditional drug responses in tolerance to the hypothermic effects of alcohol. *Psychopharmacology, 73*, 51–54.

Hinson, R. E., & Siegel, S. (1980). The contribution of Pavlovian conditioning to ethanol tolerance and dependence. In H. Rigter & J. C. Crabbe (*Eds.*), *Alcohol tolerance and dependence*. Amsterdam: Elsevier/North Holland Biomedical Press.

Jung, J.R. (2000). *Psychology of alcohol and other drugs: A research perspective*. Thousand Oaks, CA: Sage Publications.

Siegel, S. (1983). Classical conditioning, drug tolerance, and drug dependence. In F. B. Glaser et al. (Eds.), *Research advances in alcohol and drug problems* (Vol. 7). New York: Plenum.

RILEY HINSON

CONDUCT DISORDER AND DRUG USE.

In the American Psychiatric Association classification system for diagnosing mental disorder (*DSM-IV*), conduct disorder (CD) is defined as "a repetitive and persistent pattern of behavior in which the basic rights of others or major age-appropriate societal norms or rules are violated" (1994, p. 85). CD is socially disruptive and more serious in its consequences than typical childhood mischief. The duration of the behavior, its severity, and the kinds of actions involved distinguish CD from general misbehavior. In the general population of individuals under age eighteen, it occurs in 2 percent to 9 percent of females and 6 percent to 16 percent of males. Emerging evidence as of 2008 suggests, however, that the gender gap is narrowing. CD is the most common behavioral problem seen in child psychiatric settings in North America and is present in about 75 percent of emotionally disturbed youth.

DIAGNOSIS

The behaviors that characterize this disorder include: 1) aggressive conduct causing or threatening to cause physical harm to other people or animals (e.g., often bullies, threatens, or intimidates others), 2) non-aggressive conduct causing property loss or damage (e.g., has deliberately destroyed others' property), 3) deceitfulness or theft (e.g., has broken into someone else's house, building, or car), and 4) serious violation of rules (e.g., is often truant from school, beginning before age thirteen years). Criteria for a CD diagnosis are: 1) three or more symptoms in the past twelve months, with at least one symptom present in the past six months; 2) disturbance in behavior that causes clinically significant impairment in social, academic, or occupational functioning; and 3) criteria are not met for antisocial personality disorder if the individual is age eighteen years or older.

CD is one of the most valid and reliably diagnosed psychiatric disturbances. The problem behavior is trans-situational, being manifested in the home, at school, and in daily social functioning. Often, youths with CD are suspicious of others, and, consequently, they misinterpret the intentions and actions of others. By adolescence, aggression may become so severe that violent assault, rape, and homicide are committed. Precocious sexual behavior and sexual misbehavior, especially among females, are also common. Denial and minimization generally occur when the youngsters are confronted about their behavior. Typically, feelings of guilt are not experienced.

Other, less severe, types of behavior disorders are also known. The most common that resemble CD are adjustment disorder with disturbances of conduct, childhood (or adolescent) antisocial behavior, and oppositional defiant disorder. Children may manifest different combinations of CD symptoms and exhibit CD symptoms at different points of development. Substantial differences in the behavioral manifestations of CD have prompted efforts to develop subtypes. The most well known subtypes are socialized versus unsocialized, aggressive versus non-aggressive, overt versus covert, and childhood-onset versus adolescent-onset.

One variant of CD, the solitary aggressive type, characterizes approximately 50 percent of incarcerated youths; they are usually socioeconomically disadvantaged and typically come from dysfunctional families. Moral development is arrested, cognitive abilities are low, and behavior is often dangerous both to themselves and others. This CD variant should not be confused with adaptive delinquency, in which the behavior is an attempt to adjust to the manifold disadvantages of inner-city living.

NATURAL HISTORY

Other psychiatric disorders frequently occur in conjunction with CD. The most prevalent comorbid (coexisting) psychiatric disorder is attention-deficit/hyperactivity disorder. By adolescence, there is also significant comorbidity with substance use disorders and depressive disorders.

The age of onset is earlier and the behavior problems are more severe among children with comorbid CD and attention-deficit/hyperactivity disorder than in children with either disorder alone. Children with both disorders are also at greater risk for developing criminal behavior and substance abuse by adolescence or young adulthood.

The co-occurrence of CD and substance use disorders has been observed frequently. It is estimated that as many as 50 percent of serious offenders are substance abusers. In these cases, CD usually precedes the onset of substance abuse. There is some evidence that substance use disorders and CD are the overt expressions of a common underlying predisposition. Drug use during adolescence, by virtue of its pattern of illegal behavior plus association with non-normative peers, increases the risk for violent assault as well as for getting arrested and convicted for drug possession or distribution.

Among the childhood psychiatric disorders, CD is the most likely to remain stable. One study found that 54 percent of boys with a childhood diagnosis of CD were diagnosed with antisocial personality disorder in early adulthood. Persistence of conduct problems into adulthood is most likely if the behavior problems are serious, are generalized across multiple environments or situations, have an early age of onset, and lead the person into the criminal-justice system.

ETIOLOGY

The etiology of CD is considered multifactorial. Risk factors believed to contribute to its development include difficult temperament and a family history of antisocial personality disorder and/or alcohol dependence. Mild central nervous system abnormalities have been found in children with a history of violent behavior, and these are thought to contribute to the children's impulsivity. Neurologic injuries (e.g., secondary to head trauma) and neurodevelopmental disability (e.g., dyslexia) can exacerbate the expression of CD. Adoption, family, and twin studies implicate a genetic predisposition for the development of antisocial behavior. Several studies also indicate that there are common genetic influences between CD and ADHD, oppositional defiant disorder, and substance use disorders. However, a genetic propensity does not invariably ensure this adverse outcome. Some studies suggest that the interaction between genes and the environment may be important in the etiology of CD. Potential environmental risk factors for CD include poor parenting skills and family dysfunction (e.g., abusive, neglectful, and absent parents). Physically abusive and alcoholic parents frequently have had CD in their own childhoods. Socioeconomic factors (e.g., poverty, participation in street gangs) also influence the development of CD.

TREATMENT

Treatment of CD in children and adolescents can include family therapy, parent management training, behavioral and cognitive therapies, residential treatment programs, and, less frequently, pharmacotherapy. The most promising approaches as of 2008 include parent management training, which trains parents to reinforce prosocial behavior rather than aggressive behavior. Studies using random assignment show that parent management training is effective in improving parenting skills and reducing aggressive behavior in children.

See also **Adolescents and Drug Use; Crime and Drugs; Families and Drug Use; Intimate Partner Violence and Alcohol/Substance Use; Risk Factors for Substance Use, Abuse, and Dependence.**

BIBLIOGRAPHY

American Psychiatric Association (1994). *Diagnostic and statistical manual of mental disorders* (4th ed.). Washington, DC: Author.

Beers, M. H., & Berkow, R. (Eds.). (1999). *The Merck Manual of Diagnosis and Therapy* (17th ed.). Whitehouse Station, NJ: Merck Research Laboratories.

Brestan, E. V., & Eyberg, S. M. (1998). Effective psychosocial treatments of conduct-disordered children and adolescents: 29 years, 82 studies, and 5,272 kids. *Journal of Clinical Child Psychology, 27,* 180–189.

Button, T. M. M., Hewitt, J. K., Rhee, S. H., Young, S. E., Corley, R. P., & Stallings, M. C. (2006). Examination of the causes of covariation between conduct disorder symptoms and vulnerability to drug dependence. *Twin Research and Human Genetics, 9,* 38–45.

Cantwell, D. P. (1989). Conduct disorder. In H. I. Kaplan & B. J. Sadock (Eds.), *Comprehensive textbook of psychiatry* (5th ed., vol. 2, pp. 1821–1827). Baltimore, MD: Williams & Wilkins.

Caspi, A., McClay, J., Moffitt, T. E., Mill, J., Martin, J., Craig, I. W., et al. (2002). Role of genotype in the cycle of violence in maltreated children. *Science, 297,* 851–854.

Chamberlain, C., & Steinhauer, P. D. (1983). Conduct disorders and delinquency. In P. D. Steinhauer & Q. R. Grant (Eds.), *Psychological problems of the child in the family* (2nd ed., rev., pp. 258–276). New York: Basic Books.

Connor, D. F., Barkley, R. A., & Davis, H. T. (2000). A pilot study of methylphenidate, clonidine, or the combination in ADHD comorbid with aggressive oppositional defiant or conduct disorder. *Clinical Pediatrics (Philadelphia), 39*(1), 15–25.

Dick, D. M., Viken, R. J., Kaprio, J., Pulkkinen, L. & Rose, R. J. (2005). Understanding the covariation among childhood externalizing symptoms: Genetic and environmental influences on conduct disorder, attention deficit hyperactivity disorder, and oppositional defiant disorder symptoms. *Journal of Abnormal Child Psychology, 33,* 219–229.

Kazdin, A. E., Esveldt-Dawson, K., French, N. H., & Unis, A. S. (1987). Effects of parent management training and problem-solving skills combined in the treatment of antisocial child behavior. *Journal of the American Academy of Child and Adolescent Psychiatry, 26,* 416–424.

Kim-Cohen, J., Caspi, A., Taylor, A., Williams, B., Newcombe, R., Craig, I. W., et al. (2006). MAOA, maltreatment, and gene-environment interaction predicting children's mental health: New evidence and a meta-analysis. *Molecular Psychiatry, 11,* 903–913.

Lahey, B. B., Loeber, R., Burke, J. D., & Applegate, B. (2005). Predicting future antisocial personality disorder in males from a clinical assessment in childhood. *Journal of Consulting and Clinical Psychology, 73,* 389–399.

Loeber, R. (1991). Antisocial behavior: More enduring than changeable? *Journal of the American Academy of Child and Adolescent Psychiatry, 30,* 393–397.

Malone, R. P., Delaney, M. A., Luebbert, J. F., Cater, J., & Campbell, M. (2000). A double-blind placebo-controlled study of lithium in hospitalized aggressive children and adolescents with conduct disorder. *Archives of General Psychiatry, 57*(7), 649–654.

Office of the Surgeon General. (2000). Mental Health: A Report of the Surgeon General. Washington, DC: U. S. Government Printing Office.

Rutter, M. (1984). Psychopathology and development. Childhood antecedents of adult psychiatric disorder. *Australian and New Zealand Journal of Psychiatry, 18*, 225–234.

Schubiner, H., Tzelepis, A., Milberger, S., Lockhart, N., Kruger, M., Kelley, B. J., et al. (2000). Prevalence of attention-deficit/hyperactivity disorder and conduct disorder among substance abusers. *Journal of Clinical Psychiatry, 61*(4), 244–251.

Weinberg, N. Z., & Glantz, M. D. (1999). Child psychopathology risk factors for drug abuse: Overview. *Journal of Clinical Child Psychology, 28*(3), 290–297.

Zeitlin, H. (1999). Psychiatric comorbidity with substance misuse in children and teenagers. *Drug and Alcohol Dependence, 55*(3), 225–234.

ADA C. MEZZICH
RALPH E. TARTER
MYROSLAVA ROMACH
KAREN PARKER
REVISED BY MARY CARVLIN (2001)
REBECCA J. FREY (2001)
SOO HYUN RHEE (2009)

CONTROLLED SUBSTANCES ACT OF 1970. Until 1970, psychoactive drugs were regulated at the federal level by a patchwork of statutes enacted since the turn of the century. These statutes were shaped by an evolving conception of congressional power under the U.S. Constitution. The first federal law on the subject was the Pure Food and Drug Act of 1906, which required the labeling of substances such as patent medicines if they included designated narcotics (e.g., opiates and cocaine) and were shipped in interstate commerce. In 1909, Congress banned the importation of smoking opium. Then in 1914, in the Harrison Narcotics Act, Congress deployed its taxing power as a device for prohibiting the distribution and use of narcotics for nonmedical purposes. (The taxing power was used because U.S. Supreme Court decisions implied that Congress would not be permitted to use its power to regulate interstate commerce in banning "local" activities, such as the production and distribution of narcotics.) The scheme established by the Harrison

Act required the registration and payment of an occupational tax by all persons who imported, produced, or distributed narcotics; it imposed a tax on each transaction; and it made it a crime to engage in a transaction without paying the tax. Mere possession of narcotics without a prescription was presumptive evidence of a violation of the act. The Marihuana Tax Act of 1937 utilized the same model.

In 1965, Congress prohibited the manufacture and distribution of "dangerous drugs" (stimulants, depressants, and hallucinogens) for nonmedical purposes. By this time, Congress's constitutional authority to enact such legislation under the commerce clause was no longer in doubt. (In 1968, Congress made simple possession of the drugs a misdemeanor.) An all-important feature of the 1965 "dangerous drug" legislation was its delegation of authority to the secretary of Health, Education and Welfare (HEW) to control previously uncontrolled drugs if they had a "potential for abuse" due to their depressant, stimulant, or hallucinogenic properties. (In 1968, this scheduling authority was transferred to the U.S. attorney general.)

All this legislation was replaced by a comprehensive regulatory structure in the 1970 Controlled Substances Act (CSA). Under the new statutory scheme, all previously controlled substances were classified—in five schedules—according to their potential for abuse and accepted medical utility; an administrative process was then established for scheduling new substances, building on the model of the 1965 act. Schedule I lists drugs that have no traditional recognized medical use, such as heroin, LSD, and cannabis (marijuana). Schedule II lists the drugs with medical uses that have the greatest potential for abuse and dependence, such as morphine and cocaine. The remaining schedules use a sliding scale that balances each drug's abuse potential and its legitimate medical uses.

Different degrees of control are applied to manufacturers, distributors, and prescribers—depending on the schedule in which the drug has been placed. The regulatory structure of the Controlled Substances Act is predicated on the assumption that tighter controls on legitimate transactions will prevent diversion of these substances and will thereby reduce the availability of these substances for nonmedical use.

The drafting of the Controlled Substances Act reflected a continuing controversy regarding the locus of administrative authority for scheduling new drugs and for rescheduling previously controlled drugs. Under the bill passed by the Senate, this responsibility would have rested with the U.S. attorney general, who was required only to "request the advice" of the secretary of HEW (now Health and Human Services, HHS) and of a scientific advisory committee; the attorney general was not required to follow this advice although the various criteria in the act require primarily scientific and medical judgments. The Senate rejected an amendment that would have made the recommendations of the "advisor" binding on the attorney general. Under the bill passed in the House of Representatives, however, the secretary's decision declining to schedule a new drug was binding on the attorney general, and the secretary's recommendation concerning rescheduling was binding as to its medical and scientific aspects. The House version prevailed in the 1970 law as it was finally adopted.

After enactment of the federal Controlled Substances Act, the National Conference of Commissioners on Uniform State Laws promulgated a Uniform Controlled Substances Act, which was modeled after the federal act. (Earlier state laws were modeled on the 1934 Uniform Narcotic Drug Act, which had also been promulgated by the National Conference.) Every state has enacted the Uniform Controlled Substances Act.

See also **Anslinger, Harry Jacob, and U.S. Drug Policy; Controls: Scheduled Drugs/Drug Schedules, U.S; Legal Regulation of Drugs and Alcohol.**

BIBLIOGRAPHY

Bonnie, R. J., & Whitebread, C. H., II. (1974). *The marihuana conviction.* Charlottesville, VA: University Press of Virginia.

Courtwright, D. T. (2004). The Controlled Substances Act: How a "big tent" reform became a punitive drug law. *Drug and Alcohol Dependence, 76,* 1, 9–15.

Musto, D. F. (1987). *The American disease.* New York: Oxford University Press.

Sonnenreich, M. R., Roccograndi, A. J., & Bogomolny, R. L. (1975). *Handbook on the 1970 federal drug act.* Springfield, IL: Charles C. Thomas.

Spillane, J. F. (2004). Debating the Controlled Substances Act. *Drug and Alcohol Dependence, 76,* 1, 17–29.

RICHARD BONNIE

CONTROLS: SCHEDULED DRUGS/ DRUG SCHEDULES, U.S.

The Comprehensive Drug Abuse Prevention and Control Act of 1970, commonly known as the Controlled Substance Act (CSA) establishes the procedures that must be followed by drug manufacturers, researchers, physicians, pharmacists, and others involved in the legal manufacturing, distributing, prescribing, and dispensing of controlled drugs. These procedures provide accountability for a drug from its initial production through distribution to the patient to reduce widespread diversion of controlled drugs from legitimate medical or scientific use.

DRUG CONTROL AND SCHEDULING CRITERIA

Several factors are considered before a drug is controlled under this act. These factors include the potential for abuse (i.e., history, magnitude, duration, and significance), risk to public health, and potential of physical or psychological dependence. Drugs controlled under this act are divided into five Schedules (I–V) according to their potential for abuse, ability to produce dependence, and medical utility. Drugs in Schedule I have a high potential for abuse and/or dependence with no accepted medical use, or they lack demonstrated clinical safety. Those in Schedules II–V have a high potential for abuse or an ability to produce dependence but also have an accepted medical use. (However, some substances that have no accepted medical use but are precursors to clinically useful substances may also be found in Schedules II–V. For example, thebaine, found naturally in opium, has no medical use but it is a substance used in the manufacture of codeine and a series of potent opioid compounds as well as opioid antagonists.) The potential for abuse and the ability to produce dependence is the greatest for Schedule I and II drugs and progressively less for Schedule III, IV, and V (see Table 1).

The amount of controlled drug in a product can also determine the schedule in which it is placed. For example, amphetamine, methamphetamine, and codeine, as pure substances, are placed in Schedule II; however, these same drugs in limited quantities and in combination with a noncontrolled drug are placed in Schedules III and V. Drugs in Schedule V

DEA schedule	Abuse potential	Examples of drugs covered	Some of the effects	Medical use
I	highest	heroin, LSD, hashish, marijuana, methaqualone	unpredictable effects, severe psychological or physical dependence, or death	no accepted use: some are legal for limited research use only
II	high	morphine, PCP, cocaine, methadone, methamphetamine	may lead to severe psychological or physical dependence	accepted use with restrictions
III	medium	codeine with aspirin or Tylenol®, some barbiturates, anabolic steroids	may lead to moderate or low physical dependence or high psychological dependence	accepted use
IV	low	Darvon®, Talwin®, Equanil® Valium®, Xanax®	may lead to limited physical or psychological dependence	accepted use
V	lowest	over-the-counter or prescription cough medicines with codeine	may lead to limited physical or psychological dependence	accepted use

Table 1. Drugs are scheduled under federal law according to their effects, medical use, and potential for abuse. (Adapted from *Drugs of Abuse* (2005), Drug Enforcement Administration, U.S. Department of Justice.) ILLUSTRATION BY GGS INFORMATION SERVICES. GALE, CENGAGE LEARNING

Schedule	Potential for: Abuse	Potential for: Dependence	Medical use & safety
I	+ + + +	+ + + +	No
II	+ + + +	+ + + +	Yes
III	+ + +	+ + +	Yes
IV	+ +	+ +	Yes
V	+	+	Yes

Table 2. Criteria for U.S. drug scheduling. (Adapted from *Drugs of Abuse* (2005), Drug Enforcement Administration, U.S. Department of Justice.) ILLUSTRATION BY GGS INFORMATION SERVICES. GALE, CENGAGE LEARNING

generally contain limited quantities of certain narcotic drugs used for cough and antidiarrheal purposes and can only be distributed or dispensed for medical purposes.

LISTS OF SCHEDULED DRUGS

Drugs controlled under the CSA are listed by schedule and drug class in Table 2 (Schedules I and II) and Table 3 (Schedules III, IV, and V). A listing of controlled chemical derivatives, immediate precursors (chemical that precedes the active drug), and chemicals essential for making a controlled drug, along with drugs exempt from control can be found in the most current edition of the *Controlled Substances Handbook*. Some brand names for drugs in Schedules II–V are not included in the tables, but can be found in the latest edition of the *Controlled Substances Handbook*.

PRESCRIBING AND DISPENSING CONTROLLED DRUGS

Medical practitioners have to follow specific rules for each schedule when prescribing or dispensing controlled drugs. Drugs in Schedule I can only be obtained, prescribed, and dispensed to an individual after special approval is obtained from the Food and Drug Administration (FDA). Drugs in Schedule II cannot be refilled or dispensed without a written prescription from a practitioner, except in an emergency. When they are dispensed in an emergency, a written prescription must be obtained within 72 hours. Drugs in Schedule III and in Schedule IV may not be dispensed without a written or an oral prescription. Prescriptions for these drugs may not be filled or refilled more than six months after their issue date or refilled more than five times unless authorized by a licensed practitioner. Drugs in Schedule V can be refilled, with a practitioner's authorization, without a limitation on number of refills or amount of time. Certain Schedule V drugs may be purchased directly from a pharmacist, in limited quantities, without a prescription. The purchaser must be at least 18 years of age and furnish appropriate identification, and these transactions must be recorded by the dispensing pharmacist.

When drugs in Schedule II, III, and IV are dispensed, a warning label stating, "Caution: Federal law prohibits the transfer of this drug to any person other than the patient for whom it was prescribed," must be affixed to the dispensing container. The warning label regarding transfer does not apply to Schedule V drugs.

Schedule—I					
Opiates		**Opium derivatives**	**Hallucinogens**	**Depressants**	**Stimulants**
Acetyl-alpha-methylfentanyl	Hydroxypethidine	Acetorphine	Alpha-ethyltryptamine	Mecloqualone	Aminorex Cathinone
Acetylmethadol	Ketobemidone	Acetyldihydrocodeine	4-bromo-2.5-DMA	Methaqualone	Fenethylline
Allylprodine	Levomoramide	Benzylmorphine	Alpha-desmethyl DOB		Metheathinone
Alphameprodine	Levophenacylmorphan	Codeine methylbromide	2.5-DMA		(±) cis-4-
Alphamethadol	3-methylfentanyl	Codeine-N-Oxide	DOET		methylaminorex
Alpha-methylfentanyl	3-methylthiofentanyl	Cyprenorphine	PMA		N-ethylamphetamine
Alpha-methylthiofentanyl	Morpheridine	Desomorphine	5-methoxy-3,4-methylene-		N.N-dimethyl-
Benzethidine	MPPP	Dihydromorphine	dioxyamphetamine		amphetamine
Betacetylmethadol	Noracymethadol	Drotebanol	MMDA		
Beta-hydroxyfentanyl	Norlevorphanol	Etorphine (except HCI salt)	DOM, STP		
Beta-hydroxy-3-methylfentanyl	Normethadone	Heroin	MDA		
Betameprodine	Norpipanone	Hydromorphinol	MDMA		
Betamethadol	Para-fluorofentanyl	Methyldesorphine	MDEA		
Betaprodine	PEPAP	Methyldihydromorphine	N-hydroxy MDA		
Clonitazene	Phenadoxone	Morphine methylbromide	3,4,5-trimethoxy amphetamine		
Dextromocamide	Phenampromide	Morphine methylsulfonate	Bufotenine		
Diampromide	Phenomorphan	Morphine-N-Oxide	DET		
Diethylthiambutene	Phenoperidine	Myrophine	DMT		
Difenoxin	Piritramide	Nicocodeine	Ibogaine		
Dimenoxadol	Proheptazine	Nicomorphine	LSD		
Dimepheptanol	Properidine	Normorphine	Marijuana		
Dimethylthiambutene	Propiram	Pholcodine	Mescaline		
Dioxaphetyl butyrate	Raccmoramide	Thebacon	N-ethyl-3-piperidyl benzilate		
Dipipanone	Thiofentanyl		N-methyl-3-piperidyl benzilate		
Ethylmethylthiambatene	Tilidine		Peyote		
Etonitazene	Trimeperidine		Pheneyelidine analogs		
Etoxeridine			PCE, PCPy, TCP, TCPy		
Furethidine			Psilocybin		
			Psilocyn		
			Tetrahydrocannabinols		

Table 3. List of controlled drugs, Schedule I. (Source: Drug Scheduling, Drug Enforcement Administration, U.S. Department of Justice.) ILLUSTRATION BY GGS INFORMATION SERVICES. GALE, CENGAGE LEARNING

REGISTRATION, ORDERING, QUOTAS, AND RECORDS

Each individual or institution engaged in manufacturing, distributing, or dispensing any controlled drug must be authorized by and register annually with federal and state drug-enforcement agencies, unless specifically exempted. A unique registration number is assigned to each individual or institution registered under the act. A separate registration is required for practitioners who dispense narcotic drugs to individuals for the purpose of addiction treatment (such as Methadone and LAAM [l-Alpha-Acetylmethadol] for opioid detoxification or maintenance).

All orders for Schedule I and II drugs must be made using a special narcotic order form. Proof of registration is required when ordering Schedule III–V drugs. Annual production quotas are established for drugs in Schedule I and Schedule II. Everyone registered to handle controlled drugs must maintain records, conduct inventories, and file periodic reports specific to their business or professional activity.

The Controlled Substances Act of 1970 also created the requirement for manufacturers and distributors to report their controlled substances transactions to the Attorney General. The Attorney General delegates this authority to the Drug Enforcement Administration (DEA). ARCOS (Automation of Reports and Consolidated Orders System) is an automated, comprehensive drug-reporting system that monitors the flow of DEA-controlled substances from their point of manufacture through commercial distribution channels to point of sale or distribution at the dispensing/retail level. ARCOS tracks transactions involving all Schedules I and II materials, Schedule III narcotic and gama-hydroxybutyric acid (GHB) materials, and selected Schedule III and IV psychotropic drugs (manufacturers only). ARCOS summarizes these transactions into reports that give federal and state investigators information that can be used to identify the diversion of controlled substances into illicit channels of distribution.

Schedule–II					
Opiates	**Opium & derivatives**	**Hallucinogens**	**Depressants**	**Stimulants**	**Others**
Alfentanil	Raw opium	Nabilone	Amobarbital	Amphetamine	Opium poppy
Alphaprodine	Opium extracts		Glutethimide	Methamphetamine	Poppy straw
Anileridine	Opium fluid extract		Pentobarbital	Phenmetrazine	Coca leaves
Bezitramide	Powdered opium		Phencyclidine	Methylphenidate	Immediate precursors to:
Carfentanil	Granulated opium		Secobarbital		Amphetamine
Dextroprophene, bulk	Tincture of opium				Methamphetamine
Dihydrocodeine	Codeine				Phencyclidine
Diphenoxylate	Ethylmorphine				
Fentanyl	Etorphine hydrochloride				
Isomethadone	Hydrocodone				
Levo-alphacetylmethadol	Hydromorphone				
Levomethorphan	Metopon				
Levorphanol	Morphine				
Meperidine Intermediate-A	Oxycodone				
Meperidine Intermediate-B	Oxymorphone				
Meperidine Intermediate-C	Thebaine				
Metazocine					
Methadone					
Methadone-Intermediate					
Moramide-Intermediate					
Pethidine					
Phenazocine					
Piminodine					
Racemethorphan					
Racemorphan					
Remifentanil					
Sufentanil					

Table 4. List of controlled drugs, Schedule II. (Source: Drug Scheduling, Drug Enforcement Administration, U.S. Department of Justice.) ILLUSTRATION BY GGS INFORMATION SERVICES. GALE, CENGAGE LEARNING

Schedule–III			
Narcotics	**Depressants**	**Stimulants**	**Others**
Limited quantities of:	Mixtures of	Limited mixtures	Dronabinol in sesame oil
Codeine	Amobarbital	of Schedule II	in soft gelatin capsule
Dihydrocodeinone,	Secobarbital	amphetamines	Nalorphine
Dihydrocodeine,	Pentobarbital	Benzphetamine	All anabolic steroids
Ethylmorphine,	Derivatives of	Chlorphentermine	
Hydrocodone,	barbituric acid	Clortermine	
Opium, and	Aprobarbital	Phendimetrazine	
Morphine	Butabarbital		
in combination	Butalbital		
with nonnarcotics	Chlorhexadol		
Buprenorphine	Ketamine		
	Lysergic acid		
	Lysergic acid amide		
	Methyprylon		
	Sulfondiethylmethane		
	Sulfonethylmethane		
	Sulfonmethane		
	Talbutal		
	Thiopental		
	Tiletamine		
	Vinbarbital		
	Zolazepam		

Table 5. List of controlled drugs, Schedule III. (Source: Drug Scheduling, Drug Enforcement Administration, U.S. Department of Justice.) ILLUSTRATION BY GGS INFORMATION SERVICES. GALE, CENGAGE LEARNING

Schedule–IV				
Narcotics	**Depressants**		**Stimulants**	**Others**
Limited quantity of difenoxin in combination with atropine sulfate	Alprazolam	Loprasolam	Cathine	Butorphanol
	Barbital	Lorazepam	Dexfenfluramine	Fenfluramine
	Bromazepam	Lormetazepam	Diethylpropion	Pentazocine
Dextropropoxyphere	Camazepam	Mebutamate	Fencamfamin	
	Chloral betaine	Medazepam	Fenproporex	
	Chloral hydrate	Meprobamate	Mazindol	
	Chlordiazepoxide	Methohexital	Mefenorex	
	Clobazam	Methylphenobarbital	Modafinil	
	Clonazepam	Midazolam	Pemoline	
	Clorazepate	Nimetazepam	Phentermine	
	Clotiazepam	Nitrazepam	Pipradrol	
	Cloxazolam	Nordiazepam	Sibutramine	
	Delorazepam	Oxazepam	SPA	
	Diazepam	Oxazolam		
	Dichloralphenazone	Paraldehyde		
	Estazolam	Petrichloral		
	Ethchlorvynol	Phenobarbital		
	Ethinamate	Pinazepam		
	Ethyl loflazepate	Prazepam		
	Fludiazepam	Quazepam		
	Flunitrazepam	Temazepam		
	Flurazepam	Tetrazepam		
	Halazepam	Triazolam		
	Haloxazolam	Zaleplon		
	Ketazolam	Zolpidem		

Table 6. List of controlled drugs, Schedule IV. (Source: Drug Scheduling, Drug Enforcement Administration, U.S. Department of Justice.) ILLUSTRATION BY GGS INFORMATION SERVICES. GALE, CENGAGE LEARNING

Schedule–V	
Narcotics	**Stimulants**
Buprenorphine	Pyrovalcrone
Limited quantities (less than Schedules III & IV) of: Codeine, Dihydrocodeine, Ethylmorphine, Dipehnoxylate, Opium, and Difenoxin in combination with nonnarcotics	

Table 7. List of controlled drugs, Schedule V. (Source: Drug Scheduling, Drug Enforcement Administration, U.S. Department of Justice.) ILLUSTRATION BY GGS INFORMATION SERVICES. GALE, CENGAGE LEARNING

SPECIAL ISSUES

The development of designer drugs has raised many concerns about policing drugs of abuse. Underground chemists who develop designer drugs seek to achieve two results: the creation of marketable drugs that mimic the effects of restricted drugs of abuse and the creation of drugs that are not specifically listed as controlled substances by the Drug Enforcement Administration. The most popular designer drug of the late 1990s was MDMA (methylenedioxymethamphetamine), popularly known as Ecstasy. Despite efforts to evade federal drug laws, the designers of these drugs eventually see them added to the CSA. For example, MDMA was placed on Schedule I on an emergency basis in 1985 because of its neurotoxic effects and abuse potential. In 2007 the synthetic drug fentanyl, a synthetic opiate that is 30 to 50 times more powerful than heroin, had become a popular drug; it too was placed on Schedule I.

The abuse of prescription drugs for nonmedical purposes is the second largest form of illegal drug abuse in the United States. The federal government estimates that in 2007 approximately 6.4 million people use controlled-substance prescription drugs for nonmedical purposes, with 4.7 million misusing pain relievers. Policing prescription drugs has become more difficult with the advent of online pharmacies. Active drug cases involving the Internet increased by 25 percent in 2006, rising from 194 to 242 cases (*National Drug Control Strategy: 2007 Annual Report*, p. 31.)

State and local laws either parallel the federal regulations as described by the CSA or impose additional restrictions. Individuals registered to handle controlled drugs must abide by the law (state or federal) that is most stringent in governing their business or professional activity. Examples of where state law may be more stringent than federal law include the requirement for Triplicate Prescription forms or the placing of a drug in a higher schedule.

See also **Addiction: Concepts and Definitions; Legal Regulation of Drugs and Alcohol.**

BIBLIOGRAPHY

Baumgartner, K., & Hoffman, D. (Eds.). (1993). Schedules of controlled substances. In *Controlled substances handbook*. Arlington, VA: Government Information Services, J. J. Marshall Publisher.

Code of Federal Regulations (21 CFR Parts 1301–1308). (1992). *Food and drugs—Drug Enforcement Administration, Department of Justice*. Washington, DC: U.S. Government Printing Office.

Office of Diversion Control, Department of Justice, (2008, May 22) *ARCOS—Automation of Reports and Consolidated Orders System*. Available from http://www.deadiversion.usdoj.gov/.

Simonsmeier, L. M., & Fink, J. L. (1990). The comprehensive drug abuse prevention and control act of 1970. In A. R. Gennaro (Ed.), *Remington's pharmaceutical sciences* (18th ed.). Easton, PA: Mack Publishing.

White House Office of National Drug Control Policy. (2007). *National Drug Control Strategy: 2007 Annual Report*. Washington, DC.

ROLLEY E. JOHNSON
ANASTASIA E. NASIS
REVISED BY FREDERICK K. GRITTNER (2009)

COPING AND DRUG USE. Coping is the strategy used to manage stress. This process consists of two facets: *Coping style* refers to the tactics used to attenuate ongoing stress or to avoid anticipated stress. *Coping competence* refers to the cognitive, emotional, and behavioral resources deployed to manage stress.

Adaptive coping buffers the risk of developing stress-related medical illnesses and psychological disorder. An exercise routine is one example of adaptive coping because it reduces stress and improves mental and physical fitness. Maladaptive coping abates stress but at the cost of potential future adverse consequences. Because of the ubiquity of

drugs that have abuse potential, substance consumption is a maladaptive coping strategy. Habitual use may lead to addiction, organ-system injury and disease, psychiatric disorders, legal problems, and social maladjustment.

Many chemicals contained naturally in plants and animals, and in modern times synthesized, are consumed to potentiate well-being in healthy individuals (e.g., vitamins, herbs, minerals, fish oil). In addition, an enormous number of chemicals are used to treat disease. From this ever-expanding pharmacopeia, a subset of chemicals acts on the neuroanatomical substrate subserving the experience of reward by affecting the release of dopamine. Accordingly, drug consumption results in the experience of pleasure (positive reinforcement) and relief from discomfort (negative reinforcement). Drugs are consumed as a coping strategy to reduce discomfort; however, both positive and negative reinforcement can occur together as, for example, during so-called happy hour when alcohol dampens stress at the end of the workday while enhancing pleasure through convivial social interaction.

Repetitive consumption results in adaptation to the drug by the brain. This process, termed *tolerance*, leads to the progressive need for increasingly higher doses to alleviate stress. Thus, as tolerance increases, drug use as a coping strategy is motivated by both the desire to reduce stress and the desire to avoid the symptoms of withdrawal.

The likelihood of using drugs as a coping strategy depends on three sets of factors: 1) characteristics of the individual; 2) number, severity, and chronicity of stressors; and, 3) availability, cost, and legal sanctions determining accessibility and desirability of compounds having addictive potential.

Many individual characteristics, albeit no specific personality type, predispose to habitual substance use. Within the population of substance users, individuals who have a constellation of characteristics indicative of stress susceptibility are, however, prone to using abusable drugs as a coping strategy. These characteristics include but are not limited to anxiety, panic reaction, phobia, and depression.

Stress is the necessary condition required to be present to promote drug use as a coping strategy. The quality of relationship with parents and peers, capacity to perform adequately and adjust to school, and concern about physical appearance are common stressors in adolescents. Stress related to work, dissatisfaction with the intimate partner, and psychiatric disturbance frequently trigger substance use during middle adulthood. As aging progresses, declining health (including chronic pain and insomnia), depression following death of family members and friends, boredom from loss of routine following retirement, and social isolation are stressors that frequently result in psychiatric disturbance and are managed by prescription medications that have addictive potential or other compounds, especially alcohol.

Stimulants and depressants are used to manage stress. Caffeine, the most widely used psychoactive drug, boosts mood and elevates energy. Nicotine is commonly used to cope with stress. Both drugs are stimulants, indicating that pharmacokinetic and pharmacodynamic properties, along with social learning, beliefs, and attitudes contribute to drug use as a coping strategy. Alcohol, a depressant, is used to cope with a variety of stressors and accordingly is consumed for its perceived properties as an aphrodisiac, analgesic, sedative, and hypnotic.

Because stress is only one of many reasons for substance use, the presence of this association needs to be determined on a case-by-case basis. Stress can be ascertained by querying the individual about the motivation for consuming drugs. A response pointing to a desire to manage an aversive physical or emotional condition or a threatening social situation reveals that the substance is used as a coping strategy. In formal evaluation, the revised Drug Use Screening Inventory (Tarter, 1990) is an efficient method of evaluating severity of substance use in relation to psychiatric disorder, behavior patterns, health status, family system, work, and psychosocial adjustment. Obtaining information about coping style and competence can be objectively evaluated using the Ways of Coping Scale (Lazarus & Folkman, 1984). Once it is established that the person consumes drugs to cope with stress, a treatment plan can be designed to inculcate healthier strategies. Notably, prognosis is improved by enhancing coping competence in alcoholics (Getter et al., 1992) and a treatment protocol has been developed for this population (Kadden et al., 1992). Good coping skills have been shown to be predictive of abstinence from drugs in youths

(Anderson et al., 2007) and adults (Hser, 2007). Thus, when substance use is a coping strategy, prognosis is enhanced by inculcating more adaptive methods to manage stress.

See also **Relapse; Treatment, Behavioral Approaches to: Cognitive Therapy.**

BIBLIOGRAPHY

Anderson, K., et al. (2007). Life stress, coping, and comorbid youth: An examination of the stress-vulnerability model for substance relapse. *Journal of Psychoactive Drugs, 38,* 253–262.

Getter, H., et al. (1992). Measuring treatment process in coping skills and interactional group therapies for alcoholism. *International Journal of Group Psychotherapy, 42,* 419–430.

Hser, Y. (2007). Predicting long-term stable recovery from heroin addiction: Findings from a 33-year follow-up study. *Journal of Addictive Diseases, 28,* 251–160.

Kadden, R., et al. (1992). Cognitive behavioral coping skills therapy manual. *Project MATCH Monograph Series, Vol. 3, DHHS Publication No. (ADM),* 92–1895.

Lazarus, R., & Folkman, S. (1984). *Stress, appraisal and coping.* New York: Springer.

Tarter, R. (1990). Evaluation and treatment of adolescent substance abuse. A decision tree method. *American Journal of Drug and Alcohol Abuse, 16,* 1–46.

RALPH TARTER

CRACK. *Crack,* sometimes called *crack cocaine,* is the smokable form of cocaine. It is made by adding a base—either ammonia or, more typically, baking soda and water—to cocaine hydrochloride. The white powder called cocaine is the hydrochloride form, which is water-soluble and can be injected. It cannot be smoked, however, because it is destroyed at high temperatures. Thus, in order to be smoked, cocaine must be converted to the base state. Once the proper mixture is made, it is heated to remove the hydrochloride, resulting in a cake-like solid substance that can be smoked. This form of cocaine is generally available in small quantities, making it inexpensive and readily available for purchase "on the street." It is called "crack" because of the cracks that form in the solid mass as it dries—and because of the noise it makes when smoked.

Although crack can be smoked in tobacco or marijuana cigarettes, it is generally smoked in a special crack pipe. In its simplest form, this is a glass tube with a hole at the top of one end and a hole at the other end through which the smoke is inhaled. Most commercially available crack pipes have a small bowl at the end. The crack pellet is placed on fine wire-mesh screens that cover the hole, and a flame is applied directly to the pellet. Soda bottles, small liquor bottles, and other similar implements are all used to manufacture homemade crack pipes. What all crack pipes have in common is the fine mesh screen, which prevents the crack from being lost as it melts. A temperature of approximately 200°F (93°C) is the most efficient in providing the largest amount of cocaine to the user, as higher temperatures destroy more of the cocaine.

Smoking cocaine began with the use of "freebase" cocaine, which is prepared by its users from cocaine hydrochloride. Soon after this form of cocaine achieved its popularity in the 1980s, single doses of cocaine already prepared for smoking and known as crack became available through the illicit drug market. Unlike the process for forming freebase cocaine, the crack manufacturing process does not rid the cocaine of its adulterants. This manufactured form of smokable cocaine soon became readily available and was so convenient to use, and smoking cocaine became a popular route of administration. The levels of cocaine in the blood peak rapidly when it is smoked, because of efficient respiratory absorption, and this method yields effects (e.g., peak effects, duration of effect, half-life) comparable to the intravenous route of administration. The smoker of cocaine, however, can get the effects within about 10 seconds. This leads to a cocaine "rush" and substantial levels of cocaine in the blood. This can be done repeatedly by smoking, which is a more socially acceptable route of administration than injection and does not require the paraphernalia associated with hardcore illicit drug use (e.g., syringes, needles).

The more rapid the onset of the drug effect, the more likely it is that the drug will be abused. Thus, although the overall effects of smoking crack are no different than the effects of taking cocaine by any other route, the ready availability of small amounts of the drug for purchase and the ease with which the drug can be taken, combined with its toxicity, make this an extremely dangerous substance.

From a financial perspective, crack is more desirable for both the buyer and the seller. A gram of cocaine hydrochloride costs approximately $50 to $100. This gram can be turned into 10 to 25 crack pellets, each selling for $3 to $50. Prices vary, however, as does the purity of the crack sold. Lower prices may mean lower purity and less effect for the buyer. Still, a gram of cocaine can generate a substantial profit for the seller and make single dose units available to anyone with only a few dollars to spend.

See also **Coca Paste; Freebasing; Pharmacokinetics: General; Street Value.**

BIBLIOGRAPHY

Erickson, P. G., Adlaf, E. M., Smart, R. G. & Murray, G. F. (1994). *The steel drug: Cocaine and crack in perspective* (2nd ed.). New York: Lexington Books.

Schifano, F. (2008). Cocaine/crack cocaine consumption, treatment demand, seizures, related offences, prices, average purity levels and death in the U.K (1990–2004). *Journal of Psychopharmacology, 22*(1), 71–79.

MARIAN W. FISCHMAN
REVISED BY REG SMART (2009)

CRAVING. *Craving* is generally defined as a state of desire, longing, or urge for a drug that is responsible for ongoing drug-use behavior, as well as relapse, among drug-dependent individuals. Craving has also been used to describe desire for non-drug related substances or activities, such as food, sex, and gambling. During periods of abstinence, drug-dependent individuals often complain of intense craving for their drug. Systems for diagnosing addictive disorders include persistent desire or craving for a drug as a major symptom of drug dependence, and many pharmacological and behavioral treatments for drug addiction focus on craving reduction as a way to reduce drug-use behavior.

The belief that an addict's inability to control drug use is caused by craving was a prominent feature of descriptions of addictive disorders provided by many nineteenth-century and early twentieth-century writers. The use of craving as a key mechanism in theories of addiction peaked in the 1950s, supported largely by E. M. Jellinek (1890–1963) in his writings on the causes of alcoholism. Jellinek contended that sober alcoholics who consumed a small amount of alcohol would experience overwhelming craving that would compel them to continue to drink. Many clinicians and addiction researchers adopted the proposal that craving and loss of control over drinking were equivalent concepts. Equally popular was the position, also supported by Jellinek, that craving was a direct sign of drug withdrawal. Withdrawal-based craving was often described as physical craving, distinguishing it from a more psychological form of craving that led to relapse during long periods of abstinence after withdrawal had subsided. The craving concept was sufficiently controversial that a committee of alcoholism experts (World Health Organization Expert Committees on Mental Health and Alcohol, 1955) recommended that the term *craving* not be used to describe various aspects of drinking behavior seen in alcoholics.

The use of craving as a key process in theories of addiction decreased during the 1960s and early 1970s as a result of several factors. During this period, many studies showed that alcoholics did not necessarily engage in loss of control drinking when they drank small doses of alcohol. The failure to confirm Jellinek's conceptualization of alcoholic drinking cast doubt on the idea that *craving* was synonymous with *loss of control* over drug intake. Furthermore, withdrawal models of craving could not account for the common observation that many addicts experienced craving and relapsed long after their withdrawal had disappeared. Finally, addiction research was increasingly dominated by behavioral approaches that focused on the influence of environmental variables in the control of drug taking and avoided the use of subjective concepts, such as craving.

Even though many addiction researchers questioned the value of craving as an explanatory concept, it persisted as an important clinical issue, as many addicts complained that craving was a major barrier to their attempts to stop using drugs. Craving continued to be cited as a major symptom of drug dependence in formal diagnostic systems, and the notion that craving was responsible for compulsive drug use remained at the core of several popular conceptualizations of drug addiction. Scientific interest

in the role of craving in addictive disorders re-emerged in the middle 1970s as a result of two developments. First, behavioral theories of addiction were increasingly influenced by social-cognitive models of behavior that were more sympathetic to hypothetical entities such as craving. Second, animal research on the contribution of learning processes to drug tolerance and drug withdrawal provided support for the hypothesis that learned withdrawal effects might produce craving and relapse in abstinent addicts.

THEORIES OF CRAVING
Although in the early twenty-first century there is considerable disagreement across theories regarding the processes that supposedly control craving, nearly all models describe craving as a fundamentally subjective state. With few exceptions, modern theories of craving also assume that craving is a necessary, but probably not sufficient, condition for drug taking among addicts. These theories suppose that addicts are driven to use drugs because of their craving, and craving is generally described as the principal cause of relapse in addicts trying to remain abstinent. Most comprehensive models of craving invoke some sort of learning or cognitive process in their descriptions of the mechanisms controlling craving, and these models make little distinction between physical and psychological forms of drug craving.

Many modern theories suggest that craving may be merely a part of drug withdrawal. For example, the diagnostic system published by the American Psychiatric Association in 1987 (*Diagnostic and Statistical Manual of Mental Disorders*, 3rd ed. rev.) listed craving as one of the symptoms of withdrawal for nicotine and opioids. Other approaches assume that cravings are distinct from withdrawal but represent an addict's anticipation of, and desire for, relief from withdrawal. To explain the presence of craving following long periods of abstinence, it has been posited that learning processes are responsible for the maintenance of withdrawal effects. For example, Wikler's conditioning model of drug withdrawal hypothesizes that situations reliably paired with episodes of drug withdrawal become conditioned stimuli that can later produce conditioned withdrawal responses (Wikler, 1948). This learned-withdrawal reaction will trigger drug craving, which, in turn, may lead to relapse. A similar theory is based on the suggestion that drug-tolerance processes can become conditioned to environmental stimuli. Some have hypothesized that conditioned drug-tolerance effects will produce withdrawal-like reactions that, as in Wikler's theory, should promote craving and relapse to drug use (Poulos, Hinson, & Siegel, 1981).

Another perspective on craving is that it is strongly associated with the positively reinforcing, or stimulating, effects of drugs. For example, Marlatt (1985) suggested that craving is a subjective state produced by the expectation that use of a drug will produce euphoria, excitation, or stimulation. Similarly, Wise (1988) proposed that craving represents memories of the pleasurable or positively reinforcing effects of drugs. There are also multi-process models, in which expectancies of positive reinforcement and anticipation of withdrawal relief, as well as other factors, including mood states and access to drugs, generate craving (Baker, Morse, & Sherman, 1987).

The early twenty-first century saw a surge of cognitive accounts of craving. In general, cognitive accounts have increasingly emphasized the role of implicit processes as playing an important motivational influence on drug taking (Wiers & Stacy, 2006). One influential cognitive theory suggests that drug use may operate independently of craving (Tiffany, 1990). According to this theory, an addict's drug-use behavior becomes highly automatic due to a long history of repeated practice. Over time, drug use may be easily triggered by certain cues, difficult to stop once triggered, and carried out effortlessly with little awareness. Addicts attempting to withdraw from drug use will experience craving as they try to stop these automatized actions from going through to completion.

Other models have proposed specific neural underpinnings for craving. For instance, the incentive-sensitization view, which distinguishes drug liking from drug wanting, associates the latter with sensitized neural circuits related to the nucleus accumbens (Robinson & Berridge, 1993). This sensitization results in excessive incentive salience being attributed to drug-associated cues.

MEASURES OF CRAVING

Craving is generally measured through three types of behaviors: self-reports of craving, drug-use behavior, and physiological responding. Most often, addicts are simply asked to rate or describe their level of craving for a drug. Questionnaires have been developed that ask addicts to rate a variety of issues related to craving. These questionnaires are considerably more reliable than a single rating of craving and show that an addict's description of craving may have multiple dimensions. The most common measure of tobacco craving is the Questionnaire of Smoking Urges (Tiffany & Drobes, 1991), and the Obsessive-Compulsive Drinking Scale (Anton, Moak, & Latham, 1995) is the most widely used measure related to alcohol craving. Measures of drug-use behavior have also been used to assess drug craving, which is entirely consistent with the assumption that craving is responsible for drug use in addicts. Finally, as several theories posit that craving should be represented by particular patterns of physiological changes, physiological measures, primarily those controlled by the autonomic nervous system, have been included in several studies as an index of craving. These measures have included changes in heart rate, sweat gland activity, and salivation. In general, withdrawal-based theories predict that the physiology of craving should look like the physiology of drug withdrawal, and models that emphasize positive reinforcement would associate drug desire with physiology characteristic of the excitatory effects of drugs. A number of neuroimaging techniques (fMRI, PET) have attempted to address the neural underpinnings of craving. As of 2008, though, research had not clearly identified which neural systems are associated with craving, though it appeared that areas related to reward processing (e.g., ventral striatum, orbitofrontal cortex, amygdala) are likely involved.

RESEARCH ON CRAVING

Naturalistic and laboratory studies have been used to investigate drug craving. Naturalistic studies examine changes in addicts' descriptions of craving as they are attempting to stop using drugs. These studies generally have shown that cravings are especially strong in the first several weeks of abstinence, but decline over time as addicts stay off drugs. They also reveal that craving rarely remains at a constant level throughout the day, but grows stronger or weaker depending on the situations the addict encounters. These situations tend to be strongly associated with previous use of drugs, such as meeting drug-using friends or going to locations where the addict used drugs in the past.

Laboratory studies attempt to manipulate craving by presenting addicts with stimuli or cues that have been associated with their previous drug use. For example, a heroin addict may watch a videotape of someone injecting heroin or smokers may be asked to imagine a situation in which they would want to smoke. These cue-reactivity studies allow the measurement of self-reports of craving, drug-use behavior, and physiological reactions under controlled conditions. Results from these studies indicate that abstinence from drugs, drug-related stimuli, and negative moods can increase craving.

Findings from naturalistic and laboratory studies have presented a challenge to the dominant assumption that craving is directly responsible for drug use in addicts (Kassel & Shiffman, 1992; Tiffany, 1990). For example, there is only a weak correlation between addicts' reported levels of craving and their level of drug consumption within most cue-reactivity studies. Correlations between self-reported craving and physiological reactions also tend to be weak. Other studies reveal that, although addicts frequently complain that cravings are a major difficulty, few addicts who relapse say that they experienced craving just before their relapse episode. However, when addicts are asked about their craving in general, or over a longer period of time, these ratings tend to better predict relapse. Overall, the exact function of craving in drug dependence remains controversial.

See also **Addiction: Concepts and Definitions; Conditioned Tolerance; Research, Animal Model: An Overview; Risk Factors for Substance Use, Abuse, and Dependence: Learning.**

BIBLIOGRAPHY

American Psychiatric Association. (1987). *Diagnostic and statistical manual of mental disorders* (3rd rev. ed.). Washington, DC: Author.

Anton, R. F., Moak, D. H., & Latham, P. (1995). The obsessive compulsive drinking scale: A self-rated instrument for the quantification of thoughts about alcohol and drinking behavior. *Alcoholism: Clinical and Experimental Research, 19,* 92–99.

Baker, T. B., Morse, E., & Sherman, J. E. (1987). The motivation to use drugs: A psychobiological analysis of urges. In P. C. Rivers (Ed.), *The Nebraska symposium on motivation: Alcohol use and abuse* (pp. 257–323). Lincoln: University of Nebraska Press.

Jellinek, E. M. (1955). The "craving" for alcohol. *Quarterly Journal of Studies on Alcohol, 16,* 35–38.

Kassel, J. D., & Shiffman, S. (1992). What can hunger teach us about drug craving? A comparative analysis of the two constructs. *Advances in Behaviour Research and Therapy, 14,* 141–167.

Marlatt, G. A. (1985). Cognitive factors in the relapse process. In G. A. Marlatt & J. R. Gordon (Eds.), *Relapse prevention* (pp. 128–200). New York: Guilford Press.

Poulos, C. W., Hinson, R., & Siegel, S. (1981). The role of Pavlovian processes in drug tolerance and dependence: Implications for treatment. *Addictive Behaviors, 6,* 205–211.

Robinson, T. E., & Berridge, K. C. (1993). The neural basis of drug craving: An incentive-sensitization theory of addiction. *Brain Research Review, 18,* 247–291.

Tiffany, S. T. (1990). A cognitive model of drug urges and drug-use behavior: Role of automatic and nonautomatic behavior. *Psychological Review, 97,* 147–168.

Tiffany, S. T., & Drobes, D. J. (1991). The development and initial validation of a questionnaire on smoking urges. *British Journal of Addiction, 86,* 1467–1476.

Wiers, R. W., & Stacy, A. W. (2006). *Handbook of implicit cognition and addiction.* Thousand Oaks, CA: Sage.

Wikler, A. (1948). Recent progress on neurophysiological basis of morphine addiction. *American Journal of Psychiatry, 105,* 329–338.

Wise, R. A. (1988). The neurobiology of craving: Implications for understanding and treatment of addiction. *Journal of Abnormal Psychology, 97,* 118–132.

World Health Organization Expert Committees on Mental Health and Alcohol. (1955). Craving for alcohol: Formulation of the Joint Expert Committees on Mental Health and Alcohol. *Quarterly Journal of Studies on Alcohol, 16,* 63–64.

STEPHEN T. TIFFANY
REVISED BY STEPHEN T. TIFFANY (2009)
DAVID J. DROBES (2009)

CREATIVITY AND DRUGS. Accounts of alcohol and drug use to stimulate creativity are apocryphal and anecdotal. For example, Samuel Taylor Coleridge reportedly composed much of his unfinished poem *Kubla Khan* while in an opium dream. In ancient Greece, however, the

Pythian priestesses of the oracle at Delphi inhaled medicinal fumes to facilitate revelatory trances—as did the priests and peoples of most ancient societies. The institutionalized twentieth-century Native American Church continues to use the peyote of their ancestors to promote profound religious experiences.

Psychedelic drugs, such as lysergic acid diethylamide (LSD), mescaline, psilocybin, and methylene dioxyamphetamine (MDA) have been used—both legally and illicitly—to increase aesthetic appreciation, improve artistic techniques, and enhance creativity. Marijuana has been used to heighten the sense of meaning, foster creativity, and heighten perceptions (also both legally and illicitly); and alcohol has been employed by countless people worldwide to relieve inhibitions, increase spontaneity, and stimulate innovation and originality.

In the industrial West, the common belief in, and positive association between, alcohol or drug use and creativity is strengthened by the popular stereotypes of artists, writers, actors, and others in the creative and performing arts as heavy users or abusers of such substances. Despite these anecdotal claims, little scientific evidence supports the notion that alcohol and drug use actually increase creativity.

Part of the reason that creativity is attributed to drug use involves the actions of many psychoactive substances in producing altered states of consciousness. These altered states are characterized by some or all of the following features: (1) *alterations in thinking*, in which distinctions between cause and effect become blurred and in which logical incongruities may coexist; (2) *disturbances in time sense*, whereby the sense of time and chronology may become greatly altered; (3) a sense of *loss of control*, during which the person becomes less inhibited and self-possessed; (4) a *change in emotional expression*; (5) *body image change*, with a dissolution of boundaries between one's self and the world, resulting in transcendental or mystical experiences of "oneness" or "oceanic feelings"; (6) *perceptual distortions*, including illusions, pseudohallucinations, heightened acuity, and increased visual imagery; (7) *hypersuggestibility*, representing a decrease in the use of critical faculties; (8) a heightened *sense of meaning and significance*; (9) *sense of the ineffable*, in which the experience cannot be expressed in words; and

(10) feelings of *rebirth and rejuvenation*. When people experience such features as these, it is understandable that they attribute creativity to certain drug experiences.

The immediate problem, however, in evaluating whether this is really so depends on the definition of creativity. At the outset, three dimensions of creativity need to be distinguished: those pertaining to the creative person, those pertaining to the creative process, and those pertaining to the creative product. If creativity pertains to an attribute of the person (e.g., original thinking), then any unusual or extraordinary experiences should qualify as "creative," even if nothing of social value emerges. If creativity pertains to a process (e.g., discovery, insight), then the testing and validation of the insights must take place as well. If creativity pertains to a product, it not only should possess some measure of social utility but should embody such qualities as novelty, surprise, uniqueness, originality, beauty, simplicity, value, and/or coherence. For both the creative process and the creative product, there is no substantive evidence to indicate that alcohol or drugs have benefit, despite the ongoing belief of many that they do. The experience of the *sense of meaning or significance* produced by drugs may have no bearing on whether that experience has *true* meaning or significance. The American philosopher and psychologist William James's claim that alcohol makes things seem more "utterly utter" is especially apt. This also happens with psychedelic drugs, which have the capacity to induce a sense of profundity and epiphany (intuitive grasp of reality), but usually without any substantive or lasting benefit or practical value.

What, then, is the actual state of knowledge about the relationship between substance use and creative achievement? What few studies exist, in fact, indicate mostly detrimental effects of drugs on creativity, especially when these substances are taken in large amounts and over an extended period of time. The results of studies on the actions of alcohol typify this. As early as 1962, for example, Nash demonstrated that small doses (about equal to two martinis) of alcohol, in normal volunteers, tended to facilitate mental associations, while large doses (about equal to four martinis) had adverse effects. With the large doses, they had more trouble in discriminating and assimilating details and performing complex tasks. In another study, Hajcak (1976) found that male under-graduates permitted alcohol on an ad-lib basis (without limits or restraints) showed greater initial productivity than when not allowed to drink but showed decreased appropriateness and decreased creative problem solving when intoxicated.

In an anecdotal study with seventeen artists who drank, Roe (1946) found that all but one regarded the short-term effects of alcohol as deleterious to their work, but they sometimes used it to overcome various technical difficulties. The general sentiment was that alcohol provided the freedom for painting but impaired the discipline. In a more extensive study of thirty-four eminent writers, Ludwig (1990) found that more than 75 percent of artists or performers who drank heavily experienced negative effects from alcohol—either directly or indirectly, on creative activity, particularly when they did not refrain from drinking when they were working. More positive effects of alcohol were found in a small number of cases, among those who used it in moderate amounts early in their careers to remove certain roadblocks, to lessen depression or mania, or to modulate the effects of other drugs.

With many anecdotal accounts to the contrary, the weight of scientific and clinical evidence suggests that long-term alcohol and drug use exert mostly negative effects on creativity. That drugs and alcohol are used so widely within the creative arts professions seems to have less to do with creativity than with social expectations and other extraneous factors. In fact, people use pharmacological substances for many reasons other than the stimulation of their imaginations. These reasons include relaxation, the facilitation of sleep, self-medication, social rituals, pleasure, or simply habituation or addiction.

Because writers, artists, actors, or musicians may write about, portray, or act out certain aspects of their pharmacological experiences does not logically or necessarily mean that these experiences are essential for the creative process. Creative people often exploit all aspects of their experiences—whether pathological or healthy and whether drug-induced or not—in a creative way; they try to translate personal visions and insights within their own fields of expression into socially acceptable, useful, or scientifically testable truths. Without some measure of social utility, unique drug-induced experiences represent little more than idiosyncratic to quasi-psychotic productions, having value and meaning only, perhaps, to the substance user.

See also **Alcohol; Lysergic Acid Diethylamide (LSD) and Psychedelics; Marijuana (Cannabis); Mescaline; Peyote; Psilocybin.**

BIBLIOGRAPHY

Dobkin de Rios, M., & Janiger, O. (2003). *LSD, spirituality, and the creative process.* Rochester, VT: Park Street Press.

Hajcak, F. J. (1976). *The effects of alcohol on creativity.* Microfilm of typescript. Ann Arbor, MI: University Microfilms.

Harmon, W. W., et al. (1966). Psychedelic agents in creative problem-solving. *Psychological Reports, 19,* 211–227.

Koski-Jannes, A. (1985). Alcohol and literary creativity. *Journal of Creative Behavior, 19,* 120–136.

Krippner, S. (1969). The psychedelic state, the hypnotic trance and the creative act. In C. Tart (Ed.), *Altered states of consciousness.* New York: Wiley.

Ludwig, A. M. (1966). Altered states of consciousness. *Archives of General Psychiatry, 15,* 223–234.

Ludwig, A. M. (1989). Reflections on creativity and madness. *American Journal of Psychotherapy, 43,* 4–14.

Ludwig, A. M. (1990). Alcohol input and creative output. *British Journal of Addiction, 85,* 953–963.

McGlothlin, W., Cohen, S., and McGlothlin, M. S. (1967). Long-lasting effects of LSD on normals. *Archives of General Psychiatry, 17,* 521–532.

Nash, H. (1962). *Alcohol and caffeine: A study of their psychological effects.* Springfield, IL: Charles C. Thomas.

Roe, A. (1946). Alcohol and creative work. *Quarterly Journal of the Study of Alcohol,* 415–467.

Tart, C. T. (1971). *On being stoned.* Palo Alto. CA: Science and Behavior Books.

Wolf, P. L. (2005). The effects of diseases, drugs, and chemicals on the creativity and productivity of famous sculptors, classic painters, classic music composers, and authors. *Archives of Pathology and Laboratory Medicine 129,* 11, 1457–1464.

ARNOLD M. LUDWIG

CRIME AND ALCOHOL. The relationship between alcohol consumption and involvement in crime is not a simple one. Drinking is a very common activity, and most drinking is not followed by criminal behavior. Understanding the alcohol-crime relationship requires an identification of the drinking effects and circumstances that are related to crime. Alcohol's relationship to crime also varies by the type of crime. The major crime-type distinction is between violent personal crime (such as homicide, forcible rape, and assault) and property crime (such as burglary and larceny). In addition, driving while intoxicated is a crime, and although first offenses are usually classified as misdemeanors, repeat offenders may be charged with gross misdemeanors and felonies. Certain variables also come into play in the alcohol-crime relationship. Age and gender, for example, have a bearing on whether drinking leads to criminal behavior. Young adult males are more likely than older adult males and females of all ages to engage in alcohol-related offenses. Moreover, underage drinking is a criminal offense, as is providing alcohol to minors.

According to the available evidence, drinking is more likely to be implicated in violent crime than in property crime. Moreover, violent offenses are often thought of as "expressive" or "instrumental." Expressive violent offenses are typically those resulting from interpersonal conflict that escalates from verbal abuse to physical aggression. Such violence often involves a drinking offender or drinking by both (or multiple) parties involved. Instrumental offenses have rational goals, typified by stealing to realize the value of the stolen money or goods. Alcohol is not thought to be an important causal factor in acquisitive crimes such as theft.

Research has shown that alcohol is an important factor in the occurrence of expressive interpersonal violence, that alcohol use increases the risk of being a crime victim, that the alcohol-crime relationship is complex (involving multiple factors in addition to alcohol), and that alcohol is often blamed without justification for criminal offenses.

DRINKING AS A PRECEDENT TO CRIME
The Bureau of Justice Statistics (BJS), an agency of the U.S. Department of Justice, reviewed the role alcohol played in crime by looking at convicted offender data from 1996 (Greenfield, 1998). On an average day in 1996, an estimated 5.3 million convicted offenders were under the supervision of criminal justice authorities. Nearly 40 percent of these offenders, or about two million persons,

had been using alcohol at the time of the offense for which they were convicted. Whether the offender was on probation or was incarcerated in a local jail or a state prison, all the offenders were about equally likely to have been drinking at the time of the crime. What they consumed was similar as well, with beer being the most commonly consumed alcoholic beverage—30 percent of probationers, 32 percent of jail inmates, and 23 percent of state prisoners said that they had been drinking beer either on its own or in combination with liquor prior to the commission of the current offense. Consumption of wine alone was comparatively rare among the surveyed offender populations.

Surveys of crime victims also indicate that offenders had often been drinking. The National Crime Victimization Survey (NCVS) is one of two statistical series maintained by the Department of Justice to learn about the extent to which crime is occurring. The NCVS, which gathers data on criminal victimization from a national sample of household respondents, provides annual estimates of crimes experienced by the public without regard to whether a law enforcement agency was called about the crime. Initiated in 1972, the NCVS was designed to complement what is known about crimes reported to local law enforcement agencies under the FBI's annual compilation known as the Uniform Crime Reporting (UCR) Program. Estimates from the 1998 NCVS indicate that victims of about three million violent crimes each year, or about a quarter of all violent crimes, perceived the offenders to have been drinking.

Most studies of alcohol and crime focus on offenses known to the police or on offenders serving sentences for crimes that resulted in a conviction. A notable exception is a community study done in Thunder Bay, in the province of Ontario, Canada. Pernanen (1976, 1981, 1991) collected information from a representative sample of 1,100 community residents. Among those who had been victimized, the assailant had been drinking in 51 percent of the cases in which violence occurred, and 68 percent of the time the assailant was judged to have been "drunk." Pernanen notes that the findings from the Thunder Bay study are consistent with many other North American studies using police records. Generally, half of all violent offenders have been found to have been drinking at the time of their offense.

The most common pattern found in studies of violent crimes is that 60 percent or more of the events involve drinking by the offender, by both the offender and the victim, or by the victim alone. The results of a classic 1958 study by Wolfgang indicate that the most common pattern in a survey of homicides involved the presence of alcohol for both the victim and offender.

If these findings indicated the extent to which drinking was causally implicated in violent crime, it would be remarkable. It could then be argued that alcohol accounts for a majority of violent offenses. But neither the presence of alcohol in a crime nor the intoxication of an offender is necessarily an indication that alcohol influenced the occurrence of the crime. Because drinking is such a common activity, it is likely that alcohol is sometimes simply present but not causally relevant. Drinking is also sometimes offered by offenders as an excuse for the crime, as a way of avoiding being held accountable.

ALCOHOL USE AND CRIME VICTIMIZATION

Alcohol use raises the likelihood that the drinker will be a victim of violent crime. Substantial percentages of homicide, assault, and robbery victims were drinking just before their victimization. Medical examiners have done a significant number of homicide studies by running toxicological tests of the body fluids of homicide victims. Separate reviews by Greenberg (1981) and Murdoch, Pihl, and Ross (1990) found that the percentage of homicide victims who had been drinking ranges widely, but is usually about 50 percent. Goodman et al. (1986) tested the alcohol levels of several thousand homicide victims and found that 46 percent of the victims had consumed alcohol in the period before being killed, and that three out of ten victims had alcohol levels beyond the legal intoxication level.

Roizen (1993) examined studies of alcohol use by robbery and rape victims. The percentage who had been drinking before their victimization ranged widely—from 12 to 16 percent for robbery victims and from 6 to 36 percent for rape victims. Abbey (1991) and Muehlenhard and Linton (1987) also found in their studies of date rape that both offenders and victims had commonly been drinking. Abbey suggested that drinking by either the offender or the victim contributes to rape

because of the impaired communication and misperception that results from alcohol's effects on cognitive ability (among other contributing factors). Males who have been drinking, for example, may mistakenly attribute sexual intent to women whom they date.

Alcohol may increase the risk that the drinker will be a crime victim because of effects that alcohol has on judgment and demeanor. Someone who has been drinking may take risks that might not be taken when sober, such as walking in a dangerous area of a city at night. Alcohol also causes some individuals to be loud and verbally aggressive. Such a demeanor can be offensive and might sometimes precipitate physical attack.

DRINKING AND FAMILY VIOLENCE

Unfortunately, violence is common in American households, and alcohol is a contributing factor, according to research done by Kantor and Straus (1989) and Straus, Gelles, and Steinmetz (1980), among others. Hotaling and Sugarman (1986) found that alcohol appears to be most relevant to the occurrence of husband-against-wife violence. Hamilton and Collins (1981) reviewed about 25 studies that examined the role of alcohol in spouse and child abuse. They found alcohol to be most relevant to wife beating, where it was present in one-quarter to one-half of all such events. (Alcohol was present in less than one in five incidents of child abuse, however.) The most common patterns were for only the husband to be drinking or for both parties to have consumed alcohol. It was uncommon for only the wife to have been drinking. Studies also indicate that husbands or intimate partners with alcohol problems are more likely to be violent against their wives or partners.

A 1998 BJS study on the relationship between crime and alcohol found that two-thirds of victims who suffered violence by an "intimate" (a current or former spouse, boyfriend, or girlfriend) reported that alcohol had been a factor. Among spouse victims, three out of four incidents were reported to have involved an offender who had been drinking. By contrast, an estimated 31 percent of stranger victimizations where the victim could determine the absence or presence of alcohol were perceived to be alcohol-related.

Research by Jones and Schecter (1992) and Barnett and Fagan (1993) on family violence suggests that violence against women may lead to their own use of alcohol and drugs as a coping mechanism. Both drinking and drug use may be a response to the physical and emotional pain and fear that result from living in a violent relationship. Miller, Downs, and Testa (1993) found that women in alcohol-treatment programs had higher rates of father-to-daughter violence than did the women in a comparison group. These findings underline the importance of interpreting the meaning of alcohol's association with family violence (and other forms of violence) carefully. As previously noted, alcohol is often present but irrelevant to the occurrence of violence. Some recent literature on family violence indicates that alcohol use may sometimes be a response to violent victimization.

ALCOHOL AND ITS CONTRIBUTION TO CRIME

There are a number of possible explanations offered for alcohol's role in crime:

- The need for money to support drinking may cause some individuals to commit crimes to generate cash to support their habit.
- The pharmacological effects of alcohol can compromise drinkers' cognitive ability and judgment and raise the likelihood of physical aggression.
- Expectations that alcohol makes drinkers aggressive may increase the chance of violence.
- Standards of conduct and accountability for behavior may differ for sober and drunken activities, and these differences can result in an increase in the likelihood of criminal behavior after drinking.

These possible explanations are not mutually exclusive, and they all may sometimes accurately describe how drinking causes crime. Two or more of the explanations may even apply to the same incident.

Committing "income crimes," or crimes to obtain money for drinking, is not thought to be an important explanation. Although the cost of maintaining an addiction to relatively expensive drugs (e.g., heroin and cocaine) is high, the price tag for supporting heavy drinking is usually modest. In most of the United States, for example, one can support a habit of daily heavy drinking for 10 dollars a day or less. The majority of individuals could maintain such a habit without resorting to crime, although many heavy drinkers spend more than this minimal amount on alcohol. There is virtually no information in the research literature about the likelihood or frequency of involvement in income crime to support drinking, but alcohol is not thought to be a major factor in income crimes. This does not mean it never happens, however, only that it is uncommon.

If alcohol is not an important factor in the occurrence of income-generating crime, why do so many property offenders (approximately 30 percent of inmates in 1996) report they were under the influence of alcohol at the time they committed such offenses? At least two explanations are possible for the high correlation between drinking and property crime. The first suggests that the correlation is simply coincidental, not causal. A second reason (put forward by both Collins, 1988, and Cordilia, 1985) is that a property offender who has been drinking is more likely to be caught than one who is sober. This reason makes sense, based on the known impairment effects of alcohol. A drinking offender may not be as competent or careful as a sober one, so drinking offenders may be overrepresented among offenders who are caught, and thus known to criminal-justice officials.

Alcohol impairs one's cognitive abilities, including the capacity to communicate clearly and the capacity to understand the verbal and behavioral cues of others. In addition, a person whose abilities have been impaired by alcohol is less able to make decisions and carry out appropriate and effective actions. Pernanen, in his early work (1976), discussed how alcohol-impaired cognitive ability can lead to violence. When one or both parties who are interacting have been drinking, there is an increased potential for misunderstanding that can lead to conflict and that may in turn escalate to violence. One factor in such a scenario is what may be called a "reduced behavioral response repertoire." Alcohol impairs a drinker's capacity to conceive and utilize the wide range of verbal and other behavioral options that are available to sober individuals. Alcohol-induced cognitive impairment may also diminish the drinker's capacity to foresee the negative implications of violent actions. In summary, one way that alcohol increases the likelihood of violence is through its negative effects on cognitive capacities, and these effects lead to an increased risk of violence.

It has been demonstrated in laboratory experiments that both actual alcohol use and the belief that alcohol has been consumed can raise levels of aggression. In laboratory experiments using competitive encounters between opponents in which the winner could apply an electrical shock to the loser, subjects who had been given alcohol behaved more aggressively. Evidence gathered by Bushman and Cooper (1990) and by Hull and Bond (1986) also indicates that subjects who have been told they have received alcohol, but who actually have been given a placebo, are more aggressive in their administration of electrical shocks. These findings suggest that beliefs about alcohol's behavioral effects can themselves affect behavior.

Expectations that alcohol use leads to aggressive behavior probably have sociocultural roots. Anthropologists such as Heath (1976a, 1976b) and MacAndrew and Edgerton (1969), for example, note that societies differ in the behavior that occurs after drinking. Some of these differences may be attributable to racial or ethnic differences in physiological reactions to alcohol, but it is also clear that there are normative variations in what behaviors are expected or acceptable after drinking. In fact, behavioral norms after drinking may vary within societies. MacAndrew and Edgerton note that during certain "time-out" periods, usual standards of behavior are suspended. For example, festivals or Mardi Gras celebrations are often characterized by high levels of drinking and behavior that is considered deviant or criminal during normal times.

Alcohol appears to be implicated in violence in another indirect way. Drinking is sometimes used as an excuse for crime or as a way to avoid accountability after the fact. McCaghy (1968) refers to this phenomenon as "deviance disavowal." The deviance disavowal potential of alcohol can account for a drinker's involvement in crime in two ways: Individuals may drink or say that they have been drinking as an advance excuse for their conduct, or drinking may be offered as an excuse after the fact.

CRIME AND ALCOHOL: SUMMARY

Drinking alcohol and involvement in criminal behavior frequently occur together. Some of the time alcohol has a causal role in crime, but often it is merely present. Drinking is most likely to be relevant causally to expressive interpersonal violence—including family violence. Drinking can increase the risk of being victimized as well. Drinking may also sometimes help account for the commission of crimes to obtain money to support the habit, but alcohol is not a major factor in the occurrence of income crime. Drinking leads to criminal behavior in a number of ways, including having an impact on cognition and the rules that govern behavior and accountability for behavior. The alcohol-crime relationship is complex. It is clear that drinking is rarely the only cause of criminal behavior, and that when it does contribute, it is usually only one of a number of relevant factors.

See also **Complications: Cardiovascular System (Alcohol and Cocaine); Complications: Cognition; Crime and Drugs; Driving, Alcohol, and Drugs; Driving Under the Influence (DUI); Economic Costs of Alcohol and Drug Abuse; Expectancies; Intimate Partner Violence and Alcohol/Substance Use; Social Costs of Alcohol and Drug Abuse.**

BIBLIOGRAPHY

Abbey, A. (1991). Acquaintance rape and alcohol consumption on college campuses: How are they linked? *Journal of American College Health, 39*(4), 165–169.

Barnett, O. W., & Fagan, R. W. (1993). Alcohol use in male spouse abusers and their female partners. *Journal of Family Violence, 8*(1), 1–25.

Baum, K., & Baum, P. (2005). Violent victimization of college students, 1995–2002 (NCJ-206836). Washington, DC: U.S. Department of Justice, Office of Justice Programs, Bureau of Justice Statistics.

Beck, A., et al. (1993). Survey of state prison inmates, 1991 (NCJ-136949). Washington, DC: U.S. Department of Justice, Office of Justice Programs, Bureau of Justice Statistics. Available from http://ojp.usdoj.gov/.

Bushman, B. J., & Cooper, H. M. (1990). Effects of alcohol on human aggression: An integrative research review. *Psychological Bulletin, 107*(3), 341–354.

Collins, J. J. (1988). Alcohol and interpersonal violence: Less than meets the eye. In N. A. Weiner & M. E. Wolfgang (Eds.), *Pathways to criminal violence*. Newbury Park, CA: Sage Publications.

Cordilia, A. (1985). Alcohol and property crime: Exploring the causal nexus. *Journal of Studies on Alcohol, 46*(2), 161–171.

Goodman, R. A., et al. (1986). Alcohol use and interpersonal violence: Alcohol detected in homicide victims. *American Journal of Public Health, 76*(2), 144–149.

Greenberg, S. W. (1981). Alcohol and crime: A methodological critique of the literature. In J. J. Collins, Jr. (Ed.), *Drinking and crime: Perspectives on the relationships between alcohol consumption and criminal behavior.* New York: Guilford Press.

Greenfield, L. A. (1998). Alcohol and crime: An analysis of national data on the prevalence of alcohol involvement in crime (NCJ 168632). Washington, DC: U.S. Department of Justice, Office of Justice Programs, Bureau of Justice Statistics. Available from http://ojp.usdoj.gov/.

Greenfield, L. A., & Hennenberg, M. A. (2001). Victim and offender self-reports of alcohol involvement in crime. *Alcohol Research & Health, 25*(1), 20–31. Available from http://pubs.niaaa.nih.gov/.

Gruenwald, P. J., Friesthler, B., Remer, L., LaScala, E. A., & Treno, A. (2006) Ecological models of alcohol outlets and violent assaults: Crime potentials and geospatial analysis. *Addiction 101*(5), 666–677.

Hamilton, C. J., & Collins, J. J., Jr. (1981). The role of alcohol in wife beating and child abuse: A review of the literature. In J. J. Collins, Jr. (Ed.), *Drinking and crime: Perspectives on the relationship between alcohol consumption and criminal behavior.* New York: Guilford Press.

Heath, D. B. (1976a). Anthropological perspectives on alcohol: An historical review. In M. W. Everett, J. O. Waddell, & D. B. Heath (Eds.), *Cross-cultural approaches to the study of alcohol.* The Hague: Mauton.

Heath, D. B. (1976b). Anthropological perspectives on the social biology of alcohol: An introduction to the literature. In B. Kissin & H. Begleiter (Eds.), *The biology of alcoholism: Vol. 4. Social aspects of alcoholism.* New York: Plenum.

Hotaling, G., & Sugarman, D. (1986). An analysis of risk markers in husband to wife violence: The current state of knowledge. *Violence and Victims, 1*(2), 101–124.

Hull, J. G., & Bond, C. F., Jr. (1986). Social and behavioral consequences of alcohol consumption and expectancy: A meta-analysis. *Psychological Bulletin, 99*(3), 347–360.

Jones, A., & Schecter, S. (1992). *When love goes wrong: What to do when you can't do anything right.* New York: HarperCollins.

Kantor, G.-K., & Straus, M. A. (1989). Substance abuse as a precipitant of wife abuse victimizations. *American Journal of Drug and Alcohol Abuse, 15*(2), 173–189.

MacAndrew, C., & Edgerton, R. B. (1969). *Drunken comportment: A social explanation.* Chicago: Aldine.

McCaghy, C. (1968). *Drinking and deviance disavowal: The case of child molesters. Social Problems,* 16, 43–49.

Miller, B. A., Downs, W. R., & Testa, M. (1993). Interrelationships between victimization experiences and women's alcohol/drug use. *Journal of Studies on Alcohol,* (Suppl. 11), 109–117.

Muehlenhard, C. L., & Linton, M. A. (1987). Date rape and sexual aggression in dating situations: Incidence and risk factors. *Journal of Counseling Psychology, 34,* 186–196.

Murdoch, D., Pihl, R. O., & Ross, D. (1990). Alcohol and crimes of violence: Present issues. *International Journal of the Addictions, 25*(9), 1065–1081.

Pernanen, K. (1976). Alcohol and crimes of violence. In B. Kissin & H. Begleiter (Eds.), *The biology of alcoholism:* Vol. 4. *Social aspects of alcoholism.* New York: Plenum.

Pernanen, K. (1981). Theoretical aspects of the relationship between alcohol use and crime. In J. J. Collins, Jr. (Ed.), *Drinking and crime: Perspectives on the relationships between alcohol consumption and criminal behavior.* New York: Guilford Press.

Pernanen, K. (1991). *Alcohol in human violence.* New York: Guilford Press.

Quigley, B. M., & Leonard, K. E. (2005). Alcohol use and violence among young adults. *Alcohol Research & Health, 28,* 191–194. Available from http://pubs.niaaa.nih.gov/.

Roizen, J. (1993). Issues in the epidemiology of alcohol and violence. In S. E. Martin (Ed.), *Alcohol and interpersonal violence: Fostering multidisciplinary perspectives* (NIH Publication No. 93-3496, Research Monograph 24). Rockville, MD: U.S. Department of Health and Human Services.

Straus, M. A., Gelles, R. J., & Steinmetz, S. K. (1980). *Behind closed doors: Violence in the American family.* Garden City, NY: Anchor-Doubleday.

Widom, C. S. & Hiller-Sturmhofel, S. (2001). Alcohol abuse as a risk factor for and consequence of child abuse. *Alcohol Research & Health, 25,* 52–57.

Wolfgang, M. E. (1958). *Patterns of criminal homicide.* Philadelphia: University of Pennsylvania Press.

Zawitz, M. W., et al. (1993). Highlights from 20 years of surveying crime victims: The National Crime Victimization Survey, 1973–92 (NCJ-144525). Washington, DC: U.S. Department of Justice, Office of Justice Programs, Bureau of Justice Statistics.

JAMES J. COLLINS
REVISED BY FREDERICK K. GRITTNER (2009)

CRIME AND DRUGS.

Because of widespread public and political concern over drug-related crime, there has been an urgent need to understand the relationship between drugs and crime. However, despite numerous studies on this topic, only since the 1980s have significant empirical advances in understanding this relationship emerged.

In a comprehensive literature review, Gandossy et al. (1980) concluded that the drugs-crime relationship was far more complex than originally believed. While acknowledging the significant contributions of previous research, the authors argued that methodological problems in the studies they reviewed had obscured an understanding of the linkage between drugs and crime. As these and other reviewers have observed, perhaps the most serious of these weaknesses was the use of official arrest records as indicators of criminal activity. Studies using confidential self-report methods in settings in which there is immunity from prosecution have consistently documented that less than 1 percent of offenses committed by drug abusers result in arrest.

Studies conducted since 1980 have relied more on such confidential self-report data, which has permitted more realistic estimates of the extent of criminality among drug abusers. In addition, victims of violent crime are now being asked whether they perceived the offender to be under the influence of drugs or alcohol. The annual Bureau of Justice Statistics (BJS) National Crime Victimization Survey asks this question of crime victims. Though a subjective inquiry, the 1998 survey revealed that 30 percent of victims could not determine whether the offender was under the influence of a substance. Of those who could make a determination, about 31 percent reported that the offender was under the influence of drugs or alcohol.

From 1987 to 2003, the National Institute of Justice (NIJ) conducted a program that obtained urine specimens from and interviewed close to half a million arrestees at 44 locations across the country. Originally called Drug Use Forecasting (DUF), in 1997 it was renamed the Arrestee Drug Abuse Monitoring (ADAM) program. The program was designed to measure drug use among arrestees by calculating the percentage of arrestees with positive urine tests for drug use. The samples were collected voluntarily and anonymously at the time of arrest in booking facilities. The ADAM program has given researchers a powerful tool for obtaining empirical evidence of patterns of drug abuse. ADAM is the only national research program studying drug use that employs both drug testing and interviews, thus giving analysts the means of assessing the validity of self-report data. Therefore, ADAM data are less susceptible to either exaggeration or denial of drug use than many other surveys. Moreover, ADAM is the only national drug research program built upon data collection at the local level. This data has revealed that there is no single national drug problem, but rather different local drug problems that vary from city to city. Unfortunately, the program ended in January 2004 due to budget problems.

THE CRIMINALITY OF DRUG ABUSERS

In examining the criminality of drug abusers, it is important to note that the onset of illicit drug use typically does not result in the onset of criminal behavior. Rather, it is the frequency, not the onset, of drug use that increases criminal activity. Furthermore, the positive relationship between drug-use frequency and crime frequency is not consistent across all types of drug use and all types of crime. Such a relationship has been observed with respect to only three types of drug abuse: heroin addiction, cocaine abuse, and multiple-drug use. In addition, such associations are more common for property crime than for violent crime.

Narcotic Drug Use. Much of the current knowledge about the relationship between drugs and crime comes from detailed self-report information on the type, extent, and severity of criminal activity of narcotic (mainly heroin) addicts. Large-scale, independently conducted studies have convincingly shown that increases in property crime and robbery, which has components of both property crime and violence, are associated with increased heroin use. Such a relationship, however, is less clear for violent crimes other than robbery.

Prevalence and Scope of Property and Violent Crime. Several key studies have revealed an exceptionally high prevalence of property crime among narcotic addicts. Anglin and Speckart (1988) found that 82 percent of a sample of 386 California male narcotic addicts reported involvement in property crime over an average five-year period of daily narcotic use. Anglin and Hser (1987) reported that 77 percent of a sample of 196 female narcotic addicts from California admitted to involvement in property crime during an average six-year narcotic addiction period. Inciardi (1986) noted that almost all of a sample of 573 male and female narcotic abusers from Miami had reportedly engaged in theft during the year prior to interview. Inciardi also found that these individuals reported involvement in more than 77,000 property crimes (averaging 135 per subject) over a 12-month period while at large in the community. This figure included 6,669 burglaries, 841 vehicle thefts, 25,045 instances of shoplifting, and 17,240 instances of fencing stolen merchandise. While these studies varied in sampling methods and definitions of property crime (e.g., including and not including robbery), they provide evidence that a substantial majority of narcotic abusers routinely engage in property crime.

Property crime comprises a considerable portion of the crime, other than drug distribution, committed by narcotic addicts. For instance, Nurco et al. (1991a) found that of the nondistribution crimes committed by a sample of 250 male narcotic addicts during an average 7.5-year addiction period, approximately 48 percent were property crimes. Research has also consistently documented that violent crime is less prevalent and occurs with less frequency than property crime among heroin addicts. Earlier studies noted that addicts tend to prefer property crime to violent crime, and that they appear to be less violent than other offenders. While findings from later studies have continued to show that violence accounts for only a small proportion of all addict crime (approximately 1% to 3%, a rate that is much smaller than the property-crime figure), the actual number of violent crimes is still quite large because addicts commit so many crimes. For example, in Inciardi's 1986 sample of 573 Miami narcotic abusers, violent crime made up only 2.8 percent of all offenses (5% of nondistribution offenses) committed by the subjects in the year prior to interview. However, this relatively small percentage amounted to 6,000 incidents of violent crime (or 10.4 per subject, on average), since a total of 215,105 offenses were committed.

Researchers have also suggested that heavy heroin use and, more recently, heavy cocaine abuse have contributed to record numbers of homicides in large cities in the United States. The ways in which drugs can contribute to violence is the basis for a prominent theory in the drugs-crime field, discussed below.

Crime and Frequency of Heroin Use. Studies have provided consistent evidence of a direct, functional relationship between the frequency of narcotic drug use (primarily heroin) and the frequency of property crime. These investigations have employed a unique longitudinal design in which crime data are obtained for each subject over periods during which the frequency of narcotic use may vary. These studies of addiction careers reveal that property-crime rates are significantly higher during narcotic addiction periods than during periods of nonaddiction. Such a relationship tends to be linear, with the highest property-crime rates occurring during the highest levels of narcotic use (three or more times per day). In addition, although most addicts commit property crime prior to addiction, the frequency of such crime increases significantly from preaddiction to addiction, and it remains high over subsequent addiction periods and low during any intervening nonaddiction periods. While other factors also influence property-crime rates, the simplest explanation for these results is that property crime is functionally related to narcotic addiction (since addicts need cash to support their habits).

Evidence of a similar relationship between heroin use and violent crime is less conclusive. Studies have consistently shown that rates for robbery, in which there are property-crime features, are considerably higher during addiction periods than during either preaddiction or nonaddiction periods. However, when rates for composite measures of violence and rates of assault alone are examined, the relationship appears less clear.

In compiling composite measures of violence, Ball et al. (1983) found that for a sample of 243 male Baltimore addicts, the number of days on which violent crime was committed was considerably higher during the first addiction period than during the first nonaddiction period. However, in subsequent studies of 250 male addicts from Baltimore and New York City, most of whom had multiple periods of addiction, more complex relationships were observed. Over an addiction career, violent-crime rates for the total sample were significantly higher for combined addiction periods than for combined nonaddiction periods (Nurco et al., 1986; Nurco et al., 1988a). This result stemmed largely from high levels of crime committed during the first addiction period, and violent crime actually decreased over subsequent periods of addiction, a finding that appeared to be age-related. The fact that mean rates for violence were found to be even higher for preaddiction (10 days per year) than for addiction periods (8 days per year) also reflects an inverse relationship between age and violent criminal activity.

The 1999 ADAM report on U.S. drug use of arrestees revealed that opiate use among adult arrestees was relatively low compared to the prevalence of cocaine and marijuana in the overall sample. For female arrestees, the median rate for testing positive to opiates was 8 percent in 1999, and for male arrestees it was 6 percent.

Nonnarcotic Drug Use. Investigation of the nonnarcotic drugs-crime relationship only emerged as a major research question in the 1980s. In their literature review, Gandossy and associates (1980) found that in the few studies conducted on the nonnarcotic drug-crime relationship, evidence linking the use of various nonnarcotic substances to either property crime or violent crime was weak. Another reason for the unclear relationship between nonnarcotic drug use and criminal behavior is that various narcotic and nonnarcotic drugs are often used in combination. Thus, disentangling their separate relationships to criminal activity, let alone determining cause and effect, is especially problematic. Despite these difficulties, significant advances have been made in understanding the nonnarcotic drugs-crime relationship since that time.

Cocaine. Data analyses by Johnson et al. (1991) on a nationwide probability sample of 1,725 adolescents strongly supported a cocaine-crime connection. Adolescents who reported using cocaine in the year preceding the interview (comprising only 1.3% of the sample) were responsible for a disproportionately large share of the property and violent crime committed by the sample during this period. The cocaine users accounted for 60 percent of all minor thefts, 57 percent of felony thefts, 41 percent of all robberies, and 28 percent of felony assaults committed by the entire sample.

In typological studies involving seriously delinquent youth and female crack-cocaine abusers, those subjects who reported the heaviest levels of cocaine use also engaged in substantially higher rates of property and violent crime than subjects who used crack less frequently. Among a sample of 254 youth identified by Inciardi and coworkers (1993a) as serious delinquents, the 184 crack dealers (86% of whom were daily crack users) were responsible for 45,563 property crimes (an average of 231 per user) during the year preceding the interview. In contrast, the 70 subjects who were not crack dealers and who used crack less frequently (approximately three times per week) averaged 135 property crimes per year. In addition, the heavy cocaine users averaged ten robberies per year, compared with only one per year for the remaining subjects. Similar results were reported for a sample of 197 female crack abusers (Inciardi et al., 1993b). The average adjusted annual rates for the 58 subjects classified as heavy cocaine users (8 or more doses per day) were 12 for violent crime, 14 for major property offenses, and 320 for minor property crimes. These rates were substantially higher than rates for the 90 subjects classified as "typical" users (4–7.99 doses per day). For those 49 users who took less than four doses per day, the average adjusted annual rates for violence and major property crime were less than one, and the rate for minor property offenses was 24.

Increased cocaine use among narcotic addicts has also been associated with increased property and violent-crime rates. Both Nurco et al. (1988b) and Shaffer et al. (1985) found that male narcotic addicts who had higher rates of cocaine use tended to have higher rates of property and violent crime than addicts who did not abuse cocaine.

The 1999 ADAM report found that cocaine use among adult arrestees remained high, with cocaine found in more than one-third of adult arrestees in 20 sites. There was substantial variation in the proportion of those testing positive for cocaine in the various sites, however. In three sites (Atlanta, Chicago, New York City), more than 60 percent of adult female arrestees tested positive for cocaine. In six other sites, however, cocaine use was less than 25 percent.

Other Nonnarcotic Drugs. The use of other nonnarcotic drugs appears to be unrelated to increased criminal activity. While there is considerable evidence that frequent users of multiple nonnarcotic substances, including amphetamines, barbiturates, marijuana, and PCP, typically have high crime rates (although somewhat lower than the rates for heroin addicts), such is not the case for users of single non-narcotic drugs. Although such usage may be related to offenses such as disorderly conduct or driving while impaired, it is not generally associated with predatory crime.

Marijuana. Research on the relationship between marijuana use and crime has found that the use of marijuana is not associated with an increase in crime—with the possible exception of the sale of the drug, disorderly conduct, and driving while impaired. Some studies have reported that marijuana use may actually reduce inclinations toward violent crime.

A major problem in studying the association between marijuana use and criminal behavior is that the exclusive use of marijuana is generally short-lived. Further, like other illicit nonnarcotic substances, marijuana is often used in combination with other drugs. Under such circumstances, it is difficult to isolate the effects of heavy marijuana use from those associated with the use of various drug combinations.

The 1999 ADAM report disclosed that marijuana remained a very popular drug for adult arrestees, particularly among young males between 15 and 20 years of age. The median rate of marijuana positives for this group of arrestees in 1999 was 63 percent, compared to the overall adult male arrestee median rate of 39 percent and the overall adult female arrestee median rate of 26 percent.

Amphetamines. Literature reviews published during the late 1970s and early 1980s (e.g., Gandossy et al., 1980; Greenberg, 1976) reported that the association between amphetamine use and crime was difficult to determine because of the diversity of amphetamine users, among other factors. More recent ethnographic studies of drug abusers (e.g., Goldstein, 1986) have reported that amphetamine use is related to violent crime in some individuals. In the general population, however, the association between amphetamine use and crime is not readily apparent. Despite assertions of the media in the 1960s and 1970s, the prevalence of amphetamine-related violence among American youth is likely to be quite low.

The 1999 ADAM report indicated that methamphetamine use among ADAM arrestees was concentrated mainly in the western part of the United States. A large number of sites had virtually no presence of methamphetamine. However, prevalence rates exceeded 10 percent both for adult female arrestees in 12 sites and for adult male arrestees in 9 sites.

Psychedelic Substances. Most studies investigating the relationship between psychedelic-substance abuse and crime have involved phencyclidine (PCP). Much of this research has examined the relationship between PCP and violence. As in the coverage of many other nonnarcotic drugs, media reports, principally in the 1970s and early 1980s, have emphasized a perceived link between PCP use and violent behavior. However, the actual extent of this link has been greatly exaggerated. In his report on the subject, Kinlock (1991) noted that serious methodological problems in some studies, as well as contradictory findings in others, disallowed a conclusive answer to the question of whether PCP use increases violent crime. Nevertheless, researchers have suggested that the inconsistency of study findings may indicate that PCP use facilitates violence in a small proportion of users (see Inciardi, 1986; Kinlock, 1991). There is agreement that biological, psychological, situational, and other factors underlying seemingly drug-related aggressive behavior should be examined in future research.

THEORIES ON THE DRUGS-CRIME RELATIONSHIP

Inciardi (1986) has noted that numerous theories have been posited to explain the drugs-crime relationship. Many of these theories deal with the etiology of drug use and crime. Early etiological theories tended to be overly simplistic, focusing on what Inciardi termed the "chicken-egg" question: Which came first, drugs or crime? This question polarized the drugs-crime field for over 50 years. It typically reflected two mutually exclusive positions, with one side arguing that addicts were criminals to begin with and that addiction was simply another manifestation of a deviant lifestyle, and the other side positing that addicts were not criminals but were simply forced into committing crime to support their drug habits.

Reflecting a middle-ground position, more recent theories have argued for a diversity among narcotic addicts with regard to the predispositional characteristics and motives underlying drug-related criminal behavior. For example, based on their research with narcotic addicts, Nurco and his associates (1991b) concluded that there is considerable variation among addicts in their propensity toward criminal activity: Some addicts were heavily involved in crime prior to addiction, whereas others are extensively involved in crime only when addicted.

In the late 1970s, drugs-crime theories became increasingly complex, partly because studies tended to have fewer methodological problems that could interfere with the measurement of both drug use and crime. With improvements in techniques, researchers gradually become more aware of heterogeneity among drug abusers on many dimensions, including the type and severity of drug-use patterns and related criminal activity. In addition, more recent studies have found that drug use and crime, in most instances, do not initially have a causal relationship but are often the joint result of multiple influences. Among the many factors contributing to drug use and crime are negative family dynamics (e.g., lack of parental supervision, parental rejection, family conflict, lack of discipline, and parental deviance); association with deviant peers; school dropout, failure, and discipline problems; and early antisocial behavior. Consistent with the notion that all drug abusers are not alike, varying combinations of factors probably contribute to different patterns of deviant behavior in individuals at risk.

However, as Inciardi et al. (1993a) have noted, these theories still have some limitations. Most theories discuss drug abuse only as one of several manifestations of delinquency. Furthermore, as in earlier studies, the primary concern has been with the etiology of deviant behavior. Very little attention has been paid to explaining events that occur after the onset of drug use and criminal behavior, specifically how certain types of drug abuse increase the frequency of criminal activity. Finally, theories have typically focused on adolescence, without incorporating attributes and events that influence behavior during childhood and adulthood.

Among the most prominent theories in the drugs-crime field is that of Paul Goldstein regarding the relationship between drugs and violence. Goldstein's theory is based on his numerous ethnographic accounts of violent drug-related acts obtained from both perpetrators and victims in New York City. According to this theory, drugs and violence can be related in three separate ways: psychopharmacologically, economic-compulsively, and systemically. Within the psychopharmacological model, violent crime results from the short- or long-term effects of the ingestion of particular substances, most notably crack-cocaine and heroin. According to the economic-compulsive model, violent crime is committed as a means to obtain money to purchase drugs, primarily expensive addictive drugs such as heroin and cocaine. The systemic model posits that drug-related violence results from the traditionally aggressive patterns of interaction found at various levels within systems of illicit-drug distribution. Examples include killing or assaulting someone for failure to pay debts; for selling "bad," or adulterated, drugs; or for transgression on one's drug-dealing "turf."

Several key studies have analyzed data in the light of Goldstein's concepts. In a study of 578 homicides in Manhattan in 1981, 38 percent of male victims and 14 percent of female victims were murdered as a result of drug-related activity (Tardiff et al., 1986). The investigators contended that these percentages were higher than those previously reported in the United States. In a subsequent study by Goldstein and his coworkers (1989) involving 414 homicides in New York City that occurred over an eight-month period, 53 percent were classified by the police and researchers as being drug-related. In both studies, most of the drug-related homicides were attributed to systemic causes. Interestingly, in the former study most of the homicides involved heroin, whereas in the latter study most involved crack-cocaine.

Drug Use and High-Rate, Serious Criminality. As indicated earlier, the onset of illicit drug use does not typically result in the onset of criminal behavior. In most cases, both drug use and crime begin in the early teens. Generally, the less serious the drug or crime, the earlier the age at onset of involvement. For example, among illicit drugs, marijuana is more commonly used at a younger age than are sedatives or tranquilizers, and these drugs, in turn, are typically used at a younger age than "hard" drugs such as heroin and cocaine. Similarly, minor forms of crime (e.g., shoplifting, vandalism) have an earlier onset than more serious types of crimes, such as assault, robbery, and drug dealing.

Most marijuana users do not become heroin addicts, and most youths who commit minor property crimes do not subsequently become involved in more serious offenses. In both instances, the salient variable appears to be age of onset: the younger the individual is when first using a "soft" drug or committing a minor crime, the more likely he or she will be to move on to more serious forms of deviance. In general, the more deviant the environment (i.e., family, peers, community), the earlier the onset of deviance.

Since 1980, independent studies have identified several core characteristics of high-rate, serious offenders. According to Chaiken and Chaiken (1990), these studies have consistently found that predatory individuals tend to commit many different types of crime, including violent crime, at high rates, and that they tend to abuse many types of drugs, including heroin and cocaine. Research findings have consistently reported that among heroin addicts, prisoners, and seriously delinquent youth, the younger a person is at onset of heroin or cocaine addiction, the more frequent, persistent, and severe that person's criminal activity tends to be. In these studies, individuals with early onsets of addiction (typically before age 16) tended to abuse several types of drugs and have disproportionately high rates of several types of crime, regardless of addiction status. Such findings have been observed in various geographic locations and are independent of ethnic group. These results are also similar for both males and females, with one notable exception: females with an early onset of addiction are more likely to commit prostitution, shoplifting, and other property crimes at high rates, whereas males with an early onset are more likely to commit violent acts.

Chaiken and Chaiken's 1982 study of over 2,000 male prisoners in three states was significant for at least two reasons. First, it challenged the long-held perception that drug abusers were less violent than other arrestees. While 65 percent of Chaiken and Chaiken's sample reported having used illicit drugs during the one- to two-year period preceding the arrest leading to the most recent incarceration, an even higher proportion (83%) of high-rate, serious offenders, who were identified as "violent predators," had used drugs during the same period. Among the offenders studied, violent predators were also most likely to have had histories of "hard" drug use (including heavy multiple-drug use and heroin addiction) and to have had an early onset of several types of drug use and criminal activity. Second, and perhaps more important, the information on an offender's drug history was more likely than official arrest records to be related to the amount and seriousness of self-reported criminal activity. As in the results of drug-crime studies discussed earlier, official arrest data were poor indicators of the type, amount, and severity of crime committed by these respondents.

These findings suggest a potential for using an individual's history of illicit drug use, including age of onset, in identifying high-rate, dangerous offenders. However, this approach has several limitations. First, a general caution is in order whenever findings based on aggregate data are applied to an individual case. Second, although self-reports of drug use and crime are generally valid when obtained from individuals who are either at large in the community, entering a drug-abuse treatment program, or already incarcerated, they tend to be less accurate for individuals being evaluated for initial disposition in the criminal-justice system. Approximately one out of every two new arrestees identified as drug users by urine testing will conceal their recent drug use, even in a voluntary, confidential interview having no bearing on their correctional status.

See also **Antisocial Personality Disorder; Arrestee Drug Abuse Monitoring (ADAM and ADAM II); Cocaine; Conduct Disorder and Drug Use; Crime and Alcohol; Criminal Justice System, Treatment in the; Families and Drug Use; Heroin; Intimate Partner Violence and Alcohol/Substance Use; Marijuana (Cannabis); Myths About Addiction and Its Treatment; Narcotic; Phencyclidine (PCP); U.S. Government Agencies: Office of National Drug Control Policy.**

BIBLIOGRAPHY

Anglin, M. D., & Hser, Y. (1987). Addicted women and crime. *Criminology, 25,* 359–397.

Anglin, M. D., & Speckart, G. (1988). Narcotics use and crime: A multisample, multimethod analysis. *Criminology, 26*(2), 197–233.

Ball, J. C., Shaffer, J. W., & Nurco, D. N. (1983). The day-to-day criminality of heroin addicts in Baltimore: A study in the continuity of offense rates. *Drug and Alcohol Dependence, 12*(2), 119–142.

Bennet, T., & Holloway, K. (2007). *Drug-crime Connections.* New York: Cambridge University Press.

Chaiken, J. M., & Chaiken, M. R. (1982). *Varieties of criminal behavior.* Santa Monica, CA: Rand.

Chaiken, J. M., & Chaiken, M. R. (1990). Drugs and predatory crime. In M. Tonry & J. Q. Wilson (Eds.), *Crime and justice: A review of research: Vol. 13. Drugs and crime.* Chicago: University of Chicago Press.

Elliott, D. S., et al. (1989). *Multiple problem youth: Delinquency, substance use, and mental health problems.* New York: Springer-Verlag.

Gandossy, R. P., et al. (1980). *Drugs and crime: A survey and analysis of the literature.* Washington, DC: National Institute of Justice.

Goldstein, P. J. (1986). Homicide related to drug traffic. *Bulletin of the New York Academy of Medicine, 62*(5), 509–516.

Goldstein, P. J. (1989a). Drugs and violent crime. In N. A. Weiner & M. E. Wolfgang (Eds.), *Pathways to criminal violence.* Newbury Park, CA: Sage.

Goldstein, P. J., et al. (1989b). Crack and homicide in New York City, 1988: A conceptually based event analysis. *Contemporary Drug Problems, 16,* 651–687.

Greenberg, S. W. (1976). The relationship between crime and amphetamine abuse: An empirical review of the literature. *Contemporary Drug Problems, 5*(2), 101–103.

Hunt, D. E. (2006). Methamphetamine Abuse: Challenges for Law Enforcement and Communities (NCJ 214117). *NIJ Journal, 254,* 24–27. Washington, DC: National Institute of Justice. http://www.ojp.usdoj.gov/.

Inciardi, J. A. (Ed.). (1981). *The drugs-crime connection* (Sage Annual Reviews of Drug and Alcohol Abuse, Vol. 5). Beverly Hills, CA: Sage.

Inciardi, J. A. (1986). *The war on drugs: Heroin, cocaine, and public policy.* Palo Alto, CA: Mayfield.

Inciardi, J. A., et al. (1993a). *Street kids, street drugs, street crime: An examination of drug use and serious delinquency in Miami.* Belmont, CA: Wadsworth.

Inciardi, J. A., et al. (1993b). *Women and crack-cocaine.* New York: Macmillan.

Johnson, B. D., et al. (1991). Concentration of delinquent offending: Serious drug involvement and high delinquency rates. *Journal of Drug Issues, 21,* 205–229.

Kinlock, T. W. (1991). Does phencyclidine (PCP) use increase violent crime? *Journal of Drug Issues, 21*(4), 795–816.

National Institute of Justice. (1999). *1999 annual report on drug use among adult and juvenile arrestees.* Washington, DC: Author.

Nurco, D. N., et al. (1986). A comparison by ethnic group and city of the criminal activities of narcotic addicts. *Journal of Nervous and Mental Disease, 174*(2), 112–116.

Nurco, D. N., et al. (1988a). Differential criminal patterns of narcotic addicts over an addiction career. *Criminology, 26*(3), 407–423.

Nurco, D. N., et al. (1988b). Nonnarcotic drug use over an addiction career: A study of heroin addicts in Baltimore and New York City. *Comprehensive Psychiatry, 29*(5), 450–459.

Nurco, D. N., et al. (1991a). A classification of narcotic addicts based on type, amount, and severity of crime. *Journal of Drug Issues, 21*(2), 429–448.

Nurco, D. N., et al. (1991b). Recent research on the relationship between illicit drug use and crime. *Behavioral Sciences and the Law, 9*(3), 221–242.

Office of National Drug Control Policy. (2007). *Drug related-crime* (fact sheet). Washington, DC: Author.

Office of National Drug Control Policy. (2007). *National drug control strategy: 2007 annual report.* Washington, DC: Author.

Shaffer, J. W., et al. (1985). The frequency of nonnarcotic drug use and its relationship to criminal activity among narcotic addicts. *Comprehensive Psychiatry, 26*(6), 558–566.

Sharps, P., et al. (2003). Risky Mix: Drinking, Drug Use, and Homicide (NCJ 196546). *NIJ Journal, 250,* 2–13. Washington, DC: National Institute of Justice.

Tardiff, K., et al. (1986). A study of homicide in Manhattan, 1981. *American Journal of Public Health, 76*(2), 139–143.

Walker, S. (2005). *Sense and nonsense about crime and drugs: A policy guide.* 6th ed. San Francisco: Wadsworth Press.

DAVID N. NURCO
TIMOTHY W. KINLOCK
REVISED BY THOMAS E. HANLON (2001)
FREDERICK K. GRITTNER (2009)

CRIMINAL JUSTICE SYSTEM, TREATMENT IN THE.

In the United States, approximately 80 percent of prison and jail inmates have a history of drug or alcohol abuse and nearly one-half meet diagnostic criteria for current substance abuse or dependence. Roughly 60 percent of arrestees test positive for illicit drugs at booking. Conversely, two-thirds of clients in residential drug abuse treatment and one-half in outpatient drug abuse treatment have some current involvement with the criminal justice system.

One-sided strategies that have emphasized either punishment or treatment for drug offenders have typically met with disappointing results. Upon release from prison, over 60 percent of drug offenders are re-arrested for a new crime, more than half are re-incarcerated, and 95 percent return to substance abuse. Moreover, simply diverting these individuals into treatment with insufficient correctional supervision has produced equally lackluster results. Nearly 70 percent drop out of treatment or attend irregularly within a few months, often well before receiving a minimally adequate dosage of treatment, and crime rates have increased in some instances.

Programs that reliably produce the most beneficial results are those that combine community-based substance abuse treatment with continuous monitoring by the criminal justice system and certain and immediate consequences for clients' failure to comply with treatment or other supervisory obligations. The basic elements of effective programs include:

Treatment in the community. For treatment gains to generalize and be sustained, clients need opportunities to practice new skills (for example, drug-refusal strategies) in the community where those behaviors must ultimately occur.

Opportunity to avoid a criminal record or incarceration. Treatment completion and abstinence are most attractive to clients when they are rewarded with the opportunity to avoid a serious criminal sanction and possibly the stigma of a criminal record.

Close supervision. Programs are most effective when they can rapidly and reliably detect substance use and other infractions, when clients' progress is regularly reviewed by staff, and when team members share important information with each other, including information about treatment attendance, abstinence, and rule infractions.

Certain and immediate consequences. The more rapidly and reliably rewards and sanctions are applied for achievements and infractions, the more effective the program.

COMMUNITY DISPOSITIONS

The unprecedented expansion of the U.S. inmate population that ensued from the War on Drugs led to spiraling correctional costs and severe prison overcrowding. This situation has left many jurisdictions with little choice but to divert large numbers of nonviolent, drug-possession offenders from incarceration to community-based correctional programs.

A relatively new but successful example of such a diversionary program is drug courts. Drug courts are special criminal court dockets that offer a judicially supervised regimen of substance abuse treatment and other needed services in lieu of criminal prosecution or incarceration. Clients in drug courts must attend frequent court hearings in which the judge reviews their progress in treatment and the results of random weekly urine drug testing and can administer punitive sanctions for infractions and rewards for accomplishments. Common examples of sanctions include verbal reprimands, writing assignments, increased drug testing, fines, community service, and brief intervals of jail detention. Common examples of rewards include praise; applause; small, token gifts; certificates of recognition; and reductions in treatment or supervisory obligations. In pre-plea or pre-adjudication drug courts, successful graduates have their charges dropped and may have the record expunged, making the arrest a legal non-event for many purposes. In post-adjudication drug courts, the conviction stands but graduates can avoid incarceration or have their probation term reduced in length or severity.

Several rigorous meta-analyses and systematic review articles have concluded that drug courts reduce substance use and crime by an average of 20 to 30 percent while participants are in the programs and reduce re-arrest rates after discharge by about 10 to 15 percent as compared to probation or adjudication as usual. The positive effects on crime have been shown in several studies to last several years after the program. Outcomes other than re-arrests (for example, substance use or employment) are difficult and costly to assess after discharge.

Other community programs have been studied less intensively than drug courts but are showing promising evidence of success. *Seamless probation* unites probation officers and clinicians as a team in the treatment and management of probationers.

The probation department might, for example, maintain office space at the treatment program and vice versa, thus reducing the likelihood of clients falling through the cracks and eluding deserved consequences, permitting a more efficient exchange of information, and allowing for co-facilitation of certain group interventions by probation officers and clinicians. Emerging evidence suggests outcomes may be substantially improved by such an arrangement; however, more research is needed to identify best practices for this approach. Some types of clients might respond well to this integrated strategy, whereas others might respond better to more traditional clinical interventions that maintain stricter confidentiality and separation of boundaries between treatment and the criminal justice system.

Coerced abstinence refers to a straightforward arrangement in which drug offenders are required to deliver randomly timed urine specimens on at least a weekly basis. They receive negative sanctions that gradually escalate in magnitude in response to successive drug-positive specimens. At higher magnitudes, the sanctions could include jail detention of up to a few days but eventually could result in a custodial sentence. Significant reductions in substance use, technical violations, and new offenses have been reported in at least two randomized experimental studies contrasting outcomes to standard probation or pre-trial supervision. More research is needed, however, to determine what types of drug offenders are aptly suited to such an arrangement. Presumably, individuals who are compulsively addicted to drugs or alcohol would have considerable difficulty stopping their usage even in response to threatened sanctions. However, individuals whose use has not yet progressed to the point of addiction and is still under voluntary control might respond sufficiently to this relatively simple and inexpensive procedure. Evidence also suggests that the use of punishment alone rarely leads to sustained improvements over the long term, and it may be as important or more important to reward offenders for engaging in productive and socially desirable behaviors in order to maintain abstinence after the coercive control of the criminal justice system has been lifted.

RE-ENTRY PROGRAMS
Less is known about successful re-entry strategies to assist inmates in returning to their communities following imprisonment. What is clear is that offering treatment behind bars without continuity of care in the community rarely elicits lasting change. The effects of in-custody treatment degrade rapidly soon after release. Importantly, however, in-custody treatment does offer important benefits. First, it is associated with fewer disciplinary infractions by inmates and greater job satisfaction by correctional officers. More importantly, it is associated with better compliance with treatment in the community following release. In-prison programming can prepare inmates to make better use of treatment services upon release, when they are at the greatest risk for relapse. In the first several months after release from prison, constraints have suddenly been lifted, the individual faces major challenges to re-engage with others, and a criminal record may pose a serious obstacle to successful re-integration (for instance, making it difficult to obtain a job or housing). Under such circumstances, a resumption of substance use or crime is often looming and a seamless transfer from in-custody to community-based treatment may be critically important to guard against impending relapse or criminal recidivism.

Unfortunately, evidence suggests the most commonly available treatments in prisons and jails are not very effective. Often going by names such as *psychoeducational groups* or *drug-focused group counseling*, the average effects of the interventions are not appreciably better than zero. Further, substantial proportions of inmates with identified substance abuse problems may receive little or no services at all. Many facilities target their scarce treatment slots to inmates who are scheduled to be released in the not-too-distant future, but who still have sufficient time left on their sentences to permit them to complete the intervention. This narrow time window, coupled with slow turnover of available slots, means that many needy individuals never gain access to the programs. In addition, it is not uncommon for some prisons to conduct "criminogenic risk assessments" of inmates and to exclude higher risk offenders (those with more serious criminal backgrounds) from participation in treatment programs. Although this may make sense from the standpoint of maintaining institutional order and control, it can also have the effect of excluding some of the most drug-addicted and impaired individuals from needed services.

The most widely studied re-entry programs are correctional *therapeutic communities* (TCs). TCs are residential programs that isolate clients from drugs and alcohol. Peers influence one another by confronting negative traits and behaviors, rewarding good performance, and offering mentorship and camaraderie. Clinical interventions commonly include process groups, milieu therapies, and community meetings, and more recently TCs have begun integrating behavioral and cognitive-behavioral components into their programs. Research reveals that in-prison TC treatment alone is insufficient to produce lasting improvements; however, offenders who begin TC treatment in prison and continue in a work-release TC program followed by outpatient aftercare have substantial reductions in crime and re-arrest rates. This step-down approach from institutional treatment to treatment in a halfway house or work-release center to outpatient treatment appears to be the most effective approach for the large proportion of inmates who may lack adequate social supports and access to sober living arrangements in the community.

MEDICATIONS

The criminal justice system has traditionally been wary about the use of anti-addiction medications. In part, this attitude may be due to ethical concerns about the coercive use of medications with prisoners and also to the fact that some anti-addiction medications, such as methadone, have psychoactive properties and are addictive themselves. However, research consistently demonstrates that maintaining addicts on appropriately prescribed medication can substantially reduce illicit drug use, crime, and HIV-risk behaviors such as needle sharing. For individuals who were prescribed medication prior to their arrest, the sudden discontinuation of treatment, substitution of a different medication, and/or lower dosage are problematic, but not uncommon, occurrences when individuals enter the criminal justice system. Moreover, for the relatively large proportion of offenders who have co-occurring psychiatric disorders, such as major depression or bipolar disorder, it may be tantamount to malpractice to discontinue prescribed psychotropic medications without a thorough psychiatric re-evaluation and medically indicated reason for doing so.

Fortunately, newer classes of medications are being developed that have less or no addictive properties and that can assist in reducing cravings or blocking the psychoactive effects of illicit drugs. Examples include naltrexone and buprenorphine, which are used to treat opioid dependence. Greater use of such medications is critically important for intervening with the large numbers of drug-addicted individuals entering and leaving U.S. jails and prisons each year.

See also **Coerced Treatment for Substance Offenders; Prisons and Jails; Prisons and Jails, Drug Treatment in.**

BIBLIOGRAPHY

Belenko, S., & Peugh, J. (1998). *Behind bars: Substance abuse and America's prison population.* New York: National Center on Addiction & Substance Abuse at Columbia University.

Farrington, D. P., & Welsh, B. C. (Eds.). (2001). What works in preventing crime? Systematic reviews of experimental and quasi-experimental research [special issue]. *Annals of the American Academy of Political & Social Science, 578.*

Knight, K., & Farabee, D. (Eds.). (2007). *Treating addicted offenders: A continuum of effective practices* (Vol. II). Kingston, NJ: Civic Research Institute.

Leukefeld, C. G., Tims, F., & Farabee, D. (Eds.). (2002). *Treatment of drug offenders: Policies and issues.* New York: Springer.

Marlowe, D. B. (2003). Integrating substance abuse treatment and criminal justice supervision. *NIDA Science & Practice Perspectives, 2* (1), 4–14.

National Association of Drug Court Professionals. (2008). *Principles of evidence-based sentencing and other court dispositions for substance abusing individuals.* Alexandria, VA: Author.

National Institute on Drug Abuse. (2006). *Principles of drug abuse treatment for criminal justice populations: A research-based guide.* Bethesda, MD: Author.

Petersilia, J. (2003). *When prisoners come home: Parole and prisoner reentry.* Oxford and New York: Oxford University Press.

DOUGLAS B. MARLOWE

CROP CONTROL POLICIES. The

crops that produce heroin, cocaine, and cannabis are respectively the opium poppy, *Papaver somniferum*; the coca bush, *Erythroxylum coca*; and the three cannabis plants—*Cannabis sativa, Cannabis indica,* and *Cannabis ruderalis,* the most widely grown of which is *Cannabis sativa.* Crop control policies have included a wide range of strategies, from diplomatic pressure to enforced eradication.

The most difficult crop to control is cannabis because it can grow almost anywhere in the world, even in altitudes of up to 8,000 feet. Its life cycle is only three to five months, so it is quick to grow and easy to harvest. Modern techniques mean that it can be grown indoors hydroponically, as well as outdoors, but for increased potency, it needs full sun and warmth. There has recently been a dramatic change in the illicit cannabis market as the drug is increasingly produced locally rather than trafficked from one country to another. Vietnamese gangs have been found in the United States, Canada, and the United Kingdom running massive indoor cannabis farms with as many as 17,000 plants. Eradication of cannabis is therefore more of a domestic or national problem.

The opium poppy is similarly ubiquitous, although yield varies with weather and conditions, and it needs enough sun and water for maximum yield. Turkey was the traditional supplier for Europe and the North American eastern seaboard via the infamous French Connection, where Turkish opium was processed by French criminals based in Marseilles. When Presidents Nixon and Pompidou acted in concert to close down the trafficking route, production increased elsewhere, particularly in Mexico and in the *golden triangle* of Laos, Thailand, Myanmar (Burma), and part of the bordering Yunnan province of China. Other contributors were the *golden crescent* countries of Iran, Pakistan, and Afghanistan, although Iranian production all but ceased after the United States and Britain made this a condition of restoring the Shah of Iran to the Peacock Throne. Political pressure on Thailand produced the same result. This left Afghanistan and Pakistan the major producers at that time.

By contrast, the coca bush—a perennial with a life span of up to forty years and up to six harvests a year of its leaves—is geographically specific, with the warm, humid eastern slopes of the Andes at between 4,500 and 6,000 feet ideal for growing, either in open spaces or as understory in the forest. Peru and Bolivia were the major producers with a small amount grown in Ecuador until Colombian cocaine drug trafficking cartels in Medellin and Cali

started taking control of distribution and then began growing it themselves. They later diversified into opium poppies and heroin.

Two other plants are less widely used as mild stimulants, namely khat (sometimes spelled qat), *Catha edulis*, and ephedra, *Ephhedra equisetina*. Khat contains the alkaloid cathinone, which itself is under international control, but in many countries the khat tree and its leaves are not. It is grown in Yemen and Somalia and, because it has become more profitable than coffee, Kenya. Its use is mainly limited to the Yemeni and Somali communities, and little if any effort is made to control its growth since the active ingredients disappear little more than a day after picking: Customs officers can merely delay shipments for a week before releasing them. There is also relatively little concern about the ephedra plant, a source of ephedrine, because ephedrine and amphetamine are made predominantly in laboratories.

Although there are also thousands of plants, roots, leaves, flowers, nuts, and mushrooms with psychoactive and hallucinogenic properties, most often they are gathered rather than farmed. Only the poppy, coca bush, and cannabis plant are illegal in volume production. As of the early twenty-first century, the main world producers of heroin and cocaine were Afghanistan and Colombia respectively.

EARLY EFFORTS TO STOP OPIUM PRODUCTION

There are two direct examples of opium poppy eradication as a result of political pressure, namely in Turkey and Iran, but in neither case was the eradication sustained.

Turkey's Exit from Opium Production. In 1969 two new presidents took office, Richard Nixon in the United States and Georges Pompidou in France. Pompidou wanted to repair relations with the United States and at the same time clean up the Service de Documentation Extérieure et de Contre-Espionnage (SDECE), the French intelligence service, and the Service d'Action Civique (SAC), a force originally set up to protect President Charles de Gaulle. The latter employed men involved in the heroin trade for dirty work. After a slow start, arrests accelerated after a man who had worked for SDECE was found with 45 kilos of heroin in his campervan in New Jersey.

Meanwhile, the United States had launched Operation Intercept in September 1969 to stop cannabis and heroin from coming into the country through Mexico. At the time, the Mexican ruling elite were tied to the French heroin business. However, almost no drugs were seized, and the operation proved a diplomatic disaster with Latin America as a whole, so the operation was quietly dropped (Musto & Korsmeyer, 2002).

Eager to make a political impact on illicit drugs, Nixon turned his attention to Turkey, a NATO ally that grew no more than eight percent of the world's total opium, but was diplomatically, politically, and physically accessible in a way that opium producers such as Afghanistan, Burma (Myanmar), India, Pakistan, and Thailand were not. Following a military coup in 1971, the new regime, headed by Nihat Erim, traded arms and American aid in exchange for suppressing poppy growing. The package included $35 million in compensation to farmers. The policy worked through a combination of military control and easily accessible growing areas. There was little global effect, however: Production increased in Mexico and the Far East to fill the gap in the market. Nor was Turkey's expertise lost. In July 1974 it resumed production under government control because of a world shortage of codeine. Controllability was the key here. Australia also helped fill the medical gap by offering Tasmania as a safe and secure place to grow legal opium.

Iran, the Shah, and Oil. In 1953 Mohammad Mosaddeq, the prime minister of Iran, was ousted in a western-backed coup, and Shah Mohammad Reza Pahlavi was restored to the ancient Peacock Throne that he had occupied since 1941, thus safeguarding Western interests in the country. Abolition of opium poppy cultivation was a condition of his restoration, and this was achieved in 1955 using military force. The Shah, however, decided in 1969 to replant 20,000 hectares with opium poppies for sale to registered addicts to control a developing problem. Opium had been coming into the country from other producers and turned into heroin, thus creating heroin addicts instead of opium smokers and opium addicts. The fall of the Shah in 1979 and the takeover by religious leaders meant that, once again, opium production was eradicated and therefore no estimates exist of any illegal opium growing. Anecdotal evidence suggests a small but increasing amount might be grown, but Iran's contiguous borders with Afghanistan and Pakistan means there is no difficulty in getting supplies of illicit opiates into the country.

THAILAND AND PAKISTAN

Political pressure was also exerted on Thailand and Pakistan to reduce illicit opium production. In Thailand peasants grew opium in the highlands, but the Nationalist Chinese Army, the Kuomintang (KMT), the remnants of Chiang Kai-shek's army defeated by Mao Tse-tung in 1948, controlled the trade. Heavily involved in the opium trade in China, they trafficked opium from Burma until 1961, when they were forced out and moved to Thailand. Mule caravans moved the opium grown in northern Thailand to Bangkok, where it was processed into heroin. Thailand announced an anti-opium program in 1969 but, due to the communist insurgency and widespread corruption throughout the government, it took 30 years to get production down to nine metric tons in 2001, the last year for which figures are available (World Drug Report, 2008). Only after the insurgents were defeated and widespread alternative livelihoods programs put in place was eradication of the opium poppy possible.

In Pakistan numerous alternative development programs were tried, particularly in the Dir valley, but the net result was that the valley became depopulated. In 1990 it produced 7,488 metric tons. This fell to 260 metric tons by 2000, but production began rising again and reached 1,701 metric tons in 2007, mainly in tribal areas near the Afghan border.

AFGHANISTANI RISE IN OPIUM PRODUCTION

Afghanistan produced 8,200 metric tons of opium in 2007, compared with 460 from Myanmar, 9.2 from Laos, and only 3.2 from Thailand. Afghanistan topping the opium production table is largely an unintended consequence of U.S. foreign policy. The United States backed Mujahideen resistance to the Soviet Union invasion of Afghanistan in 1979 by using drugs, which had undermined U.S. forces in Vietnam, as a weapon. With Saudi Arabian financial backing and logistical support from a strongly Islamist Pakistan, production of opium and cannabis was encouraged at the expense of traditional crops such as wheat and apricots; the Afghans even halted fighting invaders to harvest the crop (Cooley, 1999). When the Soviet Union withdrew in 1989, civil war broke out between Afghan warlords, and in 1994 the Taliban moved in with the connivance of the Pakistan intelligence service, the Directorate for Inter-Services Intelligence (ISI), and Saudi financial support. In the hope of gaining international recognition for their regime, Taliban leaders stopped all opium growing in 2001, on pain of death, so farmers starved and/or went into serious debt. But when international recognition did not come, the Taliban let production resume.

The net result is that Afghanistan has become a narco-state, with an estimated 60 percent of gross domestic product (GDP) generated by drugs. Partly because of history, trying to eradicate opium production posed major problems that were compounded by the complex nature of the country. There is no one common language, although Pushtu, Dari, and Urdu are most common, and the country has nine different ethnic groups or tribes—Uzbegs, Hazaras, Turkmen, Tajiks, Aimaq, Kirgiz, Nuristani and Pashtoons (or Pathans), five of which straddle the borders. There are also nomadic groups such as the Ghilzai. The border with Pakistan is a particular problem: Drawn by the British in 1893, it placed all defensible foothills in what is now Pakistan. This cut the Pashtoon (Pathan) nation in two, so the border is not recognized by the Pashtoon, and its mountain ranges are completely porous and unpoliceable. In addition, in some tribal areas in Pakistan along the Afghan border, local leaders rule themselves.

With widespread poverty and many farmers dependent on the opium poppy, the effects of eradication would be devastating. Therefore the issues surrounding the eradication (physical destruction of the standing crop) or elimination (no longer grow the crop) are intimately tied to the role of opium in the economy.

ERADICATION, CROP SUBSTITUTION, AND ALTERNATIVE DEVELOPMENT

The United Nations Fund for Drug Abuse Control (UNFDAC), one of the predecessor bodies of what is now the United Nations Office on Drugs and Crime (UNODC), was set up in 1971 to control the supply of drugs and establish crop substitution programs in Pakistan and Latin America. For many reasons these programs were a complete failure,

with farmers either taking the money for not growing the crop, then growing the illicit crop in different areas, or finding the alternative crop impossible to market. Examples include truckloads of tomatoes rotting because a landslide prevented the trucks from reaching the market, or fruit ripening during a glut in the market, or a cheese factory being set up where people do not eat cheese or keep goats or cows.

The concept changed to *alternative development* (AD) which "sought to create an economic and social environment in which households can attain an acceptable standard of living without the need for drug crop cultivation" (Mansfield & Sage, 1997, p. 166). However, implementation suffered from a too uniform approach that failed to take into account the diversity of the population such as land ownership, or lack of it, the mobility of some workers, and the role of opium in households. In addition, the idea had been based on the simplistic assumption that behavior is driven only by economic rationality, with other factors playing no part (Mansfield, 2007).

Conditional on giving aid for alternative development, the United States has often argued for a parallel program of poppy eradication by spraying with glycosaphate, or Round Up, as is done in Colombia. However, there is little evidence that eradication reduces cultivation in the long term— drug crops move, production technologies evolve, and total production decreases very slowly if at all. It damages communities without undermining the reasons why people choose to grow drugs, and "there is no evidence... that it is possible to rebuild economies quickly" (UNODC, 2005, p. 23). In other words, this *conditional development* has failed.

The UNODC (2005), therefore, says alternative development should be used in four different ways, namely as a "multifaceted holistic, systemic, strategic approach to a complex problem... (as) the leg of a stool with interdiction, policing, eradication and education as the other legs... (as) a series of discrete development projects or pilot projects... (and) no more than a new name for crop substitution" (UNODC, 2005, p. 18). It notes that in Lao People's Democratic Republic, Pakistan, Vietnam, and Latin America poorly designed alternative development projects led to an increase in cultivation so that the farmers could earn enough to participate in projects to reduce the drug crop. Similar faults were evident from the 1970s UNFDAC projects in Pakistan and the Hindu Kush.

SUSTAINABLE LIVELIHOODS

The concept of sustainable livelihoods dates from 1987 and was developed by Chambers and Conway in 1991 and then taken up by the U.K. Department for International Development (DFID) and later by the U.S. International Narcotics and Law Enforcement Bureau (INL). The DFID definition (1999–2001) is that "a livelihood comprises the capabilities, assets, and activities required for a means of living. A livelihood is sustainable when it can cope with and recover from stresses and shocks and maintain or enhance its capabilities and assets both now and in the future, while not undermining the natural resource base" (DFID, 1999–2001). As a concept it has been endorsed by the World Bank with the proviso that it is mainstreamed into rural development programs (Ward & Byrd, 2004).

AFGHANISTAN NATIONAL DEVELOPMENT STRATEGY

The Afghan government has proposed the systematic integration of the counter-narcotics dimension into all policies, strategies, programs, projects, studies, and technical assistance. They argue that alternative livelihoods and law enforcement against traffickers and processors must go together but that eradication should only come in once these have been established (Afghanistan National Development Strategy, 2006). How realistic this is when set against a likely unachievable goal of a 70 percent reduction in production by 2008 and elimination by 2013 remains to be seen as pressure to eradicate runs ahead of establishing alternative livelihoods. However, it is clear that this strategy will take many years to implement, but it seems to be the only viable one. There is also the problem of how to deal with powerful local warlords or clan chiefs, who might wish to undermine all the central government's initiatives. One way might be to incorporate them into the antidrug effort through economic support, in return for aid in implementing the strategy.

AID DIFFICULTIES IN AFGHANISTAN

With international aid accounting for 90 percent of all public expenditure funding in the early 2000s, the Afghan government does not know how some

$5 billion has been spent, owing to a lack of communication and coordination. More than two-thirds of all aid bypasses the Afghan government. In addition, many countries pledged funding for projects but have not honored their commitments, causing a $10 billion shortfall on promised aid. Additionally, over half the aid is tied, requiring the procurement of donor-country goods and services. Thus, 45 percent of tied aid goes back to donor countries in corporate revenues and consultant salaries, where the profit margins range from 20 percent to 50 percent (Waldman, 2008). There are substantial "aid gaps," and many donors are suspicious of giving aid because of corruption within the government and among the governors in the country.

A further complication is the lack of a legitimate banking system, which makes aid difficult to distribute and the proceeds of drug trafficking impossible to trace. There is monetary exchange, but via the Hawala system, an informal network of trusted individuals who guarantee receipts and payments among themselves. This system operates also in Pakistan, Bangladesh, China, and Saudi Arabia (Maimbo, 2003, Thompson 2007). A government controlled banking system that works and that users trust is needed, possibly combining the advantages of the familiar Hawala system, but providing transparency for the transfer of funds.

ALTERNATE SOLUTIONS TO OPIUM PROBLEMS

A number of methods have been proposed to curb the production of illegal opium crops, but none of these approaches has met with long-term success.

Specially Bred Weevils. Numerous diseases (mildew, blight) and insects (aphids, thrips, and cutworms) attack the opium poppy (Kapoor, 1995), but the strangest story associated with opium parasites is that of the screwworm. In 1971 President Nixon appointed Jerome Jaffe, a noted treatment specialist and pharmacologist, as the first national Drug Czar to head the Special Action Office on Drug Abuse Prevention (SAODAP). The president suggested that they find an insect that could consume poppy crops. To limit proliferation, it would have to die after intercourse, so it was dubbed the screwworm. The job was given to the Department of

Agriculture Stoneville (Mississippi) laboratories, where scientists experimented with various weevil life cycles. Two problems occurred: First, no one could guarantee that the weevil would be specific to opium poppies and would not eradicate wheat or rice crops as well; second, it could not be confined to illegal crops, but could spread to legal opium crops, the source of morphine, thebaine, and codeine. This could cause a worldwide health crisis in pain control, with international repercussions. "The screwworm was relegated to a long-term experimental program which would be made operational only if it produced a categorically host-specific weevil that would also stop at international borders" (Epstein, 1977, p. 151).

Pay Farmers Not to Grow. In 2002 the United Kingdom offered Afghan farmers $1,235 per hectare not to grow opium poppies. If they had grown wheat instead, they would have added an income of $390 per hectare. Even in a bad year—2004, for example—gross income per hectare from opium was still $4,600. In 2003, a good year, the yield was $12,700. Also, many farmers never received the promised money for not growing opium, resulting in a legacy of a long-term lack of trust.

Buy the Opium Crop. The recent suggestion of the Senlis Group (2005), which licenses exports of opium for pain relief in Africa, would offer a short-term solution, but is based on a false assumption that there is a world shortage of such opiate-based analgesic medicines. According to the International Narcotics Control Board (INCB), which licenses controlled opium production for medical purposes, this is no longer true, although it might have been in 1989, when a joint WHO-INCB report looked at the problem. But by 2007 the same organizations concluded that the current supply of legal opium was adequate to meet world demand. Although more painkilling drugs might be needed in Africa, they are not being used or prescribed for various other reasons. To change this culture would take years, and the lack of a regulatory framework or a secure distribution network in many less-developed countries could lead to drug diversion into illicit markets.

Moreover, if Afghanistan were to overprovide for the opiate needs of the world, what would happen to the Tasmanian, Turkish and Indian farmers who have licences to supply medical markets already? Would their livelihoods be taken away?

Seed with Low-Morphine Poppies. Another suggestion involved sowing poppies with lower morphine yields, such as *Papaver bracteatum* (now called *orientale*), which has a high yield of thebaine and low morphine content. Also it does not fall under the control of the 1961 Single Narcotic Convention or its amended 1972 list. However, thebaine is source of the so-called Bentley compounds, discovered in 1963 by the pharmacist K. W. Bentley. One of these, etorphine, is 1,000 times more powerful than morphine. This plan was not pursued.

Close Down Laboratories. One idea favored by the United Kingdom is to use Special Forces to target the laboratories where opium is converted into heroin. However, a laboratory can be a room in a house, a courtyard, or a cave. All producers need are filtering cloths, two barrels, and various easy-to-obtain chemicals (Zerrell et al., 2005). The only one that may be difficult to obtain is acetic anhydride, but drug refiners appear to have no problem procuring this. Heroin can be processed easily in small batches using hundreds of makeshift, temporary laboratories, each operating for a few days at a time. With risks spread in this way, closure of a few small units, when found, would have little impact on total production.

Spray the Poppy Fields. The fungus that attacks poppies, *Pleosporum papaveracea*, has been well researched, but there is a fear that it may well damage other crops. *Denryphion penicillatum* is also a pathogen for poppies. But the fungi that attack poppies, coca, and cannabis have been genetically modified, so these agents might also attack other vegetation and possibly damage human and animal life, leading to a consequent reluctance to use them.

COLOMBIA, COCA, AND HEROIN

Similar arguments to those in Afghanistan apply to Latin America, where, in 2007, Colombia had 99,000 hectares under coca cultivation; Peru, 53,700; and Bolivia, 28,900; producing 600 metric tons, 290 metric tons, and 104 metric tons, respectively to produce a grand total of 994 metric tons (UNODC, 2008). Colombia also produced 14 metric tons of opium. Claims of reduced cocaine production though eradication are difficult to prove. With no obvious shortage of cocaine on the world markets, many commentators suggest that the coca bush is simply being planted in new areas (National Drug Intelligence Center, 2007).

Alternative development. Alternative development has been tried in Colombia, particularly in the Chapare region and Upper Huallaga Valley. However, projects were individual rather than systematic and rounded packages of aid and were not linked with long-term development plans. The result in some places has been a disproportionately negative impact on the poor, forcing many people from their farms and villages into the favelas of the towns.

Spray with Herbicide or Fungus. As part of Plan Colombia, funded by the U.S. government in 2000, the herbicide *glyphosate*, or Round Up, was used to kill the coca bush. The U.S. government also had an agreement with the government of Peru to test tebuthiuron—Spike or Graslon—but concern about its wider impact has inhibited its use.

Environmentalists argue that Spike is a particular risk to the ecosystem (Solomon et al., 2005). Moreover, eradication usually leads to more forest clearing and burning, as well as the displacement of farmers, to enable illegal coca bush cultivation elsewhere (AIDA, 2005; Transnational Institute [TNI], 2005). Meanwhile, the U.S. government is growing coca bushes to test means of eradication.

The fungus *Fusarum oxysporum*, which has also been genetically modified for greater impact, is fatal to both coca bushes and cannabis plants. It has been used to spray coca bushes, but the practice was banned by Latin American countries and was stopped by President Clinton. However, the United States is talking about using it again.

UNITED STATES INFLUENCE
The United States has always had more important international goals—such as the suppression of communism or the fight against terrorism—than trying to control the international drug trade. Paradoxically then, the United States has sometimes been more instrumental in the growth of drug production and drug trade than in its suppression. The United States has long supported people and

states involved in illegal drugs when this has been politically expedient, going back to the invasion of Sicily in World War II, when Lucky Luciano negotiated with the Mafia for Patton's troops to pass through the island unhindered, with his eventual reward being deportation to Italy. The Mafia, who had been purged by Mussolini, was able to regain its grip and establish a postwar heroin empire (McCoy, 2003). Three other major interventions that resulted in increased opium production were in Laos in the 1960s, Vietnam in the 1970s, and Afghanistan in the 1980s. In Laos and Vietnam, the CIA were directly involved in the heroin trade, and when the agency withdrew in 1971–1972, the trade expanded to fill the Turkish gap. In Afghanistan, after the Russian invasion of 1979, the trainers of the Mujahideen (mainly the Pakistan intelligence service, the ISI, with U.S. backing) encouraged the expansion of opium and cannabis cultivation to undermine the Russian troops as the Americans had been undermined in Vietnam (Cooley, 1999). The active role of the CIA between 1981 and 1986, when cocaine trafficking helped finance the Contras in fighting the left-wing government of Nicaragua, is well laid out in the Kerry Report (1989), ranging from protecting informants, even if they were serious drug traffickers, to actively helping their activities (McCoy, 2003).

CONCLUSIONS
The provision of alternative livelihoods seems the only, but very long-term, solution to stopping cultivation of illicit drug-producing crops. If farmers' incomes increase through other means, there would be a disincentive to grow illicit crops. Simple eradication by hand or by using fungi or herbicides has not worked in the past, though there remains strong support for such policies in the United States. Experience also shows that insurgencies must be overcome before alternative development can take place, which has clear lessons for Afghanistan and Colombia in the early 2000s. One risk is that a long-term strategy based on alternative livelihoods may not survive if eradication is not carefully controlled, particularly if spraying is used. Aerial spraying of crops in Afghanistan, for example, might result in both mass starvation and an uprising. Meanwhile, simple crop substitution has proved uneconomic for farmers. Other indirect

means to reduce the drug supply are to control the precursor chemicals used in the processing of the crop and to close down processing laboratories. In Afghanistan, the lack of a formal banking system adds to the problems. In other countries the Hawala banking system or the Black Peso (its Latin American equivalent) frustrate attempts to damage drug profits through control of money laundering. Economists talk of a 10- to 20-year time frame to get rid of illicit crops, but this will require a commitment from donor countries, one that many do not think can be sustained.

See also **Afghanistan; Amphetamine; Bolivia; Cannabis, International Overview; Cannabis Sativa; Coca Plant; Coca/Cocaine, International; Cocaine; Codeine; Colombia; Foreign Policy and Drugs, United States; France; Golden Triangle as Drug Source; Hallucinogenic Plants; Heroin; India and Pakistan; International Control Policies; International Drug Supply Systems; Kenya; Khat; Mexico; Morphine; Operation Intercept; Opiates/Opioids; Opium: International Overview; Peru; Plants, Drugs From; Psychoactive; Vietnam War: Drug Use in U.S. Military; World Health Organization Expert Committee on Drug Dependence.**

BIBLIOGRAPHY

Afghanistan National Development Strategy. (2006). *Summary Report: An interim strategy for security, governance, economic growth, and poverty reduction.* Kabul: Author. Available from http://www.aisa.org.af/.

Asociación Interamericana para la Defensa del Ambiente (AIDA) [Interamerican Association for Environmental Defense]. (2005). *Rethinking Plan Colombia: Critical Omissions in the CICAD Environmental and Health Assessment of the Aerial Eradication Program in Colombia.* Available from http://www.aida-americas.org/.

Brown, A., Bechstedt, H.-D., Muthoo, R., Hernandez, T., Sibanda, B., Miranda, E., et al. Independent Evaluation Unit. (2005). *Thematic evaluation of UNODC's alternative development initiatives.* Vienna: United Nations Office on Drugs and Crime (UNODC).

Chambers, R., & Conway, G. R. (1991). *Sustainable rural livelihoods: Practical concepts for the 21st Century.* (Discussion Paper 296). London: Institute of Development Studies. Available from http://www.livelihoods.org/.

Cooley, J. K. (1999). *Unholy wars: Afghanistan, America, and international terrorism.* Sterling, VA: Pluto Press.

Department for International Development, U.K. (1999–2001). *Sustainable livelihoods guidance sheets.* London.

International Narcotics Control Board. (2005). *Report of the International Narcotics Control Board for 2004.* New York: United Nations.

Kapoor, L. D. (1995). *Opium poppy botany, chemistry, and pharmacology.* London: Haworth Press.

Kerry, J. (Senator). (1989). *Drugs, law enforcement and foreign policy: A report prepared by the subcommittee on terrorism, narcotics and international operations of the committee on foreign relations United State senate.* Washington: U.S. Government Printing Office.

MacDonald, D. (2007). *Drugs in Afghanistan: Opium, outlaws and scorpion tales.* London: Pluto Press.

Maimbo, S. M. (2003). *The money exchange dealers of Kabul.* (Working Paper No. 13). Washington: World Bank.

Mansfield, M., & Sage, C. (1998). Drug crop producing countries: A development perspective. In R. Coomber (Ed.), *The control of drugs and drug users: Reason or reaction?* Boca Raton, FL: CRC Press.

Mansfield, D. (2006) *Exploring the 'shades of grey': An assessment of the factors influencing decisions to cultivate opium poppy in 2005/06.* Vienna: United Nations Office on Drugs and Crime.

Mansfield, D. (2007). Responding to the challenge of diversity in opium poppy cultivation in Afghanistan (pp. 47–76). In D. Buddenberg and W. A. Byrd (Eds.), *Afghanistan's drug industry: Structure, functioning, dynamics, and implications for counter narcotics policy.* Vienna: United Nations Office on Drugs and Crime. Available from http://www.unodc.org/.

McCoy, A. W. (2003). *The politics of heroin: CIA complicity in the global drug trade.* (Rev. ed.). Chicago: Lawrence Hill Books.

Musto, D. F., & Korsmeyer, P. (2002). The quest for drug control: Politics and federal policy in a period of increasing substance abuse, 1963–1981. New Haven: Yale University Press.

National Drug Intelligence Center. U.S. Department Of Justice. (2007). *National drug threat assessment 2008.* Available from http://www.usdoj.gov/.

Solomon, K. R., Anadon, A., Cerdeira, A. L., Marshall, J., & Sanin, L.-H. (2005). *Environmental and human health assessment of the aerial spray program for coca and poppy control in Colombia.* Washington: Inter-American Drug Abuse Control Commission (CICAD).

Thompson, E. A. (2007). The nexus of drug trafficking and hawala in Afghanistan. In D. Buddenberg and W. A. Byrd, (Eds.), *Afghanistan's drug industry: Structure, functioning, dynamics, and implications for counter narcotics policy.* (pp. 155–188). Vienna: United Nations Office on Drugs and Crime (UNODC). Available from http://www.unodc.org/.

Transnational Institute (TNI). (2005). *The politics of glyphosate*. TNI Policy Briefing 14. Available from http://www.tni.org/.

United Nations Office on Drugs and Crime (UNODC). (2008). *World drug report 2008*. Vienna: Author.

Waldman, M. (2008). *Falling short: Aid effectiveness in Afghanistan. Kabul, Afghanistan, Agency Coordinating Body for Afghan Relief (ACBAR)*. Afghanistan: Oxfam International. Available from http://www.acbar.org/.

Ward, C., & Byrd, W. (2004). *Afghanistan's opium drug economy*. Washington: The World Bank.

Zerell, U., Ahrens, B., Gerz, P. (2005) Documentation of a heroin manufacturing process in Afghanistan. *Bulletin on Narcotic Drugs. 57*,(1–2), 11–31.

CINDY FAZEY

CULTS AND DRUG USE. *Cult* most commonly denotes a small, extremist offshoot from an established religion or other ideology. The term has pejorative connotations. Groups that are termed cults usually have a dogmatic ideology, are isolated from the outside world, have charismatic (and sometimes messianic and grandiose) leadership, and induce altered states of consciousness via exhaustion and other privation. Member identity is greatly transformed, often through a religious conversion experience, and it is expected that members will make a significant commitment. Cult is also used alternatively with the term *sect*. In recent decades the concept of sects and cults has been expanded to include nonreligious groups such as political cults (for example, the Symbionese Liberation Army) or psychotherapy cults. It is difficult at times to recognize a cult in the early activities of what will later become an established religion, and to distinguish full-fledged cults from organizations and movements that have some cultlike features.

HISTORICAL BACKGROUND
In Islam, alcohol is forbidden, but medieval Islamic sects were formed that used hashish (a form of Cannabis sativa or marijuana). The drug came into use in the Islamic Middle East only centuries after the Prophet Muhammad (who lived from approximately 570 CE to 632 CE) and his followers founded the Muslim faith. Hashish was allegedly used to offer a taste of the paradise to come.

In pre-Columbian America, drugs of a wide variety were utilized in religious rituals. The Native American Church continues to use the hallucinogens peyote and mescaline (both derived from the small cactus Lophophora williamsii). Recent court decisions have protected and reaffirmed the right of this church to use these drugs in religious ceremonies. As Preston and Hammerschlag (1983) have noted, this use of hallucinogens is rigidly controlled—part of a transcendent experience, accompanied by rituals of purification, and not lending itself to use on a promiscuous basis. Some Native American drug counselors have been members of the Native American Church, and peyotism has been a pathway from alcoholism within several tribal cultures.

Recovery from alcoholism occurred in *revitalization* movements or cults such as that founded by Seneca prophet Handsome Lake in upper New York State in 1799. Among such tribes depression and excessive drinking were endemic as they faced the humiliation and stress of deculturation under European rule.

Bohemian and countercultural subcultures have favored using psychoactive substances to alter consciousness. These groups ranged from the Parisian bohemians of the mid-nineteenth century, through the Greenwich Village bohemias at the turn of the twentieth century, the Beats of the 1950s, and, most famously, to the hippie counterculture of the 1960s and early 1970s, which overlapped with various guru-led Hindu and Buddhist philosophies.

The 1960s and 1970s were characterized by a youth movement (the baby boomer generation of the early twenty-first century) that developed an intense interest in the cultic and the occult—and by a popularization of drug use within mainstream American society. Some of this interest was fueled by the philosophies and practices of Asia, especially Southeast Asia, where the Vietnam War raged; some of it was inspired by the Shangri-La nature of the lands of the Himalayas, where Buddhism was practiced in secluded monasteries and nirvana was sought. As the greening of America proceeded throughout these two decades, mind-altering substances joined alcohol and nicotine as drugs of choice, at once available on the street and no longer confined to the disenfranchised or marginal.

More than 900 members of the People's Temple died by mass suicide/murder on November 18, 1979, in Jonestown, Guyana. The leader, Jim Jones, had lured many people into the cult by claiming he would cure their drug abuse problems. © BETTMANN/CORBIS

Increasingly, the so-called transcendent or mind-expanding religious experience was juxtaposed with drug use that often evolved into drug abuse. There was a paradoxical, parallel development of inner exploration and discovery in the then popular encounter group culture, and in the mind-altering, sleep-deprived marathon group therapy sessions that flourished in both the encounter culture and the therapeutic community's drug rehabilitation settings, which sometimes in their emotional extremism served to isolate members in a subcultural, cultish cocoon.

By combining aspects of their own experimentation with hallucinogenic drugs with elements of transcendental meditation in their 1967 song "Lucy in the Sky with Diamonds," the much beloved Beatles (who performed as a group from 1960 to 1969) both mirrored and promoted the use of hallucinogens as providing a readily accessible transcendental experience—although in Buddhism the goal

of all existence is a state of complete redemption (and nirvana is a state achieved by righteous living not drugs). Unlike Aldous Huxley (1894–1963), who combined his interest in Vedanta (an orthodox system of Hindu philosophy) with the use of mescaline, the Beatles and their spiritual mentor, the Maharishi Mahesh Yogi, proclaimed the desirability of enlightening the masses rather than restricting enlightenment to a righteous educated elite.

The relationship of such cults to drug use is paradoxical. Deutsch (1983) has noted that prolonged drug use may encourage this type of cult affiliation, and many cult groups offer themselves to the public and to those most vulnerable as quasi-therapeutic environments where individuals will be able to transcend the need for drugs. A variety of cult and cultlike pathways out of substance abuse exist. In the 1960s many drug abusers overcame their addiction after joining the Hare Krishna cult, and in the 1970s many others quit by responding to the evangelical appeals of the ultra-Orthodox Lubavitcher branch of Judaism. The Hare Krishna experience was a cult alternative to drugs that incorporated certain aspects of the counterculture valued by youth. Other movements that prospered in recruiting confused and burned-out drug users were fundamentalist Protestant groups (so-called Jesus freaks), the crypto-Protestant Children of God, and the Reverend Sun Myung Moon's Unification Church. For adolescents in the mid- to late twentieth century cult affiliation often offered a resolution of ambiguity, ambivalence, and dissonance; a small and manageable, nurturing social universe; the structured regulation of impulsivity; and a higher purpose, meaning, and identity as opposed to malaise and drift.

One charismatic cult leader was the Reverend Jim Jones, leader of the People's Temple. His claim of curing drug abuse was only one of the cult's lures. After moving around in the United States, he brought his followers to Guyana, South America. There, in a remote location, one of Jones's former substance abusers mixed a massive batch of poisoned Kool-Aid for the cult's final event—a mass suicide.

Scientology has its own chain of drug treatment programs, Narcanon, that is easy to confuse with Nar-Anon (a fellowship of relatives and significant others of addicts) or mistake as an abbreviation for Narcotics Anonymous. Its treatment of substance abusers reflects the Dianetics-based teachings of L. Ron Hubbard (born Lafayette Ronald Hubbard, 1911–1986), an American science fiction writer, whose Scientology movement expanded in the 1950s when he moved to England (he was subsequently banned from reentering England in 1968). Scientology is a quasi-philosophical system that claims to improve its followers' mental and physical well-being as they advance within the cult after completing (and paying handsomely for) a series of courses.

TWELVE-STEP PROGRAMS
Intense religious commitment is a significant aspect of much of the twelve-step recovery movement. As a result, some observers have expressed concern that this level of commitment to a program can lead to a kind of cult affiliation. Alcoholics Anonymous (AA), the oldest, most constructive, and most respected of the twelve-step

programs, is not considered a cult by most, although there are several critics who so define it (Bufe, 1998). Another, more nuanced view is that for some individuals only, AA (or its sister organization Narcotics Anonymous, NA) becomes the functional equivalent of a cult affiliation, where any and all competing philosophies are defined as heretical, and all behavior is interpreted through a dogmatic lens.

THERAPEUTIC COMMUNITIES
Rebhun (1983) and many others have noted the danger that drug treatment programs can turn into cults. One such example is Synanon. Founded in 1958 by Charles A. Dederich, Synanon involved an insular, dogmatic, and rigid subculture, one ruled by an absolutist leader. Dissent was not tolerated, and violence against critics eventually resulted in the downfall of the organization. Synanon was not unique; the history of residential drug treatment centers includes a number of insular, authoritarian and hierarchical organizations. Recovering substance abusers often found it very difficult to leave the protection of a therapeutic community to become independent members of mainstream society. The therapeutic communities of the early twenty-first century have greatly modified the harsh practices of decades ago—they embrace professionalism and evidence-based practices, and encourage reentry into society via vocational and educational training. Psychotherapeutic programs through which persons have ended substance use but which former members allege to be cults or cultlike include the Upper West Side Sullivanians, Erhard Skills Training (EST), Landmark, Harvey Jackin's Re-evaluation Counseling, and Fred Newman's Social Therapy.

ASSESSMENT
Drugs and other mind-altering substances have formed an integral part of some cultic or religious rituals from very ancient times. In the mid- to late twentieth century the structure provided by groups that mobilize intense religious or quasi-religious feelings has sometimes enabled vulnerable individuals to transcend their personal difficulties such as drug and alcohol use. However, this may come at the cost of losing personal identity, fusion with an

authoritarian and charismatic leader, and loss of contact with mainstream society, family, and peers.

See also **Religion and Drug Use.**

BIBLIOGRAPHY

Bufe, C. (1998). *A.A.: Cult or cure?* Phoenix, AZ: SeeSharp Press. Available from http://www.morerevealed.com/.

Deutsch, A. (1983). Psychiatric perspectives on an Eastern-style cult. In David A. Halperin (Ed.), *Psychodynamic perspectives on religion, sect, and cult.* Littleton, MA: James Wright-PSG.

Madsen, W. (Spring 1974). Alcoholics Anonymous as a crisis cult. *Alcohol Health and Research World.* Spring, pp. 27–30.

Myers, P. L. (1991). Cult and cult-like pathways out of adolescent addiction. In Eileen Smith Sweet (Ed.), *Special problems in counseling the chemically dependent adolescent.* New York: Haworth Press, pp. 115–137.

Ottenberg, D. J. (1982). Therapeutic community and the danger of the cult phenomenon. *Marriage and Family Review,* 4(^{3}/$_4$), 151–173.

Preston, R., & Hammerschlag, C. (1983). The Native American Church. In David A. Halperin (Ed.), *Psychodynamic perspectives on religion, sect, and cult.* Littleton, MA: James Wright-PSG, pp. 93–104.

Rebhun, J. (1983). The drug rehabilitation program: Cults in formation? In David A. Halperin (Ed.), *Psychodynamic perspectives on religion, sect, and cult.* Littleton, MA: James Wright-PSG.

Reich, C. A. (1970). *The greening of America.* New York: Random House.

DAVID A. HALPERIN
REVISED BY JAMES T. MCDONOUGH JR. (2001)
PETER L. MYERS (2009)